STRATEGIC

Concepts & Cases

MANAGEMENT

Arthur A. Thompson, Jr.

A. J. Strickland III

Both of the University of Alabama

Ninth Edition

IRWIN

Chicago • Bogotá • Boston • Buenos Aires • Caracas
London • Madrid • Mexico City • Sydney • Toronto

To Hasseline and Kitty

© Richard D. Irwin, a Times Mirror Higher Education Group, Inc. company, 1978, 1981, 1984, 1987, 1990, 1992, 1993, 1995, and 1996

Irwin Book Team

Publisher: *Rob Zwettler*
Executive editor: *Kurt L. Strand*
Senior developmental editor: *Laura Hurst Spell*
Marketing manager: *Michael Campbell*
Production supervisor: *Lara Feinberg*
Assistant manager, graphics: *Charlene R. Perez*
Project editor: *Mary Conzachi*
Senior designer: *Heidi J. Baughman*
Compositor: *Weimer Graphics, Inc., Division of Shepard Poorman Communications Corp.*
Typeface: *10/12 Times Roman*
Printer: *Von Hoffman Press, Inc.*

◤◥ **Times Mirror**
◣◢ **Higher Education Group**

Library of Congress Cataloging-in-Publication Data

Thompson, Arthur A.,
   Strategic management : concepts and cases / Arthur A. Thompson and
A. J. Strickland — 9th ed.
     p.   cm.
   Includes bibliographical references and indexes.
   ISBN 0-256-16205-0
   1. Strategic planning. 2. Strategic planning—Case studies.
3. Strategic planning. 4. Strategic planning—Case studies.
I. Strickland, A. J. (Alonzo J.) II. Title
HD30.28.T53   1996
658.4′012—dc20   95–36378

Printed in the United States of America
1 2 3 4 5 6 7 8 9 0 VH 2 1 0 9 8 7 6 5

Preface

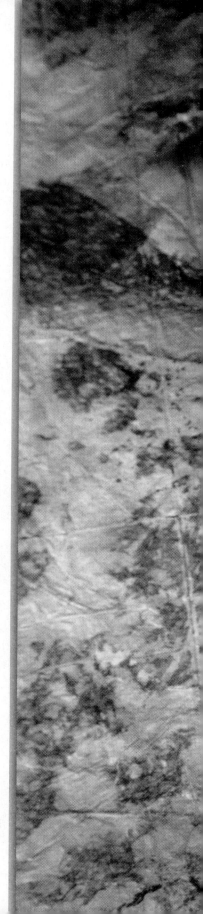

This ninth edition, following on the heels of last year's eighth edition, continues our response to the market's unrelenting appetite for fresh, interesting cases. Even though the pace of new developments in the literature of strategic management doesn't warrant an ultra-short text revision cycle, keeping readers well-supplied with a stream of timely, newly researched cases satisfies a legitimate market need. With so many business schools offering the strategic management course every term, the case collection in any one edition "wears out" after a few terms—we've all experienced the speed with which case files sprout and circulate; moreover, fast-changing company circumstances can prematurely render an otherwise good case obsolete. The strong desire of adopters for fresh cases, together with welcome and much-needed growth in the supply of first-rate cases being developed each year, has again prompted us to institute a short *case* revision cycle and provide a second collection of 36 cases to choose from. We've carried over only the classic two-page Robin Hood case; the other 35 cases in this edition all differ from those contained in the eighth edition. Aside from the new cases, however, the content of this ninth edition matches the eighth edition; the 11 chapters of text material remain untouched except for redesigned artwork and minor editing.

If you are a user of the eighth edition, shifting to the ninth edition merits consideration (1) as soon as you deem it's time to incorporate a new case collection into your course offering and/or (2) if you are intrigued with the pedagogical possibilities of our new Strat-Tutor software supplement for students. If you haven't been an adopter of the eighth edition, we suggest giving priority to the ninth edition and seeing what enthusiasm your students have for the new Strat-Tutor courseware. Because only the cases and the optional Strat-Tutor software differentiate the ninth from the eighth edition, both editions will simultaneously remain available from the publisher, thus allowing adopters free rein to select whichever case lineup and software option is preferred.

THE CASE COLLECTION IN THE NINTH EDITION

The 36 cases in this edition include 23 new cases not appearing in any of our previous editions, 7 popular cases mostly from the seventh edition that have been thoroughly revised and updated, 1 carryover case from the eighth edition, and 5 carryover cases from the seventh edition. We've tried to strike a good balance between fresh cases and proven favorites. To highlight the close link between the cases and strategic management concepts, we have grouped the cases under 5 chapter-related and topical headings. In the first grouping are 5 cases spotlighting the role and tasks of the manager as chief strategy-maker and chief strategy-implementer (these cases convincingly demonstrate why the discussions in Chapters 1 and 2 are relevant to a company's long-term market success). There's a 14-case grouping where the central issues deal with analyzing industry and competitive situations and crafting business-level strategy; these cases call upon students to apply the text material in Chapters 3–6. There are 4 cases involving strategy assessments and strategy-making in diversified companies that make nice follow-ons to the coverage of Chapters 7 and 8. A 10-case grouping covering the managerial challenges of implementing strategy match well with the concepts presented in Chapters 9, 10, and 11. The last section contains 3 cases highlighting the links between strategy, ethics, and social responsibility.

The cases in this ninth edition reflect our ongoing preference for situations that feature interesting products and companies and that trigger lively classroom discussions. At least 22 of the cases involve companies, products, or people that students will have heard of, know about from personal experience, or can easily identify with. Scattered throughout the lineup are 7 cases concerning international companies, globally competitive industries, and cross-cultural situations; these cases, in conjunction with the globalized content of the chapters, permit solid international coverage—in keeping with AACSB standards and the ongoing globalization of the world economy. Then there are 7 cases where the central figures are women, 9 cases dealing with the strategic problems of family-owned or relatively small entrepreneurial businesses, 1 nonprofit organization case, and 17 cases involving public companies about which students can do further research in the library or on the Internet. Eight of the cases have videotape segments that are available from the publisher or can be ordered from other services.

The case researchers whose work appears in this edition have done an absolutely first-class job of preparing cases that contain valuable teaching points, that illustrate the important kinds of strategic challenges managers face, and that allow students to apply the tools of strategic analysis. We believe you will find the ninth edition's collection of 36 cases exceptionally appealing, eminently teachable, and very suitable for drilling students in the use of concepts and analytical treatments in Chapters 1–11. It is a solid, attractive, and stimulating case lineup from beginning to end.

THE NEW STRAT-TUTOR™ SOFTWARE SUPPLEMENT

Available with this ninth edition is an innovative software option called Strat-Tutor that goes well beyond the number-crunching assistance and analytical conveniences incorporated in the Strat-Analyst software accompanying our previous five editions. The new Strat-Tutor courseware is, in effect, a full-fledged, computer-assisted, interactive study guide for the entire text. Strat-Tutor has two main sections:

- A 25-question test for each text chapter that students can use to measure their comprehension of the material presented.
- A set of custom-designed case preparation exercises for 18 of the 36 cases in the ninth edition; these exercises lead students through the needed analysis, provide number-crunching assistance, and tutor students in use of the concepts and tools in the text chapters.

The Self-Testing Feature

Each chapter's test consists of 25 questions—some multiple-answer, some true–false, some fill-in-the-blank, some that test understanding of figures and diagrams in the text chapters. We've tried to be creative in developing the tests, varying the formats from chapter to chapter (to heighten interest), and building in as much opportunity for student interaction and input as we could dream up. When the student completes each test, Strat-TUTOR automatically grades the answers, provides a test score, and directs students to the text pages where the correct answers can be found. Questions incorrectly answered can be attempted as many times as needed to arrive at the right answer. *None of the questions on Strat-TUTOR correspond to those on the instructor's test bank.* We believe students will find these chapter-by-chapter self-tests a welcome and effective way to gauge their readiness for the course instructor's examinations.

The Case Preparation Guides

We've all experienced poor and uneven student preparation of cases for class discussion. Sometimes it's because of inadequate effort, but more often it is because of confusion over exactly what analysis to do and/or inexperience in translating the results of strategic analysis into solid recommendations. Strat-TUTOR aims at significantly boosting the quality of student preparation of assigned cases by providing a set of well-conceived study questions for each of the 36 cases and comprehensive case preparation exercises for a select subset of 18 cases (those marked with an asterisk in the Table of Contents). The 18 case preparation exercises coach students in the discipline of thinking strategically, walk them step-by-step through proper use of the analytical techniques described in the text chapters, provide assistance in doing routine calculations, and help develop their business judgment. Each exercise has been *tailored* to fit the specific issues/problems and analytical requirements posed by the case. We have scrupulously avoided creating one generic study guide because cases in strategic management cut across a broad range of issues/problems and entail diverse analytical requirements (strategy analysis in single-business situations is fundamentally different from strategy analysis of diversified companies; cases where the spotlight is on developing a strategy are fundamentally different from cases where the main issues revolve around strategy implementation and execution).

The Strat-TUTOR case preparation exercises consist of the following:

- *Study questions* for each case (to trigger the process of thinking strategically and to point students toward the analysis needed to arrive at sound recommendations).

- A series of *interactive screens that coach students in the use of whatever analytical tools are appropriate* (five-forces analysis, strategic group mapping, identification of key success factors, SWOT analysis, value chain analysis, competitive strength assessments, construction of business portfolio matrixes, and so on).

- *Follow-on questions* to prod students to think clearly about what conclusions flow from the analysis they have done.

- *Calculations* of financial ratios, compound average growth rates, common-size income statements and balance sheets, and any other statistics useful in evaluating industry data, company financial statements, and company operating performance (similar to what was provided on the former Strat-

Analyst software, but with added questions that prompt students to contemplate the relevance of the calculations provided).

- *What-iffing capability* that allows students to readily develop projections of company financial performance (when such projections are germane to the case).
- *Reminders* of strategy principles and generic strategic options to help students arrive at a set of pragmatic action recommendations.
- *Printouts* of the work done (to serve as notes students can use in the class discussion).

The design of the 18 case preparation exercises keeps the ball squarely in the student's court to do the analysis, to decide what story the numbers tell about a company's situation and performance, and to think through the options to arrive at recommendations. Strat-TUTOR is thus not a crutch or "answer-file" for the cases; rather, it is a tool for bringing the PC deeper into the teaching of strategic management. We've endeavored to design the case preparation exercises to *tutor* students— to coach them in how to think strategically about business problems/issues, to drill them in the methods of strategic analysis, and to promote sound reasoning. You can be assured that *the case notes students develop with the aid of Strat-TUTOR will represent their work, not ours.*

To decide whether Strat-TUTOR makes sense as a requirement or recommended option in your course, we suggest loading your set of Strat-TUTOR disks and perusing several of the chapter tests and case preparation exercises. Strat-TUTOR is programmed in the familiar, user-friendly Windows format and runs on both Windows 3.1 or Windows 95.

HOW THE TEXT CHAPTERS DIFFER FROM THE SIXTH AND SEVENTH EDITIONS

New concepts, analytical tools, and methods of managing continue to appear in the strategic management literature at a speed that mandates important edition-to-edition changes to keep the content of the text chapters close to the cutting edge. But whereas the text changes in earlier editions were concentrated more heavily in the chapters relating to strategic analysis and strategy formation (because advances in the literature have, for many years running, come faster in strategy formulation than in implementation), the most numerous changes in the eighth and ninth editions are in the chapters pertaining to strategy implementation. Since our last text revision, it has become clear that there are revolutionary developments underway in how to manage. Books, journals, and the business press are full of research studies and reports describing new tools and management approaches for restoring competitiveness, streamlining operations, and enhancing stakeholder satisfaction in one way or another. Across the world, companies are organizing the work effort around teams, totally reengineering core business processes, competing on organizational capabilities (as much as on differentiated product attributes), and installing leaner, flatter organization structures.

These new developments are not only durable, fundamental additions to the conventional wisdom about how to manage, but they represent valuable new methodologies for improving the caliber of strategy implementation and execution.

Incorporating them into the current presentation drove us to undertake a comprehensive overhaul of our prior treatment of the strategy implementation process. We expanded the presentation to three solid chapters, introduced a more compelling conceptual framework for thinking strategically about the tasks of implementation, and weaved in new material on employee empowerment, team and process organization, delayering and flattening organizational structure, ways to build core competencies and hard-to-match organizational capabilities, reengineering, best practice programs, total quality management, and healthy versus unhealthy corporate cultures. The outcome is a fresh, common-sense approach to implementing and executing strategy that is very much in sync with both recent contributions to the literature and contemporary management practice.

In the other text chapters, you'll find up-to-date sections dealing with benchmarking techniques, value-chain analysis, competence-based competitive advantage, activity-based costing (which dovetails perfectly with value-chain concepts and strategic cost analysis), outsourcing of noncritical activities, vertical integration, and why strategy is partly planned and partly reactive. Once again, there's front-to-back coverage of global issues in strategic management and prominent treatment of ethical and social responsibility issues. Extensive rewriting to sharpen the presentations in every chapter has allowed us to include the new material and still cover everything in less than 320 pages—something that readers and adopters ought to welcome, given the jam-packed content of the course.

Specific Content Changes versus the Sixth and Seventh Editions

While the overall organizational arrangement of chapters and topical sequences in this edition parallels the sequencing in prior editions, you'll find several noteworthy refinements in content and emphasis:

- Chapters 1 and 2 contain better explanations of how and why a company's strategy emerges from (*a*) the deliberate and purposeful actions of management and (*b*) as-needed reactions to unanticipated developments and fresh competitive pressures. We've also introduced the concept of a strategy-making pyramid to underscore that a company's strategic plan is a collection of strategies devised by different managers at different levels in the organizational hierarchy; the effect is to build a stronger case for why all managers are on a company's strategy-making, strategy-implementing team and thus need to know about and be skilled in using the concepts and tools of strategic management.

- The roles of *core competencies* and organizational capabilities in creating customer value and helping build competitive advantage have been given added prominence in the discussions concerning company strengths, crafting strategy around what a company does best, and building a capable organization (Chapters 2, 4, and 9).

- The treatment of value-chain analysis has been recast and expanded, new graphics added, and emphasis placed on benchmarking costs and the performance of key value-chain activities to help determine a company's cost competitiveness and overall competitive strength (Chapter 4). There are new sections describing benchmarking techniques and activity-based costing that take value-chain analysis to a new plateau of understanding and application.

- We've couched the discussion of competitive strategy around five generic approaches rather than three—overall low-cost leadership, focused low-cost, broad differentiation, focused differentiation, and being the best-cost producer—see Figure 5–1 on page 117.
- We continue to believe that global competition and global strategy issues are best dealt with by integrating the relevant discussions into each chapter rather than partitioning the treatment off in a separate chapter. The globalization of each chapter, a prominent feature of the previous edition, is carried over and strengthened in this edition, plus we've added more illustration capsules to highlight the strategies of non-U.S. companies.
- The new three-chapter module (Chapters 9–11) on strategy implementation is structured around eight tasks: (1) building an organization capable of carrying out the strategy successfully; (2) developing budgets to steer ample resources into those value-chain activities critical to strategic success; (3) establishing strategically appropriate policies and procedures; (4) instituting best practices and mechanisms for continuous improvement; (5) installing support systems that enable company personnel to carry out their strategic roles successfully day-in and day-out; (6) tying rewards and incentives tightly to the achievement of performance objectives and good strategy execution; (7) creating a strategy-supportive work environment and corporate culture; and (8) exerting the internal leadership needed to drive implementation forward and to keep improving on how the strategy is being executed.
- The eight-task framework for understanding the managerial components of strategy implementation and execution is explained in the first section of Chapter 9. The remainder of Chapter 9 is devoted exclusively to the management tasks of building a capable organization—featuring new coverage of building core competencies and unique organizational capabilities; developing the dominating depth in competence-related activities needed for competitive advantage; making strategy-critical value-chain activities the main building blocks in the organization structure; the pros and cons of outsourcing noncritical activities, downsizing and delayering hierarchical structures; employee empowerment, reengineering of core business processes; and using cross-functional and self-contained work teams. The result is a much-revised treatment of organization-building that ties together and makes strategic sense out of all the revolutionary organizational changes sweeping through today's corporations.
- Chapter 10 surveys the role of strategy-supportive budgets, policies, reward structures, and internal support systems and explains why the benchmarking of best practices, total quality management, reengineering, and continuous improvement programs are important managerial tools for enhancing organizational competency in executing strategy.
- Chapter 11 deals with creating a strategy-supportive corporate culture and exercising the internal leadership needed to drive implementation forward. There's all-new coverage of strong versus weak cultures, low performance and unhealthy cultures, adaptive cultures, and the sustained leadership commitment it takes to change a company with a problem culture, plus sections on ethics management and what managers can do to improve the calibre of strategy execution.
- There are 18 new Illustration Capsules.

The use of margin notes to highlight basic concepts, major conclusions, and "core truths" about strategic behavior in competitive markets was well-received in the previous three editions and remains a feature of this edition. Most of these notes represent an effort to distill the subject matter into a series of concise principles expressing what every student should know about strategic management. The margin notes bring the text discussion into sharper focus for readers, point them to what is important, and promote clearer strategic thinking.

Diligent attention has been paid to improving content, clarity, and writing style. We've tried to take dead aim on creating a text presentation that is crisply written, clear and convincing, interesting to read, comfortably mainstream, and as close to the frontiers of theory and practice as a basic textbook should be. Our objective continues to be one of satisfying the market's legitimate need for a book that squarely targets what every student needs to know about crafting, implementing, and executing business strategies.

THE BUSINESS STRATEGY GAME OPTION ————————

Version three of *The Business Strategy Game*, offered as an optional accompaniment to this ninth edition, represents a major step-up in capability and performance over versions one and two. It incorporates an array of new and better features, cuts instructor processing times, and greatly reduces the potential for operator error. Our objective in preparing the new version was to make the use of a simulation as attractive and as convenient as possible. Instructor gear-up time is minimal, processing of decisions is straightforward, and the administrative requirements are modest. Version three is definitely more streamlined and user-friendly than versions one and two—thanks to some excellent feedback and suggestions from users, faster and more versatile computers, and expedited programming on our end.

The Business Strategy Game has five features that make it an uncommonly effective teaching–learning aid for strategic management courses: (1) *the product and the industry*—producing and marketing athletic footwear is a business that students can readily identify with and understand; (2) *the industry environment is global*—providing students with up-close exposure to what global competition is like and the kinds of strategic issues that managers in global industries have to address; (3) *the realistic quality of the simulation exercise*—we've designed the simulation to be as faithful as possible to real world markets, competitive conditions, and revenue-cost-profit relationships; (4) *the wide degree of strategic freedom students have in managing their companies*—we've gone to great lengths to make the game free of bias as concerns one strategy versus another; and (5) *the five-year planning and decision-making capability it incorporates as an integral part of the exercise of running a company*. These features, wrapped together as a package, provide an exciting and valuable bridge between concept and practice, the classroom and real-life management, and reading conventional wisdom about management and learning-by-doing.

The Value a Simulation Adds

Our own experiences with simulation games, along with hours of discussions with users, have convinced us that simulation games are the single best exercise available for helping students understand how the functional pieces of a business fit together and giving them an integrated, capstone experience.

First, the exercise of running a simulated company over a number of decision periods helps develop students' business judgment. Simulation games provide a live case situation where events unfold and circumstances change as the game progresses. Their special hook is an ability to get students personally involved in the subject matter. *The Business Strategy Game* quickly immerses students in the entrepreneurial aspects of running a business. In plotting their competitive strategies each decision period, students learn about risk-taking. They have to respond to changing market conditions, react to the moves of competitors, and choose among alternative courses of action. They get valuable practice in reading the signs of industry change, spotting market opportunities, evaluating threats to their company's competitive position, weighing the tradeoffs between profits now and profits later, and assessing the long-term consequences of short-term decisions. They chart a long-term direction, set strategic and financial objectives, and try out different strategies in pursuit of competitive advantage. They become active strategic thinkers, planners, analysts, and decision-makers. And by having to live with the decisions they make, they experience what it means to be accountable for decisions and responsible for achieving satisfactory results. All this serves to drill students in responsible decision making and improve their business acumen and managerial judgment.

Second, students learn from working with the numbers, exploring options, and trying to unite production, marketing, finance, and human resource decisions into a coherent strategy. They begin to see ways to apply knowledge from prior courses and figure out what really makes a business tick. The effect is to help students integrate a lot of material, look at decisions from the standpoint of the company as a whole, and see the importance of thinking strategically about a company's competitive position and future prospects. Since a simulation game is, by its very nature, a hands-on exercise, the lessons learned are forcefully planted in students' minds—the impact is far more lasting than what is remembered from lectures.

Third, students' entrepreneurial instincts blossom as they get caught up in the competitive spirit of the game. The resulting entertainment value helps maintain an unusually high level of student motivation and emotional involvement in the course throughout the term.

About the Simulation

We designed *The Business Strategy Game* around athletic footwear because it is a product students can understand and because the athletic footwear market displays the characteristics of globally competitive industries in the 1990s—fast growth, worldwide use of the product, competition among companies from several continents, production located in low-wage locations, and ample room for a variety of competitive approaches and business strategies. The simulation allows companies to manufacture and sell their brands in North America, Europe, and Asia, plus there's the option to compete for supplying private-label sales to chain discounters. Competition is head-to-head—each team of students must match their strategic wits against the other company teams. Companies can focus their branded marketing efforts on one geographic market or two or all three or they can deemphasize branded sales and specialize in private-label production (an attractive strategy for low-cost producers). They can establish a one-country production base or they can manufacture in all three of the geographic markets. Low-cost leadership, differentiation strategies, best-cost producer strategies, and focus strategies are all viable competitive options. Companies can position their products in the low end of the market, the high end, or stick close to the middle on price, quality, and service; they can have a wide or narrow product line, small or big dealer networks, extensive or limited advertising. Company market shares are based on how each company's competitive effort stacks up against the efforts of rivals. Demand conditions, tariffs, and wage rates vary between geographic areas. Raw materials used in footwear production are purchased in a worldwide commodity market at prices that move up or down in response to supply–demand conditions.

The company that students manage has plants to operate, a workforce to compensate, distribution expenses and inventories to control, capital expenditure decisions to make, marketing and sales campaigns to wage, sales forecasts to consider, and ups and downs in exchange rates, interest rates, and the stock market to take into account. Students must weave functional decisions in production, distribution, marketing, finance, and human resources into a cohesive action plan. They have to react to changing market and competitive conditions, initiate moves to try to build competitive advantage, and decide how to defend against aggressive actions by competitors. And they must endeavor to maximize shareholder wealth via increased dividend payments and stock price appreciation. Each team of students is challenged to use their entrepreneurial and strategic skills to become the next Nike or Reebok and ride the wave of growth to the top of the worldwide athletic footwear industry. The whole exercise is representative of a real world competitive market where companies try to outcompete and outperform rivals—things are every bit as realistic and true to actual business practice as we could make them.

There are built-in planning and analysis features that allow students to (1) craft a five-year strategic plan, (2) gauge the long-range financial impact of current decisions, (3) do the number-crunching to make informed short-run versus long-run tradeoffs, (4) assess the revenue-cost-profit consequences of alternative strategic actions, and (5) build different strategy scenarios. Calculations at the bottom of each decision screen provide instantly updated projections of sales revenues, profits, return on equity, cash flow, and other key outcomes as each decision entry is made. The sensitivity of financial and operating outcomes to different decision entries is easily observed on the screen and on detailed printouts of projections. With the speed of today's personal computers, the relevant number-crunching is done in a second. The game is designed throughout to lead students to decisions based on "My analysis shows . . . " and away from the quicksand of decisions based on "I think," "It sounds good," "Maybe, it will work out," and other such seat-of-the-pants approaches.

The Business Strategy Game can be used with any IBM or compatible PC with 640K memory and it is suitable for both senior-level and MBA courses. The game is programmed to accommodate a wide variety of computer setups as concerns disk drives, monitors, and printers.

Features of the Third Edition

This much-upgraded version of *The Business Strategy Game* makes things easier and better for both the players and the game administrator:

- **New decision variables.** Four new decision variables have been added to enhance the game's realism and provide greater strategic latitude. Each plant can now produce different quality shoes and different numbers of models, allowing both product quality and product line breadth to vary by market segment. Portions of plants can now be sold or closed. There are more options for revamping less efficient plants to make them more cost competitive. And we've changed some decision entries to give companies more flexibility in competing simultaneously in the private-label and branded segments.

- **Expanded decision support.** We've greatly expanded the number of on-screen calculations at the bottom of each decision entry screen, achieving a quantum improvement in players' ability to do what-iffing and immediately see the sensitivity of key outcomes without having to move to a new file and consult the projected company reports.

- **The Competitor Analysis Report.** A new set of competitor analysis reports has been added that reorganizes the competitive effort information appearing in the Footwear Industry Report into formats suitable for easy diagnosis of competitors' actions and strategies, market segment-by-market segment and year-by-year. Printouts for any year and any competitor of interest are easily obtained and easily used as a diagnostic tool.

- **Other information enhancements.** In addition to the competitor analysis reports, we've improved the information in the Footwear Industry Report by including a whole page of cross-company comparisons of income statement and balance sheet statistics, additional plant construction data, and more information on the private-label segment. Plus we've beefed up the Administrator's Report with more diagnostic information and cross-company comparisons.

- **A new look.** We've given the screens a new look. The redesigned decision entry and report screens are easier to read, simpler to use, and more pleasing to the eye. There's a new menu bar that speeds access to all decision screens. It is also quicker to move from file to file.

- **The mouse.** All programs and disks used by both players and the game administrator are now "mouse aware." The mouse may be used to make menu selections and to invoke the [Enter] and [Esc] keys when necessary.

- **Error trapping and entry validation.** There's expanded error trapping capability that rejects any decision entry that falls outside the valid range or is of the wrong type [a letter versus a number].

- **Programming refinements.** We've refined the interaction among some key variables, adjusted several algorithms, improved the methodology of calculating the strategy rating, eliminated the need for students to manually update announced changes in costs and rates (it's now done automatically on the company disk during processing), relocated the what-if entries to boxes just below the relevant decision entries, and reformatted the decision screens so that all current-year decisions can be made on 6 decision screens instead of 14. There's also a more sophisticated and user friendly printer setup program.

- **Streamlined processing.** Just as in the last version, we've implemented another round of streamlining in processing decisions. Instructors/game administrators have more processing flexibility and options.

- **Improved manuals.** The *Player's Manual* has been reworked to provide better explanations of cause-effect relationships and more information on the conditions surrounding decision entries. The *Instructor's Manual* has been expanded by 20 percent to provide more details on administering a successful simulation.

At the same time, though, we've kept intact the features that users told us made them enthusiastic about the last two versions:

- There's no paperwork associated with student decisions or with returning the results. Students turn in disks with their decisions already entered. When you process the results, everything the students need is automatically written onto their company disks, and they make their own printouts. It takes only a few minutes to collect the disks and return them. A printout of the industry scoreboard and a printout of the administrator's report are automatically generated during processing.

- Decisions can be processed in 40 minutes (less than 25 minutes on a fast PC); simple procedures allow most or all of the processing to be delegated to a student assistant.

- Students will find it convenient and uncomplicated to use the PC to play *The Business Strategy Game* even if they have had no prior exposure to PCs; no programming of any kind is involved and full instructions are presented in the *Player's Manual* and on the screens themselves.

- A scoreboard of company performance is automatically calculated each decision period. Instructors determine the weights to be given to each of six performance measures—revenues, after-tax profits, return on stockholders' investment, stock value, bond rating, and strategy rating. Students always know where their company stands and how well they are doing; the overall performance score can be used to grade team performance.

- An *Instructor's Manual* describes how to integrate the game into your course, provides pointers on how to administer the game, and contains step-by-step processing instructions.

THE READINGS BOOK OPTION

For instructors who want to incorporate samples of the strategic management literature into the course, a companion *Readings in Strategic Management* containing 47 selections is available. Forty-two of the 47 readings are new to the fifth edition. Over 80 percent have appeared since 1990. All are quite readable, and all are suitable for seniors and MBA students. Most of the selections are articles reprinted from leading journals; they add in-depth treatment to important topic areas covered in the text and put readers at the cutting edge of academic thinking and research on the subject. Some of the articles are drawn from practitioner sources and stress how particular tools and concepts relate directly to actual companies and managerial practices. Seven articles examine the role of the general manager and strategy; 13 articles concern strategic analysis and strategy formation at the business unit level; 6 articles deal with strategy in diversified companies; 16 articles relate to various aspects of strategy implementation and execution; and 5 articles are about strategy and ethics management. Five articles concentrate on the international dimensions of strategic management. In tandem, the readings package provides an effective, efficient vehicle for reinforcing and expanding the text-case approach.

THE INSTRUCTOR'S PACKAGE

A full complement of instructional aids is available to assist adopters in using the ninth edition successfully. The *Instructor's Manual* contains suggestions for using the text materials, various approaches to course design and course organization, a sample syllabus, alternative course outlines, a thoroughly revised and expanded set of 940 multiple-choice and essay questions, a comprehensive teaching note for each case, plus eight "classic" cases from previous editions. There is a computerized test bank for generating examinations, a set of color transparencies depicting the figures and tables in the eleven text chapters, a set of transparency masters for lecture presentations, and a 3½-inch disk that utilizes PowerPoint software and contains a full set of slide-quality visuals for classrooms equipped with computer screen projection capability. To help instructors enrich and vary the pace of class discussions of cases, there are video supplements available from either the publisher or other sources that can be used with the Ben & Jerry's, Hamilton Technologies, Campus Designs, SEGA versus Nintendo, World Tire, Bama Pie, Titeflex, Perdue Farms, and Zetor Tractor cases.

In concert, the textbook, the three companion supplements, and the comprehensive instructor's package provide a complete, integrated lineup of teaching materials. The package offers wide latitude in course design, full access to the range of computer-assisted instructional techniques, an assortment of visual aids, and plenty of opportunity to keep the nature of student assignments varied and interesting. Our goal has been to give you everything you need to offer a course that is very much in keeping with the strategic management challenges and issues of the 1990s and that is capable of winning enthusiastic student approval.

ACKNOWLEDGMENTS

We have benefited from the help of many people during the evolution of this book. Students, adopters, and reviewers have generously supplied an untold number of insightful comments and helpful suggestions. Our intellectual debt to those academics, writers, and practicing managers who have blazed new trails in the strategy field will be obvious to any reader familiar with the literature of strategic management.

We are particularly indebted to the case researchers whose casewriting efforts appear herein and to the companies whose cooperation made the cases possible. To each one goes a very special thank you. The importance of timely, carefully researched cases cannot be overestimated in contributing to a substantive study of strategic management issues and practices. From a research standpoint, cases in strategic management are invaluable in exposing the generic kinds of strategic issues that companies face, in forming hypotheses about strategic behavior, and in drawing experienced-based generalizations about the practice of strategic management. Pedagogically, cases about strategic management give students essential practice in diagnosing and evaluating strategic situations, in learning to use the tools and concepts of strategy analysis, in sorting through various strategic options, in crafting strategic action plans, and in figuring out successful ways to implement and execute the chosen strategy. Without a continuing stream of fresh, well-researched, and well-conceived cases, the discipline of strategic management would quickly fall into disrepair, losing much of its energy and excitement. There's no questions, therefore, that first-class case research constitutes a valuable scholarly contribution.

The following reviewers provided insightful suggestions and advice regarding ways to make the eighth edition better: James Boulgarides, California State University at Los Angeles; Betty Diener, University of Massachusetts; Daniel F. Jennings, Baylor University; David Kuhn, Florida State University; Kathryn Martell, Southern Illinois University; Wilbur Mouton, University of Toledo; and Bobby Vaught, Southeast Missouri State University.

We are also indebted to Tuck Bounds, Lee Burk, Ralph Catalanello, William Crittenden, Vince Luchsinger, Stan Mendenhall, John Moore, Will Mulvaney, Sandra Richard, Ralph Roberts, Thomas Turk, Gordon VonStroh, Fred Zimmerman, S. A. Billion, Charles Byles, Gerard L. Geisler, Rose Knotts, Joseph Rosenstein, James B. Thurman, Ivan Able, W. Harvey Hegarty, Roger Evered, Charles B. Saunders, Rhae M. Swisher, Claude I. Shell, R. Thomas Lenz, Michael C. White, Dennis Callahan, R. Duane Ireland, William E. Burr II, C. W. Millard, Richard Mann, Kurt Christensen, Neil W. Jacobs, Louis W. Fry, D. Robley Wood, George J. Gore, and William R. Soukup. These reviewers were of considerable help in directing our efforts at various stages in the evolution of the manuscript through these nine editions.

Naturally, as custom properly dictates, we are responsible for whatever errors of fact, deficiencies in coverage or in exposition, and oversights that remain. As always we value your recommendations and thoughts about the book. Your comments regarding coverage and contents will be most welcome, as will your calling our attention to specific errors. Please fax us at 205-348-6695 or write us at P.O. Box 870225, Department of Management and Marketing, The University of Alabama, Tuscaloosa, Alabama 35487-0225.

A SPECIAL NOTE TO STUDENTS

The ground that strategic management covers is challenging, wide-ranging, and exciting. The center of attention is *the total enterprise*—the environment in which it operates, the direction management intends to head, management's strategic plan for getting the enterprise moving in this direction, and the managerial tasks of implementing and executing the chosen strategy successfully. We'll be examining the foremost issue in running a business enterprise: What must managers do, and do well, to make the company a winner rather than a loser in the game of business?

The answer that emerges again and again, and which becomes the theme of the course, is that good strategy making and good strategy implementing are always the most reliable signs of good management. The task of this course is to expose you to the reasons why good strategic management nearly always produces good company performance and to instruct you in the methods of crafting a well-conceived strategy and then successfully executing it.

During the course, you can expect to learn what the role and tasks of the strategy-maker are. You will grapple with what strategy means and with all the ramifications of figuring out which strategy is best in light of a company's overall situation. You will get a workout in sizing up a variety of industry and competitive situations, in using the tools of strategic analysis, in considering the pros and cons of strategic alternatives, and in crafting an attractive strategic plan. You will learn about the principal managerial tasks associated with implementing the chosen strategy successfully. You will become more skilled as a strategic thinker and you will develop your powers of business judgment. The excitement comes, believe it or not, from the extra savvy you will pick up about playing the game of business and from the blossoming of your entrepreneurial and competitive instincts.

In the midst of all this, another purpose is accomplished: to help you integrate and apply what you've learned in prior courses. Strategic management is a big picture course. It deals with the grand sweep of how to manage. Unlike your other business courses where the subject matter was narrowly aimed at a particular function or piece of the business—accounting, finance, marketing, production, human resources, or information systems—this course deals with the company's entire makeup and situation from both inside and outside. Nothing is ignored or assumed away. The task is to arrive at solid judgments about how all the relevant factors add up. This makes strategic management an integrative, capstone course in which you reach back to use concepts and techniques covered in previous courses. For perhaps the first time you'll see how the various pieces of the business puzzle fit together and why the different parts of a business need to be managed in strategic harmony for the organization to operate in winning fashion.

No matter what your major is, the content of this course has all the ingredients to be the best course you've taken—best in the sense of learning a lot about business and holding your interest from beginning to end. Dig in, get involved, and make the most of what the course has to offer. As you tackle the subject matter, ponder Ralph Waldo Emerson's observation, "Commerce is a game of skill which many people play, but which few play well." What we've put between these covers is aimed squarely at helping you become a wiser, shrewder player. Good luck!

A.A.T., A.J.S.

P.S. This edition is accompanied by a new interactive software supplement called Strat-TUTOR. The software has two main sections:

- A 25-question test for *each* of the 11 chapters that you can take to gauge your recollection and understanding of the text material.
- Study questions for each of the 36 cases in the book.
- Interactive case preparation exercises for 18 of the cases (each exercise is tailored to the content of the case and fits the specific issues/problems and analytical requirements of the case). The case preparation guides coach you in using whatever analytical techniques are appropriate, give you helpful diagnostic calculations for financial data when needed, and push you to think through and support your recommendations. The 18 cases for which there is a case-preparation exercise on Strat-TUTOR are marked with an asterisk in the Table of Contents.

We think you'll find that the Strat-TUTOR software will significantly improve your performance in the course—besides, computer-assisted learning is interesting. The software is easy to use and employs a Windows format; it runs on computers equipped with either Windows 3.1 or Windows 95. Strat-TUTOR's features and capabilities are more fully described in the Preface.

In the event your instructor has elected to make use of Strat-TUTOR optional rather than required and no copies are on the bookstore shelf, your bookstore can order a copy for you from the publisher. Consult your instructor for help in ordering the software if you encounter any problems. Instructions for installing the disks come with the software; all other instructions are provided directly on the screens. Should you misplace the instructions for booting the disk, your instructor can provide you with a replacement instruction sheet.

Contents

8   Strategic Analysis of Diversified Companies   216

9   Implementing Strategy: Core competencies, reengineering, and structure   240

10   Implementing Strategy: Budgets, policies, best practices, support systems, and rewards   275

11   Implementing Strategy: Culture and leadership   294

PART TWO   Cases in Strategic Management   321

A Guide to Case Analysis   322

---

*The new Strat-TUTOR software contains a comprehensive case preparation exercise for student use in preparing this case.

PART ONE

The Concepts and Techniques of Strategic Management

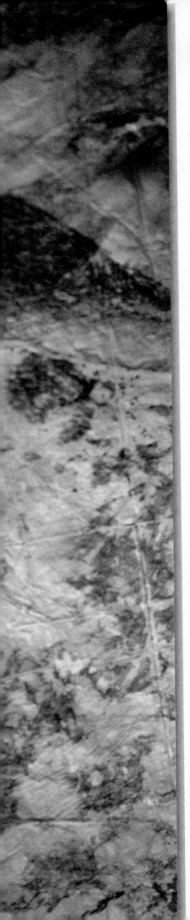

CHAPTER ONE

The Strategic Management Process: An overview

"Cheshire Puss," she [Alice] began . . . "would you please tell me which way I ought to go from here?"

"That depends on where you want to get to," said the cat.

Lewis Carroll

My job is to make sure the company has a strategy and that everybody follows it.

Kenneth H. Olsen
Former CEO, Digital Equipment Corporation

A strategy is a commitment to undertake one set of actions rather than another.
Sharon M. Oster
Professor, Yale University

This book is about the managerial tasks of crafting, implementing, and executing company strategies. Strategy is grounded in the array of competitive moves and business approaches management depends on to produce successful performance. Strategy, in effect, is management's game plan for strengthening the organization's position, pleasing customers, and achieving performance targets. Managers devise strategies to guide *how* the company's business will be conducted and to help them make reasoned, cohesive choices among alternative courses of action. The strategy managers decide on indicates that "among all the paths and actions we could have chosen, we decided to follow this route and conduct our business in this manner." Without a strategy, a manager has no thought-out course to follow, no roadmap to manage by, no unified action program to produce the intended results.

Management's game plan involves every major function and department—purchasing, production, finance, marketing, human resources, R&D. Each has a role in the strategy. The strategy-making challenge is to mold business decisions and competitive actions taken across the company into a cohesive *pattern*. The prevailing pattern of moves and approaches indicates what the current strategy is; new moves and approaches under consideration signal how the current strategy may be embellished or recast.

Crafting and implementing strategy are core management functions. Among all the things managers do, few affect company performance more fundamentally than how well its management team charts the company's long-term direction, develops competitively effective strategic moves and business approaches, and executes the strategy in ways that produce the targeted results. Indeed, *good strategy and good strategy execution are the most trustworthy signs of good management.*

There's a strong case for linking "good management" to how well managers craft and execute strategy. Some managers design shrewd strategies but fail to carry them out well. Others design mediocre strategies but execute them competently. Both situations open the door to shortfalls in performance. Managers must combine good strategy-making with good strategy execution for company performance to approach maximum potential. The better conceived a company's strategy and the more proficient its execution, the greater the chance the company will be a solid performer. Powerful execution of a powerful strategy is not only a proven recipe for business success but also the best test of excellent management.

Granted, good strategy combined with good strategy execution doesn't *guarantee* that a company will avoid periods of weak or ho-hum performance. On occasion it takes time for management's efforts to show good results. And even well-managed organizations can face adverse and unforeseen conditions. But neither the "we need more time" reason nor the bad luck of adverse events excuses mediocre performance year after year. It is management's responsibility to adjust to unexpectedly tough conditions by undertaking strategic defenses and business approaches that can overcome adversity. Indeed, the essence of good strategy-making is to build a market position strong enough and an organization capable enough to produce successful performance despite unforeseeable events, potent competition, and internal problems.

> **To qualify as excellently managed, an organization must exhibit excellent execution of an excellent strategy.**

THE FIVE TASKS OF STRATEGIC MANAGEMENT

The strategy-making, strategy-implementing process consists of five interrelated managerial tasks:

1. Deciding what business the company will be in and forming a strategic vision of where the organization needs to be headed—in effect, infusing the organization with a sense of purpose, providing long-term direction, and establishing a clear mission to be accomplished.

2. Converting the strategic vision and mission into measurable objectives and performance targets.

3. Crafting a strategy to achieve the desired results.

4. Implementing and executing the chosen strategy efficiently and effectively.

5. Evaluating performance, reviewing new developments, and initiating corrective adjustments in long-term direction, objectives, strategy, or implementation in light of actual experience, changing conditions, new ideas, and new opportunities.

Figure 1–1 illustrates this process. Together, these five components define what we mean by the term strategic management. Let's explore this framework in more detail to set the stage for all that follows.

Figure 1–1   The Five Tasks of Strategic Management

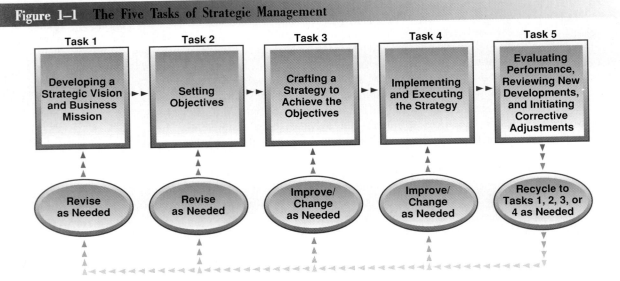

Developing a Strategic Vision and Business Mission

The foremost direction-setting question senior managers need to ask is "What is our vision for the company—what are we trying to do and to become?" Developing a carefully reasoned answer to this question pushes managers to consider what the company's business character is and should be and to develop a clear picture of where the company needs to be headed over the next 5 to 10 years. Management's answer to "who we are, what we do, and where we're headed" charts a course for the organization to take and helps establish a strong organizational identity. What a company seeks to do and to become is commonly termed the company's mission. A mission statement defines a company's business and provides a clear view of what the company is trying to accomplish for its customers. But managers also have to think strategically about where they are trying to take the company. Management's concept of the business needs to be supplemented with a concept of the company's future business makeup and long-term direction. Management's view of the kind of company it is trying to create and its intent to stake out a particular business position represent a *strategic vision* for the company. By developing and communicating a business mission and strategic vision, management infuses the workforce with a sense of purpose and a persuasive rationale for the company's future direction. Some examples of company mission and vision statements are presented in Illustration Capsule 1.

> A well-conceived strategic vision prepares a company for the future, establishes long-term direction, and indicates the company's intent to stake out a particular business position.

Setting Objectives

The purpose of setting objectives is to convert managerial statements of business mission and company direction into specific performance targets, something the organization's progress can be measured by. Objective-setting implies challenge, establishing performance targets that require stretch and disciplined effort. The challenge of trying to close the gap between actual and desired performance pushes an organization to be more inventive, to exhibit some urgency in improving both its

Illustration Capsule 1 Examples of Company Mission and Vision Statements

Otis Elevator

Our mission is to provide any customer a means of moving people and things up, down, and sideways over short distances with higher reliability than any similar enterprise in the world.

Avis Rent-a-Car

Our business is renting cars. Our mission is total customer satisfaction.

McCormick & Company

The primary mission of McCormick & Company is to expand our worldwide leadership position in the spice, seasoning, and flavoring markets.

The Saturn Division of General Motors

To market vehicles developed and manufactured in the United States that are world leaders in quality, cost, and customer satisfaction through the integration of people, technology, and business systems and to transfer knowledge, technology, and experience throughout General Motors.

Public Service Company of New Mexico

Our mission is to work for the success of people we serve by providing our customers reliable electric service, energy information, and energy options that best satisfy their needs.

American Red Cross

The mission of the American Red Cross is to improve the quality of human life; to enhance self-reliance and concern for others; and to help people avoid, prepare for, and cope with emergencies.

Eastman Kodak

To be the world's best in chemical and electronic imaging.

McCaw Cellular Communications

Develop a reliable wireless network that empowers people with the freedom to travel anywhere—across the hall or across the continent—and communicate effortlessly.

Compaq Computer

To be the leading supplier of PCs and PC servers in all customer segments.

Long John Silver's

To be America's best quick service restaurant chain. We will provide each guest great tasting, healthful, reasonably priced fish, seafood, and chicken in a fast, friendly manner on every visit.

---

financial performance and its business position, and to be more intentional and focused in its actions. Setting challenging but achievable objectives thus helps guard against complacency, drift, internal confusion over what to accomplish, and status quo organizational performance. As Mitchell Leibovitz, CEO of Pep Boys—Manny, Moe, and Jack, puts it, "If you want to have ho-hum results, have ho-hum objectives."

> **Objectives are yardsticks for tracking an organization's performance and progress.**

The objectives managers establish should ideally include both short-range and long-range performance targets. Short-range objectives spell out the immediate improvements and outcomes management desires. Long-range objectives prompt managers to consider what to do *now* to position the company to perform well over the longer term. As a rule, when tradeoffs have to be made between achieving long-run objectives and achieving short-run objectives, long-run objectives should take precedence. Rarely does a company prosper from repeated management actions that sacrifice better long-run performance for better short-term performance.

Objective-setting is required of *all* managers. Every unit in a company needs concrete, measurable performance targets that contribute meaningfully toward achieving company objectives. When companywide objectives are broken down into specific targets for each organizational unit and lower-level managers are held accountable for achieving them, a results-oriented climate builds throughout the enterprise. The ideal situation is a team effort where each organizational unit is striving hard to produce results in its area of responsibility that will help the company reach its performance targets and achieve its strategic vision.

From a companywide perspective, two types of performance yardsticks are called for: financial objectives and strategic objectives. *Financial objectives* are important because without acceptable financial performance an organization risks being denied the resources it needs to grow and prosper. *Strategic objectives* are needed to prompt managerial efforts to strengthen a company's overall business and competitive position. Financial objectives typically relate to such measures as earnings growth, return on investment, borrowing power, cash flow, and shareholder returns. Strategic objectives, however, concern a company's competitiveness and long-term business position in its markets: growing faster than the industry average, overtaking key competitors on product quality or customer service or market share, achieving lower overall costs than rivals, boosting the company's reputation with customers, winning a stronger foothold in international markets, exercising technological leadership, gaining a sustainable competitive advantage, and capturing attractive growth opportunities. Strategic objectives serve notice that management not only intends to deliver good financial performance but also to improve the organization's competitive strength and long-range business prospects.

Examples of the kinds of strategic and financial objectives companies set are shown in Illustration Capsule 2.

Companies need both financial objectives and strategic objectives.	

Crafting a Strategy

Strategy-making brings into play the critical managerial issue of *how* to achieve the targeted results in light of the organization's situation and prospects. Objectives are the "ends," and strategy is the "means" of achieving them. In effect, strategy is the pattern of actions managers employ to achieve strategic and financial performance targets. The task of crafting a strategy starts with solid diagnosis of the company's internal and external situation. Only when armed with hard analysis of the big picture are managers prepared to devise a sound strategy to achieve targeted strategic and financial results. Why? Because misdiagnosis of the situation greatly raises the risk of pursuing ill-conceived strategic actions.

A company's strategy is typically a blend of (1) deliberate and purposeful actions and (2) as-needed reactions to unanticipated developments and fresh competitive pressures. As illustrated in Figure 1–2, strategy is more than what managers have carefully plotted out in advance and *intend* to do as part of some grand strategic plan. New circumstances always emerge, whether important technological developments, rivals' successful new product introductions, newly enacted government regulations and policies, widening consumer interest in different kinds of performance features, or whatever. There's always enough uncertainty about the future that managers cannot plan every strategic action in advance and pursue their *intended strategy* without alteration. Company strategies end up, therefore, being a composite of planned actions (intended strategy) and as-needed reactions to unforeseen conditions ("unplanned" strategy responses). Consequently, *strategy is best conceived as a combination of planned actions and on-the-spot adaptive reactions to fresh developing industry and competitive events.* The strategy-making task involves developing a

An organization's strategy consists of the actions and business approaches management employs to achieve the targeted organizational performance.

Strategy is both proactive (intended) and reactive (adaptive).

Illustration Capsule 2   Strategic and Financial Objectives of Well-Known Corporations

NationsBank

To build the premier financial services company in the U.S.

Ford Motor Company

To satisfy our customers by providing quality cars and trucks, developing new products, reducing the time it takes to bring new vehicles to market, improving the efficiency of all our plants and processes, and building on our teamwork with employees, unions, dealers, and suppliers.

Exxon

To provide shareholders a secure investment with a superior return.

Alcan Aluminum

To be the lowest-cost producer of aluminum and to outperform the average return on equity of the Standard and Poor's industrial stock index.

General Electric

To become the most competitive enterprise in the world by being number one or number two in market share in every business the company is in.

Apple Computer

To offer the best possible personal computing technology, and to put that technology in the hands of as many people as possible.

Atlas Corporation

To become a low-cost, medium-size gold producer, producing in excess of 125,000 ounces of gold a year and building gold reserves of 1,500,000 ounces.

Quaker Oats Company

To achieve return on equity at 20% or above, "real" earnings growth averaging 5% or better over time; to be a leading marketer of strong consumer brands; and to improve the profitability of low-return businesses or divest them.

game plan, or intended strategy, and then adapting it as events unfold. A company's actual strategy is something managers must craft as events transpire outside and inside the company.

Strategy and Entrepreneurship   Crafting strategy is an exercise in entrepreneurship and outside-in strategic thinking. The challenge is for company managers to keep their strategies closely matched to such outside drivers as changing buyer preferences, the latest actions of rivals, market *opportunities* and threats, and newly appearing business conditions. Company strategies can't be responsive to changes in the business environment unless managers exhibit entrepreneurship in studying market trends, listening to customers, enhancing the company's competitiveness, and steering company activities in new directions in a timely manner. Good strategy-making is therefore inseparable from good business entrepreneurship. One cannot exist without the other.

A company encounters two dangers when its managers fail to exercise strategy-making entrepreneurship. One is a stale strategy. The faster a company's business environment is changing, the more critical it becomes for its managers to be good entrepreneurs in diagnosing shifting conditions and instituting strategic adjustments. Coasting along with a status quo strategy tends to be riskier than making modifications. Strategies that are increasingly out of touch with market realities make a company a good candidate for a performance crisis.

The second danger is inside-out strategic thinking. Managers with weak entrepreneurial skills are usually risk-averse and hesitant to embark on a new strategic course

> Strategy-making is fundamentally a market-driven entrepreneurial activity—risk-taking, venturesomeness, business creativity, and an eye for spotting emerging market opportunities are all involved in crafting a strategic action plan.

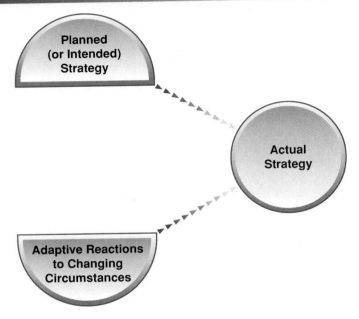

Figure 1–2   A Company's Actual Strategy Is Partly Planned and Partly Reactive to Changing Circumstances

so long as the present strategy produces acceptable results. They pay only perfunctory attention to market trends and listen to customers infrequently. Often, they either dismiss new outside developments as unimportant ("we don't think it will really affect us") or else study them to death before taking actions. Being comfortable with the present strategy, they focus their energy and attention inward on internal problem-solving, organizational processes and procedures, reports and deadlines, company politics, and the administrative demands of their jobs. Consequently the strategic actions they initiate tend to be inside-out and governed by the company's traditional approaches, what is acceptable to various internal political coalitions, what is philosophically comfortable, and what is safe, both organizationally and careerwise. Inside-out strategies, while not disconnected from industry and competitive conditions, stop short of being market-driven and customer-driven. Rather, outside considerations end up being compromised to accommodate internal considerations. The weaker a manager's entrepreneurial instincts and capabilities, the greater a manager's propensity to engage in inside-out strategizing, an outcome that raises the potential for reduced competitiveness and weakened organizational commitment to total customer satisfaction.

> **Good strategy-making is more outside-in than inside-out.**

How boldly managers embrace new strategic opportunities, how much they emphasize out-innovating the competition, and how often they lead actions to improve organizational performance are good barometers of their entrepreneurial spirit. Entrepreneurial strategy-makers are inclined to be first-movers, responding quickly and opportunistically to new developments. They are willing to take prudent risks and initiate trailblazing strategies. In contrast, reluctant entrepreneurs are risk-averse; they tend to be late-movers, hopeful about their chances of soon catching up and alert to how they can avoid whatever "mistakes" they believe first-movers have made. They prefer incremental strategic change over bold and sweeping strategic moves.

In strategy-making, all managers, not just senior executives, must take prudent risks and exercise entrepreneurship. Entrepreneurship is involved when a district customer service manager, as part of a company's commitment to better customer service, crafts a strategy to speed the response time on service calls by 25 percent and commits $15,000 to equip all service trucks with mobile telephones. Entrepreneurship is involved when a warehousing manager contributes to a company's strategic emphasis on total quality by figuring out how to reduce the error frequency on filling customer orders from one error every 100 orders to one error every 100,000. A sales manager exercises strategic entrepreneurship by deciding to run a special promotion and cut sales prices by 5 percent to wrest market share away from rivals. A manufacturing manager exercises strategic entrepreneurship in deciding, as part of a companywide emphasis on greater cost competitiveness, to source an important component from a lower-priced South Korean supplier instead of making it in-house. Company strategies can't be truly market- and customer-driven unless the strategy-related activities of managers all across the company have an outside-in entrepreneurial character and contribute to boosting customer satisfaction and achieving sustainable competitive advantage.

Why Company Strategies Evolve   Frequent finetuning and tweaking of a company's strategy, first in one department or functional area and then in another, are quite normal. On occasion, quantum changes in strategy are called for—when a competitor makes a dramatic move, when technological breakthroughs occur, or when crisis strikes and managers are forced to make radical strategy alterations very quickly. Because strategic moves and new action approaches are ongoing across the business, an organization's strategy forms over a period of time and then reforms as the number of changes begin to mount. Current strategy is typically a blend of holdover approaches, fresh actions and reactions, and potential moves in the planning stage. Except for crisis situations (where many strategic moves are often made quickly to produce a substantially new strategy almost overnight) and new company start-ups (where strategy exists mostly in the form of plans and intended actions), it is common for key elements of a company's strategy to emerge in bits and pieces as the business develops.

> A company's strategy is dynamic, emerging in bits and pieces as the enterprise develops, always subject to revision whenever managers see avenues for improvement or a need to adapt business approaches to changing conditions.

Rarely is a company's strategy so well-conceived and durable that it can withstand the test of time. Even the best-laid business plans must be adapted to shifting market conditions, altered customer needs and preferences, the strategic maneuvering of rival firms, the experience of what is working and what isn't, emerging opportunities and threats, unforeseen events, and fresh thinking about how to improve the strategy. This is why strategy-making is a dynamic process and why a manager must reevaluate strategy regularly, refining and recasting it as needed.

However, when strategy changes so fast and so fundamentally that the game plan undergoes major overhaul every few months, managers are almost certainly guilty of poor strategic analysis, erratic decision-making, and weak "strategizing." Quantum changes in strategy are needed occasionally, especially in crisis situations, but they cannot be made too often without creating undue organizational confusion and disrupting performance. Well-crafted strategies normally have a life of at least several years, requiring only minor tweaking to keep them in tune with changing circumstances.

What Does a Company's Strategy Consist Of?

Company strategies concern how: how to grow the business, how to satisfy customers, how to outcompete rivals, how to respond to changing market conditions, how to manage each functional piece of the business, how to achieve strategic and financial objectives. The hows of strategy tend to be company-specific, customized to a company's own situation and performance objectives. In the business world, companies have a wide degree of strategic freedom. They can diversify broadly or narrowly, into related or unrelated industries, via acquisition, joint venture, strategic alliances, or internal start-up. Even when a company elects to concentrate on a single business, prevailing market conditions usually offer enough strategy-making latitude that close competitors can easily avoid carbon-copy strategies—some pursue low-cost leadership, others stress various combinations of product/service attributes, and still others elect to cater to the special needs and preferences of narrow buyer segments. Hence, descriptions of the content of company strategy necessarily have to be suggestive rather than definitive.

> **Company strategies are partly visible and partly hidden to outside view.**

Figure 1–3 depicts the kinds of actions and approaches that reflect a company's overall strategy. Because many are visible to outside observers, most of a company's strategy can be deduced from its actions and public pronouncements. Yet, there's an unrevealed portion of strategy outsiders can only speculate about—the actions and moves company managers are considering. Managers often, for good reason, choose not to reveal certain elements of their strategy until the time is right.

To get a better understanding of the content of company strategies, see the overview of McDonald's strategy in Illustration Capsule 3 on page 12.

Figure 1–3   Understanding a Company's Strategy—What to Look For

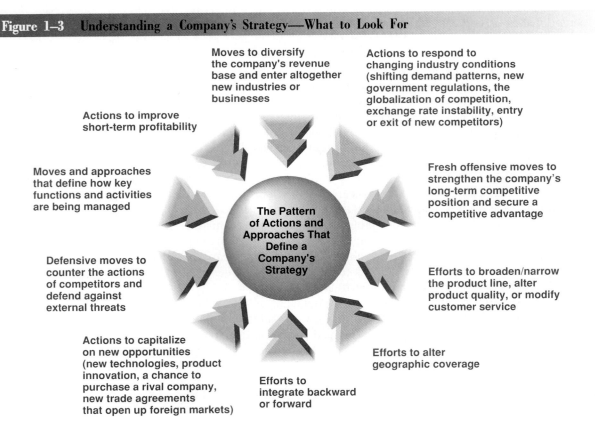

Strategy and Strategic Plans Developing a strategic vision and mission, establishing objectives, and deciding on a strategy are basic direction-setting tasks. They map out where the organization is headed, its short-range and long-range performance targets, and the competitive moves and internal action approaches to be used in achieving the targeted results. Together, they constitute a *strategic plan*. In some companies, especially large corporations committed to regular strategy reviews and formal strategic planning, a document describing the upcoming year's strategic plan is prepared and circulated to managers and employees (although parts of the plan may be omitted or expressed in general terms if they are too sensitive to reveal before they are actually undertaken). In other companies, the strategic plan is not put in writing for widespread distribution but rather exists in the form of consensus and commitments among managers about where to head, what to accomplish, and how to proceed. Organizational objectives are the part of the strategic plan most often spelled out explicitly and communicated to managers and employees.

However, annual strategic plans seldom anticipate all the strategically relevant events that will transpire in the next 12 months. Unforeseen events, unexpected opportunities or threats, plus the constant bubbling up of new proposals encourage managers to modify planned actions and forge "unplanned" reactions. Postponing the recrafting of strategy until it's time to work on next year's strategic plan is both foolish and unnecessary. Managers who confine their strategizing to the company's regularly scheduled planning cycle (when they can't avoid turning something in) have a wrongheaded concept of what their strategy-making responsibilities are. Once-a-year strategizing under "have to" conditions is not a prescription for managerial success.

Strategy Implementation and Execution

The strategy-implementing function consists of seeing what it will take to make the strategy work and to reach the targeted performance on schedule—the skill here is being good at figuring out what must be done to put the strategy in place, execute it proficiently, and produce good results. The job of implementing strategy is primarily a hands-on, close-to-the-scene administrative task that includes the following principal aspects:

- Building an organization capable of carrying out the strategy successfully.
- Developing budgets that steer resources into those internal activities critical to strategic success.
- Establishing strategy-supportive policies.
- Motivating people in ways that induce them to pursue the target objectives energetically and, if need be, modifying their duties and job behavior to better fit the requirements of successful strategy execution.
- Tying the reward structure to the achievement of targeted results.
- Creating a company culture and work climate conducive to successful strategy implementation.
- Installing internal support systems that enable company personnel to carry out their strategic roles effectively day in and day out.
- Instituting best practices and programs for continuous improvement.
- Exerting the internal leadership needed to drive implementation forward and to keep improving on how the strategy is being executed.

In 1993 McDonald's was the leading food service retailer in the global consumer marketplace, with a strong
brand name and systemwide restaurant sales exceeding
$22 billion. Two-thirds of its 13,000 restaurants were
franchised to 3,750 owner/operators around the world.
Sales had grown an average of 8 percent in the U.S. and
20 percent outside the U.S. over the past 10 years.

The company-pioneered food quality specifications,
equipment technology, marketing and training programs, operating systems, and supply systems were
considered industry standards throughout the world.
The Company's strategic priorities were continued
growth, providing exceptional customer care, remaining an efficient and quality producer, offering high
value, and effectively marketing McDonald's brand on
a global scale. McDonald's strategy had the following
core elements:

Growth Strategy

- Add 700 to 900 restaurants annually, some
  company-owned and some franchised, with
  about two-thirds outside the United States.
- Promote more frequent customer visits via the
  addition of breakfast and dinner menu items,
  low-price specials, and Extra Value Meals.

Franchising Strategy

- Be highly selective in granting franchises.
  (McDonald's approach was to recruit only
  highly motivated, talented entrepreneurs with
  integrity and business experience and train them
  to become active, on-premise owners of
  McDonald's; no franchises were granted to
  corporations, partnerships, or passive investors.)

Store Location and Construction Strategy

- Locate restaurants only on sites that offer
  convenience to customers and afford long-term
  sales growth potential. (The company utilized
  sophisticated site selection techniques to obtain
  premier locations. In the U.S., the company
  supplemented its traditional suburban and urban
  locations with outlets in food courts, major
  airports, hospitals, and universities; outside the
  U.S., the strategy was to establish an initial
  presence in center cities, then open freestanding
  units with drive-thrus outside center cities.
  Where site ownership was not practical,
  McDonald's secured long-term leases.)
- Reduce site costs and building costs by using
  standardized, cost-efficient store designs and
  consolidating purchases of equipment and
  materials via a global sourcing system. (One of
  the company's four approved designs was half
  the size of a traditional restaurant, required a
  smaller parcel of land, was about 25% cheaper,
  and could accommodate nearly the same
  volume.)
- Utilize store and site designs that are attractive
  and pleasing inside and out, and where feasible
  provide drive-thru service and play areas for
  children.

Product Line Strategy

- Offer a limited menu.
- Expand product offerings into new categories of
  fast food (chicken, Mexican, pizza, and so on)

(continued)

The administrative aim is to create "fits" between the way things are done and
what it takes for effective strategy execution. The stronger the fits, the better the
execution of strategy. The most important fits are between strategy and organizational capabilities, between strategy and the reward structure, between strategy
and internal support systems, and between strategy and the organization's culture
(the latter emerges from the values and beliefs shared by organizational members,
the company's approach to people management, and ingrained behaviors, work
practices, and ways of thinking). Fitting the ways the organization does things
internally to what it takes for effective strategy execution helps unite the organization behind the accomplishment of strategy.

The strategy-implementing task is easily the most complicated and time-consuming part of strategic management. It cuts across virtually all facets of managing and
must be initiated from many points inside the organization. The strategy-

(concluded)

and include more items for health-conscious customers.

- Do extensive testing to ensure consistent high quality and ample customer appeal before rolling out new menu items systemwide.

Store Operations

- Establish stringent product standards, strictly enforce restaurant operating procedures (especially as concerns food preparation, store cleanliness and friendly, courteous counter service), and build close working relationships with suppliers to assure that food is safe and of the highest quality. (Generally, McDonald's does not supply food, paper products, or equipment to restaurants; instead, it approves suppliers from whom these items can be purchased.)
- Develop new equipment and production systems that improve the ability to serve hotter, better-tasting food, faster and with greater accuracy.

Sales Promotion, Marketing, and Merchandising

- Enhance the McDonald's image of quality, service, cleanliness, and value globally via heavy media advertising and in-store merchandise promotions funded with fees tied to a percent of sales revenues at each restaurant.
- Continue to use value pricing and Extra Value Meals to build customer traffic.
- Use Ronald McDonald to create greater brand awareness among children and the Mc prefix to reinforce the connection of menu items and McDonald's.

Human Resources and Training

- Offer wage rates that are equitable and nondiscriminatory in every location; teach job skills; reward both individual accomplishments and teamwork; offer career opportunities.
- Hire restaurant crews with good work habits and courteous attitudes and train them to act in ways that will impress customers.
- Provide proper training on delivering customer satisfaction and running a fast-food business to franchisees, restaurant managers, and assistant managers. (Instructors at four Hamburger University campuses in Illinois, Germany, England, and Japan in 1992 trained over 3,000 students in 20 languages.)

Social Responsibility

- Operate in a socially responsible manner by supporting educational programs for student employees, Ronald McDonald Houses (at year-end 1992, there were 150 houses in nine countries providing a home-away-from-home for families of seriously ill children receiving treatment at nearby hospitals), workforce diversity and voluntary affirmative action, minority-owned franchises (McDonald's franchises included the largest and most successful group of minority entrepreneurs in the U.S.), recycling (McDonald's McRecycle USA program has won national awards), and by providing nutritional information on McDonald's products to customers.

Source: Company annual reports.

implementer's agenda for action emerges from careful assessment of what the organization must do differently and better to carry out the strategic plan proficiently. Each manager has to think through the answer to "What has to be done in my area to carry out my piece of the strategic plan, and how can I best get it done?" How much internal change is needed to put the strategy into effect depends on the degree of strategic change, how much internal practices deviate from what the strategy requires, and how well strategy and organizational culture already match. As needed changes and actions are identified, management must supervise all the details of implementation and apply enough pressure on the organization to convert objectives into results. Depending on the amount of internal change involved, full implementation can take several months to several years.

Strategy implementation is fundamentally an action-oriented, make-it-happen activity—organizing, budgeting, policy-making, motivating, culture-building, and leading are all part of achieving the target results.

Evaluating Performance, Reviewing New Developments, and Initiating Corrective Adjustments

None of the previous four tasks are one-time exercises. New circumstances call for corrective adjustments. Long-term direction may need to be altered, the business redefined, and management's vision of the organization's future course narrowed or broadened. Performance targets may need raising or lowering in light of past experience and future prospects. Strategy may need to be modified because of shifts in long-term direction, because new objectives have been set, or because of changing conditions in the environment.

The search for ever better strategy execution is also continuous. Sometimes an aspect of implementation does not go as well as intended and changes have to be made. Progress is typically uneven—faster in some areas and slower in others. Some tasks get done easily; others prove nettlesome. Implementation has to be thought of as a process, not an event. It occurs through the pooling effect of many managerial decisions and many incremental actions on the part of work groups and individuals across the organization. Budget revisions, policy changes, reorganization, personnel changes, re-engineered activities and work processes, culture—changing actions, and revised compensation practices are typical actions managers take to make a strategy work better.

> A company's mission, objectives, strategy, and approach to implementation are never final; evaluating performance, reviewing changes in the surrounding environment, and making adjustments are normal and necessary parts of the strategic management process.

WHY STRATEGIC MANAGEMENT IS AN ONGOING PROCESS

Because each one of the five tasks of strategic management requires constant evaluation and a decision whether to continue or change, a manager cannot afford distractions. Nothing about the strategic management process is final—all prior actions are subject to modification as conditions in the surrounding environment change and ideas for improvement emerge. Strategic management is a process filled with motion. Changes in the organization's situation, either from the inside or outside or both, fuel the need for strategic adjustments. This is why, in Figure 1–1, we highlight the recycling feature inherent in the strategic management process.

The task of evaluating performance and initiating corrective adjustments is both the end and the beginning of the strategic management cycle. The march of external and internal events guarantees that revisions in mission, objectives, strategy, and implementation will be needed sooner or later. It is always incumbent on management to push for better performance—to find ways to improve the existing strategy and how it is being executed. Changing external conditions add further impetus to the need for periodic revisions in a company's mission, performance objectives, strategy, and approaches to strategy execution. Adjustments usually involve fine-tuning, but occasions for major strategic reorientation do arise—sometimes prompted by significant external developments and sometimes by sharply sliding financial performance. Strategy managers must stay close enough to the situation to detect when changing conditions require a strategic response and when they don't. It is their job to sense the winds of change, recognize significant changes early, and initiate adjustments.

Characteristics of the Process

Although developing a mission, setting objectives, forming a strategy, implementing and executing the strategic plan, and evaluating performance portray what strategic management involves, actually performing these five tasks is not so cleanly divided into separate, neatly sequenced compartments. There is much interplay among the five tasks. For example, considering what strategic actions to take raises issues about whether and how the strategy can be satisfactorily implemented. Deciding on a company mission shades into setting objectives (both involve directional priorities). To establish challenging but achievable objectives, managers must consider both current performance and the strategy options available to improve performance. Deciding on a strategy is entangled with decisions about long-term direction and whether objectives have been set too high or too low. Clearly, the direction-setting tasks of developing a mission, setting objectives, and crafting strategy need to be integrated and done as a package, not individually.

> **Strategic management is a process; the boundaries between the five tasks are conceptual, not real.**

Second, the five strategic management tasks are not done in isolation from a manager's other job responsibilities—supervising day-to-day operations, dealing with crises, going to meetings, preparing reports, handling people problems, and taking on special assignments and civic duties. Thus, while the job of managing strategy is the most important managerial function insofar as organizational success or failure is concerned, it isn't all managers must do or be concerned about.

Third, crafting and implementing strategy make erratic demands on a manager's time. Change does not happen in an orderly or predictable way. Events can build quickly or gradually; they can emerge singly or in rapid-fire succession; and their implications for strategic change can be easy or hard to diagnose. Hence the task of reviewing and adjusting the strategic game plan can take up big chunks of management time in some months and little time in other months. As a practical matter, there is as much skill in knowing *when* to institute strategic changes as there is in knowing what to do.

Last, the big day in, day out time-consuming aspect of strategic management involves trying to get the best strategy-supportive performance out of every individual and trying to perfect the current strategy by refining its content and execution. Managers usually spend most of their efforts improving bits and pieces of the current strategy rather than developing and instituting radical changes. Excessive changes in strategy can be disruptive to employees and confusing to customers, and they are usually unnecessary. Most of the time, there's more to be gained from improving execution of the present strategy. Persistence in making a sound strategy work better is often the key to managing the strategy to success.

WHO PERFORMS THE FIVE TASKS OF STRATEGIC MANAGEMENT?

An organization's chief executive officer, as captain of the ship, is the most visible and important strategy manager. The title of CEO carries with it the mantles of chief direction-setter, chief objective-setter, chief strategy-maker, and chief strategy-implementer for the total enterprise. Ultimate responsibility for leading the tasks of formulating and implementing a strategic plan for the whole organization rests with the CEO, even though many other managers normally have a hand in the process. What the CEO views as strategically important usually is reflected in the company's strategy, and the CEO customarily puts a personal stamp of approval on big strategic decisions and actions.

Vice presidents for production, marketing, finance, human resources, and other functional departments have important strategy-making and strategy-implementing responsibilities as well. Normally, the production VP has a lead role in developing the company's production strategy; the marketing VP oversees the marketing strategy effort; the financial VP is in charge of devising an appropriate financial strategy; and so on. Usually, functional vice presidents are also involved in proposing key elements of the overall company strategy and developing major new strategic initiatives, working closely with the CEO to hammer out a consensus and coordinate various aspects of the strategy more effectively. Only in the smallest, owner-managed companies is the strategy-making, strategy-implementing task small enough for a single manager to handle.

All managers are involved in the strategy-making and strategy-implementing process.

But managerial positions with strategy-making and strategy-implementing responsibility are by no means restricted to CEOs, vice presidents, and owner-entrepreneurs. Every major organizational unit in a company—business unit, division, staff support group, plant, or district office—normally has a leading or supporting role in the company's strategic game plan. And the manager in charge of that organizational unit, with guidance from superiors, usually ends up doing some or most of the strategy-making for the unit and deciding how to implement whatever strategic choices are made. While managers farther down in the managerial hierarchy obviously have a narrower, more specific strategy-making/strategy-implementing role than managers closer to the top, every manager is a strategy-maker and strategy-implementer for the area he/she supervises.

One of the primary reasons why middle- and lower-echelon managers are part of the strategy-making/strategy-implementing team is that the more geographically scattered and diversified an organization's operations are, the more unwieldy it becomes for senior executives to craft and implement all the necessary actions and programs. Managers in the corporate office seldom know enough about the situation in every geographic area and operating unit to direct every move made in the field. It is common practice for top-level managers to grant some strategy-making responsibility to managerial subordinates who head the organizational subunits where specific strategic results must be achieved. Delegating a strategy-making role to on-the-scene managers charged with implementing whatever strategic moves are made in their areas fixes accountability for strategic success or failure. When the managers who implement the strategy are also its architects, it is hard for them to shift blame or make excuses if they don't achieve the target results. And since they have participated in developing the strategy they are trying to implement and execute, they ought to have strong buy-in and support for the strategy, an essential condition for effective strategy execution.

In diversified companies where the strategies of several different businesses have to be managed, there are usually four distinct levels of strategy managers:

- The chief executive officer and other senior corporation-level executives who have primary responsibility and personal authority for big strategic decisions affecting the total enterprise and the collection of individual businesses the enterprise has diversified into.

- Managers who have profit-and-loss responsibility for one specific business unit and who are delegated a major leadership role in formulating and implementing strategy for that unit.

- Functional area managers within a given business unit who have direct authority over a major piece of the business (manufacturing, marketing and sales, finance, R&D, personnel) and whose role it is to support the business unit's overall strategy with strategic actions in their own areas.

- Managers of major operating units (plants, sales districts, local offices) who have on-the-scene responsibility for developing the details of strategic efforts in their areas and for implementing and executing the overall strategic plan at the grassroots level.

Single-business enterprises need no more than three of these levels (a business-level strategy manager, functional area strategy managers, and operating-level strategy managers). In a large single-business company, the team of strategy managers consists of the chief executive, who functions as chief strategist with final authority over both strategy and its implementation; the vice presidents in charge of key functions (R&D, production, marketing, finance, human resources, and so on); plus as many operating-unit managers of the various plants, sales offices, distribution centers, and staff support departments as it takes to handle the company's scope of operations. Proprietorships, partnerships, and owner-managed enterprises, however, typically have only one or two strategy managers since in small-scale enterprises the whole strategy-making/strategy-implementing function can be handled by just a few key people.

Managerial jobs involving strategy formulation and implementation abound in not-for-profit organizations as well. In federal and state government, heads of local, district, and regional offices function as strategy managers in their efforts to respond to the needs and situations of the areas they serve (a district manager in Portland may need a slightly different strategy than a district manager in Orlando). In municipal government, the heads of various departments (fire, police, water and sewer, parks and recreation, health, and so on) are strategy managers because they have line authority for the operations of their departments and thus can influence departmental objectives, the formation of a strategy to achieve these objectives, and how the strategy is implemented.

Managerial jobs with strategy-making/strategy-implementing roles are thus the norm rather than the exception. The job of crafting and implementing strategy touches virtually every managerial job in one way or another, at one time or another. Strategic management is basic to the task of managing; it is not something just top-level managers deal with.

The Role and Tasks of Strategic Planners

If senior and middle managers have the lead roles in strategy-making and strategy-implementing in their areas of responsibility, what should strategic planners do? Is there a legitimate place in big companies for a strategic planning department staffed with specialists in planning and strategic analysis? The answer is yes. But the planning department's role and tasks should consist chiefly of helping to gather and organize information that strategy-makers need, establishing and administering an annual strategy review cycle whereby managers reconsider and refine their strategic plans, and coordinating the process of reviewing and approving the strategic plans developed for all the various parts of the company. Strategic planners can help managers at all levels crystallize the strategic issues that ought to be addressed; in addition, they can provide data, help analyze industry and competitive conditions, and distribute information on the company's strategic performance. But strategic planners should not make strategic decisions, prepare strategic plans (for someone else to implement), or make strategic action recommendations that usurp the strategy-making responsibilities of managers in charge of major operating units.

When strategic planners are asked to go beyond providing staff assistance and actually prepare a strategic plan for management's consideration, either of two adverse consequences may occur. First, some managers will gladly toss their tough strategic problems onto the desks of strategic planners and let the planners do their strategic thinking for them. The planners, not knowing as much about the situation as managers do, are in a weaker position to design a workable action plan. And they can't be held responsible for implementing what they recommend. Giving planners responsibility for strategy-making and line managers responsibility for implementation makes it hard to fix accountability for poor results. It also deludes line managers into thinking they shouldn't be held responsible for crafting a strategy for their own organizational unit or for devising solutions to strategic problems in their area of responsibility. The hard truth is that strategy-making is not a staff function, nor is it something that can be handed off to an advisory committee of lower-ranking managers. Second, when line managers have no ownership stake in or personal commitment to the strategic agenda proposed by the planners, they give it lip service, perhaps make a few token implementation efforts, and quickly get back to business as usual, knowing that the formal written plan concocted by the planners carries little weight in shaping their own action agenda and decisions. Unless the planners' written strategic plan has visible, credible top-management support, it quickly collects dust on managers' shelves. Absent belief in and commitment to the actions recommended by the planners, few managers will take the work of the strategic planning staff seriously enough to pursue implementation—strategic planning then comes to be seen as just another bureaucratic exercise.

Either consequence renders formal strategic planning efforts ineffective and opens the door for a strategy-making vacuum conducive to organizational drift or to fragmented, uncoordinated strategic decisions. The odds are that the organization will have no strong strategic rudder and insufficient top-down direction. Having staffers or advisory committees formulate strategies for areas they do not directly manage is therefore flawed in two respects: (1) they can't be held accountable if their recommendations don't produce the desired results since they don't have authority for directing implementation, and (2) there's a strong chance that what they recommend won't be well accepted or enthusiastically implemented by those who "have to sing the song the planners have written"—lukewarm buy-in is a guaranteed plan-killer.

On the other hand, when line managers are expected to be the chief strategy-makers and strategy-implementers for the areas they head, their own strategy and implementation end up being put to the test. As a consequence, their buy-in becomes a given, and they usually commit the time and resources to make the plan work (their annual performance reviews and perhaps even their future careers with the organization are at risk if the plan fails and they fail to achieve the target results!). When those who craft strategy are also those who must implement strategy, there's no question who is accountable for results. Moreover, when authority for crafting and implementing the strategy of an organizational unit is placed on the shoulders of the unit manager, it's easy to fix accountability for results and it pushes strategic decisions down to the manager closest to the action who *should* know what to do. Unit managers who consistently prove incapable of crafting and implementing good strategies and achieving target results have to be moved to less responsible positions.

Strategic Management Principle
Strategy-making is not a proper task for strategic planners.

The Strategic Role of the Board of Directors

Since lead responsibility for crafting and implementing strategy falls to key managers, the chief strategic role of an organization's board of directors is to see that the overall task of managing strategy is adequately done. Boards of directors normally review important strategic moves and officially approve the strategic plans submitted by senior management—a procedure that makes the board ultimately responsible for the strategic actions taken. But directors rarely can or should play a direct role in formulating strategy. The immediate task of directors is to ensure that all proposals have been adequately analyzed and considered and that the proposed strategic actions are superior to available alternatives; flawed proposals are customarily withdrawn for revision by management.

The longer-range task of directors is to evaluate the caliber of senior executives' strategy-making and strategy-implementing skills. The board must determine whether the current CEO is doing a good job of strategic management (as a basis for awarding salary increases and bonuses and deciding on retention or removal) and evaluate the strategic skills of other senior executives in line to succeed the CEO. In recent years, at General Motors, IBM, American Express, Goodyear, and Compaq Computer, company directors concluded that executives were not adapting their company's strategy fast enough and fully enough to the changes sweeping their markets. They pressured the CEOs to resign, and installed new leadership to provide the impetus for strategic renewal. Boards who fail to review the strategy-making, strategy-implementing skills of senior executives face embarrassment or even lawsuits when an out-dated strategy sours company performance and management fails to come up with a promising turnaround strategy.

> **Strategic Management Principle**
> A board of directors' role in the strategic management process is to critically appraise and ultimately approve strategic action plans but rarely, if ever, to develop the details.

THE BENEFITS OF A "STRATEGIC APPROACH" TO MANAGING

The message of this book is that doing a good job of managing inherently requires good strategic thinking and good strategic management. Today's managers have to think strategically about their company's position and about the impact of changing conditions. They have to monitor the external situation closely enough to know when to institute strategy change. They have to know the business well enough to know what kinds of strategic changes to initiate. Simply said, the fundamentals of strategic management need to drive the whole approach to managing organizations. The chief executive officer of one successful company put it well when he said:

> In the main, our competitors are acquainted with the same fundamental concepts and techniques and approaches that we follow, and they are as free to pursue them as we are. More often than not, the difference between their level of success and ours lies in the relative thoroughness and self-discipline with which we and they develop and execute our strategies for the future.

The advantages of first-rate strategic thinking and conscious strategy management (as opposed to freewheeling improvisation, gut feel, and drifting along) include (1) providing better guidance to the entire organization on the crucial point of "what it is we are trying to do and to achieve," (2) making managers more alert to the winds of change, new opportunities, and threatening developments, (3) providing managers with a rationale for evaluating competing budget requests for investment capital and new staff—a rationale that argues strongly for steering resources into strategy-supportive, results-producing areas, (4) helping to unify the numerous strategy-related decisions by managers across the organization, and (5) creating a more proactive management posture and counteracting tendencies for decisions to be reactive and defensive.

The advantage of being proactive is that trailblazing strategies can be the key to better long-term performance. Business history shows that high-performing enterprises often initiate and lead, not just react and defend. They launch strategic offensives to out-innovate and out-maneuver rivals and secure sustainable competitive advantage, then use their market edge to achieve superior financial performance. Aggressive pursuit of a creative, opportunistic strategy can propel a firm into a leadership position, paving the way for its products/services to become the industry standard.

Terms to Remember

In the chapters to come, we'll be using some key phrases and terms again and again. You'll find the following definitional listing helpful.

Strategic vision—a view of an organization's future direction and business course; a guiding concept for what the organization is trying to do and to become.

Organization mission—management's customized answer to the question "What is our business and what are we trying to accomplish on behalf of our customers?" A mission statement broadly outlines the organization's activities and business makeup.

Financial objectives—the targets management has established for the organization's financial performance.

Strategic objectives—the targets management has established for strengthening the organization's overall business position and competitive vitality.

Long-range objectives—the results to be achieved either within the next three to five years or else on an ongoing basis year after year.

Short-range objectives—the organization's near-term performance targets; the amount of short-term improvement signals how fast management is trying to achieve the long-range objectives.

Strategy—the pattern of actions managers employ to achieve organizational objectives; a company's actual strategy is partly planned and partly reactive to changing circumstances.

Strategic plan—a statement outlining an organization's mission and future direction, near-term and long-term performance targets, and strategy.

Strategy formulation—the entire direction-setting management function of conceptualizing an organization's mission, setting performance objectives, and crafting a strategy. The end product of strategy formulation is a strategic plan.

Strategy implementation—the full range of managerial activities associated with putting the chosen strategy into place, supervising its pursuit, and achieving the targeted results.

On the following pages, we will probe the strategy-related tasks of managers and the methods of strategic analysis much more intensively. When you get to the end of the book, we think you will see that two factors separate the best-managed organizations from the rest: (1) superior strategy-making and entrepreneurship, and (2) competent implementation and execution of the chosen strategy. There's no escaping the fact that the quality of managerial strategy-making and strategy-implementing has a significant impact on organization performance. A company that lacks clear-cut direction, has vague or undemanding objectives, has a muddled or flawed strategy, or can't seem to execute plans competently is a company whose performance is probably suffering, whose business is at long-term risk, and whose management is less than capable.

Suggested Readings

Andrews, Kenneth R. *The Concept of Corporate Strategy*. 3rd ed. Homewood, Ill.: Richard D. Irwin, 1987, chap. 1.

Gluck, Frederick W. "A Fresh Look at Strategic Management." *Journal of Business Strategy* 6, no. 2 (Fall 1985), pp. 4–21.

Hax, Arnoldo C., and Nicolas S. Majluf. *The Strategy Concept and Process: A Pragmatic Approach*. Englewood Cliffs, N.J.: Prentice-Hall, 1991, chaps. 1 and 2.

Kelley, C. Aaron. "The Three Planning Questions: A Fable." *Business Horizons* 26, no. 2 (March–April 1983), pp. 46–48.

Mintzberg, Henry. "The Strategy Concept: Five Ps for Strategy." *California Management Review* 30, no. 1 (Fall 1987), pp. 11–24.

———. "The Strategy Concept: Another Look at Why Organizations Need Strategies." *California Management Review* 30, no. 1 (Fall 1987), pp. 25–32.

———. "Crafting Strategy." *Harvard Business Review* 65, no. 4 (July–August 1987), pp. 66–75.

Quinn, James B. *Strategies for Change: Logical Incrementalism*. Homewood, Ill.: Richard D. Irwin, 1980, chaps. 2 and 3.

Ramanujam, V., and N. Venkatraman. "Planning and Performance: A New Look at an Old Question." *Business Horizons* 30, no. 3 (May–June 1987), pp. 19–25.

Yip, George S. *Total Global Strategy: Managing for Worldwide Competitive Advantage*. Englewood Cliffs, N.J.: Prentice-Hall, 1992, chap. 1.

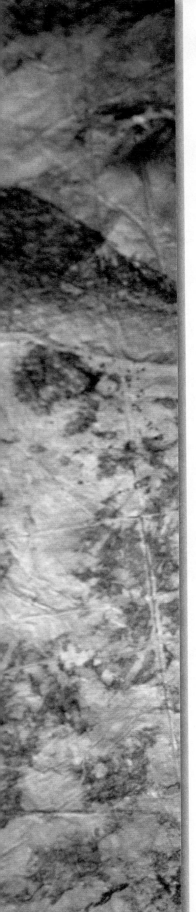

CHAPTER TWO

The Three Strategy-Making Tasks: Developing a strategic vision, setting objectives, and crafting a strategy

How can you lead if you don't know where you are going?

George Newman
The Conference Board

Management's job is not to see the company as it is . . . but as it can become.
John W. Teets
CEO, Greyhound Corporation

Once your direction becomes clear to you and fully visible to others, all the elements of winning—attitude, performance, teamwork, and competition—begin to come together.
Dennis Conner

Without a strategy the organization is like a ship without a rudder, going around in circles. It's like a tramp; it has no place to go.
Joel Ross and Michael Kami

In this chapter, we provide a more in-depth look at each of the three strategy-making tasks: developing a strategic vision and business mission, setting performance objectives, and crafting a strategy to produce the desired results. We also examine the kinds of strategic decisions made at each management level, the major determinants of a company's strategy, and four frequently used managerial approaches to forming a strategic plan.

DEVELOPING A STRATEGIC VISION AND MISSION: THE FIRST DIRECTION-SETTING TASK

Management's views about what activities the organization intends to pursue and the long-term course it charts for the future constitute a strategic vision. A *strategic vision* provides a big picture perspective of "who *we* are, what *we* do, and where *we* are headed." It leaves no doubt about the company's long-term direction and where management intends to take the company. A well-conceived strategic vision is a prerequisite to effective strategic leadership. A manager cannot function effectively as either leader or strategy-maker without a sound concept of the business, what activities to pursue, what not to pursue, and what kind of long-term competitive position to build vis-à-vis both customers and competitors.

Although we use the following terms interchangeably, we like *strategic vision* better than the more common term *business mission* or *mission statement*. Missions tend to be more concerned with the present ("What is our business?") than with the bigger issue of long-term direction (where are we headed, what new things do we intend to pursue, what will our business makeup be in 5 to 10 years, what kind of company are we trying to become, and what sort of long-term market position do we aspire to achieve?).

Strategic visions and company mission statements are always highly personalized. Generic statements, applicable to any company or to any industry, have no managerial value. A strategic vision/mission statement sets an organization apart from others in its industry and gives it its own special identity, business emphasis, and path for development. For example, the mission of a globally active New York bank like Citicorp has little in common with that of a locally owned small-town bank even though both are in the banking industry. Compaq Computer is not on the same strategic path as IBM, even though both sell personal computers. General Electric is not on the same long-term strategic course as Whirlpool Corp., even though both are leaders in the major home appliance business; while Whirlpool's business is concentrated in appliances, GE has major business positions in aircraft engines, defense electronics, engineering plastics, electric power generation equipment, factory automation, locomotives, lighting, medical diagnostic imaging, and TV broadcasting (it owns NBC). Similarly, there are important differences between the long-term strategic direction of such fierce business rivals as Intel and Motorola, Philips and Matsushita, Eastman Kodak and Fuji Photo Film Co., Michelin and Bridgestone/Firestone, Procter & Gamble and Unilever, and British Telecom and AT&T. Illustration Capsule 4 describes Delta Airlines' strategic vision.

Sometimes companies mistakenly couch their mission in terms of making a profit. However, profit is more correctly an *objective* and a *result* of what the company does. The desire to make a profit says nothing about the business arena in which profits are to be sought. Missions based on making a profit are incapable of distinguishing one type of profit-seeking enterprise from another-the business and long-term direction of Sears are plainly different from the business and long-term direction of Toyota, even though both endeavor to earn a profit. A company that says its mission is to make a profit begs the question "What will we do to make a profit?" To know anything useful about a company's business mission, we must know management's answer to "make a profit doing what and for whom?"

There are three distinct aspects involved in forming a well-conceived strategic vision and expressing it in a company mission statement:

- Understanding what business a company is really in.
- Communicating the vision and mission in ways that are clear, exciting, and inspiring.
- Deciding when to alter the company's strategic course and change its business mission.

Effective strategy-making begins with a concept of what the organization should and should not do and a vision of where the organization needs to be headed.

Visionless companies are unsure what business position they are trying to stake out.

Illustration Capsule 4   Delta Airlines' Strategic Vision

In late 1993, Ronald W. Allen, Delta's chief executive officer, described the company's vision and business mission in the following way:

. . . we want Delta to be the **Worldwide Airline of Choice**.

Worldwide, because we are and intend to remain an innovative, aggressive, ethical, and successful competitor that offers access to the world at the highest standards of customer service. We will continue to look for opportunities to extend our reach through new routes and creative global alliances.

Airline, because we intend to stay in the business we know best—air transportation and related services. We won't stray from our roots. We believe in the long-term prospects for profitable growth in the airline industry, and we will continue to focus time, attention, and investment on enhancing our place in that business environment.

Of Choice, because we value the loyalty of our customers, employees, and investors. For passengers and shippers, we will continue to provide the best service and value. For our personnel, we will continue to offer an ever more challenging, rewarding, and result-oriented workplace that recognizes and appreciates their contributions. For our shareholders, we will earn a consistent, superior financial return.

Source: *Sky Magazine*, December 1993, p. 10.

Understanding and Defining the Business

Deciding what business an organization is in is neither obvious nor easy. Is IBM in the computer business (a product-oriented definition) or the information and data processing business (a customer service or customer needs type of definition) or the advanced electronics business (a technology-based definition)? Is Coca-Cola in the soft-drink business (in which case its strategic vision can be trained narrowly on the actions of Pepsi, 7UP, Dr Pepper, Canada Dry, and Schweppes)? Or is it in the beverage industry (in which case management must think strategically about positioning Coca-Cola products in a market that includes fruit juices, alcoholic drinks, milk, bottled water, coffee, and tea)? This is not a trivial question for Coca-Cola. Many young adults get their morning caffeine fix by drinking cola instead of coffee; with a beverage industry perspective as opposed to a soft-drink industry perspective, Coca-Cola management is more likely to perceive a long-term growth opportunity in winning youthful coffee drinkers over to its colas.

Arriving at a good business definition usually requires taking three factors into account:[1]

> **A company's business is defined by what needs it is trying to satisfy, by which customer groups it is targeting, and by the technologies it will use and the functions it will perform in serving the target market.**

1. Customer needs, or *what* is being satisfied.
2. Customer groups, or *who* is being satisfied.
3. The technologies used and functions performed—*how* customers' needs are satisfied.

Defining a business in terms of what to satisfy, who to satisfy, and how the organization will go about producing the satisfaction makes a complete definition. It takes all three. Just knowing what products or services a firm provides is never enough. Products or services *per se* are not important to customers; a product or

---

[1]Derek F. Abell, *Defining the Business: The Starting Point of Strategic Planning* (Englewood Cliffs, N.J.: Prentice-Hall, 1980), p. 169.

service becomes a business when it satisfies a need or want. Without the need or want there is no business. Customer groups are relevant because they indicate the market to be served—the geographic domain to be covered and the types of buyers the firm is going after.

Technology and functions performed are important because they indicate *how* the company will satisfy the customers' needs and how much of the industry's production-distribution chain its activities will span. For instance, a firm's business can be *specialized*, concentrated in just one stage of an industry's total production-distribution chain, or *fully integrated*, spanning all parts of the industry chain. Wal-Mart, Home Depot, Toys-R-Us, and The Limited are essentially one-stage firms. Their operations focus on the retail end of the consumer goods business; they don't manufacture the items they sell. Delta Airlines is a one-stage enterprise; it doesn't manufacture the airplanes it flies, and it doesn't operate the airports where it lands. Delta made a conscious decision to limit its business mission to moving travelers from one location to another via commercial jet aircraft. Major international oil companies like Exxon, Mobil, and Chevron, however, are fully integrated. They lease drilling sites, drill wells, pump oil, transport crude oil in their own ships and pipelines to their own refineries, and sell gasoline and other refined products through their own networks of branded distributors and service station outlets. Because of the disparity in functions performed and technology employed, the business of a retailer like Lands' End or Wal-Mart is much narrower and quite different than that of a fully integrated enterprise like Exxon.

Between these two extremes, firms can stake out *partially integrated* positions, participating only in selected stages of the industry. Goodyear, for instance, both manufactures tires and operates a chain of company-owned retail tire stores, but it has not integrated backward into rubber plantations and other tire-making components. General Motors, the world's most integrated manufacturer of cars and trucks, makes between 60 and 70 percent of the parts and components used in assembling GM vehicles. But GM is moving to outsource a greater fraction of its parts and systems components, and it relies totally on a network of independent, franchised dealers to handle sales and service functions.

So one way of distinguishing a firm's business, especially among firms in the same industry, is by looking at which functions it performs in the production-distribution chain and how far its scope of operation extends across all the business activities involved in getting products to end-users.

One good example of a business definition that incorporates all three components—needs served, target market, and functions performed— is Polaroid's business definition during the early 1970s: "perfecting and marketing instant photography to satisfy the needs of more affluent U.S. and West European families for affection, friendship, fond memories, and humor." McDonald's mission is focused on "serving a limited menu of hot, tasty food quickly in a clean, friendly restaurant for a good value" to a broad base of fast-food customers worldwide (McDonald's serves approximately 25 million customers daily at some 13,000 restaurants in over 65 countries). The concepts that McDonald's uses to define its business are a limited menu, good-tasting fast-food products of consistent quality, value pricing, exceptional customer care, convenient locations, and global market coverage.

Trying to identify needs served, target market, and functions performed in a single, snappy sentence is a challenge, and many firms' mission statements fail to illuminate all three bases explicitly. The mission statements of some companies are thus better than others in terms of how they cut to the chase of what the enterprise is really about.

A Broad or Narrow Business Definition? A small Hong Kong printing company that defines its business broadly as "Asian-language communications" gains no practical guidance in making direction-setting decisions. With such a definition the company could pursue limitless courses, many well beyond its scope and capability. To have managerial value, strategic visions, business definitions, and mission statements must be narrow enough to pin down the company's real arena of business interest. Consider the following definitions based on broad-narrow scope:

Broad Definition	Narrow Definition
• Beverages	• Soft drinks
• Footwear	• Athletic footwear
• Furniture	• Wrought iron lawn furniture
• Global mail delivery	• Overnight package delivery
• Travel and tourism	• Ship cruises in the Caribbean

Broad-narrow definitions are relative, of course. Being in "the furniture business" is probably too broad a concept for a company intent on being the largest manufacturer of wrought-iron lawn furniture in North America. On the other hand, "soft drinks" has proved too narrow a scope for a growth-oriented company like Coca-Cola, which, with its beverage-industry perspective, acquired Minute-Maid and Hi-C (to capitalize on growing consumer interest in fruit-juice products) and Taylor Wine Company (using the California Cellars brand to establish a foothold in wines).[2] The U.S. Postal Service operates with a broad definition, providing global mail-delivery services to all types of senders. Federal Express, however, operates with a narrow business definition based on handling overnight package delivery for customers who have unplanned emergencies and tight deadlines.

Diversified companies have broader missions and business definitions than single-business enterprises.

Diversified firms have more sweeping business definitions than do single-business enterprises. Their mission statements typically are phrased narrowly enough to pinpoint their current customer-market-technology arenas but are open-ended and adaptable enough to incorporate expansion into new businesses. Alcan, Canada's leading aluminum company, used broad, inclusive words in expressing its strategic vision and mission:

> Alcan is determined to be the most innovative diversified aluminum company in the world. To achieve this position, Alcan will be one, global, customer-oriented enterprise committed to excellence and lowest cost in its chosen aluminum businesses, with significant resources devoted to building an array of new businesses with superior growth and profit potential.

Thermo Electron Corp., a substantially more diversified enterprise, used simultaneous broad-narrow terms to define its arenas of business interest:

> Thermo Electron Corporation develops, manufactures, and markets environmental, analytical, and test instruments, alternative-energy power plants, low-emission combustion systems, paper- and waste-recycling equipment, and biomedical products. The company also operates power plants and provides services in environmental sciences and analysis, thermal waste treatment, and specialty metals fabrication and processing, as well as research and product

---

[2]Coca-Cola's foray into wines was not viewed as successful enough to warrant continuation; the division was divested about five years after initial acquisition.

development in unconventional imaging, laser technology, and direct-energy conversion.

Times Mirror Corp., also a diversified enterprise, describes its business scope in broad but still fairly explicit terminology:

> Times Mirror is a media and information company principally engaged in newspaper publishing; book, magazine and other publishing; and cable and broadcast television.

John Hancock's mission statement communicates a shift from its long-standing base in insurance to a broader mission in insurance, banking, and diversified financial services:

> At John Hancock, we are determined not just to compete but to advance, building our market share by offering individuals and institutions the broadest possible range of products and services. Apart from insurance, John Hancock encompasses banking products, full brokerage services and institutional investment, to cite only a few of our diversified activities. We believe these new directions constitute the right moves . . . the steps that will drive our growth throughout the remainder of this century.

Mission Statements for Functional Departments   There's also a place for mission statements for key functions (R&D, marketing, finance) and support units (human resources, training, information systems). Every department can benefit from a consensus statement spelling out its contribution to the company mission, its principal role and activities, and the direction it needs to be moving. Functional and departmental managers who think through and debate with subordinates and higher-ups what their unit needs to focus on and do have a clearer view of how to lead the unit. Three examples from actual companies indicate how a functional mission statement puts the spotlight on a unit's organizational *role* and *scope*:

- The mission of the human resources department is to contribute to organizational success by developing effective leaders, creating high-performance teams, and maximizing the potential of individuals.
- The mission of the corporate claims department is to minimize the overall cost of liability, workers compensation, and property damage claims through competitive cost containment techniques and loss prevention and control programs.
- The mission of corporate security is to provide services for the protection of corporate personnel and assets through preventive measures and investigations.

Communicating the Strategic Vision

How to describe the strategic vision, word it in the form of a mission statement, and communicate it down the line to lower-level managers and employees is almost as important as the strategic soundness of the organization's business concept and long-term direction. A vision and mission couched in words that inspire and challenge help build committed effort from employees and serve as powerful motivational tools. Bland language, platitudes, and motherhood-and-apple-pie-style verbiage must be scrupulously avoided—they can be a turn-off rather than a turn-on. Managers

A well-worded mission statement creates enthusiasm for the future course management has charted; the motivational goal in communicating the mission is to pose a challenge that inspires and engages everyone in the organization.

need to communicate the vision in words that arouse a strong sense of organizational purpose, build pride, and induce employee buy-in. People are proud to be associated with a company that has a worthwhile mission and is trying to be the world's best at something competitively significant. Having an exciting mission or cause brings the workforce together, galvanizes people to act, stimulates extra effort, and causes people to live the business instead of just coming to work.[3] In organizations with freshly changed missions, executives need to provide a compelling rationale for the new direction and why things must be done differently. Unless people understand how a company's business environment is changing and why a new direction is needed, a new mission statement does little to win employees' commitment or alter work practices—outcomes that can open up a trust gap and make it harder to move the organization down the chosen path.

The best-worded mission statements are simple and concise; they speak loudly and clearly, generate enthusiasm for the firm's future course, and elicit personal effort and dedication from everyone in the organization. They have to be presented and then repeated over and over as a worthy organizational challenge, one capable of benefiting customers in a valuable and meaningful way—indeed it is crucial that the mission stress the payoff for customers and not the payoff for stockholders. It goes *without saying* that the company intends to profit shareholders from its efforts to provide real value to its customers. A crisp, clear, often-repeated, inspiring strategic vision has the power to turn heads in the intended direction and begin a new organizational march. When this occurs, the first step in organizational direction-setting is successfully completed. Illustration Capsule 5 is a good example of an inspiration-oriented company vision and mission.

When to Change the Mission—Where Entrepreneurship Comes In

A member of Maytag's board of directors summed it up well when commenting on why the company acquired a European appliance-maker and expanded its arena of business into international markets: "Times change, conditions change." The march of new events and altered circumstances make it incumbent on managers to continually reassess their company's position and prospects, always checking for *when* it's time to steer a new course and adjust the mission. The key strategic question here is "What new directions should we be moving in now to get ready for the changes we see coming in our business?"

The entrepreneurial challenge in developing a mission is to recognize when emerging opportunities and threats in the surrounding environment make it desirable to revise the organization's long-term direction.

Repositioning an enterprise in light of emerging developments and changes on the horizon lessens the chances of getting trapped in a stagnant or declining core business or letting attractive new growth opportunities slip away because of inaction. Good entrepreneurs have a sharp eye for shifting customer wants and needs, emerging technological capabilities, changing international trade conditions, and other important signs of growing or shrinking business opportunity. They attend quickly to users' problems and complaints with the industry's current products and services. They listen intently when a customer says, "If only . . ." Such clues and information tidbits stimulate them to think creatively and strategically about ways to break new ground. Appraising new customer-market-technology opportunities ultimately leads to entrepreneurial judgments about which fork in the road to take. It is the strategy-maker's

---

[3]Tom Peters, *Thriving on Chaos* (New York: Harper & Row, Perennial Library Edition, 1988), pp. 486–487; and Andrall E. Pearson, "Corporate Redemption and The Seven Deadly Sins," *Harvard Business Review* 70, no. 3 (May–June 1992), pp. 66–68.

Illustration Capsule 5　NovaCare's Business Mission and Vision

NovaCare is a fast-growing health care company specializing in providing patient rehabilitation services on a contract basis to nursing homes. Rehabilitation therapy is a $10 billion industry, of which 35 percent is provided contractually; the contract segment is highly fragmented with over 1,000 competitors. In 1990 NovaCare was a $100 million company, with a goal of being a $300 million business in 1994. The company stated its business mission and vision as follows:

> NovaCare is people committed to making a difference . . . enhancing the future of all patients . . . breaking new ground in our professions . . . achieving excellence . . . advancing human capability . . . changing the world in which we live.
>
> We lead the way with our enthusiasm, optimism, patience, drive, and commitment.
>
> We work together to enhance the quality of our patients' lives by reshaping lost abilities and teaching new skills. We heighten expectations for the patient and family. We rebuild hope, confidence, self-respect, and a desire to continue.
>
> We apply our clinical expertise to benefit our patients through creative and progressive techniques. Our ethical and performance standards require us to expend every effort to achieve the best possible results.
>
> Our customers are national and local health care providers who share our goal of enhancing the patients' quality of life. In each community, our customers consider us a partner in providing the best possible care. Our reputation is based on our responsiveness, high standards, and effective systems of quality assurance. Our relationship is open and proactive.
>
> We are advocates of our professions and patients through active participation in the professional, regulatory, educational, and research communities at national, state, and local levels.
>
> Our approach to health care fulfills our responsibility to provide investors with a high rate of return through consistent growth and profitability.
>
> Our people are our most valuable asset. We are committed to the personal, professional, and career development of each individual employee. We are proud of what we do and dedicated to our Company. We foster teamwork and create an environment conducive to productive communication among all disciplines.
>
> NovaCare is a company of people in pursuit of this Vision.

Source: Company annual report.

job to evaluate the risks and prospects of alternative paths and make direction-setting decisions to position the enterprise for success in the years ahead. *A well-chosen mission prepares a company for the future.*

Many companies in consumer electronics and telecommunications believe their future products will incorporate microprocessors and other elements of computer technology. So they are broadening their vision about industry boundaries and establishing new business positions through acquisitions, alliances, and joint ventures to gain better access to cutting-edge technology. Cable TV companies and telephone companies are in a strategic race to install fiber optics technology and position themselves to market a whole new array of services—pay-per-view TV, home shopping, electronic mail, electronic banking, home security systems, energy management systems, information services, and high-speed data transfer—to households and businesses. Numerous companies in manufacturing, seeing the collapse of trade barriers and the swing to a world economy, are broadening their strategic vision from serving domestic markets to serving global markets. Coca-Cola, Kentucky Fried Chicken, and McDonald's are pursuing market opportunities in China, Europe, Japan, and Russia. Japanese automobile companies are working to establish a much bigger presence in the European car market. CNN, Turner Broadcasting's very successful all-news cable channel, is fast winning its way into more and more homes the world over, solidifying its position as the first global all-news channel, a major shift from 10 years ago when its mission was to build a loyal U.S. audience. A company's mission has a finite life, one subject to change whenever top management concludes that the present mission is no longer adequate.

A well-conceived, well-worded mission statement has real managerial value: (1) it crystalizes senior executives' own views about the firm's long-term direction and business makeup, (2) it reduces the risk of visionless management and rudderless decision-making, (3) it conveys an organizational purpose and identity that motivate employees to go all out and do their very best work, (4) it provides a beacon lower-level managers can use to form departmental missions, set departmental objectives, and craft functional and departmental strategies that are in sync with the company's direction and strategy, and (5) it helps an organization prepare for the future.

SETTING OBJECTIVES: THE SECOND DIRECTION-SETTING TASK

Objectives represent a managerial commitment to achieving specific performance targets by a certain time.

Setting objectives converts the strategic vision and directional course into target outcomes and performance milestones. Objectives represent a managerial commitment to producing specified results in a specified time frame. They spell out *how much* of *what kind* of performance *by when*. They direct attention and energy to what needs to be accomplished.

The Managerial Value of Setting Objectives

Unless an organization's long-term direction and business mission are translated into *measurable* performance targets and managers are pressured to show progress in reaching these targets, statements about direction and mission will end up as nice words, window dressing, and unrealized dreams of accomplishment. The experiences of countless companies and managers teach that *companies whose managers set objectives for each key result area and then aggressively pursue actions calculated to achieve their performance targets typically outperform companies whose managers have good intentions, try hard, and hope for success.*

For performance objectives to have value as a management tool, they must be stated in *quantifiable* or measurable terms and they must contain a *deadline for achievement.* This means avoiding generalities like "maximize profits," "reduce costs," "become more efficient," or "increase sales," which specify neither how much or when. Objective-setting is a call for action—what to achieve, when to achieve it, and who is responsible. As Bill Hewlett, co-founder of Hewlett-Packard, once observed, "You cannot manage what you cannot measure . . . And what gets measured gets done."[4] Spelling out organization objectives in measurable terms and then holding managers accountable for reaching their assigned targets within a specified time frame (1) substitutes purposeful strategic decision-making for aimless actions and confusion over what to accomplish and (2) provides a set of benchmarks for judging the organization's performance.

---

[4]As quoted in Charles H. House and Raymond L. Price, "The Return Map: Tracking Product Teams," *Harvard Business Review* 60, no. 1 (January–February 1991), p. 93.

What Kinds of Objectives to Set

Objectives are needed for each *key result* managers deem important to success.[5] Two types of key result areas stand out: those relating to *financial performance* and those relating to *strategic performance*. Achieving acceptable financial performance is a must; otherwise the organization's survival ends up at risk. Achieving acceptable strategic performance is essential to sustaining and improving the company's long-term market position and competitiveness. Specific kinds of financial and strategic performance objectives are shown below:

Strategic Management Principle
Every company needs both strategic objectives and financial objectives.

Financial Objectives	Strategic Objectives
• Faster revenue growth	• A bigger market share
• Faster earnings growth	• A higher, more secure industry rank
• Higher dividends	• Higher product quality
• Wider profit margins	• Lower costs relative to key competitors
• Higher returns on invested capital	• Broader or more attractive product line
• Stronger bond and credit ratings	• A stronger reputation with customers
• Bigger cash flows	• Superior customer service
• A rising stock price	• Recognition as a leader in technology and/or product innovation
• Recognition as a "blue chip" company	• Increased ability to compete in international markets
• A more diversified revenue base	• Expanded growth opportunities
• Stable earnings during recessionary periods	• Total customer satisfaction

Illustration Capsule 6 provides a sampling of the strategic and financial objectives of three well-known enterprises.

Strategic Objectives versus Financial Objectives: Which Take Precedence? Both financial and strategic objectives carry top priority. However, sometimes companies under pressure to improve near-term financial performance elect to kill or postpone strategic moves that hold promise for strengthening the enterprise's business and competitive position for the long haul. The pressures on managers to opt for better near-term financial performance and to sacrifice at least some strategic moves aimed at building a stronger competitive position are especially pronounced when (1) an enterprise is struggling financially, (2) the

Strategic objectives need to be competitor-focused, usually aiming at unseating a competitor considered to be the industry's best in a particular category.

---

[5]The literature of management is filled with references to *goals* and *objectives*. These terms are used in a variety of ways, many of them conflicting. Some writers use the term goals to refer to the long-run results an organization seeks to achieve and the term objectives to refer to immediate, short-run performance targets. Some writers reverse the usage, referring to objectives as the desired long-run results and goals as the desired short-run results. Others use the terms interchangeably. And still others use the term goals to refer to broad organizationwide performance targets and the term objectives to designate specific targets set by subordinate managers in response to the broader, more inclusive goals of the whole organization. In our view, little is gained from semantic distinctions between goals and objectives. The important thing is to recognize that the results an enterprise seeks to attain vary both in scope and in time perspective. Nearly always, organizations need to have broad and narrow performance targets for both the near term and long term. It is inconsequential which targets are called goals and which objectives. To avoid a semantic jungle, we use the single term *objectives* to refer to the performance targets and results an organization seeks to attain. We use the adjectives *long-range* (or long-run) and *short-range* (or short-run) to identify the relevant time frame, and we try to describe objectives in words that indicate their intended scope and level in the organization.

Illustration Capsule 6   Examples of Corporate Objectives: McDonald's, Rubbermaid, and McCormick & Company

McDonald's

- To achieve 100 percent total customer satisfaction . . . everyday . . . in every restaurant . . . for every customer.

Rubbermaid

- To increase annual sales from $1 billion to $2 billion in five years.
- To enter a new market every 18 to 24 months.
- To have 30 percent of sales each year come from products not in the company's product line five years earlier.
- To be the lowest cost, highest quality producer in the household products industry.
- To achieve a 15 percent average annual growth in sales, profits, and earnings per share.

McCormick & Company

- To achieve a 20 percent return on equity.
- To achieve a net sales growth rate of 10 percent per year.
- To maintain an average earnings per share growth rate of 15 percent per year.
- To maintain total debt-to-total capital at 40 percent or less.
- To pay out 25 percent to 35 percent of net income in dividends.
- To make selective acquisitions which complement our current businesses and can enhance our overall returns.
- To dispose of those parts of our business which do not or cannot generate adequate returns or do not fit our business strategy.

Source: Company annual reports.

resource commitments for strategically beneficial moves will materially detract from the bottom line for several years, and (3) the proposed strategic moves are risky and have an uncertain market and competitive payoff.

Yet, there are dangers in management's succumbing time and again to the lure of immediate gains in margins and return on investment when it means paring or forgoing strategic moves that would build a stronger business position. A company that consistently passes up opportunities to strengthen its long-term competitive position in order to realize better near-term financial gains risks diluting its competitiveness, losing momentum in its markets, and impairing its ability to stave off market challenges from ambitious rivals. The business landscape is littered with ex-market leaders who put more emphasis on boosting next quarter's profit than strengthening long-term market position. The danger of trading off long-term gains in market position for near-term gains in bottom-line performance is greatest when a profit-conscious market leader has competitors who invest relentlessly in gaining market share in preparation for the time when they will be big and strong enough to outcompete the leader in a head-to-head market battle. One need look no further than Japanese companies' patient and persistent strategic efforts to gain market ground on their more profit-centered American and European rivals to appreciate the pitfall of letting short-term financial objectives dominate. The surest path to protecting and sustaining a company's profitability quarter after quarter and year after year is to pursue strategic actions that strengthen its competitiveness and business position.

Strategic Management Principle
Building a stronger long-term competitive position benefits shareholders more lastingly than improving short-term profitability.

The Concept of Strategic Intent
A company's strategic objectives are important for another reason—they indicate *strategic intent* to stake out a particular business

position.[6] The strategic intent of a large company may be industry leadership on a national or global scale. The strategic intent of a small company may be to dominate a market niche. The strategic intent of an up-and-coming enterprise may be to overtake the market leaders. The strategic intent of a technologically innovative company may be to pioneer a promising discovery and open a whole new vista of products and market opportunities—as did Xerox, Apple Computer, Microsoft, Merck, and Sony.

The time horizon underlying a company's strategic intent is long term. Companies that rise to prominence in their markets almost invariably begin with strategic intents that are out of proportion to their immediate capabilities and market positions. But they set ambitious long-term strategic objectives and then pursue them relentlessly, sometimes even obsessively, over a 10- to 20-year period. In the 1960s, Komatsu, Japan's leading earth-moving equipment company, was less than one-third the size of Caterpillar, had little market presence outside Japan, and depended on its small bulldozers for most of its revenue. Komatsu's strategic intent was to "encircle Caterpillar" with a broader product line and then compete globally against Caterpillar. By the late 1980s, Komatsu was the industry's second-ranking company, with a strong sales presence in North America, Europe, and Asia plus a product line that included industrial robots and semiconductors as well as a broad array of earth-moving equipment.

Often, a company's strategic intent takes on a heroic character, serving as a rallying cry for managers and employees alike to go all out and do their very best. Canon's strategic intent in copying equipment was to "Beat Xerox." Komatsu's motivating battle cry was "Beat Caterpillar." The strategic intent of the U.S. government's Apollo space program was to land a person on the moon ahead of the Soviet Union. Throughout the 1980s, Wal-Mart's strategic intent was to "overtake Sears" as the largest U.S. retailer (a feat accomplished in 1991). In such instances, strategic intent signals a deep-seated commitment to winning—unseating the industry leader, remaining the industry leader (and becoming more dominant in the process), or otherwise beating long odds to gain a significantly stronger business position. A capably managed enterprise whose strategic objectives exceed its present reach and resources can be a more formidable competitor than a company with modest strategic intent.

Long-Range versus Short-Range Objectives   An organization needs both long-range and short-range objectives. Long-range objectives serve two purposes. First, setting performance targets five or more years ahead pushes managers to take actions *now* in order to achieve the targeted long-range performance *later* (a company that has an objective of doubling its sales within five years can't wait until the third or fourth year of its five-year strategic plan to begin growing its sales and customer base!). Second, having explicit long-range objectives prompts managers to weigh the impact of today's decisions on longer-range performance. Without the pressure to make progress in meeting long-range performance targets, it is human nature to base decisions on what is most expedient and worry about the future later. The problem with short-sighted decisions, of course, is that they put a company's long-term business position at greater risk.

> **Basic Concept**
> A company exhibits *strategic intent* when it relentlessly pursues a certain long-term strategic objective and concentrates its strategic actions on achieving that objective.

---

[6]The concept of strategic intent is described in more detail in Gary Hamel and C. K. Pralahad, "Strategic Intent," *Harvard Business Review* 89, no. 3 (May–June 1989), pp. 63–76. This section draws upon their pioneering discussion.

Short-range objectives spell out the immediate and near-term results to be achieved. They indicate the *speed* at which management wants the organization to progress as well as the *level of performance* being aimed for over the next two or three periods. Short-range objectives can be identical to long-range objectives anytime an organization is already performing at the targeted long-term level. For instance, if a company has an ongoing objective of 15 percent profit growth every year and is currently achieving this objective, then the company's long-range and short-range profit objectives coincide. The most important situation where short-range objectives differ from long-range objectives occurs when managers are trying to elevate organizational performance and cannot reach the long-range/ongoing target in just one year. Short-range objectives then serve as stairsteps or milestones.

The "Challenging but Achievable" Test

Company performance targets should be challenging but achievable.

Objectives should not represent whatever levels of achievement management decides would be "nice." Wishful thinking has no place in objective-setting. For objectives to serve as a tool for *stretching* an organization to reach its full potential, they must be *challenging but achievable*. Satisfying this criterion means setting objectives in light of several important "inside-outside" considerations:

- What performance levels will industry and competitive conditions realistically allow?
- What results will it take for the organization to be a successful performer?
- What performance is the organization capable of *when pushed*?

To set challenging but achievable objectives, managers must judge what performance is possible in light of external conditions against what performance the organization is capable of achieving. The tasks of objective-setting and strategy-making often become intertwined at this point. Strategic choices, for example, cannot be made in a financial vacuum; the money has to be there to execute them. Consequently, decisions about strategy are contingent on setting the organization's financial performance objectives high enough to (1) execute the chosen strategy, (2) fund other needed actions, and (3) please investors and the financial community. Objectives and strategy also intertwine when it comes to matching the means (strategy) with the ends (objectives). If a company can't achieve established objectives (because the objectives are set unrealistically high or the present strategy can't deliver the desired performance), the objectives or the strategy need adjustment to produce a better fit.

The Need for Objectives at All Management Levels

For strategic thinking and strategy-driven decision-making to permeate organization behavior, performance targets must be established not only for the organization as a whole but also for each of the organization's separate businesses, product lines, functional areas, and departments.[7] Only when every manager, from the CEO to the lowest-level manager, is held accountable for achieving specific results and when each unit's objectives support achievement of company objectives is the

---

[7]Peter F. Drucker, *Management: Tasks, Responsibilities, Practices* (New York: Harper & Row, 1974), p. 100. See also Charles H. Granger, "The Hierarchy of Objectives," *Harvard Business Review* 42, no. 3 (May–June 1963), pp. 63–74.

objective-setting process complete enough to ensure that the whole organization is headed down the chosen path and that each part of the organization knows what it needs to accomplish.

The objective-setting process is more top-down than bottom-up. To see why strategic objectives at one managerial level tend to drive objectives and strategies at the next level down, consider the following example. Suppose the senior executives of a diversified corporation establish a corporate profit objective of $5 million for next year. Suppose further, after discussion between corporate management and the general managers of the firm's five different businesses, each business is given the challenging but achievable profit objective of $1 million by year-end (i.e., if the five business divisions contribute $1 million each in profit, the corporation can reach its $5 million profit objective). A concrete result has thus been agreed on and translated into measurable action commitments at two levels in the managerial hierarchy. Next, suppose the general manager of business unit X, after some analysis and discussion with functional area managers, concludes that reaching the $1 million profit objective will require selling 100,000 units at an average price of $50 and producing them at an average cost of $40 (a $10 profit margin times 100,000 units equals $1 million profit). Consequently, the general manager and the manufacturing manager settle on a production objective of 100,000 units at a unit cost of $40; and the general manager and the marketing manager agree on a sales objective of 100,000 units and a target selling price of $50. In turn, the marketing manager breaks the sales objective of 100,000 units into unit sales targets for each sales territory, each item in the product line, and each salesperson.

A top-down process of establishing performance targets for strategy-critical activities, business processes, and departmental units is a logical way of breaking down companywide targets into pieces that lower-level units and managers are responsible for achieving. Such an approach also provides a valuable degree of *unity* and *cohesion* to objective-setting and strategy-making in different parts of the organization. Generally speaking, organizationwide objectives and strategy need to be established first so they can *guide* objective-setting and strategy-making at lower levels. Top-down objective-setting and strategizing steer lower-level units toward objectives and strategies that take their cues from those of the total enterprise. When objective-setting and strategy-making begin at the bottom levels of an organization and organizationwide objectives and strategies reflect the aggregate of what has bubbled up from below, the resulting strategic action plan is likely to be inconsistent, fragmented, or uncoordinated. Bottom-up objective-setting, with no guidance from above, nearly always signals an absence of strategic leadership on the part of senior executives.

> **Strategic Management Principle**
> Objective-setting needs to be more of a top-down than a bottom-up process in order to guide lower-level managers and organizational units toward outcomes that support the achievement of overall business and company objectives.

CRAFTING A STRATEGY: THE THIRD DIRECTION-SETTING TASK

Organizations need strategies to guide *how* to achieve objectives and *how* to pursue the organization's mission. Strategy-making is all about *how*—how to reach performance targets, how to outcompete rivals, how to achieve sustainable competitive advantage, how to strengthen the enterprise's long-term business position, how to make management's strategic vision for the company a reality. A strategy is needed for the company as a whole, for each business the company is in, and for each functional piece of each business—R&D, purchasing, production, sales and marketing, finance, human resources, and so on. An organization's overall strategy and managerial game plan emerge from the *pattern* of actions already initiated and the plans managers have for fresh moves. In forming a strategy out of the many feasible options, a manager acts as a forger of responses to market change, a seeker of new opportunities, and a synthesizer of the different moves and approaches taken at various times in various parts of the organization.[8]

The strategy-making spotlight, however, needs to be kept trained on the important facets of management's game plan for running the enterprise—those actions that determine what market position the company is trying to stake out and that underpin whether the company will succeed. Low-priority issues (whether to increase the advertising budget, raise the dividend, locate a new plant in country X or country Y) and routine managerial housekeeping (whether to own or lease company vehicles, how to reduce sales force turnover) are not basic to the strategy, even though they must be dealt with. Strategy is inherently action-oriented; it concerns what to do, when to do it, and who should be involved. Unless there is action, unless something happens, unless somebody does something, strategic thinking and planning simply go to waste and, in the end, amount to nothing.

An organization's strategy evolves over time. It's seldom possible to plan all the bits and pieces of a company's strategy in advance and then go for long periods without change. Reacting and responding to happenings either inside the company or in the surrounding environment is a normal part of the strategy-making process. The dynamic and partly unpredictable character of competition, budding trends in buyer needs and expectations, unplanned increases or decreases in costs, mergers and acquisitions among major industry players, new regulations, the raising or lowering of trade barriers, and countless other events can make parts of the strategy obsolete. There is always something new to react to and some new strategic window opening up. This is why the task of crafting strategy is never ending. And it is why a company's actual strategy turns out to be a blend of its intended or planned strategy and its unplanned reactions to fresh developments.

The Strategy-Making Pyramid

As we emphasized in the opening chapter, strategy-making is not just a task for senior executives. In large enterprises, decisions about what approaches to take and what new moves to initiate involve senior executives in the corporate office, heads of business units and product divisions, the heads of major functional areas within a business or division (manufacturing, marketing and sales, finance, human resources, and the like), plant managers, product managers, district and regional sales managers, and lower-level supervisors. In diversified enterprises, strategies are initiated at four distinct organization levels. There's a strategy for the company and all of its businesses as a whole *(corporate strategy)*. There's a strategy for each separate business the company has diversified into *(business strategy)*. Then there is a strategy for each specific functional unit within a business *(functional strategy)*—each business usually has a production strategy, a marketing strategy, a finance strategy, and so on. And, finally, there are still narrower strategies for basic operating units—plants, sales

---

[8]Henry Mintzberg, "The Strategy Concept II: Another Look at Why Organizations Need Strategies," *California Management Review* 30, no. 1 (Fall 1987), pp. 25–32.

districts and regions, and departments within functional areas *(operating strategy).* Figure 2–1 shows the strategy-making pyramid for a diversified company. In single-business enterprises, there are only three levels of strategy-making (business strategy, functional strategy, and operating strategy) unless diversification into other businesses becomes an active consideration. Table 2–1 highlights the kinds of strategic actions that distinguish each of the four strategy-making levels.

Corporate Strategy

Corporate strategy is the overall managerial game plan for a diversified company. Corporate strategy extends companywide—an umbrella over all a diversified company's businesses. It consists of the moves made to establish business positions in different industries and the approaches used to manage the company's group of businesses. Figure 2–2 depicts the core elements that identify a diversified company's corporate strategy. Crafting corporate strategy for a diversified company involves four kinds of initiatives:

1. *Making the moves to accomplish diversification.* The first concern in diversification is what the company's portfolio of businesses should consist of—specifically, what industries to diversify into, and whether to enter the industries by starting a new business or acquiring another company (an established leader, an up-and-coming company, or a troubled company with turnaround potential). This piece of corporate strategy establishes whether diversification is based narrowly in a few industries or broadly in many industries, and it shapes how the company will be positioned in each of the target industries.

2. *Initiating actions to boost the combined performance of the businesses the firm has diversified into.* As positions are created in the chosen industries, corporate strategy-making concentrates on ways to get better performance out of the business-unit portfolio. Decisions must be reached about how to strengthen the long-term competitive positions and profitabilities of the businesses the firm has invested in. Corporate parents can help their business subsidiaries be more successful by financing additional capacity and efficiency improvements, by supplying missing skills and managerial know-how, by acquiring another company in the same industry and merging the two operations into a stronger business, and/or by acquiring new businesses that strongly complement existing businesses. The overall plan for managing a group of diversified businesses usually involves pursuing rapid-growth strategies in the most promising businesses, keeping the other core businesses healthy, initiating turnaround efforts in weak-performing businesses with potential, and divesting businesses that are no longer attractive or that don't fit into management's long-range plans.

3. *Finding ways to capture the synergy among related business units and turn it into competitive advantage.* When a company diversifies into businesses with related technologies, similar operating characteristics, the same distribution channels, common customers, or some other synergistic relationship, it gains competitive advantage potential not open to a company that diversifies into totally unrelated businesses. Related diversification presents opportunities to transfer skills, share expertise, or share facilities, thereby reducing overall costs, strengthening the competitiveness of some of

Basic Concept
Corporate strategy **concerns how a diversified company intends to establish business positions in different industries and the actions and approaches employed to improve the performance of the group of businesses the company has diversified into.**

Figure 2–1   The Strategy-Making Pyramid

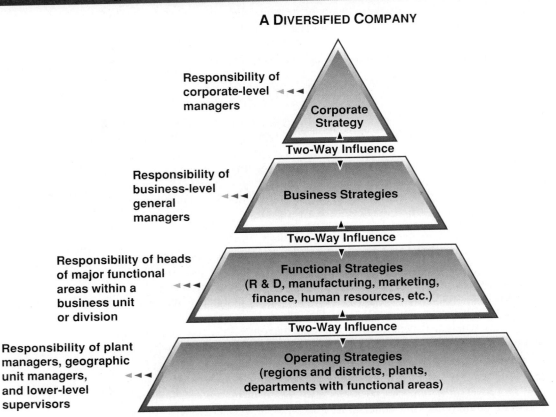

Table 2–1   How the Strategy-Making Task Tends to Be Shared

Strategy Level	Lead Responsibility	Primary Strategy-Making Concerns at Each Managerial Level
• Corporate strategy	• CEO, other key executives (decisions are typically reviewed/ approved by boards of directors)	• Building and managing a high-performing portfolio of business units (making acquisitions, strengthening existing business positions, divesting businesses that no longer fit into management's plans) • Capturing the synergy among related business units and turning it into competitive advantage • Establishing investment priorities and steering corporate resources into businesses with the most attractive opportunities • Reviewing/revising/unifying the major strategic approaches and moves proposed by business-unit managers
• Business strategies	• General manager/head of business unit (decisions are typically reviewed/approved by a senior executive or a board of directors)	• Devising moves and approaches to compete successfully and to secure a competitive advantage • Forming responses to changing external conditions • Uniting the strategic initiatives of key functional departments • Taking action to address company-specific issues and operating problems
• Functional strategies	• Functional managers (decisions are typically reviewed/approved by business-unit head)	• Crafting moves and approaches to support business strategy and to achieve functional/departmental performance objectives • Reviewing/revising/unifying strategy-related moves and approaches proposed by lower-level managers
• Operating strategies	• Field-unit heads/lower-level managers within functional areas (decisions are reviewed/ approved by functional area head/department head)	• Crafting still narrower and more specific approaches/moves aimed at supporting functional and business strategies and at achieving operating-unit objectives

the company's products, or enhancing the capabilities of particular business units—any of which can represent a significant source of competitive advantage. The greater the relatedness among the businesses of a diversified company, the greater the opportunities for skills transfer and/or sharing across businesses and the bigger the window for creating competitive advantage. Indeed, what makes related diversification so attractive is the

Figure 2–2   Identifying the Corporate Strategy of a Diversified Company

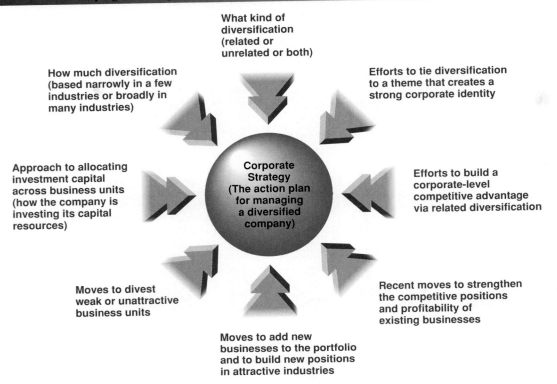

synergistic *strategic fit* across related business units that allows company resources to be leveraged into a combined performance *greater* than the units could achieve operating independently. The 2 + 2 = 5 aspect of strategic fit makes related diversification a very appealing strategy for boosting corporate performance and shareholder value.

4. *Establishing investment priorities and steering corporate resources into the most attractive business units.* A diversified company's different businesses are usually not equally attractive from the standpoint of investing additional funds. This facet of corporate strategy-making involves deciding on the priorities—that is, investing more capital in some of the businesses and channeling resources into areas where earnings potentials are higher and away from areas where they are lower. Corporate strategy may include divesting business units that are chronically poor performers or those in an increasingly unattractive industry. Divestiture frees up unproductive investments for redeployment to promising business units or for financing attractive new acquisitions.

Corporate strategy is crafted at the highest levels of management. Senior corporate executives normally have lead responsibility for devising corporate strategy and for choosing among whatever recommended actions bubble up from lower-level managers. Key business-unit heads may also be influential, especially in strategic decisions affecting the businesses they head. Major strategic decisions are usually reviewed and approved by the company's board of directors.

Business Strategy

The term *business strategy* (or business-level strategy) refers to the managerial game plan for a single business. It is mirrored in the pattern of approaches and moves crafted by management to produce successful performance in *one specific line of business*. The core elements of business strategy are illustrated in Figure 2–3. For a stand-alone single-business company, corporate strategy and business strategy are one and the same since there is only one business to form a strategy for. The distinction between corporate strategy and business strategy is relevant only for diversified firms.

The central thrust of business strategy is how to build and strengthen the company's long-term competitive position in the marketplace. Toward this end, business strategy is concerned principally with (1) forming responses to changes under way in the industry, the economy at large, the regulatory and political arena, and other

Basic Concept
Business strategy **concerns the actions and the approaches crafted by management to produce successful performance in one specific line of business; the central business strategy issue is *how* to build a stronger long-term competitive position.**

Figure 2–3   Identifying Strategy for a Single-Business Company

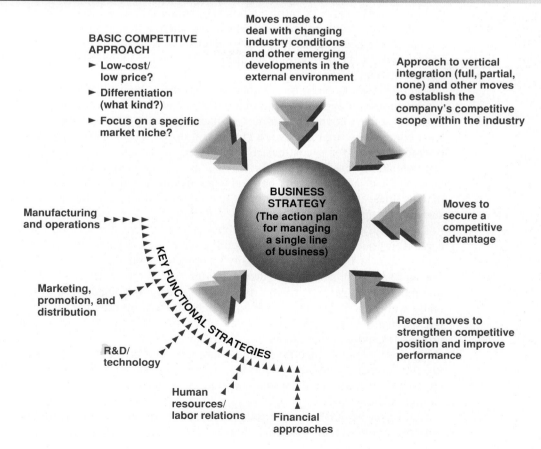

relevant areas, (2) crafting competitive moves and market approaches that can lead to sustainable competitive advantage, (3) uniting the strategic initiatives of functional departments, and (4) addressing specific strategic issues facing the company's business.

Clearly, business strategy encompasses whatever moves and new approaches managers deem prudent in light of market forces, economic trends and developments, buyer needs and demographics, new legislation and regulatory requirements, and other such broad external factors. A good strategy is well-matched to the external situation; as the external environment changes in significant ways, then adjustments in strategy are made on an as-needed basis. Whether a company's response to external change is quick or slow tends to be a function of how long events must unfold before managers can assess their implications and how much longer it then takes to form a strategic response. Some external changes, of course, require little or no response, while others call for significant strategy alterations. On occasion, external factors change in ways that pose a formidable strategic hurdle—for example, cigarette manufacturers face a tough challenge holding their own against the mounting antismoking campaign.

What separates a powerful business strategy from a weak one is the strategist's ability *to forge a series of moves and approaches capable of producing sustainable competitive advantage*. With a competitive advantage, a company has good prospects for above-average profitability and success in the industry. Without competitive advantage, a company risks being outcompeted by stronger rivals and locked into mediocre performance. Crafting a business strategy that yields sustainable competitive advantage has three facets: (1) deciding where a firm has the best chance to win a competitive edge, (2) developing product/service attributes that have strong buyer appeal and set the company apart from rivals, and (3) neutralizing the competitive moves of rival companies.

A company's strategy for competing is typically both offensive and defensive—some actions are aggressive and amount to direct challenges to competitors' market positions; others counter fresh moves made by rivals. Three of the most frequently used competitive approaches are (1) striving to be the industry's low-cost producer (thereby aiming for a cost-based competitive advantage over rivals), (2) pursuing differentiation based on such advantages as quality, performance, service, styling, technological superiority, or unusually good value, and (3) focusing on a narrow market niche and winning a competitive edge by doing a better job than rivals of serving the special needs and tastes of its buyers.

Internally, business strategy involves taking actions to develop the skills and capabilities needed to achieve competitive advantage. Successful business strategies usually aim at building the company's competence in one or more core activities crucial to strategic success and then using the core competence as a basis for winning a competitive edge over rivals. A *core competence* is something a firm does especially well in comparison to rival companies. It thus represents a source of competitive strength. Core competencies can relate to R&D, mastery of a technological process, manufacturing capability, sales and distribution, customer service, or anything else that is a competitively important aspect of creating, producing, or marketing the company's product or service. *A core competence is a basis for competitive advantage because it represents specialized expertise that rivals don't have and cannot readily match.*

On a broader internal front, business strategy must also aim at uniting strategic initiatives in the various functional areas of business (purchasing, production, R&D,

---

A business strategy is powerful if it produces a sizable and sustainable competitive advantage; it is weak if it results in competitive disadvantage.

finance, human resources, sales and marketing, and distribution). Strategic actions are needed in each functional area to *support* the company's competitive approach and overall business strategy. Strategic unity and coordination across the various functional areas add power to the business strategy.

Business strategy also extends to action plans for addressing any special strategy-related issues unique to the company's competitive position and internal situation (such as whether to add new capacity, replace an obsolete plant, increase R&D funding for a promising technology, or reduce burdensome interest expenses). Such custom tailoring of strategy to fit a company's specific situation is one of the reasons why every company in an industry has a different business strategy.

Lead responsibility for business strategy falls in the lap of the manager in charge of the business. Even if the business head does not personally wield a heavy hand in the business strategy-making process, preferring to delegate much of the task to others, he or she is still accountable for the strategy and the results it produces. The business head, as chief strategist for the business, has at least two other responsibilities. The first is seeing that supporting strategies in each of the major functional areas of the business are well-conceived and consistent with each other. The second is getting major strategic moves approved by higher authority (the board of directors and/or corporate-level officers) if needed and keeping them informed of important new developments, deviations from plan, and potential strategy revisions. In diversified companies, business-unit heads may have the additional obligation of making sure business-level objectives and strategy conform to corporate-level objectives and strategy themes.

Functional Strategy

The term *functional strategy* refers to the managerial game plan for a particular department or key functional activity within a business. A company's marketing strategy, for example, represents the managerial game plan for running the marketing part of the business. A company needs a functional strategy for every major departmental unit and piece of the business—for R&D, production, marketing, customer service, distribution, finance, human resources, and so on. Functional strategies, while narrower in scope than business strategy, add relevant detail to the overall business game plan by setting out the actions, approaches, and practices to be employed in managing a particular department or business function. The primary role of a functional strategy is to *support* the company's overall business strategy and competitive approach. A related role is to create a managerial roadmap for achieving the functional area's objectives and mission. Thus, functional strategy in the production/manufacturing area represents the game plan for *how* manufacturing activities will be managed to support business strategy and achieve the manufacturing department's objectives and mission. Functional strategy in the finance area consists of *how* financial activities will be managed in supporting business strategy and achieving the finance department's objectives and mission.

Lead responsibility for strategy-making in the functional areas of a business is normally delegated to the respective functional department heads unless the business-unit head decides to exert a strong influence. In crafting strategy, a functional department head ideally works closely with key subordinates and touches base with the heads of other functional areas and the business head often. If functional heads plot strategy independent of each other or the business head they open the door for uncoordinated or conflicting strategies. Compatible, mutually reinforcing functional

Basic Concept
Functional strategy **concerns the managerial game plan for running a major functional activity within a business— R&D, production, marketing, customer service, distribution, finance, human resources, and so on; a business needs as many functional strategies as it has major activities.**

strategies are essential for the overall business strategy to have maximum impact. Plainly, a business's marketing strategy, production strategy, finance strategy, and human resources strategy should be in sync rather than serving their own narrower purposes. Coordination across functional area strategies is best accomplished during the deliberation stage. If inconsistent functional strategies are sent up the line for final approval, the business head must spot the conflicts and get them resolved.

Operating Strategy

Operating strategies concern the even narrower strategic initiatives and approaches for managing key operating units (plants, sales districts, distribution centers) and for handling daily operating tasks with strategic significance (advertising campaigns, materials purchasing, inventory control, maintenance, shipping). Operating strategies, while of lesser scope, add further detail and completeness to functional strategies and to the overall business plan. Lead responsibility for operating strategies is usually delegated to front-line managers, subject to review and approval by higher-ranking managers.

Even though operating strategy is at the bottom of the strategy-making pyramid, its importance should not be downplayed. For example, a major plant that fails in its strategy to achieve production volume, unit cost, and quality targets can undercut the achievement of company sales and profit objectives and wreak havoc with the whole company's strategic efforts to build a quality image with customers. One cannot reliably judge the importance of a given strategic move by the organizational or managerial level where it is initiated.

Frontline managers are part of an organization's strategy-making team because many operating units have strategy-critical performance targets and need to have strategic action plans in place to achieve them. A regional manager needs a strategy customized to the region's particular situation and objectives. A plant manager needs a strategy for accomplishing the plant's objectives, carrying out the plant's part of the company's overall manufacturing game plan, and dealing with any strategy-related problems that exist at the plant. A company's advertising manager needs a strategy for getting maximum audience exposure and sales impact from the ad budget. The following two examples illustrate how operating strategy supports higher-level strategies:

- A company with a low-price, high-volume business strategy and a need to achieve low manufacturing costs launches a companywide effort to boost worker productivity by 10 percent. To contribute to the productivity-boosting objective: (1) the manager of employee recruiting develops a strategy for interviewing and testing job applicants that is thorough enough to weed out all but the most highly motivated, best-qualified candidates; (2) the manager of information systems devises a way to use office technology to boost the productivity of office workers; (3) the employee benefits manager devises an improved incentive-compensation plan to reward increased output by manufacturing employees; and (4) the purchasing manager launches a program to obtain new efficiency-increasing tools and equipment in quicker, less costly fashion.

- A distributor of plumbing equipment emphasizes quick delivery and accurate order-filling as keystones of its customer service approach. To support this strategy, the warehouse manager (1) develops an inventory stocking strategy that allows 99 percent of all orders to be completely filled

Basic Concept
Operating strategies concern how to manage key organizational units within a business (plants, sales districts, distribution centers) and how to perform strategically significant operating tasks (materials purchasing, inventory control, maintenance, shipping, advertising campaigns).

without back ordering any item and (2) institutes a warehouse staffing strategy that allows any order to be shipped within 24 hours.

Uniting the Strategy-Making Effort

The previous discussion underscores that *a company's strategic plan is a collection of strategies* devised by different managers at different levels in the organizational hierarchy. The larger the enterprise, the more points of strategic initiative it has. Management's direction-setting effort is not complete until the separate layers of strategy are unified into a coherent, supportive pattern. Ideally the pieces and layers of strategy should fit together like the pieces of a picture puzzle. Unified objectives and strategies don't emerge from an undirected process where managers at each level set objectives and craft strategies independently. Indeed, functional and operating-level managers have a duty to set performance targets and invent strategic actions that will help achieve business objectives and make business strategy more effective.

> **Objectives and strategies that are unified from an organization's top-management levels to its bottom-management levels do not come from an undirected process where managers at each level have objective-setting and strategy-making autonomy.**

Harmonizing objectives and strategies piece by piece and level by level can be tedious and frustrating, requiring numerous consultations and meetings, annual strategy review and approval processes, the experience of trial and error, and months (sometimes years) of consensus building. The politics of gaining strategic consensus and the battle of trying to keep all managers and departments focused on what's best for the total enterprise (as opposed to what's best for their departments or careers) are often big obstacles in unifying the layers of objectives and strategies.[9] Broad consensus is particularly difficult when there is ample room for opposing views and disagreement. Managerial discussions about an organization's mission, basic direction, objectives and strategies often provoke heated debate and strong differences of opinion.

Figure 2–4 portrays the networking of objectives and strategies through the managerial hierarchy. The two-way arrows indicate that there are simultaneous bottom-up and top-down influences on missions, objectives, and strategies at each level. These vertical linkages, if managed in a way that promotes coordination, can help unify the direction-setting and strategy-making activities of many managers into a mutually reinforcing pattern. The tighter that coordination is enforced, the tighter the linkages in the missions, objectives, and strategies of the various organizational units. Tight linkages safeguard against organizational units straying from the company's charted strategic course.

> **Consistency between business strategy and functional/operating strategies comes from organizationwide allegiance to business objectives; functional and operating-level managers have a duty to set performance targets and invent strategic actions that will help achieve business objectives and improve the execution of business strategy.**

As a practical matter, however, corporate and business missions, objectives, and strategies need to be clearly outlined and communicated down the line before much progress can be made in direction-setting and strategy-making at the functional and operating levels. Direction and guidance need to flow from the corporate level to the business level and from the business level to the functional and operating levels. The strategic disarray that occurs in an organization when senior managers don't exercise strong top-down direction-setting and strategic leadership is akin to what would

---

[9]Functional managers are sometimes more interested in doing what is best for their own areas, building their own empires, and consolidating their personal power and organizational influence than they are in cooperating with other functional managers to unify behind the overall business strategy. As a result, it's easy for functional area support strategies to conflict, thereby forcing the business-level general manager to spend time and energy refereeing functional strategy conflicts and building support for a more unified approach.

Figure 2–4   The Networking of Missions, Objectives, and Strategies in the Strategy–Making Pyramid

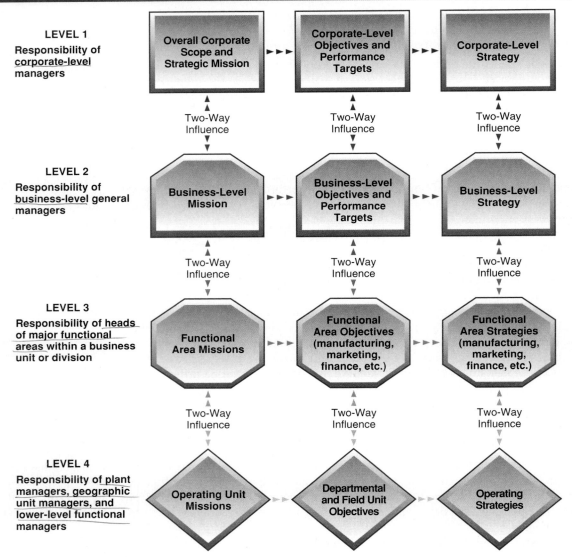

happen to a football team's offensive performance if the quarterback decided not to call a play for the team, but instead let each player pick whatever play he thought would work best at his respective position. In business, as in sports, all the strategy-makers in a company are on the same team. They are obligated to perform their strategy-making tasks in a manner that benefits the whole company, not in a manner that suits personal or departmental interests. A company's strategy is at full power only when its many pieces are united. This means that the strategizing process proceeds more from the top down than from the bottom up. Lower-level managers cannot do good strategy-making without understanding the company's long-term direction and higher-level strategies.

THE FACTORS THAT SHAPE A COMPANY'S STRATEGY ———

Many situational considerations enter into crafting strategy. Figure 2–5 depicts the primary factors that shape a company's strategic approaches. The interplay of these factors and the influence that each has on the strategy-making process vary from company to company. No two strategic choices are made in exactly the same context; even in the same industry situational factors differ enough from company to company that each company ends up pursuing a customized strategy. This is why carefully sizing up all the various situational factors, both external and internal, is the starting point in crafting strategy.

Societal, Political, Regulatory, and Citizenship Considerations

What an enterprise can and cannot do strategywise is always constrained by what is legal, by what complies with government policies and regulatory requirements, by what is socially acceptable, and by what constitutes community citizenship.

Figure 2–5   Factors Shaping the Choice of Company Strategy

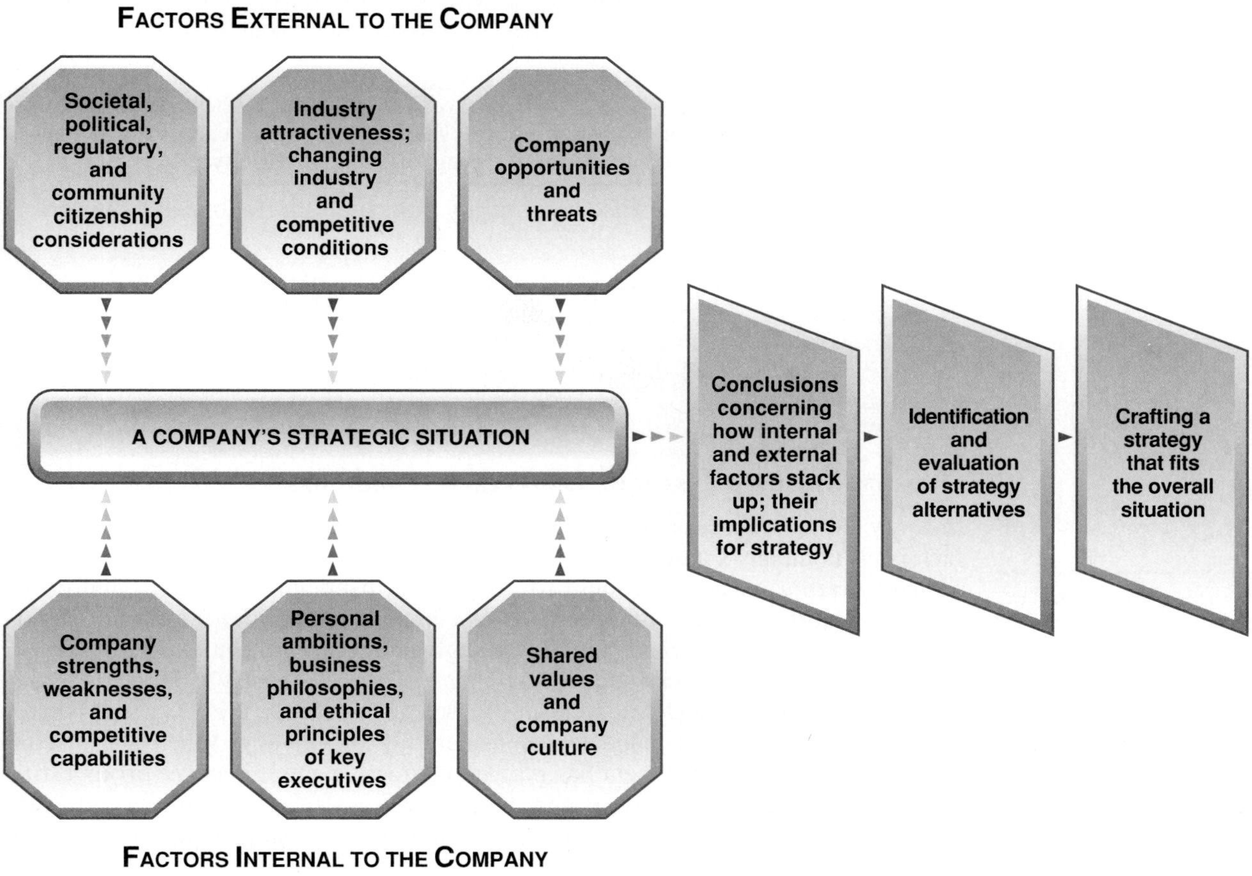

FACTORS EXTERNAL TO THE COMPANY

Societal, political, regulatory, and community citizenship considerations

Industry attractiveness; changing industry and competitive conditions

Company opportunities and threats

A COMPANY'S STRATEGIC SITUATION

Conclusions concerning how internal and external factors stack up; their implications for strategy

Identification and evaluation of strategy alternatives

Crafting a strategy that fits the overall situation

Company strengths, weaknesses, and competitive capabilities

Personal ambitions, business philosophies, and ethical principles of key executives

Shared values and company culture

FACTORS INTERNAL TO THE COMPANY

Societal, political, regulatory, and citizenship factors limit the strategic actions a company can or should take.

Outside pressures also come from other sources—special interest groups, the glare of investigative reporting, a fear of unwanted political action, and the stigma of negative opinion. Societal concerns over health and nutrition, alcohol and drug abuse, hazardous waste disposal, sexual harassment, and the impact of plant closings on local communities affect the strategies of many companies. American concerns over the size of foreign imports and political debate over whether to impose tariffs to cure the chronic U.S. trade deficit are driving forces in the strategic decisions of Japanese and European companies to locate plants in the United States. Heightened awareness of the dangers of cholesterol have prompted most food products companies to phase out high-fat ingredients and substitute low-fat ingredients, despite the extra costs.

Factoring in societal values and priorities, community concerns, and the potential for onerous legislation and regulatory requirements is a regular part of external situation analysis at more and more companies. Intense public pressure and adverse media coverage make such a practice prudent. The task of making an organization's strategy socially responsible means (1) conducting organizational activities within the bounds of what is considered ethical and in the general public interest; (2) responding positively to emerging societal priorities and expectations; (3) demonstrating a willingness to take action ahead of regulatory confrontation; (4) balancing stockholder interests against the larger interests of society as a whole; and (5) being a good citizen in the community.

Corporate social responsibility is showing up in company mission statements. John Hancock, for example, concludes its mission statement with the following sentence:

> In pursuit of this mission, we will strive to exemplify the highest standards of business ethics and personal integrity; and shall recognize our corporate obligation to the social and economic well-being of our community.

At Union Electric, a St. Louis–based utility company, the following statement is official corporate policy:

> As a private enterprise entrusted with an essential public service, we recognize our civic responsibility in the communities we serve. We shall strive to advance the growth and welfare of these communities and shall participate in civic activities which fulfill that goal—for we believe this is both good citizenship and good business.

Industry Attractiveness and Competitive Conditions

Strategic Management Principle
A company's strategy ought to be closely matched to industry and competitive conditions.

Industry attractiveness and competitive conditions are big strategy-determining factors. A company's assessment of the industry and competitive environment has a direct bearing on how it should try to position itself in the industry and on its basic competitive strategy approach. When competitive conditions intensify significantly, a company must respond with strategic actions to protect its position. Fresh moves on the part of rival companies, changes in the industry's price-cost-profit economics, and new technological developments can alter the requirements for competitive success and mandate reconsideration of strategy. When a firm concludes its industry environment has grown unattractive and it is better off investing company resources elsewhere, it may begin a strategy of disinvestment and eventual abandonment. A strategist, therefore, has to be a student of industry and competitive conditions.

Specific Market Opportunities and Threats

The particular business opportunities open to a company and the threatening external developments that it faces are key influences on strategy. They both point to the need for strategic action. A company's strategy needs to be deliberately aimed at capturing its best growth opportunities, especially the ones that hold the most promise for building sustainable competitive advantage and enhancing profitability. Likewise, strategy should be geared to providing a defense against external threats to the company's well-being and future performance. For strategy to be successful, it has to be well-matched to market opportunities and threatening external developments; this usually means crafting offensive moves to capitalize on the company's most promising market opportunities and crafting defensive moves to protect the company's competitive position and long-term profitability.

Strategic Management Principle
A well-conceived strategy aims at capturing a company's best growth opportunities and defending against external threats to its well-being and future performance.

Organizational Strengths, Weaknesses, and Competitive Capabilities

Experience shows management should build strategy around what the company does well and avoid strategies whose success depends on something the company does poorly or has never done at all. In short, *strategy must be well-matched to company strengths, weaknesses, and competitive capabilities*. Pursuing an opportunity without the organizational competencies and resources to capture it is foolish. An organization's strengths make some opportunities and strategies attractive; likewise its internal weaknesses and its present competitive market position make certain strategies risky or even out of the question.

One of the most pivotal strategy-shaping internal considerations is whether a company has or can build the core strengths or competencies needed to execute a strategy proficiently. An organization's core strengths—the things it does especially well—are an important strategy-making consideration because of (1) the skills and capabilities they provide in capitalizing on a particular opportunity, (2) the competitive edge they may give a firm in the marketplace, and (3) the potential they have for becoming a cornerstone of strategy. The best path to competitive advantage is found where a firm has core strengths in one or more of the key requirements for market success, where rivals do not have matching or offsetting competencies, and where rivals can't develop comparable strengths except at high cost and/or over an extended period of time.[10]

Even if an organization has no outstanding core competencies (and many do not), it still must shape its strategy to suit its particular skills and available resources. It never makes sense to develop a strategic plan that cannot be executed with the skills and resources a firm is able to muster.

Strategic Management Principle
A company's strategy ought to be grounded in what it is good at doing (i.e., its organizational strengths and competitive capabilities); it is perilous for success to depend on what it is not so good at doing (i.e., its organizational and competitive weaknesses).

The Personal Ambitions, Business Philosophies, and Ethical Beliefs of Managers

Managers do not dispassionately assess what strategic course to steer. Their choices are often influenced by their own vision of how to compete and how to position the enterprise and by what image and standing they want the company to have. Both casual observation and formal studies indicate that managers' ambitions, values, business philosophies, attitudes toward risk, and ethical beliefs have important

---

[10]David T. Kollat, Roger D. Blackwell, and James F. Robeson, *Strategic Marketing* (New York: Holt, Rinehart & Winston, 1972), p. 24.

The personal ambitions, business philosophies, and ethical beliefs of managers are usually stamped on the strategies they craft.

influences on strategy.[11] Sometimes the influence of a manager's personal values, experiences, and emotions is conscious and deliberate; at other times it may be unconscious. As one expert noted in explaining the relevance of personal factors to strategy, "People have to have their hearts in it."[12]

Several examples of how business philosophies and personal values enter into strategy-making are particularly noteworthy. Japanese managers are strong proponents of strategies that take a long-term view and that aim at building market share and competitive position. In contrast, some U.S. corporate executives and Wall Street financiers draw criticism for overemphasizing short-term profits at the expense of long-term competitive positioning and for being more attracted to strategies involving a financial play on assets (leveraged buyouts and stock buybacks) rather than using corporate resources to make long-term strategic investments. Japanese companies also display a quite different philosophy regarding the role of suppliers. Their preferred supplier strategy is to enter into long-term partnership arrangements with key suppliers because they believe that working closely with the same supplier year after year improves the quality and reliability of component parts, permits just-in-time delivery, and reduces inventory carrying costs. In U.S. and European companies, the traditional strategic approach has been to play suppliers off against one another, doing business on a short-term basis with whoever offers the best price and promises acceptable quality.

Attitudes toward risk also have a big influence on strategy. Risk-avoiders are inclined toward "conservative" strategies that minimize downside risk, have a quick payback, and produce sure short-term profits. Risk-takers lean more toward opportunistic strategies where visionary moves can produce a big payoff over the long term. Risk-takers prefer innovation to imitation and bold strategic offensives to defensive moves to protect the status quo.

Managerial values also shape the ethical quality of a firm's strategy. Managers with strong ethical convictions take pains to see that their companies observe a strict code of ethics in all aspects of the business. They expressly forbid such practices as accepting or giving kickbacks, badmouthing rivals' products, and buying political influence with political contributions. Instances where a company's strategic actions run afoul of high ethical standards include charging excessive interest rates on credit card balances, employing bait-and-switch sales tactics, continuing to market products suspected of having safety problems, and using ingredients that are known health hazards.

The Influence of Shared Values and Company Culture on Strategy

An organization's policies, practices, traditions, philosophical beliefs, and ways of doing things combine to give it a distinctive culture. A company's strategic actions typically reflect its cultural traits and managerial values. In some cases a company's core beliefs and culture even dominate the choice of strategic moves. This is because culture-related values and beliefs become so embedded in management's strategic

---

[11]See, for instance, William D. Guth and Renato Tagiuri, "Personal Values and Corporate Strategy," *Harvard Business Review* 43, no. 5 (September–October 1965), pp. 123–32; Kenneth R. Andrews, *The Concept of Corporate Strategy*, 3rd ed. (Homewood, Ill.: Richard D. Irwin, 1987), chap. 4; and Richard F. Vancil, "Strategy Formulation in Complex Organizations," *Sloan Management Review* 17, no. 2 (Winter 1986), pp. 4–5.

[12]Andrews, *The Concept of Corporate Strategy*, p. 63.

thinking and actions that they condition how the enterprise responds to external events. Such firms have a culture-driven bias about how to handle strategic issues and what kinds of strategic moves it will consider or reject. Strong cultural influences partly account for why companies gain reputations for such strategic traits as technological leadership, product innovation, dedication to superior craftsmanship, a proclivity for financial wheeling and dealing, a desire to grow rapidly by acquiring other companies, a strong people-orientation, or unusual emphasis on customer service and total customer satisfaction.

In recent years, more companies began to articulate the core beliefs and values underlying their business approaches. One company expressed its core beliefs and values like this:

> We are market-driven. We believe that functional excellence, combined with teamwork across functions and profit centers, is essential to achieving superb execution. We believe that people are central to everything we will accomplish. We believe that honesty, integrity, and fairness should be the cornerstone of our relationships with consumers, customers, suppliers, stockholders, and employees.

Wal-Mart's founder, Sam Walton, was a fervent believer in frugality, hard work, constant improvement, dedication to customers, and genuine care for employees. The company's commitment to these values is deeply ingrained in its strategy of low prices, good values, friendly service, productivity through the intelligent use of technology, and hard-nosed bargaining with suppliers.[13] At Hewlett-Packard, the company's basic values, known internally as "the HP Way," include sharing the company's success with employees, showing trust and respect for employees, providing customers with products and services of the greatest value, being genuinely interested in providing customers with effective solutions to their problems, making profit a high stockholder priority, avoiding the use of long-term debt to finance growth, individual initiative and creativity, teamwork, and being a good corporate citizen.[14] At both Wal-Mart and Hewlett-Packard, the value systems are deeply ingrained and widely shared by managers and employees. Whenever this happens, values and beliefs are more than an expression of nice platitudes; they become a way of life within the company.[15]

> A company's values and culture can dominate the kinds of strategic moves it considers or rejects.

LINKING STRATEGY WITH ETHICS

Strategy ought to be ethical. It should involve rightful actions, not wrongful ones; otherwise it won't pass the test of moral scrutiny. This means more than conforming to what is legal. Ethical and moral standards go beyond the prohibitions of law and the language of "thou shalt not" to the issues of *duty* and the language of "should do and should not do." Ethics concerns human duty and the principles on which this duty rests.[16]

> Every strategic action a company takes should be ethical.

[13]Sam Walton with John Huey, *Sam Walton: Made in America* (New York: Doubleday, 1992); and John P. Kotter and James L. Heskett, *Corporate Culture and Performance* (New York: Free Press, 1992), pp. 17 and 36.

[14]Kotter and Heskett, *Corporate Culture and Performance*, pp. 60–61.

[15]For another example of the impact of values and beliefs, see Richard T. Pascale, "Perspectives on Strategy: The Real Story behind Honda's Success," in Glenn Carroll and David Vogel, *Strategy and Organization: A West Coast Perspective* (Marshfield, Mass.: Pitman Publishing, 1984), p. 60.

[16]Harry Downs, "Business Ethics: The Stewardship of Power," working paper provided to the authors.

Every business has an ethical duty to each of five constituencies: owners/shareholders, employees, customers, suppliers, and the community at large. Each of these constituencies affects the organization and is affected by it. Each is a stakeholder in the enterprise, with certain expectations as to what the enterprise should do and how it should do it.[17] Owners/shareholders, for instance, rightly expect a return on their investment. Even though investors may individually differ in their preferences for profits now versus profits later, their tolerances for greater risk, and their enthusiasm for exercising social responsibility, business executives have a moral duty to pursue profitable management of the owners' investment.

> **A company has ethical duties to owners, employees, customers, suppliers, the communities where it operates, and the public at large.**

A company's duty to employees arises out of respect for the worth and dignity of individuals who devote their energies to the business and who depend on the business for their economic well-being. Principled strategy-making requires that employee-related decisions be made equitably and compassionately, with concern for due process and for the impact that strategic change has on employees' lives. At best, the chosen strategy should promote employee interests as concerns wage and salary levels, career opportunities, job security, and overall working conditions. At worst, the chosen strategy should not disadvantage employees. Even in crisis situations where adverse employee impact cannot be avoided, businesses have an ethical duty to minimize whatever hardships have to be imposed in the form of workforce reductions, plant closings, job transfers, relocations, retraining, and loss of income.

The duty to the customer arises out of expectations that attend the purchase of a good or service. Inadequate appreciation of this duty led to product liability laws and a host of regulatory agencies to protect consumers. All kinds of strategy-related ethical issues still arise here, however. Should a seller inform consumers about the contents of its product, especially if it contains ingredients that, though officially approved for use, are suspected of having potentially harmful effects? Is it ethical for the makers of alcoholic beverages to sponsor college events, given that many college students are under 21? Is it ethical for cigarette manufacturers to advertise at all (even though it is legal)? Is it ethical for manufacturers to produce and sell products they know have faulty parts or defective designs that may not become apparent until after the warranty expires?

A company's ethical duty to its suppliers arises out of the market relationship that exists between them. They are both partners and adversaries. They are partners in the sense that the quality of suppliers' parts affects the quality of a firm's own product. They are adversaries in the sense that the supplier wants the highest price and profit it can get while the buyer wants a cheaper price, better quality, and speedier service. A company confronts several ethical issues in its supplier relationships. Is it ethical to threaten to cease doing business with a supplier unless the supplier agrees not to do business with key competitors? Is it ethical to reveal one supplier's price quote to a rival supplier? Is it ethical to accept gifts from suppliers? Is it ethical to pay a supplier in cash?

A company's ethical duty to the community at large stems from its status as a citizen of the community and as an institution of society. Communities and society are reasonable in expecting businesses to be good citizens—to pay their fair share of taxes for fire and police protection, waste removal, streets and

---

[17]Ibid.

highways, and so on, and to exercise care in the impact their activities have on the environment and on the communities in which they operate. The community and public interest should be accorded the same recognition and attention as the other four constituencies. Whether a company is a good community citizen is ultimately demonstrated by the way it supports community activities, encourages employees to participate in community activities, handles the health and safety aspects of its operations, accepts responsibility for overcoming environmental pollution, relates to regulatory bodies and employee unions, and exhibits high ethical standards.

Carrying Out Ethical Responsibilities   Management, not constituent groups, is responsible for managing the enterprise. Thus, it is management's perceptions of its ethical duties and of constituents' claims that drive whether and how strategy is linked to ethical behavior. Ideally, managers weigh strategic decisions from each constituent's point of view and, where conflicts arise, strike a rational, objective, and equitable balance among the interests of all five constituencies. If any of the five constituencies conclude that management is not doing its duty, they have their own avenues for recourse. Concerned investors can act through the annual share-holders' meeting, by appealing to the board of directors, or by selling their stock. Concerned employees can unionize and bargain collectively, or they can seek employment elsewhere. Customers can switch to competitors. Suppliers can find other buyers or pursue other market alternatives. The community and society can do anything from staging protest marches to stimulating political and governmental action.[18]

   A management that truly cares about business ethics and corporate social responsibility is proactive rather than reactive in linking strategic action and ethics. It steers away from ethically or morally questionable business opportunities. It won't do business with suppliers that engage in activities the company does not condone. It produces products that are safe for its customers to use. It operates a workplace environment that is safe for employees. It recruits and hires employees whose values and behavior match the company's principles and ethical standards. It acts to reduce any environmental pollution it causes. It cares about how it does business and whether its actions reflect integrity and high ethical standards. Illustration Capsule 7 describes Harris Corporation's ethical commitments to its stakeholders.

Tests of a Winning Strategy

What are the criteria for weeding out candidate strategies? How can a manager judge which strategic option is best for the company? What are the standards for determining whether a strategy is successful or not? Three tests can be used to evaluate the merits of one strategy over another and to gauge how good a strategy is:

The Goodness of Fit Test   A good strategy is well-matched to the company's internal and external situation—without situational fit, a strategy's appropriateness is suspect.

---

[18]Ibid.

Illustration Capsule 7   Harris Corporation's Commitments to Its Stakeholders

Harris Corporation is a major supplier of information, communication, and semiconductor products, systems, and services to commercial and governmental customers throughout the world. The company utilizes advanced technologies to provide innovative and cost-effective solutions for processing and communicating data, voice, text, and video information. The company's sales exceed $2 billion, and it employs nearly 23,000 people. In a recent annual report, the company set forth its commitment to satisfying the expectations of its stakeholders:

Customers—For customers, our objective is to achieve ever-increasing levels of satisfaction by providing quality products and services with distinctive benefits on a timely and continuing basis worldwide. Our relationships with customers will be forthright and ethical, and will be conducted in a manner to build trust and confidence.

Shareholders—For shareholders, the owners of our company, our objective is to achieve sustained growth in earnings-per-share. The resulting stock-price appreciation combined with dividends should provide our shareholders with a total return on investment that is competitive with similar investment opportunities.

Employees—The people of Harris are our company's most valuable asset, and our objective

is for every employee to be personally involved in and share the success of the business. The company is committed to providing an environment which encourages all employees to make full use of their creativity and unique talents; to providing equitable compensation, good working conditions, and the opportunity for personal development and growth which is limited only by individual ability and desire.

Suppliers—Suppliers are a vital part of our resources. Our objective is to develop and maintain mutually beneficial partnerships with suppliers who share our commitment to achieving increasing levels of customer satisfaction through continuing improvements in quality, service, timeliness, and cost. Our relationships with suppliers will be sincere, ethical, and will embrace the highest principles of purchasing practice.

Communities—Our objective is to be a responsible corporate citizen. This includes support of appropriate civic, educational, and business activities, respect for the environment, and the encouragement of Harris employees to practice good citizenship and support community programs. Our greatest contribution to our communities is to be successful so that we can maintain stable employment and create new jobs.

Source: 1988 Annual Report.

The Competitive Advantage Test   A good strategy leads to sustainable competitive advantage. The bigger the competitive edge that a strategy helps build, the more powerful and effective it is.

The Performance Test   A good strategy boosts company performance. Two kinds of performance improvements are the most telling: gains in profitability and gains in the company's long-term business strength and competitive position.

Strategic Management Principle
A strategy is not a true winner unless it fits the enterprise's situation, builds sustainable competitive advantage, and improves company performance.

Strategic options judged to have low potential on one or more of these criteria are candidates to be dropped from further consideration. The strategic option judged to have the highest potential on all three counts can be regarded as the best or most attractive strategic alternative. Once a strategic commitment is made and enough time elapses to see results, these same tests can be used to assess how well a company's current strategy is performing. The bigger the margins by which a strategy satisfies all three criteria when put to test in the marketplace, the more it qualifies as a winning strategy.

There are, of course, some additional criteria for judging the merits of a particular strategy: clarity, internal consistency among all the pieces of strategy, timeliness, match to the personal values and ambitions of key executives, the degree of risk involved, and flexibility. Whenever appropriate, these can be used to supplement the three tests posed above.

APPROACHES TO PERFORMING THE STRATEGY-MAKING TASK

Companies and managers perform the strategy-making task differently. In small, owner-managed companies strategy-making is developed informally. Often the strategy is never reduced to writing but exists mainly in the entrepreneur's own mind and in oral understandings with key subordinates. Large companies, however, tend to develop their plans via an annual strategic planning cycle (complete with prescribed procedures, forms, and timetables) that includes broad management participation, lots of studies, and multiple meetings to probe and question. The larger and more diverse an enterprise, the more managers feel it is better to have a structured annual process with written plans, management scrutiny, and official approval at each level.

Along with variations in the organizational process of formulating strategy are variations in how managers personally participate in analyzing the company's situation and deliberating what strategy to pursue. The four basic strategy-making styles managers use are:[19]

The Master Strategist Approach

Here the manager functions as chief strategist and chief entrepreneur, exercising *strong* influence over assessments of the situation, over the strategy alternatives that are explored, and over the details of strategy. This does not mean that the manager personally does all the work; it means that the manager personally becomes the chief architect of strategy and wields a proactive hand in shaping some or all of the major pieces of strategy. The manager acts as strategy commander and has a big ownership stake in the chosen strategy.

The Delegate-It-to-Others Approach

Here the manager in charge delegates the exercise of strategy-making to others, perhaps a strategic planning staff or a task force of trusted subordinates. The manager then personally stays off to the side, keeps in touch with how things are progressing via reports and oral conversations, offers guidance if need be, smiles or frowns as trial balloon recommendations are informally run by him/her for reaction, then puts a stamp of approval on the strategic plan after it has been formally presented and discussed and a consensus emerges. But the manager rarely has much ownership in the recommendations and, privately, may not see much urgency in pushing *hard* to implement some or much of what has been stated in writing in the company's "official strategic plan." Also, it is generally understood that "of course, we may have to proceed a bit differently if conditions change"—which gives the manager flexibility to go slow or ignore those approaches/ moves that "on further reflection may not be the thing to do at this time." This strategy-making style has the advantage of letting the manager pick and chose from the smorgasbord of strategic ideas that bubble up from below, and it allows room for broad participation and input from many managers and areas. The weakness is that a manager can end up so detached from the process of formal strategy-making that no real strategic leadership is exercised—indeed, subordinates are likely to conclude that strategic planning isn't important enough to warrant a big claim on the boss's personal time and attention. The stage is then set for rudderless direction-setting.

---

[19]This discussion is based on David R. Brodwin and L. J. Bourgeois, "Five Steps to Strategic Action," in Glenn Carroll and David Vogel, *Strategy and Organization: A West Coast Perspective* (Marshfield, Mass.: Pitman Publishing, 1984), pp. 168–78.

Often the strategy-making that does occur is short-run oriented and reactive; it says more about today's problems than positioning the enterprise to capture tomorrow's opportunities.

The Collaborative Approach   This is a middle approach whereby the manager enlists the help of key subordinates in hammering out a consensus strategy that all the key players will back and do their best to implement successfully. The biggest strength of this strategy-making style is that those who are charged with crafting the strategy also are charged with implementing it. Giving subordinate managers such a clear-cut ownership stake in the strategy they must implement enhances commitment to successful execution. And when subordinates have had a hand in proposing their part of the overall strategy, they can be held accountable for making it work—the "I told you it was a bad idea" alibi won't fly.

The Champion Approach   In this style, the manager is interested neither in a big personal stake in the details of strategy nor in the time-consuming tedium of leading others through participative brainstorming or a collaborative "group wisdom" exercise. Rather, the idea is to encourage subordinate managers to develop, champion, and implement sound strategies. Here strategy moves upward from the "doers" and the "fast-trackers." Executives serve as judges, evaluating the strategy proposals reaching their desks. This approach works best in large diversified corporations where the CEO cannot personally orchestrate strategy-making in each of many business divisions. For headquarters executives to capitalize on having people in the enterprise who can see strategic opportunities that they cannot, they must delegate the initiative for strategy-making to managers at the business-unit level. Corporate executives may well articulate general strategic themes as organizationwide guidelines for strategic thinking, but the key to good strategy-making is stimulating and rewarding new strategic initiatives conceived by a champion who believes in the opportunity and badly wants the blessing to go after it. With this approach, the total strategy ends up being the sum of the championed initiatives that get approved.

These four basic managerial approaches to forming a strategy illuminate several aspects about how strategy emerges. In situations where the manager in charge personally functions as the chief architect of strategy, the choice of what strategic course to steer is a product of his/her own vision about how to position the enterprise and of the manager's ambitions, values, business philosophies, and sense of what moves to make next. Highly centralized strategy-making works fine when the manager in charge has a powerful, insightful vision of what needs to be done and how to do it. The primary weakness of the master strategist approach is that the caliber of the strategy depends so heavily on one person's strategy-making skills. It also breaks down in large enterprises where many strategic initiatives are needed and the strategy-making task is too complex for one person to handle alone.

> **Of the four basic approaches managers can use in crafting strategy, none is inherently superior—each has strengths and weaknesses.**

On the other hand, the group approach to strategy-making has its risks too. Sometimes, the strategy that emerges is a middle-of-the-road compromise, void of bold, creative initiative. Other times, it represents political consensus, with the outcome shaped by influential subordinates, by powerful functional departments, or by majority coalitions that have a common interest in promoting their particular version of what the strategy ought to be. Politics and the exercise of power are most likely to come into play in situations where there is no strong consensus on what strategy to adopt; this opens the door for a political solution to emerge. The collaborative approach is conducive to political strategic choices as well, since powerful departments and individuals have ample opportunity to try to build a consensus for their favored strategic approach. However, the big danger of a delegate-it-to-others approach is a serious lack of top-down direction and strategic leadership.

The strength of the champion approach is also its weakness. The value of championing is that it encourages people at lower organizational levels to make suggestions and propose innovative ideas. Individuals with attractive strategic proposals are given the latitude and resources to try them out, thus helping keep strategy fresh and renewing an organization's capacity for innovation. On the other hand, the championed actions, because they come from many places in the organization, are not likely to form a coherent pattern or promote clear strategic direction. With championing, the chief executive has to work at ensuring that what is championed adds power to the overall organization strategy; otherwise, strategic initiatives may be launched in directions that have no integrating links or overarching rationale.

All four styles of handling the strategy-making task thus have strengths and weaknesses. All four can succeed or fail depending on how well the approach is managed and depending on the strategy-making skills and judgments of the individuals involved.

Key Points

Management's direction-setting task involves developing a mission, setting objectives, and forming a strategy. Early on in the direction-setting process, managers need to form a vision of where to lead the organization and to answer the question, "What is our business and what will it be?" A well-conceived mission statement helps channel organizational efforts along the course management has charted and builds a strong sense of organizational identity. Effective visions are clear, challenging, and inspiring; they prepare a firm for the future, and they make sense in the marketplace. A well-conceived, well-said mission statement serves as a beacon of long-term direction and creates employee buy-in.

The second direction-setting step is to establish strategic and financial objectives for the organization to achieve. Objectives convert the mission statement into specific performance targets. The agreed-on objectives need to be challenging but achievable, and they need to spell out precisely how much by when. In other words, objectives should be measurable and should involve deadlines for achievement. Objectives are needed at all organizational levels.

The third direction-setting step entails forming strategies to achieve the objectives set in each area of the organization. A corporate strategy is needed to achieve corporate-level objectives; business strategies are needed to achieve business-unit performance objectives; functional strategies are needed to achieve the performance targets set for each functional department; and operating-level strategies are needed to achieve the objectives set in each operating and geographic unit. In effect, an organization's strategic plan is a collection of unified and interlocking strategies. As shown in Table 2–1, different strategic issues are addressed at each level of managerial strategy-making. Typically, the strategy-making task is more top-down than bottom-up. Lower-level strategy supports and complements higher-level strategy and contributes to the achievement of higher-level, companywide objectives.

Strategy is shaped by both outside and inside considerations. The major external considerations are societal, political, regulatory, and community factors; industry attractiveness; and the company's market opportunities and threats. The primary internal considerations are company strengths, weaknesses, and competitive capabilities;

managers' personal ambitions, philosophies, and ethics; and the company's culture and shared values. A good strategy must be well matched to all these situational considerations. In addition, a good strategy must lead to sustainable competitive advantage and improved company performance.

There are essentially four basic ways to manage the strategy formation process in an organization: the master strategist approach where the manager in charge personally functions as the chief architect of strategy, the delegate-it-to-others approach, the collaborative approach, and the champion approach. All four have strengths and weaknesses. All four can succeed or fail depending on how well the approach is managed and depending on the strategy-making skills and judgments of the individuals involved.

Suggested Readings

Andrews, Kenneth R. *The Concept of Corporate Strategy*. 3rd ed. Homewood, Ill.: Dow Jones Irwin, 1987, chaps. 2, 3, 4, and 5.

Campbell, Andrew, and Laura Nash. *A Sense of Mission: Defining Direction for the Large Corporation*. Reading, Mass.: Addison-Wesley, 1993.

Foster, Lawrence W. "From Darwin to Now: The Evolution of Organizational Strategies." *Journal of Business Strategy* 5, no. 4 (Spring 1985), pp. 94–98.

Hamel, Gary, and C. K. Prahalad. "Strategic Intent." *Harvard Business Review* 89, no. 3 (May–June 1989), pp. 63–76.

———. "Strategy as Stretch and Leverage." *Harvard Business Review* 71, no. 2 (March–April 1993), pp. 75–84.

Hammer, Michael, and James Champy. *Reengineering the Corporation*. New York: Harper Business, 1993, chap. 9.

Hax, Arnaldo C., and Nicolas S. Majluf. *The Strategy Concept and Process: A Pragmatic Approach*. Englewood Cliffs, N.J.: Prentice-Hall, 1991, chaps. 3, 4, 8, and 9.

Ireland, R. Duane, and Michael A. Hitt. "Mission Statements: Importance, Challenge, and Recommendations for Development." *Business Horizons* (May-June 1992), pp. 34–42.

Morris, Elinor. "Vision and Strategy: A Focus for the Future." *Journal of Business Strategy* 8, no. 2 (Fall 1987), pp. 51–58.

Mintzberg, Henry. "Crafting Strategy." *Harvard Business Review* 65, no. 4 (July–August 1987), pp. 66–77.

Porter, Michael E. "Toward a Dynamic Theory of Strategy." *Strategic Management Journal* 12 (1991), pp. 95–118.

Quinn, James Brian. *Strategies for Change: Logical Incrementalism*. Homewood, Ill.: Richard D. Irwin, 1980, chaps. 2 and 4.

CHAPTER THREE

Industry and Competitive Analysis

Analysis is the critical starting point of strategic thinking.

Kenichi Ohmae

Awareness of the environment is not a special project to be undertaken only when warning of change becomes deafening . . .

Kenneth R. Andrews

Crafting strategy is an analysis-driven exercise, not an activity where managers can succeed through good intentions and creativity. Judgments about what strategy to pursue have to be grounded in a probing assessment of a company's external environment and internal situation. Unless a company's strategy is well-matched to both external and internal circumstances, its suitability is suspect. The two biggest situational considerations are (1) industry and competitive conditions (these are the heart of a single-business company's "external environment") and (2) a company's own internal situation and competitive position. This chapter examines the techniques of *industry and competitive analysis*, the term commonly used to refer to external situation analysis of a single-business company. In the next chapter, we'll cover the tools of *company situation analysis*. Industry and competitive analysis looks broadly at a company's external *macroenvironment*; company situation analysis concerns a firm's immediate *microenvironment*.

Figure 3–1 illustrates the kinds of strategic thinking managers need to do to diagnose a company's situation. Note the logical flow from scrutiny of the company's external and internal situation to evaluation of alternatives to choice of strategy. Managers must have a keen grasp of the strategic aspects of a company's macro- and microenvironments to do a good job of establishing a strategic vision, setting objectives, and crafting a winning strategy. Absent such understanding, the door is wide open for managers to be seduced into a strategic game plan that doesn't fit the situation well, that holds little prospect for building competitive advantage, and that is unlikely to boost company performance.

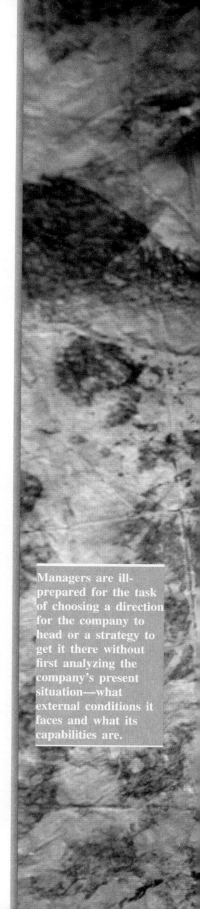

Managers are ill-prepared for the task of choosing a direction for the company to head or a strategy to get it there without first analyzing the company's present situation—what external conditions it faces and what its capabilities are.

THE METHODS OF INDUSTRY AND COMPETITIVE ANALYSIS

Industries differ widely in their economic characteristics, competitive situations, and future outlooks. The pace of technological change can range from fast to slow. Capital requirements can vary from big to small. The market can extend from local to

Figure 3–1 How Strategic Thinking and Strategic Analysis Lead to Good Strategic Choices

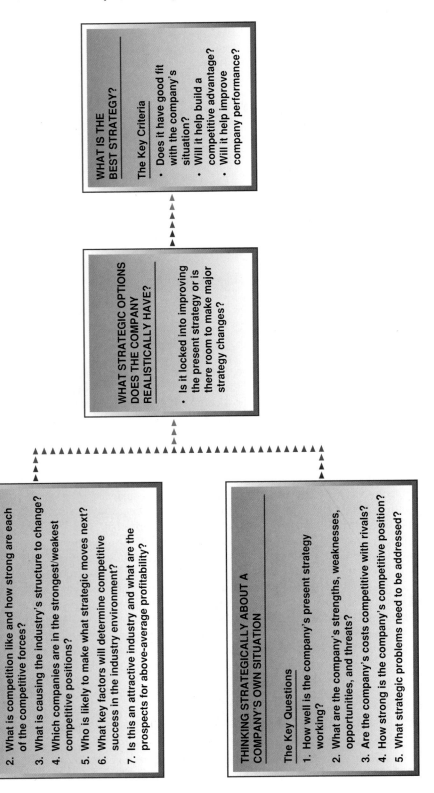

THINKING STRATEGICALLY ABOUT INDUSTRY AND COMPETITIVE CONDITIONS

The Key Questions

1. What are the industry's dominant economic traits?
2. What is competition like and how strong are each of the competitive forces?
3. What is causing the industry's structure to change?
4. Which companies are in the strongest/weakest competitive positions?
5. Who is likely to make what strategic moves next?
6. What key factors will determine competitive success in the industry environment?
7. Is this an attractive industry and what are the prospects for above-average profitability?

THINKING STRATEGICALLY ABOUT A COMPANY'S OWN SITUATION

The Key Questions

1. How well is the company's present strategy working?
2. What are the company's strengths, weaknesses, opportunities, and threats?
3. Are the company's costs competitive with rivals?
4. How strong is the company's competitive position?
5. What strategic problems need to be addressed?

WHAT STRATEGIC OPTIONS DOES THE COMPANY REALISTICALLY HAVE?

• Is it locked into improving the present strategy or is there room to make major strategy changes?

WHAT IS THE BEST STRATEGY?

The Key Criteria

• Does it have good fit with the company's situation?
• Will it help build a competitive advantage?
• Will it help improve company performance?

worldwide. Sellers' products can be standardized or highly differentiated. Competitive forces can be strong or weak and can reflect varying degrees of emphasis on price, product performance, service, promotion, and so on. Buyer demand can be rising briskly or declining. Industry conditions differ so much that leading companies in unattractive industries can find it hard to earn respectable profits, while even weak companies in attractive industries can turn in good performances. Moreover, industry conditions change continuously as one or more aspects grow or diminish in influence.

Industry and competitive analysis utilizes a toolkit of concepts and techniques to get a clear fix on changing industry conditions and on the nature and strength of competitive forces. This tool kit provides a way of thinking strategically about any industry's overall situation and drawing conclusions about whether the industry represents an attractive investment for company funds. Industry and competitive analysis aims at developing probing answers to seven questions:

1. What are the industry's dominant economic traits?
2. What competitive forces are at work in the industry and how strong are they?
3. What are the drivers of change in the industry and what impact will they have?
4. Which companies are in the strongest/weakest competitive positions?
5. Who's likely to make what competitive moves next?
6. What key factors will determine competitive success or failure?
7. How attractive is the industry in terms of its prospects for above-average profitability?

The answers to these questions build understanding of a firm's surrounding environment and, collectively, form the basis for matching its strategy to changing industry conditions and competitive realities.

Question 1: What Are the Industry's Dominant Economic Traits?

Because industries differ significantly in their basic character and structure, industry and competitive analysis begins with an overview of the industry's dominant economic traits. As a working definition, we use the word *industry* to mean a group of firms whose products have so many of the same attributes that they compete for the same buyers. The factors to consider in profiling an industry's economic features are fairly standard:

- Market size.
- Scope of competitive rivalry (local, regional, national, international, or global).
- Market growth rate and where the industry is in the growth cycle (early development, rapid growth and takeoff, early maturity, late maturity and saturation, stagnant and aging, decline and decay).
- Number of rivals and their relative sizes—is the industry fragmented with many small companies or concentrated and dominated by a few large companies?
- The number of buyers and their relative sizes.
- The prevalence of backward and forward integration.

- Ease of entry and exit.
- The pace of technological change in both production process innovation and new product introductions.
- Whether the product(s)/service(s) of rival firms are highly differentiated, weakly differentiated, or essentially identical.
- Whether companies can realize scale economies in purchasing, manufacturing, transportation, marketing, or advertising.
- Whether high rates of capacity utilization are crucial to achieving low-cost production efficiency.
- Whether the industry has a strong learning and experience curve such that average unit cost declines as *cumulative* output (and thus the experience of "learning by doing") builds up.
- Capital requirements.
- Whether industry profitability is above/below par.

Table 3-1 provides a sample profile of the economic character of the sulfuric acid industry.

An industry's economic characteristics are important because of the implications they have for strategy. For example, in capital-intensive industries where investment

---

Table 3–1   A Sample Profile of the Dominant Economic Characteristics of the Sulfuric Acid Industry

Market Size: $400–$500 million annual revenues; 4 million tons total volume.

Scope of Competitive Rivalry: Primarily regional; producers rarely sell outside a 250-mile radius of plant due to high cost of shipping long distances.

Market Growth Rate: 2–3 percent annually. **Stage in Life Cycle:** Mature.

Number of Companies in Industry: About 30 companies with 110 plant locations and capacity of 4.5 million tons. Market shares range from a low of 3 percent to a high of 21 percent.

Customers: About 2,000 buyers; most are industrial chemical firms.

Degree of Vertical Integration: Mixed; 5 of the 10 largest companies are integrated backward into mining operations and also forward in that sister industrial chemical divisions buy over 50 percent of the output of their plants; all other companies are engaged solely in manufacturing.

Ease of Entry/Exit: Moderate entry barriers exist in the form of capital requirements to construct a new plant of minimum efficient size (cost equals $10 million) and ability to build a customer base inside a 250-mile radius of plant.

Technology/Innovation: Production technology is standard and changes have been slow; biggest changes are occurring in products—1–2 newly formulated specialty chemicals products are being introduced annually, accounting for nearly all of industry growth.

Product Characteristics: Highly standardized; the brands of different producers are essentially identical (buyers perceive little real difference from seller to seller).

Scale Economies: Moderate; all companies have virtually equal manufacturing costs but scale economies exist in shipping in multiple carloads to same customer and in purchasing large quantities of raw materials.

Experience Curve Effects: Not a factor in this industry.

Capacity Utilization: Manufacturing efficiency is highest between 90–100 percent of rated capacity; below 90 percent utilization, unit costs run significantly higher.

Industry Profitability: Subpar to average; the commodity nature of the industry's product results in intense price-cutting when demand slackens, but prices firm up during periods of strong demand. Profits track the strength of demand for the industry's products.

in a single plant can run several hundred million dollars, a firm can spread the burden of high fixed costs by pursuing a strategy that promotes high utilization of fixed assets and generates more revenue per dollar of fixed-asset investment. Thus commercial airlines employ strategies to boost the revenue productivity of their multi-million dollar jets by cutting ground time at airport gates (to get in more flights per day with the same plane) and by using multi-tiered price discounts to fill up otherwise empty seats on each flight. In industries characterized by one product advance after another, companies must spend enough time and money on R&D to keep their technical prowess and innovative capability abreast of competitors—a strategy of continuous product innovation becomes a condition of survival.

In industries like semiconductors, the presence of a *learning/experience* curve effect in manufacturing causes unit costs to decline about 20 percent each time *cumulative* production volume doubles. With a 20 percent experience curve effect, if the first 1 million chips cost $100 each, by a production volume of 2 million the unit cost would be $80 (80 percent of $100), by a production volume of 4 million the unit cost would be $64 (80 percent of $80), and so on. When an industry is characterized by a strong experience curve effect in its manufacturing operations, a company that moves first to initiate production of a new-style product and develops a strategy to capture the largest market share can win the competitive advantage of being the low-cost producer. The bigger the experience curve effect, the bigger the cost advantage of the company with the largest *cumulative* production volume, as shown in Figure 3–2.

Table 3–2 presents some additional examples of how an industry's economic traits are relevant to managerial strategy-making.

> An industry's economic characteristics impose boundaries on the kinds of strategic approaches a company can pursue.

> **Basic Concept**
> When a strong learning/experience curve effect causes unit costs to decline substantially as cumulative production volume builds, a strategy to become the largest-volume manufacturer can offer the competitive advantage of being the industry's lowest-cost producer.

Question 2: What Is Competition Like and How Strong Are Each of the Competitive Forces?

One important component of industry and competitive analysis involves delving into the industry's competitive process to discover the main sources of competitive pressure and how strong each competitive force is. This analytical step is essential

Figure 3–2   Comparison of Experience Curve Effects for 10 Percent, 20 Percent, and 30 Percent Cost Reductions for Each Doubling of Cumulative Production Volume

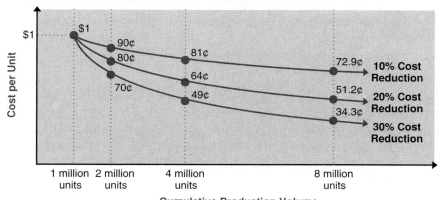

Table 3–2   **Examples of the Strategic Importance of an Industry's Key Economic Characteristics**

Factor/Characteristic	Strategic Importance
• Market size	• Small markets don't tend to attract big/new competitors; large markets often draw the interest of companies looking to acquire competitors with established positions in attractive industries.
• Market growth rate	• Fast growth breeds new entry; growth slowdowns spawn increased rivalry and a shake-out of weak competitors.
• Capacity surpluses or shortages	• Surpluses push prices and profit margins down; shortages pull them up.
• Industry profitability	• High-profit industries attract new entrants; depressed conditions encourage exit.
• Entry/exit barriers	• High barriers protect positions and profits of existing firms; low barriers make existing firms vulnerable to entry.
• Product is a big-ticket item for buyers	• More buyers will shop for lowest price.
• Standardized products	• Buyers have more power because it is easier to switch from seller to seller.
• Rapid technological change	• Raises risk factor; investments in technology facilities/equipment may become obsolete before they wear out.
• Capital requirements	• Big requirements make investment decisions critical; timing becomes important; creates a barrier to entry and exit.
• Vertical integration	• Raises capital requirements; often creates competitive differences and cost differences among fully versus partially versus nonintegrated firms.
• Economies of scale	• Increases volume and market share needed to be cost competitive.
• Rapid product innovation	• Shortens product life cycle; increases risk because of opportunities for leapfrogging.

because managers cannot devise a successful strategy without in-depth understanding of the industry's competitive character.

The Five-Forces Model of Competition   Even though competitive pressures in various industries are never precisely the same, the competitive process works similarly enough to use a common analytical framework in gauging the nature and intensity of competitive forces. As Professor Michael Porter of the Harvard Business School has convincingly demonstrated, *the state of competition in an industry is a composite of five competitive forces:*[1]

1. The rivalry among competing sellers in the industry.
2. The market attempts of companies in other industries to win customers over to their own *substitute* products.
3. The potential entry of new competitors.
4. The bargaining power and leverage exercisable by suppliers of inputs.
5. The bargaining power and leverage exercisable by buyers of the product.

Porter's *five-forces model*, as depicted in Figure 3–3, is a powerful tool for systematically diagnosing the principal competitive pressures in a market and assessing how

---

[1] For a thoroughgoing treatment of the five-forces model by its originator, see Michael E. Porter, *Competitive Strategy: Techniques for Analyzing Industries and Competitors* (New York: Free Press, 1980), chapter 1.

Figure 3–3   The "Five-Forces" Model of Competition: A Key Analytical Tool

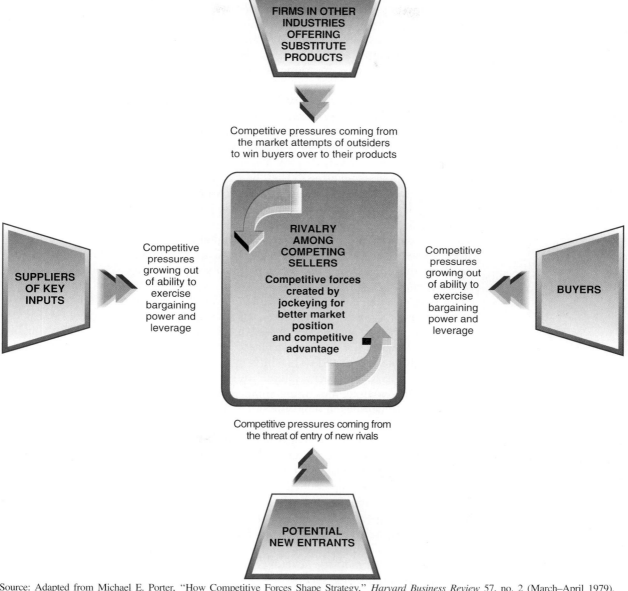

Source: Adapted from Michael E. Porter, "How Competitive Forces Shape Strategy," *Harvard Business Review* 57, no. 2 (March–April 1979), pp. 137–45.

strong and important each one is. Not only is it the most widely used technique of competition analysis, but it is also relatively easy to use.

The Rivalry among Competing Sellers   The strongest of the five competitive forces is *usually* the jockeying for position and buyer favor that goes on among rival firms. Rivalry emerges because one or more competitors sees an opportunity to better meet customer needs or is under pressure to improve its performance. The intensity of rivalry among competing sellers is reflected by how vigorously they employ such competitive tactics as lower prices, snazzier features, increased customer services, longer warranties, special promotions, and new product introductions. Rivalry can range from friendly to cutthroat, depending on how frequently and how aggressively companies undertake fresh moves that threaten rivals' profitability. Ordinarily, rivals are clever at adding new wrinkles to their product offerings that enhance buyer appeal, and they persist in trying to exploit weaknesses in each other's market approaches.

Irrespective of whether rivalry is lukewarm or heated, every company is challenged to craft a successful strategy for competing—ideally, one that *produces a competitive edge over rivals* and strengthens its position with buyers. The big complication in most industries is that the success of any one firm's strategy hinges on what strategies its rivals employ and the resources rivals are willing and able to put behind their strategic efforts. The "best" strategy for one firm in its maneuvering for competitive advantage depends, in other words, on the competitive capabilities and strategies of rival companies. Such mutual interdependence means that whenever one firm makes a strategic move, its rivals often retaliate with offensive or defensive countermoves. This pattern of action and reaction makes competitive rivalry a "war-games" type of contest that is conducted in a market setting according to the rules of fair competition. Indeed, from a strategy-making perspective, *competitive markets are economic battlefields.*

Not only do competitive contests among rival sellers assume different intensities but the kinds of competitive pressures that emerge from cross-company rivalry also vary over time. The relative emphasis that rival companies put on price, quality, performance features, customer service, warranties, advertising, dealer networks, new product innovation, and so on shifts as they try different tactics to catch buyers' attention and as competitors initiate fresh offensive and defensive maneuvers. Rivalry is thus dynamic; the current competitive scene is ever-changing as companies act and react, sometimes in rapid-fire order and sometimes methodically, and as their strategic emphasis swings from one mix of competitive tactics to another.

Principle of Competitive Markets
Competitive jockeying among rival firms is a dynamic, everchanging process as firms initiate new offensive and defensive moves and emphasis swings from one mix of competitive weapons to another.

Two facets of competitive rivalry stand out: (1) the launch of a powerful competitive strategy by one company intensifies the competitive pressures on the remaining companies and (2) the manner in which rivals employ various competitive weapons to try to outmaneuver one another shapes "the rules of competition" in the industry and determines the requirements for competitive success. Once an industry's prevailing rules of competitive rivalry are understood, managers can determine whether competitive rivalry is fierce, moderate, or attractively weak and whether it is likely to increase or diminish in strength.

Regardless of the industry, several common factors seem to influence the tempo of rivalry among competing sellers:[2]

1. *Rivalry intensifies as the number of competitors increases and as competitors become more equal in size and capability.* Up to a point, the greater the number of competitors, the greater the probability of fresh, creative strategic initiatives. In addition, when rivals are more equal in size and capability, they can usually compete on a fairly even footing,

---

[2]These indicators of what to look for in evaluating the intensity of intercompany rivalry are based on Porter, *Competitive Strategy*, pp. 17–21.

making it harder for one or two firms to "win" the competitive battle and dominate the market.

2. *Rivalry is usually stronger when demand for the product is growing slowly.* In a rapidly expanding market, there tends to be enough business for everybody to grow. Indeed, it may take all of a firm's financial and managerial resources just to keep abreast of the growth in buyer demand, much less steal rivals' customers. But when growth slows or when market demand drops unexpectedly, expansion-minded firms and/or firms with excess capacity often cut prices and deploy other sales-increasing tactics, thereby igniting a battle for market share that can result in a shake-out of the weak and less efficient firms. The industry then consolidates into a smaller, but individually stronger, number of sellers.

3. *Rivalry is more intense when industry conditions tempt competitors to use price cuts or other competitive weapons to boost unit volume.* Whenever fixed costs account for a large fraction of total cost, unit costs tend to be lowest at or near full capacity since fixed costs can be spread over more units of production. Unused capacity imposes a significant cost-increasing penalty because there are fewer units carrying the fixed cost burden. In such cases, if market demand weakens and capacity utilization begins to fall off, the pressure of rising unit costs pushes rival firms into secret price concessions, special discounts, rebates, and other sales-increasing tactics, thus heightening competition. Likewise, when a product is perishable, seasonal, or costly to hold in inventory, competitive pressures build quickly anytime one or more firms decide to dump excess supplies on the market.

4. *Rivalry is stronger when customers' costs to switch brands are low.* The lower the costs of switching, the easier it is for rival sellers to raid one another's customers. On the other hand, high switching costs give a seller some protection against the efforts of rivals to raid its customers.

5. *Rivalry is stronger when one or more competitors is dissatisfied with its market position and launches moves to bolster its standing at the expense of rivals.* Firms that are losing ground or in financial trouble often react aggressively by acquiring smaller rivals, introducing new products, boosting advertising, discounting prices, and so on. Such actions can trigger a new round of competitive maneuvering and a hotly contested battle for market share.

6. *Rivalry increases in proportion to the size of the payoff from a successful strategic move.* The more rewarding an opportunity, the more likely some firm will aggressively pursue a strategy to capture it. The size of the strategic payoff varies partly with the speed of retaliation. When competitors respond slowly (or not at all), the initiator of a fresh competitive strategy can reap benefits in the intervening period and perhaps gain a first-mover advantage that is not easily surmounted. The greater the benefits of moving first, the more likely some firm will accept the risk and try it.

7. *Rivalry tends to be more vigorous when it costs more to get out of a business than to stay in and compete.* The higher the exit barriers (and thus the more costly it is to abandon a market), the stronger the incentive for firms to remain and compete as best they can, even though they may be earning low profits or even incurring losses.

8. *Rivalry becomes more volatile and unpredictable the more diverse competitors are in terms of their strategies, personalities, corporate priorities, resources, and countries of origin.* A diverse group of sellers often contains one or more mavericks willing to rock the boat with unconventional moves and market approaches, thus generating a livelier and less predictable competitive environment. Attempts by cross-border rivals to gain stronger footholds in each other's domestic markets is a surefire factor in boosting the intensity of rivalry, especially when foreign rivals have lower costs.

9. *Rivalry increases when strong companies outside the industry acquire weak firms in the industry and launch aggressive, well-funded moves to transform their newly acquired competitors into major market contenders.* A classic example of this occurred when Philip Morris, a leading cigarette firm with excellent marketing know-how, shook up the U.S. beer industry's approach to marketing by acquiring stodgy Miller Brewing Company in the late 1960s. In short order, Philip Morris revamped the marketing of Miller High Life and pushed it to the number two best-selling brand. PM also pioneered low-calorie beers with the introduction of Miller Lite—a move that made light beer the fastest-growing segment in the beer industry.

In sizing up the competitive pressures created by rivalry among existing competitors, the strategist's job is to identify what the current weapons of competitive rivalry are, to stay on top of how the game is being played, and to judge how much pressure cross-company rivalry is going to put on profitability. Competitive rivalry is considered intense when the actions of competitors are driving down industry profits, moderate when most companies can earn acceptable profits, and weak when most companies in the industry can earn above-average returns on investment. Chronic outbreaks of cutthroat competition among rival sellers make an industry brutally competitive.

The Competitive Force of Potential Entry   New entrants to a market bring new production capacity, the desire to establish a secure place in the market, and sometimes substantial resources with which to compete.[3] Just how serious the competitive threat of entry is in a particular market depends on two classes of factors: *barriers to entry* and the *expected reaction of incumbent firms to new entry*. A barrier to entry exists whenever it is hard for a newcomer to break into the market and/or economic factors put a potential entrant at a disadvantage relative to its competitors. There are several types of entry barriers:[4]

- *Economies of scale*—Scale economies deter entry because they force potential competitors either to enter on a large-scale basis (a costly and perhaps risky move) or to accept a cost disadvantage (and consequently lower profitability). Large-scale entry is a difficult barrier to hurdle because it can create chronic overcapacity problems in the industry and it can so threaten the market shares of existing firms that they retaliate aggressively

---

[3]Michael E. Porter, "How Competitive Forces Shape Strategy," *Harvard Business Review* 57, no. 2 (March–April 1979), p. 138.
[4]Porter, *Competitive Strategy*, pp. 7–17.

(with price cuts, increased advertising and sales promotion, and similar blocking actions) to maintain their positions. Either way, a potential entrant is discouraged by the prospect of lower profits. Entrants may encounter scale-related barriers not just in production, but in advertising, marketing and distribution, financing, after-sale customer service, raw materials purchasing, and R&D as well.

- *Inability to gain access to technology and specialized know-how*—Many industries require technological capability and skills not readily available to a new entrant. Key patents can effectively bar entry as can lack of technically skilled personnel and an inability to execute complicated manufacturing techniques. Existing firms often carefully guard know-how that gives them an edge in technology and manufacturing capability. Unless new entrants can gain access to such proprietary knowledge, they will lack the technical capability to compete on a level playing field.

- *The existence of learning and experience curve effects*—When lower unit costs are partly or mostly a result of experience in producing the product and other learning curve benefits, new entrants face a cost disadvantage competing against existing firms with more accumulated know-how.

- *Brand preferences and customer loyalty*—Buyers are often attached to established brands. European consumers, for example, are fiercely loyal to European brands of major household appliances. High brand loyalty means that a potential entrant must be prepared to spend enough money on advertising and sales promotion to overcome customer loyalties and build its own clientele. Substantial time and money can be involved. In addition, if it is difficult or costly for a customer to switch to a new brand, a new entrant must persuade buyers that its brand is worth the switching costs. To overcome the switching cost barrier, new entrants may have to offer buyers a discounted price or an extra margin of quality or service. All this can mean lower expected profit margins for new entrants—something that increases the risk to start-up companies dependent on sizable, early profits to support their new investments.

- *Capital requirements*—The larger the total dollar investment needed to enter the market successfully, the more limited the pool of potential entrants. The most obvious capital requirements are associated with manufacturing plant and equipment, working capital to finance inventories and customer credit, introductory advertising and sales promotion to establish a clientele, and cash reserves to cover start-up losses.

- *Cost disadvantages independent of size*—Existing firms may have cost advantages not available to potential entrants regardless of the entrant's size. These advantages can include access to the best and cheapest raw materials, possession of patents and proprietary technology, the benefits of learning and experience curve effects, existing plants built and equipped years earlier at lower costs, favorable locations, and lower borrowing costs.

- *Access to distribution channels*—In the case of consumer goods, a potential entrant may face the barrier of gaining adequate access to distribution channels. Wholesale distributors may be reluctant to take on a product that lacks buyer recognition. A network of retail dealers may have to be set up from scratch. Retailers have to be convinced to give a new brand ample display space and an adequate trial period. The more existing producers tie up present distribution channels, the tougher entry will be. To overcome this barrier, potential entrants may have to "buy" distribution access by offering better margins to dealers and distributors or by giving advertising allowances and other promotional incentives. As a consequence, a potential entrant's profits may be squeezed unless and until its product gains enough acceptance that distributors and retailers want to carry it.

- *Regulatory policies*—Government agencies can limit or even bar entry by requiring licenses and permits. Regulated industries like cable TV, electric and gas utilities, radio and television broadcasting, liquor retailing, and railroads feature government-controlled entry. In international markets, host governments commonly limit foreign entry and must approve all foreign investment applications. Stringent government-mandated safety regulations and environmental pollution standards are entry barriers because they raise entry costs.

- *Tariffs and international trade restrictions*—National governments commonly use tariffs and trade restrictions (antidumping rules, local content requirements, and quotas) to raise entry barriers for foreign firms. In 1988, due to tariffs imposed by the South Korean government, a Ford Taurus cost South Korean car buyers over $40,000. European governments require that certain Asian products, from electronic typewriters to copying machines, contain European-made parts and labor equal to 40 percent of selling price. And to protect European chipmakers from low-cost Asian competition, European governments instituted a rigid formula for calculating floor prices for computer memory chips.

Even if a potential entrant is willing to tackle the problems of entry barriers, it still faces the issue of how existing firms will react.[5] Will incumbent firms offer only passive resistance, or will they aggressively defend their market positions using price cuts, increased advertising, new product improvements, and whatever else is calculated to give a new entrant (as well as other rivals) a hard time? A potential entrant can have second thoughts when financially strong incumbent firms send clear signals that they will stoutly defend their market positions against entry. A potential entrant may also turn away when incumbent firms can use leverage with distributors and customers to keep their business.

The best test of whether potential entry is a strong or weak competitive force is to ask if the industry's growth and profit prospects are attractive enough to induce additional entry. When the answer is no, potential entry is not a source of competitive pressure. When the answer is yes (as in industries where lower-cost foreign competitors are exploring new markets), then potential entry is a strong force. The stronger the threat of entry, the greater the motivation of incumbent firms to fortify their positions against newcomers to make entry more costly or difficult.

One additional point: the threat of entry changes as the industry's prospects grow brighter or dimmer and as entry barriers rise or fall. For example, the expiration of a key patent can greatly increase the threat of entry. A technological discovery can create an economy of scale advantage where none existed before. New actions by incumbent firms to increase advertising, strengthen distributor-dealer relations, step up R&D, or improve product quality can raise the roadblocks to entry. In international markets,

Principle of Competitive Markets
The competitive threat that outsiders will enter the market is stronger when entry barriers are low, when incumbent firms are not inclined to fight vigorously to prevent a newcomer from gaining a market foothold, and when a newcomer can expect to earn attractive profits.

---

[5]Porter, "How Competitive Forces Shape Strategy," p. 140, and Porter, *Competitive Strategy*, pp. 14–15.

entry barriers for foreign-based firms fall as tariffs are lowered, as domestic wholesalers and dealers seek out lower-cost foreign-made goods, and as domestic buyers become more willing to purchase foreign brands.

Competitive Pressures from Substitute Products Firms in one industry are, quite often, in close competition with firms in another industry because their respective products are good substitutes. The producers of eyeglasses compete with the makers of contact lenses. The producers of wood stoves compete with such substitutes as kerosene heaters and portable electric heaters. The sugar industry competes with companies that produce artificial sweeteners. The producers of plastic containers confront strong competition from manufacturers of glass bottles and jars, paperboard cartons, and tin cans and aluminum cans. Aspirin manufacturers must consider how their product compares with other pain relievers and headache remedies.

Competitive pressures from substitute products operate in several ways. First, the presence of readily available and competitively priced substitutes places a ceiling on the prices an industry can afford to charge for its product without giving customers an incentive to switch to substitutes and risking sales erosion.[6] This price ceiling, at the same time, puts a lid on the profits that industry members can earn unless they find ways to cut costs. When substitutes are cheaper than an industry's product, industry members come under heavy competitive pressure to reduce their prices and find ways to absorb the price cuts with cost reductions. Second, the availability of substitutes inevitably invites customers to compare quality and performance as well as price. For example, firms that buy glass bottles and jars from glassware manufacturers monitor whether they can just as effectively and economically package their products in plastic containers, paper cartons, or tin cans. Competitive pressures from substitute products thus push industry participants to convince customers their product is more advantageous than substitutes. Usually this requires devising a competitive strategy to differentiate the industry's product from substitute products via some combination of lower price, better quality, better service, and more desirable performance features.

Another determinant of whether substitutes are a strong or weak competitive force is how difficult or costly it is for the industry's customers to switch to substitute products.[7] Typical switching costs include employee retraining costs, the purchase costs of any additional equipment, payments for technical help in making the changeover, the time and cost in testing the quality and reliability of the substitute, and the psychic costs of severing old supplier relationships and establishing new ones. If switching costs are high, sellers of substitutes must offer a major cost or performance benefit in order to steal the industry's customers away. When switching costs are low, it's much easier for sellers of substitutes to convince buyers to change over to their products.

As a rule, then, the lower the price of substitutes, the higher their quality and performance, and the lower the user's switching costs, the more intense the competitive pressures posed by substitute products. The best indicators of the competitive strength of substitute products are the rate at which their sales are growing, the market inroads they are making, their plans for expanding production capacity, and the size of their profits.

Principle of Competitive Markets The competitive threat posed by substitute products is strong when prices of substitutes are attractive, buyers' switching costs are low, and buyers believe substitutes have equal or better features.

---

[6]Porter, "How Competitive Forces Shape Strategy," p. 142, and Porter, *Competitive Strategy*, pp. 23–24.
[7]Porter, *Competitive Strategy*, p. 10.

The Power of Suppliers   Whether the suppliers to an industry are a weak or strong competitive force depends on market conditions in the supplier industry and the significance of the item they supply.[8] The competitive force of suppliers is greatly diminished whenever the item they provide is a standard commodity available on the open market from a large number of suppliers with ample capability to fill orders. Then it is relatively simple to obtain whatever is needed from a list of capable suppliers, dividing purchases among several to promote lively competition for orders. In such cases, suppliers have market power only when supplies become tight and users are so anxious to secure what they need that they agree to terms more favorable to suppliers. Suppliers are likewise in a weak bargaining position whenever there are good substitute inputs and switching is neither costly nor difficult. For example, soft drink bottlers can effectively check the power of aluminum can suppliers by using more plastic containers and glass bottles.

Suppliers also have less leverage when the industry they are supplying is a *major* customer. In this case, the well-being of suppliers becomes closely tied to the well-being of their major customers. Suppliers then have a big incentive to protect the customer industry via reasonable prices, improved quality, and the development of new products and services that might enhance their customers' competitive positions, sales, and profits. When industry members form close working relationships with major suppliers, they may gain substantial benefit in the form of better quality components, just-in-time deliveries, and reduced inventory costs.

On the other hand, when the item suppliers provide accounts for a sizable fraction of the costs of an industry's product, is crucial to the industry's production process, and/or significantly affects the quality of the industry's product, suppliers have considerable influence on the competitive process. This is particularly true when a few large companies control most of the available supplies and have pricing leverage. Likewise, a supplier (or group of suppliers) possesses bargaining leverage the more difficult or costly it is for users to switch to alternate suppliers. Big suppliers with good reputations and growing demand for their output are harder to wring concessions from than struggling suppliers striving to broaden their customer base or more fully utilize their production capacity.

Principle of Competitive Markets The suppliers to a group of rival firms are a strong competitive force whenever they have sufficient bargaining power to put certain rivals at a competitive disadvantage based on the prices they can command, the quality and performance of the items they supply, or the reliability of their deliveries.

Suppliers are also more powerful when they can supply a component more cheaply than industry members can make it themselves. For instance, most producers of outdoor power equipment (lawnmowers, rotary tillers, snowblowers, and so on) find it cheaper to source the small engines they need from outside manufacturers rather than make their own because the quantity they need is too little to justify the investment and master the process. Specialists in small-engine manufacture, by supplying many kinds of engines to the whole power equipment industry, obtain a big enough sales volume to capture scale economies, become proficient in all the manufacturing techniques, and keep costs well below what power equipment firms could realize on their own. Small-engine suppliers then are in a position to price the item below what it would cost the user to self-manufacture but far enough above their own costs to generate an attractive profit margin. In such situations, the bargaining position of suppliers is strong *until* the volume of parts a user needs becomes large enough for the user to justify backward integration. Then the balance of power shifts from suppliers to users. The more credible the threat of backward integration into the suppliers' business becomes, the more leverage users have in negotiating favorable terms with suppliers.

---

[8]Ibid., pp. 27–28.

A final instance in which an industry's suppliers play an important competitive role is when suppliers, for one reason or another, do not have the capability or the incentive to provide items of high or consistent quality. For example, if a manufacturer's suppliers provide components that have a relatively high defect rate or that fail prematurely, they can so increase the warranty and defective goods costs of the manufacturer that its profits, reputation, and competitive position are seriously impaired.

The Power of Buyers   Just as with suppliers, the competitive strength of buyers can range from strong to weak. Buyers have substantial bargaining leverage in a number of situations.[9] The most obvious is when buyers are large and purchase a sizable percentage of the industry's output. The bigger buyers are and the larger the quantities they purchase, the more clout they have in negotiating with sellers. Often, purchasing in large quantities gives a buyer enough leverage to obtain price concessions and other favorable terms. Buyers also gain power when the costs of switching to competing brands or substitutes are relatively low. Any time buyers have the flexibility to fill their needs by sourcing from several sellers rather than having to use just one brand, they have added room to negotiate with sellers. When sellers' products are virtually identical, it is relatively easy for buyers to switch from seller to seller at little or no cost. However, if sellers' products are strongly differentiated, buyers are less able to switch without incurring sizable changeover costs.

One last point: all buyers are not likely to possess equal degrees of bargaining power with sellers, and some may be less sensitive than others to price, quality, or service. For example, in the apparel industry, major manufacturers confront significant customer power when selling to retail chains like Wal-Mart or Sears. But they can get much better prices selling to the small owner-managed apparel boutiques.

Strategic Implications of the Five Competitive Forces   The value of the five-forces model is the assist it provides in exposing the makeup of competitive forces. *To analyze the competitive environment, managers must assess the strength of each one of the five competitive forces.* The collective impact of these forces determines what competition is like in a given market. As a rule, the stronger competitive forces are, the lower is the collective profitability of participant firms. The most brutally competitive situation occurs when the five forces create market conditions tough enough to impose prolonged subpar profitability or even losses on most or all firms. The competitive structure of an industry is clearly "unattractive" from a profit-making standpoint if rivalry among sellers is very strong, entry barriers are low, competition from substitutes is strong, and both suppliers and customers are able to exercise considerable bargaining leverage. On the other hand, when competitive forces are not collectively strong, the competitive structure of the industry is "favorable" or "attractive" from the standpoint of earning superior profits. The "ideal" competitive environment from a profit-making perspective is where both suppliers and customers are in weak bargaining positions, there are no good substitutes, entry barriers are relatively high, and rivalry among present sellers is only moderate. However, even when some of the five competitive forces are strong, an industry can be competitively attractive to those firms whose market position and strategy provide a good enough defense against competitive pressures to preserve their ability to earn above-average profits.

> **Principle of Competitive Markets**
> Buyers become a stronger competitive force the more they are able to exercise bargaining leverage over price, quality, service, or other terms of sale.

> A company's competitive strategy is increasingly effective the more it provides good defenses against the five competitive forces, influences the industry's competitive rules in the company's favor, and helps create sustainable competitive advantage.

---

[9]Ibid., pp. 24–27.

To deal successfully with competitive forces, managers must craft strategies that (1) insulate the firm as much as possible from the five competitive forces, (2) influence the industry's competitive rules in the company's favor, and (3) provide a strong, secure position of advantage from which to "play the game" of competition as it unfolds in the industry. Managers cannot do this task well without a perceptive understanding of the industry's whole competitive picture. The five-forces model is a tool for gaining this understanding.

Question 3: What Is Causing the Industry's Competitive Structure and Business Environment to Change?

Industry conditions change because important forces are driving industry participants (competitors, customers, or suppliers) to alter their actions; the *driving forces* in an industry are the *major underlying causes* of changing industry and competitive conditions.

An industry's economic features and competitive structure say a lot about the basic nature of the industry environment but very little about the ways in which the environment may be changing. All industries are characterized by trends and new developments that either gradually or speedily produce changes important enough to require a strategic response from participating firms. The popular hypothesis about industries going through evolutionary phases or life-cycle stages helps explain industry change but is still incomplete.[10] The life-cycle stages are strongly keyed to the overall industry growth rate (which is why such terms as rapid growth, early maturity, saturation, and decline are used to describe the stages). Yet there are more causes of industry change than an industry's position on the growth curve.

The Concept of Driving Forces   While it is important to judge what growth stage an industry is in, there's more analytical value in identifying the specific factors causing fundamental industry and competitive adjustments. Industry and competitive conditions change *because forces are in motion that create incentives or pressures for change.*[11] The most dominant forces are called *driving forces* because they have the biggest influence on what kinds of changes will take place in the industry's structure and competitive environment. Driving forces analysis has two steps: identifying what the driving forces are and assessing the impact they will have on the industry.

The Most Common Driving Forces   Many events can affect an industry powerfully enough to qualify as driving forces. Some are one of a kind, but most fall into one of several basic categories.[12]

- *Changes in the long-term industry growth rate*—Shifts in industry growth up or down are a force for industry change because they affect the balance between industry supply and buyer demand, entry and exit, and how hard it will be for a firm to capture additional sales. An upsurge in long-term demand frequently attracts new entrants to the market and encourages established firms to invest in additional capacity. A shrinking market can cause some companies to exit the industry and induce those remaining to close their least efficient plants and retrench to a smaller production base.

---

[10]For a more extended discussion of the problems with the life-cycle hypothesis, see Porter, *Competitive Strategy*, pp. 157–62.

[11]Porter, *Competitive Strategy*, p. 162.

[12]What follows draws on the discussion in Porter, *Competitive Strategy*, pp. 164–83.

- *Changes in who buys the product and how they use it*—Shifts in buyer composition and new ways of using the product can force adjustments in customer service offerings (credit, technical assistance, maintenance and repair), open the way to market the industry's product through a different mix of dealers and retail outlets, prompt producers to broaden/narrow their product lines, increase/decrease capital requirements, and change sales and promotion approaches. The development of new cable-converter boxes is now allowing home computer service firms like Prodigy, CompuServe, and America Online to sign up cable companies to deliver their games, bulletin boards, data services, and electronic shopping services to home subscribers via cable television. Consumer enthusiasm for cordless and cellular telephones has opened a major new buyer segment for telephone equipment manufacturers.

- *Product innovation*—Product innovation can broaden an industry's customer base, rejuvenate industry growth, and widen the degree of product differentiation among rival sellers. Successful new product introductions strengthen the market position of the innovating companies, usually at the expense of companies who stick with their old products or are slow to follow with their own versions of the new product. Industries where product innovation has been a key driving force include copying equipment, cameras and photographic equipment, computers, electronic video games, toys, prescription drugs, frozen foods, and personal computer software.

- *Technological change*—Advances in technology can dramatically alter an industry's landscape, making it possible to produce new and/or better products at lower cost and opening up whole new industry frontiers. Technological developments can also produce changes in capital requirements, minimum efficient plant sizes, vertical integration benefits, and learning or experience curve effects.

- *Marketing innovation*—When firms are successful in introducing new ways to market their products, they can spark a burst of buyer interest, widen industry demand, increase product differentiation, and/or lower unit costs— any or all of which can alter the competitive positions of rival firms and force strategy revisions.

- *Entry or exit of major firms*—The entry of one or more foreign companies into a market once dominated by domestic firms nearly always shakes up competitive conditions. Likewise, when an established domestic firm from another industry attempts entry either by acquisition or by launching its own start-up venture, it usually applies its skills and resources in some innovative fashion that introduces a new element to competition. Entry by a major firm often produces a "new ballgame" not only with new key players but also with new rules for competing. Similarly, exit of a major firm changes competitive structure by reducing the number of market leaders (perhaps increasing the dominance of the leaders who remain) and causing a rush to capture the exiting firm's customers.

- *Diffusion of technical know-how*—As knowledge about how to perform a particular activity or execute a particular manufacturing technology spreads, any technically based competitive advantage held by firms originally possessing this know-how erodes. The diffusion of such know-how can occur through scientific journals, trade publications, on-site plant tours, word-of-mouth among suppliers and customers, and the hiring away of knowledgeable employees. It can also occur when the possessors of technological know-how license others to use it for a royalty fee or team up with a company interested in turning the technology into a new business venture. Quite often, technological know-how can be acquired by simply buying a company that has the wanted skills, patents, or manufacturing capabilities. In recent years technology transfer across national boundaries has emerged as one of the most important driving forces in globalizing markets and competition. As companies in more countries gain access to technical know-how, they upgrade their manufacturing capabilities in a long-term effort to compete head-on against established companies. Examples of where technology transfer has turned a largely domestic industry into an increasingly global one include automobiles, tires, consumer electronics, telecommunications, and computers.

- *Increasing globalization of the industry*—Industries move toward globalization for any of several reasons. One or more nationally prominent firms may launch aggressive long-term strategies to win a globally dominant market position. Demand for the industry's product may pop up in more and more countries. Trade barriers may drop. Technology transfer may open the door for more companies in more countries to enter the industry arena on a major scale. Significant labor cost differences among countries may create a strong reason to locate plants for labor-intensive products in low-wage countries (wages in South Korea, Taiwan, and Singapore, for example, are about one-fourth those in the U.S.). Significant cost economies may accrue to firms with world-scale volumes as opposed to national-scale volumes. Multinational companies with the ability to transfer their production, marketing, and management know-how from country to country at very low cost can sometimes gain a significant competitive advantage over domestic-only competitors. As a consequence, global competition usually shifts the pattern of competition among an industry's key players, favoring some and disadvantaging others. Such occurrences make globalization a driving force. Globalization is most likely to be a driving force in industries *(a)* based on natural resources (supplies of crude oil, copper, and cotton, for example, are geographically scattered all over the globe), *(b)* where low-cost production is a critical consideration (making it imperative to locate plant facilities in countries where the lowest costs can be achieved), and *(c)* where one or more growth-oriented, market-seeking companies are pushing hard to gain a significant competitive position in as many attractive country markets as they can.

- *Changes in cost and efficiency*—In industries where new economies of scale are emerging or where strong learning curve effects allow firms with the most production experience to undercut rivals' prices, large market share becomes such a distinct advantage that all firms must shift to volume-building strategies—triggering a "race for growth." Likewise, sharply rising costs for a key input (either raw materials or labor) can cause a scramble to either *(a)* line up reliable supplies of the input at affordable prices or *(b)* search out lower-cost substitute inputs. Any time important changes in cost or efficiency take place in an industry, widening or shrinking cost differences among key competitors can dramatically alter the state of competition.

- *Emerging buyer preferences for differentiated products instead of a commodity product (or for a more standardized product instead of strongly differentiated products)*—Sometimes growing numbers of buyers decide that a standard "one size fits all" product with a bargain price meets their needs as effectively as premium-priced brands with snappy features and options. Such a development tends to shift patronage away from sellers of more expensive differentiated products to sellers of cheaper commodity products and create a price-competitive market environment. Pronounced shifts toward greater product standardization can so dominate a market that the strategic freedom of rival producers is limited to driving costs out of the business and competing hard on price. On the other hand, a shift away from standardized products occurs when sellers are able to win a bigger and more loyal buyer following by introducing new features, making style changes, offering options and accessories, and creating image differences via advertising and packaging. Then the driver of change is the contest among rivals to cleverly outdifferentiate one another. Industries evolve differently depending on whether the market forces in motion are acting to increase or decrease the emphasis on product differentiation.

- *Regulatory influences and government policy changes*—Regulatory and governmental actions can often force significant changes in industry practices and strategic approaches. Deregulation has been a big driving force in the airline, banking, natural gas, and telecommunications industries. President Clinton's proposal for universal health insurance recently became a driving force in the health care industry. In international markets, host governments can open up their domestic markets to foreign participation or close them off to protect domestic companies, thus shaping whether the competitive struggle occurs on a level playing field or favors domestic firms (owing to government protectionism).

- *Changing societal concerns, attitudes, and lifestyles*—Emerging social issues and changing attitudes and lifestyles can be powerful instigators of industry change. Consumer concerns about salt, sugar, chemical additives, cholesterol, and nutrition have forced food producers to reexamine food processing techniques, redirect R&D efforts into the use of healthier ingredients, and engage in contests to come up with healthier products that also taste good. Safety concerns are now altering the competitive emphasis in the automobile, toy, and outdoor power equipment industries, to mention a few. Increased interest in physical fitness has spawned whole new industries to supply exercise equipment, jogging clothes and shoes, and medically supervised diet programs. Social concerns about air and water pollution are major forces in industries that discharge waste products. Growing antismoking sentiment has emerged as the major driver of change in the tobacco industry.

- *Reductions in uncertainty and business risk*—A young, emerging industry is typically characterized by an unproven cost structure and much uncertainty over potential market size, how much time and money will be needed to surmount technological problems, and what distribution channels to emphasize in accessing potential buyers. Emerging industries tend to attract only risk-taking entrepreneurial companies. Over time, however, if pioneering firms succeed and uncertainty about the industry's viability fades, more conservative firms are usually enticed to enter the industry. Often, these later entrants are larger, financially strong firms looking to invest in attractive growth industries. In international markets, conservatism is prevalent in the early stages of globalization. Firms guard against risk by relying initially on exporting, licensing, and joint ventures to enter foreign markets. Then, as experience accumulates and perceived risk levels decline, companies move more quickly and aggressively to form wholly owned subsidiaries and to pursue full-scale, multicountry competitive strategies.

The foregoing list of *potential* driving forces in an industry indicates why it is too simplistic to view industry change only in terms of the growth stages model and why it is essential to probe for the *causes* underlying the emergence of new competitive conditions.

> **The task of driving forces analysis is to separate the major causes of industry change from the minor ones; usually no more than three or four factors qualify as driving forces.**

However, while many forces of change may be at work in a given industry, no more than three or four are likely to qualify as *driving* forces in the sense that they will act as *the major determinants* of how the industry evolves and operates. Thus, strategic analysts must resist the temptation to label everything they see changing as driving forces; the analytical task is to evaluate the forces of industry and competitive change carefully enough to separate major factors from minor ones.

Sound analysis of an industry's driving forces is a prerequisite to sound strategy-making. Without keen awareness of what external factors will have the greatest effect on the company's business over the next one to three years, managers are ill-prepared to craft a strategy tightly matched to changing external conditions. Similarly, if managers are uncertain about the implications of each driving force or if their views are incomplete or off-base, it's difficult for them to craft a strategy that is responsive to the driving forces and their consequences for the industry. So driving forces analysis is not something to take lightly; it has practical strategy-making value and is basic to the task of thinking strategically about the business.

Environmental Scanning Techniques   One way to get a jump on which driving forces are likely to emerge is to utilize environmental scanning techniques for early detection of new straws in the wind. *Environmental scanning* involves studying and interpreting the sweep of social, political, economic, ecological, and technological events in an effort to spot budding trends and conditions that could eventually impact the industry. Environmental scanning involves time frames well beyond the next one to three years—for example, it could involve judgments about the demand for energy in the year 2010, what kinds of household appliances will be in the "house of the future," what people will be doing with computers 20 years from now, or what will happen to our forests in the 21st century if the demand for paper continues to grow at its present rate. Environmental scanning thus attempts to spot first-of-a-kind happenings and new ideas and approaches that are catching on and to extrapolate their possible implications 5 to 20 years into the future. The purpose and value of environmental scanning is to raise the consciousness of managers about potential developments that could have an important impact on industry conditions or pose new opportunities and threats.

> **Managers can use *environmental scanning* to spot budding trends and clues of change that could develop into new driving forces.**

Environmental scanning can be accomplished by systematically monitoring and studying current events, constructing scenarios, and employing the Delphi method (a technique for finding consensus among a group of knowledgeable experts). Environmental scanning methods are highly qualitative and subjective. The appeal of environmental scanning, notwithstanding its speculative nature, is that it helps managers lengthen their planning horizon, translate vague inklings of future opportunities or threats into clearer strategic issues (for which they can begin to develop strategic answers), and think strategically about future developments in the surrounding environment.[13] Companies that undertake formal environmental scanning on a fairly continuous and comprehensive level include General Electric, AT&T, Coca-Cola, Ford, General Motors, Du Pont, and Shell Oil.

Question 4: Which Companies Are in the Strongest/Weakest Positions?

The next step in examining the industry's competitive structure is to study the market positions of rival companies. One technique for revealing the competitive positions of industry participants is *strategic group mapping*.[14] This analytical tool is a bridge between looking at the industry as a whole and considering the standing of each firm separately. It is most useful when an industry has so many competitors that it is not practical to examine each one in depth.

Strategic group mapping is a technique for displaying the different competitive positions that rival firms occupy in the industry.

Using Strategic Group Maps to Assess the Competitive Positions of Rival Firms

A strategic group consists of those rival firms with similar competitive approaches and positions in the market.[15] Companies in the same strategic group can resemble one another in any of several ways: they may have comparable product line breadth, use the same kinds of distribution channels, be vertically integrated to much the same degree, offer buyers similar services and technical assistance, use essentially the same product attributes to appeal to similar types of buyers, emphasize the same distribution channels, depend on identical technological approaches, and/or sell in the same price/quality range. An industry contains only one strategic group when all sellers approach the market with essentially identical strategies. At the other extreme, there are as many strategic groups as there are competitors when each rival pursues a distinctively different competitive approach and occupies a substantially different competitive position in the marketplace.

The procedure for constructing a strategic group map and deciding which firms belong in which strategic group is straightforward:

- Identify the competitive characteristics that differentiate firms in the industry—typical variables are price/quality range (high, medium, low), geographic coverage (local, regional, national, global), degree of vertical integration (none, partial, full), product line breadth (wide, narrow), use of distribution channels (one, some, all), and degree of service offered (no-frills, limited, full service).
- Plot the firms on a two-variable map using pairs of these differentiating characteristics.
- Assign firms that fall in about the same strategy space to the same strategic group.

[13]For further discussion of the nature and use of environmental scanning, see Roy Amara and Andrew J. Lipinski, *Business Planning for an Uncertain Future: Scenarios and Strategies* (New York: Pergamon Press, 1983); Harold E. Klein and Robert U. Linneman, "Environmental Assessment: An International Study of Corporate Practice," *Journal of Business Strategy* 5, no. 1 (Summer 1984), pp. 55–75; and Arnoldo C. Hax and Nicolas S. Majluf, *The Strategy Concept and Process* (Englewood Cliffs, N.J.: Prentice-Hall, 1991), chapters 5 and 8.
[14]Porter, *Competitive Strategy*, chapter 7.
[15]Ibid., pp. 129–30.

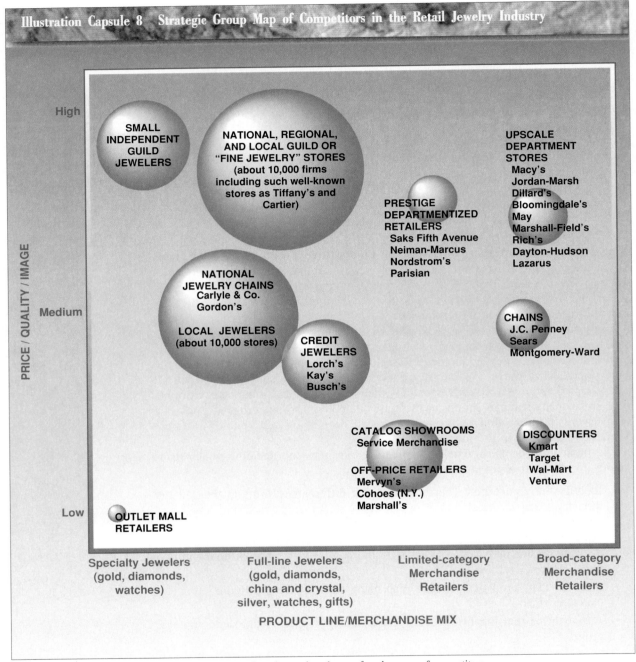

Illustration Capsule 8   Strategic Group Map of Competitors in the Retail Jewelry Industry

Note: The sizes of the circles are roughly proportional to the market shares of each group of competitors.

- Draw circles around each strategic group, making the circles proportional to the size of the group's respective share of total industry sales revenues.

This produces a two-dimensional *strategic group map* such as the one for the retail jewelry industry portrayed in Illustration Capsule 8.

To map the positions of strategic groups accurately in the industry's overall strategy space, several guidelines need to be observed.[16] First, the two variables selected as axes for the map should *not* be highly correlated; if they are, the circles on the map will fall along a diagonal and strategy-makers will learn nothing more about the relative positions of competitors than they would by considering just one of the variables. For instance, if companies with broad product lines use multiple distribution channels while companies with narrow lines use a single distribution channel, then one of the variables is redundant. Looking at broad versus narrow product lines reveals just as much about who is positioned where as adding single versus multiple distribution channels. Second, the variables chosen as axes for the map should expose big differences in how rivals position themselves to compete in the marketplace. This, of course, means analysts must identify the characteristics that differentiate rival firms and use these differences as variables for the axes and as the basis for deciding which firm belongs in which strategic group. Third, the variables used as axes don't have to be either quantitative or continuous; rather, they can be discrete variables or defined in terms of distinct classes and combinations. Fourth, drawing the sizes of the circles on the map proportional to the combined sales of the firms in each strategic group allows the map to reflect the relative sizes of each strategic group. Fifth, if more than two good competitive variables can be used as axes for the map, several maps can be drawn to give different exposures to the competitive positioning relationships present in the industry's structure. Because there is not necessarily one best map for portraying how competing firms are positioned in the market, it is advisable to experiment with different pairs of competitive variables.

Strategic group analysis helps deepen management understanding of competitive rivalry.[17] To begin with, *driving forces and competitive pressures often favor some strategic groups and hurt others.* Firms in adversely affected strategic groups may try to shift to a more favorably situated group; how hard such a move proves to be depends on whether entry barriers into the target strategic group are high or low. Attempts by rival firms to enter a new strategic group nearly always increase competitive pressures. If certain firms are known to be trying to change their competitive positions on the map, then attaching arrows to the circles showing the targeted direction helps clarify the picture of competitive jockeying among rivals.

A second thing to look for is whether *the profit potential of different strategic groups varies due to the strengths and weaknesses in each group's market position.* Differences in profitability can occur because of differing degrees of bargaining leverage with suppliers or customers and differing degrees of exposure to competition from substitute products outside the industry.

Generally speaking, *the closer strategic groups are to each other on the map, the stronger competitive rivalry among member firms tends to be.* Although firms in the same strategic group are the closest rivals, the next closest rivals are in the immediately adjacent groups. Often, firms in strategic groups that are far apart on the map hardly compete at all. For instance, Tiffany's and Wal-Mart both sell gold and silver jewelry, but the prices and perceived qualities of their products are much too different to generate any real competition between them. For the same reason, Timex is not a meaningful competitive rival of Rolex, and Subaru is not a close competitor of Lincoln or Mercedes-Benz.

Some strategic groups are usually more favorably positioned than other strategic groups because driving forces and competitive pressures do not affect each group evenly and because profit prospects vary among groups based on the relative attractiveness of their market positions.

---

[16]Ibid., pp. 152–54.
[17]Ibid., pp. 130, 132–38, and 154–55.

Question 5: What Strategic Moves Are Rivals Likely to Make Next?

Studying the actions and behavior of one's closest competitors is essential. Unless a company pays attention to what competitors are doing, it ends up flying blind into competitive battle. A company can't expect to outmaneuver its rivals without monitoring their actions and anticipating what moves they are likely to make next. As in sports, a good scouting report is invaluable. The strategies rivals are using and the actions they are likely to take next have direct bearing on a company's own best strategic moves—whether it needs to defend against specific actions taken by rivals or whether rivals' moves provide an opening for a new offensive thrust.

Successful strategists take great pains in scouting competitors— understanding their strategies, watching their actions, sizing up their strengths and weaknesses, and trying to anticipate what moves they will make next.

Identifying Competitors' Strategies   A quick profile of key competitors can be obtained by studying where they are in the industry, their strategic objectives as revealed by actions recently taken, and their basic competitive approaches. Table 3–3 provides an easy-to-use scheme for categorizing the objectives and strategies of rival companies. Such a summary, along with a strategic group map, usually suffices to diagnose the competitive intent of rivals.

Table 3–3   Categorizing the Objectives and Strategies of Competitors

Competitive Scope	Strategic Intent	Market Share Objective	Competitive Position/Situation	Strategic Posture	Competitive Strategy
• Local • Regional • National • Multicountry • Global	• Be the dominant leader • Overtake the present industry leader • Be among the industry leaders (top 5) • Move into the top 10 • Move up a notch or two in the industry rankings • Overtake a particular rival (not necessarily the leader) • Maintain position • Just survive	• Aggressive expansion via both acquisition and internal growth • Expansion via internal growth (boost market share at the expense of rival firms) • Expansion via acquisition • Hold on to present share (by growing at a rate equal to the industry average) • Give up share if necessary to achieve short-term profit objectives (stress profitability, not volume)	• Getting stronger; on the move • Well-entrenched; able to maintain its present position • Stuck in the middle of the pack • Going after a different market position (trying to move from a weaker to a stronger position) • Struggling; losing ground • Retrenching to a position that can be defended	• Mostly offensive • Mostly defensive • A combination of offense and defense • Aggressive risk-taker • Conservative follower	• Striving for low cost leadership • Mostly focusing on a market niche —High end —Low end —Geographic —Buyers with special needs —Other • Pursuing differentiation based on —Quality —Service —Technological superiority —Breadth of product line —Image and reputation —More value for the money —Other attributes

Note: Since a focus strategy can be aimed at any of several market niches and a differentiation strategy can be keyed to any of several attributes, it is best to be explicit about what kind of focus strategy or differentiation strategy a given firm is pursuing. All focusers do not pursue the same market niche, and all differentiators do not pursue the same differentiating attributes.

Evaluating Who the Industry's Major Players Are Going to Be   It's usually obvious who the *current* major contenders are, but these same firms are not necessarily positioned strongly for the future. Some may be losing ground or be ill-equipped to compete on the industry's future battleground. Smaller companies may be moving into contention and poised for an offensive against larger but vulnerable rivals. Long-standing market leaders sometimes slide quickly down the industry's ranks; others end up being acquired. Today's industry leaders don't automatically become tomorrow's.

In deciding whether a competitor is favorably or unfavorably positioned to gain market ground, attention needs to center on why there is potential for it to do better or worse than other rivals. Usually, how securely a company holds its present market share is a function of its vulnerability to driving forces and competitive pressures, whether it has a competitive advantage or disadvantage, and whether it is the likely target of offensive attack from other industry participants. Pinpointing which rivals are poised to gain market position and which rivals seem destined to lose market share helps a strategist anticipate what kinds of moves they are likely to make next.

Predicting Competitors' Next Moves   This is the hardest yet most useful part of competitor analysis. Good clues about what moves a specific company may make next come from studying its situation—understanding its strategic intent, monitoring how well it is faring in the marketplace, and determining how much pressure it is under to improve its financial performance. Aggressive rivals on the move are strong candidates for some type of new strategic initiative. Content rivals are likely to continue their present strategy with only minor fine-tuning. Ailing rivals can be performing so poorly that fresh strategic moves, either offensive or defensive, are virtually certain. Since managers generally operate from assumptions about the industry's future and beliefs about their own firm's situation, insights into their strategic thinking can be gleaned from their public pronouncements about where the industry is headed and what it will take to be successful, what they are saying about their firm's situation, information from the grapevine about what they are doing, and their past actions and leadership styles. Another thing to consider is whether a rival has the flexibility to make major strategic changes or whether it is locked into pursuing its same basic strategy with minor adjustments.

To succeed in predicting a competitor's next moves, one has to have a good feel for the rival's situation, how its managers think, and what its options are. Doing the necessary detective work can be tedious and time-consuming since the information comes in bits and pieces from many sources. But scouting competitors well enough to anticipate their next moves allows managers to prepare effective countermoves (perhaps even beat a rival to the punch!) and to take rivals' probable actions into account in designing the best course of action.

> **Managers who fail to study competitors closely risk being blindsided by "surprise" actions on the part of rivals.**

Question 6: What Are the Key Factors for Competitive Success?

An industry's *key success factors* (KSFs) are the strategy-related action approaches, competitive capabilities, and business outcomes that every firm must be competent at doing or must concentrate on achieving in order to be competitively and financially successful. KSFs are business aspects all firms in the industry must pay close attention to—the specific outcomes crucial to market success (or failure) and the competencies and competitive capabilities with the most direct bearing on company

An industry's *key success factors* spell the difference between profit and loss and, ultimately, between competitive success and failure.

Strategic Management Principle
A sound strategy incorporates industry key success factors.

profitability. In the beer industry, the KSFs are full utilization of brewing capacity (to keep manufacturing costs low), a strong network of wholesale distributors (to gain access to as many retail outlets as possible), and clever advertising (to induce beer drinkers to buy a particular brand and thereby pull beer sales through the established wholesale/retail channels). In apparel manufacturing, the KSFs are appealing designs and color combinations (to create buyer interest) and low-cost manufacturing efficiency (to permit attractive retail pricing and ample profit margins). In tin and aluminum cans, where the cost of shipping empty cans is substantial, one of the keys is having plants located close to end-use customers so that the plant's output can be marketed within economical shipping distances (regional market share is far more crucial than national share).

Determining the industry's key success factors, in light of prevailing and anticipated industry and competitive conditions, is a top-priority analytical consideration. At the very least, managers need to know the industry well enough to conclude what is more important to competitive success and what is less important. Company managers who misdiagnose what factors are truly crucial to long-term competitive success are prone to employ ill-conceived strategies or to pursue less important competitive targets. Frequently, a company with perceptive understanding of industry KSFs can gain sustainable competitive advantage by training its strategy on industry KSFs and devoting its energies to being distinctively better than rivals at succeeding on these factors. Indeed, using one or more of the industry's KSFs as *cornerstones* for the company's strategy is often a wise approach to crafting a winning managerial game plan.

Key success factors vary from industry to industry and even from time to time within the same industry as driving forces and competitive conditions change. Table 3–4 provides a shopping list of the most common types of key success factors. Only rarely does an industry have more than three or four key success factors at any one time. And even among these three or four, one or two usually outrank the others in importance. Managers, therefore, have to resist the temptation to include factors that have only minor importance on their list of key success factors—the purpose of identifying KSFs is to make judgments about what things are more important to competitive success and what things are less important. To compile a list of every factor that matters even a little bit defeats the purpose of concentrating management attention on the factors truly crucial to long-term competitive success.

Question 7: Is the Industry Attractive and What Are Its Prospects for Above-Average Profitability?

The final step of industry and competitive analysis is to review the overall industry situation and develop reasoned conclusions about the relative attractiveness or unattractiveness of the industry, both near-term and long-term. An assessment that the industry is fundamentally attractive typically suggests using an aggressive grow-and-build strategy, expanding sales efforts and investing in additional facilities and equipment as needed to strengthen the firm's long-term competitive position in the business. If the industry and competitive situation is judged relatively unattractive, more successful industry participants may choose to invest cautiously, look for ways to protect their long-term competitiveness and profitability, and perhaps acquire smaller firms if the price is right. Weaker companies may consider leaving the industry or merging with a rival. Stronger companies may consider diversification into more attractive businesses. Outsiders considering entry may decide against investing in the business and look elsewhere for opportunities.

Table 3–4 Types of Key Success Factors

Technology-Related KSFs
- Scientific research expertise (important in such fields as pharmaceuticals, medicine, space exploration, other "high-tech" industries)
- Production process innovation capability
- Product innovation capability
- Expertise in a given technology

Manufacturing-Related KSFs
- Low-cost production efficiency (achieve scale economies, capture experience curve effects)
- Quality of manufacture (fewer defects, less need for repairs)
- High utilization of fixed assets (important in capital intensive/high fixed-cost industries)
- Low-cost plant locations
- Access to adequate supplies of skilled labor
- High labor productivity (important for items with high labor content)
- Low-cost product design and engineering (reduces manufacturing costs)
- Flexibility to manufacture a range of models and sizes/take care of custom orders

Distribution-Related KSFs
- A strong network of wholesale distributors/dealers
- Gaining ample space on retailer shelves
- Having company-owned retail outlets
- Low distribution costs
- Fast delivery

Marketing-Related KSFs
- A well-trained, effective sales force
- Available, dependable service and technical assistance
- Accurate filling of buyer orders (few back orders or mistakes)
- Breadth of product line and product selection
- Merchandising skills
- Attractive styling/packaging
- Customer guarantees and warranties (important in mail-order retailing, big ticket purchases, new product introductions)

Skills-Related KSFs
- Superior talent (important in professional services)
- Quality control know-how
- Design expertise (important in fashion and apparel industries)
- Expertise in a particular technology
- Ability to come up with clever, catchy ads
- Ability to get newly developed products out of the R&D phase and into the market very quickly

Organizational Capability
- Superior information systems (important in airline travel, car rental, credit card, and lodging industries)
- Ability to respond quickly to shifting market conditions (streamlined decision-making, short lead times to bring new products to market)
- More experience and managerial know-how

Other Types of KSFs
- Favorable image/reputation with buyers
- Overall low cost (not just in manufacturing)
- Convenient locations (important in many retailing businesses)
- Pleasant, courteous employees
- Access to financial capital (important in newly emerging industries with high degrees of business risk and in capital-intensive industries)
- Patent protection

Important factors for company managers to consider in drawing conclusions about whether the industry is a good business to be in include

- The industry's growth potential.
- Whether the industry will be favorably or unfavorably impacted by the prevailing driving forces.
- The potential for the entry/exit of major firms (probable entry reduces attractiveness to existing firms; the exit of a major firm or several weak firms opens up market share growth opportunities for the remaining firms).
- The stability/dependability of demand (as affected by seasonality, the business cycle, the volatility of consumer preferences, inroads from substitutes, and the like).
- Whether competitive forces will become stronger or weaker.
- The severity of problems/issues confronting the industry as a whole.
- The degrees of risk and uncertainty in the industry's future.
- Whether competitive conditions and driving forces are conducive to rising or falling industry profitability.

As a general proposition, if an industry's overall profit prospects are above average, the industry can be considered attractive. If its profit prospects are below average, it is unattractive. However, it is a mistake to think of industries as being attractive or unattractive in an absolute sense. Attractiveness is relative, not absolute, and conclusions one way or the other are in the eye of the beholder. Companies on the outside may look at an industry's environment and conclude that it is an unattractive business for them to get into; they may see more profitable opportunities elsewhere. But a favorably positioned company already in the industry may survey the very same business environment and conclude that the industry is attractive because it has the resources and competitive capabilities to exploit the vulnerabilities of its weaker rivals, gain market share, build a strong leadership position, and grow its revenues and profits at a rapid clip. Hence industry attractiveness *always* has to be appraised from the standpoint of a particular company. Industries unattractive to outsiders may be attractive to insiders. Industry environments unattractive to weak competitors may be attractive to strong competitors.

A company that is uniquely well-situated in an otherwise unattractive industry can, under certain circumstances, still earn unusually good profits.

While companies contemplating entry into an industry can rely on the above list of factors, along with the answers to the first six questions, to draw conclusions about industry attractiveness, companies already in the industry need to consider the following additional aspects:

- The company's competitive position in the industry and whether its position is likely to grow stronger or weaker (being a well-entrenched leader in an otherwise lackluster industry can still produce good profitability).
- The company's potential to capitalize on the vulnerabilities of weaker rivals (thereby converting an unattractive *industry* situation into a potentially rewarding *company* opportunity).
- Whether the company is insulated from, or able to defend against, the factors that make the industry unattractive.
- Whether continued participation in this industry adds importantly to the firm's ability to be successful in other industries in which it has business interests.

ACTUALLY DOING AN INDUSTRY AND COMPETITIVE ANALYSIS

Table 3–5 provides a *format* for reporting the pertinent facts and conclusions of industry and competitive analysis. It pulls the relevant concepts and considerations together in systematic fashion and makes it easier to do a concise, understandable analysis of the industry and competitive environment.

Two things should be kept in mind in doing industry and competitive analysis. One, the task of analyzing a company's external situation cannot be reduced to a mechanical, formula-like exercise in which facts and data are plugged in and definitive conclusions come pouring out. There can be several appealing scenarios about how an industry will evolve and what future competitive conditions will be like. For this reason, strategic analysis always leaves room for differences of opinion about how all the factors add up and how industry and competitive conditions will change. However, while no strategy analysis methodology can guarantee a single conclusive diagnosis, it doesn't make sense to shortcut strategic analysis and rely on opinion and casual observation. Managers become better strategists when they know what analytical questions to pose, can use situation analysis techniques to find answers, and have the skills to read clues about which way the winds of industry and competitive change are blowing. This is why we concentrated on suggesting the right questions to ask, explaining concepts and analytical approaches, and indicating the kinds of things to look for.

Table 3–5 Industry and Competitive Analysis Summary Profile

1. **Dominant Economic Characteristics of the Industry Environment** (market growth, geographic scope, industry structure, scale economies, experience curve effects, capital requirements, and so on)

2. **Competition Analysis**
   - Rivalry among competing sellers (a strong, moderate, or weak force/weapons of competition)
   - Threat of potential entry (a strong, moderate, or weak force/assessment of entry barriers)
   - Competition from substitutes (a strong, moderate, or weak force/why)
   - Power of suppliers (a strong, moderate, or weak force/why)
   - Power of customers (a strong, moderate, or weak force/why)

3. **Driving Forces**

4. **Competitive Position of Major Companies/Strategic Groups**
   - Favorably positioned/why
   - Unfavorably positioned/why

5. **Competitor Analysis**
   - Strategic approaches/predicted moves of key competitors
   - Whom to watch and why

6. **Key Success Factors**

7. **Industry Prospects and Overall Attractiveness**
   - Factors making the industry attractive
   - Factors making the industry unattractive
   - Special industry issues/problems
   - Profit outlook (favorable/unfavorable)

Two, sweeping industry and competitive analyses need to be done every one to three years; in the interim, managers are obliged to continually update and reexamine their thinking as events unfold. There's no substitute for being a good student of industry and competitive conditions and staying on the cutting edge of what's happening in the industry. Anything else leaves a manager unprepared to initiate shrewd and timely strategic adjustments.

Key Points

Thinking strategically about a company's external situation involves probing for answers to the following seven questions:

1. *What are the industry's dominant economic traits?* Industries differ significantly on such factors as market size and growth rate, the scope of competitive rivalry, the number and relative sizes of both buyers and sellers, ease of entry and exit, whether sellers are vertically integrated, how fast basic technology is changing, the extent of scale economies and experience curve effects, whether the products of rival sellers are standardized or differentiated, and overall profitability. An industry's economic characteristics are important because of the implications they have for crafting strategy.

2. *What is competition like and how strong are each of the five competitive forces?* The strength of competition is a composite of five forces: the rivalry among competing sellers, the presence of attractive substitutes, the potential for new entry, the leverage major suppliers have, and the bargaining power of customers. The task of competition analysis is to assess each force, determine whether it produces strong or weak competitive pressures, and then think strategically about what sort of competitive strategy, given the "rules" of competition in the industry, the company will need to employ to (a) insulate the firm as much as possible from the five competitive forces, (b) influence the industry's competitive rules in the company's favor, and (c) gain a competitive edge.

3. *What is causing the industry's competitive structure and business environment to change?* Industry and competitive conditions change because forces are in motion that create incentives or pressures for change. The most common driving forces are changes in the long-term industry growth rate, changes in buyer composition, product innovation, entry or exit of major firms, globalization, changes in cost and efficiency, changing buyer preferences for standardized versus differentiated products or services, regulatory influences and government policy changes, changing societal and lifestyle factors, and reductions in uncertainty and business risk. Sound analysis of driving forces and their implications for the industry is a prerequisite to sound strategy-making.

4. *Which companies are in the strongest/weakest competitive positions?* Strategic group mapping is a valuable, if not necessary, tool for understanding the similarities, differences, strengths, and weaknesses inherent in the market positions of rival companies. Rivals in the same or nearby strategic group(s) are close competitors whereas companies in distant strategic groups usually pose little or no immediate threat.

5. *What strategic moves are rivals likely to make next?* This analytical step involves identifying competitors' strategies, deciding which rivals are likely to be strong contenders and which weak contenders, evaluating their competitive options, and predicting what moves they are likely to make next. Scouting competitors well enough to anticipate their actions helps prepare effective countermoves (perhaps even beat a rival to the punch) and allows managers to take rivals' probable actions into account in designing their own company's best course of action. Managers who fail to study competitors closely risk being blindsided by "surprise" actions on the part of rivals. A company can't expect to outmaneuver its rivals without monitoring their actions and anticipating what moves they may make next.

6. *What are the key factors for competitive success?* Key success factors are the strategy-related action approaches, competitive capabilities, and business outcomes which all firms in an industry must be competent at doing or must concentrate on achieving in order to be competitively and financially successful. Determining the industry's key success factors, in light of industry and competitive conditions, is a top-priority analytical consideration. Frequently, a company can gain sustainable competitive advantage by training its strategy on industry KSFs and devoting its energies to being distinctively better than rivals at succeeding on these factors. Companies that only dimly perceive what factors are truly crucial to long-term competitive success are less likely to have winning strategies.

7. *Is the industry attractive and what are its prospects for above-average profitability?* The answer to this question is a major driver of company strategy. An assessment that the industry and competitive environment is fundamentally attractive typically suggests employing an aggressive strategy to build a strong competitive position in the business, expanding sales efforts and investing in additional facilities and equipment as needed. If the industry is relatively unattractive, outsiders considering entry may decide against it and look elsewhere for opportunities, weak companies in the industry may merge with or be acquired by a rival, and strong companies may restrict further investments and employ cost-reduction strategies and/or product innovation strategies to boost long-term competitiveness and protect their profitability. On occasion, an industry that is unattractive overall is still very attractive to a favorably situated company with the skills and resources to take business away from weaker rivals.

Good industry and competitive analysis is crucial to good strategy-making. A competently done industry and competitive analysis provides the keen understanding of a company's macroenvironment managers need to craft a strategy that fits the company's external situation well.

D'Aveni, Richard A. *Hypercompetition*. New York: Free Press, 1994, chaps. 5 and 6.

Ghemawat, Pankaj. "Building Strategy on the Experience Curve." *Harvard Business Review* 64, no. 2 (March–April 1985), pp. 143–49.

Linneman, Robert E., and Harold E. Klein. "Using Scenarios in Strategic Decision Making." *Business Horizons* 28, no. 1 (January–February 1985), pp. 64–74.

Suggested Readings

Ohmae, Kenichi. *The Mind of the Strategist*. New York: Penguin Books, 1983, chaps. 3, 6, 7, and 13.

Porter, Michael E. "How Competitive Forces Shape Strategy." *Harvard Business Review* 57, no. 2 (March–April 1979), pp. 137–45.

———. *Competitive Strategy: Techniques for Analyzing Industries and Competitors*. New York: Free Press, 1980, chap. 1.

———. *Competitive Advantage*. New York: Free Press, 1985, chap. 2.

Yip, George S. *Total Global Strategy: Managing for Worldwide Competitive Advantage*. Englewood Cliffs, N.J.: Prentice-Hall, 1992, chap. 10.

Zahra, Shaker A. and Sherry S. Chaples. "Blind Spots in Competitive Analysis." *Academy of Management Executives* 7, no. 2 (May 1993), pp. 7–28.

CHAPTER FOUR

Company Situation Analysis

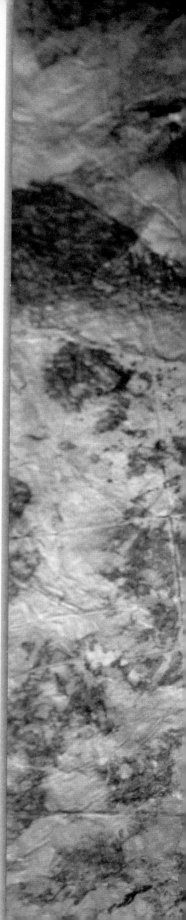

Understand what really makes a company "tick."

Charles R. Scott
CEO, Intermark Corporation

The secret of success is to be ready for opportunity when it comes.
Benjamin Disraeli

If a company is not "best in world" at a critical activity, it is sacrificing competitive advantage by performing that activity with its existing technique.
James Brian Quinn

In the previous chapter we described how to use the tools of industry and competitive analysis to think strategically about a company's external situation. In this chapter we discuss how to size up a company's strategic position in that environment. Company situation analysis centers on five questions:

1. How well is the present strategy working?
2. What are the company's strengths, weaknesses, opportunities, and threats?
3. Are the company's prices and costs competitive?
4. How strong is the company's competitive position?
5. What strategic issues does the company face?

To explore these questions, four new analytical techniques need to be mastered: SWOT analysis, value chain analysis, strategic cost analysis, and competitive strength assessment. These techniques are basic strategic management tools because they expose the pluses and minuses of a company's situation, the strength of its competitive position, and whether the present strategy needs to be modified.

QUESTION 1: HOW WELL IS THE PRESENT STRATEGY WORKING?

In evaluating how well a company's present strategy is working, a manager has to start with what the strategy is (see Figure 2–3 in Chapter 2 to refresh your recollection of the key components of business strategy) and what the company's strategic and financial objectives are. The first thing to pin down is the company's competitive approach—whether it is (1) striving to be a low-cost leader, (2) stressing ways to differentiate its product offering from rivals, or (3) concentrating its efforts on a narrow market niche. Another strategy-defining consideration is the firm's competitive scope within the industry—how many stages of the industry's production-distribution chain it operates in (one, several, or all), the size and diversity of its geographic market coverage, and the size and diversity of its customer base. The company's functional strategies in production, marketing, finance, human resources, and so on further characterize company strategy. In addition, the company may have initiated some recent strategic moves (for instance, a price cut, stepped-up advertising, entry into a new geographic area, or merger with a competitor) that are integral to its strategy and that aim at securing a particular competitive advantage and/or improved competitive position. Reviewing the rationale for each piece of the strategy—for each competitive move and each functional approach—clarifies what the present strategy is.

While there's merit in evaluating the strategy from a qualitative standpoint (its completeness, internal consistency, rationale, and suitability to the situation), the best evidence of how well a company's strategy is working comes from studying the company's recent strategic and financial performance and seeing what story the numbers tell about the results the strategy is producing. Obvious indicators of strategic and financial performance include (1) the firm's market share ranking in the industry, (2) whether the firm's profit margins are increasing or decreasing and how large they are relative to rival firms' margins, (3) trends in the firm's net profits and return on investment, (4) the company's credit rating, (5) whether the firm's sales are growing faster or slower than the market as a whole, (6) the firm's image and reputation with its customers, and (7) whether the company is regarded as a leader in technology, product innovation, product quality, customer service, and the like. The stronger a company's current overall performance, the less likely the need for radical changes in strategy. The weaker a company's strategic and financial performance, the more its current strategy must be questioned. Weak performance is usually a sign of weak strategy or weak execution or both.

> **The stronger a company's strategic and financial performance, the more likely it has a well-conceived, well-executed strategy.**

QUESTION 2: WHAT ARE THE COMPANY'S STRENGTHS, WEAKNESSES, OPPORTUNITIES, AND THREATS?

Sizing up a firm's internal strengths and weaknesses and its external opportunities and threats is commonly known as *SWOT analysis*. It is an easy-to-use technique for getting a quick *overview* of a firm's strategic situation. SWOT analysis underscores the basic principle that strategy must produce a good fit between a company's internal capability (its strengths and weaknesses) and its external situation (reflected in part by its opportunities and threats).

Identifying Internal Strengths and Weaknesses

A *strength* is something a company is good at doing or a characteristic that gives it an important capability. A strength can be a skill, important expertise, a valuable organizational resource or competitive capability, or an achievement that puts the company in a position of market advantage (like having a better product, stronger name recognition, superior technology, or better customer service). A strength can also result from alliances or cooperative ventures with a partner having expertise or capabilities that enhance a company's competitiveness.

A *weakness* is something a company lacks or does poorly (in comparison to others) or a condition that puts it at a disadvantage. A weakness may or may not make a company competitively vulnerable, depending on how much the weakness matters in the marketplace. Table 4–1 indicates the kinds of factors managers should consider in determining a company's internal strengths and weaknesses.

Once managers identify a company's internal strengths and weaknesses, the two compilations need to be carefully evaluated from a strategy-making perspective. Some strengths are more important than others because they matter more in determining performance, in competing successfully, and in forming a powerful strategy. Likewise, some internal weaknesses can prove fatal, while others are inconsequential or easily remedied. Sizing up a company's strengths and weaknesses is akin to

---

Table 4–1   SWOT Analysis—What to Look for in Sizing Up a Company's Strengths, Weaknesses, Opportunities, and Threats

Potential Internal Strength	Potential Internal Weaknesses
• Core competencies in key areas	• No clear strategic direction
• Adequate financial resources	• Obsolete facilities
• Well-thought-of by buyers	• Subpar profitability because . . .
• An acknowledged market leader	• Lack of managerial depth and talent
• Well-conceived functional area strategies	• Missing some key skills or competencies
• Access to economies of scale	• Poor track record in implementing strategy
• Insulated (at least somewhat) from strong competitive pressures	• Plagued with internal operating problems
• Proprietary technology	• Falling behind in R&D
• Cost advantages	• Too narrow a product line
• Better advertising campaigns	• Weak market image
• Product innovation skills	• Weak distribution network
• Proven management	• Below-average marketing skills
• Ahead on experience curve	• Unable to finance needed changes in strategy
• Better manufacturing capability	• Higher overall unit costs relative to key competitors
• Superior technological skills	• Other?
• Other?	

Potential External Opportunities	Potential External Threats
• Ability to serve additional customer groups or expand into new markets or segments	• Entry of lower-cost foreign competitors
• Ways to expand product line to meet broader range of customer needs	• Rising sales of substitute products
• Ability to transfer skills or technological know-how to new products or businesses	• Slower market growth
• Integrating forward or backward	• Adverse shifts in foreign exchange rates and trade policies of foreign governments
• Falling trade barriers in attractive foreign markets	• Costly regulatory requirements
• Complacency among rival firms	• Vulnerability to recession and business cycle
• Ability to grow rapidly because of strong increases in market demand	• Growing bargaining power of customers or suppliers
• Emerging new technologies	• Changing buyer needs and tastes
	• Adverse demographic changes
	• Other?

Basic Concept
A company's internal strengths usually represent competitive assets; its internal weaknesses usually represent competitive liabilities.

constructing a *strategic balance sheet* where strengths represent *competitive assets* and weaknesses represent *competitive liabilities*. The strategic issues are whether the company's strengths/assets adequately overcome its weaknesses/liabilities (50-50 balance is definitely not the desired condition!), how to meld company strengths into an effective strategy, and whether management actions are needed to tilt the company's strategic balance more toward strengths/assets and away from weaknesses/liabilities.

From a strategy-making perspective, a company's strengths are significant because they can form the cornerstones of strategy and the basis for creating competitive advantage. If a company doesn't have strong capabilities and competitive assets around which to craft an attractive strategy, managers need to take decisive remedial action to develop organizational strengths and competencies that can underpin a sound strategy. At the same time, managers have to correct competitive weaknesses that make the company vulnerable, hurt its strategic performance, or disqualify it from pursuing an attractive opportunity. The strategy-making principle here is simple: *a company's strategy should be well-suited to its strengths, weaknesses, and competitive capabilities.* It is foolhardy to pursue a strategic plan that cannot be competently executed with the skills and resources a company can marshal or that can be undermined by company weaknesses. As a rule, managers should build their strategies around what the company does best and avoid strategies that place heavy demands on areas where the company is weakest or has unproven ability.

Strategic Management Principle
Successful strategists seek to capitalize on what a company does best—its expertise, strengths, core competencies, and strongest competitive capabilities.

Core Competencies   One of the "trade secrets" of first-rate strategic management is consolidating a company's technological, production, and marketing know-how into core competencies that enhance its competitiveness. *A core competence is something a company does especially well in comparison to its competitors.*[1] In practice, there are many possible types of core competencies: excellent skills in manufacturing a high quality product, know-how in creating and operating a system for filling customer orders accurately and swiftly, the capability to provide better after-sale service, a unique formula for selecting good retail locations, unusual innovativeness in developing new products, better skills in merchandising and product display, superior mastery of an important technology, a carefully crafted process for researching customer needs and tastes and spotting new market trends, an unusually effective sales force, outstanding skills in working with customers on new applications and uses of the product, and expertise in integrating multiple technologies to create whole families of new products. Typically, a core competence relates to a set of skills, expertise in performing particular activities, or a company's scope and depth of technological know-how; it resides in a company's people, not in assets on the balance sheet.

The importance of a core competence to strategy-making rests with (1) the added capability it gives a company in going after a particular market opportunity, (2) the competitive edge it can yield in the marketplace, and (3) its potential for being a cornerstone of strategy. It is always easier to build competitive advantage when a firm has a core competence in performing activities important to market success, when rival companies do not have offsetting competencies, and when it is

Strategic Management Principle
Core competencies empower a company to build competitive advantage.

---

[1]For a fuller discussion of the core competence concept, see C. K. Prahalad and Gary Hamel, "The Core Competence of the Corporation," *Harvard Business Review* 90, no. 3 (May–June 1990), pp. 79–93.

costly and time-consuming for rivals to match the competence. Core competencies are thus valuable competitive assets, capable of being the mainsprings of a company's success.

Identifying External Opportunities and Threats

Market opportunity is a big factor in shaping a company's strategy. Indeed, managers can't match strategy to the company's situation without first identifying each industry opportunity and appraising the growth and profit potential each one holds. Depending on industry conditions, opportunities can be plentiful or scarce and can range from wildly attractive (an absolute "must" to pursue) to marginally interesting (low on the company's list of strategic priorities).

In appraising industry opportunities and ranking their attractiveness, managers have to guard against equating industry opportunities with company opportunities. Not every company in an industry is well-positioned to pursue each opportunity that exists in the industry—ome companies are more competitively situated than others and a few may be hopelessly out of contention or at least limited to a minor role. A company's strengths, weaknesses, and competitive capabilities make it better suited to pursuing some industry opportunities than others. *The industry opportunities most relevant to a particular company are those that offer important avenues for profitable growth, those where a company has the most potential for competitive advantage, and those which the company has the financial resources to pursue.* An industry opportunity that a company doesn't have the capability to capture is an illusion.

Often, certain factors in a company's external environment pose *threats* to its well-being. Threats can stem from the emergence of cheaper technologies, rivals' introduction of new or better products, the entry of low-cost foreign competitors into a company's market stronghold, new regulations that are more burdensome to a company than to its competitors, vulnerability to a rise in interest rates, the potential of a hostile takeover, unfavorable demographic shifts, adverse changes in foreign exchange rates, political upheaval in a foreign country where the company has facilities, and the like. Table 4–1 also presents a checklist of things to be alert for in identifying a company's external opportunities and threats.

Opportunities and threats not only affect the attractiveness of a company's situation but point to the need for strategic action. To be adequately matched to a company's situation, strategy must (1) be aimed at pursuing opportunities well-suited to the company's capabilities and (2) provide a defense against external threats. SWOT analysis is therefore more than an exercise in making four lists. The important part of SWOT analysis involves *evaluating* a company's strengths, weaknesses, opportunities, and threats and *drawing conclusions* about the attractiveness of the company's situation and the possible need for strategic action. Some of the pertinent strategy-making questions to consider, once the SWOT listings have been compiled, are:

- Does the company have any internal strengths or core competencies an attractive strategy can be built around?

- Do the company's weaknesses make it competitively vulnerable and/or do they disqualify the company from pursuing certain industry opportunities? Which weaknesses does strategy need to correct?

- Which industry opportunities does the company have the skills and resources to pursue with a real chance of success? Which industry

---

Strategic Management Principle
Successful strategists aim at capturing a company's best growth opportunities and creating defenses against threats to its competitive position and future performance.

opportunities are "best" from the company's standpoint? (*Remember*: Opportunity without the means to capture it is an illusion.)

- What external threats should management be worried most about and what strategic moves should be considered in crafting a good defense?

Unless management is acutely aware of the company's internal strengths and weaknesses and its external opportunities and threats, it is ill-prepared to craft a strategy tightly matched to the company's situation. SWOT analysis is therefore an essential component of thinking strategically about a company's situation.

QUESTION 3: ARE THE COMPANY'S PRICES AND COSTS COMPETITIVE?

Company managers are often stunned when a competitor cuts price to "unbelievably low" levels or when a new market entrant comes on strong with a very low price. The competitor may not, however, be "dumping," buying market share, or waging a desperate move to gain sales; it may simply have substantially lower costs. One of the most telling signs of whether a company's market position is strong or precarious is whether its prices and costs are competitive with industry rivals. Price-cost comparisons are especially critical in a commodity-product industry where the value provided to buyers is the same from seller to seller, price competition is typically the ruling market force, and lower-cost companies have the upper hand. But even in industries where products are differentiated and competition centers around the different attributes of competing brands as much as around price, rival companies have to keep their costs *in line* and make sure that any added costs they incur and price premiums they charge create ample buyer value.

> **Assessing whether a company's costs are competitive with those of its close rivals is a necessary and crucial part of company situation analysis.**

Competitors usually don't incur the same costs in supplying their products to end-users. The cost disparities can range from trivial to competitively significant and can arise from any of several factors:

- Differences in the prices paid for raw materials, components parts, energy, and other items purchased from suppliers.
- Differences in basic technology and the age of plants and equipment. (Because rival companies usually invest in plants and key pieces of equipment at different times, their facilities have somewhat different technological efficiencies and different fixed costs. Older facilities are typically less efficient, but if they were less expensive to construct or were acquired at bargain prices, they *may* still be reasonably cost competitive with modern facilities.)
- Differences in internal operating costs due to economies of scale associated with different-size plants, learning and experience curve effects, different wage rates, different productivity levels, different operating practices, different organization structures and staffing levels, different tax rates, and the like.
- Differences in rival firms' exposure to inflation rates and changes in foreign exchange rates (as can occur in global industries where competitors have plants located in different nations).
- Differences in marketing costs, sales and promotion expenditures, and advertising expenses.

- Differences in inbound transportation costs and outbound shipping costs.
- Differences in forward channel distribution costs (the costs and markups of distributors, wholesalers, and retailers associated with getting the product from the point of manufacture into the hands of end users).

For a company to be competitively successful, its costs must be in line with those of close rivals. While some cost disparity is justified so long as the products or services of closely competing companies are sufficiently differentiated, a high-cost firm's market position becomes increasingly vulnerable the more its costs exceed those of close rivals.

Strategic Cost Analysis and Value Chains

Given the numerous opportunities for cost disparities, a company must thus be alert to how its costs compare with rivals'. This is where *strategic cost analysis* comes in. *Strategic cost analysis focuses on a firm's cost position relative to its rivals'.*

The Value Chain Concept   The primary analytical tool of strategic cost analysis is a *value chain* identifying the activities, functions, and business processes that have to be performed in designing, producing, marketing, delivering, and supporting a product or service.[2] The chain of value-creating activities starts with raw materials supply and continues on through parts and components production, manufacturing and assembly, wholesale distribution, and retailing to the ultimate end-user of the product or service.

A *company's* value chain shows the linked set of activities and functions it performs internally (see Figure 4–1). The chain includes a profit margin because a markup over the cost of performing the firm's value-creating activities is customarily part of the price (or total cost) borne by buyers—creating value that exceeds the cost of doing so is a fundamental objective of business.

By disaggregating a company's operations into strategically relevant activities and business processes, it is possible to better understand the company's cost structure and to see where the major cost elements are. Each activity in the value chain incurs costs and ties up assets; assigning the company's operating costs and assets to each individual activity in the chain provides cost estimates for each activity. The costs a company incurs in performing each activity can be driven up or down by two types of factors: *structural drivers* (scale economies, experience curve effects, technology requirements, capital intensity, and product line complexity) and *executional drivers* (how committed the work force is to continuous improvement, employee attitudes and organizational capabilities regarding product quality and process quality, cycle time in getting newly developed products to market, utilization of existing capacity, whether internal business processes are efficiently designed and executed, and how effectively the firm works with suppliers and/or customers to reduce the costs of performing its activities). Understanding a company's cost structure means understanding

Principle of Competitive Markets
The higher a company's costs are above those of close rivals, the more competitively vulnerable it becomes.

Basic Concept
Strategic cost analysis involves comparing a company's cost position relative to key competitors activity by activity all the way from raw materials purchase to the price paid by ultimate customers.

Basic Concept
A company's value chain identifies the primary activities that create value for customers and the related support activities; value chains are a tool for thinking strategically about the relationships among activities performed inside and outside the firm—which ones are strategy-critical and how core competencies can be developed.

---

[2]Value chains and strategic cost analysis are described at greater length in Michael E. Porter, *Competitive Advantage* (New York: Free Press, 1985), chapters 2 and 3; Robin Cooper and Robert S. Kaplan, "Measure Costs Right: Make the Right Decisions," *Harvard Business Review* 66, no. 5 (September–October, 1988), pp. 96–103; and John K. Shank and Vijay Govindarajan, *Strategic Cost Management* (New York: Free Press, 1993), especially chapters 2–6 and 10.

- Whether it is trying to achieve a competitive advantage based on (1) lower costs (in which case managerial efforts to lower costs along the company's value chain should be highly visible) or (2) differentiation (in which case managers may deliberately spend more performing those activities responsible for creating the differentiating attributes).

Figure 4–1　Representative Company Value Chain

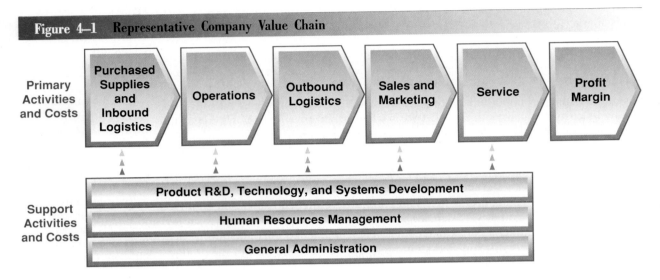

Primary Activities

- **Purchased Supplies and Inbound Logistics**—Activities, costs, and assets associated with purchasing fuel, energy, raw materials, parts components, merchandise, and consumable items from vendors; receiving storing, and disseminating inputs from suppliers; inspection; and inventory management.
- **Operations**—Activities, costs, and assets associated with converting inputs into final product form (production, assembly, packaging, equipment maintenance, facilities, operations, quality assurance, environmental protection).
- **Outbound Logistics**—Activities, costs, and assets dealing with physically distributing the product to buyers (finished goods warehousing, order processing, order picking and packing, shipping, delivery vehicle operations).
- **Sales and Marketing**—Activities, costs, and assets related to sales force efforts, advertising and promotion, market research and planning, and dealer/distributor support.
- **Service**—Activities, costs, and assets associated with providing assistance to buyers, such as installation, spare parts delivery, maintenance and repair, technical assistance, buyer inquiries, and complaints.

Support Activities

- **Research, Technology, and Systems Development**—Activities, costs, and assets relating to product R&D, process R&D, process design improvement, equipment design, computer software development, telecommunications systems, computer-assisted design and engineering, new database capabilities, and development of computerized support systems.
- **Human Resources Management**—Activities, costs, and assets associated with the recruitment, hiring, training, development, and compensation of all types of personnel; labor relations activities; development of knowledge-based skills.
- **General Administration**—Activities, costs, and assets relating to general management, accounting and finance, legal and regulatory affairs, safety and security, management information systems, and other "overhead" functions.

Source: Adapted from Michael E. Porter, *Competitive Advantage* (New York: The Free Press, 1985), pp. 37-43.

- Cost behavior in each activity in the value chain and how the costs of one activity spill over to affect the costs of others.
- Whether the linkages among activities in the company's value chain present opportunities for cost reduction (for example, Japanese VCR producers were able to reduce prices from $1,300 in 1977 to under $300 in 1984 by spotting the impact of an early step in the value chain, product design, on a later step, production, and deciding to drastically reduce the number of parts).[3]

However, there's more to strategic cost analysis and a company's cost competitiveness than just comparing the costs of activities comprising rivals' value chains. Competing companies often differ in their degrees of vertical integration. Comparing the value chain for a partially integrated rival against a fully integrated rival requires adjusting for differences in scope of activities performed. Moreover, uncompetitive prices can have their origins in activities performed by suppliers or by forward channel allies involved in getting the product to end-users. Suppliers or forward channel allies may have excessively high cost structures or profit margins that jeopardize a company's cost competitiveness even though its costs for internally performed activities are competitive.

For example, when determining Michelin's cost competitiveness vis-à-vis Goodyear and Bridgestone in supplying replacement tires to vehicle owners, one has to look at more than whether Michelin's tire manufacturing costs are above or below Goodyear's and Bridgestone's. If a buyer has to pay $400 for a set of Michelin tires and only $350 for comparable sets of Goodyear or Bridgestone tires, Michelin's $50 price disadvantage in the replacement tire marketplace can stem not only from higher manufacturing costs (reflecting, *perhaps*, the added costs of Michelin's strategic efforts to build a better quality tire with more performance features) but also from (1) differences in what the three tiremakers pay their suppliers for materials and tire-making components and (2) differences in the operating efficiencies, costs, and markups of Michelin's wholesale-retail dealer outlets versus those of Goodyear and Bridgestone. Thus, determining whether a company's prices and costs are competitive from an end-user's standpoint requires looking at the activities and costs of competitively relevant suppliers and forward allies, as well as the costs of internally performed activities.

As the tire industry example makes clear, a company's value chain is embedded in a larger system of activities that includes the value chains of its upstream suppliers and downstream customers or allies engaged in getting its product/service to end-users.[4] Accurately assessing a company's competitiveness in end-use markets requires that company managers understand the entire value delivery system, not just the company's own value chain; at the very least, this means considering the value chains of suppliers and forward channel allies (if any)—as shown in Figure 4–2. Suppliers' value chains are relevant because suppliers perform activities and incur costs in creating and delivering the purchased inputs used in a company's own value chain; the cost and quality of these inputs influence the company's cost and/or differentiation capabilities. Anything a company can do to reduce its suppliers' costs or improve suppliers' effectiveness can enhance its own competitiveness. Forward channel value chains are relevant because (1) the costs and margins of downstream companies are part of the price the ultimate end-user pays and (2) the activities forward channel allies perform

Value chains are also a tool for understanding the firm's cost structure and how costs are driven up or down within activities and across activities.

A company's cost competitiveness depends not only on the costs of internally performed activities (its own value chain) but also on costs in the value chains of suppliers and forward channel allies.

[3]M. Hegert and D. Morris, "Accounting Data for Value Chain Analysis," *Strategic Management Journal* 10 (1989), p. 183.

[4]Porter, *Competitive Advantage*, p. 34.

Figure 4–2   The Value Chain System

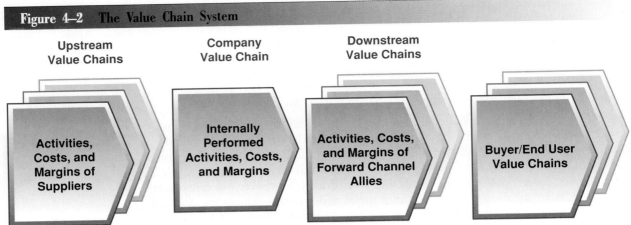

Upstream Value Chains

Activities, Costs, and Margins of Suppliers

Company Value Chain

Internally Performed Activities, Costs, and Margins

Downstream Value Chains

Activities, Costs, and Margins of Forward Channel Allies

Buyer/End User Value Chains

Source: Adapted from Michael E. Porter, *Competitive Advantage* (New York: The Free Press, 1985), p. 35.

affect the end-user's satisfaction. Furthermore, a company can often enhance its competitiveness by undertaking activities that have a beneficial impact on its customers' value chains. For instance, some aluminum can producers constructed plants next to beer breweries and delivered cans on overhead conveyors directly to brewers' can-filling lines. This resulted in significant savings in production scheduling, shipping, and inventory costs for both container producers and breweries.[5]

Although the value chains in Figures 4–1 and 4–2 are typical, the nature of the chains and the relative importance of the activities within them vary by industry and by company position in the value chain system. The value chain for the pulp and paper industry (timber farming, logging, pulp mills, papermaking, printing, and publishing) differs from the chain for the home appliance industry (parts and components manufacture, assembly, wholesale distribution, retail sales). The value chain for the soft drink industry (processing of basic ingredients, syrup manufacture, bottling and can filling, wholesale distribution, retailing) differs from the chain for the computer software industry (programming, disk loading, marketing, distribution). A producer of bathroom and kitchen faucets depends heavily on the activities of wholesale distributors and building supply retailers to represent its products to homebuilders and do-it-yourselfers; a producer of small gasoline engines markets directly to the makers of lawn and garden equipment. A wholesaler's most important activities and costs deal with purchased goods, inbound logistics, and outbound logistics. A hotel's most important activities and costs are in operations—check-in and check-out, maintenance and housekeeping, dining and room service, conventions and meetings, and accounting. A global public accounting firm's most important activities and costs revolve around customer service and human resources management (recruiting and training a highly competent professional staff). Outbound logistics is a crucial activity at Domino's Pizza but comparatively insignificant at Blockbuster. Sales and marketing are dominant activities at Coca-Cola but only minor activities at electric and gas utilities. Consequently, generic value chains like those in Figures 4–1 and 4–2 are illustrative, not absolute, and may require adaptation to fit a particular company's circumstances.

---

[5]Hegert and Morris, "Accounting Data for Value Chain Analysis," p. 180.

Developing the Data for Strategic Cost Analysis   The data requirements for value chain analysis can be formidable. Typically, the analyst must break down a firm's departmental cost accounting data into the costs of performing specific activities.[6] The appropriate degree of disaggregation depends on the economics of the activities and how valuable it is to develop cross-company cost comparisons for narrowly defined activities as opposed to broadly defined activities. A good guideline is to develop separate cost estimates for activities having different economics and for activities representing a significant or growing proportion of cost.[7]

Traditional accounting identifies costs according to broad categories of expenses—wages and salaries, employee benefits, supplies, travel, depreciation, R&D, and other fixed charges. *Activity-based costing* entails assigning these broad categories of costs to the specific tasks and activities being performed, as shown in Table 4–2.[8] It also entails developing cost estimates for activities performed in the competitively relevant portions of suppliers' and downstream customers' value chains. To benchmark the firm's cost position against rivals, costs for the same activities for each rival must be estimated—an advanced art in competitive intelligence. But despite the tediousness of developing cost estimates activity by activity and the imprecision of some of the estimates, the payoff in exposing the costs of particular internal tasks and functions and the cost competitiveness of one's position vis-â-vis rivals makes activity-based costing a valuable strategic management tool. Despite the calculation problems, every company's managers should attempt to estimate the value chain for their business.[9] Illustration Capsule 9 shows a simplified value chain comparison for two prominent brewers of beer—Anheuser-Busch (the U.S. industry leader) and Adolph Coors (the third-ranking brewer).

The most important application of value chain analysis is to expose how a particular firm's cost position compares with the cost positions of its rivals. What is needed is competitor versus competitor cost estimates for supplying a product or service to a well-defined customer group or market segment. The size of a company's cost advantage/disadvantage can vary from item to item in the product line, from customer group to customer group (if different distribution channels are used), and from geographic market to geographic market (if cost factors vary across geographic regions).

Benchmarking the Costs of Key Activities

Many companies today are benchmarking the costs of performing a given activity against competitors' costs (and/or against the costs of a noncompetitor in another industry that efficiently and effectively performs much the same activity or business process). Benchmarking focuses on cross-company comparisons of how well basic functions and processes in the value chain are performed—how materials are purchased, how suppliers are paid, how inventories are managed, how employees are trained, how payrolls are processed, how fast the company can get new products to

---

[6]For discussions of the accounting challenges in calculating the costs of value chain activities, see Shank and Govindarajan, *Strategic Cost Management*, pp. 62–72 and chapter 5, and Hegert and Morris, "Accounting Data for Value Chain Analysis," pp. 175–88.

[7]Porter, *Competitive Advantage*, p. 45.

[8]For a discussion of activity-based cost accounting, see Cooper and Kaplan, "Measure Costs Right: Make the Right Decisions," pp. 96–103; Shank and Govindarajan, *Strategic Cost Management*, Chapter 11; and Terence P. Paré, "A New Tool for Managing Costs," *Fortune*, June 14, 1993, pp. 124–29.

[9]Shank and Govindarajan, *Strategic Cost Management*, p. 62.

Table 4–2   The Difference between Traditional Cost Accounting and Activity-Based Cost Accounting

Traditional Cost Accounting Categories in Departmental Budget		Cost of Performing Specific Departmental Activities Using Activity-Based Cost Accounting	
Wages and salaries	$350,000	Evaluate supplier capabilities	$135,750
Employee benefits	115,000	Process purchase orders	82,100
Supplies	6,500	Expedite supplier deliveries	23,500
Travel	2,400	Expedite internal processing	15,840
Depreciation	17,000	Check quality of items purchased	94,300
Other fixed charges	124,000	Check incoming deliveries against purchase orders	48,450
Miscellaneous operating expenses	25,250	Resolve problems	110,000
		Internal administration	130,210
	$640,150		$640,150

Source: Adapted from information in Terence P. Paré, "A New Tool for Managing Costs," *Fortune*, June 14, 1993, pp. 124-29.

Benchmarking the performance of company activities against rivals and other best-practice companies provides hard evidence of a company's cost competitiveness.

market, how the quality control function is performed, how customer orders are filled and shipped, and how maintenance is performed.[10] The ultimate objective is to understand the best practices in performing an activity, to learn how lower costs are actually achieved, and to take action to improve a company's cost competitiveness whenever benchmarking reveals that the costs of performing an activity are out of line with what other companies (competitors or noncompetitors) have been able to achieve successfully.

In 1979, Xerox became an early pioneer in the use of benchmarking when Japanese manufacturers began selling mid-size copiers in the U.S. for $9,600 each—less than Xerox's production costs.[11] Although Xerox management suspected its Japanese competitors were dumping, it sent a team of line managers to Japan, including the head of manufacturing, to study competitors' business processes and costs. Fortunately, Xerox's joint venture partner in Japan, Fuji-Xerox, knew the competitors well. The team found that Xerox's costs were excessive due to gross inefficiencies in its manufacturing processes and business practices; the study proved instrumental in Xerox's efforts to become cost competitive and prompted Xerox to embark on a long-term program to benchmark 67 of its key work processes against companies identified as having the "best practices" in performing these processes. Xerox quickly decided not to restrict its benchmarking efforts to its office equipment rivals but to extend them to any company regarded as "world class" in performing an activity relevant to Xerox's business. Illustration Capsule 10 describes one of Ford Motor's benchmarking experiences.

Sometimes cost benchmarking can be accomplished by collecting information from published reports, trade groups, and industry research firms and by talking to knowledgeable industry analysts, customers, and suppliers (customers, suppliers, and joint-venture partners often make willing benchmarking allies). Usually, though,

---

[10]For more details, see Gregory H Watson, *Strategic Benchmarking: How to Rate Your Company's Performance Against the World's Best* (New York: John Wiley, 1993) and Robert C. Camp, *Benchmarking: The Search for Industry Best Practices That Lead to Superior Performance* (Milwaukee:ASQC Quality Press, 1989). See also Alexandra Biesada, "Strategic Benchmarking," *Financial World*, September 29, 1992, pp. 30–38.

[11]Jeremy Main, "How to Steal the Best Ideas Around," *Fortune*, October 19, 1992, pp. 102–3.

Illustration Capsule 9 Value Chains for Anheuser-Busch and Adolph Coors Beers

In the table below are average cost estimates for the combined brands of beer produced by Anheuser-Busch and Coors. The example shows raw material costs, other manufacturing costs, and forward channel distribution costs. The data are for 1982.

Value Chain Activities and Costs	Estimated Average Cost Breakdown for Combined Anheuser-Busch Brands		Estimated Average Cost Breakdown for Combined Adolph Coors Brands	
	Per 6-Pack of 12-oz Cans	Per Barrel Equivalent	Per 6-Pack of 12-oz Cans	Per Barrel Equivalent
1. Manufacturing costs				
Direct production costs:				
Raw material ingredients	$0.1384	$ 7.63	$0.1082	$ 5.96
Direct labor	0.1557	8.58	0.1257	6.93
Salaries for nonunionized personnel	0.0800	4.41	0.0568	3.13
Packaging	0.5055	27.86	0.4663	25.70
Depreciation on plant and equipment	0.0410	2.26	0.0826	4.55
Subtotal	0.9206	50.74	0.8396	46.27
Other expenses:				
Advertising	0.0477	2.63	0.0338	1.86
Other marketing costs and general administrative expenses	0.1096	6.04	0.1989	10.96
Interest	0.0147	0.81	0.0033	0.18
Research and development	0.0277	1.53	0.0195	1.07
Total manufacturing costs	$1.1203	$ 61.75	$1.0951	$ 60.34
2. Manufacturer's operating profit	0.1424	7.85	0.0709	3.91
3. Net selling price	1.2627	69.60	1.1660	64.25
4. Plus federal and state excise taxes paid by brewer	0.1873	10.32	0.1782	9.82
5. Gross manufacturer's selling price to distributor/wholesaler	1.4500	79.92	1.3442	74.07
6. Average margin over manufacturer's cost	0.5500	30.31	0.5158	28.43
7. Average wholesale price charged to retailer (inclusive of taxes in item 4 above but exclusive of other taxes)	$2.00	$110.23	$1.86	$102.50
8. Plus other assorted state and local taxes levied on wholesale and retail sales (this varies from locality to locality)	0.60		0.60	
9. Average 20% retail markup over wholesale cost	0.40		0.38	
10. Average price to consumer at retail	$3.00		$2.84	

Note: The difference in the average cost structures for Anheuser-Busch and Adolph Coors is, to a substantial extent, due to A-B's higher proportion of super-premium beer sales. A-B's super-premium brand, Michelob, was the bestseller in its category and somewhat more costly to brew than premium and popular-priced beers.

Source: Compiled by Tom McLean, Elsa Wischkaemper, and Arthur A. Thompson, Jr., from a wide variety of documents and field interviews.

Illustration Capsule 10   Ford Motor Company's Benchmarking of Its Accounts Payable Activity

In the 1980s Ford's North American accounts payable department employed more than 500 people. Clerks spent the majority of their time straightening out the relatively few situations where three documents—the purchase order issued by the purchasing department, the receiving document prepared by clerks at the receiving dock, and the invoice sent by the vendor/supplier to accounts payable—did not match. Sometimes resolving the discrepancies took weeks of time and the efforts of many people. Ford managers believed that by using computers to automate some functions performed manually, head count could be reduced to 400.

Before proceeding, Ford managers decided to visit Mazda—a company in which Ford had recently acquired a 25 percent ownership interest. To their astonishment, Mazda handled its accounts payable function with only five people. Following Mazda's lead, Ford benchmarkers created an invoiceless system where payments to suppliers were triggered automatically when the goods were received. The reengineered system allowed Ford to reduce its accounts payable staff to under 200, a lot more than Mazda but much better than would have resulted without benchmarking the accounts payable activity.

Sources: Michael Hammer and James Champy, *Reengineering the Corporation* (New York: HarperBusiness, 1993), pp. 39–43, and Jeremy Main, "How to Steal the Best Ideas Around," *Fortune*, October 19, 1992, p. 106.

benchmarking requires field trips to the facilities of competing or noncompeting companies to observe how things are done, ask questions, compare practices and processes, and perhaps exchange data on productivity, staffing levels, time requirements, and other cost components. However, benchmarking involves competitively sensitive information about how lower costs are achieved, and close rivals can't be expected to be completely open, even if they agree to host facilities tours and answer questions. But the explosive interest of companies in benchmarking costs and identifying best practices has prompted consulting organizations (for example, Andersen Consulting, A. T. Kearney, Best Practices Benchmarking & Consulting, and Towers Perrin) and several newly formed councils and associations (the International Benchmarking Clearinghouse and the Strategic Planning Institute's Council on Benchmarking) to gather benchmarking data, do benchmarking studies, and distribute information about best practices and the costs of performing activities to clients/members without identifying the sources. The ethical dimension of benchmarking is discussed in Illustration Capsule 11. Over 80 percent of *Fortune 500* companies now engage in some form of benchmarking.

Benchmarking is a manager's best tool for determining whether the company is performing particular functions and activities efficiently, whether its costs are in line with competitors, and which internal activities and business processes need to be improved. It is a way of learning which companies are best at performing certain activities and functions and then imitating—or, better still, improving on—their techniques. Toyota managers got their idea for just-in-time inventory deliveries by studying how U.S. supermarkets replenished their shelves. Southwest Airlines reduced the turnaround time of its aircraft at each scheduled stop by studying pit crews on the auto racing circuit.

Strategic Options for Achieving Cost Competitiveness

Value chain analysis can reveal a great deal about a firm's cost competitiveness. One of the fundamental insights of strategic cost analysis is that a company's competitiveness depends on how well it manages its value chain relative to how well competitors

Illustration Capsule 11 Benchmarking and Ethical Conduct

Because actions between benchmarking partners can involve competitively sensitive data and discussions, conceivably raising questions about possible restraint of trade or improper business conduct, the SPI Council on Benchmarking and The International Benchmarking Clearinghouse urge all individuals and organizations involved in benchmarking to abide by a code of conduct grounded in ethical business behavior. The code is based on the following principles and guidelines:

- In benchmarking with competitors, establish specific ground rules up front, e.g., "We don't want to talk about those things that will give either of us a competitive advantage; rather, we want to see where we both can mutually improve or gain benefit." Do not discuss costs with competitors if costs are an element of pricing.

- Do not ask competitors for sensitive data or cause the benchmarking partner to feel that sensitive data must be provided to keep the process going. Be prepared to provide the same level of information that you request. Do not share proprietary information without prior approval from the proper authorities of both parties.

- Use an ethical third party to assemble and blind competitive data, with inputs from legal counsel, for direct competitor comparisons.

- Consult with legal counsel if any information gathering procedure is in doubt, e.g., before contacting a direct competitor.

- Any information obtained from a benchmarking partner should be treated as internal, privileged information. Any external use must have the partner's permission.

- Do not:
  — Disparage a competitor's business or operations to a third party.
  — Attempt to limit competition or gain business through the benchmarking relationship.
  — Misrepresent oneself as working for another employer.

- Demonstrate commitment to the efficiency and effectiveness of the process by being adequately prepared at each step, particularly at initial contact. Be professional, honest, and courteous. Adhere to the agenda—maintain focus on benchmarking issues.

Sources: The SPI Council on Benchmarking, The International Benchmarking Clearinghouse, and conference presentation of AT&T Benchmarking Group, Des Moines, Iowa, October 1993.

manage theirs.[12] Examining the makeup of a company's own value chain and comparing it to rivals' indicates who has how much of a cost advantage/disadvantage and which cost components are responsible. Such information is vital in crafting strategies to eliminate a cost disadvantage or create a cost advantage.

Looking again at Figure 4–2, observe that there are three main areas in a company's overall value chain where important differences in the costs of competing firms can occur: in the suppliers' part of the industry value chain, in a company's own activity segments, or in the forward channel portion of the industry chain. If a firm's lack of cost competitiveness lies either in the backward (upstream) or forward (downstream) sections of the value chain, then reestablishing cost competitiveness may have to extend beyond the firm's own in-house operations. When a firm's cost disadvantage is principally associated with the costs of items purchased from suppliers (the upstream end of the industry chain), company managers can pursue any of several strategic actions to correct the problem:[13]

Strategic actions to eliminate a cost disadvantage need to be linked to the location in the value chain where the cost differences originate.

---

[12]Shank and Govindarajan, *Strategic Cost Management*, p. 50.
[13]Porter, *Competitive Advantage*, chapter 3.

- Negotiate more favorable prices with suppliers.
- Work with suppliers to help them achieve lower costs.
- Integrate backward to gain control over the costs of purchased items.
- Try to use lower-priced substitute inputs.
- Do a better job of managing the linkages between suppliers' value chains and the company's own chain; for example, close coordination between a company and its suppliers can permit just-in-time deliveries that lower a company's inventory and internal logistics costs and that may also allow its suppliers to economize on their warehousing, shipping, and production scheduling costs—a win-win outcome for both (instead of a zero-sum game where a company's gains match supplier concessions).
- Try to make up the difference by cutting costs elsewhere in the chain.

A company's strategic options for eliminating cost disadvantages in the forward end of the value chain system include[14]

- Pushing distributors and other forward channel allies to reduce their markups.
- Working closely with forward channel allies/customers to identify win-win opportunities to reduce costs. A chocolate manufacturer learned that by shipping its bulk chocolate in liquid form in tank cars instead of 10-pound molded bars, it saved its candy bar manufacturing customers the cost of unpacking and melting, and it eliminated its own costs of molding bars and packing them.
- Changing to a more economical distribution strategy, including the possibility of forward integration.
- Trying to make up the difference by cutting costs earlier in the cost chain.

When the source of a firm's cost disadvantage is internal, managers can use any of nine strategic approaches to restore cost parity:[15]

1. Initiate internal budget reductions and streamline operations.
2. Reengineer business processes and work practices (to boost employee productivity, improve the efficiency of key activities, increase the utilization of company assets, and otherwise do a better job of managing the cost drivers).
3. Try to eliminate some cost-producing activities altogether by revamping the value chain system (for example, shifting to a radically different technological approach or maybe bypassing the value chains of forward channel allies and marketing directly to end-users).
4. Relocate high-cost activities to geographic areas where they can be performed more cheaply.
5. See if certain activities can be outsourced from vendors or performed by contractors more cheaply than they can be done internally.
6. Invest in cost-saving technological improvements (automation, robotics, flexible manufacturing techniques, computerized controls).
7. Innovate around the troublesome cost components as new investments are made in plant and equipment.

---

[14]Ibid.
[15]Ibid.

8. Simplify the product design so that it can be manufactured more economically.

9. Try to make up the internal cost disadvantage by achieving savings in the backward and forward portions of the value chain system.

Value Chain Analysis, Core Competencies, and Competitive Advantage

How well a company manages its value chain activities relative to competitors is a key to building valuable core competencies and leveraging them into sustainable competitive advantage. With rare exceptions, a firm's products or services are not a basis for sustainable competitive advantage—it is too easy for a resourceful company to clone, improve on, or find an effective substitute for them.[16] Rather, a company's competitive edge is usually grounded in its skills and capabilities relative to rivals' and, more specifically, in the scope and depth of its ability to perform competitively crucial activities along the value chain better than rivals.

> **Value chain analysis is a powerful managerial tool for identifying which activities in the chain have competitive advantage potential.**

Core competencies emerge from a company's experience, learned skills, and focused efforts in performing one or more related value chain components. Merck and Glaxo, two of the world's most competitively capable pharmaceutical companies, built their strategic positions around expert performance of a few key activities: extensive R&D to achieve first discovery of new drugs, a carefully constructed approach to patenting, skill in gaining rapid and thorough clinical clearance through regulatory bodies, and unusually strong distribution and sales force capabilities.[17] To arrive at a sound diagnosis of a company's true competitive capabilities, managers need to do four things:

1. Construct a value chain of company activities.

2. Examine the linkages among internally performed activities and the linkages with suppliers' and customers' chains.

3. Identify the activities and competencies critical to customer satisfaction and market success.

4. Make appropriate internal and external benchmarking comparisons to determine how well the company performs activities (which activities represent core competencies and which ones are better performed by outsiders?) and how its cost structure compares with competitors.

The strategy-making lesson of value chain analysis is that increased company competitiveness hinges on managerial efforts to concentrate company resources and talent on those skills and activities where the company can gain dominating expertise to serve its target customers.

QUESTION 4: HOW STRONG IS THE COMPANY'S COMPETITIVE POSITION?

Using value chain concepts and the other tools of strategic cost analysis to determine a company's cost competitiveness is necessary but not sufficient. A more broad-ranging assessment needs to be made of a company's competitive position and

---

[16]James Brian Quinn, *Intelligent Enterprise* (New York: The Free Press, 1993), p. 54.
[17]Quinn, *Intelligent Enterprise*, p. 34.

Systematic assessment of whether a company's competitive position is strong or weak *relative to close rivals* is an essential step in company situation analysis.

competitive strength. Particular elements to single out for evaluation are (1) how strongly the firm holds its present competitive position, (2) whether the firm's position can be expected to improve or deteriorate if the present strategy is continued (allowing for fine-tuning), (3) how the firm ranks *relative to key rivals* on each important measure of competitive strength and industry key success factors, (4) whether the firm enjoys a competitive advantage or is currently at a disadvantage, and (5) the firm's ability to defend its position in light of industry driving forces, competitive pressures, and the anticipated moves of rivals.

Table 4–3 lists some indicators of whether a firm's competitive position is improving or slipping. But company managers need to do more than just identify the areas of competitive improvement or slippage. They have to judge whether the company has a net competitive advantage or disadvantage vis-à-vis key competitors and whether the company's market position and performance can be expected to improve or deteriorate under the current strategy.

Managers can begin the task of evaluating the company's competitive strength by using benchmarking techniques to compare the company against industry rivals not just on cost but also on such competitively important measures as product quality, customer service, customer satisfaction, financial strength, technological skills, and product cycle time (how quickly new products can be taken from idea to design to market). It is not enough to benchmark the costs of activities and identify best practices; a company should benchmark itself against competitors on all strategically and competitively important aspects of its business.

Competitive Strength Assessments

The most telling way to determine how strongly a company holds its competitive position is to quantitatively assess whether the company is stronger or weaker than close rivals on each key success factor and each important indicator of competitive strength. Much of the information for competitive position assessment comes from

---

Table 4–3   The Signs of Strength and Weakness in a Company's Competitive Position

Signs of Competitive Strength	Signs of Competitive Weakness
• Important core competencies	• Confronted with competitive disadvantages
• Strong market share (or a leading market share)	• Losing ground to rival firms
• A pacesetting or distinctive strategy	• Below-average growth in revenues
• Growing customer base and customer loyalty	• Short on financial resources
• Above-average market visibility	• A slipping reputation with customers
• In a favorably situated strategic group	• Trailing in product development
• Concentrating on fastest-growing market segments	• In a strategic group destined to lose ground
• Strongly differentiated products	• Weak in areas where there is the most market potential
• Cost advantages	• A higher-cost producer
• Above-average profit margins	• Too small to be a major factor in the marketplace
• Above-average technological and innovational capability	• Not in good position to deal with emerging threats
• A creative, entrepreneurially alert management	• Weak product quality
• In position to capitalize on opportunities	• Lacking skills and capabilities in key areas

previous analyses. Industry and competitive analysis reveals the key success factors and competitive measures that separate industry winners from losers. Competitor analysis and benchmarking data provide a basis for judging the strengths and capabilities of key rivals.

Step one is to make a list of the industry's key success factors and most telling measures of competitive strength or weakness (6 to 10 measures usually suffice). Step two is to rate the firm and its key rivals on each factor. Rating scales from 1 to 10 are best to use although ratings of stronger (+), weaker (−), and about equal (=) may be appropriate when information is scanty and assigning numerical scores conveys false precision. Step three is to sum the individual strength ratings to get an overall measure of competitive strength for each competitor. Step four is to draw conclusions about the size and extent of the company's net competitive advantage or disadvantage and to take specific note of areas where the company's competitive position is strongest and weakest.

Table 4–4 provides two examples of competitive strength assessment. The first one employs an *unweighted rating scale*; with unweighted ratings each key success factor/competitive strength measure is assumed to be equally important. Whichever company has the highest strength rating on a given measure has an implied competitive edge on that factor; the size of its edge is mirrored in the margin of difference between its rating and the ratings assigned to rivals. Summing a company's strength ratings on all the measures produces an overall strength rating. The higher a company's overall strength rating, the stronger its competitive position. The bigger the margin of difference between a company's overall rating and the scores of lower-rated rivals, the greater its implied net competitive advantage. Thus, ABC's total score of 61 (see the top half of Table 4–4) signals a greater net competitive advantage over Rival 4 (with a score of 32) than over Rival 1 (with a score of 58).

However, it is better methodology to use a weighted rating system because the different measures of competitive strength are unlikely to be equally important. In a commodity-product industry, for instance, having low unit costs relative to rivals is nearly always the most important determinant of competitive strength. In an industry with strong product differentiation the most significant measures of competitive strength may be brand awareness, amount of advertising, reputation for quality, and distribution capability. In a *weighted rating system* each measure of competitive strength is assigned a weight based on its perceived importance in shaping competitive success. The largest weight could be as high as 0.75 (maybe even higher) in situations where one particular competitive variable is overwhelmingly decisive or as low as 0.20 when two or three strength measures are more important than the rest. Lesser competitive strength indicators can carry weights of 0.05 or 0.10. No matter whether the differences between the weights are big or little, *the sum of the weights must add up to 1.0.*

Weighted strength ratings are calculated by deciding how a company stacks up on each strength measure (using the 1 to 10 rating scale) and multiplying the assigned rating by the assigned weight (a rating score of 4 times a weight of 0.20 gives a weighted rating of 0.80). Again, the company with the highest rating on a given measure has an implied competitive edge on that measure, with the size of its edge reflected in the difference between its rating and rivals' ratings. The weight attached to the measure indicates how important the edge is. Summing a company's weighted strength ratings for all the measures yields an overall strength rating. Comparisons of the weighted overall strength scores indicate which competitors are in the strongest

High competitive strength ratings signal a strong competitive position and possession of competitive advantage; low ratings signal a weak position and competitive disadvantage.

A weighted competitive strength analysis is conceptually stronger than an unweighted analysis because of the inherent weakness in assuming that all the strength measures are equally important.

Table 4–4   Illustrations of Unweighted and Weighted Competitive Strength Assessments

A. Sample of an Unweighted Competitive Strength Assessment
Rating scale: 1 = Very weak; 10 = Very strong

Key Success Factor/Strength Measure	ABC Co.	Rival 1	Rival 2	Rival 3	Rival 4
Quality/product performance	8	5	10	1	6
Reputation/image	8	7	10	1	6
Manufacturing capability	2	10	4	5	1
Technological skills	10	1	7	3	8
Dealer network	9	4	10	5	1
Marketing/advertising	9	4	10	5	1
Financial strength	5	10	7	3	1
Relative cost position	5	10	3	1	4
Customer service	5	7	10	1	4
Unweighted overall strength rating	61	58	71	25	32

B. Sample of a Weighted Competitive Strength Assessment
Rating scale: 1 = Very weak; 10 = Very strong

Key Success Factor/Strength Measure	Weight	ABC Co.	Rival 1	Rival 2	Rival 3	Rival 4
Quality/product performance	0.10	8/0.80	5/0.50	10/1.00	1/0.10	6/0.60
Reputation/image	0.10	8/0.80	7/0.70	10/1.00	1/0.10	6/0.60
Manufacturing capability	0.10	2/0.20	10/1.00	4/0.40	5/0.50	1/0.10
Technological skills	0.05	10/0.50	1/0.05	7/0.35	3/0.15	8/0.40
Dealer network	0.05	9/0.45	4/0.20	10/0.50	5/0.25	1/0.05
Marketing/advertising	0.05	9/0.45	4/0.20	10/0.50	5/0.25	1/0.05
Financial strength	0.10	5/0.50	10/1.00	7/0.70	3/0.30	1/0.10
Relative cost position	0.35	5/1.75	10/3.50	3/1.05	1/0.35	4/1.40
Customer service	0.15	5/0.75	7/1.05	10/1.50	1/0.15	4/1.60
Sum of weights	1.00					
Weighted overall strength rating		6.20	8.20	7.00	2.10	2.90

and weakest competitive positions and who has how big a net competitive advantage over whom.

The bottom half of Table 4–4 shows a sample competitive strength assessment for ABC Company using a weighted rating system. Note that the unweighted and weighted rating schemes produce a different ordering of the companies. In the weighted system, ABC Company dropped from second to third in strength, and Rival 1 jumped from third into first because of its high strength ratings on the two most important factors. Weighting the importance of the strength measures can thus make a significant difference in the outcome of the assessment.

Competitive strength assessments provide useful conclusions about a company's competitive situation. The ratings show how a company compares against rivals, factor by factor or measure by measure, thus revealing where it is strongest and weakest and against whom. Moreover, the overall competitive strength scores indicate whether the company is at a net competitive advantage or disadvantage against each rival. The firm with the largest overall competitive strength rating can be said to have a net competitive advantage over each rival.

Knowing where a company is competitively strong and where it is weak is essential in crafting a strategy to strengthen its long-term competitive position. As a general rule, a company should try to convert its competitive strengths into sustainable competitive advantage and take strategic actions to protect against its competitive weaknesses. At the same time, competitive strength ratings point to which rival companies may be vulnerable to competitive attack and the areas where they are weakest. When a company has important competitive strengths in areas where one or more rivals are weak, it makes sense to consider offensive moves to exploit rivals' competitive weaknesses.

> **Competitive strengths and competitive advantages enable a company to improve its long-term market position.**

QUESTION 5: WHAT STRATEGIC ISSUES DOES THE COMPANY FACE?

The final analytical task is to home in on the strategic issues management needs to address in forming an effective strategic action plan. Here, managers need to draw upon all the prior analysis, put the company's overall situation into perspective, and get a lock on exactly where they need to focus their strategic attention. This step should not be taken lightly. Without a precise fix on what the issues are, managers are not prepared to start crafting a strategy—a good strategy must offer a plan for dealing with all the strategic issues that need to be addressed.

> **Effective strategy-making requires thorough understanding of the strategic issues a company faces.**

To pinpoint issues for the company's strategic action agenda, managers ought to consider the following:

* Whether the present strategy is adequate in light of driving forces at work in the industry.
* How closely the present strategy matches the industry's *future* key success factors.
* How good a defense the present strategy offers against the five competitive forces—particularly those that are expected to intensify in strength.
* In what ways the present strategy may not adequately protect the company against external threats and internal weaknesses.
* Where and how the company may be vulnerable to the competitive efforts of one or more rivals.
* Whether the company has competitive advantage or must work to offset competitive disadvantage.
* Where the strong spots and weak spots are in the present strategy.
* Whether additional actions are needed to improve the company's cost position, capitalize on emerging opportunities, and strengthen the company's competitive position.

These considerations should indicate whether the company can continue the same basic strategy with minor adjustments or whether major overhaul is called for.

The better matched a company's strategy is to its external environment and internal situation, the less need there is to contemplate big shifts in strategy. On the other hand, when the present strategy is not well-suited for the road ahead, managers need to give top priority to the task of crafting a new strategy.

Table 4–5 provides a format for doing company situation analysis. It incorporates the concepts and analytical techniques discussed in this chapter and provides a way of reporting the results of company situation analysis in a systematic, concise manner.

Table 4–5   Company Situation Analysis

1. Strategic Performance Indicators

Performance Indicator	19–	19–	19–	19–	19–
Market share	___	___	___	___	___
Sales growth	___	___	___	___	___
Net profit margin	___	___	___	___	___
Return on equity investment	___	___	___	___	___
Other?	___	___	___	___	___

2. Internal Strengths

    Internal Weaknesses

    External Opportunities

    External Threats

3. Competitive Strength Assessment

Rating scale: 1 = Very weak; 10 = Very strong.

Key Success Factor/ Competitive Variable	Weight	Firm A	Firm B	Firm C	Firm D	Firm E
Quality/product performance	___	___	___	___	___	___
Reputation/image	___	___	___	___	___	___
Manufacturing capability	___	___	___	___	___	___
Technological skills	___	___	___	___	___	___
Dealer network	___	___	___	___	___	___
Marketing/advertising	___	___	___	___	___	___
Financial strength	___	___	___	___	___	___
Relative cost position	___	___	___	___	___	___
Customer service	___	___	___	___	___	___
Other?	___	___	___	___	___	___
Overall strength rating	___	___	___	___	___	___

4. Conclusions Concerning Competitive Position

(Improving/slipping? Competitive advantages/disadvantages?)

5. Major Strategic Issues/Problems the Company Must Address

There are five key questions to consider in performing company situation analysis:

1. *How well is the present strategy working?* This involves evaluating the strategy from a qualitative standpoint (completeness, internal consistency, rationale, and suitability to the situation) and also from a quantitative standpoint (the strategic and financial results the strategy is producing). The stronger a company's current overall performance, the less likely the need for radical strategy changes. The weaker a company's performance and/or the faster the changes in its external situation (which can be gleaned from industry and competitive analysis), the more its current strategy must be questioned.

2. *What are the company's strengths, weaknesses, opportunities, and threats?* A SWOT analysis provides an overview of a firm's situation and is an essential component of crafting a strategy tightly matched to the company's situation. A company's strengths, especially its core competencies, are important because they can serve as major building blocks for strategy; company weaknesses are important because they may represent vulnerabilities that need correction. External opportunities and threats come into play because a good strategy necessarily aims at capturing attractive opportunities and at defending against threats to the company's well-being.

3. *Are the company's prices and costs competitive?* One telling sign of whether a company's situation is strong or precarious is whether its prices and costs are competitive with industry rivals. Strategic cost analysis and value chain analysis are essential tools in benchmarking a company's prices and costs against rivals, determining whether the company is performing particular functions and activities cost effectively, learning whether its costs are in line with competitors, and deciding which internal activities and business processes need to be scrutinized for improvement. Value chain analysis teaches that how competently a company manages its value chain activities relative to rivals is a key to building valuable core competencies and leveraging them into sustainable competitive advantage.

4. *How strong is the company's competitive position?* The key appraisals here involve whether the company's position is likely to improve or deteriorate if the present strategy is continued, how the company matches up against key rivals on industry KSFs and other chief determinants of competitive success, and whether and why the company has a competitive advantage or disadvantage. Quantitative competitive strength assessments, using the methodology presented in Table 4–4, indicate where a company is competitively strong and weak and provide insight into the company's ability to defend or enhance its market position. As a rule a company's competitive strategy should be built on its competitive strengths and attempt to shore up areas where it is competitively vulnerable. Also, the areas where company strengths match up against competitor weaknesses represent the best potential for new offensive initiatives.

5. *What strategic issues does the company face?* The purpose of this analytical step is to develop a complete strategy-making agenda using the

results of both company situation analysis and industry and competitive analysis. The emphasis here is on drawing conclusions about the strengths and weaknesses of a company's strategy and framing the issues that strategy-makers need to consider.

Good company situation analysis, like good industry and competitive analysis, is crucial to good strategy-making. A competently done company situation analysis exposes strong and weak points in the present strategy, company capabilities and vulnerabilities, and the company's ability to protect or improve its competitive position in light of driving forces, competitive pressures, and the competitive strength of rivals. Managers need such understanding to craft a strategy that fits the company's situation well.

Suggested Readings

Abell, Derek F. *Managing with Dual Strategies*. New York: Free Press, 1993, chaps. 9 and 10.

Andrews, Kenneth R. *The Concept of Corporate Strategy*. 3rd ed. Homewood, Ill.: Richard D. Irwin, 1987, chap. 3.

Fahey, Liam, and H. Kurt Christensen. "Building Distinctive Competencies into Competitive Advantages." Reprinted in Liam Fahey, *The Strategic Planning Management Reader*, Englewood Cliffs, N.J.: Prentice-Hall, 1989, pp. 113–18.

Hax, Arnoldo C., and Nicolas S. Majluf. *Strategic Management: An Integrative Perspective*. Englewood Cliffs, N.J.: Prentice-Hall, 1984, chap. 15.

Henry, Harold W. "Appraising a Company's Strengths and Weaknesses." *Managerial Planning*, July–August 1980, pp. 31–36.

Paine, Frank T., and Leonard J. Tischler. "Evaluating Your Costs Strategically." Reprinted in Liam Fahey, *The Strategic Planning Management Reader*, Englewood Cliffs, N.J.: Prentice-Hall, 1989, pp. 118–23.

Prahalad, C. K., and Gary Hamel. "The Core Competence of the Corporation." *Harvard Business Review* 90, no. 3 (May–June 1990), pp. 79–93.

Shank, John K., and Vijay Govindarajan. *Strategic Cost Management: The New Tool for Competitive Advantage*. New York: Free Press, 1993.

Stalk, George, Philip Evans, and Lawrence E. Shulman. "Competing on Capabilities: The New Rules of Corporate Strategy." *Harvard Business Review* 70, no. 2 (March–April 1992), pp. 57–69.

Watson, Gregory H. *Strategic Benchmarking: How to Rate Your Company's Performance Against the World's Best*. New York: John Wiley & Sons, 1993.

CHAPTER FIVE

Strategy and Competitive Advantage

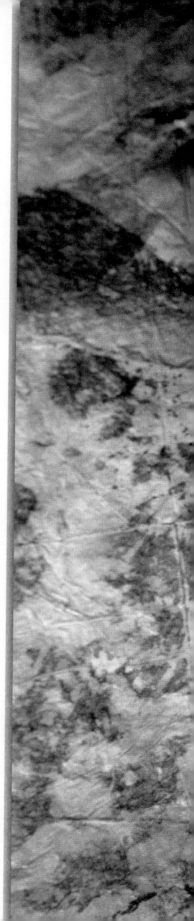

Competing in the marketplace is like war. You have injuries and casualties, and the best strategy wins.

John Collins

The essence of strategy lies in creating tomorrow's competitive advantages faster than competitors mimic the ones you possess today.

Gary Hamel and C. K. Prahalad

You've got to come up with a plan. You can't wish things will get better.

John F. Welch
CEO, General Electric

Winning business strategies are grounded in sustainable competitive advantage. A company has *competitive advantage* whenever it has an edge over rivals in attracting customers and defending against competitive forces. There are many sources of competitive advantage: having the best-made product on the market, delivering superior customer service, achieving lower costs than rivals, being in a more convenient geographic location, proprietary technology, features and styling with more buyer appeal, shorter lead times in developing and testing new products, a well-known brand name and reputation, and providing buyers more value for the money (a combination of good quality, good service, and acceptable price). Essentially, though, to succeed in building a competitive advantage, a company's strategy must aim at providing buyers with what they perceive as superior value—a good product at a lower price or a better product that is worth paying more for.

This chapter focuses on how a company can achieve or defend a competitive advantage.[1] We begin by describing the basic types of competitive strategies and then examine how these approaches rely on offensive moves to build competitive advantage and on defensive moves to protect competitive advantage. In the concluding two sections we survey the pros and cons of a vertical integration strategy and look at the competitive importance of timing strategic moves—when it is advantageous to be a first-mover and when it is better to be a late-mover.

---

[1]The definitive work on this subject is Michael E. Porter, *Competitive Advantage* (New York: Free Press, 1985). The treatment in this chapter draws heavily on Porter's pioneering contribution.

115

THE FIVE GENERIC COMPETITIVE STRATEGIES

A company's competitive strategy consists of the business approaches and initiatives it takes to attract customers, withstand competitive pressures, and strengthen its market position. The objective, quite simply, is to knock the socks off rival companies ethically and honorably, earn a competitive advantage in the marketplace, and cultivate a clientele of loyal customers. A company's strategy for competing typically contains both offensive and defensive actions, with emphasis shifting from one to the other as market conditions warrant. And it includes short-lived tactical maneuvers designed to deal with immediate conditions, as well as actions calculated to have lasting impact on the firm's long-term competitive capabilities and market position.

Investing aggressively in creating sustainable competitive advantage is a company's singlemost dependable contributor to above-average ROI.

Competitive strategy has a narrower scope than business strategy. Business strategy not only concerns the issue of how to compete but also embraces functional area strategies, how management plans to respond to changing industry conditions of all kinds (not just those that are competition-related), and how management intends to address the full range of strategic issues confronting the business. Competitive strategy deals exclusively with management's action plan for competing successfully and providing superior value to customers.

Companies the world over try every conceivable approach to attracting customers, earning their loyalty on repeat sales, outcompeting rivals, and winning an edge in the marketplace. And since managers tailor short-run tactics and long-term maneuvers to fit their company's specific situation and market environment, there are countless strategy variations and nuances. In this sense, there are as many competitive strategies as there are competitors. However, beneath the subtleties and superficial differences are impressive similarities when one considers (1) the company's market target and (2) the type of competitive advantage the company is trying to achieve. Five categories of competitive strategy approaches stand out:[2]

1. *A low-cost leadership strategy*—Striving to be the overall low-cost provider of a product or service that appeals to a broad range of customers.

2. *A broad differentiation strategy*—Seeking to differentiate the company's product offering from rivals' in ways that will appeal to a broad range of buyers.

3. *A best-cost provider strategy*—Giving customers more value for the money by combining an emphasis on low cost with an emphasis on upscale differentiation; the target is to have the best (lowest) costs and prices relative to producers of products with comparable quality and features.

4. *A focused or market niche strategy based on lower cost*—Concentrating on a narrow buyer segment and outcompeting rivals on the basis of lower cost.

5. *A focused or market niche strategy based on differentiation*—Offering niche members a product or service customized to their tastes and requirements.

---

[2]The classification scheme is an adaptation of one presented in Michael E. Porter, *Competitive Strategy: Techniques for Analyzing Industries and Competitors* (New York: Free Press, 1980), chapter 2 and especially pp. 35–39 and 44–46.

Figure 5–1 The Five Generic Competitive Strategies

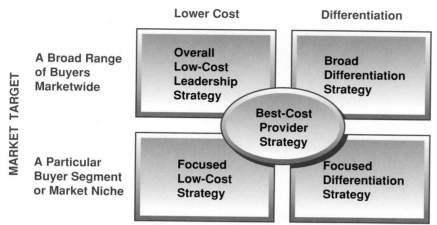

Source: Adapted from Michael E. Porter, *Competitive Strategy* (New York: Free Press, 1980), pp. 35–40.

The five generic competitive approaches are shown in Figure 5–1; each takes out a different market position and involves fundamentally different approaches to managing the business. Table 5–1 highlights the distinctive features of these generic competitive strategies (for simplicity, the two strains of focused strategies are combined under one heading since they differ only on one feature—the basis of competitive advantage).

Low-Cost Provider Strategies

Striving to be the industry's overall low-cost provider is a powerful competitive approach in markets where many buyers are price-sensitive. The aim is to open up a sustainable cost advantage over competitors and then use the company's lower-cost edge as a basis for either underpricing competitors and gaining market share at their expense or earning a higher profit margin selling at the going market price. A cost advantage generates superior profitability unless it is used up in aggressive price-cutting efforts to win sales from rivals. Achieving low-cost leadership typically means making low cost *relative to competitors* the theme of the firm's entire business strategy—though low cost cannot be pursued so zealously that a firm's offering ends up being too spartan and frills-free to generate buyer appeal. Illustration Capsule 12 describes ACX Technologies' strategy for gaining low-cost leadership in aluminum cans.

A low-cost leader's basis for competitive advantage is lower overall costs than competitors. Successful low-cost leaders are exceptionally good at finding ways to drive costs out of their businesses.

Opening Up a Cost Advantage   To achieve a cost advantage, a firm's cumulative costs across its value chain must be lower than competitors' cumulative costs. There are two ways to accomplish this:[3]

---

[3]Michael E. Porter, *Competitive Advantage* (New York: Free Press, 1985), p. 97.

Table 5–1   Distinctive Features of the Generic Competitive Strategies

Type of Feature	Low-Cost Leadership	Broad Differentiation	Best-Cost Provider	Focused Low-Cost and Focused Differentiation
• Strategic target	• A broad cross-section of the market.	• A broad cross-section of the market.	• Value-conscious buyers.	• A narrow market niche where buyer needs and preferences are distinctively different from the rest of the market.
• Basis of competitive advantage	• Lower costs than competitors.	• An ability to offer buyers something different from competitors.	• Give customers more value for the money	• Lower cost in serving the niche or an ability to offer niche buyers something customized to their requirements and tastes.
• Product line	• A good basic product with few frills (acceptable quality and limited selection).	• Many product variations, wide selection, strong emphasis on the chosen differentiating features.	• Good-to-excellent attributes, several-to-many upscale features.	• Customized to fit the specialized needs of the target segment.
• Production emphasis	• A continuous search for cost reduction without sacrificing acceptable quality and essential features.	• Invent ways to create value for buyers; strive for product superiority.	• Incorporate upscale features and attributes at low cost.	• Tailor-made for the niche.
• Marketing emphasis	• Try to make a virtue out of product features that lead to low cost.	• Build in whatever features buyers are willing to pay for. • Charge a premium price to cover the extra costs of differentiating features.	• Underprice rival brands with comparable features.	• Communicate the focuser's unique ability to satisfy the buyer's specialized requirements.
• Sustaining the strategy	• Economical prices/ good value. • All elements of strategy aim at contributing to a sustainable cost advantage—the key is to manage costs down, year after year, in every area of the business.	• Communicate the points of difference in credible ways. • Stress constant improvement and use innovation to stay ahead of imitative competitors. • Concentrate on a few key differentiating features; tout them to create a reputation and brand image.	• Unique expertise in managing costs down and product/ service caliber up simultaneously.	• Remain totally dedicated to serving the niche better than other competitors; don't blunt the firm's image and efforts by entering other segments or adding other product categories to widen market appeal.

Illustration Capsule 12   ACX Technologies' Strategy to Become a Low-Cost Producer of Aluminum Cans

ACX Technologies began as an idea of William Coors, CEO of Adolph Coors beer company, to recycle more used aluminum cans back into new cans. Typical aluminum can-making operations involved producing thick aluminum slabs from a smelter using bauxite ore combined with as much as 50% scrap aluminum, including used aluminum beverage cans; the slabs of aluminum ingot were fed into a rolling mill to achieve the required thickness. Cans were then formed by stamping pieces of thin aluminum sheet into a seamless can with the top open for filling.

Coor's idea was to produce aluminum-can sheet from 95% recycled cans. He began by purchasing rights to technology that his company had helped develop in Europe; the technology used lower-cost electric arc furnaces to melt aluminum scrap directly, short-cutting the smelter process, which required heavy capital investment and big production volumes to be competitive. Coors then built a plant in Colorado that could grind and melt used cans and pour hot aluminum through a continuous caster to make aluminum sheet suitable for the tops and tabs of beverage cans. It took seven years to develop alloys with the desired attributes and to fine-tune the process—Coors originally believed it could be done in less than two years.

In mid-1991 Coors announced it would build a new $200 million mill in Texas to make sheet aluminum for the body of the can—the product with the most exacting specifications but also the number one end use for aluminum in the United States. Production was expected to begin by mid-1992, but problems and delays soon pushed the start-up date into fall 1993. The new plant's low-cost advantages stemmed from several factors:

- Lower capital investment.
- Use of 95% recycled aluminum cans as feedstock—reducing raw material costs in producing aluminum sheet by 10 to 15.
- Lower electricity requirements—electric arc technology used only about one-fifth of the electricity of bauxite-smelter technology.
- Comparatively low electric rates at the Texas location.

- Reduced labor costs as compared to bauxite-smelter technology.

Overall, production costs were expected to be anywhere from 20 to 35% below the costs of aluminum can producers using traditionally produced aluminum sheet, depending on the prevailing market prices for aluminum ingot and scrap aluminum. In addition, the mill had greater flexibility than traditional producers to vary its alloy mixes to meet different customer specifications.

Meanwhile, in December 1992 during construction of the Texas plant, Coors decided to spin off all aluminum can operations (along with a paper-packaging operation making patented polyethylene cartons with high quality metallic graphics—packaging for Cascade boxes and Lever 2000 soapbars are examples; a ceramics unit making materials for high-tech applications; and several developmental businesses) into a new publicly-owned company called ACX Technologies. The new company had 1992 revenues of $570 million, about 28% of which were sales to Coors. The breakdown of revenues in 1992 was aluminum for cans 17%, graphics packaging 37%, ceramics materials 32%, and developmental businesses 14% (including corn wet milling, biotechnology, defense electronics, and biodegradable polymers).

In summer 1993, the Texas plant was in start-up and can makers began testing the quality of its aluminum sheet. Coors was the first to qualify ACX's output for use; at year-end 1993 four other can users were testing the suitability of the plant's output for their products. ACX expected the plant to ship close to 50 million pounds of aluminum by year-end 1993 and 100 million pounds or more in 1994 as new customers placed orders. Analysts believed that ACX, given its cost advantage, could grow its annual volume to 1.0 to 1.5 billion pounds in 10 years as it perfected the process and gained acceptance for the quality of its output.

The company's new shares were issued at $10.75 in December 1992 when it went public. In the first 20 days of trading the price climbed to $21.75. Later in 1993, shares traded as high as $46. In May 1994 they were trading in the mid-$30s.

Sources: Based on information published by The Robinson-Humphrey Company and on Marc Charlier, "ACX Strives to Become Aluminum's Low-Cost Producer," *The Wall Street Journal*, September 29, 1993, p. B2.

- Do a better job than rivals of performing internal value chain activities efficiently and of managing the factors that drive the costs of value chain activities.
- Revamp the firm's value chain to bypass some cost-producing activities altogether.

Let's look at each of the two avenues for gaining a cost advantage.

Controlling the Cost Drivers   A firm's cost position is the result of the behavior of costs in each activity in its total value chain. The major cost drivers which come into play in determining a company's costs in each activity segment of the chain fall into two categories: (1) structural determinants of cost that depend on the fundamental economic nature of the business; and (2) executional cost determinants that stem directly from how well internal activities are managed.[4]

Structural Cost Drivers

1. *Economies or diseconomies of scale*. Economies and diseconomies of scale can be found or created in virtually every segment of the value chain. For example, manufacturing economies can sometimes be achieved by simplifying the product line and scheduling longer production runs for fewer models. A geographically organized sales force can realize economies as regional sales volume grows because a salesperson can write larger orders at each sales call and/or because of reduced travel time between calls; on the other hand, a sales force organized by product line can encounter travel-related diseconomies if salespersons have to spend disproportionately more travel time calling on distantly spaced customers. In global industries, modifying products by country instead of selling a standard product worldwide tends to boost unit costs because of lost time in model changeover, shorter production runs, and inability to reach the most economic scale of production for each model. Boosting local or regional market share can lower sales and marketing costs per unit, whereas opting for a bigger national share by entering new regions can create scale diseconomies unless and until market penetration in the newly entered regions reaches efficient proportions.

2. *Learning and experience curve effects*. Experience-based cost savings can come from improved layout, gains in labor efficiency, debugging of technology, product design modifications that enhance manufacturing efficiency, redesign of machinery and equipment to gain increased operating speed, getting samples of a rival's products and having design engineers study how they are made, and tips from suppliers, consultants, and ex-employees of rival firms. Learning tends to vary with the amount of management attention devoted to capturing the benefits of experience of both the firm and outsiders. Learning benefits can be kept proprietary by building or modifying production equipment in-house, retaining key employees, limiting the dissemination of information through employee publications, and enforcing strict nondisclosure provisions in employment contracts.

---

[4]The list and explanations are condensed from Porter, *Competitive Advantage*, pp. 70–107.

3. *Linkages with other activities in the chain.* When the cost of one activity is affected by how other activities are performed, companies can lower costs of linked activities through superior coordination and/or joint optimization. Linkages with suppliers tend to center on suppliers' product-design characteristics, quality-assurance procedures, delivery and service policies, and the manner in which the supplier's product is furnished (for example, nails delivered in prepackaged 1-lb., 5-lb., and 10-lb. assortments instead of 100-lb. bulk cartons can reduce a hardware dealer's labor costs in filling individual customer orders). The easiest supplier linkages to exploit are those where both a supplier's and firm's costs fall because of coordination and/or joint optimization. Linkages with forward channels tend to center on location of warehouses, materials handling, outbound shipping, and packaging.

4. *Sharing opportunities with other business units within the enterprise.* Activities shared with a sister unit can create significant cost savings. Cost sharing can help achieve scale economies, shorten the learning curve in mastering a new technology, and/or achieve fuller capacity utilization. Sometimes the know-how gained in one division can be used to help lower costs in another; sharing know-how is significant when the activities are similar and know-how can be readily transferred from one unit to another.

5. *The benefits of vertical integration versus outsourcing.* Partially or fully integrating into the activities of either suppliers or forward channel allies can allow an enterprise to detour suppliers or buyers with considerable bargaining power. Vertical integration can also result in cost savings when it is feasible to coordinate or merge adjacent activities in the value chain. On the other hand, it is sometimes cheaper to outsource certain functions and activities to outside specialists, who by virtue of their expertise and volume can perform the activity/function more cheaply.

6. *Locational variables.* Locations differ in their prevailing wage levels, tax rates, energy costs, inbound and outbound shipping and freight costs, and so on. Opportunities may exist for reducing costs by relocating plants, field offices, warehousing, or headquarters operations. Moreover, whether sister facilities are nearby or far apart affects the costs of shipping intrafirm inventory, outbound freight on goods shipped to customers, and coordination.

Executional Cost Drivers

1. *Timing considerations associated with first-mover advantages and disadvantages.* Sometimes the first major brand in the market is able to establish and maintain its brand name at a lower cost than later brand arrivals—being a first-mover turns out to be cheaper than being a late-mover. On other occasions, such as when technology is developing fast, late-purchasers can benefit from waiting to install second- or third-generation equipment that is both cheaper and more efficient; first-generation users often incur added costs associated with debugging and learning how to use an immature and unperfected technology. Likewise, companies that follow rather than lead new product development efforts

sometimes avoid many of the costs that pioneers incur in performing pathbreaking R&D and opening up new markets.

2. *The percentage of capacity utilization.* High fixed costs as a percentage of total costs create a stiff unit-cost penalty for underutilization of existing capacity. Increased capacity utilization spreads indirect and overhead costs over a larger unit volume and enhances the efficiency of fixed assets. The more capital-intensive the business, the more important this cost driver becomes. Finding ways to minimize the ups and downs in seasonal capacity utilization can be an important source of cost advantage.[5]

3. *Strategic choices and operating decisions.* Managers at various levels affect a firm's costs through the decisions they make:

   - Increasing/decreasing the number of products offered.
   - Adding/cutting the services provided to buyers.
   - Incorporating more/fewer performance and quality features into the product.
   - Paying higher/lower wages and fringes to employees relative to rivals and firms in other industries.
   - Increasing/decreasing the number of different forward channels utilized in distributing the firm's product.
   - Raising/lowering the levels of R&D support relative to rivals.
   - Putting more/less emphasis on higher productivity and efficiency as compared to rivals.
   - Raising/lowering the specifications for purchased materials.

Managers intent on achieving low-cost leader status have to understand which structural and executional factors drive the costs of each activity in the firm's total value chain. Then they have to use their knowledge about the cost drivers to reduce costs for every activity where cost savings can be identified. The task of continuously coming up with ways to drive costs out of the business (and ways to avoid incurring some costs at all) is seldom simple or painless; rather, it is a task that managers have to attack with ingenuity and single-minded toughness.

Revamping the Makeup of the Value Chain   Dramatic cost advantages can emerge from finding innovative ways to restructure processes and tasks, cut out frills, and provide the basics more economically. The primary ways companies can achieve a cost advantage by reconfiguring their value chains include:

- Simplifying the product design.
- Stripping away the extras and offering only a basic, no-frills product or service, thereby cutting out activities and costs associated with multiple features and options.

---

[5]A firm can improve its capacity utilization by *(a)* serving a mix of accounts with peak volumes spread throughout the year, *(b)* finding off-season uses for its products, *(c)* serving private-label customers that can intermittently use the excess capacity, *(d)* selecting buyers with stable demands or demands that are counter to the normal peak/valley cycle, *(e)* letting competitors serve the buyer segments whose demands fluctuate the most, and *(f)* sharing capacity with sister units having a different pattern of needs.

- Reengineering core business processes to cut out needless work steps and low-value-added activities.
- Shifting to a simpler, less capital-intensive, or more streamlined technological process.
- Finding ways to bypass the use of high-cost raw materials or component parts.
- Using direct-to-end-user sales and marketing approaches that cut out the often large costs and margins of wholesalers and retailers (costs and margins in the wholesale-retail portions of the value chain often represent 50 percent of the price paid by final consumers).
- Relocating facilities closer to suppliers, customers, or both to curtail inbound and outbound logistics costs.
- Achieving a more economical degree of forward or backward vertical integration relative to competitors.
- Dropping the "something for everyone" approach and focusing on a limited product/service to meet a special, but important, need of the target buyer, thereby eliminating activities and costs associated with numerous product versions.

Successful low-cost producers usually achieve their cost advantages by exhaustively pursuing cost savings throughout the value chain. All avenues are used and no area of potential is overlooked. Normally, low-cost producers have a very cost-conscious corporate culture symbolically reinforced with spartan facilities, limited perks and frills for executives, intolerance of waste, intensive screening of budget requests, and broad employee participation in cost-control efforts. But while low-cost providers are champions of frugality, they are usually aggressive in committing funds to projects that promise to drive costs out of the business.

The Keys to Success   Managers intent on pursuing a low-cost-provider strategy have to scrutinize each cost-creating activity and identify what drives its cost. Then they have to use their knowledge about the cost drivers to manage the costs of each activity down further year after year. They have to be proactive in redesigning business processes, eliminating nonessential work steps, and reengineering the value chain. By totally revamping how activities are performed and coordinated, companies have been able to achieve savings of 30 to 70 percent, compared to the 5 to 10 percent possible with creative tinkering and adjusting. As the two examples in Illustration Capsule 13 indicate, companies can sometimes achieve dramatic cost advantages from restructuring their value chains and slicing out a number of cost-producing activities that produce little value added insofar as customers are concerned.

Companies that employ low-cost leadership strategies include Lincoln Electric in arc welding equipment, Briggs and Stratton in small gasoline engines, BIC in ballpoint pens, Black and Decker in power tools, Stride Rite in footwear, Beaird-Poulan in chain saws, Ford in heavy-duty trucks, General Electric in major home appliances, Wal-Mart in discount retailing, and Southwest Airlines in commercial airline travel.

The Competitive Defenses of Low-Cost Leadership   Being the low-cost provider in an industry provides some attractive defenses against the five competitive forces.

Illustration Capsule 13   Winning a Cost Advantage: Iowa Beef Packers and Federal Express

Iowa Beef Packers and Federal Express have been able to win strong competitive positions by restructuring the traditional value chains in their industries. In beef packing, the traditional cost chain involved raising cattle on scattered farms and ranches, shipping them live to labor-intensive, unionized slaughtering plants, and then transporting whole sides of beef to grocery retailers whose butcher departments cut them into smaller pieces and package them for sale to grocery shoppers.

Iowa Beef Packers revamped the traditional chain with a radically different strategy—large automated plants employing nonunion labor were built near economically transportable supplies of cattle, and the meat was partially butchered at the processing plant into smaller high-yield cuts (sometimes sealed in plastic casing ready for purchase), boxed, and shipped to retailers. IBP's inbound cattle transportation expenses, traditionally a major cost item, were cut significantly by avoiding the weight losses that occurred when live animals were shipped long distances; major outbound shipping cost savings were achieved by not having to ship whole sides of beef with their high waste factor. Iowa Beef's strategy was so successful that it was, in 1985, the largest U.S. meatpacker, surpassing the former industry leaders, Swift, Wilson, and Armour.

Federal Express innovatively redefined the value chain for rapid delivery of small parcels. Traditional firms like Emery and Airborne Express operated by collecting freight packages of varying sizes, shipping them to their destination points via air freight and commercial airlines, and then delivering them to the addressee. Federal Express opted to focus only on the market for overnight delivery of small packages and documents. These were collected at local drop points during the late afternoon hours and flown on company-owned planes during early evening hours to a central hub in Memphis where from 11 PM to 3 AM each night all parcels were sorted, then reloaded on company planes, and flown during the early morning hours to their destination points, where they were delivered the next morning by company personnel using company trucks. The cost structure so achieved by Federal Express was low enough to permit it to guarantee overnight delivery of a small parcel anywhere in the United States for a price as low as $11. In 1986, Federal Express had a 58 percent market share of the air-express package delivery market versus a 15 percent share for UPS, 11 percent for Airborne Express, and 10 percent for Emery/Purolator.

Source: Based on information in Michael E. Porter, *Competitive Advantage* (New York: Free Press, 1985), p. 109.

- In meeting the challenges of *rival competitors*, the low-cost company is in the best position to compete offensively on the basis of price, to defend against price war conditions, to use the appeal of lower price to grab sales (and market share) from rivals, and to earn above-average profits (based on bigger profit margins or greater sales volume). Low cost is a powerful defense in markets where price competition thrives.

- In defending against the power of *buyers*, low costs provide a company with partial profit-margin protection, since powerful customers are rarely able to bargain price down past the survival level of the next most cost-efficient seller.

- In countering the bargaining leverage of *suppliers*, the low-cost producer is more insulated than competitors from powerful suppliers *if* the primary source of its cost advantage is greater internal efficiency. (A low-cost provider whose cost advantage stems from being able to buy components at favorable prices from outside suppliers could be vulnerable to the actions of powerful suppliers.)

- As concerns *potential entrants*, the low-cost leader can use price-cutting to make it harder for a new rival to win customers; the pricing power of the low-cost provider acts as a barrier for new entrants.

- In competing against *substitutes*, a low-cost leader is better positioned to use low price as a defense against companies trying to gain market inroads with a substitute product or service.

A low-cost company's ability to set the industry's price floor and still earn a profit erects barriers around its market position. Anytime price competition becomes a major market force, less efficient rivals get squeezed the most. Firms in a low-cost position relative to rivals have a competitive edge in meeting the demands of buyers who want low price.

> **A low-cost leader is in the strongest position to set the floor on market price.**

When a Low-Cost Provider Strategy Works Best   A competitive strategy predicated on low-cost leadership is particularly powerful when

1. Price competition among rival sellers is especially vigorous.
2. The industry's product is essentially standardized or a commodity readily available from a host of sellers (a condition that allows buyers to shop for the best price).
3. There are few ways to achieve product differentiation that have value to buyers (put another way, the differences between brands do not matter much to buyers), thereby making buyers very sensitive to price differences.
4. Most buyers utilize the product in the same ways—with common user requirements, a standardized product can satisfy the needs of buyers, in which case low selling price, not features or quality, becomes the dominant factor in causing buyers to choose one seller's product over another's.
5. Buyers incur low switching costs in changing from one seller to another, thus giving them the flexibility to switch readily to lower-priced sellers having equally good products.
6. Buyers are large and have significant power to bargain down prices.

As a rule, the more price sensitive buyers are and the more inclined they are to base their purchasing decisions on which seller offers the best price, the more appealing a low-cost strategy becomes. In markets where rivals compete mainly on price, low cost relative to competitors is the only competitive advantage that matters.

The Risks of a Low-Cost Provider Strategy   A low-cost competitive approach has its drawbacks though. Technological breakthroughs can open up cost reductions for rivals that nullify a low-cost leader's past investments and hard-won gains in efficiency. Rival firms may find it easy and/or inexpensive to imitate the leader's low-cost methods, thus making any advantage short-lived. A company driving zealously to push its costs down can become so fixated on cost reduction that it fails to react to subtle but significant market swings—like growing buyer interest in added features or service, new developments in related products that start to alter how buyers use the product, or declining buyer sensitivity to price. The low-cost zealot risks getting left behind as buyers opt for enhanced quality, innovative performance features, faster service, and other differentiating features. Again, heavy investments in cost reduction can lock a firm into both its present technology and present strategy, leaving it vulnerable to new technologies and to growing customer interest in something other than a cheaper price.

To avoid the risks and pitfalls of a low-cost leadership strategy, managers must understand that the strategic target is *low cost relative to competitors*, not absolute low cost. In pursuing low-cost leadership, managers must take care not to strip away features and services that buyers consider essential. Furthermore, from a competitive strategy perspective, the value of a cost advantage depends on its sustainability. Sustainability, in turn, hinges on whether the company achieves its cost advantage in ways difficult for rivals to copy or match.

Differentiation Strategies

The essence of a differentiation strategy is to be unique in ways that are valuable to customers and that can be sustained.

Differentiation strategies become an attractive competitive approach whenever buyers' needs and preferences are too diverse to be fully satisfied by a standardized product. To be successful with a differentiation strategy, a company has to study buyers' needs and behavior carefully to learn what buyers consider important, what they think has value, and what they are willing to pay for. Then the company has to incorporate one, or maybe several, attributes and features with buyer appeal into its product/service offering—enough to set its offering visibly and distinctively apart. Competitive advantage results once a sufficient number of buyers become strongly attached to the differentiated attributes and features. The stronger the buyer appeal of the differentiated features, the stronger the company's competitive advantage.

Successful differentiation allows a firm to

- Command a premium price for its product, and/or
- Increase unit sales (because additional buyers are won over by the differentiating features), and/or
- Gain buyer loyalty to its brand (because some buyers are strongly attracted to the differentiating features).

Differentiation enhances profitability whenever the extra price the product commands outweighs the added costs of achieving the differentiation. Company differentiation strategies fail when buyers don't value the brand's uniqueness enough to buy it instead of rivals' brands and/or when a company's approach to differentiation is easily copied or matched by its rivals.

Types of Differentiation Themes   Companies can pursue differentiation from many angles: a different taste (Dr Pepper and Listerine), special features (Jenn Air's indoor-cooking tops with a vented built-in grill for barbecuing), superior service (Federal Express in overnight package delivery), spare parts availability (Caterpillar guarantees 48-hour spare parts delivery to any customer anywhere in the world or else the part is furnished free), more for the money (McDonald's and Wal-Mart), engineering design and performance (Mercedes in automobiles), prestige and distinctiveness (Rolex in watches), product reliability (Johnson & Johnson in baby products), quality manufacture (Karastan in carpets and Honda in automobiles), technological leadership (3M Corporation in bonding and coating products), a full range of services (Merrill Lynch), a complete line of products (Campbell's soups), and top-of-the-line image and reputation (Brooks Brothers and Ralph Lauren in menswear, Kitchen Aid in dishwashers, and Cross in writing instruments).

Activities Where Differentiation Opportunities Exist   Differentiation is not something hatched in marketing and advertising departments, nor is it limited to the catchalls of quality and service. The possibilities for successful differentiation exist in activities performed anywhere in the industry's value chain. The most common places in the chain where differentiation opportunities exist include:

1. *Purchasing and procurement activities* that ultimately spill over to affect the performance or quality of the company's end product. (McDonald's gets high ratings on its french fries partly because it has very strict specifications on the potatoes purchased from suppliers.)

2. *Product-oriented R&D activities* that hold potential for improved designs and performance features, expanded end uses and applications, wider product variety, shorter lead times in developing new models, more frequent first-on-the-market victories, added user safety, greater recycling capability, and enhanced environmental protection.

3. *Production process–oriented R&D activities* that allow custom-order manufacture, environmentally safe production methods, and improved product quality, reliability, or appearance.

4. *Manufacturing activities* that can reduce product defects, prevent premature product failure, extend product life, allow better warranty coverages, improve economy of use, result in more end-user convenience, and enhance product appearance. (The quality edge enjoyed by Japanese automakers stems from their superior performance of manufacturing and assembly-line activities.)

5. *Outbound logistics and distribution activities* that allow for faster delivery, more accurate order filling, and fewer warehouse and on-the-shelf stockouts.

6. *Marketing, sales, and customer service activities* that can result in such differentiating attributes as superior technical assistance to buyers, faster maintenance and repair services, more and better product information provided to customers, more and better training materials for end users, better credit terms, quicker order processing, more frequent sales calls, and greater customer convenience. (IBM boosts buyer value by providing its mainframe computer customers with extensive technical support and round-the-clock operating maintenance.)

Managers need a full understanding of the sources of differentiation and the activities that drive uniqueness to devise a sound differentiation strategy and evaluate various differentiation approaches.[6]

Achieving a Differentiation-Based Competitive Advantage   One key to a successful differentiation strategy is to create buyer value in ways unmatched by rivals. There are three approaches to creating buyer value. One is to incorporate product attributes and user features that lower the buyer's overall costs of using the company's product—Illustration Capsule 14 lists options for making a company's product more economical to use. A second approach is to incorporate features that raise the performance a buyer gets out of the product—Illustration Capsule 15 contains differentiation avenues that enhance product performance and buyer value.

> **A differentiator's basis for competitive advantage is a product whose attributes differ significantly from the products of rivals.**

---

[6]Porter, *Competitive Advantage*, p. 124.

A company doesn't have to lower price to make it cheaper for a buyer to use its product. An alternative is to incorporate features and attributes into the company's product/service package that

- Reduce the buyer's scrap and raw materials waste. Example of differentiating feature: cut-to-size components.
- Lower the buyer's labor costs (less time, less training, lower skill requirements). Examples of differentiating features: snap-on assembly features, modular replacement of worn-out components.
- Cut the buyer's downtime or idle time. Examples of differentiating features: greater product reliability, ready spare parts availability, or less frequent maintenance requirements.
- Reduce the buyer's inventory costs. Example of differentiating feature: just-in-time delivery.
- Reduce the buyer's pollution control costs or waste disposal costs. Example of differentiating feature: scrap pickup for use in recycling.
- Reduce the buyer's procurement and order-processing costs. Example of differentiating feature: computerized on-line ordering and billing procedures.

- Lower the buyer's maintenance and repair costs. Example of differentiating feature: superior product reliability.
- Lower the buyer's installation, delivery, or financing costs. Example of differentiating feature: 90-day payment same as cash.
- Reduce the buyer's need for other inputs (energy, safety equipment, security personnel, inspection personnel, other tools and machinery). Example of differentiating feature: fuel-efficient power equipment.
- Raise the trade-in value of used models.
- Lower the buyer's replacement or repair costs if the product unexpectedly fails later. Example of differentiating feature: longer warranty coverage.
- Lower the buyer's need for technical personnel. Example of differentiating feature: free technical support and assistance.
- Boost the efficiency of the buyer's production process. Examples of differentiating features: faster processing speeds, better interface with ancillary equipment.

Source: Adapted from Michael E. Porter, *Competitive Advantage* (New York: Free Press, 1985), pp. 135–37.

A third approach is to incorporate features that enhance buyer satisfaction in noneconomic or intangible ways. Goodyear's new Aquatread tire design appeals to safety-conscious motorists wary of slick roads in rainy weather. Wal-Mart's campaign to feature products "Made in America" appeals to customers concerned about the loss of American jobs to foreign manufacturers. Rolex, Jaguar, Cartier, Ritz-Carlton, and Gucci have differentiation-based competitive advantages linked to buyer desires for status, image, prestige, upscale fashion, superior craftsmanship, and the finer things in life. L. L. Bean makes its mail-order customers feel secure in their purchases by providing an unconditional guarantee with no time limit: "All of our products are guaranteed to give 100 percent satisfaction in every way. Return anything purchased from us at anytime if it proves otherwise. We will replace it, refund your purchase price, or credit your credit card, as you wish."

Real Value, Perceived Value, and Signals of Value   Buyers seldom pay for value they don't perceive, no matter how real the unique extras may be.[7] Thus the price

---

[7]This discussion draws from Porter, *Competitive Advantage*, pp. 138–42. Porter's insights here are particularly important to formulating differentiating strategies because they highlight the relevance of "intangibles" and "signals."

Illustration Capsule 15   Differentiating Features That Raise the Performance a User Gets

To enhance the performance a buyer gets from using its product/service, a company can incorporate features and attributes that

- Provide buyers greater reliability, durability, convenience, or ease of use.
- Make the company's product/service cleaner, safer, quieter, or more maintenance-free than rival brands.
- Exceed environmental or regulatory standards.

- Meet the buyer's needs and requirements more completely, compared to competitors' offerings.
- Give buyers the option to add on or to upgrade later as new product versions come on the market.
- Give buyers more flexibility to tailor their own products to the needs of their customers.
- Do a better job of meeting the buyer's future growth and expansion requirements.

Source: Adapted from Michael E. Porter, *Competitive Advantage*, (New York: Free Press, 1985), pp. 135–38.

premium that a differentiation strategy commands reflects *the value actually delivered* to the buyer and *the value perceived* by the buyer (even if not actually delivered). Actual and perceived value can differ whenever buyers have trouble assessing what their experience with the product will be. Incomplete knowledge on the part of buyers often causes them to judge value based on such *signals* as price (where price connotes quality), attractive packaging, extensive ad campaigns (i.e., how well-known the product is), ad content and image, the quality of brochures and sales presentations, the seller's facilities, the seller's list of customers, the firm's market share, length of time the firm has been in business, and the professionalism, appearance, and personality of the seller's employees. Such signals of value may be as important as actual value (1) when the nature of differentiation is subjective or hard to quantify, (2) when buyers are making a first-time purchase, (3) when repurchase is infrequent, and (4) when buyers are unsophisticated.

> A firm whose differentiation strategy delivers only modest extra value but clearly signals that extra value may command a higher price than a firm that actually delivers higher value but signals it poorly.

Keeping the Cost of Differentiation in Line   Once company managers identify what approach to creating buyer value and establishing a differentiation-based competitive advantage makes the most sense given the nature of the company's product/service and competitive situation, they must build the value-creating attributes into the product at an acceptable cost. Attempts to achieve differentiation usually raise costs. The trick to profitable differentiation is either to keep the costs of achieving differentiation below the price premium the differentiating attributes can command in the marketplace (thus increasing the profit margin per unit sold) or offset thinner profit margins with enough added volume to increase total profits (larger volume can make up for smaller margins provided differentiation adds enough extra sales). It usually makes sense to add extra differentiating features that are not costly but add to buyer satisfaction—fine restaurants typically provide such extras as a slice of lemon in the water glass, valet parking, and complimentary after-dinner mints. The overriding condition in pursuing differentiation is that a firm must be careful not to get its unit costs so far out of line with competitors' that it has to charge a higher price than buyers are willing to pay.

What Makes a Differentiation Strategy Attractive   Differentiation offers a buffer against the strategies of rivals when it results in enhanced buyer loyalty to a company's brand or model and greater willingness to pay a little (perhaps a lot!) more for it. In addition, successful differentiation (1) erects entry barriers in the form of customer loyalty and uniqueness that newcomers find hard to hurdle, (2) mitigates buyers' bargaining power since the products of alternative sellers are less attractive to them, and (3) helps a firm fend off threats from substitutes not having comparable features or attributes. To the extent that differentiation allows a company to charge a higher price and have bigger profit margins, it is in a stronger position to withstand the efforts of powerful vendors to get a higher price for the items they supply. Thus, as with cost leadership, successful differentiation creates lines of defense for dealing with the five competitive forces.

For the most part, differentiation strategies work best in markets where (1) there are many ways to differentiate the product or service and many buyers perceive these differences as having value, (2) buyer needs and uses of the item or service are diverse, and (3) few rival firms are following a similar differentiation approach.

The most appealing approaches to differentiation are those that are hard or expensive for rivals to duplicate. Easy-to-copy differentiating features cannot produce sustainable competitive advantage. Indeed, resourceful competitors can, in time, clone almost any product. This is why sustainable differentiation usually has to be linked to unique internal skills and core competencies. When a company has skills and capabilities that competitors cannot readily match and when its expertise can be used to perform activities in the value chain where differentiation potential exists, then it has a strong basis for sustainable differentiation. As a rule, differentiation yields a longer-lasting and more profitable competitive edge when it is based on

- Technical superiority.
- Product quality.
- Comprehensive customer service.

Such differentiating attributes are widely perceived by buyers as having value; moreover, the skills and expertise required to produce them tend to be tougher for rivals to copy or overcome profitably.

The Risks of a Differentiation Strategy   There are, of course, no guarantees that differentiation will produce a meaningful competitive advantage. If buyers see little value in uniqueness (i.e., a standard item meets their needs), then a low-cost strategy can easily defeat a differentiation strategy. In addition, differentiation can be defeated if competitors can quickly copy most or all of the appealing product attributes a company comes up with. Rapid imitation means that a firm never achieves real differentiation since competing brands keep changing in like ways each time a company makes a new move to set its offering apart from rivals'. Thus, to be successful at differentiation a firm must search out lasting sources of uniqueness that are burdensome for rivals to overcome. Aside from these considerations, other common pitfalls in pursuing differentiation include[8]

A low-cost producer strategy can defeat a differentiation strategy when buyers are satisfied with a basic product and don't think "extra" attributes are worth a higher price.

- Trying to differentiate on the basis of something that does not lower a buyer's cost or enhance a buyer's well-being, as perceived by the buyer.
- Overdifferentiating so that price is too high relative to competitors, or product quality or service levels exceed buyers' needs.

[8]Porter, *Competitive Advantage*, pp. 160–62.

- Trying to charge too high a price premium (the bigger the price differential the harder it is to keep buyers from switching to lower-priced competitors).

- Ignoring the need to signal value and depending only on intrinsic product attributes to achieve differentiation.

- Not understanding or identifying what buyers consider as value.

The Strategy of Being a Best-Cost Provider

This strategy aims at giving customers *more value for the money*. It combines a strategic emphasis on low cost with a strategic emphasis on *more than minimally acceptable* quality, service, features, and performance. The idea is to create superior value by meeting or exceeding buyers' expectations on quality-service-features-performance attributes and by beating their expectations on price. The strategic objective is to become the low-cost provider of a product or service with *good-to-excellent* attributes, then use the cost advantage to underprice brands with comparable attributes. Such a competitive approach is termed a *best-cost provider strategy* because the producer has the best (lowest) cost relative to producers whose brands are comparably positioned on the quality-service-features-performance scale.

The competitive advantage of a best-cost provider comes from matching close rivals on key quality-service-features-performance dimensions and beating them on cost. To become a best-cost provider, a company must match quality at a lower cost than rivals, match features at a lower cost than rivals, match product performance at a lower cost than rivals, and so on. What distinguishes a successful best-cost provider is expertise in incorporating upscale product or service attributes at a low cost, or, to put it a bit differently, an ability to contain the costs of providing customers with a better product. The most successful best-cost producers have the skills to simultaneously manage unit costs down and product calibre up—see Illustration Capsule 16.

A best-cost provider strategy has great appeal from the standpoint of competitive positioning. It produces superior customer value by balancing a strategic emphasis on low cost against a strategic emphasis on differentiation. In effect, it is a *hybrid* strategy that allows a company to combine the competitive advantage of both low cost and differentiation to arrive at superior buyer value. In markets where buyer diversity makes product differentiation the norm and many buyers are price and value sensitive, a best-cost producer strategy can be more advantageous than either a pure low-cost producer strategy or a pure differentiation strategy keyed to product superiority. This is because a best-cost provider can position itself near the middle of the market with either a medium-quality product at a below-average price or a very good product at a medium price. Often the majority of buyers prefer a mid-range product rather than the cheap, basic product of a low-cost producer or the expensive product of a top-of-the-line differentiator.

> The most powerful competitive approach a company can pursue is to strive relentlessly to become a lower-and-lower-cost producer of a higher-and-higher-caliber product, with the intention of eventually becoming the industry's absolute lowest-cost producer and, simultaneously, the producer of the industry's overall best product.

Focused or Market Niche Strategies

What sets focused strategies apart from low-cost or differentiation strategies is concentrated attention on a narrow piece of the total market. The target segment or niche can be defined by geographic uniqueness, by specialized requirements in using the product, or by special product attributes that appeal only to niche members. The objective is to do a better job of serving buyers in the target market niche than rival competitors. *A focuser's basis for competitive advantage is either (1) lower costs*

Illustration Capsule 16   Toyota's Best-Cost Producer Strategy for Its Lexus Line

Toyota Motor Co. is widely regarded as the leading low-cost producer among the world's motor vehicle manufacturers. Despite its emphasis on product quality, Toyota has achieved absolute low-cost leadership because of its considerable skills in efficient manufacturing techniques and because its models are positioned in the low-to-medium end of the price spectrum where high production volumes are conducive to low unit costs. But when Toyota decided to introduce its new Lexus models to compete in the luxury-car market, it employed a classic best-cost producer strategy. Toyota's Lexus strategy had three features:

- Transferring its expertise in making high-quality Toyota models at low cost to making premium quality luxury cars at costs below other luxury-car makers, especially Mercedes and BMW. Toyota executives reasoned that Toyota's manufacturing skills should allow it to incorporate high-tech performance features and upscale quality into Lexus models at less cost than other luxury-car manufacturers.

- Using its relatively lower manufacturing costs to underprice Mercedes and BMW, both of which had models selling in the $40,000 to $75,000 range (and some even higher). Toyota believed that with its cost advantage it could price attractively equipped Lexus models in the $38,000 to $42,000 range, drawing price-

conscious buyers away from Mercedes and BMW and perhaps inducing quality-conscious Lincoln and Cadillac owners to trade up to a Lexus.

- Establishing a new network of Lexus dealers, separate from Toyota dealers, dedicated to providing a level of personalized, attentive customer service unmatched in the industry.

In the 1993–94 model years, the Lexus 400 series models were priced in the $40,000 to $45,000 range and competed against Mercedes's 300/400E series, BMW's 525i/535i series, Nissan's Infiniti Q45, Cadillac Seville, Jaguar, and Lincoln's Continental Mark VIII series. The lower-priced Lexus 300 series, priced in the $30,000 to $38,000 range, competed against Cadillac Eldorado, Acura Legend, Infiniti J30, Buick Park Avenue, Mercedes's new C-Class series, BMW's 315 series, and Oldsmobile's new Aurora line.

Lexus's best-cost producer strategy was so successful that Mercedes, plagued by sagging sales and concerns about overpricing, reduced its prices significantly on its 1994 models and introduced a new C-Class series, priced in the $30,000 to $35,000 range, to become more competitive. The Lexus LS 400 models and the Lexus SC 300/400 models ranked first and second, respectively, in the widely watched J. D. Power & Associates quality survey for 1993 cars; the entry-level Lexus ES 300 model ranked eighth.

---

than competitors in serving the market niche or (2) an ability to offer niche members something different from other competitors. A focused strategy based on low cost depends on there being a buyer segment whose requirements are less costly to satisfy compared to the rest of the market. A focused strategy based on differentiation depends on there being a buyer segment that demands unique product attributes.

Examples of firms employing some version of a focused strategy include Tandem Computers (a specialist in "nonstop" computers for customers who need a "fail-safe" system), Rolls Royce (in super luxury automobiles), Cannondale (in top-of-the-line mountain bikes), Fort Howard Paper (specializing in paper products for industrial and commercial enterprises only), commuter airlines like Horizon and Atlantic Southeast (specializing in low-traffic, short-haul flights linking major airports with smaller cities 50 to 250 miles away), and Bandag (a specialist in truck tire recapping that promotes its recaps aggressively at over 1,000 truck stops). Illustration Capsule 17 describes Motel 6's focused low-cost strategy and Ritz-Carlton's focused differentiation strategy.

Using a focused strategy to compete on the basis of low cost is a fairly common business approach. Producers of private-label goods have lowered their marketing,

Motel 6 and Ritz-Carlton compete at opposite ends of the lodging industry. Motel 6 employs a focused strategy keyed to low cost; Ritz-Carlton employs a focused strategy based on differentiation.

Motel 6 caters to price-conscious travelers who want a clean, no-frills place to spend the night. To be a low-cost provider of overnight lodging, Motel 6 (1) selects relatively inexpensive sites on which to construct its units—usually near interstate exits and high traffic locations but far enough away to avoid paying prime site prices; (2) builds only basic facilities—no restaurant or bar and only rarely a swimming pool; (3) relies on standard architectural designs that incorporate inexpensive materials and low-cost construction techniques; and (4) has simple room furnishings and decorations. These approaches lower both investment costs and operating costs. Without restaurants, bars, and all kinds of guest services, a Motel 6 unit can be operated with just front desk personnel, room cleanup crews, and skeleton building-and-grounds maintenance. To promote the Motel 6 concept with travelers who have simple overnight requirements, the chain uses unique, recognizable radio ads done by nationally syndicated radio personality Tom Bodett; the ads describe Motel 6's clean rooms, no-frills facilities, friendly atmosphere, and dependably low rates (usually under $30 per night).

In contrast, the Ritz-Carlton caters to discriminating travelers and vacationers willing and able to pay for top-of-the-line accommodations and world-class personal service. Ritz-Carlton hotels feature (1) prime locations and scenic views from many rooms, (2) custom architectural designs, (3) fine dining restaurants with gourmet menus prepared by accomplished chefs, (4) elegantly appointed lobbies and bar lounges, (5) swimming pools, exercise facilities, and leisure time options, (6) upscale room accommodations, (7) an array of guest services and recreation opportunities appropriate to the location, and (8) large, well-trained professional staffs who do their utmost to make each guest's stay an enjoyable experience.

Both companies concentrate their attention on a narrow piece of the total market. Motel 6's basis for competitive advantage is lower costs than competitors in providing basic, economical overnight accommodations to price-constrained travelers. Ritz-Carlton's advantage is its capability to provide superior accommodations and unmatched personal service for a well-to-do clientele. Each is able to succeed, despite polar opposite strategies, because the market for lodging consists of diverse buyer segments with diverse preferences and abilities to pay.

distribution, and advertising costs by concentrating on direct sales to retailers and chain discounters who stock a no-frills house brand to sell at discount to name brand merchandise. Discount stock brokerage houses have lowered costs by focusing on customers who are willing to forgo the investment research, advice, and financial services offered by full-service firms like Merrill Lynch in return for 30 percent or more commission savings on their buy-sell transactions. Pursuing a cost advantage via focusing works well when a firm can find ways to lower costs significantly by limiting its customer base to a well-defined buyer segment.

At the other end of the market spectrum, companies like Ritz-Carlton, Tiffany's, Porsche, Häagen-Dazs, and W. L. Gore (the maker of Gore-tex) crafted successful differentiation-based focused strategies targeted at upscale buyers wanting products/ services with world-class attributes. Indeed, most markets contain a buyer segment willing to pay a big price premium for the very finest items available, thus opening the strategic window for some competitors to employ differentiation-based focused strategies aimed at the very top of the market pyramid.

When Focusing Is Attractive   A focused strategy based either on low cost or differentiation becomes increasingly attractive as more of the following conditions are met:

- The segment is big enough to be profitable.
- The segment has good growth potential.
- The segment is not crucial to the success of major competitors.
- The focusing firm has the skills and resources to serve the segment effectively.
- The focuser can defend itself against challengers based on the customer goodwill it has built up and its superior ability to serve buyers in the segment.

A focuser's specialized skills in serving the target market niche provide a basis for defending against the five competitive forces. Multisegment rivals may not have the same competitive capability to serve the focused firm's target clientele. The focused firm's competence in serving the market niche raises entry barriers, thus making it harder for companies outside the niche to enter. A focuser's unique capabilities in serving the niche also present a hurdle that makers of substitute products must overcome. The bargaining leverage of powerful customers is blunted somewhat by their own unwillingness to shift their business to rival companies less capable of meeting their expectations.

Focusing works best (1) when it is costly or difficult for multisegment competitors to meet the specialized needs of the target market niche, (2) when no other rival is attempting to specialize in the same target segment, (3) when a firm doesn't have the resources to go after a wider part of the total market, and (4) when the industry has many different segments, thereby allowing a focuser to pick an attractive segment suited to its strengths and capabilities.

The Risks of a Focused Strategy   Focusing carries several risks. One is the chance that competitors will find effective ways to match the focused firm in serving the narrow target market. A second is the potential for the niche buyer's preferences and needs to shift toward the product attributes desired by the market as a whole. An erosion of the differences across buyer segments lowers entry barriers into a focuser's market niche and provides an open invitation for rivals in adjacent segments to begin competing for the focuser's customers. A third risk is that the segment becomes so attractive it is soon inundated with competitors, causing segment profits to be splintered.

USING OFFENSIVE STRATEGIES TO SECURE COMPETITIVE ADVANTAGE

Competitive advantage is nearly always achieved by successful offensive strategic moves; defensive strategies can protect competitive advantage but rarely are the basis for achieving competitive advantage. How long it takes for a successful offensive to create an edge is a function of the industry's competitive characteristics.[9] The *buildup period*, shown in Figure 5–2, can be short, as in service businesses that need little in the way of equipment and distribution system support to implement a new offensive

---

[9]Ian C. MacMillan, "How Long Can You Sustain a Competitive Advantage?" reprinted in Liam Fahey, *The Strategic Planning Management Reader* (Englewood Cliffs, N.J.: Prentice-Hall, 1989), pp. 23–24.

Figure 5–2   The Building and Eroding of Competitive Advantage

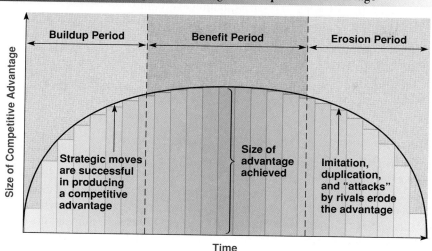

move. Or the buildup can take much longer, as in capital intensive and technologically sophisticated industries where firms may need several years to debug a new technology, bring new capacity on-line, and win consumer acceptance of a new product. Ideally, an offensive move builds competitive advantage quickly; the longer it takes, the more likely rivals will spot the move, see its potential, and begin a counter-response. The size of the advantage (indicated on the vertical scale in Figure 5–2) can be large (as in pharmaceuticals where patents on an important new drug produce a substantial advantage) or small (as in apparel where popular new designs can be imitated quickly).

> Competitive advantage is usually acquired by employing a creative offensive strategy that isn't easily thwarted by rivals.

Following a successful competitive offensive is a *benefit period* during which the fruits of competitive advantage can be enjoyed. The length of the benefit period depends on how much time it takes rivals to launch counteroffensives and begin closing the competitive gap. A lengthy benefit period gives a firm valuable time to earn above-average profits and recoup the investment made in creating the advantage. The best strategic offensives produce big competitive advantages and long benefit periods.

As competitors respond with serious counteroffensives to attack the advantage, the *erosion period* begins. Any competitive advantage a firm currently holds will eventually be eroded by the actions of competent, resourceful competitors.[10] Thus, to sustain an initially won advantage, a firm must devise a second strategic offensive. The groundwork for the second offensive needs to be laid during the benefit period so that everything is ready for launch when competitors mount efforts to cut into the leader's advantage. To successfully sustain a competitive advantage, a company must stay a step ahead of rivals by initiating one creative strategic offensive after another to improve its market position and retain customer favor.

---

[10]Ian C. MacMillan, "Controlling Competitive Dynamics by Taking Strategic Initiative," *The Academy of Management Executive* 2, no. 2 (May 1988), p. 111.

There are six basic types of strategic offensives:[11]

- Initiatives to match or exceed competitor strengths.
- Initiatives to capitalize on competitor weaknesses.
- Simultaneous initiatives on many fronts.
- End-run offensives.
- Guerrilla offensives.
- Preemptive strikes.

Initiatives to Match or Exceed Competitor Strengths

There are two good reasons to go head-to-head against rival companies, pitting one's own strengths against theirs, price for price, model for model, promotion tactic for promotion tactic, and geographic area by geographic area. The first is to try to gain market share by outcompeting weaker rivals. Challenging weaker rivals where they are strongest is attractive whenever a firm has a superior product offering and the organizational capabilities to win profitable sales and market share away from less competent and less resourceful competitors. The other reason is to whittle away at a strong rival's competitive advantage. Here success is measured by how much the competitive gap is narrowed. The merits of a strength-against-strength offensive challenge, of course, depend on how much the offensive costs compared to its competitive benefits. To succeed, the initiator needs enough competitive strength and resources to take at least some market share from the targeted rivals. Absent good prospects for long-term competitive gains and added profitability, such an offensive is ill-advised.

> **One of the most powerful offensive strategies is to challenge rivals with an equally good or better product at a lower price.**

Attacking a competitor's strengths can involve initiatives on any of several fronts—price-cutting, running comparison ads, adding new features that appeal to the rival's customers, constructing major new plant capacity in the rival's backyard, or bringing out new models to match the rival model for model. In one classic ploy, the aggressor challenges the targeted rival with an equally good offering at a lower price.[12] This can produce market share gains if the targeted rival has strong reasons for not resorting to price cuts of its own and if the challenger convinces buyers that its product is just as good. However, such a strategy increases profits only if volume gains offset the impact of thinner margins per unit sold.

Another way to mount a price-aggressive challenge is to first achieve a cost advantage and then hit competitors with a lower price.[13] Price-cutting supported by a cost advantage is perhaps the strongest basis for launching and sustaining a price-aggressive offensive. Without a cost advantage, price-cutting works only if the aggressor has more financial resources and can outlast its rivals in a war of attrition.

> **Challenging larger, entrenched competitors with aggressive price-cutting is foolhardy unless the aggressor has either a cost advantage or greater financial strength.**

Initiatives to Capitalize on Competitor Weaknesses

In this offensive approach, a company tries to gain market inroads by directing its competitive attention to the weaknesses of rivals. There are a number of ways to achieve competitive gains at the expense of rivals' weaknesses:

---

[11]Philip Kotler and Ravi Singh, "Marketing Warfare in the 1980s," *The Journal of Business Strategy* 1, no. 3 (Winter 1981), pp. 30–41; Philip Kotler, *Marketing Management*, 5th ed. (Englewood Cliffs, N.J.: Prentice-Hall, 1984), pp. 401–6; and Ian MacMillan, "Preemptive Strategies," *Journal of Business Strategy* 14, no. 2 (Fall 1983), pp. 16–26.

[12]Kotler, *Marketing Management*, p. 402.

[13]Kotler, *Marketing Management*, p. 403.

- Concentrate on geographic regions where a rival has a weak market share or is exerting less competitive effort.

- Pay special attention to buyer segments that a rival is neglecting or is weakly equipped to serve.

- Go after the customers of those rivals whose products lag on quality, features, or product performance; in such cases, a challenger with a better product can often convince the most performance-conscious customers to switch to its brand.

- Make special sales pitches to the customers of those rivals who provide subpar customer service—it may be relatively easy for a service-oriented challenger to win a rival's disenchanted customers.

- Try to move in on rivals that have weak advertising and weak brand recognition—a challenger with strong marketing skills and a recognized brand name can often win customers away from lesser-known rivals.

- Introduce new models or product versions that exploit gaps in the product lines of key rivals; sometimes "gap fillers" turn out to be a market hit and develop into new growth segments—witness Chrysler's success in minivans. This initiative works well when new product versions satisfy certain buyer needs that heretofore have been ignored or neglected.

As a rule, initiatives that exploit competitor weaknesses stand a better chance of succeeding than do those that challenge competitor strengths, especially if the weaknesses represent important vulnerabilities and the rival is caught by surprise with no ready defense.[14]

Simultaneous Initiatives on Many Fronts

On occasion a company may see merit in launching a grand competitive offensive involving multiple initiatives (price cuts, increased advertising, new product introductions, free samples, coupons, in-store promotions, rebates) across a wide geographic and competitive front. Such all-out campaigns can throw a rival off-balance, diverting its attention in many directions and forcing it to protect many pieces of its customer base simultaneously. Hunt's ketchup tried such an offensive several years ago in an attempt to wrest market share away from Heinz. The attack began when Hunt's introduced two new ketchup flavors (pizza and hickory) to disrupt consumers' taste preferences, create new flavor segments, and capture more shelf space in retail stores. Simultaneously, Hunt's lowered its price to 70 percent of Heinz's price, offered sizable trade allowances to retailers, and raised its advertising budget to over twice the level of Heinz's.[15] The offensive failed because not enough Heinz users tried the Hunt's brands, and many of those who did soon switched back to Heinz. Wide-scale offensives have their best chance of success when a challenger with an attractive product or service also has the financial resources to outspend rivals in courting customers; then it may be able to blitz the market with an array of promotional offers sufficient to entice large numbers of buyers to switch their brand allegiance.

---

[14]For a discussion of the use of surprise, see William E. Rothschild, "Surprise and the Competitive Advantage," *Journal of Business Strategy* 4, no. 3 (Winter 1984), pp. 10–18.

[15]As cited in Kotler, *Marketing Management*, p. 404.

End-Run Offensives

End-run offensives seek to avoid head-on challenges tied to aggressive price-cutting, escalated advertising, or costly efforts to outdifferentiate rivals. Instead the idea is to maneuver *around* competitors and be the first to enter unoccupied market territory. Examples of end-run offensives include moving aggressively into geographic areas where close rivals have little or no market presence, trying to create new segments by introducing products with different attributes and performance features to better meet the needs of selected buyers, and leapfrogging into next-generation technologies to supplant existing products and/or production processes. With an end-run offensive, a company can gain a significant first-mover advantage in a new arena and force competitors to play catch-up. The most successful end-runs change the rules of the competitive game in the aggressor's favor.

Guerrilla Offensives

Guerrilla offensives are particularly well-suited to small challengers who have neither the resources nor the market visibility to mount a full-fledged attack on industry leaders. A guerrilla offensive uses the hit-and-run principle, selectively attacking where and when an underdog can temporarily exploit the situation to its own advantage. There are several ways to wage a guerrilla offensive:[16]

1. Go after buyer groups that are not important to major rivals.
2. Go after buyers whose loyalty to rival brands is weakest.
3. Focus on areas where rivals are overextended and have spread their resources most thinly (possibilities include going after selected customers located in isolated geographic areas, enhancing delivery schedules at times when competitors' deliveries are running behind, adding to quality when rivals have quality control problems, and boosting technical services when buyers are confused by competitors' proliferation of models and optional features).
4. Make small, scattered, random raids on the leaders' customers with such tactics as occasional lowballing on price (to win a big order or steal a key account).
5. Surprise key rivals with sporadic but intense bursts of promotional activity to pick off buyers who might otherwise have selected rival brands.
6. If rivals employ unfair or unethical competitive tactics and the situation merits it, file legal actions charging antitrust violations, patent infringement, or unfair advertising.

Preemptive Strategies

Preemptive strategies involve moving first to secure an advantageous position that rivals are foreclosed or discouraged from duplicating. There are several ways to win a prime strategic position with preemptive moves:[17]

---

[16]For more details, see Ian MacMillan "How Business Strategists Can Use Guerrilla Warfare Tactics," *Journal of Business Strategy* 1, no. 2 (Fall 1980), pp. 63–65; Kathryn R. Harrigan, *Strategic Flexibility* (Lexington, Mass.: Lexington Books, 1985), pp. 30–45; and Liam Fahey, "Guerrilla Strategy: The Hit-and-Run Attack," in Fahey, *The Strategic Management Planning Reader*, pp. 194–97.

[17]The use of preemptive moves is treated comprehensively in Ian MacMillan, "Preemptive Strategies," *Journal of Business Strategy*, pp. 16–26. What follows in this section is based on MacMillan's article.

- Expand production capacity well ahead of market demand in hopes of discouraging rivals from following with expansions of their own. When rivals are "bluffed" out of adding capacity for fear of creating long-term excess supply and having to struggle with the bad profit economics of underutilized plants, the preemptor stands to win a bigger market share as market demand grows and it has the production capacity to take on new orders.
- Tie up the best (or the most) raw material sources and/or the most reliable, high-quality suppliers via long-term contracts or backward vertical integration. This move can relegate rivals to struggling for second-best supply positions.
- Secure the best geographic locations. An attractive first-mover advantage can often be locked up by moving to obtain the most favorable site along a heavily traveled thoroughfare, at a new interchange or intersection, in a new shopping mall, in a natural beauty spot, close to cheap transportation or raw material supplies or market outlets, and so on.
- Obtain the business of prestigious customers.
- Build a "psychological" image in the minds of consumers that is unique and hard to copy and that establishes a compelling appeal and rallying cry. Examples include Avis's well-known "We try harder" theme; Frito-Lay's guarantee to retailers of "99.5% service"; Holiday Inn's assurance of "no surprises"; and Prudential's "piece of the rock" image of safety and permanence.
- Secure exclusive or dominant access to the best distributors in an area.

General Mills's Red Lobster restaurant chain succeeded in tying up access to excellent seafood suppliers. DeBeers became the dominant world distributor of diamonds by buying up the production of most of the important diamond mines. DuPont's aggressive capacity expansions in titanium dioxide, while not blocking all competitors from expanding, did discourage enough to give it a leadership position in the titanium dioxide industry. Fox's stunning $6.2 billion preemptive bid over CBS to televise NFL games is widely regarded as a strategic move to catapult Fox into the ranks of the major TV networks alongside ABC, CBS, and NBC.

To be successful, a preemptive move doesn't have to totally block rivals from following or copying; it merely needs to give a firm a "prime" position. A prime position is one that puts rivals at a competitive disadvantage and is not easily circumvented.

Choosing Who to Attack

Aggressor firms need to analyze which of their rivals to challenge as well as how to outcompete them. Four types of firms make good targets:[18]

1. *Market leaders.* Waging an offensive against strong leaders risks squandering valuable resources in a futile effort and perhaps even precipitating a fierce and profitless industrywide battle for market share—caution is well advised. Offensive attacks on a major competitor make the best sense when the leader in terms of size and market share is not a

---

[18]Kotler, *Marketing Management*, p. 400.

"true leader" in terms of serving the market well. Signs of leader vulnerability include unhappy buyers, sliding profits, strong emotional commitment to a technology the leader has pioneered, outdated plants and equipment, a preoccupation with diversification into other industries, a product line that is clearly not superior to what several rivals have, and a competitive strategy that lacks real strength based on low-cost leadership or differentiation. Attacks on leaders can also succeed when the challenger is able to revamp its value chain or innovate to gain a fresh cost-based or differentiation-based competitive advantage.[19] Attacks on leaders need not have the objective of making the aggressor the new leader, however; a challenger may "win" by simply wresting enough sales from the leader to make the aggressor a stronger runner-up.

2. *Runner-up firms.* Launching offensives against weaker runner-up firms whose positions are vulnerable entails relatively low risk. This is an especially attractive option when a challenger's competitive strengths match the runner-up's weaknesses.

3. *Struggling enterprises that are on the verge of going under.* Challenging a hard-pressed rival in ways that further sap its financial strength and competitive position can weaken its resolve and hasten its exit from the market.

4. *Small local and regional firms.* Because these firms typically have limited expertise, a challenger with broader capabilities is well-positioned to raid their biggest and best customers—particularly those who are growing rapidly, have increasingly sophisticated requirements, and may already be thinking about switching to a supplier with more full-service capability.

As we have said, successful strategies are grounded in competitive advantage. This goes for offensive strategies too. The kinds of competitive advantages that usually offer the strongest basis for a strategic offensive include:[20]

- Having a lower-cost product design.
- Having lower-cost production capability.
- Having product features that deliver superior performance to buyers or that lower user costs.
- An ability to give buyers more responsive after-sale support.
- Having the resources to escalate the marketing effort in an undermarketed industry.
- Pioneering a new distribution channel.
- Having the capability to bypass wholesale distributors and sell direct to the end user.

Almost always, a strategic offensive should be tied to what a firm does best—its competitive strengths and capabilities. As a rule, these strengths should take the form of a *key skill* (cost reduction capabilities, customer service skills, technical expertise) a uniquely *strong functional competence* (engineering and product design, manufacturing expertise, advertising and promotion, marketing know-how) or

---

[19]Porter, *Competitive Advantage*, p. 518.
[20]Ibid., pp. 520–22.

superior ability to perform key activities in the value chain that lower cost or enhance differentiation.[21]

USING DEFENSIVE STRATEGIES TO PROTECT COMPETITIVE ADVANTAGE

In a competitive market, all firms are subject to challenges from rivals. Market offensives can come both from new entrants in the industry and from established firms seeking to improve their market positions. The purpose of defensive strategy is to lower the risk of being attacked, weaken the impact of any attack that occurs, and influence challengers to aim their efforts at other rivals. While defensive strategy usually doesn't enhance a firm's competitive advantage, it helps fortify a firm's competitive position and sustain whatever competitive advantage it does have.

The foremost purpose of defensive strategy is to protect competitive advantage and fortify the firm's competitive position.

There are several basic ways for a company to protect its competitive position. One approach involves trying to block the avenues challengers can take in mounting an offensive; the options include[22]

- Broadening the firm's product line to close off vacant niches and gaps to would-be challengers.
- Introducing models or brands that match the characteristics challengers' models already have or might have.
- Keeping prices low on models that most closely match competitors' offerings.
- Signing exclusive agreements with dealers and distributors to keep competitors from using the same ones.
- Granting dealers and distributors sizable volume discounts to discourage them from experimenting with other suppliers.
- Offering free or low-cost training to product users.
- Making it harder for competitors to get buyers to try their brands by (1) giving special price discounts to buyers who are considering trial use of rival brands, (2) resorting to high levels of couponing and sample giveaways to buyers most prone to experiment, and (3) making early announcements about impending new products or price changes to induce potential buyers to postpone switching.
- Raising the amount of financing provided to dealers and/or to buyers.
- Reducing delivery times for spare parts.
- Increasing warranty coverages.
- Patenting alternative technologies.
- Maintaining a participation in alternative technologies.
- Protecting proprietary know-how in product design, production technologies, and other strategy-critical value chain activities.
- Signing exclusive contracts with the best suppliers to block access of aggressive rivals.

---

[21]For more details, see MacMillan, "Controlling Competitive Dynamics," pp. 112–16.
[22]Porter, *Competitive Advantage*, pp. 489–94.

- Purchasing natural resource reserves ahead of present needs to keep them from competitors.
- Avoiding suppliers that also serve competitors.
- Challenging rivals' products or practices in regulatory proceedings.

Moves such as these not only buttress a firm's present position, they also present competitors with a moving target. Protecting the status quo isn't enough. A good defense entails adjusting quickly to changing industry conditions and, on occasion, being a first-mover to block or preempt moves by would-be aggressors. A mobile defense is preferable to a stationary defense.

A second approach to defensive strategy entails signaling challengers that there is a real threat of strong retaliation if a challenger attacks. The goal is to dissuade challengers from attacking at all (by raising their expectations that the resulting battle will be more costly to the challenger than it is worth) or at least divert them to options that are less threatening to the defender. Would-be challengers can be signaled by[23]

- Publicly announcing management's commitment to maintain the firm's present market share.
- Publicly announcing plans to construct adequate production capacity to meet and possibly surpass the forecasted growth in industry volume.
- Giving out advance information about a new product, technology breakthrough, or the planned introduction of important new brands or models in hopes that challengers will be induced to delay moves of their own until they see if the announced actions actually are forthcoming.
- Publicly committing the company to a policy of matching competitors' terms or prices.
- Maintaining a war chest of cash and marketable securities.
- Making an occasional strong counter-response to the moves of weak competitors to enhance the firm's image as a tough defender.

Another way to dissuade rivals is to try to lower the profit inducement for challengers to launch an offensive. When a firm's or industry's profitability is enticingly high, challengers are more willing to tackle high defensive barriers and combat strong retaliation. A defender can deflect attacks, especially from new entrants, by deliberately forgoing some short-run profits and using accounting methods that obscure profitability.

VERTICAL INTEGRATION STRATEGIES AND COMPETITIVE ADVANTAGE

Vertical integration extends a firm's competitive scope within the same industry. It involves expanding the firm's range of activities backward into sources of supply and/or forward toward end users of the final product. Thus, if a manufacturer elects to build a new plant to make certain component parts rather than purchase them from outside suppliers, it remains in essentially the same industry as before. The only

---

[23]Ibid., pp. 495–97. The listing here is selective; Porter offers a greater number of options.

change is that it has business units in two production stages in the industry's value chain system. Similarly, if a personal computer manufacturer elects to integrate forward by opening 100 retail stores to market its brands directly to users, it remains in the personal computer business even though its competitive scope extends further forward in the industry chain.

Vertical integration strategies can aim at *full integration* (participating in all stages of the industry value chain) or *partial integration* (building positions in just some stages of the industry's total value chain). A firm can accomplish vertical integration by starting its own operations in other stages in the industry's activity chain or by acquiring a company already performing the activities it wants to bring in-house.

The Strategic Advantages of Vertical Integration

The only good reason for investing company resources in vertical integration is to strengthen the firm's competitive position.[24] Unless vertical integration produces sufficient cost savings to justify the extra investment or yields a competitive advantage, it has no real payoff profitwise or strategywise.

Integrating backward generates cost savings only when the volume needed is big enough to capture the same scale economies suppliers have and when suppliers' production efficiency can be matched or exceeded. Backward integration is most advantageous when suppliers have sizable profit margins, when the item being supplied is a major cost component, and when the needed technological skills are easily mastered. Backward vertical integration can produce a differentiation-based competitive advantage when a company, by performing in-house activities that were previously outsourced, ends up with a better-quality product/service offering, improves the calibre of its customer service, or in other ways enhances the performance of its final product. On occasion, integrating into more stages along the value chain can add to a company's differentiation capabilities by allowing it to build or strengthen its core competencies, better master key skills or strategy-critical technologies, or add features that deliver greater customer value.

> A vertical integration strategy has appeal *only* if it significantly strengthens a firm's competitive position.

Backward integration can also spare a company the uncertainty of being dependent on suppliers of crucial components or support services, and it can lessen a company's vulnerability to powerful suppliers that raise prices at every opportunity. Stockpiling, fixed-price contracts, multiple-sourcing, long-term cooperative partnerships, or the use of substitute inputs are not always attractive ways for dealing with uncertain supply conditions or with economically powerful suppliers. Companies that are low on a key supplier's customer priority list can find themselves waiting on shipments every time supplies get tight. If this occurs often and wreaks havoc in a company's own production and customer relations activities, backward integration can be an advantageous strategic solution.

The strategic impetus for forward integration has much the same roots. In many industries, independent sales agents, wholesalers, and retailers handle competing brands of the same product; they have no allegiance to any one company's brand and tend to push "what sells" and earns them the biggest profits. Undependable sales and distribution channels can give rise to costly inventory pileups and frequent

---

[24]See Kathryn R. Harrigan, "Matching Vertical Integration Strategies to Competitive Conditions," *Strategic Management Journal* 7, no. 6 (November–December 1986), pp. 535–56; for a discussion of the advantages and disadvantages of vertical integration, see John Stuckey and David White, "When and When *Not* to Vertically Integrate," *Sloan Management Review* (Spring 1993), pp. 71–83.

underutilization of capacity, thereby undermining the economies of a steady, near-capacity production operation. In such cases, it can be advantageous for a manufacturer to integrate forward into wholesaling and/or retailing in order to build a committed group of dealers and outlets representing its products to end users. Sometimes even a small increase in the average rate of capacity utilization can boost manufacturing margins enough so a firm really profits from company-owned distributorships, franchised dealer networks, and/or a chain of retail stores. On other occasions, integrating forward into the activity of selling directly to end users can result in a relative cost advantage and lower selling prices to end users by eliminating many of the costs of using regular wholesale-retail channels.

For a raw materials producer, integrating forward into manufacturing may permit greater product differentiation and provide an avenue of escape from the price-oriented competition of a commodity business. Often, in the early phases of an industry's value chain, intermediate goods are commodities in the sense that they have essentially identical technical specifications irrespective of producer (as is the case with crude oil, poultry, sheet steel, cement, and textile fibers). Competition in the markets for commodity or commoditylike products is usually fiercely price competitive, with the shifting balance between supply and demand giving rise to volatile profits. However, the closer the activities in the chain get to the ultimate consumer, the greater the opportunities for a firm to break out of a commoditylike competitive environment and differentiate its end product via design, service, quality features, packaging, promotion, and so on. Product differentiation often reduces the importance of price compared to other value-creating activities and allows for improved profit margins.

The Strategic Disadvantages of Vertical Integration

The big disadvantage of vertical integration is that it locks a firm deeper into the industry; unless operating across more stages in the industry's value chain builds competitive advantage, it is a questionable strategic move.

Vertical integration has some substantial drawbacks, however. It boosts a firm's capital investment in the industry, increasing business risk (what if the industry goes sour?) and perhaps denying financial resources to more worthwhile pursuits. A vertically integrated firm has vested interests in protecting its present investments in technology and production facilities even if they are becoming obsolete. Because of the high costs of abandoning such investments before they are worn out, fully integrated firms tend to adopt new technologies slower than partially integrated or nonintegrated firms. Second, integrating forward or backward locks a firm into relying on its own in-house activities and sources of supply (that later may prove more costly than outsourcing) and potentially results in less flexibility in accommodating buyer demand for greater product variety.

Third, vertical integration can pose problems of balancing capacity at each stage in the value chain. The most efficient scale of operation at each activity link in the value chain can vary substantially. Exact self-sufficiency at each interface is the exception not the rule. Where internal capacity is deficient to supply the next stage, the difference has to be bought externally. Where internal capacity is excessive, customers need to be found for the surplus. And if by-products are generated, they require arrangements for disposal.

Fourth, integration forward or backward often calls for radically different skills and business capabilities. Manufacturing, wholesale distribution, and retailing are different businesses with different key success factors, even though the physical products are the same. Managers of a manufacturing company should consider carefully whether it makes good business sense to invest time and money in developing the expertise and merchandising skills to integrate forward into wholesaling or retailing. Many manufacturers learn the hard way that owning and operating wholesale-retail networks present many headaches, fit poorly with what they do best, and don't always add the kind of value to their core business they thought they would. Integrating backward into parts and components manufacture isn't as simple or profitable as it sometimes sounds either. Personal computer makers, for example, frequently have trouble getting timely deliveries of the latest semiconductor chips at favorable prices, but most don't come close to having the resources or capabilities to integrate backward into chip manufacture; the semiconductor business is technologically sophisticated and entails heavy capital requirements and ongoing R&D effort, and mastering the manufacturing process takes a long time.

Fifth, backward vertical integration into the production of parts and components can reduce a company's manufacturing flexibility, lengthening the time it takes to make design and model changes and to bring new products to market. Companies that alter designs and models frequently in response to shifting buyer preferences often find vertical integration into parts and components burdensome because of constant retooling and redesign costs and the time it takes to implement coordinated changes throughout the value chain. Outsourcing is often quicker and cheaper than vertical integration, allowing a company to be more flexible and more nimble in adapting its product offering to fast-changing buyer preferences. Most of the world's automakers, despite their expertise in automotive technology and manufacturing, have concluded that they are better off from the standpoints of quality, cost, and design flexibility purchasing many of their key parts and components from manufacturing specialists rather than integrating backward to supply their own needs.

Unbundling and Outsourcing Strategies   In recent years, some vertically integrated companies have found vertical integration to be so competitively burdensome that they have adopted vertical deintegration (or unbundling) strategies. Deintegration involves withdrawing from certain stages/activities in the value chain system and relying on outside vendors to supply the needed products, support services, or functional activities. Outsourcing pieces of the value chain formerly performed in-house makes strategic sense whenever

- An activity can be performed better or more cheaply by outside specialists.
- The activity is not crucial to the firm's ability to achieve sustainable competitive advantage and won't hollow out its core competencies, essential skills, or technical know-how.
- It reduces the company's risk exposure to changing technology and/or changing buyer preferences.
- It streamlines company operations in ways that improve organizational flexibility, cut cycle time, speed decision-making, and reduce coordination costs.
- It allows a company to concentrate on its core business and do what it does best.

Often, many of the advantages of vertical integration can be captured and many of the disadvantages avoided via long-term cooperative partnerships with key suppliers.

All in all, therefore, a strategy of vertical integration can have both important strengths and weaknesses. Which direction the scales tip on vertical integration depends on (1) whether it can enhance the performance of strategy-critical activities in ways that lower cost or increase differentiation, (2) whether it will impact investment costs, flexibility and response times, and administrative overheads associated with coordinating operations across more stages, and (3) whether it creates competitive advantage. Absent solid benefits, vertical integration is not likely to be an attractive competitive strategy option.

FIRST-MOVER ADVANTAGES AND DISADVANTAGES

When to make a strategic move is often as crucial as *what* move to make. Timing is especially important when *first-mover advantages* or *disadvantages* exist.[25] Being first to initiate a strategic move can have a high payoff when (1) pioneering helps build a firm's image and reputation with buyers, (2) early commitments to supplies of raw materials, new technologies, distribution channels, and so on can produce an absolute cost advantage over rivals, (3) first-time customers remain strongly loyal to pioneering firms in making repeat purchases, and (4) moving first constitutes a preemptive strike, making imitation extra hard or unlikely. The bigger the first-mover advantages, the more attractive that making the first move becomes.

However, a wait-and-see approach doesn't always carry a competitive penalty. Being a first-mover may entail greater risks than being a late-mover. First-mover disadvantages (or late-mover advantages) arise when (1) pioneering leadership is much more costly than followership and only negligible experience curve effects accrue to the leader, (2) technological change is so rapid that early investments are soon rendered obsolete (thus allowing following firms to gain the advantages of next-generation products and more efficient processes), (3) it is easy for latecomers to crack the market because customer loyalty to pioneering firms is weak, and (4) the hard-earned skills and know-how developed by the market leaders during the early competitive phase are easily copied or even surpassed by late-movers. Good timing, therefore, is an important ingredient in deciding whether to be aggressive or cautious in pursuing a particular move.

Key Points

The challenge of competitive strategy—whether it be overall low-cost, broad differentiation, best-cost, focused low-cost, or focused differentiation—is to create a competitive advantage for the firm. Competitive advantage comes from positioning a firm in the marketplace so it has an edge in coping with competitive forces and in attracting buyers.

A strategy of trying to be the low-cost provider works well in situations where

- The industry's product is essentially the same from seller to seller (brand differences are minor).
- Many buyers are price-sensitive and shop for the lowest price.
- There are only a few ways to achieve product differentiation that have much value to buyers.
- Most buyers use the product in the same ways and thus have common user requirements.

---

[25]Porter, *Competitive Strategy*, pp. 232–33.

- Buyers' costs in switching from one seller or brand to another are low (or even zero).
- Buyers are large and have significant power to negotiate pricing terms.

To achieve a low-cost advantage, a company must become more skilled than rivals in controlling structural and executional cost drivers and/or it must find innovative cost-saving ways to revamp its value chain. Successful low-cost providers usually achieve their cost advantages by imaginatively and persistently ferreting out cost savings throughout the value chain. They are good at finding ways to drive costs out of their businesses.

Differentiation strategies seek to produce a competitive edge by incorporating attributes and features into a company's product/service offering that rivals don't have. Anything a firm can do to create buyer value represents a potential basis for differentiation. Successful differentiation is usually keyed to lowering the buyer's cost of using the item, raising the performance the buyer gets, or boosting a buyer's psychological satisfaction. To be sustainable, differentiation usually has to be linked to unique internal skills and core competencies that give a company capabilities its rivals can't easily match. Differentiation tied just to unique physical features seldom is lasting because resourceful competitors are adept at cloning, improving on, or finding substitutes for almost any feature or trait that appeals to buyers.

Best-cost provider strategies combine a strategic emphasis on low cost with a strategic emphasis on more than minimal quality, service, features, or performance. The aim is to create competitive advantage by giving buyers more value for the money; this is done by matching close rivals on key quality-service-features-performance attributes and beating them on the costs of incorporating such attributes into the product or service. To be successful with a best-cost provider strategy, a company must have unique expertise in incorporating upscale product or service attributes at a lower cost than rivals; its core competencies must revolve around an ability to manage unit costs down and product/service calibre up simultaneously.

The competitive advantage of focusing is earned either by achieving lower costs in serving the target market niche or by developing an ability to offer niche buyers something different from rival competitors—in other words, it is either *cost-based* or *differentiation-based*. Focusing works best when

- Buyer needs or uses of the item are diverse.
- No other rival is attempting to specialize in the same target segment.
- A firm lacks the capability to go after a wider part of the total market.
- Buyer segments differ widely in size, growth rate, profitability, and intensity in the five competitive forces, making some segments more attractive than others.

A variety of offensive strategic moves can be used to secure a competitive advantage. Strategic offensives can be aimed either at competitors' strengths or at their weaknesses; they can involve end-runs or grand offensives on many fronts; they can be designed as guerrilla actions or as preemptive strikes; and the target of the offensive can be a market leader, a runner-up firm, or the smallest and/or weakest firms in the industry.

The strategic approaches to defending a company's position usually take the form of (1) making moves that fortify the company's present position, (2) presenting competitors with a moving target to avoid "out of date" vulnerability, and (3) dissuading rivals from even trying to attack.

Vertically integrating forward or backward makes strategic sense only if it strengthens a company's position via either cost reduction or creation of a differentiation-based advantage. Otherwise, the drawbacks of vertical integration (increased investment, greater business risk, increased vulnerability to technological changes, and less flexibility in making product changes) outweigh the advantages (better coordination of production flows and technological know-how from stage to stage, more specialized use of technology, greater internal control over operations, greater scale economies, and matching production with sales and marketing). There are ways to achieve the advantages of vertical integration without encountering the drawbacks.

The timing of strategic moves is important. First-movers sometimes gain strategic advantage; at other times, such as when technology is developing fast, it is cheaper and easier to be a follower than a leader.

Suggested Readings

Aaker, David A. "Managing Assets and Skills: The Key to a Sustainable Competitive Advantage." *California Management Review* 31, no. 2 (Winter 1989), pp. 91–106.

Cohen, William A. "War in the Marketplace." *Business Horizons* 29, no. 2 (March–April 1986), pp. 10–20.

Coyne, Kevin P. "Sustainable Competitive Advantage—What It Is, What It Isn't." *Business Horizons* 29, no. 1 (January–February 1986), pp. 54–61.

D'Aveni, Richard A. *Hypercompetition: The Dynamics of Strategic Maneuvering* (New York: Free Press, 1994), chaps. 1, 2, 3, and 4.

Harrigan, Kathryn R. "Guerrilla Strategies of Underdog Competitors." *Planning Review* 14, no. 16 (November 1986), pp. 4–11.

———. "Formulating Vertical Integration Strategies." *Academy of Management Review* 9, no. 4 (October 1984), pp. 638–52.

Hout, Thomas, Michael E. Porter, and Eileen Rudden. "How Global Companies Win Out." *Harvard Business Review* 60, no. 5 (September–October 1982), pp. 98–108.

MacMillan, Ian C. "Preemptive Strategies." *Journal of Business Strategy* 14, no. 2 (Fall 1983), pp. 16–26.

———. "Controlling Competitive Dynamics by Taking Strategic Initiative." *The Academy of Management Executive* 2, no. 2 (May 1988), pp. 111–18.

Porter, Michael E. *Competitive Advantage* (New York: Free Press, 1985), chaps. 3, 4, 5, 7, 14, and 15.

Rothschild, William E. "Surprise and the Competitive Advantage." *Journal of Business Strategy* 4, no. 3 (Winter 1984), pp. 10–18.

Stuckey, John and David White, "When and When *Not* to Vertically Integrate," *Sloan Management Review* (Spring 1993), pp. 71–83.

Venkatesan, Ravi. "Strategic Outsourcing: To Make or Not to Make." *Harvard Business Review* 7, no. 6 (November–December 1992), pp. 98–107.

CHAPTER SIX

Matching Strategy to a Company's Situation

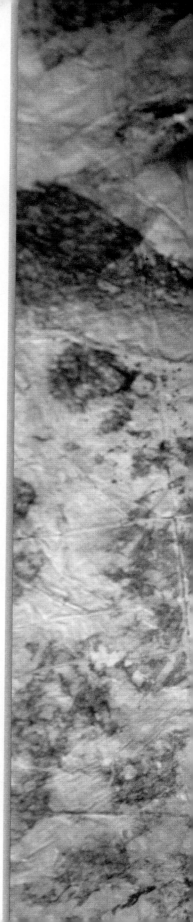

Strategy isn't something you can nail together in slapdash fashion by sitting around a conference table . . .

Terry Haller

The essence of formulating competitive strategy is relating a company to its environment . . . the best strategy for a given firm is ultimately a unique construction reflecting its particular circumstances.

Michael E. Porter

You do not choose to become global. The market chooses for you; it forces your hand.

Alain Gomez
CEO, Thomson, S.A.

The task of matching strategy to a company's situation is complicated because of the many external and internal factors managers have to weigh. However, while the number and variety of considerations is necessarily lengthy, the most important drivers shaping a company's strategic options fall into two broad categories:

- The nature of industry and competitive conditions.
- The firm's own competitive capabilities, market position, and best opportunities.

The dominant strategy-shaping industry and competitive conditions revolve around what stage in the life-cycle the industry is in (emerging, rapid growth, mature, declining), the industry's structure (fragmented versus concentrated), the nature and relative strength of the five competitive forces, and the scope of competitive rivalry (particularly whether the company's market is globally competitive). The pivotal company-specific considerations hinge on (1) whether the company is an industry leader, an up-and-coming challenger, a content runner-up, or an also-ran struggling to survive, and (2) the company's particular set of strengths, weaknesses, opportunities, and threats. But even these few categories occur in too many combinations to cover here. However, we can demonstrate what the task of matching strategy to the situation involves by considering five classic types of industry environments:

1. Competing in emerging and rapidly growing industries.
2. Competing in maturing industries.
3. Competing in stagnant or declining industries.
4. Competing in fragmented industries.
5. Competing in international markets.

and three classic types of company situations:

1. Firms in industry leadership positions.
2. Firms in runner-up positions.
3. Firms that are competitively weak or crisis-ridden.

STRATEGIES FOR COMPETING IN EMERGING INDUSTRIES ——

An emerging industry is one in the early, formative stage. Most companies in an emerging industry are in a start-up mode, adding people, acquiring or constructing facilities, gearing up production, trying to broaden distribution and gain buyer acceptance. Often, there are important product design problems and technological problems to be worked out as well. Emerging industries present managers with some unique strategy-making challenges:[1]

- Because the market is new and unproven, there are many uncertainties about how it will function, how fast it will grow, and how big it will get; the little historical data available is virtually useless in projecting future trends.
- Much of the technological know-how tends to be proprietary and closely guarded, having been developed in-house by pioneering firms; some firms may file patents in an effort to secure competitive advantage.
- Often, there is no consensus regarding which of several competing production technologies will win out or which product attributes will gain the most buyer favor. Until market forces sort these things out, wide differences in product quality and performance are typical and rivalry centers around each firm's efforts to get the market to ratify its own strategic approach to technology, product design, marketing, and distribution.
- Entry barriers tend to be relatively low, even for entrepreneurial start-up companies; well-financed, opportunity-seeking outsiders are likely to enter if the industry has promise for explosive growth.
- Experience curve effects often permit significant cost reductions as volume builds.
- Firms have little hard information about competitors, how fast products are gaining buyer acceptance, and users' experiences with the product; there are no trade associations gathering and distributing information.
- Since all buyers are first-time users, the marketing task is to induce initial purchase and to overcome customer concerns about product features, performance reliability, and conflicting claims of rival firms.

---

[1]Michael E. Porter, *Competitive Strategy* (New York: Free Press, 1980), pp. 216–23.

- Many potential buyers expect first-generation products to be rapidly improved, so they delay purchase until technology and product design mature.

- Often, firms have trouble securing ample supplies of raw materials and components (until suppliers gear up to meet the industry's needs).

- Many companies, finding themselves short of funds to support needed R&D and get through several lean years until the product catches on, end up merging with competitors or being acquired by outsiders looking to invest in a growth market.

The two critical strategic issues confronting firms in an emerging industry are (1) how to finance the start-up phase and (2) what market segments and competitive advantages to go after in trying to secure a leading industry position.[2] Competitive strategies keyed either to low cost or differentiation are usually viable. Focusing should be considered when financial resources are limited and the industry has too many technological frontiers to pursue at once; one option for financially constrained enterprises is to form a strategic alliance or joint venture with another company to gain access to needed skills and resources. Because an emerging industry has no established "rules of the game" and industry participants employ widely varying strategic approaches, a well-financed firm with a powerful strategy can shape the rules and become a recognized industry leader.

Dealing with all the risks and opportunities of an emerging industry is one of the most challenging business strategy problems. To be successful in an emerging industry, companies usually have to pursue one or more of the following strategic avenues:[3]

1. Try to win the early race for industry leadership with risk-taking entrepreneurship and a bold, creative strategy. Broad or focused differentiation strategies keyed to product superiority typically offer the best chance for early competitive advantage.

2. Push to perfect the technology, to improve product quality, and to develop attractive performance features.

3. Try to capture any first-mover advantages associated with more models, better styling, early commitments to technologies and raw materials suppliers, experience curve effects, and new distribution channels.

4. Search out new customer groups, new geographical areas to enter, and new user applications. Make it easier and cheaper for first-time buyers to try the industry's first-generation product.

5. Gradually shift the advertising emphasis from building product awareness to increasing frequency of use and creating brand loyalty.

6. As technological uncertainty clears and a dominant technology emerges, adopt it quickly. While there's merit in trying to pioneer the "dominant design" approach, such a strategy carries high risk when there are many competing technologies, R&D is costly, and rapidly moving technological developments quickly make early investments obsolete.

Strategic success in an emerging industry calls for bold entrepreneurship, a willingness to pioneer and take risks, an intuitive feel for what buyers will like, quick response to new developments, and opportunistic strategy-making.

[2]Charles W. Hofer and Dan Schendel, *Strategy Formulation: Analytical Concepts* (St. Paul, Minn.: West Publishing, 1978), pp. 164–65.

[3]Phillip Kotler, *Marketing Management*, 5th ed. (Englewood Cliffs, N.J.: Prentice-Hall, 1984), p. 366, and Porter, *Competitive Strategy*, chapter 10.

7. Use price cuts to attract the next layer of price-sensitive buyers into the market.

8. Expect well-financed outsiders to move in with aggressive strategies as industry sales start to take off and the perceived risk of investing in the industry lessens. Try to prepare for the entry of powerful competitors by forecasting *(a)* who the probable entrants will be (based on present and future entry barriers) and *(b)* the types of strategies they are likely to employ.

The short-term value of winning the early race for growth and market share leadership has to be balanced against the longer-range need to build a durable competitive edge and a defendable market position.[4] New entrants, attracted by the growth and profit potential, may crowd the market. Aggressive newcomers, aspiring to industry leadership, can quickly become major players by acquiring and merging the operations of weaker competitors. Young companies in fast-growing markets face three strategic hurdles: (1) managing their own rapid expansion, (2) defending against competitors trying to horn in on their success, and (3) building a competitive position extending beyond their initial product or market. Such companies can help their cause by selecting knowledgeable members for their boards of directors, by hiring entrepreneurial managers with experience in guiding young businesses through the start-up and takeoff stages, by concentrating on out-innovating the competition, and perhaps by merging with or acquiring another firm to gain added expertise and a stronger resource base.

STRATEGIES FOR COMPETING IN MATURING INDUSTRIES —

The rapid-growth environment of a young industry cannot go on forever. However, the transition to a slower-growth, maturing industry environment does not begin on an easily predicted schedule, and the transition can be forestalled by a steady stream of technological advances, product innovations, or other driving forces that keep rejuvenating market demand. Nonetheless, when growth rates do slacken, the transition to market maturity usually produces fundamental changes in the industry's competitive environment:[5]

1. *Slowing growth in buyer demand generates more head-to-head competition for market share.* Firms that want to continue on a rapid-growth track start looking for ways to take customers away from competitors. Outbreaks of price-cutting, increased advertising, and other aggressive tactics are common.

2. *Buyers become more sophisticated, often driving a harder bargain on repeat purchases.* Since buyers have experience with the product and are familiar with competing brands, they are better able to evaluate different brands and can use their knowledge to negotiate a better deal with sellers.

---

[4]Hofer and Schendel, *Strategy Formulation*, pp. 164–65.
[5]Porter, *Competitive Strategy*, pp. 238–40.

3. *Competition often produces a greater emphasis on cost and service.* As sellers all begin to offer the product attributes buyers prefer, buyer choices increasingly depend on which seller offers the best combination of price and service.

4. *Firms have a "topping out" problem in adding production capacity.* Slower rates of industry growth mean slowdowns in capacity expansion. Each firm has to monitor rivals' expansion plans and time its own capacity additions to minimize oversupply conditions in the industry. With slower industry growth, the mistake of adding too much capacity too soon can adversely affect company profits well into the future.

5. *Product innovation and new end-use applications are harder to come by.* Producers find it increasingly difficult to create new product features, find further uses for the product, and sustain buyer excitement.

6. *International competition increases.* Growth-minded domestic firms start to seek out sales opportunities in foreign markets. Some companies, looking for ways to cut costs, relocate plants to countries with lower wage rates. Greater product standardization and diffusion of technological know-how reduce entry barriers and make it possible for enterprising foreign companies to become serious market contenders in more countries. Industry leadership passes to companies that succeed in building strong competitive positions in most of the world's major geographic markets and in winning the biggest global market shares.

7. *Industry profitability falls temporarily or permanently.* Slower growth, increased competition, more sophisticated buyers, and occasional periods of overcapacity put pressure on industry profit margins. Weaker, less-efficient firms are usually the hardest hit.

8. *Stiffening competition induces a number of mergers and acquisitions among former competitors, drives the weakest firms out of the industry, and, in general, produces industry consolidation.* Inefficient firms and firms with weak competitive strategies can survive in a fast-growing industry with booming sales. But the intensifying competition that accompanies industry maturity exposes competitive weakness and throws second- and third-tier competitors into a survival-of-the-fittest contest.

As industry maturity begins to hit full force, and changes in the competitive environment set in, several strategic moves can strengthen firms' competitive positions.[6]

In a maturing industry, strategic emphasis needs to be on efficiency-increasing, profit-preserving measures: pruning the product line, improving production methods, reducing costs, accelerating sales promotion efforts, expanding internationally, and acquiring distressed competitors.

Pruning the Product Line   A wide selection of models, features, and product options has competitive value during the growth stage when buyers' needs are still evolving. But such variety can become too costly as price competition stiffens and profit margins are squeezed. Maintaining too many product versions prevents firms from achieving the economies of long production runs. In addition, the prices of slow-selling versions may not cover their true costs. Pruning marginal products from the line lowers costs and permits more concentration on items whose margins are highest and/or where the firm has a competitive advantage.

---

[6]The following discussion draws on Porter, *Competitive Strategy*, pp. 241–46.

More Emphasis on Process Innovations   Efforts to "reinvent" the manufacturing process can have a fourfold payoff: lower costs, better production quality, greater capability to turn out multiple product versions, and shorter design-to-market cycles. Process innovation can involve mechanizing high-cost activities, revamping production lines to improve labor efficiency, creating self-directed work teams, reengineering the manufacturing portion of the value chain, and increasing use of advanced technology (robotics, computerized controls, and automatic guided vehicles). Japanese firms have become remarkably adept at using manufacturing process innovation to become lower-cost producers of higher-quality products.

A Stronger Focus on Cost Reduction   Stiffening price competition gives firms extra incentive to reduce unit costs. Such efforts can cover a broad front: companies can push suppliers for better prices, switch to lower-priced components, develop more economical product designs, cut low-value activities out of the value chain, streamline distribution channels, and reengineer internal processes.

Increasing Sales to Present Customers   In a mature market, growing by taking customers away from rivals may not be as appealing as expanding sales to existing customers. Strategies to increase purchases by existing customers can involve providing complementary items and ancillary services, and finding more ways for customers to use the product. Convenience food stores, for example, have boosted average sales per customer by adding video rentals, automatic bank tellers, and deli counters.

Purchasing Rival Firms at Bargain Prices   Sometimes the facilities and assets of distressed rivals can be acquired cheaply. Bargain-priced acquisitions can help create a low-cost position if they also present opportunities for greater operating efficiency. In addition, an acquired firm's customer base can provide expanded market coverage. The most desirable acquisitions are those that will significantly enhance the acquiring firm's competitive strength.

> One of the greatest strategic mistakes a firm can make in a maturing industry is pursuing a compromise between low-cost, differentiation, and focusing such that it ends up "stuck in the middle" with a fuzzy strategy, an average image, an ill-defined market identity, no competitive advantage, and little prospect of becoming an industry leader.

Expanding Internationally   As its domestic market matures, a firm may seek to enter foreign markets where attractive growth potential still exists and competitive pressures are not so strong. Several manufacturers in highly industrialized nations found international expansion attractive because equipment no longer suitable for domestic operations could be used in plants in less-developed foreign markets (a condition that lowered entry costs). Such possibilities arise when (1) foreign buyers have less sophisticated needs and have simpler, old-fashioned, end-use applications, and (2) foreign competitors are smaller, less formidable, and do not employ the latest production technology. Strategies to expand internationally also make sense when a domestic firm's skills, reputation, and product are readily transferable to foreign markets. Even though the U.S. market for soft drinks is mature, Coca-Cola has remained a growth company by upping its efforts to penetrate foreign markets where soft-drink sales are expanding rapidly.

Strategic Pitfalls

Perhaps the biggest strategic mistake a company can make as an industry matures is steering a middle course between low cost, differentiation, and focusing. Such strategic compromises guarantee that a firm will end up stuck in the middle with a fuzzy strategy, a lack of commitment to winning a competitive advantage based on either low cost or differentiation, an average image with buyers, and little chance of springing into the ranks of the industry leaders. Other strategic pitfalls include sacrificing long-term competitive position for short-term profit, waiting too long to respond to price-cutting, getting caught with too much capacity as growth slows, overspending on marketing efforts to boost sales growth, and failing to pursue cost reduction soon enough and aggressively enough.

STRATEGIES FOR FIRMS IN STAGNANT OR DECLINING INDUSTRIES

Many firms operate in industries where demand is growing more slowly than the economywide average or is even declining. Although harvesting the business to obtain the greatest cash flow, selling out, or closing down are obvious end-game strategies for uncommitted competitors with dim long-term prospects, strong competitors may be able to achieve good performance in a stagnant market environment.[7] Stagnant demand by itself is not enough to make an industry unattractive. Selling out may or may not be practical, and closing operations is always a last resort.

Businesses competing in slow-growth/declining industries have to accept the difficult realities of an environment of continuing stagnation, and they must resign themselves to performance targets consistent with available market opportunities. Cash flow and return-on-investment criteria are more appropriate than growth-oriented performance measures, but sales and market share growth are by no means ruled out. Strong competitors may be able to take sales from weaker rivals, and the acquisition or exit of weaker firms creates opportunities for the remaining companies to capture greater market share.

In general, companies that succeed in stagnant industries rely heavily on one of the following three strategic themes:[8]

1. *Pursue a focused strategy by identifying, creating, and exploiting the growth segments within the industry.* Stagnant or declining markets, like other markets, are composed of numerous segments or niches. Frequently, one or more of these segments is growing rapidly, despite stagnation in the industry as a whole. An astute competitor who is first to concentrate on the attractive growth segments can escape stagnating sales and profits and possibly achieve competitive advantage in the target segments.

2. *Stress differentiation based on quality improvement and product innovation.* Either enhanced quality or innovation can rejuvenate demand by creating important new growth segments or inducing buyers to trade up. Successful product innovation opens up an avenue for competing besides meeting or beating rivals' prices. Differentiation based on successful innovation has the additional advantage of being difficult and expensive for rival firms to imitate.

> Achieving competitive advantage in stagnant or declining industries usually requires pursuing one of three competitive approaches: focusing on growing market segments within the industry, differentiating on the basis of better quality and frequent product innovation, or becoming a lower cost producer.

[7]R. G. Hamermesh and S. B. Silk, "How to Compete in Stagnant Industries," *Harvard Business Review* 57, no. 5 (September–October 1979), p. 161.
[8]Ibid., p. 162.

3. *Work diligently and persistently to drive costs down.* When increases in sales cannot be counted on to generate increases in earnings, companies can improve profit margins and return on investment by continuous productivity improvement and cost reduction year after year. Potential cost-saving actions include (a) outsourcing functions and activities that can be performed more cheaply by outsiders, (b) completely redesigning internal business processes, (c) consolidating underutilized production facilities, (d) adding more distribution channels to ensure the unit volume needed for low-cost production, (e) closing low-volume, high-cost distribution outlets, and (f) cutting marginally beneficial activities out of the value chain.

These three strategic themes are not mutually exclusive.[9] Introducing new, innovative versions of a product can *create* a fast-growing market segment. Similarly, relentless pursuit of greater operating efficiencies permits price reductions that create price-conscious growth segments. Note that all three themes are spinoffs of the generic competitive strategies, adjusted to fit the circumstances of a tough industry environment.

The most attractive declining industries are those in which sales are eroding only slowly, there is large built-in demand, and some profitable niches remain. The most common strategic mistakes companies make in stagnating or declining markets are (1) getting trapped in a profitless war of attrition, (2) diverting too much cash out of the business too quickly (thus accelerating a company's demise), and (3) being overly optimistic about the industry's future and waiting complacently for things to get better.

Illustration Capsule 18 describes the creative approach taken by Yamaha to reverse declining market demand for pianos.

STRATEGIES FOR COMPETING IN FRAGMENTED INDUSTRIES

A number of industries are populated by hundreds, even thousands, of small and medium-sized companies, many privately held and none with a substantial share of total industry sales.[10] The standout competitive feature of a fragmented industry is the absence of market leaders with king-sized market shares or widespread buyer recognition. Examples of fragmented industries include book publishing, landscaping and plant nurseries, kitchen cabinets, oil tanker shipping, auto repair, restaurants and fast-food, public accounting, women's dresses, metal foundries, meat packing, paperboard boxes, log homes, hotels and motels, and furniture.

Any of several reasons can account for why the supply side of an industry is fragmented:

- Low entry barriers allow small firms to enter quickly and cheaply.
- An absence of large-scale production economies permits small companies to compete on an equal cost footing with larger firms.

---

[9]Ibid., p. 165.
[10]This section is summarized from Porter, *Competitive Strategy*, chapter 9.

Illustration Capsule 18   Yamaha's Strategy in the Piano Industry

For some years now, worldwide demand for pianos has been declining—in the mid-1980s the decline was 10% annually. Modern-day parents have not put the same stress on music lessons for their children as prior generations of parents did. In an effort to see if it could revitalize its piano business, Yamaha conducted a market research survey to learn what use was being made of pianos in households that owned one. The survey revealed that the overwhelming majority of the 40 million pianos in American, European, and Japanese households were seldom used. In most cases, the reasons the piano had been purchased no longer applied. Children had either stopped taking piano lessons or were grown and had left the household; adult household members played their pianos sparingly, if at all—only a small percentage were accomplished piano players. Most pianos were serving as a piece of fine furniture and were in good condition despite not being tuned regularly. The survey

also confirmed that the income levels of piano owners were well above average.

Yamaha's piano strategists saw the idle pianos in these upscale households as a potential market opportunity. The strategy that emerged entailed marketing an attachment that would convert the piano into an old-fashioned automatic player piano capable of playing a wide number of selections recorded on 3½-inch floppy disks (the same kind used to store computer data). The player piano conversion attachment carried a $2,500 price tag. Concurrently, Yamaha introduced Disklavier, an upright acoustic player piano model that could play *and record* performances up to 90 minutes long; the Disklavier retailed for $8,000. At year-end 1988 Yamaha offered 30 prerecorded disks for $29.95 each and planned to release a continuing stream of new selections. Yamaha believed that these new high-tech products held potential to reverse the downtrend in piano sales.

Buyers require relatively small quantities of customized products (as in business forms, interior design, and advertising); because demand for any particular product version is small, sales volumes are not adequate to support producing, distributing, or marketing on a scale that yields advantages to a large firm.

- The market for the industry's product/service is local (dry cleaning, residential construction, medical services, automotive repair), giving competitive advantage to local businesses familiar with local buyers and local market conditions.

- Market demand is so large and so diverse that it takes very large numbers of firms to accommodate buyer requirements (restaurants, energy, apparel).

- High transportation costs limit the radius a plant can economically service—as in concrete blocks, mobile homes, milk, and gravel.

- Local regulations make each geographic area somewhat unique.

- The industry is so new that no firms have yet developed the skills and resources to command a significant market share.

Some fragmented industries consolidate naturally as they mature. The stiffer competition that accompanies slower growth produces a shake-out of weak, inefficient firms and a greater concentration of larger, more visible sellers. Other fragmented industries remain atomistically competitive because it is inherent in the nature of their businesses. And still others remain stuck in a fragmented state because existing firms lack the resources or ingenuity to employ a strategy powerful enough to drive industry consolidation.

Competitive rivalry in fragmented industries can vary from moderately strong to fierce. Low barriers make entry of new competitors an ongoing threat. Competition

In fragmented industries competitors usually have the strategic latitude (1) to compete broadly or to focus and (2) to pursue either a low-cost or a differentiation-based competitive advantage.

from substitutes may or may not be a major factor. The relatively small size of companies in fragmented industries puts them in a weak position to bargain with powerful suppliers and buyers, although sometimes they can become members of a cooperative formed for the purpose of using their combined leverage to negotiate better sales and purchase terms. In such an environment, the best a firm can expect is to cultivate a loyal customer base and grow a bit faster than the industry average. Competitive strategies based either on low cost or product differentiation are viable unless the industry's product is highly standardized. Focusing on a well-defined market niche or buyer segment usually offers more competitive advantage potential than striving for broad market appeal. Suitable competitive strategy options in a fragmented industry include

- **Constructing and operating "formula" facilities**—This strategic approach is frequently employed in restaurant and retailing businesses operating at multiple locations. It involves constructing standardized outlets in favorable locations at minimum cost and then polishing to a science how to operate all outlets in a superefficient manner. McDonald's, Home Depot, and 7-Eleven have pursued this strategy to perfection, earning excellent profits in their respective industries.

- **Becoming a low-cost operator**—When price competition is intense and profit margins are under constant pressure, companies can stress no-frills operations featuring low overhead, high-productivity/low-cost labor, lean capital budgets, and dedicated pursuit of total operating efficiency. Successful low-cost producers in a fragmented industry can play the price-cutting game and still earn profits above the industry average.

- **Increasing customer value through integration**—Backward or forward integration may contain opportunities to lower costs or enhance the value provided to customers. Examples include assembling components before shipment to customers, roviding technical advice, or opening regional distribution centers.

- **Specializing by product type**—When a fragmented industry's products include a range of styles or services, a strategy to focus on one product/service category can be very effective. Some firms in the furniture industry specialize in only one furniture type such as brass beds, rattan and wicker, lawn and garden, or early American. In auto repair, companies specialize in transmission repair, body work, or speedy oil changes.

- **Specialization by customer type**—A firm can cope with the intense competition of a fragmented industry by catering to those customers (1) who have the least bargaining leverage (because they are small in size or purchase small amounts), (2) who are the least price sensitive, or (3) who are interested in unique product attributes, a customized product/service, or other "extras."

- **Focusing on a limited geographic area**—Even though a firm in a fragmented industry can't win a big share of total industrywide sales, it can still try to dominate a local/regional geographic area. Concentrating company efforts on a limited territory can produce greater operating efficiency, speed delivery and customer services, promote strong brand awareness, and permit saturation advertising, while avoiding the diseconomies of stretching operations out over a much wider area.

Supermarkets, banks, and sporting goods retailers successfully operate multiple locations within a limited geographic area.

In fragmented industries, firms generally have the strategic freedom to pursue broad or narrow market targets and low-cost or differentiation-based competitive advantages. Many different strategic approaches can exist side by side.

STRATEGIES FOR COMPETING IN INTERNATIONAL MARKETS

Companies are motivated to expand into international markets for any of three basic reasons: a desire to seek out new markets, a competitive need to achieve lower costs, or a desire to access natural resource deposits in other countries. Whatever the reason, an international strategy has to be situation-driven. Special attention has to be paid to how national markets differ in buyer needs and habits, distribution channels, long-run growth potential, driving forces, and competitive pressures. In addition to the basic market differences from country to country, there are four other situational considerations unique to international operations: cost variations among countries, fluctuating exchange rates, host government trade policies, and the pattern of international competition.

> **Competing in international markets poses a bigger strategy-making challenge than competing in only the company's home market.**

Country-to-Country Cost Variations   Differences in wage rates, worker productivity, inflation rates, energy costs, tax rates, government regulations, and the like create sizable variations in manufacturing costs from country to country. Plants in some countries have major manufacturing cost advantages because of lower input costs (especially labor), relaxed government regulations, or unique natural resources. In such cases, the low-cost countries become principal production sites, and most of the output is exported to markets in other parts of the world. Companies with facilities in these locations (or that source their products from contract manufacturers in these countries) have a competitive advantage. The competitive role of low manufacturing costs is most evident in low-wage countries like Taiwan, South Korea, Mexico, and Brazil, which have become production havens for goods with high labor content.

Another important manufacturing cost consideration in international competition is the concept of *manufacturing share* as distinct from brand share or market share. For example, although less than 40 percent of all the video recorders sold in the United States carry a Japanese brand, Japanese companies do 100 percent of the manufacturing—all sellers source their video recorders from Japanese manufacturers.[11] In microwave ovens, Japanese brands have less than a 50 percent share of the U.S. market, but the manufacturing share of Japanese companies is over 85 percent. *Manufacturing share is significant because it is a better indicator than market share of the industry's low-cost producer.* In a globally competitive industry where some competitors are intent on global dominance, being the worldwide low-cost producer is a powerful competitive advantage. Achieving low-cost producer status often requires a company to have the largest worldwide manufacturing share, with production centralized in one or a few superefficient plants. However, important marketing and distribution economies associated with multinational operations can also yield low-cost leadership.

---

[11]C. K. Prahalad and Yves L. Doz, *The Multinational Mission* (New York: Free Press, 1987), p. 60.

Fluctuating Exchange Rates   The volatility of exchange rates greatly complicates the issue of geographic cost advantages. Exchange rates often fluctuate as much as 20 to 40 percent annually. Changes of this magnitude can totally wipe out a country's low-cost advantage or transform a former high-cost location into a competitive-cost location. A strong U.S. dollar makes it more attractive for U.S. companies to manufacture in foreign countries. Declines in the value of the dollar against foreign currencies can eliminate much of the cost advantage that foreign manufacturers have over U.S. manufacturers and can even prompt foreign companies to establish production plants in the United States.

Host Government Trade Policies   National governments enact all kinds of measures affecting international trade and the operation of foreign companies in their markets. Host governments may impose import tariffs and quotas, set local content requirements on goods made inside their borders by foreign-based companies, and regulate the prices of imported goods. In addition, outsiders may face a web of regulations regarding technical standards, product certification, prior approval of capital spending projects, withdrawal of funds from the country, and minority (sometimes majority) ownership by local citizens. Some governments also provide subsidies and low-interest loans to domestic companies to help them compete against foreign-based companies. Other governments, anxious to obtain new plants and jobs, offer foreign companies a helping hand in the form of subsidies, privileged market access, and technical assistance.

Multicountry Competition Versus Global Competition

Multicountry (or multidomestic) competition exists when competition in one national market is independent of competition in another national market— there is no "international market," just a collection of self-contained country markets.

There are important differences in the patterns of international competition from industry to industry.[12] At one extreme, competition can be termed *multicountry* or *multidomestic* because it takes place country by country; competition in each national market is essentially independent of competition in other national markets. For example, there is a banking industry in France, one in Brazil, and one in Japan, but competitive conditions in banking differ markedly in all three countries. Moreover, a bank's reputation, customer base, and competitive position in one nation have little or no bearing on its ability to compete successfully in another. In industries where multicountry competition prevails, the power of a company's strategy in any one nation and any competitive advantage it yields are largely confined to that nation and do not spill over to other countries where it operates. With multicountry competition there is no "international market," just a collection of self-contained country markets. Industries characterized by multicountry competition include beer, life insurance, apparel, metals fabrication, many types of food products (coffee, cereals, canned goods, frozen foods), and many types of retailing.

At the other extreme is *global competition* where prices and competitive conditions across country markets are strongly linked together and the term international or global market has true meaning. In a globally competitive industry, a company's competitive position in one country both affects and is affected by its position in other countries. Rival companies compete against each other in many different countries, but especially so in countries where sales volumes are large and where

---

[12]Michael E. Porter, *The Competitive Advantage of Nations* (New York: Free Press, 1990), pp. 53–54.

having a competitive presence is strategically important to building a strong global position in the industry. In global competition, a firm's overall competitive advantage grows out of its entire worldwide operations; the competitive advantage it creates at its home base is supplemented by advantages growing out of its operations in other countries (having plants in low-wage countries, a capability to serve customers with multinational operations of their own, and a brand reputation that is transferable from country to country). *A global competitor's market strength is directly proportional to its portfolio of country-based competitive advantages.* Global competition exists in automobiles, television sets, tires, telecommunications equipment, copiers, watches, and commercial aircraft.

An industry can have segments that are globally competitive and segments where competition is country by country.[13] In the hotel-motel industry, for example, the low- and medium-priced segments are characterized by multicountry competition because competitors mainly serve travelers within the same country. In the business and luxury segments, however, competition is more globalized. Companies like Nikki, Marriott, Sheraton, and Hilton have hotels at many international locations and use worldwide reservation systems and common quality and service standards to gain marketing advantages in serving businesspeople and travelers who make frequent international trips.

In lubricants, the marine engine segment is globally competitive because ships move from port to port and require the same oil everywhere they stop. Brand reputations have a global scope, and successful marine engine lubricant producers (Exxon, British Petroleum, and Shell) operate globally. In automotive motor oil, however, multicountry competition dominates. Countries have different weather conditions and driving patterns, production is subject to limited scale economies and shipping costs are high, and retail distribution channels differ markedly from country to country. Thus domestic firms, like Quaker State and Pennzoil in the U.S. and Castrol in Great Britain, can be leaders in their home markets without competing globally.

All these situational considerations, along with the obvious cultural and political differences between countries, shape a company's strategic approach in international markets.

> *Global competition exists when competitive conditions across national markets are linked strongly enough to form a true international market and when leading competitors compete head-to-head in many different countries.*

> **In multicountry competition, rival firms vie for national market leadership. In globally competitive industries, rival firms vie for worldwide leadership.**

Types of International Strategies

There are six distinct strategic options for a company participating in international markets. It can

1. *License foreign firms to use the company's technology or produce and distribute the company's products* (in which case international revenues will equal the royalty income from the licensing agreement).

2. *Maintain a national (one-country) production base and export goods to foreign markets* using either company-owned or foreign-controlled forward distribution channels.

3. *Follow a multicountry strategy* whereby a company's international strategy is crafted country by country to be responsive to buyer needs and competitive conditions in each country where it operates. Strategic

---

[13]Ibid., p. 61.

moves in one country are made independent of actions taken in another country; strategy coordination across countries is secondary to matching company strategy to individual country conditions.

4. *Follow a global low-cost strategy* where the company strives to be a low-cost supplier to buyers in most or all strategically important markets of the world. The company's strategic efforts are coordinated worldwide to achieve a low-cost position relative to all competitors.

5. *Follow a global differentiation strategy* whereby a firm differentiates its product on the same attributes in all countries to create a globally consistent image and a consistent competitive theme. The firm's strategic moves are coordinated across countries to achieve consistent differentiation worldwide.

6. *Follow a global focus strategy* where company strategy is aimed at serving the same identifiable niche in each of many strategically important country markets. Strategic actions are coordinated globally to achieve a consistent low-cost or differentiation-based competitive approach in the target niche worldwide.

Licensing makes sense when a firm with valuable technical know-how or a unique patented product has neither the internal organizational capability nor the resources in foreign markets. By licensing the technology or the production rights to foreign-based firms, the firm at least realizes income from royalties.

Using domestic plants as a production base for exporting goods to foreign markets is an excellent initial strategy for pursuing international sales. It minimizes both risk and capital requirements, and it is a conservative way to test the international waters. With an export strategy, a manufacturer can limit its involvement in foreign markets by contracting with foreign wholesalers experienced in importing to handle the entire distribution and marketing function in their countries or regions of the world. If it is more advantageous to maintain control over these functions, a manufacturer can establish its own distribution and sales organizations in some or all of the target foreign markets. Either way, a firm minimizes its direct investments in foreign countries because of its home-based production and export strategy. Such strategies are commonly favored by Korean and Italian companies—products are designed and manufactured at home and only marketing activities are performed abroad. Whether such a strategy can be pursued successfully over the long run hinges on the relative cost competitiveness of a home-country production base. In some industries, firms gain additional scale economies and experience curve benefits from centralizing production in one or several giant plants whose output capability exceeds demand in any one country market; obviously, to capture such economies a company must export to markets in other countries. However, this strategy is vulnerable when manufacturing costs in the home country are substantially higher than in foreign countries where rivals have plants.

The pros and cons of a multicountry strategy versus a global strategy are a bit more complex.

A Multicountry Strategy or a Global Strategy?

The need for a multicountry strategy derives from the sometimes vast differences in cultural, economic, political, and competitive conditions in different countries. The more diverse national market conditions are, the stronger the case for a *multicountry strategy* where the company tailors its strategic approach to fit each host country's market situation. In such cases, the company's overall international strategy is a collection of its individual country strategies.

While multicountry strategies are best suited for industries where multicountry competition dominates, global strategies are best suited for globally competitive industries. A *global strategy* is one where the company's strategy for competing is mostly the same in all countries. Although *minor* country-to-country differences in strategy do exist to accommodate specific competitive conditions in host countries, the company's fundamental competitive approach (low-cost, differentiation, or focused) remains the same worldwide. Moreover, a global strategy involves (1) integrating and coordinating the company's strategic moves worldwide and (2) selling in many if not all nations where there is significant buyer demand. Table 6–1 provides a point-by-point comparison of multicountry versus global strategies. The question of which of these two strategies to pursue is the foremost strategic issue firms face when they compete in international markets.

The strength of a multicountry strategy is that it matches the company's competitive approach to host country circumstances. A multicountry strategy is essential when there are significant country-to-country differences in customers' needs and buying habits (see Illustration Capsule 19), when buyers in a country insist on special-order or highly customized products, when buyer demand for the product exists in comparatively few national markets, when host governments enact regulations requiring that products sold locally meet strict manufacturing specifications or performance standards, and when the trade restrictions of host governments are so diverse and complicated they preclude a uniform, coordinated worldwide market approach. However, a multicountry strategy has two big drawbacks: it entails very little strategic coordination across country boundaries, and it is not tied tightly to competitive advantage. The primary orientation of a multicountry strategy is responsiveness to local country conditions, not building a multinational competitive advantage over other international competitors and the domestic companies of host countries.

A global strategy, because it is more uniform from country to country, can concentrate on securing a sustainable low-cost or differentiation-based competitive advantage over both international and domestic rivals. Whenever country-to-country differences are small enough to be accommodated within the framework of a global strategy, a global strategy is preferable to a multicountry strategy because of the value of uniting a company's competitive efforts worldwide to pursue lower cost or differentiation.

> **A multicountry strategy is appropriate for industries where multicountry competition dominates, but a global strategy works best in markets that are globally competitive or beginning to globalize.**

Global Strategy and Competitive Advantage

There are two ways in which a firm can gain competitive advantage (or offset domestic disadvantages) with a global strategy.[14] One way exploits a global competitor's ability to deploy R&D, parts manufacture, assembly, distribution centers, sales and marketing, customer service centers and other activities among nations in a manner that lowers costs or achieves greater product differentiation; the other way draws on a global competitor's ability to coordinate its dispersed activities in ways that a domestic-only competitor cannot.

---

[14]Ibid., p. 54.

Table 6–1   Differences between Multicountry and Global Strategies

	Multicountry Strategy	Global Strategy
Strategic Arena	• Selected target countries and trading areas.	• Most countries which constitute critical markets for the product, at least North America, the European Community, and the Pacific Rim (Australia, Japan, South Korea, and Southeast Asia).
Business Strategy	• Custom strategies to fit the circumstances of each host country situation; little or no strategy coordination across countries.	• Same basic strategy worldwide; minor country-by-country variations where essential.
Product-line Strategy	• Adapted to local needs.	• Mostly standardized products sold worldwide.
Production Strategy	• Plants scattered across many host countries.	• Plants located on the basis of maximum competitive advantage (in low-cost countries, close to major markets, geographically scattered to minimize shipping costs, or use of a few world-scale plants to maximize economies of scale—as most appropriate).
Source of Supply for Raw Materials and Components	• Suppliers in host country preferred (local facilities meeting local buyer needs; some local sourcing may be required by host government).	• Attractive suppliers from anywhere in the world.
Marketing and Distribution	• Adapted to practices and culture of each host country.	• Much more worldwide coordination; minor adaptation to host country situations if required.
Company Organization	• Form subsidiary companies to handle operations in each host country; each subsidiary operates more or less autonomously to fit host country conditions.	• All major strategic decisions are closely coordinated at global headquarters; a global organizational structure is used to unify the operations in each country.

A global strategy enables a firm to pursue sustainable competitive advantage by locating activities in the most advantageous nations and coordinating its strategic actions worldwide; a domestic-only competitor forfeits such opportunities.

Locating Activities   To use location to build competitive advantage, a global firm must consider two issues: (1) whether to concentrate each activity it performs in one or two countries or to disperse performance of the activity to many nations and (2) in which countries to locate particular activities. Activities tend to be concentrated in one or two locations when there are significant economies of scale in performing an activity, when there are advantages in locating related activities in the same area to achieve better coordination, and when there is a steep learning or experience curve associated with performing an activity in a single location. Thus in some industries scale economies in parts manufacture or assembly are so great that a company establishes one large plant from which it serves the world market. Where just-in-time inventory practices yield big cost savings and/or where the assembly firm has long-term partnering arrangements with its key suppliers, parts manufacturing plants may be clustered around final assembly plants.

On the other hand, dispersing activities is more advantageous than concentrating them in several instances. Buyer-related activities—such as distribution to dealers, sales and advertising, and after-sale service—usually must take place close to buyers.

Illustration Capsule 19   Nestlé's Multicountry Strategy in Instant Coffee

Nestlé is the world's largest food company with over $33 billion in revenues, market penetration on all major continents, and plants in over 60 countries. The star performer in Nestlé's food products lineup is coffee, with sales of over $5 billion and operating profits of $600 million. Nestlé is the world's largest producer of coffee. It is also the world's market leader in mineral water (Perrier), condensed milk, frozen food, candies, and infant food.

In 1992 the company's Nescafé brand was the leader in the instant coffee segment in virtually every national market but the U.S., where it ranked number two behind Maxwell House. Nestlé produced 200 types of instant coffee, from lighter blends for the U.S. market to dark espressos for Latin America. To keep its instant coffees matched to consumer tastes in different countries (and areas within some countries), Nestlé operated four coffee research labs, with a combined budget of $50 mil-lion annually, to experiment with new blends in aroma, flavor, and color. The strategy was to match the blends marketed in each country to the tastes and preferences of coffee drinkers in that country, introducing new blends to develop new segments when opportunities appeared and altering blends as needed to respond to changing tastes and buyer habits.

Although instant coffee sales were declining worldwide due to the introduction of new style automatic coffeemakers, sales were rising in two tea-drinking countries, Britain and Japan. In Britain, Nescafé was promoted extensively to build a wider base of instant coffee drinkers. In Japan, where Nescafé was considered a luxury item, the company made its Japanese blends available in fancy containers suitable for gift-giving. In 1993 Nestlé began introducing Nescafé instant coffee and Coffee-Mate creamer in several large cities in China.

Sources: Shawn Tully, "Nestlé Shows How to Gobble Markets," *Fortune*, January 16, 1989, pp. 74–78; "Nestlé: A Giant in a Hurry," *Business Week*, March 22, 1993, pp. 50–54; and company annual reports.

This means physically locating the capability to perform such activities in every country market where a global firm has major customers (unless buyers in several adjoining countries can be served quickly from a nearby central location). For example, firms that make mining and oil drilling equipment maintain operations in many international locations to support customers' needs for speedy equipment repair and technical assistance. Large public accounting firms have numerous international offices to service the foreign operations of their multinational corporate clients. A global competitor that effectively disperses its buyer-related activities can gain a service-based competitive edge in world markets over rivals whose buyer-related activities are more concentrated—this is one reason the Big Six public accounting firms have been so successful relative to second-tier firms. Dispersing activities to many locations is also competitively advantageous when high transportation costs, diseconomies of large size, and trade barriers make it too expensive to operate from a central location. Many companies distribute their products from multiple locations to shorten delivery times to customers. In addition, it is strategically advantageous to disperse activities to hedge against the risks of fluctuating exchange rates, supply interruptions (due to strikes, mechanical failures, and transportation delays), and adverse political developments. Such risks are greater when activities are concentrated in a single location.

The classic reason for locating an activity in a particular country is lower costs.[15] Even though a global firm has strong reason to disperse buyer-related activities to many international locations, such activities as materials procurement, parts manu-facture, finished goods assembly, technology research, and new-product development

---

[15]Ibid., p. 57.

can frequently be decoupled from buyer locations and performed wherever advantage lies. Components can be made in Mexico, technology research done in Frankfurt, new products developed and tested in Phoenix, and assembly plants located in Spain, Brazil, Taiwan, and South Carolina. Capital can be raised in whatever country it is available on the best terms.

Low front-end cost is not the only locational consideration, however. A research unit may be situated in a particular nation because of its pool of technically trained personnel. A customer service center or sales office may be opened in a particular country to help develop strong relationships with pivotal customers. An assembly plant may be located in a country in return for the host government's allowing freer import of components from large-scale, centralized parts plants located elsewhere.

Coordinating Activities and Strategic Moves   Aligning and coordinating company activities located in different countries contributes to sustainable competitive advantage in several different ways. If a firm learns how to assemble its product more efficiently at its Brazilian plant, the accumulated knowledge and expertise can be transferred to its assembly plant in Spain. Knowledge gained in marketing a company's product in Great Britain can be used to introduce the product in New Zealand and Australia. A company can shift production from one country to another to take advantage of exchange rate fluctuations, to enhance its leverage with host country governments, and to respond to changing wage rates, energy costs, or trade restrictions. A company can enhance its brand reputation by consistently incorporating the same differentiating attributes in its products in all worldwide markets where it competes. The reputation for quality that Honda established worldwide first in motorcycles and then in automobiles gave it competitive advantage in positioning Honda lawnmowers at the upper end of the market—the Honda name gave the company instant credibility with buyers.

A global competitor can choose where and how to challenge rivals. It may decide to retaliate against aggressive rivals in the country market where the rival has its biggest sales volume or its best profit margins in order to reduce the rival's financial resources for competing in other country markets. It may decide to wage a price-cutting offensive against weak rivals in their home markets, capturing greater market share and subsidizing any short-term losses with profits earned in other country markets.

A company that competes only in its home country has access to none of the competitive advantage opportunities associated with international locations or coordination. By shifting from a domestic strategy to a global strategy, a domestic company that finds itself at a competitive disadvantage against global companies can begin to restore its competitiveness.

Strategic Alliances

Strategic alliances are cooperative agreements between firms that go beyond normal company-to-company dealings but that fall short of merger or full partnership.[16] An alliance can involve joint research efforts, technology sharing, joint use of production facilities, marketing one another's products, or joining forces to manufacture components or assemble finished products. Strategic alliances are a means for firms in the

---

[16]Ibid., p. 65. See also Kenichi Ohmae, "The Global Logic of Strategic Alliances," *Harvard Business Review* 89, no. 2 (March–April 1989), pp. 143–54.

same industry yet based in different countries to compete on a more global scale while still preserving their independence. Historically, export minded firms in industrialized nations sought alliances with firms in less-developed countries to import and market their products locally—such arrangements were often necessary to gain access to the less-developed country's market. More recently, leading companies from different parts of the world have formed strategic alliances to strengthen their mutual ability to serve whole continental areas and move toward more global market participation. Both Japanese and American companies are actively forming alliances with European companies to strengthen their ability to compete in the 12-nation European Community and to capitalize on the opening up of Eastern European markets. Illustration Capsule 20 describes Toshiba's successful use of strategic alliances and joint ventures to pursue related technologies and product markets.

> **Strategic alliances can help companies in globally competitive industries strengthen their competitive positions while still preserving their independence.**

Companies enter into alliances for several strategically beneficial reasons.[17] The three most important are to gain economies of scale in production and/or marketing, to fill gaps in their technical and manufacturing expertise, and to acquire market access. By joining forces in producing components, assembling models, and marketing their products, companies can realize cost savings not achievable with their own small volumes. Allies learn much from one another in performing joint research, sharing technological know-how, and studying one another's manufacturing methods. Alliances are often used by outsiders to meet governmental requirements for local ownership, and allies can share distribution facilities and dealer networks, thus mutually strengthening their access to buyers. In addition, alliances affect competition; not only can alliances offset competitive disadvantages but they also can result in the allied companies' directing their competitive energies more toward mutual rivals and less toward one another. Many runner-up companies, wanting to preserve their independence, resort to alliances rather than merger to try to close the competitive gap on leading companies.

Alliances have their pitfalls, however. Achieving effective coordination between independent companies, each with different motives and perhaps conflicting objectives, is a challenging task. It requires many meetings of many people over a period of time to iron out what is to be shared, what is to remain proprietary, and how the cooperative arrangements will work. Allies may have to overcome language and cultural barriers as well. The communication, trust-building, and coordination costs are high in terms of management time. Often, once the bloom is off the rose, partners discover they have deep differences of opinion about how to proceed and conflicting objectives and strategies. Tensions build up, working relationships cool, and the hoped-for benefits never materialize.[18] Many times, allies find it difficult to collaborate effectively in competitively sensitive areas, thus raising questions about mutual trust and forthright exchanges of information and expertise. There can also be clashes of egos and company cultures. The key people on whom success or failure depends may have little personal chemistry, be unable to work closely together or form a partnership, or be unable to come to consensus.

Most important, though, is the danger of depending on another company for essential expertise and capabilities over the long term. To be a serious market contender, a company must ultimately develop internal capabilities in all areas

---

[17]Porter, *The Competitive Advantage of Nations*, p. 66; see also Jeremy Main, "Making Global Alliances Work," *Fortune*, December 17, 1990, pp. 121–26.
[18]Jeremy Main, "Making Global Alliances Work," p. 125.

Illustration Capsule 20   Toshiba's Use of Strategic Alliances and Joint Ventures

Toshiba, Japan's oldest and third largest electronics company (after Hitachi and Matsushita), over the years has made technology licensing agreements, joint ventures, and strategic alliances cornerstones of its corporate strategy. Using such partnerships to complement its own manufacturing and product innovation capabilities, it has become a $37 billion maker of electrical and electronics products—from home appliances to computer memory chips to telecommunications equipment to electric power generation equipment.

Fumio Sato, Toshiba's CEO, contends that joint ventures and strategic alliances are a necessary component of strategy for a high-tech electronics company with global ambitions:

> It is no longer an era in which a single company can dominate any technology or business by itself. The technology has become so advanced, and the markets so complex, that you simply can't expect to be the best at the whole process any longer.

Among Toshiba's two dozen major joint ventures and strategic alliances are

- A five-year-old joint venture with Motorola to design and make dynamic random access memory chips (DRAMs) for Toshiba and microprocessors for Motorola. Initially the two partners invested $125 million apiece in the venture and have since invested another $480 million each.

- A joint venture with IBM to make flat-panel liquid crystal displays in color for portable computers.

- Two other joint ventures with IBM to develop computer memory chips (one a "flash" memory chip that remembers data even after the power is turned off).

- An alliance with Sweden-based Ericsson, one of the world's biggest telecommunications manufacturers, to develop new mobile telecommunications equipment.

- A partnership with Sun Microsystems, the leading maker of microprocessor-based

workstations, to provide portable versions of the workstations to Sun and to incorporate Sun's equipment in Toshiba products to control power plants, route highway traffic, and monitor automated manufacturing processes.

- A $1 billion strategic alliance with IBM and Siemens to develop and produce the next-generation DRAM—a single chip capable of holding 256 million bits of information (approximately 8,000 typewritten pages).

- An alliance with Apple Computer to develop CD-ROM-based multimedia players that plug into a TV set.

- A joint project with the entertainment division of Time Warner to design advanced interactive cable television technology.

Other alliances and joint ventures with General Electric, United Technologies, National Semiconductor, Samsung (Korea), LSI Logic (Canada), and European companies like Olivetti, SCS-Thomson, Rhone-Poulenc, Thomson Consumer Electronics, and GEC Alstholm are turning out such products as fax machines, copiers, medical equipment, computers, rechargeable batteries, home appliances, and nuclear and steam power generating equipment.

So far, none of Toshiba's relationships with partners have gone sour despite potential conflicts among related projects with competitors (Toshiba has partnerships with nine other chip makers to develop or produce semiconductors). Toshiba attributes this to its approach to alliances: choosing partners carefully, being open about Toshiba's connections with other companies, carefully defining the role and rights of each partner in the original pact (including who gets what if the alliance doesn't work out), and cultivating easy relations and good friendships with each partner. Toshiba's management believes that strategic alliances and joint ventures are an effective way for the company to move into new businesses quickly, share the design and development costs of ambitious new products with competent partners, and achieve greater access to important geographic markets outside Japan.

Source: Based on Brenton R. Schlender, "How Toshiba Makes Alliances Work," *Fortune*, October 4, 1993, pp. 116–20.

important to strengthening its competitive position and building a sustainable competitive advantage. Where this is not feasible, merger is a better solution than strategic alliance. Strategic alliances are best used as a transitional way to combat competitive disadvantage in international markets; rarely if ever can they be relied on as a means for creating competitive advantage. Illustration Capsule 21 relates the experiences of companies with strategic alliances.

> **Strategic alliances are more effective in combating competitive disadvantage than in gaining competitive advantage.**

To realize the most from strategic alliance, companies should observe five guidelines:[19]

1. Pick a compatible partner; take the time to build strong bridges of communication and trust and don't expect immediate payoffs.

2. Choose an ally whose products and market strongholds *complement* rather than compete directly with the company's own products and customer base.

3. Learn thoroughly and rapidly about a partner's technology and management; transfer valuable ideas and practices into one's own operations promptly.

4. Be careful not to divulge competitively sensitive information to a partner.

5. View the alliance as temporary (5 to 10 years); continue longer if it's beneficial but don't hesitate to terminate the alliance and go it alone when the payoffs run out.

Strategic Intent, Profit Sanctuaries, and Cross-Subsidization

Competitors in international markets can be distinguished not only by their strategies but also by their long-term strategic objectives and strategic intent. Four types of competitors stand out:[20]

- Firms whose strategic intent is *global dominance* or, at least, high rank among the global market leaders; such firms pursue some form of global strategy.

- Firms whose primary strategic objective is *defending domestic dominance* in their home market, even though they derive some of their sales internationally (usually under 20 percent) and have operations in several or many foreign markets.

- Firms who aspire to a growing share of worldwide sales and whose primary strategic orientation is *host country responsiveness;* such firms have a multicountry strategy and may already derive a large fraction of their revenues from foreign operations.

- *Domestic-only firms* whose strategic intent does not extend beyond building a strong competitive position in their home country market; such firms base their competitive strategies on domestic market conditions and watch events in the international market only for their impact on the domestic situation.

The types of firms are *not* equally well-positioned to be successful in markets where they compete head-on. Consider the case of a purely domestic U.S. company in competition with a Japanese company operating in many country markets and

---

[19]Ibid.
[20]Prahalad and Doz, *The Multinational Mission*, p. 52.

Illustration Capsule 21   Company Experiences with Strategic Alliances

As the chairman of British Aerospace recently observed, a strategic alliance with a foreign company is "one of the quickest and cheapest ways to develop a global strategy." AT&T formed joint ventures with many of the world's largest telephone and electronics companies. Boeing, the world's premier manufacturer of commercial aircraft, partnered with Kawasaki, Mitsubishi, and Fuji to produce a long-range, wide-body jet for delivery in 1995. General Electric and Snecma, a French maker of jet engines, have a 50-50 partnership to make jet engines to power aircraft made by Boeing, McDonnell-Douglas, and Airbus Industrie (Airbus, the leading European maker of commercial aircraft, was formed by an alliance of aerospace companies from Britain, Spain, Germany, and France). The GE/Snecma alliance is regarded as a model because it existed for 17 years and it produced orders for 10,300 engines, totaling $38 billion.

Since the early 1980s, hundreds of strategic alliances have been formed in the motor vehicle industry as car and truck manufacturers and automotive parts suppliers moved aggressively to get in stronger position to compete globally. Not only have there been alliances between automakers strong in one region of the world and automakers strong in another region but there have also been strategic alliances between vehicle makers and key parts suppliers (especially those with high-quality parts and strong technological capabilities). General Motors and Toyota in 1984 formed a 50-50 partnership called New United Motor Manufacturing Inc. (NUMMI) to produce cars for both companies at an old GM plant in Fremont, California. The strategic value of the GM-Toyota alliance was that Toyota would learn how to deal with suppliers and workers in the U.S. (as a prelude to building its own plants in the U.S.) while GM would learn about Toyota's approaches to manufacturing and management. Each company sent managers to the NUMMI plant to work for two or three years to learn and absorb all they could, then transferred their NUMMI "graduates" to jobs where they could be instrumental in helping their companies apply what they learned. Toyota moved quickly to capitalize on its experiences at NUMMI. By 1991 Toyota had opened two plants on its own in North America, was constructing a third plant, and was producing 50% of the vehicles it sold in North America in its North American plants. While General Motors incorporated much of its NUMMI learning into the management practices and manufacturing methods it was using at its newly opened Saturn plant in Tennessee, it proceeded more slowly than Toyota. American and European companies are generally regarded as less skilled than the Japanese in transferring the learning from strategic alliances into their own operations.

Many alliances fail or are terminated when one partner ends up acquiring the other. A 1990 survey of 150 companies involved in terminated alliances found that three-fourths of the alliances had been taken over by Japanese partners. A nine-year alliance between Fujitsu and International Computers, Ltd., a British manufacturer, ended when Fujitsu acquired 80% of ICL. According to one observer, Fujitsu deliberately maneuvered ICL into a position of having no better choice than to sell out to its partner. Fujitsu began as a supplier of components for ICL's mainframe computers, then expanded its role over the next nine years to the point where it was ICL's only source of new technology. When ICL's parent, a large British electronics firm, saw the mainframe computer business starting to decline and decided to sell, Fujitsu was the only buyer it could find.

Source: Jeremy Main, "Making Global Alliances Work," *Fortune*, December 17, 1990, pp. 121–26.

aspiring to global dominance. The Japanese company can cut its prices in the U.S. market to gain market share at the expense of the U.S. company, subsidizing any losses with profits earned in its home sanctuary and in other foreign markets. The U.S. company has no effective way to retaliate. It is vulnerable even if it is the U.S. market leader. However, if the U.S. company is a multinational competitor and operates in Japan as well as elsewhere, it can counter Japanese pricing in the United States with retaliatory price cuts in its competitor's main profit sanctuary, Japan, and in other countries where it competes against the same Japanese company.

Thus, a domestic-only competitor is not on a level playing field in competing against a multinational rival. When aggressive global competitors enter a domestic-only company's market, one of the domestic-only competitor's best strategic defenses is to switch to a multinational or global strategy to give it the same cross-subsidizing capabilities the aggressors have.

Profit Sanctuaries and Critical Markets *Profit sanctuaries* are country markets where a company has a strong or protected market position and derives substantial profits. Japan, for example, is a profit sanctuary for most Japanese companies because trade barriers erected around Japanese industries by the Japanese government effectively block foreign companies from competing for a large share of Japanese sales. Protected from the threat of foreign competition in their home market, Japanese companies can safely charge somewhat higher prices to their Japanese customers and thus earn attractively large profits on sales made in Japan. In most cases, a company's biggest and most strategically crucial profit sanctuary is its home market, but multinational companies also have profit sanctuaries in those country markets where they have strong competitive positions, big sales volumes, and attractive profit margins.

Profit sanctuaries are valuable competitive assets in global industries. Companies with large, protected profit sanctuaries have competitive advantage over companies that don't have a dependable sanctuary. Companies with multiple profit sanctuaries are more favorably positioned than companies with a single sanctuary. Normally, a global competitor with multiple profit sanctuaries can successfully attack and beat a domestic competitor whose only profit sanctuary is its home market.

To defend against global competitors, companies don't have to compete in all or even most foreign markets, but they do have to compete in all critical markets. *Critical markets* are markets in countries

- That are the profit sanctuaries of key competitors.
- That have big sales volumes.
- That contain prestigious customers whose business it is strategically important to have.
- That offer exceptionally good profit margins due to weak competitive pressures.[21]

> A particular nation is a company's *profit sanctuary* when the company, either because of its strong competitive position or protective governmental trade policies, derives a substantial part of its total profits from sales in that nation.

The more critical markets a company participates in, the greater its ability to use cross-subsidization as a defense against competitors intent on global dominance.

The Competitive Power of Cross-Subsidization Cross-subsidization is a powerful competitive weapon. It involves using profits earned in one or more country markets to support a competitive offensive against key rivals or to gain increased penetration of a critical market. A typical offensive involves matching (or nearly matching) rivals on product quality and service, then charging a low enough price to draw customers away from rivals. While price-cutting may result in a challenger's earning lower profits (or even incurring losses) in the critical market it is attacking, it may still realize acceptable overall profits when the above-average earnings from its profit sanctuaries are added in.

Cross-subsidization is most powerful when a global firm with multiple profit sanctuaries is aggressively intent on achieving global market dominance over the

[21]Ibid., p. 61.

A competent global competitor with multiple profit sanctuaries can wage and generally win a competitive offensive against a domestic competitor whose only profit sanctuary is its home market.

long term. Both a domestic-only competitor and a multicountry competitor with no strategic coordination between its locally responsive country strategies are vulnerable to competition from rivals intent on global dominance. A global strategy can defeat a domestic-only strategy because a one-country competitor cannot effectively defend its market share over the long term against a global competitor with cross-subsidization capability. The global company can use lower prices to siphon off the domestic company's customers, all the while gaining market share, building name recognition, and supporting its strategic offensive with profits earned in its other critical markets. It can adjust the depth of its price-cutting to move in and capture market share quickly, or it can shave prices slightly to make gradual market inroads over a decade or more so as not to threaten domestic firms precipitously and perhaps trigger protectionist government actions. When attacked in this manner, a domestic company's best short-term hope is to pursue immediate and perhaps dramatic cost reduction and, if the situation warrants, to seek government protection in the form of tariff barriers, import quotas, and antidumping penalties. In the long term, the domestic company has to find ways to compete on a more equal footing—a difficult task when it must charge a price to cover full unit costs plus a margin for profit while the global competitor can charge a price only high enough to cover the incremental costs of selling in the domestic company's profit sanctuary. The best long-term strategic defenses for a domestic company are to enter into strategic alliances with foreign firms or to adopt a global approach to strategy and compete on an international scale, although sometimes it is possible to drive enough costs out of the business over the long term to survive with a domestic-only strategy. As a rule, however, competing only domestically is a perilous strategy in an industry populated with global competitors.

To defend against aggressive international competitors intent on global dominance, a domestic-only competitor usually has to abandon its domestic focus, become a multinational competitor, and craft a multinational competitive strategy.

While a company with a multicountry strategy has some cross-subsidy defense against a company with a global strategy, its vulnerability comes from a lack of competitive advantage and a probable cost disadvantage. A global competitor with a big manufacturing share and world-scale state-of-the-art plants is almost certain to be a lower-cost producer than a multicountry strategist with many small plants and short production runs turning out specialized products country by country. Companies pursuing a multicountry strategy thus need differentiation and focus-based advantages keyed to local responsiveness in order to defend against a global competitor. Such a defense is adequate in industries with significant enough national differences to impede use of a global strategy. But if an international rival can accommodate necessary local needs within a global strategy and still retain a cost edge, then a global strategy can defeat a multicountry strategy.

STRATEGIES FOR INDUSTRY LEADERS

The competitive positions of industry leaders normally range from stronger-than-average to powerful. Leaders typically are well-known, and strongly entrenched leaders have proven strategies (keyed either to low-cost leadership or to differentiation). Some of the best-known industry leaders are Anheuser-Busch (beer), IBM (mainframe computers), McDonald's (fast-food), Gillette (razor blades), Campbell's Soup (canned soups), Gerber (baby food), AT&T (long-distance telephone service), Eastman Kodak (camera film), and Levi Strauss (jeans). The main strategic concern for a leader revolves around how to sustain a leadership position, perhaps becoming the *dominant* leader as opposed to *a* leader. However, the pursuit of industry leadership and large market share per se is primarily important because of the competitive advantage and profitability that accrue to being the industry's biggest company.

Three contrasting strategic postures are open to industry leaders and dominant firms:[22]

1. **Stay-on-the-offensive strategy**—This strategy rests on the principle that the best defense is a good offense. Offensive-minded leaders stress being first-movers to sustain their competitive advantage (lower cost or differentiation) and to reinforce their reputation as *the* leader. A low-cost provider aggressively pursues cost reduction, and a differentiator constantly tries new ways to set its product apart from rivals' brands. The theme of a stay-on-the-offensive strategy is relentless pursuit of continuous improvement and innovation. Striving to be first with new products, better performance features, quality enhancements, improved customer services, or ways to cut production costs not only helps a leader avoid complacency but it also keeps rivals on the defensive scrambling to keep up. The array of offensive options can also include initiatives to expand overall industry demand—discovering new uses for the product, attracting new users of the product, and promoting more frequent use. In addition, a clever offensive leader stays alert for ways to make it easier and less costly for potential customers to switch their purchases from runner-up firms to its own products. Unless a leader's market share is already so dominant that it presents a threat of antitrust action (a market share under 60 percent is usually "safe"), a stay-on-the-offensive strategy means trying to grow *faster* than the industry as a whole and wrest market share from rivals. A leader whose growth does not equal or outpace the industry average is losing ground to competitors.

2. **Fortify-and-defend strategy**—The essence of "fortify and defend" is to make it harder for new firms to enter and for challengers to gain ground. The goals of a strong defense are to hold onto the present market share, strengthen current market position, and protect whatever competitive advantage the firm has. Specific defensive actions can include

   - Attempting to raise the competitive ante for challengers and new entrants via increased spending for advertising, higher levels of customer service, and bigger R&D outlays.
   - Introducing more of the company's own brands to match the product attributes that challenger brands have or could employ.
   - Adding personalized services and other "extras" that boost customer loyalty and make it harder or more costly for customers to switch to rival products.
   - Broadening the product line to close off possible vacant niches for competitors to slip into.

> **Industry leaders can strengthen their long-term competitive positions with strategies keyed to aggressive offense, aggressive defense, or muscling smaller rivals into a follow-the-leader role.**

---

[22]Kotler, *Marketing Management*, chapter 23; Michael E. Porter, *Competitive Advantage* (New York: Free Press, 1985), chapter 14; and Ian C. MacMillan, "Seizing Competitive Initiative," *The Journal of Business Strategy* 2, no. 4 (Spring 1982), pp. 43–57.

- Keeping prices reasonable and quality attractive.
- Building new capacity ahead of market demand to try to block the market expansion potential of smaller competitors.
- Investing enough to remain cost competitive and technologically progressive.
- Patenting the feasible alternative technologies.
- Signing exclusive contracts with the best suppliers and dealer distributors.

A fortify-and-defend strategy best suits firms that have already achieved industry dominance and don't wish to risk antitrust action. It is also well-suited to situations where a firm wishes to milk its present position for profits and cash flow because the industry's prospects for growth are low or because further gains in market share do not appear profitable enough to go after. But the fortify-and-defend strategy always entails trying to grow as fast as the market as a whole (to stave off market share slippage) and requires reinvesting enough capital in the business to protect the leader's ability to compete.

3. **Follow-the-leader strategy**—Here the leader's strategic posture involves using its competitive muscle (ethically and fairly!) to encourage runner-up firms to be content followers rather than aggressive challengers. The leader plays competitive hardball when smaller rivals rock the boat with price cuts or mount new market offensives that directly threaten its position. Specific responses can include quickly matching and perhaps exceeding challengers' price cuts, using large promotional campaigns to counter challengers' moves to gain market share, and offering better deals to the major customers of maverick firms. Leaders can also court distributors assiduously to dissuade them from carrying rivals' products, provide salespersons with documented information about the weaknesses of an aggressor's products, or try to fill any vacant positions in their own firms by making attractive offers to the better executives of rivals that "get out of line." When a leader consistently meets any moves to cut into its business with strong retaliatory tactics, it sends clear signals that offensive attacks on the leader's position will be met head-on and probably won't pay off. However, leaders pursuing this strategic approach should choose their battles. It may be more strategically productive to assume a hands-off posture and not respond in hardball fashion when smaller rivals attack each other's customer base in ways that don't affect its own.

STRATEGIES FOR RUNNER-UP FIRMS

Runner-up firms occupy weaker market positions than the industry leader(s). Some runner-up firms are up-and-coming *market challengers*, employing offensive strategies to gain market share and a stronger market position. Others behave as *content followers*, willing to coast along in their current positions because profits are adequate. Follower firms have no urgent strategic issue to confront beyond "What kinds of strategic changes are the leaders initiating and what do we need to do to follow along?''

A challenger firm interested in improving its market standing needs a strategy aimed at building a competitive advantage of its own. *Rarely can a runner-up firm improve its competitive position by imitating the strategies of leading firms. A cardinal rule in offensive strategy is to avoid attacking a leader head-on with an imitative strategy, regardless of the resources and staying power an underdog may have.*[23] Moreover, if a challenger has a 5 percent market share and needs a 20 percent share to earn attractive returns, it needs a more creative approach to competing than just "try harder."

In industries where large size yields significantly lower unit costs and gives large-share competitors an important cost advantage, small-share firms have only two viable strategic options: try to increase their market share (and achieve cost parity with larger rivals) or withdraw from the business (gradually or quickly). The competitive strategies most underdogs use to build market share are based on (1) becoming a lower-cost producer and using lower price to win customers from weak, higher-cost rivals and (2) using differentiation strategies based on quality, technological superiority, better customer service, best cost, or innovation. Achieving low-cost leadership is usually open to an underdog only when one of the market leaders is not already solidly positioned as the industry's low-cost producer. But a small-share firm may still be able to reduce its cost disadvantage by merging with or acquiring smaller firms; the combined market shares may provide the needed access to size-related economies. Other options include revamping its value chain to produce the needed cost savings and finding ways to better manage executional cost drivers.

In situations where scale economies or experience curve effects are small and a large market share produces no cost advantage, runner-up companies have more strategic flexibility and can consider any of the following six approaches:[24]

1. **Vacant-niche strategy**—This version of a focused strategy involves concentrating on customer or end-use applications that market leaders have bypassed or neglected. An ideal vacant niche is of sufficient size and scope to be profitable, has some growth potential, is well-suited to a firm's own capabilities and skills, and for one reason or another is not interesting to leading firms. Two examples where vacant-niche strategies worked successfully are regional commuter airlines serving cities with too few passengers to attract the interest of major airlines and health foods producers (like Health Valley, Hain, and Tree of Life) that cater to local health food stores—a market segment traditionally ignored by Pillsbury, Kraft General Foods, Heinz, Nabisco, Campbell's Soup, and other leading food products firms.

2. **Specialist strategy**—A specialist firm trains its competitive effort on one market segment: a single product, a particular end use, or buyers with special needs. The aim is to build competitive advantage through product uniqueness, expertise in special-purpose products, or specialized customer services. Smaller companies that successfully use a specialist focused

> **Rarely can a runner-up firm successfully challenge an industry leader with a copycat strategy.**

---

[23]Porter, *Competitive Advantage*, p. 514.

[24]For more details, see Kotler, *Marketing Management*, pp. 397–412; R. G. Hamermesh, M. J. Anderson, Jr., and J. E. Harris, "Strategies for Low Market Share Businesses," *Harvard Business Review* 56, no. 3 (May–June 1978), pp. 95–102; and Porter, *Competitive Advantage*, chapter 15.

strategy include Formby's (a specialist in stains and finishes for wood furniture, especially refinishing), Liquid Paper Co. (a leader in correction fluid for writers and typists), Canada Dry (known for its ginger ale, tonic water, and carbonated soda water), and American Tobacco (a leader in chewing tobacco and snuff).

3. **Ours-is-better-than-theirs strategy**—The approach here is to use a differentiation-based focused strategy keyed to superior product quality or unique attributes. Sales and marketing efforts are aimed directly at quality-conscious and performance-oriented buyers. Fine craftsmanship, prestige quality, frequent product innovations, and/or close contact with customers to solicit their input in developing a better product usually undergird this "superior product" approach. Some examples include Beefeater and Tanqueray in gin, Tiffany in diamonds and jewelry, Chicago Cutlery in premium-quality kitchen knives, Baccarat in fine crystal, Cannondale in mountain bikes, Bally in shoes, and Patagonia in apparel for outdoor recreation enthusiasts.

4. **Content-follower strategy**—Follower firms deliberately refrain from initiating trendsetting strategic moves and from aggressive attempts to steal customers away from the leaders. Followers prefer approaches that will not provoke competitive retaliation, often opting for focus and differentiation strategies that keep them out of the leaders' paths. They react and respond rather than initiate and challenge. They prefer defense to offense. And they rarely get out of line with the leaders on price. Union Camp (in paper products) has been a successful market follower by consciously concentrating on selected product uses and applications for specific customer groups, focused R&D, profits rather than market share, and cautious but efficient management.

5. **Growth-via-acquisition strategy**—One way to strengthen a company's position is to merge with or acquire weaker rivals to form an enterprise that has more competitive strength and a larger share of the market. Commercial airline companies such as Northwest, USAir, and Delta owe their market share growth during the past decade to acquisition of smaller, regional airlines. Likewise, the Big Six public accounting firms enhanced their national and international coverage by merging or forming alliances with smaller CPA firms at home and abroad.

6. **Distinctive-image strategy**—Some runner-up companies build their strategies around ways to make themselves stand out from competitors. A variety of strategic approaches can be used: creating a reputation for charging the lowest prices, providing prestige quality at a good price, going all out to give superior customer service, designing unique product attributes, being a leader in new product introduction, or devising unusually creative advertising. Examples include Dr Pepper's strategy in calling attention to its distinctive taste, Apple Computer's making it easier and more interesting for people to use a personal computer, and Mary Kay Cosmetics' distinctive use of the color pink.

In industries where big size is definitely a key success factor, firms with low market shares have some obstacles to overcome: (1) less access to economies of scale in manufacturing, distribution, or sales promotion; (2) difficulty in gaining customer recognition; (3) an inability to afford mass media advertising on a grand scale; and (4) difficulty in funding capital requirements.[25] But *it is erroneous to view runner-up firms as inherently less profitable or unable to hold their own against the biggest firms.* Many firms with small market shares earn healthy profits and enjoy good reputations with customers. Often, the handicaps of smaller size can be surmounted and a profitable competitive position established by (1) focusing on a few market segments where the company's strengths can yield a competitive edge; (2) developing technical expertise that will be highly valued by customers; (3) aggressively pursuing the development of new products for customers in the target market segments; and (4) using innovative/"dare to be different"/"beat the odds" entrepreneurial approaches to outmanage stodgy, slow-to-change market leaders. Runner-up companies have a golden opportunity to gain market share if they make a leapfrog technological breakthrough, if the leaders stumble or become complacent, or if they have the patience to nibble away at the leaders and build up their customer base over a long period of time.

STRATEGIES FOR WEAK BUSINESSES

A firm in an also-ran or declining competitive position has four basic strategic options. If it has the financial resources, it can launch an *offensive turnaround strategy* keyed either to low-cost or "new" differentiation themes, pouring enough money and talent into the effort to move up a notch or two in the industry rankings and become a respectable market contender within five years or so. It can employ a *fortify-and-defend* strategy, using variations of its present strategy and fighting hard to keep sales, market share, profitability, and competitive position at current levels. It can opt for an *immediate abandonment strategy* and get out of the business, either by selling out to another firm or by closing down operations if a buyer cannot be found. Or it can employ a *harvest strategy*, keeping reinvestment to a bare-bones minimum and taking actions to maximize short-term cash flows in preparation for an orderly market exit. The gist of the first three options is self-explanatory. The fourth merits more discussion.

> The strategic options for a competitively weak company include waging a modest offensive to improve its position, defending its present position, being acquired by another company, or employing a harvest strategy.

A *harvest strategy* steers a middle course between preserving the status quo and exiting as soon as possible. Harvesting is a phasing down or endgame strategy that involves sacrificing market position in return for improved cash flows or short-term profitability. The overriding financial objective is to reap the greatest possible harvest of cash to deploy to other business endeavors.

The measures taken in a harvest strategy are fairly clear-cut. The operating budget is chopped to a rock-bottom level; reinvestment in the business is held to a bare minimum. Capital expenditures for new equipment are put on hold or given low financial priority (unless replacement needs are unusually urgent); instead, efforts are made to stretch the life of existing equipment and make do with present facilities as long as possible. Price may be raised gradually, promotional expenses slowly cut, quality reduced in not-so-visible ways, nonessential customer services curtailed, and the like. Although harvesting results in shrinking sales and market share, if cash expenses can be cut even faster, then after-tax cash flows may rise (at least temporarily) and the company's profits will erode slowly rather than rapidly.

---

[25]Hamermesh, Anderson, and Harris, "Strategies for Low Market Share Businesses," p. 102.

Harvesting is a reasonable strategic option for a weak business in the following circumstances:[26]

1. When the industry's long-term prospects are unattractive.
2. When rejuvenating the business would be too costly or at best marginally profitable.
3. When the firm's market share is becoming increasingly costly to maintain or defend.
4. When reduced levels of competitive effort will not trigger an immediate or rapid falloff in sales.
5. When the enterprise can redeploy the freed resources in higher opportunity areas.
6. When the business is *not* a crucial or core component of a diversified company's portfolio of business interests (harvesting a noncore business is strategically preferable to harvesting a core business).
7. When the business does not contribute other desired features (sales stability, prestige, a well-rounded product line) to a company's overall business portfolio.

The more of these seven conditions present, the more ideal the business is for harvesting.

Harvesting strategies make the most sense for diversified companies that have sideline or noncore business units in weak competitive positions or in unattractive industries. Such companies can take the cash flows from harvesting unattractive, noncore business units and reallocate them to business units with greater profit potential or to the acquisition of new businesses.

Turnaround Strategies for Businesses in Crisis

Turnaround strategies are needed when a business worth rescuing goes into crisis; the objective is to arrest and reverse the sources of competitive and financial weakness as quickly as possible. Management's first task in formulating a suitable turnaround strategy is to diagnose what lies at the root of poor performance. Is it an unexpected downturn in sales brought on by a weak economy? An ill-chosen competitive strategy? Poor execution of an otherwise workable strategy? An overload of debt? Can the business be saved, or is the situation hopeless? Understanding what is wrong with the business and how serious its strategic problems are is essential because different diagnoses lead to different turnaround strategies.

Some of the most common causes of business trouble are taking on too much debt, overestimating the potential for sales growth, ignoring the profit-depressing effects of an overly aggressive effort to "buy" market share with deep price-cuts, being burdened with heavy fixed costs because of an inability to utilize plant capacity, betting on R&D efforts to boost competitive position and profitability and failing to come up with effective innovations, betting on technological long shots, being too optimistic about the ability to penetrate new markets, making frequent changes in strategy (because the previous strategy didn't work out), and being overpowered by

---

[26]Phillip Kotler, "Harvesting Strategies for Weak Products," *Business Horizons* 21, no. 5 (August 1978), pp. 17–18.

the competitive advantages enjoyed by more successful rivals. Curing these kinds of problems and achieving a successful business turnaround can involve any of the following actions:

- Revising the existing strategy.
- Launching efforts to boost revenues.
- Pursuing cost reduction.
- Selling off assets to raise cash to save the remaining part of the business.
- Using a combination of these efforts.

Strategy Revision   When weak performance is caused by bad strategy, the task of strategy overhaul can proceed along any of several paths: (1) shifting to a new competitive approach to rebuild the firm's market position; (2) overhauling internal operations and functional area strategies to better support the same overall business strategy; (3) merging with another firm in the industry and forging a new strategy keyed to the newly merged firm's strengths; and (4) retrenching into a reduced core of products and customers more closely matched to the firm's strengths. The most appealing path depends on prevailing industry conditions, the firm's particular strengths and weaknesses, its competitive capabilities vis-à-vis rival firms, and the severity of the crisis. Situation analysis of the industry, major competitors, and the firm's own competitive position and its skills and resources are prerequisites for action. As a rule, successful strategy revision must be tied to the ailing firm's strengths and near-term competitive capabilities and directed at its best market opportunities.

Boosting Revenues   Revenue-increasing turnaround efforts aim at generating increased sales volume. There are a number of revenue-building options: price cuts, increased promotion, a bigger sales force, added customer services, and quickly achieved product improvements. Attempts to increase revenues and sales volumes are necessary (1) when there is little or no room in the operating budget to cut expenses and still break even and (2) when the key to restoring profitability is increased utilization of existing capacity. If buyer demand is not especially price sensitive because of differentiating features, the quickest way to boost short-term revenues may be to raise prices rather than opt for volume-building price cuts.

Cutting Costs   Cost-reducing turnaround strategies work best when an ailing firm's value chain and cost structure are flexible enough to permit radical surgery, when operating inefficiencies are identifiable and readily correctable, when the firm's costs are obviously bloated and there are many places where savings can be quickly achieved, and when the firm is relatively close to its break-even point. Accompanying a general belt-tightening can be an increased emphasis on paring administrative overheads, elimination of nonessential and low value-added activities in the firm's value chain, modernization of existing plant and equipment to gain greater productivity, delay of nonessential capital expenditures, and debt restructuring to reduce interest costs and stretch out repayments.

Selling Off Assets   Assets reduction/retrenchment strategies are essential when cash flow is a critical consideration and when the most practical ways to generate cash are

(1) through sale of some of the firm's assets (plant and equipment, land, patents, inventories, or profitable subsidiaries) and (2) through retrenchment (pruning of marginal products from the product line, closing or selling older plants, reducing the workforce, withdrawing from outlying markets, cutting back customer service, and the like). Sometimes crisis-ridden companies sell off assets not so much to unload losing operations and to stem cash drains as to raise funds to save and strengthen the remaining business activities. In such cases, the choice is usually to dispose of noncore business assets to support strategy renewal in the firm's core business(es).

Combination Efforts   Combination turnaround strategies are usually essential in grim situations that require fast action on a broad front. Likewise, combination actions frequently come into play when new managers are brought in and given a free hand to make whatever changes they see fit. The tougher the problems, the more likely the solutions will involve multiple strategic initiatives.

Turnaround efforts tend to be high-risk undertakings, and they often fail. A landmark study of 64 companies found no successful turnarounds among the most troubled companies in eight basic industries.[27] Many of the troubled businesses waited too long to begin a turnaround. Others found themselves short of both the cash and entrepreneurial talent needed to compete in a slow-growth industry characterized by a fierce battle for market share. Better-positioned rivals simply proved too strong to defeat in a long, head-to-head contest. Even when successful, many troubled companies go through a series of turnaround attempts and management changes before long-term competitive viability and profitability are finally restored.

THIRTEEN COMMANDMENTS FOR CRAFTING SUCCESSFUL BUSINESS STRATEGIES

Business experiences over the years prove again and again that disastrous courses of action can be avoided by adhering to good strategy-making principles. The wisdom gained from these past experiences can be distilled into 13 commandments which, if faithfully observed, can help strategists craft better strategic action plans.

1. *Place top priority on crafting and executing strategic moves that enhance the company's competitive position for the long term.* An ever stronger competitive position pays off year after year, but the glory of meeting one quarter's and one year's financial performance targets quickly fades. Shareholders are never well-served by managers who let short-term financial performance considerations rule out strategic initiatives that will meaningfully bolster the company's long-term competitive position and competitive strength. The best way to protect a company's long-term profitability is with a strategy that strengthens the company's long-term competitiveness.

---

[27]William K. Hall, "Survival Strategies in a Hostile Environment," *Harvard Business Review* 58, no. 5 (September–October 1980), pp. 75–85. See also Frederick M. Zimmerman, *The Turnaround Experience: Real-World Lessons in Revitalizing Corporations* (New York: McGraw-Hill, 1991), and Gary J. Castrogiovanni, B. R. Baliga, and Roland E. Kidwell, "Curing Sick Businesses: Changing CEOs in Turnaround Efforts," *Academy of Management Executive* 6, no. 3 (August 1992), pp. 26–41.

2. *Understand that a clear, consistent competitive strategy, when well-crafted and well-executed, builds reputation and recognizable industry position; a frequently changed strategy aimed at capturing momentary market opportunities yields fleeting benefits.* Short-run financial opportunism, absent any long-term strategic consistency, tends to produce the worst kind of profits: one-shot rewards that are unrepeatable. Over the long haul, a company that has a well-conceived, consistent competitive strategy aimed at securing an ever stronger market position will outperform and defeat a rival whose strategic decisions are driven by a desire to meet Wall Street's short-term financial performance expectations. In an ongoing enterprise, the game of competition ought to be played for the long term, not the short term.

3. *Avoid "stuck in the middle" strategies that represent compromises between lower costs and greater differentiation and between broad and narrow market appeal.* Compromise strategies rarely produce sustainable competitive advantage or a distinctive competitive position—well-executed best-cost producer strategies are the only exception where a compromise between low cost and differentiation succeeds. Usually, companies with compromise or middle-of-the-road strategies end up with average costs, average differentiation, an average image and reputation, a middle-of-the-pack industry ranking, and little prospect of climbing into the ranks of the industry leaders.

4. *Invest in creating a sustainable competitive advantage.* It is the single most dependable contributor to above-average profitability.

5. *Play aggressive offense to build competitive advantage and aggressive defense to protect it.*

6. *Avoid strategies capable of succeeding only in the most optimistic circumstances.* Expect competitors to employ countermeasures and expect times of unfavorable market conditions.

7. *Be cautious in pursuing a rigid or inflexible strategy that locks the company in for the long term with little room to maneuver—inflexible strategies can be made obsolete by changing market conditions.* Strategies to achieve top quality or lowest cost should be interpreted as *relative to competitors'* and/or customers' needs rather than based on arbitrary management absolutes. While long-term strategic consistency is usually a virtue, strategic absolutes and constants are usually flaws—some adapting to changing circumstances and some discovery of ways to improve are normal and necessary.

8. *Don't underestimate the reactions and the commitment of rival firms.* Rivals are most dangerous when they are pushed into a corner and their well-being is threatened.

9. *Be wary of attacking strong, resourceful rivals without solid competitive advantage and ample financial strength.*

10. *Consider that attacking competitive weakness is usually more profitable than attacking competitive strength.*

11. *Be judicious in cutting prices without an established cost advantage.* Only a low-cost producer can win at price-cutting over the long term.

12. *Be aware that aggressive moves to wrest market share away from rivals often provoke aggressive retaliation in the form of a marketing "arms race" and/or price wars*—to the detriment of everyone's profits. Aggressive moves to capture a bigger market share invite cutthroat competition, particularly when the market is plagued with high inventories and excess production capacity.

13. *Strive to open up very meaningful gaps in quality or service or performance features when pursuing a differentiation strategy.* Tiny differences between rivals' product offerings may not be visible or important to buyers.

Key Points

It is not enough to understand that a company's basic competitive strategy options are overall low-cost leadership, broad differentiation, best cost, focused low cost, and focused differentiation and that there are a variety of offensive, defensive, first-mover, and late-mover initiatives and actions to choose from. Managers must also understand that the array of strategic options is narrowed and shaped by (1) the nature of industry and competitive conditions and (2) a firm's own competitive capabilities, market position, and best opportunities. Some strategic options are better suited to certain specific industry and competitive environments than others. Some strategic options are better suited to certain specific company situations than others. This chapter portrays the multifaceted task of matching strategy to a firm's external and internal situations by considering five classic types of industry environments and three classic types of company situations.

Rather than try to summarize the main points we made about choosing strategies for these eight sets of circumstances (the relevant principles can't really be encapsulated in three or four sentences each), we think it more useful to conclude by outlining a broader framework for matching strategy to *any* industry and company situation. Table 6–2 provides a summary checklist of the most important situational considerations and strategic options. Matching strategy to the situation starts with an overview of the industry environment and the firm's competitive standing in the industry (columns 1 and 2 in Table 6–2):

1. What basic type of industry environment does the company operate in (emerging, rapid growth, mature, fragmented, global, commodity-product)? What strategic options and strategic postures are usually best suited to this generic type of environment?

2. What position does the firm have in the industry (strong vs. weak vs. crisis-ridden; leader vs. runner-up vs. also-ran)? How does the firm's standing influence its strategic options given the stage of the industry's development—in particular, which options have to be ruled out?

Next, strategists need to factor in the primary external and internal situational considerations (column 3) and decide how all the factors add up. This should narrow the firm's basic market share and investment options (column 4) and strategic options (column 5).

The final step is to custom-tailor the chosen generic strategic approaches (columns 4 and 5) to fit *both* the industry environment and the firm's standing vis-à-vis competitors. Here, it is important to be sure that (1) the customized aspects of the

Table 6–2   Matching Strategy to the Situation (A checklist of optional strategies and generic situations)

Industry Environments	Company Positions/ Situations	Situational Considerations	Market Share and Investment Options	Strategy Options

• Young, emerging industry
• Rapid growth
• Consolidating to a smaller group of competitors
• Mature/slow growth
• Aging/declining
• Fragmented
• International/global
• Commodity/product orientation
• High technology/ rapid changes
	• Dominant leader
	  — Global
	  — National
	  — Regional
	  — Local
	• Leader
	• Aggressive challenger
	• Content follower
	• Weak/distressed candidate for turnaround or exit
	• "Stuck in the middle"/no clear strategy or market image
		• External
		  — Driving forces
		  — Competitive pressures
		  — Anticipated moves of key rivals
		  — Key success factors
		  — Industry attractiveness
		• Internal
		  — Current company performance
		  — Strengths and weaknesses
		  — Opportunities and threats
		  — Cost position
		  — Competitive strength
		  — Strategic issues and problems
			• Grow and build
			  — Capture a bigger market share by growing faster than industry as a whole
			  — Invest heavily to capture growth potential
			• Fortify and defend
			  — Protect market share; grow at least as fast as whole industry
			  — Invest enough resources to maintain competitive strength and market position
			• Retrench and retreat
			  — Surrender weakly held positions when forced to, but fight hard to defend core markets/customer base
			  — Maximize short-term cash flow
			  — Minimize reinvestment of capital in the business
			• Overhaul and reposition
			  — Pursue a turnaround
			• Abandon/liquidate
			  — Sell out
			  — Close down
				• Competitive approach
				  — Overall low-cost
				  — Differentiation
				  — Best-cost
				  — Focused low-cost
				  — Focused differentiation
				• Offensive initiatives
				  — Competitor strengths
				  — Competitor weaknesses
				  — End run
				  — Guerrilla warfare
				  — Preemptive strikes
				• Defensive initiatives
				  — Fortify/protect
				  — Retaliatory
				  — Harvest
				• International initiatives
				  — Licensing
				  — Export
				  — Multicountry
				  — Global
				• Vertical integration initiatives
				  — Forward
				  — Backward

proposed strategy are well-matched to the firm's competencies and competitive capabilities and (2) the strategy addresses all strategic issues the firm confronts.

In weeding out weak strategies and weighing the pros and cons of the most attractive ones, the answers to the following questions often indicate the way to go:

• What kind of competitive edge can the company realistically hope to have and what strategic moves/approaches will it need take to secure this edge?

- Does the company have the organizational capabilities and financial resources to succeed in these moves and approaches? If not, can they be acquired?
- Once built, how can the competitive advantage be protected? What defensive strategies need to be employed? Will rivals counterattack? What will it take to blunt their efforts?
- Are any rivals particularly vulnerable? Should the firm mount an offensive to capitalize on these vulnerabilities? What offensive moves need to be employed?
- What additional strategic moves are needed to deal with driving forces in the industry, specific threats and weaknesses, and any other issues/problems unique to the firm?

As the choice of strategic initiatives is developed, there are several pitfalls to avoid:

- Designing an overly ambitious strategic plan—one that calls for a lot of different strategic moves and/or that overtaxes the company's resources and capabilities.
- Selecting a strategy that represents a radical departure from or abandonment of the cornerstones of the company's prior success—a radical strategy change need not be rejected automatically, but it should be pursued only after careful risk assessment.
- Choosing a strategy that goes against the grain of the organization's culture or that conflicts with the values and philosophies of the most senior executives.

Table 6–3   Sample Format for a Strategic Action Plan

1. Strategic Vision and Mission	**5. Supporting Functional Strategies** • Production
2. Strategic Objectives • Short term	• Marketing/sales
• Long term	• Finance
3. Financial Objectives • Short term	• Personnel/human resources
• Long term	• Other
4. Overall Business Strategy	**6. Recommended Actions** • Immediate
	• Longer-range

- Being unwilling to make a decisive *choice* about how to compete. Trying to achieve competitive advantage through several means simultaneously often produces so many compromises and inconsistent actions that the company fails to achieve any of them and ends up stuck in the middle.

Table 6–3 suggests a generic format for presenting a strategic action plan for a single-business enterprise.

Suggested Readings

Bleeke, Joel A. "Strategic Choices for Newly Opened Markets." *Harvard Business Review* 68, no. 5 (September–October 1990), pp. 158–65.

Bolt, James F. "Global Competitors: Some Criteria for Success." *Business Horizons* 31, no. 1 (January–February 1988), pp. 34–41.

Cooper, Arnold C., and Clayton G. Smith. "How Established Firms Respond to Threatening Technologies." *Academy of Management Executive* 6, no. 2 (May 1992), pp. 55–57.

D'Aveni, Richard A. *Hypercompetition: Managing the Dynamics of Strategic Maneuvering.* New York: Free Press, 1994, chaps. 3 and 4.

Feldman, Lawrence P., and Albert L. Page. "Harvesting: The Misunderstood Market Exit Strategy." *Journal of Business Strategy* 5, no. 4 (Spring 1985), pp. 79–85.

Finkin, Eugene F. "Company Turnaround." *Journal of Business Strategy* 5, no. 4 (Spring 1985), pp. 14–25.

Gordon, Geoffrey L., Roger J. Calantrone, and C. Anthony di Benedetto. "Mature Markets and Revitalization Strategies: An American Fable." *Business Horizons* (May–June 1991), pp. 39–50.

Hall, William K. "Survival Strategies in a Hostile Environment." *Harvard Business Review* 58, no. 5 (September–October 1980), pp. 75–85.

Hamermesh, R. G., and S. B. Silk. "How to Compete in Stagnant Industries." *Harvard Business Review* 57, no. 5 (September–October 1979), pp. 161–68.

Heany, Donald F. "Businesses in Profit Trouble." *Journal of Business Strategy* 5, no. 4 (Spring 1985), pp. 4–13.

Hofer, Charles W. "Turnaround Strategies." *Journal of Business Strategy* 1, no. 1 (Summer 1980), pp. 19–31.

Lei, David. "Strategies for Global Competition." *Long Range Planning* 22, no. 1 (February 1989), pp. 102–9.

Mayer, Robert J. "Winning Strategies for Manufacturers in Mature Industries." *Journal of Business Strategy* 8, no. 2 (Fall 1987), pp. 23–31.

Ohmae, Kenichi. "The Global Logic of Strategic Alliances." *Harvard Business Review* 67, no. 2 (March–April 1989), pp. 143–54.

Porter, Michael E. *Competitive Strategy: Techniques for Analyzing Industries and Competitors.* New York: Free Press, 1980, chaps. 9–13.

Porter, Michael E. *The Competitive Advantage of Nations.* New York: Free Press, 1990, chap. 2.

Sugiura, Hideo, "How Honda Localizes Its Global Strategy." *Sloan Management Review* 33 (Fall 1990), pp. 77–82.

Yip, George S. *Total Global Strategy.* Englewood Cliffs, N.J.: Prentice-Hall, 1992, chaps. 1, 2, 3, 5, and 7.

Zimmerman, Frederick M. *The Turnaround Experience: Real-World Lessons in Revitalizing Corporations.* New York: McGraw-Hill, 1991.

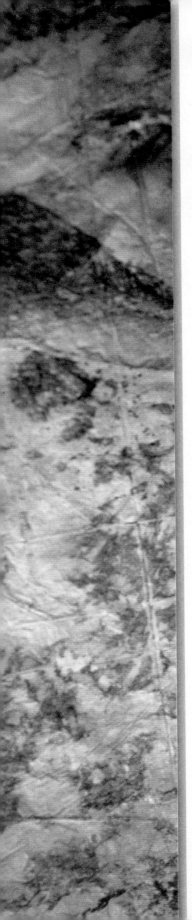

CHAPTER SEVEN

Corporate Diversification Strategies

. . . to acquire or not to acquire: that is the question.

Robert J. Terry

Strategy is a deliberate search for a plan of action that will develop a business's competitive advantage and compound it.

Bruce D. Henderson

In this chapter and the next, we move up one level in the strategy-making hierarchy. Attention shifts from formulating strategy for a single-business enterprise to formulating strategy for a diversified enterprise. Because a diversified company is a collection of individual businesses, corporate strategy-making is a bigger-picture exercise than crafting line-of-business strategy. In a single-business enterprise, management has to contend with only one industry environment and the question of how to compete successfully in it. But in a diversified company corporate managers have to craft a multibusiness, multi-industry strategic action plan for a number of different business divisions competing in diverse industry environments.

As explained in Chapter 2, the task of crafting corporate strategy for a diversified company concerns

1. Deciding on moves to position the company in the industries chosen for diversification (the basic strategic options here are to acquire a company in the target industry, form a joint venture with another company to enter the target industry, or start a new company internally and try to grow it from the ground up).

2. Devising actions to improve the long-term performance of the corporation's portfolio of businesses once diversification is achieved (helping to strengthen the competitive positions of existing businesses, divesting businesses that no longer fit into management's long-range plans, and adding new businesses to the portfolio).

3. Trying to capture whatever strategic-fit benefits exist within the portfolio of businesses and turn them into competitive advantage.

4. Evaluating the profit prospects of each business unit and steering corporate resources into the most attractive strategic opportunities.

These four tasks are sufficiently time-consuming and demanding that corporate-level decision-makers generally refrain from becoming immersed in the details of crafting and implementing business-level strategies, preferring instead to delegate lead responsibility for business strategy to the heads of each business unit.

In this chapter we survey the generic types of corporate diversification strategies and describe how a company can use diversification to create or compound competitive advantage for its business units. In Chapter 8 we will examine the techniques and procedures for assessing the strategic attractiveness of a diversified company's business portfolio.

FROM SINGLE-BUSINESS CONCENTRATION TO DIVERSIFICATION

Most companies begin as small single-business enterprises serving a local or regional market. During a company's early years, its product line tends to be limited, its capital base thin, and its competitive position vulnerable. Usually, a young company's strategic emphasis is on increasing sales volume, boosting market share, and cultivating a loyal clientele. Profits are reinvested and new debt is taken on to grow the business as fast as conditions permit. Price, quality, service, and promotion are tailored more precisely to customer needs. As soon as practical, the product line is broadened to meet variations in customer wants and to capture sales opportunities in related end-use applications.

Opportunities for geographic market expansion are normally pursued next. The natural sequence of geographic expansion proceeds from local to regional to national to international markets, though the degree of penetration may be uneven from area to area because of varying profit potentials. Geographic expansion may, of course, stop well short of global or even national proportions because of intense competition, lack of resources, or the unattractiveness of further market coverage.

Somewhere along the way, the potential of vertical integration, either backward to sources of supply or forward to the ultimate consumer, may become a strategic consideration. Generally, vertical integration makes strategic sense only if it significantly enhances a company's profitability and competitive strength.

So long as the company has its hands full trying to capitalize on profitable growth opportunities in its present industry, there is no urgency to pursue diversification. But when company growth potential starts to wane, the strategic options are either to become more aggressive in taking market share away from rivals or to pursue diversification into other lines of businesses. A decision to diversify raises the question "What kind and how much diversification?" The strategic possibilities are wide open. A company can diversify into closely related businesses or into totally unrelated businesses. It can diversify to a small extent (less than 10 percent of total revenues and profits) or to a large extent (up to 50 percent of revenues and profits). It can move into one or two large new businesses or a greater number of small ones. And once diversification is achieved, the time may come when management has to consider divesting or liquidating businesses that are no longer attractive.

Diversification doesn't need to become a strategic priority until a company begins to run out of growth opportunities in its core business.

Why a Single-Business Strategy Is Attractive

Companies that concentrate on a single business can achieve enviable success over many decades without relying upon diversification to sustain their growth. McDonald's, Delta Airlines, Coca-Cola, Domino's Pizza, Apple Computer,

Wal-Mart, Federal Express, Timex, Campbell's Soup, Anheuser-Busch, Gerber, and Polaroid all won their reputations in a single business. In the nonprofit sector, continued emphasis on a single activity has proved successful for the Red Cross, Salvation Army, Christian Children's Fund, Girl Scouts, Phi Beta Kappa, and American Civil Liberties Union.

Concentrating on a single line of business (totally or with a small dose of diversification) has some useful organizational and managerial advantages. First, single-business concentration entails less ambiguity about "who we are and what we do." The energies of the *total* organization are directed down *one* business path. There is less chance that senior management's time or limited organizational resources will be stretched too thin over too many diverse activities. Entrepreneurial efforts can be trained exclusively on keeping the firm's business strategy and competitive approach responsive to industry change and fine-tuned to customer needs. All the firm's managers, especially top executives, can have hands-on contact with the core business and in-depth knowledge of operations. Most senior officers will usually have risen through the ranks and possess firsthand experience in field operations. (In broadly diversified enterprises, corporate managers seldom have had the opportunity to work in more than one or two of the company's businesses.) Furthermore, concentrating on one business carries a heftier built-in incentive for managers to direct the company toward capturing a stronger long-term competitive position in the industry rather than pursuing the fleeting benefits of juggling corporate assets to produce higher short-term profits. The company can devote the full force of its organizational resources to becoming better at what it does. Important competencies and competitive skills are more likely to emerge. With management's attention focused exclusively on one business, the probability is higher that good ideas will emerge on how to improve production technology, better meet customer needs with innovative new product features, and enhance efficiencies or differentiation capabilities along the value chain. The more successful a single-business enterprise is, the more able it is to parlay its accumulated experience and distinctive expertise into a sustainable competitive advantage and a prominent leadership position in its industry.

> **There are important organizational and managerial advantages to concentrating on just one business.**

The Risk of a Single-Business Strategy

The big risk of single-business concentration is putting all of a firm's eggs in one industry basket. If the industry stagnates or becomes competitively unattractive, company prospects dim, and superior profit performance is much harder to achieve. At times, changing customer needs, technological innovation, or new substitute products can undermine or wipe out a single-business firm—consider, for example, what the word processing capabilities of personal computers have done to the electric typewriter business and what compact disk technology is doing to the market for cassette tapes and records. For this reason most single-business companies turn their strategic attention to diversification when their business starts to show signs of peaking out.

When Diversification Starts to Make Sense

To analyze when diversification makes the most strategic sense, consider Figure 7–1 where the variable of competitive position is plotted against various rates of market growth to create four distinct strategic situations that might be occupied by an

Figure 7–1 **Matching Corporate Strategy Alternatives to Fit an Undiversified Firm's Situation**

COMPETITIVE POSITION

WEAK · STRONG

MARKET GROWTH RATE

RAPID

STRATEGY OPTIONS
(in probable order of attractiveness)

- Reformulate single-business concentration strategy (to achieve turnaround).
- Acquire another firm in the same business (to strengthen competitive position).
- Vertical integration (forward or backward if it strengthens competitive position).
- Diversification.
- Be acquired by/sell out to a stronger rival.
- Abandonment (a last resort in the event all else fails).

STRATEGY OPTIONS
(in probable order of attractiveness)

- Continue single-business concentration
  —International expansion (if market opportunities exist).
- Vertical integration (if it strengthens the firm's competitive position).
- Related diversification (to transfer skills and expertise built up in the company's core business to adjacent businesses).

SLOW

STRATEGY OPTIONS
(in probable order of attractiveness)

- Reformulate single-business concentration strategy (to achieve turnaround).
- Merger with a rival firm (to strengthen competitive position).
- Vertical integration (only if it strengthens competitive position substantially).
- Diversification.
- Harvest/divest.
- Liquidation (a last resort in the event all else fails).

STRATEGY OPTIONS
(in probable order of attractiveness)

- International expansion (if market opportunities exist).
- Related diversification.
- Unrelated diversification.
- Joint ventures into new areas.
- Vertical integration (if it strengthens competitive position).
- Continue single-business concentration (achieve growth by taking market share from weaker rivals).

undiversified company.[1] Firms that fall into the rapid market growth/strong competitive position box have several logical strategy options, the strongest of which in the near term may be continuing to pursue single-business concentration. Given the industry's high growth rate (and implicit long-term attractiveness), it makes sense for firms in this position to push hard to maintain or increase their market shares, further

[1] C. Roland Christensen, Norman A. Berg, and Malcolm S. Salter, *Policy Formulation and Administration*, 7th ed. (Homewood, Ill.: Richard D. Irwin, 1976), pp. 16–18.

When to diversify depends partly on a company's growth opportunities in its present industry and partly on its competitive position.

develop core competencies, and make whatever capital investments are necessary to continue in a strong industry position. At some juncture, a company in this box may contemplate vertical integration if this would add to its competitive strength. Later, when market growth starts to slow, it can consider a diversification strategy to spread business risk and transfer the skills or expertise the company has built up into closely *related* businesses.

Firms in the rapid growth/weak position category should first address the questions of (1) why their current approach to the market has resulted in a weak competitive position and (2) what it will take to become an effective competitor. Second they should consider their options for rejuvenating their present competitive strategy (given the high rate of market growth). In a rapidly expanding market, even weak firms should be able to improve their performance and make headway in building a stronger market position. If the firm is young and struggling to develop, it usually has a better chance for survival in a growing market where plenty of new business is up for grabs than in a stable or declining industry. However, if a weakly positioned company in a rapid-growth market lacks the resources and skills to hold its own, its best option is merger either with another company in the industry that has the missing pieces or with an outsider having the cash and resources to support the firm's development. Vertical integration, either forward or backward or both, is an option for a weakly positioned firm whenever it can materially strengthen the firm's competitive position. A third option is diversification into related or unrelated businesses (if adequate financing can be found). If all else fails, abandonment—divestiture in the case of a multibusiness firm or liquidation in the case of a single-business firm—has to become an active strategic option. While abandonment may seem extreme because of the high growth potential, a company unable to make a profit in a booming market probably does not have the ability to make a profit at all—particularly if competition stiffens or industry conditions sour.

Companies with a weak competitive position in a relatively slow-growth market should look at (1) initiating actions to create a more attractive competitive position, (2) merging with or being acquired by a rival to build a stronger base for competing, (3) diversifying into related or unrelated areas if ample financial resources are available, (4) integrating forward or backward if such actions will boost profits and long-term competitive strength, (5) employing a harvest-then-divest strategy, and (6) liquidating their position in the business by either selling out to another firm or closing down operations.

Companies with strong competitive positions in slow-growth industries are prime candidates for diversifying into new businesses.

Companies that are strongly positioned in a slow-growth industry should consider taking the excess cash flow from their existing business to finance a diversification strategy. Diversification into businesses where a firm can leverage its core competencies and competitive strengths is usually the best strategy. But diversification into totally unrelated businesses has to be considered if none of its related business opportunities offer attractive profit prospects. Joint ventures with other organizations into new fields of endeavor are another logical possibility. Vertical integration should be a last resort (since it provides no escape from the industry's slow-growth condition) and makes strategic sense only if a firm can expect sizable profit gains. Unless it sees important growth *segments* within the industry that merit further invest-and-build actions, a strong company in a slow-growth industry usually needs to curtail new investment in its present business to free cash for new endeavors.

When to diversify is therefore partly a function of a firm's competitive position and partly a function of the remaining opportunities in its home-base industry. There really is no well-defined point at which companies in the same industry should diversify. Indeed, companies in the same industry can rationally choose different diversification approaches and launch them at different times.

BUILDING SHAREHOLDER VALUE: THE ULTIMATE JUSTIFICATION FOR DIVERSIFYING

The overriding purpose of corporate diversification is to build shareholder value. For diversification to enhance shareholder value, corporate strategy must do more than simply diversify the company's business risk by investing in more than one industry. Shareholders can achieve the same risk diversification on their own by purchasing stock in companies in different industries. Strictly speaking, *diversification does not create shareholder value unless a diversified group of businesses perform better under a single corporate umbrella than they would perform operating as independent, stand-alone businesses.* For example, if company A diversifies by purchasing company B and if A and B's consolidated profits in the years to come prove no greater than what each would have earned on its own, then A's diversification into business B won't provide its shareholders with added value. Company A's shareholders could have achieved the same 2 + 2 = 4 result on their own accord by purchasing stock in company B. Shareholder value is not *created* by diversification unless it produces a 2 + 2 = 5 effect where sister businesses perform better together as part of the same firm than they could have performed as independent companies.

> To create shareholder value, a diversifying company must get into businesses that can perform better under common management than they could perform as stand-alone enterprises.

Three Tests for Judging a Diversification Move

The problem with such a strict benchmark of whether diversification has enhanced shareholder value is that it requires speculative judgments about how well a diversified company's businesses would have performed on their own. Comparisons of actual performance against the hypothetical of what performance might have been under other circumstances are never very satisfactory and, besides, they represent after-the-fact assessments. Strategists have to base diversification decisions on future expectations. Attempts to gauge the impact of particular diversification moves on shareholder value do not have to be abandoned, however. Corporate strategists can make before-the-fact assessments of whether a particular diversification move is capable of increasing shareholder value by using three tests:[2]

1. **The attractiveness test:** The industry chosen for diversification must be attractive enough to yield consistently good returns on investment. Whether an industry is attractive depends chiefly on the presence of favorable competitive conditions and a market environment conducive to long-term profitability. Such indicators as rapid growth or a sexy product are unreliable proxies of attractiveness.

2. **The cost-of-entry test:** The cost to enter the target industry must not be so high as to erode the potential for good profitability. A catch-22 situation can prevail here, however. The more attractive the industry, the more expensive it can be to get into. Entry barriers for start-up

---

[2]Michael E. Porter, "From Competitive Advantage to Corporate Strategy," *Harvard Business Review* 45, no. 3 (May–June 1987), pp. 46–49.

companies are nearly always high—were barriers low, a rush of new entrants would soon erode the potential for high profitability. And buying a company already in the business typically entails a high acquisition cost because of the industry's strong appeal. Costly entry undermines the potential for enhancing shareholder value.

3. **The better-off test:** The diversifying company must bring some potential for competitive advantage to the new business it enters, or the new business must offer added competitive advantage potential to the company's present businesses. The opportunity to create sustainable competitive advantage where none existed before means there is also opportunity for added profitability and shareholder value.

Diversification moves that satisfy all three tests have the greatest potential to build shareholder value over the long term. Diversification moves that can pass only one or two tests are suspect.

DIVERSIFICATION STRATEGIES

Once the decision is made to pursue diversification, any of several different paths can be taken. There is plenty of room for varied strategic approaches. Figure 7–2 shows the paths a company can take in moving from a single-business enterprise to a diversified enterprise. Vertical integration strategies may or may not enter the picture depending on the extent to which forward or backward integration strengthens a firm's competitive position or helps it secure a competitive advantage. When diversification becomes a serious strategic option, a choice must be made whether to pursue related diversification, unrelated diversification, or some mix of both. Once diversification is accomplished, management's task is to figure out how to manage the collection of businesses the company has invested in—the six fundamental strategic options are shown in the last box of Figure 7–2.

We can better understand the strategic issues corporate managers face in creating and managing a diversified group of businesses by looking at six diversification-related strategies:

1. Strategies for entering new industries—acquisition, start-up, and joint ventures.
2. Related diversification strategies.
3. Unrelated diversification strategies.
4. Divestiture and liquidation strategies.
5. Corporate turnaround, retrenchment, and restructuring strategies.
6. Multinational diversification strategies.

The first three are ways to diversify; the last three are strategies to strengthen the positions and performance of companies that have already diversified.

Strategies for Entering New Businesses

Entry into new businesses can take any of three forms: acquisition, internal start-up, and joint ventures. *Acquisition of an existing business* is the most popular means of diversifying into another industry and has the advantage of much quicker entry into

Figure 7–2   Corporate Strategy Alternatives

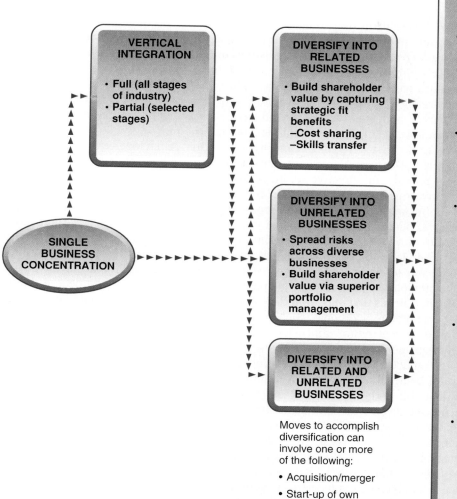

POST-DIVERSIFICATION STRATEGIC MOVE ALTERNATIVES

- Make new acquisitions (or seek merger partnerships)
  - To build positions in new related/unrelated industries
  - To strengthen the position of business units in industries where the firm already has a stake
- Divest some business units
  - To eliminate weak-performing businesses from portfolio
  - To eliminate businesses that no longer fit
- Restructure makeup of whole portfolio if many business units are performing poorly
  - By selling selected business units
  - By using cash from divestitures plus unused debt capacity to make new acquisitions
- Retrench/narrow the diversification base
  - By pruning weak businesses
  - By shedding all noncore businesses
  - By divesting one or more core businesses
- Become a multinational, multi-industry enterprise (DMNC)
  - To succeed in globally competitive core businesses against international rivals
  - To capture strategic fit benefits and win a competitive advantage via multinational diversification
- Liquidate/close down money-losing businesses that cannot be sold

VERTICAL INTEGRATION

- Full (all stages of industry)
- Partial (selected stages)

DIVERSIFY INTO RELATED BUSINESSES

- Build shareholder value by capturing strategic fit benefits
  - Cost sharing
  - Skills transfer

DIVERSIFY INTO UNRELATED BUSINESSES

- Spread risks across diverse businesses
- Build shareholder value via superior portfolio management

DIVERSIFY INTO RELATED AND UNRELATED BUSINESSES

SINGLE BUSINESS CONCENTRATION

Moves to accomplish diversification can involve one or more of the following:

- Acquisition/merger
- Start-up of own new businesses from scratch
- Joint venture partnerships

the target market.[3] At the same time, it helps a diversifier overcome such entry barriers as acquiring technological experience, establishing supplier relationships, becoming big enough to match rivals' efficiency and unit costs, having to spend large sums on introductory advertising and promotions to gain market visibility and brand recognition, and getting adequate distribution. In many industries, going the internal start-up route and trying to develop the knowledge, resources, scale of operation, and market reputation necessary to become an effective competitor can take years and entail all the problems of getting a brand new company off the ground and operating.

However, finding the right kind of company to acquire sometimes presents a challenge.[4] The big dilemma an acquisition-minded firm faces is whether to buy a successful company at a high price or a struggling company at a bargain price. If the buying firm has little knowledge of the industry but ample capital, it is often better off purchasing a capable, strongly positioned firm—unless the acquisition price is unreasonably high. On the other hand, when the acquirer sees promising ways to transform a weak firm into a strong one and has the money, the know-how, and the patience to do it, a struggling company can be the better long-term investment.

The cost-of-entry test requires that the expected profit stream of an acquired business provide an attractive return on the total acquisition cost and on any new capital investment needed to sustain or expand its operations. A high acquisition price can make meeting that test improbable or difficult. For instance, suppose that the price to purchase a company is $3 million and that the business is earning after-tax profits of $200,000 on an equity investment of $1 million (a 20 percent annual return). Simple arithmetic requires that the acquired business's profits be tripled for the purchaser to earn the same 20 percent return on the $3 million acquisition price that the previous owners were getting on their $1 million equity investment. Building the acquired firm's earnings from $200,000 to $600,000 annually could take several years—and require additional investment on which the purchaser would also have to earn a 20 percent return. Since the owners of a successful and growing company usually demand a price that reflects their business's future profit prospects, it's easy for such an acquisition to flunk the cost-of-entry test. A would-be diversifier can't count on being able to acquire a desirable company in an appealing industry at a price that still permits attractive returns on investment.

Achieving diversification through *internal start-up* involves creating a new company under the corporate umbrella to compete in the desired industry. A newly formed organization not only has to overcome entry barriers, it also has to invest in new production capacity, develop sources of supply, hire and train employees, build channels of distribution, grow a customer base, and so on. Generally, forming a start-up company to enter a new industry is more attractive when (1) there is ample time to launch the business from the ground up, (2) incumbent firms are likely to be slow or ineffective in responding to a new entrant's efforts to crack the market, (3) internal entry has lower costs than entry via acquisition, (4) the company already has in-house most or all of the skills it needs to compete effectively, (5) adding new production capacity will not adversely impact the supply-demand balance in the industry, and (6)

One of the big stumbling blocks to entering attractive industries by acquisition is the difficulty of finding a suitable company at a price that satisfies the cost-of-entry test.

The biggest drawbacks to entering an industry by forming a start-up company internally are the costs of overcoming entry barriers and the extra time it takes to build a strong and profitable competitive position.

---

[3]In recent years, hostile takeovers have become a hotly debated and sometimes abused approach to acquisition. The term *takeover* refers to the attempt (often sprung as a surprise) of one firm to acquire ownership or control over another firm against the wishes of the latter's management (and perhaps some of its stockholders).

[4]Michael E. Porter, *Competitive Strategy: Techniques for Analyzing Industries and Competitors* (New York: Free Press, 1980), p. 354–55.

the targeted industry is populated with many relatively small firms so the new start-up does not have to compete head-to-head against larger, more powerful rivals.[5]

Joint ventures are a useful way to gain access to a new business in at least three types of situations.[6] First, a joint venture is a good way to do something that is uneconomical or risky for an organization to do alone. Second, joint ventures make sense when pooling the resources and competencies of two or more independent organizations produces an organization with more of the skills needed to be a strong competitor. In such cases, each partner brings special talents or resources that the other doesn't have and that are important for success. Third, joint ventures with foreign partners are sometimes the only or best way to surmount import quotas, tariffs, nationalistic political interests, and cultural roadblocks. The economic, competitive, and political realities of nationalism often require a foreign company to team up with a domestic partner in order to gain access to the national market in which the domestic partner is located. Domestic partners offer outside companies the benefits of local knowledge, managerial and marketing personnel, and access to distribution channels. However, such joint ventures often pose complicated questions about how to divide efforts among the partners and about who has effective control.[7] Conflicts between foreign and domestic partners can arise over whether to use local sourcing of components, how much production to export, whether operating procedures should conform to the foreign company's standards or to local preferences, who has control of cash flows, and how to distribute profits.

RELATED DIVERSIFICATION STRATEGIES

In choosing which industries to diversify into, the two basic options are to pick industries *related* to or *unrelated* to the organization's core business and what the organization already does. A related diversification strategy involves diversifying into businesses that possess some kind of "strategic fit." *Strategic fit* exists when different businesses have sufficiently related value chains that there are important opportunities for (1) transferring skills and expertise from one business to another or (2) combining the related activities of separate businesses into a single operation and reducing costs.[8] *A diversified firm that exploits these value-chain interrelationships and captures the benefits of strategic fit achieves a consolidated performance greater than the sum of what the businesses can earn pursuing independent strategies.* The presence of strategic fit within a diversified firm's business portfolio, together with corporate management's deftness and skill in capturing the benefits of the interrelationships, makes related diversification a 2 + 2 = 5 phenomenon and becomes a basis for competitive advantage. The bigger the strategic-fit benefits, the bigger the competitive advantage of related diversification and the more that related diversification satisfies the better-off test for building shareholder value.

Related diversification involves diversifying into businesses whose value chains have appealing strategic fits.

[5]Ibid., pp. 344–45.

[6]Peter Drucker, *Management: Tasks, Responsibilities, Practices* (New York: Harper & Row, 1974), pp. 720–24. Strategic alliances offer much the same benefits as joint ventures, but represent a weaker commitment to entering a new business.

[7]Porter, *Competitive Strategy*, p. 340.

[8]Michael E. Porter, *Competitive Advantage* (New York: Free Press, 1985), pp. 318–19 and pp. 337–53; Kenichi Ohmae, *The Mind of the Strategist* (New York: Penguin Books, 1983), pp. 121–24; and Porter, "From Competitive Advantage to Corporate Strategy," pp. 53–57.

Strategic-fit relationships can arise out of the opportunity for technology sharing, the existence of common labor skills and requirements, use of common suppliers and raw materials sources, the potential for joint manufacture of parts and components, the presence of similar operating methods and similar managerial know-how, reliance on the same types of marketing and merchandising skills, the possibility of sharing a common sales force and using the same wholesale distributors or retail dealers, the potential for combining after-sale service activities, or the advantages and synergistic effects of a common brand name. The fit or relatedness can occur anywhere along the businesses' respective value chains. Strategic-fit relationships are important because they represent opportunities for cost-saving efficiencies, technology or skills transfers, added differentiation, or brand name advantages, all of which are avenues for gaining competitive advantages over business rivals that have not diversified or that have diversified but not in ways that give them access to such strategic-fit benefits.

> **What makes related diversification attractive is the opportunity to turn strategic fits into competitive advantage.**

Some of the most commonly used approaches to related diversification are

- Entering businesses where sales force, advertising, and distribution activities can be shared (a bread bakery buying a maker of crackers and salty snack foods).
- Exploiting closely related technologies (a marketer of agricultural seeds and fertilizers diversifying into chemicals for insect and plant disease control).
- Transferring know-how and expertise from one business to another (a successful operator of hamburger outlets acquiring a chain specializing in Mexican fast-foods).
- Transferring the organization's brand name and reputation with consumers to a new product/service (a tire manufacturer diversifying into automotive repair centers).
- Acquiring new businesses that will uniquely help the firm's position in its existing businesses (a cable TV broadcaster purchasing a sports team or purchasing a movie production company to provide original programming).

Examples of related diversification abound. BIC Pen, which pioneered inexpensive disposable ballpoint pens, used its core competencies in low-cost manufacturing and mass merchandising as its basis for diversifying into disposable cigarette lighters and disposable razors—both of which required low-cost production know-how and skilled consumer marketing for success. Tandy Corp. practiced related diversification when its chain of Radio Shack outlets, which originally handled mostly radio and stereo equipment, added telephones, intercoms, calculators, clocks, electronic and scientific toys, personal computers, and peripheral computer equipment. The Tandy strategy was to use the marketing access provided by its thousands of Radio Shack locations to become one of the world's leading retailers of electronic technology to individual consumers. Philip Morris, a leading cigarette manufacturer, employed a marketing-related diversification strategy when it purchased Miller Brewing, General Foods, and Kraft and transferred its skills in cigarette marketing to the marketing of beer and food products. Lockheed pursued a customer needs-based diversification strategy in creating business units to supply the Department of Defense with missiles, rocket engines, aircraft, electronic equipment, ships, and contract R&D for weapons. Procter & Gamble's lineup of products includes Jif peanut butter, Duncan Hines cake mixes, Folger's coffee, Tide laundry detergent, Crisco vegetable oil, Crest toothpaste, Ivory soap, Charmin toilet tissue, and Head and Shoulders shampoo—all different

---

Illustration Capsule 22   Examples of Companies with Related Business Portfolios

---

Presented below are the business portfolios of four companies that have pursued some form of related diversification:

Gillette

- Blades and razors
- Toiletries (Right Guard, Silkience, Foamy, Dry Idea, Soft & Dry, Oral-B toothbrushes, White Rain, Toni)
- Writing instruments and stationery products (Paper Mate pens, Liquid Paper correction fluids, Waterman pens)
- Braun shavers, cordless curlers, coffeemakers, alarm clocks, and electric toothbrushes

PepsiCo

- Soft drinks (Pepsi, Mountain Dew, Slice)
- Kentucky Fried Chicken
- Pizza Hut
- Taco Bell
- Frito-Lay
- 7UP International (non-US sales of 7UP)

Philip Morris Companies

- Cigarettes (Marlboro, Virginia Slims, Benson & Hedges, and Merit)
- Miller Brewing Company
- Kraft General Foods (Maxwell House, Sanka, Oscar Mayer, Kool-Aid, Jell-O, Post cereals, Birds-Eye frozen foods, Kraft cheeses, Sealtest dairy products, Breyer's ice cream)
- Mission Viejo Realty

Johnson & Johnson

- Baby products (powder, shampoo, oil, lotion)
- Disposable diapers
- Band-Aids and wound care products
- Stayfree, Carefree, Sure & Natural, and Modess feminine hygiene products
- Tylenol
- Prescription drugs
- Surgical and hospital products
- Dental products
- Oral contraceptives
- Veterinary and animal health products

Source: Company annual reports.

---

businesses with different competitors and different production requirements. But P&G's products still represent related diversification because they all move through the same wholesale distribution systems, are sold in common retail settings to the same shoppers, are advertised and promoted in the same ways, and utilize the same marketing and merchandising skills. Illustration Capsule 22 shows the business portfolios of several companies that have pursued a strategy of related diversification.

Strategic Fit, Economies of Scope, and Competitive Advantage

A related diversification strategy clearly has considerable appeal. It allows a firm to preserve a degree of unity in its business activities, reap the competitive advantage benefits of skills transfer or lower costs, and still spread investor risks over a broader business base.

Diversifying into businesses where technology, facilities, functional activities, or distribution channels can be shared can lead to lower costs because of economies of

> **Strategic fits among related businesses offer the competitive advantage potential of *(a)* lower costs, *(b)* efficient transfer of key skills, technological expertise, or managerial know-how from one business to another, or *(c)* ability to share a common brand name.**

Economies of scope arise from the ability to eliminate costs by operating two or more businesses under the same corporate umbrella; the cost-saving opportunities can stem from interrelationships anywhere along the businesses' value chains.

scope. *Economies of scope* exist whenever it is less costly for two or more businesses to be operated under centralized management than to function as independent businesses. The economies of operating over a wider range of businesses or product lines can arise from cost-saving opportunities to share resources or combine activities anywhere along the respective value chains of the businesses and from shared use of an established brand name. The greater the economies of scope associated with the particular businesses a company has diversified into, the greater the potential for creating a competitive advantage based on lower costs.

Both skills transfer and activity sharing enable the diversifier to earn greater profits from its businesses than the businesses could earn operating independently. Thus the economies of scope. The key to activity sharing and skills transfer opportunities and thus to cost saving is diversification into businesses with strategic fit. While strategic-fit relationships can occur throughout the value chain, most fall into one of three broad categories.

Market-Related Fit   When the value chains of different businesses overlap such that the products are used by the same customers, distributed through common dealers and retailers, or marketed and promoted in similar ways, then the businesses enjoy *market-related strategic fit.* A variety of cost-saving opportunities (or economies of scope) spring from market-related strategic fit: using a single sales force for all related products rather than having separate sales forces for each business, advertising the related products in the same ads and brochures, using the same brand names, coordinating delivery and shipping, combining after-sale service and repair organizations, coordinating order processing and billing, using common promotional tie-ins (cents-off couponing, free samples and trial offers, seasonal specials, and the like), and combining dealer networks. Such market-related strategic fits usually allow a firm to economize on its marketing, selling, and distribution costs.

In addition to economies of scope, market-related fit can generate opportunities to transfer selling skills, promotional skills, advertising skills, and product differentiation skills from one business to another. Moreover, a company's brand name and reputation in one product can often be transferred to other products. Honda's name in motorcycles and automobiles gave it instant credibility and recognition in entering the lawnmower business without spending large sums on advertising. Canon's reputation in photographic equipment was a competitive asset that facilitated the company's diversification into copying equipment. Panasonic's name in consumer electronics (radios, TVs) was readily transferred to microwave ovens, making it easier and cheaper for Panasonic to diversify into the microwave oven market.

Operating Fit   Different businesses have *operating fit* when there is potential for activity sharing or skills transfer in procuring materials, conducting R&D, mastering a new technology, manufacturing components, assembling finished goods, or performing administrative support functions. Sharing-related operating fits usually present cost-saving opportunities; some derive from the economies of combining activities into a larger-scale operation *(economies of scale)*, and some derive from the ability to eliminate costs by performing activities together rather than independently *(economies of scope)*. The bigger the proportion of cost that a shared activity represents, the more significant the shared cost savings become and the bigger the cost advantage that can result. With operating fit, the most important skills transfer opportunities usually relate to situations where technological or manufacturing expertise in one business has beneficial applications in another.

Management Fit   This type of fit emerges when different business units have comparable types of entrepreneurial, administrative, or operating problems, thereby allowing managerial know-how in one line of business to be transferred to another. Transfers of managerial expertise can occur anywhere in the value chain. Ford transferred its automobile financing and credit management know-how to the savings and loan industry when it acquired some failing savings and loan associations during the 1989 bailout of the crisis-ridden S&L industry. Emerson Electric transferred its skills in low-cost manufacture to its newly acquired Beaird-Poulan chain saw business division; the transfer of management know-how drove Beaird-Poulan's new strategy, changed the way its chain saws were designed and manufactured, and paved the way for new pricing and distribution emphasis.

Capturing Strategic-Fit Benefits   It is one thing to diversify into industries with strategic fit and another to actually realize the benefits. To capture the benefits of activity sharing, related activities must be merged into a single functional unit and coordinated; then the cost savings (or differentiation advantages) must be squeezed out. Merged functions and coordination can entail reorganization costs, and management must determine that the benefit of *some* centralized strategic control is great enough to warrant sacrifice of business-unit autonomy. Likewise, where skills transfer is the cornerstone of strategic fit, managers must find a way to make the transfer effective without stripping too many skilled personnel from the business with the expertise. The more a company's diversification strategy is tied to skills transfer, the more it has to develop a big enough and talented enough pool of specialized personnel not only to supply new businesses with the skill but also to master the skill sufficiently to create competitive advantage.

> **Competitive advantage achieved through strategic fits among related businesses adds to the performance potential of the firm's individual businesses; this extra source of competitive advantage allows related diversification to have a 2 + 2 = 5 effect on shareholder value.**

UNRELATED DIVERSIFICATION STRATEGIES

Despite the strategic-fit benefits associated with related diversification, a number of companies opt for unrelated diversification strategies—they exhibit a willingness to diversify into *any industry* with a good profit opportunity. Corporate managers exert no deliberate effort to seek out businesses having strategic fit with the firm's other businesses. While companies pursuing unrelated diversification may try to make certain their diversification targets meet the industry-attractiveness and cost-of-entry tests, the conditions needed for the better-off test are either disregarded or relegated to secondary status. Decisions to diversify into one industry versus another are the product of an opportunistic search for "good" companies to acquire—*the basic premise of unrelated diversification is that any company that can be acquired on good financial terms and that has satisfactory profit prospects represents a good business to diversify into.* Much time and effort goes into finding and screening acquisition candidates. Typically, corporate strategists screen candidate companies using such criteria as

> **A strategy of unrelated diversification involves diversifying into whatever industries and businesses hold promise for attractive financial gain; exploiting strategic-fit relationships is secondary.**

- Whether the business can meet corporate targets for profitability and return on investment.
- Whether the new business will require substantial infusions of capital to replace fixed assets, fund expansion, and provide working capital.
- Whether the business is in an industry with significant growth potential.

- Whether the business is big enough to contribute significantly to the parent firm's bottom line.
- Whether there is a potential for union difficulties or adverse government regulations concerning product safety or the environment.
- Whether there is industry vulnerability to recession, inflation, high interest rates, or shifts in government policy.

Sometimes, companies with unrelated diversification strategies concentrate on identifying acquisition candidates that offer quick opportunities for financial gain because of their "special situation." Three types of businesses may hold such attraction:

- *Companies whose assets are undervalued*—opportunities may exist to acquire such companies for less than full market value and make substantial capital gains by reselling their assets and businesses for more than their acquired costs.
- *Companies that are financially distressed*—such businesses can often be purchased at a bargain price, their operations turned around with the aid of the parent companies' financial resources and managerial know-how, and then either held as long-term investments in the acquirers' business portfolios (because of their strong earnings or cash flow potential) or sold at a profit, whichever is more attractive.
- *Companies that have bright growth prospects but are short on investment capital*—capital-poor, opportunity-rich companies are usually coveted diversification candidates for a financially strong, opportunity-seeking firm.

Companies that pursue unrelated diversification nearly always enter new businesses by acquiring an established company rather than by forming a start-up subsidiary within their own corporate structures. Their premise is that growth by acquisition translates into enhanced shareholder value. Suspending application of the better-off test is seen as justifiable so long as unrelated diversification results in sustained growth in corporate revenues and earnings and so long as none of the acquired businesses end up performing badly.

Illustration Capsule 23 shows the business portfolios of several companies that have pursued unrelated diversification. Such companies are frequently labeled *conglomerates* because there is no strategic theme in their diversification makeup and because their business interests range broadly across diverse industries.

The Pros and Cons of Unrelated Diversification

Unrelated or conglomerate diversification has appeal from several financial angles:

1. Business risk is scattered over a variety of industries, making the company less dependent on any one business. While the same can be said for related diversification, unrelated diversification places no restraint on how risk is spread. An argument can be made that unrelated diversification is a superior way to diversify financial risk as compared to related diversification because the company's investments can span a bigger variety of totally different businesses.

2. Capital resources can be invested in whatever industries offer the best profit prospects; cash flows from company businesses with lower profit prospects can be diverted to acquiring and expanding business units with

Illustration Capsule 23 Diversified Companies with Unrelated Business Portfolios

Union Pacific Corporation
- Railroad operations (Union Pacific Railroad Company)
- Oil and gas exploration
- Mining
- Microwave and fiber optic transportation, information, and control systems
- Hazardous waste management disposal
- Trucking (Overnite Transportation Company)
- Oil refining
- Real estate

United Technologies, Inc.
- Pratt & Whitney aircraft engines
- Carrier heating and air-conditioning equipment
- Otis elevators
- Sikorsky helicopters
- Essex wire and cable products
- Norden defense systems
- Hamilton Standard controls
- Space transportation systems
- Automotive components

Westinghouse Electric Corporation
- Electric utility power generation equipment
- Nuclear fuel
- Electric transmission and distribution products
- Commercial and residential real estate financing
- Equipment leasing
- Receivables and fixed asset financing
- Radio and television broadcasting
- Longines-Wittnauer Watch Co.
- Beverage bottling
- Elevators and escalators
- Defense electronic systems (missile launch equipment, marine propulsion)
- Commercial furniture
- Community land development

Textron, Inc.
- Bell helicopters
- Paul Revere Insurance
- Missile reentry systems
- Lycoming gas turbine engines and jet propulsion systems
- E-Z-Go golf carts
- Homelite chain saws and lawn and garden equipment
- Davidson automotive parts and trims
- Specialty fasteners
- Avco Financial Services
- Jacobsen turf care equipment
- Tanks and armored vehicles

Source: Company annual reports.

higher growth and profit potentials. Corporate financial resources are thus employed to maximum advantage.

3. Company profitability is somewhat more stable because hard times in one industry may be partially offset by good times in another—ideally, cyclical downswings in some of the company's businesses are counterbalanced by cyclical upswings in other businesses the company has diversified into.

4. To the extent that corporate managers are exceptionally astute at spotting bargain-priced companies with big upside profit potential, shareholder wealth can be enhanced.

While entry into an unrelated business can often pass the attractiveness and the cost-of-entry tests (and sometimes even the better-off test), a strategy of unrelated diversification has drawbacks. One Achilles' heel of conglomerate diversification is the big demand it places on corporate-level management to make sound decisions

The two biggest drawbacks to unrelated diversification are the difficulties of competently managing many different businesses and being without the added source of competitive advantage that strategic fit provides.

regarding fundamentally different businesses operating in fundamentally different industry and competitive environments. The greater the number of businesses a company is in and the more diverse they are, the harder it is for corporate managers to oversee each subsidiary and spot problems early, to have real expertise in evaluating the attractiveness of each business's industry and competitive environment, and to judge the calibre of strategic actions and plans proposed by business-level managers. As one president of a diversified firm expressed it:

> . . . we've got to make sure that our core businesses are properly managed for solid, long-term earnings. We can't just sit back and watch the numbers. We've got to know what the real issues are out there in the profit centers. Otherwise, we're not even in a position to check out our managers on the big decisions.[9]

With broad diversification, corporate managers have to be shrewd and talented enough to (1) discern a good acquisition from a bad acquisition, (2) select capable managers to run each of many different businesses, (3) discern when the major strategic proposals of business-unit managers are sound, and (4) know what to do if a business unit stumbles. Because every business tends to encounter rough sledding, a good way to gauge the risk of diversifying into new unrelated areas is to ask, "If the new business got into trouble, would we know how to bail it out?" When the answer is no, unrelated diversification can pose significant financial risk and the business's profit prospects are more chancy.[10] As the former chairman of a Fortune 500 company advised, "Never acquire a business you don't know how to run." It takes only one or two big strategic mistakes (misjudging industry attractiveness, encountering unexpected problems in a newly acquired business, or being too optimistic about how hard it will be to turn a struggling subsidiary around) to cause a precipitous drop in corporate earnings and crash the parent company's stock price.

Second, without the competitive advantage potential of strategic fit, consolidated performance of an unrelated multibusiness portfolio tends to be no better than the sum of what the individual business units could achieve if they were independent, and it may be worse to the extent that corporate managers meddle unwisely in business-unit operations or hamstring them with corporate policies. Except, perhaps, for the added financial backing that a cash-rich corporate parent can provide, a strategy of unrelated diversification does nothing for the competitive strength of the individual business units. Each business is on its own in trying to build a competitive edge—the unrelated nature of sister businesses offers no basis for cost reduction, skills transfer, or technology sharing. In a widely diversified firm, the value added by corporate managers depends primarily on how good they are at deciding what new businesses to add, which ones to get rid of, how best to deploy available financial resources to build a higher-performing collection of businesses, and the quality of the decision-making guidance they give to the general managers of their business subsidiaries.

Third, although in theory unrelated diversification offers the potential for greater sales-profit stability over the course of the business cycle, in practice attempts at countercyclical diversification fall short of the mark. Few attractive businesses have

---

[9]Carter F. Bales, "Strategic Control: The President's Paradox," *Business Horizons* 20, no. 4 (August 1977), p. 17.

[10]Of course, management may be willing to assume the risk that trouble will not strike before it has had time to learn the business well enough to bail it out of almost any difficulty. See Peter Drucker, *Management: Tasks, Responsibilities, Practices*, p. 709.

opposite up-and-down cycles; the great majority of businesses are similarly affected by economic good times and hard times. There's no convincing evidence that the consolidated profits of broadly diversified firms are more stable or less subject to reversal in periods of recession and economic stress than the profits of less diversified firms.[11]

Despite these drawbacks, unrelated diversification can sometimes be a desirable corporate strategy. It certainly merits consideration when a firm needs to diversify away from an endangered or unattractive industry and has no distinctive skills it can transfer to an adjacent industry. There's also a rationale for pure diversification to the extent owners have a strong preference for investing in several unrelated businesses instead of a family of related ones. Otherwise, the argument for unrelated diversification hinges on the case-by-case prospects for financial gain.

A key issue in unrelated diversification is how wide a net to cast in building the business portfolio. In other words, should the corporate portfolio contain few or many unrelated businesses? How much business diversity can corporate executives successfully manage? A reasonable way to resolve the issue of how much diversification comes from answering two questions: "What is the least diversification it will take to achieve acceptable growth and profitability?" and "What is the most diversification that can be managed given the complexity it adds?"[12] The optimal amount of diversification usually lies between these two extremes.

Unrelated Diversification and Shareholder Value

Unrelated diversification is fundamentally a finance-driven approach to creating shareholder value whereas related diversification is fundamentally strategy-driven. *Related diversification represents a strategic approach to building shareholder value* because it is predicated on exploiting the linkages between the value chains of different businesses to lower costs, transfer skills and technological expertise across businesses, and gain other strategic-fit benefits. The objective is to convert the strategic fits among the firm's businesses into an extra measure of competitive advantage that goes beyond what business subsidiaries are able to achieve on their own. The added competitive advantage a firm achieves through related diversification is the driver for building greater shareholder value.

In contrast, *unrelated diversification is principally a financial approach to creating shareholder value* because it is predicated on astute deployment of corporate financial resources and executive skill in spotting financially attractive business opportunities. Since unrelated diversification produces no strategic-fit opportunities of consequence, corporate strategists can't build shareholder value by acquiring companies that create or compound competitive advantage for its business subsidiaries—in a conglomerate, competitive advantage doesn't go beyond what each business subsidiary can achieve independently through its own competitive strategy. Consequently, for unrelated diversification to result in enhanced shareholder value (above the $2 + 2 = 4$ effect that the subsidiary businesses could produce through independent operations and that shareholders could obtain by purchasing ownership interests in a variety of businesses to spread investment risk on their own behalf), corporate

Unrelated diversification is a financial approach to creating shareholder value; related diversification, in contrast, represents a strategic approach.

For corporate strategists to build shareholder value in some way other than through strategic fits and competitive advantage, they must be smart enough to produce financial results from a group of businesses that exceed what business-level managers can produce.

---

[11]Ibid., p. 767. Research studies in the interval since 1974, when Drucker made his observation, uphold his conclusion—on the whole, broadly diversified firms do not outperform less diversified firms over the course of the business cycle.

[12]Ibid., pp. 692–93.

strategists must exhibit superior skills in creating and managing a portfolio of diversified business interests. This specifically means

- Doing a superior job of diversifying into new businesses that can produce consistently good returns on investment (satisfying the attractiveness test).
- Doing an excellent job of negotiating favorable acquisition prices (satisfying the cost-of-entry test).
- Making astute moves to sell previously acquired business subsidiaries at their peak and getting premium prices (this requires skills in discerning when a business subsidiary is on the verge of confronting adverse industry and competitive conditions and probable declines in long-term profitability).
- Being shrewd in shifting corporate financial resources out of businesses where profit opportunities are dim and into businesses where rapid earnings growth and high returns on investment are occurring.
- Doing such a good job overseeing the firm's business subsidiaries and contributing to how they are managed (by providing expert problem-solving skills, creative strategy suggestions, and decision-making guidance to business-level managers) that the businesses perform at a higher level than they would otherwise be able to do (a possible way to satisfy the better-off test).

To the extent that corporate executives are able to craft and execute a strategy of unrelated diversification that produces enough of the above outcomes for an enterprise to consistently outperform other firms in generating dividends and capital gains for stockholders, then a case can be made that shareholder value has truly been enhanced. Achieving such results consistently requires supertalented corporate executives, however. Without them, unrelated diversification is a very dubious and unreliable way to try to build shareholder value—there are far more who have tried it and failed than who have tried and succeeded.

DIVESTITURE AND LIQUIDATION STRATEGIES

> **A business needs to be considered for divestiture when corporate strategists conclude it no longer fits or is an attractive investment.**

Even a shrewd corporate diversification strategy can result in the acquisition of business units that, down the road, just do not work out. Misfits or partial fits cannot be completely avoided because it is impossible to predict precisely how getting into a new line of business will actually work out. In addition, long-term industry attractiveness changes with the times; what was once a good diversification move into an attractive industry may later turn sour. Subpar performance by some business units is bound to occur, thereby raising questions of whether to keep them or divest them. Other business units, despite adequate financial performance, may not mesh as well with the rest of the firm as was originally thought.

Sometimes, a diversification move that seems sensible from a strategic-fit standpoint turns out to lack the compatibility of values essential to a *cultural fit*.[13] Several pharmaceutical companies had just this experience. When they diversified into cosmetics and perfume, they discovered their personnel had little respect for the "frivolous" nature of such products compared to the far nobler task of developing miracle drugs to cure the ill. The absence of shared values and cultural compatibility between

---

[13]Ibid., p. 709.

the medical research and chemical-compounding expertise of the pharmaceutical companies and the fashion-marketing orientation of the cosmetics business was the undoing of what otherwise was diversification into businesses with technology-sharing potential, product-development fit, and some overlap in distribution channels.

When a particular line of business loses its appeal, the most attractive solution usually is to sell it. Normally such businesses should be divested as fast as is practical. To drag things out serves no purpose unless time is needed to get it into better shape to sell. The more business units in a diversified firm's portfolio, the more likely that it will have occasion to divest poor performers, "dogs," and misfits. A useful guide to determine if and when to divest a business subsidiary is to ask the question, "If we were not in this business today, would we want to get into it now?"[14] When the answer is no or probably not, divestiture should be considered.

Divestiture can take either of two forms. The parent can spin off a business as a financially and managerially independent company in which the parent company may or may not retain partial ownership. Or the parent may sell the unit outright, in which case a buyer needs to be found. As a rule, divestiture should not be approached from the angle of "Who can we pawn this business off on and what is the most we can get for it?"[15] Instead, it is wiser to ask "For what sort of organization would this business be a good fit, and under what conditions would it be viewed as a good deal?" Organizations for which the business is a good fit are likely to pay the highest price.

Of all the strategic alternatives, liquidation is the most unpleasant and painful, especially for a single-business enterprise where it means the organization ceases to exist. For a multi-industry, multibusiness firm to liquidate one of its lines of business is less traumatic. The hardships of job eliminations, plant closings, and so on, while not to be minimized, still leave an ongoing organization, perhaps one that is healthier after its pruning. In hopeless situations, an early liquidation effort usually serves owner-stockholder interests better than an inevitable bankruptcy. Prolonging the pursuit of a lost cause exhausts an organization's resources and leaves less to liquidate; it can also mar reputations and ruin management careers. Unfortunately, it is seldom simple for management to differentiate between when a turnaround is achievable and when it isn't. This is particularly true when emotions and pride overcome sound business judgment—as often they do.

CORPORATE TURNAROUND, RETRENCHMENT, AND PORTFOLIO RESTRUCTURING STRATEGIES

Turnaround, retrenchment, and portfolio restructuring strategies come into play when corporate management has to restore an ailing business portfolio to good health. Poor performance can be caused by large losses in one or more business units that pull the corporation's overall financial performance down, a disproportionate number of businesses in unattractive industries, a bad economy adversely impacting many of the firm's business units, an excessive debt burden, or ill-chosen acquisitions that haven't lived up to expectations.

Corporate turnaround strategies focus on efforts to restore money-losing businesses to profitability instead of divesting them. The intent is to get the whole

---

[14]Ibid., p. 94.
[15]Ibid., p. 719.

company back in the black by curing the problems of those businesses in the portfolio that are most responsible for pulling overall performance down. Turnaround strategies are most appropriate in situations where the reasons for poor performance are short-term, the ailing businesses are in attractive industries, and divesting the money-losers does not make long-term strategic sense.

Corporate retrenchment strategies involve reducing the scope of diversification to a smaller number of businesses. Retrenchment is usually undertaken when corporate management concludes that the company is in too many businesses and needs to concentrate its efforts on a few core businesses. Sometimes diversified firms retrench because they can't make certain businesses profitable after several frustrating years of trying or because they lack funds to support the investment needs of all of their business subsidiaries. More commonly, however, corporate executives conclude that the firm's diversification efforts have ranged too far afield and that the key to improved long-term performance lies in concentrating on building strong positions in a smaller number of businesses. Retrenchment is usually accomplished by divesting businesses that are too small to make a sizable contribution to earnings or that have little or no strategic fit with the company's core businesses. Divesting such businesses frees resources that can be used to reduce debt or support expansion of the company's core businesses.

Portfolio restructuring strategies involve radical surgery on the mix and percentage makeup of the types of businesses in the portfolio. For instance, one company over a two-year period divested 4 business units, closed down the operations of 4 others, and added 25 new lines of business to its portfolio, 16 through acquisition and 9 through internal start-up. Restructuring can be prompted by any of several conditions: (1) when a strategy review reveals that the firm's long-term performance prospects have become unattractive because the portfolio contains too many slow-growth, declining, or competitively weak business units; (2) when one or more of the firm's core businesses fall prey to hard times; (3) when a new CEO takes over and decides to redirect where the company is headed; (4) when "wave of the future" technologies or products emerge and a major shakeup of the portfolio is needed to build a position in a potentially big new industry; (5) when the firm has a unique opportunity to make an acquisition so big that it has to sell several existing business units to finance the new acquisition; or (6) when major businesses in the portfolio have become more and more unattractive, forcing a shakeup in the portfolio in order to produce satisfactory long-term corporate performance.

Portfolio restructuring involves bold strategic action to revamp the diversified company's business makeup through a series of divestitures and new acquisitions.

Portfolio restructuring typically involves both divestitures and new acquisitions. Candidates for divestiture include not only weak or up-and-down performers or those in unattractive industries, but also those that no longer fit (even though they may be profitable and in attractive-enough industries). Many broadly diversified companies, disenchanted with the performance of some acquisitions and having only mixed success in overseeing so many unrelated business units, restructure their business portfolios to a narrower core of activities. Business units incompatible with newly established related diversification criteria are divested, the remaining units regrouped and aligned to capture more strategic fit benefits, and new acquisitions made to strengthen the parent company's business position in the industries it has chosen to emphasize.

The recent trend among broadly diversified companies to demerge and decon-glomerate is being driven by a growing preference for building diversification around the creation of strong competitive positions in a few, well-selected industries. Indeed, in response to investor disenchantment with the conglomerate approach to diversification (evident in the fact that conglomerates often have *lower* price-earnings ratios than companies with related diversification strategies), some conglomerates have undertaken portfolio restructuring and retrenchment in a deliberate effort to escape being regarded as a conglomerate.

MULTINATIONAL DIVERSIFICATION STRATEGIES

The distinguishing characteristics of a multinational diversification strategy are a *diversity of businesses* and a *diversity of national markets*.[16] Here, corporate managers have to conceive and execute a substantial number of strategies—at least one for each industry, with as many multinational variations as is appropriate for the situation. At the same time, managers of diversified multinational corporations (DMNCs) need to be alert for beneficial ways to coordinate their firms' strategic actions across industries and countries. The goal of strategic coordination at the headquarters level is to bring the full force of corporate resources and capabilities to the task of securing sustainable competitive advantages in each business and national market.[17]

The Emergence of Multinational Diversification

Until the 1960s, multinational companies (MNCs) operated fairly autonomous subsidiaries in each host country, each catering to the special requirements of its own national market.[18] Management tasks at company headquarters primarily involved finance functions, technology transfer, and export coordination. In pursuing a national responsiveness strategy, the primary competitive advantage of an MNC was grounded in its ability to transfer technology, manufacturing know-how, brand name identification, and marketing and management skills from country to country quite efficiently, allowing them to beat out smaller host country competitors on price, quality, and management know-how. Standardized administrative procedures helped minimize overhead costs, and once an initial organization for managing foreign subsidiaries was put in place, entry into additional national markets could be accomplished at low incremental costs. Frequently, an MNC's presence and market position in a country was negotiated with the host government rather than driven by international competition.

During the 1970s, however, multicountry strategies based on national responsiveness began to lose their effectiveness. Competition broke out on a global scale in more and more industries as Japanese, European, and U.S. companies pursued international expansion in the wake of trade liberalization and the opening up of market opportunities in both industrialized and less-developed countries.[19] The relevant market arena in many industries shifted from national to global principally because the strategies of global competitors, most notably the Japanese companies, involved gaining a market foothold in host country markets via lower-priced, higher-quality offerings than established companies. To fend off global competitors, traditional MNCs were driven to integrate their operations across national borders in a quest for better efficiencies and lower manufacturing costs. Instead of separately manufacturing a complete product range in each country, plants became more specialized in their production operations to

---

[16]C. K. Prahalad and Yves L. Doz, *The Multinational Mission* (New York: Free Press, 1987), p. 2.
[17]Ibid., p. 15.
[18]Yves L. Doz, *Strategic Management in Multinational Companies* (New York: Pergamon Press, 1985), p. 1.
[19]Ibid., pp. 2–3.

gain the economies of longer production runs, to permit use of faster automated equipment, and to capture experience curve effects. Country subsidiaries obtained the rest of the product range they needed from sister plants in other countries. Gains in manufacturing efficiencies from converting to state-of-the-art, world-scale manufacturing plants more than offset increased international shipping costs, especially in light of the other advantages globalized strategies offered. With a global strategy, an MNC could locate plants in countries with low labor costs—a key consideration in industries whose products have high labor content. With a global strategy, an MNC could also exploit differences in tax rates, setting transfer prices in its integrated operations to produce higher profits in low-tax countries and lower profits in high-tax countries. Global strategic coordination also gave MNCs increased ability to take advantage of country-to-country differences in interest rates, exchange rates, credit terms, government subsidies, and export guarantees. As a consequence of these advantages, it became increasingly difficult for a company that produced and sold its product in only one country to succeed in an industry populated with aggressive competitors intent on achieving global dominance.

During the 1980s another source of competitive advantage began to emerge: using the strategic fit advantages of related diversification to build stronger competitive positions in several related global industries simultaneously. Being a diversified MNC (DMNC) became competitively superior to being a single-business MNC in cases where strategic fits existed across global industries. Related diversification is most capable of producing competitive advantage for a multinational company where expertise in a core technology can be applied in different industries (at least one of which is global) and where there are important economies of scope and brand name advantages to being in a family of related businesses.[20] Illustration Capsule 24 indicates Honda's strategy in exploiting gasoline engine technology and its well-known name by diversifying into a variety of products with engines.

A multinational corporation can gain competitive advantage by diversifying into global industries having related technologies.

Sources of Competitive Advantage for a DMNC

When a multinational company has expertise in a core technology and has diversified into a series of related products and businesses to exploit that core, a centralized R&D effort coordinated at the headquarters level holds real potential for competitive advantage. By channeling corporate resources directly into a strategically coordinated R&D/technology effort, as opposed to letting each business unit perform its own R&D function, the DMNC can launch a world-class, global-scale assault to advance the core technology, generate technology-based manufacturing economies within and across product/business lines, make across-the-board product improvements, and develop complementary products—all significant advantages in a globally competitive marketplace. In the absence of centralized coordination, R&D/technology investments are likely to be scaled down to match each business's product-market perspective, setting the stage for lost opportunity as the strategic-fit benefits of coordinated technology management slip through the cracks and go uncaptured.[21]

The second source of competitive advantage for a DMNC concerns the distribution and brand name advantages that can accrue from diversifying into related global industries. Consider, for instance, the competitive strength of such Japanese DMNCs

---

[20]Pralahad and Doz, *The Multinational Mission*, pp. 62–63.
[21]Ibid.

The Technology of Engines

At first blush anyone looking at Honda's lineup of products—cars, motorcycles, lawn mowers, power generators, outboard motors, snowmobiles, and snowblowers, and garden tillers—might conclude that Honda has pursued unrelated diversification. But underlying the obvious product diversity is a common core: the technology of engines.

The basic Honda strategy is to exploit the company's expertise in engine technology and manufacturing and to capitalize on its brand recognition. One Honda ad teases consumers with the question, "How do you put six Hondas in a two-car garage?" It then shows a garage containing a Honda car, a Honda motorcycle, a Honda snowmobile, a Honda lawnmower, a Honda power generator, and a Honda outboard motor.

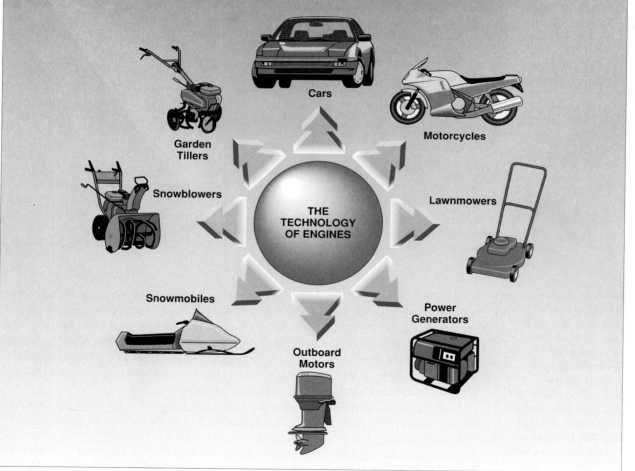

Source: Adapted from C. K. Prahalad and Yves L. Doz, *The Multinational Mission* (New York: Free Press, 1987), p. 62.

as Sanyo and Matsushita. Both have diversified into a range of globally competitive consumer goods industries—TVs, stereo equipment, radios, VCRs, small domestic appliances (microwave ovens, for example), and personal computers. By widening their scope of operations in products marketed through similar distribution channels, Sanyo and Matsushita have not only exploited related technologies but also built stronger distribution capabilities, captured logistical and distribution-related

Illustration Capsule 25   Mitsubishi: The Competitive Power of a Keiretsu

Mitsubishi is Japan's largest *keiretsu*—a family of affiliated companies. With combined 1992 sales of $175 billion, the Mitsubishi keiretsu consists of 28 core companies: Mitsubishi Corp. (the trading company), Mitsubishi Heavy Industries (the group's biggest manufacturer—shipbuilding, air conditioners, forklifts, robots, gas turbines), Mitsubishi Motors, Mitsubishi Steel, Mitsubishi Aluminum, Mitsubishi Oil, Mitsubishi Petrochemical, Mitsubishi Gas Chemical, Mitsubishi Plastics, Mitsubishi Cable, Mitsubishi Electric, Mitsubishi Construction, Mitsubishi Paper Mills, Mitsubishi Mining and Cement, Mitsubishi Rayon, Nikon, Asahi Glass, Kirin Brewery, Mitsubishi Bank (the world's fifth largest bank and the lead bank for family companies), Tokyo Marine and Fire Insurance (one of the world's largest insurance companies), and eight others. Beyond this core group are hundreds of other Mitsubishi-related subsidiaries and affiliates.

The 28 core companies of the Mitsubishi keiretsu are bound together by cross-ownership of each other's stock (the percentage of shares of each core company owned by other members ranges from 17% to 100%, with an average of 27%), by interlocking directorships (it is standard for officers of one company to sit on the boards of other keiretsu members), joint ventures, and long-term business relationships. They use each other's products and services in many instances—among the suppliers to Mitsubishi Motor's

Diamond Star plant in Bloomington, Illinois, are 25 Mitsubishi and Mitsubishi-related suppliers. It is common for them to join forces to make acquisitions—five Mitsubishi companies teamed to buy a cement plant in California; Mitsubishi Corp. bought an $880 million chemical company in Pittsburgh with financial assistance from Mitsubishi Bank and Mitsubishi Trust, then sold pieces to Mitsubishi Gas Chemical, Mitsubishi Rayon, Mitsubishi Petrochemical, and Mitsubishi Kasei. Mitsubishi Bank and occasionally other Mitsubishi financial enterprises serve as a primary financing source for new ventures and as a financial safety net if keiretsu members encounter tough market conditions or have financial problems.

Despite these links, there's no grand Mitsubishi strategy. Each company operates independently, pursuing its own strategy and markets. On occasion, group members find themselves going after the same markets competing with each other. Nor do member companies usually get sweetheart deals from other members; for example, Mitsubishi Heavy Industries lost out to Siemens in competing to supply gas turbines to a new power plant that Mitsubishi Corp.'s wholly owned Diamond Energy subsidiary constructed in Virginia. But operating independence does not prevent them from recognizing their mutual interests, cooperating voluntarily without formal controls, or turning inward to keiretsu

(continued)

A multinational corporation can also gain competitive advantage by diversifying into related global industries where the strategic fits produce economies of scope and the benefits of brand name transfer.

economies, and established greater brand awareness for their products.[22] Such competitive advantages are not available to a domestic-only company pursuing single-business concentration. Moreover, with a well-diversified product line and a multinational market base, a DMNC can enter new country markets or new product markets and gain market share via below-market pricing (and below-average cost pricing if need be), subsidizing the entry with earnings from one or more of its country market profit sanctuaries and/or earnings in other businesses.

Both a one-business multinational company and a one-business domestic company are weakly positioned to defend their market positions against a determined DMNC willing to accept lower short-term profits in order to win long-term competitive position in a desirable new market. A one-business domestic company has only one profit sanctuary—its home market. A one-business multinational company may have profit sanctuaries in several country markets but all are in the same business. Each is vulnerable to a DMNC that launches a major strategic offensive in their profit sanctuaries and low-balls its prices to win market share at their expense. A DMNC's ability to keep hammering away at competitors with low-ball prices year after year may reflect either a cost advantage growing out of its related diversification strategy or a willingness to cross-subsidize low profits or even losses with earnings from its

[22]Ibid., p. 64.

(concluded)

members for business partnerships on ventures perceived as strategically important.

A President's Council, consisting of 49 chairmen and presidents, meets monthly, usually the second Friday of the month. While the formal agenda typically includes a discussion of joint philanthropical and public relations projects and a lecture by an expert on some current topic, participants report instances where strategic problems or opportunities affecting several group members are discussed and major decisions made. It is common for a Mitsubishi company involved in a major undertaking (initiating its first foray into the U.S. or European markets or developing a new technology) to ask for support from other members. In such cases, group members who can take business actions that contribute to solutions are expected to do so. The President's Council meetings also serve to cement personal ties, exchange information, identify mutual interests, and set up follow-on actions by subordinates. Other ways that Mitsubishi uses to foster an active informal network of contacts, information sharing, cooperation, and business relationships among member companies include regular get-togethers of Mitsubishi-America and Mitsubishi-Europe executives and even a matchmaking club where member company employees can meet prospective spouses.

In recent years, Mitsubishi companies introduced a number of consumer products in the U.S. and elsewhere, all branded with a three-diamond logo derived from the crest of the founding samurai family—cars and trucks made by Mitsubishi Motors, big-screen TVs and mobile phones made by Mitsubishi Electric, and air conditioners produced by Mitsubishi Heavy Industries. Mitsubishi executives believe common logo usage has produced added brand awareness; for example, in the U.S. Mitsubishi Motors' efforts to advertise and market its cars and trucks helped boost brand awareness of Mitsubishi TVs. In several product categories one or more Mitsubishi companies operate in stages all along the industry value chain—from components production to assembly to shipping, warehousing, and distribution.

Similar practices exist in the other five of the six largest Japanese keiretsu: Dai-Ichi Kangin with 47 core companies, Mitsui Group with 24 core companies (including Toyota and Toshiba), Sanwa with 44 core companies, Sumitomo with 20 core companies (including NEC, a maker of telecommunications equipment and personal computers), and Fuyo with 29 core companies (including Nissan and Canon). Most observers agree that Japan's keiretsu model gives Japanese companies major competitive advantages in international markets. According to a Japanese economics professor at Osaka University, "Using group power, they can engage in cutthroat competition."

Source: Based on information in "Mighty Mitsubishi Is on the Move" and "Hands across America: The Rise of Mitsubishi," *Business Week*, September 24, 1990, pp. 98–107.

profit sanctuaries in other country markets and/or its earnings from other businesses. Sanyo, for example, by pursuing related diversification keyed to product-distribution-technology strategic fit and managing its product families on a global scale, has the ability to encircle domestic companies like Zenith (which manufactures TVs and small computer systems) and Maytag (which manufactures home appliances) and put them under serious competitive pressure. In Zenith's case, Sanyo can peck away at Zenith's market share in TVs and in the process weaken the loyalty of TV retailers to the Zenith brand. In Maytag's case, Sanyo can diversify into large home appliances (by acquiring an established appliance maker or manufacturing on its own) and cross-subsidize a low-priced market entry against Maytag and other less-diversified home appliance firms with earnings from its many other business and product lines. If Sanyo chooses, it can keep its prices low for several years to gain market share at the expense of domestic rivals, turning its attention to profits after the battle for market share and competitive position is won.[23] Some additional aspects of the competitive power of broadly diversified enterprises is described in Illustration Capsule 25.

> **A multinational corporation that diversifies into related global industries is well-positioned to outcompete both a one-business domestic company and a one-business multinational company.**

---

[23]Ibid.

A DMNC's most potent advantages usually derive from technology sharing, economies of scope, shared brand names, and its potential to employ cross-subsidization tactics.

The competitive principle is clear: A DMNC has a strategic arsenal capable of defeating both a single-business MNC and a single-business domestic company over the long term. The competitive advantages of a DMNC, however, depend on employing a related diversification strategy in industries that are already globally competitive or are on the verge of becoming so. Then the related businesses have to be managed so as to capture strategic-fit benefits. DMNCs have the biggest competitive advantage potential in industries with technology-sharing and technology-transfer opportunities and where there are important economies of scope and brand name benefits associated with competing in related product families.

A DMNC also has important cross-subsidization potential for winning its way into attractive new markets. However, while DMNCs have significant cross-subsidization powers, they rarely use them in the extreme. It is one thing to use a *portion* of the profits and cash flows from existing businesses to cover reasonable short-term losses to gain entry to a new business or a new country market; it is quite another to drain corporate profits indiscriminately (and thus impair overall company performance) to support either deep price discounting and quick market penetration in the short term or continuing losses over the longer term. At some juncture, every business and every market entered has to make a profit contribution or become a candidate for abandonment. Moreover, the company has to wring consistently acceptable overall performance from the whole business portfolio. So there are limits to cross-subsidization. As a general rule, cross-subsidization is justified only if there is a good chance that short-term losses can be amply recouped in some way over the long term.

COMBINATION DIVERSIFICATION STRATEGIES

The six corporate diversification approaches described above are not mutually exclusive. They can be pursued in combination and in varying sequences, allowing ample room for companies to customize their diversification strategies to fit their own circumstances. The most common business portfolios created by corporate diversification strategies are

- A dominant-business enterprise with sales concentrated in one major core business but with a modestly diversified portfolio of either related or unrelated businesses (amounting to one-third or less of total corporatewide sales).
- A narrowly diversified enterprise having a *few* (two to five) *related core* business units.
- A broadly diversified enterprise made up of *many* mostly *related* business units.
- A narrowly diversified enterprise composed of a *few* (two to five) *core* business units in *unrelated* industries.
- A broadly diversified enterprise having *many* business units in mostly *unrelated* industries.
- A multibusiness enterprise that has diversified into unrelated areas but that has a portfolio of related businesses within each area—thus giving it *several unrelated groups of related businesses.*

In each case, the geographic markets of individual businesses within the portfolio can range from local to regional to national to multinational to global. Thus, a company can be competing locally in some businesses, nationally in others, and globally in still others.

***

Most companies have their business roots in a single industry. Even though they may have since diversified into other industries, a substantial part of their revenues and profits still usually comes from the original or core business. Diversification becomes an attractive strategy when a company runs out of profitable growth opportunities in its core business (including any opportunities to integrate backward or forward to strengthen its competitive position). The purpose of diversification is to build shareholder value. Diversification builds shareholder value when a diversified group of businesses can perform better under the auspices of a single corporate parent than they would as independent, stand-alone businesses. Whether a particular diversification move is capable of increasing shareholder value hinges on the attractiveness test, the cost-of-entry test, and the better-off test.

There are two fundamental approaches to diversification—into related businesses and into unrelated businesses. The rationale for related diversification is *strategic:* diversify into businesses with strategic fit, capitalize on strategic-fit relationships to gain competitive advantage, then use competitive advantage to achieve the desired $2 + 2 = 5$ impact on shareholder value. Businesses have strategic fit when their value chains offer potential (1) for realizing economies of scope or cost-saving efficiencies associated with sharing technology, facilities, functional activities, distribution outlets, or brand names; (2) for skills transfers or technology transfers; and/or (3) for added differentiation. Such competitive advantage potentials can exist anywhere along the value chains of related businesses.

The basic premise of unrelated diversification is that any business that has good profit prospects and can be acquired on good financial terms is a good business to diversify into. Unrelated diversification is basically a *financial* approach to diversification; strategic fit is a secondary consideration compared to the expectation of financial gain. Unrelated diversification surrenders the competitive advantage potential of strategic fit in return for such advantages as (1) spreading business risk over a variety of industries and (2) gaining opportunities for quick financial gain (if candidate acquisitions have undervalued assets, are bargain-priced and have good upside potential given the right management, or need the backing of a financially strong parent to capitalize on attractive opportunities). In theory, unrelated diversification also offers greater earnings stability over the business cycle, a third advantage. However, achieving these three outcomes consistently requires corporate executives who are smart enough to avoid the considerable disadvantages of unrelated diversification. The greater the number of businesses a conglomerate company is in and the more diverse these businesses are, the more that corporate executives are stretched to know enough about each business to distinguish a good acquisition from a risky one, select capable managers to run each business, know when the major strategic proposals of business units are sound, or wisely decide what to do when a business unit stumbles. Unless corporate managers are exceptionally shrewd and talented, unrelated diversification is a dubious and unreliable approach to building shareholder value when compared to related diversification.

Once diversification is accomplished, corporate management's task is to manage the firm's business portfolio for maximum long-term performance. There are six different strategic options for improving a diversified company's performance: (1) make new acquisitions, (2) divest weak-performing business units or those that no longer fit, (3) restructure the makeup of the portfolio when overall performance is poor and future prospects are bleak, (4) retrench to a narrower diversification base, (5) pursue multinational diversification, and (6) liquidate money-losing businesses with poor turnaround potential.

The most popular option for getting out of a business that is unattractive or doesn't fit is to sell it—ideally to a buyer for whom the business has attractive fit. Sometimes a business can be divested by spinning it off as a financially and managerially independent enterprise in which the parent company may or may not retain an ownership interest.

Corporate turnaround, retrenchment, and restructuring strategies are used when corporate management has to restore an ailing business portfolio to good health. Poor performance can be caused by large losses in one or more businesses that pull overall corporate performance down, by too many business units in unattractive industries, by an excessive debt burden, or by ill-chosen acquisitions that haven't lived up to expectations. Corporate turnaround strategies aim at restoring money-losing businesses to profitability instead of divesting them. Retrenchment involves reducing the scope of diversification to a smaller number of businesses by divesting those that are too small to make a sizable contribution to corporate earnings or those that don't fit with the narrower business base on which corporate management wants to concentrate company resources and energies. Restructuring strategies involve radical portfolio shakeups, divestiture of some businesses and acquisition of others to create a group of businesses with much improved performance potential.

Multinational diversification strategies feature a diversity of businesses and a diversity of national markets. Despite the complexity of having to devise and manage so many strategies (at least one for each industry, with as many variations for country markets as may be needed), multinational diversification can be a competitively advantageous strategy. DMNCs can use the strategic-fit advantages of related diversification (economies of scope, skills transfer, and shared brand names) to build competitively strong positions in several related global industries simultaneously. Such advantages, if competently exploited, can allow a DMNC to outcompete a one-business domestic rival or a one-business multinational rival over time. A one-business domestic company has only one profit sanctuary—its home market. A single-business multinational company may have profit sanctuaries in several countries, but all are in the same business. Both are vulnerable to a DMNC that launches offensive campaigns in their profit sanctuaries. The DMNC can use its lower-cost advantage growing out of its economies of scope to underprice rivals and gain market share at their expense. Even without a cost advantage, the DMNC can decide to underprice such rivals and subsidize its lower profit margins (or even losses) with the profits earned in its other businesses. A well-financed and competently managed DMNC can sap the financial and competitive strength of one-business domestic-only and multinational rivals. DMNCs have the biggest competitive advantage potential in industries with significant economies of scope, shared brand name benefits, and technology-sharing opportunities.

Suggested Readings   Buzzell, Robert D. "Is Vertical Integration Profitable?" *Harvard Business Review* 61, no. 1 (January–February 1983), pp. 92–102.

Goold, Michael, and Kathleen Luchs. "Why Diversify? Four Decades of Management Thinking." *Academy of Management Executive* 7, no. 3 (August 1993), pp. 7–25.

Harrigan, Kathryn R. "Matching Vertical Integration Strategies to Competitive Conditions." *Strategic Management Journal* 7, no. 6 (November–December 1986), pp. 535–56.

Hax, Arnoldo, and Nicolas S. Majluf. *The Strategy Concept and Process.* Englewood Cliffs, N.J.: Prentice-Hall, 1991, chaps. 9, 11, and 15.

Hofer, Charles W. "Turnaround Strategies." *Journal of Business Strategy* 1, no. 1 (Summer 1980), pp. 19–31.

Hoffman, Richard C. "Strategies for Corporate Turnarounds: What Do We Know about Them?" *Journal of General Management* 14, no. 3 (Spring 1989), pp. 46–66.

Kumpe, Ted, and Piet T. Bolwijn. "Manufacturing: The New Case for Vertical Integration." *Harvard Business Review* 88, no. 2 (March–April 1988), pp. 75–82.

Ohmae, Kenichi. *The Mind of the Strategist.* New York: Penguin Books, 1983, chaps. 10 and 12.

Prahalad, C. K., and Yves L. Doz. *The Multinational Mission.* New York: Free Press, 1987, chaps. 1 and 2.

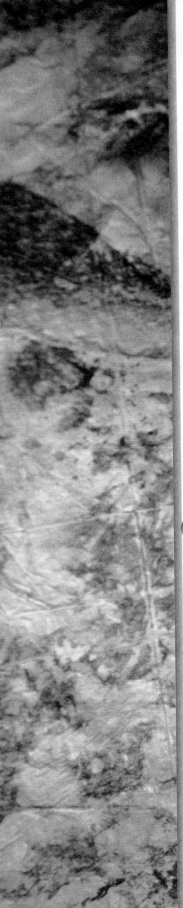

CHAPTER EIGHT

Strategic Analysis of Diversified Companies

If we can know where we are and something about how we got there, we might see where we are trending—and if the outcomes which lie naturally in our course are unacceptable, to make timely change.

Abraham Lincoln

No company can afford everything it would like to do. Resources have to be allocated. The essence of strategic planning is to allocate resources to those areas that have the greatest future potential.

Reginald Jones

Once a company diversifies, three strategic issues emerge to challenge corporate strategy-makers:

- How attractive is the group of businesses the company is in?

- Assuming the company sticks with its present lineup of businesses, how good is its performance outlook in the years ahead?
- If the previous two answers are not satisfactory, what should the company do to get out of some businesses, strengthen the positions of remaining businesses, and get into new businesses to boost the performance prospects of its business portfolio?

Crafting and implementing action plans to improve the attractiveness and competitive strength of a company's business-unit portfolio is the heart of corporate-level strategic management.

Strategic analysis of diversified companies builds on the concepts and methods used for single-business companies. But there are also new aspects to consider and additional analytical approaches to master. To evaluate the strategy of a diversified company, assess the caliber and potential of its businesses, and decide what strategic actions to take next, managers need to adhere closely to the following eight-step procedure:

1. Identify the present corporate strategy.
2. Construct one or more business portfolio matrices to reveal the character of the company's business portfolio.
3. Compare the long-term attractiveness of each industry the company is in.

216

4. Compare the competitive strength of the company's business units to see which ones are strong contenders in their respective industries.

5. Rate each business unit on the basis of its historical performance and future prospects.

6. Assess each business unit's compatibility with corporate strategy and determine the value of any strategic-fit relationships among existing business units.

7. Rank the business units in terms of priority for new capital investment and decide whether the strategic posture for each business unit should be aggressive expansion, fortify and defend, overhaul and reposition, or harvest/divest. (The task of initiating *specific* business-unit strategies to improve the business unit's competitive position is usually delegated to business-level managers, with corporate-level managers offering suggestions and having authority for final approval.)

8. Craft new strategic moves to improve overall corporate performance—change the makeup of the portfolio via acquisitions and divestitures, improve coordination among the activities of related business units to achieve greater cost-sharing and skills-transfer benefits, and steer corporate resources into the areas of greatest opportunity.

The rest of this chapter describes this eight-step process and introduces analytical techniques needed to arrive at sound corporate strategy appraisals.

IDENTIFYING THE PRESENT CORPORATE STRATEGY

Strategic analysis of a diversified company starts by probing the organization's present strategy and business makeup. Recall from Figure 2–2 in Chapter 2 that a good overall perspective of a diversified company's corporate strategy comes from looking at

Evaluating a diversified firm's business portfolio needs to begin with a clear identification of the firm's diversification strategy.

- The extent to which the firm is diversified (as measured by the proportion of total sales and operating profits contributed by each business unit and by whether the diversification base is broad or narrow).

- Whether the firm's portfolio is keyed to related or unrelated diversification, or a mixture of both.

- Whether the scope of company operations is mostly domestic, increasingly multinational, or global.

- The nature of recent moves to boost performance of key business units and/or strengthen existing business positions.

- Any moves to add new businesses to the portfolio and build positions in new industries.

- Any moves to divest weak or unattractive business units.

- Management efforts to realize the benefits of strategic-fit relationships and use diversification to create competitive advantage.

- The proportion of capital expenditures going to each business unit.

Getting a clear fix on the current corporate strategy and its rationale sets the stage for a thorough strategy analysis and, subsequently, for making whatever refinements or major alterations management deems appropriate.

MATRIX TECHNIQUES FOR EVALUATING DIVERSIFIED PORTFOLIOS

One of the most-used techniques for assessing the quality of a diversified company's businesses is portfolio matrix analysis. *A business portfolio matrix is a two-dimensional display comparing the strategic positions of each business a diversified company is in.* Matrices can be constructed using any pair of strategic position indicators. The most revealing indicators are industry growth rate, market share, long-term industry attractiveness, competitive strength, and stage of product/market evolution. Usually one dimension of the matrix relates to the attractiveness of the industry environment and the other to the strength of a business within the industry. Three types of business portfolio matrices are used most frequently—the growth-share matrix developed by the Boston Consulting Group, the industry attractiveness–business strength matrix pioneered at General Electric, and the Hofer–A. D. Little industry life-cycle matrix.

> **A business portfolio matrix is a two-dimensional display comparing the strategic positions of every business a diversified company is in.**

The Growth-Share Matrix

> **The BCG portfolio matrix compares a diversified company's businesses on the basis of industry growth rate and relative market share.**

The first business portfolio matrix to receive widespread use was a four-square grid devised by the Boston Consulting Group (BCG), a leading management consulting firm.[1] Figure 8–1 illustrates a BCG-type matrix. The matrix is formed using *industry growth rate* and *relative market share* as the axes. Each business unit in the corporate portfolio appears as a "bubble" on the four-cell matrix, with the size of each bubble or circle scaled to the percent of revenues it represents in the overall corporate portfolio.

Early BCG methodology arbitrarily placed the dividing line between "high" and "low" industry growth rates at around twice the real GNP growth rate plus inflation, but the boundary can be set at any percentage (5 percent, 10 percent, or whatever) managers consider appropriate. Business units in industries growing faster than the economy as a whole should end up in the "high-growth" cells and those in industries growing slower in the "low-growth" cells ("low-growth" industries are those that are mature, aging, stagnant, or declining). Rarely does it make sense to put the dividing line between high growth and low growth at less than 5 percent.

Relative market share is the ratio of a business's market share to the market share held by the largest rival firm in the industry, with market share measured in unit volume, not dollars. For instance, if business A has a 15 percent share of its industry's total volume and A's largest rival has 30 percent, A's relative market share is 0.5. If business B has a market-leading share of 40 percent and its largest rival has

---

[1]The original presentation is Bruce D. Henderson, "The Experience Curve—Reviewed. IV. The Growth Share Matrix of the Product Portfolio" (Boston: The Boston Consulting Group, 1973), Perspectives No. 135. For an excellent chapter-length treatment of the use of the BCG growth-share matrix in strategic portfolio analysis, see Arnoldo C. Hax and Nicolas S. Majluf, *Strategic Management: An Integrative Perspective* (Englewood Cliffs, N.J.: Prentice-Hall, 1984), chapter 7.

Figure 8–1   The BCG Growth-Share Business Portfolio Matrix

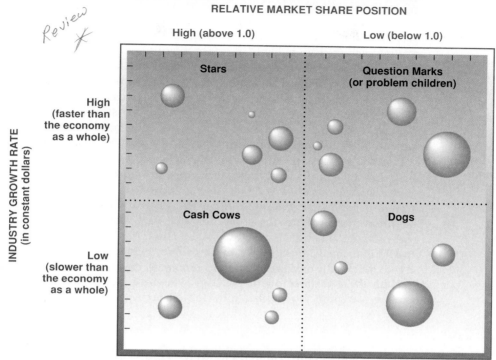

Review ✗

Note: *Relative* market share is defined by the ratio of a company's own market share to the market share held by its largest rival. When the vertical dividing line is set at 1.0, the only way a firm can achieve a star or cash cow position in the growth-share matrix is to have the largest market share in the industry. Since this is a very stringent criterion, it may be "fairer" and more revealing to locate the vertical dividing line in the matrix at about 0.75 or 0.80.

30 percent, B's relative market share is 1.33. Given this definition, only business units that are market share leaders in their respective industries will have relative market shares greater than 1.0. Business units that trail rivals in market share will have ratios below 1.0.

BCG's original standard put the border between "high" and "low" relative market share at 1.0, as shown in Figure 8–1. When the boundary is set at 1.0, circles in the two left-side cells of the matrix represent businesses that are market share leaders in their industries. Circles in the two right-side cells identify businesses that are runners-up in their industries. The degree to which they trail is indicated by the size of the relative market share ratio. A ratio of 0.10 indicates that the business has a market share only one-tenth that of the largest firm in the market; a ratio of 0.80 indicates a market share four-fifths or 80 percent as big as the leading firm's. Many portfolio analysts think that putting the boundary between high and low relative market share at 1.0 is unreasonably stringent because only businesses with the largest market share in their industry qualify for the two left-side cells of the matrix. They advocate putting the boundary at about 0.75 or 0.80 so businesses to the left have *strong* or above-average market positions (even though they are not *the* leader) and businesses to the right are clearly in underdog or below-average positions.

Using *relative* market share instead of *actual* market share to construct the growth-share matrix is analytically superior because the former measure is a better indicator of comparative market strength and competitive position. A 10 percent market share is much stronger if the leader's share is 12 percent than if it is 50 percent; the use of relative market share captures this difference. Equally important, relative market share is likely to reflect relative cost based on experience in producing the product and economies of large-scale production. Large businesses may be able to operate at lower unit costs than smaller firms because of technological and efficiency gains that attach to larger size. But the Boston Consulting Group accumulated evidence that the phenomenon of lower unit costs went beyond just the effects of scale economies; they found that, as the cumulative volume of production increased, the knowledge gained from the firm's growing production experience often led to the discovery of additional efficiencies and ways to reduce costs even further. BCG labeled the relationship between *cumulative production volume* and lower unit costs *the experience curve effect* (for more details, see Figure 3–1 in Chapter 3). A sizable experience curve effect in an industry's value chain places a strategic premium on market share: the competitor that gains the largest market share tends to realize important cost advantages which, in turn, can be used to lower prices and gain still additional customers, sales, market share, and profit. The stronger the experience curve effect in a business, the more dominant its role in strategy-making.[2]

With these features of the BCG growth-share matrix in mind, we are ready to explore the portfolio implications for businesses in each cell of the matrix in Figure 8–1.

> **Relative market share is a better indicator of a business's competitive strength and market position than a simple percentage measure of market share.**

Question Marks and Problem Children   Business units in the upper-right quadrant of the growth-share matrix were labeled by BCG as "question marks" or "problem children." Rapid market growth makes such business units attractive from an industry standpoint. But their low relative market share (and thus reduced access to experience curve effects) raises a question about whether they have the strength to compete successfully against larger, more cost-efficient rivals—hence, the question mark or problem child designation. Question mark businesses, moreover, are typically "cash hogs"—so labeled because their cash needs are high (owing to the large investment needed to finance rapid growth and new product development) and their internal cash generation is low (owing to low market share, less access to experience curve effects and scale economies, and consequently thinner profit margins). A question mark/cash hog business in a fast-growing industry may require large infusions of cash just to keep up with rapid market growth—and even bigger cash infusions if it must outgrow the market and gain enough market share to become an industry leader. The corporate parent of a cash hog/question mark has to decide whether it is worthwhile to fund the perhaps considerable investment requirements of such a business.

BCG has argued that the two best strategic options for a question mark business are (1) an aggressive invest-and-expand strategy to capitalize on the industry's rapid-growth opportunities or (2) divestiture, in the event that the costs of expanding

> **A "cash hog" business is one whose internal cash flows are inadequate to fully fund its needs for working capital and new capital investment.**

---

[2]For two insightful discussions of the strategic importance of the experience curve, see Pankaj Ghemawat, "Building Strategy on the Experience Curve," *Harvard Business Review* 64, no. 2 (March–April 1985), pp. 143–49, and Bruce D. Henderson, "The Application and Misapplication of the Experience Curve," *Journal of Business Strategy* 4, no. 3 (Winter 1984), pp. 3–9.

capacity and building market share outweigh the potential payoff and financial risk. Pursuit of a fast-growth strategy is imperative any time an attractive question mark business is in an industry characterized by a strong experience curve effect; in such cases it takes major gains in market share to begin to match the lower costs of firms with greater cumulative production experience and bigger market shares. The stronger the experience curve effect, the more potent the cost advantages of rivals with larger relative market shares. Consequently, so the BCG thesis goes, unless a question mark/problem child business can successfully pursue a fast-growth strategy and win major market share gains, it cannot hope to become cost competitive with large-volume firms that are further down the experience curve. Divestiture then becomes the only other viable long-run alternative. BCG's corporate strategy prescriptions for question mark/problem child businesses are straightforward: divest those that are weaker and have less chance to catch the leaders on the experience curve; invest heavily in high-potential question marks and groom them to become tomorrow's "stars."

Stars   Businesses with high relative market share positions in high-growth markets rank as stars in the BCG grid because they offer excellent profit and growth opportunities. They are the business units an enterprise depends on to boost overall performance of the total portfolio.

Given their dominant market-share position and rapid growth environment, stars typically require large cash investments to expand production facilities and meet working capital needs. But they also tend to generate their own large internal cash flows due to the low-cost advantage of scale economies and cumulative production experience. Star businesses vary as to their cash hog status. Some can cover their investment needs with self-generated cash flows; others require capital infusions from their corporate parents to stay abreast of rapid industry growth. Normally, strongly positioned star businesses in industries where growth is beginning to slow tend to be self-sustaining in terms of cash flow and make little claim on the corporate parent's treasury. Young stars, however, typically require substantial investment capital *beyond what they can generate on their own* and are thus cash hogs.

Cash Cows   Businesses with a high relative market share in a low growth market are designated "cash cows" in the BCG scheme. A *cash cow business* generates substantial cash surpluses over what is needed for reinvestment and growth. There are two reasons why a business in this box tends to be a cash cow. Because of the business's high relative market share and industry leadership position, it has the sales volumes and reputation to earn attractive profits. Because it is in a slow-growth industry, cash flows from current operations typically exceed what is needed for capital reinvestment and competitive maneuvers to sustain its present market position.

Many of today's cash cows are yesterday's stars, having gradually moved down on the vertical scale (dropping from the top cell into the bottom cell) as industry demand matured. Cash cows, though less attractive from a growth standpoint, are valuable businesses. The surplus cash flows they generate can be used to pay corporate dividends, finance acquisitions, and provide funds for investing in emerging stars and problem children being groomed as future stars. Every effort should be made to keep strong cash cow businesses in healthy condition to preserve their cash-generating capability over the long term. The goal should be to fortify and defend a cash cow's

---

The standard strategy prescriptions for a "question mark" business are to either invest aggressively and grow it into a star performer or else divest it and shift resources to businesses with better prospects.

"Star" businesses have strong competitive positions in rapidly growing industries, are major contributors to corporate revenue and profit growth, and may or may not be cash hogs.

A "cash cow" business is a valuable part of a diversified company's business portfolio because it generates cash for financing new acquisitions, funding the capital requirements of cash hog businesses, and paying dividends.

market position while efficiently generating dollars to redeploy elsewhere. Weakening cash cows (those drifting toward the lower right corner of the cash cow cell) may become candidates for harvesting and eventual divestiture if stiffer competition or increased capital requirements (stemming from new technology) cause cash flow surpluses to dry up or, in the worst case, become negative.

Dogs   Businesses with a low relative market share in a slow-growth industry are called "dogs" because of their dim growth prospects, their trailing market position, and the squeeze that trailing the experience curve leaders puts on their profit margins. Weak dog businesses (those positioned in the lower right corner of the dog cell) often cannot generate attractive long-term cash flows. Sometimes they cannot produce enough cash to support a rear-guard fortify-and-defend strategy—especially if competition is brutal and profit margins are chronically thin. Consequently, except in unusual cases, BCG prescribes that weaker-performing dog businesses be harvested, divested, or liquidated, depending on which alternative yields the most cash.

Implications for Corporate Strategy   The chief contribution of the BCG growth-share matrix is the attention it draws to the cash flow and investment characteristics of various types of businesses and how corporate financial resources can be shifted between business subsidiaries to optimize the performance of the whole corporate portfolio. According to BCG analysis, a sound, long-term corporate strategy should utilize the excess cash generated by cash cow business units to finance market share increases for cash hog businesses—the young stars unable to finance their own growth internally and problem children with the best potential to grow into stars. If successful, the cash hogs eventually become self-supporting stars. Then, when stars' markets begin to mature and their growth slows, they become cash cows. The "success sequence" is thus problem child/question mark to young star (but perhaps still a cash hog) to self-supporting star to cash cow.

Weaker, less-attractive question mark businesses unworthy of a long-term invest-and-expand strategy are often a liability to a diversified company because of the high cost economics associated with their low relative market share and because their cash hog nature typically requires the corporate parent to keep pumping more capital into the business to keep abreast of fast-paced market growth. According to BCG prescriptions, weaker question marks should be prime divestiture candidates *unless* (1) they can be kept profitable and viable with their own internally generated funds or (2) the capital infusions needed from the corporate parent are quite modest.

Not every question mark business is a cash hog or a disadvantaged competitor, however. Those in industries with small capital requirements, few scale economies, and weak experience curve effects can often compete ably against larger industry leaders and contribute enough to corporate earnings and return on investment to justify retention. Clearly, though, weaker question marks still have a low-priority claim on corporate resources and a tenuous role in the portfolio. Question mark businesses unable to become stars are destined to drift vertically downward in the matrix, becoming dogs as their industry growth slows and market demand matures.

Dogs should be retained only as long as they contribute adequately to overall company performance. Strong dogs may produce a positive cash flow and show average profitability. But the further a dog business moves toward the bottom right corner of the BCG matrix, the more likely it is tying up assets that could be redeployed more profitably elsewhere. BCG recommends harvesting a weakening or

---

Weaker "dog" businesses should be harvested, divested, or liquidated; stronger dogs can be retained as long as their profits and cash flows remain acceptable.

The BCG growth-share matrix highlights the cash flow, investment, and profitability characteristics of various types of businesses and the benefits of shifting a diversified company's financial resources between them to optimize the whole portfolio's performance.

already weak dog. When a harvesting strategy is no longer attractive, a weak dog should be eliminated from the portfolio.

There are two "disaster sequences" in the BCG scheme of things: (1) when a star's position in the matrix erodes over time to that of a problem child and then is dragged by slowing industry growth into the dog category and (2) when a cash cow loses market leadership to the point where it becomes a dog on the decline. Other strategic mistakes include overinvesting in a safe cash cow; underinvesting in a high-potential question mark so instead of moving into the star category it tumbles into a dog; and scattering resources thinly over many question marks rather than concentrating on the best question marks to boost their chances of becoming stars.

Strengths and Weaknesses in the Growth-Share Matrix Approach   The BCG business portfolio matrix makes a definite contribution to the corporate strategist's toolkit when it comes to evaluating the attractiveness of a diversified company's businesses and devising general prescriptions for strategy and direction for each business unit in the portfolio. Viewing a diversified group of businesses as a collection of cash flows and cash requirements (present and future) is a major step forward in understanding the financial aspects of corporate strategy. The BCG matrix highlights the financial interaction within a corporate portfolio, shows the kinds of financial considerations that must be dealt with, and explains why priorities for corporate resource allocation can differ from business to business. It also provides good rationalizations for both invest-and-expand strategies and divestiture. Yet, it is analytically incomplete and potentially misleading:

> **The growth-share matrix has significant shortcomings.**

1. A four-cell matrix based on high-low classifications hides the fact that many businesses (the majority?) are in markets with an average growth rate and have relative market shares that are neither high nor low but in between or intermediate. In which cells do these average businesses belong?

2. While viewing businesses as stars, cash cows, dogs, or question marks does have communicative appeal, it is a misleading simplification to classify all businesses into one of four categories. Some market-share leaders are never really stars in terms of profitability. All businesses with low relative market shares are not dogs or question marks—in many cases, runner-up firms have proven track records in terms of growth, profitability, and competitive ability, even gaining on the so-called leaders. Hence, a key characteristic to assess is the *trend* in a firm's relative market share. Is it gaining ground or losing ground and why? This weakness of the matrix can be solved by placing directional arrows on each of the circles in the matrix—see Figure 8–2.

3. The BCG matrix is not a reliable indicator of relative investment opportunities across business units.[3] For example, investing in a star is not necessarily more attractive than investing in a lucrative cash cow. The matrix doesn't indicate if a question mark business is a potential winner or a likely loser. It says nothing about whether shrewd investment can turn a strong dog into a cash cow.

---

[3]Derek F. Abell and John S. Hammond, *Strategic Market Planning* (Englewood Cliffs, N.J.: Prentice-Hall, 1979), p. 212.

Figure 8–2   Present versus Future Positions in the Portfolio Matrix

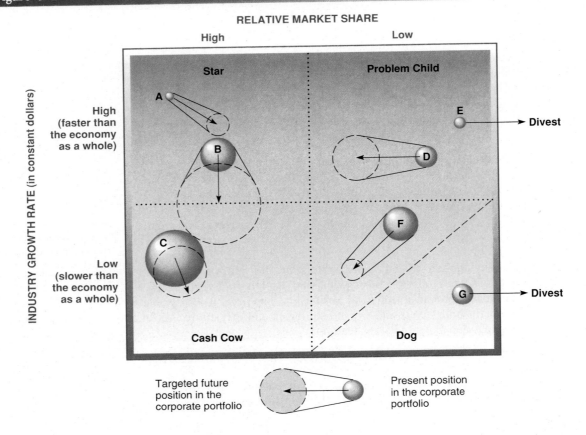

4. Being a market leader in a slow-growth industry does not guarantee cash cow status because (a) the investment requirements of a fortify-and-defend strategy, given the impact of inflation and changing technology on the costs of replacing worn-out facilities and equipment, can soak up much or all of the available internal cash flows and (b) as markets mature, competitive forces often stiffen and the ensuing vigorous battle for volume and market share can shrink profit margins and wipe out any surplus cash flows.

5. To thoroughly assess the relative long-term attractiveness of a group of businesses, corporate strategists need to examine more than just industry growth and relative market share—as our discussion in Chapter 3 clearly indicated.

6. The connection between relative market share and profitability is not as tight as the experience curve effect implies. The importance of cumulative production experience in lowering unit costs varies from industry to industry. Sometimes, a larger market share translates into a unit-cost advantage; sometimes it doesn't. Hence, it is wise to be cautious when prescribing strategy based on the assumption that experience curve effects are strong enough and cost differences among competitors big enough to

totally drive competitive advantage (there are more sources of competitive advantage than just experience curve economics).

The Industry Attractiveness–Business Strength Matrix

An alternative approach that avoids some of the shortcomings of the BCG growth-share matrix was pioneered by General Electric with help from the consulting firm of McKinsey and Company. GE's effort to analyze its broadly diversified portfolio produced a nine-cell matrix based on the two dimensions of long-term industry attractiveness and business strength/competitive position (see Figure 8–3).[4] Both dimensions of the matrix are a composite of several factors as opposed to a single factor. The criteria for determining long-term industry attractiveness include market size and growth rate; technological requirements; the intensity of competition; entry and exit barriers; seasonality and cyclical influences; capital requirements; emerging industry threats and opportunities; historical and projected industry profitability; and social, environmental, and regulatory influences. To arrive at a formal, quantitative measure of long-term industry attractiveness, the chosen measures are assigned weights based on their importance to corporate management and their role in the diversification strategy. The sum of the weights must add up to 1.0. Weighted attractiveness ratings are calculated by multiplying the industry's rating on each factor (using a 1 to 5 or 1 to 10 rating scale) by the factor's weight. For example, a rating score of 8 times a weight of 0.25 gives a weighted rating of 2.0. The sum of weighted ratings for all the attractiveness factors yields the industry's long-term attractiveness. The procedure is shown below:

> **In the attractiveness-strength matrix, each business's location is plotted using quantitative measures of long-term industry attractiveness and business strength/competitive position.**

Industry Attractiveness Factor	Weight	Rating	Weighted Industry Rating
Market size and projected growth	0.15	5	0.75
Seasonality and cyclical influences	0.10	8	0.80
Technological considerations	0.10	1	0.10
Intensity of competition	0.25	4	1.00
Emerging opportunities and threats	0.15	1	0.15
Capital requirements	0.05	2	0.10
Industry profitability	0.10	3	0.30
Social, political, regulatory, and environmental factors	0.10	7	0.70
Industry Attractiveness Rating	1.00		3.90

Attractiveness ratings are calculated for each industry represented in the corporate portfolio. Each industry's attractiveness score determines its position on the vertical scale in Figure 8–3.

To arrive at a quantitative measure of business strength/competitive position, each business in the corporate portfolio is rated using the same kind of approach as for industry attractiveness. The factors used to assess business strength/competitive

---

[4]For an expanded treatment, see Michael G. Allen, "Diagramming GE's Planning for What's WATT," in *Corporate Planning: Techniques and Applications*, ed. Robert J. Allio and Malcolm W. Pennington (New York: AMACOM, 1979), and Hax and Majluf, *Strategic Management: An Integrative Perspective*, chapter 8.

Figure 8–3   General Electric's Industry Attractiveness–Business Strength Matrix

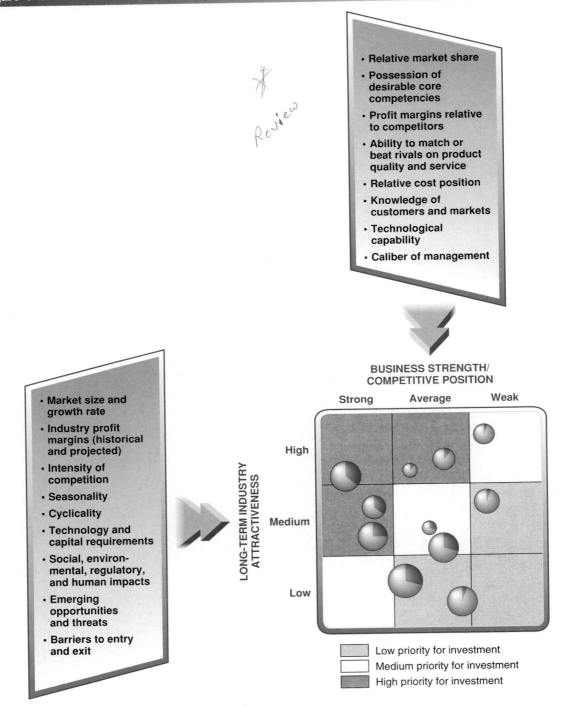

position include such criteria as market share, relative cost position, ability to match rival firms on product quality, knowledge of customers and markets, possession of desirable core competencies, adequacy of technological know-how, caliber of management, and profitability relative to competitors (as specified in the box in Figure 8–3). Analysts have a choice between rating each business unit on the same generic factors (which strengthens the basis for interindustry comparisons) or rating each business unit's strength on the factors most pertinent to its industry (which gives a sharper measure of competitive position than a generic set of factors). Each business's strength/position rating determines its position along the horizontal axis of the matrix—that is, whether it merits a strong, average, or weak designation.[5]

The industry attractiveness and business strength scores provide the basis for locating a business in one of the nine cells of the matrix. In the GE attractiveness-strength matrix, the area of the circles is proportional to the size of the industry, and the pie slices within the circle reflect the business's market share.

Corporate Strategy Implications   The most important strategic implications from the attractiveness-strength matrix concern the assignment of investment priorities to each of the company's business units. Businesses in the three cells at the upper left, where long-term industry attractiveness and business strength/competitive position are favorable, are accorded top investment priority. The strategic prescription for businesses falling in these three cells is "grow and build," with businesses in the high-strong cell having the highest claim on investment funds. Next in priority come businesses positioned in the three diagonal cells stretching from the lower left to the upper right. These businesses are usually given medium priority. They merit steady reinvestment to maintain and protect their industry positions; however, if such a business has an unusually attractive opportunity, it can win a higher investment priority and be given the go-ahead to employ a more aggressive strategic approach. The strategy prescription for businesses in the three cells in the lower right corner of the matrix is typically harvest or divest (in exceptional cases where good turnaround potential exists, it can be "overhaul and reposition" using some type of turnaround approach).[6]

The nine-cell attractiveness-strength approach has three desirable attributes. First, it allows for intermediate rankings between high and low and between strong and weak. Second, it incorporates explicit consideration of a much wider variety of strategically relevant variables. The BCG matrix is based on only two considerations—industry growth rate and relative market share; the nine-cell GE matrix takes many factors into account to determine long-term industry attractiveness and business strength/competitive position. Third, and most important, the nine-cell matrix stresses the channeling of corporate resources to businesses with the greatest probability of achieving competitive advantage and superior performance. It is hard to argue against the logic of concentrating resources in those businesses that enjoy a

---

[5]Essentially the same procedure is used in company situation analysis to do a competitive strength assessment (see Table 4–3 in Chapter 4). The only difference is that in the GE methodology the same set of competitive strength factors is used for every industry to provide a common benchmark for making comparisons across industries. In strategic analysis at the business level, the strength measures are *always* industry specific, never generic generalizations.

[6]At General Electric, each business actually ended up in one of five types of categories: (1) *high-growth potential* businesses deserving top investment priority, (2) *stable base* businesses deserving steady reinvestment to maintain position, (3) *support* businesses deserving periodic investment funding, (4) *selective pruning or rejuvenation* businesses deserving reduced investment funding, and (5) *venture* businesses deserving heavy R&D investment.

The nine-cell attractiveness-strength matrix has a stronger conceptual basis than the four-cell growth-share matrix.

higher degree of attractiveness and competitive strength, being very selective in making investments in businesses with intermediate positions, and withdrawing resources from businesses that are lower in attractiveness and strength unless they offer exceptional turnaround potential.

However, the nine-cell GE matrix, like the four-cell growth-share matrix, provides no real guidance on the specifics of business strategy; the most that can be concluded from the GE matrix analysis is what *general* strategic posture to take: aggressive expansion, fortify and defend, or harvest-divest. Such prescriptions, though valuable from an overall portfolio management perspective, ignore the issue of strategic coordination across related businesses as well as the issue of what specific competitive approaches and strategic actions to take at the business-unit level. Another weakness is that the attractiveness-strength matrix effectively hides businesses that are about to emerge as winners because their industries are entering the takeoff stage.[7]

The Life-Cycle Matrix

The life-cycle matrix highlights how a diversified firm's businesses are distributed across the stages of the industry life-cycle.

To better identify a *developing winner* business, analysts can use a 15-cell matrix where business units are plotted based on stage of industry evolution and strength of competitive position, as shown in Figure 8–4.[8] Again, the circles represent the sizes of the industries involved, and pie wedges denote the business's market share. In Figure 8–4, business A could be labeled a *developing winner;* business C a *potential loser;* business E an *established winner,* business F a cash cow, and business G a loser or a dog. The power of the life-cycle matrix is the story it tells about the distribution of a diversified company's businesses across the stages of industry evolution.

Deciding Which Portfolio Matrix to Construct

Restricting portfolio analysis to just one type of matrix is unwise. Each matrix has its pros and cons, and each tells a different story about the portfolio's strengths and weaknesses. Provided adequate data is available, all three matrices should be constructed since there's merit in assessing the company's business portfolio from different perspectives. Corporate managers need to understand the mix of industries represented in the portfolio, the strategic position each business has in its industry, the portfolio's performance potential, and the kinds of financial and resource allocation considerations that have to be dealt with. Using all three matrices to view a diversified portfolio enhances such understanding.

COMPARING INDUSTRY ATTRACTIVENESS

The more attractive the industries that a company has diversified into, the better its performance prospects.

A principal consideration in evaluating a diversified company's strategy is the attractiveness of the industries it has diversified into. The more attractive these industries, the better the company's long-term profit prospects. Industry attractiveness needs to be evaluated from three perspectives:

---

[7]Charles W. Hofer and Dan Schendel, *Strategy Formulation: Analytical Concepts* (St. Paul, Minn.: West Publishing, 1978), p. 33.

[8]Ibid., p. 34. This approach to business portfolio analysis was reportedly first used in actual practice by consultants at Arthur D. Little, Inc. For a full-scale review of this portfolio matrix approach, see Hax and Majluf, *Strategic Management: An Integrative Perspective,* chapter 9.

Figure 8–4   The Life-Cycle Portfolio Matrix

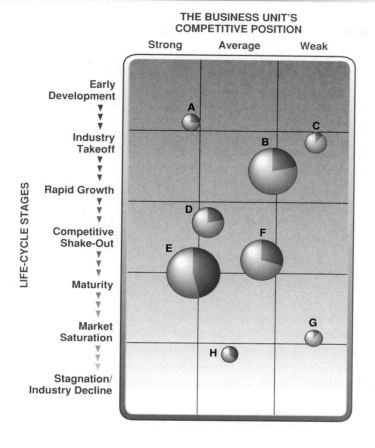

1. *The attractiveness of each industry represented in the business portfolio.*
   The relevant question is "Is this a good industry for the company to be
   in?" Ideally, each industry the firm has diversified into can pass the
   attractiveness test.

2. *Each industry's attractiveness relative to the others.* The question to
   answer here is "Which industries in the portfolio are the most attractive
   and which are the least attractive?" Ranking the industries from most
   attractive to least attractive is a prerequisite for deciding how to allocate
   corporate resources.

3. *The attractiveness of all the industries as a group.* The question here is
   "How appealing is the mix of industries?" A company whose revenues
   and profits come chiefly from businesses in unattractive industries
   probably needs to consider restructuring its business portfolio.

All the industry attractiveness considerations discussed in Chapter 3 have application in this analytical phase.

An industry attractiveness-business strength portfolio matrix provides a strong,
systematic basis for judging which business units are in the most attractive industries.
If such a matrix has not been constructed, quantitative rankings of industry attractiveness can be developed using the same procedure described earlier for the nine-cell

GE portfolio matrix. As a rule, all the industries represented in the business portfolio should, at minimum, be judged on the following attractiveness factors:

- *Market size and projected growth rate*—faster-growing industries tend to be more attractive than slow-growing industries, other things being equal.
- *The intensity of competition*—industries where competitive pressures are relatively weak are more attractive than industries where competitive pressures are strong.
- *Technological and production skills required*—industries where the skill requirements are closely matched to company capabilities are more attractive than industries where the company's technical and/or manufacturing know-how is limited.
- *Capital requirements*—industries with low capital requirements (or amounts within the company's reach) are relatively more attractive than industries where investment requirements could strain corporate financial resources.
- *Seasonal and cyclical factors*—industries where demand is relatively stable and dependable are more attractive than industries where there are wide swings in buyer demand.
- *Industry profitability*—industries with healthy profit margins and high rates of return on investment are generally more attractive than industries where profits have historically been low or where the business risks are high.
- *Social, political, regulatory, and environmental factors*—industries with significant problems in these areas are less attractive than industries where such problems are no worse than most businesses encounter.
- *Strategic fits with other industries the firm has diversified into*—an industry can be attractive simply because it has valuable strategic-fit relationships with other industries represented in the portfolio.

Calculation of industry attractiveness ratings for all industries in the corporate portfolio provides a basis for ranking the industries from most to least attractive. If formal industry attractiveness ratings seem too cumbersome or tedious to calculate, corporate managers can rely on their knowledge of conditions in each industry to classify individual industries as having "high," "medium," or "low" attractiveness. However, the validity of such subjective assessments depends on whether management has probed industry conditions sufficiently to make dependable judgments.

For a diversified company to be a strong performer, a substantial portion of its revenues and profits must come from business units judged to be in attractive industries. It is particularly important that core businesses be in industries with a good outlook for growth and above-average profitability. Business units in the least attractive industries may be divestiture candidates, unless they are positioned strongly enough to overcome the adverse industry environment or they are a strategically important component of the portfolio.

COMPARING BUSINESS-UNIT STRENGTH

Doing an appraisal of each business unit's strength and competitive position in its industry helps corporate managers judge a business unit's chances for success. The task here is to evaluate whether the business is well-positioned in its industry and the extent to which it already is or can become a strong market contender. The two most revealing techniques for evaluating a business's position in its industry are SWOT analysis and competitive strength assessment. Quantitative rankings of the strength/position of the various business units in the corporate portfolio can be calculated using either the procedure described in constructing the attractiveness-strength matrix or the procedure presented in Chapter 4. Assessments of how a diversified company's business subsidiaries compare in competitive strength should be based on such factors as

- *Relative market share*—business units with higher relative market shares normally have greater competitive strength than those with lower shares.
- *Ability to compete on price and/or quality*—business units that are very cost competitive and/or have established brand names and reputations for excellent product quality tend to be more strongly positioned in their industries than business units struggling to establish recognized names or to achieve cost parity with major rivals.
- *Technology and innovation capabilities*—business units recognized for their technological leadership and track record in innovation are usually strong competitors in their industry.
- *How well the business unit's skills and competences match industry key success factors*—the more a business unit's strengths match the industry's key success factors, the stronger its competitive position tends to be.
- *Profitability relative to competitors*—business units that consistently earn above-average returns on investment and have bigger profit margins than their rivals usually have stronger competitive positions than business units with below-average profitability for their industry. Moreover, above-average profitability signals competitive advantage while below-average profitability usually denotes competitive disadvantage.

Other competitive strength indicators that can be employed include knowledge of customers and markets, production capabilities, marketing skills, reputation and brand name awareness, and the caliber of management.

Calculation of competitive strength ratings for each business unit provides a basis for judging which ones are in strong positions in their industries and which are in weak positions. If analysts lack sufficient data, they can rely on their knowledge of each business unit's competitive situation to classify it as being in a "strong," "average," or "weak" competitive position. If trustworthy, such subjective assessments of business-unit strength can substitute for quantitative measures.

Managerial evaluations of which businesses in the portfolio enjoy the strongest competitive positions add further rationale and justification for corporate resource allocation. A company may earn larger profits over the long term by investing in a business with a competitively strong position in a moderately attractive industry than by investing in a weak business in a glamour industry. This is why a diversified company needs to consider *both* industry attractiveness and business strength in deciding where to steer resources.

Shareholder interests are generally best served by concentrating corporate resources on businesses that can contend for market leadership in their industries.

Many diversified companies concentrate their resources on industries where they can be strong market contenders and divest businesses that are not good candidates for becoming leaders. At General Electric, the whole thrust of corporate strategy and corporate resource allocation is to put GE's businesses into a number one or two position in both the United States and globally—see Illustration Capsule 26.

When Jack Welch became CEO of General Electric in 1981, he launched a corporate strategy effort to reshape the company's diversified business portfolio. Early on he issued a challenge to GE's business-unit managers to become number one or number two in their industry; failing that, the business units either had to capture a decided technological advantage translatable into a competitive edge or face possible divestiture.

By 1989, GE was a different company. Under Welch's prodding, GE divested operations worth $9 billion—TV operations, small appliances, a mining business, and computer chips. It spent a total of $24 billion acquiring new businesses, most notably RCA, Roper (a maker of major appliances whose biggest customer was Sears), and Kidder Peabody (a Wall Street investment banking firm). Internally, many of the company's smaller business operations were put under the direction of larger "strategic business units." But, most significantly, in 1989, 12 of GE's 14 strategic business units were market leaders in the United States and globally (the company's financial services and communications units served markets too fragmented to rank).

In 1989, having divested most of the weak businesses and having built existing businesses into leading contenders, Welch launched a new initiative within GE to dramatically boost productivity and reduce the size of GE's bureaucracy. Welch argued that for GE to continue to be successful in a global marketplace, the company had to press hard for continuous cost reduction in each of its businesses and cut through bureaucratic procedures to shorten response times to changing market conditions.

GE Strategic Business Units	Market Standing in the United States	Market Standing in the World
Aircraft Engines	First	First
Broadcasting (NBC)	First	Not applicable
Circuit breakers	Tied for first with two others	Tied for first with three others
Defense electronics	Second	Second
Electric motors	First	First
Engineering plastics	First	First
Factory automation	Second	Third
Industrial and power systems	First	First
Lighting	First	Second
Locomotives	First	Tied for first
Major home appliances	First	Tied for second
Medical diagnostic imaging	First	First

Source: Developed from information in Stratford P. Sherman, "Inside the Mind of Jack Welch," *Fortune*, March 27, 1989, pp. 39–50.

COMPARING BUSINESS-UNIT PERFORMANCE

Once each business subsidiary is rated on the basis of industry attractiveness and competitive strength, the next step is to evaluate which businesses have the best performance prospects and which ones the worst. The most important considerations in judging business-unit performance are sales growth, profit growth, contribution to company earnings, and the return on capital invested in the business; sometimes, cash flow generation is a big consideration, especially for cash cow businesses or businesses with potential for harvesting. Information on each business's past performance can be gleaned from financial records. While past performance is not necessarily a good predictor of future performance, it does signal which businesses have been strong performers and which have been weak performers. The industry attractiveness-business strength evaluations should provide a solid basis for judging future prospects. Normally, strong business units in attractive industries have significantly better prospects than weak businesses in unattractive industries.

The growth and profit outlooks for the company's core businesses generally determine whether the portfolio as a whole will turn in a strong or weak performance. Noncore businesses with subpar track records and little expectation for improvement are logical candidates for divestiture. Business subsidiaries with the brightest profit and growth prospects generally should head the list for capital investment.

STRATEGIC-FIT ANALYSIS

The next analytical step is to determine how well each business unit fits into the company's overall business picture. Fit needs to be looked at from two angles: (1) whether a business unit has valuable strategic fit with other businesses the firm has diversified into (or has an opportunity to diversify into) and (2) whether the business unit meshes well with corporate strategy or adds a beneficial dimension to the corporate portfolio. A business is more attractive *strategically* when it has activity-sharing, skills transfer, or brand-name transfer opportunities that enhance competitive advantage, and when it fits in with the firm's strategic direction. A business is more valuable *financially* when it is capable of contributing heavily to corporate performance objectives (sales growth, profit growth, above-average return on investment, and so on) and when it materially enhances the company's overall worth. Just as businesses with poor profit prospects ought to become divestiture candidates, so should businesses that don't fit strategically into the company's overall business picture. Firms that emphasize related diversification probably should divest businesses with little or no strategic fit unless such businesses are unusually good financial performers or offer superior growth opportunities.

> **Business subsidiaries that don't fit strategically should be considered for divestiture unless their financial performance is outstanding.**

RANKING THE BUSINESS UNITS ON INVESTMENT PRIORITY

Using the information and results of the preceding evaluation steps, corporate strategists can rank business units in terms of priority for new capital investment and decide on a general strategic direction for each business unit. The task is to determine where the corporation should be investing its financial resources. Which business units should have top priority for new capital investment and financial support? Which business units should carry the lowest priority for new investment? The ranking process should clarify management thinking about what the basic strategic approach for each business unit should be—invest-and-grow (aggressive expansion), fortify-and-defend (protect current position with new investments as needed), overhaul-and-reposition (try to move the business into a more desirable industry position and to a better spot in the business portfolio matrix), or harvest-divest. In deciding whether to divest a business unit, corporate managers should rely on a number of evaluating criteria: industry attractiveness, competitive strength, strategic fit with other businesses, performance potential (profit, return on capital employed, contribution to cash flow), compatibility with corporate priorities, capital requirements, and value to the overall portfolio.

Improving a diversified company's long-term financial performance entails concentrating company resources on businesses with good to excellent prospects and investing minimally, if at all, in businesses with subpar prospects.

In ranking the business units on investment priority, consideration needs to be given to whether and how corporate resources and skills can be used to enhance the competitive standing of particular business units.[9] The potential for skills transfer and infusion of new capital becomes especially important when the firm has business units in less than desirable competitive positions and/or where improvement in some key success area could make a big difference to the business unit's performance. It is also important when corporate strategy is predicated on strategic fits that involve transferring corporate skills to recently acquired business units to strengthen their competitive capabilities.[10]

CRAFTING A CORPORATE STRATEGY

The preceding analysis sets the stage for crafting strategic moves to improve a diversified company's overall performance. The basic issue of "what to do" hinges on the conclusions drawn about the overall mix of businesses in the portfolio.[11] Key considerations here are: Does the portfolio contain enough businesses in very attractive industries? Does the portfolio contain too many marginal businesses or question marks? Is the proportion of mature or declining businesses so great that corporate growth will be sluggish? Does the firm have enough cash cows to finance the stars and emerging winners? Can the company's core businesses be counted on to generate dependable profits and/or cash flow? Is the portfolio overly vulnerable to seasonal or recessionary influences? Does the portfolio contain businesses that the company really doesn't need to be in? Is the firm burdened with too many businesses in average-to-weak competitive positions? Does the makeup of the business portfolio put the company in good position for the future? Answers to these questions indicate whether corporate strategists should consider divesting certain businesses, making new acquisitions, or restructuring the makeup of the portfolio.

The Performance Test

A good test of the strategic and financial attractiveness of a diversified firm's business portfolio is whether the company can attain its performance objectives with its current lineup of businesses. If so, no major corporate strategy changes are indicated. However, if a performance shortfall is probable, corporate strategists can take any of several actions to close the gap:[12]

1. *Alter the strategic plans for some (or all) of the businesses in the portfolio.* This option involves renewed corporate efforts to get better performance out of its present business units. Corporate managers can push business-level managers for better business-unit performance. However, pursuing better short-term performance, if done too zealously, can impair a business's potential for performing better over the long term. Cancelling expenditures that will bolster a business's long-term

---

[9]Hofer and Schendel, *Strategy Formulation: Analytical Concepts*, p. 80.
[10]Michael E. Porter, *Competitive Advantage* (New York: Free Press, 1985), chapter 9.
[11]Barry Hedley, "Strategy and the Business Portfolio," *Long Range Planning* 10, no. 1 (February 1977), p. 13; and Hofer and Schendel, *Strategy Formulation*, pp. 82–86.
[12]Hofer and Schendel, *Strategy Formulation: Analytical Concepts*, pp. 93–100.

competitive position in order to squeeze out better short-term financial performance is a perilous strategy. In any case there are limits on how much extra performance can be squeezed out to reach established targets.

2. *Add new business units to the corporate portfolio.* Boosting overall performance by making new acquisitions and/or starting new businesses internally raises some new strategy issues. Expanding the corporate portfolio means taking a close look at *(a)* whether to acquire related or unrelated businesses, *(b)* what size acquisition(s) to make, *(c)* how the new unit(s) will fit into the present corporate structure, *(d)* what specific features to look for in an acquisition candidate, and *(e)* whether acquisitions can be financed without shortchanging present business units on their new investment requirements. Nonetheless, adding new businesses is a major strategic option, one frequently used by diversified companies to escape sluggish earnings performance.

3. *Divest weak-performing or money-losing businesses.* The most likely candidates for divestiture are businesses in a weak competitive position, in a relatively unattractive industry, or in an industry that does not "fit." Funds from divestitures can, of course, be used to finance new acquisitions, pay down corporate debt, or fund new strategic thrusts in the remaining businesses.

4. *Form alliances to try to alter conditions responsible for subpar performance potentials.* In some situations, alliances with domestic or foreign firms, trade associations, suppliers, customers, or special interest groups may help ameliorate adverse performance prospects.[13] Forming or supporting a political action group may be an effective way of lobbying for solutions to import-export problems, tax disincentives, and onerous regulatory requirements.

5. *Lower corporate performance objectives.* Adverse market circumstances or declining fortunes in one or more core business units can render companywide performance targets unreachable. So can overly ambitious objective-setting. Closing the gap between actual and desired performance may then require revision of corporate objectives to bring them more in line with reality. Lowering performance objectives is usually a "last resort" option, used only after other options come up short.

Finding Additional Diversification Opportunities

One of the major corporate strategy-making concerns in a diversified company is whether to pursue further diversification and, if so, how to identify the "right" kinds of industries and businesses to get into. For firms pursuing unrelated diversification, the issue of where to diversify next always remains wide open—the search for acquisition candidates is based more on financial criteria than on industry or strategic criteria. Decisions to add unrelated businesses to the firm's portfolio are usually based on such considerations as whether the firm has the financial ability to make another acquisition, whether new acquisitions are badly needed to boost overall

---

[13]For an excellent discussion of the benefits of alliances among competitors in global industries, see Kenichi Ohmae, "The Global Logic of Strategic Alliances," *Harvard Business Review* 67, no. 2 (March–April 1989), pp. 143–54.

Firms with unrelated diversification strategies hunt for businesses that offer attractive financial returns—regardless of what industry they're in.

Firms with related diversification strategies look for an attractive industry with good strategic fit.

corporate performance, whether one or more acquisition opportunities have to be acted on before they are purchased by other firms, and whether the timing is right for another acquisition (corporate management may have its hands full dealing with the current portfolio of businesses).

With a related diversification strategy, however, the search for new industries is aimed at identifying industries whose value chains have fits with the value chains of one or more businesses represented in the company's business portfolio.[14] The interrelationships can concern (1) product or process R&D, (2) opportunities for joint manufacturing and assembly, (3) marketing, distribution channel, or common brand-name usage, (4) customer overlaps, (5) opportunities for joint after-sale service, or (6) common managerial know-how requirements—essentially any area where market-related, operating, or management fits can occur.

Once strategic-fit opportunities outside a diversified firm's related business portfolio are identified, corporate strategists have to distinguish between opportunities where important competitive advantage potential exists (through cost savings, skill transfers, and so on) and those where the strategic-fit benefits are minor. The size of the competitive advantage potential depends on whether the strategic-fit benefits are competitively significant, how much it will cost to capture the benefits, and how difficult it will be to merge or coordinate the business unit interrelationships.[15] Often, careful analysis reveals that while there are many actual and potential business unit interrelationships and linkages, only a few have enough strategic importance to generate meaningful competitive advantage.

Deploying Corporate Resources

To get ever-higher levels of performance out of a diversified company's business portfolio, corporate managers also have to do an effective job of allocating corporate resources. They have to steer resources out of low-opportunity areas into high-opportunity areas. Divesting marginal businesses is one of the best ways of freeing unproductive assets for redeployment. Surplus funds from cash cow businesses and businesses being harvested also add to the corporate treasury. Options for allocating these funds include (1) investing in ways to strengthen or expand existing businesses, (2) making acquisitions to establish positions in new industries, (3) funding long-range R&D ventures, (4) paying off existing long-term debt, (5) increasing dividends, and (6) repurchasing the company's stock. The first three are *strategic* actions; the last three are *financial* moves. Ideally, a company will have enough funds to serve both its strategic and financial purposes. If not, strategic uses of corporate resources should take precedence over financial uses except in unusual and compelling circumstances.

GUIDELINES FOR MANAGING THE PROCESS OF CRAFTING CORPORATE STRATEGY

Although formal analysis and entrepreneurial brainstorming normally undergird the corporate strategy-making process, there is more to where corporate strategy comes from and how it evolves. Rarely is there an all-inclusive grand formulation of the

---

[14]Porter, *Competitive Advantage*, pp. 370–371.
[15]Ibid., pp. 371–72.

total corporate strategy. Instead, corporate strategy in major enterprises emerges incrementally from the unfolding of many different internal and external events, the result of probing the future, experimenting, gathering more information, sensing problems, building awareness of the various options, spotting new opportunities, developing ad hoc responses to unexpected crises, communicating consensus as it emerges, and acquiring a feel for all the strategically relevant factors, their importance, and their interrelationships.[16]

Strategic analysis is not something that the executives of diversified companies do all at once in comprehensive fashion. Such big reviews are sometimes scheduled, but research indicates that major strategic decisions emerge gradually rather than from periodic, full-scale analysis followed by prompt decision. Typically, top executives approach major strategic decisions a step at a time, often starting from broad, intuitive conceptions and then embellishing, fine-tuning, and modifying their original thinking as more information is gathered, as formal analysis confirms or modifies their judgments about the situation, and as confidence and consensus build for what strategic moves need to be made. Often attention and resources are concentrated on a few critical strategic thrusts that illuminate and integrate corporate direction, objectives, and strategies.

Key Points

Strategic analysis in diversified companies is an eight-step process:

Step 1: *Get a clear fix on the present strategy*—whether the emphasis is on related or unrelated diversification; whether the scope of company operations is mostly domestic, increasingly multinational, or global; recent moves to add new businesses and build positions in new industries; recent divestitures; any efforts to capture strategic fits and create competitive advantage based on economies of scope, skills transfer, or shared brand name; and how much capital is being invested in each business. This step sets the stage for thorough evaluation of the need for strategy changes.

Step 2: *Construct a four-cell growth-share matrix, a nine-cell attractiveness-business strength matrix, and/or a life-cycle matrix to expose the strategic quality of the company's portfolio and the relative positions of its different businesses.* The nine-cell attractiveness-business strength matrix is conceptually and methodologically superior to the four-cell growth-share matrix, mainly because it incorporates consideration of a richer variety of strategically relevant considerations.

Step 3: *Evaluate the relative attractiveness of each industry represented in the company's portfolio.* If a nine-cell industry attractiveness-business strength matrix was constructed in Step 2, then the information is already available. Quantitative ratings of industry attractiveness, using the methodology described, are more systematic and reliable than qualitative subjective judgments.

Step 4: *Evaluate the relative competitive positions and business strength of each of the company's business units.* Again, this is a simple step if

---

[16]Ibid., pp. 58 and 196.

a nine-cell industry attractiveness-business strength matrix has been constructed. As always, quantitative ratings of competitive strength, using the same methodology as for industry attractiveness or the methodology presented in Table 4–4 in Chapter 4, are preferable to subjective judgments.

Step 5: *Rank the past performance of different business units from best to worst and rank their future performance prospects from best to worst.* Normally, strong business units in attractive industries have significantly better prospects than weak businesses or businesses in unattractive industries. This step provides a basis for concluding how well the portfolio as a whole should perform in the future.

Step 6: *Determine which businesses have important strategic fits with other businesses in the portfolio and how well each business fits in with the parent company's direction and strategy.* A business is more attractive *strategically* if it contributes economies of scope, skills transfer opportunities, and shared brand-name opportunities and if it is a business the parent company should be in for the foreseeable future. A business is more attractive *financially* if it is capable of contributing heavily to the firm's future financial performance.

Step 7: *Rank the business units from highest to lowest in investment priority,* thereby determining where the parent company should concentrate new capital investments. Also, determine a general strategic direction for each business unit (invest-and-expand, fortify-and-defend, overhaul-and-reposition, harvest, or divest).

Step 8: *Use the preceding analysis to craft a series of moves to improve overall corporate performance.* The most advantageous actions include

- Making acquisitions, starting new businesses from within, and divesting marginal businesses or businesses that no longer match the corporate direction and strategy.

- Devising moves to strengthen the long-term competitive positions of the company's core businesses.

- Acting to create strategic-fit opportunities and turn them into long-term competitive advantage.

- Steering corporate resources out of low-opportunity areas into high-opportunity areas.

Suggested Readings   Bettis, Richard A., and William K. Hall. "Strategic Portfolio Management in the Multibusiness Firm." *California Management Review* 24 (Fall 1981), pp. 23–38.

———. "The Business Portfolio Approach—Where It Falls Down in Practice." *Long Range Planning* 16, no. 2 (April 1983), pp. 95–104.

Christensen, H. Kurt, Arnold C. Cooper, and Cornelius A. Dekluyuer. "The Dog Business: A Reexamination." *Business Horizons* 25, no. 6 (November–December 1982), pp. 12–18.

Haspeslagh, Phillippe. "Portfolio Planning: Uses and Limits." *Harvard Business Review* 60, no. 1 (January–February 1982), pp. 58–73.

Haspeslagh, Phillippe C., and David B. Jamison. *Managing Acquisitions: Creating Value through Corporate Renewal.* New York: Free Press, 1991.

Hax, Arnoldo, and Nicolas S. Majluf. *Strategic Management: An Integrative Perspective.* Englewood Cliffs, N.J.: Prentice-Hall, 1984, chaps. 7–9.

———. *The Strategy Concept and Process.* Englewood Cliffs, N.J.: Prentice-Hall, 1991, chaps. 8–11 and 15.

Henderson, Bruce D. "The Application and Misapplication of the Experience Curve." *Journal of Business Strategy* 4, no. 3 (Winter 1984), pp. 3–9.

Naugle, David G., and Garret A. Davies. "Strategic-Skill Pools and Competitive Advantage." *Business Horizons* 30, no. 6 (November–December 1987), pp. 35–42.

Porter, Michael E. *Competitive Advantage.* New York: Free Press, 1985, chaps. 9–11.

———. "From Competitive Advantage to Corporate Strategy." *Harvard Business Review* 65, no. 3 (May–June 1987), pp. 43–59.

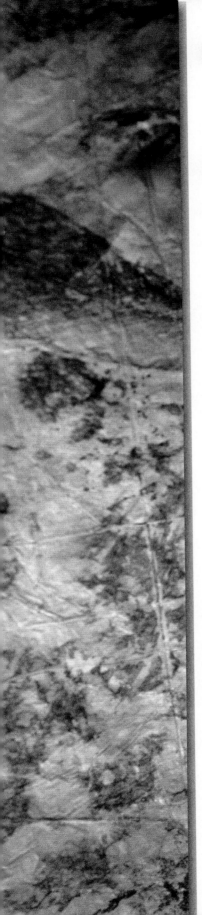

CHAPTER NINE

Implementing Strategy: Core competencies, reengineering, and structure

We strategize beautifully, we implement pathetically.

An auto-parts firm executive

Just being able to conceive bold new strategies is not enough. The general manager must also be able to translate his or her strategic vision into concrete steps that "get things done."

Richard G. Hamermesh

Organizing is what you do before you do something, so that when you do it, it is not all mixed up.

A. A. Milne

Once managers have decided on a strategy, the next step is to convert it into actions and good results. Putting a strategy into place and getting the organization to execute it well call for a different set of managerial tasks and skills. Whereas crafting strategy is largely a market-driven entrepreneurial activity, implementing strategy is primarily an operations-driven activity revolving around the management of people and business processes. Whereas successful strategy-making depends on business vision, shrewd industry and competitive analysis, and entrepreneurial creativity, successful strategy implementation depends on leading, motivating, and working with and through others to create strong "fits" between how the organization performs its core business activities and the requirements for good strategy execution. Implementing strategy is an action-oriented, make-things-happen task that tests a manager's ability to direct organizational change, design and supervise business processes, motivate people, and achieve performance targets.

Experienced managers, savvy in strategy-making and strategy-implementing, are emphatic in declaring that it is a whole lot easier to develop a sound strategic plan than it is to make it happen. According to one executive, "It's been rather easy for us to decide where we wanted to go. The hard part is to get the organization to act on the new priorities."[1] What makes strategy implementation a tougher, more time-consuming management challenge than crafting strategy is the wide array of managerial activities that have to be attended to, the many ways managers can proceed, the demanding people-management skills required, the perseverance it takes to get a variety of initiatives launched and moving, the number of bedeviling issues that must be worked out, and the resistance to change that must be overcome. *Just because managers announce a new strategy doesn't mean that subordinates will agree with it or cooperate in implementing it.* Some may be skeptical about the merits of the strategy, seeing it as contrary to the organization's best interests, unlikely to succeed, or threatening to their own careers. Moreover, company personnel may interpret the new strategy differently, be uncertain about how their departments will fare, and have different ideas about the internal changes the new strategy will entail. Long-standing attitudes, vested interests, inertia, and ingrained organizational practices don't melt away when managers decide on a new strategy and start to implement it. It takes adept managerial leadership to overcome pockets of doubt and disagreement, build consensus for how to proceed, secure the commitment and cooperation of concerned parties, and get all the implementation pieces into place. Depending on how much consensus building and organizational change is involved, the implementation process can take several months to several years.

> **The strategy-implementer's task is to convert the strategic plan into action and get on with what needs to be done to achieve the targeted strategic and financial objectives.**

> **Companies don't implement strategies, people do.**

A FRAMEWORK FOR IMPLEMENTING STRATEGY

Implementing strategy entails converting the organization's strategic plan into action and then into results. Like crafting strategy, it's a job for the whole management team, not a few senior managers. While an organization's chief executive officer and the heads of major organizational units (business divisions, functional departments, and key operating units) are ultimately responsible for seeing that strategy is implemented successfully, the implementation process typically impacts every part of the organizational structure, from the biggest operating unit to the smallest frontline work group. Every manager has to think through the answer to "What has to be done in my area to implement our part of the strategic plan, and what should I do to get these things accomplished?" In this sense, all managers become strategy-implementers in their areas of authority and responsibility, and all employees are participants. One of the keys to successful implementation is communication. Management must present the case for organizational change so clearly and persuasively that there is determined commitment throughout the ranks to carry out the strategy and meet performance targets. Ideally, managers turn the implementation process into a companywide crusade. When they achieve the strategic objectives and financial and operating performance targets, they can consider the implementation successful.

> **Every manager has an active role in the process of implementing and executing the firm's strategic plan.**

Unfortunately, there are no 10-step checklists, no proven paths, and few concrete guidelines for tackling the job—strategy implementation is the least charted, most open-ended part of strategic management. The best evidence on do's and don'ts comes from personal experiences, anecdotal reports, and case studies—and the wisdom they yield is inconsistent. What's worked well for some managers has been tried by others and found lacking. The reasons are understandable. Not only are some

> **Managing strategy implementation is more art than science.**

---

[1]As quoted in Steven W. Floyd and Bill Wooldridge, "Managing Strategic Consensus: The Foundation of Effective Implementation," *Academy of Management Executive* 6, no. 4 (November 1992), p. 27.

managers more effective than others in employing this or that recommended approach to organizational change but each instance of strategy implementation takes place in a different organizational context. Different business practices and competitive circumstances, different work environments and cultures, different policies, different compensation incentives, and different mixes of personalities and organizational histories require a customized approach to strategy implementation—one based on individual situations and circumstances, the strategy-implementer's best judgment, and the implementer's ability to use particular change techniques adeptly.

The Principal Tasks

While managers' approaches should be tailor-made for the situation, certain bases have to be covered no matter what the organization's circumstances; these include

- Building an organization capable of carrying out the strategy successfully.
- Developing budgets to steer ample resources into those value-chain activities critical to strategic success.
- Establishing strategically appropriate policies and procedures.
- Instituting best practices and mechanisms for continuous improvement.
- Installing support systems that enable company personnel to carry out their strategic roles successfully day in and day out.
- Tying rewards and incentives to the achievement of performance objectives and good strategy execution.
- Creating a strategy-supportive work environment and corporate culture.
- Exerting the internal leadership needed to drive implementation forward and to keep improving on how the strategy is being executed.

These managerial tasks crop up repeatedly in the strategy implementation process, no matter what the specifics of the situation, and drive the priorities on the strategy-implementer's agenda—as depicted in Figure 9–1. One or two of these tasks usually end up being more crucial or time-consuming than others, depending on the organization's financial condition and competitive capabilities, the nature and extent of the strategic change involved, the requirements for creating sustainable competitive advantage, the strength of ingrained behavior patterns that have to be changed, whether there are important weaknesses to correct or new competencies to develop, the configuration of personal and organizational relationships in the firm's history, any pressures for quick results and near-term financial improvements, and all other relevant factors.

In devising an action agenda, strategy-implementers should begin with a probing assessment of what the organization must do differently and better to carry out the strategy successfully, then consider how to make the necessary internal changes as rapidly as practical. The strategy-implementer's action priorities should concentrate on fitting how the organization performs its value-chain activities and conducts its internal business to what it takes for first-rate strategy execution. A series of "fits" are needed. Organizational skills and capabilities must be carefully matched to the requirements of strategy—especially if the chosen strategy is predicated on a competence-based competitive advantage. Resources must be allocated in a manner calculated to provide departments with the people and operating budgets needed to execute their strategic roles effectively. The company's reward structure, policies, information systems, and operating practices need to push for strategy execution,

Figure 9–1   The Eight Big Managerial Components of Implementing Strategy

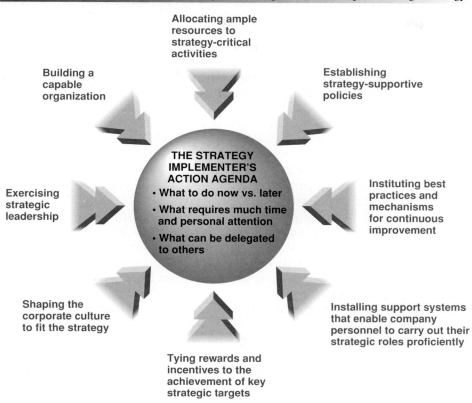

Allocating ample resources to strategy-critical activities

Building a capable organization

Establishing strategy-supportive policies

THE STRATEGY IMPLEMENTER'S ACTION AGENDA
- What to do now vs. later
- What requires much time and personal attention
- What can be delegated to others

Exercising strategic leadership

Instituting best practices and mechanisms for continuous improvement

Shaping the corporate culture to fit the strategy

Installing support systems that enable company personnel to carry out their strategic roles proficiently

Tying rewards and incentives to the achievement of key strategic targets

rather than playing a merely passive role or, even worse, acting as obstacles. Equally important, is the need for managers to do things in a manner and style that create and nurture a strategy-supportive work environment and corporate culture. The stronger such fits, the better the chances for successful strategy implementation. Systematic management efforts to match how the organization goes about its business with the needs of good strategy execution help unite the organization in a team effort to achieve the intended performance outcomes. Successful strategy-implementers have a knack for diagnosing what their organizations need to do to execute the chosen strategy well, and they are creative in finding ways to perform key value-chain activities effectively.

Leading the Implementation Process

One make-or-break determinant of successful strategy implementation is how well management leads the process. Managers can exercise leadership in many ways. They can play an active, visible role or a low-key, behind-the-scenes one. They can make decisions authoritatively or on the basis of consensus; delegate much or little; be personally involved in the details of implementation or stand on the sidelines and coach others; proceed swiftly (launching implementation initiatives on many fronts) or deliberately (remaining content with gradual progress over a long time frame).

How managers lead the implementation task tends to be a function of (1) their experience and knowledge about the business; (2) whether they are new to the job or veterans; (3) their network of personal relationships with others in the organization; (4) their own diagnostic, administrative, interpersonal, and problem-solving skills; (5) the authority they've been given; (6) the leadership style they're comfortable with; and (7) their view of the role they need to play to get things done.

Although major initiatives to implement corporate and business strategies usually have to be led by the CEO and other senior officers, top-level managers still have to rely on the active support and cooperation of middle and lower managers to push strategy changes into functional areas and operating units and to carry out the strategy effectively on a daily basis. Middle- and lower-level managers not only are responsible for initiating and supervising the implementation process in their areas of authority but they also are instrumental in seeing that performance targets are met and in working closely with employees to improve strategy execution on the front lines where key value-chain activities are performed.

The action agenda of senior-level strategy-implementers, especially in big organizations with geographically scattered operating units, mostly involves communicating the case for change to others, building consensus for how to proceed, installing strong allies in positions where they can push implementation along in key organizational units, urging and empowering subordinates to get the process moving, establishing measures of progress and deadlines, recognizing and rewarding those who achieve implementation milestones, reallocating resources, and personally presiding over the strategic change process. Thus, the bigger the organization, the more the success of the chief strategy-implementer depends on the cooperation and implementing skills of operating managers who can push needed changes at the lowest organizational levels. In small organizations, the chief strategy-implementer doesn't have to work through middle managers and can deal directly with frontline managers and employees, personally orchestrating the action steps and implementation sequence, observing firsthand how implementation is progressing, and deciding how hard and how fast to push the process along. Irrespective of organization size and whether implementation involves sweeping or minor changes, the most important leadership trait is a strong, confident sense of "what to do" to achieve the desired results. Knowing "what to do" comes from a savvy understanding of the business and the organization's circumstances.

In the remainder of this chapter and the next two chapters, we survey the ins and outs of the manager's role as chief strategy-implementer. The discussion is framed around the eight managerial components of the strategy implementation process and the most often-encountered issues associated with each. This chapter explores the management tasks of building a capable organization. Chapter 10 looks at budget allocations, policies, best practices, internal support systems, and strategically appropriate reward structures. Chapter 11 deals with creating a strategy-supportive corporate culture and exercising strategic leadership.

> **The real strategy-implementing skill is being good at figuring out what it will take to execute the strategy proficiently.**

BUILDING A CAPABLE ORGANIZATION ———————————

Proficient strategy execution depends heavily on competent personnel, better-than-adequate skills and competitive capabilities, and effective internal organization. Building a capable organization is thus always a top strategy-implementing priority. Three types of organization-building actions are paramount:

1. Selecting able people for key positions.

2. Making certain that the organization has the skills, core competencies, managerial talents, technical know-how, and competitive capabilities it needs.

3. Organizing business processes and decision-making in a manner that is conducive to successful strategy execution.

Selecting People for Key Positions

Assembling a capable management team is one of the first cornerstones of the organization-building task. Strategy-implementers must determine the kind of core management team they need to execute the strategy successfully and then find the right people to fill each slot. Sometimes the existing management team is suitable; sometimes it needs to be strengthened and/or expanded by promoting qualified people from within or by bringing in outsiders whose backgrounds, ways of thinking, and leadership styles suit the situation. In turnaround and rapid-growth situations, and in instances when a company doesn't have insiders with the requisite experience and management know-how, filling key management slots from the outside is a fairly standard organization-building approach.

The important skill in assembling a core executive group is discerning what mix of backgrounds, experiences, know-how, values, beliefs, management styles, and personalities will reinforce and contribute to successful strategy execution. As with any kind of team-building exercise, it is important to put together a compatible group of managers who possess the full set of skills to get things done. The personal chemistry needs to be right, and the talent base needs to be appropriate for the chosen strategy. Picking a solid management team is an essential organization-building function—often the first strategy implementation step to take.[2] Until key slots are filled with able people, it is hard for strategy implementation to proceed at full speed.

> Putting together a strong management team with the right personal chemistry and mix of skills is one of the first strategy-implementing steps.

Building Core Competencies

An equally important organization-building concern is that of staffing operating units with the specialized talents, skills, and technical expertise needed to give the firm a competitive edge over rivals in performing one or more critical activities in the value chain. When it is difficult or impossible to outstrategize rivals (beat them on the basis of a superior strategy), the other main avenue to industry leadership is to outexecute them (beat them with superior strategy implementation). Superior strategy execution is essential in situations where rival firms have very similar strategies and can readily imitate one another's strategic maneuvers. Building core competencies and organizational capabilities that rivals can't match is one of the best ways to outexecute them. This is why one of management's most important strategy-implementing tasks is to guide the building of core competencies in competitively advantageous ways.

> Building core competencies and organizational capabilities that rivals can't match is a sound foundation for sustainable competitive advantage.

Core competencies can relate to any strategically relevant factor: greater proficiency in product development, better manufacturing know-how, the capability to provide customers better after-sale services, faster response to changing customer

---

[2]For an analytical framework in top-management team analysis, see Donald C. Hambrick, "The Top Management Team: Key to Strategic Success," *California Management Review* 30, no. 1 (Fall 1987), pp. 88–108.

requirements, superior performance in minimizing costs, the capacity to reengineer and redesign products faster than rivals, superior inventory management systems, strong marketing and merchandising skills, specialized depth in unique technologies, or greater effectiveness in promoting union-management cooperation. Honda's core competence is its depth of expertise in gasoline engine technology and small engine design. Intel's is in the design of complex chips for personal computers. Procter & Gamble's core competencies reside in its superb marketing-distribution skills and its R&D capabilities in five core technologies—fats, oils, skin chemistry, surfactants, and emulsifiers.[3] Sony's core competencies are its expertise in electronic technology and its ability to translate that expertise into innovative products (miniaturized radios and video cameras, TVs and VCRs with unique features). Most often, a company's core competencies emerge incrementally as it moves either to bolster skills that contributed to earlier successes or to respond to customer problems, new technological and market opportunities, and the competitive maneuverings of rivals.[4] Occasionally, company managers may foresee coming changes in customer-market requirements and proactively build up new sets of competencies that offer a competitive edge.

Four traits concerning core competencies are important to a strategy-implementer's organization-building task:[5]

- Core competencies rarely consist of narrow skills or the work efforts of a single department. Rather, they are composites of skills and activities performed at different locations in the firm's value chain that, when linked, create unique organizational capability.

- Because core competencies typically originate in the combined efforts of different work groups and departments, individual supervisors and department heads can't be expected to see building the overall corporation's core competencies as their responsibility.

- The key to leveraging a company's core competencies into long-term competitive advantage is concentrating more effort and more talent than rivals on deepening and strengthening these competencies.

- Because customers' needs change in often unpredictable ways and the specific skills needed for competitive success cannot always be accurately forecasted, a company's selected bases of competence need to be broad enough and flexible enough to respond to an unknown future.

The multiskill, multiactivity character of core competencies makes building and strengthening them an exercise in (1) managing human skills, knowledge bases, and intellect and (2) coordinating and networking the efforts of different work groups and departments at every related place in the value chain. It's an exercise best orchestrated by senior managers who understand how the organization's core competencies are created and who can enforce the necessary networking and cooperation among functional departments and managers protective of their turf. Moreover, organization builders have to concentrate enough resources and management attention on core competence-related activities to achieve the *dominating depth* needed for competitive

[3]James Brian Quinn, *Intelligent Enterprise* (New York: Free Press, 1992), p. 76.
[4]Ibid.
[5]Quinn, *Intelligent Enterprise*, pp. 52–53, 55, 73, and 76.

advantage.[6] This does not necessarily mean spending more money on competence-related activities than present or potential competitors. It does mean consciously focusing more talent on them and making appropriate internal and external bench-marking comparisons to move toward best-in-industry, if not best-in-world, status. To achieve dominance on lean financial resources, companies like Cray in large computers, Lotus in software, and Honda in small engines leveraged the expertise of their talent pool by frequently re-forming high-intensity teams and reusing key people on special projects.[7] In leveraging internal knowledge and skills rather than physical assets or market position, it is superior selection, training, powerful cultural influences, cooperative networking, motivation, empowerment, attractive incentives, organizational flexibility, short deadlines, and good databases—not big operating budgets—that are the usual keys to success.[8]

Strategy-implementers can't afford to become complacent once core competencies are in place and functioning. It's a constant organization-building challenge to broaden, deepen, or modify them in response to ongoing customer-market changes. But it's a task worth pursuing. Core competencies that are finely honed and kept current with shifting circumstances can provide a big executional advantage. Distinctive core competencies and organizational capabilities are not easily duplicated by rival firms; thus any competitive advantage that results from them is likely to be sustainable, paving the way for above-average organizational performance. Dedicated management attention to the task of building strategically relevant internal skills and capabilities is always one of the keys to of effective strategy implementation.

Employee Training   Training and retraining are important parts of the strategy implementation process when a company shifts to a strategy requiring different skills, managerial approaches, and operating methods. Training is also strategically important in organizational efforts to build skills-based competencies. And it is a key activity in businesses where technical know-how is changing so rapidly that a company loses its ability to compete unless its skilled people have cutting-edge knowledge and expertise. Successful strategy-implementers see that the training function is adequately funded and that effective training programs are in place. If the chosen strategy calls for new skills or different know-how, training should be placed near the top of the action agenda because it needs to be done early in the strategy implementation process.

Matching Organization Structure to Strategy

There are few hard-and-fast rules for organizing the work effort in a strategy-supportive fashion. Every firm's organization chart is idiosyncratic, reflecting prior organizational patterns, executive judgments about how best to arrange reporting relationships, the politics of who to give which assignments, and varying internal circumstances. Moreover, every strategy is grounded in its own set of key success factors and value-chain activities. So a customized organization structure is appropriate. The following four guidelines can be helpful in fitting structure to strategy:

> Core competencies don't come into being or reach strategic fruition without conscious management attention.

---

[6]Ibid., p. 73.
[7]Ibid.
[8]Ibid., pp. 73–74.

1. Pinpoint the primary activities and key tasks in the value chain that are pivotal to successful strategy execution and make them the main building blocks in the organization structure.

2. If all facets of a strategy-related activity cannot, for some reason, be placed under the authority of a single manager, establish ways to bridge departmental lines and achieve the necessary coordination.

3. Determine the degrees of authority needed to manage each organizational unit, endeavoring to strike an effective balance between capturing the advantages of both centralization and decentralization.

4. Determine whether noncritical activities can be outsourced more efficiently or effectively than they can be performed internally.

Pinpointing Strategy-Critical Activities   In any business, some activities in the value chain are always more critical to strategic success than others. From a strategy perspective, a certain portion of an organization's work involves routine administrative housekeeping (doing the payroll, managing cash flows, handling grievances and the usual assortment of people problems, providing corporate security, managing stockholder relations, maintaining fleet vehicles, and complying with regulations). Other activities are support functions (data processing, accounting, training, public relations, market research, legal and legislative affairs, and purchasing). Among the primary value-chain activities are certain crucial business processes that have to be performed exceedingly well for the strategy succeed. For instance, hotel/motel enterprises have to be good at fast check in/check out, room maintenance, food service, and creating a pleasant ambiance. A manufacturer of chocolate bars must be skilled in purchasing quality cocoa beans at low prices, efficient production (a fraction of a cent in cost savings per bar can mean seven-figure improvement in the bottom line), merchandising, and promotional activities. In discount stock brokerage, the strategy-critical activities are fast access to information, accurate order execution, efficient record-keeping and transactions processing, and good customer service. In specialty chemicals, the critical activities are R&D, product innovation, getting new products onto the market quickly, effective marketing, and expertise in assisting customers. Strategy-critical activities vary according to the particulars of a firm's strategy, value-chain makeup, and competitive requirements.

Two questions help identify what an organization's strategy-critical activities are: "What functions have to be performed extra well or in timely fashion to achieve sustainable competitive advantage?" and "In what value-chain activities would malperformance seriously endanger strategic success?"[9] The answers generally point to the crucial activities and organizational areas on which to concentrate organization-building efforts.

The rationale for making strategy-critical activities the main building blocks in the organization structure is compelling: if activities crucial to strategic success are to get the attention and organizational support they merit, they have to be centerpieces in the organizational scheme. When key business units and strategy-critical functions are put on a par with or, worse, superseded by less important activities, they usually end up with fewer resources and less clout in the organization's power

---

[9]Peter F. Drucker, *Management: Tasks, Responsibilities, Practices* (New York: Harper & Row, 1974), pp. 530, 535.

structure than they deserve. On the other hand, when the primary value-creating activities form the core of a company's organization structure and their managers hold key positions on the organization chart, their role and power is ingrained in daily operations and decision-making. Senior executives seldom send a stronger signal about what is strategically important than by making key business units and critical activities prominent organizational building blocks and, further, giving the managers of these units a visible, influential position in the organizational pecking order. In many cases, there is merit in operating each of these main organizational units as profit centers.

In deciding how to graft routine and staff support activities onto the basic building block structure, company managers must understand the strategic relationships among the primary and support functions that make up its value chain. Activities can be related by the flow of work along the value chain, by the type of customer served, by the distribution channels used, by the technical skills and know-how needed to perform them, by their contribution to building a core competence, by their role in a work process that spans traditional departmental lines, by their role in how customer value is created, by their sequence in the value chain, by the skills-transfer opportunities they present, and by the potential for combining or coordinating them in a manner that will reduce total costs, to mention some of the most obvious. Such relationships are important because one or more such linkages usually signal how to structure reporting relationships and where there's a need for close cross-functional coordination. If the needs of successful strategy execution are to drive organization design, then the relationships to look for are those that (1) link one work unit's performance to another and (2) can be melded into a core competence.

Managers need to be particularly alert to the fact that in traditional functionally organized structures, pieces of strategically relevant activities are often scattered across many departments. The process of filling customer orders accurately and promptly is a case in point. The order fulfillment process begins when a customer places an order, ends when the goods are delivered, and typically includes a dozen or so steps performed by different people in different departments.[10] Someone in customer service receives the order, logs it in, and checks it for accuracy and completeness. It may then go to the finance department, where someone runs a credit check on the customer. Another person may be needed to approve credit terms or special financing. Someone in sales calculates or verifies the correct pricing. When the order gets to inventory control, someone has to determine if the goods are in stock. If not, a back order may be issued or the order routed to production planning so that it can be factored into the production schedule. When the goods are ready, warehouse operations prepares a shipment schedule. Personnel in the traffic department determine the shipment method (rail, truck, air, water) and choose the route and carrier. Product handling picks the product from the warehouse, verifies the picking against the order, and packages the goods for shipment. Traffic releases the goods to the carrier, which takes responsibility for delivery to the customer. Each handoff from one department to the next entails queues and wait times. Although such organization incorporates Adam Smith's division of labor principle (every person involved has specific responsibility for performing one simple task) and allows for tight management control (everyone in the process is accountable to a manager for efficiency and adherence to

Strategic Management Principle
Matching structure to strategy requires making strategy-critical activities and strategy-critical organizational units the main building blocks in the organization structure.

Functional specialization can result in the pieces of strategically relevant activities being scattered across many different departments.

---

[10]Michael Hammer and James Champy, *Reengineering the Corporation* (New York: HarperBusiness, 1993), pp. 26–27.

procedures), *no one oversees the whole process and its result.*[11] Accurate, timely order fulfillment, despite its relevance to effective strategy execution, ends up being neither a single person's job nor the job of any one functional department.[12]

Managers have to guard against organization designs that unduly fragment strategically relevant activities. Parceling strategy-critical work efforts across many specialized departments contributes to an obsession with activity (performing the assigned tasks in the prescribed manner) rather than result (customer satisfaction, competitive advantage, lower costs). So many handoffs lengthen completion time and frequently drive up overhead costs since coordinating the fragmented pieces can soak up hours of effort on the parts of many people. Nonetheless, some fragmentation is necessary, even desirable, in the case of support activities like finance and accounting, human resource management, engineering, technology development, and information systems where functional centralization works to good advantage. The key in weaving support activities into the organization design is to establish reporting and coordinating arrangements that

- Maximize how support activities contribute to enhanced performance of the primary, strategy-critical tasks in the firm's value chain.
- Contain the costs of support activities and minimize the time and energy internal units have to spend doing business with each other.

Without such arrangements, the cost of transacting business internally becomes excessive, and functional managers, forever diligent in guarding their turf and protecting their prerogatives to run their areas as they see fit, can weaken the strategy execution effort and become part of the strategy-implementing problem rather than part of the solution.

Reporting Relationships and Cross-Functional Coordination   The classic way to coordinate the activities of organizational units is to position them in the hierarchy so that those most closely related report to a single person. Managers higher up in the pecking order generally have authority over more organizational units and thus the clout to coordinate, integrate, and arrange for the cooperation of units under their supervision. In such structures, the chief executive officer, chief operating officer, and business-level managers end up as central points of coordination because of their positions of authority over the whole unit. When a firm is pursuing a related diversification strategy, coordinating the related activities of independent business units often requires the centralizing authority of a single corporate-level officer. Also, companies with either related or unrelated diversification strategies commonly centralize such staff support functions as public relations, finance and accounting, employee benefits, and data processing at the corporate level.

But, as the customer order fulfillment example illustrates, it isn't always feasible to position closely related value-chain activities and/or organizational units vertically under the coordinating authority of a single executive. Formal reporting relationships have to be supplemented. Options for unifying the strategic efforts of interrelated organizational units include the use of coordinating teams, cross-functional task forces, dual reporting relationships, informal organizational networking, voluntary

---

[11]Ibid.
[12]Ibid., pp. 27–28.

cooperation, incentive compensation tied to group performance measures, and strong executive-level insistence on teamwork and interdepartmental cooperation (including removal of recalcitrant managers who stonewall cooperative efforts).

Determining the Degree of Authority and Independence to Give Each Unit

Companies must decide how much authority and decision-making latitude to give managers of each organization unit, especially the heads of business subsidiaries and functional departments. In a highly centralized organization structure, top executives retain authority for most strategic and operating decisions and keep a tight rein on business-unit heads and department heads; comparatively little discretionary authority is granted to subordinate managers. The weakness of centralized organization is that its vertical, hierarchical character tends to foster excessive bureaucracy and stall decision-making until the review-approval process runs its course through the management layers. In a highly decentralized organization, managers (and, increasingly, many nonmanagerial employees) are empowered to act on their own in their areas of responsibility. In a diversified company operating on the principle of decentralized decision-making, for example, business unit heads have broad authority to run the subsidiary with comparatively little interference from corporate headquarters. Moreover, the business head gives functional department heads considerable decision-making latitude. Employees with customer contact are empowered to do what it takes to please customers.

> **Resolving which decisions to centralize and which to decentralize is always a big issue in organization design.**

Delegating greater authority to subordinate managers and employees creates a more horizontal organization structure with fewer management layers. Whereas in a centralized vertical structure managers and workers have to go up the ladder of authority for an answer, in a decentralized horizontal structure they develop their own answers and action plans—making decisions and being accountable for results is part of their job. Streamlining the decision-making process usually shortens the time it takes to respond to competitors' actions, changing customer preferences, and other market developments. And it spurs new ideas, creative thinking, innovation, and greater involvement on the part of subordinate managers and employees.

In recent years, there's been a decided shift from authoritarian, multilayered hierarchical structures to flatter, more decentralized structures that stress employee empowerment. The new preference for leaner management structures and empowered employees is grounded in two tenets. (1) Decision-making authority should be pushed down to the lowest organizational level capable of making timely, informed, competent decisions—those people (managers or nonmanagers) nearest the scene who are knowledgeable about the issues and trained to weigh all the factors. Insofar as strategic management is concerned, decentralization means that the managers of each organizational unit should not only lead the crafting of their unit's strategy but also lead the decision-making on how to implement it. Decentralization thus requires selecting strong managers to head each organizational unit and holding them accountable for crafting and executing appropriate strategies for their units. Managers who consistently produce unsatisfactory results and have poor track records in strategy-making and strategy-implementing have to be weeded out. (2) Employees below the management ranks should be empowered to exercise judgement on matters pertaining to their jobs. The case for empowering employees to make decisions and be accountable for their performance is based on the belief that a company that draws on the combined brainpower of all its employees can outperform a company where the approach to people management consists of transferring ideas from the heads of bosses into the actions of workers-doers. To ensure that the decisions of empowered people are as well-informed as possible, great pains have to be taken to put accurate, timely data into everyone's hands and make sure they understand the links between their performance and company performance. Delayered corporate hierarchies and rapid diffusion of information technologies make greater empowerment feasible. It's possible now to create "a wired company" where people have direct electronic access to data and other employees and managers, allowing them to access information quickly, check with superiors as needed and take responsible action. Typically, there are genuine morale gains when people are well-informed and allowed to operate in a self-directed way.

One of the biggest exceptions to decentralizing strategy-related decisions and giving lower-level managers more operating rein arises in diversified companies with related businesses. In such cases, strategic-fit benefits are often best captured by either centralizing decision-making authority or enforcing close cooperation and shared decision-making. For example, if businesses with overlapping process and product technologies have their own independent R&D departments, each pursuing their own priorities, projects, and strategic agendas, it's hard for the corporate parent to prevent duplication of effort, capture either economies of scale or economies of scope, or broaden the vision of the company's R&D efforts to include new technological pathways, product families, end-use applications, and customer groups. Likewise, centralizing control over the related activities of separate businesses makes sense when there are opportunities to share a common sales force, utilize common distribution channels, rely upon a common field service organization to handle customer requests for technical assistance or provide maintenance and repair services, and so on. And for reasons previously discussed, limits also have to be placed on the independence of functional managers when pieces of strategy-critical processes are located in different organizational units and require close coordination for maximum effectiveness.

Centralizing strategy-implementing authority at the corporate level has merit when the related activities of related businesses need to be tightly coordinated.

Reasons to Consider Outsourcing Noncritical Activities   Each supporting activity in a firm's value chain and within its traditional staff groups can be considered a "service."[13] Most overheads, for example, are just services the company chooses to produce internally. Often, such services can be readily purchased from outside vendors. An outsider, by concentrating specialists and technology in its area of expertise, can sometimes perform these services better or more cheaply than a company that performs the activities only for itself. Outsourcing activities not crucial to its strategy allows a company to concentrate its own energies and resources on those value-chain activities where it can create unique value, where it can be best in the industry (or, better still, best in the world), and where it needs strategic control to build core competencies, achieve competitive advantage, and manage key customer-supplier relationships.[14] Managers too often spend inordinate amounts of time, psychic energy, and resources wrestling with functional support groups and other internal bureaucracies, diverting attention from the company's strategy-critical activities. Approached from a strategic point of view, outsourcing noncrucial support activities (and maybe a few selected primary activities in the value chain if they are not a basis for competitive advantage) can decrease internal bureaucracies, flatten the

Outsourcing noncritical activities has many advantages.

[13]Quinn, *Intelligent Enterprise*, p. 32.
[14]Ibid., p. 37.

organization structure, provide the company with heightened strategic focus, and increase competitive responsiveness.[15]

Critics contend that extensive outsourcing can hollow out a company, leaving it at the mercy of outside suppliers and barren of the skills and organizational capabilities needed to be master of its own destiny.[16] However, a number of companies have successfully relied on outside components suppliers, product designers, distribution channels, advertising agencies, and financial services firms. For years Polaroid Corporation bought its film medium from Eastman Kodak, its electronics from Texas Instruments, and its cameras from Timex and others, while it concentrated on producing its unique self-developing film packets and designing its next generation of cameras and films. Nike concentrates on design, marketing, and distribution to retailers, while outsourcing virtually all production of its shoes and sporting apparel. Many mining companies outsource geological work, assaying, and drilling. Ernest and Julio Gallo Winery outsources 95 percent of its grape production, letting farmers take on the weather and other grape-growing risks while it concentrates on wine production and the marketing-sales function.[17] The major airlines outsource their in-flight meals even though food quality is important to travelers' perception of overall service quality. Eastman Kodak, Ford, Exxon, Merrill Lynch, and Chevron have outsourced their data processing activities to computer service firms, believing that outside specialists can perform the needed services at lower costs and equal or better quality. Outsourcing certain value-chain activities makes strategic sense whenever outsiders can perform them at lower cost and/or with higher value-added than the buyer company can perform them internally.[18]

Why Structure Follows Strategy

Research confirms the merits of matching organization design and structure to the particular needs of strategy. A landmark study by Alfred Chandler found that changes in an organization's strategy bring about new administrative problems which, in turn, require a new or refashioned structure for the new strategy to be successfully implemented.[19] Chandler's study of 70 large corporations revealed that structure tends to follow the growth strategy of the firm—but often not until inefficiency and internal operating problems provoke a structural adjustment. The experiences of these firms followed a consistent sequential pattern: new strategy creation, emergence of new administrative problems, a decline in profitability and performance, a shift to a more appropriate organizational structure, and then recovery to more profitable levels and improved strategy execution. That managers should reassess their company's internal organization whenever strategy changes is pretty much

> **Strategic Management Principle**
> **Attempting to carry out a new strategy with an old organizational structure is usually unwise.**

---

[15]Ibid., pp. 33 and 89.
[16]Ibid., pp. 39–40.
[17]Ibid., p. 43.
[18]Ibid., p. 47.
[19]Alfred Chandler, *Strategy and Structure* (Cambridge, Mass.: MIT Press, 1962). Although the stress here is on matching structure to strategy, it is worth noting that structure can and does influence the choice of strategy. A good strategy must be doable. When an organization's present structure is so far out of line with the requirements of a particular strategy that the organization would have to be turned upside down to implement it, the strategy may not be doable and should not be given further consideration. In such cases, structure shapes the choice of strategy. The point here, however, is that once strategy is chosen, structure must be modified to fit the strategy if, in fact, an approximate fit does not already exist. Any influences of structure on strategy should, logically, come before the point of strategy selection rather than after it.

common sense. A new strategy is likely to entail new or different skills and key activities; if these go unrecognized, the resulting mismatch between strategy and structure can open the door to implementation and performance problems.

How Structure Evolves as Strategy Evolves   As firms develop from small, single-business companies into more complex enterprises employing vertical integration, geographic expansion, and diversification strategies, their organizational structures tend to evolve from one-person management to functional departments to divisions to decentralized business units. Single-business companies are usually organized around functional departments. In vertically integrated firms, the major building blocks are divisional units, each of which performs one (or more) of the major processing steps along the value chain (raw materials production, components manufacture, assembly, wholesale distribution, retail store operations); each division in the value-chain sequence may operate as a profit center for performance measurement purposes. Companies with broad geographic coverage typically are divided into regional operating units, each of which has profit-loss responsibility for its assigned geographic area. The typical building blocks of a diversified company are its individual businesses; the authority for business-unit decisions is delegated to business-level managers. Each business unit operates as an independent profit center, with corporate headquarters performing assorted support functions for all the businesses.

The Strategic Advantages and Disadvantages of Different Organizational Structures

There are five formal approaches to matching structure to strategy: (1) functional specialization, (2) geographic organization, (3) decentralized business divisions, (4) strategic business units, and (5) matrix structures featuring dual lines of authority and strategic priority. Each has strategic advantages and disadvantages, and each usually needs to be supplemented with formal or informal organizational arrangements to fully coordinate the work effort.

Functional Organization Structures   Organizational structures anchored around functionally specialized departments are far and away the most popular form for matching structure to strategy in single-business enterprises. However, just what form the functional specialization takes varies according to customer-product-technology considerations. For instance, a technical instruments manufacturer may be organized around research and development, engineering, production, technical services, quality control, marketing, personnel, and finance and accounting. A hotel may have an organization based on front-desk operations, housekeeping, building maintenance, food service, convention services and special events, guest services, personnel and training, and accounting. A discount retailer may divide its organizational units into purchasing, warehousing and distribution, store operations, advertising, merchandising and promotion, and corporate administrative services. Two types of functional organizational approaches are diagrammed in Figure 9–2.

Making specialized functions the main organizational building blocks works best when a firm's value chain consists of a series of discipline-specific activities, each requiring a fairly extensive set of specialized skills, experience, and know-how. In such instances, departmental units staffed with experts in every facet of the activity is an attractive way (1) to exploit any learning/experience curve benefits or economy-

Figure 9–2 Functional Organizational Structures

A. The Building Blocks of a "Typical" Functional Organizational Structure

B. The Building Blocks of a Process-Oriented Functional Structure

STRATEGIC ADVANTAGES	STRATEGIC DISADVANTAGES
• Centralized control of strategic results.	• Excessive fragmentation of strategy-critical processes.
• Very well-suited for structuring a single business.	• Can lead to interfunctional rivalry and conflict, rather than team-play and cooperation—GM must referee functional politics.
• Structure is linked tightly to strategy by designating key activities as functional departments.	• Multilayered management bureaucracies and centralized decision-making slow response times.
• Promotes in-depth functional expertise.	• Hinders development of managers with cross-functional experience because the ladder of advancement is up the ranks within the same functional area.
• Well-suited to developing functional skills and functional-based competencies.	• Forces profit responsibility to the top.
• Conducive to exploiting learning/experience curve effects associated with functional specialization.	• Functional specialists often attach more importance to what's best for the functional area than to what's best for the whole business—can lead to functional empire-building.
• Enhances operating efficiency where tasks are routine and repetitive.	• Functional myopia often works against creative entrepreneurship, adapting to change, and attempts to create cross-functional core competencies.

of-scale opportunities associated with division of labor and the use of specialized technology and equipment and (2) to develop deep expertise in an important business function. When dominating depth in one or more functional specialties enhances operating efficiency and/or organizational know-how, it becomes a basis for competitive advantage (lower cost or unique capability). Functional structures work quite satisfactorily so long as strategy-critical activities closely match functional specialties, there's minimal need for interdepartmental cooperation, and top-level management is able to short-circuit departmental rivalries and create a spirit of teamwork, trust, and interdepartmental cooperation.

A functional structure has two Achilles' heels: excessive functional myopia and fragmentation of strategy-critical business processes across traditional departmental lines. It's tough to achieve tight strategic coordination across strongly entrenched functional bureaucracies that don't "talk the same language" and that prefer to do their own thing without outside interference. Functional specialists are prone to focus inward on departmental matters and upward at their boss's priorities but not outward on the business, the customer, or the industry.[20] Members of functional departments usually have strong departmental loyalties and are protective of departmental interests. There's a natural tendency for each functional department to push for solutions and decisions that advance its well-being and organizational influence (despite the lip service given to cooperation and "what's best for the company"). All this creates an organizational environment where functional departments operate as vertical silos, or stovepipes, and a breeding ground for departmental bureaucracies, excessive layers of management, authoritarian decision-making, and narrow perspectives. In addition, functionally dominated structures, because of preoccupation with developing deeper expertise and improving functional performance, have tunnel vision when it comes to devising entrepreneurially creative responses to major customer-market-technological changes. They are quick to kill ideas or discard alternatives that aren't compatible with the present functional structure. Classical functional structures also exacerbate the problems of process fragmentation whenever a firm's value chain includes strategy-critical activities that, by their very nature, are cross-functional rather than discipline specific. Process fragmentation not only complicates the problems of achieving interdepartmental coordination but also poses serious hurdles to developing cross-functional core competencies.

Interdepartmental politics, functional empire-building, functional myopia, and process fragmentation can impose a time-consuming administrative burden on the general manager, who is the only person on the organization chart with authority to resolve cross-functional differences and to enforce interdepartmental cooperation. In a functional structure, much of a GM's time and energy is spent opening lines of communication across departments, tempering departmental rivalries, convincing stovepipe thinkers of the merits of broader solutions, devising ways to secure cooperation, and working to mold desirable cross-functional core competencies. To be successful, a GM has to be tough and uncompromising in insisting that department heads be team players and that functional specialists work together closely as needed; failure to cooperate fully has to carry negative consequences (specifically, a lower job performance evaluation and maybe even reassignment).

To strike a good balance between being function-driven and team-driven, the formal functional structure has to be supplemented with coordinating mechanisms—

> **Functional departments develop strong functional mindsets and are prone to approach strategic issues more from a functional than a business perspective.**

---

[20]Hammer and Champy, *Reengineering the Corporation*, p. 28.

frequent use of interdisciplinary task forces to work out procedures for coordinating fragmented processes and strategy-critical activities, incentive compensation schemes tied to joint performance measures, empowerment of cross-functional teams that possess all the skills needed to perform strategy-critical processes in a unified, timely manner, and the formation of interdisciplinary teams charged with building the internal organizational bridges needed to create cross-functional organizational capabilities. On occasion, rather than continuing to scatter related pieces of a business process across several functional departments and scrambling to integrate their efforts, it may be better to reengineer the work effort and create process departments by pulling the people who performed the pieces in functional departments into a group that works together to perform the whole process.[21] Bell Atlantic did so in cutting through its bureaucratic procedures for connecting a telephone customer to its long-distance carrier.[22] In Bell Atlantic's functional structure, when a business customer requested a connection between its telephone system and a long-distance carrier for data services, the request traveled from department to department, taking two to four weeks to complete all the internal processing steps. In reengineering that process, Bell Atlantic pulled workers doing the pieces of the process from the many functional departments and put them on teams that, working together, could handle most customer requests in a matter of days and sometimes hours. Because the work was recurring—similar customer requests had to be processed daily—the teams were permanently grouped into a "process department."

Geographic Forms of Organization   Organizing on the basis of geographic areas or territories is a common structural form for enterprises operating in diverse geographic markets or serving an expansive geographic area. As indicated in Figure 9–3, geographic organization has advantages and disadvantages, but the chief reason for its popularity is that it promotes improved performance.

> **A geographic organization structure is well-suited to firms pursuing different strategies in different geographic regions.**

In the private sector, a territorial structure is typically utilized by discount retailers, power companies, cement firms, restaurant chains, and dairy products enterprises. In the public sector, such organizations as the Internal Revenue Service, the Social Security Administration, the federal courts, the U.S. Postal Service, state troopers, and the Red Cross have adopted territorial structures in order to be directly accessible to geographically dispersed clienteles. Multinational enterprises use geographic structures to manage the diversity they encounter operating across national boundaries.

Raymond Corey and Steven Star cite Pfizer International as a good example of a company whose strategic requirements made geographic decentralization advantageous:

> Pfizer International operated plants in 27 countries and marketed in more than 100 countries. Its product lines included pharmaceuticals (antibiotics and other ethical prescription drugs), agricultural and veterinary products (such as animal feed supplements and vaccines and pesticides), chemicals (fine chemicals, bulk pharmaceuticals, petrochemicals, and plastics), and consumer products (cosmetics and toiletries).
>
> Ten geographic Area Managers reported directly to the President of Pfizer International and exercised line supervision over Country Managers. According

---

[21]Ibid., p. 66.
[22]Ibid., pp. 66–67.

Figure 9–3   Geographic Organizational Structure

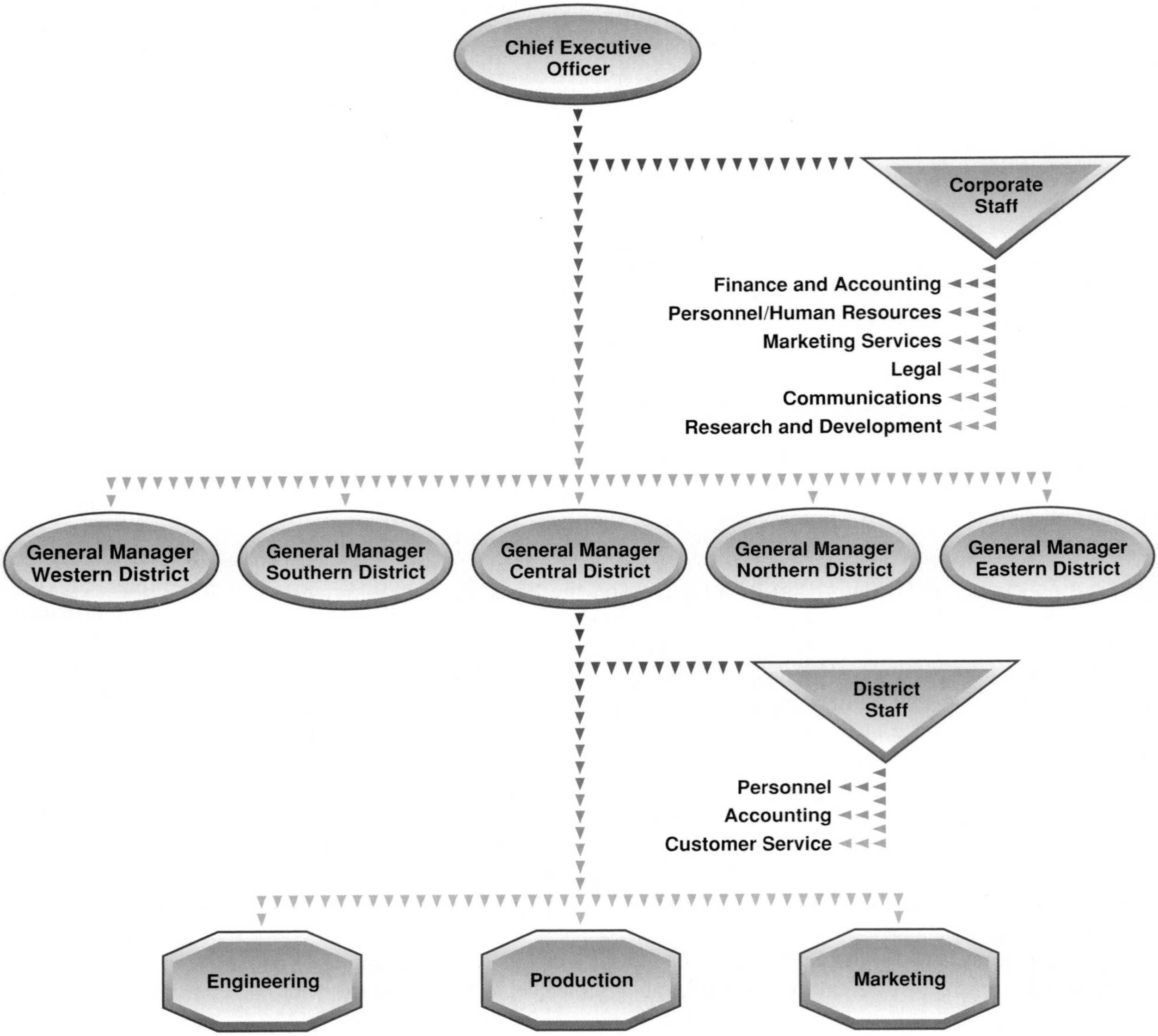

STRATEGIC ADVANTAGES

- Allows tailoring of strategy to needs of each geographical market.
- Delegates profit/loss responsibility to lowest strategic level.
- Improves functional coordination within the target market.
- Takes advantage of economies of local operations.
- Area units make an excellent training ground for higher-level general managers.

STRATEGIC DISADVANTAGES

- Poses a problem of how much geographic uniformity headquarters should impose versus how much geographic diversity should be allowed.
- Greater difficulty in maintaining consistent company image/reputation from area to area when area managers exercise much strategic freedom.
- Adds another layer of management to run the geographic units.
- Can result in duplication of staff services at headquarters and district levels, creating a cost disadvantage.

to a company position description, it was "the responsibility of each Area Manager to plan, develop, and carry out Pfizer International's business in the assigned foreign area in keeping with company policies and goals."

Country Managers had profit responsibility. In most cases a single Country Manager managed all Pfizer activities in his country. In some of the larger, well-developed countries of Europe there were separate Country Managers for pharmaceutical and agricultural products and for consumer lines.

Except for the fact that New York headquarters exercised control over the to-the-market prices of certain products, especially prices of widely used pharmaceuticals, Area and Country Managers had considerable autonomy in planning and managing the Pfizer International business in their respective geographic areas. This was appropriate because each area, and some countries within areas, provided unique market and regulatory environments. In the case of pharmaceuticals and agricultural and veterinary products (Pfizer International's most important lines), national laws affected formulations, dosages, labeling, distribution, and often price. Trade restrictions affected the flow of bulk pharmaceuticals and chemicals and packaged products, and might in effect require the establishment of manufacturing plants to supply local markets. Competition, too, varied significantly from area to area.[23]

Decentralized Business Units Grouping activities along business and product lines has been a favored organizing device among diversified enterprises for the past 70 years, beginning with the pioneering efforts of DuPont and General Motors in the 1920s. Separate business/product divisions emerged because diversification made a functionally specialized manager's job incredibly complex. Imagine the problems a manufacturing executive and his/her staff would have if put in charge of, say, 50 different plants using 20 different technologies to produce 30 different products in eight different businesses/industries. In a multibusiness enterprise, the practical organizational sequence is corporate to business to functional area within a business rather than corporate to functional area (aggregated for all businesses).

Thus while functional departments and geographic divisions are the standard organizational building blocks in a single-business enterprise, in a multibusiness corporation the basic building blocks are the individual businesses. Authority over each business unit is typically delegated to a business-level manager. The approach is to put entrepreneurial general managers in charge of each business unit, give them authority to formulate and implement a business strategy, motivate them with performance-based incentives, and hold them accountable for results. Each business unit then operates as a stand-alone profit center and is organized around whatever functional departments and geographic units suit the business's strategy, key activities, and operating requirements.

> In a diversified firm, the basic organizational building blocks are its business units; each business is operated as a stand-alone profit center.

Fully independent business units, however, pose an organizational obstacle to companies pursuing related diversification: *there is no mechanism for coordinating related activities across business units.* It can be tough to get autonomy-conscious business-unit managers to coordinate and share related activities. They are prone to argue about turf and about being held accountable for activities outside their control. To capture strategic-fit benefits in a diversified company, corporate headquarters must devise some internal organizational means for achieving strategic coordination across

[23]Raymond Corey and Steven H. Star, *Organization Strategy: A Marketing Approach* (Boston: Harvard Business School, 1971), pp. 23–24.

related business-unit activities. One option is to centralize related functions at the corporate level—for example, maintaining a corporate R&D department if there are technology and product development fits, creating a special corporate sales force to call on customers who purchase from several of the company's business units, combining the dealer networks and sales force organizations of closely related businesses, merging the order processing and shipping functions of businesses with common customers, and consolidating the production of related components and products into fewer, more efficient plants. Alternatively, corporate officers can develop bonus arrangements that give business-unit managers strong incentives to work together to achieve the full benefits of strategic fit. If the strategic-fit relationships involve skills or technology transfers across businesses, corporate headquarters can arrange to transfer people with the requisite skills and know-how from one business to another and can create interbusiness teams to open the flow of proprietary technology, managerial know-how, and related skills between businesses.

A typical line-of-business organization structure is shown in Figure 9–4, along with the strategy-related pros and cons of this organizational form.

Strategic Business Units   In broadly diversified companies, the number of decentralized business units can be so great that the span of control is too much for a single chief executive. Then it may be useful to group related businesses and to delegate authority over them to a senior executive who reports directly to the chief executive officer. While this imposes a layer of management between business-level managers and the chief executive, it may nonetheless improve strategic planning and top-management coordination of diverse business interests. This explains both the popularity of the group vice president concept among multibusiness companies and the creation of strategic business units.

A *strategic business unit* (SBU) is a grouping of business subsidiaries based on some important strategic elements common to all. The elements can be an overlapping set of competitors, closely related value-chain activities, a common need to compete globally, emphasis on the same kind of competitive advantage (low cost or differentiation), common key success factors, or technologically related growth opportunities. At General Electric, a pioneer in the concept of SBUs, 190 businesses were grouped into 43 SBUs and then aggregated further into six "sectors."[24] At Union Carbide, 15 groups and divisions were decomposed into 150 "strategic planning units" and then regrouped and combined into 9 new "aggregate planning units." At General Foods, SBUs were originally defined on a product-line basis but were later redefined according to menu segments (breakfast foods, beverages, main meal products, desserts, and pet foods). SBUs make headquarters' reviews of the strategies of lower-level units less imposing (there is no practical way for a CEO to conduct in-depth reviews of a hundred or more different businesses). A CEO can, however, effectively review the strategic plans of a lesser number of SBUs, leaving detailed business strategy reviews and direct supervision of individual businesses to the SBU heads. Figure 9–5 illustrates the SBU form of organization, along with its strategy-related pros and cons.

---

[24]William K. Hall, "SBUs: Hot, New Topic in the Management of Diversification," *Business Horizons* 21, no. 1 (February 1978), p. 19. For an excellent discussion of the problems of implementing the SBU concept at 13 companies, see Richard A. Bettis and William K. Hall, "The Business Portfolio Approach— Where It Falls Down in Practice," *Long Range Planning* 16, no. 2 (April 1983), pp. 95–104.

Figure 9–4 A Decentralized Line-of-Business Organization Structure

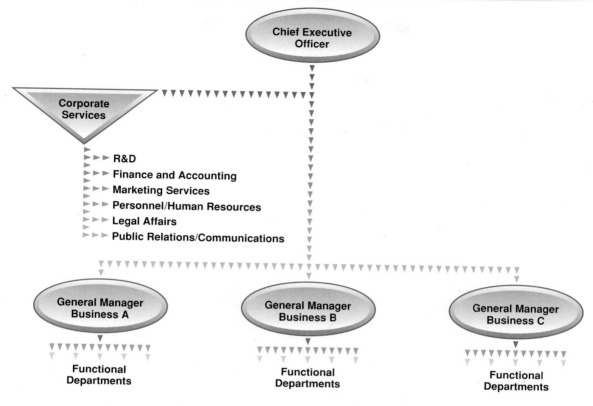

STRATEGIC ADVANTAGES

- Offers a logical and workable means of decentralizing responsibility and delegating authority in diversified organizations.

- Puts responsibility for business strategy in closer proximity to each business's unique environment.

- Allows each business unit to organize around its own value chain system, key activities and functional requirements.

- Frees CEO to handle corporate strategy issues.

- Puts clear profit/loss accountability on shoulders of business-unit managers.

STRATEGIC DISADVANTAGES

- May lead to costly duplication of staff functions at corporate and business-unit levels, thus raising administrative overhead costs.

- Poses a problem of what decisions to centralize and what decisions to decentralize (business managers need enough authority to get the job done, but not so much that corporate management loses control of key business-level decisions).

- May lead to excessive division rivalry for corporate resources and attention.

- Business/division autonomy works against achieving coordination of related activities in different business units, thus blocking to some extent the capture of strategic-fit benefits.

- Corporate management becomes heavily dependent on business-unit managers.

- Corporate managers can lose touch with business-unit situations, end up surprised when problems arise, and not know much about how to fix such problems.

Figure 9–5   An SBU Organization Structure

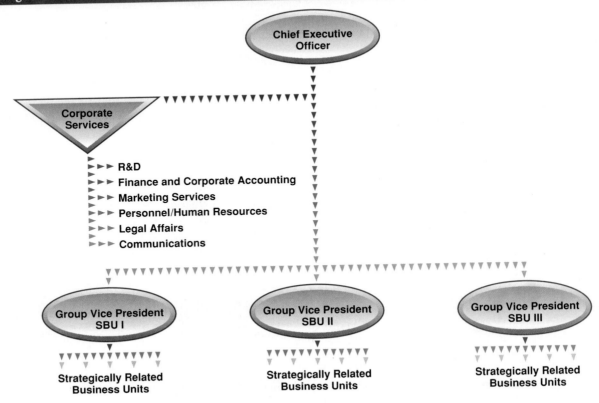

STRATEGIC ADVANTAGES

- Provides a strategically relevant way to organize the business-unit portfolio of a broadly diversified company.

- Facilitates the coordination of related activities within an SBU, thus helping to capture the benefits of strategic fits in the SBU.

- Promotes more cohesiveness among the new initiatives of separate but related businesses.

- Allows strategic planning to be done at the most relevant level within the total enterprise.

- Makes the task of strategic review by top executives more objective and more effective.

- Helps allocate corporate resources to areas with greatest growth opportunities.

STRATEGIC DISADVANTAGES

- It is easy for the definition and grouping of businesses into SBUs to be so arbitrary that the SBU serves no other purpose than administrative convenience. If the criteria for defining SBUs are rationalizations and have little to do with the nitty-gritty of strategy coordination, then the groupings lose real strategic significance.

- The SBUs can still be myopic in charting their future direction.

- Adds another layer to top management.

- The roles and authority of the CEO, the group vice president, and the business-unit manager have to be carefully worked out or the group vice president gets trapped in the middle with ill-defined authority.

- Unless the SBU head is strong willed, very little strategy coordination is likely to occur across business units in the SBU.

- Performance recognition gets blurred; credit for successful business units tends to go to corporate CEO, then to business-unit head, last to group vice president.

The SBU concept provides broadly diversified companies with a way to rationalize the organization of many different businesses and a management arrangement for capturing strategic-fit benefits and streamlining strategic planning and budgeting processes. The strategic function of the group vice president is to provide the SBU with some cohesive direction, enforce strategic coordination across related businesses, and keep an eye out for trouble at the business-unit level, providing counsel and additional corporate support as needed. The group vice president, as strategic coordinator for all businesses in the SBU, can facilitate resource sharing and skills transfers where appropriate and unify the strategic decisions and actions of businesses in the SBU. The SBU, in effect, becomes a strategy-making, strategy-implementing unit with a wider field of vision and operations than a single business unit. It serves as a diversified company's organizational mechanism for capturing strategic-fit benefits across businesses and adding to the competitive advantage that each business in the SBU is able to build on its own. Moreover, it affords opportunity to "cross-pollinate" the activities of separate businesses, ideally creating enough new capability to stretch a company's strategic reach into adjacent products, technologies, and markets. Aggressive pursuit of resource-sharing, skills-transfer, and cross-pollination opportunities is one of the best avenues companies can use to develop the internal capabilities needed to enter new business areas.

> **SBU structures are a means for managing broad diversification and enforcing strategic coordination across related businesses.**

Matrix Forms of Organization   A matrix organization is a structure with two (or more) channels of command, two lines of budget authority, and two sources of performance and reward. The key feature of the matrix is that authority for a business/product/project/venture and authority for a function or business process are overlaid (to form a matrix or grid), and decision-making responsibility in each unit/cell of the matrix is shared between the business/project/venture team manager and the functional/process manager—as shown in Figure 9–6. In a matrix structure, subordinates have a continuing dual assignment: to the business/project/process/venture and to their home-base function. The outcome is a compromise between functional specialization (engineering, R&D, manufacturing, marketing, finance) and product line, project, process, line-of-business or special venture divisions (where all of the specialized talent needed for the product line/project/line-of-business/venture are assigned to the same divisional or departmental unit).

> **Matrix structures, although complex to manage and sometimes unwieldy, allow a firm to be organized in two different strategy-supportive ways at the same time.**

A matrix-type organization is a genuinely different structural form and represents a "new way of life." It breaks the unity-of-command principle; two reporting channels, two bosses, and shared authority create a new kind of organizational climate. In essence, the matrix is a conflict resolution system through which strategic and operating priorities are negotiated, power is shared, and resources are allocated internally on the basis of "strongest case for what is best overall for the unit.[25]

The impetus for matrix organizations stems from growing use of strategies that create a simultaneous need for process teams, special project managers, product managers, functional managers, geographic area managers, new-venture managers, and business-level managers—all of whom have important strategic responsibilities. When at least two of several variables (product, customer, technology, geography,

---

[25]For two excellent critiques of matrix organizations, see Stanley M. Davis and Paul R. Lawrence, "Problems of Matrix Organizations," *Harvard Business Review* 56, no. 3 (May–June 1978), pp. 131–42, and Erik W. Larson and David H. Gobeli, "Matrix Management: Contradictions and Insights," *California Management Review* 29, no. 4 (Summer 1987), pp. 126–38.

Figure 9–6   A Matrix Organization Structure

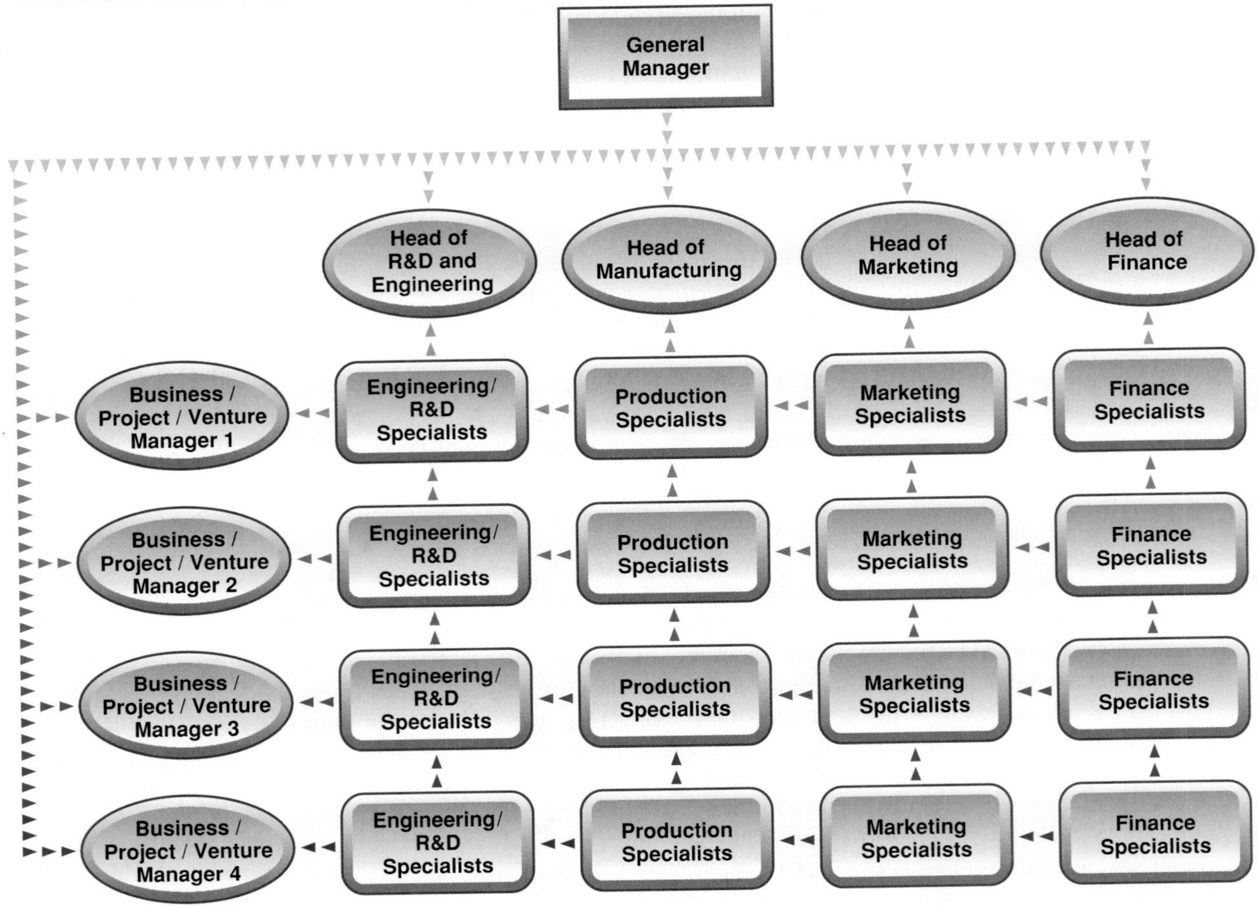

STRATEGIC ADVANTAGES

- Gives formal attention to each dimension of strategic priority.
- Creates checks and balances among competing viewpoints.
- Facilitates capture of functionally based strategic fits in diversified companies.
- Promotes making trade-off decisions on the basis of "what's best for the organization as a whole."
- Encourages cooperation, consensus-building, conflict resolution, and coordination of related activities.

STRATEGIC DISADVANTAGES

- Very complex to manage.
- Hard to maintain "balance" between the two lines of authority.
- So much shared authority can result in a transactions logjam and disproportionate amounts of time being spent on communications.
- It is hard to move quickly and decisively without getting clearance from many other people.
- Promotes an organizational bureaucracy and hamstrings creative entrepreneurship.

*Arrows indicate reporting channels.

functional area, business process, and market segment) have roughly equal strategic priorities, a matrix organization can be an effective structural form. A matrix structure promotes internal checks and balances among competing viewpoints and perspectives, with separate managers for different dimensions of strategic initiative. A matrix arrangement thus allows each of several strategic considerations to be managed directly and to be formally represented in the organization structure. In this sense, it helps middle managers make trade-off decisions from an organizationwide perspective.[26] The other big advantage of matrix organization is that it can serve as a mechanism for capturing strategic fit. When the strategic fits in a diversified company are related to a specific functional area (R&D, technology, marketing), or cross traditional functional lines, matrix organization can be a reasonable structural arrangement for coordinating activity sharing and skills transfer.

Companies using matrix structures include General Electric, Texas Instruments, Citibank, Shell Oil, TRW, Bechtel, Boeing, and Dow Chemical. Illustration Capsule 27 on pages 266–267 describes how one broadly diversified company with global strategies in each of its businesses developed a matrix-type structure to manage its operations worldwide. However, in most companies, use of matrix organization is confined to a portion of what the firm does (certain important functions) rather than its whole organizing scheme.

Many companies and managers shun matrix organization because of its chief weaknesses.[27] It is a complex structure to manage; people end up confused or frustrated over who to report to for what. Moreover, because the matrix signals a need for communication and consensus, a "transactions logjam" can result. People in one area are pushed into transacting business with people in another area and networking their way through internal bureaucracies. Action turns into paralysis since, with shared authority, it is hard to move decisively without first checking with other people and getting clearance. Much time and psychic energy get eaten up in meetings and communicating back and forth. Sizable transactions costs and longer decision times can result with little value-added work accomplished. Even so, in some situations the benefits of conflict resolution, consensus building, and coordination outweigh these weaknesses, as the ABB example in Illustration Capsule 27 indicates.

Supplementing the Basic Organization Structure   None of the basic structural designs is wholly adequate for organizing the total work effort in strategy-supportive ways. Some weaknesses can be corrected by using two or more of the structural designs simultaneously—many companies are large enough and diverse enough to have SBUs, functionally organized business units, geographic organizational structures in one or more businesses, units employing matrix principles, and several functionally specialized departments. But in many companies strategy-supportive organization requires supplementing the formal structure with special coordinating mechanisms and "creative disorganization"—cross-functional task forces, project teams, venture teams, self-sufficient work teams to perform whole processes, and special empowerment of key individuals to cut through red tape and get things done

---

[26]Davis and Lawrence, "Problems of Matrix Organizations," p. 132.
[27]Thomas J. Peters and Robert H. Waterman, Jr., *In Search of Excellence* (New York: Harper & Row, 1982), pp. 306–7.

Illustration Capsule 27   Matrix Organization in a Diversified Global Company The Case of Asea Brown Boveri

Asea Brown Boveri (ABB) is a diversified multinational corporation headquartered in Zurich, Switzerland. ABB was formed in 1987 through the merger of Asea, one of Sweden's largest industrial enterprises, and Brown Boveri, a major Swiss company. Both companies manufactured electrical products and equipment. Following the merger, ABB acquired or took minority positions in 60 companies, mostly outside Europe. In 1991 ABB had annual revenues of $25 billion and employed 240,000 people around the world, including 150,000 in Western Europe, 40,000 in North America, 10,000 in South America, and 10,000 in India. The company was a world leader in the global markets for electrical products, electrical installations and service, and power-generation equipment and was the dominant European producer. European sales accounted for 60% of revenues, while North America accounted for 30% and Asia 15%.

To manage its global operations, ABB had devised a matrix organization that leveraged its core competencies in electrical-power technologies and its ability to achieve global economies of scale while, at the same time, maximizing its national market visibility and responsiveness. At the top of ABB's corporate organization structure was an executive committee composed of the CEO, Percy Barnevik, and 12 colleagues; the committee consisted of

Swedes, Swiss, Germans, and Americans, several of whom were based outside Switzerland. The group, which met every three weeks at various locations around the world, was responsible for ABB's corporate strategy and performance.

Along one dimension of ABB's global matrix were 50 or so business areas (BAs), each representing a closely related set of products and services. The BAs were grouped into eight "business segments"; each segment was supervised by a different member of the executive committee. Each BA had a leader charged with responsibility for (1) devising and championing a global strategy, (2) setting quality and cost standards for the BA's factories worldwide, (3) deciding which factories would export to which country markets, (4) rotating people across borders to share technical expertise, create mixed-nationality teams to solve BA problems, and build a culture of trust and communication, and (5) pooling expertise and research funds for the benefit of the BA worldwide. BA leaders worked out of whatever world location made the most sense for their BA. For example, the BA leader for power transformers, who had responsibility for 25 factories in 16 countries, was a Swede who worked out of Mannheim, Germany; the BA leader for electric metering was an American based in North Carolina.

(continued)

quickly when necessary. Six of the most frequently used devices for supplementing the formal organization structure are:

1. *Special project teams*—creating a separate, largely self-sufficient work group to oversee the completion of a special activity (setting up a new technological process, bringing out a new product, starting up a new venture, consummating a merger with another company, seeing through the completion of a government contract, supervising the construction and opening of a new plant). Project teams are especially suitable for one-of-a-kind situations with a finite life expectancy when the normal organization is not equipped to achieve the same results in addition to regular duties.

2. *Cross-functional task forces*—bringing a number of top-level executives and/or specialists together to solve problems requiring specialized expertise from several parts of the organization, coordinating strategy-related activities that span departmental boundaries, or exploring ways to leverage the skills of different functional specialists into broader core competencies. Task forces seem to be most effective when they have less than 10 members, membership is voluntary, the seniority of the members is proportional to the importance of the problem, the task force moves swiftly

(concluded)

Along the other dimension of the matrix was a group of national enterprises with presidents, boards of directors, financial statements, and career ladders. The presidents of ABB's national enterprises had responsibility for maximizing the performance and effectiveness of all ABB activities within their country's borders. Country presidents worked closely with the BA leaders to evaluate and improve what was happening in ABB's business areas in their countries.

Inside the matrix were 1,200 "local" ABB companies with an average of 200 employees, each headed by a president. The local company president reported both to the national president in whose country the local company operated and to the leader of the BA to which its products/services were assigned. Each local company was a subsidiary of the ABB national enterprise where it was located. Thus, all of ABB's local companies in Norway were subsidiaries of ABB Norway, the national company for Norway; all ABB operations in Portugal were subsidiaries of ABB Portugal, and so on. The 1,200 presidents of ABB's local companies were expected to be excellent profit center managers, able to answer to two bosses effectively. The local president's global boss was the BA manager who established the local company's role in ABB's global strategy and, also,

the rules a local company had to observe in supporting this strategy. The local president's country boss was the national CEO, with whom it was necessary to cooperate on local issues.

ABB believed that its matrix structure allowed it to optimize its pursuit of global business strategies and, at the same time, maximize its performance in every country market where it operated. The matrix was a way of being global and big strategically, yet small and local operationally. Decision-making was decentralized (to BA leaders, country presidents, and local company presidents), but reporting and control was centralized (through the BA leaders, the country presidents, and the executive committee). ABB saw itself as a federation of national companies with a global coordination center.

Only 100 professionals were located in ABB's corporate headquarters in Zurich. A management information system collected data on all profit centers monthly, comparing actual performance against budgets and forecasts. Data was collected in local currencies but translated into U.S. dollars to allow for cross-border analysis. ABB's corporate financial statements were reported in U.S. dollars, and English was ABB's official language. All high-level meetings were conducted in English.

Source: Compiled from information in William Taylor, "The Logic of Global Business: An Interview with ABB's Percy Barnevik," *Harvard Business Review* 69, no. 2 (March–April 1991), pp. 90–105.

to deal with its assignment, they are used sparingly—only on an as-needed basis, no staff is assigned, and documentation is scant.[28] Companies that have used task forces successfully form them to solve pressing problems, produce some solutions efficiently, and then disband them.

3. *Venture teams*—forming a group of individuals to manage the launch of a new product, entry into a new geographic market, or creation of a specific new business. Dow, General Mills, Westinghouse, General Electric, and Monsanto used the venture-team approach to regenerate an entrepreneurial spirit. The difficulties with venture teams include deciding who the venture manager should report to; whether funding for ventures should come from corporate, business, or departmental budgets; how to keep the venture clear of bureaucratic and vested interests; and how to coordinate large numbers of different ventures.

4. *Self-contained work teams*—forming a group of people drawn from different disciplines who work together on a semipermanent basis to continuously improve organizational performance in specific strategy-

---

[28]Ibid., pp. 127–32.

related areas—shortening the lab-to-market cycle time, boosting product quality, improving customer service, cutting delivery times, eliminating stockouts, reducing the costs of purchased materials and components, increasing assembly-line productivity, trimming equipment downtime and maintenance expenses, or designing new models. American Express cut out three layers of hierarchy when it developed self-managed teams to handle all types of customer inquiries in a single-call, quick-resolution manner.[29]

5. *Process teams*—putting functional specialists who perform pieces of a business process together on a team instead of assigning them to their home-base functional department. Such teams can be empowered to reengineer the process, held accountable for results, and rewarded on the basis of how well the process is performed. Much of Chrysler's revitalization is due to dramatically revamping its new-model development process using "platform teams."[30] Each platform team consists of members from engineering, design, finance, purchasing, and marketing. The team is responsible for the car's design from beginning to end, has broad decision-making power, and is held accountable for the success or failure of their design. Teams coordinate their designs with manufacturing so that the models will be easier to build and consult regularly with purchasing agents regarding parts quality. In one case Chrysler purchasing agents elected to pay 30 percent more for a better part because the engineer on the platform team believed the added cost would be offset by the time saved during assembly.

6. *Contact managers*—providing a single point of contact for customers when the steps of a process either are so complex or are dispersed in such a way that integrating them for a single person or team to perform is impractical.[31] Acting as a buffer between internal processes and the customer, the contact person endeavors to answer customer questions and solve customer problems as if he or she were responsible for performing the called-for activities. To perform this role, contact persons need access to all the information systems that the persons actually performing the process use and the ability to contact those people with questions and requests for further assistance when necessary. The best results are achieved when contact persons are empowered to use their own judgment to get things done in a manner that will please customers. Duke Power, a Charlotte-based electric utility, uses empowered customer service representatives to resolve the problems of residential customers while shielding them from whatever goes on "behind the scenes" to produce solutions.

Perspectives on Organizing the Work Effort

There's no perfect or ideal organization structure. All the basic designs have their strategy-related strengths and weaknesses. To do a good job of matching structure to strategy, strategy-implementers have to pick a basic design, modify it as needed to fit

---

[29]Quinn, *Intelligent Enterprise*, p. 163.
[30]"Can Jack Smith Fix GM?" *Business Week*, November 1, 1993, pp. 130–31.
[31]Hammer and Champy, *Reengineering the Corporation*, pp. 62–63.

the company's particular business makeup, and then supplement it with whatever coordinating mechanisms and communication arrangements it takes to support effective execution of the firm's strategy. While practical realities often dictate giving some consideration to existing reporting relationships, to the personalities involved, to internal politics, and to other situational idiosyncrasies, strategy-structure factors have to predominate.

Peter Drucker, one of the foremost authorities on managing, sums up the intricacies of organization design:

> The simplest organization structure that will do the job is the best one. What makes an organization structure "good" is the problems it does not create. The simpler the structure, the less that can go wrong.
>
> Some design principles are more difficult and problematic than others. But none is without difficulties and problems. None is primarily people-focused rather than task-focused; none is more "creative," "free," or "democratic." Design principles are tools; and tools are neither good nor bad in themselves. They can be used properly or improperly; and that is all. To obtain both the greatest possible simplicity and the greatest "fit," organization design has to start out with a clear focus on *key activities* needed to produce *key results*. They have to be structured and positioned in the simplest possible design. Above all, the architect of organization needs to keep in mind the purpose of the structure he is designing.[32]

Current Organizational Trends   Many of today's companies are remodeling their traditional hierarchical structures built around functional specialization and centralized authority. Such structures make good strategic and organizational sense so long as (1) activities can be divided into simple, repeatable tasks that can be mastered quickly and then efficiently performed in mass quantity, (2) there are important benefits to deep functional expertise in each managerial discipline, and (3) customer needs are sufficiently standardized that it is easy to prescribe procedures for satisfying them. But traditional hierarchies become a liability in businesses where customer preferences are shifting from standardized products to custom orders and special features, product life-cycles are growing shorter, flexible manufacturing methods are replacing mass production techniques, customers want to be treated as individuals, the pace of technological change is accelerating, and market conditions are fluid. Multilayered management hierarchies and functionalized bureaucracies that require people to look upward in the organizational structure for answers tend to bog down in such environments. They can't deliver responsive customer service or adapt fast enough to changing conditions. Functional silos, task-oriented work, process fragmentation, layered management hierarchies, centralized decision-making, growing functional and middle-management bureaucracies, lots of checks and controls, and long response times can undermine competitive success in fluid or volatile business environments. Success in fast-changing markets depends on strategies featuring important organizational capabilities: quick response to shifting customer preferences, short design-to-market cycles, make-it-right-the-first-time quality, custom-order and multiversion production, expedited delivery, personalized customer service, accurate order filling, rapid assimilation of new technologies, creativity and innovativeness, and speedy reactions to external competitive developments.

---

[32]Drucker, *Management: Tasks, Responsibilities, Practices,* pp. 601–2.

These new components of business strategy are driving a revolution in corporate organization.[33] Much of the corporate downsizing movement is aimed at busting up functional and middle management bureaucracies and recasting authoritarian pyramidal organizational structures into flatter, decentralized structures. The latest organizational designs for matching structure to strategy feature fewer layers of management authority, small-scale business units, reengineered work processes to cut back on fragmentation across functional department lines, creation of process teams and interdisciplinary work groups, lean staffing of corporate support functions, partnerships with key suppliers, empowerment of firstline supervisors and nonmanagement employees, open communications vertically and laterally, computers and telecommunications technologies to provide fast access to and dissemination of information, and accountability for results rather than emphasis on activity. The new organizational themes are lean, flat, responsive, and innovative. The new tools of organizational design are managers and workers empowered to act on their own judgments, reengineered work processes, and self-directed work teams.

The command-and-control paradigm of vertically layered structures assumes that the people actually performing work have neither the time nor the inclination to monitor and control it and that they lack the knowledge to make informed decisions about how best to do it; hence, the need for prescribed procedures, close supervision, and managerial control of decision-making. In flat, decentralized structures, these assumptions are discarded. Jobs are defined more broadly; several tasks are integrated into a single job where possible. People operate in a more self-directed fashion, armed with the information they need to get things done. Fewer managers are needed because deciding how to do things becomes part of each person's or team's job.

Reengineering Can Promote Better Implementation   Reengineering strategy-critical business processes to reduce fragmentation across traditional departmental lines and cut bureaucratic overheads has proven to be a legitimate organization design tool. It's not a passing fad or another management program of the month. Process organization is every bit as valid an organizing principle as functional specialization. Strategy execution is improved when the pieces of strategy-critical activities and core business processes performed by different departments are properly integrated and coordinated.

Companies that have reengineered some of their business processes have ended up compressing formerly separate steps and tasks into jobs performed by a single person and integrating jobs into team activities. Reorganization then follows, a natural consequence of task synthesis and job redesign. The experiences of companies that have successfully reengineered and restructured their operations in strategy-supportive ways suggest attacking process fragmentation and overhead reduction in the following fashion:[34]

- Develop a flow chart of the total business process, including its interfaces with other value-chain activities.

---

[33]Evidence to this effect is contained in the scores of examples reported in Tom Peters, *Liberation Management* (New York: Alfred A. Knopf, 1992); Quinn, *Intelligent Enterprise;* and Hammer and Champy, *Reengineering the Corporation.*
[34]Quinn, *Intelligent Enterprise,* p. 162.

- Try to simplify the process first, eliminating tasks and steps where possible and analyzing how to streamline the performance of what remains.

- Determine which parts of the process can be automated (usually those that are repetitive, time-consuming, and require little thought or decision); consider introducing advanced technologies that can be upgraded to achieve next-generation capability and provide a basis for further productivity gains down the road.

- Evaluate each activity in the process to determine whether it is strategy-critical or not. Strategy-critical activities are candidates for benchmarking to achieve best-in-industry or best-in-world performance status.

- Weigh the pros and cons of outsourcing activities that are noncritical or that contribute little to organizational capabilities and core competencies.

- Design a structure for performing the activities that remain; reorganize the personnel and groups who perform these activities into the new structure.

Reengineer, then reorganize.

Reengineering can produce dramatic gains in productivity and organizational capability when done properly. In the order-processing section of General Electric's circuit breaker division, elapsed time from order receipt to delivery was cut from three weeks to three days by consolidating six production units into one, reducing a variety of former inventory and handling steps, automating the design system to replace a human custom-design process, and cutting the organizational layers between managers and workers from three to one.[35] Productivity rose 20 percent in one year, and unit manufacturing costs dropped 30 percent.

There's no escaping the conclusion that reengineering, in concert with advanced office technologies, empowerment, and the use of self-directed work teams, provides company managers with important new organization design options. Organizational hierarchies can be flattened and middle-management layers removed. Responsibility and decision-making authority can be pushed downward and outward to those places in the organization where customer contacts are made. Strategy-critical processes can be unified, performed more quickly and at lower cost, and made more responsive to changing customer preferences and expectations. Used properly, these new design approaches can trigger big gains in organizational creativity and employee productivity.

Illustration Capsule 28 reports the results of a study of trends in organizational arrangements in multinational and global companies.

The job of strategy implementation is to convert strategic plans into actions and good results. The test of successful strategy implementation is whether actual organization performance matches or exceeds the targets spelled out in the strategic plan. Shortfalls in performance signal weak strategy, weak implementation, or both.

In deciding how to implement strategy, managers have to determine what internal conditions are needed to execute the strategic plan successfully. Then they must create these conditions as rapidly as practical. The process involves creating a series of tight fits:

Key Points

---

[35]T. Stuart, "GE Keeps Those Ideas Coming," *Fortune*, August 12, 1991. For other examples, see Gene Hall, Jim Rosenthal, and Judy Wade, "How to Make Reengineering Really Work," *Harvard Business Review* 71, no. 6 (November–December 1993), pp. 119–31.

A 1993 study of 43 large U.S.-based consumer products companies conducted by McKinsey & Co., a leading management consulting firm, identified internal organizational actions with the strongest and weakest links to rapidly growing sales and profits in international and global markets.

Organizational Actions Strongly Linked to International Success

- Centralizing international decision-making in every area except new product development.
- Having a worldwide management development program and more foreigners in senior management posts.
- Requiring international experience for advancement into top management.
- Linking global managers with video-conferencing and electronic mail.
- Having product managers of foreign subsidiaries report to a country general manager.
- Using local executives to head operations in foreign countries (however, this is rapidly ceasing to distinguish successful companies

because nearly everyone has implemented such a practice).

Organizational Actions Weakly Linked to International Success

- Creating global divisions.
- Forming international strategic business units.
- Establishing centers of excellence (where a single company facility takes global responsibility for a key product or emerging technology (too new to evaluate pro or con).
- Using cross-border task forces to resolve problems and issues.
- Creating globally-integrated management information systems.

However, the lists of organizational do's and don'ts are far from decisive. In general, the study found that internal organizational structure "doesn't matter that much" as compared to having products with attractive prices and features. It is wrong to expect good results just because of good organization. Moreover, certain organizational arrangements, such as centers of excellence, are too new to determine whether they positively affect sales and profit growth.

Source: Based on information reported by Joann S. Lublin, "Study Sees U.S. Businesses Stumbling on the Road to Globalization," *The Wall Street Journal*, March 22, 1993, p. B4B.

- Between strategy and the organization's skills, competencies, and structure.
- Between strategy and budgetary allocations.
- Between strategy and policy.
- Between strategy and internal support systems.
- Between strategy and the reward structure.
- Between strategy and the corporate culture.

The tighter the fits, the more powerful strategy execution becomes and the more likely targeted performance can actually be achieved.

Implementing strategy is not just a top-management function; it is a job for the whole management team. All managers function as strategy-implementers in their respective areas of authority and responsibility. All managers have to consider what actions to take in their areas to achieve the intended results—they each need an *action agenda*.

The three major organization-building actions are (1) filling key positions with able people, (2) seeing that the organization has the skills, know-how, core competencies, and internal capabilities needed to perform its value-chain activities proficiently, and (3) structuring the work effort and deciding what the organization chart should look like. Selecting able people for key positions tends to be one of the earliest strategy implementation steps because it takes a full complement of capable managers to get changes in place and functioning smoothly.

Building strategy-critical core competencies is one of the best ways to outexecute rivals with similar strategies. Core competencies emerge from skills and activities performed at different points in the value chain that, when linked, create unique organizational capability. The key to leveraging a company's core competencies into long-term competitive advantage is to concentrate more effort and more talent than rivals do on strengthening and deepening these competencies. The multiskill, multi-activity character of core competencies makes achieving dominating depth an exercise in (1) managing human skills, knowledge bases, and intellect and (2) coordinating and networking the efforts of different work groups and departments at every place in the value chain related to such competencies.

Matching structure to strategy centers around making strategy-critical activities the main organizational building blocks and finding effective ways to bridge organizational lines of authority and coordinate the related efforts of separate units and individuals. Other big considerations include what decisions to centralize and what decisions to decentralize and whether noncritical activities can be outsourced more effectively or efficiently than they can be performed internally.

All organization structures have strategic advantages and disadvantages; there is no one best way to organize. Functionally specialized organization structures have traditionally been the most popular way to organize single-business companies. Functional organization works well where strategy-critical activities closely match discipline-specific activities and minimal interdepartmental cooperation is needed. But it has significant drawbacks: functional myopia and empire-building, interdepartmental rivalries, excessive process fragmentation, and vertically layered management hierarchies.

Geographic organization structures are favored by enterprises operating in diverse geographic markets or across expansive geographic areas. SBU structures are well-suited to companies pursuing related diversification. Decentralized business-unit structures are well-suited to companies pursuing unrelated diversification. Matrix structures work well for companies that need separate lines of authority and managers for each of several strategic dimensions (products, buyer segments, functional departments, projects or ventures, technologies, core business processes, geographic areas) yet also need close cooperation between these managers to coordinate related value-chain activities, share or transfer skills, and perform certain related activities jointly.

Whatever formal organization structure is chosen, it usually has to be supplemented with interdisciplinary task forces, incentive compensation schemes tied to measures of joint performance, empowerment of cross-functional teams to perform and unify fragmented processes and strategy-critical activities, special project and venture teams, self-contained work teams, and contact managers.

New strategic priorities like short design-to-market cycles, multiversion production, and personalized customer service are promoting a revolution in organization-building featuring lean, flat, horizontal structures that are responsive and innovative. Such designs for matching structure to strategy involve fewer layers of management authority, small-scale business units, reengineering work processes to reduce fragmentation across departmental lines, the creation of process teams and cross-functional work groups, managers and workers empowered to act on their own judgments, partnerships with key suppliers and increased outsourcing of noncritical activities, lean staffing of internal support functions, and use of computers and telecommunications technologies to provide fast access to and information.

SUGGESTED READINGS

Aaker, David A. "Managing Assets and Skills: The Key to a Sustainable Competitive Advantage." *California Management Review* 31 (Winter 1989), pp. 91–106.

Bartlett, Christopher A., and Sumantra Ghoshal. "Matrix Management: Not a Structure, a Frame of Mind." *Harvard Business Review* 68, no. 4 (July–August 1990), pp. 138–45.

Bettis, Richard A., and William K. Hall. "The Business Portfolio Approach—Where It Falls Down in Practice." *Long Range Planning* 16, no. 2 (April 1983), pp. 95–104.

Chandler, Alfred D. *Strategy and Structure*. Cambridge, Mass.: MIT Press, 1962.

Hall, Gene, Jim Rosenthal, and Judy Wade. "How to Make Reengineering Really Work." *Harvard Business Review* 71, no. 6 (November–December 1993), pp. 119–31.

Hambrick, Donald C. "The Top Management Team: Key to Strategic Success." *California Management Review* 30, no. 1 (Fall 1987), pp. 88–108.

Hammer, Michael, and James Champy. *Reengineering the Corporation*. New York: HarperBusiness, 1993, chaps. 2 and 3.

Howard, Robert. "The CEO as Organizational Architect: An Interview with Xerox's Paul Allaire." *Harvard Business Review* 70, no. 5 (September–October 1992), pp. 107–19.

Katzenbach, Jon R., and Douglas K. Smith. "The Discipline of Teams." *Harvard Business Review* 71, no. 2 (March–April 1993), pp. 111–24.

Larson, Erik W., and David H. Gobeli. "Matrix Management: Contradictions and Insights." *California Management Review* 29, no. 4 (Summer 1987), pp. 126–27.

Powell, Walter W. "Hybrid Organizational Arrangements: New Form or Transitional Development?" *California Management Review* 30, no. 1 (Fall 1987), pp. 67–87.

Prahalad, C. K., and Gary Hamel. "The Core Competence of the Corporation." *Harvard Business Review* 68 (May–June 1990), pp. 79–93.

Quinn, James Brian. *Intelligent Enterprise*. New York: Free Press, 1992, chaps. 2 and 3.

Stalk, George, Philip Evans, and Lawrence E. Shulman. "Competing on Capabilities: The New Rules of Corporate Strategy." *Harvard Business Review* 70, no. 2 (March–April 1992), pp. 57–69.

Yip, George S. *Total Global Strategy: Managing for Worldwide Competitive Advantage*. Englewood Cliffs, N.J.: Prentice-Hall, 1992, chap. 8.

CHAPTER TEN

Implementing Strategy:
Budgets, policies, best practices, support systems, and rewards

If you talk about change but don't change the reward and recognition system, nothing changes.

Paul Allaire
CEO, Xerox Corporation

. . . Winning companies know how to do their work better.
Michael Hammer and James Champy

. . . While a corporation can come up with a plan for the future, it takes everybody's help—and commitment—to implement it.

Ronald W. Allen
CEO, Delta Airlines

In the previous chapter we emphasized the importance of building an organization capable of performing strategy-critical activities in a coordinated and highly competent manner. In this chapter we discuss five additional strategy-implementing tasks:

1. Reallocating resources to match the budgetary and staffing requirements of the new strategy.

2. Establishing strategy-supportive policies.

3. Instituting best practices and mechanisms for continuous improvement.

4. Installing support systems that enable company personnel to carry out their strategic roles proficiently day in and day out.

5. Employing motivational practices and incentive compensation methods that enhance organizationwide commitment to good strategy execution.

275

LINKING BUDGETS TO STRATEGY ————————————

Implementing strategy forces a manager into the budget-making process. Organizational units need enough resources to carry out their parts of the strategic plan. This includes having enough of the right kinds of people and having sufficient operating funds for organizational units to do their work successfully. Strategy-implementers must screen subordinates' requests for new capital projects and bigger operating budgets, distinguishing between what would be nice and what can make a cost-justified contribution to strategy execution. Moreover, implementers have to make a persuasive, documented case to superiors on what additional resources, if any, it will take to execute their assigned pieces of company strategy.

How well a strategy-implementer links budget allocations to the needs of strategy can either promote or impede the implementation process. Too little funding slows progress and impedes the ability of organizational units to execute their pieces of the strategic plan proficiently. Too much funding wastes organizational resources and reduces financial performance. Both outcomes argue for the strategy-implementer to be deeply involved in the budgeting process, closely reviewing the programs and budget proposals of strategy-critical organization units.

Implementers must also be willing to shift resources from one area to another to support new strategic initiatives and priorities. A change in strategy nearly always calls for budget reallocations. Units important in the old strategy may now be oversized and overfunded. Units that now have a bigger and more critical strategic role may need more people, new equipment, additional facilities, and above-average increases in their operating budgets. Strategy-implementers need to be active and forceful in shifting resources, downsizing some areas, upsizing others, and amply funding activities with a critical role in the new strategy. They have to exercise their power to allocate resources to make things happen and make the tough decisions to kill projects and activities that are no longer justified. The essential condition is that the funding requirements of the new strategy must drive how capital allocations are made and the size of each unit's operating budgets. Underfunding organizational units and activities pivotal to strategic success can defeat the whole implementation process.

Aggressive resource reallocation can have a positive strategic payoff. For example, at Harris Corporation where the strategy was to diffuse research ideas into areas that were commercially viable, top management regularly shifted groups of engineers out of government projects and moved them (as a group) into new commercial venture divisions. Boeing used a similar approach to reallocating ideas and talent; according to one Boeing officer, "We can do it (create a big new unit) in two weeks. We couldn't do it in two years at International Harvester."[1] Forceful actions to reallocate operating funds and move people into new organizational units signal a strong commitment to implementing strategic change and are frequently needed to catalyze the implementation process and give it credibility.

Fine-tuning the implementation of a company's existing strategy seldom requires big movements of people and money from one area to another. The desired improvements can usually be accomplished through above-average budget increases to organizational units where new initiatives are contemplated and below-average increases

---

Strategic Management Principle

Depriving strategy-critical groups of the funds needed to execute their pieces of the strategy can undermine the implementation process.

New strategies usually call for significant budget reallocations.

---

[1]Thomas J. Peters and Robert H. Waterman, Jr., *In Search of Excellence* (New York: Harper & Row, 1980), p. 125.

(or even small cuts) for the remaining organizational units. The chief exception occurs where a prime ingredient of corporate/business strategy is to generate fresh, new products and business opportunities within the existing budget. Then, as proposals and business plans worth pursuing bubble up from below, decisions have to be made regarding where the needed capital expenditures, operating budgets, and personnel will come from. Companies like 3M, GE, and Boeing shift resources and people from area to area on an as-needed basis to support the launch of new products and new business ventures. They empower "product champions" and small bands of would-be entrepreneurs by giving them financial and technical support and by setting up organizational units and programs to help new ventures blossom more quickly.

CREATING STRATEGY-SUPPORTIVE POLICIES AND PROCEDURES

Changes in strategy generally call for some changes in work practices and how internal operations are conducted. Asking people to alter established procedures and behavior always upsets the internal order of things. It is normal for pockets of resistance to develop and for people to exhibit some degree of stress and anxiety about how the changes will affect them, especially when the changes may eliminate jobs. Questions are also likely to arise over what needs to be done in like fashion and where there ought to be leeway for independent action.

Prescribing policies and operating procedures aids the task of implementing strategy in several ways:

1. New or freshly revised policies and procedures provide top-down guidance to operating managers, supervisory personnel, and employees regarding how certain things now need to be done and what behavior is expected, thus establishing some degree of regularity, stability, and dependability in how management has decided to try to execute the strategy and operate the business on a daily basis.

2. Policies and procedures help align actions and behavior with strategy throughout the organization, placing limits on independent action and channeling individual and group efforts along the intended path. Policies and procedures counteract tendencies for some people to resist or reject common approaches—most people refrain from violating company policy or ignoring established practices without first gaining clearance or having strong justification.

3. Policies and standardized operating procedures help enforce needed consistency in how particular strategy-critical activities are performed in geographically scattered operating units (different plants, sales regions, customer service centers, or the individual outlets in a chain operation). Eliminating significant differences in the operating practices and procedures of organizational units performing common functions is necessary to avoid sending mixed messages to internal personnel and to customers who do business with the company at multiple locations.

4. Because dismantling old policies and procedures and instituting new ones invariably alter the character of the internal work climate, strategy-implementers can use the policy-changing process as a powerful lever for

Illustration Capsule 29   Nike's Manufacturing Policies and Practices

When Nike decided on a strategy of outsourcing 100% of its athletic footwear from independent manufacturers (all of which turned out, for reasons of low cost, to be located in Taiwan, South Korea, Thailand, Indonesia, and China), it developed a series of policies and production practices to govern its working relationships with its "production partners" (a term Nike carefully nurtured because it implied joint responsibilities):

- Nike personnel were stationed on-site at all key manufacturing facilities; each Nike representative tended to stay at the same factory site for several years to get to know the partner's people and processes in detail. They functioned as liaisons with Nike headquarters, working to match Nike's R&D and new product design efforts with factory capabilities and to keep monthly orders for new production in line with the latest sales forecasts.

- Nike instituted a quality assurance program at each factory site to enforce up-to-date and effective quality management practices.

- Nike endeavored to minimize ups and downs in monthly production orders at factory sites making Nike's premium-priced top-of-the-line models (volumes typically ran 20,000 to 25,000 pairs daily); the policy was to keep month-to-month variations in order quantity under 20%. These factories made Nike footwear exclusively and were expected to codevelop new models and to coinvest in new technologies.

- Factory sites that made mid-to-low-end Nike products in large quantities (usually 70,000 to 85,000 pairs per day), known as "volume producers," were expected to handle most ups and downs in monthly orders themselves; these factories usually produced shoes for five to eight other buyers, giving them the flexibility to juggle orders and stabilize their production.

- It was strict Nike policy to pay its bills from production partners on time, providing them with predictable cash flows.

Source: Based on information in James Brian Quinn, *Intelligent Enterprise* (New York: Free Press, 1992), pp. 60–64.

changing the corporate culture in ways that produce a stronger fit with the new strategy.

From a strategy implementation perspective, therefore, company managers need to be inventive in devising policies and practices that can provide vital support to effective strategy implementation. McDonald's policy manual, in an attempt to steer "crew members" into stronger quality and service behavior patterns, spells out such detailed procedures as "Cooks must turn, never flip, hamburgers. If they haven't been purchased, Big Macs must be discarded in 10 minutes after being cooked and french fries in 7 minutes. Cashiers must make eye contact with and smile at every customer." At Delta Airlines, it is corporate policy to test the aptitudes of all applicants for flight attendants' positions for friendliness, cooperativeness, and teamwork. Caterpillar Tractor has a policy of guaranteeing its customers 24-hour parts delivery anywhere in the world; if it fails to fulfill the promise, it supplies the part free. Hewlett-Packard requires R&D people to make regular visits to customers to learn about their problems, talk about new product applications, and, in general, keep the company's R&D programs customer-oriented. Illustration Capsule 29 describes Nike's manufacturing policies and practices in some detail.

> **Well-conceived policies and procedures aid implementation; out-of-sync policies are barriers.**

Thus there is a definite role for new and revised policies and procedures in the strategy implementation process. Wisely constructed policies and procedures help enforce strategy implementation by channeling actions, behavior, decisions, and practices in directions that improve strategy execution. When policies and practices aren't strategy-supportive, they become a barrier to the kinds of attitudinal and behavioral changes strategy-implementers are trying to promote. Often, people opposed to certain elements of the strategy or certain implementation approaches will hide behind or vigorously defend long-standing policies and operating procedures in an effort to stall implementation or divert the approach to implementation along a different route. Any time a company alters its strategy, managers should review existing policies and operating procedures, proactively revise or discard those that are out of sync, and formulate new ones to facilitate execution of new strategic initiatives.

None of this implies that companies need huge policy manuals. Too much policy can be as stifling as wrong policy or as chaotic as no policy. Sometimes, the best policy for implementing strategy is a willingness to empower subordinates and let them do it any way they want if it makes sense and works. A little "structured chaos" can be a good thing when individual creativity and initiative are more essential to good strategy execution than standardization and strict conformity. When Rene McPherson became CEO at Dana Corp., he dramatically threw out 22½ inches of policy manuals and replaced them with a one-page statement of philosophy focusing on "productive people."[2] Creating a strong supportive fit between strategy and policy can mean more policies, less policies, or different policies. It can mean policies that require things to be done a certain way or policies that give employees leeway to do activities the way they think best.

INSTITUTING BEST PRACTICES AND A COMMITMENT TO CONTINUOUS IMPROVEMENT

If value-chain activities are to be performed as effectively and efficiently as possible, each department and organizational unit needs to benchmark how it performs specific tasks and activities against best-in-industry or best-in-world performers. A strong commitment to searching out and adopting best practices is integral to effective strategy implementation—especially for strategy-critical and big-dollar activities where better quality performance or lower costs can translate into a sizable bottom-line impact.

Identifying and implementing best practices is a journey not a destination.

The benchmarking movement to search out, study, and implement best practices has spawned a number of spinoff efforts—reengineering (the redesign of business processes), continuous improvement programs, and total quality management (TQM). A 1991 survey by The Conference Board showed 93 percent of manufacturing companies and 69 percent of service companies have implemented some form of quality improvement program.[3] Another survey found that 55 percent of American executives and 70 percent of Japanese executives used quality improvement information at least monthly as part of their assessment of overall business performance.[4] Indeed, quality improvement processes have now become part of the fabric of implementing strategies keyed to defect-free manufacture, superior product quality, superior customer service, and total customer satisfaction.

Management interest in quality improvement programs typically originates in a company's production areas—fabrication and assembly in manufacturing enterprises,

---

[2]Ibid., p. 65.
[3]Judy D. Olian and Sara L. Rynes, "Making Total Quality Work: Aligning Organizational Processes, Performance Measures, and Stakeholders," *Human Resource Management* 30, no. 3 (Fall 1991), p. 303.
[4]Ibid.

teller transactions in banks, order picking and shipping at catalog firms, or customer-contact interfaces in service organizations. Other times, initial interest begins with executives who hear TQM presentations, read about TQM, or talk to people in other companies that have benefited from total quality programs. Usually, interested managers have quality and customer-satisfaction problems they are struggling to solve.

TQM entails creating a total quality culture bent on continuously improving the performance of every task and value-chain activity.

While TQM concentrates on the production of quality goods and the delivery of excellent customer service, to succeed it must extend organizationwide to employee efforts in all departments—HR, billing, R&D, engineering, accounting and records, and information systems—that may lack less-pressing customer-driven incentives to improve. This is because the institution of best practices and continuous improvement programs involves reforming the corporate culture and shifting to a total quality/continuous improvement business philosophy that permeates every facet of the organization. TQM aims at instilling enthusiasm and commitment to doing things right from top to bottom of the organization. It entails a restless search for continuing improvement, the little steps forward each day that the Japanese call *kaizen*. TQM is a race without a finish. The managerial objective is to kindle an innate, burning desire in people to use their ingenuity and initiative to progressively improve on how tasks and value-chain activities are performed. TQM preaches that there's no such thing as good enough and that everyone has a responsibility to participate in continuous improvement—see Illustration Capsule 30 describing Motorola's approach to involving employees in the TQM effort.

Reengineering seeks one-time quantum improvement; TQM seeks ongoing incremental improvement.

Best practices, reengineering, and continuous improvement efforts like TQM all aim at improved efficiency and reduced costs, better product quality, and greater customer satisfaction. The essential difference between reengineering and TQM is that reengineering aims at quantum gains on the order of 30 to 50 percent or more whereas total quality programs stress incremental progress, striving for inch-by-inch gains again and again in a never-ending stream. The two approaches to improved performance of value-chain activities are not mutually exclusive; it makes sense to use them in tandem. Reengineering can be used first to produce a good basic design that yields dramatic improvements in performing a business process. Total quality programs can then be used as a follow-on to work out bugs, perfect the process, and gradually improve both efficiency and effectiveness. Such a two-pronged approach to implementing organizational change is like a marathon race where you run the first four laps as fast as you can, then gradually pick up speed the remainder of the way.

When best practices, reengineering, and TQM are not part of a wider-scale effort to improve strategy execution and business performance, they deteriorate into strategy-blind efforts to manage better.

Surveys indicate that some companies benefit from reengineering and TQM and some do not.[5] Usually, the biggest beneficiaries are companies that view such programs not as ends in themselves but as tools for implementing and executing company strategy more effectively. The skimpiest payoffs from best practices, TQM, and reengineering occur when company managers seize them as something worth trying, novel ideas that could improve things; in most such instances, they result in strategy-blind efforts to simply manage better. There's an important lesson here. Best practices, TQM, and reengineering all need to be seen and used as part of a bigger-picture effort to execute strategy proficiently. Only strategy can point to which activities matter and what performance targets make the most sense. Absent a

[5]See, for example, Gene Hall, Jim Rosenthal, and Judy Wade, "How to Make Reengineering Really Work," *Harvard Business Review* 71, no. 6 (November–December 1993), pp. 119–31.

Motorola is rated as one of the best companies in measuring performance against its strategic targets and in promoting total quality practices that lead to continuous improvement. Motorola was selected in 1988 as one of the first winners of the Malcolm Baldrige Quality Award and has since improved on its own award-winning efforts. In 1993, the company estimated it was saving about $2.2 billion annually from its team-oriented approach to TQM and continuous improvement.

A central feature of Motorola's approach is a year-long contest highlighting the successes of employee teams from around the world in improving internal company practices, making better products, saving money, pleasing customers, and sharing best practices with other Motorola groups. The contest, known as the Total Customer Satisfaction Team Competition, in 1992 attracted entries from nearly 4,000 teams involving nearly 40,000 of Motorola's 107,000 employees. Preliminary judging eventually reduced the 1992 finalists to 24 teams from around the world, all of which were invited to Chicago in January 1993 to make a 12–minute presentation to a panel of 15 senior executives, including the CEO. Twelve teams were awarded gold medals and 12 silver medals. The gold medalists are listed below.

Motorola does not track the costs of the contest because "the benefits are so overwhelming." It has sent hundreds of videos about the contests to other companies wanting details. However, TQM consultants are skeptical whether other companies have progressed far enough in establishing a team-based quality culture to benefit from a companywide contest. The downsides to such elaborate contests, they say, are the added costs (preparation, travel, presentation, and judging) and the risks to the morale of those who don't win.

Gold Medal Teams	Work Location	Achievement
B.E.A.P. Goes On	Florida	Removed bottleneck in testing pagers by using robots.
The Expedition	Malaysia	Designed and delivered a new chip for Apple Computer in six months.
Operation Paging Storm	Singapore	Eliminated component alignment defect in pagers.
ET/EV=1	Illinois	Streamlined order process for auto electronics.
The Mission	Arizona	Developed quality system for design of iridium satellites.
Class Act	Illinois	Cut training program from 5 years to 2 with better results.
Dyna-Attackers	Dublin	Cut production time and defect rate on new battery part.
Orient Express	Malaysia	Cut response time on tooling orders from 23 days to 4.
The Dandles	Japan	Improved efficiency of boiler operations.
Cool Blue Racers	Arizona	Cut product development time in half to win IBM contract.
IO Plastics Misload	Manila	Eliminated resin seepage in modulator assembly.

Source: Based on information reported in Barnaby J. Feder, "At Motorola, Quality Is a Team Sport," *New York Times*, January 21, 1993, pp. C1 and C6.

strategic framework, managers lack the context in which to fix things that really matter to business-unit performance and competitive success.

To get the most from benchmarking, best practices, reengineering, TQM, and related tools for enhancing organizational competence in executing strategy, managers have to start with a clear fix on the indicators of successful strategy execution—defect-free manufacture, on-time delivery, low overall costs, exceeding customers' expectations, faster cycle time, increased product innovation, or some other specific performance measure. Benchmarking best-in-industry and best-in-world performance of most or all value-chain activities provides a realistic basis for setting internal performance milestones and longer-range targets.

Then comes the managerial task of building a total quality culture and instilling the necessary commitment to achieving the targets and performance measures that the strategy requires. The action steps managers can take include[6]

- Visible, unequivocal, and unyielding commitment to total quality and continuous improvement, including a quality vision and specific, measurable quality goals.
- Nudging people toward TQ-supportive behaviors by initiating such organizational programs as

  — Screening job applicants rigorously and hiring only those with attitudes and aptitudes right for quality-based performance.
  — Quality training for most employees.
  — Using teams and team-building exercises to reinforce and nurture individual effort (expansion of a TQ culture is facilitated when teams become more cross-functional, multitask, and increasingly self-managed).
  — Recognizing and rewarding individual and team efforts regularly and systematically.
  — Stressing prevention (doing it right the first time) not inspection (instituting ways to correct mistakes).

- Empowering employees so that authority for delivering great service or improving products is in the hands of the doers rather than the overseers.
- Providing quick electronic information access to doers so that real-time data can drive actions and decisions and feedback can continuously improve value-chain activities.
- Preaching that performance can, and must, be improved because competitors are not resting on past laurels and customers are always looking for something better.

If the targeted performance measures are appropriate to the strategy and if all organizational members (top executives, middle managers, professional staff, and line employees) buy into the process of continuous improvement, then the work climate will be conducive to proficient strategy execution and good bottom-line business performance.

INSTALLING SUPPORT SYSTEMS

Company strategies can't be implemented or executed well without a number of support systems for business operations. American, United, Delta, and other major airlines cannot hope to provide world-class passenger service without a computerized reservation system, an accurate and expeditious baggage handling system, and a strong aircraft maintenance program. Federal Express has a computerized parcel-tracking system that can instantly report the location of any given package in its transit-delivery process; it has communication systems that allow it to coordinate its

---

[6]Olian and Rynes, "Making Total Quality Work," pp. 305–6 and 310–11.

21,000 vans nationwide to make an average of 720,000 stops per day to pick up customer packages; and it has leading-edge flight operations systems that allow a single controller to direct as many as 200 FedEx aircraft simultaneously, overriding their flight plans should weather or special emergencies arise—all these operations essential to FedEx's strategy of next-day delivery of a package that "absolutely, positively has to be there."[7]

Otis Elevator has a sophisticated support system called OtisLine to coordinate its maintenance efforts nationwide.[8] Trained operators take all trouble calls, input critical information on a computer screen, and dispatch people directly via a beeper system to the local trouble spot. From the trouble-call inputs, problem patterns can be identified nationally and the information communicated to design and manufacturing personnel, allowing them to quickly alter design specifications or manufacturing procedures when needed to correct recurring problems. Also, much of the information needed for repairs is provided directly from faulty elevators through internally installed microcomputer monitors, further lowering outage time.

Procter & Gamble codes the more than 900,000 call-in inquiries it receives annually on its toll-free 800 number to obtain early warning signals of product problems and changing tastes.[9] Domino's Pizza has computerized systems at each outlet to facilitate ordering, inventory, payroll, cash flow, and work control functions, thereby freeing managers to spend more time on supervision, customer service, and business development activities.[10] Most telephone companies, electric utilities, and TV broadcasting systems have on-line monitoring systems to spot transmission problems within seconds and increase the reliability of their services. At Mrs. Fields' Cookies, systems can monitor sales at 15-minute intervals and suggest product mix changes, promotional tactics, or operating adjustments to improve customer response—see Illustration Capsule 31.

Well-conceived, state-of-the art support systems not only facilitate better strategy execution, they also can strengthen organizational capabilities enough to provide a competitive edge over rivals. For example, a company with a differentiation strategy based on superior quality needs systems for training personnel in quality techniques, tracking product quality at each production step, and ensuring that all goods shipped meet quality standards. A company striving to be a low-cost provider needs systems that exploit opportunities to drive costs out of the business. Fast-growing companies need employee recruiting systems to attract and hire qualified employees in large numbers. In businesses such as public accounting and management consulting where large numbers of professional staffers need cutting-edge technical know-how, companies have to install systems to train and retrain employees regularly and keep them supplied with up-to-date information.

Strategic Management Principle
Innovative, state-of-the-art support systems can be a basis for competitive advantage if they give a firm capabilities that rivals can't match.

Instituting Formal Reporting of Strategic Information

Accurate information is an essential guide to action. Every organization needs systems for gathering and reporting strategy-critical information and tracking key performance measures over time. Telephone companies have elaborate information

---

[7]James Brian Quinn, *Intelligent Enterprise* (New York: Free Press, 1992) pp. 114–15.
[8]Ibid., p. 181.
[9]Ibid., p. 186.
[10]Ibid., p. 111.

Illustration Capsule 31   Operating Practices and Support Systems at Mrs. Fields' Cookies, Inc.

Mrs. Fields' Cookies is one of the best known specialty foods companies in the United States with over 500 outlets in operation in malls, airports, and other high pedestrian-traffic locations; the company also has over 250 outlets retailing other bakery and cookie products. Debbi Fields, age 37, is the company's founder and CEO. Her business concept for Mrs. Fields' Cookies is "to serve absolutely fresh, warm cookies as though you'd stopped by my house and caught me just taking a batch from the oven." Cookies not sold within two hours are removed from the case and given to charity. The company's major form of advertising is sampling; store employees walk around the shopping mall giving away cookie samples. People are hired for store crews on the basis of warmth, friendliness, and the ability to have a good time giving away samples, baking fresh batches, and talking to customers during the course of a sale.

To implement its strategy, the company developed several novel practices and a customized computer support system. One key practice is giving each store an *hourly* sales quota. Another is for Fields to make unannounced visits to her stores, where she masquerades as a casual shopper to test the enthusiasm and sales techniques of store crews, sample the quality of the cookies they are baking, and observe customer reactions.

Debbi's husband Randy developed a software program that keeps headquarters and stores in close contact. Via the computer network, each store manager receives a daily sales goal (broken down by the hour) based on the store's recent performance history and on such special factors as special promotions, mall activities, weekdays vs. weekends, holiday shopping patterns, and the weather forecast. With the hourly sales quotas also comes a schedule of the number of cookies to bake and when to bake them. As the day progresses, store managers type in actual hourly sales figures and customer counts. If customer counts are up but sales are lagging, the computer is programmed to recommend more aggressive sampling or more suggestive selling. If it becomes obvious the day is going to be a bust for the store, the computer automatically revises the sales projections for the day, reducing hourly quotas and instructing how much to cut back cookie baking. To facilitate crew scheduling by the store manager, sales projections are also provided for two weeks in advance. All job applicants must sit at the store's terminal and answer a computerized set of questions as part of the interview process.

In addition, the computer software contains a menu giving store staff immediate access to company personnel policies, maintenance schedules for store equipment, and repair instructions. If a store manager has a specific problem, it can be entered on the system and routed to the appropriate person. Messages can be sent directly to Debbi Fields via the computer; even if she is on a store inspection trip, her promise is to respond to all inquiries within 48 hours.

The computerized information support system serves several objectives: (1) it gives store managers more time to work with their crews and achieve sales quotas as opposed to handling administrative chores and (2) it gives headquarters instantaneous information on store performance and a means of controlling store operations. Debbi Fields sees the system as a tool for projecting her influence and enthusiasm into more stores more frequently than she could otherwise reach.

Source: Developed from information in Mike Korologos, "Debbi Fields," *Sky Magazine*, July 1988, pp. 42–50.

Accurate, timely information allows organizational members to monitor progress and take corrective action promptly.

systems to measure signal quality, connection times, interrupts, wrong connections, billing errors, and other measures of reliability. To track and manage the quality of passenger service, airlines have information systems to monitor gate delays, on-time departures and arrivals, baggage handling times, lost baggage complaints, stockouts on meals and drinks, overbookings, and maintenance delays and failures. Many companies have provided customer-contact personnel with instant electronic access to customer databases so that they can respond effectively to customer inquiries and personalize customer services.

To properly oversee strategy implementation, company managers need prompt feedback on implementation initiatives to steer them to a successful conclusion in case early steps don't produce the expected progress or things seem to be drifting off course. Such monitoring (1) allows managers to detect problems early and adjust either the strategy or how it is being implemented and (2) provides some assurance that things are moving ahead as planned.[11] Early experiences are sometimes difficult to assess, but they yield the first hard data and should be closely scrutinized as a basis for corrective action.

Information systems need to cover four broad areas: (1) customer data, (2) operations data, (3) employee data, and (4) financial performance data. All key strategic performance indicators have to be measured as often as practical. Many retail companies generate daily sales reports for each store and maintain up-to-the-minute inventory and sales records on each item. Manufacturing plants typically generate daily production reports and track labor productivity on every shift. Monthly profit-and-loss statements are common, as are monthly statistical summaries.

In designing formal reports to monitor strategic progress, five guidelines should be observed:[12]

1. Information and reporting systems should involve no more data and reporting than is needed to give a reliable picture. The data gathered should emphasize strategically meaningful outcomes and symptoms of potentially significant developments. Temptations to supplement "what managers need to know" with other "interesting" but marginally useful information should be avoided.

2. Reports and statistical data-gathering have to be timely—not too late to take corrective action or so often as to overburden.

3. The flow of information and statistics should be kept simple. Complicated reports confound readers and divert attention to methodological issues; long or overly-detailed reports run the risk of going unread; and too many reports consume unnecessary amounts of managerial time.

4. Information and reporting systems should aim at "no surprises"; that is, they should point out early warning signs rather than just produce information. It is debatable whether reports should receive wide distribution ("for your information"); but they should always be provided to managers who are in a position to act when trouble signs appear.

5. Statistical reports should flag exceptions and big or unusual variances from plan, thus directing management attention to significant departures from targeted performance.

Statistical information gives the strategy-implementer a feel for the numbers; reports and meetings provide a feel for new developments and problems; and personal contacts add a feel for the people dimension. All are good barometers of overall performance and good indicators of which things are on and off track. Managers have to identify problem areas and deviations from plan before they can take actions either to improve implementation or fine-tune strategy.

---

[11]Boris Yavitz and William H. Newman, *Strategy in Action* (New York: Free Press, 1982), pp. 209–10.
[12]Peter F. Drucker, *Management: Tasks, Responsibilities, Practices* (New York: Harper & Row, 1974), pp. 498–504; Harold Koontz, "Management Control: A Suggested Formulation of Principles," *California Management Review* 2, no. 2 (Winter 1959), pp. 50–55; and William H. Sihler, "Toward Better Management Control Systems," *California Management Review* 14, no. 2 (Winter 1971), pp. 33–39.

DESIGNING STRATEGY-SUPPORTIVE REWARD SYSTEMS ———

It is important for organizational subunits and for individuals to be committed to implementing strategy and achieving performance targets. Company managers typically try to enlist organizationwide commitment to carrying out the strategic plan by motivating people and rewarding them for good performance. The range of options includes offering people the chance to be part of something exciting, giving them an opportunity for greater personal satisfaction, challenging them with ambitious performance targets for them, using the carrot of promotion and the stick of being "sidelined" in a routine or dead-end job, giving praise, recognition, constructive criticism, more (or less) responsibility, increased (or decreased) job control and decision-making autonomy, offering a better shot at assignments in attractive locations, the intangible bonds of group acceptance, greater job security, and the promise of sizable financial rewards (salary increases, performance bonuses, stock options, and retirement packages). But motivational techniques and rewards have to be used *creatively* and linked tightly to the factors and targets necessary for good strategy execution.

Motivational Practices

One of the biggest strategy-implementing challenges is to employ motivational techniques that build wholehearted commitment and winning attitudes among employees.

Successful strategy-implementers inspire and challenge employees to do their best. They get employees to buy into the strategy and commit to making it work. They allow employees to participate in making decisions about how to perform their jobs, and they try to make jobs interesting and satisfying. As Frederick Herzberg said, "If you want people motivated to do a good job, give them a good job to do." They structure individual efforts into teams and work groups in order to facilitate an exchange of ideas and a climate of support. They devise strategy-supportive motivational approaches and use them effectively. Consider some actual examples:[13]

- At Mars Inc. (best known for its candy bars), every employee, including the president, gets a weekly 10 percent bonus by coming to work on time each day that week. This on-time incentive is designed to minimize absenteeism and tardiness and to boost worker productivity in order to produce the greatest number of candy bars during each available minute of machine time.

- In a number of Japanese companies, employees meet regularly to hear inspirational speeches, sing company songs, and chant the corporate litany. In the United States, Tupperware conducts a weekly Monday night rally to honor, applaud, and fire up its salespeople who conduct Tupperware parties. Amway and Mary Kay Cosmetics hold similar inspirational get-togethers for their sales force organizations.

- A San Diego area company assembles its 2,000 employees at its six plants the first thing every workday to listen to a management talk about the state of the company. Then they engage in brisk calisthenics. This company's management believes "that by doing one thing together each day, it reinforces the unity of the company. It's also fun. It gets the blood up." Managers take turns making the presentations. Many of the speeches "are

---

[13]Alfie Kohn, "Rethinking Rewards," *Harvard Business Review* 71, no. 6 (November–December 1993), p. 49.

very personal and emotional, not approved beforehand or screened by anybody."

- Texas Instruments and Dana Corp. insist that teams and divisions set their own goals and have regular peer reviews.

- Procter & Gamble's brand managers are asked to compete fiercely against each other; the official policy is "a free-for-all among brands with no holds barred." P&G's system of purposeful internal competition breeds people who love to compete and excel. Those who win become corporate heroes, and around them emerges a folklore of war stories of valiant brand managers who waged uphill struggles against great odds and made market successes out of their brands.

These motivational approaches accentuate the positive; others blend positive and negative features. Consider the way Harold Geneen, former president and chief executive officer of ITT, allegedly combined the use of money, tension, and fear:

Geneen provides his managers with enough incentives to make them tolerate the system. Salaries all the way through ITT are higher than average—Geneen reckons 10 percent higher—so that few people can leave without taking a drop. As one employee put it: "We're all paid just a bit more than we think we're worth." At the very top, where the demands are greatest, the salaries and stock options are sufficient to compensate for the rigors. As someone said, "He's got them by their limousines."

Having bound his [managers] to him with chains of gold, Geneen can induce the tension that drives the machine. "The key to the system," one of his [managers] explains, "is the profit forecast. Once the forecast has been gone over, revised, and agreed on, the managing director has a personal commitment to Geneen to carry it out. That's how he produces the tension on which the success depends." The tension goes through the company, inducing ambition, perhaps exhilaration, but always with some sense of fear: what happens if the target is missed?[14]

If a strategy-implementer's motivational approach and reward structure induces too much stress, internal competitiveness, and job insecurity, the results can be counterproductive. For a healthy work environment, positive reinforcement needs to outweigh negative reinforcement. Yet it is unwise to completely eliminate pressure for performance and the anxiety it evokes. There is no evidence that a no-pressure work environment leads to superior strategy execution or sustained high performance. As the CEO of a major bank put it, "There's a deliberate policy here to create a level of anxiety. Winners usually play like they're one touchdown behind."[15] High-performing organizations need a cadre of ambitious people who relish the opportunity to climb the ladder of success, love a challenge, thrive in a performance-oriented environment, and find some competition and pressure useful to satisfy their own drives for personal recognition, accomplishment, and self-satisfaction. Unless meaningful incentive and career consequences are associated with successfully implementing strategic initiatives and hitting strategic performance targets, few people will attach much significance to the company's strategic plan.

Positive motivational approaches generally work better than negative ones.

[14]Anthony Sampson, *The Sovereign State of ITT* (New York: Stein and Day, 1973), p. 132.
[15]As quoted in John P. Kotter and James L. Heskett, *Corporate Culture and Performance* (New York: Free Press, 1992), p. 91.

Rewards and Incentives

The conventional view is that a manager's push for strategy implementation should incorporate more positive than negative motivational elements because when cooperation is positively enlisted and rewarded, rather than strong-armed by a boss's orders, people tend to respond with more enthusiasm and more effort. Nevertheless, how much of which incentives to use depends on how hard the task of strategy implementation will be. A manager has to do more than just talk to everyone about how important new strategic practices and performance targets are to the organization's future well-being. No matter how inspiring, talk seldom commands people's best efforts for long. To get employees' sustained, energetic commitment, management has to be resourceful in designing and using motivational incentives—both monetary and nonmonetary. The more a manager understands what motivates subordinates and the more he or she relies on motivational incentives as a tool for implementing strategy, the greater will be employees' commitment to good day in, day out execution of their roles in the company's strategic plan.

Linking Work Assignments to Performance Targets

The first step in creating a strategy-supportive system of rewards and incentives is to define jobs and assignments in terms of the results to be accomplished, not the duties and functions to be performed. Focusing the jobholder's attention and energy on what to achieve as opposed to what activities to perform boosts the chances of reaching agreed-on outcomes. It is flawed thinking to stress duties and activities in job descriptions in hopes that the by-products will be the desired kinds of accomplishments. In any job, performing assigned tasks is not equivalent to achieving intended outcomes. Working hard, staying busy, and diligently attending to assigned duties do not guarantee results. Stressing "what to accomplish" instead of "what to do" is an important difference. As any student knows, just because an instructor teaches doesn't mean students are learning. Teaching and learning are different things—the first is an activity and the second is a result.

Job assignments should stress the results to be achieved rather than the duties and activities to be performed.

Emphasizing what to accomplish—that is, performance targets for individual jobs, work groups, departments, businesses, and the entire company—has the larger purpose of making the work environment results-oriented. Without target objectives, individuals and work groups can become so engrossed in the details of performing assigned functions on schedule that they lose sight of what the tasks are intended to accomplish. By regularly tracking actual achievement versus targeted performance (monthly, weekly, or daily if need be), managers can proactively concentrate on making the right things happen rather than supervising people closely in hopes that the right outcomes will materialize if every activity is performed according to the book. Making the right things happen is what results-oriented management is all about.

To create a tight fit between carrying out work assignments and accomplishing the strategic plan, managers must use strategic and financial objectives as the basis for incentive compensation. If the details of strategy have been fleshed out thoroughly from the corporate level down to the operating level, appropriate measures of performance either exist or can be developed for the whole company, for each business unit, for each functional department, for each operating unit, and for each work group. These become the targets that strategy-implementers aim at achieving, and they form the basis for deciding on the necessary jobs, skills, expertise, funding, and time frame.

Usually a number of performance measures are needed at each level. At the corporate and line-of-business levels, performance objectives typically revolve around measures of profitability (total profit, return on equity investment, return on total assets, return on sales, operating profit, and so on), sales and earnings growth, market share, product quality, customer satisfaction, and other hard measures that market position, overall competitiveness, and future prospects have improved. In the manufacturing area, the strategy-relevant performance measures may focus on unit manufacturing costs, employee productivity, on-time production and shipping, defect rates, the number and extent of work stoppages due to labor disagreements and equipment breakdowns, and so on. In the marketing area, measures may include unit selling costs, dollar sales and unit volume, sales penetration of each target customer group, market share, the fate of newly introduced products, the frequency of customer complaints, the number of new accounts acquired, and customer satisfaction surveys. While most performance measures are quantitative, several may have elements of subjectivity—the state of labor-management relations, employee morale, the effectiveness of advertising campaigns, and how far the firm is ahead of or behind rivals on quality, service, and technological capability.

Rewarding Performance   The most dependable way to keep people focused on the objectives laid out in the strategic plan and to make achieving these objectives a way of life up and down the organization is to generously reward individuals and groups who achieve their assigned targets and deny rewards to those who don't. For strategy-implementers, doing a good job needs to mean one thing: achieving the agreed-on performance targets. Any other standard undermines implementation of the strategic plan and condones the diversion of time and energy into activities that don't much matter (if such activities are really important, they deserve a place in the strategic plan). The pressure to achieve the targeted strategic performance should be unrelenting. A "no excuses" standard has to prevail.[16]

With the pressure to perform must come deserving and meaningful rewards. Without an ample payoff, the system breaks down, and the strategy-implementer is left with the unworkable option of barking orders and pleading for compliance. Some of the best performing companies—Wal-Mart, Nucor Steel, Lincoln Electric, Electronic Data Systems, Remington Products, and Mary Kay Cosmetics—owe much of their success to a set of incentives and rewards that induce people to do the things needed to hit performance targets and execute strategy well enough for the companies to become leaders in their industries.

Nucor's strategy was (and is) to be *the* low-cost producer of steel products. Because labor costs are a significant fraction of total cost in the steel business, successful implementation of Nucor's low-cost strategy requires achieving lower labor costs per ton of steel than competitors'. To drive its labor costs per ton below rivals', Nucor management utilizes production incentives that give workers bonuses roughly equal to their regular wages if their production teams meet or exceed weekly production targets; the regular wage scale is set at levels comparable to wages for similar manufacturing jobs in the local areas where Nucor has plants. Bonuses are paid every two weeks based on the prior weeks' actual production levels measured against the targets. The results of Nucor's piece-rate incentive plan are impressive. Nucor's labor productivity

> **Strategic Management Principle**
> The strategy-implementer's standard for judging whether individuals and organizational units have done a good job must be whether they achieved their performance targets.

---

[16]Tom Peters and Nancy Austin, *A Passion for Excellence* (New York: Random House, 1985), p. xix.

(in output per worker) runs over 50 percent above the average of the unionized workforces of the industry's major producers. Nucor enjoys about a $50 to $75 per ton cost advantage over large, integrated steel producers like U.S. Steel and Bethlehem Steel (a substantial part of which comes from its labor cost advantage), and Nucor workers are the highest-paid workers in the steel industry.

At Remington Products, only 65 percent of factory workers' paychecks is salary; the rest is based on piece-work incentives. The company conducts 100 percent inspections of products, and rejected items are counted against incentive pay for the responsible worker. Top-level managers earn more from bonuses than from their salaries. During the first four years of Remington's incentive program, productivity rose 17 percent.

These and other experiences demonstrate some important lessons about designing rewards and incentives:

1. *The performance payoff must be a major, not minor, piece of the total compensation package.* Incentives that amount to 20 percent or more of total compensation are big attention-getters and are capable of driving individual effort.

2. *The incentive plan should extend to all managers and all workers*, not just be restricted to top management. It is a gross miscalculation to expect that lower-level managers and employees will work their tails off to hit performance targets just so a few senior executives can get lucrative rewards!

3. *The reward system must be administered with scrupulous care and fairness.* If performance standards are set unrealistically high or if individual performance evaluations are not accurate and well-documented, dissatisfaction and disgruntlement with the system will overcome any positive benefits.

4. *The incentives must be tightly linked to achieving only those performance targets spelled out in the strategic plan* and not to any other factors that get thrown in because they are thought to be nice occurrences. Performance evaluation based on factors not related to the strategy signal that either the strategic plan is incomplete (because important performance targets were left out) or management's real agenda is something other than what was stated in the strategic plan.

5. *The performance targets each individual is expected to achieve should involve outcomes that the individual can personally affect.* The role of incentives is to enhance individual commitment and channel behavior in beneficial directions. This role is not well-served when the performance measures an individual is judged by are outside his/her arena of influence.

Aside from these general guidelines it is hard to prescribe what kinds of incentives and rewards to develop except to say that the payoff must be directly attached to performance measures that indicate the strategy is working and implementation is on track. If the company's strategy is to be a low-cost provider, the incentive system must reward performance that lowers costs. If the company has a differentiation strategy predicated on superior quality and service, the incentive system must reward such outcomes as zero defects, infrequent need for product repair, low numbers of customer complaints, and speedy order processing and delivery. If a company's growth is predicated on a strategy of new product innovation, incentives should be tied to factors such as the percentages of revenues and profits coming from newly introduced products.

Why the Performance-Reward Link Is Important

The use of incentives and rewards is the single most powerful tool management has to win strong employee commitment to carrying out the strategic plan. Failure to use this tool wisely and powerfully will weaken the entire implementation process. *Decisions on salary increases, incentive compensation, promotions, who gets which key assignments, and the ways and means of awarding praise and recognition are the strategy-implementer's foremost attention-getting, commitment-generating devices.* How a company's incentives are structured signals what sorts of behavior and performance management wants; how managers parcel out raises, promotions, and praise says more about who is considered to be doing a good job than any other factor. Such matters seldom escape the closest employee scrutiny. A company's system of incentives and rewards thus ends up being the vehicle by which its strategy is emotionally ratified in the form of real commitment. Incentives make it in employees' self-interest to do what is needed to achieve the performance targets spelled out in the strategic plan.

> **Strategic Management Principle**
> **The reward structure is management's most powerful strategy-implementing tool.**

Making Performance-Driven Compensation Work

Creating a tight fit between strategy and the reward structure is generally best accomplished by agreeing on strategy-critical performance objectives, fixing responsibility and deadlines for achieving them, and treating their achievement as a pay-for-performance *contract*. From a strategy-implementation perspective, the key is to make strategically relevant measures of performance the dominating basis for designing incentives, evaluating individual efforts, and handing out rewards. Every organizational unit, every manager, every team or work group, and ideally every employee needs to have clearly defined performance targets to aim at that reflect measurable progress in implementing the strategic game plan, and then they must be held accountable for achieving them. For example, at Banc One, the fifth largest U.S. bank and the second most profitable bank in the world (based on return on assets), a high level of customer satisfaction is a key performance objective. To enhance employee commitment to the task of pleasing customers, Banc One ties the pay scales in each branch office to that branch's customer satisfaction rating—the higher the branch's ratings, the higher that branch's pay scales. By shifting from a theme of equal pay for equal work to one of equal pay for equal performance, Banc One has focused the attention of branch employees on the task of pleasing, even delighting, their customers.

To prevent undermining and undoing pay-for-performance approaches to strategy implementation, companies must be scrupulously fair in comparing actual performance against agreed-on performance targets. Everybody needs to understand how their incentive compensation is calculated and how their individual performance targets contribute to organizational performance targets. The reasons for anyone's failure or deviations from targets have to be explored fully to determine whether the causes are attributable to poor individual performance or to circumstances beyond the individual's control. Skirting the system to find ways to reward nonperformers must be absolutely avoided. It is debatable whether exceptions should be made for people who've tried hard, gone the extra mile, yet still come up short because of circumstances beyond their control—a good case can be made either way. The problem with making exceptions for unknowable, uncontrollable, or unforeseeable circumstances is that once "good" excuses start to creep into justifying rewards for nonperformers, the door is open for all kinds of "legitimate" reasons why actual performance failed to match targeted performance. In short, people at all levels have to be held accountable for carrying out their assigned parts of the strategic plan, and they have to know their rewards are based on the caliber of their strategic accomplishments.

Key Points

A change in strategy nearly always calls for budget reallocations. Reworking the budget to make it more strategy-supportive is a crucial part of the implementation process because every organization unit needs to have the people, equipment, facilities, and other resources to carry out its part of the strategic plan (but no more than what it really needs!). Implementing a new strategy often entails shifting resources from one area to another—downsizing units that are overstaffed and overfunded, upsizing those more critical to strategic success, and killing projects and activities that are no longer justified.

Anytime a company alters its strategy, company managers are well-advised to review existing policies and operating procedures, revising those that are out of sync and devising new ones. Prescribing new or freshly revised policies and operating procedures aids the task of implementation (1) by providing top-down guidance to operating managers, supervisory personnel, and employees regarding how certain things now need to be done and what behavior is expected; (2) by placing limits on independent actions and decisions; (3) by enforcing needed consistency in how particular strategy-critical activities are performed in geographically scattered operating units; and (4) by helping to create a strategy-supportive work climate and corporate culture. Huge policy manuals are uncalled for. Indeed, when individual creativity and initiative are more essential to good execution than standardization and conformity, it is often wise to give people the freedom to do things however they see fit and hold them accountable for good results. Hence, creating a supportive fit between strategy and policy can mean more policies, fewer policies, or different policies.

Competent strategy execution entails visible, unyielding managerial commitment to best practices and continuous improvement. Benchmarking, instituting best practices, reengineering core business processes, and total quality management programs all aim at improved efficiency, lower costs, better product quality, and greater customer satisfaction. All these techniques are important tools for learning how to execute a strategy more proficiently. Benchmarking provides a realistic basis for setting performance targets. Instituting "best-in-industry" or "best-in-world" operating practices in most or all value-chain activities is essential to create a total quality, high-performance work environment. Reengineering is a way to make quantum progress in being world class while TQM instills a commitment to continuous improvement. Typically, such techniques involve organizing the work effort around cross-functional, multitask teams and work groups that are self-directed and/or self-managed.

Company strategies can't be implemented or executed well without a number of support systems to carry on business operations. Well-conceived, state-of-the-art support systems not only facilitate better strategy execution, they can also strengthen organizational capabilities enough to provide a competitive edge over rivals. In an age of computers, computerized monitoring and control systems, and expanding communications capabilities, companies can't hope to outexecute their competitors without elaborate information systems and technologically sophisticated operating capabilities that allow people to perform their jobs effectively and efficiently.

Strategy-supportive motivational practices and reward systems are powerful management tools for gaining employee buy-in and commitment. Positive motivational practices generally work better than negative ones, but there is a place for both. There's also a place for both monetary and nonmonetary incentives. For monetary incentives to work well (1) the monetary payoff should be a major percentage of the compensation package, (2) the incentive plan should extend to all managers and workers, (3) the system should be administered with care and fairness, (4) the incentives should be linked to performance targets spelled out in the strategic plan, and (5) each individual's performance targets should involve outcomes the person can personally affect.

Suggested Readings

Grant, Robert M., Rami Shani, and R. Krishnan, "TQM's Challenge to Management Theory and Practice." *Sloan Management Review* (Winter 1994), pp. 25–35.

Herzberg, Frederick. "One More Time: How Do You Motivate Employees?" *Harvard Business Review* 65, no. 4 (September–October 1987), pp. 109–20.

Johnson, H. Thomas. *Relevance Regained.* New York: Free Press, 1992.

Kiernan, Matthew J. "The New Strategic Architecture: Learning to Compete in the Twenty-First Century." *Academy of Management Executive* 7, no. 1 (February 1993), pp. 7–21.

Kohn, Alfie. "Why Incentive Plans Cannot Work." *Harvard Business Review* 71, no. 5 (September-October 1993), pp. 54–63.

Olian, Judy D. and Sara L. Rynes, "Making Total Quality Work: Aligning Organizational Processes, Performance Measures, and Stakeholders," *Human Resource Management* 30, no. 3 (Fall 1991), pp. 303–333.

Wiley, Carolyn. "Incentive Plan Pushes Production." *Personnel Journal* (August 1993), pp. 86–91.

Quinn, James Brian. *Intelligent Enterprise.* New York: Free Press, 1992, chap. 4.

Shetty, Y. K. "Aiming High: Competitive Benchmarking for Superior Performance." *Long-Range Planning* 26, no. 1 (February 1993), pp. 39–44.

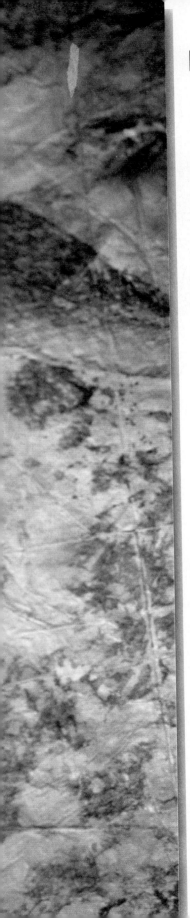

CHAPTER ELEVEN

Implementing Strategy:
Culture and leadership

Weak leadership can wreck the soundest strategy; forceful execution of even a poor plan can often bring victory.

Sun Zi

Effective leaders do not just reward achievement, they celebrate it.

Shelley A. Kirkpatrick and Edwin A. Locke

Ethics is the moral courage to do what we know is right, and not to do what we know is wrong.

C. J. Silas
CEO, Philips Petroleum

. . . A leader lives in the field with his troops.

H. Ross Perot

In the previous two chapters we examined six of the strategy-implementer's tasks—building a capable organization, steering ample resources into strategy-critical activities and operating units, establishing strategy-supportive policies, instituting best practices and programs for continuous improvement, creating internal support systems to enable better execution, and employing appropriate motivational practices and compensation incentives. In this chapter we explore the two remaining implementation tasks: creating a strategy-supportive corporate culture and exerting the internal leadership needed to drive implementation forward.

BUILDING A STRATEGY-SUPPORTIVE CORPORATE CULTURE

Every company has a unique organizational culture. Each has its own business philosophy and principles, its own ways of approaching problems and making decisions, its own embedded patterns of "how we do things around here," its own lore (stories told over and over to illustrate company values and what they mean to employees), its own taboos and political don'ts—in other words, its own ingrained beliefs, behavior and thought patterns, business practices, and personality. The

---

Illustration Capsule 32   The Culture at Nordstrom

The culture at Nordstrom, a department store retailer noted for exceptional commitment to its customers, revolves around the company's motto: "Respond to Unreasonable Customer Requests." Living up to the company's motto is so strongly ingrained in behavior that employees learn to relish the challenges that some customer requests pose. Usually, meeting customer demands in pleasing fashion entails little more than gracious compliance and a little extra personal attention. But occasionally it means paying a customer's parking ticket when in-store gift wrapping takes longer than normal or hand delivering items purchased by phone to the airport for a customer with an emergency need.

At Nordstrom, each out-of-the-ordinary customer request is seen as an opportunity for a "heroic" act by an employee and a way to build the company's reputation for great service. Nordstrom encourages these acts by promoting employees noted for outstanding service, keeping scrapbooks of "heroic" acts, and paying its salespeople entirely on commission (it is not unusual for good salespeople at Nordstrom to earn double what they would at other department store retailers). For go-getters who truly enjoy retail selling and pleasing customers, Nordstrom is a great company to work for. But the culture weeds out those who can't meet Nordstrom's demanding standards and rewards those who are prepared to be what Nordstrom stands for.

Source: Based on information in Tracy Goss, Richard Pascale, and Anthony Athos, "Risking the Present for a Powerful Future," *Harvard Business Review* 71, no. 6 (November–December 1993), pp. 101–2.

---

bedrock of Wal-Mart's culture is dedication to customer satisfaction, zealous pursuit of low costs, a strong work ethic, Sam Walton's legendary frugality, the ritualistic Saturday morning headquarters meetings to exchange ideas and review problems, and company executives' commitment to visiting stores, talking to customers, and soliciting suggestions from employees. At Frito-Lay, stories abound of potato chip route salesmen slogging through mud and snow to uphold the company's 99.5 percent service level. At McDonald's the constant message from management is the overriding importance of quality, service, cleanliness, and value; employees are drilled over and over on the need for attention to detail and perfection in every fundamental of the business. Illustration Capsule 32 describes the culture of Nordstrom.

> **Corporate culture refers to a company's values, beliefs, traditions, operating style, and internal work environment.**

Where Does Corporate Culture Come From?

The taproot of corporate culture is the organization's beliefs and philosophy about how its affairs ought to be conducted—the reasons why it does things the way it does. A company's culture is manifested in the values and business principles that management preaches and practices, in its ethical standards and official policies, in its stakeholder relationships (especially its dealings with employees, unions, stockholders, vendors, and the communities in which it operates), in the traditions the organization maintains, in its supervisory practices, in employees' attitudes and behavior, in the legends people repeat about happenings in the organization, in the peer pressures that exist, in the organization's politics, and in the "chemistry" and the "vibrations" that permeate the work environment. All these sociological forces, some of which operate quite subtly, combine to define an organization's culture.

Beliefs and practices that become embedded in a company's culture can originate anywhere: from one influential individual, work group, department, or division, from the bottom of the organizational hierarchy or the top.[1] Very often, many components of the culture are associated with a founder or other early leaders who articulated them as a company philosophy, a set of principles which the organization should rigidly adhere to, company policies, a vision, a business strategy, or a combination of these. Over time, these cultural underpinnings come to be shared by company managers and employees and then persist as new employees are encouraged to adopt and follow the professed values and practices. A company's culture is a product of internal social forces; it represents an interdependent set of values and behavioral norms that prevail across the organization.

Once established, company cultures can be perpetuated by continuity of leadership, by screening and selecting new group members according to how well their values and behavior fit in, by systematic indoctrination of new members in the culture's fundamentals, by the efforts of senior group members to reiterate core values in daily conversations and pronouncements, by the telling and retelling of company legends, by regular ceremonies honoring members who display cultural ideals, and by visibly rewarding those who follow cultural norms and penalizing those who don't.[2] However, even stable cultures aren't static. Crises and new challenges evolve into new ways of doing things. Arrival of new leaders and turnover of key members often spawn new or different values and practices that alter the culture. Diversification into new businesses, expansion into different geographical areas, and rapid growth that adds new employees can all cause a culture to evolve.

Although it is common to speak about corporate culture in the singular, companies typically have multiple cultures (or subcultures).[3] Values, beliefs, and practices can vary significantly by department, geographic location, division, or business unit. A company's subcultures can clash, or at least not mesh well, if recently acquired business units have not yet been assimilated or if different organizational units have conflicting managerial styles, business philosophies, and operating approaches.

The Power of Culture

Most managers, as a consequence of their own experiences and of reading case studies in the business press, accept that an organization's culture is an important contributor (or obstacle) to successful strategy execution. Thomas Watson, Jr., who succeeded his father as CEO at IBM, stated the case for a culture-performance link eloquently in a 1962 speech at Columbia University:

> The basic philosophy, spirit, and desire of an organization have far more to do with its relative achievements than do technological or economic resources, organization structure, innovation, and timing. All these things weigh heavily on success. But they are, I think, transcended by how strongly the people in the organization believe in its basic precepts and how faithfully they carry them out.[4]

---

[1]John P. Kotter and James L. Heskett, *Corporate Culture and Performance* (New York: Free Press, 1992), p. 7.

[2]Ibid., pp. 7–8.

[3]Ibid., p. 5.

[4]"A Business and Its Beliefs," McKinsey Foundation Lecture (New York: McGraw-Hill, 1963), as quoted in Kotter and Heskett, *Corporate Culture and Performance*, p. 17.

The beliefs, goals, and practices called for in a strategy may be compatible with a firm's culture or they may not. When they are not, a company usually finds it difficult to implement the strategy successfully.[5] A close culture-strategy match that energizes people throughout the company to do their jobs in a strategy-supportive manner adds significantly to the power and effectiveness of strategy execution. Strong cultures promote good long-term performance when there's fit and hurt performance when there's little fit. When a company's culture is out of sync with what is needed for strategic success, the culture has to be changed as rapidly as can be managed; the more entrenched the culture, the greater the difficulty of implementing new or different strategies. A sizable and prolonged strategy-culture conflict weakens and may even defeat managerial efforts to make the strategy work.

A tight culture-strategy alignment is a powerful lever for channeling behavior and helping employees do their jobs in a more strategy-supportive manner; this occurs in two ways:[6]

> **A strong culture and a tight strategy-culture fit are powerful levers for influencing people to do their jobs better.**

- *A work environment where the culture matches well with the conditions for good strategy execution provides a system of informal rules and peer pressures regarding how to conduct business internally and how to go about doing one's job.* Culturally approved behavior thrives, while culturally disapproved behavior gets squashed and often penalized. In a company where strategy and culture are misaligned, ingrained values and operating philosophies don't cultivate strategy-supportive work habits; often, the very kinds of behavior needed to execute strategy successfully run afoul of the culture and attract negative recognition rather than praise and reward.

- *A strong strategy-supportive culture nurtures and motivates people to their best; it provides structure, standards, and a value system in which to operate; and it promotes strong company identification among employees.* All this makes employees feel genuinely better about their jobs and work environment and, more often than not, stimulates them to perform closer to the best of their abilities.

This says something important about the task of leading strategy implementation: *anything so fundamental as implementing a strategic plan involves moving the organization's culture into close alignment with the requirements for proficient strategy execution.* The optimal condition is a work environment that enlists and encourages people to perform strategy-critical activities in superior fashion. As one observer noted:

> It has not been just strategy that led to big Japanese wins in the American auto market. It is a culture that enspirits workers to excel at fits and finishes, to produce moldings that match and doors that don't sag. It is a culture in which Toyota can use that most sophisticated of management tools, the suggestion box, and in two years increase the number of worker suggestions from under 10,000 to over 1 million with resultant savings of $250 million.[7]

---

[5]Kotter and Heskett, *Corporate Culture and Performance*, p. 5.
[6]Ibid., pp. 15–16.
[7]Robert H. Waterman, Jr., "The Seven Elements of Strategic Fit," *Journal of Business Strategy* 2, no. 3 (Winter 1982), p. 70.

Strong versus Weak Cultures

Company cultures vary widely in the degree to which they are embedded in company practices and behavioral norms. A company's culture can be weak and fragmented in the sense that many subcultures exist, few values and behavioral norms are widely shared, and there are few traditions. In such cases, organizational.members typically have no deeply felt sense of company identity; they view their company as merely a place to work and their job only as a way to make a living. While they may have some feelings of loyalty toward their department, their colleagues, their union, or their boss, they usually have no strong emotional allegiance to the company or its business mission. On the other hand, a company's culture can be strong and cohesive in the sense that the company conducts its business according to a clear and explicit set of principles and values, that management devotes considerable time to communicating these principles and values to organizational members and explaining how they relate to its business environment, and that the values are shared widely across the company—by senior executives and rank-and-file employees alike.[8] Strong-culture companies typically have creeds or values statements, and executives regularly stress the importance of using these values and principles as the basis for decisions and actions taken throughout the organization. In strong culture companies values and behavioral norms are so deeply rooted that they don't change much when a new CEO takes over—although they can erode over time if the CEO ceases to nurture them.

A strong culture is a valuable asset when it matches strategy and a dreaded liability when it doesn't.

Three factors contribute to the development of strategically supportive strong cultures: (1) a founder or strong leader who establishes values, principles, and practices that are consistent and sensible in light of customer needs, competitive conditions, and strategic requirements; (2) a sincere, long-standing company commitment to operating the business according to these established traditions, thereby creating an internal environment that supports decision-making based on cultural norms; and (3) a genuine concern for the well-being of the organization's three biggest constituencies—customers, employees, and shareholders. Continuity of leadership, small group size, stable group membership, geographic concentration, and considerable success all contribute to the emergence of a strong culture.[9]

Low-Performance or Unhealthy Cultures

There are a number of unhealthy cultural characteristics that can undermine a company's business performance.[10] One unhealthy organizational trait is a politicized internal environment that allows influential managers to operate their fiefdoms autonomously and resist needed change. In politically dominated cultures, many issues get resolved on the basis of turf, vocal support or opposition by powerful executives, personal lobbying by a key executive, and coalitions among individuals or departments with vested interests in a particular outcome. What's best for the company plays second fiddle to personal aggrandizement.

A second unhealthy cultural trait, one that can plague companies suddenly confronted with fast-changing business conditions, is hostility to change and to people who champion new ways of doing things. Executives who don't value managers or

---

[8]Terrence E. Deal and Allen A. Kennedy, *Corporate Cultures* (Reading, Mass.: Addison-Wesley, 1982), p. 22.
[9]Vijay Sathe, *Culture and Related Corporate Realities* (Homewood, Ill.: Richard D. Irwin, 1985).
[10]Kotter and Heskett, *Corporate Culture and Performance*, chapter 6.

employees with initiative or new ideas put a damper on experimentation and on efforts to improve the status quo. Avoiding risks and not screwing up become more important to a person's career advancement than entrepreneurial successes and innovative accomplishments. This trait is most often found in companies with multilayered management bureaucracies that have enjoyed considerable market success and whose business environments have been hit with accelerating change. General Motors, IBM, Sears, and Eastman Kodak are classic examples; all four gradually became burdened by a stifling bureaucracy that rejected innovation. Now, they are struggling to reinvent the cultural approaches that caused them to succeed in the first place.

A third unhealthy characteristic is promoting managers who understand structures, systems, budgets, and controls better than they understand vision, strategies, inspiration, and culture-building. While the former are adept at solving internal organizational challenges, if they ascend to senior executive positions, the company can find itself short on the entrepreneurial skills and leadership needed to manage strategic change—a condition that ultimately erodes long-term performance.

A fourth characteristic of low-performance cultures is an aversion to looking outside the company for superior practices and approaches. Sometimes a company enjoys such great market success and reigns as an industry leader for so long that its management becomes inbred and arrogant. It believes it has all the answers or can develop them on its own. Insular thinking, inward-looking solutions, and a must-be-invented-here syndrome often precede a decline in company performance. Kotter and Heskett cite Avon, BankAmerica, Citicorp, Coors, Ford, General Motors, Kmart, Kroger, Sears, Texaco, and Xerox as examples of companies that had low-performance cultures during the late 1970s and early 1980s.[11]

Changing problem cultures is very difficult because of the heavy anchor of deeply held values, habits, and the emotional clinging of people to the old and familiar. Sometimes executives succeed in changing the values and behaviors of small groups of managers and even whole departments or divisions, only to find the changes eroded over time by the actions of the rest of the organization. What is communicated, praised, supported, and penalized by the entrenched majority undermines the new emergent culture and halts its progress. Executives can revamp formal organization charts, announce new strategies, bring in managers from the outside, introduce new technologies, and open new plants, yet fail at altering embedded cultural traits and behaviors because of skepticism about the new directions and covert resistance to altering traditional methods.

Adaptive Cultures

In fast-changing business environments, the capacity to introduce new strategies and organizational practices is a necessity if a company is to achieve superior performance over long periods of time.[12] This requires a culture that helps the company adapt to environmental change rather than a culture that has to be coaxed and cajoled to change. The hallmarks of an adaptive culture are: (1) leaders who have a greater commitment to timeless business principles and to organizational stakeholders—customers, employees, shareowners, suppliers, and the communities where the

---

[11]Ibid., p. 68.
[12]This section draws heavily from Kotter and Heskett, *Corporate Culture and Performance*, chapter 4.

company operates—than to any specific business strategy or operating practice; and (2) group members who are receptive to risk-taking, experimentation, innovation, and changing strategies and practices whenever necessary to satisfy the legitimate interests of stakeholders.

In adaptive cultures, members share a feeling of confidence that the organization can deal with whatever threats and opportunities come down the pike. Hence, members willingly embrace a proactive approach to identifying issues, evaluating the implications and options, and implementing workable solutions—there's a spirit of doing what's necessary to ensure long-term organizational success *provided core values and business principles are upheld in the process*. Managers habitually fund product development initiatives, evaluate new ideas openly, and take prudent risks to create new business positions. Entrepreneurship is encouraged and rewarded. Strategies and traditional operating practices are modified as needed to adjust to or take advantage of changes in the business environment. The leaders of adaptive cultures are adept at changing the right things in the right ways, not changing for the sake of change and not compromising core values or business principles. Adaptive cultures are very supportive of managers and employees at all ranks who propose or help initiate useful change; indeed, executives consciously seek, train, and promote individuals who display these leadership traits.

In adaptive cultures, top management genuinely cares about the well-being of all key constituencies—customers, employees, stockholders, major suppliers, and the communities where the company operates—and tries to satisfy all their legitimate interests simultaneously. No group is ignored, and fairness to all constituencies is a decision-making principle—a commitment often described as "doing the right thing."[13] In less-adaptive cultures where resistance to change is the norm, managers often behave conservatively and politically to protect or advance their own careers, the interests of their immediate work groups, or their pet projects. They avoid risk-taking and prefer following to leading when it comes to technological change and new product innovation.[14]

> **Adaptive cultures are a strategy-implementer's best ally.**

Creating the Fit between Strategy and Culture

It is the *strategy-maker's* responsibility to select a strategy compatible with the "sacred" or unchangeable parts of prevailing corporate culture. It is the *strategy-implementer's* task, once strategy is chosen, to change whatever facets of the corporate culture hinder effective execution.

Changing a company's culture and aligning it with strategy are among the toughest management tasks—easier to talk about than do. The first step is to diagnose which facets of the present culture are strategy-supportive and which are not. Then, managers have to talk openly and forthrightly to all concerned about those aspects of the culture that have to be changed. The talk has to be followed swiftly by visible, forceful actions to modify the culture—actions that everyone will understand are intended to establish a new culture more in tune with the strategy.

Symbolic Actions and Substantive Actions   Managerial actions to tighten the culture-strategy fit need to be both symbolic and substantive. Symbolic actions are

---

[13]Ibid., p. 52.
[14]Ibid., p. 50.

valuable for the signals they send about the kinds of behavior and performance strategy-implementers wish to encourage. The most important symbolic actions are those that top executives take to serve as role models—leading cost reduction efforts by curtailing executive perks; emphasizing the importance of responding to customers' needs by requiring all officers and executives to spend a significant portion of each week talking with customers and understanding their requirements; and initiating efforts to alter policies and practices identified as hindrances in executing the new strategy. Another category of symbolic actions includes the events organizations hold to designate and honor people whose actions and performance exemplify what is called for in the new culture. Many universities give outstanding teacher awards each year to symbolize their commitment to and esteem for instructors who display exceptional classroom talents. Numerous businesses have employee-of-the-month awards. The military has a long-standing custom of awarding ribbons and medals for exemplary actions. Mary Kay Cosmetics awards an array of prizes—from ribbons to pink automobiles—to its beauty consultants for reaching various sales plateaus.

The best companies and the best executives expertly use symbols, role models, ceremonial occasions, and group gatherings to tighten the strategy-culture fit. Low-cost leaders like Wal-Mart and Nucor are renowned for their Spartan facilities, executive frugality, intolerance of waste, and zealous control of costs. Executives sensitive to their role in promoting strategy-culture fits make a habit of appearing at ceremonial functions to praise individuals and groups that "get with the program." They honor individuals who exhibit cultural norms and reward those who achieve strategic milestones. They participate in employee training programs to stress strategic priorities, values, ethical principles, and cultural norms. Every group gathering is seen as an opportunity to implant values, praise good deeds, reinforce cultural norms, and promote changes that assist strategy implementation. Sensitive executives make sure that current decisions and policy changes will be construed by organizational members as consistent with and supportive of the company's new strategic direction.[15]

Awards ceremonies, role models, and symbols are a fundamental part of a strategy-implementer's culture-shaping effort.

In addition to being out front personally and symbolically leading the push for new behaviors and communicating the reasons for new approaches, strategy-implementers have to convince all those concerned that the effort is more than cosmetic. Talk and plans have to be complemented by substantive actions and real movement. The actions taken have to be credible, highly visible, and unmistakably indicative of the seriousness of management's commitment to new strategic initiatives and the associated cultural changes. There are several ways to accomplish this. One is to engineer some quick successes that highlight the benefits of strategy-culture changes, thus making enthusiasm for the changes contagious. However, instant results are usually not as important as having the will and patience to create a solid, competent team psychologically committed to pursuing the strategy in a superior fashion. The strongest signs that management is truly committed to creating a new culture include: replacing old-culture traditionalist managers with "new breed" managers, changing long-standing policies and operating practices that are dysfunctional or that impede new initiatives, undertaking major reorganizational moves that bring structure into better alignment with strategy, tying compensation incentives directly to the new measures of strategic performance, and making major budgetary reallocations that shift substantial resources from old-strategy projects and programs to new-strategy projects and programs.

---

[15]Judy D. Olian and Sara L. Rynes, "Making Total Quality Work: Aligning Organizational Processes, Performance Measures, and Stakeholders," *Human Resource Management* 30, no. 3 (Fall 1991), p. 324.

Senior executives must personally lead efforts to align culture with strategy.

At the same time, chief strategy-implementers must be careful to *lead by example*. For instance, if the organization's strategy involves a drive to become the industry's low-cost producer, senior managers must display frugality in their own actions and decisions: Spartan decorations in the executive suite, conservative expense accounts and entertainment allowances, a lean staff in the corporate office, scrutiny of budget requests, and so on. The CEO of SAS Airlines, Jan Carlzon, symbolically reinforced the primacy of quality service for business customers by flying coach instead of first class and by giving up his seat to waitlisted travelers.[16]

Implanting the needed culture-building values and behavior depends on a sincere, sustained commitment by the chief executive coupled with extraordinary persistence in reinforcing the culture at every opportunity through both word and deed. Neither charisma nor personal magnetism are essential. However, personally talking to many departmental groups about the reasons for change *is* essential; organizational changes are seldom accomplished successfully from an office. Moreover, creating and sustaining a strategy-supportive culture is a job for the whole management team. Major cultural change requires many initiatives from many people. Senior officers, department heads, and middle managers have to reiterate values, "walk the talk," and translate the organization's philosophy into everyday practice. In addition, for the culture-building effort to be successful, strategy-implementers must enlist the support of firstline supervisors and employee opinion-leaders, convincing them of the merits of practicing and enforcing cultural norms at the lowest levels in the organization. Until a big majority of employees join the new culture and share an emotional commitment to its basic values and behavioral norms, there's considerably more work to be done in both instilling the culture and tightening the culture-strategy fit.

The task of making culture supportive of strategy is not a short-term exercise. It takes time for a new culture to emerge and prevail; it's unrealistic to expect an overnight transformation. The bigger the organization and the greater the cultural shift needed to produce a culture-strategy fit, the longer it takes. In large companies, changing the corporate culture in significant ways can take three to five years at minimum. In fact, it is usually tougher to reshape a deeply ingrained culture that is not strategy-supportive than it is to instill a strategy-supportive culture from scratch in a brand new organization.

Establishing Ethical Standards and Values

An ethical corporate culture has a positive impact on a company's long-term strategic success; an unethical culture can undermine it.

A strong corporate culture founded on ethical business principles and moral values is a vital driving force behind continued strategic success. Many executives are convinced that a company must care about how it does business; otherwise a company's reputation, and ultimately its performance, is put at risk. Corporate ethics and values programs are not window dressing; they are undertaken to create an environment of strongly held values and convictions and to make ethical conduct a way of life. Morally upstanding values and high ethical standards nurture the corporate culture in a very positive way—they connote integrity, "doing the right thing," and genuine concern for stakeholders.

Companies establish values and ethical standards in a number of different ways.[17] Companies steeped in tradition with a rich folklore to draw on rely on

---

[16]Ibid.

[17]The Business Roundtable, *Corporate Ethics: A Prime Asset*, February 1988, pp. 4–10.

Table 11–1 Topics Generally Covered in Value Statements and Codes of Ethics

Topics Covered in Values Statements	Topics Covered in Codes of Ethics
• Importance of customers and customer service	• Honesty and observance of the law
• Commitment to quality	• Conflicts of interest
• Commitment to innovation	• Fairness in selling and marketing practices
• Respect for the individual employee and the duty the company has to employees	• Using inside information and securities trading
• Importance of honesty, integrity, and ethical standards	• Supplier relationships and purchasing practices
• Duty to stockholders	• Payments to obtain business/Foreign Corrupt Practices Act
• Duty to suppliers	• Acquiring and using information about others
• Corporate citizenship	• Political activities
• Importance of protecting the environment	• Use of company assets, resources, and property
	• Protection of proprietary information
	• Pricing, contracting, and billing

word-of-mouth indoctrination and the power of tradition to instill values and enforce ethical conduct. But many companies today set forth their values and codes of ethics in written documents. Table 11–1 indicates the kinds of topics such statements cover. Written statements have the advantage of explicitly stating what the company intends and expects, and they serve as benchmarks for judging both company policies and actions and individual conduct. They put a stake in the ground and define the company's position. Value statements serve as a cornerstone for culture-building; a code of ethics serves as a cornerstone for developing a corporate conscience. Illustration Capsule 33 presents the Johnson & Johnson Credo, the most publicized and celebrated code of ethics and values among U.S. companies. J&J's CEO calls the credo "the unifying force for our corporation." Illustration Capsule 34 presents the pledge that Bristol-Myers Squibb makes to all of its stakeholders.

Once values and ethical standards have been formally set forth, they must be institutionalized and ingrained in the company's policies, practices, and actual conduct. Implementing the values and code of ethics entails several actions:

Values and ethical standards must not only be explicitly stated but they must also be ingrained into the corporate culture.

- Incorporation of the statement of values and the code of ethics into employee training and educational programs.
- Explicit attention to values and ethics in recruiting and hiring to screen out applicants who do not exhibit compatible character traits.
- Communication of the values and ethics code to all employees and explaining compliance procedures.
- Management involvement and oversight, from the CEO down to firstline supervisors.
- Strong endorsements by the CEO.
- Word-of-mouth indoctrination.

In the case of codes of ethics, special attention must be given to sections of the company that are particularly sensitive and vulnerable—purchasing, sales, and political

Illustration Capsule 33   The Johnson & Johnson Credo

- We believe our first responsibility is to the doctors, nurses, and patients, to mothers and all others who use our products and services.
- In meeting their needs everything we do must be of high quality.
- We must constantly strive to reduce our costs in order to maintain reasonable prices.
- Customers' orders must be serviced promptly and accurately.
- Our suppliers and distributors must have an opportunity to make a fair profit.
- We are responsible to our employees, the men and women who work with us throughout the world.
- Everyone must be considered as an individual.
- We must respect their dignity and recognize their merit.
- They must have a sense of security in their jobs.
- Compensation must be fair and adequate, and working conditions clean, orderly, and safe.
- Employees must feel free to make suggestions and complaints.
- There must be equal opportunity for employment, development, and advancement for those qualified.

- We must provide competent management, and their actions must be just and ethical.
- We are responsible to the communities in which we live and work and to the world community as well.
- We must be good citizens—support good works and charities and bear our fair share of taxes.
- We must encourage civic improvements and better health and education.
- We must maintain in good order the property we are privileged to use, protecting the environment and natural resources.
- Our final responsibility is to our stockholders.
- Business must make a sound profit.
- We must experiment with new ideas.
- Research must be carried on, innovative programs developed, and mistakes paid for.
- New equipment must be purchased, new facilities provided, and new products launched.
- Reserves must be created to provide for adverse times.
- When we operate according to these principles, the stockholders should realize a fair return.

Source: 1982 Annual Report.

lobbying.[18] Employees who deal with external parties are in ethically sensitive positions and often are drawn into compromising situations. Procedures for enforcing ethical standards and handling potential violations have to be developed.

The compliance effort must permeate the company, extending into every organizational unit. The attitudes, character, and work history of prospective employees must be scrutinized. Every employee must receive adequate training. Line managers at all levels must give serious and continuous attention to the task of explaining how the values and ethical code apply in their areas. In addition, they must insist that company values and ethical standards become a way of life. In general, instilling values and insisting on ethical conduct must be looked on as a continuous culture-building, culture-nurturing exercise. Whether the effort succeeds or fails depends largely on how well corporate values and ethical standards are visibly integrated into company policies, managerial practices, and actions at all levels.

---

[18]Ibid, p. 7.

Illustration Capsule 34   The Bristol-Myers Squibb Pledge

To those who use our products . . .

We affirm Bristol-Myers Squibb's commitment to the highest standards of excellence, safety, and reliability in everything we make. We pledge to offer products of the highest quality and to work diligently to keep improving them.

To our employees and those who may join us . . .

We pledge personal respect, fair compensation, and equal treatment. We acknowledge our obligation to provide able and humane leadership throughout the organization, within a clean and safe working environment. To all who qualify for advancement, we will make every effort to provide opportunity.

To our suppliers and customers . . .

We pledge an open door, courteous, efficient, and ethical dealing, and appreciation for their right to a fair profit.

To our shareholders . . .

We pledge a companywide dedication to continued profitable growth, sustained by strong finances, a high level of research and development, and facilities second to none.

To the communities where we have plants and offices . . .

We pledge conscientious citizenship, a helping hand for worthwhile causes, and constructive action in support of civic and environmental progress.

To the countries where we do business . . .

We pledge ourselves to be a good citizen and to show full consideration for the rights of others while reserving the right to stand up for our own.

Above all, to the world we live in . . .

We pledge Bristol-Myers Squibb to policies and practices which fully embody the responsibility, integrity, and decency required of free enterprise if it is to merit and maintain the confidence of our society.

Source: 1990 Annual Report.

Building a Spirit of High Performance into the Culture

An ability to instill strong individual commitment to strategic success and to create an atmosphere in which there is constructive pressure to perform is one of the most valuable strategy-implementing skills. When an organization performs consistently at or near peak capability, the outcome is not only improved strategic success but also an organizational culture permeated with a spirit of high performance. Such a spirit of performance should not be confused with whether employees are "happy" or "satisfied" or whether they "get along well together." An organization with a spirit of high performance emphasizes achievement and excellence. Its culture is results-oriented, and its management pursues policies and practices that inspire people to do their best.

> A results-oriented culture that inspires people to do their best is conducive to superior strategy execution.

Companies with a spirit of high performance typically are intensely people-oriented, and they reinforce their concern for individual employees on every conceivable occasion in every conceivable way. They treat employees with dignity and respect, train each employee thoroughly, encourage employees to use their own initiative and creativity in performing their work, set reasonable and clear performance expectations, utilize the full range of rewards and punishment to enforce high-performance standards, hold managers at every level responsible for developing the people who report to them, and grant employees enough autonomy to stand out, excel, and contribute. To create a results-oriented organizational culture, a company must make champions out of the people who turn in winning performances:[19]

---

[19]Thomas J. Peters and Robert H. Waterman, Jr., *In Search of Excellence* (New York: Harper & Row, 1982), pp. xviii, 240, and 269, and Thomas J. Peters and Nancy Austin, *A Passion for Excellence* (New York: Random House, 1985), pp. 304–7.

- At Boeing, General Electric, and 3M Corporation, top executives make a point of ceremoniously honoring individuals who believe so strongly in their ideas that they take it on themselves to hurdle the bureaucracy, maneuver their projects through the system, and turn them into improved services, new products, or even new businesses. In these companies, "product champions" are given high visibility, room to push their ideas, and strong executive support. Champions whose ideas prove out are usually handsomely rewarded; those whose ideas don't pan out still have secure jobs and are given chances to try again.

- The manager of a New York area sales office rented the Meadowlands Stadium (home field of the New York Giants) for an evening. After work, the salespeople were all assembled at the stadium and asked to run one at a time through the players' tunnel onto the field. As each one emerged, the electronic scoreboard flashed the person's name to those gathered in the stands—executives from corporate headquarters, employees from the office, family, and friends. Their role was to cheer loudly in honor of the individual's sales accomplishments. The company involved was IBM. The occasion for this action was to reaffirm IBM's commitment to satisfy an individual's need to be part of something great and to reiterate IBM's concern for championing individual accomplishment.

- Some companies upgrade the importance and status of individual employees by referring to them as Cast Members (Disney), crew members (McDonald's), or associates (Wal-Mart and J. C. Penney). Companies like Mary Kay Cosmetics, Tupperware, and McDonald's actively seek out reasons and opportunities to give pins, buttons, badges, and medals for good showings by average performers—the idea being to express appreciation and give a motivational boost to people who stand out doing "ordinary" jobs.

- McDonald's has a contest to determine the best hamburger cooker in its entire chain. It begins with a competition to determine the best hamburger cooker in each store. Store winners go on to compete in regional championships, and regional winners go on to the "All-American" contest. The winners get trophies and an All-American patch to wear on their shirts.

- Milliken & Co. holds Corporate Sharing Rallies once every three months; teams come from all over the company to swap success stories and ideas. A hundred or more teams make five-minute presentations over a two-day period. Each rally has a major theme—quality, cost reduction, and so on. No criticisms and negatives are allowed, and there is no such thing as a big idea or a small one. Quantitative measures of success are used to gauge improvement. All those present vote on the best presentation and several ascending grades of awards are handed out. Everyone, however, receives a framed certificate for participating.

What makes a spirit of high performance come alive is a complex network of practices, words, symbols, styles, values, and policies pulling together that produces extraordinary results with ordinary people. The drivers of the system are a belief in the worth of the individual, strong company commitment to job security and promotion from within, managerial practices that encourage employees to exercise individual initiative and creativity in doing their jobs, and pride in doing the "itty-bitty, teeny-tiny things" right. A company that treats its employees well generally benefits from increased teamwork, higher morale, and greater employee loyalty.

While emphasizing a spirit of high performance nearly always accentuates the positive, there are negative reinforcers too. Managers whose units consistently perform poorly have to be removed. Aside from the organizational benefits, weak-performing managers should be reassigned for their own good—people who find themselves in a job they cannot handle are usually frustrated, anxiety-ridden, harassed, and unhappy.[20] Moreover, subordinates have a right to be managed with competence, dedication, and achievement. Unless their boss performs well, they themselves cannot perform well. In addition, weak-performing workers and people who reject the cultural emphasis on dedication and high performance have to be weeded out. Recruitment practices need to aim at selecting highly motivated, ambitious applicants whose attitudes and work habits mesh well with a results-oriented corporate culture.

EXERTING STRATEGIC LEADERSHIP

The litany of good strategic management is simple enough: formulate a sound strategic plan, implement it, execute it to the fullest, win! But it's easier said than done. Exerting take-charge leadership, being a "spark plug," ramrodding things through, and getting things done by coaching others to do them are difficult tasks. Moreover, a strategy manager has many different leadership roles to play: chief entrepreneur and strategist, chief administrator and strategy-implementer, culture builder, supervisor, crisis solver, taskmaster, spokesperson, resource allocator, negotiator, motivator, adviser, arbitrator, consensus builder, policymaker, policy enforcer, mentor, and head cheerleader. Sometimes it is useful to be authoritarian and hard-nosed; sometimes it is best to be a perceptive listener and a compromising decision-maker; and sometimes a strongly participative, collegial approach works best. Many occasions call for a highly visible role and extensive time commitments, while others entail a brief ceremonial performance with the details delegated to subordinates.

In general, the problem of strategic leadership is one of diagnosing the situation and choosing from any of several ways to handle it. Six leadership roles dominate the strategy-implementer's action agenda:

1. Staying on top of what is happening and how well things are going.
2. Promoting a culture in which the organization is "energized" to accomplish strategy and perform at a high level.
3. Keeping the organization responsive to changing conditions, alert for new opportunities, and bubbling with innovative ideas.
4. Building consensus, containing "power struggles," and dealing with the politics of crafting and implementing strategy.
5. Enforcing ethical standards.
6. Pushing corrective actions to improve strategy execution and overall strategic performance.

---

[20]Peter Drucker, *Management: Tasks, Responsibilities, Practices* (New York: Harper & Row, 1974), p. 457.

Managing by Walking Around (MBWA)

To stay on top of how well the implementation process is going, a manager needs to develop a broad network of contacts and sources of information, both formal and informal. The regular channels include talking with key subordinates, reviewing reports and the latest operating results, talking to customers, watching the competitive reactions of rival firms, tapping into the grapevine, listening to rank-and-file employees, and observing the situation firsthand. However, some information tends to be more trustworthy than the rest. Written reports may represent "the truth but not the whole truth." Bad news may be covered up, minimized, or not reported at all. Sometimes subordinates delay conveying failures and problems in hopes that more time will give them room to turn things around. As information flows up an organization, there is a tendency for it to get censored and sterilized to the point that it may fail to reveal strategy-critical information. Hence, there is reason for strategy managers to guard against major surprises by making sure that they have accurate information and a "feel" for the existing situation. The chief way this is done is by regular visits "to the field" and talking with many different people at many different levels. The technique of *managing by walking around* (MBWA) is practiced in a variety of styles:[21]

MBWA is one of the techniques effective leaders use.

- At Hewlett-Packard, there are weekly beer busts in each division, attended by both executives and employees, to create a regular opportunity to keep in touch. Tidbits of information flow freely between down-the-line employees and executives—facilitated in part because "the HP Way" is for people at all ranks to be addressed by their first names. Bill Hewlett, one of HP's cofounders, had a companywide reputation for getting out of his office and "wandering around" the plant greeting people, listening to what was on their minds, and asking questions. He found this so valuable that he made MBWA a standard practice for all HP managers. Furthermore, ad hoc meetings of people from different departments spontaneously arise; they gather in rooms with blackboards and work out solutions informally.

- McDonald's founder Ray Kroc regularly visited store units and did his own personal inspection on Q.S.C.&V. (Quality, Service, Cleanliness, and Value)—the themes he preached regularly. There are stories of his pulling into a unit's parking lot, seeing litter lying on the pavement, getting out of his limousine to pick it up himself, and then lecturing the store staff at length on the subject of cleanliness.

- The CEO of a small manufacturing company spends much of his time riding around the factory in a golf cart, waving to and joking with workers, listening to them, and calling all 2,000 employees by their first names. In addition, he spends a lot of time with union officials, inviting them to meetings and keeping them well-informed about what is going on.

- Wal-Mart executives have had a long-standing practice of spending two to three days every week visiting Wal-Mart's stores and talking with store managers and employees. Sam Walton, Wal-Mart's founder, insisted "The key is to get out into the store and listen to what the associates have to say. Our best ideas come from clerks and stockboys."

---

[21]Ibid., pp. xx, 15, 120–23, 191, 242–43, 246–47, 287–90. For an extensive report on the benefits of MBWA, see Peters and Austin, *A Passion for Excellence*, chapters 2, 3, and 19.

- When Ed Carlson became CEO of United Airlines, he traveled about 200,000 miles a year talking with United's employees. He observed, "I wanted these people to identify me and to feel sufficiently comfortable to make suggestions or even argue with me if that's what they felt like doing . . . Whenever I picked up some information, I would call the senior officer of the division and say that I had just gotten back from visiting Oakland, Reno, and Las Vegas, and here is what I found."
- At Marriott Corp. Bill Marriott personally inspects Marriott hotels. He also invites all Marriott guests to send him their evaluations of Marriott's facilities and services; he personally reads every customer complaint and has been known to telephone hotel managers about them.

Managers at many companies attach great importance to informal communications. They report that it is essential to have a "feel" for situations and to have the ability to gain quick, easy access to information. When executives stay in their offices, they tend to become isolated and often surround themselves with people who are not likely to offer criticism and different perspectives. The information they get is secondhand, screened and filtered, and sometimes dated.

Fostering a Strategy-Supportive Climate and Culture

Strategy-implementers have to be out front in promoting a strategy-supportive organizational climate and culture. When major strategic changes are being implemented, a manager's time is best spent personally leading the changes and promoting needed cultural adjustments. In general, organizational cultures need major overhaul every 5 to 25 years, depending on how fast events in the company's business environment move.[22] When only strategic fine-tuning is being implemented, it takes less time and effort to bring values and culture into alignment with strategy, but there is still a lead role for the manager to play in pushing ahead and prodding for continuous improvements. Successful strategy leaders recognize it is their responsibility to convince people that the chosen strategy is right and that implementing it to the best of the organization's ability is top priority.

The single most visible factor that distinguishes successful culture-change efforts from failed attempts is competent leadership at the top. Effective management action to match culture and strategy has several attributes:[23]

- A stakeholders-are-king philosophy that links the need to change to the need to serve the long-term best interests of all key constituencies.
- An openness to new ideas.
- Challenging the status quo with very basic questions: Are we giving customers what they really need and want? How can we be more competitive on cost? Why can't design-to-market cycle time be halved? How can we grow the company instead of downsizing it? Where will the company be five years from now if it sticks with just its present business?
- Persuading individuals and groups to commit themselves to the new direction and energizing individuals and departments sufficiently to make it happen despite the obstacles.

---

[22]Kotter and Heskett, *Corporate Culture and Performance*, p. 91.
[23]Ibid., pp. 84, 144, and 148.

- Repeating the new messages again and again, explaining the rationale for change, and convincing skeptics that all is not well and things must be changed.
- Recognizing and generously rewarding those who exhibit new cultural norms and who lead successful change efforts—this helps cultivate expansion of the coalition for change.
- Creating events where everyone in management is forced to listen to angry customers, dissatisfied stockholders, and alienated employees to keep management informed and to help them realistically assess organizational strengths and weaknesses.

Only top management has the power to bring about major cultural change.

Great power is needed to force major cultural change—to overcome the springback resistance of entrenched cultures—and great power normally resides only at the top. Moreover, the interdependence of values, strategies, practices, and behaviors inside organizations makes it difficult to change anything fundamental without simultaneously undertaking wider-scale changes. Usually the people with the power to effect change of that scope are those at the top.

Both words and deeds play a part in strategic leadership. Words inspire people, infuse spirit and drive, define strategy-supportive cultural norms and values, articulate the reasons for strategic and organizational change, legitimize new viewpoints and new priorities, urge and reinforce commitment, and arouse confidence in the new strategy. Deeds add credibility to the words, create strategy-supportive symbols, set examples, give meaning and content to the language, and teach the organization what sort of behavior is needed and expected.

Highly visible symbols and imagery are needed to complement substantive actions. One General Motors manager explained how symbolism and managerial style accounted for the striking difference in performance between two large plants:[24]

> At the poorly performing plant, the plant manager probably ventured out on the floor once a week, always in a suit. His comments were distant and perfunctory. At South Gate, the better plant, the plant manager was on the floor all the time. He wore a baseball cap and a UAW jacket. By the way, whose plant do you think was spotless? Whose looked like a junkyard?

As a rule, the greater the degree of strategic change being implemented and/or the greater the shift in cultural norms needed to accommodate a new strategy, the more visible and unequivocal the strategy-implementer's words and deeds need to be. Lessons from well-managed companies show that what the strategy leader says and does has a significant bearing on down-the-line strategy implementation and execution.[25] According to one view, "It is not so much the articulation . . . about what an [organization] should be doing that creates new practice. It's the imagery that creates the understanding, the compelling moral necessity that the new way is right."[26] Moreover, the actions and images, both substantive and symbolic, have to be hammered out regularly, not just restricted to ceremonial speeches and special occasions. This is where a high profile and "managing by walking around" come into play. As a Hewlett-Packard official expresses it in the company publication *The HP Way*:

---

[24]As quoted in Peters and Waterman, *In Search of Excellence*, p. 262.
[25]Ibid., chapter 9.
[26]Warren Bennis, *The Unconscious Conspiracy: Why Leaders Can't Lead* (New York: AMACOM, 1987), p. 93.

Once a division or department has developed a plan of its own—a set of working objectives—it's important for managers and supervisors to keep it in operating condition. This is where observation, measurement, feedback, and guidance come in. It's our "management by wandering around." That's how you find out whether you're on track and heading at the right speed and in the right direction. If you don't constantly monitor how people are operating, not only will they tend to wander off track but also they will begin to believe you weren't serious about the plan in the first place. It has the extra benefit of getting you off your chair and moving around your area. By wandering around, I literally mean moving around and talking to people. It's all done on a very informal and spontaneous basis, but it's important in the course of time to cover the whole territory. You start out by being accessible and approachable, but the main thing is to realize you're there to listen. The second reason for MBWA is that it is vital to keep people informed about what's going on in the company, especially those things that are important to them. The third reason for doing this is because it is just plain fun.

Such contacts give the manager a "feel" for how things are progressing, and they provide opportunity to speak with encouragement, lift spirits, shift attention from the old to the new priorities, create some excitement, and project an atmosphere of informality and fun—all of which drive implementation in a positive fashion and intensify the organizational energy behind strategy execution. John Welch of General Electric sums up the hands-on role and motivational approach well: "I'm here every day, or out into a factory, smelling it, feeling it, touching it, challenging the people."[27]

The vast majority of companies probably don't have strong, adaptive cultures capable of producing excellent long-term performance in a fast-paced market and competitive environment. In such companies, managers have to do more than show incremental progress. Conservative incrementalism seldom leads to major cultural adaptations; more usually, gradualism is defeated by the resilience of entrenched cultures and the ability of vested interests to thwart or minimize the impact of piecemeal change. Only with bold leadership and concerted action on many fronts can a company succeed in tackling so large and difficult a task as major cultural change.

Keeping the Internal Organization Responsive and Innovative

While formulating and implementing strategy is a manager's responsibility, the task of generating fresh ideas, identifying new opportunities, and being responsive to changing conditions cannot be accomplished by a single person. It is an organizationwide task, particularly in large corporations. One of the toughest parts of exerting strategic leadership is generating a dependable supply of fresh ideas from the rank and file, managers and employees alike, and promoting an entrepreneurial, opportunistic spirit that permits continuous adaptation to changing conditions. A flexible, responsive, innovative internal environment is critical in fast-moving high-technology industries, in businesses where products have short life-cycles and growth depends on new product innovation, in companies with widely diversified business portfolios (where opportunities are varied and scattered), in markets where successful product differentiation depends on out-innovating the competition, and in situations where low-cost

---

[27]As quoted in Ann M. Morrison, "Trying to Bring GE to Life," *Fortune*, January 25, 1982, p. 52.

leadership hinges on continuous improvement and new ways to drive costs out of the business. Managers cannot mandate such an environment by simply exhorting people to "be creative."

One useful leadership approach is to take special pains to foster, nourish, and support people who are willing to champion new ideas, better services, new products, and new product applications and are eager for a chance to try turning their ideas into new divisions, new businesses, and even new industries. When Texas Instruments reviewed 50 or so successful and unsuccessful new product introductions, one factor marked every failure: "Without exception we found we hadn't had a volunteer champion. There was someone we had cajoled into taking on the task."[28] The rule seems to be that an idea either finds a champion or dies. The best champions are persistent, competitive, tenacious, committed, and fanatic about the idea and seeing it through to success.

Empowering Champions   In order to promote an organizational climate where champion innovators can blossom and thrive, strategy managers need to do several things. First, individuals and groups have to be encouraged to bring their ideas forward, be creative, and exercise initiative. The culture has to nurture, even celebrate, experimentation and innovation. Everybody must be expected to contribute ideas and seek out continuous improvement. The trick is to keep a sense of urgency alive in the business so that people see change and innovation as a necessity. Second, the champion's maverick style has to be tolerated and given room to operate. People's imaginations need to be encouraged to fly in all directions. Freedom to experiment and a practice of informal brainstorming sessions need to become ingrained. Above all, people with creative ideas must not be looked on as disruptive or troublesome. Third, managers have to induce and promote lots of "tries" and be willing to tolerate mistakes and failures. Most ideas don't pan out, but the organization learns from a good attempt even when it fails. Fourth, strategy managers should be willing to use all kinds of ad hoc organizational forms to support ideas and experimentation—venture teams, task forces, "performance shootouts" among different groups working on competing approaches, informal "bootlegged" projects composed of volunteers, and so on. Fifth, strategy managers have to see that the rewards for successful champions are large and visible and that people who champion an unsuccessful idea are encouraged to try again rather than punished or sidelined. In effect, the leadership task is to create an adaptive, innovative culture that embraces organizational responses to changing conditions rather than fearing the new conditions or seeking to minimize them. Companies with conspicuously innovative cultures include Sony, 3M, Motorola, and Levi Strauss. All four inspire their employees with strategic visions to excel and be world-class at what they do.

Dealing with Company Politics

A manager can't effectively formulate and implement strategy without being perceptive about company politics and being adept at political maneuvering.[29] Politics virtually always comes into play in formulating the strategic plan. Inevitably, key

> **High-performance cultures make champions out of people who excel.**

> **The faster a company's business environment changes, the more attention managers must pay to keeping the organization innovative and responsive.**

---

[28]As quoted in Peters and Waterman, *In Search of Excellence*, pp. 203–4.
[29]For further discussion of this point see Abraham Zaleznik, "Power and Politics in Organizational Life," *Harvard Business Review* 48, no. 3 (May–June 1970), pp. 47–60; R. M. Cyert, H. A. Simon, and D. B.

individuals and groups form coalitions, and each group presses the benefits and potential of its own ideas and vested interests. Political considerations enter into decisions about which objectives take precedence and which lines of business in the corporate portfolio have top priority in resource allocation. Internal politics is a factor in building a consensus for one strategic option over another.

As a rule, there is even more politics in implementing strategy than in formulating it. Typically, internal political considerations affect practical issues such as whose areas of responsibility get reorganized, who reports to whom, who has how much authority over subunits, what individuals should fill key positions and head strategy-critical activities, and which organizational units will get the biggest budget increases. As a case in point, Quinn cites a situation where three strong managers who fought each other constantly formed a potent coalition to resist a reorganization scheme that would have coordinated the very things that caused their friction.[30]

In short, political considerations and the forming of individual and group alliances are integral parts of building organizationwide support for the strategic plan and gaining consensus on how to implement it. Political skills are a definite, maybe even necessary, asset for managers in orchestrating the whole strategic process.

A strategy manager must understand how an organization's power structure works, who wields influence in the executive ranks, which groups and individuals are "activists" and which are defenders of the status quo, who can be helpful and who may not be in a showdown on key decisions, and which direction the political winds are blowing on a given issue. When major decisions have to be made, strategy managers need to be especially sensitive to the politics of managing coalitions and reaching consensus. As the chairman of a major British corporation expressed it:

> I've never taken a major decision without consulting my colleagues. It would be unimaginable to me, unimaginable. First, they help me make a better decision in most cases. Second, if they know about it and agree with it, they'll back it. Otherwise, they might challenge it, not openly, but subconsciously.[31]

The politics of strategy centers chiefly around stimulating options, nurturing support for strong proposals and killing weak ones, guiding the formation of coalitions on particular issues, and achieving consensus and commitment. A recent study of strategy management in nine large corporations showed that successful executives relied upon the following political tactics:[32]

- Letting weakly supported ideas and proposals die through inaction.
- Establishing additional hurdles or tests for strongly supported ideas that the manager views as unacceptable but that are best not opposed openly.
- Keeping a low political profile on unacceptable proposals by getting subordinate managers to say no.
- Letting most negative decisions come from a group consensus that the manager merely confirms, thereby reserving personal veto for big issues and crucial moments.

Company politics presents strategy leaders with the challenge of building consensus for the strategy and how to implement it.

Trow, "Observation of a Business Decision," *Journal of Business*, October 1956, pp. 237–48; and James Brian Quinn, *Strategies for Change: Logical Incrementalism* (Homewood, Ill.: Richard D. Irwin, 1980).
[30]Quinn, *Strategies for Change*, p. 68.
[31]Ibid., p. 65. This statement was made by Sir Alastair Pilkington, Chairman, Pilkington Brothers, Ltd.
[32]Ibid., pp. 128–45. ·

- Leading the strategy but not dictating it—giving few orders, announcing few decisions, depending heavily on informal questioning, and seeking to probe and clarify until a consensus emerges.

- Staying alert to the symbolic impact of one's actions and statements lest a false signal stimulate proposals and movements in unwanted directions.

- Ensuring that all major power bases within the organization have representation in or access to top management.

- Injecting new faces and new views into considerations of major changes to preclude those involved from coming to see the world the same way and then acting as systematic screens against other views.

- Minimizing political exposure on issues that are highly controversial and in circumstances where opposition from major power centers can trigger a "shootout."

The politics of strategy implementation is especially critical when it comes to introducing a new strategy against the resistance of those who support the old one. Except for crisis situations where the old strategy is plainly revealed as out-of-date, it is usually bad politics to push the new strategy via attacks on the old one.[33] Bad-mouthing old strategy can easily be interpreted as an attack on those who formulated it and those who supported it. The old strategy and the judgments behind it may have been well-suited to the organization's earlier circumstances, and the people who made these judgments may still be influential.

In addition, the new strategy and/or the plans for implementing it may not have been the first choices of others, and lingering doubts may remain. Good arguments may exist for pursuing other actions. Consequently, in trying to surmount resistance, nothing is gained by knocking the arguments for alternative approaches. Such attacks often produce alienation instead of cooperation.

In short, to bring the full force of an organization behind a strategic plan, the strategy manager must assess and deal with the most important centers of potential support for and opposition to new strategic thrusts.[34] He or she needs to secure the support of key people, co-opt or neutralize serious opposition and resistance when and where necessary, learn where the zones of indifference are, and build as much consensus as possible.

Enforcing Ethical Behavior

For an organization to display consistently high ethical standards, the CEO and those around the CEO must be openly and unequivocally committed to ethical and moral conduct.[35] In companies that strive hard to make high ethical standards a reality, top management communicates its commitment in a code of ethics, in speeches and company publications, in policies concerning the consequences of unethical behavior, in the deeds of senior executives, and in the actions taken to ensure compliance. Senior management iterates and reiterates to employees that it is not only their duty to observe ethical codes but also to report ethical violations. While such companies have provisions for disciplining violators, the main purpose of enforcement is to

---

[33]Ibid., pp. 118–19.
[34]Ibid., p. 205.
[35]The Business Roundtable, *Corporate Ethics*, pp. 4–10.

encourage compliance rather than administer punishment. Although the CEO leads the enforcement process, all managers are expected to make a personal contribution by stressing ethical conduct with their subordinates and by involving themselves in the process of monitoring compliance with the code of ethics. "Gray areas" must be identified and openly discussed with employees, and procedures created for offering guidance when issues arise, for investigating possible violations, and for resolving individual cases. The lesson from these companies is that it is never enough to assume activities are being conducted ethically, nor can it be assumed that employees understand they are expected to act with integrity.

There are several concrete things managers can do to exercise ethics leadership.[36] First and foremost, they must set an excellent ethical example in their own behavior and establish a tradition of integrity. Company decisions have to be seen as ethical— "actions speak louder than words." Second, managers and employees have to be educated about what is ethical and what is not; ethics training programs may have to be established and gray areas pointed out and discussed. Everyone must be encouraged to raise issues with ethical dimensions, and such discussions should be treated as a legitimate topic. Third, top management should regularly reiterate its unequivocal support of the company's ethical code and take a strong stand on ethical issues. Fourth, top management must be prepared to act as the final arbiter on hard calls; this means removing people from a key position or terminating them when they are guilty of a violation. It also means reprimanding those who have been lax in monitoring and enforcing ethical compliance. Failure to act swiftly and decisively in punishing ethical misconduct is interpreted as a lack of real commitment.

A well-developed program to ensure compliance with ethical standards typically includes (1) an oversight committee of the board of directors, usually made up of outside directors; (2) a committee of senior managers to direct ongoing training, implementation, and compliance; (3) an annual audit of each manager's efforts to uphold ethical standards and formal reports on the actions taken by managers to remedy deficient conduct; and (4) periodically requiring people to sign documents certifying compliance with ethical standards.[37]

High ethical standards cannot be enforced without the open and unequivocal commitment of the chief executive.

Leading the Process of Making Corrective Adjustments

No strategic plan and no scheme for strategy implementation can foresee all the events and problems that will arise. Making adjustments and mid-course corrections is a normal and necessary part of strategic management.

When responding to new conditions involving either the strategy or its implementation, prompt action is often needed. In a crisis, the typical approach is to push key subordinates to gather information and formulate recommendations, personally preside over extended discussions of the proposed responses, and try to build a quick consensus among members of the executive inner circle. If no consensus emerges or if several key subordinates remain divided, the burden falls on the strategy manager to choose the response and urge its support.

When time permits a full-fledged evaluation, strategy managers seem to prefer a process of incrementally solidifying commitment to a response.[38] The approach involves

Corrective adjustments in the company's approach to strategy implementation should be made on an as-needed basis.

---

[36]Ibid.
[37]Ibid.
[38]Quinn, *Strategies for Change*, pp. 20–22.

1. Staying flexible and keeping a number of options open.
2. Asking a lot of questions.
3. Gaining in-depth information from specialists.
4. Encouraging subordinates to participate in developing alternatives and proposing solutions.
5. Getting the reactions of many different people to proposed solutions to test their potential and political acceptability.
6. Seeking to build commitment to a response by gradually moving toward a consensus solution.

The governing principle seems to be to make a final decision as late as possible to (1) bring as much information to bear as needed, (2) let the situation clarify enough to know what to do, and (3) allow the various political constituencies and power bases within the organization to move toward a consensus solution. Executives are often wary of committing themselves to a major change too soon because it limits the time for further fact-finding and analysis, discourages others from asking questions that need to be raised, and precludes thorough airing of all the options.

Strategy leaders should be proactive as well as reactive in reshaping strategy and how it is implemented.

Corrective adjustments to strategy need not be just reactive, however. Proactive adjustments can improve the strategy or its implementation. The distinctive feature of a proactive adjustment is that it arises from management initiatives rather than from forced reactions. Successful strategy managers employ a variety of proactive tactics:[39]

1. Commissioning studies to explore and amplify areas where they have a "gut feeling" or sense a need exists.
2. Shopping ideas among trusted colleagues and putting forth trial concepts.
3. Teaming people with different skills, interests, and experiences and letting them push and tug on interesting ideas to expand the variety of approaches considered.
4. Contacting a variety of people inside and outside the organization to sample viewpoints, probe, and listen, thereby deliberating short-circuiting all the careful screens of information flowing up from below.
5. Stimulating proposals for improvement from lower levels, encouraging the development of competing ideas and approaches, and letting the momentum for change come from below, with final choices postponed until it is apparent which option best matches the organization's situation.
6. Seeking new options and solutions that go beyond extrapolations from the status quo.
7. Accepting and committing to partial steps forward as a way of building comfort levels before going on ahead.
8. Managing the politics of change to promote managerial consensus and solidify management's commitment to whatever course of action is chosen.

The process leaders go through in deciding on corrective adjustments is essentially the same for both proactive and reactive changes; they sense needs, gather information, amplify understanding and awareness, put forth trial concepts, develop options,

---

[39]Ibid., chapter 4.

explore the pros and cons, test proposals, generate partial (comfort-level) solutions, empower champions, build a managerial consensus, and finally formally adopt an agreed-on course of action.[40] The ultimate managerial prescription may have been given by Rene McPherson, former CEO at Dana Corporation. Speaking to a class of students at Stanford University, he said, "You just keep pushing. You just keep pushing. I made every mistake that could be made. But I just kept pushing."[41]

All this, once again, highlights the fundamental nature of strategic management: the job of formulating and implementing strategy is not one of steering a clear-cut, linear course while carrying out the original strategy intact according to some preconceived and highly detailed implementation plan. Rather, it is one of creatively (1) adapting and reshaping strategy to unfolding events and (2) drawing upon whatever managerial techniques are needed to align internal activities and behaviors with strategy. The process is interactive, with much looping and recycling to fine-tune and adjust visions, objectives, strategies, implementation approaches, and cultures to one another in a continuously evolving process where the conceptually separate acts of crafting and implementing strategy blur and join together.

Key Points

Building a strategy-supportive corporate culture is important to successful implementation because it produces a work climate and organizational esprit de corps that thrive on meeting performance targets and being part of a winning effort. An organization's culture emerges from why and how it does things the way it does, the values and beliefs that senior managers espouse, the ethical standards expected of all, the tone and philosophy underlying key policies, and the traditions the organization maintains. Culture thus concerns the atmosphere and "feeling" a company has and the style in which it gets things done.

Very often, the elements of company culture originate with a founder or other early influential leaders who articulate certain values, beliefs, and principles the company should adhere to, which then get incorporated into company policies, a creed or values statement, strategies, and operating practices. Over time, these values and practices become shared by company employees and managers. Cultures are perpetuated as new leaders act to reinforce them, as new employees are encouraged to adopt and follow them, as legendary stories that exemplify them are told and retold, and as organizational members are honored and rewarded for displaying the cultural norms.

Company cultures vary widely in strength and in makeup. Some cultures are strongly embedded, while others are weak and fragmented in the sense that many subcultures exist, few values and behavioral norms are shared companywide, and there are few strong traditions. Some cultures are unhealthy, dominated by self-serving politics, resistant to change, and too inwardly focused; such cultural traits are often precursors to declining company performance. In fast-changing business environments, adaptive cultures are best because the internal environment is receptive to change, experimentation, innovation, new strategies, and new operating practices needed to respond to changing stakeholder requirements. One significant defining trait of adaptive cultures is that top management genuinely cares about the well-being of all key constituencies—customers, employees, stockholders, major suppliers, and

[40]Ibid., p. 146.

[41]As quoted in Peters and Waterman, *In Search of Excellence*, p. 319.

the communities where it operates—and tries to satisfy all their legitimate interests simultaneously.

The philosophy, goals, and practices implicit or explicit in a new strategy may or may not be compatible with a firm's culture. A close strategy-culture alignment promotes implementation and good execution; a mismatch poses real obstacles. Changing a company's culture, especially a strong one with traits that don't fit a new strategy's requirements, is one of the toughest management challenges. Changing a culture requires competent leadership at the top. It requires symbolic actions (leading by example) and substantive actions that unmistakably indicate top management is seriously committed. The stronger the fit between culture and strategy, the less managers have to depend on policies, rules, procedures, and supervision to enforce what people should and should not do; rather, cultural norms are so well-observed that they automatically guide behavior.

Healthy corporate cultures are also grounded in ethical business principles and moral values. Such standards connote integrity, "doing the right thing," and genuine concern for stakeholders and for how the company does business. To be effective, corporate ethics and values programs have to become a way of life through training, strict compliance and enforcement procedures, and reiterated management endorsements.

Successful strategy-implementers exercise an important leadership role. They stay on top of how well things are going by spending considerable time outside their offices, wandering around the organization, listening, coaching, cheerleading, picking up important information, and keeping their fingers on the organization's pulse. They take pains to reinforce the corporate culture through the things they say and do. They encourage people to be creative and innovative in order to keep the organization responsive to changing conditions, alert to new opportunities, and anxious to pursue fresh initiatives. They support "champions" of new approaches or ideas who are willing to stick their necks out and try something innovative. They work hard at building consensus on how to proceed, on what to change and what not to change. They enforce high ethical standards. And they push corrective action to improve strategy execution and overall strategic performance.

A manager's action agenda for implementing and executing strategy is thus expansive and creative. As we indicated at the beginning of our discussion of strategy implementation (Chapter 9), eight bases need to be covered:

1.   Building an organization capable of carrying out the strategy successfully.
2.   Developing budgets to steer ample resources into those value-chain activities critical to strategic success.
3.   Establishing strategically appropriate policies and procedures.
4.   Instituting best practices and mechanisms for continuous improvement.
5.   Installing support systems that enable company personnel to carry out their strategic roles successfully day in and day out.
6.   Tying rewards and incentives tightly to the achievement of performance objectives and good strategy execution.
7.   Creating a strategy-supportive work environment and corporate culture.
8.   Leading and monitoring the process of driving implementation forward and improving on how the strategy is being executed.

Making progress on these eight tasks sweeps broadly across virtually every aspect of administrative and managerial work.

Because each instance of strategy implementation occurs under different organizational circumstances, a strategy-implementer's action agenda always needs to be situation specific—there's no neat generic procedure to follow. And, as we said at the beginning, implementing strategy is an action-oriented, make-the-right-things-happen task that challenges a manager's ability to lead and direct organizational change, create or reinvent business processes, manage and motivate people, and achieve performance targets. If you now better understand the nature of the challenge, the range of available approaches, and the issues that need to be considered, we will look upon our discussion in these last three chapter as a success.

Suggested Readings

Bettinger, Cass. "Use Corporate Culture to Trigger High Performance." *Journal of Business Strategy* 10, no. 2 (March–April 1989), pp. 38–42.

Bower, Joseph L., and Martha W. Weinberg. "Statecraft, Strategy, and Corporate Leadership." *California Management Review* 30, no. 2 (Winter 1988), pp. 39–56.

Deal, Terrence E., and Allen A. Kennedy. *Corporate Cultures*. Reading, Mass.: Addison-Wesley, 1982, especially chaps. 1 and 2.

Eccles, Robert G. "The Performance Measurement Manifesto." *Harvard Business Review* 69 (January–February 1991), pp. 131–37.

Floyd, Steven W., and Bill Wooldridge. "Managing Strategic Consensus: The Foundation of Effective Implementation." *Academy of Management Executive* 6, no. 4 (November 1992), pp. 27–39.

Freeman, R. Edward, and Daniel R. Gilbert, Jr. *Corporate Strategy and the Search for Ethics*. Englewood Cliffs, N.J.: Prentice-Hall, 1988.

Gabarro, J. J. "When a New Manager Takes Charge." *Harvard Business Review* 64, no. 3 (May–June 1985), pp. 110–23.

Ginsburg, Lee and Neil Miller, "Value-Driven Management," *Business Horizons* (May–June 1992), pp. 25–27.

Green, Sebastian. "Strategy, Organizational Culture, and Symbolism." *Long Range Planning* 21, no. 4 (August 1988), pp. 121–29.

Kirkpatrick, Shelley A., and Edwin A. Locke. "Leadership: Do Traits Matter?" *Academy of Management Executive* 5, no. 2 (May 1991), pp. 48–60.

Kotter, John P. "What Leaders Really Do." *Harvard Business Review* 68 (May–June 1990), pp. 103–11.

Kotter, John P., and James L. Heskett. *Corporate Culture and Performance*. New York: Free Press, 1992.

O'Toole, James. "Employee Practices at the Best-Managed Companies." *California Management Review* 28, no. 1 (Fall 1985), pp. 35–66.

Paine, Lynn Sharp. "Managing for Organizational Integrity." *Harvard Business Review* 72, no. 2 (March–April 1994), pp. 106–117.

Pascale, Richard. "The Paradox of 'Corporate Culture': Reconciling Ourselves to Socialization." *California Management Review* 27, no. 2 (Winter 1985), pp. 26–41.

Quinn, James Brian. *Strategies for Change: Logical Incrementalism*. Homewood, Ill.: Richard D. Irwin, 1980, chap. 4.

———. "Managing Innovation: Controlled Chaos." *Harvard Business Review* 64, no. 3 (May–June 1985), pp. 73–84.

Reimann, Bernard C., and Yoash Wiener. "Corporate Culture: Avoiding the Elitest Trap." *Business Horizons* 31, no. 2 (March–April 1988), pp. 36–44.

Scholz, Christian. "Corporate Culture and Strategy—The Problem of Strategic Fit." *Long Range Planning* 20 (August 1987), pp. 78–87.

PART TWO

Cases in Strategic Management

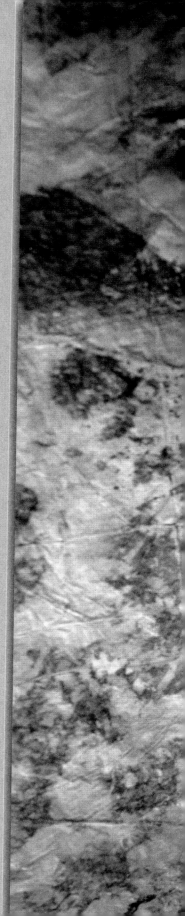

A Guide to Case Analysis

I keep six honest serving men
(They taught me all I knew);
Their names are What and Why and When;
And How and Where and Who.

Rudyard Kipling

In most courses in strategic management, students use cases about actual companies to practice strategic analysis and to gain some experience in the tasks of crafting and implementing strategy. A case sets forth, in a factual manner, the events and organizational circumstances surrounding a particular managerial situation. It puts readers at the scene of the action and familiarizes them with all the relevant circumstances. A case on strategic management can concern a whole industry, a single organization, or some part of an organization; the organization involved can be either profit seeking or not-for-profit. The essence of the student's role in case analysis is to *diagnose* and *size up* the situation described in the case and then to *recommend* appropriate action steps.

WHY USE CASES TO PRACTICE STRATEGIC MANAGEMENT?

A student of business with tact
Absorbed many answers he lacked.
But acquiring a job,
He said with a sob,
"How does one fit answer to fact?"

The foregoing limerick was used some years ago by Professor Charles Gragg to characterize the plight of business students who had no exposure to cases.[1] Gragg observed that the mere act of listening to lectures and sound advice about managing does little for anyone's management skills and that the accumulated managerial wisdom cannot effectively be passed on by lectures and assigned readings alone. Gragg suggested that if anything had been learned about the practice of management, it is that a storehouse of ready-made textbook answers does not exist. Each managerial situation has unique aspects, requiring its own diagnosis, judgment, and tailor-made actions. Cases provide would-be managers with a valuable way to practice wrestling with the actual problems of actual managers in actual companies.

The case approach to strategic analysis is, first and foremost, an exercise in learning by doing. Because cases provide you with detailed information about

---

[1]Charles I. Gragg, "Because Wisdom Can't Be Told," in *The Case Method at the Harvard Business School,* ed. M. P. McNair (New York: McGraw-Hill, 1954), p. 11.

conditions and problems of different industries and companies, your task of analyzing company after company and situation after situation has the twin benefit of boosting your analytical skills and exposing you to the ways companies and managers actually do things. Most college students have limited managerial backgrounds and only fragmented knowledge about companies and real-life strategic situations. Cases help substitute for on-the-job experience by (1) giving you broader exposure to a variety of industries, organizations, and strategic problems; (2) forcing you to assume a managerial role (as opposed to that of just an onlooker); (3) providing a test of how to apply the tools and techniques of strategic management; and (4) asking you to come up with pragmatic managerial action plans to deal with the issues at hand.

OBJECTIVES OF CASE ANALYSIS

Using cases to learn about the practice of strategic management is a powerful way for you to accomplish five things:[2]

1. Increase your understanding of what managers should and should not do in guiding a business to success.
2. Build your skills in conducting strategic analysis in a variety of industries, competitive situations, and company circumstances.
3. Get valuable practice in diagnosing strategic issues, evaluating strategic alternatives, and formulating workable plans of action.
4. Enhance your sense of business judgment, as opposed to uncritically accepting the authoritative crutch of the professor or "back-of-the-book" answers.
5. Gaining in-depth exposure to different industries and companies, thereby gaining something close to actual business experience.

If you understand that these are the objectives of case analysis, you are less likely to be consumed with curiosity about "the answer to the case." Students who have grown comfortable with and accustomed to textbook statements of fact and definitive lecture notes are often frustrated when discussions about a case do not produce concrete answers. Usually, case discussions produce good arguments for more than one course of action. Differences of opinion nearly always exist. Thus, should a class discussion conclude without a strong, unambiguous consensus on what do to, don't grumble too much when you are *not* told what the answer is or what the company actually did. Just remember that in the business world answers don't come in conclusive black-and-white terms. There are nearly always several feasible courses of action and approaches, each of which may work out satisfactorily. Moreover, in the business world, when one elects a particular course of action, there is no peeking at the back of a book to see if you have chosen the best thing to do and no one to turn to for a provably correct answer. The only valid test of management action is *results*. If the results of an action turn out to be "good," the decision to take it may be presumed "right." If not, then the action chosen was "wrong" in the sense that it didn't work out.

Hence, the important thing for a student to understand in case analysis is that the managerial exercise of identifying, diagnosing, and recommending builds your skills;

---

[2]Ibid., pp. 12–14; and D. R. Schoen and Philip A. Sprague, "What Is the Case Method?" in *The Case Method at the Harvard Business School*, ed. M. P. McNair, pp. 78–79.

discovering the right answer or finding out what actually happened is no more than frosting on the cake. Even if you learn what the company did, you can't conclude that it was necessarily right or best. All that can be said is "here is what they did. . . "

The point is this: *The purpose of giving you a case assignment is not to cause you to run to the library to look up what the company actually did but, rather, to enhance your skills in sizing up situations and developing your managerial judgment about what needs to be done and how to do it.* The aim of case analysis is for *you* to bear the strains of thinking actively, of offering your analysis, of proposing action plans, and of explaining and defending your assessments—this is how cases provide you with meaningful practice at being a manager.

PREPARING A CASE FOR CLASS DISCUSSION

If this is your first experience with the case method, you may have to reorient your study habits. Unlike lecture courses where you can get by without preparing intensively for each class and where you have latitude to work assigned readings and reviews of lecture notes into your schedule, a case assignment requires conscientious preparation before class. You will not get much out of hearing the class discuss a case you haven't read, and you certainly won't be able to contribute anything yourself to the discussion. What you have got to do to get ready for class discussion of a case is to study the case, reflect carefully on the situation presented, and develop some reasoned thoughts. Your goal in preparing the case should be to end up with what you think is a sound, well-supported analysis of the situation and a sound, defensible set of recommendations about which managerial actions need to be taken. The Strat-TUTOR software package that accompanies this edition will assist you in preparing the cases—it contains a set of study questions for each case and step-by-step tutorials to walk you through the process of analyzing and developing reasonable recommendations.

To prepare a case for class discussion, we suggest the following approach:

1. *Read the case through rather quickly for familiarity.* The initial reading should give you the general flavor of the situation and indicate which issue or issues are involved. If your instructor has provided you with study questions for the case, now is the time to read them carefully.

2. *Read the case a second time.* On this reading, try to gain full command of the facts. Begin to develop some tentative answers to the study questions your instructor has provided or that are provided on the Strat-TUTOR software package. If your instructor has elected not to give you assignment questions or has elected to not use Strat-TUTOR, then start forming your own picture of the overall situation being described.

3. *Study all the exhibits carefully.* Often, there is an important story in the numbers contained in the exhibits. Expect the information in the case exhibits to be crucial enough to materially affect your diagnosis of the situation.

4. *Decide what the strategic issues are.* Until you have identified the strategic issues and problems in the case, you don't know what to analyze, which tools and analytical techniques are called for, or otherwise how to proceed. At times the strategic issues are clear—either being stated in the case or else obvious from reading the case. At other times you will have to dig them out from all the information given; if so, the study questions and the case preparation outlines on Strat-TUTOR will guide you.

5. *Start your analysis of the issues with some number crunching.* A big majority of strategy cases call for some kind of number crunching—calculating assorted financial ratios to check out the company's financial condition and recent performance, calculating growth rates of sales or profits or unit volume, checking out profit margins and the makeup of the cost structure, and understanding whatever revenue-cost-profit relationships are present. See Table 1 for a summary of key financial ratios, how they are calculated, and what they show. If you are using Strat-Tutor, much of the number-crunching has been computerized and you'll spend most of your time interpreting the growth rates, financial ratios, and other calculations provided.

6. *Use whichever tools and techniques of strategic analysis are called for.* Strategic analysis is not just a collection of opinions; rather, it entails application of a growing number of powerful tools and techniques that cut beneath the surface and produce important insight and understanding of strategic situations. Every case assigned is strategy related and contains an opportunity to usefully apply the weapons of strategic analysis. Your instructor is looking for you to demonstrate that you know *how* and *when* to use the strategic management concepts presented in the text chapters. The case preparation guides on Strat-Tutor will point you toward the proper analytical tools needed to analyze the case situation.

7. *Check out conflicting opinions and make some judgments about the validity of all the data and information provided.* Many times cases report views and contradictory opinions (after all, people don't always agree on things, and different people see the same things in different ways). Forcing you to evaluate the data and information presented in the case helps you develop your powers of inference and judgment. Asking you to resolve conflicting information "comes with the territory" because a great many managerial situations entail opposing points of view, conflicting trends, and sketchy information.

8. *Support your diagnosis and opinions with reasons and evidence.* The most important things to prepare for are your answers to the question "Why?" For instance, if after studying the case you are of the opinion that the company's managers are doing a poor job, then it is your answer to "Why?" that establishes just how good your analysis of the situation is. If your instructor has provided you with specific study questions for the case or if you are using the case preparation guides on Strat-Tutor, by all means prepare answers that include all the reasons and number-crunching evidence you can muster to support your diagnosis. Work through the case preparation outlines on Strat-Tutor *conscientiously* or, if you are using study questions provided by the instructor, *generate at least two pages of notes!*

9. *Develop an appropriate action plan and set of recommendations.* Diagnosis divorced from corrective action is sterile. The test of a manager is always to convert sound analysis into sound actions—actions that will produce the desired results. Hence, the final and most telling step in preparing a case is to develop an action agenda for management that lays out a set of specific recommendations on what to do. Bear in mind that proposing realistic, workable solutions is far preferable to casually tossing out off-the-top-of-your-head suggestions. Be prepared to argue why your recommendations are more attractive than other courses of action that are open. You'll find Strat-Tutor's case preparation guides helpful in performing this step, too.

Table 1   A Summary of Key Financial Ratios, How They Are Calculated, and What They Show

Ratio	How Calculated	What It Shows
Profitability Ratios		
1. Gross profit margin	$$\frac{\text{Sales} - \text{Cost of goods sold}}{\text{Sales}}$$	An indication of the total margin available to cover operating expenses and yield a profit.
2. Operating profit margin (or return on sales)	$$\frac{\text{Profits before taxes and before interest}}{\text{Sales}}$$	An indication of the firm's profitability from current operations without regard to the interest charges accruing from the capital structure.
3. Net profit margin (or net return on sales)	$$\frac{\text{Profits after taxes}}{\text{Sales}}$$	Shows after tax profits per dollar of sales. Subpar profit margins indicate that the firm's sales prices are relatively low or that costs are relatively high, or both.
4. Return on total assets	$$\frac{\text{Profits after taxes}}{\text{Total assets}}$$ or $$\frac{\text{Profits after taxes} + \text{interest}}{\text{Total assets}}$$	A measure of the return on total investment in the enterprise. It is sometimes desirable to add interest to aftertax profits to form the numerator of the ratio since total assets are financed by creditors as well as by stockholders; hence, it is accurate to measure the productivity of assets by the returns provided to both classes of investors.
5. Return on stockholder's equity (or return on net worth)	$$\frac{\text{Profits after taxes}}{\text{Total stockholders' equity}}$$	A measure of the rate of return on stockholders' investment in the enterprise.
6. Return on common equity	$$\frac{\text{Profits after taxes} - \text{Preferred stock dividends}}{\text{Total stockholders' equity} - \text{Par value of preferred stock}}$$	A measure of the rate of return on the investment the owners of the common stock have made in the enterprise.
7. Earnings per share	$$\frac{\text{Profits after taxes} - \text{Preferred stock dividends}}{\text{Number of shares of common stock outstanding}}$$	Shows the earnings available to the owners of each share of common stock.
Liquidity Ratios		
1. Current ratio	$$\frac{\text{Current assets}}{\text{Current liabilities}}$$	Indicates the extent to which the claims of short-term creditors are covered by assets that are expected to be converted to cash in a period roughly corresponding to the maturity of the liabilities.
2. Quick ratio (or acid-test ratio)	$$\frac{\text{Current assets} - \text{Inventory}}{\text{Current liabilities}}$$	A measure of the firm's ability to pay off short-term obligations without relying on the sale of its inventories.
3. Inventory to net working capital	$$\frac{\text{Inventory}}{\text{Current assets} - \text{Current liabilities}}$$	A measure of the extent to which the firm's working capital is tied up in inventory.
Leverage Ratios		
1. Debt-to-assets ratio	$$\frac{\text{Total debt}}{\text{Total assets}}$$	Measures the extent to which borrowed funds have been used to finance the firm's operations.
2. Debt-to-equity ratio	$$\frac{\text{Total debt}}{\text{Total stockholders' equity}}$$	Provides another measure of the funds provided by creditors versus the funds provided by owners.

Table 1   A Summary of Key Financial Ratios, How They Are Calculated, and What They Show (*cont.*)

Ratio	How Calculated	What It Shows
Leverage Ratios (*cont.*)		
3. Long-term debt-to-equity ratio	$$\frac{\text{Long-term debt}}{\text{Total shareholders' equity}}$$	A widely used measure of the balance between debt and equity in the firm's long-term capital structure.
4. Times-interest-earned (or coverage) ratio	$$\frac{\text{Profits before interest and taxes}}{\text{Total interest charges}}$$	Measures the extent to which earnings can decline without the firm becoming unable to meet its annual interest costs.
5. Fixed-charge coverage	$$\frac{\text{Profits before taxes and interest} + \text{Lease obligations}}{\text{Total interest charges} + \text{Lease obligations}}$$	A more inclusive indication of the firm's ability to meet all of its fixed-charge obligations.
Activity Ratios		
1. Inventory turnover	$$\frac{\text{Sales}}{\text{Inventory of finished goods}}$$	When compared to industry averages, it provides an indication of whether a company has excessive or perhaps inadequate finished goods inventory.
2. Fixed assets turnover	$$\frac{\text{Sales}}{\text{Fixed Assets}}$$	A measure of the sales productivity and utilization of plant and equipment.
3. Total assets turnover	$$\frac{\text{Sales}}{\text{Total Assets}}$$	A measure of the utilization of all the firm's assets; a ratio below the industry average indicates the company is not generating a sufficient volume of business, given the size of its asset investment.
4. Accounts receivable turnover	$$\frac{\text{Annual credit sales}}{\text{Accounts receivable}}$$	A measure of the average length of time it takes the firm to collect the sales made on credit.
5. Average collection period	$$\frac{\text{Accounts receivable}}{\text{Total sales} \div 365}$$ or $$\frac{\text{Accounts receivable}}{\text{Average daily sales}}$$	Indicates the average length of time the firm must wait after making a sale before it receives payment.
Other Ratios		
1. Dividend yield on common stock	$$\frac{\text{Annual dividends per share}}{\text{Current market price per share}}$$	A measure of the return to owners received in the form of dividends.
2. Price-earnings ratio	$$\frac{\text{Current market price per share}}{\text{After tax earnings per share}}$$	Faster-growing or less-risky firms tend to have higher price-earnings ratios than slower-growing or more-risky firms.
3. Dividend payout ratio	$$\frac{\text{Annual dividends per share}}{\text{After tax earnings per share}}$$	Indicates the percentage of profits paid out as dividends.
4. Cash flow per share	$$\frac{\text{After tax profits} + \text{Depreciation}}{\text{Number of common shares outstanding}}$$	A measure of the discretionary funds over and above expenses that are available for use by the firm.

Note: Industry-average ratios against which a particular company's ratios may be judged are available in *Modern Industry* and *Dun's Reviews* published by Dun & Bradstreet (14 ratios for 125 lines of business activities), Robert Morris Associates' Annual Statement Studies (11 ratios for 156 lines of business), and the FTC-SEC's *Quarterly Financial Report* for manufacturing corporations.

As long as you are conscientious in preparing your analysis and recommendations, and have ample reasons, evidence, and arguments to support your views, you shouldn't fret unduly about whether what you've prepared is the right answer to the case. In case analysis there is rarely just one right approach or set of recommendations. Managing companies and devising and implementing strategies are not such exact sciences that there exists a single provably correct analysis and action plan for each strategic situation. Of course, some analyses and action plans are better than others; but, in truth, there's nearly always more than one good way to analyze a situation and more than one good plan of action. So, if you have carefully prepared the case using either the Strat-Tutor case preparation guides or your instructor's assignment questions, don't lose confidence in the correctness of your work and judgment.

PARTICIPATING IN CLASS DISCUSSION OF A CASE

Classroom discussions of cases are sharply different from attending a lecture class. In a case class students do most of the talking. The instructor's role is to solicit student participation, keep the discussion on track, ask "Why?" often, offer alternative views, play the devil's advocate (if no students jump in to offer opposing views), and otherwise lead the discussion. The students in the class carry the burden for analyzing the situation and for being prepared to present and defend their diagnoses and recommendations. Expect a classroom environment, therefore, that calls for *your* size-up of the situation, *your* analysis, what actions *you* would take, and why *you* would take them. Do not be dismayed if, as the class discussion unfolds, some insightful things are said by your fellow classmates that you did not think of. It is normal for views and analyses to differ and for the comments of others in the class to expand your own thinking about the case. As the old adage goes, "Two heads are better than one." So it is to be expected that the class as a whole will do a more penetrating and searching job of case analysis than will any one person working alone. This is the power of group effort, and its virtues are that it will help you see more analytical applications, let you test your analyses and judgments against those of your peers, and force you to wrestle with differences of opinion and approaches.

To orient you to the classroom environment on the days a case discussion is scheduled, we compiled the following list of things to expect:

1. Expect students to dominate the discussion and do most of the talking. The case method enlists a maximum of individual participation in class discussion. It is not enough to be present as a silent observer; if every student took this approach, there would be no discussion. (Thus, expect a portion of your grade to be based on your participation in case discussions.)

2. Expect the instructor to assume the role of extensive questioner and listener.

3. Be prepared for the instructor to probe for reasons and supporting analysis.

4. Expect and tolerate challenges to the views expressed. All students have to be willing to submit their conclusions for scrutiny and rebuttal. Each student needs to learn to state his or her views without fear of disapproval and to overcome the hesitation of speaking out. Learning

respect for the views and approaches of others is an integral part of case analysis exercises. But there are times when it is OK to swim against the tide of majority opinion. In the practice of management, there is always room for originality and unorthodox approaches. So while discussion of a case is a group process, there is no compulsion for you or anyone else to cave in and conform to group opinions and group consensus.

5. Don't be surprised if you change your mind about some things as the discussion unfolds. Be alert to how these changes affect your analysis and recommendations (in the event you get called on).

6. Expect to learn a lot from each case discussion; use what you learned to be better prepared for the next case discussion.

There are several things you can do on your own to be good and look good as a participant in class discussions:

- Although you should do your own independent work and independent thinking, don't hesitate before (and after) class to discuss the case with other students. In real life, managers often discuss the company's problems and situation with other people to refine their own thinking.

- In participating in the discussion, make a conscious effort to contribute, rather than just talk. There is a big difference between saying something that builds the discussion and offering a long-winded, off-the-cuff remark that leaves the class wondering what the point was.

- Avoid the use of "I think," "I believe," and "I feel"; instead, say, "My analysis shows . . ." and "The company should do . . . because . . ." Always give supporting reasons and evidence for your views; then your instructor won't have to ask you "Why?" every time you make a comment.

- In making your points, assume that everyone has read the case and knows what it says; avoid reciting and rehashing information in the case—instead, use the data and information to explain your assessment of the situation and to support your position.

- Bring the printouts of the work you've done on Strat-TUTOR or the notes you've prepared (usually two or three pages' worth) to class and rely on them extensively when you speak. There's no way you can remember everything off the top of your head—especially the results of your number crunching. To reel off the numbers or to present all five reasons why, instead of one, you will need good notes. When you have prepared thoughtful answers to the study questions and use them as the basis for your comments, *everybody* in the room will know you are well prepared, and your contribution to the case discussion will stand out.

PREPARING A WRITTEN CASE ANALYSIS

Preparing a written case analysis is much like preparing a case for class discussion, except that your analysis must be more complete and put in report form. Unfortunately, though, there is no ironclad procedure for doing a written case analysis. All we can offer are some general guidelines and words of wisdom—this is because company situations and management problems are so diverse that no one mechanical way to approach a written case assignment always works.

Your instructor may assign you a specific topic around which to prepare your written report. Or, alternatively, you may be asked to do a comprehensive written case analysis, where the expectation is that you will (1) *identify* all the pertinent issues that management needs to address, (2) perform whatever *analysis* and *evaluation* is appropriate, and (3) propose an *action plan* and *set of recommendations* addressing the issues you have identified. In going through the exercise of identify, evaluate, and recommend, keep the following pointers in mind.[3]

Identification   It is essential early on in your paper that you provide a sharply focused diagnosis of strategic issues and key problems and that you demonstrate a good grasp of the company's present situation. Make sure you can identify the firm's strategy (use the concepts and tools in Chapters 1–8 as diagnostic aids) and that you can pinpoint whatever strategy implementation issues may exist (again, consult the material in Chapters 9–11 for diagnostic help). Consult the key points we have provided at the end of each chapter for further diagnostic suggestions. Work through the case preparation exercise on Strat-TUTOR. Consider beginning your paper by sizing up the company's situation, its strategy, and the significant problems and issues that confront management. State problems/issues as clearly and precisely as you can. Unless it is necessary to do so for emphasis, avoid recounting facts and history about the company (assume your professor has read the case and is familiar with the organization).

Analysis and Evaluation   This is usually the hardest part of the report. Analysis is hard work! Check out the firm's financial ratios, its profit margins and rates of return, and its capital structure, and decide how strong the firm is financially. Table 1 contains a summary of various financial ratios and how they are calculated. Use it to assist in your financial diagnosis. Similarly, look at marketing, production, managerial competence, and other factors underlying the organization's strategic successes and failures. Decide whether the firm has core skills and competencies and, if so, whether it is capitalizing on them.

Check to see if the firm's strategy is producing satisfactory results and determine the reasons why or why not. Probe the nature and strength of the competitive forces confronting the company. Decide whether and why the firm's competitive position is getting stronger or weaker. Use the tools and concepts you have learned about to perform whatever analysis and evaluation is appropriate. Work through the case preparation exercise on Strat-TUTOR.

In writing your analysis and evaluation, bear in mind four things:

1.   You are obliged to offer analysis and evidence to back up your conclusions. Do not rely on unsupported opinions, over-generalizations, and platitudes as a substitute for tight, logical argument backed up with facts and figures.

2.   If your analysis involves some important quantitative calculations, use tables and charts to present the calculations clearly and efficiently. Don't just tack the exhibits on at the end of your report and let the reader figure out what they mean and why they were included. Instead, in the

---

[3]For some additional ideas and viewpoints, you may wish to consult Thomas J. Raymond, "Written Analysis of Cases," in *The Case Method at the Harvard Business School*, ed. M. P. McNair, pp. 139–63. Raymond's article includes an actual case, a sample analysis of the case, and a sample of a student's written report on the case.

body of your report cite some of the key numbers, highlight the conclusions to be drawn from the exhibits, and refer the reader to your charts and exhibits for more details.

3. Demonstrate that you have command of the strategic concepts and analytical tools to which you have been exposed. Use them in your report.

4. Your interpretation of the evidence should be reasonable and objective. Be wary of preparing a one-sided argument that omits all aspects not favorable to your conclusions. Likewise, try not to exaggerate or overdramatize. Endeavor to inject balance into your analysis and to avoid emotional rhetoric. Strike phrases such as "I think," "I feel," and "I believe" when you edit your first draft and write in "My analysis shows," instead.

Recommendations   The final section of the written case analysis should consist of a set of definite recommendations and a plan of action. Your set of recommendations should address all of the problems/issues you identified and analyzed. If the recommendations come as a surprise or do not follow logically from the analysis, the effect is to weaken greatly your suggestions of what to do. Obviously, your recommendations for actions should offer a reasonable prospect of success. High-risk, bet-the-company recommendations should be made with caution. State how your recommendations will solve the problems you identified. Be sure the company is financially able to carry out what you recommend; also check to see if your recommendations are workable in terms of acceptance by the persons involved, the organization's competence to implement them, and prevailing market and environmental constraints. Try not to hedge or weasel on the actions you believe should be taken.

By all means state your recommendations in sufficient detail to be meaningful—get down to some definite nitty-gritty specifics. Avoid such unhelpful statements as "the organization should do more planning" or "the company should be more aggressive in marketing its product." For instance, do not simply say "the firm should improve its market position" but state exactly how you think this should be done. Offer a definite agenda for action, stipulating a timetable and sequence for initiating actions, indicating priorities, and suggesting who should be responsible for doing what.

In proposing an action plan, remember there is a great deal of difference between, on the one hand, being responsible for a decision that may be costly if it proves in error and, on the other hand, casually suggesting courses of action that might be taken when you do not have to bear the responsibility for any of the consequences. A good rule to follow in making your recommendations is: *Avoid recommending anything you would not yourself be willing to do if you were in management's shoes.* The importance of learning to develop good judgment in a managerial situation is indicated by the fact that, even though the same information and operating data may be available to every manager or executive in an organization, the quality of the judgments about what the information means and which actions need to be taken does vary from person to person.[4]

---

[4]Gragg, "Because Wisdom Can't Be Told," p. 10.

Table 2 The Ten Commandments of Case Analysis

To be observed in written reports and oral presentations, and while participating in class discussions.

1. Read the case twice, once for an overview and once to gain full command of the facts; then take care to explore every one of the exhibits.
2. Make a list of the problems and issues that have to be confronted.
3. Do enough number crunching to discover the story told by the data presented in the case. (To help you comply with this commandment, consult Table 1 to guide your probing of a company's financial condition and financial performance.)
4. Look for opportunities to apply the concepts and analytical tools in the text chapters.
5. Be thorough in your diagnosis of the situation (either make a one- or two-page outline of your assessment or work through the exercises on Strat-TUTOR).
6. Support any and all opinions with well-reasoned arguments and numerical evidence; don't stop until you can purge "I think" and "I feel" from your assessment and, instead, are able to rely completely on "My analysis shows."
7. Develop charts, tables, and graphs to expose more clearly the main points of your analysis.
8. Prioritize your recommendations and make sure they can be carried out in an acceptable time frame with the available skills and financial resources.
9. Review your recommended action plan to see if it addresses all of the problems and issues you identified.
10. Avoid recommending any course of action that could have disastrous consequences if it doesn't work out as planned; therefore, be as alert to the downside risks of your recommendations as you are to their upside potential and appeal.

It goes without saying that your report should be well organized and well written. Great ideas amount to little unless others can be convinced of their merit—this takes tight logic, the presentation of convincing evidence, and persuasively written arguments.

THE TEN COMMANDMENTS OF CASE ANALYSIS

As a way of summarizing our suggestions about how to approach the task of case analysis, we have compiled what we like to call "The Ten Commandments of Case Analysis." They are shown in Table 2. If you observe all or even most of these commandments faithfully as you prepare a case either for class discussion or for a written report, your chances of doing a good job on the assigned cases will be much improved. Hang in there, give it your best shot, and have some fun exploring what the real world of strategic management is all about.

Ben & Jerry's Homemade, Inc.
Arthur A. Thompson, The University of Alabama

In 1963, Bennett Cohen and Jerry Greenfield, the two slowest, chubbiest kids in their seventh-grade gym class, started to hang out together. They had just gone through the common experience of being chewed out for not being able to run a mile around their Long Island, New York, junior high school track in less than seven minutes. Three years later, as high school classmates, their friendship truly began. Jerry, a self-described social nerd, was academically bright, graduating 3rd in a class of over 600.[1] Ben was an independent spirit who was motivated to do things he initiated or was interested in and who was turned off by required assignments, prescribed conduct, and parental authority.

After high school, Jerry enrolled at Oberlin College and graduated in premed; Ben decided to go to Colgate University, but he rebelled against the structured collegiate atmosphere, had little interest in the courses he took, and made poor grades. During the summer between his freshman and sophomore year, Ben worked for an ice cream distributor in his hometown, driving through neighborhoods selling ice cream out of a truck. When he drew a high enough number in the draft lottery to be safe from having to serve in the Vietnam War, Ben dropped out of Colgate and started through a progression of menial jobs to cover living expenses, including jobs in an ice cream parlor and an ice cream plant. Jerry, who was never really committed to becoming a doctor, worked in several jobs as a hospital lab technician. Both qualified as hippies, in their personal appearance (beards, long hair, jeans, T-shirts) and in their counter-culture beliefs and life-style.

By 1977, both Ben and Jerry were anxious for a change in careers and began to discuss starting their own business. Their first choice, a bagel delivery service, didn't pan out. Their second choice was an ice cream shop. Cohen and Greenfield researched the business by visiting scoop shops and split the tuition on a $5 correspondence course in ice cream making offered by Penn State. They began looking for suitable communities and for used equipment in mid-1977. Both wanted to live in rural New England surroundings compatible with their 1960s counterculture life-style and perspective. By late 1977, they settled on Burlington, Vermont. In December, they formed a corporation and opened the first Ben & Jerry's scoop shop in a renovated gas station in downtown Burlington on May 5, 1978. Their $12,000 investment was financed in part by a loan from Cohen's father who, according to Ben, "saw this as a transition from my being a hippie to becoming a businessman." The two cofounders decided Jerry should assume the title of company president since Ben's name came first in the company's name. According to Greenfield:

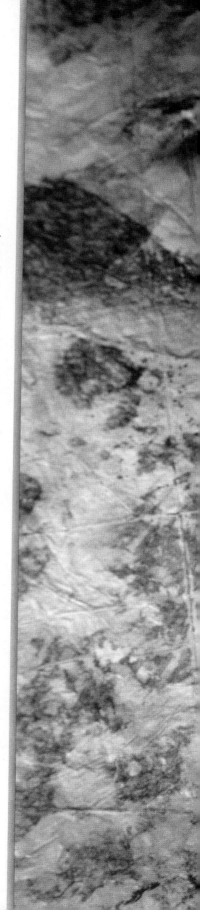

[1]Fred "Chico" Lager, *Ben & Jerry's: The Inside Scoop* (New York: Crown Publishers, 1994), p. 3.

We didn't have a whole lot going for us. We had no assets or collateral to speak of. We were new to the area. We were young. We weren't married. And we had no business experience.[2]

Because of his biochemistry background, Jerry took on the task of figuring out the formula for their ice cream mix. With the aid of a calculator and an industry guide on making ice cream, Jerry started making test batches using cream, milk, cane sugar, egg yolks, and natural stabilizers. The cofounders' business concept was to make the best ice cream available (using only the highest-quality ingredients they could find) and to sell it at a price that everyone could afford. The shop attracted an ample clientele from the start, but slow wintertime sales prompted Cohen and Greenfield in 1979 to begin wholesaling their ice cream brand in 2½-gallon tubs to area restaurants. Jerry supervised production and Ben spent most of his time on the road making deliveries and selling new accounts; a manager was hired to run the scoop shop.

After a few months, it became apparent that restaurant sales alone wouldn't be enough to make the truck routes Ben was driving profitable. Then Ben hit on an idea that ultimately would transform the business: They would package the ice cream in pint cartons and wholesale them to area groceries and mom-and-pop stores along his truck route. Jerry was skeptical but Ben prevailed. A friend worked on the design for the pint carton; the end result was an oval logo featuring a man making ice cream, a slogan "Vermont's Finest All Natural Ice Cream" below the logo, a picture of the cofounders on the lid, and a sales pitch signed by Ben and Jerry to persuade consumers to buy the ice cream:

> This carton contains some of the finest ice cream available anywhere. We know because we're the guys who make it. We start with lots of fresh Vermont cream and the finest flavorings available. We never use any fillers or artificial ingredients of any kind. With our specially modified equipment, we stir less air into the ice cream creating a denser, richer, creamier product of uncompromisingly high quality. It costs more and it's worth it.[3]

Underneath was an offer to refund the purchase price to any unsatisfied customer. A big contributor to the company's image was the decision to use mostly hand-lettering and draw lines with just enough of a wiggle to look hand-drawn; the visual impact fit nicely with the "homemade" impression that Ben and Jerry wanted the company's products to project.

Ben found that the best way to get small grocery stores to put Ben & Jerry's pint cartons in their freezer cases was to let them taste the product and then offer to refund the store's money if the stock didn't sell.[4] Within a few months Ben was able to increase distribution from 35 accounts to more than 200 accounts. Next, Ben approached several supermarket chains and eventually persuaded Grand Union to test-market Ben & Jerry's in nine stores. To promote the product, Jerry and Ben set up a dip case and scooped free samples for store shoppers. Sales proved brisk, and soon other supermarket chains elected to stock the Ben & Jerry's line.

Sales had grown enough by 1981 to require expanding production into a second building. Then *Time* magazine ran an August 1981 cover story on infatuation with superpremium ice cream; the article started off with the statement, "What you must

---

[2]Ibid., p. 15.
[3]Ibid., p. 41.
[4]Ibid., p. 42.

understand is that Ben & Jerry's in Burlington, Vermont, makes the best ice cream in the world." Even though the article went on to state that other brands were equally great-tasting, sales of Ben & Jerry's pint cartons and customer counts at the scoop shop immediately took off. Cohen and Greenfield viewed the company's growth as both a lucky fluke and an adventure into the future.

Company revenues climbed from under $300,000 in 1980 to almost $10 million in 1985 to $78 million in 1990 and to nearly $150 million in 1994 (Exhibit 1). Growth came from expanding distribution into more metropolitan areas and states, stimulating buyer interest with an ongoing stream of exotic flavors (Chocolate Chip Cookie Dough, Cherry Garcia, Chunky Monkey), opening additional scoop shops (reaching a total of 100 in 1994), and adding a frozen yogurt line. To help raise additional capital to finance growth, the company went public in 1985. The Small Business Administration named cofounders Cohen and Greenfield as Small Business Persons of the Year in 1988. Going into the 1990s, the Ben & Jerry's brand was available in most major U.S. markets and was stocked in a sizable fraction of the supermarkets and retail outlets that sold ice cream in take-home cartons. By 1994, Ben & Jerry's products were distributed in all 50 states and the company was marketing 29 flavors in pint cartons and over 45 flavors in bulk. The company's 100 scoop shops were located in New England, New York, the mid-Atlantic region, Georgia, Florida, Ohio, Indiana, Illinois, and California. It also had 4 licensed shops in Canada, 3 in Russia, and 10 in Israel. In mid-1994, Ben & Jerry's became the market leader in the luxury/gourmet or superpremium ice cream segment, surpassing Häagen-Dazs.

Along the way, the company became something of a business phenomenon—partly because of its ice cream, partly because of the two cofounders' hippie backgrounds and iconoclastic business approaches, and partly because the company gained a reputation for social responsibility virtually unmatched in American business circles.

THE ICE CREAM AND FROZEN YOGURT INDUSTRY IN 1995 —

Ice cream, frozen yogurt, and related frozen dessert novelties constituted a $10 billion retail market going into 1995. With the exception of frozen yogurt, new low-fat ice creams, and certain novelty items, industry growth was sluggish if not stagnant. Per capita consumption had been stuck in the 13 to 15 quarts per year range for four decades. Although over 90 percent of U.S. households purchased ice cream and frozen yogurt products, consumption was highest among families with young children and persons over 55 years old. Consumption patterns were only somewhat seasonal: about 30 percent of annual sales occurred during the summer months.

Market Trends and Consumer Preferences

The market for frozen dairy desserts consisted of many segments and product categories: superpremium (or luxury/gourmet) ice creams and frozen yogurt brands; premium ice cream, ice milk, and frozen yogurt products; economy and private-label ice cream, ice milk, and frozen yogurt products; low-fat ice cream products of a superpremium, premium, economy, or private-label nature; fruit sherbets and sorbets; and a growing array of bars and sandwich-type products containing ice cream, ice milk, frozen yogurt, and perhaps chocolate, fruits, cookies, nuts, and other mix-in items (generally

Exhibit 1   **Financial Summary, Ben & Jerry's Homemade, Inc., 1987–1994**   *(in millions of dollars, except for per share data)*

	1987	1988	1989	1990	1991	1992	1993	1994
Income Statement Data								
Net sales	$31.8	$47.6	$58.5	$77.0	$97.0	$132.0	$140.3	$148.8
Cost of sales	22.7	33.9	41.7	54.2	68.5	94.4	100.2	109.8
Gross profit	9.2	13.6	16.8	22.8	28.5	37.6	40.1	39.0
Selling, delivery and administrative expense	6.8	10.7	13.0	17.6	21.3	26.2	28.3	36.3
Operating income	2.4	3.0	3.8	5.2	7.2	11.3	11.9	2.7
Interest income	0.2	0.4	0.2	0.3	0.1	0.4	0.8	1.0
Interest expense	0.1	0.8	0.8	0.9	0.7	0.2	0.1	0.3
Other income (expense)	0.2	0.1	0.2	(0.1)	(0.1)	(0.2)	(0.5)	(7.2)†
Income before taxes	2.7	2.7	3.4	4.5	6.5	11.3	12.0	(3.8)
Income taxes	1.3	1.1	1.4	1.9	2.8	4.6	4.8	(1.9)
Net income	$ 1.4	$ 1.6	$ 2.1	$ 2.6	$ 3.7	$ 6.7	$ 7.2	(1.9)
Earnings per share	$ 0.28	$ 0.32	$ 0.40	$ 0.50	$ 0.67	$ 1.07	$ 1.01	$ (0.26)
Balance Sheet Data								
Current assets		$10.3	$10.5	$16.4	$23.7	$ 35.5	$ 42.4	$ 51.9
Current liabilities		4.7	4.7	8.2	12.7	17.5	13.1	14.5
Net property, plant, equipment		15.3	17.0	17.3	19.3	26.7	40.3	58.0
Total assets		26.3	28.1	34.3	43.1	88.2	106.4	120.3
Long-term debt		9.7	9.3	8.9	2.8	2.6	18.0	32.4
Stockholders' equity*		11.2	13.4	16.1	26.3	66.8	74.3	72.5

* No cash dividends have been paid since the company's founding. The company has stated it intends to reinvest earnings for use in its business and to finance future growth. The company's board of directors does not anticipate declaring any cash dividends in the foreseeable future.

† Includes a writedown of $6.8 million to replace certain of the software and equipment installed at the company's newly opened St. Albans, Vermont, plant.

Source: Company annual reports.

lumped together in a category called frozen novelties). Superpremium ice creams traditionally were distinguished from premium ice creams by their higher butterfat content, the use of all-natural and other more expensive ingredients, and a lower level of "overrun" or air content. Superpremium brands, like Ben & Jerry's Homemade and Häagen-Dazs, tended to be more expensively packaged and usually carried prices double those of premium brands and triple those of economy and private-label brands. However, high butterfat content was becoming a questionable attribute on which to hang the superpremium designation, since a growing number of low-fat ice creams (like ConAgra's new Healthy Choice brand) were trying to win a "superpremium" image and "light" and low-fat varieties of high-end name brands were becoming common. For the most part, consumers were only dimly aware of the butterfat and overrun specifications that technically separated superpremium from premium and premium from economy/private-label designations. Instead, consumer opinions about where different brands ranked on the quality scale related chiefly to price, taste, flavors, selection, and brand image rather than to butterfat content and overrun.

Starting in the late 1980s, consumer concerns about fat, cholesterol, and artificial additives spawned a wave of new low-fat and nonfat frozen yogurt products and light and fat-free ice creams. At the same time, though, demand for rich superpremium brands like Häagen-Dazs, Ben & Jerry's, and Frusen Glädje continued to mushroom on into the early 1990s, as consumers looked for "the very best" or gave into desires for a special treat. By the second half of 1992, however, growth in the sales of high-fat, high-calorie frozen dairy products started tapering off. Then, when new government-mandated nutritional labels appeared on food products in mid-1994, consumers found it easier to compare the calories, fat, and cholesterol content of brands and flavors. Sales of rich ice cream and frozen novelties plateaued over the next six months, even declining in several instances, as some label-reading consumers switched to low-fat or nonfat ice cream and frozen yogurt products.

Historically, consumers tended to be more loyal to their favorite flavors than to any particular brand. If they were not committed to a particular flavor, buyers were likely to peruse several brands, check out the flavors available in the freezer case, and choose an appealing flavor at an acceptable price. Most ice cream purchasers were willing to try new brands and new flavors. The best way for ice cream producers to cultivate brand loyalty was to maintain a broad selection of flavors in the freezer case and introduce new flavors frequently.

Competition

The supply side of the U.S. frozen dairy dessert market was fragmented, consisting of several hundred local and regional companies plus a few competitors whose brands were available in most major markets nationally. In 1995, the major players included:

Brand	Marketer
Ben & Jerry's	Ben & Jerry's Homemade, Inc.
Häagen-Dazs	Pillsbury/Grand Metropolitan
Healthy Choice	ConAgra
TCBY	TCBY Enterprises, Inc.
Baskin-Robbins	Allied-Lyons North America
Breyers	Unilever
Colombo	General Mills
Dreyer's/Edy's	Dreyer's Grand Ice Cream
Kemps	BolsWessanen

Some ice cream/frozen yogurt marketers competed only in the on-premise retail scoop shop market segment (the most notable was Baskin-Robbins); some competed in both the on-premise and take-home segments (Ben & Jerry's, Häagen-Dazs, and TCBY operated a chain of scoop shops and had supermarket distribution as well); and the remainder—a big majority—competed exclusively in the take-home segment, selling through supermarkets, convenience stores, health-food stores, and assorted other retailers. A growing number of ice cream marketers were introducing frozen yogurt lines to stake out a position in the flourishing frozen yogurt segment and to avoid being totally dependent on the ice cream segment where the signs of long-term sales erosion and intensifying competition were much in evidence.

Marketers of ice creams were scrambling to introduce light/low-fat ice creams, frozen yogurt, and frozen novelties that had lower fat, lower cholesterol, and lower calories, yet tasted as good as the traditional products with rich ingredients. These new products vied with existing products for shelf space and had triggered a competitive shakeout among brands and flavors in freezer cases as retailers made room for increasingly popular products that appealed to health-conscious buyers.

Production   Manufacturing involved ingredients preparation, mixing, packaging, and freezing—about a six-hour process. Superpremium brands and brands with mix-ins cost the most to produce. Mix-in flavors usually consisted of a vanilla or chocolate base to which fruits, nuts, fudge or caramel syrups, or chunks of cookies or candy bars were added. The cost of mix-ins could range up to a third of cost of goods sold for some varieties. A brand's selling prices, however, were usually the same for all flavors, resulting in higher profit margins for traditional plain flavors than mix-in flavors. Superpremium brands were usually packaged in more expensive round pint containers with decorative colors and graphics; premium and economy brands were typically sold in half-gallon round or rectangular cartons. Manufacturing cost differences between brands were chiefly a function of the kinds of basic ingredients used, type and percentage of mix-ins used, packaging, labor costs, and depreciation. Some manufacturers had recently invested in large, automated plants (which increased depreciation costs but which trimmed labor costs and permitted greater output of a wider flavor variety.)

A number of marketers owned no manufacturing facilities, opting instead to have local or regional producers with excess capacity handle production on a contract basis. Such marketers also usually relied on the contract producer, often a dairy products company, to handle distribution to local retailers.

Distribution   Due to the importance of convincing retailers to stock a company's brand and of gaining favorable shelf locations in the freezer case, distribution capability was one of the keys to market and competitive success. Retailers preferred to allocate their limited freezer space to the best-selling brands and flavors. Large retailers stocked one or two superpremium brands, two (maybe three) premium brands, and one or two local brands; smaller retailers usually stocked just one superpremium brand, a local premium or economy brand, and perhaps one other brand. Supermarket chains almost always supplemented their name brand offerings with a selection of private-label or economy ice cream, ice milk, and frozen yogurt products. Both large and small retailers stocked an assortment of frozen novelties, with the range of selection depending on store size and customer mix.

The preferred method of distribution was to have an area distributor representative deliver supplies by truck to each retail location and stock the retailer's shelves. It was the distributor's job to sell retailers on a brand, help the retailer determine the number of shelf facings each brand should be allocated based on sales turnover and profit margins, and choose how many units of which flavors should be stocked. Häagen-Dazs had created a national network of distributors at considerable cost, getting about 50 percent of its products into stores with company-owned distributors and 50 percent with independent distributors. Ben & Jerry's utilized two primary distributors, Sut's Premium Ice Cream for much of New England and Dreyer's Grand Ice Cream for states in the Midwest and West; the company had a number of other local distributors that serviced limited market areas to round out its coverage of most geographic areas nationwide. Dreyer's accounted for 52 percent ($77.6 million) of Ben & Jerry's net sales in 1994, up from 49 percent ($65 million) in 1992.

Competitive Rivalry   In the 1990s, rivalry among competing ice cream and frozen yogurt brands centered around ingredients (all-natural versus artificial, high-fat versus low-fat and fat-free, cholesterol levels), taste, flavor selection and variety, distribution capability, retail price, and brand image/reputation. Price competition was more a factor across categories (superpremium versus premium versus regular/economy versus private-label) than within categories. Market share gains were being made primarily by brands that (1) had succeeded in making their product offerings healthier without sacrificing taste, and/or (2) had captured buyer interest with a stream of new flavors, and/or (3) were adding new distributors to gain wider geographic coverage. Competition for shelf space was so intense that retailers were able to raise "slotting fees" (cash payments or off-price allowances that manufacturers customarily paid chain retailers, ostensibly to offset retailers' costs of slotting the product into their warehouses and getting it into their pricing, inventory, and ordering systems). Nor was it unusual for manufacturers and distributors to make payments (referred to as "grease") to individual buyers and purchasers to ensure that the people making decisions on which brands to stock were predisposed to their brands.

By 1994, supermarket sales of frozen yogurt had become a $600 million category. Market shares based on supermarket sales during the 52 weeks ended April 24, 1994, were as follows:[5]

Brand	Dollar Sales (in millions)	Percentage Share
Dreyer's/Edy's	$ 74.5	12.5%
Kemps	61.7	10.4
Ben & Jerry's	44.1	7.4
Breyers	36.3	6.1
Colombo	27.4	4.6
Häagen-Dazs	27.0	4.6
All private-label brands	94.0	15.8
All others	229.0	38.6
	$594.0	100.0%

In 1994, Dannon Co., a unit of BSN Groupe, began introducing two frozen yogurt versions: Dannon Light and Dannon Pure Indulgence. Häagen-Dazs was placing more marketing emphasis on its lower-fat offerings such as Strawberry Duet and Orange Tango. TCBY Enterprises' new supermarket line of frozen yogurt included Honey Almond Vanilla and Brazil & Cashew Nut Crunch. ConAgra's Healthy Choice line included Peanut Butter Fudge and Caramel Pecan Crisp.

BEN & JERRY'S MARKET POSITION AND STRATEGY ————

During 1994, Ben & Jerry's overtook Häagen-Dazs as the market leader of the superpremium ice cream market nationwide. The company ranked among the top five marketers of ice cream and frozen yogurt. The Ben & Jerry's brand was sold in bulk

---

[5]Compiled by Information Resources Inc., a market research company, and reported in *The Wall Street Journal.*

to the Ben & Jerry's chain of retail scoop shops and to food-service enterprises, but the big majority of its sales were pint containers sold through supermarkets, convenience stores, delicatessens, and related food outlets. In 1988, the company introduced Peace Pops and Brownie Bars to supplement its product line and to gain more freezer case exposure. In 1989, it introduced Ben & Jerry's Light, with one-third less fat and 40 percent less cholesterol than its regular superpremium line, but Light was soon dropped due to poor sales. The frozen yogurt line was introduced in 1991. In early 1994, Ben & Jerry's introduced a "Smooth, No Chunks" line consisting of eight flavors.

Competitive Strategy

The company competed on the basis of its product quality (chatty messages on the pint container boasted of great taste, delectable ingredients, and generous amounts of mix-ins), its ability to sustain buyer interest by creating innovative flavors, the product's Vermont-made character and the use of dairy ingredients coming only from Vermont family farms (which the company believed conveyed an image of quality and purity), its nationwide distribution capability, and its reputation for being an offbeat, funky, antiestablishment company. Customers were guaranteed satisfaction or their money back. Ben & Jerry's claimed its products contained 1½ to 2½ times more flavorings and chunks of mix-ins than rival brands (this was an outgrowth of Ben's insistence on personally approving all flavors and varieties—his sinus problems prevented him from distinguishing subtle flavors, plus he wanted different products to vary in texture and "mouth feel").[6] Also, the company's ice cream contained no preservatives or artificial ingredients except for those in some of the mix-in cookies and candies. Even though the company produced 30 flavors in packaged pints, it was the company's policy to distribute only about 12 to 18 flavors at any one time in any one area because of limited retailer shelf space; when a new flavor was introduced in an area, one of the less popular flavors was dropped. However, the company's product line for its scoop shops included an array of over 40 flavors.

Ben & Jerry's operated three plants in Vermont. Ben Cohen was passionate about the importance of making a high-quality product and was largely successful in instilling a strong commitment to quality throughout the production process. The company's most bedeviling production problem was getting the right amount of chunks into every pint. From the company's earliest days, Cohen insisted on adding generous proportions of mix-ins and using big chunks instead of small pieces. but the available ice cream-making equipment did not accommodate large chunks easily; spouts on the pint-filling machines jammed frequently and it was virtually impossible to ensure that each pint contained the same number of chunks. The company's most frequent customer complaint was that a particular pint didn't have enough chunks in it. The company had received an average of about 11.75 complaints per 80,000 pints since 1991. In 1993, the company received a batch of bad chocolate from one of its vendors that unknowingly was used in two flavors; rather than totally recalling the product, the company did a partial recall—retrieving unsold pints from distributors but not from retail stores. Responsibility for quality assurance was divided among four departments; quality managers reported to plant and production managers.

---

[6]Lager, *Ben & Jerry's: The Inside Scoop,* p. 22.

Conventional approaches to marketing and promotion were not employed. The company did no formal market research and no test-marketing; only a minimal amount of media advertising was done to promote the company's product line—a reflection of the cofounders' disapproval of commercialism and Madison Avenue glitz. The big majority of the company's media expenditures were for ads to introduce Ben & Jerry's products in new markets; otherwise, the company relied primarily on giving away free samples and word-of-mouth advertising by satisfied customers. Where needed, the company paid slotting fees to gain shelf space and wider market exposure.

Ben Cohen, who took a personal interest in and, in effect, dominated the company's approach to marketing, decided that the company's selling and promotional activities should revolve mainly around distributing free samples, hosting fun-oriented special attractions and educational events, and participating in or sponsoring campaigns that drew attention to social issues. A converted bus with solar-powered systems, known as the Cowmobile, carried traveling vaudeville acts around the country and served free scoops of ice cream. Labeling on the company's pint containers promoted campaigns to ban Bovine Growth Hormone and to promote support for the family farm (over 500 farms in Vermont supplied the company's dairy ingredients). Summer music festivals were sponsored at locations around the country. On one occasion Cohen and another company officer drove a truck containing Peace Pops and ice cream to a rally in Concord, New Hampshire, protesting the licensing of the Seabrook nuclear plant; Ben spoke at the rally and, afterward, passed out free Peace Pops and ice cream to the protesters. The company's annual shareholder meetings (which lasted several days) and factory tours at the Waterbury plant (the second most popular tourist attraction in Vermont) were utilized as promotional vehicles. Publicity surrounding these events broadened consumer awareness of the company's products and gave the company a certain mystique. Where Häagen-Dazs presented itself as a worldly, elegant, sophisticated, and snobbish product, Ben & Jerry's endeavored to be unpretentious, genuine, and down-home. Ben Cohen wanted consumers' image of the company to be one of "two real guys, Ben and Jerry, who live in Vermont, the land of green grass, blue sky, and black-and-white cows and who make world class ice cream in some really unusual flavors."[7]

In 1984, a few years after Pillsbury purchased Häagen-Dazs from Reuben Mattus (the New York City entrepreneur who in 1960 created the brand and spawned the birth of the superpremium segment), Pillsbury brought pressure on Häagen-Dazs's distributors in New England that also carried Ben & Jerry's to either drop Ben & Jerry's or risk losing their distribution rights for Häagen-Dazs. Ben & Jerry's filed for a restraining order in federal court and fashioned a PR campaign against Pillsbury using the slogan "What's the Doughboy Afraid of?" Jerry Greenfield picketed Pillsbury's Minneapolis headquarters and handed out leaflets describing Pillsbury's attempt to keep Ben & Jerry's off supermarket shelves:

> They are not content to compete with us based on product, price, or marketing . . . Do you think that maybe the Doughboy is afraid of the American Dream? We only want to make our ice cream in Vermont and let the people of Boston and New England make their choice in the supermarket . . . Next time you're in your local market, pick up a pint of Ben & Jerry's and give it a taste. Because to tell you the truth, *that's* what the Doughboy is really afraid of.

[7]Lager, *Ben & Jerry's: The Inside Scoop*, pp. 81–82.

Ben & Jerry's also developed a kit that supporters could use to write protest letters, printed T-shirts with the Doughboy slogan, affixed labels with the Doughboy slogan on pint containers, set up an 800 phone number for callers wanting information, ran an ad in *Rolling Stone* magazine to sell Doughboy bumper stickers for $1, and rented a billboard on a busy Boston route that headlined, "Don't Let Pillsbury Put the Squeeze on Ben & Jerry's." The campaign was cast as Pillsbury, a $4 billion Fortune 500 company, against two hippies. The media picked up the story, and after a few months Pillsbury signed a legal agreement to cease its loyalty program.

In late 1992, Häagen-Dazs introduced a line of chunky flavors designed to compete against the chunky flavors that were so much a part of Ben & Jerry's success. During the first half of 1993, Häagen-Dazs promoted these flavors with heavy media advertising and deep price discounting. In several key markets, Häagen-Dazs pints were retailing for half the regular price. Ben & Jerry's chose not to match the discounted prices, although it did offer distributors and retailers more promotional deals. While the company lost some market share during the discounting period, Ben & Jerry's market share was four points higher at the end of 1993 than at the beginning of the year.

Starting in March 1994, Ben & Jerry's introduced a new eight-flavor "Smooth, No Chunks" line to broaden its ability to satisfy consumer tastes for ice cream. Prior to the Smooth line (which included vanilla, vanilla bean, deep dark chocolate, and mocha fudge), the company had not competed in the traditional flavor area, preferring to set itself apart with its trendsetting chunky flavors. Management considered the Smooth, No Chunks line to be the company's most significant new product launch since the 1991 introduction of the frozen yogurt line. Launch of the new line was supported with national TV and print advertising, outdoor billboards in selected regions, and cents-off coupons. The Smooth, No Chunks line captured an estimated 6 percent national market share in 1994. Also in 1994, the company began marketing Ben & Jerry's pints and Peace Pops in gourmet stores and selected supermarkets in and around London, England.

Pint sales represented 84 percent of total revenues in 1993. Sales of 2½-gallon bulk containers to scoop shops accounted for 8 percent of revenues. Novelty products generated 5 percent of revenues, and sales of company-owned scoop shops represented 3 percent of revenues. Franchised scoop shops averaged $300,000 in sales annually, well above the industry average of $200,000.

One of the company's competitive strengths—product quality and creamy taste—turned out to be a source of competitive weakness starting in 1994. Its superpremium ice cream products contained comparatively high amounts of calories, saturated fat, and cholesterol. Exhibits 2 and 3 provide comparative nutrition statistics on selected brands of ice creams and frozen yogurts. Many consumers who bought upscale products like Ben & Jerry's were exactly the type likely to read the newly instituted nutritional labels. The new federal labeling requirements were said to be at the root of the company's January 1995 announcement that fourth-quarter 1994 sales had declined and that the company expected to post its first quarterly loss since it went public in 1985. Until recently, company management had expressed doubts about medical research linking excessive cholesterol and fat intake to a variety of heart, circulation, and other health-related problems. A 1989 *Washington Post* story quoted Ben Cohen as stating that cholesterol concerns were a fad; he went on to say:

> Ice cream in moderation is an incredibly healthy thing. We are not recommending that people eat a pint a day . . . Some people do, and I appreciate it.[8]

---

[8]From Daniel Seligman, "Ben & Jerry Save the World," *Fortune*, June 1, 1991, p. 248.

Exhibit 2   Comparative Nutrition Statistics of Selected Ice Cream Brands, January 1995

Nutritional Attribute	Ben & Jerry's Peanut Butter Cup	Ben & Jerry's Chocolate Chip Cookie Dough	Ben & Jerry's Rain Forest Crunch	Ben & Jerry's Cherry Garcia	Ben & Jerry's Wavy Gravy	Häagen-Dazs Macadamia Brittle	Häagen-Dazs Vanilla	Dreyer's Grand Rocky Road	Dreyer's Grand Light, Vanilla	Dreyer's Grand No Sugar Added Chocolate Chip	Barber's Best Rum Raisin
Calories ($\frac{1}{2}$-cup serving)	340	280	300	250	310	300	270	170	110	100	190
Calories from fat	220	150	200	140	200	180	160	90	35	40	90
Total fat (grams)	24	17	22	16	22	20	18	10	4	5	10
Percent of daily value	37	26	34	25	34	31	28	16	6	7	16
Saturated fat (grams)	11	9	11	10	9	11	11	5	2.5	2.5	7
Percent of daily value	55	45	55	50	45	56	54	27	12	13	33
Cholesterol (milligrams)	70	80	85	75	75	110	120	25	25	15	40
Percent of daily value	23	27	28	25	25	36	40	9	8	5	14

Nutritional Attribute	Edy's Grand Cherry Chocolate Chip	Edy's Grand Light Rocky Road	Four Winds Fudge Royale	Breyers Deluxe Rocky Road	Breyers Cookies in Cream	Breyers Reduced Fat Praline Almond Crunch	Kemps Kids Ice Cream, Dinosaur Egg Crunch	City Market Vanilla	Healthy Choice Rocky Road	Healthy Choice Black Forest	Meadow Gold Low Fat Cherry Vanilla
Calories ($\frac{1}{2}$-cup serving)	150	120	130	190	170	140	140	140	140	120	110
Calories from fat	80	40	60	80	80	45	60	70	20	20	20
Total fat (grams)	8	5	6	9	9	5	7	7	2	2	2
Percent of daily value	13	7	10	14	14	8	11	11	3	3	3
Saturated fat (grams)	5	25	4	5	6	3	4.5	4.5	1	1	1
Percent of daily value	23	12	20	25	30	15	23	23	5	5	5
Cholesterol (milligrams)	25	25	25	25	30	35	25	30	<5	5	10
Percent of daily value	8	8	8	8	10	12	8	10	1	3	3

Source: Compiled by the case author from nutritional labels of respective products.

A section in the company's 1994 annual report took issue with critics who insisted that selling a high-fat, high-sugar product was inherently irresponsible:

> the criticism that a company which makes full-fat ice cream is socially irresponsible seems a bit sanctimonious. Each person must decide whether to eat some foods for pleasure, foods that do not pretend to be nutritionally balanced staples. It is no secret that ice cream, if eaten excessively or obsessively, can cause nutritional problems. But to maintain that foods that give us cheap thrills and are fun to eat should not be sold by "responsible" companies is more puritanical than progressive. Ben & Jerry's is founded on fun, even mischief, and most people hope it doesn't stray far from the frivolous, the inane, the hilarious, and the quixotic. Providing healthy alternatives to its original super premium ice cream will go a long way toward satisfying customers' various needs.

Exhibit 3　Comparative Nutrition Statistics of Selected Frozen Yogurt Brands, January 1995

Nutritional Attribute	Ben & Jerry's Toffee Crunch	Ben & Jerry's Coffee Almond Fudge	Häagen-Dazs Exträas Strawberry Cheesecake Craze	Häagen-Dazs Chocolate	Dreyer's Marble Fudge	Dreyer's Raspberry Vanilla Swirl	Dreyer's Fat Free Vanilla Chocolate Swirl	I Can't Believe It's Yogurt Nonfat Not Just Plain Vanilla
Calories ($\frac{1}{2}$-cup serving)	190	200	220	160	110	100	90	90
Calories from fat	50	60	70	25	25	25	0	0
Total fat (grams)	6	7	8	2.5	3	2.5	0	0
Percent of daily value	9	11	12	4	4	4	0	0
Saturated fat (grams)	2.5	2	4	1.5	1.5	1.5	0	0
Percent of daily value	13	11	19	7	8	8	0	0
Cholesterol (milligrams)	10	15	65	30	10	10	0	0
Percent of daily value	4	4	22	11	3	3	0	0

Nutritional Attribute	Kemps M&M's Brownie Fudge	Kemps Nonfat Chocolate Toffee Sundae	Edy's Chocolate	Edy's Fat Free Chocolate	Edy's Heath Toffee Crunch	Breyers Natural Black Cherry	Breyers Chocolate	TCBY Classic Vanilla	TCBY Dutch Chocolate
Calories ($\frac{1}{2}$-cup serving)	150	120	100	90	120	140	150	110	100
Calories from fat	35	0	25	0	35	30	25	10	10
Total fat (grams)	4	0	3	0	4	3	3	1.5	1.5
Percent of daily value	6	0	4	0	6	5	5	2	2
Saturated fat (grams)	2	0	15	0	2	2.5	2	1	1
Percent of daily value	10	0	8	0	10	13	10	6	6
Cholesterol (milligrams)	10	0	10	0	10	15	15	5	5
Percent of daily value	3	0	3	0	3	5	5	1	1

Source: Compiled by the case author from nutritional labels of respective products.

BEN & JERRY'S STATEMENT OF MISSION

Growing Ben & Jerry's ice cream business in Burlington into a $100 million–plus public corporation had never been an objective or even a dim hope in the minds of the two cofounders. All Cohen and Greenfield were looking to do originally was create a business that would provide them a living wage. Their antiwar, antibusiness convictions, ingrained during the Vietnam protest era, made both cofounders uncomfortable managing a multimillion-dollar company with well-known products and a built-in profit orientation. As sales headed toward $1 million in 1982 and with managerial responsibilities escalating, Jerry announced his intention to leave the company at year-end, partly because of burnout from working 12- to 16-hour days, seven days a week, partly because he wanted to be with his girlfriend who was moving to Arizona, partly because he disliked the problems that came with supervising 20 employees, and partly because he wanted to get away from the growing pressures to think and act like a businessperson. During 1982, Ben also struggled with his future role, concerned that his socially activist beliefs and laidback approach to life clashed with how businesses were normally run.

For a while in 1982, the two cofounders flirted with selling the company, even going so far as to list the company with a Vermont broker that specialized in selling rural businesses. Ben was seriously ambivalent about selling out, however. When a friend convinced him that a large company could indeed be run in a compassionate and socially progressive manner, Ben canceled the planned sale and decided to hold onto his 50 percent ownership in the company. Jerry ended up keeping a 10 percent stake; the remainder of his share was later sold in small-share lots to 1,800 Vermont investors. When Jerry left at the end of 1982, Ben took over as CEO, becoming the dominant influence on the company's culture, leading its marketing and promotion efforts, and orchestrating company undertakings to enrich the quality of life for suppliers, employees, the communities where the company operated, and society at large. After living in Arizona for a little over two years, Jerry returned to Vermont in 1985. For a time thereafter, he served as a paid consultant to the company on a variety of issues, and then rejoined the company full time in 1987 as director of promotions.

Company policies and programs to promote the cofounders' sense of social mission were collectively referred to internally as "caring capitalism." Fervent in his conviction that business had a responsibility to give back to the community, Cohen diligently ferreted out ways for the company to pursue a social mission and a business mission simultaneously. Cohen described the kind of joint commitment he wanted the company to display:

> It's not a question of making great ice cream, making some money, and then going and doing socially responsible things. Caring about the community has to be imbued throughout the organization so that it impacts every decision we make.[9]

With Cohen's prodding (and sometimes authoritarian insistence), Ben & Jerry's instituted an assortment of practices and actions that were deemed worthy:

- Ingredients were sourced to serve social purposes. A Yonkers, New York, bakery that provided jobs for the homeless, the former homeless, and the hard-core unemployed was chosen to supply the brownies used as a mix-in for the company's Chocolate Fudge Brownie flavor; a portion of the bakery's profits were used for transitional housing, counseling, and training its employees. The blueberries for a flavor called Wild Maine Blueberry were all purchased from a Passamaquoddy Indian farming group in Maine. Cashew and Brazil nuts for the Rain Forest Crunch flavor were sourced in part from native forest people in Brazil, allowing them to earn 3 to 10 times their previous income and helping encourage preservation of the Brazilian rain forest. The apple pie mix-in for Apple Pie frozen yogurt was

[9]Lager, *Ben & Jerry's: The Inside Scoop,* p. 181.

baked by recovering addicts and alcoholics who worked at a New Jersey bakery that donated 10 percent of profits to Operation Mustard Seed—a community-based ministry for people in recovery. The company's pint labels for these flavors carried messages to consumers telling them about the sources of such ingredients.

- When federal subsidies to dairy farmers were trimmed back, resulting in declining milk prices, Ben & Jerry's continued to pay its Vermont milk suppliers above-market rates that added about $500,000 annually to the company's cost. Ben Cohen explained, "We refuse to profit off the misfortune of our dairy suppliers due to some antiquated, misguided, convoluted federal system."[10]

- The company was actively committed to working with farmers to produce milk without the use of rBGH (recombinant Bovine Growth Hormone), a synthetic hormone developed by Monsanto that could increase milk production by as much as 20 percent when injected into cows. The company's opposition to rBGH was based on concerns about its effect on the health of dairy cows and an expected adverse impact on the economic viability of small family farms if rBGH came into widespread use. Ben Cohen testified at Federal Drug Administration hearings in May 1993 against FDA approval of rBGH and, assuming FDA approval, for full disclosure to consumers. The company agreed to pay a premium of about $500,000 to its Vermont dairy suppliers in exchange for their pledge not to use rBGH.

- The company's new 17 million–gallon per year plant was deliberately located in an economically distressed area of Vermont.

- When a production line had to be closed for three and a half months, the affected employees (roughly 35) were not laid off but instead were kept on the payroll to do odd jobs around the plant and in the community.[11] Their assignments included painting all the fire hydrants in North Springfield, doing yard work, winterizing homes for the elderly and disabled, and putting on a Halloween benefit for local children's causes.

- In 1985, the company established the Ben & Jerry's Foundation to fund community-oriented projects that were models for social change, approached societal problems in nontraditional ways, incorporated a spirit of hope and generosity, or enhanced people's quality of life. The activities of the Foundation were funded by annual contributions from the company equal to 7.5 percent of the company's pretax profits; Ben Cohen gave the foundation 50,000 shares of his Ben & Jerry's stock as an initial endowment. In 1993, the Foundation distributed $808,000 to 142 projects. The Foundation had a policy of granting no more than $15,000 to any one project.

- In 1988, the two cofounders organized 400 companies into a group called "1% for Peace," which sought to redirect 1 percent of the national defense budget into activities promoting peace through understanding. The Ben & Jerry's Foundation agreed to donate the equivalent of 1 percent of the

[10]Ibid.

[11]Jennifer J. Laabs, "Ben & Jerry's Caring Capitalism," *Personnel Journal,* November 1992, p. 55.

company's pretax profits to support the organization's cause. To promote the effort, Ben decided to name one of the company's frozen novelties "Peace Pops."

- Admissions proceeds from factory tours at the Waterbury plant were allocated 50 percent to the Employee Community Fund, which supported local causes, and 50 percent to the company's Entrepreneurial Fund, which awarded low-interest loans to people starting new businesses, including employees.[12]

- Believing that environmental issues had to be taken seriously, the company appointed an environmental affairs director and invested in state-of-the-art greenhouse technology for treating wastewater at its plants. Ice cream waste was donated to a pig farm in Stowe, Vermont. Five-gallon white plastic buckets containing ingredients from suppliers were shredded into "regrind," which was recycled into other plastic products; starting in 1994, the company switched to returnable containers to eliminate the need to grind and recycle 1 million bulk containers annually. The company used office supplies made from recycled materials where possible. In 1994, two environmental consultants were brought in to evaluate how the company could improve on the adverse impacts its operations had as concerned waste, energy use, packaging, transportation, and chemical use.

- A Ben & Jerry's scoop shop in Harlem, New York, employed 12 homeless workers; 75 percent of the store's profits were donated to a Harlem shelter and drug-crisis center. A Baltimore scoop shop employed people in a rehabilitation program for the psychiatrically disabled. An Ithaca, New York, scoop shop was partnered with a youth services organization to provide job experience and business training for disadvantaged teenagers. In all three cases, Ben & Jerry's waived its usual franchise fee and provided extra management assistance to get the businesses up and running.[13]

- The company supported the Burlington Peace & Justice Coalition, which opposed the Gulf War and joined with 18 other companies in sponsoring a full-page ad in the *New York Times* urging President Bush and Congress to give economic sanctions against Iraq more time to work.

- The company took a public stand against a large Canadian hydroelectric project that would flood lands on which Cree Indians resided.

- Truckloads of ice cream seconds were sent to flood victims along the Mississippi River in 1993.

- In 1992 and 1993, the company focused most of its social mission efforts and resources on supporting the Children's Defense Fund's "Leave No Child Behind" campaign.

- Ben & Jerry's annual shareholder meetings included promotions for world peace, environmental causes, and efforts to solve social ills.

- Management believed that efforts to create a richer quality of life for society began with employees. The company provided a comprehensive employee benefits package, offered a minimum wage of $8 an hour, and went to great lengths to provide a progressive, caring work environment.

---

[12]Ibid., p. 55.
[13]Lager, *Ben & Jerry's: The Inside Scoop*, p. 188.

- The company donated $1,240,000 to help renovate a 652-unit apartment complex in Times Square in New York City that provided housing for low-income and homeless single adults, including people who were AIDS patients or had a history of mental illness.

- In 1994, grants were made to the Boreal Forest Advocacy Project in Alaska to help halt efforts to open up the pristine interior region of Alaska to timber operations and to the Farm Labor Research Project to improve the working conditions and wages for farm workers in North Carolina's pickle industry.

As the company developed and its involvement in political and social causes became integral to the company's culture and policies, the need to formalize the role of social activism in the company became a concern to the cofounders, other senior managers, and outside board members. A series of discussions to develop a mission statement was initiated in 1988. A three-part mission statement emerged (see Exhibit 4), but a heated debate ensued over what weight was to be given each part.[14] Some argued for greater weight being given to the economic mission on grounds that rewards for shareholders and employees were integral to the company's long-term success and its ability to give something back to the community and society at large. Others, led by Ben Cohen, argued for the greatest weight being placed on the social mission. In the end, the company's board of directors agreed to equal weighting for the three mission elements and to recognize that the elements were interdependent. Following adoption of the mission statement in 1988, a review of the company's social performance, compiled and/or verified by an independent auditor, was included in the annual report to shareholders. The auditor's first report commended the company on its charitable contributions and societal improvement efforts but criticized the company's nutritional labels, the high-fat and high-cholesterol content of its products, and its failure to offer products for health-conscious consumers. In the company's 1992 annual report to shareholders, Ben Cohen wrote:

> The most amazing thing is that our social values—that part of our company mission statement that calls us to use our power as a business to improve the quality of life in our local, national and international communities—have actually helped us to become a stable, profitable, high-growth company. This is especially interesting because it flies in the face of those business theorists who state that publicly held corporations cannot make a profit and help the community at the same time, and moreover that such companies have no business trying to do so. The issues here are heart, soul, love and spirituality. Corporations which exist solely to maximize profit become disconnected from their soul—the spiritual interconnectedness of humanity. Like individuals, businesses can conduct themselves with the knowledge that the hearts, souls and spirits of all people are interconnected; so that as we help others, we cannot help helping ourselves.

The unusually prominent role of the social mission resulted in considerable free publicity for the company and its products, as interested reporters regularly developed stories on the company's latest social program and demonstrations of "caring capitalism." Moreover, the company's strong social component was a source of pride and motivation for those employees who were of liberal political and social

---

[14]Ibid., pp. 183–84.

Exhibit 4	Ben & Jerry's Statement of Mission

Ben & Jerry's is dedicated to the creation and demonstration of a new corporate concept of linked prosperity. Our mission consists of three interrelated parts:

Product Mission

To make, distribute and sell the finest-quality all-natural ice cream and related products in a wide variety of innovative flavors made from Vermont dairy products.

Social Mission

To operate the company in a way that actively recognizes the central role that business plays in the structure of society by initiating innovative ways to improve the quality of life of a broad community: local, national and international.

Economic Mission

To operate the company on a sound financial basis of profitable growth, increasing value for our shareholders and creating career opportunities and financial rewards for our employees.

Underlying the mission of Ben & Jerry's is the determination to seek new and creative ways of addressing all three parts, while holding a deep respect for individuals, inside and outside the company, and for the communities of which they are a part.

Source: Company annual report.

persuasion. Liberal elements within the general population were likewise attracted by Ben & Jerry's attempt to balance financial and market success against the need to contribute meaningfully to society's overall well-being; management believed many of the company's customers patronized the Ben & Jerry's brand because they knew about and approved of the company's record of social responsibility.

HUMAN RESOURCE PRACTICES

Ben & Jerry's compensation philosophy was based on the concept of linked prosperity—every employee was seen as a contributor to the company's success; thus, if the company prospered, so should employees.

The Salary Ratio Policy

Until 1992, the company's policy was that the salary of the company's highest-paid executive could not be more than five times what the lowest-paid employee could earn annually; the ratio was adjusted to 7:1 in 1992, after heated debate and much reluctance on Ben Cohen's part, because the company's salary cap was making it difficult to attract and retain capable executives. Ben & Jerry's policy of tying top management compensation to the pay scale for entry-level jobs had drawn more attention, internally and externally, than any other company practice. The policy was a source of great pride to the cofounders and many employees because it made a strong philosophical statement that corporate America tended to overcompensate top executives relative to the earnings and contribution of entry-level employees and that salary ranges from top to bottom should be reduced (the ratio in the largest corporations typically exceeded 50 to 1). Cohen, several board members, and numerous employees believed the policy symbolized values that were the soul of the company's culture.

Yet, the policy, even after the 7:1 adjustment, was a source of problems and continuing controversy. The 7:1 salary cap meant that the top salary was always tied to the pay scale for entry-level jobs. Raising either the top salary or the entry-level salary had repercussions throughout the company's salary structure, as well as having significant bottom-line impact. The company raised its minimum wage for entry-level jobs to $8 an hour in 1992. In 1994, the lowest salary plus benefits equaled about $23,000 a year. Still, the highest executive salary in 1994 was under $160,000, quite low for a $150 million company. Salary compression generated a morale problem among middle and upper-level managers; the small salary differences dampened individual incentives to excel and produce superior results. Furthermore, many employees did not agree that tying compensation levels to an arbitrary ratio was inherently more equitable or fair than paying market rates for jobs performed. Exhibit 5 shows compensation for the company's senior executives as of early 1994. The average salary of the top 10 percent of the company's best-paid employees in 1994 was $83,617, including benefits; the pay of the lowest-paid 10 percent averaged $25,472. Also in 1994, the average pay of the company's 299 male employees was $33,392; pay for the 215 female employees averaged $32,128.

Profit Sharing

Ben & Jerry's concept of linked prosperity also included a stock purchase plan and a profit-sharing plan. Five percent of the company's pretax profits were set aside for profit sharing. The size of each employee's profit-sharing bonus was a function of length of service. The formula was straightforward: The dollars in the profit-sharing pool (equal to 5 percent of pretax profits) were divided by the combined number of months everybody employed had worked for the company; this yielded the bonus amount per month employed. That number was multiplied by the number of months each individual had been employed at Ben & Jerry's to get the size of the individual's bonus. Profit-sharing payouts to the company's 500 employees totaled $1,148,839 in 1992, $671,675 in 1993, and $247,000 in 1994. Going into 1994, employees (excluding founders and top management) owned only 0.04 percent of the company's stock. In 1994, the company began to grant stock options to employees at all levels.

The Employee Benefits Package

All full-time employees received the same basic benefit package, regardless of salary or wage level—see Exhibit 6. When looking at changes in the employee benefits program, the company *first* considered the impact they would have on workers and *then* the impact on the budget.[15] All changes were examined by an advisory group of employees; advisory group members were allotted ample time to discuss proposals with fellow workers. Some special benefits, such as stock options or stock grants, were based on salary level; for example, it was normal for stock options to be granted in proportion to an employee's annual salary or wage.

The Work Environment

The work environment at Ben & Jerry's was characterized by casual dress, informality, attempts to make the atmosphere fun and pleasurable, and frequent communication between employees and top management. There was no dress code—T-shirts

---

[15]Laabs, "Ben & Jerry's Caring Capitalism," p. 54.

Exhibit 5   Compensation of Executive Officers and Directors of Ben & Jerry's Homemade, Inc., 1993

| Name and Principal Position | Year | Annual Compensation | | Other Annual Compensation‡ | Long-Term Compensation | |
		Salary	Bonus†		Restricted Stock Awards	All Other Compensation§
Ben Cohen, chairperson and CEO	1993	$133,212	—			$2,664
	1992	123,173	$600			2,469
	1991	100,000	300			2,006
Jerry Greenfield, vice chairperson	1993	132,517	—			2,650
	1992	123,173	600			2,469
	1991	95,567	300			1,911
Charles Lacy, president and COO	1993	150,262	1,970			3,045
	1992	131,346	2,714	$20,498		2,635
	1991	98,462	1,529		$96,250	1,998
Frances Rathke, CFO, treasurer, and secretary	1993	110,000	1,581			2,232
	1992	97,557	2,206	8,078		1,959
	1991	75,000	1,155		19,250	1,523
Elizabeth Bankowski,* director of social mission development	1993	105,000	694			2,114
	1992	87,691	1,041			—
	1991	3,077	—			—

Note: Directors who are not employees of the company receive $9,000 per year plus expenses.

* Bankowski's 1991 compensation is exclusive of $36,000 paid by the company for consulting services prior to her becoming a full-time employee.

† "Bonus" includes the $600 bonus paid to all employees in 1992 ($300 in 1991) and also includes discretionary distributions under the Company's profit-sharing plan pursuant to which a cash bonus was awarded to all employees (other than cofounders Ben Cohen and Jerry Greenfield) in 1993 based on a percentage of the profits of the company and the employee's length of service.

‡ "Other Annual Compensation" includes tax reimbursement on stock awards and gross up.

§ "All Other Compensation" includes company contributions to 401(K) plans.

Source: 1993 10-K Report.

and jeans were a wardrobe must. Ben Cohen was noted for not owning a suit. Managers believed that dressing casually made it easier to communicate with and relate to workers (70 percent of Ben & Jerry's employees worked in the company's three manufacturing plants). Top management believed it was important to recognize and celebrate achievements throughout the organization and for managers to coach employees and listen to their views and criticisms without getting defensive. Ben Cohen had some definite views about what the company's culture should be like.[16]

I want our people to love their work and have positive feelings about the company. Everyone should feel taken care of and listened to. This should be a company that gives generously, and where people feel joy, warmth, support, and accomplishment.

People were treated with fairness and respect. Employee opinions were sought out and given serious consideration, and employees were expected to take responsibility for doing their jobs well. No organization chart existed, yet people generally understood the division of responsibilities. Rank and hierarchy were viewed with distaste; people preferred to get things done cooperatively rather than by authoritarian means.

[16]Lager, *Ben & Jerry's: The Inside Scoop,* p. 166.

Exhibit 6   Summary of Ben & Jerry's Employee Benefits Package

- Short-term disability plan pays 60% of salary for six months.
- Long-term disability plan pays 60% of salary after 6 months for duration of disability.
- Women who have new babies receive six weeks' full pay after delivery and 60% of salary for the next six weeks.
- Fathers may take a 12-week paternity leave; the first two weeks are paid in full; the remaining 10 are unpaid.
- A parent who adopts a child may take four weeks off with full pay if he or she is the primary caregiver, or take two weeks off with pay if he or she is the secondary caregiver.
- Children's center.
- Health and dental insurance for hourly and salaried workers (health coverage includes mammograms and well-baby care); coverage begins on the first day of employment. Dependent coverage for children, spouses, or gay or lesbian partners was available for $2.10 per week, or $4.93 per family. Employees could contribute up to $5,000 per year pretax to an account that would pay for noncovered medical expenses.
- The company contributes $1,500 toward adoption costs.
- Financial counseling, including home ownership workshops.
- Cholesterol and blood pressure screening on-site.
- Smoking cessation classes.
- Life insurance (two times salary); additional coverage up to five times annual pay could be obtained at low rates.
- Tuition reimbursement (three classes a year).
- Profit-sharing plan.
- Free health club access.
- 401(k) plan (the company matched employee contributions up to 2% of salary).
- Employee stock purchase plan.
- A housing loan program where employees with three or more years of service could borrow up to $6,000 for down payments on new home purchases (the company established a loan pool of $250,000 to fund the program).
- Sabbatical leave program.
- Employee assistance program to help workers with drug, alcohol, marital, and other family problems (106 employees had used this program as of 1993).
- Free ice cream.

Sources: Jennifer J. Laabs, "Ben & Jerry's Caring Capitalism," *Personnel Journal*, November 1991, p. 57; 1994 company annual report, pp. 13–14.

Staff meetings were held every six weeks to two months; the two cofounders frequently attended, listening to employees, relating plans and the latest information, and telling jokes. The meetings were also a forum for discussing issues raised by employees (topics included plant safety, burnout from long work schedules, or whether to have Coca-Cola or Pepsi in the lunchroom vending machines). To foster more two-way communication at the staff meetings, the attendees would sometimes be divided into representative groups of five to eight people to discuss specific issues intensively and then present their conclusions to the whole group; typical topics for such discussions included cutting expenses, enhancing factory tours, and which fringe benefits ought to be added. The staff meetings were used not only to involve employees in the decision-making process but also to articulate the company's operating philosophy, expound on core values and beliefs, and build commitment to the culture.

Starting in 1990, a 10-page employee-opinion survey was conducted every two years; results indicated that roughly 60 percent believed the company's social mission was in tune with their own values (12 percent believed the social mission was too conservative and 27 percent saw it as too radical).[17] The 1992 survey revealed that 93 percent of the employees liked working at Ben & Jerry's; 84 percent thought the social mission was important to the company's success.[18] To ensure that no employee was offended by the language used in company communication, the vocabulary in all company memos, handbooks, and other literature was gender- and sexual-orientation neutral. For example, the company used the term partner instead of spouse. According to one employee:

> It wasn't until I actually got into the company that I really came to appreciate it, but this is a very, very open company, where you can work and be yourself. No one here is in the closet—and I mean that in the literal sense. I'm an openly gay person, and my partner works in the marketing department. This is a company that's very open and accepting; there aren't any lines drawn. I can't imagine any typical company making me feel this comfortable.[19]

Personnel Journal gave Ben & Jerry's its 1992 Optimas Award in the Quality of Life category for creating a supportive environment for employees.[20]

There were indications that the cultures at the company's three plants, distribution center, and central administrative office were becoming more distinct as opposed to growing more homogenous. Morale at the Waterbury plant was lowest, partly because of a series of managers with less than exemplary leadership and delegation skills. Workers at the Springfield plant were quite active in supporting the company's social mission in their community. At the newly opened St. Albans plant, morale was high; a strong team approach to problem solving made people feel involved and respected. The company's distribution center, with 19 employees and 8 truck drivers engaged in shipping 40 truckloads per work, was the first to implement team organization and a total quality management process. Following criticism from the social auditor in 1993 that safety needed more attention, company managers undertook initiatives to address safety issues. A companywide committee had been formed to oversee implementation of safety policies, and on-site committees were formed to recommend actions to improve and monitor safety procedures.

The 1994 employee survey revealed a somewhat surprising amount of employee dissatisfaction and concerns. Satisfaction with pay was down; only 49 percent of salaried employees felt pay levels were fair, compared to 69 percent for hourly employees. There were concerns about job classifications, the job review process, a lack of training opportunities, a lack of enough promotion opportunities, the influx of professional managers, and expanded use of part-time and temporary employees. Performance appraisals, working conditions, job safety, responsiveness to complaints or suggestions, and training and development received overall negative ratings from employees. Many people working in administration expressed concern that decisions were ill-founded or badly communicated, that top management was remote and overworked, and that the company was drifting. People felt that executives had not formed a strong strategic vision, not created a workable growth strategy, and not made timely decisions.

---

[17]Ibid., p. 214.
[18]Ibid., p. 228.
[19]Laab, "Ben & Jerry's Caring Capitalism," p. 52.
[20]Ibid., p. 50.

The Joy Gang   In 1988, Jerry Greenfield created the Joy Gang, a roving band of six employees from different departments whose sole mission was to promote fun and enjoyment in the workplace. Greenfield, the company's self-proclaimed minister of joy, often remarked, "If it's not fun, why do it."[21] The Joy Gang sponsored company celebrations of lesser holidays, like national clash-dressing day that provided workers a chance to dress in outrageous outfits and compete for prizes, and put on monthly events for either the entire company or a department. On one occasion, the Joy Gang cooked an Italian meal for third shift (11:30 PM to 8:00 AM) production workers and brought in a DJ to play songs on request.[22] On another occasion, the Joy Gang purchased a stereo and, using speakers mounted on the ceiling, arranged for music from local radio stations to be heard daily throughout a plant's production area. When company parties were held, arrangements were made for child care on-site so that parents who wished could attend.

BEN & JERRY'S MANAGEMENT TEAM

Jerry Greenfield served as company president from 1977 until January 1983, when he elected to withdraw from company operations and temporarily moved to Arizona.[23] Ben Cohen succeeded Greenfield as president and CEO. Cohen emerged as the company's spiritual leader, espousing the values he believed the company should champion, leading efforts to support the social mission, and directing marketing and promotion. But the administrative tedium of overseeing daily operations never appealed to him.

Fred "Chico" Lager was brought in as treasurer, general manager, and member of the board of directors in November 1982; previously, he had been owner/operator of a Burlington restaurant and nightclub. Lager, age 28 at the time, had an MBA, a talent for professional management, and philosophically believed in the merits of the company's social mission; as general manager, he assumed primary responsibility for day-to-day operations and functioned as unofficial leader of the company's economic mission. Over the next several years, Ben Cohen's presence diminished from a daily operations standpoint; a marketing director was hired in 1986 to assume duties Cohen had always taken responsibility for. In February 1989, Chico Lager was named president and CEO; Cohen retained the title of chairperson of the board and, as the company's spiritual leader and biggest stockholder, continued to wield a heavy hand in major decisions and policies.

Without Cohen's on-the-scene daily involvement, the company's focus under Lager drifted more to developing and strengthening the company's market position. Concerned about reduced attention to the social mission, Cohen applied increasing pressure on Lager and the company's other board members, eventually winning the board's approval of the mission statement (Exhibit 4). Lager never was given the leeway as CEO to run the company as he saw fit. Ben quickly intervened whenever he believed company managers were not running the business in accordance with his values and vision for the company.

---

[21]Ibid., p. 51.
[22]Ibid., p. 52.
[23]Greenfield moved back to Vermont in 1985 and through 1986 was a consultant to the company on promotional activities, special projects, and various policy decisions. In January 1987 he rejoined the company full-time as director of promotions.

In January 1991, Chico Lager relinquished the title of president and CEO. Charles "Chuck" Lacy was named president and chief operating officer; Lacy had joined the company in 1988 as director of special projects, moving up to general manager when Chico Lager became president. Lacy had a background as a social activist, once being arrested for civil disobedience at a rally protesting construction of the Seabrook nuclear plant in New Hampshire. Ben Cohen reassumed the title of CEO in January 1991, involving himself in projects and issues that interested him. Jerry Greenfield took on the title of vice chairperson, soon becoming as much of a presence and a force in the business as Cohen and Lacy. In early 1992, Ben was so pleased with how well things were going, he decided to take a six-month sabbatical leave; a *Forbes* article attributed his leave to "a bad case of the guilties" over his and the company's financial success.

Ironically, Ben Cohen's management style frequently clashed with his beliefs about the merits of participatory decision making and how subordinates should be treated. He exercised personal authority over virtually all major decisions, was a taskmaster and perfectionist who held everyone to very high standards, rarely praised the work and efforts of others, and was quick to stress what was wrong or had fallen through the cracks. While Ben believed in soliciting employees' input, it was more a matter of getting their ideas on how to achieve certain objectives rather than on what the company's objectives, strategies, and policies should be. According to Chico Lager:[24]

> Ben was usually so single-mindedly convinced that he was right about something that he often didn't even acknowledge the legitimacy of alternative points of view . . . criticism from Ben, particularly given his role in the company, was powerful and demoralizing.
>
> Once Ben made a decision, it was usually only a matter of time until he changed his mind . . . Operating in a last-minute crisis mode was the norm if it was something in which Ben was involved, and as a result, the organization was in a constant state of turmoil . . . In his mind, he was just improving on whatever decision he'd made, all for the greater good of the business, and in fact, more often than not, he was.
>
> "Ben is Ben," was the saying most managers used to explain the phenomena, which essentially meant that you should just expect him to change his mind or come up with some seemingly whacked-out idea, and not be surprised when he did. Of course, a lot of Ben's seemingly whacked-out ideas weren't so wacky, once they were implemented.
>
> A large part of my job was insulating the rest of the organization from Ben, a role I'd inherited from Jerry. People who couldn't challenge Ben face to face would come into my office, leaving it to me to take their case to Ben. It was also my job to soften what Ben said to people, taking out the bite and getting them focused on the message.
>
> As a result of being second-guessed all the time, people were reluctant to proceed with anything until they had Ben's input . . .
>
> Ben was always trying to convince people that when things didn't get fixed, it only meant they had to shout louder or in a different direction, but that under no circumstances should they give up and accept things that weren't right.
>
> When Ben told the staff to shout louder, he was mostly referring to people who didn't report to him. As in other companies led by strong-willed visionary entrepreneurs, there were no areas that had been managed more from the top down than those Ben had direct responsibility for.

---

[24]Lager, *Ben & Jerry's: The Inside Scoop*, pp. 150–151, 163.

Exhibit 7   Profile of Key Executives of Ben & Jerry's Homemade, Inc., 1994

Ben Cohen, age 42, a founder of the company, was president and chief executive officer from January 1983 until February 1989, when he became chairperson. He resumed the position of chief executive officer of the company as of January 1, 1991, and spends the principal portion of his time on new product development and marketing strategy, in addition to those matters considered by the board of directors at its monthly meetings.

Cohen first became involved with ice cream in 1968 as an independent mobile ice cream retailer with Pied Piper Distributors, Inc., Hempstead, New York, during three summers. He was promoted within the Pied Piper organization, and his responsibilities were broadened to include warehousing, inventory control, and driver training. He spent three years, from 1974 to 1977, as a crafts teacher at Highland Community, Paradox, New York, a residential school for disturbed adolescents, before moving to Vermont to form the company with Jerry Greenfield. Cohen has been a director of the company since 1977. Cohen is a director of Community Products, Inc., manufacturer of Rain Forest Crunch candy, a director of Oxfam America, and a trustee of Hampshire College.

Jerry Greenfield, age 42, became a director and vice chairperson on the board in 1990 and spends the principal portion of his time on sales, promotion, and distribution. Greenfield is a founder of the company and was president from 1977 until January 1983. After graduating from Oberlin College in 1973 with a BA in biology, Greenfield engaged in biochemical research at the Public Health Research Institute in New York City and then at the University of North Carolina, Chapel Hill. Greenfield moved to Vermont to establish the company with Cohen in 1977. Effective in January 1983, Greenfield elected to withdraw from the daily operations of the company and moved to Arizona. Greenfield moved back to Vermont in 1985 and through 1986 was a consultant to the company, participating in promotional activities, special projects, and certain major policy decisions. Effective January 1, 1987, Greenfield became a full-time employee of the company.

Charles Lacy, age 37, has been president and chief operating officer of the company since January 1, 1991. He became a director in 1991. He first joined the company in 1988 as director of Special Projects and became general manager in February 1989. Lacy is responsible for the day-to-day operations and for long-term strategic planning of the company. From 1984 until joining Ben & Jerry's, Lacy was a finance and business development executive with United Health Services, a chain of nonprofit hospitals and clinics in upstate New York. He has a BA from Amherst College and an MBA from Cornell University.

Elizabeth Bankowski, age 46, became a director of the company in 1990, having served as a consultant to the company since earlier that year. She joined the company as an employee and director of Social Mission Development in December 1991. Bankowski was chief of staff to the governor of Vermont from 1985 through 1989. She held the office of secretary of Civil and Military Affairs.

Fred "Chico" Lager, age 39, has been a director and consultant to or officer of the company since 1982. He joined the company as treasurer and general manager in November 1982. From February 1989 until his resignation in early 1991, he was president and chief executive officer of the company. Lager is a director of Seventh Generation, Inc., a mail-order marketer, and Working Assets. Lager serves as chairperson of the Compensation Committee of the board of directors and as a member of the Audit Committee of the board of directors.

Frances Rathke was named chief financial officer and chief accounting officer of the company in April 1990, and secretary and treasurer effective January 1, 1991. Rathke joined the company in April 1989 as its controller. From September 1982 to March 1989, she was a manager at Coopers & Lybrand, independent public accountants, in Boston, Massachusetts. Rathke is a certified public accountant.

Holly Alves, age 38, joined the company as director of marketing in April 1990. From 1986 to 1990, she was the marketing director of ESPRIT, Inc., a worldwide manufacturer and retailer of clothing. Prior to that, Alves worked for Hannaford Brothers, Inc., a food distributor and supermarket company, as the director of advertising.

Exhibit 7   Profile of Key Executives of Ben & Jerry's Homemade, Inc., 1994 (*continued*)

Bruce Dillingham, age 50, joined the company as director of manufacturing in January 1993. He had been with Digital Equipment Corporation since 1966. Dillingham has held many manufacturing management positions, including production manager, manufacturing business manager for Industrial Products, plant manager in Kanata, Canada, and startup plant manager in Enfield, Connecticut. Dillingham introduced the High Performance Work System concept to Digital. Digital's Enfield plant has been recognized for its pioneering efforts in the integration of people and technology.

Keith Hunt, age 43, joined the company as director of Human Resources in February 1993. From 1982 to 1993 Hunt was with Scott Paper Company. His most recent position was manager, Human Resources. He also held positions as manager, Manufacturing, and as manager of Organizational Effectiveness, providing leadership in a large system change. From 1975 to 1982, Hunt worked for Procter & Gamble as senior consultant/Organizational Development for Research and Development, Manufacturing, and engineering organizations.

John Stigmon, age 45, joined the company in July 1991 as director of Retail Operations. From 1989 until 1991 he was employed by Circle K, a convenience store chain, as national product manager of Food Service. From 1987 until 1989 Stigmon was self-employed, assisting entrepreneurial companies in the development of franchise programs. From 1976 until 1987 Stigmon was employed by Swensen's Ice Cream Co. in various management positions, including group vice president of Franchise Operations from 1984 to 1987.

Rei Tanaka, age 50, joined the company in late March 1994 as director of sales. From 1991 to March 1994, Tanaka was a marketing and sales consultant to Meteor Publishing Corporation, a division of Hosiery Corporation of America. From 1990 until 1991 Tanaka was senior vice president, Marketing and Sales/Circulation, for Marvel Entertainment Group, Inc. From 1978 until 1989 Tanaka was employed by Harlequin Enterprises Ltd., a division of Torstar Corporation, in various management positions in North America and international sales and distribution divisions, including executive vice president, North American Retail Division.

Source: 1993 10-K Report.

The Search for a New CEO.   In June 1994, Ben Cohen announced he was stepping down as Ben & Jerry's chief executive officer and that the company was launching a six-month search for a replacement (see Exhibit 7 for a description of the company's top-management team at the time of Cohen's announcement). Chuck Lacy was to retain his title of president and CEO. Ben Cohen, 43 years old, while resigning as CEO, planned to remain chairperson of the board and concentrate on "the fun stuff—product development and promotion." Cohen indicated that the company was looking for candidates with "gentleness of spirit" who had the experience in international marketing to launch the Ben & Jerry's brand in overseas markets or experience in franchising to expand its chain of 100 scoop shops. Cohen said:

This is a great opportunity for someone who cares about people, has the skills and vision to see around the corners of our future business development, and has always wanted to wear jeans to work.

There's a tremendous amount of potential in ice cream novelty and single-portion servings. There's growth by expanding franchised scoop shops and other food-service venues. The potential internationally is quite large.[25]

---

[25]As quoted in *The Wall Street Journal,* June 14, 1994, p. B1, and January 10, 1995, p. B1.

As part of its wide-ranging search for a new CEO, the company conducted an essay contest in which aspirants were asked to state in 100 words or less "why I would be a great CEO for Ben & Jerry's." All interested persons were invited to enter the essay contest. If the essay contest failed to turn up attractive candidates, the board of directors planned to retain an executive search firm. To attract top corporate talent, the company said it was abandoning its policy of limiting the salary of the highest paid officer to seven times that of the lowest paid full-time worker, instead placing no cap on executive pay.

The Faith Mountain Company

James J. Dowd, Michael D. Atchison, and John H. Lindgren, Jr.,
University of Virginia

Having passed the $5 million mark in annual sales, the Faith Mountain Company recorded its first profit in July 1991. Based on the prior experiences of other industry participants, it was right on schedule, but it still came as something of a surprise to Cheri and Martin Woodard. It had been a remarkable year on several counts: the all-important catalog customer list had grown 31 percent, to 251,771 names; despite the recession, sales were up 41 percent; and, best of all, from a loss of $185,791 in fiscal year 1990, the company had posted a net profit of $161,476 for fiscal year 1991.

By December 1991, it was clear that Faith Mountain was on its way to another record-breaking year. When they stopped to reflect on the growth of their business, however, Cheri and Martin admitted they faced some tough questions. What next? Could they count on continued growth at this rate, and if so, could they manage it and remain profitable? Where should they grow, and how? What financial and human resources would be required, and would this small company in the Blue Ridge Mountains be able to attract and retain them?

In their first business plan, completed only last year in conjunction with a major effort to raise capital, they had set ambitious goals: by the year 1995, $10 million in sales from the Faith Mountain catalog, $5 million from the retail division, and an additional $10 million from acquisitions or development of another catalog company. Even as they struggled to keep pace with customer demand in their busiest time of the year, they knew they soon would have to find the time to review that plan, examine their goals, and renew their efforts to make them reality.

HISTORY OF THE FAITH MOUNTAIN COMPANY

Cheri Faith Woodard

Cheri Faith Woodard grew up, in her own words, "a product of the 70s—I wasn't a radical, but I had a vision of a better society, and a belief that things could be different." She left college before graduating, married, had a son, and helped found a cooperative natural foods store near College Park, Maryland. After a divorce in 1974, she moved to Sperryville, Virginia, a small town of about 500 people at the foot of the Blue Ridge Mountains. Only 69 miles from Washington, D.C., the natural beauty and very low cost of living in Rappahannock County attracted many young people to the area.

This case was prepared for the 11th McIntire Commerce Invitational (MCI XI) held at the University of Virginia on February 13–15, 1992. The authors gratefully acknowledge the General Electric Foundation and the McIntire School of Commerce for their support.

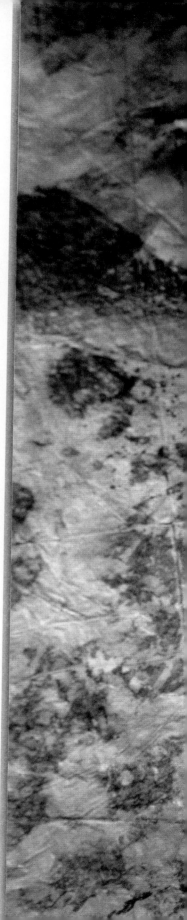

To support herself and her young son, Cheri worked in an antique shop. At the time, the best connecting route between two major state highways went through Sperryville, right around the corner from the antique shop. During vacation seasons, with heavy tourist traffic to and from the Shenandoah National Park, the shop did extremely good business. Cheri learned much about antiques and furniture restoration, and she enjoyed bargaining with customers.

Soon after arriving in Sperryville, Cheri met Florence Williamson, known throughout the area as "the herb lady." She knew how to grow all kinds of herbs and how to use them in recipes, medicines, and gardens. Many people, from local families to the directors of the National Herb Garden in Washington, D.C., sought her advice.

Cheri became interested in herbs while working at the natural foods store in Maryland, and she was eager to learn more. Mrs. Williamson was always busy, but as she approached 75, she decided she needed a helper, so she was willing to teach Cheri. The two began working together as teacher and apprentice.

In 1975, Cheri met Martin Woodard at a square dance. Martin had graduated from Vanderbilt University with a degree in sociology and history. He too was drawn to the quality of life in Rappahannock County and had established a successful masonry contracting business. In 1977, they were married.

Opening the Store

Meanwhile, Cheri began contemplating opening her own business. She had learned a great deal about herbs, and she sensed that more and more people were becoming interested in growing and using them. She always wanted to work at home to be near her son. She decided she would open a store to sell herbs, related products, and antiques. She discussed her ideas with Martin and Mrs. Williams, and both gave their full support. Cheri remembered:

> Martin and I had faith in each other and in ourselves—we said, "We can do this!" And we were here in the Blue Ridge Mountains—so that's how we got our name. A business started on faith at the foot of the mountains: The Faith Mountain Herbs and Antique Shop.

The Woodards found a house for sale on Main Street in Sperryville, just a block down the street from the antique shop in which Cheri had worked. The front part of the house was built in 1790 and had been used as a doctor's office, a tavern, and a guest house. There was room in the backyard for an herb garden, and there were small outbuildings for storage or workshops. Even better, the house was big enough to serve as both home and store. With owner financing, the Woodards bought the house for $26,000, assumed a $200 monthly mortgage, and set about restoring the old house.

The family lived in the back of the house and used the four front rooms for the store. Cheri grew her own herbs in the backyard and bought others locally to sell in the store. The business grew slowly; herbs were inexpensive, and small amounts lasted a long time. Local businesspeople, suspicious of herbs and of the young couple, predicted the store would fail. With the full support of "the herb lady," however, Cheri began to establish a strong reputation as an "herb lady" in her own right, giving local talks and workshops on cooking with herbs, making wreaths of dried flowers, and the like.

Between 1977 and 1980, she slowly increased the variety of products offered, adding herb blends, dried flowers, simple garden supplies, books, kitchen tools, preserves, and handicrafts. She displayed the products on antique furniture she bought, restored, and offered for sale. Encouraged by praise from customers who had driven from Washington, D.C., for a day in the country, Cheri purchased her first ads in the *Washington Post* in 1979.

Birth of the Mail-Order Business

In 1980, construction was completed in Interstate 66, a highway connection eliminating most of the east–west traffic passing through Sperryville. Like the other businesses in Sperryville, Faith Mountain suffered, and its antique sales all but disappeared. Even though Cheri kept the store open all weekend to capture any possible business, she could not make the store profitable.

Faith Mountain was no longer merely an interesting way for Cheri to be able to work at home. She felt she deserved more reward for all her hard work, and she began to consider a mail-order catalog.

Tourists from around the country had stopped to shop at Faith Mountain on their way to Shenandoah National Park, so she knew her products appealed to a wide market. Further, more and more customers were writing to her, asking if she could send them a wreath or another product they remembered seeing in the store.

Confident that she had a market, she created the first Faith Mountain Herbs and Antiques catalog in the spring of 1980. The 12-page catalog offered mostly herbs and herbal products and featured simple line drawings and text. She was able to get the catalog printed and copied for free as a test of new machines by a friend who worked for Xerox Corporation. Her greatest difficulty was with the local post office, which had never worked with bulk mailings before. With advice from a cousin in the mail-order business, she obtained bulk rate permit No. 1 from the Sperryville post office and mailed her first 1,000 catalogs.

As the mail-order business began to grow, the Woodard family realized they had to move out of the house. They bought a local farm, grew more than 20 kinds of herbs and flowers, and dried them in their barn. Cheri hired part-time employees to help with the store and the catalog. In 1983, the first color photo catalog was mailed, with a press run of 110,000 copies.

Incorporation and Growth

Until that time, Martin Woodard had concentrated on his masonry business, helping out occasionally with the store and the catalog. Increasingly frustrated by problems with his employees and aware of the growing burden on Cheri, he began thinking about working with Faith Mountain full-time.

By 1984, Faith Mountain's annual sales had reached $400,000. At a Direct Marketing Association meeting in Washington, D.C., the Woodards were referred to Don Press, director of the Smithsonian Museum Gift Catalog and part-time mail-order consultant. They asked him two questions: "Does our business have a future? If so, what is our next step?" Martin recalled what happened next:

> Don looked at everything, and then he told us: "Yes, you have something here. It's not going to be easy, but you do have a future with this business." So there was the validation, and I had to make a decision. I sold the masonry business and came on full time at Faith Mountain in the fall of 1984.

Martin became catalog director, with responsibility for merchandise selection, catalog production and marketing, and also for financial planning. Cheri retained responsibility for the store, for manufacturing and warehouse operations, customer service, and all personnel matters. Martin was very clear from the start he wanted no responsibility for people.

Working closely with their consultant, Cheri recalled, "We really started to get serious about the business and slowly put together a real company." They incorporated in 1985 and offered Don Press a seat on the board of directors. He referred them to more professional services for catalog production and helped them manage their finances by teaching them benchmark ratios for catalog operations' budgets and income statements. They bought some small buildings in 1985 to accommodate the growing business and rented additional space as needed.

In the same year, Cheri was elected to a three-year term as president of the Sperryville Business Council. She organized a Sperryville Spring Festival to correspond with the anniversary of the Faith Mountain Herbs and Antiques Store, and it became an annual event, drawing thousands to the town. That year, Faith Mountain printed 500,000 catalogs and annual sales exceeded $1.5 million.

By 1988, Faith Mountain was running out of room, and there was no more space to rent. Later that year, the Woodards' barn burned. It was clear that the company needed more space, and it would improve operations if all parts of the business, now scattered in several buildings throughout Sperryville, could be brought together under one big roof.

At the suggestion of their banker, the Woodards applied for funding from the U.S. Small Business Administration under a special loan program assisting small business expansions. With a "504 loan," the SBA would finance 40 percent of the expansion project, secured by a second deed of trust. A conventional lending institution would finance 50 percent of the project, with a first deed of trust, and the company would pay the remaining 10 percent.

The Woodards located a 1.75-acre site on Route 211 that would support construction of a 10,000-square-foot facility for offices, a warehouse, and possibly a retail outlet. The SBA loan package would include the land and the building, the warehouse equipment and shelves, the phone system, hardware and software improvements, and office furniture and partitions, for a total cost of $425,000. Cheri remembered:

> It was a *big leap* to spend that much money. We hadn't had much of a business plan, and now we had to show one to get the money. We had to get the site rezoned for commercial use, and then we just went ahead. In April 1989, we signed contracts to buy the land and contracts to begin construction on the building—this was before we had even gotten approval on the SBA loan! I remember Martin said, "We have to have faith." Almost a full month later, on May 10, we got the call from the SBA: We had the loan. Thank God—we had already spent it!

THE FAITH MOUNTAIN COMPANY IN 1991

Location

In 1991, the Faith Mountain Company operated out of that 10,000-square-foot site. The building had about 4,000 square feet of office space and 6,000 square feet of warehouse space. The company was then paying about $5,000 per month in principal and interest for the facility. The roof was constructed to permit addition of an mezzanine level, which would double the storage space in the warehouse area, and the entire building was designed to facilitate an addition of 10,000 to 15,000 square feet. The retail store still operated in its original location, about two miles away.

Organization and Staffing

As the company ended its 1991 fiscal year, it employed 39 people, 25 of those full time. The organization chart (Exhibit 1) shows that Cheri and Martin still shared responsibilities as they had in 1984.

As chief financial officer, Martin supervised Debbie Jenkins, the accounting supervisor. With one full-time clerk, Jenkins took care of day-to-day financial bookkeeping, including payables, receivables, and all internal financial reports. Payroll was handled by an outside firm. Martin was responsible for long-term financial planning. The current fiscal year (1992) was the first year in which monthly and year-to-date budget reports were created and used.

As catalog director, Martin was responsible for all aspects of the Faith Mountain Company catalogs. The past year was the first in which Faith Mountain had produced four different catalogs, one for each season; previously, the summer catalog had been essentially the spring catalog with sale prices. The 1991 spring catalog, featuring Easter gift items, was 40 pages and mailed at the end of December 1990. The summer catalog, at 32 pages, was mailed in mid-April. The 40-page fall catalog, featuring Halloween, Thanksgiving, and some Christmas items, was mailed at the end of June. And the Christmas catalog, at 48 pages their biggest ever, was mailed in mid-September.

Kim Baader, merchandising manager, was charged with selecting and promoting items for the catalogs. She and Martin went to gift, apparel, and other trade shows throughout the year, seeking vendors with quality products and a reputation for reliability in shipping. They brought potential catalog items back to the office, where Martin and Cheri, Baader and her assistant, and Margie Ellis, the store manager, would examine each piece and argue for or against offering it to Faith Mountain customers.

Having selected the catalog merchandise, under Martin's direction, Baader worked closely with a contract copywriter while Martin worked with the professional service firms contracted to design and produce the catalog, including layout, photography, and printing. Interviewing, inspecting, selecting, negotiating, and managing these vendors demanded so much time that, in the summer of 1991, the former accounting clerk was promoted to catalog production manager to assume primary responsibility for these areas. Finally, before catalogs were mailed, Baader briefed the customer service and telemarketing staff on each catalog item, and she prepared summary product descriptions for easy reference on the automated entry system. By the time a catalog was mailed, work was already under way on the next.

As president, Cheri was responsible for overall direction of the company, and she was involved in all major decisions in all areas. Responsible for all aspects of human resource management in the firm, Cheri decided all personnel policies and practices and described them all in the Faith Mountain employee handbook. She had hired every employee in the company until September 1991, when the store manager hired a part-time sales associate, with Cheri's knowledge, but without her prior approval. Cheri stated, "That was a funny feeling, and I'm not sure I like it."

As director of operations, Cheri supervised the following people and areas:

Exhibit 1 Organization Chart for the Faith Mountain Company, 1992

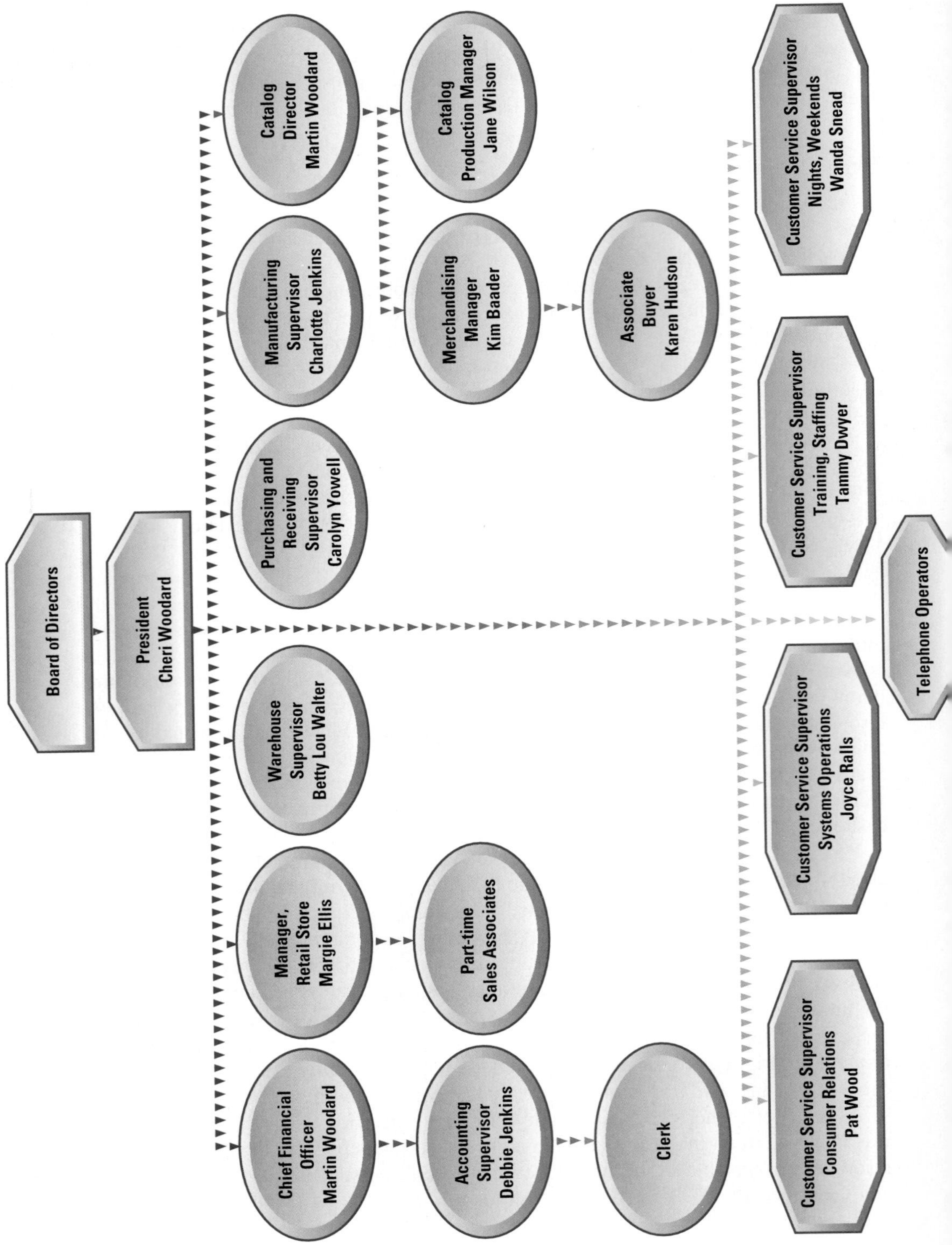

Board of Directors

President
Cheri Woodard

Chief Financial Officer
Martin Woodard

Manager, Retail Store
Margie Ellis

Warehouse Supervisor
Betty Lou Walter

Purchasing and Receiving Supervisor
Carolyn Yowell

Manufacturing Supervisor
Charlotte Jenkins

Catalog Director
Martin Woodard

Accounting Supervisor
Debbie Jenkins

Part-time Sales Associates

Merchandising Manager
Kim Baader

Catalog Production Manager
Jane Wilson

Clerk

Associate Buyer
Karen Hudson

Customer Service Supervisor Consumer Relations
Pat Wood

Customer Service Supervisor Systems Operations
Joyce Ralls

Customer Service Supervisor Training, Staffing
Tammy Dwyer

Customer Service Supervisor Nights, Weekends
Wanda Snead

Telephone Operators

Margie Ellis, manager of the retail store: Responsible for store sales, merchandising, staffing, and customer service.

Betty Lou Walker, warehouse supervisor: Responsible for product flow and shipping accuracy and timeliness.

Carolyn Yowell, purchasing and receiving supervisor: Responsible for receiving merchandise, forecasting, and managing back orders and overstocks.

Charlotte Jenkins, manufacturing supervisor: Responsible for design and production of Faith Mountain products (wreaths, herb mixtures, etc.), including purchasing, scheduling, and inventory control.

In addition, Cheri supervised the customer service and telephone operations areas. Four customer service supervisors rotated primary responsibility for customer service calls each day, and each had her own special area of responsibility:

Pat Wood: Responsible for Wednesday and Friday, handled all customer correspondence (not including mail orders).

Joyce Ralls: Responsible for Tuesday, handled system hardware and software, including local maintenance and system planning.

Tammy Dwyer: Responsible for Monday and Thursday, was responsible for training and staffing of telephone operators.

Wanda Snead: Responsible for customer service in the evening (5–8:30) and on weekends, generated day-end activity reports.

Finally, Cheri also directly supervised the telephone operators. Eight regular part-time employees (more part-timers were hired for peak season) were responsible for taking customer orders by phone, referring any customer complaints or problems to the customer service supervisor. The phone operators also opened and sorted mail orders each day, forwarding checks to the accounting department and verifying order forms for entry into the system.

Financial Position

Exhibits 2 and 3 provide information on the company's financial position in 1991. Other than the Small Business Administration loan described earlier, financing was primarily short term. R.R. Donnelly, the catalog printer, extended the firm $350,000 in credit with lenient terms. Inventory moved through the warehouse quickly, and trade payables to vendors were small. About 10 percent of catalog orders were handled as "drop shipments," where vendors shipped directly to the customer. Inventory financing was handled through a line of credit, recently increased from $350,000 to $500,000.

The Faith Mountain Mail-Order Strategy

In 1991, the Faith Mountain Company developed, manufactured, and marketed high-quality gifts, apparel, and home accessories, distributing them through its mail-order catalog and its retail store.

The company focused on the needs of women between ages 30 and 50 who owned their own homes and had family incomes of $40,000 to $60,000. Faith Mountain believed female homemakers sought traditional, nostalgic, whimsical, and romantic gifts, apparel, and home accessories to enhance the quality of their homes and family

Exhibit 2   Balance Sheet of the Faith Mountain Company, 1987–1991 *(fiscal years ending June 30; dollar amounts in thousands)*

	1987	1988	1989	1990	1991
Assets					
Cash	$ 3	$ 3	$ 15	$ 1	$ 48
Net accounts receivable	8	14	26	25	55
Inventories	114	176	183	320	410
Unamortized catalog costs	32	53	150	198	400
Total current assets	$157	$246	$374	$ 544	$ 913
Net property	35	69	203	511	489
Intangibles				10	9
Other noncurrent assets			3	2	4
Total assets	$192	$315	$580	$1,067	$1,415
Liabilities and Net Worth					
Bank loans—short-term (see Note 1)	$ 42	$ 46	$114	$ 212	$ 333
Current maturities of long-term debt				30	29
Other notes payable			135		
Accounts payable	60	84	113	321	304
Accruals	3	4	3	11	11
Advance from stockholder				15	
Total current liabilities	$105	$134	$365	$ 589	$ 677
Long-term bank debt (see Note 2)		42	28	417	399
Total liabilities	$105	$176	$393	$1,006	$1,076
Preferred stock	42				
Common stock (see Note 3)	92	264	310	370	518
Capital surplus					
Retained earnings	(47)	(125)	(123)	(309)	(179)
Total liabilities and net worth	$192	$315	$580	$1,067	$1,415

Note 1: Notes Payable, Bank

Notes payable, bank at June 30, 1991, consists of $333,000 drawn from an available line of credit of $350,000 with C&S/Sovran Bank.

The note is secured by a first security interest in all accounts receivables, inventory, and property and equipment and bears interest at C&S/Sovran Bank's prime rate plus 1½% (10.0% at June 30, 1991). The note is payable on demand, with interest payable monthly. The line expires on October 30, 1991.

Under the requirements of the note agreement the company has agreed, among other things, to: (1) maintain its ratio of debt to net worth at no more than 5 to 1, measured at fiscal years end; (2) maintain all of its primary deposit relationships with C&S/Sovran as long as this commitment is outstanding; and (3) not incur any indebtedness so long as this commitment remains outstanding without the prior written consent of the bank. The note is guaranteed by Martin Woodard and Cheri Woodard, shareholders of the company.

lives. Although increasing numbers of these women balanced their family responsibilities with work outside the home, they held traditional family values, and time spent at home with their families dominated their nonworking hours. Even as they sought products and gift items that reflected those values, they were reluctant to spend time driving through congested urban or suburban areas to shop in "glitzy" commercialized malls. Instead, these women were increasingly likely to turn to mail-order catalogs, which offered the option of shopping at their own convenience, in their own homes, 24 hours a day.

Exhibit 2 (concluded)

Note 2: Long-Term Debt

A summary of the company's long-term debt, and collateral pledged thereon, consist of the following:

	June 30	
	1991	**1990**
C&S/Sovran Bank, note due in monthly installments of $456, including interest at 12.5% through January 1995, collateralized by truck	$ 15,903	$ 18,906
Signet Bank, capitalized lease obligation, discounted at a rate of 11.5% due in monthly installments of $1,034 to October 1993	24,356	24,163
Marathon Bank, note due in monthly installments of $944, plus interest at Marathon Bank's prime rate plus 1% through November 1999, collateralized by real estate	208,510	220,242
Virginia Asset Financing Corporation, note due in monthly installments of $1,741, including interest at 8.9% through January 2010, collateralized by the personal guarantees of Martin Woodard and Cheri Woodard, shareholders of the company, and a second deed of trust on real estate	179,439	183,110
Other	107	667
	$428,315	$447,088
Less current maturities	29,483	29,610
Long-term portion	$398,832	$417,478

Aggregate maturities required on long-term debt at June 30, 1991, are due in future fiscal years ending June 30 as follows:

1992	$ 29,483
1993	30,224
1994	24,933
1995	19,435
1996	16,580
Thereafter	307,660
	$428,315

Interest expense for the years ended June 30, 1991 and 1990, was $65,824 and $35,297, respectively.

Note 3: Stockholders' Equity

For year ended June 30, 1991, the company issued 1,150 units, which comprised 1,150 shares of common stock and 1,150 warrants to purchase common stock. The gross proceeds of the issue was $115,000. Each warrant entitles the holder to purchase one share of common stock at a price of $90 per share, subject to certain conditions through June 30, 1992.

Competition   The Woodards estimated approximately 50 catalog companies sold gifts, apparel, or home accessories. Within its own niche of "traditional" products in those categories, Faith Mountain had targeted four significant competitors. Based on knowledge they had gained from industry analysts and other sources, the Woodards described them in their 1990 business plan as follows:

Potpourri: Founded in the late 1960s and run by Bill and Sue Knowles and their two sons, the company is an institution in the industry. Industry sources estimate Potpourri prints 40 million catalogs per year, with annual sales in the $50 million range, and an average order size of $60. Bill and Sue are widely respected for their business sense and marketing/merchandising abilities, but as they approach their 70s, it is unclear whether the sons will be able to carry on their successful merchandising. We believe the quality of Potpourri's merchandise and customer service is inferior to Faith Mountain's.

Charles Keath: With sales estimated in the $35 million range, this company is also widely respected for its excellent merchandising. It is owned by Charles

Exhibit 3   Income Statement for the Faith Mountain Company, 1987–1991 *(fiscal years ending June 30; dollar amounts in thousands)*

	1987	1988	1989	1990	1991
Net sales	$1,234	$1,654	$2,429	$3,554	$5,025
Less: Cost of sales	496	780	1,249	1,936	2,900
Gross profit	$ 738	$ 874	$1,249	$1,936	$2,125
Percentage of net sales	59.81%	52.84%	51.42%	54.47%	57.71%
Less: Operating expenses	366	247	545	835	1,030
Catalog production and promotional expense	382	705	753	1,346	1,784
Depreciation		23	25	33	44
Operating profit	(10)	(101)	(74)	(278)	42
Other income	14	40	88	127	185
Less: Interest expense		11	12	35	66
Net profit before tax	4	(72)	2	(186)	161
Profit after tax	4	(72)	2	(186)	161
Net profit (loss)	$ 4	$ (72)	$ 2	$ (186)	$ 161
Net after dividends	4	(72)	2	(186)	161
Add: Beginning retained earnings	(51)	(47)	(125)	(123)	(340)
Less: Other		6			
Ending retained earnings	$ (47)	$ (125)	$ (123)	$ (309)	$ (179)

Edmundson, who has built the company from the ashes of a failed catalog company. We believe Faith Mountain's catalog features higher-quality photographs and copywriting and we rate Faith Mountain's customer service more highly than that offered by Charles Keath.

W.M. Green: Only seven years old, the company is run by two sisters, Marianne Caron and Beth Everitt, and their brother, Mark Green, out of North Carolina. Annual sales are estimated at $4.5 million, with an average order size of about $110. Like Faith Mountain, this company features handmade traditional gifts, with some home accessories, but W.M. Green does not sell apparel. We respect the quality and customer service of W.M. Green but believe Faith Mountain's experience with a broader product line is a distinct advantage.

Sturbridge Yankee: Offering home accessories with a distinct American "country" flavor, this company has about $8 million in annual sales. It has opened three retail stores in New England, leading many to believe the company will emphasize retail stores over catalog operations. In any event, we believe the narrow focus on "Americana" will limit the company's growth.

For its own part, Faith Mountain adopted a mail-order strategy that focused on three key areas: merchandise, quality, and service.

Merchandise   Faith Mountain offered a broad range of high-quality products to its customers, united by "a life-style theme of traditional, cozy, and family-oriented life." In 1991, the company rotated over 500 products through its catalogs, including its own manufactured products, herbs and floral arrangements, sportswear, jewelry, gifts, and home and garden decorations. Exhibit 4 provides summary product line descriptions as contained in Faith Mountain's 1990 business plan.

Exhibit 4   Summary Descriptions of Faith Mountain's Major Product Lines

Faith Mountain herb and floral arrangements, designed by Cheri Woodard and staff and created in the Sperryville studio, were the traditional core of the business. Faith Mountain was one of the original manufacturers of these products, and its creations were regularly copied for sale in other catalogs. Especially popular were the chain of flowers, eucalyptus arrangements, and the herb wreath, the best seller in every fall catalog since 1981.

Updated casual sportswear, including sweaters, skirts, dresses, and novelty items, appealed to women who sought high-quality classic designs with a stylish flair, suitable for entertaining, parties, church, and weekends, and to a limited extent, for work. Obtained from vendors such as Lanz, Susan Bristol, and The Eagle's Eye, these products were not exclusive to Faith Mountain, although the Woodards knew of no other catalog devoted to such "country fashions."

Unique jewelry, such as pins, earrings, belts, necklaces, and bracelets, sold well as impulse purchases. They were price blind and were easy to ship and warehouse.

Children's products, including puzzles, toys, and mazes, were selected to appeal to mothers, grandmothers, or other relatives who sought "wholesome, old-fashioned fun with educational value" as gifts for children 2–8. In addition, the company sold lamps, rugs, and other accessories to bring a traditional or nostalgic appearance to children's bedrooms.

Seasonal decorative accessories, especially items for Halloween, Thanksgiving, Christmas, and Easter, were offered to help families decorate their homes for these holidays, according to old traditions and to create new ones. The line excluded "cheap plastic decorations, glitzy tinsel, or poorly constructed merchandise" to focus on long-lasting, high-quality items to keep and use every year, such as evergreen wreaths, advent calendars, and centerpieces.

Collectibles, limited edition series of handcrafted figurines, plates, dolls, cottages, and the like were increasingly popular among Faith Mountain customers. These items were created in series to inspire collecting every individual item in the set. Secondary markets sometimes developed for these items, which could bring prices far above the original purchase price. The items were ideal for catalogs because these generated repeated purchases, enhancing the responsiveness of the customer list, but manufacturers were selective in choosing catalog outlets.

Gifts, especially sentimental, inspirational, or symbolic items that reflect the customer's traditional values, were selected for the catalog. Faith Mountain did not offer "standard giftware" of silver, china, or glass, as these were easily available in many retail outlets. Instead, the catalog featured unusual items.

American crafts, or artistic handmade goods, were another way in which Faith Mountain could distinguish itself from ordinary retail outlets. To source and offer these goods, the company had to deal with artists, not vendors, and because the items were one of a kind, customers had to be educated about the use and value of these pieces. Because Faith Mountain was itself a small manufacturer, it was able to work effectively with artisans other outlets viewed as difficult or unreliable, and it offered these crafts as gifts and as decorative accessories.

Home and garden accessories, or items to decorate and personalize one's "living space," were sold to help customers create "comfortable, secure, cozy home environments." The vast array of items were available through manufacturers' representatives, trade shows, and personal contacts.

Merchandise selection was a critical ingredient in the success of the company. The Woodards attributed their success in this area to the fact that they both "lived the life-style" of their customers and to the contacts they had developed in the gift industry over the past 14 years. They sought exclusive marketing rights for products and had begun to move more aggressively to private labeling. Finding and developing quality merchandise before the competition did was the driving force of the merchandising function at Faith Mountain.

Quality   The Woodards prided themselves on offering the best-quality herb and floral products in America, and they sought to offer only merchandise of the highest quality, representing the best value available. Because Faith Mountain manufactured approximately 20 percent of the merchandise it sold, it could personalize and customize products to individual customer needs. Cheri and Martin stressed the importance of doing a quality job in all aspects of the company, from producing the catalog through taking, packing, and shipping an order. Incentive plans for both warehouse and customer service employees rewarded error-free performance. Even more important, however, the Woodards believed their own dedication to quality in all phases of the company resulted in a highly motivated staff who took great pride in their jobs. The pride and quality, they believed, would show through to customers and make them believe they were dealing with a first-class organization.

Service   Finally, Faith Mountain set for itself the goal of quality customer service unsurpassed in the mail-order industry. The company had a toll-free telephone number for placing orders and for customer service inquiries and complaints. Its telephone system, a Siemens 20/40, could support 20 incoming lines and 40 phone sets and had automatic call distribution features and activity reporting capability. Order entry and product inquiry were handled on an ADDS minicomputer with the on-line Nashbar QOP system. Designed by a mail-order bicycle company, the system allowed for speedy order placement and easy access to product reference guides, so operators could answer questions with the customer still on the phone.

The phones in Sperryville were staffed from 8 AM to 8:30 PM seven days a week. After 8:30 PM, calls were switched to a vendor who followed Faith Mountain protocol, took orders, and sent completed order forms to Sperryville by Federal Express the next morning. The average Faith Mountain order was about $75. Operators answered calls, "Faith Mountain; this is [first name]. May I help you?" They would place orders directly on the system, and if callers wanted customer service, they would transfer the call to the customer service supervisor on duty. The system was designed to answer 90 percent of all customer inquiries within two minutes, and customer service supervisors were authorized to do whatever was necessary to keep a customer happy.

From their research and experience in the industry, the Woodards knew the biggest obstacle to catalog shopping was the question of what to do with an order if the customer didn't like it. In such cases, after a customer service supervisor had talked with the customer, and if the customer was still dissatisfied, Faith Mountain would send United Parcel Service to the customer's home to retrieve the order at company expense. This policy was extremely rare in the industry and cost Faith Mountain approximately $8,000 in 1991. Other customer service policies included guaranteed lowest prices, optional Federal Express delivery, and extremely quick shipping from receipt of the order. Faith Mountain also enclosed coupons and the company history with every order.

The Faith Mountain Retail Store Strategy

Although small in comparison to the catalog business, Faith Mountain's retail store revenues totaled almost $300,000 in fiscal year 1991. The store was run by a full-time manager, Margie Ellis. She ordered merchandise for the store, hired, scheduled, and supervised the sales help, and made all the operating decisions at the store. The store employed two women part time during the week and three young women from the high school who worked part time on weekends. The store was open from 10 AM to 6 PM seven days a week.

The store had about 2,000 square feet of selling space on two floors. Its merchandise reflected the same product lines featured in the catalog, but not all items from the catalog were sold in the store, and about 20 percent of the store merchandise was not offered in the catalog. (There was some storage space in an attic and in a back room/office that the store manager rarely used.)

Customers walked in the front door of a very old house filled with antiques and the smell of herbs. The front of the store was the "food room," with the herbs and oils, potpourri, and jewelry. Straight ahead to the right was the breezeway, where collectibles and dolls were kept. In the back and side room, customers found clothes, books, lotions, and products made in Virginia. Upstairs were two rooms—a year-round Christmas room and a room for children's products. One of the outbuildings on the property was used as an outlet for catalog overstocks, which were sold at a slightly lower price.

By 1991, the store had become an important part of the town. Where once Faith Mountain had hoped to capitalize on traffic drawn to the area, it had become a draw in its own right, and other businesses hoped to grow from the Faith Mountain traffic. Local people shopped at Faith Mountain, too. Margie Ellis described the store's community role in this way:

> There are lots of tourists in the fall—the peak weekend is in October, and then people might grumble a bit about the traffic, but there is no real resentment. This store is very important to the town. This is one of the few stores in the area you can *count on* being open. That doesn't mean much in some areas, but here it means a lot. A lot of local people know about it, depend on it for birthday presents, for clothes, for herbs.
>
> You know, in terms of volume or of profit margin, those herbs are nothing. I had moved them out of the front room back into the kitchen, and you should have seen the customers react! "How could you move them to the kitchen? You can't do that!" So now we know: In the front room we have to have the herbs.
>
> The biggest sellers are the clothes and gifts. For the most part, the clothes are bought by local people. Busy tourists coming through won't buy an outfit; they might buy a sweatshirt. For the local people to get this quality apparel, they would have to drive to a mall in Culpepper, or to Manassas, and they *do not* want to drive in northern Virginia traffic.

The Woodards believe the store served another valuable but intangible purpose—it gave Faith Mountain credibility and integrity. Customers who would not buy from the company by mail were able to drive to the store and see and touch products before ordering them; traffic in the store always surged after a catalog mailing. The location of the store—in Sperryville, in Rappahannock County, Virginia, at the foot of the Blue Ridge Mountains—gave an aura of authenticity to the products offered in the catalog. Being able to give directions to the store and to invite customers to visit was part of the company's image as a good, hardworking, honest family business. Many customers arrived and asked people to point out which of the Blue Ridge peaks was "Faith Mountain."

In September 1991, Margie Ellis and Martin Woodard developed the first annual budget for the retail store. Because the previous year had been so good, but the economy was not strong, they agreed to set the previous year's numbers for the current year's targets. Margie reported directly to Cheri but met monthly with

Exhibit 5 Faith Mountain Company's Store Budget, 1992 Fiscal Year

	First Quarter	Second Quarter	Third Quarter	Fourth Quarter	Total
Sales	$79,861	$99,284	$ 41,494	$77,059	$297,698
Cost of goods sold	35,770	44,469	18,586	34,515	133,340
Gross profit	44,091	54,815	22,908	42,544	164,358
Promotional costs:					
Retail advertising	1,650	2,300	1,650	1,500	7,100
Special events	250	2,000	200	1,400	3,850
Catalog costs	14,434	15,378	8,815	7,926	46,553
Total	16,334	19,678	10,665	10,826	57,503
Operating expense	4,114	6,303	3,275	2,481	16,173
General and administrative	18,653	21,741	20,114	20,148	80,656
Net income	$ 4,990	$ 7,093	$(11,146)	$ 9,089	$ 10,026

Martin to review progress against the budget. Summary budget data appear in Exhibit 5.

THE MAIL ORDER INDUSTRY

The Market in 1990

The July 1991 issue of *Direct Marketing* magazine reported highlights of the *1990 Guide to Mail Order Sales*, the 10th annual study by Arnold Fishman of Marketing Logistics. According to that study, the total mail-order sales in the United States in 1990 topped $200 billion, with consumer mail order at $98.2 billion, business mail order at $53.4 billion, and charitable contributions by mail at $49 billion. The consumer mail-order total was further defined as follows: $40.7 billion on services, $44.5 billion on products from specialty merchandisers, and $13 billion on products from general merchandisers.

According to the Fishman study, total mail-order sales for 1990 reflected 10.1 percent of general merchandise sales, 3.2 percent of retail sales, 2.1 percent of consumer services, and 1.8 percent of gross national product for the year. The following data on growth in the industry are excerpted from the same study:

- Overall growth for consumer mail order in 1990 is between 4 and 8 percent in money (current dollar) terms and −1 to +3 percent in real (adjusted for inflation) terms, somewhat higher than growth in overall retail or in department store chain sales.
- Among specific sales segments, growth was above average for sportswear (apparel), videocassettes (audio/video), libraries and school supplies (business specialties), television and videotex (general merchandising), drugs/vitamins and physical fitness (health).
- Growth was below average for footwear (apparel), auto clubs, automotive/ aviation, full-line business supplies, consumer electronics products,

Exhibit 6   U.S. Mail-Order Sales Growth, 1981–1990

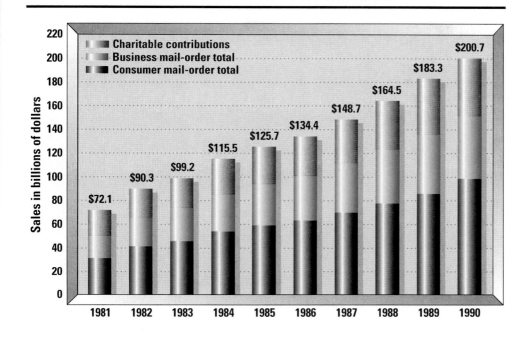

cosmetics, crafts, catalog retailers (general merchandise), low-end gifts, hardware/tools, fashion jewelry, photofinishing, photographic equipment, and apparel-oriented sporting goods.

- Among individual companies, major-size companies with 20 percent growth included American Association of Retired Persons Insurance, Cabela's, Compu-Serve, J. Crew, Current Domestications, Frederick's, Hamilton Mint, Home Shopping Network, International Masters Publishers, Medco Containment, Prodigy, Tweeds, United Services Automobile Association, and Viking Office Products.

- Limited growth was experienced by L.L. Bean, Cincinnati Microwave, Collector's Guild, Cosmetique, GRI, Horchow, Quill, Reliable, Royal Silk, Sears, Roebuck & Company, Shopsmith, and Warshawsky.

Additional data from the *1990 Guide to Mail Order Sales* excerpted from the *Direct Marketing* article appear as Exhibits 6 through 8.

Trends for the Future

Over 100 years ago, Sears, Roebuck & Company set the industry standard for general merchandise marketing through catalogs. As Exhibit 6 shows, the continuing growth through the 1980s enticed many entrepreneurs to enter the industry. In addition, several retailers had responded to the mail-order threat by developing their own catalogs. In 1986, the U.S. Postal Service sent out 11.8 billion copies of 8,500

Exhibit 7   Facts about the Mail-Order Catalog Business in the United States, 1990

- On a per capita basis, Americans spent an average of $393 on mail-order purchases in 1990.
- Specialty mail-order vendors enjoy a substantially greater share of consumer mail-order product sales (77 percent) than do general merchandising mail-order vendors (23 percent).
- U.S. business mail-order sales in 1990 were $53.4 billion and charitable contributions were $45.9 billion. The total of U.S. mail-order/sales and contributions was $200.3 billion.
- While U.S. consumer mail-order product sales may appear modest on the overall scale of gross national product, retail sales, or general merchandise sales, they are immense as a source of sales. Consumer mail-order product sales are equivalent to 82% of sales of the top 100 department stores ($70 billion), more than catalog showrooms, direct selling, and vending machines combined ($45.7 billion), and as much as any single consumer selling channel except mass general merchandisers and supermarkets. It is a leading consumer selling channel for specialty merchandise with prices under $1,000.
- U.S. consumer mail-order sales of products and services were $98.2 billion in 1990, $57.5 billion in products and $40.7 billion in services. This represents:

1.8 percent of gross national product.	3.2 percent of retail sales.
10.1 percent of general merchandise sales.	2.1 percent of consumer service sales.

Source: *Direct Marketing*, July 1991.

different catalogs. In the same year, the Direct Marketing Association surveyed these catalogers and found that 93 percent were increasing their mailings.

Some marketers argued the catalog industry was peaking. One 1984 study pointed to the fact that although the number of catalogs issued in the United States increased 68 percent in 1983, the customer base increased only 24 percent. It seemed unlikely that this customer group would increase its consumption sufficiently to support the additional catalogs entering the market and sustain the growth rates of current catalog companies.[1] In addition, a 1983 Stone-Adler market study had found that 43 percent of all U.S. households were against catalogs. Some experts expected this number to increase as mail-order companies continued to trade customer lists and a select number of people received an inordinate number of catalogs.

On the other hand, population projections for the United States (Exhibit 9) seemed to support those who predicted continued strong growth in the industry. Although many older people were not accustomed to credit card use, today's younger generations have been exposed to credit cards all their lives. As these generations grow older and their income increases, the ease of making credit card purchases through the mail would certainly improve the prospects of catalog purchasing. A 1989 study reported that 7 out of 10 families had no adult buyer home during the day to go shopping.[2] Jay Walker, chairman of Catalog Media Corporations, stated:

> Only 5 percent of retail sales are through catalogs. Now it is hard for you to tell me that a channel is mature at 5 percent penetration, when the underlying demographics of the population at large favor the channel. More working

[1]Maggie McComas, "Catalog Fallout," *Fortune*, January 20, 1986, pp. 63–64.
[2]Rayna Skolnik, "Selling Via Catalog," *Stores*, October 1989, pp. 47–50.

Exhibit 8 Specialty Vendors of Consumer Products

	Sales (Millions)	Number of Vendors	Percent of Sales
Animal care	$ 70	120	0%
Apparel	4,250	570	10
Audio/video	630	370	1
Automotive aviation	620	540	1
Books	2,760	—	6
Collectibles	1,690	520	4
Consumer electronics/science	710	100	2
Cosmetic/toiletries	450	110	1
Crafts	840	780	2
Food	1,310	940	3
Gardening	850	700	2
Gifts	2,020	630	5
Hardware/tools	530	240	1
Health products	2,480	410	6
Home construction	310	490	1
Housewares	1,220	820	3
Jewelry	500	150	1
Magazines	6,020	5,000	14
Multiproducts	7,410	340	17
Newspapers	3,020	1,700	7
Photographic products	410	90	1
Records	780	—	2
Sporting goods	3,460	1,140	8
Stationery	440	80	1
Tobacco	30	30	0
Toys/games/children's products	710	380	2
Computer software	650	60+	1
Computer hardware	350	100+	1
Total	$44,520	16,410+	100%

Consumer products specialty vendor sales segments (vendors classified by major product category) fall into three tiers:

Top Size ($1 billion+)	Middle Size ($.5 billion–1 billion)	Moderate Size (Less than $.5 billion)
Multiproducts, gifts, collectibles, magazines, books, apparel, food, newspapers, housewares, health, sporting goods	Automotive/aviation, gardening, children's products, toys/games, records, computer software, jewelry, hardware/tools, audio/video, consumer electronics/science, crafts	Cosmetics/toiletries, computer hardware, stationery, tobacco, photographic products, home construction

Excluding books, magazines, newspapers, computer software, computer hardware, and records, 9,520 businesses account for $30.9 billion in sales, or an average of $3.25 million in sales per business.

Source: *Direct Marketing*, July 1991.

Exhibit 9 Actual and Projected Population of the United States, 1990, 1995, and 2000

Male (in thousands)	1990	1995	2000
Under 5	9,426	9,118	8,661
5–17	23,377	24,787	25,027
18–24	13,216	12,290	12,770
25–34	22,078	20,579	18,662
35–44	18,785	21,104	21,945
45–54	12,406	15,292	18,296
55–64	10,103	10,149	11,557
65–74	8,171	8,476	8,242
Over 74	4,681	5,326	6,032
Total	122,243	127,121	131,192

Female (in thousands)	1990	1995	2000
Under 5	8,982	8,681	8,237
5–17	22,253	23,587	23,788
18–24	12,924	11,991	12,461
25–34	21,848	20,384	18,487
35–44	19,112	21,233	21,966
45–54	13,081	16,005	18,927
55–64	11,260	11,175	12,601
65–74	10,201	10,454	10,001
Over 74	8,505	9,507	10,607
Total	128,166	133,017	137,075

Total (in thousands)	1990	1995	2000
Under 5	18,408	17,799	16,898
5–17	45,630	48,374	48,815
18–24	26,140	24,281	25,231
25–34	43,926	40,963	37,149
35–44	37,897	42,337	43,911
45–54	25,487	31,297	37,223
55–64	21,363	21,324	24,158
65–74	18,372	18,930	18,243
Over 74	13,186	14,833	16,639
Total	250,409	260,138	268,267

women, less time, more credit cards, 800 numbers—all of these things favor the catalog industry continuing as a major growth trend.[3]

"Specialogs" One significant trend in the industry was the increasing use of "specialogs"—catalogs focused on a particular market segment. During the 1980s,

---

[3]Janice Steinberg, "Special Report: Direct Marketing," *Advertising Age*, October 26, 1987, pp. 51–51G.

many large, general merchandise catalog companies like Alden's and Montgomery Ward went out of business. In 1987, J. C. Penney began to provide catalogs targeted at petite women, extra-size women, tall women, big and tall men, nurses, brides, and other special groups. Advanced computer technology allows companies to identify, target, and track the purchases of their customers and then to develop special catalogs for groups sharing key characteristics. Then, highly sophisticated printing technology permits companies to prepare customized catalogs for particular clients. Some analysts predicted it would soon be common—and cost effective—for a mail-order company to send two different catalogs to neighboring households, depending on their past purchasing patterns.[4]

Credit Card Competition Increased competition between Visa USA and Master-Card for the mail-order market in 1991 resulted in new inducements to consumers who shop by mail. For example, Visa announced in June it would be offering a "Visa Catalog Collection": Consumers would be offered 40 catalogs at a nominal fee, and those who ordered catalogs through Visa would receive certificates good for up to 20 percent off their purchases. In response, MasterCard announced its "Forests for Our Future" green marketing approach: trees would be planted in the consumer's name for merchandise bought through certain catalogs. This promotion was designed to downplay the image of catalogers as tree killers. In essence, both companies were to provide free advertising for catalog companies, and the support of these two financial giants would likely boost sales.[5]

Government Regulations Catalogs remained vulnerable to the increasing costs of paper and postage. According to the *1990 Guide to Mail Order Sales,* a 1989 postage rate increase for third-class mail was still being felt in 1990. In addition, recent rulings from the Federal Trade Commission had increased legal risks for catalog companies. Previously, the FTC had held that manufacturers were liable for false product claims; in 1990, the FTC shifted that responsibility to the mail-order firms.[6]

On another front, mail-order firms awaited a decision from the U.S. Supreme Court concerning state taxes on mail-order goods. Targeting mail-order firms in particular, the state of North Dakota was attempting to collect sales taxes from any company that "regularly and continuously" solicited business in the state. Current practice, established by a 1967 Supreme Court case *(National Bellas Hess, Inc.* v. *Department of Revenue,* 386 U.S. 753), prohibited states from collecting taxes on companies without a physical presence in the state. The Direct Marketing Association and many mail-order firms had filed briefs arguing against the North Dakota standard, citing the excessive administrative burden such a change would impose on them.

Catalog Company Failures Even in a growing market, mail-order firms failed. A 1984 study of 35 failed catalog companies cited the following key contributing factors:

- Lack of market research; failure to evaluate the market and offer desired goods.

---

[4]Ibid.

[5]Alison Fahey, "Credit Cards Tie In with Catalogs," *Advertising Age,* June 3, 1991, p. 50.

[6]Laurie Freeman and Janet Meyers, "FTC Gets Tough on Catalog Claims," *Advertising Age,* November 12, 1990, p. 73.

- Overuse of popular mailing lists.
- Undercapitalization.
- Oversaturated marketplace.[7]

Most industry experts pointed to merchandise selection as the *sine qua non* of success in the mail-order business. Harold Schwartz, president of Hanover House Industries, noted that you cannot "fall in love with your catalog."[8] Mail-order firms had to be objective in determining what works and then be able to change their catalogs to meet new demands and to exit saturated markets.

THE FUTURE OF THE FAITH MOUNTAIN COMPANY ────────

Confident that fundamental market forces were very positive for their company, Cheri and Martin Woodard believed the key strategic question for Faith Mountain was how to grow.

Overall Company Goals

The Faith Mountain Company intended to establish itself as the industry leader in quality, high-value gifts, apparel, and home accessories. To that end, top management had set for itself the overall goal of $25 million in annual sales by 1995, with $10 million from the Faith Mountain catalog, $5 million from the retail division, and an additional $10 million from the acquisition or development of another catalog company. The Woodards intended to achieve these targets and at the same time accomplish the following objectives:

- Grow as quickly as possible, yet maintain profitability.
- Grow at a rate that does not hurt product quality and customer service.
- Aggressively develop new products and exclusive vendor relationships.
- Stay close to our customers through surveys, the store, and personal contact.
- Provide the best quality and value in unique and unusual products.
- Be the best company to do business with.
- Provide a work environment that allows employees personal and professional growth, to ensure the highest levels of motivation and knowledge among our people, and therefore the highest level of quality in all aspects of the company.

Growth for the Faith Mountain Catalog

Performance projections for the Faith Mountain catalog through 1995 appear in Exhibits 10 and 11. Martin estimated capital expenditures of $350,000 to $400,000 would be needed to increase catalog sales to $10 million.

---

[7]New York University Advanced Catalog Seminar, "Successes and Failures Examined by Catalog Leaders," *Direct Marketing*, July 1984, pp. 98–101.
[8]Ibid.

The typical percentage breakdown of a catalog company's income statement in 1991 was as follows:

Net sales	100%
Cost of goods sold	45%
Gross margin	55%
Promotional costs	30%
Operating expenses	19%
Net profit	6%
Other income	1–3%

The relationship between net sales and promotional costs was the most important dynamic in the catalog business. Promotional costs include design and layout of the catalog, photography, color separations, printing and mailing, postage, list rental, and associated computer costs. Based on his experience, Martin worked by rule of thumb requiring that increases in promotional costs increase sales by more than three times the additional costs.

Increasing the "House List"   Growth in the mail-order catalog industry was fueled by the company's customer list. An industry rule of thumb required a catalog company to mail 1,250,000 catalogs four times a year to reach critical mass and attain profitability. Accordingly, each mail-order company sought to built its "house list"—names and addresses of customers who had actually purchased product(s) from the catalog. Most smaller companies supplemented their house list by renting (for one-time use) outside lists, the house lists of other companies (through a broker), at an average price of $110 per thousand names. Any person from the rented list who purchased a product automatically went on the house list. Even the best outside list, however, was not as responsive to a mailing as the company's house list. When measured on a dollar-income-per-catalog-mailed basis, the response of the house list would be three to four times greater than any outside list.

The larger the house list, the less the company needed to rent other lists. Companies with larger lists exchange lists with each other rather than pay each other rental fees. Accordingly, as the house list grows, promotional costs decrease percentage wise as net sales increase. (In addition, the company earns additional money from the rental of its own house list; in fiscal year 1991, Faith Mountain earned $130,000 in this way.)

The most marketable segment of any list was the group who had purchased product(s) within the previous six months. A key component of Faith Mountain's growth strategy was to increase its six-month buyer list to 60,000 names. Martin explained the logic:

We regularly exchange lists with approximately 15 other catalog companies. Assuming a mailing of 1 million catalogs and an entire house list of 150,000 names, we need to use 850,000 names from these other companies. A six-month buyer list of 56,700 names would allow us to incur no rental fees (850,000 names divided by 15 companies equals 56,700 names).

Our six-month buyers typically respond with $4 in sales for every catalog mailed versus the outside response of approximately $1.10 per catalog mailed. In the most recent catalog promotion, we had approximately 20,000 six-month buyers. If this segment were tripled, we would see approximately

Exhibit 10 Catalog Sales Forecast for Faith Mountain Company, Fiscal Years 1991–1995

Season	Source of Names for Catalog Mailings	Quantity of Catalogs Mailed	Projected Sales
Fall 90	Rented lists	825,000	$ 990,000
	In-house	242,600	477,922
Holiday 90	Rented lists	980,000	1,244,600
	In-house	267,300	526,581
Spring 91	Rented lists	637,000	713,440
	In-house	295,750	553,052
Summer 91	Rented lists	300,000	276,000
	In-house	200,000	200,000
Totals	Rented lists	2,742,000	$ 3,224,000
	In-house	1,005,650	$ 1,757,555
1991 total		3,747,650	$ 4,981,595
Fall 91	Rented lists	990,000	$ 1,188,000
	In-house	322,095	653,852
Holiday 91	Rented lists	1,080,000	1,371,600
	In-house	351,500	713,545
Spring 92	Rented lists	765,000	856,800
	In-house	385,500	744,015
Summer 92	Rented lists	360,000	331,200
	In-house	300,000	318,000
Totals	Rented lists	3,195,000	$ 3,747,600
	In-house	1,359,095	$ 2,429,412
1992 total		4,554,095	$ 6,177,012
Fall 92	Rented lists	1,200,000	$ 1,584,000
	In-house	414,260	969,369
Holiday 92	Rented lists	1,300,000	1,820,000
	In-house	449,660	1,052,204
Spring 93	Rented lists	920,000	1,030,400
	In-house	490,560	995,836
Summer 93	Rented lists	300,000	276,000
	In-house	300,000	330,000
Totals	Rented lists	3,720,000	$ 4,710,400
	In-house	1,654,480	$ 3,347,409
1993 total		5,374,480	$ 8,057,809

$50,000 in savings due to exchanging lists rather than renting and $120,000 in increased sales from the larger number of responsive buyers. Assuming four such catalog promotions per year, Faith Mountain would realize $200,000 in savings and $480,000 in increased sales solely from the larger six-month-buyer house list.

To increase the buyer list, we will have to increase the catalog circulation to approximately 7 million every 12 months. Working with our list brokers, we can develop mail plans—testing list segments by monitoring coded responses—to raise the rate of response and reduce the number of catalogs required for circulation.

Exhibit 10 (*concluded*)

Season	Source of Names for Catalog Mailings	Quantity of Catalogs Mailed	Projected Sales
Fall 93	Rented lists	1,400,000	$ 1,848,000
	In-house	519,000	1,245,600
Holiday 93	Rented lists	1,500,000	2,100,000
	In-house	566,400	1,359,360
Spring 94	Rented lists	1,020,000	1,142,400
	In-house	620,200	1,290,016
Summer 94	Rented lists	300,000	276,000
	In-house	450,000	513,000
Totals	Rented lists	4,220,000	$ 5,366,400
	In-house	2,155,600	$ 4,407,976
1994 total		6,375,600	$ 9,774,376
Fall 94	Rented lists	1,400,000	$ 1,848,000
	In-house	651,000	1,562,400
Holiday 94	Rented lists	1,500,000	2,100,000
	In-house	698,286	1,675,887
Spring 95	Rented lists	1,020,000	1,142,400
	In-house	742,086	1,543,539
Summer 95	Rented lists	300,000	276,000
	In-house	500,000	570,000
Totals	Rented lists	4,220,000	$ 5,366,400
	In-house	2,591,372	$ 4,351,826
1995 total		6,811,372	$10,718,226

Moving to Private-Label Sportswear   A second strategy for growth in the Faith Mountain catalog was to change the merchandise mix, particularly in the apparel lines, to reflect half Faith Mountain designs, with private labels, and half items from better manufacturers, to retain the quality brand-name recognition. Martin gave an example of the benefits of this strategy:

> In general, the apparel industry has *no* flexibility on price, but smaller companies will do lots of deals if you are willing to commit to large quantities. For example, a vest: we paid $24 each and sold a *bunch*—somewhere between 750 and 1,000 of them—in last year's catalog for $49. The company we bought them from went out of business this year, taken down when the *Sporting Life* catalog went under. So Cheri called this guy, and he set her up with the factory in China where he had bought them. Now they have our own label, and they cost us $12.50. It's not easy to do that—you have to take a substantial position—but on this vest, we were willing to, due to last year's sales.

Growth through Acquisition of Another Catalog

Demand for the gifts, home accessories, and apparel carried in the Faith Mountain catalog was seasonal. There were two peaks in the sales calendar: the first began in September and dropped off in late December, and the second began in January and ended in February. Although the company did significant business in the other

Exhibit 11   Projected Income Statements, the Faith Mountain Company, Fiscal Years 1992–1995

	1992		1993		1994		1995	
	$	%	$	%	$	%	$	%
Gross sales	$6,433,012	107.5%	$8,325,809	107.5%	$10,056,616	107.5%	$11,014,578	107.5%
Returns and allowances	482,476	7.5	624,436	7.5	754,246	7.5	826,093	7.5
Net sales	5,950,536	100.0	7,701,373	100.0	9,302,370	100.0	10,188,485	100.0
Cost of goods sold	2,814,604	47.3	3,645,587	47.3	4,390,719	47.2	4,798,776	47.1
Gross profit	3,135,932	52.7	4,055,786	52.7	4,911,651	52.8	5,389,709	52.9
Promotional costs	1,951,776	32.8	2,502,946	32.5	2,995,363	32.2	3,250,127	31.9
Operating expense	720,015	12.1	931,866	12.1	1,125,587	12.1	1,232,807	12.1
General and administrative	410,000	6.9	475,000	6.2	565,000	6.1	615,000	6.0
Operating income	54,141	0.9	145,974	1.9	225,701	2.4	291,775	2.7
Other income	230,000	3.9	250,000	3.2	270,000	2.9	310,000	3.0
Net income	$ 284,141	4.8%	$ 395,974	5.1%	$ 495,701	5.3%	$ 601,775	5.9%

Includes catalog and the Sperryville retail store.

months, this seasonality caused rapid shifts in demand on the company's staff and system capabilities and depressed overall operating earnings.

Cheri and Martin knew they could make more efficient use of company facilities, systems, and human resources if they could acquire or develop another business countercyclical to the existing catalog. Fixed costs would be amortized over a larger and more constant flow of business. Acquiring another catalog would be the quickest and safest method to realize these efficiencies. They believed the ideal acquisition would offer small, easy-to-handle products, whose sales would peak in the first half of the year.

Growth in the Retail Division

In 1991, the retail division consisted of the one original store on Main Street in Sperryville, but Cheri and Martin had discussed opening additional retail outlets. Martin favored exploration of possible sites. Referring to Williams Sonoma, Eddie Bauer, The Sharper Image, and other retailers that had taken this route, he stressed the synergy between the catalog and retail outlets, especially as the mailings continued to increase. Cheri was slightly less sanguine about opening additional stores. Margie Ellis, the store manager in Sperryville, also had doubts:

> This store was really the birthplace of the company—here since 1790, here in the Civil War, right by the Blue Ridge Mountains—you can't re-create that. You can buy an old house somewhere and put herbs in it, but that won't be Faith Mountain.

Based on casual discussions with real estate specialists, the Woodards estimated the cost of turning an old house into a "high-end" store (gutting the inside) at approximately $18 a square foot. The average space in a shopping center mall was 1,600 to 2,000 square feet. Simply taking over an existing space and doing minor leasehold improvements might cost as little as $3,000, however; and in the 1991 market, many of these costs could be negotiated with landlords. For example, the Woodards had heard of one outlet chain that had recently spent $18,000 to open a store in Norfolk, Virginia, and the landlord reimbursed them $15,000.

Managing Projected Growth: Issues for Management

Financial Implications   The continuing economic recession in late 1991 seemed to have little effect on Faith Mountain sales, but in dealings with suppliers, Faith Mountain could feel the economic pinch. As Martin put it:

> Companies that used to offer terms of 75 to 90 days now insist on 30 days net, but we still try to negotiate terms. It's really hard to get anyone to listen to you in the apparel industry—you have to be *golden* to get those guys to listen. The name of the game for survival in this business is *credit rating*. We can't be turned in, we can't be late, we can't be delinquent.

Achieving the sales goals would require additional capital, but it was not clear where this capital would be best obtained. In November 1991, Sovran Bank increased the company's line of credit to $500,000. To increase its equity capital, in the spring of 1991, the company had offered 1,500 shares and sold 1,150. The Woodard family retained 55 percent interest in the company, but Prime Capital Group, a venture capital firm, was now the largest shareholder outside the family. Cheri and Martin were aware that outside shareholders would place different pressures on them; already Martin sensed some pressure from stockholders to start paying dividends. Exhibit 12 describes the company's board of directors.

Support Systems Implications   Faith Mountain's current hardware configuration was capable of supporting 96 terminals with two simple upgrades—an additional 380 megabyte disc drive and a 4 megabyte RAM unit. The upgrade cost was $28,319 and was scheduled to occur in 1992. Additional workstations were available for $400. With these upgrades, the computer system could support projected growth through 1995. It appeared the Siemens phone system would be adequate through 1993. Finally, with the addition of a mezzanine level and with some new equipment and technical improvements in the warehouse, the current building would also support the projected $10 million in catalog sales by 1995.

Human Resources Implications   Cheri and Martin agreed that one of the greatest challenges facing Faith Mountain was in hiring, training, and managing the new people: operators, customer service supervisors, buyers, warehouse people, and managers necessary to achieve their goals. Even now, the two knew they were working at capacity. Martin described the situation this way:

> We need to identify the key positions and put good people in them. There are lots of little jobs that go begging now, but little things become much more important with size—if you can get .5 percent of sales with X change, that's a lot more significant at $10 million than at $500,000 in sales. For example, that might pay a salary—that person could add to the bottom line *and* carry his or her own weight. You have to think about who, and when, and how much more we can do of this before we can't do any more of it.

Exhibit 12   Board of Directors and Supporting Professional Services

Faith Mountain Board of Directors

Peter Elliman: A partner in Prime Capital, a private venture capital fund in Warrenton, Virginia, brought over 25 years of financial and corporate development experience to the board.

Don Press: Past director of the Smithsonian Museum Gift Catalog, currently a catalog consultant, had helped the Woodards since 1984.

Joan Litle: A catalog consultant specializing in the creative and merchandising aspects of the industry.

James Jamieson: A member of the board of directors of several companies, had extensive experience in corporate finance and investment banking.

Linda Dietel: A local community activist with many business and community contacts.

Cheri Woodard: President of Faith Mountain.

Martin Woodard: Secretary/treasurer of Faith Mountain.

Supporting Professional Services

Legal: Bill Sharp, senior partner of Kates and Sharp, in Front Royal, Virginia, sat in on all board meetings.

Accounting: Gary Lee, of Young, Hyde and Barbour in Winchester, Virginia, assisted in monthly accounting and performed a year-end financial review.

Banking: Marathon Bank in Stephens City, Virginia, held company accounts in connection with the SBA loan, and Sovran Bank in Charlottesville, Virginia, extended the company a $500,000 line of credit.

Advertising: Forgit & White of New Hampshire designed the catalog, and Faith Mountain operated an in-house advertising agency named Telesis.

Printing: R. R. Donnelly, the largest commercial printer in the world, had printed the company's catalogs since 1988.

I have people reporting to me now, but I still have a tendency to tell them what I want them to do and then expect them to go do it. Cheri has to tell people who work for me that they need to be self-starters, motivated people. I want to be able to tell them, "Go to the show and find me stuff that will sell"— not "Go find me six mugs and four blankets."

Cheri took her responsibility for all human resources matters very seriously. She had established the company's employee evaluation/self-evaluation process, initiated the training program, and prepared the company handbook of personnel policies. In 1991, she had started a new program for ongoing education and training through a local community college, and at year-end she was developing the company's first pension plan and an employee stock option program. At the same time, however, she had misgivings about continuing to handle all aspects of human resource management as the company grew. She said:

For a long time, people answered only to me—Martin didn't want to deal with them. Now he has people who report to him. There's a changing orientation now to *us*, not just to *me*. Martin made me the president. He said, "You're so good with people, with public relations—you be the figurehead." So *Working Women* did a feature story on me, and there is just my picture in the catalog— we're selling to women, and he said they would relate better to me. And I've grown into that role, and now I like it, provided he gets the recognition he deserves in public—and that's *my* job.

Martin is more the gambler, more of a risk-taker, a visionary, while I'm more of a people person—I run the business; I see that the orders go out the door; I manage the order flow. But as we get ready to add more positions—add more people—I ask myself, what about initiation and indoctrination? I can't train them all—the management people need to be trained, too. How do you get that management time?

The Woodards had had their first serious personnel problem in 1991. In January 1991, they had hired an assistant buyer to work for the merchandising manager. In late August, they had to fire her. Martin explained:

It just didn't work out. She was not working as hard as what we were used to, and she was more of a drain on people's time than a help. It wasn't clear to this person who her boss was—I should have told Kim, "Look, this is your assistant, you tell her what to do," but she didn't want to have Kim for a boss, either. We also couldn't pay her what she thought she was worth—and even then what we did pay was too close to Kim's salary, and Kim wasn't happy about that because she was doing *far more*.

So we sat down with her, both Cheri and I, after three months, and we said we were having troubles. We talked things through with her, had her sign papers acknowledging the evaluation, and then we told Kim, "Look, you have to be the boss." Three months later, this person still wasn't coming around. We sat down with her again then and told her she had three more months, and if she hadn't improved by the end of October she'd have to leave. One month later I said, "Look, this isn't working, it's never going to work, let's get rid of her. We don't have that many people here, we might as well have the best." It was clear she was never going to be the best. We gave her four months' severance pay— so she ended up with a year's salary for eight months of work.

As Cheri and Martin considered adding staff in the company, Cheri emphasized the importance of strong human resources systems to train and support the new hires, while Martin stressed simply hiring the right people. They talked frequently about hiring an operations manager or a marketing manager to handle order taking, data processing, the warehouse, and human resources, including hiring, compensation, education, and morale. Cheri knew she would find it hard to give up responsibility for those areas. Martin described the requirements for such a person:

They'd have to come in and work hard and fast. They'd have to have the entrepreneurial spirit and be willing to get out there and pack boxes with us on Saturdays, get their hands dirty. And they'd have to be willing to work for nothing, move out here in the middle of nowhere, and have an office in a corner in a warehouse.

Personal Implications   As they considered their own futures with Faith Mountain, both Martin and Cheri realized the projected growth of their business would have significant implications on their own lives. Martin described their work/family life together:

I don't know what's work and what's not. We work a lot—we're in the building from 8 AM to 7 PM and on Saturday and Sunday. It's unusual for us to take an entire day off. Now that our son is away from home, half of our home conversation is about work. Who should we keep when we have to lay off the seasonal phone operators after Christmas? Should we do X or Y?

Every now and then, Cheri and I take off an entire day, not coming in. And we try to take an extra day on business trips. And two times a year we get away for four to six days.

In the long run, I'll still be involved with the business, but I'd like something without so much stress—there are times when cash is tight, people call and ask why they can't be paid right now—I'd like to avoid those pressures. I'd like to not be so hands-on, to be able to step back and know that the wheels won't fall off the wagon. We need some cushions, though—so we can ride through hard times. Right now we don't have the cushion. There is no margin for error, no room for major mistakes.

I enjoy all this on a theoretical level, though. There's something about keeping score. What are the greatest strengths? What are your weaknesses? Adults can compete in the business world—that appeals to me—there's something about keeping score.

For her part, Cheri had many questions about the future:

I see a goal for the business as making us a life—a life-style better than our parents'. But money is now what drives us. We want to avoid worries and be comfortable. But if we wanted money, we wouldn't have settled in Rappahannock County.

What I really like is growing a business and feeling like I can make a difference in the lives of our employees and the lives of our customers. The challenge to me is building a corporate structure that allows the individual to excel and yet be part of the team. If we get very large, will we be able to have the same esprit de corps?

Fraser River Plastics Ltd.

Christopher K. Bart and Marvin G. Ryder, McMaster University

It was early 1993. Elinore Wickham-Jones, president of British Columbia–based Fraser River Plastics Ltd., was uneasy about the crosscurrents of opinion that were developing regarding the company's future direction. Although the differences of view had perhaps been held for some time, they had surfaced in recent weeks as the merits of several projects—among them a move toward international expansion and an acquisition—were being reviewed. There was, Wickham-Jones felt, more than normal agitation in the atmosphere. Lines were hardening on the questions of how aggressively, and in what direction, the company should proceed.

THE CANADIAN PLASTICS PROCESSING INDUSTRY IN 1993

Although the history of plastics and plastics products goes back over 100 years, in 1993 the industry was still generally regarded in North America as young and growing. In fact, it had only been since World War II that plastic had begun to achieve its status as a major primary or substitute manufacturing material.

In 1993, there were over 1,400 firms engaged in plastics processing in Canada, with most of the companies located in Ontario and Quebec. Of these Canadian firms, the majority had sales of less than $2 million. The bulk of company shipments constituted proprietary products. The remainder were either produced on a custom basis or as "captive operations" for a larger manufacturing entity. This breakdown, however, was difficult to confirm precisely due to the variety of business practices in which any one manufacturing concern engaged.

In terms of the future, world shipments in the plastics processing industry were estimated in 1993 to be moderately "favorable" given the tentative signals of economic recovery. The factors contributing to this projection were an anticipated moderate level of economic growth; a continuing substitution of plastics for traditional materials; and the emergent growth in the manufacturing sector. Costs depended largely on the type of process used. For instance, reinforced plastic products (e.g., boats and storage tanks) were relatively labor-intensive, whereas extrusion products (e.g., pipes, films, etc.) were relatively capital-intensive.

In comparison with other global industries, the plastics industry was still considered a labor-intensive area. For example, in plastics the capital investment per production-related employee ranged between Cdn$5,000 and $42,000, while in petrochemicals it was about Cdn$200,000.

It was anticipated that Canadian plastics manufacturing capacity would be sufficient to meet Canadian demands. In addition, Canadian resin prices, which at one time exceeded world prices by 10 percent, were seen as becoming more competitive with U.S. and other international prices given the recent Canada–U.S. Free Trade Agreement. The prospect, in 1993, of a potential free trade agreement between Canada, the United States, and Mexico was expected to result in significant downward pressure on world prices and consolidation of the North American industry participants through mergers and bankruptcies.

CORPORATE HISTORY

The Early Years: 1984 to 1988

In the fall of 1984, two Vancouver, British Columbia, businessmen, Herbert Rudd and Oliver Farthingham, visited Portland, Oregon, on a tour sponsored by the Vancouver Board of Trade. Of the several plants they visited, one facility, Damian Plastics Inc., particularly caught their attention. This plant used an injection-molding process to manufacture heavy plastic products such as utility crates, garbage cans, and packing cartons. Damian used advanced techniques to minimize the raw material weight in the large products it produced, while retaining, through unique design, the essential rigidity and toughness. Both men, especially Farthingham, who had experience in plastics, felt there was a ready market for the products in Canada because (1) they would have a competitive edge over comparable but more expensive plastic products and (2) they could be marketed as substitutes for more expensive metal containers. The two men returned home with a tentative licensing agreement for all of Canada that included technical assistance from Damian and access to all mold designs.

The immediate problem facing Rudd and Farthingham was raising the $160,000 equity needed to build a plant and get into operation. By November, they had put together a group of local businesspeople and raised the required funds. Some of the backers, like Elinore Wickham-Jones, were associated with wholesale and industrial supply firms through which a sizable portion of the new plant's output could be marketed. On December 9, 1984, the company was incorporated under the name Fraser River Plastics Ltd. Its three major shareholders were Farthingham (20 percent), Wickham-Jones (18 percent), and Rudd (13 percent). Farthingham became Fraser River's first president. Rudd was made secretary–treasurer, and Wickham-Jones became a vice president.

Rudd located a 2-acre site for the company's manufacturing plant in Chilliwack, British Columbia—a small town near Vancouver. Bids were accepted on the building's construction in February 1985, and manufacturing equipment was ordered. During this early period, the company was being run by the three officers on a part-time basis, since all had their own full-time businesses as well. On April 1, 1985, Gunther Heinzman, a former plant manager of a Victoria plastics firm, was hired as general manager of Fraser River.

Heinzman recalled:

Elinore took me out to the site in Chilliwack. It was just a ploughed field! A few days later we did the first public showing of our products at a trade fair in

Victoria. All that I had available was two plastic garbage cans, three sizes of the packing cartons, and six pieces of Damian's literature.

One week later, the first carload of products arrived from Portland. Most of it had to be stored in a small warehoused owned by one of our shareholders since there were no storage facilities yet.

In August 1985, production began at Chilliwack while finishing touches were made on the plant. There was a ready and substantial demand for the products. FRP's prices, although high, gained customer acceptance, and the products proved to be good substitutes for conventional products. It was not long before the company was operating in the black.

Through 1986, the company's operations expanded dramatically. A temporary office annex was erected at the Chilliwack site, and the plant's capacity was increased to accommodate demand. Substantial orders for the company's products also came in from Alberta. To cut transportation costs and get local exposure, Fraser River purchased an empty plant in Calgary, ordered equipment, and hired a general manager to take charge there. The Calgary plant was in full operation by June 1986.

In time, Fraser River's success became known among those familiar with plastics processing. Not surprisingly, in 1987 another group of entrepreneurs set up a facility to produce similar injection-molding products; their plant was in Prince Rupert, British Columbia. Fraser River had no legal remedy, since the products and processes it licensed from Damian were poorly protected by patents. In addition, the initial barriers to entry—such as the special molds and know-how—started to crumble. Although the new firm marketed its products under its own name, there was little, save some cosmetic design differences, to distinguish the Prince Rupert products from those manufactured by Fraser River. As one company executive put it, "The plant in Prince Rupert was the first time we really experienced direct competition."

Fraser River's response was an offer to purchase the Prince Rupert competitor. This offer was accepted in November 1987, and Fraser River retained the old company's major shareholder as general manager. The purchase was not well received, however, by the Prince Rupert company's minority shareholders. They took their proceeds from the sale and shortly thereafter set up another injection-molding plant in Nanaimo, British Columbia.

By 1988, Wickham-Jones and Farthingham had become concerned about the limitations of the present three-person board in light of the company's growth and changing external circumstances. There were also signs, particularly in relation to the acquisition of the Prince Rupert company, that some of Fraser River's minority shareholders were disturbed and would like to see a broader representation of views at the board level. As a consequence, three new members were added to Fraser River's board: Owen Palmer, head of a local supermarket chain; Joanna Young, a management consultant who ran the local office of a large national firm; and Michelle O'Reilly, Fraser River's legal counsel.

Up to this point, the organization of the company had been loosely structured. Each of the firm's plants—in Chilliwack, Calgary, and Prince Rupert—had its own managers and field sales force reporting to Gunther Heinzman, the company's general manager. Wickham-Jones, Farthingham, and Rudd were considered the overall management committee. They had the primary responsibility for major decisions such as site selection, price, expansion, and capital investments, but they were also involved on an ad hoc basis in many overlapping operating functions.

The First Transition: 1989 to 1992

At the suggestion of Farthingham, Joanna Young reviewed the company's organization in early 1989 to "assess the marketing strengths and weaknesses of the company and to suggest desirable changes." Her principal recommendation was as follows:

> There is a clear need for greater continuity, consistency and detail in the top supervision of overall operations. The current dispersed nature of responsibilities among the company's executives should be focused in the hands of a single chief executive with time for close day-to-day contact with the organization. As chief executive officer, this person would be responsible for all company operations and for initiating and implementing policy changes with the concurrence of the board.

Prior to submitting her report, Young reviewed its content with Farthingham and discussed the need for a full-time president. Farthingham agreed with the notion but noted that his own commitments in other companies prevented him from assuming this expanded role. It was not, in any case, his cup of tea: "I've always considered myself a front man, an entrepreneur, a hustler." As a consequence, Farthingham suggested that he become chair and Wickham-Jones become president. In taking on the president's role, Wickham-Jones agreed to reduce the time spent on her family business and to run Fraser River on a full-time basis.

At the time of the reorganization, Gunther Heinzman was made manufacturing vice president. Although his title changed, his operating duties with respect to plant operation and supervision remained the same.

Heinzman commented on the reorganization:

> It was an inevitable change. As general manager, I didn't have the time needed to run the sales organization. I didn't like the pressure at the top. Besides, my strength is manufacturing. That's what I know best and that's where I'm most comfortable.

Shortly after the reorganization, Lucas Feck was hired for the position of marketing vice president. Feck recounted his early days:

> I suppose it was the entrepreneurial attitude and capabilities of the people at Fraser River which attracted me to the company. It was like running my own business; there was freedom to run things as I thought they should be.
>
> When I joined, Fraser River had experienced no stiff competition from new entrants yet. The company was begging for more structure and policies in its administration. For instance, at Calgary, the sales manager had no fixed sales price. Hell, there wasn't even a price list, so no one in the marketplace—including our customers—knew what the prices of the products were from one day to the next. There was no fixed collection policy for the company, and there was a high turnover in sales personnel.
>
> During my first 18 months, I restructured the sales organization. I set up the company's first sales forecast and budgets for each territory and established a reporting system so that salespeople knew how they and their region were doing on a monthly basis. I even instituted an advertising budget—another first!

Throughout 1989, the company continued to grow. Demand was strong and prices were reasonable in spite of the advent of significant competition and an emerging economic recession. The year was also marked by two acquisitions: Beaver Plastics in Vancouver, British Columbia, and Simcoe Plastics of Kamloops, British Columbia.

Beaver Plastics was a company owned by Farthingham that manufactured plastic pipe using an extrusion-molding process. In late 1989, Farthingham expressed concern over having to wear two hats in promoting the products of both Fraser River and Beaver. Even customers were associating the two firms as one. Sales representatives from the two companies often called on the same wholesaler/distributor accounts. In fact, some of Fraser River's fittings were made to fit the plastic pipe produced by Beaver. At the same time, Fraser River was looking for opportunities to expand its product lines. With this in mind, in early 1990 Farthingham offered his company for sale to the board of Fraser River. The sale was negotiated for cash and debt, and by year's end Wickham-Jones reported that the sales, profits, and growth resulting from the acquisition were "very encouraging."

Simcoe Plastics was a family-owned operation that manufactured plastic shower curtains and raincoats using a manufacturing process known as calendering. In October 1989, Wickham-Jones heard the company was for sale. She believed that the purchase of Simcoe would provide Fraser River with instant product diversification as well as give Fraser River the capability of producing other items, such as plastic wall coverings and backing for upholstery fabrics.

Fraser River completed its purchase of Simcoe by November 1989. The most significant operational change involved experimentation with the production of plastic-coated wall coverings. By doing so, the company hoped to take up the apparent slack in Simcoe's manufacturing facilities.

Despite the worsening recession, Fraser River concluded its 1990 fiscal year on a particularly strong note (see Exhibits 1 and 2). The strong profit showing, however, did not completely compensate for a number of developing problems:

1. The plant manager in the Calgary manufacturing facility was fired because of a failure to reduce inefficiencies and waste in the plant.

2. Inefficiency was also a problem at Simcoe, although the waste factor had been reduced substantially since the company's acquisition. Simcoe was experimenting with production of new plastic products. Costs there were mounting rapidly, a matter of increasing concern to Fraser River executives. Some blamed these problems on overreliance on the management that Fraser River had inherited when it bought Simcoe. For example, the plant manager, who had remained when the firm was acquired by Fraser River, did not have the necessary qualifications to successfully oversee the plant's experimental work. As a consequence, he was fired in May 1990, and Heinzman was instructed to supervise more closely the operation of the plant and its product development activities.

3. Two large competitors had entered Fraser River's traditional markets. One, Moldform Ltd., was a subsidiary of a large conglomerate organization. The other, Plastech Ltd., was a division of a company involved in other plastic-processing operations. Both operated in British Columbia and Alberta. Market shares were unknown. But a rough estimate gave Fraser River about 40 percent of the western Canada market and 15 percent each to Moldform and Plastech. The balance of 30 percent was shared by a variety of small companies manufacturing limited product lines and capitalizing on low overheads and local contracts to operate.

In 1991, the demand for Fraser River products in British Columbia softened, due mostly to increased competition and local market saturation.

Exhibit 1   Fraser River Plastics, Consolidated Balance Sheets, 1988–1992 (in thousands of Canadian dollars)

	1992	1991	1990	1989	1988
Assets					
Current assets:					
Cash	$ 25	$ 30	$ 5	$ 565	$ 110
Term deposits and marketable securities	—	583	2	—	690
Accounts receivable	2,453	1,155	1,215	423	540
Inventories	3,827	2,625	1,923	2,163	357
Deposits	13	25	140	2	3
Total current assets	6,318	4,428	3,285	3,153	1,700
Property, plant, and equipment, at cost less accumulated depreciation	4,453	2,935	2,743	1,940	1,468
Other assets	17	28	7	15	60
Excess of cost of subsidiaries over the net book value of acquired assets, at cost less amortization	105	145	185	105	130
Total assets	$10,893	$7,536	$6,220	$5,213	$3,358
Liabilities and Shareholders' Equity					
Current liabilities:					
Bank overdraft and loan	$ 2,348	$ 863	$ 515		
Accounts payable and accrued charges	892	1,042	338	$1,063	$ 145
Income and other taxes payable	618	738	962	1,065	260
Royalty payable	—	—	70	90	400
Total current liabilities	3,858	2,643	1,885	2,198	805
Deferred revenue	28	33	33		
Long-term debt	3,150	1,120	1,282	715	875
Total liabilities	7,036	3,796	3,200	2,913	1,680
Shareholders' equity:					
Preferred shares	—	—	—	—	253
Common shares	205	205	205	32	32
Contributed surplus	70	70	70	70	70
Retained earnings	3,582	3,465	2,745	2,198	1,323
Total shareholders' equity	3,857	3,740	3,020	2,300	1,678
Total liabilities and shareholders' equity	$10,893	$7,536	$6,220	$5,213	$3,358

To expand the company's geographic market, the company built a manufacturing facility in Winnipeg, Manitoba. Sales of Fraser River's products in mid-Western Canada had risen during the past several years, but transportation costs had reduced the firm's competitive position and profit margin. The risk of entering the region against established competition was accepted by company executives. The company also had encouraging internal projections covering the size and future growth of the market in eastern Canada. (Exhibit 3 shows financial results by separate facilities, through 1992.)

Exhibit 2 Fraser River Plastics, Ltd., Statement of Income and Selected Financial Ratios, 1988 *(in thousands of Canadian dollars)*

	1992	1991	1990	1989	1988
Net sales	$16,445	$15,750	$10,903	$7,835	$5,403
Cost of sales	11,228	10,765	7,178	3,990	3,455
Gross profit	5,217	4,985	3,725	3,845	1,948
Selling, general, and administrative expenses	3,605	2,750	1,898	838	655
Royalty expenses	332	332	332	625	338
Total operating expenses	3,937	3,082	2,230	1,463	993
Operating profit	1,280	1,903	1,495	2,382	955
Interest and other income	128	135	40	163	80
	1,408	2,038	1,535	2,545	1,035
Interest, long-term debt	493	138	92	70	77
Amortization of excess cost of subsidiaries over net book value of acquired assets	40	40	35	27	
	533	178	127	97	77
Earnings before income taxes	875	1,860	1,408	2,448	958
Income taxes	480	825	610	1,208	453
Net earnings	$ 395	$ 1,035	$ 798	$1,240	$ 505
Earnings per common share	$ 0.08	$ 0.20	$ 0.15	$ 0.24	$ 0.10
Dividends paid	278	315	251	365	
Dividends per common share	.05	.06	.05	.07	
Selected financial ratios:					
Current assets/current liabilities	1.6	1.7	1.7	1.4	2.1
Total assets/total liabilities	1.5	2.0	1.9	1.8	2.0
Long-term debt/equity	0.8	0.3	0.4	0.3	0.5
Gross profit/net sales	0.32	0.32	0.34	0.49	0.36
Inventory turnover	2.9	4.1	3.7	1.8	9.7
SG&A expense/gross profit	0.69	0.55	0.51	0.22	0.34
EBIT/gross profit	0.17	0.37	0.38	0.64	0.49

At a board meeting, Wickham-Jones later informed the other members that because of the decline in market growth and increasing competition, particularly in British Columbia, she and Marketing VP Lucas Feck were investigating numerous potential corporate acquisitions for Fraser River, including a car dealership, a precision tool manufacturing operation, a hotel, and a corrugated steel manufacturing operation. To date, no deal had been consummated.

In September 1992, Wickham-Jones hired Clayton Dunwood as Fraser River's vice president for administration. Dunwood assumed complete responsibility for the accounting and financial affairs of the company. Wickham-Jones felt that Dunwood would be of particular help to her in the area of investigation of future corporate acquisitions. However, Lucas Feck continued to be especially disappointed with Fraser River's efforts in this area. He commented on Fraser River's need for new companies:

Exhibit 3   Operating Performance of Fraser River's Plants and Business Segments, 1990–1992 *(in thousands of Canadian dollars)*

	Chilliwack and Prince Rupert			Calgary			Winnipeg and Toronto†			Beaver Plastics		Simcoe Plastics	
	1992	1991	1990	1992	1991	1990	1992	1991	1990	1992	1991	1992	1991
Dollar sales	$6,365	$6,790	$6,115	$6,710	$5,180	$4,365	$ 335	$403	$ 75	$2,950	$3,660	$1,303	$1,318
Discounts	275	220	310	153	183	175	20	33	5	57	50	28	20
Net sales	6,090	6,570	5,805	6,557	4,997	4,190	315	370	70	2,893	3,610	1,275	1,298
Cost of goods sold	4,148	4,420	4,075	4,412	3,332	2,748	312	280	50	2,265	2,765	930	1,073
Gross margin	1,942	2,150	1,730	2,145	1,665	1,442	3	90	20	628	845	345	225
Operating costs	1,382	1,093	920	1,190	847	657	153	95	48	733	580	278	313
Royalty*	165	192	192	167	140	137							
Pretax profit (loss)	$ 395	$ 865	$ 618	$ 788	$ 678	$ 648	$ (150)	$ (5)	$ (28)	$ (105)	$ 265	$ 47	$ (88)

* Each of the plants producing injection-molded products pays a royalty fee internally to Fraser River Plastics Ltd. The parent company in turn pays a royalty fee to its licensor (Damian) based on the total company production of such products, but to a limit of $332,000 as of 1991.

† Toronto sales operations have been supplied with production from Manitoba and British Columbia plants.

Since 1989 I have been pushing other senior managers to find new areas for investment and growth. Fraser River's bread-and-butter products have become commodity items. The industry is easy to enter. We have to have other businesses to support the overheads which have built up in the company. When I look at our markets here in British Columbia, I don't see anywhere to go. . .and it looks like it's going to be an uphill battle to crack the Eastern market. That's why I firmly believe that we should be planning our growth more—with, say, 20 percent coming from new acquisitions.

We haven't had a new company here in some time. It's very frustrating when you consider the number of firms that we've looked at. Of course, you get people like Joanna Young and that lawyer, O'Reilly. Whenever we bring a good acquisition to the board, they're always harping on how there are better deals around. Yet, they can't suggest any themselves.

Through 1992, Wickham-Jones also pursued another venture. Through various publications, she was aware of the need for the type of products produced by Fraser River in other parts of the world, particularly in the lesser developed countries (LDCs) in Asia. She believed this represented an opportunity for Fraser River, with its accumulated expertise in plastic products. Wickham-Jones concentrated her efforts on finding a partner to provide the international expertise and contacts that Fraser River lacked. Preliminary discussions were held with one such partner—a Canadian manufacturer of logging and sawmill equipment with sales offices in a number of foreign countries and a record of joint venture projects with nationals of those countries (mainly to set up logging and sawmill operations). The proposed agreement was for the two companies to form a joint venture limited partnership supplying capital, equipment, and expertise for new ventures in the manufacture of plastic products. Hopefully, Canadian-based resin suppliers could be brought into the deal. Conscious of the reactions multinationals received when they "invaded the LDCs," the joint venture company was to keep a low profile in its international undertakings.

By December, Wickham-Jones reported that she had identified several countries in Asia as possible sites for a first undertaking. The pursuit of the joint venture's arrangements was, for the most part, being conducted by Wickham-Jones alone. She was, many felt, personally committed to the project and was devoting more and more of her time to it. Wickham-Jones commented:

Sure, I'm committed. I really believe we can turn Fraser River into a worldwide organization and provide a useful service to other countries at the same time.

And, yes, this project is taking up a lot of my time. But that's because we don't know anything about operating on an international level. Once I know what's involved, I'll probably hire another vice president and put him in charge of our international operations. In addition, the universities are full of young aggressive people who can be brought on board to help "fill the gaps" created in Fraser River. . .We should also be able to buy talent either from the market or other organizations.

Exhibit 4 shows Fraser River's corporate structure as of the end of 1992, and Exhibit 5 is an unofficial organization chart for corporate headquarters.

THE SITUATION IN EARLY 1993

In January 1993, Wickham-Jones received drafts of Fraser River's financial statements for the 1992 fiscal year (see Exhibits 1–3). Overall, growth in company sales was sluggish, as a result of sharper competition—in particular, from smaller local

Exhibit 4   Fraser River Plastics Ltd. Corporate Structure *(Case writers' summary. No official organization charts existed at the company.)*

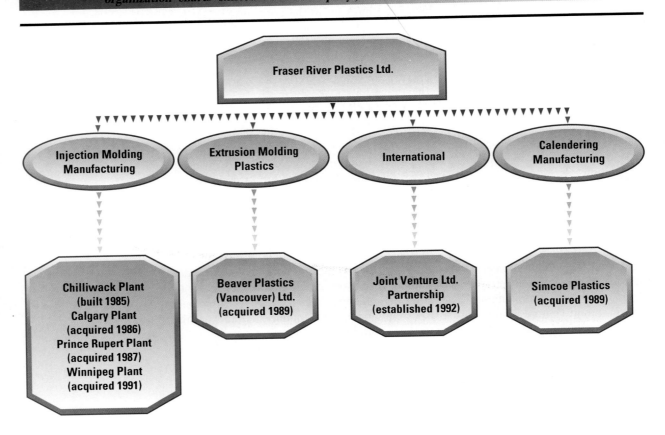

Fraser River Plastics Ltd.

Injection Molding Manufacturing

Extrusion Molding Plastics

International

Calendering Manufacturing

Chilliwack Plant (built 1985) Calgary Plant (acquired 1986) Prince Rupert Plant (acquired 1987) Winnipeg Plant (acquired 1991)

Beaver Plastics (Vancouver) Ltd. (acquired 1989)

Joint Venture Ltd. Partnership (established 1992)

Simcoe Plastics (acquired 1989)

Notes:
All companies 100% owned by Fraser River Plastics Ltd. except potential joint venture (50%).
It was a general corporate policy to incorporate a separate company for each plant and business to ensure maximum limited liability.

plastic manufacturing plants. These plants had contributed to the considerable market erosion experienced by Fraser River, especially in British Columbia. The company's share in Alberta, on the other hand, had remained strong. Profits had slipped a bit due to interest payments.

Unfortunately, Simcoe Plastics had not made much progress. To improve the situation, a qualified and experienced plastics engineer had been hired in late 1992 to take over the plant. The board considered making Simcoe more independent, by hiring a general manager, but that action had been deferred for the moment.

Beaver Plastics was also in trouble. The British Columbia market for extruded pipe was saturated and extremely competitive. At present, there were few growth prospects unless the international and eastern projects began to take off. Unfortunately, the eastern market had become a sore spot. Acceptance of Fraser River's products had not been as favorable as initially thought. Despite this, Wickham-Jones forecast that within two years the Winnipeg plant would be self-supporting.

Exhibit 5   **Fraser River Plastics Ltd. Corporate Headquarters Organization, 1992**   *(Case writers'*
summary. No official organization charts existed at the company.

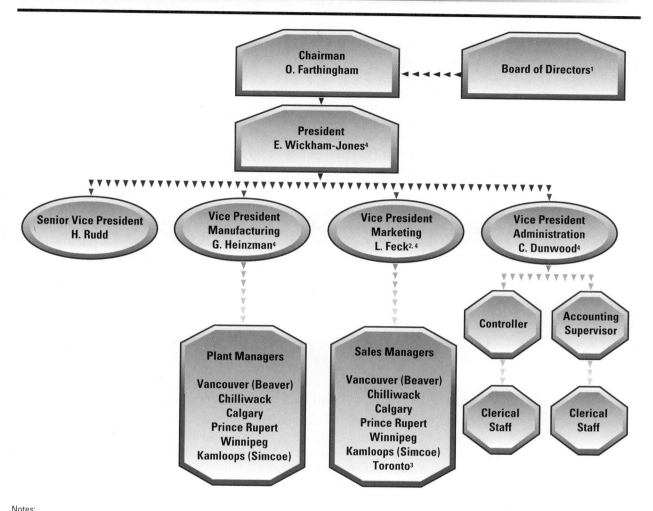

Notes:

1. Board members include O. Farthingham (chairman), E. Wickham-Jones, H. Rudd, J. Young, M. J. O'Reilly, and Grant Ackerfeldt.

2. Feck was also president of Beaver Plastics Ltd.

3. One sales representative only.

4. Wickham-Jones's and Feck's offices are located in one corner of a wholesale warehouse owned by Wickham-Jones in Vancouver. Heinzman and Fraser River's accounting staff, on the other hand, are situated one hour's drive away at the Chilliwack plant. This arrangement suited Feck because he had been made president of Beaver Plastics—which was also located in Vancouver.

In the meantime, two specific issues had arisen that required action. The first concerned the proposed international joint venture. Fraser River's potential partner in that venture had reported that preliminary inquiries conducted by its office in Indonesia had revealed substantial interest on the part of both government officials and local businesspeople. A request had been made for Fraser River to sent an investigative team to Indonesia. Wickham-Jones felt that if she delayed a response too long, the "partner" might begin to doubt Fraser River's good faith or abilities to proceed.

In addition, Wickham-Jones had heard of another plastics company that was for sale and that, if acquired, might serve to strengthen and broaden Fraser River's product line. The company involved, Plasti-Weave, was located in Kelowna, British Columbia—approximately 80 kilometers away from the Chilliwack facility. Plasti-Weave was a very small operation with sales of less than $1 million in 1992 (see Exhibit 6). It had developed a significant and potentially patentable process of "weaving" plastic strips into strong sheets that could be used as substitutes for jute in carpet backing, furniture manufacture, and so on. In 1992, Plasti-Weave realized that a major expansion would be required to exploit the potential of the new product. A new plant and warehouse would have to be built in Kelowna at an approximate cost of $750,000. The owner of Plasti-Weave, Clifford Bell, who was also the inventor of the manufacturing process, did not want to commit himself to this level of debt at the age of 62, or to be responsible for managing the company. Two recent heart attacks had resulted in his decision to sell, if the price was right. However, one of the conditions of sale was that he be retained as a consultant to the company for at least 10 years.

Wickham-Jones was enthusiastic about acquiring Plasti-Weave, but was unsure what the board's reaction would be in light of the $1 million asking price. She was confident, nevertheless, that the board would approve the deal—if she pushed hard enough for it.

FRASER RIVER'S EXECUTIVES LOOK TO THE FUTURE

As the company considered 1992 results and considered the various paths it might follow in 1993, key executives voiced their own points of view.

Oliver Farthingham—Chairman of the Board

Oliver Farthingham began his own business on graduation from high school. He had interests in an automotive body repair business and a partnership in a Canadian distributorship for narrow-aisle forklift trucks. As chairman of the board, Farthingham's day-to-day involvement with Fraser River was limited, but this did not stop him from doing what he liked to do best—promote the Fraser River name. In fact, he was regarded as one of the most outspoken people in the company. Farthingham commented on Fraser River and its operations:

> As chairman, I'm a "positive thinker." I'm sure not a worrier. . . . I'm a doer and a real strategist. I also think that I have an ability to persuade people and inspire confidence.
>
> Although my job and title around here have changed, I still have the reputation for being a "high price" zealot. Fraser River's prices have generally been the highest in the industry. Sometimes our shareholders question me on this point. I always tell them that we're not in business to make plastic products—but rather to make profits. People respect me for that.
>
> The world is full of pessimists and timid people. That's not my style. I'm quite innovative and have a knack for foresight. Look at our acquisitions. For instance, there's our plant in Prince Rupert. It made us look strong in our clients' and competitors' eyes. Sure it's not as strong today due to the competition, but that's because the guy we having running the show there has lost his aggressiveness.

Exhibit 6 Plasti-Weave Financial Statements, 1991 and 1992 *(in thousands of Canadian dollars)*

Balance Sheet Data	1992	1991
Current assets	$800	$619
Fixed assets (net)	70	57
Other assets	9	7
Total assets	$879	$683
Current liabilities	$183	$114
Deferred taxes	1	—
Long-term shareholder loan	77	64
Capital stock	1	1
Retained earnings	617	504
Total liabilities and equity	$879	$683

Income Statement Data	1992	1991
Sales	$950	$616
Other income—interest	4	2
Cost of goods sold	556	345
Expenses	192	148
Income taxes	77	28
Net income	$129	$ 97
Dividends paid	$ 16	$ 12
Selected financial ratios:		
Current assets/current liabilities	4.4	5.4
Total assets/total liabilities	3.4	3.8
Long-term debt/equity	0.12	0.13
Gross profit/net sales	0.41	0.44

As for the purchase of Simcoe, I don't buy the stories about our failure in developing new products there. The problem is that we've just been fooling around and haven't devoted our full efforts to these experimental projects.

Plastics, unfortunately, is a cyclical industry where profits are driven by the economy, crude oil supplies, and costs. This means, therefore, that we have to look for new products and new companies. We should especially be considering more exciting ventures like sports bars, cappuccino kiosks, or even roller blade rinks. They're the rage in the U.S. right now. Market demand is phenomenal—200 percent growth annually. Competition is low. We can get in on the ground floor. And we can buy the managerial talent we need to run them for us. They are opportunities that won't wait for us.

The pessimists, however, say that we don't have the resources to handle these deals. Well, Fraser River has been in this position in the past and we've survived. Look at how we originally got started. To be an entrepreneur takes guts! I'm a risk taker and I know when the odds are in our favor. We can't afford to burden ourselves with negative thoughts.

I feel I have a personal obligation to all of our shareholders to keep our reputation and profits the most attractive in the industry. After all, we still have the same number of shareholders we started out with. To keep them, we have to show them that their investment is better left in the company and to reward them with bigger dividends. We also have to provide them with some vehicle for eventually cashing out. So, I guess this means we'll have to consider going public. I think it would enhance our image greatly too.

Elinore Wickham-Jones—President

Elinore Wickham-Jones had accomplished two of the major objectives in her life—she was financially well off and she had built a company "from the ground up." Wickham-Jones had used most of her personal savings to invest in the formation of Fraser River. As vice president, she had been known for her analytical brilliance. When she became president, she committed herself to making the company grow into a national plastic manufacturing concern.

From 1985 to 1991, we managed to grow in spite of ourselves and our mistakes. To our credit, though, we moved quickly, we were flexible, and did not get bogged down in bureaucracy or paperwork.

Today, not all of our operations are as strong as we'd like, but there is still potential in them. Take Beaver Plastics, for instance. It was a natural combination with Fraser River. Sure, things are slow right now, but once we establish ourselves out east or in other new territories, we will be all right.

Simcoe Plastics is another case in point—and there, our plant manager was not as good as we thought he was. We've learned a lot from our R&D work at Simcoe—even though it cost us $200,000.

I'd like to see Fraser River grow on an even-keel basis through acquisitions and internal expansion. Of course, we're only interested in profitable and growing ventures. But we can't afford to be in it just for the money. We need to maintain our profits so that we can fund other projects as opportunities present themselves.

That's why I'm particularly keen on both our Plasti-Weave acquisition proposal and the joint venture. Right now, we're heavily committed to what are essentially simple plastic products in just one market, Canada. Consequently, we have to reduce the associated risk. We haven't begun to exploit the American market opened to us through the Canada–U.S. Free Trade Agreement, and with a North American Free Trade Agreement soon to be completed, markets in Central and South America are becoming available.

Unfortunately, these new programs always seem to bring us back to the issue of financing. So, we need more capital and that probably means an equity issue. The question, however, becomes one of when and how?

Herbert Rudd—Senior Vice President

Herbert Rudd completed his schooling in the 10th grade, but left because his parents needed him to work on the family farm. Like most farmers, Rudd became an expert in home repairs. After he left home, he worked for a small home contractor until he decided to start his own construction business.

As senior vice president, Rudd's primary responsibility had been to represent the company at industry and trade fairs and exhibits both in Canada and abroad. He commented:

Oliver and I are the real entrepreneurs in this company. So, we make decisions primarily on gut-feel. But I do think I have a good business sense and that's what I use to guide me in my judgments.

Looking back, I feel our biggest mistake has been the operation of large plants such as we have in Chilliwack and Calgary. Right now, small competitors have lower overhead and transportation costs and a more competitive price.

The joint venture project is a fantastic concept with unlimited potential for our company. I can't give any firm projections, but something tells me that this is the right road to go on. Look at Mexico. There are more people earning over $50,000 per year than there are living in Canada. I expect a western hemisphere free trade agreement by the year 2000. Some people are worried about staffing international ventures. Heck, there's a lot of talent in this company that's just not being used. After all, a boy doesn't become a man until he has a man's job to do.

Looking at the products we manufacture, though, I can't honestly say if they're better than everybody else's. I know they do the same job. But, looking at them, there's nothing to distinguish them from your ordinary loaf of bread. I also think that we have a problem communicating to our customers. Our salesmen could do a better job finding out what our customers want and what new products we should be producing.

Another major concern of mine is that we're just a limited product company and there's too much risk in it. That's why I'm in favor of diversification. And I really don't care what sort of companies we acquire. We can always hire someone to run them for us.

Lucas Feck—Vice President (Marketing)

Lucas Feck received his bachelor's degree in commerce from a large American university. Upon graduation he joined a multinational chemical company that operated a subsidiary in Canada. Within four years, he became its general manager. After the subsidiary was purchased by another multinational conglomerate, Feck became disenchanted and resigned to start his own small business. Despite the new company's success, Feck became bored and sold his interest. He went back to school and earned an MBA. After graduating, he contacted several large executive placement firms looking for a position in a small to medium-sized growth business. This led to his being hired as marketing vice president for Fraser River Plastics.

Feck was by far the most avid promoter of expanding the company by means of acquisitions. Because Feck had been actively involved in a number of acquisition investigations that had failed to result in a concrete purchase, he had come to believe that the company's present structure was standing in the way of its ability to make acquisitions.

Our neck is really in the noose today because of the competition we're up against, especially in British Columbia. So I'm pretty strong on the idea of acquisitions. They're the key to our future. Personally, I believe we could run or manage any type of company—hotels, food processing, even steel corrugation plants. Others don't.

Take this Plasti-Weave acquisition. It's a natural combination with our business—plastics. But, better still, it represents a real chance for Fraser River to latch onto a proprietary item. It involves a new technology. We can get the jump on the industry and at the same time start moving out of "commodity product" lines.

As for the joint venture idea, I think we have some real problems because we've never considered: (1) who's going to be moving from Fraser River to staff the project, and (2) who we're going to find to fill the gaps created in Fraser River. I've been pushing Elinore on this point, but she keeps saying, "not to worry."

I think our biggest problem around here, however, has to be that senior management is perpetually caught up 110 percent with day-to-day tasks. I don't think that we'll ever find any new growth or good acquisitions as long as we don't free up some of our time. Elinore Wickham-Jones has a problem divorcing herself from finance and administration. She's also been spending a lot of her time these days on the joint venture project. . . That's her style though.

Oliver Farthingham's style, however, is to "represent" the company. He shouldn't be doing that as chairman of the company. He should be setting goals. After all, isn't the board responsible for the overall direction of the company? So what if "management" wants to do one thing. The board can just overturn it.

I do know this . . . I only get my kicks from challenges. Day-to-day work is a necessity, of course, but it's not challenging to me. I'm not interested in managing a division. I just want senior management responsibility and exciting work. Otherwise, I get bored.

Gunther Heinzman—Vice President (Production)

Heinzman was in charge of the company's six plants located in Chilliwack, Vancouver (Beaver), Prince Rupert, Calgary, Winnipeg, and Kamloops (Simcoe). Each plant had its own production manager reporting directly to Heinzman.

A native of Germany, Heinzman had emigrated to Canada with his parents. His first job was in a small manufacturing concern, working on the production line. Since then, he had spent most of his life in production.

I learned this business from the ground up. Every free moment I had during the day and at night was spent reading every trade journal I could get my hands on. But, I guess you could say that even today, I'm kept pretty busy just keeping my end under control.

I've never been a frivolous person. I suppose it comes from my German background. That's why I have always run a tight ship. If Elinore ever told me to cut costs, I wouldn't know where to start because I think we're already at maximum efficiency. And I've tried to instill this objective into each one of my plant managers. I've trained every one of them, except the Simcoe manager, and I'm very proud of them. Naturally, I'm a little more liberal today but I like to do things as cheap as possible. Sometimes, Elinore has to say to me: "Don't hold the penny so close to your eye Gunther, that you can't see the dollar behind it."

When I look at our acquisitions, there are some real lessons to be learned. I don't regret our purchase of the Prince Rupert plant because it has always supported itself. The manager there runs the company as if it was his own. After all, it used to be his own. Simcoe, however, should be a warning to future acquisitions. And, as for this Plasti-Weave deal, I won't say anything about it because I don't know anything about it. And that's because I haven't been involved in the discussions.

I'm not opposed to acquisitions but I'm naturally afraid of things that I don't know too much about. Elinore, of course, is more enthusiastic about acquisitions. Me, I'm a little more nervous about them. We have three different kinds of production processes here already—for injection, extrusion, and calendering—and I'm not sure how much more work I could handle.

As for this joint venture, Elinore is again playing her cards close to the vest and I don't think it's such a good idea. It's a big responsibility for her to be carrying alone. Besides, I'm a nationalist. Canada has been good to me and to this company. I think we could spend our dollars much wiser here."

Hamilton Technologies, Inc.

John A. Seeger, Bentley College
John H. Friar, Northeastern University
Raymond M. Kinnunen, Northeastern University

Some people in the industry call it a holy grail product. They just can't believe what this can do. Many experts—people who are deeply familiar with systems and software development—are stunned when they see "001" (pronounced "double—oh—one") working.

It was June 1993, and Margaret Hamilton sat in the cluttered first-floor kitchen/office of her two-story Victorian home in Cambridge, Massachusetts. Hamilton Technologies, Inc. (HTI), was bringing to market a powerful set of tools for automating the processes of systems engineering and software development. HTI's 001 product was, in lay terms, a software system for developing software—any kind of software. Margaret Hamilton described the fundamental problem that haunted the software industry:

> Large-scale software projects are notorious: they come in over budget, over deadline, under performance, and full of operating problems. These problems are inherent in the system engineering and software development process, where traditional techniques begin by defining system requirements with a myriad of disjointed and informal techniques. The result: limitations that inherently preclude high degrees of reliability and productivity. Problems are defined into the system and most of the developers' time goes into taking them out, usually by trial and error. The larger and more complex a project is, and the more people involved in it, the more likely it is to fail.

Instead of working to take problems *out* of a system under development, Hamilton Technologies' 001 prevented them from getting *in*. "001 concentrates on doing things right the first time, rather than fixing wrong things after the fact," said Margaret Hamilton. Using 001's own proprietary language to define the desired system, designers produced a complete specification. Then 001 automatically generated complete and fully production-ready code—for any kind of application. The result was a reliable, flexible, and reusable system. "If you need to change something," said Hamilton, "you alter the system specification and let 001 automatically generate the new code. No programmer ever touches the code."

The company was proud to point out that 001[1] had been used to define and generate itself. The current version of 001 encompassed approximately 750,000 lines

[1]"001" is a trademark of Hamilton Technologies, Inc., as are *development before the fact*, the 001 Axes Language, the Analyzer, the Resource Allocation Toolset, RAT, the OMap Editor, FMaps, TMaps, the Xecutor, and Requirements Traceability module (RT(x)).

of automatically generated code on each of three platforms. During its development and applications so far, 001 had automatically produced over 6 million lines of tested, working code—in "C" or in the defense systems language called Ada. As new customers required it, HTI could reconfigure the automatic code generator to let 001 produce its output in any programming language.

Hamilton Technologies in 1993 still operated on a shoestring budget, as it had from the day its doors opened. Through its first six years, HTI's sales were primarily from consulting and contract applications, rather than sales of the 001 product. Prospective customers who wanted demonstrations of 001's capabilities would occasionally fund a development project, and HTI's own staff would produce the desired system. "We were our own best beta site," said Margaret Hamilton. "Our own people would use the product; then they would work at enhancing it or making it easier to use. Real product sales only began late last year, when we released the Unix system with a windows and mouse Motif graphics interface. Now our people use 001 for developing applications and come back saying, 'This is awesome.'"

Projections for the future anticipated sales of $32 million for 1999 with a profit of $8.4 million. (Historic and projected financial results are shown in Table 1.) Margaret Hamilton pondered over the best route to follow to reach the rich future that seemed more and more possible as 001 attracted attention from the major corporations and government agencies that comprised its potential market. Given recent success in competitive product trials, she felt a market share of 20 percent was a realistic possibility. The firm would need working capital; Hamilton estimated some $1.5 to $3 million. Potential investors, however, demanded information about HTI's management team, and there was at yet no team to tell about. Some venture capitalists expressed willingness to bring in a traditional top management group to support her, but Hamilton differed over what would be best for her company:

> We are talking with some very well-known people—investors and managers who have shown outstanding success in the industry—in hardware or software or services. But none of their products were like 001. They solved different problems than the ones we have, and it's hard to tell whether they can see the differences. Experience with traditional systems approaches or organizations, for example, may not help much here. I've dealt with venture capitalists before; this is a crucial choice because traditional structures may not cut it for HTI.

MARGARET HAMILTON: A CAREER HISTORY

Margaret Hamilton arrived in Boston expecting to enroll in a doctoral program in mathematics, but instead took a job at MIT, where her earliest computer experiences came on a meteorology project working with (among others) one of Digital Equipment Corporation's first machines (a PDP-1). She worked at the SAGE air defense program at the Lincoln Laboratories, and from 1965 to 1976 she directed the development of on-board flight software for the Apollo and Space Shuttle programs at the Charles Stark Draper Laboratories, then attached to MIT. As Draper's youngest division director and the only woman to reach that level, she oversaw the work of 100 professional programmers and some 300 indirect staff, with an annual budget (in 1993 dollars) of some $300 million.

It was one of Hamilton's people at Division 15-Z who faced and resolved the crisis when the Apollo XIII space capsule suffered an on-board explosion, threatening its ability to return to earth. Within a 2-hour window, the programmer wrote new computer

Table 1   Hamilton Technologies, Inc., Unaudited Financial Results and Business Plan Projections   *(dollar amounts in thousands)*

Fiscal Year Ending 3/31	Consulting/ Applications Revenues	Product Revenues	Total Expenses	Net Income (Loss)
1987–93	$1,318†		1,507	(189)
1994	?	?	660	(4)
1995*		1,979	3,260	(1,281)
1996*		3,965	3,139	826
1997*		8,768	6,355	2,413
1998*		17,900	13,233	4,667
1999*		32,630	24,238	8,392

Note: Corresponding balance sheets were not used in routine company decision making.

* Projected results, based on capital influx in fiscal year 1994.

† Includes sales of beta and prerelease copies of 001 in later years.

code to plot a safe trajectory home, simulated the program, found a bug, corrected it, and simulated the operation again. When the crippled spacecraft emerged from behind the moon, Division 15-Z was ready with new instructions for manually firing the capsule's retrorockets to find its last-chance reentry window back to earth.

"That programmer was a hero," said Hamilton, "but he wasn't one of our most popular people with management. He was intensely creative, but he was a rebel against the system and when his picture hit Rolling Stone after Apollo XIII some people thought he didn't make the lab look good. Good computer people are often . . . well . . . a little different; many are more at home with machines than with people. They resist red tape and bureaucracy. For example, my staff thought my office needed a change. They bought paint and did the job themselves. They painted the office—all of it—black. They knew it was my favorite color," smiled Hamilton.

At Draper Lab, Hamilton studied the software development process as well as the immediate problems of guidance and control. She monitored the errors that delayed large-scale system development and measured the costs of correcting them. A major share of the budget, she found, went to correcting mistakes that never should have been made, and then to correcting the corrections. Proper system development, she felt, would arrive at a full set of definitions and specifications before coding began, avoid the errors instead of tackling them after the fact.

HIGHER ORDER SOFTWARE, INC.

In 1976, Hamilton left Draper Labs and formed her own company, Higher Order Software, Inc. (HOS), to develop a set of tools to assist system designers. Her product, called "Use.It," was the first entrant in the new computer-aided software engineering (CASE) industry; annual sales had reached $5 million by 1984. At its peak, the company employed 100 people and its engineering-oriented product had an installed base of 80 VAX customers. Hamilton had raised $15 million and had the involvement of several major venture capital firms; she retained approximately 30 percent of the stock. Looking toward the future, her board of directors pressed for conversion of Use.It to the commercial environment, which was oriented toward IBM mainframes and minicomputers.

For several years, Electronic Data Systems, the software/services firm of H. Ross Perot, had expressed an interest in buying HOS. Hamilton, sensing impending changes, responded to EDS in 1984, when the giant firm had sales of some $900 million per year and profits of $80 million. Hamilton described the sequence of events:

> We shook hands on an agreement and drank a champagne toast: EDS would buy us for $37 million. Some of my board members had been disappointed to find I would go below their concept of a $100 million value for the company. And then EDS got into its own acquisition talks with General Motors. When the dust settled, EDS said their own technical people could develop a system like Use.It for only $30 million, so that was the highest they would pay for HOS. So much for "done deals." EDS did try to develop a system similar to ours, I think, but they never brought one to market. After the EDS deal fell through, the board brought in new management to run day-to-day operations. They insisted we stop developing VAX-based software and concentrate instead on the IBM market.

A year and a half after Hamilton was removed from daily management, she left HOS. Within another two years, essentially all the company's VAX customers were gone and the IBM system had found no buyers. HOS went into Chapter 7 bankruptcy proceedings, rendering Margaret Hamilton's HOS stock and loans owed her by the company worthless.

HAMILTON TECHNOLOGIES, INC.

HTI's Cambridge offices were in Margaret Hamilton's home, a nondescript gray-green Victorian house whose front stairs were slightly unsteady underfoot. No sign announced this was home to a company. Just inside the front door, an ornate bentwood coat tree stood beside four stone rabbits. On opposite sides of the door, two theater seats (folded up) were available for waiting guests. A grand mahogany staircase led upward from the entry, but the first three steps were piled with paper. A limp stuffed leopard occupied the top of the ornately carved newel post, and a large German Shepherd dog named Clark ("nearly always friendly") greeted newcomers. Archways to the left and right sides of the entry hall led to large rooms filled with books, boxes, papers, desks, and computers. An upright piano, topped with art deco sculptures, lined the hallway past the butler's pantry to the kitchen/conference room/office of Margaret Hamilton. Here a huge Benjamin Franklin cast iron stove, dated 1859 and recessed into a ceiling-high brick fireplace wall, dominated the room. "They built the house around that, I think," she said.

HTI was founded in 1986, with no initial capital. For its first two years, as Hamilton and her people labored to develop the new 001 technology, Hamilton paid royalties to her prior firm. She admitted to having sold personal possessions to start the new venture, and seven years later it still ran in a lean mode of operations. Many employees were paid little cash—as little as they could afford; the balance was in stock options. The company's standard response to sales inquiries from out-of-town prospects was an invitation to Cambridge, to see what 001 could do; to gain a full understanding of the system, the prospects' people could attend HTI's 1-week training course, at $3,500 per person. (Exhibit 1 shows the training course registration form.) Only if the interested firm paid all travel expenses in advance would HTI consider sending people on the road, even for the largest prospects.

Exhibit 1   The 001™ Training Course

001 seamlessly integrates all phases of system engineering and software development from requirements to fully production ready code generation.

TOPICS:
- Introduction to the concepts of 001 technology
- Learning to design any system using 001 technology
- Modeling for real-time and distributed application
- Capitalizing on reusability with structures
- Making the most of object-oriented techniques
- Using the 001 Tool Suite
- Automatic generation of fully production ready source code
- Regenerating a specification into multiple languages (e.g., C to Ada)
- Performance testing of a 001-developed system
- Team development of a 001 system

REGISTRATION FORM (All classes are 5-day and held in the Boston area)

☐ Dec. 7–11   ☐ Jan. 18–22   ☐ Feb. 22–26

Dates and course availability subject to change. Private courses for individual organizations are also available. Courses should be scheduled no later than 30 days in advance. We recommend scheduling 60 days in advance to secure the reservation.

Name: _____

Organization: _____

Address: _____

Number of 001 Training Course Attendees*: _____ @ $3,500.00 per person

Purchase Order Number (or equivalent): _____

Authorized Signature**: _____

Title: _____

Phone: _____

* Check here if an exclusive course is preferred: ☐

** By signing and submitting this form, the above-named organization accepts the terms and conditions above. Tuition is due no later than two weeks prior to the course start date.

Mail or Fax to: Hamilton Technologies, Inc., 17 Inman Street, Cambridge, MA 02139
(617) 492-0058   Fax (617) 492-1727

In June 1993, eight full-time employees and a couple of part-timers constituted the staff. In the Boston area, HTI had experimented with a full-time salesperson—a man who had retired after a successful career running software sales for a large consulting firm. In Albuquerque, another salesperson—a former 001 customer—represented HTI to the government research laboratories and defense contractors of the area.

Support functions for the business—accounting, legal, promotional, and professional work—were sometimes handled by "friends of the firm," who took full compensation in stock options because they knew Margaret Hamilton and had faith in her eventual success. "I do everything I can without help, and then ask the lawyers to bless it," said the CEO of HTI. "At this size, it's easier to get things done that way." She estimated her own time involvement at approximately 40 hours per week in marketing and sales, and at least another 40 hours in matters relating to technical development and project management.

Margaret Hamilton herself handled most telephone inquiries from prospects who had heard of 001 by word-of-mouth, had read about it, or had attended conferences where HTI presented papers. Incoming calls were screened by the secretary, Hannah Gold, who handled routine requests herself but was free to interrupt Hamilton when important calls required it. Detailed responses to requests for proposals were handled by the technical staff, as were customer support, product demonstrations, and training sessions.

THE INDUSTRY

Computer-aided systems engineering in 1993 was a thriving, churning industry without a standard definition. System design approaches called *artificial intelligence, expert systems,* and *object-oriented design* were treated as separate industries by some analysts, while others considered them part of computer-aided systems engineering or what was known as integrated CASE. Since the 001 product line combined elements from several of these different technical worlds, analysts frequently had difficulty classifying the company. "The industry is like a moving target," said Margaret Hamilton. "New-sounding buzzwords or fads come in every two years or so, and we have to show how our product is related to the newest approach."

The industry had grown as system designers and software developers generally recognized the same problems Margaret Hamilton had analyzed in the Draper Laboratory two decades earlier: Large-scale software projects defied management, regardless of the resources devoted to their accomplishment. The traditional sequence of steps in the development process (shown in Exhibit 2) was often referred to as the "waterfall model." It resulted in problems such as lack of traceability, internal inconsistencies, and incompatibilities—created in the early steps—being implemented in code, resulting in extensive testing and maintenance in the last step.

Erin Murphy, associated editor of the *IEEE Spectrum,* described the traditional process:

Whatever the programming technique used, software development tends to follow the basic waterfall mode: requirements, specification, design, implementation, testing, and maintenance. The requirements are usually stated in narrative fashion, rather than in a formal computer language, and express what the software must be able to do. They are translated into functional specifications, preferably written in a computer executable language. The design encapsulates the structure of the software system, detailing how the different parts of the program are connected. Then the design is turned into code, written in a computer language, and tested to ferret out bugs. But it is not until the maintenance phase—which consists primarily of fixing errors and implementing changes in the design—that the real work begins; it generally accounts for 60 to

Exhibit 2 Software Development Process: Traditional Waterfall Model

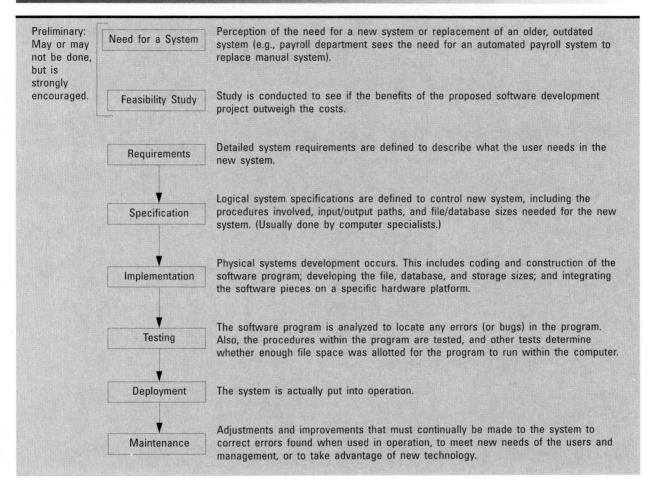

Preliminary: May or may not be done, but is strongly encouraged.

Need for a System — Perception of the need for a new system or replacement of an older, outdated system (e.g., payroll department sees the need for an automated payroll system to replace manual system).

Feasibility Study — Study is conducted to see if the benefits of the proposed software development project outweigh the costs.

Requirements — Detailed system requirements are defined to describe what the user needs in the new system.

Specification — Logical system specifications are defined to control new system, including the procedures involved, input/output paths, and file/database sizes needed for the new system. (Usually done by computer specialists.)

Implementation — Physical systems development occurs. This includes coding and construction of the software program; developing the file, database, and storage sizes; and integrating the software pieces on a specific hardware platform.

Testing — The software program is analyzed to locate any errors (or bugs) in the program. Also, the procedures within the program are tested, and other tests determine whether enough file space was allotted for the program to run within the computer.

Deployment — The system is actually put into operation.

Maintenance — Adjustments and improvements that must continually be made to the system to correct errors found when used in operation, to meet new needs of the users and management, or to take advantage of new technology.

80 percent of the time and money spent on a program, a far larger share than for hardware.[2]

The traditional, brute force development approach was vividly described in a *Wall Street Journal* story[3] on Microsoft's new operating system, Windows NT; 200 people in three organizational units, each with 5 to 10 subdivisions, had fought continuously among themselves for four years in producing 4.3 million lines of code at a cost of $150 million, missing their deadline by six months. Even within 60 days of its revised shipping deadline, the NT team was finding hundreds of new bugs each week. Not all would be fixed before the software's release.

Efforts to automate the development process in the early 1980s sought to replicate the waterfall process, (see Exhibit 3), but they failed because the whole process

[2]Erin E. Murphy, "Software R&D: From an Art to a Science," *IEEE Spectrum*, October 1990, p. 44.
[3]G. Pascal Zachary, "Agony and Ecstasy of 200 Code Writers Beget Windows NT." *The Wall Street Journal*, May 26, 1993, p. 1.

Exhibit 3 The Conventional Approach to Computer-Aided Software Engineering (CASE)

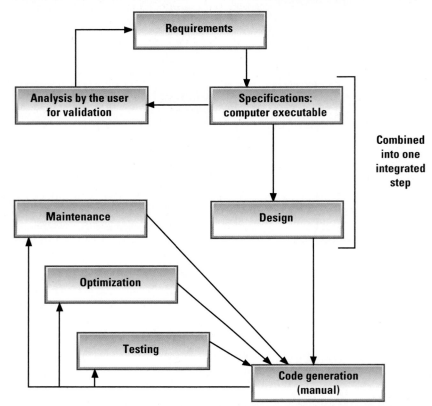

Source: Adapted from "Software R&D: From an Art to a Science," *IEEE Spectrum*, October 1990.

proved "too big a job for most tool vendors," wrote Jessica Keyes in *Corporate Computing*. She continued:

> So CASE companies began biting off chewable chunks, or modules, that attempted to break down CASE functionality into more manageable units. These modules were assigned names such as "upper CASE," which concentrated on the analytical and design components of the system development process, and "lower CASE," which tackled code generation. But the general lament of users was—and still is—that these disparate components refuse to talk to each other.[4]

By 1985, a number of firms had introduced linkages between various CASE tools under names such as *integrated CASE, technical CASE*, or *SuperCASE*. But still, wrote Keyes in 1992, "fewer than 15 percent of IS shops use CASE tools . . . and

[4]Jessica Keyes, "The Case for Super CASE: Programs That Write Themselves," *Corporate Computing*, October 1992, pp. 183–86.

worse, a mere 5 percent of programmers use CASE effectively." In mid-1993, according to Margaret Hamilton, several competitors offered tools to do parts of the system development process, but none had an integrated "suite" of tools that could automate the entire design cycle.

A 1990 census of the CASE industry by International Data Corporation (IDC) reported a 45 percent average growth rate in aggregate revenues and a 62 percent compounded annual growth in installations between 1984 and 1989. The census found 83 vendors with 101 separate CASE products and an estimated base of 380,000 installations by 1990. The average installation cost was over $32,000, and cumulative industry revenues to date were over $580 million. (Exhibit 4 shows the detail of the census.)

Volpe, Welty & Company, a San Francisco investment banking firm that followed the CASE industry, defined nine separate segments of the CASE market. In a May 1991 report, the firm's Paul Bloom summarized the market status of all nine segments (see Exhibit 5) and listed the leading suppliers in each. In March 1992, *Datamation* commented on the "stunning array of product types" available in CASE offerings. Elizabeth Lindholm wrote:

> Integrating these tools so that they work with each other—not to mention merely locating the ones that will run on your computer system—can be a considerable challenge. To make the task of investigating CASE a little easier, we've compiled below a resource list of more than 400 CASE products and the operating systems on which they run.[5]

Datamation then listed 167 firms, 9 of which offered 10 or more different products. Hamilton Technologies did not appear in the list. In September 1992, Hamilton Technologies was included as one of 24 "representative Knowledge-Based Development Tool" suppliers in a *Software Magazine* article.[6] In January 1993, HTI was one of five vendors listed as supplying "Integrated Object-Oriented CASE products" in *Object-Oriented Strategies*.[7] In April 1993, *CASE Trends* included 001 as 1 of 16 "representative Ada CASE tools."[8] Hamilton Technologies was the only vendor appearing in all three lists. One other company appeared in two; with those two exceptions, the three listings seemed to show three different populations of software development firms.

CASE Associates, Inc., a market research and consulting firm in Clackamas, Oregon, estimated the 1993 worldwide market for Integrated Project Support Environment and I-CASE tools at $800 million in the information systems market and at $600 million in the aerospace, defense, and commercial engineering market. The firm believed this segment of the CASE industry would grow at 39 percent per year until 1997, reaching $5.7 billion in total worldwide sales at that point. (see Exhibit 6).

THE HTI PRODUCT: 001 ────────────────────────────

HTI departed from the industry's traditional practice of software development. In her work on Apollo, Hamilton had found that approximately 75 percent of the errors stemmed from ambiguities in the software. As she continued to develop the

---

[5]Elizabeth Lindholm, "A World of CASE Tools," *Datamation*, March 1, 1992, pp. 75–81.
[6]Jessica Keyes, "Knowledge-Based Systems and CASE Converging," *Software Magazine*, September 1992, p. 47.
[7]Paul Harmon, ed., *Object-Oriented Strategies*, vol. III, no. 1, Cutter Information Corporation, January, 1993, p. 11.
[8]Charles Shrontz, "Ada's History and CASE Future," *CASE Trends*, April 1993, p. 52.

Exhibit 4   Worldwide CASE Installations of U.S. Vendors, through 1990

Vendor	Product Name	Date Intro	Installs thru 1989*	Installs thru 1990*	% Install in U.S.	Average Install Value	1990 Total CASE Sales
ADPAC Computing Language	Design	1984	230	240	NA	$ 25,000	$ 250,000
ADPAC Computing Language	DFCP	1981	100	112	80	$ 17,500	$ 210,000
ADPAC Computing Language	PMSS	1984	100	111	65	$ 37,000	$ 407,000
Advanced Logical Software, Inc.	Anatool Workbench	1987	1500	2000	70	$ 710	$ 355,000
Advanced Tech. Int'l	SuperCASE	1988	51	72	51	$ 48,500	$ 1,018,500
AGS Mngt Systems	First-CASE	1987	200	220	90	$ 5,000	$ 100,000
Andersen Consulting	Foundation-Design/1	1988	585	1000	48	$ 17,000	$ 7,055,000
Andersen Consulting	Foundation-Install/1	1988	55	110	51	$206,000	$11,330,000
Andersen Consulting	Foundation-Method/1	1988	588	1000	53	$ 15,000	$ 8,180,000
Arthur D. Little	IRMA	1985	40	45	40	$ 20,000	$ 100,000
Asyst.Technologies Inc.	Developer	1985	3000	4500	60	$ 8,500	$ 9,750,000
Atherton Technology	Software Backplane	1988	200	300	100	$ 13,450	$ 1,345,000
Bachman Info Sys. Inc.	Data Admin./Analyst	1987	350	1050	NA	$ 25,000	$17,500,000
Cadre Technologies	Teamwork	1985	13090	16000	75	$ 8,000	$17,460,000
Cadre Technologies	Testing for Embedded Sys	1984	4000	4800	75	$ 14,000	$11,200,000
Cadware Group Ltd.	Sylva-Sys. Developer	1984	4900	5100	60	$ 2,000	$ 2,400,000
Caseware	Amplify Control	1987	30	50	100	$ 35,000	$ 700,000
CGI Sys. Inc.	PacLAN	1989	1	50	50	$ 140	$ 6,860
CGI Sys. Inc.	PacBASE	1983	630	690	20	$235,000	$14,100,000
Chen & Associates	ERmodeler	1986	275	370	64	$ 495	$ 47,025
Clear Software Inc.	Clear for C	1989	7000	10000	90	$ 170	$ 510,000
Clear Software Inc.	Clear for DBase	1987	10000	15000	90	$ 170	$ 850,000
Cognos Inc.	Powerhouse Link Excelerator	1987	45	50	NA	$ 2,000	$ 10,000
Computer Associates	CA-O8: Architect	1986	855	1000	54	$ 8,400	$ 1,218,000
Computer Associates	Design Generator	1988	100	150	90	$ 995	$ 49,750
Computer Systems Advisors	Picture Oriented Engineering	1988	2000	2500	80	$ 850	$ 425,000
Cortex	Corvision	1987	500	600	70	$ 42,000	$ 4,200,000
Interport Software Corp.	Intercase Reverse Eng. Workbench	1989	1	NA	100	$ 98,000	
DEFT	DEFT	1986	1050	1200	80	$ 3,045	$ 456,750
Easyspec, Inc.	Object Plus	1986	55	60	100	$ 13,200	$ 66,000
Eden Systems Corp.	Q/Auditor	1985	75	82	89	$ 33,272	$ 232,904
Expertware	CVF	1986	105	150	62	$ 30,000	$ 1,350,000
Future Tech Sys., Inc.	Envision	1987	500	750	75	$ 6,500	$ 1,625,000
Hamilton Technologies, Inc.	001	1990					
Impulse Engineering	Documenter/Diagrammer	1987	2100	2200	90	$ 165	$ 16,500
Index Technology	Excelerator	1984	19648	24000	62	$ 4,575	$19,910,400
Integrated Systems, Inc.	Auto Code	1988	90	150	75	$ 27,000	$ 1,620,000
Interactive Development	Software Thru Pictures	1984	2400	3000	82	$ 8,700	$ 4,020,000
Interactive Software Eng.	Eiffel	1986	1200	2000	30	$ 3,035	$ 2,428,000
Intermetrics, Inc.	Byron	1984	105	120	67	$ 11,000	$ 165,000
D. Appleton Co.	IDEF Leverage	1985	55	65	95	$ 45,300	$ 453,000
Knowledgeware, Inc.	IEW	1986	25753	35000	60	$ 3,157	$29,192,779
Knowledgeware, Inc.	ADW	1990		10000	NA	NA	
Language Technology	Recoder	1984	144	230	90	$110,000	$ 9,460,000
LBMS, Inc.	Automate Plus	1987	7500	12000	40	$ 2,000	$ 9,000,000
M. Bryce and Assoc.	Pride-ISEM	1971	1400	1500	50	$100,000	$10,000,000
Magec Software	Magec	1981	464	570	98	$ 10,000	$ 1,060,000
McDonnell-Douglas	Prokit Workbench	1987	2500	3000	85	$ 8,500	$ 3,250,000
McDonnell-Douglas	SC Draw	1986	900	1200	90	$ 800	$ 180,000
McDonnell-Douglas	DED Draw	1984	2400	2700	95	$ 800	$ 180,000
Menlo Business Systems	Foundation Vista	1987	300	410	85	$ 54,000	$ 5,940,000
Mentor Graphics	CASE Station	1989	100	200	50	$ 9,000	$ 900,000
Mentor Graphics	TekCASE	1985	2100	2500	80	$ 5,040	$ 2,016,000

(continued)

Exhibit 4 (concluded)

Vendor	Product Name	Date Intro	Installs thru 1989*	Installs thru 1990*	% Install in U.S.	Average Install Value	1990 Total CASE Sales
Meta Software Corp.	Meta Design	1986	6500	9000	80	$ 300	$ 750,000
Meta Systems	Rslipsa	1983	500	500	90	$ 55,000	
Meta Systems	Structured Architect	1988	400	650	90	$ 1,595	$ 398,750
Mcrofocus	Workbench	1985	11000	17000	55	$ 3,000	$ 18,000,000
Oracle Corp.	CASE	1985	2400	2500	45	$ 17,750	$ 3,550,000
Pansophic	Telon	1983	600	750	58	$250,000	$ 37,500,000
PC-Systems	Model-S	1988	500	700	50	$ 149	$ 29,800
Popkin	System Architect	1988	2700	4000	81	$ 1,200	$ 1,560,000
Programmed Intelligence	Intelligent Query	1985	45000	60000	95	$ 260	$ 3,900,000
Promod Inc.	Promod Family	1985	437	750	40	$ 27,500	$ 8,607,500
Quantitative Tech.	Math Advantage	1986	1500	2000	98	$ 1,925	$ 962,500
Quicktek Corp	Q-Coner	1988	100	150	70	$ 350	$ 17,500
Rand Info Systems	Rand Devel Center	1985	40	48	85	$ 50,000	$ 400,000
Ready Systems	Card Tools	1987	425	600	50	$ 33,000	$ 5,775,000
Reasoning Systems, Inc.	Refne	1985	125	150	NA	$ 16,200	$ 405,000
Sage Software	APS Devel. Conter	1984	328	508	77	$124,500	$ 22,410,000
Sage Software	Config. Mgmt. Control	1987	4360	7360	80	$ 2,210	$ 6,630,000
Sage Software	Other Products*	1988	2050	3650	72	$ 1,800	$ 2,880,000
Sandura Intelligent Sys.	Prodoc	1988	110	120	50	$ 4,800	$ 48,000
Sherpa Corp.	Design Mngt. Systems	1986	158	300	70	$ 80,000	$ 8,520,000
Softlab	Maestro	1975	26000	29000	20	$ 12,000	$ 36,000,000
Softool Corp.	Change and Config. Control	1982	1400	1800	85	$ 33,000	$ 13,200,000
Software AG	Predict CASE	1990		55	10	$175,000	$ 9,625,000
Software Design Tools	X-Tools	1983	5000	6100	NA	$ 850	$ 715,000
Software Innovations	Proto-C	1982	6	8	100	$ 1,200	$ 2,400
Software Prod. and Services	Epos	1980	3200	3500	25	$ 12,000	$ 3,600,000
Software Prod. and Services	Respec	1989	127	50	NA	$ 6,000	$ 138,000
Software Research Inc.	Fasport, D8M	1984	2500	3500	90	$ 1,000	$ 1,000,000
Software Research Inc.	Microcaps	1984	2950	2950	90	$ 1,200	
Spectrum Int'l	Spectrum Manager	1987	42	50	50	$100,000	$ 800,000
Starsys. Inc.	MacBubbles	1987	140	200	85	$ 730	$ 43,800
Structosoft	TurboCASE	1989	500	700	80	$ 950	$ 190,000
SLN	Network Software Environment	1987	12000	18000	70	$ 1,250	$ 7,500,000
Synon	Sysnon/2E	1986	1500	2500	30	$ 48,000	$ 48,000,000
Synoptic Consult. Inc.	Rapid Automatic Programmer	1986	540	560	50	$ 2,995	$ 59,900
Syscorp. Int'l	Microstep	1988	170	250	90	$ 6,000	$ 480,000
Synthesis Computer Tech.	Syntek CASE/AP	1986	132	200	1	$ 43,000	$ 2,924,000
Tasc	Adagraph	1986	50	55	96	$ 10,000	$ 50,000
Telesoft	SDT	1989	250	NA	5	$ 8,150	
Texas Instruments, Inc.	Information Engin. Facility	1985	200	320	60	$300,000	$ 36,000,000
Transform Logic Corp.	Transform	1985	60	75	90	$225,000	$ 3,375,000
Unisys	Linc	1982	5130	7100	NA	$ 31,330	$ 61,720,100
Varnet Corp.	Power Tools	1983	5000	5200	50	$ 7,600	$ 1,520,000
Viasoft, Inc.	Via/Insight	1986	400	600	80	$ 75,000	$ 15,000,000
Viasoft, Inc.	Smart Test	1989	245	NA	80	$ 55,000	
Visible Sys. Corp.	Visible Anal. Workbench	1985	7000	10000	70	$ 1,025	$ 3,075,000
Xanalog	Graphics To Fortran Generator	1986	60	100	70	$ 7,000	$ 280,000
Yourdon, Inc.	Anal. Designer Toolkit	1986	35000	5500	63	$ 1,400	$ 2,800,000
Yourdon, Inc.	Cradle	1989	35	50	11	$ 75	$ 1,125
TOTALS			278640	380468		$32,168†	$582,742,843

* These figures are total installations through 1989 and 1990 to date, not for that single year.

† This figure, $32,168, is the average installation value of all CASE vendors.

Source: International Data Corporation Software Marketing Planning Services, 1990 Computer-Aided Software Engineering (CASE) Census. Used with permission.

Exhibit 5   CASE Market Segmentation

Market Segment	Nature of Problem	Example of Problem	Opportunity	Penetration of Opportunity		Representative Vendors
				Now	In Three Years	
Planning, analysis, and design	Initial errors doom system to high maintenance or failure	BofA spends $50 million and fails to implement trust system	Front-end CASE products, 40%+ savings	Low $445 million	High $935 million	KnowledgeWare, Intersolv, Texas Instruments, Softlab
Application code generators	Hand coding causes errors and slow development	Modest improvement in programmer productivity over past 10 years	Back-end CASE products, 50% savings	Very low $100 million	Medium $220 million	Intersolv, Pansophic, IBM
Maintenance/reengineering	Large corporations spend 70% of programmer resources on maintenance	Every 6 months a TWA flight does not have a flight crew	Reengineering products, 30%+ savings	Very low $55 million	Medium $185 million	VIASOFT, XA Systems, Language Technology, BACHMAN
4GL-CASE	Complex design of transaction processing application	End-users don't get systems they need	Specialized development, 50%+ savings	Medium $775 million	High $1,515 million	Cognos, Oracle, Progress, Ingres, Unify, Cortex, Synon
Knowledge-based expert systems	Scarcity of experts, lengthens activities, allows mistakes	Three Mile Island nuclear power plant accident	Knowledge-based systems, no economical alternative	Low $310 million	Medium $680 million	AICorp, Alon, Carnegie Group, Inference Corp. IntelliCorp
Technical CASE	Large system, complexity	B-1 bomber—$1.2 billion to upgrade capability	Front-end CASE, 40% savings	Low $150 million	High $385 million	Cadre, IDE, Ready Systems, Integrated Systems
Cross Lifecycle	Difficult to manage large systems	New systems are always late	Required to manage large systems	Low $130 million	Medium $320 million	ABT, Intersolv, LEGENT, Softool
Languages and development environments	Too many mistakes in hand coding	Code error makes AT&T long distance network crash	Interactive development, 20%+ savings	High $310 million	High $615 million	LIANT, Rational Micro Focus, Saber Microtec Research
Object-oriented programming	Virtually no improvement in programmer productivity	Unacceptable time to market for new products	Code reuse, 50%+ savings	Very low $50 million	Medium $170 million	AT&T, Digitalk, IntelliCorp, ParcPlace

Source: Volpe, Welty & Company, CASE Industry Investment Report, May 1991.

Exhibit 6 Worldwide CASE Market Results and Projections *(dollar amounts in millions)*

Segment	1990	1991	1992	1993 ...	1997	1992–97* CAGR
Information Systems (IS) Market Only						
Analysis and design tools†	300	340	360	450 ...	900	20%
Code and application generators includes 4GLs‡	520	600	650	800 ...	2,000	25%
IPSEs and I-CASE tools§	400	500	600	800 ...	3,300	41%
Editors, compilers, debuggers, testing tools	750	900	1,050	1,300 ...	2,700	21%
Reverse/reengineering tools	85	105	135	190 ...	600	35%
Total segment	2,055	2,445	2,795	3,540	9,500	28%
Aerospace, Defense, and Commercial Engineering (ADE) Market Only						
Analysis and design tools	170	210	250	300 ...	800	26%
Code and application generators	110	150	200	250 ...	1,000	38%
IPSEs and I-CASE tools	300	400	500	600 ...	2,400	37%
Editors, compilers, debuggers, testing tools	500	600	750	900 ...	2,400	26%
Reverse/reengineering tools	15	15	35	55 ...	220	45%
Total segment	1,095	1,385	1,735	2,105	6,820	31%
IS + ADE = Total Market						
Analysis and design tools	470	550	610	750 ...	1,700	23%
Code and application generators	630	750	850	1,050 ...	3,000	29%
IPSEs and I-CASE tools	700	900	1,100	1,400 ...	5,700	39%
Editors, compilers, debuggers, testing tools	1,250	1,500	1,800	2,200 ...	5,100	23%
Reverse/reengineering tools	100	130	170	245 ...	820	37%
Total market	3,150	3,830	4,530	5,645 ...	16,320	29%

* CAGR = Compounded annual growth rate

† Analysis and design tools include structured, object-oriented, and all other methods.

‡ Code and application generations includes client/server, GUI development tools, 4GLs, AI, and traditional code application generators.

§ IPSE and I-CASE tools include integrated toolset environments, frameworks, tool integration utilities, repositories, and individual tools for process management, software project management, configuration management, requirements management, and documentation management. If I-CASE tools include analysis and design and code generation, they are counted here and not in their respective categories.

Source: © 1993 CASE Associates Inc. Used by permission.

theory, Hamilton recognized that real-world systems had traditionally been developed "after the fact," as analysts and engineers sought ways around roadblocks they discovered when the system was tested.

In her earlier research she realized that the solution of one serious problem (i.e., the prevention of most errors) was in the way a system is defined. She continued to work on ways of defining systems such as to address other major issues of systems engineering and software development as well. These issues included those having to do with flexibility; integration; traceability; capitalizing on automation, open architecture, and distributed processing to the fullest extent possible; reusability; and object-oriented thinking. The result was a new paradigm for defining and developing software-based systems that addressed these issues with properties of the 001 language. HTI's 001 was based on this new philosophy: development *before* the fact.

Exhibit 7, which may be contrasted with Exhibit 3, shows an example of the fundamental difference: with 001, changes or corrections were not made to the code, but to the original statements of system requirements. When those requirements were changed, 001 generated new code to implement the newly defined system.

HTI's literature stressed the major customer benefit from the use of 001: vastly increased productivity from everyone involved in the software development process. "Documented gains have varied from 10:1 to over 50:1 when compared to traditional developmental techniques," one leaflet said. A book author was quoted as saying about 001:

> [I]t makes sure that from the very beginning, system definitions exclude ambiguities and that module interfaces can't clash . . . a miraculous methodology.[9]

HTI's price sheet (Exhibit 8) gave the list price of 001 as $24,000 per seat, while maintenance was priced at 20 percent of the then-going price for each year. For each seat purchased, the customer would receive a tape or disk containing the 001 system and its documentation—all the software needed for a single user. A three-seat license would permit a maximum of three simultaneous users. Maintenance included updates as well as the assurance of round-the-clock telephone support. Margaret Hamilton estimated that one customer support engineer was needed for each 10 seats in the field.

A brief overview of how the product was used is given in the Appendix (see page 428).

HTI MARKETING

"We Don't Sell Monoliths the Way They Sell Soap," shouted a fall, 1990 full-page ad announcing 001's prerelease on its first platform, the VAX/VMS. The ad called the product "an indestructible, prescient, self-generating and fully operational monolith," and invited interested prospects to visit Cambridge to learn about 001. "Forget the glossy brochure," the ad said. "We don't have one." Only in the third day of its training program would most people begin to believe the product claims, the ad said. But by the fifth day, trainees would have created their own new application programs. In 1993, HTI's approach to selling still relied on prospects attending the training session. No customer could buy 001 without first going through the training course, and HTI was proud of gaining commitments from virtually all of the companies that sent people to its training sessions.

Target Market Diversity

Because it was such a general-purpose set of tools, 001 could be targeted at a huge number of submarkets, all with quite different characteristics. Each submarket might have its own technological history and biases, its own diffusion process for new innovations, its own advertising media, and its own preferences for platforms, languages, and so on. For example, government aerospace organizations and the military originally tended toward the VAX/VMS platform but now required Unix, the Ada language, and the arcane documentation of Department of Defense Standard

---

[9] Max Schindler, *Computer-Aided Software Design* (New York: John Wiley & Sons, 1990).

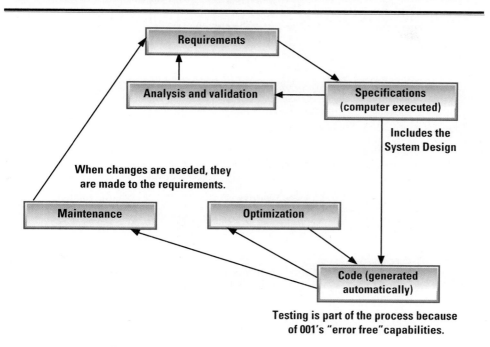

Exhibit 7   The 001 Approach to Fully Integrated CASE

Adapted from "Software R&D: From an Art to a Science," *IEEE Spectrum*, October 1990.

2167A. A marketing program geared toward this environment would mean little to major organizations in finance and banking, insurance, consumer product manufacturing, or health care, where documentation standards were entirely different and DOS or OS/2 or NT might be the required platforms. (Exhibit 9 lists target market segments as defined by HTI in 1992.)

In the face of this diversity, Hamilton Technologies had to decide on how to position its product. Potential investors in the firm asked for assurances of "focus"; they wanted to see programs concentrating HTI's limited resources on specific market opportunities. To Margaret Hamilton, this presented a problem:

> It's virtually impossible to forecast what segment of the market may take off first. The people calling us are the leading edge in their own markets, whatever those markets might be. They're the innovators. Should I refuse to talk to the systems director of a major bank, just because I'm focusing today on aerospace? Besides, the engineering and commercial markets are merging.

Enterprise Selling

Broad adoption of a fundamentally new approach to systems development within a major organization could only happen if top-level management recognized that new techniques could help the organization fulfill its strategic mission or could provide it with a real competitive advantage. This kind of selling takes place at senior management levels, and it was the kind of selling that occupied much of the time of Margaret Hamilton and Ron Hackler, HTI's director of development.

Exhibit 8   001™ Pricing (U.S.)—Effective October 1, 1992

Seat license	$24,000 (3-seat minimum purchase)
Includes	One set of 001 User Manuals C or Ada target language RAT X Window/Motif interface
Maintenance	20% of the then-current license price per year
Platforms supported	HP 700 Series, Sun 3, Sun SPARC, Solbourne, IBM RS6K, DECstation, VAX/VMS
Site/Corporate license	Available
Training	
5-day basic course	$3,500 per person
Internships	$3,500 per person/week
Consulting	
Short-term	$1,500 per person/day plus expenses
Long-term	Available

17 Inman Street, Cambridge, MA 02139 USA   617-492-0058   Fax 617-492-1727
200 State Street, Boston, MA 02109 USA   617-492-0058   Fax 617-720-4546
7328 Lew Wallace Drive NE, Albuquerque, NM 87109 USA   505-821-7029   Fax 505-821-8102

Many of the major customers targeted by Margaret Hamilton had already sent people through the HTI training program. Some—including beta test sites Martin Marietta and IBM—were conducting product demonstrations and training programs of their own, inside their organizations. Very large organizations like these might have hundreds or even thousands of analysts and programmers at work on complex systems. The potential savings to these companies from improved productivity and reliability were immense, but the required organizational and financial investments in the new tools were also large and investments at this scale were not made casually.

Typically, the technical people who saw the product's benefits did not control the purchase decisions for the enterprise as a whole. They might have purchase authority for specific programs or subunits of their organizations, but outside their areas the choice of technology fell to others. Sales on the enterprise level faced two distinct barriers: headquarters system development people would have to reject much of their own traditional knowledge about technology in order to adopt 001, and then financial people would have to commit the required funds. HTD's minimum purchase (for three design seats) was $72,000; a major customer might face an investment of many millions. Thus, the sale of a few design seats to technical staff did not automatically lead to a customer's adopting 001 as an organizationwide design approach. Margaret Hamilton commented:

> Purchase decisions for 001 are not made overnight. Some prospects take several years. One major customer was near closing, but then the key inside person left the company. In effect, we have to start over there. There is a side benefit to that, however, because the same person is now considering 001 for his new company—a big organization that hadn't been a prospect before. There is a lot of mobility in this industry, and people who know us tend to spread the word. There is a common problem, though, in selling to such large operations. We

Exhibit 9   Potential Vertical and Horizontal Markets for 001

Horizontal Markets

Computer platform and language
independence are the key.

PCs, Workstations, Minicomputers, and Mainframes

1. IBM
2. Digital (Alpha)
3. SUN
4. NCR
5. Hewlett-Packard
6. CRAY
7. APPLE Macintosh
8. Windows NT
9. OS/2

Software Development Vendors (System Integrators)

1. EDS (GM)
2. Boeing
3. CCA
4. General Electric
5. Hughes
6. Digital
7. Singer Link
8. McDonnell-Douglas
9. Martin Marietta
10. Rockwell
11. Lockheed
12. IBM
13. SAIC

Languages

1. C
2. COBOL
3. Ada
4. C++
5. Objective C

Vertical Markets

1. Banking
2. Insurance
3. Manufacturing
4. Oil
5. Retail
6. Automotive
7. Financial Services
8. Accounting Firms
9. Universities
10. Government Agencies
11. Aerospace
12. Medical

Software Product Vendors

1. Digital
2. Arthur Andersen
3. CCA
4. IBM
5. Sybase
6. Microsoft
7. Apple

Evolving Industry Trends and Market Concerns

1. Open systems (X-Open, OSI, OSF)
2. Graphical user interfaces
3. Price/performance
4. Functionality and flexibility
5. Commercial strength
6. Object oriented
7. Client server
8. Technical/commercial integration
9. Massively parallel processing

often talk to people who love the product but who can't bring themselves to
bank their futures on a company as small as ours. People bet their careers when
they choose 001. High-productivity tools can be a threat to a lot of people
lower down in the organization.

Alliances

Many independent systems integrators and software tool vendors were anxious to
help HTI sell 001. They did not act as sales representatives and they would gain no
commissions from the sales, but they saw great opportunities to help their own
customers and gain new ones. A Washington systems integrator had set up a
demonstration there for the systems heads from a dozen of the largest government

organizations, including the patent office, the various armed services, and NASA. Some of these people were people who knew of Margaret Hamilton from the old days at Apollo; many of their agencies had been following HTI's progress. The meeting went very well, Hamilton said.

> The system integrators feel we'll be swamped by demand. When things finally click, they want to be in position to run training courses for us, or to subcontract for projects using the 001 tools. Sometimes customers help us in the sales process. For example, Martin Marietta and IBM have demoed to prospects for us. Martin Marietta has about 20 people trained; we may ask them to take on an 18 man-year project that a prospect wants done.

HTI people recognized that their small size and the huge scope of the market for 001 dictated the need for finding partners or alliances. Finding the right people to reach the right markets, however, and at the same time making the relationships work and maximizing the benefits to HTI, were daunting tasks. More and more often, HTI was receiving inquiries from potential allies. Many of Margaret Hamilton's advisers urged her to seek the funds to invest heavily in marketing, but she felt the timing was premature. "Articles have to come first," she said.

Interest in Hamilton Technologies was increasing in mid-1993, for two reasons. The technical press had begun to notice 001, and favorable stories had appeared in a number of computer journals. Margaret Hamilton gave credit to a new promotion consultant in New York. In the same week an article appeared in a new magazine, *Corporate Computing*, 50 new inquiries were received in Cambridge—10 times the normal weekly tally. More important, though, to the major prospects and government agencies involved in intensive system development was HTI's performance in a government-sponsored benchmarking effort.

THE NATIONAL SOFTWARE ENGINEERING TOOL EXPERIMENT

Within the U.S. federal government, one of the agencies most affected by the problems of software development was the Defense Department's Strategic Defense Initiative Organization (SDIO), commonly referred to as the Star Wars program. Rigorous testing of all its products was fundamental to SDIO's mission of detecting and destroying intercontinental ballistic missiles threatening U.S. targets, and the agency had established a National Test Bed (NTB) to provide a realistic environment for testing the work of its contractors. In November 1991, the NTB director approved an experiment to test the utility and effectiveness of computer-aided software engineering tools.

Three tool suites were selected as finalists to be evaluated in the test. The first was an amalgam of Ascent Logic's RDD-100 and the U.S. Army's Distributed Computing Design System (DCDS), supported by TRW Systems. The second was CADRE Corporation's Teamwork, and the third was Hamilton Technologies' 001. "We were chosen for the competition in spite of our not having a commercial presence," Margaret Hamilton said. "We had spent four years working with the major contractors to SDIO, and people knew we were there."

The test was a six-week lifelike trial, with each tool vendor team working for a selected defense contracting firm to jointly develop a missile warning command system. In the first week, each contractor's team attended the training course of its own tool vendor. Then the problem was assigned and for five weeks the vendor and contractor people worked together on project planning, installation of the tools at the contractor site, design, development, and integration. Vendors and contractors worked separately at their own offices, communicating face to face only at two design review meetings. Neutral monitors observed and reported on the way all teams worked together throughout the design process.

The aim was to produce a fully functioning system written in the government's Ada language and documented according to the government's rigorous 2167A standards. The entire tool experiment, whose total budget was close to $1 million, was designed and administered by MITRE Corporation, under contract to SDIO. MITRE estimated that the entire problem might require 200 subtasks and 838 days of staff effort using normal technologies. After months of planning, the test (called "the shootout" by Hamilton staff members) was held in May and June 1992.

The government's formal five-volume report of results was not issued until May 1993, but initial drafts were circulating for several months before its final release. HTI had succeeded in automatically generating 21,000 lines of code in the C language, and then regenerating the system to produce the required documentation and a running system of 24,000 lines of Ada code. (For reference, most aerospace contractors expected productivity of two to three lines of code per day from skilled staff people on similar work.) The system was in testing when the NTB's six-week test period ended. HTI's work was judged as 90 percent complete by the monitors.

In contrast, CADRE's team had completed a detailed system design and produced some Ada skeleton code, but it had not progressed to code generation. CADRE's work was judged 75 percent complete. Ascent Logic and TRW finished the experiment with a partly completed design but no code; their work was 50 percent complete. It appeared to the staff at Hamilton Technologies that the shootout had produced a clear winner. Table 2 reproduces the tabulated results from the SDIO report.

HAMILTON TECHNOLOGIES: OPERATIONS —————————

Systems programming, maintenance, customer service, sales demonstrations, and training were all handled by everyone on the technical staff at HTI. The technical staff was led by Director of Development Ron Hackler, who had been in charge of research at Margaret Hamilton's first company, Higher Order Software. His was the only desk visible from the entry foyer of HTI's headquarters; others were sandwiched in between several Hewlett-Packard workstations and Macintoshes. (An RS-6000, a Sun SPARC, and more HP workstations and Macs occupied the large room on the opposite side of the entry hall.) Behind Ron's desk, an ornate archway led to another room, but the opening had been closed with a partition and bookshelves to shield Hackler and the others from the noise of a large VAX computer that now had the back room to itself. All the computers were networked together.

Seven people made up the technical staff and customer support. Most had been with HTI for four to six years, starting as students at Boston University or Harvard or MIT and simply staying on after graduation. An exception was Marc, whose previous work at McDonnell Douglas had made him the first customer for the 001 product; he had moved to Boston in 1991 to join HTI. Other staff members were Sam, Pooter, Robert, Nils, and Joshua (a Harvard freshman joining the staff for the summer.) All

Table 2   National Test Bed Overview

Area	Estimate	Teamwork	HTI 001	RDD/DCDS
Software requirements	200	151	86	87 + 10 Derived
Documentation		SRS, IRS, SDDD	SRS, IRS, SDDD	SRS, IRS, SEN, SDDD
SLOC			21,000 C 24,000 ADA	
Staff days	838 worker-days	140	140	120
Amount of system completed		Detailed design complete, some Ada skeletons produced	Code generated and executed; not fully tested	Detail design partially completed
Percent complete		75%	90%	50%

Source: Department of Defense, Strategic Defense Initiative, *Software Engineering Tools Experiment,* Volume 1, *Experiment Summary,* table 1, p. 9, Washington, D.C.

development people carried part of the customer service load when they were needed. New service calls came to Nils, who could seek help from whoever was currently working on the subject area where the problem arose. Since the staff worked within earshot of each other, requests for mutual assistance were easily negotiated on the spot. When longer-range problems or topics arose, they were listed for consideration at that afternoon's product meeting. The staff had found a solution to the problem of unwanted interruptions when total concentration on the job was necessary. Walkman headsets indicated that the wearer wanted to be screened from noise and distraction and was not to be bothered.

Marc, Ron, and Pooter shouldered most of the load of training. Sessions for customers and prospects were scheduled as far ahead as possible and were held in HTI's conference rooms in a major office building on State Street, in downtown Boston. When those quarters were not large enough, the meeting rooms at Hewlett-Packard's local office could be used. All the computer manufacturers were anxious to support HTI; they supplied hardware in order to ease the job of porting the 001 tools to their own computers, and cooperated wherever possible.

Office hours at HTI were flexible. Because the development staff was often on site until late at night, the firm in effect provided immediate 24-hour service coverage. Staff members took turns sleeping over or working through the night when Margaret Hamilton was out of town. Clark, the German Shepherd, was welcome company on such occasions, said Hannah Gold.

PRODUCT MEETINGS

Development work at HTI was coordinated in a daily product meeting, where each staff member reported on the day's accomplishments or problems and on plans for tomorrow. These meetings were chaired by Margaret Hamilton when she was in the city; when on the road, she would telephone the Cambridge office every afternoon. "People report progress to whoever will be talking to me," she said. Meetings ranged in length from 30 minutes to four hours and often generated animated discussion. "We shout a lot," said Hackler, "but we have to do that, sometimes." A traditional battleground was over the degree of risk involved in developing new product features. Some staff members, seeing new possibilities to enhance capabilities, would advocate changes that others felt would jeopardize the stable, reliable base of the whole tool suite.

Illustrative of the HTI meeting process are the brief excerpts below, taken from a meeting just four days before Ron Hackler and Margaret Hamilton were to travel to New York for a customer demonstration. A new front-end interface was under development and was supposed to be ready for the New York trip. The meeting began:

MH: All right, what have we done today, and what for tomorrow? Sam?

Sam: I've done nothing, really. I struggled with the pop-out feature, and should have had it done earlier today.

MH: So you're feeling frustrated?

Sam: Yeah, I hit something I really didn't understand in the behavior of Motif . . .

MH: Do you think if we had the later Motif it would go away?

Sam: I really don't know enough about the problem. I just tried to make it work.

MH: Was Pooter on this?

Sam: Yeah, I tried out a couple of his suggestions and narrowed it down to one particular scenario. I get it from the debugger. I can avoid it by eliminating one primitive.

Pooter: Regardless of what version of Motif we have.

Sam: The good part is these rules are accumulating in my mind. I can work around them.

MH: Are you getting set to move to the demo machine?

Sam: Not until this is finished. The behavior wasn't acceptable until I fixed the problem.

Ron: But with it fixed, you could link right after this meeting?

Sam: Yes . . .

MH: So we'll know about the demo?

Sam: I'll need one or two hours to do a new version of Xecutor . . .

Robert: The link only takes 10 minutes.

MH: [*to Robert*] Great productivity, Robert.

[*to Sam*] Another thing, Sam, is you weren't at yesterday's meeting. Did you see Pooter's plan?

Sam: Yes. That showed clearly I wasn't at the meeting. What are the functions that constitute the alpha level? It's not clear—not well enough defined.

Pooter: Well, that's what we need by tomorrow night.

MH: We need the typemap. At the very minimum, the typemap sketch.

Sam: Then I need more detailed requirements . . . more feedback from other people.

Pooter: Am I remembering a conversation we didn't have? About primary guidance?

Sam: That was a pretty broad conversation.

MH: [*to Pooter*] Sam mustn't be afraid to ask questions.

[*to group*] Not that Sam is afraid of anything.

Ron: We need something tomorrow, so Robert and Marc can move ahead. Even if it's temporary.

Sam: Oh! Well, all right.

MH: So what you'll do next is finish up the data facer for the demo . . .

Sam: I guess tomorrow I'm in hard core design mode.

*   *   *   *   *

MH: Marc, anything else done today? I want to catch up on the status of documentation.

Marc: Well, the manual now takes 10 1.4-meg disks . . .

MH: 10??

Marc: We're adding graphics, and that takes space.

MH: OK, what's next . . . ?

*   *   *   *   *

MH: OK, thanks. Ron, you're last.

Ron: I modified the product this morning so I could use overloading.

[*General laughter*]

Pooter: Does that mean we'll all find these files named "Lucretia" floating around again?

MH: Does it work? Is it tested?

Ron: I don't have to test it. Because it won't have an impact . . .

Pooter: I do have a less facetious question: Will you put it back, so we can remain set?

Ron: Well, the baseline hasn't been made yet. I don't know the state of the system, beyond my piece of the product. It's just one file, and yes, I will roll it back. But the rest of the product version to be baselined hasn't been approved yet.

Pooter: That stuff is part of the . . . link.

MH: Part of the product we shipped? When did we ship it?

Pooter: Last Friday we shipped the product.

Ron: It needs the link. I want it.

MH: I don't think you do.

Ron: I asked it . . .

Pooter: Then you don't get Sam's database.

Ron: Well, that's true. But that's not been tested yet.

Pooter: I know it hasn't been tested. My point is that those are experimental areas, not part of the tool as released. I'm much more adamant about getting a good snapshot of the next official release—the session manager, which I know can be snapshotted right now. Like the link system, which Robert believes can be snapshotted right now. We need to coordinate on that, databases aside.

MH: We took a baseline last Friday.

Ron: That was the best one we've had all year.

Pooter: This probably won't be as good as that.

MH: Why can't we recreate from that one?

Ron: What we made last Friday was a full-documentation *tape*, not an operating copy of the system.

MH: Starting from the original FMaps and TMaps?

Pooter: Yes, but I don't consider that a baseline per se because it's more work to recover.

Ron: It's a master archive. It would take five hours to get an operating system from it. So forget about that one for daily use. It is a master archive so we know we're safe.

Pooter: What I'm worried about is some customer calling with a really tough problem we need to address. We can't replicate it, if all we have on line is a system undergoing brain surgery.

MH: So the question is what we're baselining to.

Ron: That's a good point. The Archive really should contain everything the customer has. I can take the overloader out in 30 seconds . . . right after the meeting.

Pooter: While I'm turning off network override pop-up windows.

Ron: And we'll make the tape. Everybody make sure their piece is executable—that it matches what we put on Clark.

MH: Did you spend the day on overloading, Ron?

Ron: No. About 10 minutes putting it in, and two hours arguing about it. But we're coming to a way of handling it.

MH: Is that it? There's lots to do.

Ron: For tomorrow, I'll finalize the typemap for Robert by 11:00. Then I'll test some and prepare for the New York demo. Then if there's time I'll start Backbone.

HAMILTON TECHNOLOGIES: FINANCE

At several points in its seven years of close-to-the-bone operation, Hamilton had considered seeking outside investors. Available capital would help accelerate the development of 001 as well as bring the product to market, she thought. In 1992, placing a value of $12 million on the company as a whole before the addition of new capital, she asked some "friends of the firm" to help prepare a business plan, aimed at selling 20 percent of the company for $3 million.

Valuation of the company did not seem to be at issue as potential investors considered the opportunity, in spite of the lack of formal balance sheets. One venture capitalist offered to purchase a controlling 51 percent of the firm—implicitly accepting the $12 million value. But the control issue was an important one for Margaret Hamilton, and she was hesitant to risk repeating the experience of her previous firm, Higher Order Software. Bringing in a new CEO or COO at the appropriate time was less of a problem. "I don't have to run operations forever," said Margaret Hamilton. "But I'd want somebody I could trust—somebody who has the humility and the confidence to learn the company and the industry from me and others."

Even with employee cash salaries artificially reduced by the "part-pay-in-stock-rights" plan, however, cash flow requirements began to exceed available balances. Early in 1992, as pressures mounted to speed up 001's development, a local firm called Environmental Power invested $250,000. Environmental Power accepted a full-firm valuation of $15 million, and received an option to invest another $750,000 within a year at a valuation of $22 million. Margaret Hamilton herself defined HTI's worth at any given time, as she had in setting the company value for purposes of calculating employee stock rights.

As 1992 progressed and market prospects improved (along with the favorable press and the word of favorable results in the National Test Bed benchmark tests),

Hamilton's sense of urgency in finding other outside investors diminished. She began thinking of other alternatives, including licensing the product to some of the larger computer industry firms who had well-established distribution channels. "Even one of those agreements at half a million dollars would make a difference," said Margaret Hamilton. Two major hardware giants had voiced interest in offering 001 as an element in their own product lines. "Not just as a catalog item, but as an active partner," Hamilton said. Negotiations for this kind of partnership can move slowly, however. Hamilton commented:

> It's like negotiating for a thousand-seat order for 001. Things move very slowly, and the smallest quirk can set you back to ground zero. Even for the very large prospects, we have to start with one-seat sales instead of hoping for the jackpot at the start of the relationship. Too many things can go wrong. One person decides to change jobs, and all your progress to date goes out the window.

By early 1993, Hamilton's interest had turned toward private placement with individual investors or corporate venture funds. A friend of the firm from her old Higher Order Software days, now associated with a New York investment firm, was updating the business plan for that purpose.

What would HTI do with the money if it suddenly received $1 million? Hamilton responded:

> To start with, we would pay more of their salaries in cash, to any of our people who need it. And we could pay down part of the home equity loan and personal debt. Then we'd bring in new people—developers—more Rons, more Sams. Not professional salespeople, though. I'd rather train the technical people to sell. I'm starting to think the marketers are limited for the present phase of the company; all they do at this stage is bring in technical people to talk to our technical people. In a later phase, as the sale becomes less technical, marketing people will be helpful.

VIEWS OF THE FUTURE

Margaret Hamilton mused on the long-range picture for HTI as she stood in the entry foyer at the end of a long day:

> What should it be like 5 to 10 years from now? Research will still be here, in the Victorian house. 001 will be a standard in Unix, NT, and OS-2 environments, as well as in targets we don't even know of today. We will continue to lead the way. With time and funding, we can develop a reverse engineering system that will have our Resource Allocation Tool as a major component. You feed legacy code into it—in any language—and get out system specifications, which can then go through the 001 development process. We call that the "Anti-RAT." Think of the millions of lines of code out there that need to be reprogrammed for new languages or platforms. We will respond to that need.

001 could also solve the bottleneck of development for massively parallel processing (MPP) environments, Hamilton thought. MPPs divide up the processing work among many processors working in parallel, as opposed to doing the work on a single central processor. MPPs could reside in one box or be created from networks; many industry analysts felt their superior price and performance characteristics would bring them to dominate the long-range market. A stumbling block, however,

was adapting existing code and creating new code for the parallel environment. "People haven't figured out how to divide up systems easily for running in parallel blocks," said Margaret Hamilton. "001 can create that kind of code inherently, and we'll take advantage of that as MPP grows." She added:

> Five years from now we'll be working with many systems integrators, and we'll have a sales force of our own. A number of people want to be involved; they either want to have a good time, or make money, or both. One man, a former aerospace customer, is a student at Carnegie Mellon now; he wants to set up mechanisms for handling large numbers of customers for us. A number of competitors want to work with us, too—including one from the NTB test.
>
> The product is bundled as a fixed suite of tools now. We will unbundle it, selling the separate tools to compete with the separate offerings of other vendors. But the total 001 package will provide a discount from the cumulative cost of the separate tools, and we'll still have an obvious price advantage over the total packages of other vendors.
>
> As far as structure and people go, we'll be more like a normal company. I don't know whether we can pull that off; will product meetings still be possible when we're bigger?

Ron Hackler scratched the ears of Clark, the German Shepherd, and added his input to the vision:

> The less fun work will be at some other location, but research and new technology will still be here. We'll have about the same crew size at this location, but there will be a different mix: this will be the heavy-duty research center, separated from customer service. That bookcase [he pointed at the temporary partition behind his desk] will be gone, and we'll have people in the VAX room.

Pooter joined in musing about the future:

> It's hard to visualize. I haven't even been here five years. ["Yes, he has," claimed Ron.] If HTI changes at its old velocity—no, it'll be faster change. The house and the dog and the stone rabbits will still be here. There might be two or three other offices—clones of this one—networked with telephones and conference calls.
>
> There will be an imperfect interface to our training center and sales offices at the State Street tower. No way will HTI still be a small company; we'll be huge. How would we maintain the small company mechanisms? There will be a way, but it may be strange. Robert calls it a "melted hierarchy" of some sort—strongly internetworked.
>
> The velocity of change itself will grow. It's exponential in structure, and we're walking up the e-curve; the slope is getting steeper. It's like Frankenstein reinventing himself.

Appendix   Technical Characteristics of 001

Margaret Hamilton described the core technology of her seven-year-old company, Hamilton Technologies, Inc. (HTI):

> 001 is an integrated systems engineering and software development environment for automatically developing ultra-reliable models, simulations, and software systems. It combines elements of Computer Aided Systems Engineering (CASE), artificial intelligence, and object-oriented analysis. It integrates and automates the whole systems development life cycle, from definition of requirements to the automated generation of complete and fully production-ready code for any kind of system. Some people are calling it "SuperCASE."

HTI's literature in 1992 described the tool:

> No ordinary CASE tool, 001 defines, analyzes and then generates complete and fully production-ready, reusable, well-integrated, and significantly error-reduced systems that can be ported across all hardware and software platforms including, but not limited to: all operating systems, *all databases, all graphical environments, and all programming languages.*
>
> Because it was self-generated . . . 001 itself is a reliable and well-integrated superCASE tool . . . 001 is available today on a wide array of platforms within the Unix, X-Window, and Motif environments: HP 700 series, IBM RS6000, and Sun SPARC.

To use 001, an analyst first defines the system in HTI's special specification language, the 001 Axes Language. Real-world objects and processes are defined as a series of interlocking and interconnecting hierarchies, using TMaps to describe types and FMaps to describe functions. HTI literature said that the language "captures data flows, data dependencies, timing, priority, ordering, and parallelism as well as the structure and characteristics of all objects in the system."

001's Analyzer tool uses HTI's mathematical axioms and theorems to isolate problems in the defined system properties and suggest to the analyst how those problems might be fixed. Then the Resource Allocation Toolset (or RAT) generates "complete, production-ready, quality code in any language, under any operating system, using any database, using any GUI (graphical user interface). And at any time." Delivered with a language set of Ada, C, and English, the RAT could be programmed to produce other languages as well—from COBOL to Fortran to Swahili. The RAT also generated automatic tests to locate coding that might produce run-time errors. Other 001 tools produced documentation and user-defined measurements of the system's operating characteristics.

Campus Designs, Inc., in 1994

Barbara Allison, The University of Alabama
Arthur A. Thompson, The University of Alabama

Campus Designs, Inc., a vendor of collegiate licensed products located in Tuscaloosa, Alabama, was started in the spring of 1986 by four University of Alabama fraternity brothers, Seth Chapman, Billy and Tom Pittman, and David Gross, with an investment of $200 each. The fourth member, David Gross, was soon bought out by the other three because he was not contributing to the enterprise. Seth Chapman described how Campus Designs, Inc. (CDI), got started:

> Noticing that [there were] a lot of T-shirts out on the market, I came up with an idea of my own design, and, since I have no artistic ability, I went to two fraternity brothers who used to do all our fraternity T-shirts . . . and, I asked them if it was feasible to do this wraparound design that I had for a shirt. So, they got together, did a design, and we had it printed up.

Billy Pittman and his younger brother Tom were responsible for that first design, which featured banner-clad red and white elephants jovially parading around the bottom of a white T-shirt. Seth and Tom set up a credit account with a Tuscaloosa screen-printing company, Promotional Pullovers, and had 25 of these original T-shirts printed up, which they sold out of a bedroom in their fraternity house.

By 1989, Campus Designs had grown from a fledgling company selling a specially designed T-shirt with a University of Alabama logo into a supplier of (1) two collegiate designs, bearing the trademarked logos of over 35 colleges and universities around the country, (2) a full line of fraternity and sorority designs, (3) "game day" T-shirt designs for University of Alabama football games, and (4) customized T-shirts, sweatshirts, and tank tops for local organizations.

At the start of 1990, Seth, Billy, and Tom set some growth objectives for their young company. The objectives related to developing additional trademarked designs for more colleges and universities and extending their product line to include a line of children's clothing and additional adult-sized apparel items. Their vision was essentially to grow the business by doing what they were already doing on an even bigger scale.

Soon thereafter, however, the three co-owners began instituting changes that ultimately altered the company's long-term direction and business makeup. By 1994, the company was no longer chiefly engaged in designing and marketing collegiate-licensed products. Instead, the three partners had refashioned their company into a contractor of screen-printed apparel and a retailer of apparel and other items that appealed to University of Alabama students. Sales were approaching $2 million annually, fueled by demand for apparel items commemorating The University of Alabama football team's 1992 national championship season. See Exhibits 1–4 for

Exhibit 1   Income Statement for Campus Designs, Inc., 1988–1989

	1988	1989
Sales	$225,857	$329,548
Cost of sales:		
Purchases	102,565	130,139
Freight in	3,891	2,783
Printing	33,480	54,474
Total cost of sales	139,936	187,396
Gross profit	85,921	142,152
General and administrative expenses:		
Accounting and legal fees	1,244	9,085
Advertising	4,686	9,237
Commissions	3,119	20,101
Depreciation	882	1,847
Dues and subscriptions	2,528	1,079
Insurance—liability	3,317	2,661
Interest	7,218	5,731
Market expense	3,989	9,438
Office supplies	1,422	2,808
Postage and freight	6,923	8,303
Rent	3,021	5,883
Royalties	9,323	14,582
Salaries—officers	1,891	27,277
Supplies	1,387	3,420
Taxes and licenses	1,141	4,884
Telephone	6,016	4,907
Travel and entertainment	6,328	5,952
Utilities	533	1,934
Collection cost	0	2,815
Miscellaneous	0	227
Total general and administrative expenses	64,968	142,171
Income (loss) from operations	20,953	(19)
Income taxes	2,637	0
Net income (loss)	$ 18,316	$ (19)

Source: Campus Designs, Inc.

information regarding the company's financial performance during the 1988–93 period.

THE COLLEGIATE LICENSING INDUSTRY

The collegiate licensing industry consisted of any object embellished with the trademarked logos, designs, and emblems of a collegiate institution. Initially, licensed products consisted mostly of apparel items such as T-shirts, sweats, caps, and jackets,

Exhibit 2 Balance Sheet for Campus Designs, Inc., 1988–1989

	1988	1989
Assets		
Current assets		
Cash	$ 6,331	$ 793
Accounts receivable—net	42,292	50,511
Inventory	17,279	23,809
Total current assets	65,902	75,113
Property, plant, and equipment		
Furniture and fixtures	6,003	9,236
Less: accumulated depreciation	882	2,730
Net property, plant, and equipment	5,121	6,506
Total assets	$71,023	$81,125
Liabilities and Stockholders' Equity		
Current liabilities		
Accounts payable	$ 6,382	$15,590
Accrued interest and taxes	2,798	5,708
Note payable	2,655	5,798
Current portion long-term debt	10,134	10,134
Total current liabilities	21,969	37,230
Long-term liabilities		
Notes payable	47,681	43,043
Less: current portion	10,134	10,134
Total long-term liabilities	37,547	32,909
Total liabilities	59,516	70,139
Stockholders' equity		
Common stock	840	840
Treasury stock	(2,520)	(2,520)
Retained earnings	13,187	12,666
Total stockholders' equity	11,507	10,986
Total liabilities and stockholders' equity	$71,023	$81,125

Source: Campus Designs, Inc.

but as sales flourished in the 1980s, suppliers began to make more types of collegiate products available to consumers, including license plate emblems, glassware, coffee mugs, stuffed animals, hats, jackets, calendars, blankets, furniture, jewelry, and insulated beverage holders.

Collegiate licensing was a neophyte industry in 1981 when Bill and Pat Battle (father and son) organized a centralized licensing agency named Collegiate Concepts International (CCI). Bill Battle was formerly the head football coach at the University of Tennessee and had won All-American honors playing for Paul "Bear" Bryant's 1961 national championship team at The University of Alabama.

The Battles decided to form CCI to relieve university officials from the legal and business formalities associated with licensing, to aid suppliers in obtaining licensing agreements, and to furnish retailers with the names of suppliers of "officially

Exhibit 3   Income and Cash Flow Statements for Campus Designs, 1990–1993

Income statement:	1990	1991	1992	1993
Sales (net)	$381,378	$451,289	$882,076	$1,720,250
Cost of goods sold	233,074	276,519	538,396	1,012,918
Gross profit				
—dollars	148,304	174,769	343,680	707,331
—percent	38.9%	38.7%	39.0%	41.1%
Expenses:				
Commissions	22,276	13,722	54,209	143,400
Advertising	3,588	750	2,270	34,548
Officers' compensation	34,897	37,781	50,683	84,708
Rent and lease expense	11,540	24,985	25,186	36,426
Other occupancy (telephone/utilities)	14,608	19,608	26,602	31,992
Depreciation	3,166	3,474	18,996	51,761
Miscellaneous	1,641	1,426	5,621	4,311
All other overhead (including equipment leases)	92,737	94,554	96,688	147,022
Total expenses	184,452	196,299	280,254	534,167
Net operating income	(36,148)	(21,529)	63,426	173,164
Interest expense on debt	(10,371)	(12,366)	(11,777)	(19,089)
Pretax income	(46,519)	(33,895)	51,649	154,075
Income taxes	0	0	0	(37,473)
Net profit (loss)	$(46,519)	$(33,895)	$ 51,649	$ 116,602
Cash flow statement:				
Net profit plus depreciation	$(43,354)	$(30,421)	$ 70,645	$ 168,363
Accounts receivable (increase) decrease	(37,770)	20,687	(195,555)	(130,116)
Inventory (increase) decrease	189	2,761	(14,461)	(81,697)
Accounts payable increase (decrease)	28,556	(5,500)	172,862	10,738
Accrued expenses increase (decrease)	(4,623)	11,684	4,680	98
Other current liabilities increase (decrease)	0	0	0	0
Cash from (to) operations	(57,002)	(789)	38,171	(32,614)
Cash from (to) fixed assets	(3,791)	(3,396)	(41,291)	(40,700)
Cash from (to) debt				
AmSouth notes	73,853	40,544	62,572	130,000
Repayment of debt	(21,900)	(34,419)	(68,075)	(33,428)
From (to) shareholder debt	6,923	1,365	6,448	(9,493)
Cash from (to) debt	58,876	7,491	945	87,079
Cash flow for period	(1,917)	3,306	(2,175)	13,764
Cash—beginning of period	917	(1,001)	2,305	130
Cash—end of period	$ (1,001)	$ 2,305	$ 130	$ 13,894

Source: Campus Designs, Inc.

licensed collegiate products." Officially licensed products were identified by a red, white, and blue hang-tag or label attached to every item approved by CCI and the universities it signed on.

Over the next nine years, the market for collegiate licensed products grew from a $1 million a year industry in 1981 to a $1 billion a year industry in 1989 to a $2 billion a year industry in 1993.

Exhibit 4   Balance Sheet Data for Campus Designs, 1990–1993

| | Years ending December 31 | | | |
	1990	1991	1992	1993
Assets				
Cash	$ (1,001)	$ 2,305	$ 130	$ 13,894
Receivables	96,087	75,400	270,955	401,071
Inventory	27,300	24,539	39,000	120,697
Total current assets	122,386	102,244	310,085	535,662
Gross fixed assets	14,455	17,850	117,641	158,341
Less: accumulated depreciation	(6,318)	(9,792)	(28,787)	(80,548)
Net fixed assets	8,137	8,059	88,854	77,793
Total assets	130,523	110,302	398,939	613,456
Liabilities and Equity				
Bank notes	108,343	110,000	92,570	78,122
Line of credit	0	0	0	130,000
Accounts payable trade	46,557	41,057	213,919	224,656
Accrued expenses	1,968	13,653	18,333	18,431
Other current liabilities	0	0	0	12,935
Total current liabilities	156,868	164,709	324,822	464,144
Printer lease	0	0	57,255	48,222
Other long-term debt	6,923	12,754	32,377	0
Total liabilities	163,791	177,463	414,453	512,366
Common stock	975	975	975	975
(Treasury stock)	(2,925)	(2,925)	(2,925)	(2,925)
Retained earnings	(31,318)	(65,211)	(13,564)	103,039
Total equity	(33,268)	(67,161)	(15,514)	101,089
Total liabilities and equity	$130,523	$110,302	$398,939	$613,456
Key Ratios				
Debt to equity (times)	−4.9	−2.6	−26.7	5.1
Working capital	(34,482)	(62,465)	(14,737)	71,518
Current ratio	0.8	0.6	1.0	1.2
Quick ratio	0.6	0.5	0.8	0.9

Source: Campus Designs, Inc.

In August 1983, CCI merged with International Collegiate Enterprises and formed a consortium called CCI/ICE (referred to as either CCI/ICE or CCI). By 1989, the consortium had generated licensing agreements with approximately 1,500 suppliers (200 providing national service and the remaining 1,300 providing regional, state, or local service) and was the exclusive agent for 108 major universities, 10 football bowl games, and the Southeastern Conference. In 1993, the company changed its name to Collegiate Licensing Company (CLC). Once a licensing agreement was established between CLC and a supplier, it was CLC's responsibility to act as a liaison between that supplier and the colleges and universities CLC represented. See Exhibit 5 for the retail sales of products bearing the logos and trademarks of CLC-represented institutions.

Exhibit 5   Retail Sales of Products Bearing the Trademarks of CLC-Represented Institutions, 1983–1993

Year	Overall Retail Sales	Retail Sales of CLC-Represented Institutions
1983–84	NA	$ 26,000,000
1984–85	NA	42,000,000
1985–86	NA	78,100,000
1986–87	NA	156,800,000
1987–88	NA	221,000,000
1988–89	$1,000,000,000	347,300,000
1989–90	1,250,000,000	490,000,000
1990–91	1,500,000,000	595,000,000
1991–92	1,700,000,000	700,000,000
1992–93	2,000,000,000	825,000,000

Source: *The Sporting Goods Dealer*, August 1989, p. L-2, for 1983–89 data; Dianne Shoemake, CLC, for 1990–93 data.

By 1991, the majority of colleges and universities had raised their royalty fees from 6.5 to 7.5 percent; by comparison, the royalty rates charged by the National Football League, Major League Baseball, the National Hockey League, and the National Basketball Association ran anywhere from 9 to 11 percent. Ensuring that member institutions received these royalty fees was one of the major services provided by the CLC consortium. CLC-affiliated suppliers were required to mail the royalty fees they owed member institutions directly to CLC headquarters. CLC then retained a percentage of the gross royalties owed to its member institutions as compensation for services rendered. The basic fee CLC charged an institution was based on the wholesale dollar amount of licensed products bearing the trademarked logos, designs, and emblems of that institution that were sold by the various CLC-affiliated suppliers to retailers. As a rule, the greater the dollar volume, the smaller the percentage fee, but the service was negotiable and could vary based on other factors. Approximately 80 to 85 percent of the royalties received by CLC-member institutions came from suppliers' sales of apparel items; the remainder came from suppliers' sales of chairs, clocks, glassware, bumper stickers, car tags, pennants, watches, and other such items.

In 1994, the industry was still being driven by much the same factors as it was in the 1980s. Interest in collegiate sports remained high among alumni and students as well as the general public, television and radio broadcasts of athletic events were on the rise, and fan interest was not necessarily confined to one team but often extended to a number of favored teams. Between 1989 and 1994, the major suppliers of collegiate licensed products jockeyed for position at the top of the industry. Based on CLC-related retail sales, in 1993, Starter led the industry with a 6 percent share of the market, followed by Champion at 4.2 percent. Relative newcomers like Team Edition and Trau & Loevner (which was ranked as the 35th-largest CLC-affiliated supplier in 1989) had fought their way into the top 10 suppliers (see Exhibit 6).

To contend with growing competitive pressures, companies had merged or made strategic acquisitions in order to fortify their industry positions. In 1993, The Game was bought out by Russell Athletic for an estimated $45 million. Russell, who

Exhibit 6   Top 10 CLC-Affiliated Suppliers of Collegiate Licensed Products, 1989 and 1993

1989	Market Share	1993	Market Share
Champion Products, Inc.	8.0%	Starter	6.0%
Galt Sand	5.0	Champion Products, Inc.	4.2
Nutmeg Mills	4.7	The Game	3.6
Game Sports Novelties	3.4	Nutmeg Mills	3.1
Artex	3.3	Galt Sand	2.5
Logo 7	3.1	Team Edition	2.2
Russell Athletic	2.9	Crable Sportswear	2.2
H. Wolf & Sons, Inc.	2.8	Trau & Loevner	2.1
Rah-Rah Sales	2.1	Russell	1.8
Chalk Line	1.9	Top of the World	1.6

Source: Pat Battle, CLC, for 1989 data; Dianne Shoemake, CLC, for 1993 data.

already held licenses with Major League Baseball and the NFL, purchased The Game because it had licenses with the NHL and the NBA and made products (like head wear) that Russell did not.

Other apparel suppliers extended their positions forward in the licensed apparel business by acquiring screen-printing companies that had the capability to print designs on their "blank" apparel products. Fruit of the Loom had acquired Salem; according to a Fruit of the Loom spokesperson:

> While Fruit will supply the blanks, Salem will continue to be responsible for graphic design, printing, sales and shipping. We will provide them with financial strength, marketing expertise, and good-quality blanks at a very low price, but we will not jump in and tell them how to design.

Vanity Fair Corp., a Pennsylvania-based billion dollar conglomerate whose brands included Wrangler, Jantzen, and JanSport, bought out H. H. Cutler, a Michigan-based producer of licensed apparel for children. A Vanity Fair official explained:

> [The acquisition] allowed us to expand our position in youthwear, which, when combined with other kidswear, gives us a volume of several hundred million dollars. It also gives us an entry into the growing licensed sports apparel industry.

In January 1994, Vanity Fair also made a bid to buy out Nutmeg Mills, a $200 million company that was a major player in the collegiate licensing industry (Exhibit 6).

Royalties

Large on-campus enrollments and total number of alumni played a major part in the popularity of merchandise with a respective college's logos/designs and the royalties generated. Success in the athletic arena was another key factor in licensed products demand. Exhibit 7 shows the 25 schools and universities with the biggest royalty receipts in 1989 and 1993.

Exhibit 7   Top 25 Royalty Recipients, 1988–1989 and 1992–1993

School	1988–1989 Enrollment	1988–1989 Total Alumni	1988–1989 Ranking	1992–1993 Ranking
Michigan	32,432	323,025	1	1
North Carolina	20,300	174,000	2	5
Indiana	32,550	290,367	3	*
Alabama	16,000	150,000	4	6
Georgia	26,000	170,000	5	10
Kentucky	21,500	76,967	6	9
Georgetown	11,967	70,000	7	2
Florida State	22,550	140,479	8	4
Tennessee	25,842	180,000	9	7
Auburn	19,000	115,217	10	15
Nebraska	22,730	204,000	11	18
Purdue	32,243	235,000	12	23
Illinois	34,854	391,652	13	11
Arizona State	41,470	115,000	19	25
Arizona	23,943	117,778	15	22
Clemson	13,062	NA	16	17
South Carolina	22,685	174,000	17	*
North Carolina State	24,558	NA	18	24
Kansas	26,500	185,000	19	*
Yale	5,151	115,000	20	21
Duke	5,100	80,000	21	3
Virginia	17,629	110,000	22	16
Louisville	21,087	68,000	23	*
Maryland	32,528	300,000	24	*
Wisconsin	44,584	226,159	25	20
UNLV	NA	NA	*	8
Georgia Tech	NA	NA	*	12
LSU	NA	NA	*	13
Colorado	NA	NA	*	14
Arkansas	NA	NA	*	19

NA—Not Available

* = Not ranked among top 25 royalty recipients for the indicated period.

Source: *The Sporting Goods Dealer,* August 1989, p. L-4, for 1988–89 data; *The Collegiate Retailer,* Summer 1993, p. 4.

Products/Trends

Some licensed suppliers of collegiate products had broad product lines consisting of apparel items, glassware, mugs, pennants, blankets, license plates, and so on. Others specialized in just one or a few closely related items. Still others, mainly larger companies, had recently diversified into collegiate-licensed products because of the growing sales prospects and had products that covered other consumer market segments. Champion Products, for instance, also produced and marketed athletic uniforms, recreational and leisure wear, cycling clothes, Lycra workout outfits, and athletic shoes.

One of the major trends taking place in the collegiate licensing industry was the subtle modification of basic garment designs. Oversized T-shirts were especially popular among teenagers and college students and, in the case of some females, doubled as both daywear and sleepwear. Another trend involved cross-licensing of cartoon and animated characters (such as Snoopy, Bugs Bunny, and Elmer Fudd) with collegiate or professional sports teams; Nutmeg Mills, Artex, Chalk Line, and several others had acquired licensing rights to various cartoon and animated characters. David Mitchell, director of retail licensing for NFL Properties, explained the synergism created when cartoon and sport licensees teamed up:

> People who might not think of buying a Snoopy garment by itself would consider buying it if it had an NFL or college logo on it . . . The reverse is also true. Someone who wouldn't buy an NFL- (or college-) licensed item by itself, like a grandmother buying for a grandchild, would buy it if it had Snoopy on it because of the element of cuteness.

In addition, there were growing numbers of hard-goods and soft-goods products embellished with the trademarked logos, designs, and emblems of colleges and universities—rear window brakelights in cars, telephones, underwear, towels, bean-bag chairs, and jewelry. Suppliers were endeavoring to differentiate their designs through the use of metallic and neon ink and screen-printing processes that made their designs resemble newsprint, appear to be three dimensional, or otherwise be unique and eye-catching. A trend, popular among college students, was the game-day T-shirt displaying the date, location, and names of the competing teams in a multicolored design; smaller companies were more likely to provide such specialized products than were larger companies, mainly because of the small production runs and localized markets.

Manufacturing

Producers of collegiate licensed apparel products ranged from fully integrated manufacturers to those manufacturers who were only responsible for the graphic designs that embellished the end products. Exhibit 8 provides information on the various types of manufacturers of collegiate licensed products.

The quality of these collegiate licensed apparel products and the time required to produce these products continued to be influenced by advancements in computer graphics programs. More powerful PCs and more sophisticated software had made it easier and faster to develop new and more intricate designs, shortening the design-to-market cycle. Although advancements in automated and computerized screen-printing processes were ongoing, the fundamental nature of the screen-printing process (the steps that were required to imprint a design) had remained essentially the same.

Distribution and Marketing

In the early 1980s, between 30 and 40 percent of collegiate licensed products were sold at campus bookstores, college athletic events, and off-campus bookstores. By 1990, however, the suppliers of collegiate licensed products had expanded their distribution channels to include J. C. Penney, Wal-Mart, Sears, sporting goods stores, and upscale and specialty apparel stores, driving the market share of campus-related retailers down to under 5 percent. Even so, the volume of collegiate licensed products being sold at campus bookstores, college athletic events, and off-campus bookstores was rising due to rapidly growing sales industrywide.

Exhibit 8   Types of Suppliers of Collegiate Licensed Products

	Estimated Percent of Total
Supplier types as a percentage of licensees	
Fully integrated manufacturer (makes own garments, does own designs, does own screen printing, and may have own in-house sales force).	5%
Do own designs and own screen printing (or contract screen printing to outsiders) on garments having the supplier's private label.	10
Do own designs and screen printing on garments having the manufacturer's label.	70
Design only; purchase garments from manufacturer and contract out screen printing.	15
Supplier types as a percentage of total sales	
Fully integrated manufacturer (makes own garments, does own designs, does own screen printing, and may have own in-house sales force).	15
Do own designs and own screen printing (or contract screen printing to outsiders) on garments having the supplier's private label.	50
Do own designs and screen printing on garments having the manufacturer's label.	30
Design only; purchase garments from manufacturer and contract out screen printing.	5

Source: Dianne Shoemake, CLC.

For the most part, suppliers with broad geographic coverage and wide product lines had a competitive advantage over narrow-line and local suppliers because of the caliber of service they offered retailers, the larger selection of merchandise they carried, and the relatively lower prices they could offer due to scale economies.

In 1990, Pat Battle commented that CLC picked up about 30 new suppliers per month and lost about 10 suppliers per month. The chief reason suppliers withdrew was their poorly developed distribution system and inability to generate a profitable volume of orders from retail outlets. Battle cited instances where mediocre products thrived in the industry because companies had succeeded in convincing retailers to carry their line while potential gold mine products failed miserably because suppliers were unable to secure adequate wholesale or retail distribution. It was common for the larger suppliers to market their collegiate licensed products nationally through a variety of distribution channels, and several advertised their licensed products in popular men's and women's fashion and sports magazines and trade journals. A few suppliers had developed point-of-sale displays for in-store use by retailers carrying their line; this was more common for hard-good items than for apparel wear.

Although some smaller producers sold their wares directly to customers via street-corner and stadium vending stands, the majority of collegiate licensed products were channeled to retailers by way of in-house sales staffs or independent manufacturers' representatives. For companies with the resources, utilizing an in-house sales staff was preferable to selling through independent manufacturers' representatives because manufacturers' reps typically handled competing product lines, were inclined to push whichever lines proved popular (and generated the greatest commissions), didn't always take enough time to learn much about the lines and suppliers they represented, and sometimes lacked good understanding of what retailers and customers wanted.

Issues in the Collegiate Licensing Industry

Unauthorized sales of unlicensed products was a significant and ongoing problem. CLC had taken steps to enforce its exclusive right to license the trademarked logos, designs, and emblems of those entities it represented. The consortium's present course of action when dealing with a supplier or retailer of unlicensed goods was to first ask the company to discontinue the unauthorized use of the university's trademarked logos, designs, and emblem; follow the initial request with a cease-and-desist letter, personal visits, and telephone calls; and a last resort, to proceed with litigation. Litigation required that a university whose trademarked logos, designs, and emblems were being infringed on initiate legal action. CLC guided the process, and CLC attorneys prosecuted the case if the university so desired.

CLC representatives worked with city officials to halt the selling of unlicensed goods, promoting the passage of infringement ordinances that supplemented existing trademark laws and helping create enforcement teams to check retail stores and especially stadium vendors who sold their products to sporting fans as they approached sporting events. If unlicensed products were found, a number of things could happen to the merchant: (1) the merchant could be asked to remove all unlicensed products from sale, (2) the business could be closed down, or (3) the merchant could be arrested. Some retailers were not aware of the licensing programs that were in effect. CLC believed that its best long-run strategy for stopping the sale of unlicensed products was to promote and enforce universal use of the "officially licensed collegiate products" hang-tag.

Another issue confronting the collegiate licensing industry was that of copyright infringement. In order to combat the problem of competitors pirating their designs, many suppliers copyrighted their designs. Suppliers who did not have their designs copyrighted were at the mercy of suppliers who did "knockoffs."

The collegiate licensing industry as a whole did not endorse the selling of products imprinted with offensive language, derogatory messages, inappropriate graphics, or messages that reflected adversely on a university institution.

CLC, along with university officials, had been stepping up measures to ensure that knockoffs and offensive products were kept out of the marketplace. This was not an easy task and, according to one licensing official, "The consumer needs to be educated about licensed goods . . . they should be cautioned to only buy those items bearing collegiate markings items which have the 'official licensed collegiate products' hang-tag." The hang-tag did not, however, guarantee a quality product; rather, it signified only that a product was being marketed under legal, university-sanctioned conditions.

SCREEN PRINTING

Companies in the business of producing collegiate licensed products typically relied on screen-printing technology to imprint the collegiate designs on apparel, pennants, and other such items. Some companies did their own screen printing; others had the screen-printing performed by outside specialists.

Screen printing could be done using a manual process or an automated process. With the manual process, film positives of the design to be screen printed were shot onto screens of clear plastic acetate. Separate film positives were taken for the various parts of the designs that were to appear in different colors. The individual screens, with their black images, were then exposed to ultraviolet light. After the screens were exposed to ultraviolet light for 15 to 20 minutes, they were removed and rinsed down with tap water. The black images on the screens created porous surfaces through which the inks used in screen printing could flow. Next, the screens were clamped securely into place in a screen-printing apparatus with a revolving base; depending on the equipment, anywhere from two to six screens could be accommodated simultaneously. The arms of the apparatus onto which the screens were clamped had an area above them into which colors of ink, corresponding to the design on the screen, were poured. The item to be printed was stretched smooth over a stationary base, and the various arms of the screen-printing apparatus were lowered in sequence over the base. A squeegee was then pulled across the encasement of ink, dispersing ink through the porous sections of the individual screens and onto the item. The inking procedure was done one screen at a time and one item at a time. When the design was complete, the item being printed was removed from the stationary base and placed on a conveyor belt that carried it through a large dryer set at 270° Fahrenheit. The drying process took two and a half minutes to complete.

In automated processes, the items to be imprinted were sent along a conveyor belt driven by a hydraulic timing chain. The screens with their various designs and ink colors were hydraulically lowered in sequence onto each item. When the design was complete, the printed items were sent through a dryer. In automated screen printing, the process had to be done under supervision and the changing of screens had to be done manually.

Manual screen printing was strenuous, and the workers needed to take periodic breaks. However, for relatively small print jobs; the manual process was more economical and faster than an automated process. Automated processing could be done on a small scale for an investment of $30,000 to $40,000; manual processing involved an investment of $200 to $2,000.

CAMPUS DESIGNS: THE EARLY YEARS, 1986–1989

Early on, when the three campus bookstores and a couple of local sporting goods stores readily bought stocks of the T-shirt design that Seth, Tom, and Billy had come up with and sales began to go well as these retail outlets, Seth Chapman remembered, "that's when we realized that this might amount to something a little bit more than making a little extra money to buy beer or whatever on." By June 1986, the three cofounders had secured a licensing agreement from The University of Alabama to use its trademarked logos, emblems, name, and mascot in CD's designs. Shortly thereafter, Campus Designs signed on with the Collegiate Licensing Company and launched efforts to market its T-shirt products at more retail locations across Alabama. A number of retailers agreed to take on Campus Designs' line, and several started asking for shirts imprinted with logos and designs for other schools besides The University of Alabama. Tom and Billy Pittman used their creative talents and came up with a version of their original wraparound front and back print design for three other universities in the Southeastern Conference—Auburn, Georgia, and Florida.

By the fall of 1986, Campus Designs had severed its ties with its original screen printer, Promotional Pullovers, and was utilizing the services of a newly established screen-printing operation—Art Works. Art Works was run by three individuals: Brian Johnson, owner; Mark Gambel, office manager; and Tom LaBee, production manager. All were former employees of Promotional Pullovers.

During the spring and summer of 1986, Campus Designs ran its business out of Tom's bedroom at the fraternity house and a rented house where Seth was living. T-shirt shipments were received at the rented house, while Tom's room at the fraternity functioned as storage space for the T-shirts and the address for important business mail. As sales began to grow, so did the need for a more functional place of business. In the fall of 1986, the cofounders transferred their operations to a rented apartment where Tom and Seth had begun living. This arrangement remained until the spring of 1988. According to Seth:

> We moved in an apartment about a mile away, fairly close to campus and that got really bad because I ended up sleeping with sweatshirts. My apartment, when Tom was living with me, was just covered with sweatshirts and T-shirts and paper. We had salesmen coming in there, so it was really a tight scene. And then we realized that we needed to move our office somewhere where we would just do our office work so we'd have a place to sleep and be able to live comfortable and get away from things.

In early 1988, the company decided to share an office in downtown Tuscaloosa with Art Works; the rent was split 50–50.

By mid-1988, CDI was starting to make a profit (see Exhibit 1). Tom and Seth had set up a joint account at Central Bank of Tuscaloosa through which business operations were handled. As the business continued to grow, so did their need for working capital to finance inventories and accounts receivable. They found it necessary, as Seth put it, to start "hitting our parents up for money." Their parents agreed to cosign a loan. The bank loan gave Campus Designs the financial ability to operate on a bigger scale. The company was able to purchase blanks in greater volume, cover screen-printing costs, and expand its geographic market coverage to other southeastern universities.

Before long, CDI began to outgrow the office space that it shared with Art Works; office space adjacent to Art Works was rented, providing 1,400 square feet of storage, drafting, and office space for Campus Designs to operate in. By early 1990, the business had grown to the point where more space was needed and the owners were looking for a location that would provide greater operating room.

Campus Designs' Product Line

By 1989, the young company's product line consisted of two trademarked lines of apparel, Campus Rapp™ and Circle-M™, a complete line of fraternity and sorority designs, game-day shirts, and custom designs for special events sponsored by local organizations. Apparel items were limited to T-shirts, sweatshirts, and tank tops available in adult sizes only. All production requirements, other than design, were contracted out to other organizations.

Billy Pittman believed that it was very important for CDI to develop designs that were distinctive enough to set Campus Designs apart from bigger companies. Unique designs were critical because Campus Designs could not compete with large-scale suppliers on price, quantity, and product line breadth. Apart from design uniqueness,

Campus Designs believed it could sustain a competitive edge over many of its competitors, especially larger rivals, because the owners were personally tuned into the university scene. Tom Pittman elaborated:

> Because we're so young still, we're not very far removed from the university market itself, especially since we live here in Tuscaloosa. It's kind of hard to become that far removed from it . . . We can stay in touch with what the students like and I think we can be a little more responsive to the types of designs that the students like. Likewise we can pick up on what's on students' minds, what's happening on campus, what students like and don't like because we talk to them all the time and we spend a lot of our time on campuses. This puts us in position to respond quicker than some big gigantic company . . . even though we're small.

The owners' personal experiences allowed them to spot opportunities and trends that larger suppliers had not or could not react to. For instance, Campus Designs had the ability to supply the increasingly popular game-day shirts for all University of Alabama athletic events, a market niche that larger suppliers such as Russell Athletic found too small and specialized to be of interest.

In order to stay on the cutting edge of design technology, Campus Designs began using computer graphics to enhance the speed, quality, and creativeness of the designs it turned out. The company monitored the costs and capabilities of software programs that could perform such tasks as typesetting, a very time-consuming and expensive process if done without the aid of computers. These software programs were expensive and usually required that the user have a special computer system (costing approximately $10,000) in order to utilize the software package effectively. In 1989, Campus Designs had its typesetting done by an outside source at a cost of $20 to $30 per design. Billy summed up CDI's design strategy:

> For the newer lines of designs that we come up with, we're going to have to be very creative . . . use our minds and work on something that not really sets a trend but is in step with what the larger companies are doing—but maybe just half a step beyond what they are doing, so that we can retain our little niche in the marketplace.

A promising design developed in 1989 called the Big Play fizzled and was dropped from the company's product line in less than a year's time. Billy noted:

> The design just never really caught on. Aesthetically, it was a fine design and had a lot of potential. But, we didn't market it properly. We didn't push it hard enough.
>
> Actually, we tried to do it for too many different sports—football, basketball, lacrosse. It would have been a nightmare trying to market it properly. So, we kind of just let it die—put it out of its misery, so to speak.

The company also abandoned the development of a children's line of clothing, opting instead to remain focused on the college and young adult market.

Campus Designs' Suppliers of Blanks and Private-Label Apparel

Originally Promotional Pullovers supplied Campus Designs with all its manufacturing needs, from supplying blank apparel items to performing the screen-printing process. Promotional Pullovers charged CDI the normal screen-printing price for its services. However, as sales grew, the three co-owners began to look for ways to lower costs. Finding reliable, low-cost suppliers of blank T-shirts was complicated by the fact that the industry was undergoing a cotton shortage, prices were high, and supplies of all-cotton garments were tight.

In the summer of 1987, Campus Designs investigated the possibility of establishing an account with Hanes, Inc., to supply blanks, but found the asking prices too high. A few months later, the company decided to use Fruit of the Loom as its principal supplier. Accounts with several other wholesalers were maintained as backups in case Fruit of the Loom was unable to fill the company's orders on a timely basis.

In late 1989, Fruit of the Loom announced price increases for the coming year that were substantial enough for CDI to consider changing suppliers. In shopping the market for alternative sources of supply, Campus Designs learned that blank apparel items could be obtained from Hanes at prices comparable to the new prices being charged by Fruit of the Loom. However, the three owners concluded that the business relationship they had established with Fruit of the Loom, considering their dependable service and quality products, justified continuation with the company's present supplier.

Campus Designs' Approach to Screen Printing

The ties the co-owners had established with Promotional Pullovers, its original screen printer, paid off when Brian Johnson, a former Promotional Pullover employee, established Art Works. Brian, along with Mark Gambel and Tom LaBee, broke with Promotional Pullovers because of conflicts with its management. CDI began using the screen-printing services of Art Works as soon as it was operational early the fall of 1986. Initially, Campus Designs relied on Art Works for the entire screen-printing process. Beginning in mid-1988, Campus Designs began supplying film positives to Art Works, significantly reducing screen-printing costs.

Campus Designs became concerned when Art Works announced new screen-printing prices starting in 1990. Charges for small orders, the majority of orders placed by CDI, were scheduled to go up more than 30 percent, and in some cases as much as 200 percent, plus the surcharge on rush orders was to be increased from 10 to 20 percent. With this news and on the advice of their accountant, the owners of CDI began actively seeking alternative screen-printing options. It was Campus Designs' practice to have a design screen printed as orders for the design were placed. This had resulted in CDI placing many relatively small screen-printing orders for the same designs with Art Works, a condition that imposed higher setup costs on Art Works. About 75 percent of the orders placed were for less than 100 units.

Distribution and Marketing

CDI's strategy during its first five years was to market its designs to as many schools as possible. It had therefore become a major undertaking to do anything new. Billy expounded:

> Our rep groups, who have done very well for us in the South, in the Northeast . . . need new things constantly. If we can supply those designs, something that's a little bit different, then we'll remain competitive . . . and be able to increase our volume and that's our goal—to constantly be building the volume and getting the new product out.

A disadvantage that CDI had in gaining wider distribution was its practice of charging buyers the full wholesale price. Larger suppliers generally had three pricing advantages available to them that were unavailable to Campus Designs and other small suppliers: (1) scale economies, (2) purchase discounts, such as 2 percent for payment within 30 days, and (3) price breaks on big volume orders. Although larger companies provided price breaks, Tom believed that CDI's customer service was superior:

> Larger companies can have . . . hundreds of people working in a customer service department. Well, we are the customer service department, so we can be a little more responsive to something. [Since] there are only three of us working, our customers know us all by first name.

CDI distributed its products through independent manufacturers' representative groups; the reps called on bookstores, wholesalers, and retailers who stocked collegiate apparel. The various rep groups were generally obtained through contacts made at industry trade shows. The wider geographic distribution capability afforded by the use of manufacturers' reps had enabled Campus Designs to expand its product line to include designs for over 30 colleges and universities (see Exhibit 9).

The manufacturers' reps CDI used (see Exhibit 10) were independent contractors and handled several lines of apparel. CDI had no guarantee that its reps would push CDI's line harder than any other line they handled. Since reps worked totally on commission, they tended to be loyal to whatever products that were selling the best. The three co-owners were not satisfied with the current distribution setup because some reps were unreliable and depending on only five reps did not give Campus Designs strong enough market coverage.

CDI game-day T-shirts for University of Alabama athletic events were sold exclusively through an account with The Supe Store, The University of Alabama's on-campus bookstore. Campus Designs' fraternity and sorority shirts were sold mostly at industry trade shows and by one independent manufacturers' representative, Jack Kirch. In 1989, Campus Designs was looking for a manufacturers' rep that could give its fraternity and sorority designs wider market exposure.

In addition, Campus Designs' marketing efforts in 1989 included a direct mail campaign to retailers who had either inquired about the company or who were believed to be potential customers. The company also did limited advertising in trade journals such as *Sports Trends* and *Impressions*.

Tom and Billy pointed out that many times retailers would simply say no to their products; the two most significant reasons were that (1) CDI did not offer price breaks on quantity orders as did larger suppliers and (2) they were already stocking a similar design. Billy related an instance where a buyer claimed that CDI's Alabama Campus Rapp design was almost identical to a design she was already carrying. Billy used such episodes as a reminder that CDI's success depended on coming up with new and creative designs.

Dealing with Knockoffs of CDI's Designs

"Copying is the highest form of flattery and the lowest form of doing business," noted Billy Pittman following three incidents in which other companies had copied CDI's designs. In one incident in the fall of 1987, Artex, a leading supplier of collegiate licensed products, developed a knockoff of CDI's University of North Carolina Tarheels Campus Rapp design. CDI contacted CLC, who turned the matter

Exhibit 9   Universities Represented in Campus Designs' Product Line, 1989

Circle-M Designs		Campus Rapp Designs	
Alabama	Maryland	Alabama	Michigan
Auburn	Miami	Arizona	Michigan State
Duke	Michigan	Auburn	Minnesota
Florida	Michigan State	Baylor	Nebraska
Florida State	North Carolina	Duke	North Carolina
Georgetown	North Carolina State	Florida	North Carolina State
Georgia	Ohio State	Florida State	Ohio State
Georgia Tech	Penn State	Georgia	Oregon State
Indiana	Pittsburgh	Georgetown	Penn State
Kentucky	Syracuse	Georgia Tech	Pittsburgh
LSU	UNC Charlotte	Illinois State	Purdue
Louisville		Indiana	Seton Hall
		Kansas	South Carolina
		Kansas State	Syracuse
		Kentucky	Tennessee
		LSU	Texas
		Louisville	UNLV
		Maryland	Washington
		Miami	West Virginia

Circle-M designs are not available on tank tops.
Source: Campus Designs, Inc.

over to university officials. Artex's penalty for copying the CDI design consisted of a small monetary fine and a mandate to destroy their screens of the design.

Other CDI designs that had been copied were its University of Alabama Campus Rapp design and the Syracuse University Circle-M design. These incidents provoked CDI to institute legal action, but as Tom put it:

> As we continue to grow, it's going to continue to happen. Taking legal action against a company that does it is very expensive but it's something we feel we have to do. We can't be seen as a company that lets others get by with knocking off our designs. We're small and we're fresh meat out there for all those sharks.

Company Organization

Campus Designs' owners did not want to become locked into a particular job function. Decisions were made by group consensus. All three were familiar with every aspect of company operations and functioned as equals. Seth commented on the assignment of job titles and the philosophy behind their rotation of job titles:

> The job titles are basically meaningless; they are just assigned for outside business purposes. We rotate jobs so that everyone can get a better feel for the various responsibilities involved in running a company . . . but as I said earlier the titles really don't mean anything to us. Everyone is responsible for any business situation that might come up whether they're the secretary, the vice president, or the president—it doesn't matter.

Exhibit 10   Manufacturers' Representatives Handling Campus Designs' Products, 1990

Manufacturers' Representatives	Geographic Coverage	Products	Commission
Cole-Harris	Alabama, Mississippi, Georgia, Tennessee, North and South Carolina	Circle-M, Campus Rapp	10%
Earl Williams	Florida	Circle-M, Campus Rapp	10
Pat and Dan O'Connell	Eastern Pennsylvania, Delaware, Virginia, Washington, D.C., Maryland	Circle-M, Campus Rapp	10
Bonnie Ross	Upstate New York, Syracuse	Circle-M, Campus Rapp, Greek Shirts	10
Herman Thompson and Wells	New York City	Circle-M, Campus Rapp	10

Going into 1990, the three co-owners each had a vision of where the company would be in 1995:

Seth: I see us having top-quality facilities. I also see all aspects of our business, such as production, marketing, and designing, being top-notch. I believe that we will be involved in the production of other licensed products like professionally licensed products and maybe even some other fashion type things.

Tom: In five years I see us having our own private label, a better system of distribution, and a larger staff. Hopefully, we will be working fewer hours and not having to pull all-nighters. I also see Campus Designs having better name recognition.

Billy: I see us being more in control of the various facets of the business—not relying so much on outside sources—internalizing more of the aspects of the business. I also see us responding quicker to market opportunities—getting out new designs faster. I also hope to see all three of us become more skilled in the management and training side of the business.

When asked if they were having fun creating and running their own company, the three co-owners replied:

Seth: I don't know if you'd call it fun . . . but there is just something here that keeps you going. A business of your own allows you to come and go as you please—I like that. I also like the people I am working with.

Tom: I wouldn't be doing it if it wasn't fun. It is nice to be in a position where you are responsible for everything. The success of Campus Designs depends on us and there is always room for improvement. I find that to be an exciting challenge.

Billy: I'd rather be doing this than anything else.

CAMPUS DESIGNS, 1990–1994

By 1990, CDI had outgrown the space it shared with its screen printer and relocated to a 4,000-square-foot facility in Tuscaloosa. This new location allowed the company to integrate backward to do its own screen printing, and Tom LaBee, Art Work's production manager, was recruited to manage Campus Designs' screen-printing operations. This was the company's first major step towards independence in making its products, and it resulted in better cost control, improved product quality, and greater production flexibility. In the new location, approximately 1,200 square feet were allocated to the production of screen-printed apparel; 2,000 square feet to administrative activities, product design, and storage; and 800 square feet to shipping, receiving, and primary storage.

The move to the larger facility was accompanied by the acquisition (through leasing) of one six-arm and one four-arm manual screen printer and a 4-foot wide, medium-length dryer. The dryer was bigger than what the company needed at the time, but the rationale behind its purchase was that the company sales would soon grow enough to permit full utilization. In November 1992, the company began leasing new production equipment consisting of an air compressor for the dryer, an exposure unit and printing press for the production of screens, and a 12-station automatic screen printer. In addition to these purchases and the purchase of other screen-printing material, the dryer was expanded by another 15 feet in length. This equipment, which cost in excess of $100,000, was obtained when it became apparent that the undefeated, second-ranked Alabama Crimson Tide would play the undefeated, first-ranked University of Miami Hurricanes for the NCAA national championship in football in the Sugar Bowl on January 1, 1993. The co-owners were well aware that the frenzy of excitement over the championship game, and especially the aftermath if Alabama won, would trigger an explosion of demand for UA products all across Alabama.

By February 1993, the company was in need of additional production space, so it rented 1,500 square feet of space connected to the existing facility. The new space was converted into a larger production arena, as well as storage, distribution, and receiving space, and the newer section was reserved for administrative and design activities. According to Tom Pittman, neither the move in 1990 nor the expansion in 1993 were the owners' first choices as far as location and space, but Tom stated that they had to take what they could get at the time. In retrospect, the co-owners believed their decision to expand versus move in 1993 was for the best because it kept the company from having to face all the complications associated with a full-fledged relocation of activities. Nonetheless, by early 1994, the three young entrepreneurs were contemplating relocating to an existing 11,500 square feet location approximately 20 miles outside of Tuscaloosa.

Campus Designs' Product Line

During the 1990–1992 period, Campus Designs scaled back its collegiate licensed product line, including the number of universities it supplied, and changed its focus regarding screen-printing products in general. The company abandoned its concentration on its two trademarked designs, the Circle-M and Campus Rapp, and reduced the geographic area over which its products were marketed. Although the company was licensed to produce collegiate designs for approximately 50 different colleges and universities around the country, the owners decided to focus their efforts on schools in the Southeast. According to Tom:

We scaled back so we could learn how to "get it right" before expanding into other areas. Billy and Seth and I felt that we just didn't know our product or our buyers well enough to be a national or seminational supplier. So, we have scaled back and concentrated primarily on schools located in the Southeast. We would like to expand in the future, but, for now, we want to concentrate on a limited number of schools.

In addition, CDI emphasized producing different designs for different schools. As Seth put it:

We no longer have the mind-set that what is good for Alabama is good for Tennessee, and Auburn, and Georgia, and LSU. We shy away from doing a preset, or predetermined, design for the schools we service. Instead, we have gotten into more contract-oriented work. For example, a sports shop that carries sports-related apparel for Tennessee fans will request an order of T-shirts for a special event such as the university's homecoming or a big game, and we will design a shirt especially for that event. We are definitely more contract-oriented. This generally requires that the orders be high volume.

In 1994, the company's product line consisted of (1) two basic designs for both fraternities and sororities that were generic enough to be sold everywhere around the country; (2) an array of custom-designed collegiate licensed products for bowl games and schools in general; and (3) noncollegiate licensed products for special events such as music festivals, community sports activities, state government projects, and corporate-sponsored events. These products were supplied in regular Ts, long-sleeved Ts, and sweatshirts. The company no longer printed its designs on tank tops because the demand simply wasn't there anymore. As Tom put it, "We dropped tanks like a hot potato—they just became a bad item." In 1992, the company began limited production and distribution of screen-printed shorts and also began supplying designs in long-sleeved T-shirts. The decision to print designs on long-sleeved T-shirts proved extremely successful, and, in 1994, designs on long-sleeved blanks were a popular item in the product line. In 1994, CDI's product mix was approximately 70 percent licensed and 30 percent unlicensed goods, as compared to nearly 100 percent licensed products (not including the company's Greek designs) in prior years.

Campus Designs' Suppliers of Blanks and Private-Label Apparel

By the early 1990s, CDI's credit was strong enough that it was able to open up accounts with several large suppliers of blank T-shirts and sweatshirts. In 1994, the company had accounts with Fruit of the Loom (its original supplier), Hanes, and Soffie, to name a few. Billy indicated that having accounts with a number of suppliers was not an indication that a design company had significant buying power. In fact, in Campus Designs' case, doing business with a number of suppliers was simply a way to ensure that the company had an adequate supply of blanks to fill its orders—it was by no means the most economical or efficient way to purchase blanks. According to Billy:

The bigger we got, the more T-shirts we needed. And, we found that, as small as we were, some of our orders were not being filled in as timely a manner as we felt was necessary. Our credit had improved to the point that companies, other than Fruit of the Loom, were willing to open up accounts with us—we were no longer considered a credit risk. But, having more suppliers isn't an advantage for us as much as it is a necessity.

If we could get away with one or two suppliers we would. It's not that some suppliers charge us that much more than other suppliers for blank apparel items—the prices have a way of evening out—but that, administratively, it is more costly and time-consuming to deal with a larger number of suppliers.

The industry has become so competitive at this point that a blank costs about as much today as it did six years ago—about $2.40.

In 1991, CDI began producing designs on blanks that carried Campus Designs' own private label. The introduction of apparel items with a Campus Designs label did not have the desired effect on sales or name recognition that the three owners anticipated. Many retailers saw little value in a Campus Designs label (because the name was unknown to buyers) and felt that buyer confidence in product quality was greater with a name-brand label. In 1994, apparel items carrying the Campus Designs label accounted for just 30 percent of company sales, while items with name-brand labels comprised the remaining 70 percent of sales.

Graphic Designs

In order to turn out new designs more quickly and easily, Campus Designs in 1990 purchased a computer system and software packages that allowed Billy and Tom to develop more interesting and more complex graphic designs at an economical cost. The new equipment also eliminated the need to use the services of other companies for the typesetting of designs, plus it greatly facilitated the switch to greater emphasis on custom and single-event designs. Additional graphics-related computer equipment was purchased in 1994 at a cost of $10,000. The company's computer and production capabilities enabled it to perform its entire design and production processes in-house—except for four-color processing, which had to be contracted out.

Distribution and Marketing

Frustrated by continuing problems in dealing with manufacturers' sales representatives between 1986 and 1991, the company decided to sever its ties with manufacturers' representatives and take over more or less complete control of the marketing and distribution of its products. Since Seth had maintained the most direct contact with the company's distributors and buyers (retailers and wholesalers), he was the standout choice for assuming lead responsibility for sales and marketing.

By mid-1992, all of CDI's distribution activities were handled directly by the company except for the distribution of its Greek lines (sorority and fraternity designs) which were handled by Sidney Moss and Associates, a distributor that, according to Tom, was "just all over the place. A great distributor with lots of contacts." Billy's marketing activities consisted mainly of one-on-one personal calls on retail store buyers and over-the-phone sales spiels.

The 1993 Sales Bonanza

Billy, Tom, and Seth looked on with some 50,000 other jubilant Alabama fans on New Years night 1993 in the Sugar Bowl as the fourth quarter wound to a close. The scoreboard showed the Alabama Crimson Tide safely ahead of the highly favored Miami Hurricanes, 34 to 13, giving Alabama its 12th national championship in the 100th year of its football history. Some 300 miles away, in Campus Designs' newly expanded production facilities in Tuscaloosa, the production of custom-designed apparel items commemorating a 13–0 season and an undisputed national champion-ship was beginning. By dawn on January 2, the first production runs were being readied for shipment to retailers in Tuscaloosa and across the state. Billy and Tom had prepared several designs before they left for New Orleans; only the game's final score had to be added before production began. The victory sparked a wave of orders—sales totaled nearly $400,000 in the month of January alone. Sales for 1993 were almost 100 percent above 1992 levels (see Exhibit 3), chiefly due to the burst of demand for apparel items heralding Alabama's championship season. Alabama's national title provided enough incremental sales volume to justify the recent expan-sion in facilities, equipment, and personnel.

The Pachyderm

The three owners of CDI opened a small retail shop called the Pachyderm adjacent to The University of Alabama campus in late summer of 1991. Tom readily admitted that, while in the early spring of 1994 the store was holding its own, the decision to open the retail establishment was not very well-thought-out and came at a time when company finances were strained and the future of the company was uncertain at best.

> Looking back, I would have never done the thing. But, when Kinko's Copies moved down the street, the space became available, and we had been talking about opening a T-shirt shop. We knew it was a long shot. But when the space became available, it seemed like a good time to make our move.
>
> The decision to open the store was made in early spring 1991, and we let the thing just sit there for three months before we opened it.
>
> At first, we primarily used it to move excess inventory and take screen-printing orders from local organizations for upcoming events such as sorority and fraternity socials, baseball leagues, and university events—it was primar-ily a T-shirt shop. It has evolved to the point now where you would consider it a gift shop, or a college shop to be more exact. We sell very little of our own designs now, and only about 40 percent of the store's sales are generated by T-shirts.

The Pachyderm, which offered its patrons soft goods (shirts, shorts, bandannas, and caps) and hard goods (picture frames, postcards, candles, and purses), doubled as a retail establishment and screen print–ordering facility. The establishment was flanked by a number of student bars, restaurants, and bookstores lining the main retail strip by The University of Alabama. The University had 19,000 students, about 4,000 of whom belonged to fraternities and sororities. The Pachyderm was in direct competition with a T-shirt shop and one of the three main campus bookstores, both located within 50 yards. In the summer of 1993, the store's original facade got a face lift—a fresh coat of paint and a new awning—and the store's windows were con-stantly dressed with trendy, eye-catching merchandising. The Pachyderm accounted for 10 percent of Campus Designs' sales revenues in 1993. To increase the shop's sales and attract more customer traffic, the three co-owners had spent considerable time revising and tuning the establishment's merchandising and marketing strategies.

Company Organization

Between 1989 and 1994, CDI grew from a four-man organization (the three co-owners and a production manager, Tom LaBee) to an organization with approxi-mately 12 full-time and 6 part-time employees. In 1994, Tom, Billy and Seth were still engaging in the practice of rotating their organizational titles. This rotation took place every third Saturday in October following the Alabama/Tennessee football game. As before, their titles were considered to be basically meaningless; the possession and rotation of titles was an organizational necessity borne out of the fact that CDI was incorporated. In 1994, Billy's primary duties included handling royalties and creating designs; Tom conducted the company's payroll services and was also responsible for design creation; and Seth's primary job was product distribution.

Salomon: The Monocoque Ski

Francis Bidault, International Management Development Institute

Yes, it's excellent . . . I really love this prototype. You have all done a truly superb job! But, we are still only half way into this venture. There is a lot more work to do . . . I would say you will probably need another four years before we can see Salomon skis, as well as boots and bindings, on the slopes. But, it is time to discuss an action plan and I would like to present it at next month's New Product Committee meeting! So, I'd appreciate it if you could let us have your plan a few days beforehand.

Georges Salomon, the 62-year-old president of Salomon S.A., was stroking, with visible excitement, the new prototype that the development team had just presented during one of his regular meetings with them. It was November 15, 1987, and he was glad to see the progress made by the team on this truly strategic project which he had initiated in July 1984: to design a Salomon ski as an addition to the company's successful product portfolio.

As Georges Salomon was making his concluding comments, the project team had mixed feelings. They were happy that their work had gained such positive recognition from the president, but they also felt under pressure, knowing what remained to be done. Until now, the development of the first Salomon ski had been a very exciting adventure: unlimited creativity, daring solutions, and generous support. That was the easy part. Now, the time had come to try and make the "dream" come true: They would have to work hard to complete the development and prepare a commercial launch. The real challenge was still ahead.

As they were leaving the meeting room, each member of the team was recollecting the key events that had led to this development and considering the significance of this project for the company and for the overall ski market.

SALOMON S.A.

Salomon, a fast-growing company with headquarters in Annecy in the French Rhône-Alpes region, was proud of being the world leader (based on its sales) in winter sports equipment (refer to Exhibits 1–3). The company, always aiming for the top, had regularly improved its position in each of its market areas: number one in ski

Exhibit 1   Salomon S.A., Sales and Profits   *(FF Million)*

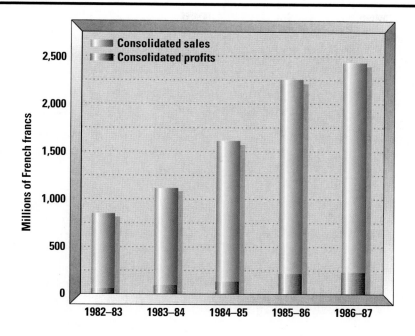

bindings with a 46 percent market share; number one in cross-country ski boot-bindings with a 30 percent market share; and number two in alpine ski boots where it was just a few percentage points behind Nordica. A line of accessories—clothes, bags, caps, etc. ("Club-Line")—completed its winter sports offerings. In addition, Salomon owned Taylor-Made, a successful firm in the golf equipment business (clubs and accessories).

Salomon's sales were distributed around the globe: 30 percent in North America, 22 percent in Japan, 40 percent in Europe, and 8 percent in the rest of the world. Salomon had fully owned subsidiaries in 12 countries, including Japan, which was the largest in terms of sales.

The company was heavily involved in competitive events in winter sports as well as in golf. Success in competition was considered very important for establishing the credibility and reputation of Salomon and Taylor-Made products. The company invested a significant amount of money (some FF 50 million annually) in amateur and professional sporting events.

Salomon's management philosophy revolved around three basic principles:

- Partnership with employees.
- Cooperation with suppliers and distributors.
- Innovation for customers.

The partnership with the company's workforce was founded on the premise that success could only come if the employees were competent and felt associated with the future of the firm. Therefore, training was regarded as a key driver in the

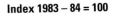

Exhibit 2   Growth of Sales and R&D Expenditures

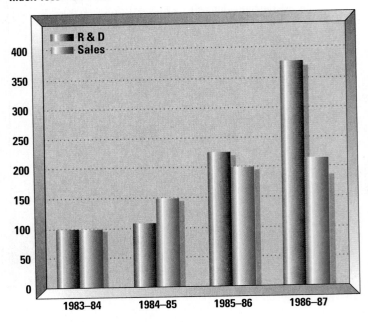

Index 1983 – 84 = 100

company's effectiveness, with over 5 percent of the payroll "invested" in this activity. In addition, employees benefited from the company's success by receiving bonuses, based on annual results, and a regular distribution of shares. The 1986–1987 annual report[1] mentioned that 3 percent of the company's common stock was held by its employees.

Salomon recognized that cooperation with suppliers and distributors was needed in order to have effective high-quality support for delivering its products. The company relied on numerous subcontractors to manufacture up to 60 percent of its production of bindings and boots, and all of its "Club-Line" products. There was also a worldwide network of retailers offering the necessary service to the customer (advice, testing, adjustments, etc.). For both the subcontractors and the retailers, Salomon provided continuous information and training to ensure the quality of their contribution. Recently, the company had taken a further step by introducing the concept of the "Salomon Authorized Dealer," whereby the rights and duties of retailers vis-à-vis the company were specified.

The third principle was no less essential: ongoing innovation and investment in new technology that would serve the needs of sports enthusiasts in increasingly better ways! Salomon spent some 4 percent of its consolidated sales on research and development, and registered around 100 patents worldwide every year. From the very beginning, innovation had always been a key word at Salomon.

---

[1]Salomon's annual report covered the time period from April 1 to March 31 of the following year.

Exhibit 3   Salomon S.A. Five-Year Financial Summary, 1983–1987   (Thousands of French Francs)

			Year Ended March 31		
Operations	**1983**	**1984**	**1985**	**1986**	**1987**
Net sales	FF817,170	FF1,109,263	FF1,666,277	FF2,220,686	FF2,241,700
Other revenues	8,656	22,182	19,462	25,200	21,307
Total revenues	825,826	1,131,445	1,685,739	2,245,886	2,443,077
Cost of sales—materials	(271,272)	(351,540)	(578,712)	(772,247)	(869,233)
Payroll expenses	(165,757)	(209,256)	(250,565)	(303,253)	(346,977)
Depreciation charge	(33,870)	(49,553)	(66,354)	(108,338)	(128,585)
Other operating expenses	(188,466)	(274,867)	(379,315)	(526,268)	(569,116)
Operating profit	166,461	246,229	410,793	535,780	529,166
Interest expense, net	(36,965)	(38,385)	(47,368)	(84,361)	(90,959)
Nonoperating items	(10,383)	(10,487)	(38,124)	(36,759)	(79,407)
Pretax net income	119,113	197,357	325,301	414,660	358,800
Provision for income taxes	(53,700)	(96,651)	(156,655)	(197,625)	(135,637)
Net income	FF 65,143	FF 100,706	FF 168,646	FF 217,035	FF 223,163
Financial Position					
Cash and marketable securities	FF169,037	FF 263,258	FF 363,854	FF 830,126	FF 656,544
Accounts receivable	174,527	185,191	279,927	350,293	414,537
Inventories	158,951	260,536	381,093	562,221	601,505
Other current assets	37,382	157,758	58,414	77,719	195,184
Total current assets	539,897	866,743	1,083,288	1,820,359	1,877,770
Property, plant and equipment, net	94,666	145,575	197,614	364,432	445,694
Other noncurrent assets	5,993	5,493	47,100	13,645	12,134
Total assets	640,556	1,017,811	1,328,002	2,196,436	2,325,598
Loans payable	108,893	300,230	302,329	646,597*	532,222*
Accounts payable and accrued expenses	326,462	300,943	381,830	496,495	568,546
Other liabilities	13,055	4,231	49,144	55,634	42,067
Shareholders' equity	192,146	412,407	594,699	997,710	1,182,763
Total liabilities and shareholders' equity	FF640,556	FF1,017,811	FF1,328,002	FF2,196,436	FF2,325,598

* Including capital lease obligations.
Source: Company annual report for 1987.

SALOMON: THE FIRST FORTY YEARS ——————

In 1947, François Salomon and his wife, Jeanne, set up a small firm that performed metal processing activities. Initially, it made saw blades and steel edges for skis, a technology for which François owned a patent. At that time, the edges were attached to the wooden skis by the retailers.

The Salomons' son Georges decided to give up his job as a schoolmaster and to join the family firm. Soon afterward, Georges invented a machine to improve the processing of steel for ski edges.[2] However, in only a few years, the Salomons

---

[2]Salomon S.A., Case Study, Jim Whyte, Department of Management, Napier College, Edinburgh, 1986.

realized that the ski manufacturers were integrating this process and that they needed to look for other activities to prepare for the future.

In the early 50s, Georges was approached by a Parisian inventor with a new type of ski binding that no manufacturer was interested in. Georges immediately saw its potential and decided to buy the technology. This innovative device filled a real need at a time when the market was developing quickly. Orders came soon and sales grew fast, particularly in North America. Thus, the firm was able to benefit from the post–World War II growth of skiing as a major leisure activity, at an international level right from the beginning. In 1962, Georges realized that the growth of his company needed to address the world market. From then on, the commercial development of Salomon S.A. was based on two pillars: new products and international presence.

Georges, however, did not become complacent with success and systematically continued to look for ways to improve the protection of skiers against accidents. In 1967, he introduced the first ski binding without a cable. This innovation was a real breakthrough, one that radically changed skiing safety and comfort, and also resulted in a profound restructuring of the bindings industry. Such an accomplishment had only occurred because Georges was determined to concentrate on product innovation, devoting much of his time to it—as he preferred that activity to administrative tasks.

By 1972, Salomon had gained a real presence in foreign markets, surpassing Tyrolia and Marker to become the world leader in bindings—a position the company has since maintained.

In the early 70s, Salomon began to look for new products beyond ski bindings. Several options were studied, among them the markets for ski boots and skis. In 1974, the decision was made to pursue the former. Georges Salomon had a clear objective: to come up with a boot that was not only better but would also offer a significant and visible improvement. In 1979, Salomon introduced a truly innovative boot design—the rear-entry boot—which addressed a key frustration for skiers: lack of comfort. This "revolutionary" ski boot concept was reasonably well accepted. However, in spite of success with Giradelli, the industry (racers, journalists, ski instructors, etc.) gave it a lukewarm welcome. They claimed that it was not tight enough on the foot and gave it the uncomplimentary nickname, *"la pantoufle."*[3] Even though sales were significant, they did not develop as quickly as expected. Salomon gradually adapted its design, keeping rear entry for only one part of the line and, in this way, eventually was able to gain a steady market share. By 1987, the company held second place, close behind Nordica (of Italy).

During this same time period, starting in 1978, Salomon undertook to enter the cross-country ski market. Again, the ambition was to offer a clearly superior product. In 1980, Salomon made the headlines when it introduced a unique system: a cross-country boot and binding combination. This was definitely a superior concept, which took off very quickly and put Salomon at the top with an amazing 30 percent of the market in 1987.

Meanwhile, being dependent on winter sports had become a major concern for Salomon's management. The company considered several activities that could provide a counterbalance. One option was windsurfing, which was turned down because it did not offer enough potential and was already suffering from a huge overcapacity. Eventually, the golfing business was chosen, an industry twice as big as winter sports: about FF 12 billion. In 1984, Salomon purchased the entire shareholdings of the American company,

---

[3]"The slipper."

Taylor-Made, which manufactured and sold upmarket golf clubs. The choice of Taylor-Made was based on its similarity to Salomon: the philosophy of providing excellence through innovation.

Over the years, Salomon's progressive product diversification reflected ambitious goals for each market entry, which had its roots in the corporate culture and, especially, in the personality of the president.

MANAGEMENT, STRUCTURE, AND CULTURE

In the mid-80s, Salomon had become a mini-multinational with subsidiaries in 12 countries. The headquarters in the suburb of Annecy also had a definite international feeling, with managers coming from around the world (Canada, Norway, the United States). Like Philips and Bosch, Salomon had a matrix organization that was structured around its products (bindings, shoes, cross-country equipment, etc.) and their respective markets (using national sales organizations). The company had come a long way from the little workshop that made ski edges to become a multi-line sports equipment firm.

At Salomon S.A., recruitment was considered a particularly important task. The company was very demanding and therefore selective, and could afford to be so because its sporty and dynamic image made it a very attractive employer. Early on, it had recruited engineers and technicians from the best schools. It also was able to attract the most senior managers from top companies. The majority of the people working at Salomon had a double profile: highly skilled in their discipline and expert in a sport. Indeed, several of them were former ski champions. Consequently, Salomon was managed with state-of-the-art technology and highly skilled motivated teams who, literally, "loved" their products.

The personality of Georges Salomon as an individual had a big impact on the culture of the company. Even though he did not have a technical education, he spent a lot of his time looking for ways that new technology could bring value to products. He had personally developed several products, which gave him credibility with his team. He was the one mainly responsible for the goal to launch only products that were clearly and visibly superior. Also essential to the company's successful product development record was its impeccable use of extreme caution in all decision making. This prudence came, in large part, from Georges's anxiety about the outcome of each company product. Everyone who managed a major project knew that he must be thoroughly prepared with an answer for all of Georges's concerns. Above all, Georges was a mountaineer and a careful climber who was aware that "rushing tends to be dangerous."

Georges Salomon's daily behavior also carried some messages to his organization; he made no secret about where his priorities were. Even though he had received countless awards in Paris for the company's performance (in design, innovation, exports), Georges avoided personal publicity. He did not care much about pleasing the establishment, either. He much preferred walking around the company's workshops discussing new products, contributing ideas, even occasionally drawing a quick sketch. When he had to meet with bankers or high-ranking officials, he would insist on inviting them to the company canteen.

Georges's personal life-style reflected his passion for his job and dedication to the company. In his dress, he was informal and casual—preferring mountaineer clothing. For a long time, he drove a rusty Renault 5, which was a frequent topic of discussion. His chalet, on a slope overlooking Annecy, was considered spacious but not luxurious.

He played a central role in company strategy, particularly when it came to market entry decisions. Georges was very demanding, systematically wanting to ensure that every product would really make a difference and that the strategy concerning its development and launch was optimal. He often reminded the project team that he would "pull the plug" at any time if he had any doubts about the project's success. And he meant it; indeed, he had actually canceled some projects a few weeks before their official launch.

THE DECISION TO ENTER THE SKI MARKET

By 1984, Georges Salomon had come to the conclusion that it was time to enter the ski market. In his view, Salomon, the world's largest company in the winter sports industry, could no longer ignore such an essential piece of equipment for skiers.

Skis, as a product, had several characteristics that made them attractive to Salomon. First of all, they were the most visible piece of equipment. In practical terms, in a photograph of a skier in action, it was the skis that one could see most clearly; the boot and the binding were usually not so easily distinguishable. Hence, from a communication point of view, skis offered better support to the brand name. Secondly, skis were the most expensive item bought by skiers and, therefore, the market size was bigger (about twice the amount of the bindings market). Finally, skis were the piece of equipment most talked about by skiers, the focus of an enthusiast's passion, in a way that boots and bindings could not equal. Consequently, skis were a powerful contributor to brand awareness. As Georges Salomon explained to his staff: "Ski companies that are much smaller than Salomon in terms of sales enjoy a greater brand recognition by the public . . . which is why this ski development challenge is so important for our firm."

Salomon's management felt that it had the capability to enter the ski market successfully. The company had adequate experience, it was argued, to take on this new activity, given its track record and current situation. For example, Salomon had:

- A **mastery of innovation**, thanks to the most advanced design tools, and databases on skiers' needs and desires, and on the behavior and reaction of various materials.

- A **know-how in automation**, which allowed it to achieve higher-quality levels and competitive production costs.

- A **financially healthy situation**, which made it possible for the corporation to afford the high R&D expenditures and the necessary financial investment at the manufacturing stage.

- A **strong brand image and distribution network**, which could quickly promote sales of this new ski and generate economies of scale at the same time.

In a survey conducted in 1984 to learn about Salomon's brand image, it appeared that the market was definitely anticipating such a move: in fact, a significant proportion of interviewees believed that Salomon was already making skis! This surprising piece of information provided even more motivation to enter this market, in spite of the risks.

Salomon's management was conscious that moving into skis was not a risk-free operation. After all, the company's bindings were being mounted on other manufacturers' skis. Even though the ski-binding assembly was done at the retail level, some feared that large ski competitors might try to retaliate by joining forces with some other bindings producers—for example, "ski X prefers bindings Y." Also, this move could prompt a countermove into Salomon's own territory, with other ski manufacturers deciding to compete in bindings and boots. Finally, the issue of branding was also raised. Salomon was planning to offer all three products (skis, bindings, and boots) under its own brand name. It would be the first company to make such an offering. Clearly, there were some risks associated with this strategy—that is, if a customer had a bad experience with one of the products, the other products could be affected as well.

These concerns, however, did not prevent the company from going ahead with the diversification. By 1985, Salomon's top management had set up ambitious objectives for the ski business:

1. To become a world leader, in five or six years, in the medium to top segments of the market.
2. To reach, at "cruising speed," a net profitability of the same order of magnitude as bindings and boots (around 9 percent of sales).

In order to pursue these demanding objectives, the following strategic principles were established:

- To give skiers a piece of equipment with a "plus," based on some visible innovation that would be identified through market surveys and technical research.
- To emphasize partnership with distributors in order to provide optimal quality service.
- To gain recognition through success in competition, with the Winter Olympics in Albertville (Winter 1992) being used to enhance the impact.

THE SKI MARKET IN 1987

There were some 55 million skiers in the world in 1987. Most of them were in Western Europe (around 30 million), North America (9 million), and Japan (the single largest national market with over 12 million skiers). There were also some minor markets in Eastern Europe (particularly Yugoslavia, Poland, Czechoslovakia, and the USSR) and in Australia. The proportion of skiers to the total population varied tremendously from country to country and was partly a function of local skiing possibilities. Switzerland was clearly the highest (with a ratio of 30.4 percent), followed by Austria (27.7 percent) and Sweden (23.8 percent), then Germany, Italy, and France (in the 10–12 percent range). The United States, although a large market of 5.4 million skiers, had a very low ratio (2.2 percent) compared to Japan (9.9 percent).

Skiing as a sport was being influenced by several important trends. First of all, skiing had become affordable and accessible to an increasing number of consumers, but the relative time spent participating in winter sports had been diminishing.

Secondly, skiers tended to be less "fanatic" than in the past, especially as the competitive pressure of other leisure activities (golfing, cruising, tourism in exotic countries) grew stronger. Thirdly, skiing had become an increasingly diversified sport—with "off-piste" (off the official groomed trails), mogul, freestyle, acrobatic, and speed skiing, as well as the introduction of new types of equipment (monoskis and surfboards). The final factor was fashion: Colors in equipment and clothing were becoming brighter and more dramatic, and styles and shapes were ever changing.

The Market

The international ski market was already mature. It was expected to plateau at around 6.5 million pairs (refer to Exhibit 4) with possible ups and downs following business cycles and the amount of snowfall. The world market was estimated at FF 4.5 billion, compared to FF 3.5 billion for ski boots and FF 2 billion for bindings. The largest national markets were (in rank order) Japan, the United States, Germany, and France (refer to Exhibit 5). Some markets still seemed to be growing (North America), while others were flattening (Japan, Western Europe) or even declining (Scandinavia) over the short to medium term.

The price structure of the market was somewhat peculiar. In most markets, the distribution of sales along the price range could be seen as a pyramid, with sales of the most expensive segment being the smallest. The ski market, however, presented a different pattern, as the most expensive products sold more than the medium-priced ones (refer to Exhibit 6).

The traditional market segmentation made a first distinction between rental (10 percent of the volume), junior (another 20 percent) and adult (the remainder). Within the adult segment, there were three types of users: leisure (55 percent of the volume), sport (20 percent) and performance (25 percent). Leisure skiers tended to be people who skied for recreation and to have fun, not for "records." The second segment included skiers that were more "aggressive" on the slopes, but not competing in any way. The last segment were those skiers who were involved in some form of competition. The last two segments (sport and performance), sometimes called "medium" and "top," represented around 2 million pairs of skis.

The Competitors

The number of competitors was much higher in skis than in bindings or boots. Some 80 different brands were competing worldwide (21 in Japan, 15 in the United States, 12 in Austria, 6 in France, and 20 more in other countries). Most companies owned one brand, except large players like the world leader Rossignol (France) which controlled Dynastar (also in France). On the average, the number of brands present in each country was about twice as large as in bindings.

In addition, skis were sold under private label. The estimate was that, worldwide, this represented around 50 percent of volume, with the proportion varying considerably from country to country.

The market was dominated by Rossignol (France), Atomic (Austria), Elan (Yugoslavia), Head (United States), Dynastar (France), and Blizzard (Austria), which all sold more than half a million pairs every year (refer to Exhibit 7). Most Japanese manufacturers were relatively small (100 to 150,000 pairs), except for Yamaha, which barely passed the 200,000 pair threshold. While the Western brands were present in Europe, the Japanese producers were virtually nonexistent outside Japan.

Exhibit 4   Ski Sales in the 1980s

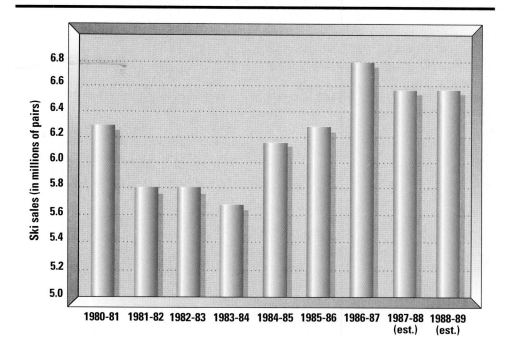

Competitors differed in their approach to the ski market in many ways. A few strategic dimensions seemed to be critical in discriminating among industry players. The first dimension was overall product positioning. Some companies, such as Rossignol and Atomic, offered skis for all levels—from beginners to racers—while others focused on a specific market niche (the upmarket: Völkl, Fischer, K2; the low to medium end: Head, Elan). Participation in ski competition also affected a company's positioning. Brands that addressed the top end of the market (Rossignol, Völkl, K2) sponsored ski racers in an effort to enhance the visibility of their products, while companies focusing on the lower niches did not pursue this activity. Another important dimension was the scope of market presence. Most of the 80 ski manufacturers around the world were only local players that marketed their products in their own country. This situation was particularly true for the Japanese brands. Among the companies that had "gone international," the scope of market coverage differed. The leaders (Rossignol, Atomic, Elan, Head, Dynastar) were present in all significant markets; other companies (like Blizzard) had substantial international sales, but were not represented in all national markets.

The Manufacturing of Skis

Skis, which had been in existence for at least 5,000 years, only were considered "sports equipment" at the beginning of the 20th century, when they were brought to Switzerland by British tourists. The first skis were very simple, made out of ordinary wood. In order to achieve a more solidly constructed ski, one of the first innovations was to use laminates of wood that were glued together, thus gaining greater flexibility

Exhibit 5   Sales of Skis, by Country, 1986–1987 Winter Season

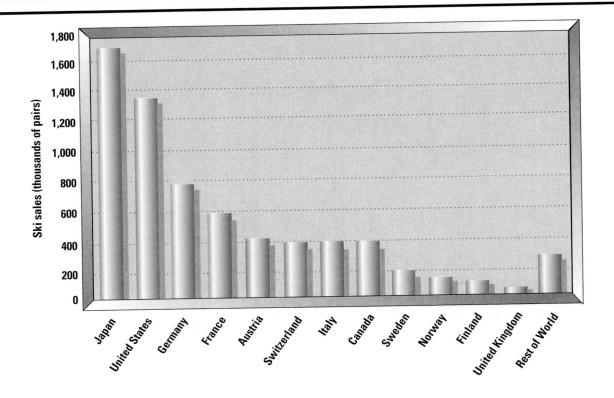

and a longer ski. Metal edges were introduced later in order to reduce deterioration of the sole of the ski and provide a better grip. After World War II, plastic soles were added to enhance the ski's sliding capability. In 1950, Head introduced the metal sandwich ski, which irreversibly changed ski technology. Metal was later replaced by the various plastic and composite materials that dominated the market in the 80s.

At this point in time, several types of design were used in the construction of skis. The most common structures were the sandwich ski and the torsion box ski (refer to Exhibit 8). A sandwich ski was essentially made of various materials arranged in layers, with the more rigid and resistant layers on the top and the bottom of the ski. This technology, which increased resistance to flexion and shock absorption, was the most widely used (75 percent of skis). In a torsion box ski, the resistance was obtained from a box located in the core of the ski. It gave a better grip in the snow, as well as a quicker reaction. Together, the sandwich and torsion box technologies represented 90 percent of the skis manufactured. There were a few other technologies—for example, the "omega" structure—but most of them had only a very limited production.

The Production Cycle

The production of skis started a full year before the winter season, in November. For instance, skis sold by retailers between November 1985 and March 1986 had been produced between November 1984 and November 1985. This production phase had

Exhibit 6   The Market Price Structure in the Ski Market

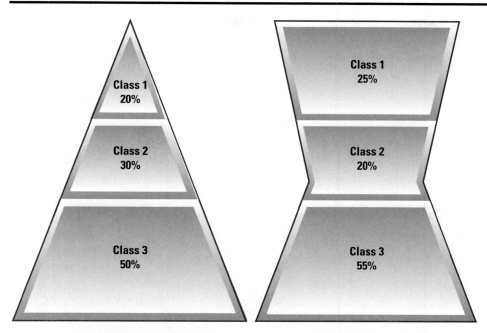

Conventional Market Price Structure   **Ski Market in the late 80s**

Salomon Winter Sports Marketing Department defined three price-based segments: Class 1 was the least expensive skis (roughly less than FF 1,000); Class 2 was medium-priced skis (1,000 to 2,000); and Class 3 included the most expensive skis (2,000 to 3,000). FF 3,000 or US $800 was considered the upper limit.

been preceded by development work on shape, materials, and art work. The duration of the development phase depended on the importance of the work involved, from four years for a major ski innovation to a few months for a cosmetic change, which was being done every year in recent years (colors and art work).

The production plan, initially made during the preceding summer, could be adjusted at three points. The first occasion was ISPO, the annual sports industry exhibition in Munich, in the second part of February every year when distributors started to order. Later, in May, when the number of orders was better known, a second adjustment would be made. Lastly, in September–October, as orders were being completed, it was possible to fine-tune production to market demand (volume and mix).

Over time, manufacturing had become a complex process. In the 80s, it involved the assembly of several kinds of material (steel, fibers, resins, plastic sheets) which represented around 13 percent of the retail price. Each material was carefully selected, as it played a role in the performance of the ski. Production workers would typically put together the different materials needed (the sole, the edges, the various layers, polyester resin, the upper platform) into a mold, which would then be put into a press with warm plates. Because of the material and equipment involved, which

Exhibit 7   Sales by Manufacturers

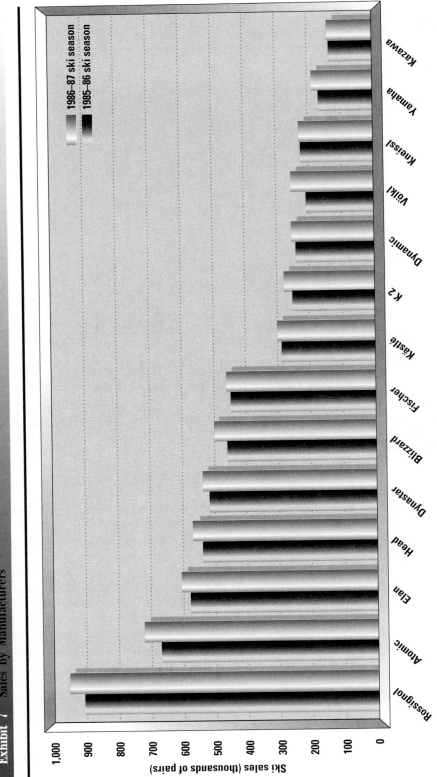

Exhibit 8 Types of Ski Structures

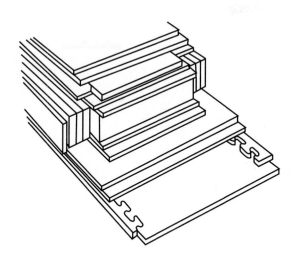

Sandwich Structure

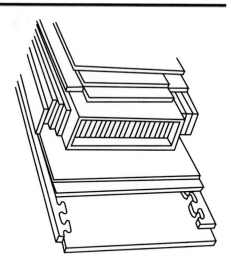

Torsion Box Structure

generated both heat and odor, working conditions were difficult. Manufacturing costs represented 19.5 percent of the retail price.

Distribution

Skis were sold through a network of wholesalers and retailers, which was organized by the manufacturers. Small brands tended to rely on local independent distributors (one per country), while large manufacturers often had their own sales organization for major countries. It was estimated that the cost of the wholesale function amounted to 17.5 percent of the retail price.

Retailing was shared between independent outlets and distribution chains. In ski resorts, independent retailers—usually also managing a large rental activity—were dominant. In major towns and cities, large retail chains (such as Intersport in Germany and Decathlon in France) represented the major portion of the market. Non-specialized chains (hypermarkets) had a limited participation, mostly selling inexpensive products. On average, the retailers' margin was 50 percent of the final price, including sales tax.

Depending on the country, retailers offered 5 to 10 different brands,[4] with 4–5 models in each one. There were some real technical differences, in terms of materials, structure, and shape, that needed to be evaluated in the selection process, along with more superficial considerations. Consumers thus had an enormous choice. The selection of a ski was often made through the recommendation of a salesperson, on the basis of physical characteristics, skiing style, ability, and budget (refer to Exhibit 9).

---

[4]Except in Japan, where retailers typically stored 25 different brands.

Exhibit 9   The Ski Purchasing Process

The following table presents the distribution of answers to the question below asked to a sample of ski buyers: "What do you think is the best way to choose skis when buying them?" Respondents could give more than one answer so the percentages do not add to 100%.

	Total	France	Germany	United States	Japan
1. Pick a brand with a good reputation.	26%	27%	21%	31%	25%
2. Select a brand you have already used.	17	16	27	15	9
3. Listen to other people's advice.	44	35	45	39	56
4. Be guided by a ski salesman.	26	31	30	15	28
5. It is a personal decision. Choose the ski you like.	16	12	5	19	26
6. Gather information, read reviews, study technical tests.	20	14	23	23	18
7. Follow advice from ski instructors.	8	12	8	4	7
8. Rent a ski and test it before buying.	16	16	23	18	6
9. Pick the brand a champion uses.	2%	*%	2%	5%	*%
Sample size (total respondents)	n=1444	n=350	n=373	n=361	n=360

* Negligible

Therefore, the sales process required having capable, often technical, explanations by the retail staff, a situation which called for training. Although makers of the best-selling brands made a genuine effort to provide technical information to their network, product descriptions and performance data provided to retailers sometimes tended to be unclear, with an overemphasis on jargon. Ill-founded rumors and myths were not uncommon.

Communication with the consumer was done through advertising in specialized magazines and point-of-sale material (catalogs, leaflets). In addition, magazines published articles appraising new products coming onto the market and were another channel of information, mostly for the high end of the market.

THE MONOCOQUE PROJECT

The origin of the monocoque[5] project could be traced to early 1984 when Georges Salomon entered the office of Roger Pascal, the director of the Bindings Division, and said: "Pascal, you have to make me a ski!"

Roger Pascal, then 46 years old, had worked with Salomon since 1969. He was an engineer by training (INSA, Lyon), but he was also an expert skier, having been a ski instructor (École du Ski Français) while he was a student. He had started in the engineering department and eventually had become manager, before heading the ski boot engineering department.

Initial Steps

Georges Salomon and Roger Pascal agreed that there could be no meaningful entry into the ski business without an in-depth knowledge of the ski market and industry. They reckoned that, even though Salomon was selling in related markets, its

---

[5]Pronounced *mon-oh-caulk.*

information on consumers' needs, technological solutions, and marketing processes was not sufficient to make a difference in the ski market.

The ski project got underway with the appointment of Jean-Luc Diard in July 1984. Jean-Luc had just completed his studies at the ESC Paris, one of the top business schools in France. He was also an excellent skier, having won the annual French student ski championship. Recruited as a special kind of trainee,[6] he was sent to Salomon's Austrian subsidiary to study the ski market and industry. He focused on making an international study of the best products available at the time, and traveled extensively to meet and interview the world's experts. The information he gathered was encouraging for Salomon: There were still ways to improve on existing ski technologies.

At the same time, a series of market surveys were launched in order to appraise the level of satisfaction among skiers. The first results came as a surprise. While Salomon had detected significant frustration with ski boots in earlier surveys, it seemed that consumers were generally satisfied with skis. These results renewed Georges Salomon's conviction that the new ski must be radically better if it were to make a difference in the marketplace. In order to have a specific goal and objective for the team, Georges and Roger agreed that the ski should be able to sell at a 15 percent premium above the market price.

The Project Team

In the summer of 1985, Georges Salomon was able to convince two technology experts—Maurice Legrand and Yves Gagneux—to join the ski development team. Maurice Legrand, the former head of Rossignol's engineering department, was in charge of product technology. Yves Gagneux, the former head of manufacturing at Dynamic, was made responsible for process technology.

The team—Roger, Jean-Luc, Maurice, and Yves—functioned like a "commando operation"—that is, a group of highly skilled volunteers who were totally devoted to their "secret mission." The team was maintained out of the normal organization, in an effort to preserve confidentiality as long as possible. Their work was kept secret, even to insiders, as Salomon did not want its competitors to know about it. Also, like a commando group, there was a sense of close community among the members, with each one knowing what the others were doing. Indeed, the competence of all the team members was truly exceptional: each individual was outstanding in his field and all were excellent skiers as well. In addition, the interaction was so interconnected that their disciplinary boundaries were blurred. Thus, Jean-Luc, in charge of marketing, also contributed technical solutions, while Maurice came up with marketing ideas.

Project Management

The activity of the ski development team was characterized by a high energy level, thanks to the enthusiasm and the sense of challenge that surrounded their mission. This project, however, was not a "skunk works" operation.[7] Quite the contrary. Yves Gagneux explained: "Maurice Legrand and myself were able to bring the

---

[6] A program that allowed a graduate to be a trainee in a French firm or public organization outside of France, as a replacement for military service.

[7] A "skunk works" project typically operated with a minimum budget and no real facilities.

technical knowledge that Salomon was lacking. But, Salomon provided us with a superb project management approach without which our expertise, as good as it was, would have been a lot less effective. Clearly, that was a strong point at Salomon!"

The management of the project actually used the whole gamut of modern techniques. At the very beginning, Georges Salomon had set the goal: to introduce a ski in five or six years, with excellent and visible advantages over existing products. The team translated this objective into a very detailed action plan, specifying the milestones, the resources needed, the tools used—Quality Function Deployment, Design to Manufacturing, Consumer Clinics. Early on, the team had worked on a business plan that outlined expenditures and income on a yearly basis, from the project's inception to the "cruising speed" period in the mid-90s.

The team reported regularly to the Executive Committee for major investment or expenditure decisions. It also presented a progress report to the New Model Committee on implementation issues. However, more important than the formal reporting were the team's meetings, which Georges Salomon personally attended. In summing up his style, one individual commented: "Georges Salomon isn't usually found behind his desk . . . he is more likely to be in the product development lab . . . clomping around in ski boots and baggy sweater . . . doing what he likes best . . . devising ways to frustrate his competition."[8] In order to answer all the probing questions that an anxious Georges Salomon inevitably asked, the team had to be well prepared—an exercise that obviously took time. *"Se hâter lentement"*[9] could have been the motto for this project.

The Concept Development

Between July 1985 and January 1987, Roger Pascal asked the team, which over time had progressively been enlarged, to systematically study all aspects of ski technology: measurements, the core, the sole, printing techniques, the spatula, edges, polishing, wax. The mandate was for each team member to come up with two or three ideas for improving every aspect studied. The team leaders would meet regularly to review these ideas and seek ways to incorporate them into a concept. In fact, they succeeded in producing the first plaster model by the second semester of 1985.

The shape of the ski gradually emerged as a result of these systematic experiments. The team realized early on that little could be done to the shape of the sole, which had been already optimized over time to the point where skiers were accustomed to it. However, alternatives for the walls on both sides and for the surface of the ski could be considered. The team started to challenge the verticality of the side walls. Were they optimum? Could other settings be better? In a very creative fashion, they explored the various options: from being slanted outward to slanted inward. A close examination revealed that the best solution was actually a progressive profile, with nearly vertical walls under the ski boots to provide an optimum grip where it was most needed, and side walls slanted inward to ensure optimum cutting into the snow at both extremes. These changes, in addition, had the required characteristics of being visible, one of the conditions set clearly by Georges Salomon (refer to Exhibit 10).

---

[8]*Business Week,* April 19, 1989.
[9]A French saying that means "rushing slowly."

Exhibit 10   The Ski Concept: Progressive Profile

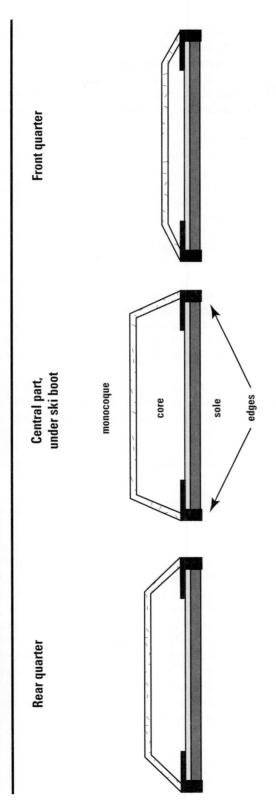

Front quarter

Central part,
under ski boot

monocoque

core

sole

edges

Rear quarter

This initial idea naturally led to another important discovery: the side walls and surface of the ski should be made of a unique shell that would carry a major part of the stress. In conventional skis, the action of the skier passed from the steel edges through a succession of layers, particularly in the sandwich ski. This method of transmission was more indirect and resulted in less precision. The monocoque structure (the unique piece linking the surface to the edges) would thus provide a better control of the ski.

The team was supplied with the best computer-assisted design (CAD) system available in the industry at the time (ComputerVision and Sun Microsystems). The ideas were quickly converted into drawings in the engineering lab. Molds for prototypes were machined directly from the CAD system, which allowed them to create a large number of shapes for testing. By the middle of 1986, the first prototypes were available. They were tested in labs as well as on the snow, with test engineers and expert skiers hired as consultants with a confidentiality agreement. The team at that time comprised around 35 people.

Several ideas for improving the manufacturing process were conceived. While most ski manufacturers applied composite material in a tacky state, the team found a new way to handle this step more satisfactorily. Yves Gagneux explored the "dry process," which consisted of using fibers that had already been impregnated with resin and dried, which were therefore not only much easier to manipulate but had the additional advantage of not smelling strongly, as the "wet process" did. It was expected that these enhanced working conditions would produce a much higher level of quality as well.

By November 1987, the engineering studies were providing interesting results. The team had developed a detailed understanding of the ski market. It knew the strengths and weaknesses of the best competitors. It had identified a long list of possible improvement areas. It had even singled out the particular areas where it wanted the new ski to make a difference. The prototypes that had been developed, through numerous trials and tests, were showing very promising potential.

THE DECISION

There were, of course, still a number of issues that needed to be clarified. In one sense, it was obvious that the team had done a good job, considering that the project had started from scratch in 1984. They had gone a long way toward the development of a radically new ski. Some of the detailed engineering still needed for the ski's final development was clearly going to be even more demanding. In order to proceed, the New Product Committee would have to release a budget for engineering work, testing, and for the construction of a new plant. Given the technology required, some of it actually calling for custom-made equipment, the budget would amount to some FF 300 million. Additionally, using a full-time team that would be expanded to 50 people would increase the operating costs.

The team's next challenge was to prepare a clear action-plan for finalizing the development of Salomon's monocoque ski and launching it into the already crowded and mature ski market.

The Whistler Golf Course

Bryan Andrews, University of Guelph
Robert C. Lewis, University of Guelph

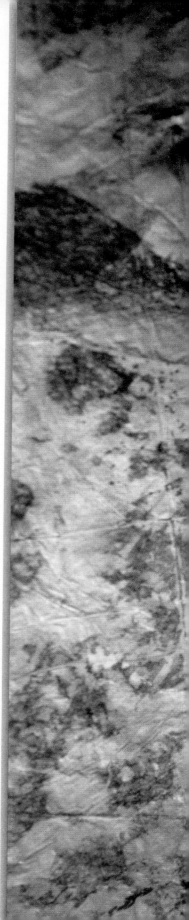

In January 1993, Jim Watson, vice president of the Whistler Resort and Conference Centre, settled in a chairlift headed for the top of the mountain. Jim was thinking about the Whistler Golf Course, one of the divisions under his control. He shook his head and chuckled, "Where else in the world would a person ski powder snow at lunch while thinking about the golf season?"

Appointed VP Finance in 1987, Jim directed company accounting and financing functions as well as managing the golf course and conference centre. He was a chartered accountant with 25 years of financial experience at McDonald's of Canada and Vancouver's World Exposition.

The golf course's sales and profits over the last three years pleased Jim. The course was running at near capacity of 30,000 rounds a season. He knew this was due to the steadily increasing popularity of the sport on the west coast. Associates at other top clubs had told him their courses were also approaching capacity. The result had been annual increases in British Columbia greens fees over the last five years. Jim realized, however, that to maintain or enhance the Whistler Golf Course's position, various long-term strategic decisions would be required.

Competition was emerging in the Whistler market. The Canadian Pacific (CP) hotel golf course had opened in 1992. A third Whistler area course with hotel, Green Lakes, was in the planning stage and would open in 1994 about four miles from the village. Seven other new courses were also planned between Vancouver (80 miles to the south) and Whistler as well as a Bjorn Borg Whistler Resort including a 17-court tennis complex, but no golf.

Since opening day in 1983, the Whistler Golf Course had operated profitably without a clubhouse. A 20-foot by 60-foot temporary trailer contained retail space, storage, washrooms, and an office. Food, mostly snacks, was served from 20-foot by 25-foot wooden huts. Jim was convinced that a new clubhouse was essential to enhance the Whistler golf product and stave off the competition.

Jim's earlier presentation had received a positive response from the Whistler Resort Association Board. The board members had approved the hiring of consultants to study the feasibility (including architectural site plans) of building a new clubhouse. When the consultant's report was presented, the approval to build was turned down. "Is our timing off?" they said. "With the continuing recession in North America why should we spend a million dollars when the Whistler Resort Association's primary function is to market Whistler?" Jim was deciding what his next move should be . . .

THE WHISTLER RESORT AREA ———————————————

Whistler began as a summer wilderness resort located 80 miles north of Vancouver in the coastal mountains of British Columbia, Canada. Lodges were built in the early 1900s as fishing and holiday retreats. The evolution to winter recreation came in 1965. That was the year Whistler Mountain Ski Corp. opened five ski lifts. By the early 1980s, an Alpine village consisting of hotels, restaurants, and shops was built and opened for business. Exhibits 1 and 2 show the route to Whistler and layout of the village. This beautiful village was nestled in the valley among five lakes and surrounded by mile-high mountains. By 1993, Whistler was North America's top ski resort as rated by *Snow Magazine*. Based on a survey of its readers, Whistler was number one for skiing terrain and facilities, village design, and amenities.

In the past 12 years, Whistler had enjoyed economic growth of 6 percent per year. A world-class, year-round international resort had arisen from dreams and hopes in the 1970s. The permanent population had grown from 400 in 1970 to 4,500 in 1992 (7,500 in winter). The community population was young (85 percent were 44 or less) and well educated (30 percent had university degrees).

The Village of Whistler had won a number of architectural design awards. A pedestrian-oriented town, automobiles were prohibited on village streets. Vehicles were parked in a vast underground lot located below the town. The buildings and walkways were designed for maximum exposure to sunshine and provided wonderful mountain views. All summer resort amenities (Exhibit 3) were integrated into the village and were within five minutes' walking distance. Whistler had 60 tourist accommodation properties, 52 restaurants, and 23 lounges and clubs. Total investment in Whistler over the last five years had been $500 million. The municipality forecasted $100 million investment per year for the next 10 years.

Blackcomb Ski Corp. and Whistler Ski Corp. operated on two separate mountains and were the dominant businesses in Whistler. The companies offered customers a full range of services. Skiers were carried by chairlift up the mountains and provided with groomed and patrolled trails and runs. The companies operated food and beverage services, retail shops, and ski schools for adults and children. Together, Blackcomb Ski Corp. and Whistler Ski Corp. operated over 200 ski runs with the largest high-speed lift system in North America. In 1992, Blackcomb and Whistler Ski Corp. reported 1.3 million ski visits during the winter season from mid-November to mid-May. Blackcomb also opened in the summer for glacier skiing from mid-July to mid-August.

The two largest hotels in Whistler were Canadian Pacific's Chateau Whistler and the Delta Mountain Inn. The Chateau Whistler was a 343-room luxury resort hotel. Its facilities included convention and meeting rooms for up to 500, tennis, swimming, and a brand-new 18-hole championship golf course. The hotel grossed over $5 million in 1992. Delta Mountain Inn was second largest with 292 rooms. The Delta had some small meeting rooms, indoor tennis and squash courts, and over 10 retail shops. This hotel was located in the village beside the Whistler Mountain gondola and the Whistler Golf Course driving range. The third largest was the Fairways Hotel with 194 rooms, located beside the Whistler Golf Course. This hotel's restaurant and sports bar were popular with golfers and tournament groups. Many hotels, lodges, and condominiums were scattered throughout the area.

Whistler Resort Association

The Whistler Resort Association (WRA) was incorporated by the landowners of Whistler to promote the development and operation of the resort lands. The organization's activities were controlled through bylaws approved by the municipality. The

Exhibit 1   Location of Whistler Resort

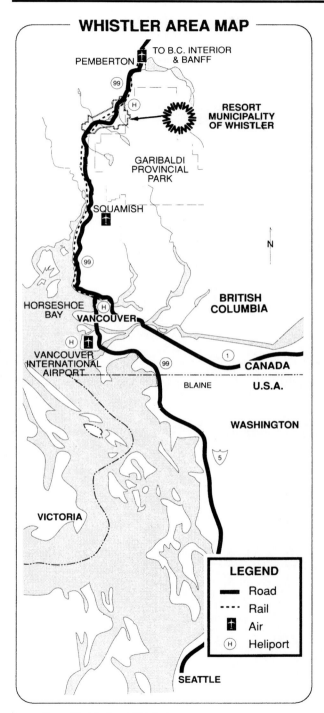

WHISTLER AREA MAP

PEMBERTON

TO B.C. INTERIOR & BANFF

99

RESORT MUNICIPALITY OF WHISTLER

GARIBALDI PROVINCIAL PARK

SQUAMISH

N

99

BRITISH COLUMBIA

HORSESHOE BAY

VANCOUVER

VANCOUVER INTERNATIONAL AIRPORT

99

CANADA

BLAINE   U.S.A.

1

WASHINGTON

5

VICTORIA

SEATTLE

LEGEND
━━━	Road
-----	Rail
✈	Air
Ⓗ	Heliport

•WHISTLER

TRANSPORTATION TO WHISTLER

ROAD   Car: Whistler is a two-hour drive from Vancouver via Highway 99 and a five-hour drive from Seattle.

Bus: Daily scheduled bus service is provided from downtown Vancouver and Vancouver International Airport. Whistler is packaged by tour operators worldwide.

Rent-a-Car: Rental cars and trucks are available in Whistler and Vancouver.

Taxi /   Companies offer transport to Whistler
Limousine: from Vancouver International Airport.

Services: B.C. Rail provides daily rail service
RAIL   from North Vancouver.

Facilities: Vancouver International Airport,
AIR   Squamish Airport, Whistler Heliport, Green Lake Floatplane Base, and Pemberton Airport.

Services: Chartered helicopter and floatplane service is offered from Whistler to Vancouver and surrounding areas.

Driving Times / Mileage from Whistler to Surrounding Towns / Cities

To:			
	Pemberton	35 km/22 mi.	25 min.
	Squamish	50 km/31 mi.	45 min.
	Vancouver	120 km/75 mi.	2 hr.
	Seattle	354 km/218 mi.	5 hr.

Source: Resort Municipality of Whistler.

Exhibit 2 Map of Whistler Village

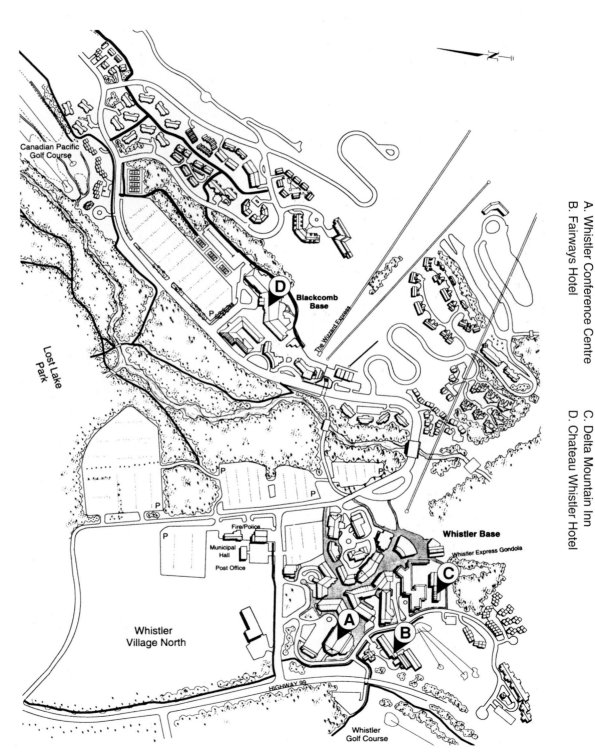

A. Whistler Conference Centre
B. Fairways Hotel
C. Delta Mountain Inn
D. Chateau Whistler Hotel

Source: Resort Municipality of Whistler.

Exhibit 3   Whistler Summer/Fall Activities

SUMMER/FALL ACTIVITIES

- Baseball
- Bicycling
- Camping
- Canoeing
- Chairlift and gondola rides
- Concerts and music festivals
- Fishing
- Floatplane tours
- Golfing
- Hay rides
- Helicopter rides and tours
- Helihiking
- Hiking

- Historical exhibits
- Horseback riding
- Hot air ballooning
- Ice climbing
- Jogging/running
- Kayaking
- Marathons
- Minigolf
- Mountain biking/racing
- Mountain climbing
- Paragliding
- Photography
- Rockclimbing

- Rollerblading
- Sailing
- Sightseeing
- Skateboarding
- Ski camps
- Skiing
- Snowboarding
- Street entertainment
- Swimming
- Tennis
- Walking
- White water rafting
- Windsurfing

WHISTLER AREA PARKS AND RECREATION

1. Alpha Lake Park
   - Beach
   - Tennis
   - Volleyball
   - Concession
   - Picnic
   - Fishing
   - Canoe rental

2. Whistler Creek
   - Information center
   - Train tours

3. Wayside Park
   - Beach
   - Canoe rentals
   - Sailboat rentals and lessons
   - Picnic
   - Fishing
   - Concession

4. Lakeside Park
   - Beach
   - Canoe rentals
   - Windsurfing rentals and lessons
   - Picnic
   - Fishing
   - Concession

5. Rainbow Park
   - Canoe launch
   - Picnic
   - Volleyball
   - Beach
   - Fishing
   - Windsurfing

6. Whistler Golf Course
   - 18-hole championship course
   - Golf lessons
   - Cart rentals
   - Putting green
   - Pro shop
   - Equipment rentals
   - Practice fairway

7. Whistler Village
   - Information booths
   - Bicycle rentals
   - Movie Theater
   - Helihiking
   - Bicycle tours
   - River rafting
   - Mountain sightseeing
   - Indoor entertainment center and arcade
   - Aerobics classes
   - Fishing trips (guided)
   - Fishing licenses

8. Fitzsimmons Creek Park
   - Picnic
   - Skateboard bowl
   - Walking trails

9. Lost Lake Park
   - Beach
   - Hiking trails
   - Fishing
   - Picnic
   - Bicycle trails

10. Balsam Park
    - Picnic
    - Children's playground

11. Meadow Park
    - Tennis
    - Children's water park
    - Softball
    - Canoe launch

12. Emerald Park
    - Tennis
    - Children's playground

13. Green Lake Park
    - Picnic
    - Beach

14. Emerald Water Access
    - Boat launch

Source: Resort Municipality of Whistler.

board of directors in 1992 included the mayor and alderman of Whistler, the president of the WRA, the president of Blackcomb Ski Corp., the president of Whistler Ski Corp., a representative of Commercial Properties, a representative of Hotel Properties, and an elected official. Membership (2,200 in 1993) was mandatory for any business in the resort. The association was funded by dues computed on a percentage of members' business revenues. The four largest dues-paying members were Blackcomb Ski Corp., Whistler Ski Corp., Canadian Pacific Whistler Chateau Hotel, and Delta Mountain Inn.

The mission of the Whistler Resort Association was to market Whistler as a year-round international resort area. The WRA operated a central reservation system for resort accommodations. Through one toll-free number, anyone anywhere in the world could book a room in Whistler. Tourist information centers, providing the latest information on current events in Whistler, were run by the Association. Summer festivals, special events, and concerts were offered by the WRA, and the Association advertised the resort extensively in Canadian, American, Japanese, and European markets. In 1985, the WRA took over the operations of the Whistler Convention Centre (WCC). In conjunction with the WCC, the WRA operated the Whistler Golf Course.

Whistler Convention Centre

The Whistler Convention Centre (WCC) was located in Whistler Village adjacent to the Whistler Golf Course. Built in 1985 to provide meeting and convention services, the Centre accommodated groups of up to 1,200 delegates. It was equipped with the latest audiovisual equipment, some of which was housed in the 300-seat movie theater. The Centre was Whistler's only movie house and was also used for stage performances and lectures.

WCC catering provided a full range of services on site. Banquets could serve groups of 10 to 1,000. The catering department had successfully hosted many large high-profile events—for example, the Premiers of Canada Dinner, the World Cup Downhill Ski Dinner, and the PepsiCo International Conference. WCC kitchens and staff also provided golf tournament catering needs. Foods prepared in the Centre were transported to the golf course.

Whistler Golf Course

The Whistler Golf Course opened in 1983, and until 1992 it was Whistler's only 18-hole championship golf course. It was designed by Arnold Palmer, a renowned golf professional, and had been chosen as one of the best in the world by *Golf Magazine*. The fairways and greens were set among five ponds and two winding creeks. The golf course was a source of pride in the community. The *Whistler Question,* a local newspaper, often ran articles about the current conditions and developments at the golf course. In 1992, the newspaper reported the WRA's intention to build a new clubhouse facility. The article was generally supportive of the plans and quoted a number of golfers it had surveyed on the issue; the responses included requests for improved membership facilities and services. The local season passholders felt a clubhouse would provide a needed place to "suit up" before a game—that is, put on golf shoes and clothing, and purchase golf balls, tees, and equipment. They also said a clubhouse would be a facility to relax in after a game or when weather stopped play. The consensus was that an attractive clubhouse would enhance the image of Whistler Resort in general, and of Whistler Golf Course in particular, in the eyes of the tourist market.

Interviews were conducted with other avid golfers who were asked why a clubhouse was important. All commented that a clubhouse provided a desirable meeting place for golfers beyond the various services needed to play a game of golf—for example, golf club rentals. A clubhouse was a place where they could organize their golfing groups. Many felt that a clubhouse provided an opportunity to socialize and network with club members. As well, families and friends could meet over dinner and/or drinks to talk and celebrate special occasions or holidays; businesspeople could make contacts, finalize deals, or reward a valued employee. At least one owner of a medium-sized business said he would use a clubhouse to hold company events along with golf tournaments. These events would be to reward employees and provide a chance for people to exchange ideas and make contacts before and after enjoying a game of golf. Other golfers said a clubhouse was the first indication of the type and quality of a golf club and golf course because it reflected the values of the individual members and their life-styles, as well as the traditions and history of the course. In sum, the respondents largely felt that a club's culture was reflected in the design, services, and operating methods of its clubhouse. Overall, they agreed that a quality clubhouse was an essential part of a quality golf course.

Whistler Golf Course facilities already included a pro shop, snack shops, club and cart rentals, a driving range, and practice greens. The Pro Shop was located in a 1,200-square-foot trailer. Food services were housed in two 500-square-foot log structures and were operated by the same outside contractor that ran the WCC catering. The only seating was on benches and the first tee deck. In return for the right to operate the snack shops on the golf course, the WGC received 15 percent of the gross food and beverage sales.

The limited take-away menu included hot dogs, sandwiches, and beverages (including beer and wine). Annual food cost in 1992 was 35 percent and beverage cost was 30 percent. Beer and wine accounted for 25 percent of total sales. The golf course food manager especially liked the higher sales generated by tournament business; they helped to increase the annual check average to $3.75 per golfer. Business generated from tournaments generally averaged 10 percent of sales. In 1992, one-third of tournament group members bought food and beverage packages (lunches for $10 to $15 per golfer). These higher average checks reduced the average labor cost to 32 percent of sales. They also lowered total other costs (excluding the leasing fees) to 10 percent of gross sales.

Adjoining the first tee snack bar was a 30-seat deck. On sunny days the deck was converted into a self-service barbecue area. Snack bar staff would sell hamburgers, hot dogs, and beer. A mobile golf cart was outfitted to provide nonalcoholic beverage service on the course. The golf course discouraged drinking alcoholic beverages while golfers were playing golf.

A driving range and training center were located in front of the Delta Mountain Inn across the highway from the course. The range consisted of 10 tees for golfers to practice their swing. The golf pro conducted individual and group golfing lessons at the training center. The driving range was very popular with hotel guests and was most frequently used by golfers waiting for a tee-off time.

Fairways and greens of the golf course were maintained in top condition subject to vagaries of the weather. The Whistler climate was temperate for Canada. Winter temperatures in the valley averaged –6 C to –1 C, while summer (June–August) temperatures ranged from 7 C to 21 C. Annual snowfall in the Alpine was 30 feet and days of rain averaged 120. Although the golf season ran from May to October, the winter climate could be harsh on the course environment. In 1986, for example, the course was severely damaged by "winter kill." Thirteen greens were unplayable, resulting in poor sales and profits that season.

To maximize capacity, course policy encouraged an average 18-hole round of golf in four hours, with tee-off times spaced every 10 minutes. The first start time was sunrise, approximately 6:30 AM, and the last was approximately 5:00 PM. The practical approximate maximum number of rounds per season was 30,000. According to the golf course manager, this held true for almost all golf courses in similar climates. Like all northern golf courses, Whistler had high and low seasons (Exhibit 4). Exhibit 5 shows actual and forecasted golf rounds from 1991 to 2000, according to the consultants' report, by golf course and by segment demand. By 1994, the course would reach its 30,000 capacity. After that, revenue growth would have to come in other ways.

WHISTLER GOLF MARKET

Demand for Whistler by tourists had grown rapidly. Especially fast growth came from the Japanese market. In 1992, the Japanese tourist represented 25 percent of the destination's total winter ski customer. The WRA projected a continued 6 percent growth rate per year for the next 10 years, an estimate consistent with historical growth figures. Summer lodging occupancies had increased five percentage points from 40 to 45 percent over the last four years. This growth rate was expected to continue because most of the new developments, such as tennis and golf resorts, would attract summer tourists.

Over 1,000 golfers were surveyed in a 1992 study of the Whistler golfing market. Almost one-quarter (24.2 percent) of the golfers questioned resided in either North or West Vancouver, making these golfers the largest market source. The rest of Vancouver was home to 21.5 percent of the golfers. The third largest group was the Whistler local market at 13.3 percent, followed by golfers from the state of Washington (9.8 percent); 17.3 percent came from other parts of Canada.

Most golfers were young and high-income earners. Fifty-three percent were between the ages of 25 and 44, and 25 percent were from 45 to 54; 65 percent of these reported incomes of $50,000 and over. Almost half (49 percent) were married with no dependents, and 19 percent were singles. Visiting golfers participated in a variety of activities while at the resort (e.g., dining out, visiting the bars and clubs, and shopping). Sightseeing, visits to local parks, and riding the chairlift to the mountain tops were also popular.

Of golfers surveyed, 45 percent of the visiting golfers and 66 percent of resident golfers cited clubhouse facilities as their first need in improving the golf club. The other highest needs for all respondents were "no changes needed" (18.4 percent) and "course design changes" (10.9 percent). All other needs were mentioned by fewer than 5 percent.

The golfing market was segmented into the following four target groups:

1. *Season's pass holder and resident nonpass holder.* The season's pass holder group, with a maximum membership of 120, paid a fee of approximately $1,000 for the right to unlimited weekday golfing. On average, they played 40 rounds of golf per person per season. Pass holders were the most frequent users of the golf course. Resident nonpass holders were Whistlerites who golfed on a pay-as-you-go-basis. Both groups combined represented 13.2 percent of total golfers. Increased interest in

Exhibit 4   Whistler Golf Course Green Fee Revenue

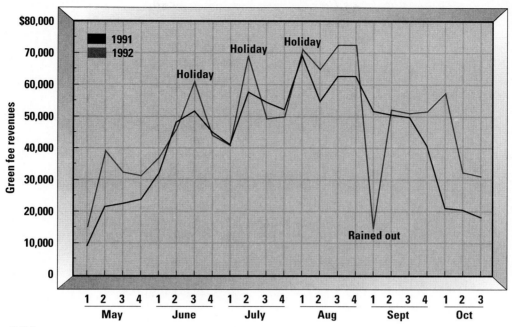

Source: Whistler Golf Course.

golfing by nonpass holders was anticipated as more courses opened and access to tee times expanded.

2.   *Day visitors.* This group were golfers that visited Whistler for the day and did not stay overnight (11 percent of total golfers). Increased demand from this segment was a direct result of decreased driving time from Vancouver. As Whistler road upgrades neared completion, the reduction of road closures would further decrease the drive time. In addition, the provincial government was studying the feasibility of building a second highway from Vancouver.

3.   *Summer second home.* This market represented 13 percent of total golfers. The second home market grew from 4,724 in 1988 to 7,273 in 1992, a 54 percent increase over five years. The municipality forecast the development of 20,000 bed-units over the next 10 years (bed-units were defined in the Whistler market as the number of beds per residential or commercial property). This appeared to be a growing market for the golf courses.

4.   *Summer visitors.* This group of vacation golfers (62.8 percent of the total golfing market) generally booked accommodations for at least one or two nights in summer (50 percent); 35 percent stayed three to seven nights, while 4 percent stayed eight nights or more. The other 11 percent made day trips. Twenty-four percent of these golfers were repeat visitors, 41 percent came by word-of-mouth, 23 percent were drawn by various media, 4 percent came through travel agents, 3 percent through brochures, and 5 percent from special events listings.

Summer hotel occupancy in 1992 reported by the WRA was 45 percent, with a room inventory of 2,756. The rate of increase in rooms inventory was forecast at

Exhibit 5   Golf Rounds

Actual and Forecasted Rounds by Golf Course

	Actual		Forecasted							
	1991	1992	1993	1994	1995	1996	1997	1998	1999	2000
Whistler Golf Course										
Green fees	24,533	24,358	23,710	27,690	25,234	29,150	29,150	29,150	29,150	29,150
Season pass holders	3,450	3,600	3,300	2,850	2,850	2,850	2,850	2,850	2,850	2,850
	27,983	27,958	27,010	30,540	28,084	32,000	32,000	32,000	32,000	32,000
Chateau Whistler										
Green fees		8,200	20,400	22,913	24,769	26,400	26,400	26,400	26,400	26,400
Members		1,800	3,600	3,600	3,600	3,600	3,600	3,600	3,600	3,600
		10,000	24,000	26,513	28,369	30,000	30,000	30,000	30,000	30,000
Green Lake										
Green fees				6,400	15,821	19,800	22,800	22,800	22,800	22,800
Members				3,600	7,200	7,200	7,200	7,200	7,200	7,200
				10,000	23,021	27,000	30,000	30,000	30,000	30,000

Actual and Forecasted Rounds by Supply and Segment Demand

	Actual		Forecasted							
	1991	1992	1993	1994	1995	1996	1997	1998	1999	2000
Demand for rounds										
Summer hotel visits	20,419	26,610	37,980	50,376	58,432	67,717	74,438	78,904	83,639	88,657
Summer second home visits	1,670	2,053	2,176	2,437	2,730	3,057	3,424	3,835	4,295	4,810
Nonpass holder permanent population	600	636	500	530	562	596	631	669	709	752
Day visits	1,844	3,258	3,454	3,661	4,101	4,593	5,144	5,761	6,452	7,227
Total demand for green fee rounds	24,533	32,558	44,110	57,004	65,824	75,962	83,637	89,169	95,095	101,446
Season pass holders	3,450	3,600	3,300	2,850	2,850	2,850	2,850	2,850	2,850	2,850
Semiprivate members		1,800	3,600	7,200	10,800	10,800	10,800	10,800	10,800	10,800
Total demand for member rounds	3,450	5,400	6,900	10,050	13,650	13,650	13,650	13,650	13,650	13,650
Total demand for rounds	27,983	37,958	51,010	67,054	79,474	89,612	97,287	102,819	108,745	115,096
Supply of rounds										
Green fees	24,533	36,600	49,100	58,950	72,350	75,350	78,350	78,350	78,350	78,350
Season pass holders	3,450	3,600	3,300	2,850	2,850	2,850	2,850	2,850	2,850	2,850
Semiprivate	0	1,800	3,600	7,200	10,800	10,800	10,800	10,800	10,800	10,800
	3,450	5,400	6,900	10,050	13,650	13,650	13,650	13,650	13,650	13,650
Total supply of rounds	27,983	42,000	56,000	69,000	86,000	89,000	92,000	92,000	92,000	92,000
Surplus/(shortfall) of supply of rounds	0	4,042	4,990	1,946	6,526	(612)	(5,287)	(10,819)	(16,745)	(23,096)

Source: Consultants' report.

Exhibit 6   Open Ended Responses in Survey of Whistler Golfers

COURSE CONDITION

- Allow carts on fairways to speed up play
- Speed up slower players
- Need 90° rule on carts
- Quicker rounds—5½ hours too long
- Add more toilets before 9th hole
- More bathrooms
- 3 difficult holes in a row (8, 10, 11) tend to cause slow play for below average/average players
- Is yardage correct? Seems short on 17
- Need course marshall
- Better marshalling
- Slow play a real problem

- Let the rough grow higher
- Flags difficult to see on greens
- Pave cart paths
- Have a sign on the course marshall so he/she will be more recognizable
- Allow carts on paths, will speed up play
- Speed up play
- Clean up after Canada Geese
- Longer green pins
- Paved cart paths
- Green was like the Rock of Gibraltar

PRICING

- Beer at $4 each is ridiculous = $48 per case!
- Second round of golf same day is too expensive
- Lower fees on practice tee
- $4 for a beer on the 19th is excessive
- Poor/expensive practice range
- $4 for beer on 19th tee is expensive

- Reduce rates for seniors
- Golf Shop merchandise is expensive
- Cost of golf round is expensive
- Golf rentals are expensive compared to some resorts
- Reduce prices

FOOD AND BEVERAGE

- Better hot dogs
- Better food at halfway house

MISCELLANEOUS

- Clear shields on cart front to shield out wind and rain
- Multimillion dollar project and NO CLUBHOUSE?!
- Have a computer-generated standby list to call if cancellations received
- Change rooms needed
- Course fully occupied by groups, not good as I was playing as a single

- Too many beginners on course
- Night driving range
- Don't fix something that isn't broken
- No clubhouse
- Require clubhouse/pro shop facility parallel to that of a world-class golf course

OVERALL EXPERIENCE

- Compared to previous years, we have noticed a great improvement in all areas
- It's been a pleasure
- It's been pretty good

- Beautiful
- Very memorable
- Nicer clubhouse would be nice

BOOKING

- Make booking easier
- Easier booking for residents/locals
- Lack of tee times available

Source: Whistler Golf Course.

Exhibit 7   1993 Rate Structure of Whistler Greens Fees

Season	Whistler Golf Course	CP Golf Course (includes cart)*
Early season (May 8–June 14)	$35	$61
High season (June 15–Sept 30)	$45	$73
Weekends/Holidays	$55	
Late season (Oct 1–Oct 12)	$35	$61
Twilight (after 4 PM)		
Low season	$20	$39
High season	$25	$45
Power cart	$22	
Pull cart	$ 4	

* CP tournament rates were $10 higher and included amenities such as club cleaning and storage.

6 percent per year. The opportunity for growth appeared significant as summer/fall commercial room-nights had increased 121 percent from 1987 to 1992. The WGC allocated booking privileges to this group so that hotels could book up to 80 percent of the total tee times available. By 1992, the hotels were booking, on average, 73 percent of the available tee times.

Of all groups, 74 percent said the Whistler Golf Course met the standards of any other North American course; 21 percent said it exceeded them. Almost three-fourths (73 percent) said the Whistler course was good to very good value for the money, while 91 percent said it was a good to very good experience. For 60 percent, the primary reason for their visit was to play golf. Open-ended responses to the survey are shown in Exhibit 6.

COMPETITION

The Canadian Pacific Whistler Chateau Hotel had opened a new golf course adjacent to its hotel in 1992. Designed by professional golf champion Robert Trent Jones, this 6,605-yard course would be a strong competitor. It was owned by Canadian Pacific Hotels, the largest Canadian resort golf operator. The greens fees at the CP golf course included the cost of mandatory power cart rental. The green fees were comparable to WGC fees with the power cart rental subtracted. The 1993 greens fees for both courses are shown in Exhibit 7.

The new course was to be heavily marketed but would develop gradually. As the head greens keeper stated:

> The first five years of a golf course are critical. The turf is maturing and must be protected from the weather. Not only does the climate have an effect but also the golfer traffic. You have to use several methods, including restricting play in the first five years, so the grassroots develop into a strong foundation.

The Chateau had the advantage of Canadian Pacific's international reservations system and the ready market of a 365-room hotel. Ninety golf memberships would also be offered to Whistler residents. The course had clubhouse facilities with retail space of 900 square feet and a 90-seat bar/grill.

The Greens Lakes golf course was scheduled to open in 1994. This tournament-standard course was being designed by famed professional Jack Nicklaus and would be able to accommodate major professional tournaments. The marketing effort would include the unique qualities of a Nicklaus course. It would be one of only three Nicklaus courses in western Canada. Typically, Nicklaus-designed courses charged greens fees between $90 and $120 without power carts. The clubhouse, at 17,000 square feet, was being designed to serve the large residential and hotel facilities that were part of the development. Investors planned to sell memberships to the 180 owners of residences in the development. This could affect Whistler's memberships.

The Whistler golf course, CP golf course, and the Green Lakes golf course would be the three competitors in Whistler. In 1995, the three clubs combined were forecasting maximum rounds of 900 golfers per day, or a total of almost 90,000 rounds of golf per season.

Within a half hour drive of Whistler, three additional 18-hole courses were planned to open by 1994, with two more in the planning stage, making five in all. All would be championship level and designed by top names in the business. Twenty minutes north of Whistler, a 9-hole course was being expanded to an 18-hole course and would charge a $35 greens fee.

In the Seattle/Vancouver corridor, there were seven significant golf facilities—"significant" meaning able to attract customers from Whistler's market segments and offering similar golfing products. Of particular interest was the day visitor market, which was most easily persuaded by promotional campaigns. They were the most mobile and therefore able to make an impulse buy decision.

MARKETING

During its 10 years of operation, the Whistler Golf Course had held a monopoly on the Whistler golf product. Until 1993, the course had never been actively marketed, but Jim planned to change this in 1993. He designed five new pieces of golf collateral, an advertising plan and new marketing efforts aimed to increase the focus of tournament business, a golf school at the practice facility, a retail outlet, and better overall customer service.

This was a short-term plan. Over the next year, the proposed addition of the clubhouse facility, the introduction of the Whistler Golf School, continuing market research, and the competition from the new Chateau Whistler course would change the scope of the plan. In 1993, a new era in the resort's golfing product would begin, with new designer courses open and coming. With the completion of three courses, Whistler could target marketing efforts at the destination golfer who was a more avid golfer than the recreational golfer.

The primary objective of the short-term plan was to increase the rounds of golf and food and beverage revenue and to work with the Whistler hotels to promote golf packages. Emphasis was to be put on increasing the number of tournament players, as this would increase rounds of golf, add revenue to food and beverage and retail outlets, and fill hotel rooms.

The long-term goal was to increase the awareness level and sales of the golf product available in the "Sea to Sky Corridor" (Seattle to Whistler) to the Vancouver area, Washington, and Oregon markets, and the emerging target markets of Southern California and Japan. Jim envisioned working with golf clubs throughout the corridor to produce a regional golf brochure. The mission statement of the WGC, however, would remain unchanged as:

> The Whistler Golf Course strives to be the premier golf course in the Sea to Sky Corridor through a comprehensive program of service that will offer a golfing experience comparable or superior to any other championship design resort golf course in North America. This is achieved by maximizing operating efficiency and revenue opportunities while maintaining the highest level of golf resort experience for our guests.

CONSULTANTS' REPORT

The recommendation by the consultants to build a clubhouse on the Whistler Golf Course was based on the increasing number of high-quality competitors. The thrust of the argument was that the next three years would see an oversupply in the Whistler golf market. Starting in 1996, demand would exceed supply. Initially, the new competition would create an opportunity for present WGC customers to try out the new courses and switch loyalty. The clubhouse was seen as an essential part of the golf product and, were it to be omitted, the course would be in a weak competitive position. The consultants argued that without the clubhouse, the WGC would not be offering a comparable product. The size and features of the proposed clubhouse are compared with other golf courses in Exhibit 8. The consultants developed financial statements comparing the golf course with and without a clubhouse (Exhibit 9). They assumed that the WGC greens fees and operating costs would be the same with or without a clubhouse—that is, number of rounds played and rentals of carts and clubs would be the same in both scenarios.

BOARD OF DIRECTORS MEETING

David Thompson, president of the Whistler Resort Association, had outlined the clubhouse proposal to the WRA board of directors. He told the group the project must go ahead in order to maintain the Whistler Golf Course position consistent with the promotion of Whistler as a world-class golf destination resort. He stated:

> Without the clubhouse the competitive situation will deteriorate against the other courses. Several issues have affected the funds available for the project, especially the purchase of a local business and the unanticipated increased winter advertising spending. The latter was a result of the provincial government's reduced spending on tourism. However, we have enough money in the WRA reserves to fund this project, but not much left for any contingencies.

The final tenders on the clubhouse indicated a cost of approximately $1 million. The construction costs were extensively reviewed to reduce costs. No further reduction in the costs was judged possible.

David outlined a number of financing options available to pay for the clubhouse:

1. Fund the full amount. This leaves one-half million to fund other WRA projects. The golf course will contribute additional reserves in the future.

Exhibit 8 Comparison of Clubhouse Facilities

Proposed Whistler Golf Course clubhouse

- Total of 6,500 square feet
- 1,500 square feet of retail space
- 80 seat bar/grill area plus 40 seats on the deck; 150-seat patio
- Golf lockers, showers, washrooms
- Administrative and reservations offices

Existing CP Golf clubhouse

- Total of 5,000 square feet
- 900 square feet of retail space
- 90 seat bar/grill; 25-seat patio
- Washrooms, lockers, showers, guest information counter

Proposed Green Lakes clubhouse

- 17,000 square feet
- Formal dining room and full lounge facilities
- Banquet and meeting facilities
- Membership locker rooms with showers
- 2,500 square feet of retail space
- Washrooms and administrative office

2. Fund half the amount and finance the rest at 7 percent over five years at a cost of about $100,000. This would leave the WRA with double the reserve of option 1.

3. Proceed with only part of the project. Build the food and beverage component first and build the pro shop later. This would result in a higher cost and a longer payback period.

The board argued against this capital expense, based on the consultants' forecast of golf rounds, but softened a little after David's insistence. They agreed to meet again in 30 days to hear any new arguments.

Vice President's Views

Jim knew the board understood the importance of the clubhouse to the golf club business. Still, how could he present the needed arguments to the board to persuade them to build? He knew the board's concern with approving a million dollar expenditure in recessionary times, especially money spent on facilities rather than marketing all of Whistler as a resort area. Alternatively, the board could use the funds for other projects. The Convention Centre was in need of major repairs. The roof, which had leaked from opening day, required some $300,000 to permanently fix. Until now, however makeshift repairs had been sufficient. Second, a Health Club facility could be built in the Convention Centre for $500,000. The Health Club would include squash courts, gym, whirlpool, and steamroom that not all Whistler hotels offered. Jim wondered if they should scale down the clubhouse project or, possibly, phase it in over a number of years to reduce the immediate cost involved? Or, possibly, could

Exhibit 9 Actual and Consultants' Projected Statements with and without Clubhouse

	Actual					Forecasted (With Clubhouse)				
	1991	1992	1993	1994	1995	1996	1997	1998	1999	2000
Average green fee	$ 35.00	$ 33.00	$ 36.00	$ 39.00	$ 42.00	$ 44.10	$ 46.31	$ 48.62	$ 51.05	$ 53.60
Revenue										
Green fees	959,839	909,398	955,187	1,172,093	1,156,626	1,387,131	1,456,488	1,529,312	1,605,778	1,686,067
Retail sales	209,869	223,660	459,164	545,145	526,373	629,748	661,235	694,297	729,012	765,463
Equipment rental	52,898	55,220	56,349	68,635	65,798	79,583	83,562	87,740	92,127	96,733
Driving range	76,173	90,134	92,957	103,861	103,084	118,232	124,144	130,351	136,869	143,712
License revenue	27,983	27,958	74,000	77,700	81,585	85,664	89,947	94,445	99,167	104,125
Commission revenue	39,298	41,049	41,856	50,816	48,760	58,894	61,839	64,931	68,177	71,586
Sponsorship	10,000	10,500	11,025	11,576	12,155	12,763	13,401	14,071	14,775	15,513
	$1,376,060	$1,357,919	$1,690,539	$2,029,827	$1,994,381	$2,372,015	$2,490,616	$2,615,147	$2,745,904	$2,883,199
Cost of retail sales	115,428	123,013	252,540	299,830	289,505	346,361	363,679	381,863	400,957	421,004
Gross margin	$1,260,632	$1,234,906	$1,437,998	$1,729,997	$1,704,876	$2,025,654	$2,126,937	$2,233,283	$2,344,948	$2,462,195
General expenses										
Administration	85,000	89,250	93,713	98,398	103,318	108,484	113,908	119,604	125,584	131,863
Marketing	3,000	20,000	21,000	22,050	23,153	24,310	25,526	26,802	28,142	29,549
Clubhouse maintenance			26,250	27,563	28,941	30,388	31,907	33,502	35,178	36,936
Building maintenance	70,000	73,500	77,175	81,034	85,085	89,340	93,807	98,497	103,422	108,593
Guest services	85,000	89,250	93,713	98,398	103,318	108,484	113,908	119,604	125,584	131,863
Course maintenance	250,000	262,500	275,625	289,406	303,877	319,070	335,024	351,775	369,364	387,832
Power carts	130,000	136,500	143,325	150,491	158,016	165,917	174,212	182,923	192,069	201,673
Pro shop	25,000	26,250	27,563	28,941	30,388	31,907	33,502	35,178	36,936	38,783
Practice fairway	$ 648,000	$ 697,250	$ 758,363	$ 796,281	$ 836,095	$ 877,899	$ 921,794	$ 967,884	$1,016,278	$1,067,092
Net revenue	$ 612,632	$ 537,656	$ 679,636	$ 933,716	$ 868,781	$1,147,754	$1,205,142	$1,265,399	$1,328,669	$1,395,103

Exhibit 9 Concluded

	Actual			No Clubhouse		Forecasted				
	1991	1992	1993	1994	1995	1996	1997	1998	1999	2000
Average green fee	$ 35.00	$ 33.00	$ 36.00	$ 39.00	$ 42.00	$ 44.10	$ 46.31	$ 48.62	$ 51.05	$ 53.60
Green fees	959,839	909,398	955,187	1,172,093	1,156,626	1,387,131	1,456,488	1,529,312	1,605,778	1,686,067
Retail sales	209,869	223,660	226,881	269,366	260,090	311,170	326,728	343,064	360,218	378,229
Equipment rental	52,898	55,220	56,349	68,635	65,798	79,583	83,562	87,740	92,127	96,733
Driving range	76,173	90,134	92,957	103,861	103,084	118,232	124,144	130,351	136,869	143,712
License revenue	27,983	27,958	27,010	30,540	28,084	32,000	32,000	32,000	32,000	32,000
Commission revenue	39,298	41,049	41,856	50,816	48,760	58,894	61,839	64,931	68,177	71,586
Sponsorship	10,000	10,500	11,025	11,576	12,155	12,763	13,401	14,071	14,775	15,513
	$1,376,060	$1,357,919	$1,411,265	$1,706,888	$1,674,598	$1,999,773	$2,098,161	$2,201,469	$2,309,943	$2,423,840
Cost of retail sales	115,428	123,013	124,785	148,151	143,050	171,143	179,700	188,685	198,120	208,026
Gross margin	$1,260,632	$1,234,906	$1,286,481	$1,558,737	$1,531,548	$1,828,629	$1,918,461	$2,012,784	2,111,823	$2,215,814
General expenses										
Administration	85,000	89,250	93,713	98,398	103,318	108,484	113,908	119,604	125,584	131,863
Marketing	3,000	20,000	21,000	22,050	23,153	24,310	25,526	26,802	28,142	29,549
Building maintenance	70,000	73,500	77,175	81,034	85,085	89,340	93,807	98,497	103,422	108,593
Guest services	85,000	89,250	93,713	98,398	103,318	108,484	113,908	119,604	125,584	131,863
Course maintenance	250,000	262,500	275,625	289,406	303,877	319,070	335,024	351,775	369,364	387,832
Power carts										
Pro shop	130,000	136,500	143,325	150,491	158,016	165,917	174,212	182,923	192,069	201,673
Practice fairway	25,000	26,250	27,563	28,941	30,388	31,907	33,502	35,178	36,936	38,783
	$ 648,000	$ 697,250	$ 732,113	$ 768,718	$ 807,154	$ 847,512	$ 889,887	$ 934,382	$ 981,101	$1,030,156
Net revenue	$ 612,632	$ 537,656	$ 554,368	$ 790,018	$ 724,394	$ 981,118	$1,028,573	$1,078,402	$1,130,722	$1,185,658

Notes: Projected average retail sales per golfer to increase from $7.50 to $17.00 with addition of clubhouse based on consultants' survey of six western Canada resort clubs.

License revenue is food and beverage revenue based on 15% of caterer's sales.

Commission revenue is corporate sponsorships plus a small amount of commissions paid by the golf pro.

Sponsorship revenue is corporate or group sponsorship of tournaments, usually charities.

Revenue drop in 1991 and 1992 due to recession and poor weather conditions.

Marketing expense shown here is largely collateral and local advertising projected by consultants.

Assumed other maintenance costs the same with/without clubhouse; expenses forecasted to increase 5% a year.

he buy an existing facility and move it to Whistler? On the other hand, he wondered, how accurate was the consultants' report?

Jim believed that to cope with the competition, he would have to develop several marketing strategies. Whistler would become a destination golf resort offering three distinct golf products by the mid-1990s. To position the WGC in this market, management would have to strive to be the premier golf course from Whistler to Vancouver. Jim felt the golf course should offer a comprehensive package of services that would create a golfing experience superior to any other championship resort golf course in North America. On top of his mind, also, was the catering contract that was up for renewal on May 1.

Jim also envisioned a network of clubs from Vancouver to Whistler, all connected by a computer network. The destination golfer would be able to book a two-week golfing holiday and play at a different top-notch club everyday. The whole trip would be paid in advance by credit card. Those were plans for the future; what about now? He had three weeks left to prepare new arguments for the board, he thought, as he barrelled down the mountain in waist-high powder snow.

Kentucky Fried Chicken and the Global Fast-Food Industry

Jeffrey Krug, University of Memphis
Harvey Hegarty, Indiana University

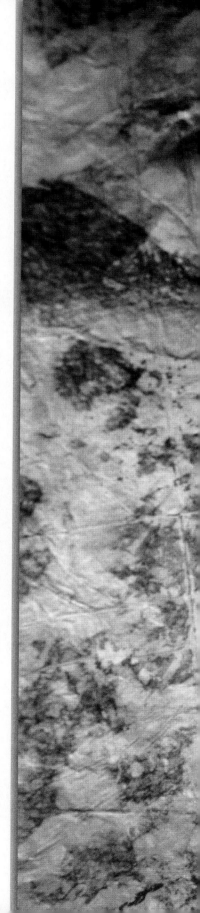

During the 1960s and 1970s, Kentucky Fried Chicken Corporation (KFC) pursued an aggressive strategy of restaurant expansion, quickly establishing itself as one of the largest fast-food restaurant chains in the United States (see Exhibit 1). KFC was also one of the first U.S. fast-food restaurant chains to expand overseas. By 1990, restaurants located outside of the United States were generating over 50 percent of KFC's total profits. By the end of 1993, KFC was operating in over 63 foreign countries and was one of the three largest fast-food restaurant chains operating outside of the United States.

Japan, Australia, and the United Kingdom accounted for the greatest share of KFC's international expansion during the 1970s and 1980s. However, as KFC entered the 1990s, a number of other international markets offered significant opportunities for growth. China, with a population of over 1 billion, and Europe, with a population roughly equal to that of the United States, offered such opportunities. Latin America also offered a unique opportunity because of the size of its markets, its common language and culture, and its geographic proximity to the United States.

By 1994, KFC was operating successful subsidiaries in Mexico and Puerto Rico. A third subsidiary was established in Venezuela in 1993. The majority of KFC's restaurants in Mexico and Puerto Rico were company-owned. However, KFC had established 21 new franchises in Mexico by the end of 1993, following enactment of Mexico's new franchise law in 1990. KFC anticipated that much of its future growth in Mexico would be through franchises rather than through company-owned restaurants. KFC was only one of many U.S. fast-food, retail, and hotel chains to begin franchising in Mexico following the new franchise law. In addition to Mexico, KFC was operating franchises in 42 other countries throughout the Caribbean, and in Central and South America by mid-1994.

COMPANY HISTORY

Fast-food franchising was still in its infancy in 1954 when Harland Sanders began his travels across the United States to speak with prospective franchisees about his "Colonel Sanders Recipe Kentucky Fried Chicken." By 1960, "Colonel" Sanders had granted KFC franchises to over 200 take-home retail outlets and restaurants across the United States. He had also succeeded in establishing a number of franchises in Canada. By 1963, the number of KFC franchises had risen to over 300 and revenues from franchise fees and royalties had reached $500,000.

Exhibit 1   Leading U.S. Fast-Food and Restaurant Chains

Chain	Parent	U.S. Sales ($ millions)		Percent Change	1992 Units
		1993*	1992		
McDonald's	McDonald's Corporation	$13,992	$13,243	5.7%	8,959
Burger King	Grand Metropolitan PLC	6,500	6,400	1.6	5,705
Pizza Hut	PepsiCo, Inc.	4,781	4,265	12.1	7,608
Hardee's	Imasco Ltd.	4,149	3,898	6.4	3,313
Taco Bell	PepsiCo, Inc.	3,643	3,139	16.1	4,078
Wendy's	Wendy's International Inc.	3,608	3,289	9.7	3,607
KFC	PepsiCo, Inc.	3,600	3,400	5.9	5,089
Little Caesars	Little Caesar Enterprises	2,311	2,160	7.0	4,575
Domino's Pizza	Domino's Pizza Inc.	2,201	2,358	−6.7	5,301
Subway	Doctor's Associates Inc.	2,200	1,800	22.2	7,000
Dairy Queen	International Dairy Queen	2,114	2,091	1.1	4,780
Denny's	Flagstar Cos. Inc.	1,730	1,600	8.1	1,391
Red Lobster	General Mills Inc.	1,688	1,610	4.9	581
Arby's	DWG Corp.	1,536	1,452	5.8	2,382
Shoney's	Shoney's Inc.	1,345	1,218	10.4	855
Dunkin' Donuts	Allied-Lyons PLC	1,228	1,076	14.1	2,342
Olive Garden	General Mills Inc.	1,091	928	17.5	379
Big Boy	Elias Bros. Restaurants	1,064	1,118	−4.8	934
Jack in the Box	Foodmaker Inc.	1,008	1,049	−3.9	1,155
Long John Silver's	Long John Silver's Rest.	946	889	6.4	1,437
Chili's	Brinker International	786	684	14.9	314
Sizzler	Sizzler International Inc.	775	764	1.5	597
Ponderosa	Metromedia Steakhouses	762	756	0.8	792
Roy Rogers	Imasco Ltd.	751	702	7.0	650
Sonic Drive-In	Sonic Corp.	690	600	15.0	1,191
T.G.I. Friday's	Carlson Cos.	676	577	17.1	195
Carl's Jr.	Carl Karcher Enterprises	625	599	4.4	623
Cracker Barrel	Cracker Barrel	575	515	11.7	152
Applebee's	Applebee's Int'l Inc.	575	404	42.3	250
Perkins	Tennessee Rest. Cos.	572	543	5.3	413
Total		$67,521	$63,125	7.0%	76,648

* 1993 sales estimated.

Source: *Nation's Restaurant News.*

By 1964, at the age of 74, the Colonel had tired of running the day-to-day operations of his business and was eager to concentrate on public relations issues. Therefore, he sought out potential buyers, eventually deciding to sell the business to two Louisville businessmen—Jack Massey and John Young Brown, Jr.—for $2 million. Massey was named chairman of the board and Brown, who would later become governor of Kentucky, was named president. The Colonel stayed on as a public relations man and goodwill ambassador for the company.

During the next five years, Massey and Brown concentrated on growing KFC's franchise system across the United States. In 1966, they took KFC public and the company was listed on the New York Stock Exchange. By the late 1960s, a strong foothold had been established in the United States, and Massey and Brown turned their attention to international markets. In 1969, a joint venture was signed with Mitsubishi Shoji Kaisha, Ltd., in Japan, and the rights to operate 14 existing KFC franchises in England were acquired. Subsidiaries were also established in Hong Kong, South Africa, Australia, New Zealand, and Mexico. By 1971, KFC had 2,450 franchises and 600 company-owned restaurants worldwide and was operating in 48 countries.

Heublein Acquires KFC

In 1971, KFC entered negotiations with Heublein, Inc., to discuss a possible merger. The decision to seek a merger candidate was partially driven by Brown's desire to pursue other interests, including a political career (Brown was elected governor of Kentucky in 1977). On April 10, Heublein announced that an agreement had been reached. Shareholders approved the merger on May 27, and KFC was merged into a subsidiary of Heublein.

Heublein was in the business of producing vodka, mixed cocktails, dry gin, cordials, beer, and other alcoholic beverages. It was also the exclusive distributor of a variety of imported alcoholic beverages. Heublein had little experience in the restaurant business. Conflicts quickly erupted between Colonel Sanders, who continued to act in a public relations capacity, and Heublein management. In particular, Colonel Sanders became increasingly distraught over quality control issues and restaurant cleanliness. By 1977, new restaurant openings had slowed to about 20 per year (in 1993, KFC opened a new restaurant on average every two days). Restaurants were not being remodeled and service quality was declining.

In 1977, Heublein sent in a new management team to redirect KFC's strategy. Richard P. Mayer, who later became chairman and chief executive officer, was part of this team (Mayer remained with KFC until 1989, when he left to become president of General Foods USA). A "back to the basics" strategy was immediately implemented. New unit construction was discontinued until existing restaurants could be upgraded and operating problems eliminated. Restaurants were refurbished, an emphasis was placed on cleanliness and service, marginal products were eliminated, and product consistency was reestablished. By 1982, KFC had succeeded in establishing a successful strategic focus and was again aggressively building new units.

R. J. Reynolds Industries Acquires Heublein

On October 12, 1982, R. J. Reynolds Industries, Inc. (RJR), announced that it would acquire Heublein and operate it as a wholly owned subsidiary. The Heublein acquisition represented part of RJR's overall corporate strategy of diversifying into businesses unrelated to cigarettes, its main sales and profit producer. RJR's objective was to reduce its dependence on the tobacco industry, which had driven RJR sales since its founding in North Carolina in 1875. Sales of cigarettes and tobacco products, while profitable, were declining in the United States, due mainly to the increased awareness among Americans regarding the negative health consequences of smoking.

RJR's diversification strategy included the acquisition of a variety of companies in the energy, transportation, and food and restaurant industries. RJR had no more experience in the restaurant business than did Heublein when Heublein purchased

KFC in 1971. RJR decided to take a hands-off approach to managing KFC. Whereas Heublein had installed its own top management at KFC headquarters, RJR left KFC management largely intact, believing that existing KFC managers were better qualified to operate KFC's businesses than were its own managers. By doing so, RJR avoided many of the operating problems that Heublein had experienced during its management of KFC. This strategy paid off for RJR, as KFC continued to expand aggressively and profitably under RJR's ownership.

In 1985, RJR acquired Nabisco Corporation for $4.9 billion. Nabisco sold a variety of well-known cookies, crackers, cereals, confectioneries, snacks, and other grocery products. In October 1986, Kentucky Fried Chicken was sold to PepsiCo, Inc.

PEPSICO, INC.

Corporate Strategy

PepsiCo, Inc. (PepsiCo), grew out of a small company first incorporated in Delaware in 1919 as Loft, Inc. In 1938, Loft acquired the Pepsi-Cola Co., a manufacturer of soft drinks and soft drink concentrates. Shortly after its acquisition of Pepsi-Cola, Loft changed its name to Pepsi-Cola Co. Pepsi-Cola's business over the next 30 years focused on the production and marketing of soft drink concentrates to licensed independent and company-owned bottlers, which produced, packaged, and distributed Pepsi-Cola, Diet Pepsi, Mountain Dew, and Slice. On June 30, 1965, Pepsi-Cola Co. acquired Frito-Lay Inc. for 3 million shares, thereby creating one of the largest consumer companies in the United States. At that time, the present name of PepsiCo, Inc., was adopted. Frito-Lay manufactures and sells a variety of snack foods. Its best known products are Fritos brand corn chips, Lay's and Ruffles brand potato chips, Doritos and Tostitos chips, and Chee-tos brand cheese flavored snacks. In 1992, 63 percent of PepsiCo's net sales were generated by its soft drink and snack food businesses (see Exhibit 2).

Beginning in the late 1960s, PepsiCo began an aggressive acquisition program, buying a number of companies in areas unrelated to its major businesses. North American Van Lines was acquired in June 1968, Wilson Sporting Goods was acquired in 1972, and Lee Way Motor Freight was acquired in 1976. However, success these businesses failed to live up to expectations, mainly because the management skills required to guide and direct these businesses were far removed from PepsiCo's area of expertise. PepsiCo fared much better with its acquisitions of Pizza Hut (1977) and Taco Bell (1978).

In 1984, then-chairman and chief executive officer Don Kendall decided to restructure PepsiCo's operations and divest those businesses that did not support PepsiCo's consumer product orientation. PepsiCo sold Lee Way Motor Freight in 1984. In 1985, Wilson Sporting Goods and North American Van Lines were sold. Additionally, PepsiCo's foreign bottling operations were sold to local businesspeople who better understood the cultural and business conditions operating in their respective countries. Lastly, Kendall reorganized PepsiCo along three lines: soft drinks, snack foods, and fast-food restaurants (see Exhibit 3). All future investment would be directed at strengthening PepsiCo's competitive position and performance in these three business arenas.

Exhibit 2   PepsiCo, Inc.—1992 Operating Results ($ millions)

	Beverages	Snack Foods	Restaurants	Total
Net sales	$7,605.6	$6,132.1	$8,232.2	$21,970.0
Operating profit	798.6	984.7	718.5	2,501.8
Percent net sales	10.5%	16.1%	8.7%	11.4%
Assets	$7,857.5	$4,628.0	$5,097.1	$17,582.6
Capital spending	343.7	446.2	757.2	1,565.1*

* Includes corporate spending of $18.0 million.

Exhibit 3   PepsiCo, Inc.—Principal Divisions

Executive Offices: Purchase, New York

Beverage Segment	Snack Food Segment	Restaurants
Pepsi-Cola North America Somers, New York	PepsiCo Worldwide Foods Plano, Texas	Kentucky Fried Chicken Louisville, Kentucky
Pepsi-Cola International Somers, New York	Frito-Lay, Inc. Plano, Texas	Pizza Hut Worldwide Wichita, Kansas
	PepsiCo Foods International Plano, Texas	Taco Bell Worldwide Irvine, California
		PepsiCo Food Systems Dallas, Texas

Restaurant Business and Acquisition of Kentucky Fried Chicken

PepsiCo first entered the quick-service restaurant business in 1977 when it acquired Pizza Hut's 3,200-unit restaurant system and promptly expanded its menu line-up with the follow-on acquisition of Taco Bell in 1978. Management believed the fast-food restaurant business complemented PepsiCo's consumer product orientation. The marketing of fast-food drew on many of the same marketing skills and techniques as the marketing of soft drinks and snack foods. This permitted PepsiCo to transfer experience and know-how gained in one business to the others and fit nicely with PepsiCo's practice of frequently moving managers among its business units as a way of developing future top executives. PepsiCo's restaurant chains also provided an additional outlet for the sale of Pepsi soft drink products. In addition, Pepsi soft drinks and fast-food products could be advertised together on the same company-sponsored television and radio programs, thereby providing higher returns for each advertising dollar.

To complete its diversification into the restaurant segment, PepsiCo acquired Kentucky Fried Chicken Corporation from RJR Nabisco in 1986 for $841 million. The acquisition of KFC gave PepsiCo the leading market share in three of the four largest and fastest-growing segments within the U.S. quick-service restaurant industry. At the end of 1992, Pizza Hut held a 25 percent share of the $16 billion U.S. pizza segment, Taco Bell held 70 percent of the $4.6 billion Mexican food segment, and KFC held 49 percent of the $7.0 billion U.S. chicken segment. In an analysis of PepsiCo's restaurant business in 1989, Shearson Lehman Hutton analyst Caroline Levy commented that

Exhibit 4   PepsiCo, Inc.——Number of Units Worldwide

Year	KFC	Pizza Hut	Taco Bell*	Total
1987	7,522	6,210	2,738	16,470
1988	7,761	6,662	2,930	17,353
1989	7,948	7,502	3,125	18,575
1990	8,187	8,220	3,349	19,756
1991	8,480	8,837	3,670	20,987
1992	8,729	9,454	4,153	22,336
Five-Year Compounded Annual Growth Rate				
	3.0%	8.8%	8.7%	6.3%

* Taco Bell units include the Hot 'n Now chain, acquired in 1990.

"on balance, PepsiCo's restaurants are clearly outperforming the industry and most of the major chains." (See Exhibits 2 and 4 for business segment financial data and restaurant count.)

PepsiCo's success during the late 1980s and early 1990s was mirrored by its upward trend in *Fortune* magazine's annual survey of "America's Most Admired Corporations." By 1991, PepsiCo ranked as the 5th most admired corporation overall (of 306 corporations included in the survey), up from a 25th place finish in 1986. In particular, PepsiCo ranked highest for its value as a long-term investment, innovativeness, wise use of corporate assets, quality of management, and quality of products/services offered.

PepsiCo	Ranking
1994	26
1993	14
1992	9
1991	5
1990	6
1989	7
1988	14
1987	24
1986	25

However, PepsiCo's ranking fell to 9th place in 1992, 14th place in 1993, and 26th place in 1994. PepsiCo's decline in the 1994 rankings resulted partly from changes *Fortune* made in its 1994 survey. In particular, *Fortune* increased the number of companies surveyed from 311 to 404, increased the number of industry groups from 32 to 42 (e.g., by adding computer services and entertainment), and divided some industry groups up into their components (e.g., by dividing the transportation group into airlines, trucking, and railroads). Home Depot, Microsoft, and Walt Disney, which were added to the survey in 1994, were all ranked in the top 10 most admired corporations in America.

FAST-FOOD INDUSTRY

U.S. Quick-Service Market

According to the National Restaurant Association (NRA), 1994 food-service sales topped $275 billion for the approximately 500,000 restaurants and other food outlets making up the U.S. restaurant industry. The NRA estimated that sales in the fast-food segment of the food industry grew 6.3 percent to approximately $86 billion in the United States in 1994, up from $81 billion in 1993. This marked the first time that fast-food sales exceeded sales in the full-service segment, which totaled about $85.5 billion in 1994. The growth in fast-food sales reflects the long, gradual change in the restaurant industry from an industry once dominated by independently operated sit-down restaurants to an industry fast becoming dominated by quick-service restaurant chains. The U.S. restaurant industry as a whole was projected to grow by 3 to 4 percent annually over the next several years.

Sales data for the top 30 fast-food restaurant chains are shown in Exhibit 1. Most striking is the dominance of McDonald's. Its sales for 1993 were approximately $14.0 billion, equal to 17.3 percent of industry sales, or 20.7 percent of sales of the top 30 fast-food chains. U.S. sales for the PepsiCo system, which included KFC, Pizza Hut, and Taco Bell, were about $12.0 billion in 1993, equal to 14.9 percent of the fast-food industry and 17.8 percent of the top 30 fast-food chains. The PepsiCo system included 16,775 restaurants by the end of 1992. McDonald's held the number one spot in the hamburger segment, while PepsiCo held the leading market share in the chicken (KFC), Mexican (Taco Bell), and pizza (Pizza Hut) segments.

Major Business Segments

Six major business segments make up the fast-food market within the food-service industry. Exhibit 5 shows sales for the top 64 fast-food chains in the six major segments for the years 1991 through 1993, as compiled by *Nation's Restaurant News*. Sandwich chains make up the largest segment, reaching estimated sales in 1993 of $42.4 billion. Of the 17 restaurant chains making up the sandwich segment, McDonald's had a 33 percent market share. Sandwich chains, faced with slowing sales growth, were turning to new menu offerings, emphasizing customer service, and establishing nontraditional units in unconventional locations to beef up sales. Hardee's and McDonald's had successfully introduced fried chicken items to challenge KFC, the chicken chain market share leader. Burger King had introduced fried clams and shrimp to its dinner menu in some locations, and Jack in the Box had introduced chicken and teriyaki with rice in its Sacramento, California, units to appeal to its Asian-American audience. Other issues of growing importance for the sandwich chains were franchise relations, increasingly tough government regulations (e.g., secondhand smoke), and food safety and handling.

The second largest fast-food segment is pizza, long dominated by Pizza Hut. Pizza Hut had sales approaching $4.8 billion in 1993, equal to a 44 percent market share among the eight competitors making up the pizza segment. Little Caesars had now overtaken Domino's as the second largest pizza chain, despite the fact that Domino's operated more outlets. Little Caesars was the only pizza chain to remain exclusively a takeout chain. Increased competition within the pizza segment and pressures to appeal to a wider customer base had led pizza chains to diversify into nonpizza menu items, to develop nontraditional units (e.g., airport kiosks), and to offer special

Exhibit 5   U.S. Sales of the Top Fast-Food Chains by Business Segment ($ billions)

Business Segment	Number of Chains	1991	1992	1993*
Sandwich chains	17	$36.7	$39.7	$42.4
McDonald's, Burger King, Hardee's, Taco Bell, Wendy's, Subway, Dairy Queen, Arby's, Jack in the Box, Roy Rogers, Sonic Drive-In, Carl's Jr., Rally's, Whataburger, White Castle, Krystal, Del Taco				
Pizza chains	8	9.6	10.4	10.8
Pizza Hut, Little Caesars, Domino's, Chuck E. Cheese's, Sbarro, Round Table Pizza, Godfather's Pizza, Pizza Inn				
Family restaurants	13	7.0	7.7	8.2
Denny's, Shoney's, Big Boy, Cracker Barrel, Perkins, Friendly's, International House of Pancakes, Bob Evan's, Bakers Square, Waffle House, Village Inn, Marie Callender's, Country Kitchen				
Dinner houses	15	6.3	6.9	7.8
Red Lobster, Olive Garden, Chili's, T.G.I. Friday's, Applebee's, Bennigan's, Chi-Chi's, Outback Steakhouse, Ruby Tuesday, Ground Round, El Torito, Stuart Anderson's Black Angus, Steak and Ale, Tony Roma's, Red Robin				
Chicken chains	4	4.5	4.7	5.0
KFC, Popeyes, Church's, Chick-fil-A				
Steak Restaurants	7	3.5	3.3	3.4
Sizzler, Ponderosa, Golden Corral, Ryan's, Western Sizzlin', Quincy's, Bonanza				
Top fast-food chains	64	$67.6	$72.7	$77.6

* 1993 sales figures estimated.
Source: *Nation's Restaurant News.*

promotions. Among the many new product offerings, Domino's had introduced submarine sandwiches, Little Caesars was offering spaghetti and bread sticks, and Pizza Hut had rolled out deep-dish pizza. Many of the pizza chains had also begun intensive advertising for giant-sized pizzas. Godfather's was the first pizza chain to introduce a giant pizza—its 18-inch Jumbo Combo. The top three pizza chains quickly followed suit: Pizza Hut introduced its 24-slice Big Foot (1 foot by 2 feet), Little Caesars offered its Big, Big deal 24-slice pizza made of two pies, and Domino's introduced The Dominator, a 30-slice pizza.

The highest growth business segment in 1992 was the dinner house segment, for which 1992 sales exceeded 1991 sales by 10.4 percent. The dinner house segment was again expected to lead all food segments in 1993, growing by an estimated 12.5 percent, about twice as fast as the next fastest-growing segment. Red Lobster was the largest dinner house chain and was expected to surpass $1.7 billion in sales for its fiscal year ending May 1994. This would make Red Lobster the 15th largest chain among the top 100. Olive Garden was expected to hit the $1 billion sales mark when its fiscal year ended May 1994. Olive Garden was currently running a strong second place within the dinner house segment behind Red Lobster. Olive Garden's sales in 1993–94 were expected to grow by 12.5 percent over the previous year, compared to a growth rate of 4.9 percent for the segment leader.

The dinner house segment should continue to outgrow the other five fast-food segments for a variety of reasons. Major chains still have low penetration in this segment, though General Mills (Red Lobster and Olive Garden) and PepsiCo, Inc. (Fresh-Mex) are poised to dominate a large portion of this segment. A maturing population is already increasing demand for full-service, sit-down restaurants. Seven of the 15 dinner houses in this segment posted growth rates in sales of over 14 percent in 1992. Outback Steakhouse, Applebee's Neighborhood Grill & Bar, Red Robin Burger & Spirits Emporium, and Chili's Grill & Bar grew at rates of 114, 40, 19, and 19 percent in 1992, respectively.

KFC continued to dominate the chicken segment, with projected 1993 sales of $3.6 billion. Its nearest competitor, Popeyes, was a distant second with projected sales of $568.8 million. Church's and Chick-fil-A follow with projected sales of $428.1 and $375.0 million, respectively. KFC accounted for about one-half of all sales by chicken franchises. Other competitors within the chicken segment were Bojangle's, El Pollo Loco, Grandy's, Pudgie's, and Boston Market.

Industry Consolidation

Although the restaurant industry has outpaced the overall economy in recent years, there are indications that the U.S. market is slowly becoming saturated. According to the U.S. Bureau of Labor, sales of U.S. eating and drinking establishments increased by 2.7 percent in 1992. Following a period of rapid expansion and intense restaurant building in the United States during the 1970s and 1980s, the fast-food industry was displaying signs of a competitive shakeout. In January 1990, Grand Metropolitan, a British company, purchased Pillsbury Co. for $5.7 billion. Included in the purchase was Pillsbury's Burger King chain. Grand Met moved to strengthen the franchise by upgrading existing restaurants and eliminated several levels of management in order to cut costs. In 1988, Grand Met purchased Wienerwald, a West German chicken chain, and the Spaghetti Factory, a Swiss chain.

Within the chicken segment, a number of acquisitions intensified competition behind KFC. The second largest chicken segment restaurant chain, Church's, was acquired by Al Copeland Enterprises in 1989 for $392 million. Copeland also owned Popeyes Famous Fried Chicken, which has since replaced Church's as the second largest restaurant in the chicken segment. In 1992, Popeye's had worldwide sales of $580 million, compared to KFC's worldwide sales of $6.7 billion and Church's worldwide sales of $510 million. Following the Church's acquisition, Copeland converted 303 of Church's 1,368 restaurants into Popeyes franchises, bringing the Popeyes restaurant system to a total of 1,030. This made Popeyes the second largest chicken chain in the United States. Several hundred Church's units were scheduled to be sold to raise cash to pay for the Church's acquisition. Although the Church's acquisition enlarged the competitive base controlled by Copeland, the Copeland restaurant system was still dwarfed by KFC, which ended 1992 with 8,729 restaurants worldwide.

Perhaps more important to KFC was Hardee's acquisition of 600 Roy Rogers restaurants from Marriott Corporation in early 1990. Hardee's immediately began to convert these restaurants to Hardee's units and quickly introduced "Roy Rogers" fried chicken to its menu. By the end of 1993, Hardee's had introduced fried chicken into most of its 3,313 domestic restaurants. While Hardee's was unlikely to outmatch the customer loyalty that KFC has long enjoyed, its wider menu selection appealed to a variety of family eating preferences and cut into the sales potential of chicken-only chains like KFC.

The effect of these and other recent mergers and acquisitions on the industry has been powerful. The top 10 restaurant chains now control over 50 percent of all fast-food sales in the United States. The acquisition of a number of quick-service restaurant chains by larger, financially more powerful firms was expected to give the acquired restaurant chains the financial and managerial resources needed to outgrow their smaller competitors.

Demographic Trends

Intense marketing by the leading fast-food chains was expected to stimulate demand for fast-food in the United States during the 1990s. However, a number of demographic and societal changes were affecting the future demand for fast-food in different directions. One such change was the rise in single-person households, which had steadily increased from 17 percent of all U.S. households in 1970 to approximately 25 percent in 1994. In addition, disposable household income was projected to increase, mainly because of more women working than ever before. According to Standard & Poor's *Industry Surveys*, Americans spent 52 percent of their food dollars at restaurants in 1992, up from 34 percent in 1970. Most of this increase came from dining out more frequently, while the balance came mainly from higher prices.

In addition to these demographic trends, a number of societal changes were projected to affect future demand for fast-food. For example, microwaves were in approximately 70 percent of all U.S. homes, producing a significant shift in the types of products sold in supermarkets and convenience restaurants. A variety of products had been introduced that could be prepared quickly and easily in microwaves, lessening the need to dine out as a time-saving convenience. Growing numbers of diet-conscious consumers were avoiding meals at fast-food chains because many of the menu selections were regarded as less healthy (high-fat, high-cholesterol, high-calorie). In addition, some observers believed the aging of America's baby boomers would increase the frequency with which people patronized more upscale restaurants. Lastly, birthrates were projected to rise in the 1990s. This was likely to affect whether families ate out or stayed home. Therefore, there were factors working both to increase and decrease the future demand for fast-food.

International Quick-Service Market

Because of the aggressive pace of new restaurant construction in the United States during the 1970s and 1980s, future growth resulting from new restaurant construction in the United States was expected to be limited. In any case, the cost of finding prime locations was rising, increasing the pressure on restaurant chains to increase per restaurant sales in order to cover higher initial investment costs. One alternative to continued investment in the U.S. market was expansion into international markets, which offered large customer bases and comparatively little competition. However, few U.S. restaurant chains had aggressive strategies for penetrating international markets.

Three restaurant chains that had established aggressive international strategies were McDonald's, Pizza Hut, and Kentucky Fried Chicken. McDonald's currently operates the most units within the U.S. market. McDonald's also operates the largest number of fast-food chains outside of the United States (4,041), recently overtaking KFC, which long dominated the fast-food industry outside of the United States. KFC ended 1992 with 3,640 restaurants outside of the United States, 401 restaurants fewer than McDonald's. However, KFC remains the most internationalized of all fast-food chains, operating almost 42 percent of its total units outside of the United States. In comparison, McDonald's operates slightly more than 31 percent of its units outside of the United States. Pizza Hut presently operates in the most countries (73). However, over 83 percent of its units are still located in the United States.

Exhibit 6 shows *Hotels'* 1993 list of the world's 20 largest fast-food restaurant chains. Several important observations may be made from these data. First, 18 of the 20 largest restaurant chains are headquartered in the United States. Only one non-U.S. company appears in the largest 18 restaurant chains. This may be partially explained by the fact that U.S. firms account for over 25 percent of the world's foreign direct investment. As a result U.S. firms have historically been more likely to invest assets abroad. However, while both Kentucky Fried Chicken and McDonald's operate over 3,600 units abroad, no other restaurant chain, U.S. or foreign, has more than 1,500 units outside of the United States. In fact, most chains have fewer than 500 foreign units and operate in fewer than 20 countries.

There are a number of possible explanations for the relative scarcity of fast-food restaurant chains outside of the United States. First, the United States represents the largest consumer market in the world, accounting for almost one-fourth of the world's GNP. Therefore, the United States has traditionally been the strategic focus of the largest restaurant chains. In addition, Americans have been more quick to accept the fast-food concept. Many other cultures have strong culinary traditions that have not been easy to break down. The Europeans, for example, have long histories of frequenting more midscale restaurants, where they may spend several hours in a formal setting enjoying native dishes and beverages. While KFC is again building restaurants in Germany, it previously failed to penetrate the German market because Germans were not accustomed to takeout food or to ordering food over the counter. McDonald's has had greater success penetrating the German market because it has made a number of changes in its menu and operating procedures in order to better appeal to German culture. For example, German beer is served in all of McDonald's German restaurants. KFC has had more success in Asia, where chicken is a traditional dish.

Aside from cultural factors, international business carries risks not present in the U.S. market. Long distances between headquarters and foreign franchises often make it difficult to control the quality of individual franchises. Large distances can also cause servicing and support problems. Transportation and other resource costs may also be higher than in the domestic market. In addition, time, cultural, and language differences can increase communication and operational problems. Therefore, it is reasonable to expect U.S. restaurant chains to expand domestically as long as they can achieve corporate profit and growth objectives. However, as the U.S. market became more saturated and companies gained additional expertise in international business, fast-food companies were expected to turn to profitable international markets as a means of expanding their restaurant bases and increasing sales, profits, and market share.

KENTUCKY FRIED CHICKEN CORPORATION

Management

One of PepsiCo's greatest challenges when it acquired Kentucky Fried Chicken in 1986 was how to blend two distinct corporate cultures. When R. J. Reynolds acquired KFC in 1982, it realized that it knew very little about the fast-food business.

Exhibit 6   The World's 20 Largest Fast-Food Chains (year-end 1992)

Franchise	Location	Units	Countries
1. McDonald's	Oakbrook, IL	13,000	65
2. Pizza Hut	Wichita, KS	9,078	73
3. Kentucky Fried Chicken	Louisville, KY	8,729	63
4. Subway Sandwiches	Milford, CT	7,327	15
5. Burger King	Miami, FL	6,648	47
6. Domino's Pizza	Ann Arbor, MI	5,300	31
7. Dairy Queen	Minneapolis, MN	5,293	20
8. Whitbread	Luton, U.K.	4,943	7
9. Little Caesars Pizza	Detroit, MI	4,500	3
10. Hardee's	Rocky Mount, NC	4,015	11
11. Wendy's International	Dublin, OH	4,000	29
12. Taco Bell	Irvine, CA	4,000	15
13. Baskin-Robbins	Glendale, CA	3,484	45
14. Dunkin' Donuts	Randolph, MA	3,000	24
15. Arby's Roast Beef	Miami Beach, FL	2,606	12
16. Long John Silvers	Lexington, KY	1,461	4
17. Denny's	Spartansburg, SC	1,460	9
18. Jack in the Box	San Diego, CA	1,155	3
19. Kyotaru Co	Tokyo, Japan	1,144	3
20. Church's Fried Chicken	Atlanta, GA	1,072	4

Source: *Hotels*, May 1993.

Therefore, it relied on existing KFC management to manage the company. As a result, there was little need for mixing the cultures of the two companies. However, one of PepsiCo's major concerns when considering the purchase of KFC was whether it had the management skills required to successfully operate KFC using PepsiCo managers. PepsiCo had already acquired considerable experience managing fast-food businesses through its Pizza Hut and Taco Bell operations. Therefore, it was anxious to pursue strategic changes within KFC that would improve performance. However, replacing KFC managers with PepsiCo managers could easily cause conflicts between managers in both companies, who were accustomed to different operating procedures and working conditions.

PepsiCo's corporate culture had long been based heavily on a "fast-track" New York approach to management. It hired the country's top business and engineering graduates and promoted them based on performance. As a result, top performers expected to move up through the ranks quickly and to be paid well for their efforts. However, this competitive environment often resulted in intense rivalries among young managers. If one failed to perform, there was always another top performer waiting in the wings. As a result, employee loyalty was sometimes lost and turnover tended to be higher than in other companies.

The corporate culture at Kentucky Fried Chicken in 1986 contrasted sharply with that at PepsiCo. KFC's culture was built largely on Colonel Sander's laid-back approach to management. As well, employees enjoyed relatively good employment stability and security. Over the years, a strong loyalty had been created among KFC employees and franchisees, mainly because of the efforts of Colonel Sanders to provide for his employees' benefits, pension, and other nonincome needs. In addition, the Southern environment of Louisville resulted in a friendly, relaxed atmosphere at KFC's corporate offices. This corporate culture was left essentially unchanged during the Heublein and RJR years.

When PepsiCo acquired KFC, it began to restructure the KFC organization, replacing most of KFC's top managers with its own. By the summer of 1990, all of KFC's top positions were occupied by PepsiCo executives. In July 1989, KFC's president and chief executive officer, Richard P. Mayer, left KFC to become president of General Foods USA. Mayer had been at KFC since 1977, when KFC was still owned by Heublein. PepsiCo replaced Mayer with John Cranor III, the former president of Pepsi-Cola East, a Pepsi-Cola unit. In November 1989, Martin Redgrave moved from PepsiCo to become KFC's new chief financial officer. In the summer of 1990, Bill McDonald, a Pizza Hut and Frito-Lay marketing executive, was named senior vice president of marketing. Two months before, PepsiCo had named Kyle Craig, a former Pillsbury executive, as president of KFC's USA operations.

Most of PepsiCo's initial management changes in 1987 focused on KFC's corporate offices and USA operations. In 1988, attention was turned to KFC's international division. During 1988, PepsiCo replaced KFC International's top managers with its own. First, it lured Don Pierce away from Burger King and made Pierce president of KFC International. However, Pierce left KFC in early 1990 to become president of Pentagram Corporation, a restaurant operation in Hawaii. Pierce commented that he wished to change jobs partly to decrease the amount of time he spent traveling. PepsiCo replaced Pierce with Allan Huston, who was formerly senior vice president of operations at Pizza Hut. In late 1988, PepsiCo also brought in Robert Briggs, former director of finance at Pepsi-Cola International, as vice president of international finance. Briggs left KFC for a position at Arby's in 1993. (See Exhibit 7 for current organizational chart.)

An example of the type of conflict faced by PepsiCo in attempting to implement changes within KFC occurred in August 1989. A month after becoming president and chief executive officer, Cranor addressed KFC's franchisees in Louisville to explain the details of a new franchise contract. This was the first contract change in 13 years. The new contract gave PepsiCo management greater power to take over weak franchises, relocate restaurants, and make changes in existing restaurants. In addition, existing restaurants would no longer be protected from competition from new KFC restaurants. The contract also gave management the right to raise royalty fees on existing restaurants as contracts came up for renewal. After Cranor finished his address, there was an uproar among the attending franchisees, who jumped to their feet to protest the changes. The franchisees had long been accustomed to relatively little interference from management in their day-to-day operations. Moving quickly and forcefully to initiate needed changes in operations and policies was, of course, an integral part of PepsiCo's "take charge and produce results" philosophy.

Operating Results

KFC's recent operating results are shown in Exhibit 8. In 1992, worldwide sales, which represent sales of both company-owned and franchised restaurants, reached $6.7 billion. Since 1987, worldwide sales had grown at a compounded annual growth rate of 10.3 percent. KFC's market share remained at about one-half of the $7 billion

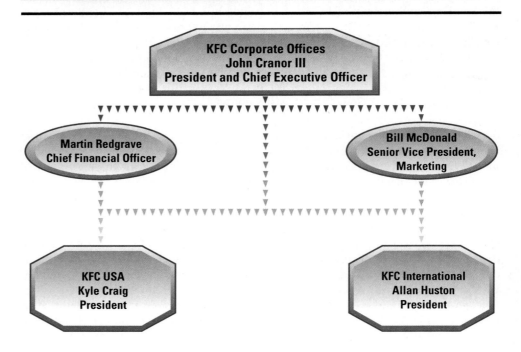

Exhibit 7   KFC Organizational Chart

KFC Corporate Offices
John Cranor III
President and Chief Executive Officer

Martin Redgrave
Chief Financial Officer

Bill McDonald
Senior Vice President,
Marketing

KFC USA
Kyle Craig
President

KFC International
Allan Huston
President

U.S. market in 1992. KFC corporate sales, which include company-owned restaurants and royalties from franchised units, reached $2.2 billion, up 18 percent from 1991 sales of $1.8 billion. New restaurants contributed $345 million to sales, while the translation effects of a weaker dollar lowered reported sales by $22 million.

KFC's worldwide profits increased by 110 percent to $169 million in 1992. KFC's operating profits were split equally between its domestic and international operations. Domestically, KFC's profits rose as a result of additional units, lower headquarters administrative expenses from a restructuring program implemented in early 1992, a sales mix change to higher margin products such as Popcorn Chicken, and higher volumes. Domestic profits were lowered slightly as a result of a higher level of sales promotions. Internationally, profits benefited from higher franchise royalty revenues and growth in Canada and Mexico. Profits were partially offset by lower profits in Australia, mainly the result of lower volumes and a negative currency translation effect.

KFC's Strategy

As KFC entered 1994, it grappled with a number of important issues. During the 1980s, consumers began to demand healthier foods and KFC was faced with a limited menu consisting mainly of fried foods. In order to reduce KFC's image as a fried chicken chain, it changed its logo from Kentucky Fried Chicken to KFC in 1991. In addition, it responded to consumer desires for greater menu variety by introducing new products. Consumers were also attracted by the convenience of

Exhibit 8   KFC Operating Results

	Worldwide Sales ($ billions)	KFC Corp.* Sales ($ billions)	KFC Corp.* Profit ($ millions)	Percent of Sales
1987	$4.1	$1.1	$ 90.0	8.3%
1988	5.0	1.2	116.5	9.6
1989	5.4	1.3	100.0	7.5
1990	5.8	1.5	126.9	8.3
1991	6.2	1.8	80.5	4.4
1992	6.7	2.2	168.8	7.8

* KFC corporate figures include company restaurants and franchise royalties and fees.
Source: PepsiCo annual reports for 1988, 1989, 1990, 1991, and 1992.

fast-food in such nontraditional locations as grocery stores, service stations, hospitals, discount warehouses, airports, and university campuses. This forced KFC management to investigate nontraditional distribution channels and restaurant designs. Management was also exploring ways to attract budget-conscious consumers with value-priced meals and special promotions.

Many of KFC's problems during the late 1980s surrounded its limited menu and its inability to quickly bring new products to market. The popularity of its Original Recipe fried chicken allowed KFC to expand through the 1980s without significant competition from other chicken competitors. As a result, new product introductions were never an important part of KFC strategy. However, the introduction of chicken sandwiches and fried chicken by hamburger chains required a competitive response and meant that they were now in more direct competition with KFC. For example, McDonald's introduced its McChicken sandwich in the U.S. market in 1989 while KFC was still testing its new sandwich.

The increased popularity of healthier foods and consumers' increasing demand for better variety prompted a number of changes in KFC's menu offerings. In 1992, KFC introduced Oriental Wings, Popcorn Chicken, and Honey BBQ Chicken as alternatives to its Original Recipe fried chicken. It also introduced a dessert menu, which included a variety of pies and cookies. In 1993, KFC rolled out its Rotisserie Chicken and began to promote its lunch and dinner buffet. The buffet, which included 30 items, was introduced into almost 1,600 KFC restaurants in 27 states by the end of 1993.

One of KFC's most aggressive strategies was the introduction of its "Neighborhood Program." By mid-1993, almost 500 company-owned restaurants in New York, Chicago, Philadelphia, Washington, D.C., St. Louis, Los Angeles, Houston, and Dallas had been outfitted with special menu offerings to appeal exclusively to the black community. Menus were beefed up with side dishes such as greens, macaroni and cheese, peach cobbler, sweet potato pie, and red beans and rice. In addition, restaurant employees were outfitted with African-inspired uniforms. The introduction of the Neighborhood Program increased sales by 5 to 30 percent in restaurants appealing directly to the black community. KFC was also testing 13 Hispanic-oriented restaurants in the Miami area, featuring such side dishes as fried plantains, flan, and tres leches.

KFC was testing a variety of nontraditional outlets, including drive-through and carryout units; snack shops in cafeterias; kiosks in airports, stadiums, amusement parks, and office buildings; mobile units that could be transported to outdoor concerts and fairs; and scaled-down outlets for supermarkets. In order to help its KFC, Taco Bell, and Pizza Hut units more quickly expand into the these nontraditional distribution channels, PepsiCo acquired a partial share of Carts of Colorado, Inc., a manufacturer of mobile merchandising carts, in 1992. KFC expected sales in such nontraditional locations to provide much of its future growth.

Operating Efficiencies

In 1989, KFC reorganized its U.S. operations in order to reduce overhead costs and to increase efficiency. Included in this reorganization was a revision of KFC's crew-training programs and operating standards. A renewed emphasis was placed on improving customer service, cleaner restaurants, faster and friendlier service, and continued high-quality products. In 1992, KFC reorganized its middle management ranks, eliminating 250 of the 1,500 management positions at KFC's corporate headquarters. More responsibility was assigned to restaurant franchisees and marketing managers and pay was more closely aligned with customer service and restaurant performance.

Restaurant Expansion and International Operations

Internationally, KFC was operating 3,640 restaurants outside of the United States at the end of 1992. In 1993, KFC expanded into two new countries—France and Brazil—bringing the total number of countries in which KFC has a presence to 63 and making KFC the third largest quick-service and largest chicken restaurant system in the world. In 1992, KFC's international operations contributed 50 percent to KFC's overall operating profit. In the future, KFC's international operations were expected to provide an increasing percentage of KFC's overall sales and profit growth as the U.S. market approached saturation.

MEXICO AND LATIN AMERICA ————————————————

KFC was one of the first restaurant chains to recognize the importance of international markets. In Latin America, KFC was operating 187 company-owned restaurants in Mexico, Puerto Rico, the Virgin Islands, and Trinidad as of April 1994. In addition, KFC had 108 franchisees in 42 countries throughout Latin America, bringing the total number of KFC restaurants in operation in Latin America to 295 (see Exhibit 9).

Through 1990, KFC concentrated its company operations in Mexico and Puerto Rico and focused its franchised operations in the Caribbean and Central America. However, by 1994, KFC had altered its Latin American strategy in a number of ways. First, it began franchising in Mexico, mainly as a result of Mexico's new franchise law, which was enacted in 1990. Second, it expanded its company-owned restaurants into the Virgin Islands and Trinidad. Third, it reestablished a subsidiary in Venezuela in 1993—KFC had closed its Venezuelan operations in 1989 because of the high fixed costs associated with running the small subsidiary. Last, it decided to expand its franchise operations beyond Central America. In 1990, a franchise was opened in Chile, and in 1993, a new franchise was opened in Brazil.

Exhibit 9 KFC Latin America Restaurant Count of January 31, 1994

	Company Restaurants	Franchise Restaurants	Total Restaurants
Mexico	108	21	129
Puerto Rico	55	0	55
Virgin Islands	7	0	7
Trinidad	17	0	17
Franchises	—	87	87
Total	187	108	295

Franchising

Through 1989, KFC relied exclusively on the operation of company-owned restaurants in Mexico. While franchising was popular in the United States, it was virtually unknown in Mexico until 1990, mainly because of the absence of a law protecting patents, information, and technology transferred to a Mexican franchise. In addition, royalties were limited. As a result, most fast-food chains opted to invest in Mexico using company-owned restaurants rather than through franchising.

In January 1990, Mexico enacted a new law that provided for the protection of technology transferred into Mexico. Under the new legislation, the franchisor and franchisee were free to set their own terms. Royalties were also allowed under the new law. Royalties were taxed at a 15 percent rate on technology assistance and know-how and 35 percent for other royalty categories. The advent of the new franchise law resulted in an explosion of franchises in fast-food, services, hotels, and retail outlets. In 1992, franchises had an estimated $750 million in sales in over 1,200 outlets throughout Mexico.

At the end of 1989, KFC was operating company-owned restaurants in three regions: Mexico City, Guadalajara, and Monterrey. By limiting operations to company-owned restaurants in these three regions, KFC was better able to coordinate operations and minimize costs of distribution to individual restaurants. However, the new franchise legislation gave KFC and other fast-food chains the opportunity to more easily expand their restaurant bases to other regions of Mexico, where responsibility for management could be handled by individual franchisees.

Economic and Political Environment

Many factors have made Mexico a potentially profitable location for U.S. direct investment and trade. Mexico's population of 89.5 million people is approximately one-third as large as that of the United States. This represents a large market for U.S. goods. Because of its geographic proximity to the United States, transportation costs from the United States have been minimal. This has increased the competitiveness of U.S. goods in comparison with European and Asian goods, which must be transported at substantial cost across the Atlantic or Pacific oceans. The passage of the North American Free Trade Agreement (NAFTA) has resulted in further opportunities as tariffs and nontarriff barriers are eliminated and restrictions on foreign investment are eased. The United States has been Mexico's largest trading partner. Over 65 percent of Mexico's imports have come from the United States, while 69 percent of Mexico's exports have been to the U.S. market (see Exhibit 10). In addition, low wage rates have made Mexico an attractive location for production. By producing in Mexico, U.S. firms could reduce labor costs and increase the cost competitiveness of their goods in world markets.

Despite the importance of the U.S. market to Mexico, Mexico still has represented a small percentage of overall U.S. trade and investment. Since the early 1900s, the portion of U.S. exports to Latin America has declined. Instead, U.S. exports to Canada and Asia, where economic growth has outpaced growth in Mexico, have increased more quickly. Canada has been the largest importer of U.S. goods. Japan has been the largest exporter of goods to the United States, with Canada close behind. The value of Mexico's exports to the United States has increased during the last two decades, mainly because of the rise in the price of oil.

The lack of U.S. investment in and trade with Mexico during this century has been partly the result of Mexico's long history of restricting trade and foreign direct investment and partly the result of political instability and governmental corruption. The Institutional Revolutionary Party (PRI), which came to power in Mexico during the 1930s, traditionally pursued protectionist economic policies in order to shield its people and economy from foreign firms and goods. Industries were predominately government-owned or controlled and production was pursued for the domestic market only. High tariffs and other trade barriers restricted imports into Mexico, and foreign ownership of assets in Mexico was largely prohibited or heavily restricted.

In addition, a dictatorial and entrenched government bureaucracy, corrupt labor unions, and a long tradition of anti-Americanism among many government officials and intellectuals reduced the motivation of U.S. firms for investing in Mexico. Further, the 1982 nationalization of Mexico's banks led to higher real interest rates and lower investor confidence. Since then, the Mexican government has battled high inflation, high interest rates, labor unrest, and lost consumer purchasing power (see Exhibit 11). Total foreign debt, which stood at $125.9 billion at the end of 1993, has remained a problem.

Investor confidence in Mexico, however, improved when Carlos Salinas de Gortari was elected president of Mexico. Following his election, Salinas embarked on an ambitious restructuring of the Mexican economy. Salinas initiated policies to strengthen the free market components of the economy. Top marginal tax rates were lowered to 36 percent in 1990, down from 60 percent in 1986, and new legislation eliminated many restrictions on foreign investment. Foreign firms were allowed to buy up to 100 percent of the equity in many Mexico firms. Previously, foreign ownership of Mexican firms was limited to 49 percent. Many government-owned companies were sold to private investors in order to eliminate government bureaucracy and improve efficiency. In addition, the elimination of trade barriers and interest surrounding NAFTA resulted in increased trade with the United States; U.S. exports to Mexico reached $40 billion in 1992, while imports from Mexico exceeded $42 billion.

Import Controls

Prior to 1989, Mexico levied high tariffs on most imported goods. In addition, many other goods were subjected to quotas, licensing requirements, and other nontariff trade barriers. In 1986, Mexico joined the General Agreement on Tariffs and Trade

Exhibit 10   Mexico's Major Trading Partners (percent total exports and imports)

	1988		1990		1992	
	Percent Total Exports	Percent Total Imports	Percent Total Exports	Percent Total Imports	Percent Total Exports	Percent Total Imports
United States	72.9%	74.9%	69.3%	68.0%	68.7%	65.2%
Japan	4.9	6.4	5.8	4.5	3.2	6.3
West Germany	1.3	3.5	1.4*	4.2*	N/A	5.1
France	1.8	2.0	3.5	2.3	2.0	2.7
Other	19.1	13.2	20.0	21.0	26.1	20.7
Percent total	100.0%	100.0%	100.0%	100.0%	100.0%	100.0%
Value ($ millions)	20,658	18,903	26,773	29,799	46,196	62,129

* Includes East Germany.
Source: Business International, 1994.

Exhibit 11   Economic Data for Mexico

	1989	1990	1991	1992
Population (millions)	84.5	86.2	87.8	89.5
GDP (billions of new pesos)	507.5	686.4	865.2	1,033.2
Real GDP growth rate (%)	3.3	4.4	3.6	2.7
Exchange rate (new pesos/$)	2.641	2.945	3.071	3.115
Inflation (%)	20.0	26.7	22.7	15.5

Source: *International Financial Statistics*, International Monetary Fund.

(GATT), a world trade organization designed to eliminate barriers to trade among member nations. As a member of GATT, Mexico was obligated to apply its system of tariffs to all member nations equally. As a result of its membership in GATT, Mexico dropped tariff rates on a variety of imported goods. In addition, import license requirements were dropped for all but 300 imported items. Since President Salinas took office in 1988, tariffs have fallen from 100 percent on some items to an average of 11 percent.

Privatization

The privatization of government-owned companies has come to symbolize the restructuring of Mexico's economy. On May 14, 1990, legislation was passed to privatize all government-run banks. By the end of 1992, over 800 of some 1,200 government-owned companies had been sold, including Mexicana and AeroMexico, the two largest airline companies in Mexico. At least 40 more companies were scheduled to be privatized in 1993. However, more than 350 companies remained under government ownership. These represented a significant portion of the assets owned by the state at the start of 1988. A large percentage of the remaining government-owned assets were in certain strategic industries such as steel, electricity, and petroleum. However, in 1993, President Salinas opened up the electricity sector to independent power producers and Petroleos Mexicanos (Pemex), the state-run petrochemical monopoly, initiated a program to sell off many of its nonstrategic assets to private and foreign buyers. This was motivated mainly by a desire by Pemex to concentrate on its basic petrochemical businesses.

Prices, Wages, and Foreign Exchange

Between December 20, 1982, and November 11, 1991, a two-tiered exchange rate system was in force in Mexico. The system consisted of a controlled rate and a free market rate. A controlled rate was used for imports, foreign debt payments, and conversion of export proceeds. An estimated 70 percent of all foreign transactions were covered by the controlled rate. A free market rate was used for other transactions. On January 1, 1989, President Salinas instituted a policy of allowing the peso to depreciate against the dollar by 1 peso per day. The result was a grossly overvalued peso. This lowered the price of imports and led to an increase in imports of over 23 percent in 1989. At the same time, Mexican exports became less competitive on world markets.

Effective November 11, 1991, the controlled rate was abolished and replaced with an official free rate. In order to limit the range of fluctuations in the value of the peso, the government fixed the rate at which it would buy or sell pesos. A floor (the maximum price at which pesos may be purchased) was initially established at Ps 3056.20 and remained fixed. A ceiling (the maximum price at which the peso may be sold) was initially established at Ps 3,056.40 and allowed to move upward by Ps 0.20 per day. This was later revised to Ps 0.40 per day. On January 1, 1993, a new currency was issued—called the new peso—with three fewer zeros. The new currency was designed to simplify transactions and to reduce the cost of printing currency.

Labor Problems

One of KFC's primary concerns was the stability of Mexico's labor markets. Labor was relatively plentiful and cheap in Mexico, though much of the work force is still relatively unskilled. While KFC benefitted from lower labor costs, labor unrest, low job retention, absenteeism, and punctuality continue to be significant problems. A good part of the problem with absenteeism and punctuality was cultural. However, problems with worker retention and labor unrest were mainly the result of workers' frustration over the loss of their purchasing power due to inflation and past government controls on wage increases. *Business Latin America* estimated that purchasing power fell by 35 percent in Mexico between January 1988 and June 1990. Though absenteeism was on the decline due to job security fears, it was still high at approximately 8 to 14 percent of the labor force. Turnover also continued to be a problem. Turnover of production line personnel was running at 5 to 12 percent per month.

RISKS AND OPPORTUNITIES

Managers in KFC Mexico were hopeful that the government's new economic policies would continue to keep inflation under control and promote growth in Mexico's economy. They also hoped that greater economic stability would help eliminate much of the labor unrest that has plagued Mexico during the last several years. Of greatest concern was KFC's market share in Mexico, which stood at around 10 percent in 1990. McDonald's and Arby's both signed franchise agreements in early 1990. While neither company had a significant market share in Mexico at that time, KFC feared that its market share gains could easily be lost if it were to slow its building program in Mexico. KFC planned to counter McDonald's and other competitors by expanding its franchise base in Mexico and relying less heavily on company-owned restaurants as it had in the past. By 1994, KFC had 21 franchised outlets in Mexico.

KFC also worried that the gains by President Salinas during the last five years, namely in stabilizing the Mexican economy, reducing restrictions on foreign investment in Mexico, and privatizing government assets, might be lost. On January 1, 1994, the day the North American Free Trade Agreement (NAFTA) went into effect, rebels (descendants of the Mayans) rebelled in the southern Mexican province of Chiapas on the Guatemalan border. After four days of fighting, Mexican troops had driven the rebels out of several towns earlier seized by the rebels. Around 150—mostly rebels—were killed. The uprising symbolized many of the fears of the poor in Mexico. While Salinas's economic programs had increased economic growth and wealth in Mexico, many of Mexico's poorest felt left out. Lower tariffs on imported agricultural goods from the United States threatened to drive many Mexican farmers out of business. Observers believed social unrest from Mexico's Indians, farmers, and the poor could unravel much of the success that Salinas had had economically by creating a politically and socially unstable environment in Mexico.

Further, Salinas's hand-picked successor for president, Luis Donaldo Colosio, was assassinated on March 23, 1994, while campaigning in Tijuana. Of greatest concern to Salinas and his Institutional Revolutionary Party was the possibility that the assassin—Mario Aburto Martinez, a 23-year-old mechanic and migrant worker—was affiliated with a dissident group upset with the PRI's economic reforms and the fact that the PRI had not lost a presidential election in seven decades. The possible existence of a dissident group raised fears of further political violence in the future. The PRI quickly named Ernesto Zedillo, a 42-year-old economist with little political experience or name recognition, as their new presidential candidate. Presidential elections were scheduled for August 1994. Further political violence by dissident groups, discontentment among the poor, fear among Mexico's farmers that NAFTA will destroy their businesses, and the lack of name recognition of the PRI's new presidential candidate meant that a PRI victory in the August elections was no longer a certainty. A victory by the Party of the Democratic Revolution (PRD), the main opposition party of the left, could result in the reversal of many of the free market reforms pursued by President Salinas since 1988.

KFC's alternative was to approach investment in Mexico more conservatively, until greater economic and political stability could be achieved. Instead, resources could be directed at other investment areas with less risk, such as Japan, Australia,

China, and Europe. At the same time, significant opportunities existed for KFC to expand its franchise base throughout the Caribbean and South America. However, PepsiCo's commitments to these other markets were unlikely to be affected by its investment decisions in Mexico, as PepsiCo's large internal cash flows could satisfy the investment needs of KFC's other international subsidiaries, regardless of its investments in Mexico. The danger in taking a conservative approach in Mexico was the potential loss of market share in a large market where KFC enjoyed enormous popularity.

The Quaker Oats Company, Gatorade, and Snapple Beverage

Arthur A. Thompson, Jr., The University of Alabama
John E. Gamble, Auburn University of Montgomery

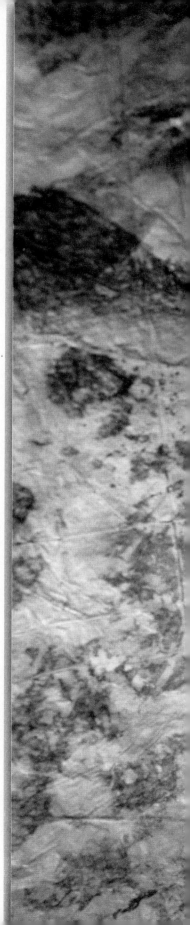

In November 1994, Quaker Oats Co. negotiated a deal to acquire iced tea and fruit drink marketer Snapple Beverage Corp. for $1.7 billion in cash, a move that took Quaker off the list of rumored takeover targets and greatly strengthened its position as a producer-marketer of beverage substitutes for soft drinks. Quaker's Gatorade brand commanded 85 percent of the sports drink segment in the United States, generated worldwide sales of almost $1.2 billion, and was Quaker's fastest-growing, most lucrative product. Snapple had 1993 sales of $516 million, up from $95 million in 1991, and was the clear-cut market leader in New Age or alternative beverages, with national distribution capability and growing brand awareness among consumers. Quaker's acquisition of Snapple elevated it into a nonalcoholic beverage powerhouse, with nearly $2 billion in sales, trailing only Coca-Cola and PepsiCo.

Quaker agreed to pay Snapple shareholders $14 a share for the 121,620,000 shares outstanding, a price roughly equal to the $13.75–$14.25 trading range of Snapple stock in the few days before the agreement was announced. Shares of Snapple, which had traded in the $28–$32 range in late 1993 and early 1994, had fallen in recent months when its sales growth during the first three quarters of 1994 slowed significantly and ready-to-drink tea products carrying the Lipton and Nestea brands began to capture almost 50 percent of sales in supermarkets. The Lipton line was jointly produced and marketed by PepsiCo and Unilever's Thomas J. Lipton subsidiary; the Nestea line was the product of an alliance between Coca-Cola and Nestlé (Nestlé was the world's largest food products company and the producer of Nestea-brand teas).

Hours before the Quaker–Snapple agreement was announced, Snapple reported a third-quarter earnings drop of 74 percent, which analysts attributed to oversized inventories and intensifying competition. In NYSE trading on the following day, Quaker's stock fell nearly 10 percent, from $74.50 to $67.125. The drop in price was said to be a combination of Snapple's poor earnings report, the reduced likelihood that Quaker would be a takeover target, and the rich acquisition price Quaker was paying for Snapple. Wall Street analysts regarded the outlook for Snapple's future sales and earnings as very uncertain. Whereas Snapple management indicated in May 1994 that it was comfortable with a 1994 earnings per share projection of 86 cents a share, the confidential business plan Snapple gave Quaker during their negotiations contained a projection of only 55 cents a share; in a filing with the Securities and Exchange Commission in the week following the acquisition announcement, Snapple indicated that 1994 earnings of 40 cents a share appeared more reasonable.[1] The $14 acquisition price represented a multiple of 35 times Snapple's latest 40 cents per share earnings projection and a multiple of nearly 20 times Snapple's estimated 1994 operating earnings (the latter multiple was well above the multiples of 10 and 11 that other recently acquired beverage companies had commanded).[2]

To finance the Snapple acquisition, Quaker borrowed $2.4 billion from NationsBank. Quaker planned to use the loan proceeds to (1) make cash payments of $1.7 billion to Snapple's shareholders for the outstanding 121,620,000 shares, (2) pay off $100 million in Snapple debt, (3) refinance $350 million in Quaker's debt, and (4) retain $250 million for working capital. Quaker management was reportedly seeking buyers for its European pet foods business and Mexican chocolate subsidiary (combined sales of $900 million) as part of an ongoing restructuring of its food products lineup and, presumably, to raise cash to pay down debt associated with the Snapple acquisition.

THE QUAKER OATS COMPANY

In 1994, Quaker Oats was the 12th largest food and beverage company in the United States, with worldwide sales of $6 billion (see Exhibit 1). The company operated 54 manufacturing plants in 16 states and 13 foreign countries and had distribution centers and sales offices in 21 states and 18 foreign countries. Nearly one-third of corporate revenues came from sales outside the United States. Quaker's worldwide grocery product portfolio included such well-known brands as Quaker Oats, Cap'n Crunch, Rice-A-Roni, Gatorade, Aunt Jemima, Ken-L Ration pet foods, and Van Camp's bean products; 81 percent of the company's sales came from brands holding the number one or number two position in their respective categories. Moreover, 82 percent of Quaker's worldwide sales came from brands positioned in categories where sales volumes were growing. Hot cereals were Quaker's oldest, best-known, and most profitable products. Of the top-25-selling cereal brands, Quaker had four: Instant Quaker Oatmeal, Cap'n Crunch, Old Fashioned and Quick Quaker Oats, and Life Cereal.

Quaker's top management was committed to achieving real earnings growth of 7 percent and providing total shareholder returns (dividends plus share price appreciation) that exceeded the S&P 500 stock index over time. Management also believed it could enhance shareholder value by prudently using leverage. Prior to the Snapple acquisition, Quaker issued $200 million in medium-term notes, increasing total debt to $1 billion. In fiscal 1994, Quaker used its debt proceeds and cash flows from operations to repurchase 3 million shares of common stock, make four small acquisitions, extend the company's record of consecutive dividend increases to 27 years, and make $175 million in capital investments to support growth and efficiency improvements. Exhibit 2 provides a 10-year financial summary of Quaker Oats corporate performance.

---

[1]Reported in *The Wall Street Journal*, November 7, 1994, p. A4.
[2]*The Wall Street Journal*, November 3, 1994, pp. A3 and A4.

Exhibit 1   The 25 Largest Food and Beverage Companies in the United States (ranked by 1993 food and beverage sales, in millions of dollars)

Company	1992	1993
1. Philip Morris	$33,024	$34,526
2. ConAgra Inc.	16,201	16,499
3. PepsiCo	13,738	15,665
4. Coca-Cola	13,039	13,937
5. IBP Inc.	11,128	11,671
6. Anheuser-Busch	10,741	10,792
7. Sara Lee	6,622	7,206
8. H.J. Heinz	6,582	7,103
9. RJR Nabisco	6,707	7,025
10. Campbell Soup	6,263	6,586
11. Kellogg	6,191	6,295
12. Quaker Oats	5,576	5,731
13. CPC International	5,502	5,636
14. General Mills	5,234	5,397
15. Seagram Company	5,214	5,227
16. Tyson Foods	4,169	4,707
17. Ralston Purina	4,558	4,526
18. Borden Inc.	4,056	3,674
19. Hershey Foods	3,220	3,488
20. Procter & Gamble	3,709	3,271
21. Dole Foods	3,120	3,108
22. Hormel Food	2,814	2,854
23. Chiquita Brands	2,723	2,522
24. Dean Foods	2,220	2,243
25. International Multifoods	2,281	2,224

Source: The Food Institute.

Quaker's Corporate Organization and Brand Portfolio

Quaker Oats' worldwide production and sales operations were structured around two broad geographic groups: U.S. and Canadian Grocery Products and International Grocery Products. The U.S. and Canadian Grocery group was subdivided into four product divisions: Breakfast Foods, Gatorade Worldwide, Diversified Grocery Products (pet foods and grain products), and Convenience Foods. The International Grocery Products group had three geographic operating divisions: Europe, Latin America, and Pacific. Exhibit 3 shows the financial performance of the two major product groups. Exhibit 4 shows the brands and sales of the divisional units.

The Gatorade Worldwide Division

Gatorade was developed in 1965 for the University of Florida Gators; it was sold to Stokely-Van Camp in 1967. Quaker acquired the Gatorade brand in 1983 when it bought Stokely-Van Camp. At the time, Gatorade sales were about $100 million.

Exhibit 2 Financial Summary for Quaker Oats Company, 1984–1994 (dollars in millions, except per share data)

Year Ended June 30	5-Year CAGR*	10-Year CAGR*	1994	1993	1992	1991	1990	1989	1988	1987	1986	1985	1984
Operating Results**, †													
Net sales	4.1%	7.7%	$5,955.0	$5,730.6	$5,576.4	$5,491.2	$5,030.6	$4,879.4	$4,508.0	$3,823.9	$2,968.6	$2,925.6	$2,830.9
Gross profit	6.3%	10.8%	3,028.8	2,860.6	2,745.3	2,652.7	2,350.3	2,229.0	2,114.6	1,750.7	1,298.7	1,174.7	1,085.7
Income from continuing operations before income taxes and cumulative effect of accounting changes	9.6%	6.0%	378.7	467.6	421.5	411.5	382.4	239.1	314.6	295.9	255.8	238.8	211.3
Provision for income taxes	10.3%	4.0%	147.2	180.8	173.9	175.7	153.5	90.2	118.1	141.3	113.4	110.3	99.0
Income from continuing operations before cumulative effect of account changes	9.2%	7.5%	231.5	286.8	247.6	235.8	228.9	148.9	196.5	154.6	142.4	128.5	112.3
Income (loss) from discontinued operations—net of tax			—	—	—	(30.0)	(59.9)	54.1	59.2	33.5	37.2	28.1	26.4
Income from the disposal of discontinued operations—net of tax			—	—	—	—	—	—	—	55.8	—	—	—
Cumulative effect of accounting changes—net of tax			—	(115.5)	—	—	—	—	—	—	—	—	—
Net income	2.7%	5.3%	$ 231.5	$ 171.3	$ 247.6	$ 205.8	$ 169.0	$ 203.0	$ 255.7	$ 243.9	$ 179.6	$ 156.6	$ 138.7
Per common share:													
Income from continuing operations for cumulative effect of accounting changes	12.3%	9.5%	$ 3.36	$ 3.93	$ 3.25	$ 3.05	$ 2.93	$ 1.88	$ 2.46	$ 1.96	$ 1.77	$ 1.53	$ 1.35
Income (loss) from discontinued operations			—	—	—	(0.40)	(0.78)	0.68	0.74	0.43	0.47	0.35	0.32
Income from the disposal of discontinued operations			—	—	—	—	—	—	—	0.71	—	—	—
Cumulative effect of accounting changes			—	(1.59)	—	—	—	—	—	—	—	—	—
Net income	5.6%	7.2%	$ 3.36	$ 2.34	$ 3.25	$ 2.65	$ 2.15	$ 2.56	$ 3.20	$ 3.10	$ 2.24	$ 1.88	$ 1.67
Dividends declared:													
Common stock	8.1%	12.2%	$ 140.6	$ 136.1	$ 128.6	$ 118.7	$ 106.9	$ 95.2	$ 79.9	$ 63.2	$ 55.3	$ 50.5	$ 44.4
Per common share	12.1%	14.4%	$ 2.12	$ 1.92	$ 1.72	$ 1.56	$ 1.40	$ 1.20	$ 1.00	$ 0.80	$ 0.70	$ 0.62	$ 0.55
Convertible preferred and redeemable preference stock			$ 4.0	$ 4.2	$ 4.2	$ 4.3	$ 3.6	—	—	—	$ 2.3	$ 3.6	$ 3.9
Average number of common shares outstanding (in thousands)			67,618	71,974	74,881	75,904	76,537	79,307	79,835	78,812	79,060	81,492	80,412

Exhibit 2 Concluded

Year Ended June 30	5-Year CAGR*	10-Year CAGR*	1994	1993	1992	1991	1990	1989	1988	1987	1986	1985	1984
Financial Statistics‡, §													
Current ratio			1.0	1.0	1.2	1.3	1.3	1.8	1.4	1.4	1.4	1.7	1.6
Working capital			$ (5.5)	$ (37.5)	$ 168.7	$ 317.8	$ 342.8	$ 695.8	$ 417.5	$ 507.9	$ 296.8	$ 400.7	$ 316.8
Property, plant and equipment—net			$1,214.2	$1,228.2	$1,273.3	$1,232.7	$1,154.1	$ 959.6	$ 922.5	$ 898.6	$ 691.0	$ 616.5	$ 650.1
Depreciation expense			$ 133.3	$ 129.9	$ 129.7	$ 125.2	$ 103.5	$ 94.2	$ 88.3	$ 81.6	$ 59.1	$ 56.3	$ 57.4
Total assets			$3,043.3	$2,815.9	$3,039.9	$3,060.5	$3,377.4	$3,125.9	$2,886.1	$3,136.5	$1,944.5	$1,760.3	$1,726.5
Long-term debt			$ 759.5	$ 632.6	$ 688.7	$ 701.2	$ 740.3	$ 766.8	$ 299.1	$ 527.7	$ 160.9	$ 168.2	$ 200.1
Preferred stock (net of deferred compensation) and redeemable preference stock			$ 15.3	$ 11.4	$ 7.9	$ 4.8	$ 1.8	—	—	—	—	$ 37.9	$ 38.5
Common shareholders' equity			$ 445.8	$ 551.1	$ 842.1	$ 901.0	$1,017.5	$1,137.1	$1,251.1	$1,087.5	$ 831.7	$ 786.9	$ 720.1
Net cash provided by operating activities			$ 450.8	$ 558.2	$ 581.3	$ 543.2	$ 460.0	$ 408.3	$ 320.8	$ 375.1	$ 266.9	$ 295.5	$ 263.6
Operating return on assets″			19.9%	21.1%	18.9%	18.8%	20.4%	14.4%	18.3%	22.1%	25.8%	24.5%	24.4%
Gross profit as a percentage of sales			50.9%	49.9%	49.2%	48.3%	46.7%	45.7%	46.9%	45.8%	43.7%	40.2%	38.4%
Advertising and merchandising as a percentage of sales			26.6%	25.7%	26.0%	25.6%	23.8%	23.4%	24.9%	22.9%	21.7%	19.4%	18.4%
Income from continuing operations before cumulative effect of accounting changes as a percentage of sales			3.9%	5.0%	4.4%	4.3%	4.6%	3.1%	4.4%	4.0%	4.8%	4.4%	4.0%
Total debt-to-total capitalization ratio#			68.8%	59.0%	48.7%	47.4%	52.3%	44.2%	33.8%	50.2%	35.7%	28.9%	35.4%
Common dividends as a percentage of income available for common shares (excluding cumulative effect of accounting changes)			63.1%	48.9%	52.9%	58.9%	65.1%	46.9%	31.3%	25.9%	31.2%	33.0%	32.9%
Number of common shareholders			28,197	33,154	33,580	33,603	33,859	34,347	34,231	32,358	27,068	26,670	26,785
Number of employees worldwide			20,000	20,200	21,100	20,900	28,200	31,700	31,300	30,800	29,500	28,700	28,400
Market price range of common stock—High			$ 82	$ 77	$ 75¼	$ 64⅞	$ 68⅛	$ 66¼	$ 57⅛	$ 57⅝	$ 39¼	$ 26⅛	$ 16⅛
—Low			$ 61⅞	$ 56⅛	$ 50¼	$ 41¾	$ 45⅛	$ 42⅝	$ 31	$ 32⅝	$ 23½	$ 14¼	$ 10¾

* CAGR—compound average growth rate.

** Fiscal 1994 results include a pretax restructuring charge of $118.4 million, or $1.09 per share, for workforce reductions, plant consolidations, and product discontinuations and a pretax gain of $9.8 million, or $0.13 per share, for the sale of a business in Venezuela.

& dagger;Fiscal 1989 results include a pretax restructuring charge of $124.3 million, or $1.00 per share, for plant consolidations and overhead reductions and a pretax charge of $25.6 million, or $0.20 per share, for a change to the LIFO method of accounting for the majority of U.S. Grocery Products inventories.

‡ Income-related statistics exclude the results of businesses reported as discontinued operations. Balance sheet amounts and related statistics have not been restated for discontinued operations, other than Fisher-Price, due to materiality.

§ Effective fiscal 1991, common shareholders' equity and number of employees worldwide were reduced as a result of the Fisher-Price spinoff.

″ Operating income divided by average identifiable assets of U.S. and Canadian and International Grocery Products.

Total debt divided by total debt plus total shareholders' equity including preferred stock (net of deferred compensation) and redeemable preference stock.

Source: 1994 Annual Report.

Exhibit 3   Financial Performance of Quaker's Two Major Grocery Products Groups, 1989–1994
(dollars in millions)

Product Group	Fiscal Year Ended June 30					
	1989	**1990**	**1991**	**1992**	**1993**	**1994**
U.S. and Canadian Grocery Products						
Net sales	$3,630	$3,610	$3,860	$3,842	$3,930	$4,253
Operating income	256	373	429	435	447	431
Identifiable assets	2,055	2,150	2,229	1,998	1,877	1,999
Return on net sales	7.1%	10.3%	11.1%	11.3%	11.4%	10.1%
Return on assets	13.1%	17.7%	19.6%	20.6%	23.1%	22.2%
International Grocery Products						
Net sales	$1,250	$1,421	$1,631	$1,734	$1,800	$1,702
Operating income	93	172	104	105	128	106
Identifiable assets	482	638	656	842	745	786
Return on net sales	7.5%	12.1%	6.4%	6.1%	7.1%	6.2%
Return on assets	20.0%	30.7%	16.1%	14.0%	16.2%	13.9%

Source: 1994 Annual Report.

Since the acquisition, sales of Gatorade had grown at an average annual compound rate of 22 percent, spurred by the addition of flavor and package-size variety as well as wider geographic distribution. Worldwide sales were just over $1.1 billion in 1994, up 21 percent over fiscal 1993. U.S. and Canadian volume increased 19 percent; international volume was up 31 percent. According to Quaker estimates, Gatorade held a 77 percent share of the $1.3 billion U.S. sports beverage category as of mid-1994 (down from 90 percent-plus in 1990–91) and more than 40 percent of the global sports drink market. Quaker management believed that Gatorade's science-based rehydration capability to replace salts and fluids lost during exercise, its strong identity with sports, and its leading position domestically and globally made it an exceptionally profitable growth opportunity worldwide. Gatorade was Quaker's number one growth priority, and the stated mission of the Gatorade Worldwide division was "to quench hot and thirsty consumers in every corner of the world."

Gatorade's Market Scope   In 1994, Gatorade was marketed in 26 countries on five continents and had the leading market position in most locations. The brand's biggest markets in 1994 were the United States, Mexico, South Korea, Canada, Venezuela, Italy, Germany, and Taiwan. In 1994, sales of Gatorade totaled nearly $900 million in the United States and approximately $220 million in the remaining 25 countries where it was marketed. Management's objective was to increase sales in Latin America, Europe, and the Pacific to $1 billion by the year 2000.

In Latin America, Gatorade's share of the sports beverage segment was in the 90 percent range in all countries where it was available. Mexico was Gatorade's second largest market after the United States. In 1994, sales in Brazil increased fourfold as Gatorade was successfully relaunched in the Sao Paulo region. Sales volumes continued to rise in Venezuela and the Caribbean, and Gatorade was introduced into Chile.

| Exhibit 4 | Quaker's Brands and Sales, by Division, 1989–1994 | *(dollars in millions)* |

Division/Category	Brands/Products	Sales in Fiscal Year Ending June 30					
		1989	1990	1991	1992	1993	1994
Breakfast Foods	Quaker Oatmeal, Cap'n Crunch, Life, Quaker rice cakes, Quaker Chewy granola bars, Quaker grits, Aunt Jemima cornmeal	$1,292	$1,280	$1,322	$1,313	$1,425	$1,573
Pet Foods	Ken-L Ration, Gaines, Kibbles 'n Bits, Puss 'n Boots, Cycle	608	518	531	531	529	539
Golden Grain	Rice-A-Roni, Noodle Roni, Near East Golden Grain, Mission	283	275	297	309	269	305
Convenience Foods	Aunt Jemima breakfast products, Celeste frozen pizza, Van Camp's canned beans, Wolf chili, Burry cookies, Maryland Club coffee, Proof & Bake frozen products, Petrofsky's bakery products	857	901	978	953	949	924
Gatorade (U.S. and Canada)	Gatorade	584	630	724	727	750	906
Europe	Quaker cereals, Gatorade, Felix cat food, Bonzo dog food, Cuore corn oil	969	1,085	1,326	1,355	1,336	1,164
Latin America and Pacific	Quaker cereals, Gatorade	281	336	305	380	465	538

Source: 1994 Annual Report.

To meet the growing sales volume in Latin America, Quaker was investing in additional production facilities.

Competition in the sports beverage market in Europe was fierce because in a number of important countries the market was already developed. When Gatorade was introduced in these country markets, it had to win sales and market share away from established brands. Quaker had pulled Gatorade out of the competitive U.K. and French markets. Given the varying competitive intensity from country to country, Quaker's Gatorade division was focusing its marketing resources on the most promising European country markets. Sales were currently biggest in Germany and Italy. In 1994, Gatorade was introduced in Holland and Austria. Quaker management anticipated that Gatorade sales in Europe would evolve more slowly than other global locations. In 1994, volume grew 9 percent in Europe but sales revenue was lower because of weaker European currencies against the U.S. dollar.

Throughout most of the Pacific, Gatorade was sold primarily via licensing agreements. Quaker's most successful licensing agreement was with Cheil Foods in South Korea, where Gatorade was a strong second in the sports beverage segment. Gatorade volume in South Korea ranked third, behind the United States and Mexico. In fiscal 1994, Gatorade was introduced in Australia (where the brand was sold through an arrangement with Pepsi-Cola bottlers of Australia), Singapore, and Hong Kong. Although Gatorade was not the first sports drink marketed in Australia, the brand captured the leading share by mid-1994, less than 12 months after it was introduced.

The expense of underwriting Gatorade's entry into new country markets had pinched Gatorade's international profit margins. Quaker's profits from international sales of Gatorade were expected to remain subpar as the company pushed for expanded penetration of international markets. Quaker management believed that increased consumer interest in healthy foods and beverages, growing sports participation, expanded sports competition in the world arena, increasing acceptance of international brands, and a growing population in warm climate countries and in youthful age segments—especially in Latin America and the Asian Pacific—all bode well for Gatorade's continued sales growth in international markets.

The U.S. Market Situation   The Gatorade brand was coming under increased competition pressure in the U.S. market as a number of companies introduced their own sports beverage brand:

Brand	Marketer
Powerade	Coca-Cola Co.
All Sport	Pepsi-Cola Co.
10-K	Suntory (Japan)
Everlast	A&W Brands
Nautilus Plus	Dr Pepper/Seven Up
Snap-Up (renamed Snapple Sport in April 1994)	Snapple Beverage Co.

Soft-drink companies were looking for new market segments because the $47 billion retail soft drink market had grown less than 3 percent annually since 1980. Both Coca-Cola and Pepsi were moving to market their brands directly against Gatorade's well-developed connections to sports teams, coaches, trainers, and celebrity athletes (Michael Jordan was Gatorade's athlete spokesman). Coca-Cola had maneuvered successfully to get Powerade named as the official sports drink of the 1996 Olympic Games in Atlanta and was running Powerade ads to sponsor World Cup Soccer. Coca-Cola's Powerade ads on local TV and radio carried the tag line "More power to ya." Coca-Cola had signed pro basketball–football star Deion Sanders to appear in Powerade ads. Pepsi-Cola's commercials for All Sport touted the theme "Fuel the fire" and showed gritty scenes of youths playing fast-action sports like blacktop basketball. Pepsi had also enlisted pro basketball's Shaquille O'Neal to appear in its ads and was sponsoring telecasts of NCAA basketball games. Snapple's ads for Snap-Up/Snapple Sport featured tennis celebrities Ivan Lendl and Jennifer Capriati. Suntory was seeking to attract preteens to its 10-K brand with ads featuring a 12-year-old boy who played five sports. Gatorade rivals were expected to spend $30 million to $40 million advertising their brands in 1994. Pepsi's All Sport and Coca-Cola's Powerade were considered particularly formidable brands because they were backed by nationwide networks of local soft drink bottlers who delivered daily to major supermarkets (and at least weekly to other soft drink retailers and vending machine outlets) and who typically stocked the shelves of retailers and set up in-store aisle displays. With such distribution muscle both Powerade and All Sport could gain market exposure everywhere soft drinks were available.

To counter rivals' efforts to horn in on Gatorade's market share, Quaker doubled its 1994 ad budget to nearly $50 million and created ads that reduced Michael Jordan's role in favor of product-benefit claims. Quaker also expanded Gatorade's line to eight flavors, compared to four for Powerade and All Sport. Still, Gatorade's estimated market share was 5 percentage points lower in fall 1994 than a year earlier.

In an attempt to develop a new beverage category, the Gatorade division was test-marketing a new product named SunBolt Energy Drink, designed for morning consumption or any time consumers wanted a "pick-me-up." Sunbolt contained three carbohydrate sources, caffeine, and vitamin C equivalent to a whole orange; it was offered in four flavors. SunBolt was positioned in juice aisles of grocery stores where Gatorade was shelved.

Despite the entry of other sports beverages, Quaker management regarded water as Gatorade's biggest competitor as a "thirst quencher." Moreover, in many supermarkets, Gatorade was located alongside fruit juices, whereas Powerade and All Sport were often located in the soft drink section, something Gatorade executives believed was an advantage. Gatorade executives also believed that the entry of competing sports drink brands would help grow the category enough so that Gatorade sales would grow despite a declining market share. According to Quaker President Phil Marineau:[3]

> When you have a 90 percent share of a category and competitors like Coke and Pepsi moving in, you're not foolish enough to think you won't lose some market share. But we're going to keep our position as the dominant force among sports drinks. Greater availability is the key to the U.S. success of Gatorade.

Gatorade's Marketing and Distribution Strategies   Quaker executives concluded as of early 1994 that U.S. sales of Gatorade were approaching the limits of its traditional grocery channel delivery system—Gatorade was shipped from plants to retailer warehouses, and stores ordered what they needed to keep shelves stocked. Sustaining Gatorade's sales growth in the United States meant stretching the distribution strategy for Gatorade to include other channels. Donald R. Uzzi, a Pepsi executive, was hired in March 1994 as president of Gatorade's U.S. and Canada geographic unit. Uzzi's top strategic priority was to develop additional sales outlets for Gatorade; the options included fountain service for restaurants and fast-food outlets, vending machines, direct deliveries to nongrocery retail outlets, and point-of-sweat locations such as sports gyms and golf courses. The customary way of accessing such outlets was by building a network of independent distributors who would market to and service such accounts. In 1994, Gatorade's strongest markets were in the South and Southwest.

In foreign markets, Gatorade relied on several strategies to establish its market presence:

- Shipping the product in, handling the marketing and advertising in-house, and partnering with a local distributor to sell retail accounts, gain shelf space, and make deliveries. This approach was being utilized in Greece with a food distribution company.

- Handling the marketing and advertising in-house and having a local partner take care of manufacturing, sales, and distribution. This approach was being used in Australia.

- Contracting with a soft drink bottler to handle production, packaging, and distribution, with Gatorade taking care of marketing functions and

---

[3]As quoted in "Gatorade Growth Seen Outside U.S.," *Advertising Age*, November 15, 1993, p. 46.

- supervising the contractor. This strategy was used in Spain, where the contractor was a Pepsi-owned bottler.

- Handling all functions in-house—manufacturing, marketing, sales, and distribution. Such was the case in Venezuela where Quaker had built facilities to produce Gatorade.

SNAPPLE BEVERAGE CORP.

Snapple Beverage Corp. originated as a subchapter S corporation in 1972. The company, operating as Mr. Natural, Inc., was the brainchild of three streetwise entrepreneurs: Leonard Marsh, Arnold Greenberg, and Hyman Golden. March and Greenberg were lifelong friends, having gone to grade school and high school together; Golden was Marsh's brother-in-law. Mr. Natural, headquartered in Brooklyn, marketed and distributed a line of specialty beverages for the New York City area; the company's products were supplied by contract manufacturers and bottlers. The company's sales and operating scope grew gradually. Its all-natural products sold well in health food stores; later, delicatessens and convenience stores began to take on the line. By 1988, the company had become a regional distributor and headquarters operations were moved to East Meadow on Long Island (N.Y.). Exhibit 5 summarizes key events in the company's history.

Capitalizing on consumers' growing interest in natural and healthy beverage products, the three entrepreneurs launched an all-natural beverage line under the Snapple name in 1980. Over the years, more flavors and varieties were added; Snapple iced teas were introduced in 1987. Introduction of the Snapple iced tea line was supported with a creative and catchy advertising campaign stressing the message, "Try this, you'll love the taste, and it's good for you." Snapple's recipe for making a good-tasting iced tea involved making it hot and then bottling it; artificial preservatives or colors were avoided. Snapple's strategy was simple: make all-natural beverages that taste great, and keep introducing new and exciting flavors. As sales grew (principally because devoted health-conscious consumers spread the word among friends and acquaintances), company principals Leonard Marsh, Arnold Greenberg, and Hyman Golden plowed their profits back into the Snapple brand. Wider geographic distribution was attained by signing new distributors and granting them exclusive rights to distribute the Snapple line across a defined territory.

By 1991, sales had reached $95 million. Revenues jumped to $205.5 million in 1992 and to $516.0 million in 1993, as distribution widened and more consumers were attracted to try the line. Snapple's sales in 1993 ranked it no. 35 on the top 50 beverage companies list. Exhibits 6 and 7 present Snapple's financial statements. The company went public in December 1992 as Snapple Beverage Corp., with the three founders retaining 23.1 percent of the stock (7.7 percent each). After the initial public offering at a split-adjusted price of $5, the stock traded as high as $32.25 in late 1993 before trading as low as $11.50 in mid-1994. Responding to concerns of investors and Wall Street analysts as to whether the company's rapid growth was sustainable, Leonard Marsh said:

> For those of you who might have heard mumblings that we've grown too far, too fast, I suggest you consider Snapple in the proper context. The average

Exhibit 5   Summary of Key Events in Snapple Beverage Corporation's History

1972
Marsh, Golden, and Greenberg formed a company in association with a California juice manufacturer to distribute 100% natural fruit juices in New York City, primarily via health food distributors.

1979
A production plant is purchased in upstate New York to produce a line of pure, natural fruit juices.

1980
The name "Snapple" makes in first appearance when Snapple Beverage Corporation became the first company to manufacture a complete line of all-natural beverages.

1982
Snapple introduces Natural Sodas and pioneers the natural soft drink category.

1986
All Natural Fruit Drinks join the Snapple family, including Lemonade, Orangeade, Grapeade, and more.

1987
Snapple launches its All Natural Real Brewed Ice Tea and revolutionizes the beverage industry with the first tea to be brewed hot instead of mixed from cold concentrate. Snapple's signature wide-mouth bottle also makes its first appearance.

1990
Snapple introduces Snapple Sport, the first isotonic sports drink with the great taste of Snapple.

1991
Snapple recruits its first international distributor in Norway.

1992
The Thomas H. Lee Investment Company buys Snapple and leads an effort to take the company public. The stock triples in the first three months and is listed among the hottest stocks in the country. The three cofounders retain 23.1% of Snapple's common stock and Thomas H. Lee ends up owning 47.5% of Snapple's common shares.

1992/1993
Fruit Drink line expands to include such exotic flavors as Kiwi-Strawberry Cocktail, Mango Madness Cocktail, and Melonberry Cocktail.

1993
Snapple goes international, signing on distributors in the United Kingdom, Canada, Mexico, the Caribbean, Hong Kong, and elsewhere.

1994
Snapple introduces seven new products including Guava Mania Cocktail, Mango Tea, Amazin Grape Soda, Kiwi Strawberry Soda, and Mango Madness Soda as well as new diet versions of some bestsellers—Diet Kiwi Strawberry Cocktail, Diet Mango Madness Cocktail, and Diet Pink Lemonade.

Source: Company promotional materials.

American drank 500 soft drinks last year (1993) . . . and the average American drank only five Snapples last year. That's a 1 percent share of a $64 billion pie.[4]

During the summer months of 1994, Snapple marketed 75 varieties and flavors in five categories (ready-to-drink iced teas, fruit drinks, natural sodas and seltzers, fruit juices, and sports drinks) and had distributors in all 50 states. Despite sales of more than $500 million, Snapple had fewer than 200 employees; production, bottling,

---
[4]As quoted in Beverage World's *Periscope*, February 28, 1994, p. 21.

Exhibit 6   Snapple's Income Statement, 1992 and 1993

	1992	1993
Net sales	$205,465,595	$516,005,327
Cost of goods sold	127,098,086	298,724,646
Gross profit	78,367,509	217,280,681
Selling, general, and administrative expenses	45,455,818	105,693,741
Nonoperating expenses	10,626,742	9,116,664
Interest expense	19,086,213	2,459,297
Income before tax	3,198,736	100,010,070
Provisions for income taxes	1,262,919	32,387,498
Net income before extraordinary items	1,935,817	67,623,481
Extraordinary item	(2,632,904)	0
Net income	$ (697,087)	$ 67,623,481

Source: Company annual report.

packaging, and distribution were handled by contractors and independent distributors. Company activities were focused on marketing, new product development (the company had expertise in flavor technology), and overall management of contractors and distributors. In May 1994, however, management initiated construction of the company's first production facility—a $25 million plant in Arizona, scheduled to begin operations in 1995 and employ 100 people.

Snapple was widely credited with catalyzing a more pronounced consumer trend toward New Age beverages, spurring added sales growth in bottled waters, sports drinks, and juices as well as its own line of flavored teas and fruit drinks. In 1993, New Age or "alternative" beverages constituted a $3 billion product category. Exhibit 8 shows trends in the per capita consumption of liquid beverages in the United States during the 1983–94 period.

Snapple's Marketing and Distribution Strategies

In Snapple's early days, the product wasn't selling well; market research revealed consumers thought the bottles were ugly and difficult to store. A packaging redesign followed, resulting in the use of clear wide-mouth 16-ounce glass bottles—a container that management said was "perfectly suited to the hot-brewed process we use to make Snapple beverages." The new bottles were affixed with redesigned labels. Sales perked up quickly, buoyed by an offbeat and catchy media campaign.

The company sparked demand for Snapple products with offbeat, witty ads and catchy themes. Snapple had gotten the greatest mileage out of an ad featuring a stereotypical receptionist, "Wendy the Snapple Lady" (who was actually employed in the company's marketing department), responding to customer inquiries. Snapple ads sometimes poked fun at things. Print ads compared Snapple sales to "hot cakes" and "greased lightning" with "more flavors than you can shake a stick at." Ivan Lendl and Rush Limbaugh appeared in Snapple TV ads as celebrity endorsers. Most of Snapple's distributors were local soft drink bottlers/distributors who had third-place or fourth-place market shares (usually behind Coca-Cola and Pepsi) and who were eager to take on product lines where competition was less

Exhibit 7 Snapple Beverage Corporation Balance Sheet, 1992 and 1993

	1992	1993
Assets		
Cash	$ 97,486,632	$ 13,396,949
Receivables	17,428,379	53,010,325
Inventories	16,166,183	40,922,888
Other current assets	6,788,585	4,192,759
Total current assets	137,869,779	111,522,921
Net property, plant, and equipment	1,053,399	10,751,597
Deferred charges	3,705,001	18,552,625
Intangibles	82,770,827	97,819,997
Other assets	1,338,166	304,745
Total assets	$226,737,172	$238,951,885
Liabilities and Shareholders' Equity		
Accounts payable	$ 6,100,345	$ 7,326,411
Current long-term debt	150,469	8,949,665
Accrued expenses	16,999,258	17,573,454
Income taxes	446,892	6,034,860
Other current liabilities	90,000,000	3,860,844
Total current liabilities	113,696,964	43,745,234
Long-term debt	18,226,138	26,218,911
Other long-term liabilities	4,000,000	5,011,000
Total liabilities	135,923,102	74,975,145
Minority interest	0	1,499,717
Common stock net	1,213,766	1,216,096
Capital surplus	90,297,391	94,334,533
Retained earnings	(697,087)	66,926,394
Total shareholders' equity	90,814,070	162,477,023
Total liabilities and shareholders' equity	$226,737,172	$238,951,885

Source: Company annual report.

intense and profit margins were bigger. The average price per case for New Age beverages was around $9 to $11 versus $5 to $6 per case for soft drinks. On average, soft drinks offered bottlers and distributors $1 margin per case compared with about $3 per case for New Age products. These distributors delivered Snapple directly to supermarkets, convenience stores, delicatessen outlets, and up-and-down the street retailers, on trucks carrying an assortment of branded beverages (low-volume soft drink brands, bottled waters, club soda, tonic water, ginger ale, and perhaps canned Gatorade). Snapple's distributors were responsible for every-thing—selling retail accounts, keeping shelves stocked, handling point-of-sale dis-plays, and setting prices. Retail prices for a 16-ounce bottle were typically around 75 cents. Snapple's surging sales in 1992 and 1993—a boom that reportedly began in convenience stores and delicatessens where trend-setting consumers bought Snapple from the cooler and drank it straight from the bottle—helped it recruit distributors willing to commit time and resources to the Snapple line. Snapple

Exhibit 8   Per Capita Consumption of Liquid Beverages in the United States, 1983–1994   (in gallons)

	1983	1984	1985	1986	1987	1988	1989	1990	1991	1992	1993E	1994P
Soft drinks	37.0	38.8	41.0	42.3	44.3	46.2	46.7	47.6	47.8	48.0	48.9	49.6
Coffee*	26.1	26.3	26.8	27.1	27.1	26.5	26.4	26.4	26.5	26.1	25.9	26.0
Beer	24.3	23.9	23.9	24.2	24.0	23.8	23.6	24.0	23.3	23.0	22.8	22.5
Milk	19.7	19.8	20.0	19.9	19.8	19.4	19.6	19.4	19.4	19.1	18.9	19.1
Tea*	7.2	7.2	7.3	7.3	7.3	7.4	7.2	7.0	6.7	6.8	6.9	7.0
Bottled water	3.4	4.0	5.2	5.8	6.4	7.3	8.1	9.2	9.6	9.9	10.5	11.2
Juices	8.2	7.0	7.9	7.8	8.3	7.7	8.0	7.1	7.6	7.1	7.0	7.0
Powdered drinks	6.5	6.4	6.3	5.2	4.9	5.3	5.4	5.7	5.9	6.1	6.0	5.9
Wine†	2.2	2.3	2.4	2.4	2.4	2.3	2.1	2.0	1.9	2.0	1.7	1.6
Distilled spirits	1.9	1.9	1.8	1.8	1.6	1.5	1.5	1.5	1.4	1.3	1.3	1.3
Subtotal	136.5	137.6	142.6	142.6	146.1	147.4	148.6	149.9	150.1	149.4	149.9	151.2
Imputed water consumption‡	46.0	44.9	39.9	39.9	36.4	35.1	33.9	32.6	32.4	33.1	32.6	31.3
Total	182.5	182.5	182.5	182.5	182.5	182.5	182.5	182.5	182.5	182.5	182.5	182.5

* Coffee and tea data are based on a three-year moving average to counterbalance inventory swings, thereby portraying consumption more realistically.

† Includes wine coolers beginning in 1984.

‡ Includes all others.

E = estimated; P = projected.

Source: John C. Maxwell, "Annual Soft Drink Report," *Beverage Industry Supplement*, March 1994, p. 6.

established a nationwide network of distributors in a matter of months—something few alternative beverage brands had been able to do. The attractive profit margins distributors earned on Snapple sales were a key factor underlying the company's ability to recruit distributors willing to invest time and resources in building the Snapple brand. Snapple's market research showed that half the U.S. population had tried Snapple by the end of October 1993. Snapple's sales were biggest in California and the Northeast; sales were weakest in the South and Southwest. By mid-1994, Snapple had begun introducing its brands in Europe. Launches in Britain, Ireland, and Norway came first, followed by Sweden and Denmark. Test-marketing was underway in France and Spain. As of November 1994, only 1 percent of Snapple's sales were derived from overseas markets.

In April 1994, Snapple announced it had developed an exclusive, glass-front vending machine capable of offering 54 different flavors simultaneously; the machine held 18 cases of the company's 16-ounce wide-mouth bottles. The company expected to place 10,000 units in service by year-end to broaden its distribution beyond supermarkets, convenience stores, and delicatessens.

Competition in the Iced Tea/New Age Segment

Snapple's success in developing consumer interest in ready-to-drink iced teas and teas spiked with fruit juices attracted other competitors quickly. In 1993, Coca-Cola, Pepsi-Cola, Dr Pepper/Seven-Up, and Cadbury Schweppes/A&W Beverages all launched New Age offerings. Several regional products, most notably Arizona Iced Tea (packaged in distinctive tall cans with a Southwestern motif), also entered the market. As of 1994, the major players in the ready-to-drink iced tea segment were:

Brand	Marketer
Snapple	Snapple Beverage Corp.
Lipton	Pepsi-Cola and the Thomas J. Lipton division of Unilever
Nestea	Coca-Cola Nestlé Refreshments (a joint venture of the Coca-Cola Company and Nestlé)
Tetley	A&W Brands and Tetley Tea Co. partnership
Luzianne	Barq's Inc. and Wm. B. Reily partnership
All Seasons	Cadbury Beverages and Omni Industries
Celestial Seasonings	Perrier Group of America and Celestial Seasonings
Arizona	Ferolito, Vultaggio and Sons

Besides the major players, there were 5 to 10 niche brands of bottled teas. In addition, Pepsi-Cola had teamed with Ocean Spray Cranberries, Inc., to introduce a line of juices and lemonade. Minute Maid had announced a new line of juices, Very Fine and Tradewinds were planning lemonade entries, and Gatorade introduced its eighth flavor, Gatorade Iced Tea Cooler. An Information Resources survey of supermarket sales of canned and bottled iced teas during the 12 weeks ended April 17, 1994, showed the following:[5]

Brand	Case Volume (in millions)	Dollar Volume (in millions)
Snapple	2.5	$22.3
Lipton	2.3	14.9
Nestea	1.0	7.8
Arizona	0.5	5.0

Snapple's market share (based on dollars) was 17 percentage points lower in this survey than the comparable year-earlier period. The Arizona brand was gaining share and had edged out Snapple as the market leader in several markets in the West. However, Snapple's market share of convenience store sales was estimated to be in the 75 percent range. Exhibit 9 presents estimated case sales of alternative beverage companies.

Industry analysts estimated that wholesale volume for iced tea flavors grew from $500 million in 1992 to more than $1 billion in 1993. Alternative beverage sales were breaking out into 40 percent take-home purchases and 60 percent single-service and on-premise consumption. Ready-to-drink teas and juice-based drinks were the fastest-growing products in the New Age category, while sales of "clear" products dropped to the 8 to 9 percent range (down from 44 percent growth in 1992). Analysts were divided in their assessments about how long the booming growth in ready-to-drink teas and fruit beverages would last. Some analysts believed that teas and fruit drinks would enjoy continued growth because of their healthy, "all-natural" image with consumers and because the proliferation of brands and varieties would help develop greater buyer interest. Others were skeptical, observing that trendy products had comparatively short life-cycles and that three or four growth years were all many

---

[5]As reported in *The Wall Street Journal*, June 9, 1994, p. B6.

Exhibit 9   Estimated Case Sales of Alternative Beverage Companies, 1992–1993

Company/Brand	Case Sales (in millions)	
	1992	1993
Snapple Beverage Company		
Snapple Iced Tea	28.33	52.63
Snapple drinks	19.73	45.41
Snapple sodas	1.52	3.10
Snapple Snap-Up/Sport	0.51	1.03
Snapple juices	0.51	1.03
Total	50.60	103.20
Coca-Cola Company		
Nestea	14.00	33.00
Powerade	1.20	10.00
Minute Maid Juices-to-Go	5.00	15.00
Total	20.20	58.00
PepsiCo		
Ocean Spray	6.50	16.00
Lipton	—	33.00
All Sport	2.00	3.00
H2 Oh!	0.50	0.63
Total	9.00	52.63
Perrier Group		
15-Brand totals	30.40	36.70
Cadbury beverages/A&W brands		
Tetley	2.90	4.30
Everlast	—	—
Others	17.30	17.30
Total	20.20	21.60
Ferolito, Vultaggio and Sons		
Arizona	—	2.00
All others	169.60	175.37
Segment totals	300.00	449.50

Source: Compiled from "Annual Soft Drink Report," *Beverage Industry Supplement*, March 1994, pp. 22–23.

product categories ever experienced. While some cola bottlers had derisively referred to Snapple as a member of the "brand of the day" club, unconvinced of its power to sustain broad consumer interest, market research indicated that younger consumers (who had fueled the growth in New Age beverages) had gravitated to Snapple, Arizona, and unusual niche brands with distinctive packaging and a certain mystique. In fall 1994, industry observers saw bottled tea as becoming increasingly complex to market successfully because the market was overcrowded, costs to support a brand were rising, shelf space was harder to obtain, and image was such a dominant factor in a brand's success or failure.

In late August 1994, Coca-Cola and Nestlé unexpectedly announced dissolution of their iced tea alliance; in recent weeks, Nestea sales had been disappointing, falling well behind supermarket sales of both Snapple and Lipton. It was not clear whether Nestlé would continue to market Nestea bottled teas on its own. Meanwhile, Pepsi–Lipton had begun running a series of radio ads attacking Snapple as being "mixed up from a tea powder." The announcer said, "Snapple. Isn't that a cute name. Kinda snappy. I bet they call it Snapple 'cause it's iced tea made in a snap." The spot went on to boast that Lipton Original varieties were "real brewed," a trait that Pepsi–Lipton believed was its best weapon against rivals.[6] Pepsi had also run Super Bowl ads for Lipton Original and promoted Lipton Original heavily in supermarkets, including a 99-cent value pack containing one bottle each of Lipton Original, All Sport, and Ocean Spray Lemonade.

Snapple management indicated its iced teas were made from "the finest tea leaves in India" but wouldn't specify how it was produced. Arnold Greenberg said:

> Pepsi would die to make tea taste so great. People don't care how it's made. They just care that it tastes good.[7]

Snapple management also pointed out that the less expensive Lipton Brisk varieties, sold in cans and 64-ounce bottles, were not "real brewed." Analysts estimated that during the first five months of 1994, about 60 percent of Pepsi's prepared iced teas were Lipton Brisk varieties. To counter the increased competition from rival teas, Snapple more than doubled its 1994 advertising budget and launched a new $65 million media campaign in April 1994.

---

[6]As quoted in *The Wall Street Journal*, June 9, 1994, p. B6.
[7]*Ibid.*

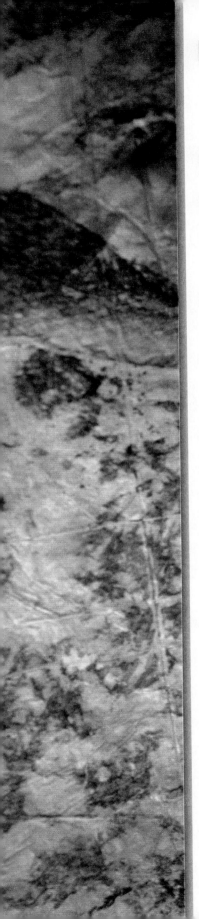

Supra Boats and the Competition Ski Boat Industry

Aimee Hagedorn and A. J. Strickland, The University of Alabama

In 1992, the competition ski boat industry was confronting several major strategic issues. Since early 1990, demand had fallen drastically in the United States as boat prices steadily increased and a severe recession virtually paralyzed the country's economy. At the same time, manufacturers had to respond to a widening array of user needs and preferences; it was becoming harder and harder to accommodate all the preferences of different buyers by offering just a few different boat models. Producers were trying to decide whether to broaden their product line or simply choose to differentiate their existing product line. To bolster sagging sales, some boat manufacturers had pursued related diversification, getting into the business of producing sportswear and other associated items to supplement their competition ski boat operations.

Supra Boats was a growing, dynamic company. Having entered the ski boat industry in the family segment and moved into the competition segment, Supra had a strong presence in both inboard ski boat markets, with approximately the third-largest market share. George Fowler, chief executive officer of Supra, wanted to take the company's present two-year plan and turn it into a five-year plan for making Supra the market share leader by the year 2000. Doing this would mean crafting a strategy to capture sales from and compete more effectively against the two current industry leaders, MasterCraft and Correct Craft.

HISTORY OF THE COMPETITION SKI BOAT INDUSTRY

Waterskiing dates back to 1922, when Ralph Samuelson became the first American to invent and ride a pair of water skis. The skis, simplistic by today's standards, were crude wooden boards with rubber footstraps and were roughly twice the length and width of today's skis. Throughout the 1920s and 30s, enthusiasm for waterskiing spread; in 1939, the American Water Ski Association (AWSA) was formed as a nonprofit organization to promote the sport. That same year, the first National Water Ski Championships were held. The towboat for this competition was an open wooden boat built of overlapping boards or strakes (similar to a wood johnboat) and powered by a four-cylinder outboard engine. The national championships were not held during World War II, and boat building was minimal during this time; after the war, however, the economy boomed, as did interest and activity in the boating industry.

During the late 1940s and early 1950s, wooden inboard boats were made by ChrisCrafts, Century Resorters, and the Atom Skier by Correct Craft were favored by most skiers. These boats were the most powerful ski boat of the times, yet performance suffered due to the boats' large wakes. Outboards offered a smaller wake but did not have enough power—until the advent of the twin-rig concept in the early 1950s (see Exhibit 1).

The twin-rig outboards quickly gained popularity among competition skiers and dominated the scene for the rest of the decade and into the 60s. Companies such as Mercury Marine, Evinrude, and Johnson recognized the potential market in waterskiing and invented the concept of promotional boats whereby manufacturers provided specially equipped boats for use in tournaments. Twin rigs, however, were difficult to set up and had high fuel consumption.

In search of the "perfect" ski boat, Leo Bentz, who operated a ski school in Florida, designed and built an inboard boat specifically for waterskiing. In the spring of 1960, the first Ski Nautique was displayed at the southern regionals in Birmingham, Alabama. It was the first inboard made of fiberglass and had a hull design that produced a smaller wake than its predecessors. Originally marketed and sold by Glass Craft Boat Company, the Ski Nautique concept was sold to Correct Craft the next year, after Bentz approached the company's owners to sell them his mold. Correct Craft refined the Ski Nautique, and the boat became a standard for others to emulate. The boat was highly successful, and boats with inboard motors made a resurgence in the sport.

In 1968, Rob Shirley, a competitive skier, noticed the growing market and absence of competition, so he designed and built his own ski boat, known as MasterCraft. Throughout the 1970s and early 1980s, Correct Craft and MasterCraft dominated the market and led the industry in innovations and technology. By the 1980s, inboards came to be used almost exclusively in AWSA-sanctioned tournaments, and many new start-up companies tried to compete with the two leaders. Yet, there still existed an opportunity for outboards as other water ski sport disciplines such as barefooting, kneeboarding, and show skiing were emerging.[1]

INDUSTRY STRUCTURE

In 1991, the National Marine Manufacturers Association (NMMA) estimated retail sales of all new and used boats and related products (including motors and engines, accessories and safety equipment, docking and storage) to be $10.5 billion, a 23 percent decrease from 1990. These results came on the heels of a similarly dismal 1990 when total industry sales dropped to $13.7 billion, down from $17.1 billion in 1989 and $17.9 billion in 1988.[2] Exhibit 2 presents estimated retail expenditures for recreational boating activities.

There were over 16.2 million recreational boats in use in 1991 (Exhibit 3) and 73.5 million people participating in recreational boating activities (Exhibit 4). The number of water-skiers grew only slightly in 1991 to 11.02 million, while the number of registered boats in the United States rose to nearly 11 million. Exhibit 4 presents additional statistics on recreational boating.

The Great Lakes region accounted for the greatest percentage of registered boats, with 28 percent of the U.S. total, followed by the Middle Atlantic, 20 percent; Gulf

---

[1]Drawn heavily from *WaterSki,* March 1991, and *The Water Skier,* April 1989.
[2]NMMA; *Boating Industry,* January 1992.

Exhibit 1   Types of Ski Boats

Twin rig

Open-bow inboard

Closed-bow inboard

Coast, 18 percent; West Coast, 11 percent; Midwestern Mountains, 10 percent; East Central, 8 percent; and New England, 5 percent. The United States was the largest boating/waterskiing nation in the world, followed by Australia and Canada.

Exhibit 2 Estimated Retail Expenditure on Boating (in millions of $)

Total Industry Dollars at Retail

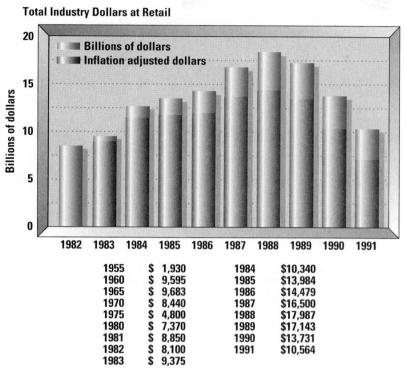

1955	$ 1,930	1984	$10,340
1960	$ 9,595	1985	$13,984
1965	$ 9,683	1986	$14,479
1970	$ 8,440	1987	$16,500
1975	$ 4,800	1988	$17,987
1980	$ 7,370	1989	$17,143
1981	$ 8,850	1990	$13,731
1982	$ 8,100	1991	$10,564
1983	$ 9,375		

Sources: National Marine Manufacturers' Association, *Boating,* 1991; *Boating Industry,* January 1992.

Segment Sales

The $4.3 billion pleasure and ski boat market had three main segments: inboards, outboards, and stern drives (inboard/outboards). Inboards were further classified as either runabouts or cruisers, and runabouts could have an open or closed bow (see Exhibit 1). Outboards, stern drives, and inboard runabouts were generally 16 to 25 feet long, while cruisers were anywhere from 30 to 50 feet long. Traditionally, outboards were the biggest sellers, followed by stern drives and inboards, although outboard and stern-drive manufacturers had always outnumbered inboard manufacturers. Over the past 20 years, sales for each segment had fluctuated, with each segment experiencing intermittent periods of increasing and decreasing sales (Exhibit 5).

During the recessions of both the early 1980s and 1990s, the inboard and stern-drive markets were the most affected. In the early 1980s, both suffered an average 36 percent initial drop in sales, while outboard sales fell only 10 percent. In both 1990 and 1991, sales fell drastically—30 and 35 percent for inboards, 27 and 25 percent for stern drives, compared to 22 and 14 percent for outboards. However, both the inboard and stern-drive segments recovered nicely from the early 1980s recession, with sales picking up by 35 to 40 percent on average, respectively. The inboard market sustained its sales growth through 1989, while stern-drive sales peaked in 1988. Exhibit 6 presents additional sales statistics.

Exhibit 3   Estimated Number of Recreational Boats Owned, 1982–1991

1982	12,820,000
1983	13,041,000
1984	13,455,000
1985	13,778,000
1986	14,318,000
1987	14,515,000
1988	15,093,000
1989	15,658,000
1990	15,987,000
1991	16,248,000

Source: National Marine Manufacturers' Association, *Boating,* 1991.

Although sales of competition ski boats in the international market were negligible, exports of pleasure boats had risen sharply the past few years (Exhibit 7). For the first time since 1980, exports had exceeded imports by approximately $225 million in 1989. In 1990, that figure more than doubled to nearly $528 million. The trend was a direct result of a decline in the value of the U.S. dollar against foreign currencies, making foreign purchases of U.S.-made boats more attractive.

Boat Shows

For both boat manufacturers and retail dealers, boat shows were an occasion to compare competitive products and test buyer response. Based on the amount of consumer interest generated at national and regional shows, manufacturers would decide how many of each model boat to manufacture for the upcoming year, how best to market each product, and where to focus advertising efforts. Dealers would also base their orders on the consumer interest indicated at regional and local shows. Interest level was gauged by the percentage of people coming and going through a dealer's or manufacturer's booth at a show and expressing an interest to buy as well as by the number of boats sold at the show.

Also of interest to competition ski boat manufacturers was the Waterski Expo, a new trade show for the water-ski industry, held in September 1991. While the ski boat industry and the water-ski industry in general tended to get overlooked at the large marine trade shows such as IMTEC (International Marine Trades Exhibit and Convention), the Waterski Expo focused on these two industries. Manufacturers were able to network and introduce their new products to dealers and retailers without getting lost in the crowd.

Entry Barriers and Manufacturing Costs

Entry into boat manufacture required a company to meet several financial hurdles. For inboard boats, the cost to produce just one prototype was over $100,000. A plug (shape) had to be built and then a mold. According to industry sources, a plug and mold both cost $3,000 to $40,000 or more, and a design could cost thousands more, as well. Once a company had the necessary tooling and equipment and had begun

Exhibit 4 Selected Boating Statistics, 1990 and 1991

	1991	1990
People participating in recreational boating	73,480,000	73,370,000
Water-skiers	11,022,000	11,006,000
All boats in use	16,248,000	15,987,000
Outboard boats owned	7,992,000	7,885,000
Inboard boats owned (includes auxiliary-powered sailboats)	558,000	555,000
Nonpowered sailboats (excluding sailboards)	1,298,000	1,298,000
Inboard/outdrive boats	1,721,000	1,659,000

Source: National Marine Manufacturers' Association, *Boating,* 1990 and 1991 issues.

production, economies of scale became critical. Construction time for one boat was approximately 10 to 13 days, depending on the model being built. Because of the capital requirements and manufacturing and design know-how, actual and potential participants in the competition ski boat market were usually large existing boat manufacturers that had tracked the growth of the ski boat market and determined that it was an attractive market arena. One new entrant was Sea Ray, which introduced its own model of a competition ski boat—the Ski Ray—in 1991.

Demographics and Economic Conditions

In a 1990 National Sporting Goods Association (NSGA) sports participation study, fishing was America's fourth most popular pastime, while motorboating and water-skiing ranked 8th and 29th, respectively. It was estimated that interest in waterskiing would double if competition skiing became an Olympic event. It was first on the list of new sports to be admitted to the Olympic Games, but it was being delayed due to a serious influential factor—the boat driver. A skier's performance could be affected by a boat driver's error and/or bias. The "cruise control" concept for the throttle and speedometer was being tested in hopes of eliminating driver error (driving slower than or faster than actual speed), and videotaping the driver's boat path had already been implemented to control bias (moving the boat to either help or hurt the skier).

Before the 1991 recession, the rising popularity of waterskiing and recreational boating was attributed in part to the growing number of baby boomers who were buying lakefront homes and adopting outdoor-oriented life-styles. Statistics indicated a dramatic rise in the boat buying population among the baby boomers, who had reached prime boat buying age. According to sales data of the NMMA, the typical boat buyer was between the ages of 25 and 54. In the NSGA study, for both boating and skiing, the greatest number of participants had a threshold income greater than or equal to $50,000 and lived in highly populated areas.

Because boats were luxury items, the boating industry suffered during periods of economic decline. The ski boat industry had escaped a 10 percent luxury tax enacted by Congress for boats costing over $100,000. Still, new federal user fees required boaters using certain bodies of water to pay from $25 for 16- to 19-foot boats up to $100 for boats over 40 feet.

In the wake of the Persian Gulf War, the United States experienced its worst economic recession in a decade. Consumer confidence dipped to its lowest level

Exhibit 5   Estimated Number of Pleasure and Ski Boats Sold at Retail, 1971–1991

Calendar Year	Outboard Boats Sold	Inboard Boats Sold	Inboard/ Outdrive Boats Sold
1971	278,000	22,500	44,000
1972	375,000	23,000	63,000
1973	448,000	12,000	78,000
1974	425,000	11,000	70,000
1975	328,000	10,200	70,000
1976	341,000	11,000	80,000
1977	336,000	11,500	84,000
1978	331,000	12,100	90,000
1979	322,000	12,600	89,000
1980	290,000	8,200	56,000
1981	281,000	8,400	51,000
1982	236,000	8,395	55,000
1983	273,000	11,385	79,000
1984	317,000	15,280	108,000
1985	305,000	16,700	115,000
1986	314,000	18,000	120,000
1987	342,000	19,700	144,000
1988	355,000	20,900	148,000
1989	291,000	21,400	133,000
1990	227,000	15,000	97,000
1991	195,000	9,800	73,000

Source: National Marine Manufacturers' Association, *Boating,* 1990 and 1991 issues.

since 1982, while sales of new cars and trucks reached their lowest level since 1983. Although housing starts were the lowest since 1945 and unemployment was an alarming 7.1 percent, inflation was only 3.1 percent. To help revive the economy and prompt consumers to spend again, the Federal Reserve pursued easy money policies that drove down banks' prime rate from 10 percent before the recession to 6.5 percent in the first quarter of 1992.

Leading Factors in Choosing a Ski Boat

For the majority of consumers, the quality of a ski boat was judged according to several factors: reliability and durability, wake and spray characteristics, and performance (tracking and turning ability, speed control, and engine power).

A market tracking study conducted by the Water Sports Industry Association (WSIA) revealed price and quality were the most important factors in the brand selection of boats and water-ski products for the general population of water-skiers; quality and brand reputation were more important for experienced skiers. Of the households that responded to the survey, about 82 percent owned a boat at the time, with the family runabout being the most popular. If they were to replace a boat soon,

Exhibit 6 Retail Sales Statistics for the Boating Market, 1986–1991

	1986	1987	1988	1989	1990	1991
Outboard Boats						
Total units sold	314,000	342,000	355,000	291,000	227,000	195,000
Retail value	$834,600,000	$1,001,003,000	$1,224,750,000	$1,134,027,000	$978,143,000	$871,260,000
Average unit cost	$2,658	$2,927	$3,450	$3,897	$4,309	$4,468
Inboard Boats—Runabouts						
Total units sold	5,300	6,600	7,400	9,100	7,500	6,200
Retail value	$85,473,000	$107,382,000	$130,610,000	$179,152,000	$139,600,000	$116,442,000
Average unit cost	$16,127	$16,270	$17,650	$19,687	$17,684	$18,781
Inboard Boats—Cruisers						
Total units sold	12,700	13,100	13,500	12,300	7,500	3,600
Retail value	$1,421,130,000	$1,665,860,000	$1,884,600,000	$1,908,960,000	$1,383,015,000	$668,412,000
Average unit cost	$111,900	$127,165	$139,600	$155,200	$184,402	$185,670
Inboard/Outdrive Boats						
Total units sold	120,000	144,000	148,000	133,000	97,000	73,000
Retail value	$1,860,960,000	$2,450,160,000	$2,584,672,000	$2,354,100,000	$1,794,306,000	$1,292,903,000
Average unit cost	$15,508	$17,015	$17,464	$17,700	$18,498	$17,711

Source: National Marine Manufacturers' Association, *Boating,* 1988 and 1991 issues.

most indicated a shift from the runabout to a more special-purpose boat. Fifty-eight percent of those who responded owned an outboard; for skiing, however, stern-drive and inboard engines were preferred, especially among experienced skiers. Eight percent of the respondents said they would buy a tournament ski boat, double the level of existing ownership.

Mergers, Acquisitions, and Industry Consolidation

By 1991, a number of manufacturers had either been acquired by or merged with another company. In 1984, MasterCraft was bought by the Coleman Company; in 1989, Ski Supreme was acquired by Genmar, Inc.; in 1989, Malibu Boats purchased Flightcraft, an Australian ski boat manufacturer; and in 1991, American Skier was purchased by WESMAR Marine Holdings. Also, in 1990, Supra Boats merged with Marine Sports, Inc. In 1991, Supra/Marine Sports created the Moomba Boat Company as a subsidiary.

Regulatory Developments

As the number of boating and waterskiing participants grew, the nation's waterways became increasingly crowded. Safety, courtesy, and environmental issues became more prevalent, sometimes drawing debate and controversy. Speed limit laws, noise limits, and environmental laws to protect against erosion by regulating boat wakes had been imposed on boaters/skiers by virtually every state. In 1991, Florida's

Exhibit 7   Trends in U.S. Export-Import of Pleasure Boats, 1985–1990

	Dollar Volume					
	1985	1986	1987	1988	1989	1990
Exports	$60,596,000	$110,984,000	$219,871,000	$414,467,000	$616,469,000	$792,716,000
Imports	$367,935,000	$370,890,000	$397,519,000	$509,701,000	$409,965,000	$265,160,000

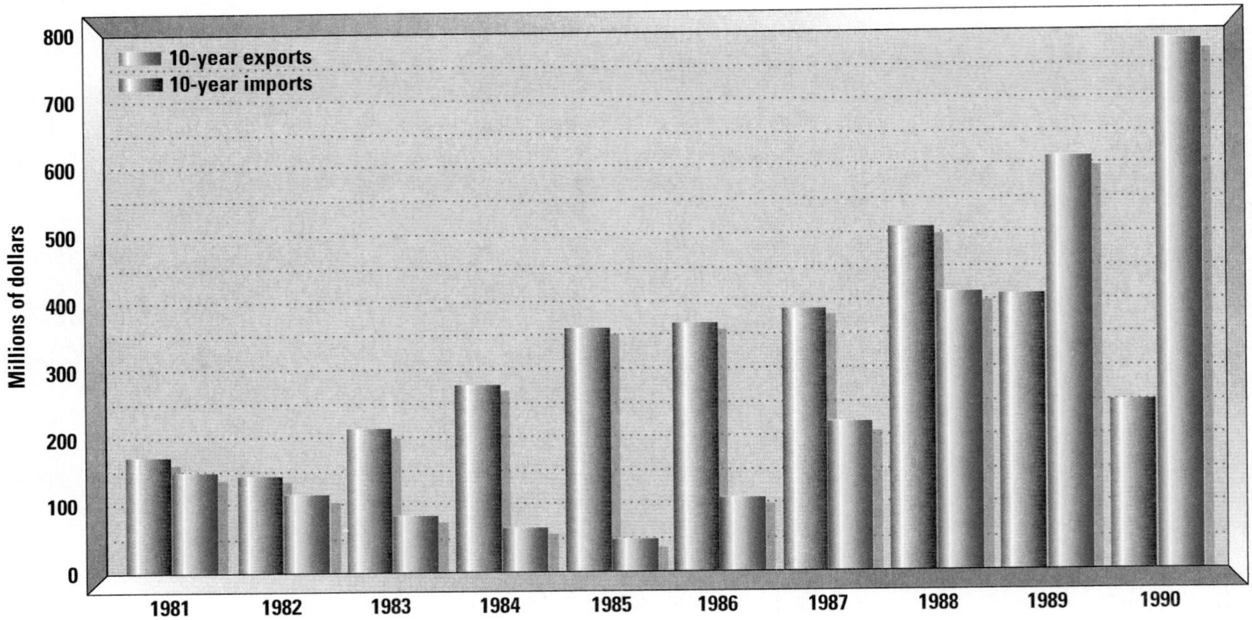

Sources: National Marine Manufacturers' Association, *Boating*, 1988 and 1990; and *Boating Industry*, January 1992.

Department of Natural Resources proposed legislation to establish a statewide boating speed limit of 30 mph for *all* waters. The boating industry feared that if such a bill was passed, other states might follow suit.

In response to such actions, the American Water Ski Association (AWSA) created a Waterways Education Committee focused on educating skiers about legislation and teaching them how to organize to fight adverse legislation and burdensome regulations. The committee compiled a database of each state's laws and regulations concerning use of the waterways, produced a manual on how to lobby legislatures, and explored the development of a lawyer/lobby referral service made up of AWSA members.

SUBSTITUTES

Personal watercraft (PWC) were an economic and fun alternative for water sports enthusiasts. Also known as "jet skies" and "waverunners," PWCs were originally introduced as standup models. Manufacturers soon introduced sitdown models to appeal to a larger group of potential customers. Sitdown models proved immensely successful as sales quickly overtook sales of standup models (Exhibit 8).

Exhibit 8 Sales of Personal Watercraft, Standup and Sitdown Models, 1988–1991

	Total	Standup	Percent	Sitdown	Percent	Retail Value	Average Unit Cost
1988	50,000	30,000	60	20,000	40	NA	NA
1989	80,000	35,200	44	44,800	56	NA	NA
1990	72,000	22,320	31	49,680	69	NA	NA
1991	68,000	16,320	24	51,680	76	$355,104,000	$4,928

Source: *Boating Industry,* January 1991 and 1992 issues.

Initially, PWCs were thought of as water toys for the young, but as models became larger and more accommodating for the entire family, their appeal spread. A few new models could carry up to three people, while one manufacturer even had a model where two people could ride side by side. Some of the larger PWCs could even pull skiers.[3]

PWCs were popular not just for personal use but for rental use also. Many lakes, resorts, and tourist areas had PWC rentals available. Even some police departments had begun to use the vehicles to patrol coastal waterways and other bodies of water.

By 1990, over 200,000 PWCs were in use, and it was a $250 million industry. Although the popularity of the PWC exploded in the late 1980s, sales fell 10 percent in 1990 and 5.5 percent in 1991.[4] Retail prices ranged from $2,300 to $8,000, depending on the model. In 1991, 39 models were produced by 11 companies, including the "big three"—Kawasaki, Yamaha, and Bombardier.[5] Seventy to 80 percent of PWCs were sold through motorcycle dealers, but the number of marine dealers increased slightly with the introduction of the sitdown models.

Apparently still in the growth stage, the PWC market seemed ripe for new entrants. Despite the 10 percent decline in 1990 sales, Polaris Industries LP, a major snowmobile manufacturer, introduced a model late in 1991, while Brunswick Corporation's U.S. Marine division was also eyeing the market. John Flowers, director of product planning and development for U.S. Marine, commented that whenever a segment competing with pleasure boats achieved sales volume, the market was enticing. Another industry source saw PWCs' greatest growth potential in the traditional boating market via marine dealers.

Yet, the PWC market was being challenged by the new, untested miniboat segment. Miniboats were hybrids of PWCs and small boats. Although Kawasaki (the only one of the big three with a miniboat product) and a few other smaller companies manufactured miniboats, the majority of competitors discounted the miniboat market.

The use of the PWC was being challenged also. Because of numerous accidents (mostly from lack of product use education), many regulations had been imposed on the vehicles. Also, because of the rowdy manner in which some PWCs were operated, the vehicles had earned a bad reputation among boaters and skiers alike for

---

[3]*WaterSki,*, September–October 1991.
[4]*Boating Industry,* January 1992.
[5]*1992 ABOS Marine Blue Book.*

being extremely annoying. In some locations this had resulted in the enactment of additional restrictive legislation.[6]

SUPPLIERS

The major suppliers to the inboard boat industry were engine manufacturers. Engines were offered in a variety of models based on General Motors, Ford, and Chrysler blocks and components (to date, no foreign manufacturers produced inboard engines); 250- to 285-horsepower engines with separate hydraulic transmissions were most common among the competition inboards. The big three automakers' marine divisions built the base engines (same engines as for cars), and marine engine manufacturers marinized (treated for marine use) and customized the engines to suit their needs.

In the mid-1980s, automakers were challenged by legislation requiring that auto engines be made to tighter fuel efficiency and pollution control standards. This affected marinized engines because pollution control devices entailed a slight decrease in power. One solution to this problem was found in geared-drive transmission (rather than direct drive), thus allowing the engine to churn the prop at a rate just faster than one revolution per second. Yet another solution was presented when, in 1991, Ford introduced its new 5.8-liter 351 HO (high output) block with 285 horsepower, a 20 percent increase in power over the standard 351.

In the early 1990s, three marine engine companies dominated the inboard market: Indmar, MerCruiser, and Pleasurecraft Marine (PCM). According to industry sources, inboard engines comprised roughly 98 percent of both Indmar and PCM's production volumes and only about 2 percent of MerCruiser's. Both Indmar and PCM specialized in inboards, while MerCruiser concentrated primarily on stern drives and produced a much larger quantity of engines than the other two manufacturers.

Indmar was one of the first to utilize Ford's new engine, adding features such as electronic ignition and an oversized exhaust manifold to make it the best inboard power product of all the company's small-block (351 or less cubic inches) engines. Indmar also used engines built by GM, and in 1991, Indmar agreed to marinize Chrysler's marine engines exclusively under the name Tri Power Indmar. In addition, Indmar built private-label versions of its engines for use by boat manufacturers. By producing both small- and big-block (454 or more cubic inches) models based on Ford and GM engines, Indmar had one of the broadest product lines of any inboard marinizer; its agreement with Chrysler virtually assured Indmar of having the most comprehensive line of inboard power products in the industry.

Although MerCruiser's specialty was in outdrive power, the company began stepping up its production of inboard engines. MerCruiser's inboard line included both small- and big-block GM engines, with two 5.7-liter 350 cubic-inch models specifically for use in competition inboards. The Competition Ski engine offered 250 horsepower, while the new Magnum Tournament Ski engine produced 265 horsepower. Both products were equipped with MerCruiser's Thunderbolt IV High-Energy ignition system and the PowerPlus exhaust system with oversized manifolds, among other features.

PCM was well known for its leadership and innovation in marine engine technology. With the introduction of its Pro Boss engine, based on the new Ford 351 HO, the

---

[6]*Boating Industry,* June 1991.

company boasted of having the only electronic management system (EMS) in the inboard power industry. Pro Tec, PCM's name for the system, controlled spark advance, corrected engine knock, and monitored all vital engine functions, including oil pressure, temperature, and engine revving. It could detect problems and would lower engine revolutions to protect the engine from potential damage. Like Indmar and MerCruiser's competition ski boat engines, the Pro Boss had larger exhaust system manifolds than standard, which PCM called the Pro Flo system. In addition, the Power Plus transmission system featured a 1.23:1 geared-drive ratio to further boost power. Like the other manufacturers, PCM had a well-rounded product line with both small- and big-block engines suitable for all types of inboard ski boats.

Of the 15 inboard block manufacturers whose boats were reviewed in *WaterSki* magazine's 1992 Boat Buyer's Guide, four powered their products with PCM engines, five with Indmar, and six with MerCruiser.[7]

TECHNOLOGY AND CHARACTERISTICS OF THE SKI BOAT SEGMENTS

All boats were constructed in a somewhat similar manner. They all had a hull, deck, floor, console, seats, and engine. They were all built from a mold from the outside in, and virtually all were made from fiberglass, a material far superior than wood for strength and reliability. Yet, both the other materials used and the methods of construction varied widely among manufacturers according to the type of boat being built.

One of the most distinctive and important differences in the construction of ski boats had to do with hull configuration. Basically, there were two types of hull designs for inboard ski boats: a deep V and a modified V. A deep V hull was one in which the degree of dead rise (usually 15 to 35 degrees) from bow to stern remained the same. With a deep V design, less hull was actually in the water, thereby causing a boat to ride higher and better in rough water, yet also have a somewhat larger wake. The modified V configuration was a hull having more than 15 degrees of dead rise at the bow and less than 15 degrees at the stern. In effect, it was a deep V that tapered off to a shallow V, resulting in more surface area on top of the water, a smaller wake, and generally better tracking.

Another fundamental element of the hull was the chine, or the point where the bottom and sides came together. A boat's turning, handling, stability, planning, tracking, and spray control characteristics were all affected by the degree of angle to the chine.[8]

Outboards

Perhaps the greatest advantage of outboards was that they had excellent maneuverability, especially at low speeds. Also, with the trim function, they had the ability to cruise through shallow waters with little difficulty. Outboards generally had good power at top speeds and relatively low noise levels. Power steering was offered on some models, with power trimming usually a standard feature. Engines could be

[7]*WaterSki,* January 1992.
[8]*World Waterskiing,* June 1984.

easily upgraded. Outboards were roomy, as well, with plenty of walk-around and storage room.

However, outboards did not make very good ski boats for several reasons. First, they had turbulent wakes and a rough table (the flat part in between wakes); second, they had marginal handling ability in ski sites with tight dimensions; and third, their controls lacked the smoothness and precision needed for skiing. They were not as naturally balanced as inboards, and they had no platform on the back of the boat for the convenience and ease of putting on skis.

Another disadvantage of outboards was that they required a specially trained mechanic for tune-ups, adjustments, and repairs. Typically, outboards did not come "packaged" from the manufacturer; that is, the controls for steering, throttle, shift, and trim had to be set by a mechanic, although some manufacturers had begun prepackaging their products. One of the greatest complaints of outboard owners concerned having to mix the oil with the gas; however, automatic mixing had increasingly become a standard feature.[9]

Closed-Bow, Tournament Inboards

These 19- to 20-foot-long boats were excellent performers, designed with the serious skier's needs and demands in mind. When riding in one, its most noticeable aspects were its "sports car" feel and "fingertip" control. Competition inboards had quick and easy handling in tight dimensions, excellent tracking ability, and low steering effort and play, resulting in easy operator effort. Standard features on inboards included two precise speedometers and a tachometer, a large dash-mounted mirror, platform, and ski pylon (an upright steel bar mounted in front of the engine to which ski ropes can be attached).

Engine installation for inboards was simpler than for outboards and stern drives and was easily built into the overall design of the boat. Inboard engines were mounted in the center of the boat and therefore were easily serviceable. Inboards had tremendous "get up" and adequate "go" acceleration. The traditional direct-drive ratio for gear transmissions was 1:1, although some models were offered with an optional 1.23:1 or 1.5:1 ratio, providing additional power and increased propeller efficiency. The propeller was fixed; therefore there was no trimming function. Wakes were defined at lower speeds and small at higher speeds, making them suitable (and desirable) for slalom, tricking, and jumping, while spray coming from the back of the boat was minimal.

The greatest drawbacks of inboards included less than adequate slow-speed handling (because only the rudder was being turned), high interior and drive-by noise level, less interior and storage space due to the centrally mounted engine, and high retail prices. Yet, the resale value of inboards in general, whether open or closed bow, was the highest of all the markets. This could be attributed to the high quality, durability, and long life of inboards, as well as to the fact that the inboard market was the smallest of the three segments.[10]

Open-Bow, Family/Pleasure Inboards

These boats began appearing in the early 1980s in response to demand from both recreational and serious skiers who had growing families but also wanted a quality water-ski boat with more room and luxury features. Open-bow inboards were nearly

---

[9]*WaterSki,* May 1988 and 1989.
[10]*WaterSki,* March 1989.

comparable to their closed-bow counterparts in performance and standard features, yet they were longer (20 to 24 feet) and wider than the closed bow, thus offering increased roominess and comfort. Because of differing demands, the family inboards usually came in a variety of models and styles. Perhaps the only complaint of the open bow was that the ride in the front of the boat was not as smooth as in the back of the boat, resulting in a sometimes "wet ride." Many new buyers of family inboards included those who, after skiing behind an inboard, decided to convert from a stern-drive boat.[11]

Stern Drives (Inboard/Outboard)

Stern drives combine attributes of both inboards and outboards. There was the runabout-sized boat ranging in length from 17 to 20 feet and family-sized boat at lengths of 20 to 23 feet. These boats had historically been aimed at recreational boaters and skiers by not providing such "serious" skier necessities as a rearview mirror, ski pylon, platform, and precise speedometers and steering/tracking ability. In 1991, however, many stern-drive manufacturers were making serious inroads toward "skier-izing" their products.

Like the outboard, stern-drive boats had excellent maneuverability and low-speed control, as well as power steering and the trimming function to aid in speed, tracking and acceleration control, and shallow water operations. They were also relatively quiet and roomy, with plenty of walk-about room and storage capacity. As in inboards, stern drives had automotive, marinized engines allowing for easy service-ability. The bow usually stayed dry, yet it had a high planing attitude, thereby impairing visibility at the start of the ride. Such planing attitude resulted in a well-defined wake for tricking but turbulent wakes for slalom.[12]

TRENDS IN COMPETITION INBOARDS

Year after year, the pursuit of the "ultimate" tournament ski boat was relentless. Manufacturers were constantly striving to improve their products and differentiate themselves, mainly through innovation and price. In the early 1990s, the most common industrywide trends were in hull design, interior styling and design, drivability, and ski-ability.[13]

Hull Design   There were several noticeable trends in hull design. The first was that hulls were becoming longer and wider. Correct Craft was the first to initiate this move in its 1990 Ski Nautique (it was the first hull design change since the inception of the 2001 model in 1982). The company abandoned the old industry standards of 18 to 18.5 feet in length and 80-inch beam (width) to produce a 19.5-foot model with 91-inch beam. Since then, virtually all companies had followed suit with 19- to 20-foot by 85- to 92-inch beam models. MasterCraft's 1991 model incorporated the company's first hull design change since 1977.

---

[11] *WaterSki,* June 1990.
[12] *WaterSki,* April 1989.
[13] *WaterSki,* March 1991.

Second, hulls were being designed so as to drastically reduce the amount of spray from the boat. In 1991, there were more "deep short-line" slalom skiers than ever before, and spray from the back of the boat could hurt a skier's performance. The manufacturers' goal was to produce a model with little or no spray. Once again, Correct Craft, with its 1990 Ski Nautique models, led the industry in seriously (and successfully) attacking this problem. Slim tunnels (or spray chines) in the rear of the hull helped displace the water so there was virtually no spray. Other manufacturers had made significant improvements in their models as well. Several companies re-created their hull designs for 1992 and obtained patents for their new designs. Most of the shapes were modifications and refinements of the existing hull designs, although a few innovative concepts were introduced.

Yet another trend had to do with hull warranties; they were becoming longer and more comprehensive. Many companies now offered a limited lifetime warranty on the hull, deck, and structural components of some or all of their products. This was a welcome addition for the consumer, not just for product liability but also for peace of mind.

Styling and Design   For both hulls and interiors, different types of styling and decor were cropping up. For instance, California and European styling were gaining popularity. The California style incorporated multicolor graphics and upholstery for a sleeker, racier appearance, while the European style created a more contemporary look through flowing, aesthetic lines. There was also more foot and hip room, a direct result of the increased length and width. And, industrywide, there was a general increase in the quality of workmanship in interior features such as upholstery, dash, storage, and engine compartments.

Drivability   Tournament inboards were beginning to follow some automotive trends such as adjustable, more supportive seats (a few companies even offered lumbar support) and foot wells. Tilt steering, once unheard of, was practically an industry standard by 1991. Perhaps the best new feature was better instrumentation. Malibu Boats invented MEMS (Malibu Electronic Management System), a high-tech system control center at the driver's fingertips. And some engines, such as PCM, implemented electronic controls to improve performance and help prevent damage. All companies, in one way or another, were considering ergonomics in their seating and control layout.

Ski-Ability   The biggest performance improvement was found in straight-line tracking ability. For a world record in slalom to be accepted, the boat path could not deviate more than eight inches from the center line of its course. The shorter the slalom line gets, the more force a skier exerts, and therefore the more important tracking becomes.

Another seemingly small yet significant improvement was made in the tops of ski pylons, thanks to a MasterCraft innovation. New antichafing designs where the ski rope is attached reduced wear and tear for longer rope life. Platforms had been enhanced, also, by making them a more integral part of the overall design of the boat.

Overall, the trend in recreational boats was toward better ski-ability and instrumentation. In tournament boats, the trend was toward greater comfort, luxury touches, and improved ski-ability. A fine line existed between family and tournament ski boats, but it seemed as though manufacturers were trying to reach two markets with essentially the same basic design.

THE AMERICAN WATER SKI ASSOCIATION

The American Water Ski Association was the nation's governing body of the sport of waterskiing. As a nonprofit organization, its purpose was "to organize, develop, and promote the sport, coordinate and sanction local and national competitions and clinics, select national and world teams, and train and certify coaches and officials." In 1990, some 640 tournaments were held. Additionally, AWSA was a member of the International Water Ski Federation, the world governing body of waterskiing, and an Affiliated Sports Organization member of the United States Olympic Committee.

As of 1990, there were 24,400 AWSA members. In 1991, membership increased 16.8 percent, largely because of a new membership approach and the hiring of a director of membership development. There were over 28,500 members (of which only one-third were competitive skiers) in 1991 in six official sport divisions: traditional three-event waterskiing, the American Barefoot Club (ABC), the American Kneeboard Association (AKA), the National Collegiate Water Ski Association (NCWSA), the National Show Ski Association (NSSA), and the National Speedboat and Water Ski Association (NSWSA). In addition, a National Disabled Skiers' Committee was formed, and the AWSA sanctioned three-event competitions for this group.

The backbone of AWSA was the numerous water-ski clubs that existed nationwide. In 1991, there were over 550 affiliated active clubs in the United States. It was mainly through the clubs that AWSA continued its growth. Clubs put on ski shows, hosted tournaments, and held clinics for water-ski instruction, as well as instruction for tournament officials.

Yet another supporting branch of AWSA was the American Water Ski Educational Foundation (AWSEF). This entity maintained the Water Ski Museum/Hall of Fame, supervised college scholarship programs, and helped support U.S. water-ski teams in recognized international competitions.

To compete in AWSA-sanctioned tournaments, one had to be an active AWSA member. Active membership was $35 per year and included $100,000 secondary medical accident insurance during club skiing activities (including practice), tournaments, and ski shows; a subscription to *The Water Skier* magazine (published seven times a year); and eligibility for special offers and programs sponsored by AWSA, such as legislative/regulatory assistance concerning the waterways, water-ski instructor certification, and towboat insurance. A $20 per year supporting membership included only a subscription to *The Water Skier* and eligibility for special offers and programs.

For traditional three-event water skiing, the largest of AWSA's sport divisions, skiers competed in one of five regions based on where they lived or skied: West, Midwest, South, South Central, or East. Based on numbers of AWSA members, the Midwest was the largest region, with 8,338 members in 10 states. The western region, by far the largest in land mass, had 7,150 members in 15 states (including Alaska and Hawaii). The southern region had 5,415 members in 7 states, the eastern region had 4,020 members in 13 states, and the South Central region had 3,584 members in 5 states. Only seven states had over 1,000 AWSA members: California

(3,700), Florida (2,532), Texas (2,450), Wisconsin (1,911), Illinois (1,306), Michigan (1,118), and Washington (1,021). Ten states had under 100 members, six of which had fewer than 50 (New Mexico, North and South Dakota, Montana, Wyoming, and Rhode Island).[14]

BOAT TESTS

In 1983, AWSA began testing ski boats to encourage manufacturers to strive for continuous improvement in their products and to certify towboats for use in AWSA-sanctioned tournaments, including traditional three-event, kneeboard, barefoot, show ski, collegiate, and disabled tournaments. Tests were conducted under the supervision of AWSA and U.S. Olympic Committee officials, and boats were tested on the following characteristics:

- Distance required to pull a skier out of the water to 36 MPH.
- Amount of spray in the slalom course.
- Wake characteristics for slalom and trick.
- Straightness of boat path in the slalom and jump courses; deviation from center line.
- Handling and maneuverability.
- Human engineering—how well the boat was functionally designed.

To receive certification, each boat had to pass AWSA standards. One of three rankings was given to each boat passing the evaluations: eligible towboat, approved towboat, or national tournament towboat. Each one was eligible to participate in AWSA-sanctioned tournaments and programs. In addition, an approved towboat had participated in 20-plus AWSA sponsored events the previous year, while a national tournament towboat had pulled four out of the five (prior-year) regional championships for three-event skiing, as well as the national championships.

In 1982, only four towboats were in use at competitions. Since the inception of the boat tests in 1983, the number of manufacturers participating in the tests and the number of boats tested has steadily increased (see Exhibit 9). For 1992, 29 boats from 14 manufacturers were tested; 25 passed as eligible towboats. Of these, 22 were inboards, and only one boat was dually certified for use in traditional and barefoot tournaments. There were 15 approved towboats and 3 national tournament towboats.[15]

COMPETITIVE RIVALRY

Rivalry in the competition ski boat industry was almost purely national. One industry expert noted, "As long as our (boat-building) technology stays within the U.S., competition will remain on the national level. No one else has the capabilities we do—not even Japan." Competition was not likely to go global until after the turn of

---

[14]Drawn heavily from *The Water Skier,* April 1989, March–April 1991, June 1991, and the AWSA membership pamphlet.
[15]*The Water Skier,* May 1983 and January–February 1984–1992.

Exhibit 9	Participation and Results of AWSA Testing of Competition Ski Boats, 1983–1992		

Year	Number of Participating Manufacturers	Number of Boats Tested	Number of Boats Passing
1983	6	8	6
1984	11	16	11
1985	12	18	15
1986	12	18	15
1987	15	22	21
1988	11	19	18
1989	16	25	22
1990	16	26	25
1991	14	26	23
1992	14	29	25

Source: *The Water Skier,* May 1983 and January–February 1984–1992.

the century. Before U.S. companies could take advantage of the cheap labor available in foreign countries and produce abroad, technological advances and manufacturing capabilities still needed further development. Furthermore, companies needed to grow and strengthen their financial condition to be able to operate efficiently in a global marketplace.

Competition in inboard ski boats centered mainly around differentiation, innovation, and quality, while some companies also relied on their tenure in the industry and others competed on the basis of lower prices. As of 1991, there had been no price wars, but it remained a possibility as the industry matured. The battle for market share was fierce, and many companies simply expanded their product line to fulfill the varied demands of consumers.

Manufacturers sold their products to retail dealers, who in turn sold to the general product. *Boating Industry* surveys revealed that in 1991 the average dealer grossed slightly under $1 million with 60 percent of sales in boats, motors, and trailers (compared to 70 percent in 1990); 12 percent in parts and accessories; 11 percent in service; 14 percent in used boats (compared to just 5 percent in 1990); and 3 percent in financing and insurance. The decline in new boat sales was attributed mainly to the deepening recession.[16]

In 1990, a marketing research firm surveyed ski boat dealers from all over the United States. Results indicated no one brand was carried by more than 6 percent of the dealers and the average dealer carried 1.5 lines of ski boats. When dealers were asked which ski boat manufacturers came to mind first, MasterCraft ranked first with 26 percent, Correct Craft second with 25 percent, and Supra third with 11 percent. This measure, called unaided awareness, was important because studies had shown that as unaided awareness increased, so did market share and "favorable predisposition" (which brands of boats dealers would either most prefer to carry or would consider carrying). The survey showed that MasterCraft ranked first in favorable

[16]*Boating Industry,* January 1992.

predisposition with 33 percent, followed by WellCraft (28 percent), Four Winns (27 percent), Correct Craft (26 percent), and Sea Ray (25 percent).

The dealers surveyed were categorized into one of three positions according to the quality and value of the product(s) they carried: Position I for low quality/moderate value, position II for high quality/high value, and position III for moderate quality/low value. Twenty-seven percent of the dealers were in position I and favored Four Winns, Bayliner, and WellCraft; 29 percent were in position II and favored Supra, Malibu, and Cobalt; the remaining 44 percent were in position III and favored MasterCraft, Correct Craft, and Sea Ray. Exhibit 10 displays these results in matrix form. When deciding which ski boats to carry, the most influential characteristics included having a nationally known brand, multiple-use models, and wide product line; a company's size and length of time in business were also important.[17]

Most companies did the majority of their advertising in boating and waterskiing magazines, and they promoted their products at boat shows, major pro tournaments, and amateur tournaments. Many also had a promotional boat program in which the company chose certain interested individuals with some degree of influence in their skiing community to use its product as a "promo" boat and take it to local and regional tournaments for use and exposure. A promo person received a new boat each year at a discounted price under an agreement to use it in a specified number of tournaments within his or her region. The skier was reimbursed for charges incurred to transport the boat and also received a stipend for each tournament in which the boat participated. However, the user was usually responsible for the sale of the boat at the end of the competition season.

MASTERCRAFT

MasterCraft, along with Correct Craft, dominated the competition ski boat industry during the 1970s and early 1980s. In 1984, the company was acquired by the Coleman Company and became part of Coleman's water recreation operations division. Although MasterCraft had eight models for 1992, most advertising and promotional efforts went toward the ProStar 190 model, its best-selling, top-of-the-line competition inboard. The ProStar 190 came standard with an Indmar engine having a 1:1 gear ratio or with an optional 1.5:1 ratio called a Power Slot. (MasterCraft was the first in the industry to introduce such an option.) The other models included the ProStar 205 and ProSport 205 (both open-bow versions of the ProStar 190); the Barefoot 200, an outboard ski boat for barefooting; two versions (open and closed bow) of a more spacious family boat called the MariStar 210; and two versions of a 25-foot cruiser (one with a cabin and the other one open bow with room for 11 people) called the MariStar 240. In 1991, the open-bow MariStar 210 received *Powerboat* magazine's Award for Product Excellence by being voted the 1991 Ski Boat of the Year. Both versions of the ProStar 190 (the 1:1 and the Power Slot) and the ProStar 205 and Barefoot 200 were AWSA-approved towboats for 1992, and the ProStar 190 was one of only three boats to be used to pull the 1991 National Water Ski Championships and U.S. Open. In addition, MasterCraft was the sole towboat sponsor of Cypress Gardens in Winter Haven, Florida, and the Professional Water Ski Tour.

---

[17]Strength and Weakness Analysis for Supra Sports conducted by Message Factors, Inc., June 1990.

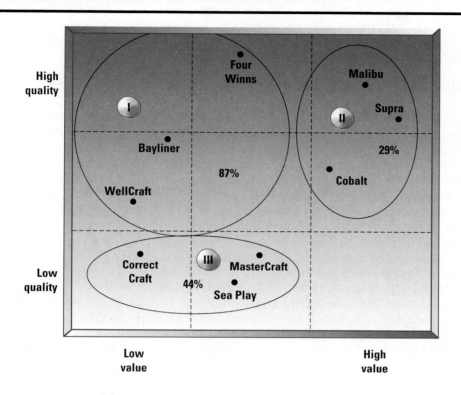

Exhibit 10   Quality-Value Perceptions of Competition Ski Boat Manufacturers, Dealer Survey Results, 1990

MasterCraft entered the industry in the competition ski boat market, going mainly after the family segment during the 1980s. By 1989, MasterCraft was the market share leader in competition ski boats with approximately 26.6 percent. For years, MasterCraft boasted of having the only 10-year hull and engine warranty in the industry. But after negotiating with Mobil Oil Company, MasterCraft upgraded its warranty in 1991 to a limited lifetime warranty. The hull warranty was covered by MasterCraft while all lubricated engine parts were covered by Mobil as long as Mobil 1 engine oil was used in the care and maintenance of the engine.

MasterCraft had the strongest and most extensive promo boat program in the industry, according to industry experts. The company had an estimated 105 dealers nationwide, as well as 10 distributors abroad. MasterCraft products were endorsed by 17 professional water-skiers who formed the official "MasterCraft Pro Ski Team."

Retail prices for the MasterCraft line ranged from $23,000 to $35,800 (including trailer), while resale values after one year of use ranged from $17,700 to $27,500.

In a 1989 study of magazine expenditures for 16 ski boat manufacturers, MasterCraft spent more than any other company (17 percent of expenditures for all 16 companies) and was the only company to advertise in all eight magazines reviewed (six boating, two waterskiing). MasterCraft was the only major competition ski boat manufacturer to advertise in *Boating* magazine, where it spent the greatest percentage of its magazine advertising dollars. *WaterSki* magazine was allotted the next largest sum in MasterCraft's advertising budget. By heavily advertising the fact that the ProStar 190 held more world records than all other ski boats combined, MasterCraft advertisements consistently focused on quality and superiority over its competition. Exhibit 11 contains sample MasterCraft ads.

CORRECT CRAFT

Correct Craft was owned by the fourth generation of the original founding family. "On the waters of the world since 1925" as their slogan went, Correct Craft was the oldest of the competition ski boat companies. Correct Craft had always concentrated on having a quality image, yet before 1990, skiers complained that the company's Ski Nautique models had a larger wake than other ski boats. In 1990, Correct Craft solved this problem with new models having a new hull design. The new Ski Nautique all but revolutionized the industry, with its radically longer and wider hull and virtually "no spray" characteristic.

In 1992, Correct Craft offered buyers five models: the closed-bow tournament Ski Nautique (in which a PCM Power Plus engine with 1.23:1 gear ratio was standard) and an open-bow version (both AWSA approved for 1992); the family-oriented Sport Nautique with walk-through bowrider; and both an open- and closed-bow version of its barefoot boat, the Nautique Excel (also called the Barefoot Nautique). The Excel was different from the other models (and all other inboard ski boats) in that the engine was placed astern to maximize seating and storage capacity. Also new for the Excel was a deep V hull configuration designed for boating in larger bodies of water and for barefooting; the closed-bow Excel was also AWSA approved.

All Correct Craft hulls were covered by a limited lifetime warranty and a transferable limited five-year warranty for those who frequently sold boats to buy a new one. Engine parts were covered by the engine manufacturer.

In 1989, Correct Craft still occupied the second position in market share with an estimated 22.2 percent, but it had slipped from 28 percent in 1985. Like most major ski boat companies, Correct Craft had a promotional program, although it tended to be more selective than others. There were approximately 100 Correct Craft dealers in the United States and several distributors abroad. About one-third of Correct Craft's sales were overseas. Retail prices ranged from $23,900 to $26,800, and, like MasterCraft, Correct Craft products had high resale value after one year ($18,400 to $20,600). The company also had a pro ski team comprising 10 world-class professional skiers to endorse its products.

Correct Craft had contracts with a couple of notable ski show and tournament sites to use Ski Nautiques exclusively. The Masters at Callaway Gardens, the most prestigious ski tournament in the United States, had never used any boat other than Ski Nautique; likewise for Sea World of Orlando. In addition, the Ski Nautique was another of the three towboats used to pull the 1991 Nationals and U.S. Open.

In magazine expenditures, Correct Craft spent approximately 8 percent of expenditures for all 16 companies in the previously mentioned study—less than half what MasterCraft spent—and advertised in only one boating magazine and both water-ski magazines. Basically, Correct Craft advertisements were similar to those of MasterCraft, focusing on quality and competitive superiority (see Exhibit 12).

Exhibit 11   Sample MasterCraft Ad

Exhibit 12   Sample Correct Craft Ad

Deena Mapple   Andy Mapple   Tory Baggiano

World Record Holders
Ski Nautique

Capturing a world record doesn't come easy. It's definitely hard work. Putting in a few hours at a tournament is a mere drop in the bucket compared to the years of practice it takes to get there.

Home is where the real work gets done - practice, evaluation, perfection. For every world record set at a tournament, it is exceeded *tenfold* on the home course.

CURRENT WORLD RECORD HOLDERS*

MEN SLALOM
Andy Mapple

WOMEN SLALOM
Deena Mapple

MEN TRICKS
Tory Baggiano

WOMEN JUMP
Deena Mapple

FREESTYLE
Dave Reinhart

BAREFOOT WOMEN SLALOM
Jennifer Calleri

BAREFOOT MEN TRICKS
Rick Powell

BAREFOOT WOMEN TRICKS
Jennifer Calleri

*As of 4/1/91

More world records are set by skiers using Correct Crafts than all other manufacturers combined. These skiers count on Correct Craft for strong, consistent world record pulls, day after day.

During a tournament, it wouldn't matter if these pros were pulled by a milk truck. They've done their homework.

They practice behind the best and it shows.

Given a *choice*, world record holders chose a Nautique.

on the waters of the world since 1925

6100 South Orange Avenue
Orlando, FL 32809
407/855-4141

For the name of your local dealer,
call: 1-800-346-2092

MALIBU

Malibu Boats was formed in 1982 by an ex-plant manager of the Ski Centurion boat company, Robert Alkema. Alkema's philosophy was to manufacture a higher value boat to meet the beginning to advanced skier's needs and budget. In 10 years, the company went from being a small upstart venture to being a recognized player in the inboard ski boat industry. Malibu's sales were boosted in 1989 when it purchased Flightcraft, an Australian ski boat company. By 1991, the company was battling it out with Supra Boats for the number three position in market share.

In 1992, Malibu had eight models in its product line—six Malibu and two Flightcraft models, all equipped with MerCruiser's Competition Ski engine. The Malibu line consisted of both a European and California series. There were four European models: the closed-bow Malibu Skier Euro-f3, now the company's premiere tournament ski boat; the open-bow Malibu Sunsetter Euro-f3; and the Mystere 215 (closed bow)/Mystere 215LX (open bow) Euro-f3. The California series included the closed-bow Malibu Skier, formerly the company's traditional top-rated competition ski boat, and the open-bow Malibu Sunsetter. The Australian series was comprised of the two closed-bow Flightcraft models: the 18XLT inboard and the 20XLOB (outboard) for barefooting. Both of these boats, as well as the Skier and Sunsetter Euro-f3, were AWSA approved for 1992. In 1989 and 1991, the Skier Euro-f3 was named Tournament Ski Boat of the Year by *Hotboat* magazine, while the Malibu Skier (California series) was voted Best Value Boat of the Year by *Powerboat* magazine in 1989.

Malibu boats had more standard features than other boats in the industry, and its models sold for a relatively lower price. Malibu did not engage in extensive marketing efforts; rather, the company concentrated on developing a superb dealer network and word-of-mouth advertising from satisfied users. Malibu spent only 7 percent of the total expenditures for the 16 companies in the 1989 advertising study, placing almost 70 percent of its advertisements in the two waterskiing publications and the rest in two boating magazines. In its ad, Malibu emphasized the high value of its products, as well as quality (see Exhibit 13 for sample ads).

Malibu was known for its innovativeness. The company's latest models had several new and different features—most notably the Malibu Electronic Management System (MEMS). MEMS was a control center that housed 18 monitoring and actuating functions within the driver's reach. The company had also developed a pivoting ski pylon to reduce rope wear and was one of the first to have introduced an air cushion system in the driver's seat for contour and lumbar support.

One characteristic that distinguished Malibu from its competitors was its employee stock ownership program; in 1989, employees were awarded stock equal to 10 percent of their annual salary. Malibu operated with a worker-oriented environment in order to promote quality workmanship, reduce defects and warranty costs, and instill greater pride and job satisfaction.

Malibu had 120 dealers nationwide, two distributors in Europe, approximately 100 promo boaters, and four world-class water-skiers endorsing its products. Also, Malibu was the only manufacturer with two production facilities—one in California and one in Tennessee. Malibu offered a lifetime limited warranty on all its products and a lower retail price than its competitors. Retail prices for the Malibu and Flightcraft lines were $17,700 to $22,000, while resale values after one year's use were $13,600 to $16,900.

Exhibit 13   Sample Malibu Ad

SUPRA BOATS

George Fowler had been general manager of MasterCraft for six years and then founded, and subsequently sold, Supreme Industries (manufacturer of Ski Supreme inboards). Fowler was one of the first people in the inboard ski boat industry to recognize the market opportunities of a roomier, more luxurious family/pleasure boat with tournament ski boat performance. He founded Supra Boats in 1980 and decided to establish the company in the family ski boat market before moving into the competition ski boat segment. Fowler's expertise and experience in the boating industry were instrumental in positioning Supra as a viable market leader and innovator.

In 1982, Supra introduced the industry's first open-bow inboard, and by 1985, the company had a 10 percent share of the market. By 1989, Supra's market share had increased to 18.3 percent—the third largest in the industry. From 1984 to 1989, Supra enjoyed a 29.5 percent annual growth rate, with sales increasing from $7.4 million to $26.9 million. In 1990, the company was acquired by Marine Sports, Inc., a publicly held company. With Marine Sports' added financial strength, Supra planned to add new models, acquire additional subsidiary companies, and explore the possibility of building a new state-of-the-art manufacturing facility.

Supra likened its boats to Porsche and Mercedes-Benz automobiles, and it targeted the discriminating, upscale buyer who sought both quality and performance in a ski boat. In 1992, the company had 11 models, one of the most comprehensive product lines in the industry. Eight of the 1992 models were carried over from 1991 with only slight changes. The open-bow Saltare and closed-bow, cuddy cabin Pirata were the biggest family boats, holding up to 10 people in their 23-foot-long, 99-inch-wide frames; these models offered special amenities such as a double bucket driver's seat and a bar complete with glasses. The open-bow Mariah and closed-bow (cuddy cabin) Bravura held up to eight people and were 21 feet long by 95 inches wide. The open-bow SunSport and closed-bow Marauder also had eight-person capacity and were 20 feet long, 96 inches wide. The rest of the original line included the 19.5-foot-by-85.5-inch open-bow Conbrio and closed-bow Comp ts6m, both of which held six people. The latter was Supra's tournament skiing model, AWSA approved and twice heralded Ski Boat of the Year by *Powerboat* magazine. The Comp had been the exclusive towboat for the 1987 World Waterskiing Championships and the 1986, 1988, and 1990 World Cup. The PCM Power Plus engine (1.23:1 gear transmission) was standard in these eight models, and retail prices ranged from $22,900 to $30,400, while one-year resale values started at $17,600 and topped out at $23,300.

New for 1992 was a lower-priced line, comprising three models, called the 3000 Series. This line was created for those who wanted the same ride and luxuries as in the original Supra line, but a more competitive price. The closed-bow, AWSA-approved Impulse and open-bow Espirit both had the same dimensions and capacity as the Comp and Conbrio, while the Spirit had the SunSport/Marauder specifications. Other than the warranty and the engine (a PCM with 1:1 transmission), the 3000 Series offered basically the same standard features and options as did the higher priced line. Whereas all Supra products were backed by a limited lifetime warranty for the hull and deck, the 3000 Series had only a 6-year/600-hour limited warranty. Past annual warranty costs for Supra were approximately 2.19 percent of sales.

In addition to the 3000 Series, Supra had another, even lower priced product by its sister company, Moomba Sports. Using a hull design licensed from an Australian

Exhibit 14   Sample Supra Ad

boat company, the Moomba Boomerang retailed for $15,000 and targeted first-time ski boat buyers. It was a bare-bones type of ski boat that offered a decent ski pull and ride for a modest price.

One of the factors contributing to Supra's success was its technology. According to one issue of *Powerboat* magazine, "The company is an industry leader when it comes to building strong, sturdy hulls." Supra boats featured a unique hull design. The SupraTrac™ hull design incorporated a semimodified V-shape at the bow that tapered to a flat planing surface near the middle of the hull. Supra applied technology developed for the aerospace industry and used the highest quality construction materials such as Kevlar, Coremat, and biaxial fiberglass bonded with AME 4000 resin to produce the strongest possible hulls.

Supra had approximately 175 dealers worldwide and 50 promotional boats. With the majority of promotional programs, the boat owner was responsible for selling the boat each year before obtaining a new promo boat, but with Supra's program, a Supra dealer was responsible for finding a buyer. Unlike the other top companies, Supra chose not to have professional skiers endorse its products because of the added cost. Since Supra's strongest presence was in the family market, the company preferred to invest more in the quality of its products and in advertising. Of the 16 major competitors, Supra was fourth in advertising expenditures, according to the 1989 advertising study. One-third of Supra's advertising funds were for ads in *WaterSki* magazine while the rest were for AWSA's publication and various boating magazines. Supra's ads focused on the high quality and luxuriousness of its products (Exhibit 14).

Management's immediate priority was to develop a strategic plan for becoming the industry's market share leader by the year 2000. George Fowler, Supra's CEO, wondered what strategic approach made the most sense.

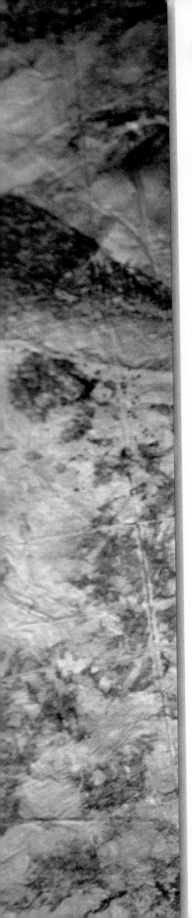

Nintendo versus SEGA (A):
The videogame industry[1]

Romuald A. Stone, James Madison University

Video and computer games have emerged as a great unforeseen by-product of the electronic age. As technological advances make simulation increasingly more realistic, videogames allow the player to set sail for the New World with a boatload of colonists, to take command of a WWII German U-boat, to fly air-to-air and ground strike missions as a pilot on board the USS Eisenhower, to enter several mystical worlds to untangle an ancient web of treachery and deceit, or to match wits with seven PGA golfers on tour. Half the top 100 games of 1994 (categories included party, family, trivia, word, puzzles, arcade, real-life strategy, abstract strategy, adventure, and war games) were for computers or videogames, up from 37 percent in 1993. For the first time ever, an electronic game ("Myst" by Broderbund) was named 1994 Game of the Year by *Games* magazine.[2]

Videogames are a $5 billion a year business in the United States (a $4 billion market in Japan, $15 billion worldwide). Nearly 10 years ago, the industry hit rock bottom with retail videogame sales less than $100 million in 1985 (see Exhibit 1). The rebirth of the industry exceeded everyone's expectations. Since then, Nintendo and SEGA have dominated the industry with over 150 million of their game machines sold worldwide (over 50 million are in U.S. households). Nearly two-thirds of the kids in North America between the ages of 6 and 14 play videogames. Worldwide, Nintendo generated net sales of $4.7 billion and SEGA $4 billion in fiscal year 1994 (ended March 31, 1994).

After years of steady growth, videogame industry revenues were expected to decline slightly in 1994 and 1995. Industry analysts attributed the decline to a maturing market, although new game systems were expected to offset some of the decline.

INDUSTRY BACKGROUND[3]

The first home videogame system was the Odyssey, released by Magnavox in 1972. The Odyssey required that plastic overlays be attached to the television set. Despite

---

[1]The generous cooperation of David Cole, president, DFC Intelligence Research, in providing information on the U.S. videogame industry is greatly appreciated. Used with permission.
[2]B. Hochberg, ed., "Games 100," *Games* (December 1994), pp. 67–76.
[3]Extracted from Standard & Poor's *Industry Surveys* (Toys), 1991, pp. L46–47; and DFC Intelligence Research, *The U.S. Market for Video Games and Interactive Electronic Entertainment* (San Diego, 1995).

Exhibit 1   Size of the U.S. Market for Videogames: Hardware and Software, 1977–1994

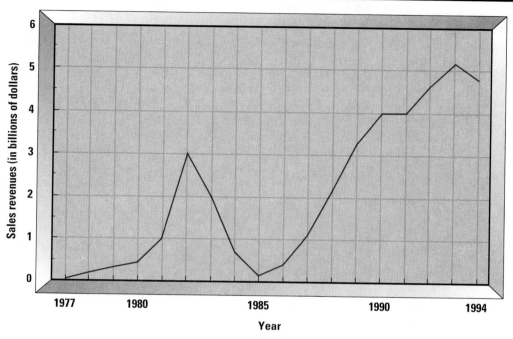

Sources: Nintendo of America and Gerard Klauer Mattison & Co.

an extensive marketing campaign by Magnavox, the Odyssey never caught on and it died after a year on the market.

It took a successful arcade game to build demand for the first home videogame systems. In 1972, Nolan Bushnell created the first electronic arcade videogame, "Pong." Pong was a simple coin-operated table-tennis game that caught on in bars and arcades. With $500, Bushnell and a buddy formed Atari in 1972 to manufacture Pong machines. The success of Pong did not go unnoticed and brought numerous imitators to the newly emerging industry, a trend that characterizes the industry to this day. By 1973, 90 percent of all Pong machines in arcades were clones manufactured by 25 competitors of Atari. Home versions quickly followed.

In 1976, Fairfield Camera & Instrument released the "Channel F," the first home system to accept interchangeable cartridges. Previously, home videogame systems played only a limited number of preprogrammed games. Once a player tired of those games the systems were relegated to a back closet and forgotten. With interchangeable cartridges, the software became separated from the hardware. By buying a new cartridge, a system played entirely new games.

Nolan Bushnell realized that interchangeable cartridges were the wave of the future. Two months after the release of Channel F, he sold Atari to Warner Communications for $27 million for the purpose of raising capital to release a new game system. Warner's Chairman and CEO Steven Ross saw the revolutionary potential of videogames. The company's 1976 annual report observed:

> Toys and games of skill go back to the early history of human life. Stones, bones, and wood were early materials for games, and many of those are still

highly salable product today. As technology advanced, games were spring driven, later battery powered, and now they have begun to incorporate electronics. Each new development somewhat eclipsed the past, but virtually every game that was ever enjoyed by a lot of people is still made and sold. Electronic games are a logical step in this historic process.

In 1977, Atari released its "video computer system" (VCS) or 2600 home system. Over the next few years, Atari established the 2600 as the dominant videogame system. Industry growth got a booster shot with the introduction in arcades of "Space Invaders" in 1979 and "Pac-Man" in 1981. Atari was the first company to license an arcade game for a home system when it licensed "Space Invaders" for the 2600. The 1980s release of "Space Invaders" on the 2600 was such a smash hit that sales doubled and Atari became the fastest-growing company in the history of American business. Atari followed with the equally successful home version of "Pac-Man" in 1982. Atari remained the undisputed industry leader through 1982, consistently maintaining a 70 to 80 percent share of the home videogame market.

While Atari was enjoying its success, competitive rivalry was intensifying. In 1982, 350 new game titles were released by a growing number of competitors. Mattel had joined the fray with Intellivision in late 1979, and Coleco made a splash in early 1983 by introducing ColecoVision (both second-generation systems with improved graphics). Other entrants included Milton Bradley (its Vectrex system flopped) and the toy subsidiaries of Quaker Oats and General Mills.[4]

But by the mid-1980s, the bloom was already fading from the rose. According to Warner Communications' 1983 annual report, in December 1981 there was only one other manufacturer of Atari-compatible cartridges; a year later, there were more than 20. The report observed, "Throughout 1983 and into 1984, unsuccessful software manufacturers liquidated their factory inventories at close-out prices, causing damaging price competition and compounding retailers' inventory problems at a time when demand fell from the peak of 1982." In fact, Warner Communications was ultimately to bury truckloads of videogame cartridges in the Arizona desert. The bottom line for Warner was a $539 million loss on its consumer electronics segment in 1983.

In 1984, Warner Communications and Mattel were nearly driven to bankruptcy by the losses of their videogame subsidiaries. Warner sold its Atari division that year, and Mattel and Coleco announced they were leaving the videogame business in 1985. Industry game sales had declined to $100 million in 1985 from its previous high of $3 billion in 1982 (see Exhibit 1). The home videogame market had collapsed; it seemed that the videogame business was dying a rapid death.

Enter Nintendo and SEGA

Nintendo proved industry observers wrong when it introduced its Nintendo Entertainment System (NES) in 1985. Encouraged by earlier success with its Famicom game system in Japan, Nintendo ignored analysts who felt that the videogame business was a fad whose time had passed and began selling its NES in New York in the fall of 1985. In 1986, the company sold 1.1 million NES units, largely on the strength of "Super Mario Brothers," a game that eventually sold 40 million copies. Sales of game systems and game cartridges took off. By 1988, Nintendo held an 80 percent share of the $2.3 billion U.S. videogame industry.

---

[4]S. P. Schnaars, *Managing Imitation Strategies* (New York: Simon & Schuster, 1994).

In his review of the videogame industry, Steven Schnaars noted the position of American competitors regarding Nintendo's entry and early success:

> Domestic observers were skeptical of the market's staying power, and the American sellers were reluctant to commit heavily for fear of being burned again. *Business Week* echoed the timidity of the industry in 1988: The "current video game revival may already be past its prime." An Atari executive acknowledged that "we're not overextending ourselves on a category that might go south again." Nintendo, some seemed to think, was repeating past mistakes. It simply did not know the risks inherent in the American market.[5]

However, Nintendo learned a valuable lesson from Warner's failure: it was important to control the supply of game cartridges to ensure quality and prevent fierce price competition. To this end, Nintendo required game developers to follow strict rules. Prior to release, Nintendo had to approve the content of the games. In addition, the agreement required licensees to order games from Nintendo. The licensee developed a game and then placed an order with Nintendo who became the sole manufacturer of cartridges. The minimum order was for 10,000 cartridges, paid in advance. Licensees were charged about twice the cost of manufacturing. This included a royalty to Nintendo, but did not include distribution and marketing costs. Nintendo made money whether or not the game sold. Licensees were also limited to developing five NES games a year, and they could not release a NES game on a competing system for a period of two years.[6]

But Nintendo had done more than just manage inventories successfully. The company also established one of the strongest brand names in the industry. The "Official Nintendo Seal of Quality," familiar to children throughout America, was prominently displayed on all of its products. Nintendo also provided "game counselors"—videogame experts available to players by phone, which helped maintain customer loyalty. In 1993, Nintendo's game counselors handled 8 million phone calls and letters, with cumulative contacts surpassing the 30 million mark.[7]

SEGA first entered the American videogame market in 1986 with its 8-bit Master System. Although the system was generally considered to have better graphics than Nintendo, it achieved only a 15 percent market share. Nintendo's early lead had allowed it to develop a high level of brand awareness and a more extensive library of games. In addition, Nintendo's success gave it the money to fund an aggressive program of game introductions and advertising that SEGA couldn't match with its limited sales. SEGA, however, remained committed to the U.S. market and, in late 1989, introduced its 16-bit Genesis system. While 1989 sales of Genesis were respectable, Nintendo remained the dominant player with a market share of approximately 85 percent, despite the fact that it was competing with the older technology contained in its 8-bit system.[8]

Videogames in the 1990s

In the early 1990s, Nintendo lost its grip on the videogame market due to complacency and slow reaction to SEGA's competitive moves. Nintendo, for example, waited 18 months before coming out with its 16-bit system to compete with Genesis.[9]

[5]Ibid., p. 178.
[6]DFC Intelligence Research.
[7]Extracted from Standard & Poor's *Industry Surveys* (Toys), 1993, pp. L46–47.
[8]Ibid.
[9]J. Carlton, "Video Games Sell in Record Numbers This Christmas," *The Wall Street Journal*, December 20, 1993, p. B3.

The NES was doing so well that Nintendo did not want to cannibalize sales by introducing a more advanced system. By the time Nintendo did release its Super NES (16-bit), SEGA had even more games available, including the popular "Sonic the Hedgehog." In addition, Nintendo's high fees alienated retailers and software developers; SEGA's license fees were lower. Finally, Nintendo's effort to maintain enthusiasm for its games by limiting supply backfired when retailers lost sales and began looking for other suppliers. SEGA also targeted a broader market than Nintendo, focusing on adults as well as teenagers. Its marketing included TV ads that disparaged Nintendo as a system for ninnies.[10]

Helping SEGA's sales was the explosive popularity of its uncensored version of the explicitly violent game, "Mortal Kombat," which Nintendo also released but without the explicit violence.[11] Howard Lincoln, Nintendo's then senior vice president, acknowledged losing tens of thousands of "Mortal Kombat" sales by not releasing the violent version. But he supported the decision by reiterating Nintendo's commitment to social responsibility.

By the early 1990s, SEGA's Genesis held a competitive, if not commanding, market share for 16-bit systems, a small but growing segment of the overall market. SEGA's mid-1992 decision to offer its lightning fast "Sonic the Hedgehog" game with the customer's purchase of the company's 16-bit Genesis system further eroded Nintendo's position. When SEGA introduced a CD-ROM attachment for its Genesis machine in November 1992, it gained further momentum. SEGA's strength in the 16-bit market continued to grow throughout 1993, ending with a 51 percent share and the segment leadership (see Exhibit 2). Through the end of fiscal year 1994, SEGA had sold over 17 million Genesis players since its debut in 1989; Nintendo had sold over 18 million Super NES system players. SEGA was projected to be the videogame leader in the 16-bit segment in 1995 with about 52 percent of overall sales. According to one observer, "SEGA has succeeded in positioning itself as the cooler machine. . . . The MTV generation plays SEGA and your little brother plays Nintendo."[12]

Beyond 2000[13]

Observers believe the outcome of the current videogame wars will determine the future for the next generation of videogames. The long-term outlook for videogame systems is unclear. There is no way to predict how long the next generation game systems will last before they are replaced with still another wave of new products.

Trying to forecast video gaming beyond the next generation is pure speculation; however, analysts have offered several observations. The ideal videogame system should have the power of a computer at an inexpensive price. Most importantly, it should be "plug and play," not only in the ease of installing software but also in the sense that a consumer does not have to worry about whether a given piece of software will play on his or her system. In other words, a given title should play on any machine, whether it is manufactured by SEGA, Nintendo, 3DO, Sony, or another company. Future advances in technology will most likely facilitate releasing titles across multiple platforms.

---

[10]Ibid.

[11]The potential for licensing titles increased significantly in 1991 after Nintendo ceased requiring its software developers to license titles exclusively to Nintendo.

[12]A. Pollack, "Sega Takes Aim at Disney World," *New York Times*, July 4, 1993, pp. 1, 6.

[13]Extracted largely from DFC Intelligence Research report.

Exhibit 2   Estimated Sales and Market Share Summary Data: 16-Bit Hardware, Software, and Add-Ons, 1992–1996 *(in millions)*

	1992	1993	1994	1995	1996
Nintendo Super NES	$1,733	$1,890	$1,728	$1,000	$ 720
EGA Genesis and CD	1,151	1,938	1,710	1,073	719
Total 16-bit	$2,884	$3,828	$3,438	$2,073	$1,439
Percent change		33%	−10%	−40%	−31%
Market Share					
Nintendo Super NES	60%	49%	50%	48%	50%
SEGA Genesis and CD	40	51	50	52	50
Total 16-bit	100%	100%	100%	100%	100%

Source: Gerard Klauer Mattison & Co.

However, the idea of having one common platform excites everyone except the hardware manufacturers. It would make life easier on developers, retailers, and consumers. Despite this, there seems to be little chance of that happening within the next five years. So far, no platform has emerged as dominant. Some experts expect the next generation of games could likely entail three or four relatively popular platforms.

It has been also difficult to speculate about the type of machine that will dominate in the future. Would it be a system dedicated solely to entertainment, or would the videogame machine of the future be multipurpose, more like today's computers? Some believe videogame machines could be replaced by an all-purpose electronic device that will deliver not only games but television programs, movies, and computer data. According to Nat Goldhaber, president of Kaleida Labs, "Once they no longer control the box, and once digital distribution of games becomes possible, how then will SEGA and Nintendo continue to be successful?"[14]

THE INTERACTIVE MULTIMEDIA MARKET[15] ————————

Consumers have demonstrated a strong interest in interactive multimedia forms of entertainment. In 1991, for example, consumers spent more (approximately $7 billion) on interactive coin-operated arcade games than they spent on tickets to movies (approximately $5.1 billion). Although videogame players and typical personal computers offer only limited graphics performance, over 150 million households worldwide have been consumers of interactive entertainment and education software. In 1991, U.S. consumers spent approximately $3 billion on interactive game software.

The potential customers for interactive multimedia systems form a consumer pyramid roughly divided into four tiers, consisting of innovators, early adopters, other current interactive system users, and mass market consumers (see Exhibit 3).

Products that have penetrated the first three tiers include both personal computers and SEGA and Nintendo videogame consoles. SEGA introduced its 16-bit Genesis

---

[14]Pollack, "Sega Takes Aim," p. 6.
[15]Extracted from The 3DO Company 10-K, 1993.

Exhibit 3   Multimedia Market Pyramid

Innovators have a history of buying new systems that offer significant technological improvements over existing alternatives and are generally insensitive to price, software availability, brand identification, breath of distribution, and factory support. It is believed that the class of innovators for home interactive media products consists of approximately 500,000 consumers.

Early adopters are similar to innovators except that they consider price/performance and software availability more carefully. Like innovators, they are motivated consumers who learn about a product through word-of-mouth even if it is not advertised heavily. It is believed the class of early adopters consists of several million consumers.

Interactive system users are consumers who currently own at least one interactive system such as a videogame console or a personal computer. These consumers base their purchase decisions on value, software availability, and price. It is believed that there are approximately 50 million households worldwide who are consumers of interactive entertainment and education software.

Mass market consumers are those who have televisions but are not current users of interactive multimedia products.

Source: 3DO 10-K.

system in the United States in 1989. This system offered a significant increase in performance and visual realism over existing 8-bit systems. (Think of the bits as the width of the highway along which game data travels; more bits allow better, faster, more dynamic games.)[16] Prior to Genesis, Nintendo had the dominant market share, brand recognition, broad distribution, and over 60 independent software companies supplying software exclusively for its 8-bit format, while SEGA had limited market share, distribution, or independent software support. Moreover, the price of SEGA's new 16-bit system was approximately twice that of Nintendo's 8-bit system. Despite these considerable obstacles, the superior characteristics of the Genesis system enabled SEGA to rapidly penetrate the first tier, selling an estimated 400,000 systems in the first year alone. By 1992, Genesis had entered the third tier, with an estimated worldwide base of approximately 9 million systems, and captured 40 percent of the U.S. 16-bit market.

Although some videogame consoles and personal computers have penetrated the third tier of interactive customers, no interactive multimedia system to date has gained acceptance as a mass market standard equivalent to that of the VCR and audio CD player in the consumer electronics market. To be successful in reaching the mass market, it is believed that any new interactive platform must provide several enhancements over existing systems: (1) a dramatic increase in audiovisual realism to appeal to innovators, (2) the broad-based support of hardware system manufacturers and software developers required to reach early adopters and achieve acceptance as a standard platform, and (3) sufficient value and affordability to reach current interactive system users and address the mass market. Existing interactive multimedia devices have not achieved full mass market penetration because they have not satisfied all of these criteria.

Advances in digital processing, storage, graphics, compression, and communication technologies are enabling a new generation of devices to address the home interactive

---

[16]M. Snider, "Video Market No Longer a 2-Player Game," *USA Today*, November 4, 1993, p. 1D.

multimedia market. Initial attempts focused on adding CD-ROM drives to existing videogames and PC-like architectures. Several large Japanese companies developed interactive video devices that utilize a CD-ROM drive. Some of the major computer product manufacturers, including Apple Computer, Inc., Microsoft Corporation, Silicon Graphics, Inc., International Business Machines Corporation, and Sony Corporation, are believed to be developing interactive video products.

Several major companies in the cable and telecommunications industry are developing methods to deliver interactive multimedia products and services through existing or planned cable and telephone networks. Additional strategic alliances and partnerships are expected to emerge as this segment of the industry develops further.

VIDEOGAME TECHNOLOGY[17]

There are seven principal types of hardware platforms (the systems that drive the videogame software): 8-bit, 16-bit, 32-bit, and 64-bit consoles, portable systems, CD-based systems, and home computers. Videogame machines are actually small computers. For example, the 16-bit chip that powers the SEGA Genesis also ran Apple's first Macintosh. The most popular 8-bit, 16-bit, and portable hardware systems are manufactured and marketed by Nintendo and SEGA. While videogame software has been marketed primarily in cartridge form for 8-, 16-, and 32-bit types of videogame systems, software products in the CD form are expected to replace cartridge-based products as the primary format during the next several years. Companies such as 3DO Company, SEGA, and Atari developed and are currently marketing CD-based delivery systems. In addition, a number of companies have announced the development of 32-bit or 64-bit game systems, collectively referred to as "next generation" players. Currently, there are more than 20 consumer computing and gaming formats available in the United States, all of which are incompatible. Exhibit 4 shows estimated sales and market shares for the 8-bit, 16-bit, portable, and next generation segments.

8-Bit Videogame Systems   Home entertainment systems based on 8-bit microprocessors were introduced in the early 1980s. Nintendo introduced the NES in the United States in 1985. It was estimated that at the end of 1993, the installed base of 8-bit videogame systems in the United States was approximately 35 million units, with approximately 700-plus software titles available for use with such videogame systems. Currently, software cartridges available for use on NES are developed by Nintendo as well as approximately 65 authorized Nintendo licensees worldwide.

Sales in recent years of 8-bit videogame systems and software cartridges for such systems have declined significantly. It is not expected that significant growth opportunities remain in this segment (see Exhibit 4). Nintendo recently announced it would discontinue manufacture of its NES.

16-Bit Videogame Systems   In 1989, SEGA introduced the 16-bit Genesis videogame system in the United States. The Genesis features a more powerful microprocessor, more colors, and superior graphics, animation, and sound relative to the NES.

---

[17]Extracted from Activision, Inc., 10-K, March 31, 1994.

**Exhibit 4   Estimated Sales and Market Share
Summary by Segment, 1992–1996   (in millions)**

	1992	1993	1994	1995	1996
8-bit	$ 720	$ 370	$ 124	$ 62	$ 30
16-bit	2,884	3,828	3,438	2,073	1,439
Portables	967	795	805	645	389
Next generation	49	115	658	2,030	4,014
Total industry	$4,620	$5,108	$5,025	$4,810	$5,872
Market Share					
8-bit	16%	7%	2%	1%	1%
16-bit	62	75	68	43	25
Portables	21	16	16	13	7
Next generation	1	2	13	42	68
Total industry	100%	100%	100%*	100%*	100%*

* Does not equal 100% due to rounding.
Source: Gerard Klauer Mattison & Co.

Nintendo introduced its 16-bit Super NES, with similar capabilities to Genesis, in the United States in September 1991. The 16-bit systems, because of their use of software cartridges, larger memories, and more advanced hardware, offer more realistic video images, natural sounds, and synthesized music. The challenge for software developers and publishers was to produce compelling products that took advantage of the game-playing capacity of the 16-bit systems. Suggested U.S. retail prices for both 16-bit consoles started at less than $100, and prices for the software products to be used on such consoles ranged from $19.95 to $79.95. It has been estimated that the installed base of 16-bit game systems in the United States is approximately 35 million (SEGA had 17 million) and the number of software titles available for use with the Genesis and the Super NES is more than 500 and 350, respectively.

Opportunities for 16-bit cartridge-based software are declining, as sales of both 16-bit hardware and software continue to weaken in the United States (see Exhibit 4). Declining 8-bit and 16-bit sales in Japan—which has historically been an early indicator of market changes in the interactive entertainment software industry—have led analysts to predict that strong sales of 16-bit software in the United States would not continue beyond calendar year 1995. It has been anticipated that 32-bit and 64-bit hardware and CD-based systems will displace 16-bit hardware.

32-Bit Videogame Systems   In November 1994, SEGA launched its Genesis 32-X adapter, which converts 16-bit Genesis videogame players into a more powerful 32-bit machine. The upgrade was designed to provide the more than 17 million Genesis owners a way to move to the next level in videogames (arcade-quality graphics and speed) at a reasonable cost. Other 32-bit systems include SEGA's Saturn and Sony's Playstation, both released in Japan in 1994 and expected to be released sometime in 1995 in the United States. Nintendo's portable Virtual Boy player was also intro-duced in the United States in early 1995. Combined sales for the three nonportable

32-bit players (SEGA 32-X, Saturn, and Playstation) were expected to reach $664 million in 1995, or about 33 percent of the market (see Exhibit 5). Both Nintendo and SEGA and their competitors announced plans to introduce 64-bit machines sometime in 1995 that would eclipse the 32-bit players.

64-Bit Videogame Systems   In November 1993, Atari introduced the Atari Jaguar, a 64-bit multimedia entertainment system at a suggested retail price of $249.95. The Jaguar features two proprietary chips (named "Tom" and "Jerry") developed in its own facilities, video with 24-bit graphics with up to 16 million colors, and a 3-D engine that can render 3-D shaded or texture map polygons in real time. The system also supports real-time texture mapping that allows for realistic surfaces to be applied over the 3-D polygons. Atari believed the graphics of the Jaguar video were equal to or superior to any other system currently available. Jaguar incorporates a 16-bit CD quality sound system, which provides realistic sounds in the software and includes human voices. The Jaguar also has a high-speed serial port that would allow for future connection into telephone networks as well as modem-based, two-player games over telephone lines.

Both Nintendo and SEGA were expected to introduce 64-bit players for home use in 1995, the Ultra 64 and Saturn. Nintendo's Ultra 64 was being designed by Silicon Graphics Inc., whose computer workstations had been used to design the 3-D special effects in such movies as *Jurassic Park, Terminator 2*, and *The Abyss*.[18] Estimated sales and market share positions for each of the major next generation machines are shown in Exhibit 5.

Handheld (Portable) Game Systems   Nintendo's release in 1989 of the Game Boy, a battery-operated, handheld interactive entertainment system incorporating an 8-bit microprocessor, revolutionized the handheld game machine market. Previously, the only handheld games available were dedicated to a single game. Game Boy offered a portable gaming system—a take-along Nintendo that allows players to insert any number of different game cartridges. SEGA's color Game Gear handheld system, released in 1991, competes directly with the Nintendo Game Boy. Atari offers a color portable handheld game system called the Atari Lynx, released in 1992. The Lynx provides 16-bit color graphics, stereo sound, fast action, and depth of game play, and comes complete with a built-in, eight-directional joypad and a 3.5-inch full color LCD offering up to 16 colors at one time from a palette of over 4,000 colors. At the end of 1993, the purchased base of handheld game systems was approximately 13 million and the numbers of software titles available for use with the Game Boy, the Game Gear, and the Atari Lynx were over 320, 100, and 65, respectively. For 1994, sales of portable systems were expected to peak at $806 million (see Exhibit 6), representing a 16 percent share of the market (see Exhibit 4).

CD-Based Systems[19]   With the introduction in recent years of computer disk drives that read optical laser disks, or "CDs," the ability to deliver complex entertainment software made significant technological advances. A CD has over 600 times more memory capacity than an 8-bit standard cartridge, enabling CD systems to incorporate

---

[18]Snider, "Video Market."
[19]Extracted from Activision Form 10-K, p. 8.

Exhibit 5   Estimated Sales and Market Share Summary: "Next Generation" Hardware and Software, 1993–1996   *(in millions)*

	1993	1994	1995	1996
3DO-based	$ 29	$370	$ 680	$1,260
Atari Jaguar	7	66	157	118
SEGA 32-X	—	158	218	133
Philips CD-I	78	64	54	171
SEGA Saturn	—	—	230	570
Sony Playstation	—	—	216	570
Nintendo Ultra-64	—	—	475	1,193
Total next generation	$114	$658	$2,030	$4,015
Market Share				
3DO-based	25%	56%	34%	31%
Atari-Juguar	6%	10%	8%	3%
SEGA 32-X	—	24%	11%	3%
Philips CD-I	68%	10%	3%	4%
SEGA Saturn	—	—	11%	14%
Sony Playstation	—	—	11%	14%
Nintendo Ultra-64	—	—	23%	30%
Total next generation	100%	100%	100%*	100%*

* Does not equal 100% due to rounding.
Source: Gerard Klauer Mattison & Co.

Exhibit 6   Estimated Sales and Market Share Summary: Portable Game Players, 1992–1996   *(in millions)*

	1992	1993	1994	1995	1996
Nintendo Game Boy	$770	$563	$415	$298	$220
SEGA Game Gear	162	219	388	348	169
Atari Lynx	35	13	3	—	—
Total portables	$967	$795	$806	$646	$389
Percent change		−18%	1%	−20%	−40%
Market Share					
Nintendo Game Boy	80%	71%	52%	46%	57%
SEGA Game Gear	17	28	48	54	43
Atari Lynx	4	2	0	—	—
Total portables	100%*	100%*	100%	100%	100%

* Does not equal 100% due to rounding.
Source: Gerard Klauer Mattison & Co.

large amounts of data, full motion video, and high-quality sound, thus creating vivid multimedia experiences.

In addition to personal computer disk drives that read CDs, known as CD-ROM drives, several CD-based videogame systems have been introduced by videogame hardware manufacturers: SEGA introduced its SEGA CD in 1992; 3DO released the

3DO Multiplayer in 1993; and Sony Corporation has a CD-based game system under development. Nintendo's new Ultra 64 does not employ CD capability. As the installed base of CD-ROM drives for personal computers increases and as the videogame industry moves more toward CD-based delivery systems, it is believed that the traditional differentiation between the videogame market and the personal computer market will become less distinct.

The market for entertainment software in a CD format is at an early stage of development. As industry standards are developed and prices for CD-based hardware decline, analysts estimate that the 1.4 million CD-ROM-equipped videogame machines in play at the close of 1993 could more than triple to 4.9 million units by the end of 1995. However, the CD-based market presents particular challenges for software developers and publishers. Entertainment software would have to incorporate increasingly sophisticated graphics (video and animation), data, and interactive capabilities, resulting in higher development costs and requiring successful software developers to coordinate talent from a variety of programming and technology disciplines in the development process.

CD-based delivery systems do, however, present advantages to software publishers. CDs are less expensive to manufacture ($1 to $2) than videogame cartridges and, unlike floppy disks, cannot yet be readily copied. Publishers could therefore expect to achieve higher profit margins from the sale of CDs than are currently the norm in the cartridge-based videogame or floppy disk–based computer software market. In addition, once a master copy is made, extra copies can be produced in small batch lots as needed. With a cartridge game, the manufacturing process takes about two months and costs from $10 to $20 (not including licensing fees).

Despite all the advantages, CD-ROM technology is far from ideal. The biggest problem related to playing videogames is speed. Compared to a cartridge system, it takes longer to access data on a compact disk. Access times are important, as most videogames require fast-paced action. Any slowdown in the access and processing of data negatively affects game play. However, as the technology advances and game developers become more experienced with CD-ROM, speed is expected to become less of a concern. Another related problem with CD-ROM technology is that the hardware is more expensive to manufacture. Currently, there is no standalone CD player under $200. Interviews of consumers have revealed that CDs are easily damaged by users. A single scratch could make a CD unreadable. Finally, there are a number of CD-ROM formats; a title written for one format will not necessarily work on another system.[20]

Exhibit 7 compares the major cartridge and CD-based systems.

Home Computers Approximately 36 percent of U.S. households have home computers. In 1994 alone, American consumers spent $9 billion to buy nearly 7 million personal computers. This has presented a new threat for videogame marketers. Industry analysts estimated that the home computer market was already siphoning off nearly 15 percent of videogame sales.

Although millions of Americans use home computers for spreadsheets and word processing, home computers are also taking on a different role. Most PCs sold feature multimedia packages that include faster processors, more memory and storage capacity, CD-ROM drives, and sound cards, all of which serve to make

---

[20]DFC Intelligence Research.

Exhibit 7   Comparative Data for Selected Video Game Systems, 1994

	Nintendo NES	SEGA Genesis	Nintendo SNES	Philips CD-I	SEGA CD	3DO	Atari Jaguar	SEGA Genesis 32-X
Release date	10/85	1/90	9/91	1991	10/92	10/93	11/93	11/94
U.S. installed base	35 million	17 million	18 million	250,000	1.5 million	200,000	125,000	500,000
Retail price	No longer manufactured	$90 to $120 (depending on bundled software)	$90 to $120 (depending on bundled software)	$300 (basic system); $500 (full system)	$220	$400	$250	$160
Available titles 1/95	700+	500+	350+	150+	50+	100+	<20	<10
Software unit sales (1994)	4 million (estimated)	23 million (estimated)	22 million (estimated)	<2 million	5 million (estimated)	<2 million	<1 million	NA
System type	Cartridge	Cartridge	Cartridge	Compact disc	CD	CD	Cartridge	Cartridge
System capabilities	8-bit processor, 1.79 MHz, 16 colors Resolution 256 × 240	16-bit processor, 7.6 MHz, 64 colors Resolution 320 × 224	16-bit processor, 3.58 MHz, 256 colors Resolution 512 × 418	16-bit processor, 15.5 MHz, 16.7 million colors	16-bit processor, Genesis processor, 12.7 MHz	32-bit RISC processor, 12.5 MHz, 16.7 million colors, Resolution 640 × 480	64-bit RISC processor, 16.7 million colors, Resolution 720 × 480	32-bit RISC processor (2), 23 MHz, 50,000 polygons/second, 32,768 colors

Sources: DFC Intelligence estimates based on company reports and various industry sources. 1994 software sales are preliminary estimates and intended to be ballpark figures only.

home computers a complete family entertainment center and all-purpose appliance for the Information Age.[21] The number of home computers with multimedia CD-ROMs was predicted to be more than 17 million by the end of 1995. It is expected that most homes in the United States will have home computers by the end of the century.

COIN-OPERATED ARCADE GAMES/THEME PARKS

Americans spend approximately $7 billion on arcade games each year. With the $5 billion spent on home versions for videogame hardware and software, the outcome is a combined market nearly two and one-half times the size of the $5 billion movie box office. Arcades have experienced a resurgence in interest in recent years, which may be partly attributed to the image of arcades becoming more "family-friendly." Although many arcades are still dark, smoky, scary dens located in shopping malls, a newer breed of family entertainment centers offers batting cages, bumper cars, fast food, and so on to draw the whole family rather than just teen-aged boys.[22] The video arcade has traditionally been the launching ground for games designed for home use and it has become clear that videogame buyers also like to sharpen their game-playing skills in arcades before buying home versions of the game.

SEGA currently operates two miniature theme parks in Japan, featuring both traditional videogames and larger virtual-reality and interactive rides that take players on adventures such as space battles or ghost hunts.[23] The company plans to open as many as 50 high-tech theme parks in the United States by the end of the century and is aggressively looking for partners to help. The first U.S. park has been scheduled to be built in Los Angeles at an estimated cost of $25 million.

SOFTWARE

Since 1988, the number of available videogame titles has increased substantially. The increase is attributed to the large number of SEGA and Nintendo licensees. At the end of 1994, for example, Nintendo had a library of 466 titles; SEGA had more than 500 titles for Genesis, 175 CD titles, and more than 200 titles for the Game Gear player.

Competitive forces in the entertainment software and videogame marketplace have increased the need for higher quality, distinctive entertainment software concepts. Competition for titles, themes, and characters from television, motion picture, and other media as the basis for "hits" has resulted in higher development costs for software producers. Substantial nonrefundable advance licensing fees and significant advertising expenses also increase the financial risk involved. Moreover, the ability to incorporate compelling story lines or game experiences with full motion video,

[21]L. Armstrong et al., "Home Computers," *Business Week*, November 28, 1994, pp. 89–94.
[22]Gerard Klauer Mattison & Co., Inc., *Interactive Electronic Industry: Entertainment Industry Overview* (New York, 1993), p. 9.
[23]D. P. Hamilton, "SEGA Looks Abroad for Partners to Open Theme Parks in U.S.," *The Wall Street Journal*, August 16, 1994, p. B6.

digital sound, other lifelike technology, and ease of use present artistic as well as technical challenges that add to the cost equation.[24]

Software is priced to generate most of the profit; the hardware typically sells for less than $200. Game software for most machines runs between $40 and $60. Software developer costs to develop a new videogame have ranged from $75,000 to $300,000, with some CD titles costing $1 million to develop.[25] The cost to manufacture an interactive CD selling for $40 is approximately $1 to $2. A software publisher could produce a videogame cartridge (including royalties) for between $15 to $25 per unit.[26] To compensate for games that turn out to be duds, companies need some megahits.[27] In 1992, SEGA earned $450 million on worldwide sales on one game, "Sonic 2." In August 1993, the top five videogames accounted for 27 percent of industry sales, with the next five games accounting for about 8.3 percent. Sales are even more concentrated among the top titles during the holiday season.

Both SEGA and Nintendo each have more than 65 companies licensed to develop software for use with their respective systems. Typically, the software developer submits a prototype for evaluation and approval from Nintendo or SEGA, including all artwork to be used in packaging and marketing the product. With several kinds of CD players, all incompatible, software developers trying to penetrate the entire market must incur additional expense to re-create their games for each different system.[28]

Several motion picture companies have joined the interactive entertainment software segment. Paramount created Paramount Interactive in 1993 to develop products based on Paramount's motion pictures, television, and sports properties. Early game titles included "*Viper:* Assault on the Outfit," a futuristic car adventure based on the television series, and "*Star Trek: Deep Space Nine*—The Hunt," a role-playing adventure. In an exclusive agreement with Paramount, software publishers Spectrum HoloByte released several titles based on *Star Trek: The Next Generation.* Warner Bros. teamed up with game publisher Konami to release *Batman—The Animated Series* for Super NES. Warner also worked with Konami and Virgin Interactive Entertainment (VIE) to feature over 1,500 original animations within game play. According to Martin Alper, CEO of VIE, "This level of collaboration between a major studio and a game company is unique and, no doubt, will become a benchmark for future products of this nature."[29]

Capital Cities/ABC Inc. formed a joint venture in December 1994 with Electronic Arts, a pioneer in interactive software, to develop software and videogames based on ABC's children and news TV shows. The new venture was expected to produce about 12 titles a year, starting in December 1995, mostly on CD-ROM, and expand eventually to about 25 titles a year.[30] In December 1994, the Walt Disney Co. also announced formation of a new computer software unit that would produce educational programs and videogames inspired by its movies. The division intended to

[24]Ibid.

[25]T. Abate, "Atari Wants Back in the Game," *San Francisco Examiner*, February 13, 1994, p. E5.

[26]3DO Company 10-K, 1993, p. 6.

[27]N. Hutheesing, "Platform Battle," *Forbes*, May 9, 1994, pp. 168–170.

[28]Ibid.

[29]Much of this section is extracted from J. Abrams, "Hollywood Comes to Las Vegas," *Dealerscope*, February 1994, pp. 24, 26.

[30]E. Jensen, "Capital Cities and Electronic Arts Plan Venture in Software and Video Games," *The Wall Street Journal*, December 6, 1994, p. B4.

focus initially on SEGA and Nintendo videogames and CD-ROM educational software linked to its animated musicals, including *Pocahontas*.[31]

Earlier attempts to link movies and games had failed, most notably Walt Disney's film based on "Super Mario Bros.," the best-selling videogame series ever. However, more efforts to create movies bringing the best-selling arcade games to the silver screen were underway. *Double Dragon* was released in November 1994; *Street Fighter* (at a cost of $40 million) was released in December 1994;[32] *Mortal Kombat* ($36 million) was released in April 1995. Also on the horizon are movies based on "Doom," "Myst," "King's Quest," and "Leisure Suit Larry."

VIDEOGAME DEVELOPMENT ISSUES ———————————

Firms must resolve four key considerations in developing a videogame: (1) what development and distribution agreement to arrange, (2) whether to acquire content or create original content, (3) which platform to develop for, and (4) future employment concerns. Each of these issues is discussed in the following sections.[33]

Development and Distribution Agreements   The distribution channels for videogames and other multimedia are constantly evolving. The common method is for a publisher to hire a developer to create a title. The developer is responsible for ensuring the quality of the product. The publisher handles manufacturing, packaging, marketing, and distribution issues. The publisher bears the risk if the product fails. Generally, developers are paid a royalty based on wholesale revenues. This royalty varies greatly, but typically ranges from 5 to 15 percent.

Many developers attempt to publish their own titles. Affiliated label and copublishing programs have become a popular means for small companies to publish their own titles and maintain their independence. Under an affiliated label program, a developer handles marketing and publishing, while a copublisher deals with distribution. In return, the developer receives a royalty of up to 75 percent of wholesale revenue. A variation on the affiliated label program is expected to become the distribution method of choice.

Acquiring Content   In the past, companies that owned popular intellectual property would license that property for use in videogames in return for a modest royalty. But the vast market potential for games had made content-owners reluctant to license their properties, and acquiring high-potential creative content was becoming difficult and time-consuming. Many large entertainment conglomerates have set up interactive divisions to create titles based on their own intellectual creations and titles. In the future, more publishers will be forced to base their games on original content or else rely on works in the public domain.

---

[31]J. Horn, "Disney Forms Interactive Unit Division to Create Computer Software Linked to Its Movies," *San Francisco Chronicle*, December 6, 1994, p. D3.

[32]J. Carlton, "Capcom Bets That Stars and a Story Can Turn a Hot Game into a Hit Film," *The Wall Street Journal*, October 6, 1994, pp. B1, B6.

[33]This section extracted from DFC Intelligence Research.

Platform Considerations   The videogame market is fast reaching the point where it is essential that a software title be released for a number of different hardware platforms. Even worse, the number of hardware platforms is growing. Each platform is incompatible and requires a different set of development tools. The personal computer is the easiest platform to develop for, but personal computer titles so far have had limited revenue potential. Creating titles for the dedicated systems is more time-consuming and difficult. As a general rule, it takes 12 to 18 months to develop a software title for the first platform, and 3 to 6 months for each additional platform.

The manufacturers of the dedicated systems (platform providers) control who can develop for their system. A license from the platform provider is required to develop a dedicated system. Licensees pay the platform provider royalty fees based on sales volume. Platform providers often regulate content and limit the number of titles that can be released. Nintendo and SEGA have high licensing fees and are strict about what titles can be released for their systems. 3DO has lower licensing fees and is not as strict about regulating content.

Publishers must carefully consider which platforms to develop for. Currently, no CD-ROM platform has a large enough installed base to make it feasible to publish a title for just one platform. In making the decision of which platform to choose, development costs, installed base figures, licensing fees, and player demographics must be studied.

Employment Concerns   Top development talent is a rare commodity. In the future, developers are expected to have significant bargaining power. Hollywood guilds and agents are just now starting to organize multimedia developers. As this trend continues, development costs are projected to rise.

THE VIDEOGAME DEVELOPMENT PROCESS[34]

The development of videogames requires a blend of technology and creative talent. Typically, a development team is formed consisting of a producer, designers, programmers, musicians, and graphic artists. The average cartridge game involves the efforts of 10 to 15 individuals, although it is not unusual for many more people to be involved.

The producer oversees the project and is responsible for coordinating the efforts of the development team. Designers come up with the basic concepts for the game, draft the script, and are responsible for the characters, plot, and overall objectives of the game. Graphic artists draw the characters and objects in the game. Programmers write the computer code that incorporates all the various elements into a form that can be used on the appropriate hardware platform.

Once a workable version of the game has been created, preliminary testing is done to evaluate the computer code and to ensure all the game elements are in place. If all has gone well, the game is play-tested to find any hidden bugs. The next level involves bringing in a group of outside players to test the game's reception with the general public. Only after the completion of all testing can a product be sent off for manufacturing and packaging.

---

[34]Extracted from DFC Intelligence Research.

Because it takes 10 to 15 months to complete an original game and then another 3 to 6 months to port that game to another platform development risks are quite high. A lot could change between the time a design was started and the time it is launched in the marketplace. A platform that was popular last year could be out of fashion 12 months later.

DEMOGRAPHICS

Videogames are in 69 percent of homes with kids 12 to 17; computers are in 18 percent of homes with kids under 18.[35] Not all videogame customers are teenagers, however. Adults—mostly men—rent sports games like "Bill Walsh College Football" and "NBA Jam." Men in their 20s and 30s represent a growing portion of the videogame market.[36] Nintendo's U.S. player demographics are shown in Exhibit 8. The U.S. population of 10- to 20-year-olds and 30- to 50-year-olds is shown in Exhibit 9.

Studies have indicated that many children who grew up playing videogames continue to do so as adults. There are several key differences between adult and younger players. Adolescents are more concerned with what is "in" and "hot." The adult market is composed of numerous niches, each with an interest in a different type of game. Adults like titles that fit in with their life-styles and interests. It is difficult to create one title that appeals to the entire adult market. In addition, the biggest complaint among adults is that most games take too much time to play. Adults prefer to play games in short bursts during free moments.[37]

Generally, videogames have not been popular with women. Many of the most popular games deal with such activities as street fighting, car racing, and football. According to the Software Publishers Association, about 28 percent of computer game and 21 percent of videogame players are female. Only one top videogame, Nintendo's "Super Metroid," has a female lead character. Software developers are slowly responding to this untapped market and rolling out games for girls. SEGA, for example, formed a task force composed of the top female marketers and game developers in the company to develop software products that appeal to female tastes.

A clue to what videogames appeal to women comes from Nintendo's experience with its Game Boy handheld players. The company found that women accounted for 40 percent of the 27 million worldwide buyers of Game Boy, a figure double the percentage of women buying its other machines. For some unknown reason, women liked "Tetris," a geometric videogame that was packaged with Game Boy. One 14-year-old boy wrote Nintendo about his mother, saying, "Almost 24 hours a day she plays Tetris . . . I can't hardly play more than one game a day."[38] Nintendo has hired experts to study adult Game Boy habits.

In another study of 10,000 children playing video and computer games over two years, Electronic Arts found that girls (1) identify with characters in videogames, (2) like fast action and competitive games less than boys, (3) prefer something they can learn from, and (4) really enjoy puzzle solving and cooperative games that allow them to create and design.

---

[35]"Electronic Games Look to Untapped Girls' Market," *San Jose Mercury News*, November 11, 1994, p. 2D.
[36]D. Wharton, "Video Legions," *Los Angeles Times* (Valley Edition), November 18, 1994, p. 10.
[37]DFC Intelligence Research.
[38]J. Carlton, "Game Makers Study How Tetris Hooks Women," *The Wall Street Journal*, May 10, 1994, p. B1.

Exhibit 8   Nintendo SNES U.S. Player Demographics

Age	Percent of Players
Under 6	2%
6–14	48
15–17	11
18+	39

Gender	Percent of SNES Players	Percent of Game Boy Players
Male	82%	59%
Female	18%	41%

Source: Nintendo.

The biggest challenge in the videogame industry is to get more adults and females to play videogames. Although numerous studies are underway, no especially successful approaches has emerged.

MARKETING[39]

In the past, the marketing of videogames was unsophisticated. Demand was created from the advertising campaigns of platform providers such as Nintendo and SEGA. Demand was so strong that publishers merely had to get their product into the store and it would sell. Advertising was an attempt to gain word-of-mouth publicity and might have consisted of a few pages in the leading videogame consumer magazines and a booth at the Consumer Electronics Show.

As of 1994 videogame marketing is big business. As retail space has become crowded, the industry witnessed a marked shift in marketing strategy. The major videogame releases are now marketed much like a release from a major movie studio. Television advertising, promotional tie-ins, merchandising, direct mail, and special launch parties are now commonplace. A well-planned marketing campaign is now a must for a hit game.

Many industry observers believe the videogame industry is becoming a "hits"-driven business as marketing costs escalate and access to retail space becomes tighter. Small game publishers without the resources of the big players in the industry face an uphill battle. These publishers are likely to be caught in a Catch-22 situation. Retailers only take their product if they have a strong brand name, backed with advertising dollars. But without shelf space, it is hard for small publishers to build a brand image and start generating the revenue necessary to fund large-scale marketing campaigns.

Toy stores and computer software stores have been the traditional retailers of videogames. However, as the videogame business has grown, other retailers have begun carrying high-margin product. In 1994, over 20,000 stores in the United States

---

[39]Extracted from DFC Intelligence Report.

Exhibit 9 U.S. Population Data, 1984–2000

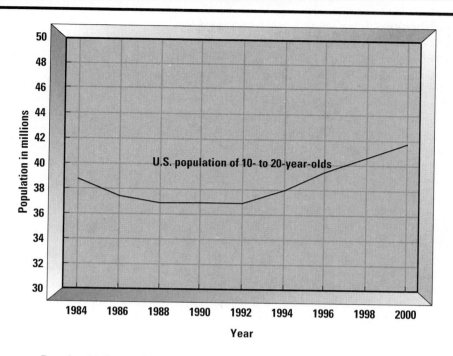

Based on birth rates from U.S. Census Bureau. Does not account for immigration.

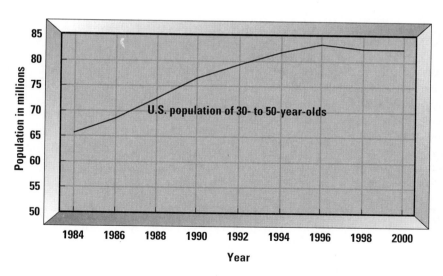

Based on birth rates from U.S. Census Bureau. Does not account for immigration.

Source: Gerard Klauer Mattison & Co.

carried videogames. Toys "Я" Us was the leading retailer with an estimated 20 percent of the U.S. market; mass merchandisers (e.g., Wal-Mart and Kmart) captured about 35 percent of all videogame sales. Exhibit 10 shows estimated market share by retail outlet.

Industry growth has created new competitive challenges for retailers. It was only a few years ago that demand for games was so high that a retailer could sell whatever was put on the shelf: Even the bad games sold. The major complaint of retailers was not having enough products. Nintendo went so far as to ration games in 1988 and 1989. All this changed as the market became flooded with product and Nintendo began to face increased competition from SEGA. In 1994, retailers found many of the 16-bit cartridges sitting unsold on the shelf; sales seem to be concentrated in a handful of hit titles. Moreover, most videogames had a shelf life of 30 to 60 days, after which they were sold at a discount. With retailers holding excess inventory, it was not uncommon to see games that originally listed for $60 discounted to the $15 to $20 range. The net effect was a substantial decline in profit margins. DFC Intelligence Research identified that retailers were most concerned about the difficulty of deciding what to buy, the lack of a return policy, and heavy discounting from increased competition. Consequently, retailers became very careful about what they would stock. Retail buyers looked at three things when deciding what product to stock: the quality of the game, the amount of advertising the publisher planned to do, and the reputation of the publisher.

Despite overcrowding of traditional distribution channels, analysts expected new channels of distribution to emerge. Technology was making new forms of distribution possible. Several companies are engaging in experiments that could revolutionize distribution. These experiments involve such things as direct marketing, electronic distribution in retail, on demand via cable television, and on-line distribution through networks such as the Internet. Finally, there is the potential that the increased bandwidth of phone and cable systems could make multiplayer networked gaming possible.

SEASONALITY[40]

Retail sales for videogames are quite slow between May and August. Analysts attribute the sales slowdown to several factors. First, teenagers spend much more time outside rather than indoors playing videogames. They watch less TV, thus making them less reachable via advertising. In addition, because they are out of school, there is less "I got to level 10, how far did you get?" to spur sales. Finally, sales are slower because the publishers put out fewer games. Two-thirds of the videogame sales occur during the year-end holiday season.

THE INFORMATION SUPERHIGHWAY[41]

According to best estimates, there are approximately 25 million people on the Internet, with the number of users growing by about 2.5 million each month. While American media companies scramble to develop strategies to put themselves on the

---

[40]This section was extracted from Gerard Klauer Mattison Industry Overview, 1993.
[41]This section was extracted from M. Schrage, "Why Sonic the Hedgehog Needs to Jump onto the Info Highway," *Los Angeles Times* (Business Section), November 3, 1994, p. 1.

Exhibit 10   Estimated U.S. Retail Outlet Market Shares for Videogames, 1994

Toys "Я" Us	20%
Other toy stores (e.g., Kay Bee Toys)	10
Computer software (e.g., Babbages)	15
Video and music stores (e.g., Blockbuster)	15
Consumer electronics (e.g., Best Buy)	5
Mass Merchants (e.g., Wal-Mart)	35
	100%

Source: DFC Intelligence estimates based on various industry sources.

Internet, both Nintendo and SEGA nixed any plan to put their games on-line even though on-line services are one of the fastest-growing segments in the global media market. Companies like America Online, CompuServe, Delphi, and Prodigy have all enjoyed double-digit growth. Microsoft planned to introduce its Marvel on-line service in 1995. On-line services had also taken off in Japan. Most observers believed that games would become an important ingredient in all these services. In fact, one observer predicted that in the not-too-distant future, people miles apart would play tennis, golf, and perhaps Virtuality Boxing together on global information highways.[42] George Lucas, creator of the *Star Wars* and *Indiana Jones* film trilogies, in an interview in the *Wall Street Journal*, commented on the future interaction of entertainment and technology:

> "Well, I have a game company, and I think view-on-demand games will take off pretty quickly. It's a little bit problematical about how it's going to work, but it seems obvious that home delivery of games is a natural . . . Interactive games that involve more than one player . . . will be popular. You're playing with two or three other people at the same time at various places over the phone . . ."[43]

Nintendo and SEGA pursued radically different strategies for bringing telecommunications to their game machines, neither of which included the telephone. Nintendo elected to go the satellite route. In 1993, Nintendo paid $8 million for a 20 percent stake in St. Giga, a troubled Japanese satellite broadcaster, for the purpose of downloading games by satellite to Japan's 14 million Nintendo game players. Although considered a novel distribution concept, this approach does not support any opportunity for networked games people can play with or against each other.

SEGA began test-marketing its SEGA Channel in the United States in early 1994, and formed SEGA Digital Communications Ltd. in July 1994 to put videogames on cable in Japan. However, the technology is such that the system does not allow for interpersonal interactivity.

New services are springing up to deliver games over phone lines. Catapult Entertainment, Inc., is selling Xband Videogame Network, which matches players of

---

[42]J. Guyon, "Virtual Center," *The Wall Street Journal* (Entertainment & Technology), March 21, 1994, p. R18.
[43]T. R. King, "Lucasvision," *The Wall Street Journal* (Entertainment & Technology), March 21, 1994, p. R20.

similar skill levels to play SEGA with people around the country. The service requires use of a $70 Xband modem available in toy and computer stores. A similar on-line service is available for computer games users from ImagiNation that connects evenly matched players who pay a base fee of $9.95 for five hours of play. Microsoft plans to offer PlayersNet, a software package that also allows PC users to compete against each other over computer networks or telephone lines using a modem.

Some industry analysts predicted that videogame companies were well positioned to take advantage of future opportunities related to the "information superhighway." They argued that a videogame machine could evolve into a set-top box that connects to fiber-optic cable networks and delivers interactive services into the home. Companies with the skills to develop and market such hardware at prices well below the cost of home computers could then offer interactive products with the potential to become an important part of the future.[44]

PROFILES OF SELECTED VIDEOGAME COMPETITORS

Nintendo and SEGA's key competitors in the videogame industry included Sony, 3DO, Atari, and Philips Electronics NV. Commodore reentered the videogame industry with a CDTV system in 1991, and more recently with the Amiga CD32; however, sales were less than expected, and the company was not considered a significant player. Neither was NEC Corporation. In late 1994, Apple Computer, Inc., formed an alliance with Japan's largest toy maker (Bandai Co., Ltd.) to build a low-cost CD-ROM videogame player, which was expected to be available worldwide for the 1995 holiday season. Exhibit 11 summarizes estimated U.S. videogame industry retail sales and market share statistics for each of the key competitors.

Nintendo Company, Ltd.[45]

Nintendo began as a playing card manufacturer in 1889 in Kyoto, Japan. In 1994, the company was headed by the great grandson of Nintendo's founder, Hiroshi Yamauchi. Yamauchi had been in charge since becoming the company's president in 1922 at the age of 22.

Under Yamauchi's leadership the company began to expand into the toy business. Nintendo became NCL, Nintendo Company, Ltd., and went public in the early 1960s. In 1975, Nintendo made its first venture into videogames when it got a license to sell Magnavox's videogame system in Japan. Nintendo released its own home videogame system in 1977 and soon began to develop arcade games.

Nintendo eventually designed a game system that could use interchangeable cartridges. The machine, called the Famicom (short for Family Computer), was released in Japan in 1983. The 8-bit Famicom sold for about $100, considerably less than the $250 to $300 most game systems cost at that time. Nintendo sold 500,000 units in the Famicom's first two months. The 14 competing systems soon withdrew from the market and Nintendo became the home videogame leader in Japan.

---

[44]DFC Intelligence Research.
[45]Nintendo's company background provided by DFC Intelligence Research.

Exhibit 11 Estimated U.S. Videogame Industry Sales and Market Share Data: Retail Sales of Hardware and Software, 1992–1996 (in millions)

	1992	Share	1993	Share	1994	Share	1995	Share	1996	Share
Nintendo										
NES Hardware	$ 180	4%	$ 120	2%	$ 49	1%	$ 25	1%	$ 10	0%
NES Software	540	12	250	5	75	1	38	1	20	0
Game Boy Hardware	320	7	263	5	165	3	138	3	100	2
Game Boy Software	450	10	300	6	250	5	160	3	120	2
Super NES Hardware	743	16	625	12	518	10	250	5	180	3
Super NES Software	990	21	1,265	25	1,210	24	750	16	540	9
Ultra 64 Hardware	—	—	—	—	—	—	125	3	563	10
Ultra 64 Software	—	—	—	—	—	—	350	7	630	11
Total Nintendo	$3,223	70%	$2,823	55%	$2,267	45%	$1,835	38%	$2,162	37%
SEGA										
Genesis Hardware	$ 440	$10	$ 550	$11	$ 400	$ 8	$ 223	$ 5	$ 170	$ 3
Genesis Software	650	14	1,156	23	1,000	20	675	14	480	8
Game Gear Hardware	72	2	99	2	223	4	223	5	89	2
Game Gear Software	90	2	120	2	165	3	125	3	80	1
SEGA CD Hardware	45	1	150	3	173	3	100	2	36	1
SEGA CD Software	17	0	83	2	138	3	75	2	33	1
32-X Hardware	—	—	—	—	75	1	94	2	50	1
32-X Software	—	—	—	—	83	2	124	3	83	1
Saturn Hardware	—	—	—	—	—	—	164	—	350	6
Saturn Software	—	—	—	—	—	—	66	—	220	4
Total SEGA	$1,313	$28	$2,157	$42	$2,255	$45	$1,868	$39	$1,591	$27
Atari										
Jaguar Hardware	—	—	$ 5	$0.1	$ 42	$ 1	$ 80	$ 2	$ 48	$ 1
Jaguar Software	—	—	2	0.0	24	0	60	1	38	1
Lynx Hardware	$ 20	$ 0	9	0.2	2	0	—	—	—	—
Lynx Software	15	0	4	0.1	1	0	—	—	—	—
Jaguar CD Hardware	—	—	—	—	—	—	10	0	18	0
Jaguar CD Software	—	—	—	—	—	—	8	0	15	0
Total Atari	$ 35	$ 1	$ 20	$0.4	$ 69	$ 1	$ 157	$ 3	$ 118	$ 2
3DO-based										
Hardware	—	—	$ 21	$ 0	$ 167	$ 3	$ 350	$ 7	$ 600	$10
Software	—	—	8	0	204	4	330	7	660	11
Total 3DO-based	—	—	$ 29	$ 1	$ 370	$ 7	$ 680	$14	$1,260	$21
Sony										
Playstation Hardware	—	—	—	—	—	—	$ 150	$ 3	$ 350	$ 6
Playstation Software	—	—	—	—	—	—	66	1	220	4
Total Sony	—	—	—	—	—	—	$ 216	$ 4	$ 570	$10
CD-I										
CD-I Hardware	$ 35	$ 1	$ 50	$ 1	$ 40	$ 1	$ 39	$ 1	$ 105	$ 2
CD-I Software	14	0	28	1	24	0	15	0	66	1
Total CD-I	$ 49	$ 1	$ 78	$ 2	$ 64	$ 1	$ 54	$ 1	$ 171	$ 3
Total Industry	$4,619	100%	$5,107	100%	$5,024	100%	$4,809	100%	$5,872	100%
Percent change from prior year			10.6%		−1.6%		−4.3%		22.1%	

In 1980, Nintendo decided to enter the U.S. market and Nintendo of America (NOA) was established as an independent subsidiary. The first president of NOA was Minoru Arakawa, Hiroshi Yamauchi's son-in-law. The original goal of NOA was to break into the $8 billion a year arcade business. Arcade games from Japan were shipped to the United States and distributed by NOA.

At first, business for NOA was slow, mainly because Nintendo did not have a hit game. That changed in 1981 with the release of "Donkey Kong," created by legendary Nintendo game developer, Sigeru Miyamota. Donkey Kong was such a success in the United States that NOA ended its second year in business with over $100 million in sales.

In 1984, Nintendo began to think about bringing the Famicom to the United States. But, because the U.S. home videogame market had crashed in 1983, no manufacturers, distributors, or retailers would have anything to do with videogames. Nintendo decided to proceed cautiously and began to test the Famicom in New York in 1985. For the U.S. release, the Famicom was renamed the Nintendo Entertainment System (NES). Slowly orders began to come in, and over Christmas 1985, 50,000 units were sold.

As noted earlier, the NES went on sale nationwide in 1986. By the end of its first year more than 1 million units had been sold in the United States. Three million units had been sold by the end of 1987, and "The Legend of Zelda" became the first game to sell over a million copies. Nintendo mania had begun.

As the NES gained momentum, sales increased from $1 billion in 1987 to over $5 billion in 1992. Game Boy, a portable videogame system released in 1989, sold 40,000 units the first day it was available in the United States. The Super Nintendo Entertainment System (SNES) was released in the United States in 1991. Sales of the SNES took off in 1992 fueled by Nintendo's marketing expertise and the release of Capcoms's "Street Fighter II." The SNES then became Nintendo's top-selling system.

As of 1994, Nintendo had been forced to undergo some significant changes. Nintendo had had to deal with increased competition and a declining 16-bit market. Nintendo received a wake-up call in 1993 when SEGA passed Nintendo in sales of 16-bit systems. Nintendo suddenly realized it no longer had the monopoly it once enjoyed. Unhappy with the performance of his U.S. subsidiary, Yamauchi replaced his son-in-law as the leader of NOA and installed Howard Lincoln, a senior vice president, as chairman.

Exhibit 12 presents summary financial data on Nintendo. During fiscal year 1994, Nintendo sold more videogame cartridges than in any previous year. However, consolidated net sales fell to $4.714 billion, a 23.5 percent decline from the previous year, and the company's consolidated net income of $511 million decreased by 40 percent from 1993. This represented Nintendo's first decline in sales and net income since it introduced the Famicom in Japan in 1983. Nintendo's stock had fallen from a high of ¥17,500 ($150.86) in 1992 to a low of ¥6,140 ($59.61) in 1994.

Sales in Nintendo's home sanctuary were healthy in fiscal 1994, but the strong yen seriously affected the company's performance around the globe. A weak economy in Europe and a soft market in the United States, coupled with increased competition, further hurt export sales. The fact that Nintendo did not introduce any new product categories in 1994 did not help its performance. However, Nintendo's overall financial position remained quite strong. The company had cash and cash equivalents of over $3.334 billion, no debt, and total liabilities of only $1.427 billion. Nintendo's liabilities-to-equity ratio was 0.33 at the end of fiscal year 1994, down from 0.51 the previous year.

Exhibit 12   Consolidated Financial Summary for Nintendo Co., Ltd., 1992–1994   (in thousands of $)

	Year Ended March 31		
	1994	1993	1992
Net sales	$4,714,675	$6,161,840	$4,843,475
Cost of goods sold	2,887,106	3,758,376	2,926,885
Gross profit	$1,827,569	$2,403,464	$1,916,590
Selling, general, and administrative expenses	693,507	650,360	483,115
Operating income	$1,134,062	$1,753,104	$1,433,475
Other income/(expenses):			
Interest income	110,392	175,380	206,823
Other	(230,727)	(104,973)	(81,971)
Total	(120,335)	70,407	124,852
Income before income taxes	$1,013,727	$1,823,511	$1,558,327
Income taxes	576,497	967,261	807,653
Foreign currency translation adjustments	73,968	4,031	224
Net income	$ 511,198	$ 860,281	$ 750,898
Net income per share	$ 3.61	$ 6.08	$ 5.30
Cash dividend	0.68	0.68	0.52
Cash and cash equivalents	3,334,679	3,425,000	2,549,144
Current assets	5,037,417	4,638,570	3,968,830
Total assets	5,740,070	5,248,012	4,458,664
Current liabilities	1,355,426	1,693,274	1,587,965
Total liabilities	1,427,515	1,762,738	1,626,353
Stockholders' equity	4,312,555	3,485,274	2,832,311

Source: Company annual reports.

For the six-month period ending September 30, 1994 (fiscal year 1995), Nintendo reported that earnings slipped 17 percent to $520 million from $623 million in the same period the previous year. Weak demand for its old games coupled with a strong yen against the dollar hurt sales revenue. Nintendo projected selling 6.5 million units of software worldwide in 1995, but later revised its estimate to a more realistic 2.5 million. Nintendo counted on Virtual Boy and Ultra 64 to reverse declining profits and help fuel sales growth in 1995.[46]

SEGA Enterprises, Ltd.[47]

SEGA Enterprises, Ltd. (SEGA) was one of the few Japanese companies started by Americans. In 1951, two Americans in Tokyo, Raymond Lemaire and Richard Stewart, began importing jukeboxes to supply American military bases in Japan. Their company eventually expanded into amusement game imports and adopted the

---

[46]"Tough Year Crimps Nintendo Earnings," *USA Today*, November 22, 1994, p. 08B.
[47]Portions of SEGA's company history extracted from DFC Intelligence Research.

slogan "service and games."[48] The modern SEGA began to take shape in 1956 when a Brooklyn-born entrepreneur named David Rosen, who had been stationed in Japan with the Air Force, returned to Japan and began importing mechanical coin-operated amusement machines as Rosen Enterprises. In 1965, the "service and games" company merged with Rosen Enterprises. Not happy with the game machines available from U.S. manufacturers, Rosen decided to make his own and acquired a Japanese factory that made jukeboxes and slot machines. The company stamped SEGA on its games—short for service games—and Rosen adopted the brand name that persists today.[49] The next year it began its transformation from importer to manufacturer, producing a submarine warfare arcade game called "Periscope," which became a worldwide hit.

SEGA was acquired by Gulf & Western (G&W) in 1969 and went public in 1974. Hayao Nakayama, a Japanese entrepreneur and former SEGA distributor, was recruited to head SEGA's Japanese operation; Rosen headed the U.S. operation. Through the 1970s and early 1980s, the videogame industry went through a boom period. SEGA's revenues reached $214 million in 1982. The overall game industry hit $3 billion in 1982, but collapsed three years later with sales of $100 million. G&W became anxious to divest SEGA. Nakayama and Rosen organized a buyout of SEGA's assets for $38 million in 1984 and SEGA Enterprises, Ltd., was formed. The deal was backed by CSK, a large Japanese software company that now owns 20 percent of SEGA. Nakayama became the chief executive and Rosen headed the U.S. subsidiary. SEGA went public in 1986. Rosen was later made a director of SEGA and cochairman of its American subsidiary.

SEGA of America was formed in 1986. Its first task was to market SEGA's first home videogame system, the 8-bit Master System. SEGA had been beaten to the punch in Japan by Nintendo, which got a jump on the market with its 1983 release of the 8-bit Famicom. Unfortunately for SEGA, Nintendo also won the 8-bit war in the United States and the Master System slowly died out. Meanwhile, Nintendo essentially grabbed the entire home videogame market share in the United States and Japan.

Europe was a different story. SEGA systems achieved success in Europe, while Nintendo sales were slow. SEGA of Europe accounted for a large share of SEGA's revenues, and some of SEGA's recent sales declines were due to the slumping European market.

SEGA did not begin to see mass-scale success until the release of its 16-bit Genesis system in 1989. The Genesis system was not an immediate hit. It took the release of "Sonic the Hedgehog" in 1991 for sales to take off. In 1994, the Genesis was challenging Nintendo's SNES as the leading 16-bit system in the United States, and SEGA was considered Nintendo's equal in the videogame industry.

Fiscal 1994 was a lackluster year for SEGA as well as Nintendo. A weak Japanese economy and a dismal consumer market in Europe coupled with an unexpectedly sharp appreciation of the yen against other major currencies resulted in a 12.8 percent increase in net consolidated sales from fiscal 1993 to $4 billion but a 58.9 percent decline in net income to $108.7 million (see Exhibit 13). The sharp decrease in net income was caused by a net loss from SEGA's European operations. From a high of ¥11,000 in 1992, SEGA's stock price declined to a low of ¥7,010 at the end of 1994.

---

[48]"Sega's American Roots," *The New York Times*, July 4, 1993, p. 6.
[49]R. Brandt, R. D. Hof, and P. Coy, "SEGA!" *Business Week*, February 21, 1994, pp. 66–74.

Exhibit 13 — Consolidated Financial Summary for SEGA Enterprises, Ltd., 1993–1994 *(in thousands of $)*

	Year Ended March 31	
	1994	1993
Net sales	$4,038,197	$3,578,968
Cost of goods sold	2,916,161	2,301,496
Gross profit	$1,122,036	$1,277,472
Selling, general and administrative expenses	831,837	697,988
Operating income	$ 290,199	$ 579,484
Other income/(expenses):		
Interest income	47,561	33,353
Other	(78,865)	(104,024)
Total	(31,304)	(70,671)
Income before income taxes	$ 258,895	$ 508,813
Income taxes	249,259	267,102
Foreign currency statements translation	99,089	22,752
Net income	$ 108,725	$ 264,463
Net income per share	$ 1.09	$ 2.72
Cash dividend	0.37	0.21
Cash and cash equivalents	1,000,262	963,646
Current assets	2,398,652	2,185,073
Total assets	3,482,821	3,026,354
Current liabilities	1,261,454	1,084,437
Total liabilities	1,973,999	2,001,006
Stockholders' equity	1,508,822	1,025,348
Effective tax rate	0.52	0.52

Source: Company annual reports.

Exhibit 14 depicts SEGA's sales by division (nonconsolidated). Sales of consumer products in 1994 reached $2.3 billion, a 16 percent increase, and accounted for 66.6 percent of net sales. Strong overseas demand for SEGA's products, particularly in the United States, offset the falloff in sales to Europe. Revenues from amusement center operations increased by 18.1 percent to $598.5 million, or about 17.4 percent of net sales. Revenue from amusement machine sales increased by 2.1 percent to $505.5 million, or 14.7 percent of net sales. Royalties on game software were up 302 percent to $41.4 million.

In the first six months of fiscal 1995 (ending September 1994), SEGA's unconsolidated pretax profit fell 43 percent to ¥16.33 billion ($166.97 million), down from ¥28.58 billion the previous year. Sales fell 25 percent, to ¥151.07 billion, from ¥200.65 billion. Analysts said the declines were expected due to slumping global demand for videogames and the soaring yen, which made Japanese products less competitive abroad.[50]

---

[50] "Video-Game Maker's Profit Plunged in Fiscal First Half," *The Wall Street Journal*, November 14, 1994, p. B5.

Exhibit 14 SEGA Sales by Division (nonconsolidated) *(in millions)*

	1994	1993
Net sales:	$3,432.2	$2,983.1
Consumer products	2,286.8	1,971.4
Domestic sales	249.7	166.2
Exports	2,037.1	1,805.2
Amusement center operations	598.5	506.6
Amusement machine sales:	505.5	494.9
Domestic sales	377.9	398.4
Exports	127.6	96.5
Royalties on game software	41.4	10.3

Source: Company annual reports.

In its home market of Japan, SEGA was being badly outcompeted by Nintendo (90 percent of all game sales in Japan went to Nintendo), in part because of distribution problems and in part because SEGA's sports-oriented games were not as popular in Japan. SEGA's market strength was in its American and European operations, which had some autonomy from Tokyo. It was reported (unconfirmed) in the press that SEGA of America contributed about 25 percent to the parent company's overall revenue.

Sony Corporation[51]

Sony Corporation was established in Japan in May 1946 as Tokyo Tsushin Kogyo Kabushiki Kaisha. In January 1958, it changed its name to Sony Kabushiki Kaisha (Sony Corporation in English). Sony Corporation of America was formed in 1960. Sony engages in the development, manufacture, and sale of various kinds of electronic equipment, instruments, and devices. In addition, Sony has a strong presence in the entertainment industry. Its music group (Sony Music Entertainment, Inc.) includes such companies as Columbia Records Group, Epic Records Group, TriStar Music Group, and others. Sony's Pictures Group includes four motion picture companies: Columbia Pictures, TriStar Pictures, Sony Pictures Classics, and Triumph Releasing Corporation.

Eager to claim a stake in the fast-growing videogame business, Sony Corp. set up a new division in May 1994, Sony Computer Entertainment of America, to develop and market a next generation home videogame, called the Sony Playstation (PSX). The PSX had been under development for more than four years and represented an important element in Sony's strategy to dominate the entertainment markets for hardware and software.[52] According to Sony, the game player, powered by a 32-bit microprocessor, provides three-dimensional animated graphics, compact-disc quality sound, and digital full-motion video. The system was released in Japan in December 1994; a U.S. and European release was scheduled for sometime in 1995.

---

[51]Extracted largely from Sony Corporation *Annual Report*, 1993.
[52]McGowan and S. Ciccarelli, Interactive Entertainment Industry Overview (New York: Gerard Klauer Mattison & Co., 1994).

As a new entrant in the stable of next generation systems, PSX faced heavy competition from 3DO, the Atari Jaguar, systems planned by Nintendo and SEGA, as well as multimedia PCs. The PSX was not compatible with any existing hardware standard. Sony reported that more than 160 videogame developers and publishers in Japan had agreed to support the Playstation.[53]

Despite Sony's lack of history in videogame hardware, and no particular success in software, the company was considered a formidable competitor in areas such as distribution of both hardware and software, a well-known brand name and image with U.S. consumers, and access to Columbia and Tri-Star film libraries.

Sony's entrance did not go unnoticed by SEGA Enterprises Ltd. President Hayao Nakayama who candidly expressed his view that Sony Corp. was likely to become SEGA's biggest adversary in home videogames in the coming year. "Sony is a much stronger company than another company I cannot name [Nintendo] . . . [Sony] has much more experience in the consumer market."[54] It was also rumored that SEGA delayed introducing Saturn from 1994 to 1995 in order to reengineer its system to compete better against Sony's new PSX system.

Exhibit 15 presents selected financial data for Sony Corp. For the fiscal year ended March 31, 1994, Sony reported consolidated net income of $148.5 million on total sales of $36.25 billion. Although sales increased by 5.3 percent over the previous year, net income was down by 52.5 percent due to factors including the appreciation of the yen (approximately 16 percent, 24 percent, and 31 percent against the U.S. dollar, the German mark, and the pound sterling, respectively), intensified price competition, and disappointing performance of a number of Sony Pictures Entertainment's motion pictures. Sony estimated that if the value of the yen had remained the same as in the previous fiscal year, corporate sales would have been $4.8 billion over the reported figure.

Sony did not anticipate a better year in 1995. The company expected a continued unfavorable operating environment due to uncertainty in the foreign currency market, delayed economic recovery in Japan and Europe, and intensifying price competition in audiovisual equipment markets in Japan and overseas. For the nine months ending December 31, 1994, Sony reported a net loss of $2.8 billion on net sales of $29.8 billion.

To counter the unfavorable forces in its environment, Sony's strategy called for aggressively moving forward to develop appealing electronics products and to promote its activities in the entertainment business. Sony also planned to reshape its corporate structure by eliminating product groups and establishing eight new companies within its organization. Finally, the company planned to make every effort to enhance overall performance by reviewing every activity in an effort to reduce costs and streamline company operations.

The 3DO Company[55]

3DO has been a relatively new player in the videogame industry. The company was initially formed in 1989 when the principals of NTG Engineering, Inc., launched an effort to create a new home interactive multimedia platform by

---

[53]DFC Intelligence Research.

[54]"SEGA Now Considers Sony, Not Nintendo, as Top Rival," *The Wall Street Journal*, September 15, 1994, p. B5.

[55]Extracted from The 3DO Company's Form 10-K, 1993 and 1994.

Exhibit 15   Selected Financial Data for Sony Corp., 1993–1994
(in millions of $)

	1994	1993
Statement of Operations Data		
Total revenue	$36,250	$34,422
Cost and expenses:		
Cost of sales	26,756	25,249
Selling, general administrative expenses	8,526	8,082
	35,282	33,331
Operating income	968	1,090
Other income:		
Interest and dividends	373	397
Foreign exchange gain, net	344	193
Other	450	376
	1,167	966
Other expenses:		
Interest	672	788
Other	470	472
	1,142	1,260
Income before taxes	993	796
Income taxes	763	718
Income before minority interest	229	369
Minority interest in consolidated subsidiaries	80	56
Net income	$ 149	$ 313
Net income per depositary share	$ 0.41	$ 0.79
Balance Sheet Data		
Cash and cash equivalents	$ 5,486	$ 4,970
Current assets	19,647	18,189
Working capital	5,982	3,164
Total assets	41,455	39,050
Current liabilities	13,366	15,025
Long-term obligations	13,947	10,974
Total stockholders' equity	12,908	12,312

Source: Annual reports and Form 20-F.

developing technology that achieved a breakthrough in audiovisual realism. In September 1991, the company was incorporated as SMSG, Inc., in California and changed its name to The 3DO Company in September 1992. In May 1993, 3DO had an initial public offering of $48.6 million. In June 1994, the company raised $37 million through a private placement.

The company's initial product design was the 3DO Interactive Multiplayer, which runs interactive entertainment, education, and information applications developed specifically for the 3DO format. It also plays conventional CDs and displays photo CDs, but it is not compatible with other commercially available software formats.

3DO's goal was to license its technology to manufacturers of consumer electronics and personal computer systems. Six global electronics companies were licensed to manufacture the 3DO Interactive Multiplayer system. Panasonic Company, a division of Matsushita Electric Corporation of America, had marketed a version of the 3DO system in the United States since October 1993 and introduced a version in Japan in March 1994. More than 500,000 3DO systems had been sold worldwide through 1994. Other companies licensed to use 3DO's technology included AT&T, Sanyo Electric Co., Goldstar and Samsung Electronics Co., Ltd., Creative Technology, Ltd., and Toshiba Corporation. The Goldstar 3DO system was launched in November 1994. 3DO systems were available at over 6,500 retail locations.

While early reports indicated videogame sales were flat for other systems, retailers reported 3DO games were selling well during the 1994 holiday season. No doubt contributing to 3DO's success were several recent awards, which included "Best System of 1994" from *DieHard GameFan* magazine and best overall game system from the *Los Angeles Daily News* (December 11, 1994). The 3DO system was also recommended as the game system to buy for the holidays by the *Miami Herald* (December 2, 1994).

3DO and its licensees were expanding the available base of software titles (over 135 titles released through 1994) in a variety of application areas, including action/strategy, sports, simulations, interactive movies, information, education, and music/arts. However, 3DO's ability to offer more game titles was hampered by a fracas with software developers over licensing fees. 3DO required developers to pay a $3 surcharge on top of the current royalty of $3 a copy for every CD produced. According to Tom Zito, president of Digital Pictures Inc., a software developer that has created four games for 3DO, "This is going to make me seriously think about investing company resources in developing more titles for their platform."[56] 3DO systems retailed for approximately $399 and were bundled with two free titles through the 1994 holiday season.

In an effort to gain a performance edge over its competitors, 3DO planned to introduce in late 1995 a peripheral upgrade, the M2 Accelerator, which promised to introduce movielike graphics and sound to its videogame players. The add-on accessory utilized a new Motorola PowerPC microprocessor and was expected to hit the market just as Nintendo and SEGA introduced their new machines. The company had not disclosed the price.

Management expected to incur substantial operating losses as it continued to develop its product, promote growth, and develop and publish software titles. For fiscal years ended March 31, 1994 and 1993, 3DO incurred net losses of $51.4 million and $15.4 million, respectively. Revenue for 1994 totaled $10.3 million. There was no revenue for 1993. Exhibit 16 presents selected financial data for 3DO since start-up operations began.

For the first nine months of fiscal year 1995 ended December 31, 1994, 3DO generated $22 million in total revenues, or a 262 percent increase over the same period in 1993. The company incurred a loss of $38.3 million as compared to a loss of $44 million in 1993.

In December 1994, the company announced a corporate restructuring. The company consolidated its technology, advanced development, product management,

---

[56]J. A. Trachtenberg, "Should Santa Bring a Nintendo, SEGA, Atari or What?" *The Wall Street Journal*, December 6, 1994, p. B1.

Exhibit 16   Selected Financial Data for 3DO, 1992–1993 *(in thousands, except per share data)*

	1994	1993	1992*
Statement of Operations Data			
Total revenue	$ 10,295	$ 0	$ 0
Cost of development systems	3,464	0	0
Gross profit	6,831	0	0
Operating expenses:			
Research and development	23,412	11,434	1,146
Sales and marketing	8,248	1,993	64
General and administrative expenses	6,175	2,008	552
Acquisitions of NTG royalty rights	21,353	0	0
Total operating expenses	59,188	15,435	2,762
Operating loss	(52,357)	(15,435)	(2,762)
Interest income	949	50	29
Other income	27	0	0
Loss before provision for income taxes	(51,381)	(15,385)	(2,733)
Provision for income taxes	50	1	1
Net loss	$(51,431)	$(15,386)	$(2,734)
Net loss per share	$ (2.60)	$ (1.02)	$ (0.18)
Shares used in per share calculations	19,747	15,018	15,014

	March 31	
	1994	1993
Balance Sheet Data		
Cash, cash equivalents, and short-term investments	$14,301	$ 2,827
Current assets	18,333	3,301
Working capital	9,960	(1,175)
Total assets	25,870	6,437
Current liabilities	8,373	4,476
Note payable to stockholder	474	474
Total liabilities	9,991	6,396
Total stockholders' equity (deficit)	15,879	(959)

* Period from October 1, 1991 (inception), to March 31, 1992.
Source: 3DO 10-K.

licensing, and business development groups into a new business operations department. Analysts said the move signaled the firm's desire to conserve cash and put off another public offering since its stock continued to drift downward.

Atari Corporation[57]

Atari Corporation (Atari) designs and markets interactive multimedia entertainment systems and related software and peripheral products. Atari's principal products were

---

[57]Extracted from Atari Corporation *Annual Report*, 1993 and 1994.

Jaguar, a 64-bit interactive multimedia entertainment system, along with related game software and peripheral products; Lynx, a 16-bit portable color handheld videogame; and the Falcon 030 series of personal computers. Manufacture of these products was performed by subcontractors. The principal methods of distribution were through mass market retailers, consumer electronic specialty stores, and distributors of electronic products. Atari had approximately 117 employees worldwide.

Management recognized in the fall of 1991 that the computer and videogame products it was marketing were rapidly becoming technologically obsolete. Intense competitive rivalry from larger competitors and shrinking margins in computer products profits led Atari to exit this line of products and to refocus itself as an interactive media entertainment company. In an effort to ensure its competitive advantage in this new market, Atari developed a 64-bit videogame system called Jaguar, which it began shipping in the fourth quarter of 1993. Jaguar is assembled by IBM in the United States, and currently sells for $249.

The Atari Jaguar was named the industry's "Best New Game System" (*Video-Games Magazine*), "Best New Hardware System" (*Game Informer*), and "1993 Technical Achievement of the Year" (*DieHard GameFan*). In April 1994, the Jaguar was given the European Computer Trade Show Award for "Best Hardware of the Year."

With the hardware developed (Atari is already working on a second-generation Jaguar system), Atari was busy developing more software titles such as "Alien vs. Predator," "Kasumi Ninja," and "Star Raiders 2000." To ensure a good supply of software titles for Jaguar, Atari licensed more than 125 third-party publishers and developers. By early 1995, Atari was expected to have more than 50 software titles available to users.

Atari planned to introduce a peripheral unit in the fall of 1995 that would enable the Jaguar to play CD-ROM games and regular audio CDs. The expected retail price was $149. Also in development was a full motion video cartridge that would enable the CD-ROM to play movies. The company was also funding development of a virtual reality system for Jaguar. In addition, Atari had decided to enter the PC software market, citing economies of scale benefits in developing a title for both the Jaguar and personal computer.

Atari's president, Sam Trmiel, was upbeat in his message to shareholders in the company's 1993 annual report: "We have completed our restructuring and consolidation around the world. As the business grows, we will reap the benefits of our streamlined central distribution in Europe and consolidation of U.S. operations." In his 1994 message he ended by saying: "The video game industry is now 20 years old and has provided millions of players with challenging and enjoyable experiences. We are well positioned for the next surge, the 32/64 bit generation."

Exhibit 17 presents selected financial data for Atari. In fiscal year 1994, Atari generated net sales of $38.4 million as compared to $28.8 million in 1993, an increase of 33 percent. The increased sales were primarily a result of Atari's national rollout of its new 64-bit Jaguar entertainment system and related software. Sales of Jaguar represented 77 percent of total sales in 1994 as compared to 13 percent in 1993. The Jaguar was launched in two markets in the fall of 1993, and approximately 100,000 units were sold by the end of 1994. Jaguar game players were sold with little or no margin, but significantly higher margins were achieved on software sales. Sales of Lynx and Falcon 030 computers and other older products represented 23 percent of sales in 1994 as compared to 87 percent in 1993. Atari paid no income taxes in 1994 because of operating loss carryforwards.

Exhibit 17   Selected Financial Data for Atari, 1992–1994   (in thousands, except per share data)

	1994	1993	1992
Statement of Operations Data			
Net sales	$ 38,444	$ 28,805	$127,340
Cost of sales	35,093	42,550	132,455
Gross profit	3,351	(13,745)	(5,115)
Operating expenses:			
Research and development	5,775	4,876	9,171
Sales and distribution	14,454	8,895	31,125
General and administrative expenses	7,169	7,558	16,544
Restructuring charges	0	12,425	17,053
Total operating expenses	27,398	33,754	73,893
Operating loss	(24,047)	(47,499)	(79,008)
Settlements of patent litigation	32,062	0	0
Exchange gain (loss)	1,184	(2,234)	(5,589)
Interest income	2,015	2,039	4,039
Other income	484	854	927
Interest expense	(2,304)	(2,290)	(3,522)
Loss before provision for income taxes	9,394	(49,130)	(83,153)
Income tax credit	0	264	434
Income (loss) before extraordinary credit	9,394	(48,866)	(82,719)
Discontinued operations	0	0	9,000
Income (loss) before extraordinary credit	$ 9,394	$(49,394)	$ (73,719)
Extraordinary credit	0	0	104
Income (loss)	$ 9,394	$(49,394)	$ (73,615)
Net profit (loss) per share	$ 0.16	$ (0.85)	$ (1.28)
Shares used in per share calculations	58,962	57,148	57,365

	December 31		
	1994	1993	1992
Balance Sheet Data			
Cash, cash equivalents, and short-term investments	$ 22,592	$23,059	$ 39,290
Current assets	113,188	50,599	109,551
Working capital	92,670	33,107	75,563
Total assets	131,042	74,833	138,508
Current liabilities	20,518	17,492	33,988
Total long-term obligations	43,454	52,987	53,937
Total stockholders' equity	67,070	4,354	50,583

Source: Atari Corporation 10-K.

Overall, Atari reported net income for 1994 of $9.4 million as compared to a net loss of $48.9 million in 1993.

Atari's future financial performance hinged on how successful the company's management would be in implementing its turnaround strategy and adapting to future changes in the highly competitive market. Atari's net sales in 1994 were largely dependent on the success of the Jaguar system and related software. Management felt that until such time as Jaguar achieved broad market acceptance and hardware and related software products were sold in substantial volume, the company would not achieve profitability. Margins on Jaguar hardware were expected to be relatively low.

In November 1994, Atari announced it completed a deal with SEGA that included a licensing agreement and an equity investment in Atari. The company received $50 million from SEGA in exchange for a license covering the use of a library of patents. SEGA also made an equity investment in Atari of $40 million to acquire common stock equal to a 7 percent interest. Both companies entered into cross-licensing agreements through the year 2001, which allow them to publish on each of their respective game platforms.

Philips Electronics NV

Founded in 1891, Philips Electronics NV (Philips) was Europe's largest consumer electronics company. The Dutch electronics giant also produces semiconductors and PCs and is a world leader in lightbulb manufacturing. Philips owns 79 percent of PolyGram (recordings), 35 percent of Matsushita Electronics (component venture with Matsushita), and 32 percent of Grundig (electronics, Germany). For inventing the digital audio technology used in CD players, Philips and Sony receive royalties on each one sold.

The company was number 32 in *Fortune's* 1994 Global 500 ranking of the world's largest industrial corporations and was listed among the top eight companies in the global electronics industry that included Hitachi, Matsushita Electric, GE, Samsung, Sony, and NEC. In fiscal 1994, Philips earned a net profit of $1.176 billion on total sales of $33.7 billion (see Exhibit 18). By the end of 1994, the company had several hundred subsidiaries in over 60 countries and employed 238,500 people worldwide.

Philips is organized into six product divisions, one of which includes "Other Consumer Products." Within this division is Philips Media, which has operations in four key business areas: software development in entertainment and electronic publishing applications, systems development and hardware/software distribution, cable TV, and media-based services. Philips Media is responsible for the CD-I game platform and software.

Philips was one of the first companies in the world to market a CD-based interactive entertainment system (called CD-I). The basic machine looks like a simplified VCR; it can play interactive movies and encyclopedias, regular movie videos, videogames, and conventional music CDs.

By its own admission Philips's marketing of its CD-I was confused and unfocused before 1993. Until the company decided to stress the machine's ability to play games and movies, consumers didn't know whether it was a video player, a home computer, a game console, or a toy. Limited game titles left consumers unconvinced that the format would last. Sales were dismal. After several years on the market, the installed base of CD-I machines in the United States at the end of 1994 was estimated at 250,000.

Philips tried to build market visibility by improving its marketing effort. A lengthy, high-quality, soft-sell infomercial began running in 1994. Hardware prices were slashed, with some units selling below $300. The company beefed up its software library with top-shelf feature films, music titles (from its Polygram recordings subsidiary), and games; Philips also signed on several leading developers in PC-

Exhibit 18   Selected Financial Data for Philips Electronics N.V., 1993–1994
(in millions of $)

	1994	1993
Statement of Operations Data		
Net sales	$33,689	$31,626
Direct costs of sales	(24,461)	(23,154)
Gross income	9,228	8,472
Selling expenses	(6,484)	(6,438)
General and administrative expenses	(815)	(766)
Other business income	148	110
Income from operations	2,077	1,378
Financial income and expenses	(478)	(559)
Income before taxes	1,599	819
Income taxes	(330)	(185)
Income after taxes	1,269	634
Equity in income of unconsolidated companies	72	(24)
Group income	1,341	610
Share of other group equity in group income	(207)	(151)
Net income from normal business operations	1,134	459
Extraordinary items—net	42	596
Net income	$ 1,176	$ 1,055
Balance Sheet Data		
Cash and cash equivalents	$ 1,560	$ 1,248
Current assets	16,517	14,840
Working capital	6,348	5,987
Total assets	26,586	24,884
Current liabilities	10,169	8,853
Long-term obligations	3,316	2,898
Total stockholders' equity	7,007	6,155

Source: Annual reports.

based CD-ROM games. In 1994, the company introduced over 100 new CD-I software titles; the software catalog now carries close to 300 titles.

Analysts projected modest sales of CD-I hardware and software. The CD-I was simply another platform with a chance of carving out a small share of the market for compact disc game players. Moreover, because the CD-I used a 16-bit processor, some perceived the machine as being based on outdated technology. However, Philips seemed to recognize the problems with the CD-I and has been focusing a lot of resources on software development for other platforms as well as the CD-I.

Nintendo versus SEGA (B):
The videogame wars

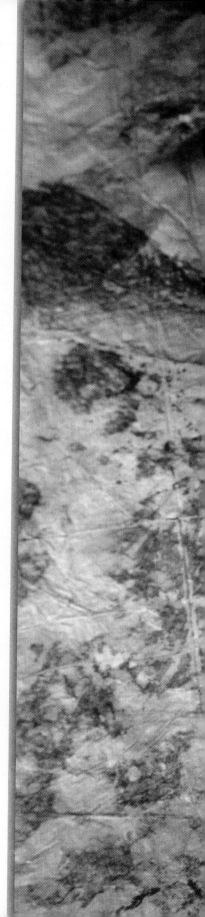

Romuald A. Stone, James Madison University

Once upon a time (1988, to be exact), Nintendo sat alone atop the mountain, master of its domain. Then came SEGA, scraping and clawing up the slope. The two stood precariously together—plumber vs. hedgehog—each trying to elbow the other off the peak. Today, if they pause and look down, the two will see new videogame challengers approaching on all sides, each promising a higher level of technology . . . Suddenly, the game's wide open again. And Nintendo's—and SEGA's—grip may be slipping . . . This is all-out war.[1]

Nintendo and SEGA had been the giants in the videogame industry for the past decade. During this period, the two competitors engaged in an ever increasing rivalry that was labeled the "Videogame Wars." The fight was intensifying, with SEGA winning some crucial engagements in the battle for market share.

Despite generally flat sales in 1994, the videogame wars were taking on a new dimension in 1995 as "next generation" game players were being released worldwide by Nintendo, SEGA, and new competitors. The entries included Nintendo's Ultra 64, SEGA's Saturn, and Sony Corp.'s Playstation, joining 3DO's Interactive Multiplayer and Atari Corp.'s Jaguar already on the market. All of these game players were not expected to survive because there was not a big enough market. The challenge for competitors was getting limited shelf space and lining up software developers. One industry observer predicted that consumers would become "very, very confused about what videogame player to buy: Sony versus Atari versus 3DO versus Nintendo versus SEGA? Sixteen-bit versus 32-bit versus 64-bit?"[2] The rapidly growing base of home computers equipped with high-tech entertainment options and CD-ROMs further added to the confusion.

Sales were expected to improve significantly once the next generation systems were fully on line in 1996, but profits were expected to be weak. Hardware margins were thin because low retail hardware prices were imperative for building a base to generate software demand. Software sales entailed much higher gross margins. But with the shift to newer game playing systems in 1995–96, margins were expected to be depressed by a rising percent of low-margin hardware sales. For software publishers and developers, increased competition had driven up the cost of securing licenses and

---

[1]M. Snider, "Video Market No Longer a 2-Player Game," *USA Today*, November 4, 1993, p. 1D.
[2]A. Harmon, "What's Coming, When, and Why It's a Big Deal," *Los Angeles Times*, December 18, 1994, p. 6.

developing games for an audience that sought out newer, more action-packed, or more interesting games with better visual graphics.[3] Moreover, software publishers and developers had to decide whether to incur the costs of programming their games to run on all or most of the different types/brands of games players or to gamble on developing software compatible with only one or two game platforms that might fail to win a significant share of the hardware systems purchased by consumers. Consumers, also, were in somewhat of a quandary because if they purchased a new game-playing hardware system that failed to attract many software developers then the system wouldn't run many of the games on the market.[4]

NINTENDO AND SEGA PROFILES

Nintendo Company, Ltd.

Background[5]   Nintendo in 1994 was one of the world's largest hardware manufacturers and software developers for interactive entertainment. A profile of Nintendo's first 100 years is presented in Exhibit 1. Exhibit 2 shows a time line of Nintendo's milestones since 1983.

Nintendo was credited with singlehandedly reviving the videogame industry after the industry collapsed in the early 1980s due to the weight of too many bad games (such as Atari's ET), poor marketing, and overproduction. In order to get a handle on what kids really wanted, Nintendo sent its representatives to video arcades around the country to learn firsthand why young people went to the arcades rather than playing at home for free. What they discovered set the stage for the eventual Nintendo-led recovery of the videogame industry.

> It wasn't the games themselves or a fickle market, but the arcade-quality, full-animation, imaginative play of the arcade games that the videogame providers—in their gold-rush, sucker-born-every-minute mentality—could not or would not provide for the home player. So Nintendo introduced a game system that was not simply a "player," but a sophisticated device with the power of a personal computer, able to reproduce near arcade-quality games on the home screen.[6]

Nintendo's arcade-quality machine was its Nintendo Entertainment System (NES). The NES was far superior to those of the Atari generation. In 1985, when the NES was introduced, 1.1 million units were sold. At the end of 1988, Nintendo accounted for $1.7 billion of the $2.3 billion videogame business. Nintendo sold its game players at cost and made money on the software. Through 1994, Nintendo had sold more than 100 million hardware systems and more than 750 million game packs

---

[3]S. McGowan and S. Ciccarelli, Interactive Entertainment Industry Overview (New York: Gerard Klauer Mattison & Co., 1994).

[4]DFC Intelligence Research, *The U.S. Market for Video Games and Interactive Electronic Entertainment* (San Diego, 1995).

[5]Additional background information is contained in Case 11, Nintendo versus SEGA (A).

[6]S. Wolpin, "How Nintendo Revived a Dying Industry," *Marketing Communications* 14, no. 5, (1989), p. 38.

Exhibit 1   Nintendo's 100-Year History

1889 Fusajiro Yamauchi, great-grandfather of the present president, began manufacturing "Hanafuda," Japanese playing cards, in Kyoto.

1933 Established an unlimited partnership, Yamauchi Nintendo & Co.

1947 Began a distribution company, Marufuku Co. Ltd.

1950 Changed the company name from Marufuku Co. Ltd. to Nintendo Playing Card Co. Ltd. Hiroshi Yamauchi took office as president. Absorbed the manufacturing operation of Yamauchi Nintendo & Co.

1952 Consolidated factories were dispersed in Kyoto.

1953 Became the first to succeed in manufacturing mass-produced plastic playing cards in Japan.

1959 Started selling cards printed with Walt Disney characters, opening a new market in children's playing cards. The card department boomed!

1962 In January, listed stock on the second section of the Osaka Stock Exchange and on the Kyoto Stock Exchange.

1963 Changed company name to Nintendo Co. Ltd. and started manufacturing games in addition to playing cards.

1969 Expanded and reinforced the game department; built a production plant in Uji City, a suburb of Kyoto.

1970 Stock listing was changed to the first section of the Osaka Stock Exchange. Reconstruction and enlargement of corporate headquarters was completed. Started selling the Beam gun Series, employing opto-electronics. Introduced electronic technology into the toy industry for the first time in Japan.

1973 Developed laser clay shooting system to succeed bowling as a major pastime.

1974 Developed image projection system employing 16mm film projector for amusement arcades. Began exporting them to America and Europe.

1975 In cooperation with Mitsubishi Electric, developed videogame system using electronic video recording (EVR) player. Introduced the microprocessor into the videogame system the next year.

1977 Developed home-use videogames in cooperation with Mitsubishi Electric.

1978 Created and started selling coin-operated videogames using microcomputers.

1979 Started an operations division for coin-operated games.

1980 Announced a wholly owned subsidiary, Nintendo of America Inc. in New York. Started selling "GAME & WATCH" product line.

1981 Developed and began distribution of the coin-operated videogame "Donkey Kong." This videogame enjoyed great popularity.

1982 Merged New York subsidiary into Nintendo of America Inc., a wholly owned subsidiary headquartered in Seattle, Washington, with a capital investment of $600,000.

1983 Built a new plant in Uji City to increase production capacity and to allow for business expansion. Established Nintendo Entertainment Centers Ltd. In Vancouver, B.C., Canada, to operate a family entertainment center. Raised authorized capital of Nintendo of America Inc. to $10 million. In July, listed stock on the first section of the Tokyo Stock Exchange. Started selling the home videogame console "Family Computer" (Famicom), employing a custom CPU (custom processing unit) and PPU (picture processing unit).

1984 Developed and started selling the unique two-screen interactive coin-operated videogame "VS. System."

1985 Started to sell the U.S. version of Family Computer "Nintendo Entertainment System" in America. Developed and started selling game software "Super Mario Bros." for the family computer.

1986 Developed and started selling the "Family Computer Disk Drive System" to expand the functions of the Family Computer. Began installation of the "Disk Writer" to rewrite game software.

1987 Sponsored a Family Computer "Golf Tournament" as a communications test using the public telephone network and Disk Faxes to aid in building a Family Computer network.

1988 Nintendo of America Inc. published the first issue of *Nintendo Power* magazine in July. Researched and developed the Hands Free controller, making the Nintendo Entertainment System accessible to many more Nintendo fans.

1989 Released "The Adventure of Link," sequel to the top-selling game "The Legend of Zelda" in the United States. Started "World of Nintendo" displays in the United States to help market Nintendo products. Studies show that children are as familiar with "Mario" as they are with Mickey Mouse and Bugs Bunny!

1990 Introduced Game Boy, the first portable, handheld game system with interchangeable game paks. Nintendo Power Fest featuring the Nintendo World Championships tours the country. Japan enters the 16-bit market by releasing the Super Famicom in the fall.

1991 Nintendo introduces World Class Service Center locations across the United States. The 16-bit Super NES, along with "Super Mario World," is released in the United States.

1992 The Super NES Super Scope and Mario Paint with the Super NES Mouse Accessory were released. The long-awaited "Zelda" sequel, "The Legend of Zelda: A Link to the Past," arrived for the Super NES.

1993 Nintendo announces the advent of the Super FX Chip, breakthrough technology for home video systems. The first game using the Super FX Chip, "Star Fox," is released in April.

Source: Nintendo of America.

Exhibit 2 Nintendo Time Line of Significant Events, 1983–1994

1983	1985	1986	1987	1988	1989	1990	1991	1992	1993	1994

Nintendo Co., Ltd., introduces Family Computer System (Famicom) in Japan

Nintendo

More than 6.5 million Nintendo Famicoms sold in Japan

Nintendo test markets NES in New York

NINTENDO ENTERTAINMENT SYSTEM®

More than one million NES units sold; more than 70 percent of industry sales captured

Home video game industry sells 4.1 million hardware units; Nintendo's share—three million

The Legend of Zelda becomes the first million seller

The Legend of ZELDA

The Legend of Zelda and *Mike Tyson's Punch-Out!* hit sales of two million units

NINTENDO POWER®

Nintendo Power magazine reaches one million subscribers, most for its age category

GAME BOY®

Game Boy and *Tetris* introduced

Super Mario Bros. 3, introduced; sells seven million units to become best-selling video game of all-time

SUPER NINTENDO ENTERTAINMENT SYSTEM

16-bit Super NES launched in the U.S.

Third-party developers grow; 61 for the NES; 62 for Game Boy; more than 100 for Super NES

An unprecedented 175 titles released in second half

Mario Paint introduced; features first-ever Super NES Mouse

SUPER NES MOUSE

STAR FOX

First Super FX game (*Star Fox*) introduced

Consumer service department logs its 30 millionth contact

100 million Mario-titled Game Paks sold worldwide

More than five million *Super Mario Land 2* Game Paks sold worldwide

750 million Game Paks sold worldwide

Nintendo Gateway System™ launched

SiliconGraphics Computer Systems

"Project Reality," joint venture with Silicon Graphics, Inc.,

SUPER FX

Cartridge-based systems and software to reach record high sales in 1994—more than 95 percent of all video game sales

Super FX 2, second generation chip, technology introduced

Ken Griffey Jr. Presents: Major League Baseball introduced for Super NES

"Project Reality" previewed in arcades in 1994; available for the home in 1995

Nintendo Gateway projected to reach 20 million travelers

worldwide. During most of the 1980s, Nintendo was the undisputed leader in the videogame industry, controlling 80 percent of the market at the end of the decade. By 1994, however, Nintendo's market share had declined to about 45 percent and was expected to decline further as SEGA continued its "take no prisoners" strategy.

Financial performance[7] For the six-month period ending September 30, 1994 (fiscal year 1995), Nintendo's earnings slipped 17 percent to $520 million from $623 million in the same period the previous year. Weak demand for its old games coupled with a strong yen against the dollar hurt sales revenue. Nintendo projected selling 6.5 million units of software worldwide in 1995, but later revised its estimate down to 2.5 million. Nintendo was counting on Virtual Boy and Ultra 64 to reverse declining profits and help fuel sales growth in 1995.[8]

During fiscal year 1994 (April 1993–March 1994), Nintendo sold more videogame cartridges than in any previous year. However, consolidated net sales fell to $4.714 billion, a 23.5 percent decline from the previous year, and the company's consolidated net income of $511 million decreased by 40 percent from 1993 (see Exhibit 3). This represented Nintendo's first decline in sales and net income since it introduced the Famicom in Japan in 1983. Nintendo's stock fell from a high of ¥17,500 ($150.86) in 1992 to a low of ¥6,140 ($59.61) in 1994.

Sales in Nintendo's home Japanese market sanctuary were strong in fiscal 1994, but the rising value of the yen seriously affected the company's performance around the globe. A weak economy in Europe and a soft market in the United States, coupled with increased competition, eroded export sales. Moreover, Nintendo did not introduce any new product categories in 1994.

Nintendo's Strategy and Product Development

A New Strategy Responding to SEGA's advances, Nintendo appointed Howard Lincoln as head of Nintendo of America and began to make changes in its strategy in 1994. Nintendo historically had demanded that third-party software developers sign exclusive deals and pay 30 percent royalties for the privilege of writing games for its systems. SEGA slowly began taking the top independent software developers away from Nintendo and into its own camp. To counter SEGA's moves, Nintendo started paying companies to write software exclusively for it. Sources reported that Nintendo paid a development fee plus royalties of 2 percent to 12 percent, worth millions of dollars for a hit game.[9] Nintendo also planned to increase the amount spent for in-house game development and production from its current 35 percent of software sales.

While other companies embraced CD-ROM technology, Nintendo elected to stay out of the multimedia end of the business. Its Ultra 64 player plays only cartridges, not CD-ROMs. According to Takashi Kawaguchi, assistant manager at Nintendo's public relations department, "The video game market is a big market that already exists and is still growing, but the multimedia market still remains an illusion that so far has no

---

[7]This section is reprinted from Case 11, Nintendo versus SEGA (A), to provide financial data for users of this case who may not have previously reviewed part (A).
[8]"Tough Year Crimps Nintendo Earnings," *USA Today*, November 22, 1994, p. O8B.
[9]R. Brandt, "Is Nintendo a Street Fighter Now?" *Business Week*, August 29, 1994, p. 35.

Exhibit 3   Consolidated Financial Summary for Nintendo Co., Ltd., 1992–1994 (in thousands of $)

	Year Ended March 31		
	1994	1993	1992
Net sales	$4,714,675	$6,161,840	$4,843,475
Cost of goods sold	2,887,106	3,758,376	2,926,885
Gross profit	$1,827,569	$2,403,464	$1,916,590
Selling, general, and administrative expenses	693,507	650,360	483,115
Operating income	$1,134,062	$1,753,104	$1,433,475
Other income/(expenses):			
Interest income	110,392	175,380	206,823
Other	(230,727)	(104,973)	(81,971)
Total	(120,335)	70,407	124,852
Income before income taxes	$1,013,727	$1,823,511	$1,558,327
Income taxes	576,497	967,261	807,653
Foreign currency translation adjustments	73,968	4,031	224
Net income	$ 511,198	$ 860,281	$ 750,898
Net income per share	$ 3.61	$ 6.08	$ 5.30
Cash dividend per share	0.68	0.68	0.52
Cash and cash equivalents	3,334,679	3,425,000	2,549,144
Current assets	5,037,417	4,638,570	3,968,830
Total assets	5,740,070	5,248,012	4,458,664
Current liabilities	1,355,426	1,693,274	1,587,965
Total liabilities	1,427,515	1,762,738	1,626,353
Stockholders' equity	4,312,555	3,485,274	2,832,311

Source: Company annual reports.

substance, and we see no point in going into what does not exist."[10] Some observers believed that Nintendo had lost the technological edge to SEGA and the newer, smaller videogame makers offering CD-ROM, virtual reality, and multimedia options.

When Nintendo saw in early 1994 that it was losing market share to SEGA, the company quickly concluded it needed both a management and an image overhaul. Nintendo President Yamauchi laid part of the blame on his son-in-law, Nintendo of America Inc. President Minoru Arakawa (whose authority was reduced by the appointment of Howard Lincoln as chairman in early 1994). When SEGA ran comparative ads in 1990, Nintendo did not respond. According to Yamauchi, Arakawa "allowed SEGA to brand our games as children's toys. It was a serious mistake."[11] Arakawa subsequently issued a statement saying that 1994 would be the most aggressive marketing year Nintendo of America had ever seen. Leo Burnett USA, a Chicago ad agency, was selected to design Nintendo's first TV image campaign.

---

[10]M. Nashima, "Next-Generation Machines Taking On Sega, Nintendo," *The Japan Times Weekly International Edition*, 34, no. 9 (1994), p. 13.
[11]N. Gross and R. D. Hof, "Nintendo's Yamauchi: No More Playing Around," *Business Week*, February 21, 1994, p. 71.

Previously, Nintendo had limited advertising to its own magazine, *Nintendo Power*, circulated to 1 million Nintendo owners. Sean McGowan, a toy analyst with Gerard Klauer Mattison, characterized Nintendo's situation:

> Nintendo has a lot of catching up to do, both in advertising and corporate strategy. The next generation of videogames is being decided now, and Nintendo has lost the edge. That will be hard to recapture with newcomers as powerful as Sony entering the game.[12]

Nintendo made another about-face in early 1994 when it changed its strategy of not selling videogames directly to video rental dealers. With the videogame rental business representing more than $1 billion a year, Nintendo decided it needed to be a competitor in that segment as well. Nintendo did not plan to require royalties on rental transactions. However, when the law prohibiting rental of computer software expires in 1997, Nintendo hopes to have the law amended to allow the company to collect royalties on game rentals.[13]

Nintendo was closely watching development of SEGA's cable TV game channel in the United States and its recent efforts to provide the same service in Japan. In January 1995, Nintendo announced the formation of an alliance with GTE Interactive Media to develop, market, and distribute videogames over telephone lines into interactive television sets. Commenting on the venture, Nintendo's chairman noted, "I think we recognize the market is changing and I don't think it's wise to go it alone in circumstances like that."[14] For Nintendo, the alliance gave the company access to GTE's telephone customer network. For GTE, the alliance provided access to entertainment media that GTE felt would drive initial consumer interest in interactive TV. Initial games were to be developed for Nintendo's Super NES and then later for Ultra 64.

Other moves included introducing more (and better) software titles, including the hotly anticipated "Donkey Kong Country." Nintendo also softened its opposition to the depiction of violence in Nintendo-licensed videogames. The company began manufacturing Game Boy systems in the People's Republic of China in order to gain access to that large and new market and opened two new subsidiaries in Spain and Australia.

Overall, Nintendo had a substantial customer base, experience in the industry, and was dedicated to providing the consumer with a quality experience. Observers believed Nintendo was positioned to be a major player in the next generation of videogame systems.[15]

New Product Development   In August 1993, Nintendo introduced the Nintendo Gateway System, a sophisticated computer designed as an interactive, multimedia information and entertainment system for travelers in airplanes, cruise ships, and hotels. The system was powered by the 16-bit Super NES. At the end of 1994, Nintendo expected to have the systems installed on 170 planes belonging to Northwest Airlines, China Air, Virgin Atlantic, and several other airlines. Nintendo also

---

[12]K. Fitzgerald, "Nintendo's Task for Burnett: Image Overhaul," *Advertising Age*, February 28, 1994, pp. 3, 45.

[13]J. Greenstein, "In About-Face, Nintendo Turns to Rental Stores," *Video Business*, April 29, 1994, pp. 1, 12.

[14]J. Carlton, "Nintendo, GTE Unit Offer Games for Interactive TV," *The Wall Street Journal*, January 4, 1995, p. B7.

[15]DFC Intelligence Research.

expanded the system to selected hotels and Holland America cruise ships in 1994. Nintendo expected the Gateway System to ultimately provide a full spectrum of entertainment and information services to 20 million travelers worldwide. With 15 million Super NES units in American homes, Nintendo believed it would be doubling its reach and expanding its audience as well.[16]

In early 1994, Nintendo introduced an adapter that let users of its Game Boy machines play their games on Nintendo's 16-bit system. The company then took 16-bit game machines to a new level when it launched a turbo-charged chip, the Super FX 2, for its 16-bit NES system. The Super FX 2 was a proprietary custom chip, which Nintendo incorporated into its software game cartridges to enhance graphic and speed capabilities, essentially offering players realistic simulation experiences. The Super NES with the FX 2 chip was the most advanced cartridge-based 16-bit game machine in the industry.

Nintendo had recently teamed up with Silicon Graphics, Inc., to design a new game system called Ultra 64. Silicon Graphics had developed the special effects in *Jurassic Park* and *Aladdin*. The technology, called Reality Immersion Technology, allowed videogame players to interact with virtual game environments (a computer-generated 3-D world). This new generation of entertainment created infinitely evolving worlds that instantly and continuously reacted to the commands and whims of individual players. With Reality Immersion Technology, videogame players, for the first time ever, became part of the game itself. Nintendo's strategy was to skip the transition to 32-bit machines (nonportable) and go directly to 64-bit technology. Nintendo planned for the Ultra 64 to be on the market by the end of 1995.

In early 1995, Nintendo introduced a new low-priced virtual reality game system in the United States and Japan. The new game system, called ''Virtual Boy,'' is a portable, table-top unit that does not connect to a TV. The game uses 32-bit technology designed to produce a 3-D experience not possible on conventional television or LCD screens. The new system sold for under $200.[17]

Outlook[18]

Nintendo's strategy was characterized by industry observers as ''slow and steady wins the race.'' Whereas SEGA was releasing products and expanding into new areas, Nintendo's strategy focused on making quality videogames. While industry observers suspected that Nintendo had ambitions of being a leading provider of services for the interactive age, its present strategic posture was seen as ''wait and see.''

Until the release of Ultra 64, Nintendo was working hard to keep the 16-bit Super NES alive. Still, recent sales were slumping, in part because of slowing demand for 16-bit systems as consumers waited for the next generation systems to come on line in 1995.

SEGA Enterprises, Ltd.

SEGA considered itself a leader in interactive digital entertainment media, with operations on five continents competing in three core business segments: consumer products, amusement center operations, and amusement machines. SEGA produced

---

[16]Nintendo Press Release, ''Nintendo Gateway System Takes Off,'' January 6, 1994.
[17]''Nintendo to Begin Selling 'Virtual Reality' System,'' *The Wall Street Journal*, November 15, 1994, p. B6.
[18]Extracted from DFC Intelligence Research report.

both hardware and software in these areas. Since 1989, SEGA had quadrupled in size from more than $800 million in annual sales to $4 billion in fiscal year 1994. SEGA, which once controlled only 10 percent of the U.S. videogame market, had emerged to contend for market leadership with Nintendo. The two companies in 1994 had approximately equal shares in the U.S. market. In Europe, SEGA had more than a 66 percent share but it trailed Nintendo by a 9 to 1 margin in Japan. A summary of SEGA's company history is presented in Case 11, Nintendo versus SEGA (A).

Positioning for the 1990s   Some critics questioned whether Hayao Nakayama, SEGA's president and CEO, had the leadership and managerial skills to continue to strengthen SEGA's position in the industry. He had been characterized as an American-style decision-making manager with a good sense of humor. He spoke very rapidly, was opinionated, and impatiently ordered subordinates around. Some said he was obsessed with competing with Nintendo. Like his counterpart at Nintendo, Hiroshi Yamauchi, he did not play videogames.

In 1990, SEGA hired a new chief executive, Thomas Kalinske, to run its U.S. subsidiary, SEGA America Inc. Nakayama specifically hired Kalinske to beat Nintendo and gave Kalinske unprecedented autonomy to do just that. Kalinske was an experienced marketer, with stints as CEO of toymaker Matchbook International Inc. and 15 years with Mattel Inc. earlier in his career. To catch Nintendo, Kalinske took decisive and bold steps that included cutting the price of Genesis 25 percent to $149, recruiting software developers to create new games, and accepting lower royalties, sometimes 15 percent below Nintendo's.[19] The strategy worked. SEGA managed to zap Nintendo's 90 percent market share in 1990 to about 50 percent in 1993, increasing its own market position from a meager 7 percent to almost 50 percent in the process. Sales from SEGA's U.S. subsidiary increased from an estimated $280 million in 1990 to more than $1 billion in 1994. Kalinske offered a hint of SEGA's future strategic direction when he said, "I see us as a new form of entertainment company . . . I don't think we should be happy until there are more people using our products than sitting down to watch "Melrose Place" or "Beverly Hills 90210."[20]

Financial Performance[21]   Fiscal 1994 was a lackluster year for SEGA as well as Nintendo. A weak Japanese economy and a dismal consumer market in Europe, coupled with an unexpectedly sharp appreciation of the yen against other major currencies, resulted in a 12.8 percent increase in net consolidated sales from fiscal 1993 to $4 billion and a 58.9 percent decline in net income to $108.7 million (see Exhibit 4). The sharp decrease in net income was precipitated by losses in SEGA's European operations. From a high of ¥11,000 in 1992, SEGA's stock price declined to a low of ¥7,010 at the end of 1994. Exhibit 5 depicts SEGA's sales by division.

In the first six months of fiscal 1995 (ending September 1994), SEGA's unconsolidated pretax profit fell 43 percent to ¥16.33 billion ($166.97 million), down from ¥28.58 billion the previous year. Sales fell 25 percent, to ¥151.07 billion, from ¥200.65 billion. Analysts said the declines were expected due to slumping global

[19]N. Hutheesing, "How a Cool Sega Zapped Nintendo," *Forbes* 15, no. 42 (1993), pp. 72–73.
[20]Brandt, "Is Nintendo a Street Fighter Now?", p. 69.
[21]This section reprinted from Case 11, Nintendo versus SEGA (A).

**Exhibit 4   Consolidated Financial Summary for SEGA Enterprises, Ltd., 1993–1994   *(in thousands of $)*

	Year Ended March 31	
	1994	1993
Net sales	$4,038,197	$3,578,968
Cost of goods sold	2,916,161	2,301,496
Gross profit	$1,122,036	$1,277,472
Selling, general, and administrative expenses	831,837	697,988
Operating income	$ 290,199	$ 579,484
Other income/(expenses):		
Interest income	47,561	33,353
Other	(78,865)	(104,024)
Total	(31,304)	(70,671)
Income before income taxes	$ 258,895	$ 508,813
Income taxes	249,259	267,102
Foreign currency statements translation	99,089	22,752
Net income	$ 108,725	$ 264,463
Net income per share	$ 1.09	$ 2.72
Cash dividend per share	0.37	0.21
Cash and cash equivalents	1,000,262	963,646
Current assets	2,398,652	2,185,073
Total assets	3,482,821	3,026,354
Current liabilities	1,261,454	1,084,437
Total liabilities	1,973,999	2,001,006
Stockholders' equity	1,508,822	1,025,348
Effective tax rate	52%	52%

Source: Company annual reports.

demand for videogames and the soaring yen, which made Japanese products less competitive abroad.[22]

In Japan, SEGA was being badly beaten by Nintendo (90 percent of all game sales were Nintendo), in part because of distribution problems and also because SEGA's sports-oriented games were not as popular in Japan. SEGA's performance was helped by its American and European operations, which had some autonomy from Tokyo. SEGA of America contributed about 25 percent to the parent company's overall revenue.

SEGA's Strategy and Product Development

Grand Strategy   SEGA's president had made no secret of his strategic intent: to build an entertainment empire. "We'd like to resemble a combination of Sony and

---

[22]"Video-Game Maker's Profit Plunged in Fiscal First Half," *The Wall Street Journal*, November 14, 1994, p. B5.

Exhibit 5   SEGA Sales by Division (nonconsolidated)   *(in millions)*

	1994	1993
Net sales:	$3,432.2	$2,983.1
Consumer products	2,286.8	1,971.4
Domestic sales	249.7	166.2
Exports	2,037.1	1,805.2
Amusement center operations	598.5	506.6
Amusement machine sales:	505.5	494.9
Domestic sales	377.9	398.4
Exports	127.6	96.5
Royalties on game software	41.4	10.3

Source: Company annual reports.

Disneyland by the 21st century."[23] To achieve this goal, SEGA had adopted a technology-oriented strategic plan that focused on acquiring and maintaining competitive advantage in such fields as multimedia, computer graphics, virtual reality, and high-tech amusement theme parks. Anticipating the convergence of the worlds of computers, communications, and entertainment, SEGA had stepped up R&D spending in multimedia, "edutainment," and audiovisual products. The company had approximately 850 employees working on interactive amusements for homes, arcade, and theme parks, representing the highest investment in R&D in the industry. SEGA's drive to achieve and maintain its goal of industry dominance led the company to make alliances with AT&T in communications, Hitachi in chips, Yamaha in sound, JVC in game machines, and perhaps Microsoft in future software developments.

In an effort to deal with competition from inexpensive multimedia home computers, SEGA has explored the possibility of making some of its popular videogame software available for PCs equipped with CD-ROM drives. According to the *Wall Street Journal:*

> If SEGA does decide to embrace the PC, the company will be making a major break with tradition. Up to now, SEGA has developed its own software mainly for use on its own proprietary game systems. Unlike its archrival Nintendo Co., which relies heavily on outside software developers, SEGA develops roughly 45 percent of the software for its game machines in-house.[24]

Since SEGA competes in both home and arcade games (Nintendo is only in home games), it was able to develop expensive technology for arcade machines and then transition the technology to home machines when the price of computer chips fell. Additionally, SEGA planned to move beyond auto racing and action games, at which it excelled, to more general multimedia entertainment featuring full motion video, drama, and characters besides Sonic that could be as popular as Mickey Mouse.[25]

[23]"The High-Tech Art of Having Fun," *Asia Week* 18, no. 36 (1992), p. 65.
[24]D. P. Hamilton, "SEGA May Make Some Video Games Available for PCs," *The Wall Street Journal*, May 16, 1994, p. B6.
[25]A. Pollack, "SEGA Takes Aim at Disney World," *New York Times*, July 4, 1993, p. 6.

One component of SEGA's strategic move into more general multimedia entertainment was its formation in 1994 of the SEGA Club, a vehicle for attracting some of the nearly 32 million kids aged 3 to 11. SEGA's objective was to be an industry leader in bringing good, clean videogame entertainment and educational products to the videogame market for teens and pre-teens.

Because domestic sales have been more profitable than its overseas sales, SEGA planned to increase the contribution of its Japanese home sanctuary to overall net sales. Specifically, the company planned to expand sales of new products through heavy advertising and marketing efforts.

The company expected to make a complete review of its operations in Europe in order to respond more effectively to the needs of local European markets and to improve sales and gross margins. To stimulate demand for its high-tech entertainment products, SEGA planned to release PICO, Saturn, and the 32-X adapter in Europe.

SEGA viewed Asia both as a high-potential market and as a center for manufacturing. The company produced all of its videogame players in Japan in cooperation with a subsidiary of Hitachi Ltd. Localizing production in this part of the world was expected to result in an increased ratio of non-Japan manufacturing, lower costs, and decreased risks associated with fluctuations in the value of the Japanese yen. To lower production costs in Japan, SEGA planned to increase imports of raw materials.

SEGA's future strategy aims at capturing some of the $6 billion U.S. theme park industry. Plans call for constructing small theme parks that combine high-tech amusement center machines using state-of-the-art computer graphics with virtual-reality technologies to make customers believe they are somewhere they are not. SEGA's strategy is not to imitate Disney but to reinvent the amusement park:

> Whereas Disney built huge amusement parks with roller coasters and log flume rides, SEGA wants to build small theme parks that will provide the same thrills using computer simulations known as virtual reality—a Disney-land in a box.[26]

Noting that Disney has only three huge parks to attract patrons, SEGA said it would build 50 parks in Japan and another 50 in the United States over the next several years. Unlike the Disney attractions that remained fixed for decades, a virtual reality attraction could be changed just by changing the software. The same simulator could be used for a space battle or a police chase.[27] According to Tom Kalinske, "We want consumers to spend their time and money with SEGA entertainment when they're out of the home and when they're inside the home . . . we want to provide entertainment that you'd rather do with us than any of the alternative forms, whether TV, local TV, or whatever."[28]

Currently, SEGA derives about one-sixth of its consolidated revenue from amusement center operations. One analyst predicted that SEGA would enjoy gross margins above 30 percent, compared to Disney's 25 percent for its two stateside theme parks. On the downside, SEGA has no experience running amusement parks; however, it does know how to provide "experiences"—it has more than 1,200 video arcades in Japan.

---

[26]Ibid.
[27]"Big Plans for Theme Parks," *New York Times*, July 4, 1993, p. 6.
[28]J. Battle and B. Johnstone, "Seizing the Next Level," *Wired*, December 1993, p. 126.

New Product Development   For the home market, SEGA focused on multimedia, introducing its new $399 CDX player in April 1994. This player uses Genesis cartridges and SEGA CD games in one portable module that also functions as a compact disc player. American Telephone & Telegraph planned to introduce the Edge 16, an under-$150 modem, to permit two Genesis machines to communicate over phone lines.

In November 1994, SEGA introduced in Japan its newest entry in the multimedia field, the 32-bit Saturn console; the model was scheduled for release in the United States in the fall of 1995. This game unit has a built-in CD-ROM player (quadruple-speed) and enough processing power to reproduce movielike sound and visual effects.

To enhance demand for the firm's 16-bit game players, SEGA developed a hardware booster (Super Genesis 32-X) that enabled 32-bit game cartridges to play on its 16-bit players. SEGA expected to have more than 120 games specifically designed for the 32-X by December 1995.

One problem SEGA faced, however, was the numerous game system formats it had on the market. The feeling among some observers was that SEGA was trying to cover too many bases at one time. The result could be consumer confusion, with the various systems cannibalizing each other. SEGA management was aware of this potential.

In 1994, SEGA test-marketed its SEGA Channel via cable TV in the United States. Genesis owners could pay $12 to $20 per month for unlimited playing time. Subscribers could choose from a wide selection of popular Genesis games, special versions of soon to be released titles, gameplay tips, news, contests, and promotions. SEGA hoped to have 1 million subscribers in 1995 and 2 million by the end of 1996. The SEGA Channel was cited by the editors of *Science Magazine* as one of 1994's innovative products and achievements in science and technology in the magazine's seventh annual "Best of What's New" special awards section in its December issue. SEGA was also gearing up to introduce a similar game channel in Japan. However, the number of Japanese homes wired for cable was small at 1.6 million (a 5 percent penetration rate) compared to the United States with more than 60 percent of U.S. homes wired for cable. The diffusion of cable systems in Japan had been hurt by the widespread use of satellite systems.

SEGA's strategy included diversification into toy lines that included books that interacted with a TV through an electronic pen. The booklike toy, called "PICO" (about $160), involves touching a pen to a picture in a book that then appears on the TV screen. This product, released in Japan in June 1993, represented SEGA's first entry into the emerging edutainment market.

Both Nintendo and SEGA started offering videogame systems that could be attached to exercise equipment in the fall of 1994. SEGA offered add-on units, while Nintendo's product was built into a Life Fitness exercise bike. The systems were designed so that videogame characters reflected the user's speed and effort during the workout, offering entertainment and distraction while motivating exercise. Analysts believed these so called exertainment systems could become a $2 billion business in a few years.[29]

Outlook[30]   Whereas Nintendo's strategy reflected a posture of "slow and steady wins the race," SEGA appeared to operate on the principle of "first at all costs."

---

[29]K. Fitzgerald, "It's Sonic vs. The Stairmaster," *Advertising Age*, June 13, 1994, p. 26.
[30]Extracted from DFC Intelligence Research report.

SEGA had been burned badly by entering the 8-bit market after Nintendo and seemed determined not to let such a delay happen again.

The SEGA Genesis was the first 16-bit system on the market, 18 months before Nintendo's 16-bit Super NES. The SEGA CD was released well before any competing systems. Recently, SEGA got the Genesis 32-X out a full year before similar systems from Nintendo and Sony.

So far, the strategy of being first had served SEGA well. Nintendo was forced into playing catch-up and SEGA was challenging Nintendo for the lead in the U.S. videogame market. Sales of the SEGA CD had been less than spectacular, but the system had gone a long way toward enhancing SEGA's reputation.

PRICING

Price is a key competitive weapon in the battle of the game boxes. 3DO learned a hard lesson when it introduced its interactive player in the United States at an initial price of $699 with disappointing results. According to one Japanese consumer-electronics official, 3DO is "an object lesson in how not to approach the U.S. market . . . For our company we would only enter the U.S. market if we could price our machines at under $200."[31] 3DO eventually dropped the price of its system to $399, but many parents still considered that too expensive for a toy.

One sales tactic that had proven successful in the past was getting consumers to buy a new system in installments. This has been SEGA's strategy and one that others appeared to be following. For example, a fully loaded Genesis system contains a $100 game player, a $200 SEGA CD, and a $150 Genesis 32-X. The cost of such a system exceeds the $399 price tag of a 3DO player, even though a 3DO system has superior performance.[32]

Widespread emergence of a videogame cartridge rental market has the potential of cannibalizing retail sales of game cartridges and ultimately resulting in a significant increase in competition for retail shelf space and pricing and margin pressures.[33] The shift to a CD-ROM format for games also holds potential for significant reduction in production costs. A CD-ROM game could be pressed and packaged for less than $4, as compared to a cartridge-based system where chip costs and manufacturing expenses could push the cost to make a top-quality cartridge over $20. The cost advantage of the CD-ROM format, coupled with greater ability to match production with demand, offers game marketers a significant improvement in the structure of their value chain systems.

ADVERTISING AND MARKETING

Growing advertising budgets for new game titles signalled just how competitive the industry was becoming. Acclaim Entertainment spent $10 million in its marketing campaign to launch "Mortal Kombat II" in September 1994. The original version

---

[31]S. Mansfield, "Sony, NEC Video Game Entries No Threat to Sega, Nintendo," *Electronic Business Buyer*, 1994, pp. 30, 32.
[32]DFC Intelligence Research.
[33]Activision's Form 10-K, 1994, p. 15.

had sold more than 6 million games since it was introduced in September 1993. The game, in which players rip out the hearts of their enemies, was manufactured for the Nintendo and SEGA home systems. SEGA reportedly spent $45 million on a world-wide marketing blitz to promote its recently introduced game, "Sonic & Knuckles." Nintendo spent $17 million to promote its new game "Donkey Kong Country" for the 1994 holiday season. Good Times Entertainment undertook a $3 million to $5 million campaign for its October 1994 launch of "Doom II," a follow-up to "Doom," one of the industry's most successful computer software titles.[34] Video-game industry analysts predicted that advertising could be the deciding factor in the 1994 race between Nintendo and SEGA to keep their sales pumped up until their newer, more powerful videogame systems came on the market. In 1993 alone, Nintendo spent more than $165 million on marketing support. Despite the big dollars expended on advertising and marketing, word-of-mouth, rental, and borrowing games continued as powerful influences on unit sales volumes. Many game players preferred to try a game before they purchased it.

THE FUTURE

The intensifying rivalry between Nintendo and SEGA heightens the need for each company to develop a viable long-term competitive strategy. While it seems clear that videogames have staying power in the entertainment industry, neither company's future success is assured as computers, telecommunications technologies, and enter-tainment merge to create a vista of new multimedia options—some of which repre-sent opportunities and some of which pose threats. The challenges for Nintendo and SEGA are how to capitalize on their prior successes and market reputations, what directions to pursue, and how to exploit the opportunities before them and win a sustainable competitive advantage. Where will Nintendo and SEGA be in five years? Who will emerge as the dominant provider of videogames?

---

[34]J. A. Trachtenberg, "Zap! Smash! Aggressive Ads Plug Game Sequels," *The Wall Street Journal*, August 24, 1994, p. B1.

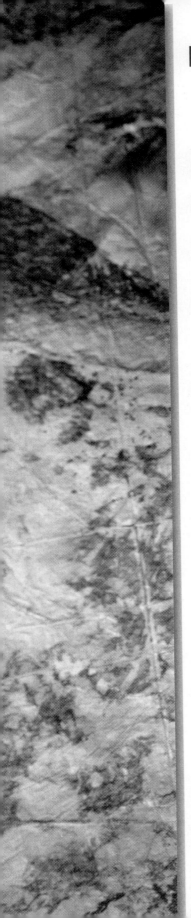

Briggs & Stratton Corporation: Competing in the Outdoor Power Equipment Industry

Richard C. Hoffman, Salisbury State University
John E. Gamble, Auburn University at Montgomery
Edwin W. Arnold, Auburn University at Montgomery

Since introducing its first small aluminum engine in 1953, Briggs & Stratton had consistently led the industry in manufacturing small gasoline engines for outdoor power equipment such as lawn mowers, rotary tillers, snow throwers, and lawn vacuums (see Exhibit 1). During the 1980s, Briggs & Stratton, like many other U.S. manufacturing companies, found itself confronted with a new group of rivals—Japanese companies with the strategic intent of capturing the U.S. market. In 1994, Briggs & Stratton President and Chief Executive Officer Frederick P. Stratton observed:

> We began the 1980s as the world's leading producer of small engines. We began the 1990s as the world's leading producer. These two statements belie the intervening difficulties . . . Responding to reduced demand and a weakening yen, the four Japanese motorcycle manufacturers threw resources into an effort to conquer the small engine market. We recognized that we had to do a lot of things differently if we were to maintain our leadership position in the face of this threat. The combination of a stronger yen and the things we did stemmed the tide. The Japanese thrust has been parried, and the experience made us in many ways a stronger company.

To maintain its leadership position, the company broadened its product line, reduced costs, improved quality, and invested in new plants and processes. One of the outcomes combating the Japanese invasion was a clearer vision of the firm's strategy in a period characterized by strong competitive rivalry. As Stratton described it:

> We reaffirmed our traditional strategic direction, agreeing to commit major resources only to our traditional mass market core business and to serve other market segments with limited resources or in partnerships with other companies with appropriate capabilities.

COMPANY HISTORY

Briggs & Stratton (B&S) began conducting business in Milwaukee in 1908. The company's first product was a six-cylinder, two-cycle engine that Stephen F. Briggs had developed during his engineering courses at South Dakota State

Exhibit 1	Outdoor Power Equipment Products

Lawn mowers	Lawn edger-trimmers
Garden tractors	Shredder-grinders
Rotary tillers	Lawn vacuums
Snow throwers	Leaf blowers
Flexible line trimmers	

Source: *Profile of the Outdoor Power Equipment Industry,* 1993.

College. After he graduated in 1907, he was eager to produce his engine and enter the rapidly expanding automobile industry. Through a mutual friend, Stephen F. Briggs, the inventor, met Harold M. Stratton, the successful businessman. With that introduction, the Briggs & Stratton Corporation was born. Unfortunately, the engine cost too much to produce, as did their second product, an automobile called the Superior. The partners were out of money and out of the automobile assembly business.

However, in 1909 Briggs filed a patent for a gas engine igniter to replace the existing magneto ignition system in automobiles. This product set the stage for the company to later become the largest U.S. producer of switch and lock apparatus used in automobiles. By 1920, the company was widely recognized as a major producer of ignition switches for cars and trucks.

In 1920, Briggs & Stratton acquired the patents and manufacturing rights to the Smith motor wheel and the Flyer, a buckboardlike motor vehicle powered by the Smith motor wheel. The Smith motor wheel was a wheel with a small engine attached for propulsion. It could also be used on bicycles. The price for the two-passenger Flyer was $150, but it still could not compete with Ford's Model T. The Model T was higher priced but also more technologically advanced.

As sales of the motor wheel slowed, the company found that a stationary version, the model PB, provided a good power source for washing machines, garden tractors, and lawn mowers. By 1936, engines were being mass produced at the rate of 120 units per hour. During World War II, Briggs & Stratton produced bomb fuses and aircraft ignitions.

After the war, Briggs & Stratton set out to capture a larger share of the growing lawn and garden equipment market. Recognizing the lawn mower market as a potential growth area, the company set out to make a lighter weight, low-cost engine. Briggs developed and introduced the aluminum alloy engine in 1953, which achieved a 40 percent reduction for both weight and price. The aluminum engine was a huge success, with initial demand outstripping supply. In response to demand, the company opened a new engine plant in Wauwatosa, Wisconsin, on an 85-acre site.

In November 1975, some 56 years after the motor wheel opened the way into the small engine business, the 100 millionth Briggs & Stratton engine came off the assembly line. In 1990, revenues reached $1 billion for the first time, and in 1995, B&S ranked 717th in sales on the Fortune 1000 list of the largest U.S. industrial and service corporations. Over 90 percent of the company's revenues came from the sale of small gasoline-powered engines; the remainder came from selling ignition switches and locks for motor vehicles to the auto manufacturers. Exhibits 2–5 present the company's recent financial performance.

Exhibit 2   Briggs & Stratton Corporation Income Statements, 1992–1994

	1994	1993	1992
Net sales	$1,285,517,000	$1,139,462,000	$1,041,828,000
Cost of goods sold	1,018,977,000	926,861,000	867,780,000
Gross profit on sales	266,540,000	212,601,000	174,048,000
Engineering, selling, general, and administrative expenses	94,795,000	83,176,000	78,736,000
Income from operations	171,745,000	129,425,000	95,312,000
Interest expense	(8,997,000)	(11,283,000)	(11,246,000)
Other income (expense), net	6,973,000	(3,737,000)	(3,863,000)
Income before provision for income taxes	169,721,000	114,405,000	80,203,000
Provision for income taxes	67,240,000	44,060,000	28,700,000
Net income before cumulative effect of accounting changes	102,481,000	70,345,000	51,503,000
Cumulative effect of accounting changes for:			
Postretirement health care, net of income taxes of $25,722,000	(40,232,000)	—	—
Postemployment benefits, net of income taxes of $430,000	(672,000)	—	—
Deferred income taxes	8,346,000	—	—
	(32,558,000)	—	—
Net income	$ 69,923,000	$ 70,345,000	$ 51,503,000

Source: 1994 company annual report.

OUTDOOR POWER EQUIPMENT INDUSTRY

In 1995, the outdoor power equipment (OPE) industry consisted of a diverse group of various-sized manufacturers of finished goods and components. The $7.5 billion industry had experienced considerable attrition and consolidation since the mid-1970s. The number of lawn mower manufacturers had declined from around 80 competitors in the mid-1970s to 25 major manufacturers of walk-behind lawn mowers and 15 manufacturers of garden tractors in 1995. The four largest companies accounted for nearly 70 percent of total outdoor power equipment production. The surviving OPE manufacturers were faced with consumers demanding value—higher quality products with greater horsepower at a relatively low price.

Outdoor power equipment manufacturing was not vertically integrated to any significant extent. Industry members manufactured components or assembled finished goods. Component manufacturers supplied one or more of the parts listed in Exhibit 6 to the OPE finished goods manufacturers. Most OPE manufacturers fabricated the metal housings and frames of the lawn mowers, garden tractors, snow throwers, and other outdoor power equipment and then assembled their products from the various parts supplied by the components manufacturers. The cost of components accounted for 47 percent of the value of all finished OPE shipments. Honda and Toro were the only power equipment manufacturers that had vertically

Exhibit 3 Briggs & Stratton Corporation, Consolidated Balance Sheets, 1993 and 1994

	July 3, 1994	June 27, 1993
Assets		
Current assets:		
Cash and cash equivalents	$221,101,000	$ 39,501,000
Short-term investments	—	70,422,000
Receivables, less reserves of $1,678,000 and $754,000, respectively	122,597,000	124,981,000
Inventories:		
Finished products and parts	55,847,000	46,061,000
Work in process	27,078,000	25,320,000
Raw materials	2,745,000	2,684,000
Total inventories	85,670,000	74,065,000
Future income tax benefits	32,868,000	27,457,000
Prepaid expenses	20,548,000	16,537,000
Total current assets	482,784,000	352,963,000
Prepaid pension cost	8,681,000	7,602,000
Plant and equipment:		
Land and land improvements	10,279,000	10,991,000
Buildings	111,966,000	114,066,000
Machinery and equipment	530,701,000	516,565,000
Construction in progress	16,647,000	16,498,000
Less: Accumulated depreciation and unamortized investment tax credit	383,703,000	362,578,000
Total plant and equipment, net	285,890,000	295,542,000
Total assets	$777,355,000	$656,107,000
Liabilities and Shareholders' Investment		
Current liabilities:		
Accounts payable	$ 56,364,000	$ 39,357,000
Foreign loans	21,323,000	15,927,000
Accrued liabilities:		
Wages and salaries	48,545,000	34,668,000
Warranty	29,800,000	28,318,000
Taxes, other than income taxes	6,772,000	6,003,000
Other	34,837,000	23,079,000
Total accrued liabilities	119,954,000	92,068,000
Federal and state income taxes	9,103,000	10,592,000
Total current liabilities	206,744,000	157,944,000
Deferred income taxes	12,317,000	49,900,000
Accrued employee benefits	15,423,000	13,305,000
Accrued postretirement health care obligation	64,079,000	—
Long-term debt	75,000,000	75,000,000
Shareholders' investment:		
Common stock—authorized 30 million shares $0.01 par value, issued and outstanding 14,463,500 shares in 1994 and 1993	145,000	145,000
Additional paid-in capital	42,358,000	42,883,000
Retained earnings	362,136,000	318,247,000
Cumulative translation adjustments	(847,000)	(1,317,000)
Total shareholders' investment	403,792,000	359,958,000
Total liabilities and shareholders' investment	$777,355,000	$656,107,000

Source: 1994 company annual report.

Exhibit 4   Briggs & Stratton's Performance by Business Segment, 1990–1994 (in thousands of dollars)

	Year Ended June 30				
	1994	**1993**	**1992**	**1991**	**1990**
Sales					
Engines and parts	$1,197,744	$1,066,053	$ 967,802	$885,930	$ 931,638
Locks	87,773	73,409	74,026	64,817	71,219
	$1,285,517	$1,139,462	$1,041,828	$950,747	$1,022,857
Operating Income					
Engines and parts	$ 158,900	$ 128,079	$ 90,781	$ 61,081	$ 61,246
Locks	12,845	1,346	4,531	2,335	5,035
	$ 171,745	$ 129,425	$ 95,312	$ 63,416	$ 66,281
Assets					
Engines and parts	$ 467,561	$ 458,369	$ 455,691	$432,345	$ 456,927
Locks	46,832	49,557	45,713	46,994	39,698
Unallocated	262,962	148,181	112,449	77,452	38,415
	$ 777,355	$ 656,107	$ 613,853	$556,791	$ 535,040
Depreciation Expense					
Engines and parts	$ 40,605	$ 44,895	$ 38,808	$ 34,521	$ 38,080
Locks	2,345	2,327	2,305	1,926	1,809
	$ 42,950	$ 47,222	$ 41,113	$ 36,447	$ 39,889
Expenditures for Plant and Equipment					
Engines and parts	$ 37,398	$ 34,251	$ 37,035	$ 28,760	$ 35,010
Locks	3,406	3,859	3,189	3,276	2,787
	$ 40,804	$ 38,110	$ 40,224	$ 32,036	$ 37,797

Source: 1994 company annual report.

integrated backward into components. Honda manufactured engines, housings, frames, and components at its Sweponsville, North Carolina, lawn mower assembly plant. Toro's vertical integration resulted from its 1989 acquisition of Lawn-Boy from Outdoor Marine Corporation. Most Lawn-Boy models were equipped with the brand's own two-cycle engines. Exhibit 7 presents industry-average costs and profit margins for outdoor power equipment manufacturers.

Distribution in the industry had undergone a major shift during the late 1980s and early 1990s. Traditionally, approximately 50 percent of outdoor power equipment produced by manufacturers was shipped to independent wholesalers who in turn distributed it to general merchandisers, home centers, lawn and garden stores, and other OPE retailers. By 1992, only 20 percent of OPE products on their way to market passed through wholesalers, 18 percent were handled by exporters, and the balance were shipped factory-direct to the retailer. At the retail level, home centers (Home Depot, Lowe's), national merchandisers such as Sears, and discounters (Wal-Mart, Kmart, and Target) were gaining a larger share of the OPE market. The five largest retailers of OPE products accounted for nearly half of all walk-behind and

Exhibit 5 **Briggs & Stratton's Sales, Earnings, and Statistical Data, 1985–1994** *(in thousands of dollars except per share data)*

	For the Years Ended June 30									
	1994	1993	1992	1991	1990	1989	1988	1987	1986	1985
Summary of Operations										
Net sales	$1,285,517	$1,139,462	$1,041,828	$950,747	$1,002,857	$876,379	$914,057	$784,665	$745,831	$717,773
Gross profit on sales	266,540	212,601	174,048	132,431	132,438	59,629	115,113	111,618	124,408	111,248
Provision for income taxes	67,240	44,060	28,700	16,500	18,290	(13,980)	12,950	18,950	27,850	28,990
Net income	$ 69,923	$ 70,345	$ 51,503	$ 36,453	$ 35,375	$ (20,032)	$ 30,211	$ 26,614	$ 34,080	$ 33,517
Average number of shares of common stock outstanding	14,464	14,464	14,464	14,464	14,464	14,464	14,464	14,464	14,464	14,464
Per share of common stock:										
Net income	$ 4.84	$ 4.86	$ 3.56	$ 2.52	$ 2.45	$ (1.39)	$ 2.09	$ 1.84	$ 2.36	$ 2.32
Cash dividends	1.80	1.70	1.60	1.60	1.60	1.60	1.60	1.60	1.60	1.60
Shareholders' investment	27.92	24.89	21.60	19.69	18.76	17.92	20.97	20.48	20.29	19.59
Other Data										
Shareholders' investment	$ 403,792	$ 359,958	$ 312,404	$284,715	$ 271,383	$259,226	$303,305	$296,260	$293,517	$283,399
Total assets	777,355	656,107	637,853	556,791	535,040	560,816	510,600	451,879	436,622	411,598
Plant and equipment	669,593	658,120	643,433	632,488	606,863	580,184	513,700	470,586	427,672	390,657
Plant and equipment net of reserves	285,890	295,542	309,698	320,364	326,288	330,198	295,573	273,903	248,347	230,240
Provision for depreciation	42,950	47,222	41,113	36,447	39,889	38,995	29,955	24,502	21,508	17,914
Expenditures for plant and equipment	40,804	38,110	40,224	32,036	37,797	79,513	57,001	52,235	46,288	58,443
Working capital	276,040	195,019	137,008	105,298	84,082	63,757	63,372	77,281	93,854	92,522
Current ratio	2.3 to 1	2.2 to 1	1.9 to 1	1.8 to 1	1.7 to 1	1.4 to 1	1.4 to 1	1.8 to 1	2.0 to 1	2.0 to 1
Number of employees at year-end	8,628	7,950	7,799	7,242	7,994	7,316	9,827	8,611	8,299	8,203
Number of shareholders at year-end	6,228	6,651	7,118	7,943	8,466	9,222	6,923	7,206	7,924	8,959
Quoted market price:										
High	$ 90¼	$ 68⅝	$ 54¾	$ 33¾	$ 34	$ 34¾	$ 41⅞	$ 42	$ 40¼	$ 31⅛
Low	64⅞	42⅛	32⅞	20½	24⅛	24¾	20¼	31½	25¾	25½

Source: 1994 company annual report.

Exhibit 6   Components Used in the Assembly of Outdoor Power Equipment, 1992, 1988, and 1983

Component	Percent of Total Value of Components Sold to OPE Finished Goods Assemblers		
	1992	1988	1983
Engines	50.6%	52.4%	58.0%
Wheels	4.2	4.6	6.0
Transmissions	8.9	7.6	9.0
Blades	1.1	NA	NA
Brakes/steering	1.0	NA	NA
Belts	1.3	1.8	NA
Tires	3.1	2.9	NA
Plugs/filters	0.6	NA	NA
Grass-catching bags	1.4	1.2	2.0
Seats	1.3	1.4	NA
Batteries	1.4	1.4	2.0
Decks	2.9	NA	NA
Engine parts	1.3	NA	NA
Electrical motor parts	1.2	NA	NA
Pulleys	1.3	NA	NA
Tines and augers	0.6	NA	NA
Fuel tanks	0.8	NA	NA
Cables and controls	1.6	NA	NA
Other	15.4	26.7	23.0
Total	100.0%	100.0%	100.0%

Source: *Profile of the Outdoor Power Equipment Industry,* 1993.

riding mowers sold in the United States. Outdoor power equipment market share by retail channel is presented in Exhibit 8.

Retail sales of outdoor power equipment tended to vary with the ups and downs in housing starts and the general condition of the national economy. During the late 1970s, industry sales had grown rapidly, driven by the growth in new housing starts and the U.S. economy, allowing many components producers and OPE makers to prosper. Shipments of walk-behind rotary lawn mowers approached 6 million units in 1979 and then tumbled to 4.4 million in 1983 as a result of recessionary effects on the U.S. economy. As the economy improved, sales of walk-behind mowers improved to 5 million units throughout the late 1980s. Exhibit 9 provides shipments of outdoor power equipment by category for recent years and shipment forecasts for 1995 and 1996.

In 1974, U.S. exports of OPE products amounted to $85 million versus imports of a meager $2 million. By 1985, U.S. exports had grown to $127 million, with imports reaching $118 million—giving the U.S. OPE industry a slim $9 million trade surplus. While most of the 1985 exports were to Canada, over 40 percent of the imports were from Japan. Imports of OPE products peaked in 1988 at $273 million and were only $74 million in 1991. Exports by the U.S. OPE industry in 1991 were $539 million,

Exhibit 7   Costs and Profit Margins for Outdoor Power Equipment, 1992

Cost Area	Percent
Materials	9.6%
Components	47.6
Wages and benefits	18.3
Transportation	1.7
Advertising	2.8
Selling and administration	9.2
Other	7.5
Total costs	96.7
Net income before taxes	3.3
Total	100.0%

Source: *Profile of the Outdoor Power Equipment Industry,* 1993.

Exhibit 8   U.S. Outdoor Power Equipment Retail Distribution, 1995, 1992, and 1983

Retail Outlet	1995	1992	1983
Hardware stores	5.0%	6.3%	12.0%
Home centers	12.0	8.7	3.0
National merchandisers	30.0	27.2	22.0
Discount department stores	17.0	12.0	8.0
Lawn and garden stores	15.0	16.9	17.0
OPE/farm equipment stores	16.0	20.2	19.0
Other	5.0	8.7	19.0
Total	100.0%	100.0%	100.0%

Sources: Compiled by the case researchers from a number of sources, including interviews with company personnel; 1983 and 1992 data is based on information contained in the *Profile of the Outdoor Power Equipment Industry,* 1993.

giving U.S. manufacturers a $465 trade surplus. Exhibit 10 summarizes trade patterns for outdoor power equipment in 1991. Exchange rates played a big role in whether foreign-made OPE products could be price competitive in the U.S. market and whether U.S.-made OPE products could compete in foreign markets. Currency exchange rates for selected countries for the years 1985 and 1990–95 are displayed in Exhibit 11.

Industry Regulation

Prior to 1982, manufacturers of OPE were not regulated by the Consumer Products Safety Commission (CPSC); compliance was voluntary. Voluntary standards were promulgated by the Outdoor Power Equipment Institute (OPEI) and had been supported by the industry trade association since the mid-1950s. The standards were primarily concerned with improved product performance and safety. Safety

Exhibit 9   Shipments of Outdoor Power Equipment, 1985, 1990–1994, with Forecasts for 1995–1996   (units in thousands)

| | Equipment | | | | | |
| | Walk-Behind | | | Riding | | |
Year	Rotary Mowers	Rotary Tillers	Snow Throwers	Rear-Engine Mowers	Front-Engine Mowers	Garden Tractors
1985	5,015	430	258	322	479	153
1990	5,700	300	355	247	885	156
1991	5,350	296	285	209	840	128
1992	5,150	343	285	205	847	133
1993	5,720	343	265	185	1,060	163
1994*	6,030	315	248	177	1,086	189
Extended Forecasts						
1995	6,170	341	NA	158	1,168	199
1996	6,078	352	NA	149	1,170	207

* Estimated.
Source: Outdoor Power Equipment Institute.

Exhibit 10   U.S. Trade Patterns for the Outdoor Power Equipment Industry, 1991   (in millions of dollars)

| | U.S. Exports of OPE Products | | Source of U.S. Imports of OPE Products | |
Country	Dollar Value	Percent	Dollar Value	Percent
Canada and Mexico	$166	30.8%	$27	36.9%
European Community	223	41.4	7	10.1
Japan	20	3.6	29	39.5
East Asia	15	2.8	6	7.7
South America	11	2.0	1	1.7
Other	104	19.4	3	4.1
World total	$539	100.0%	$74	100.0%

Source: *Profile of the Outdoor Power Equipment Industry*, 1993.

standards involved both the protection from thrown objects and noise level. About 90 percent of the industry's products were in compliance with these voluntary standards. Products complying with the standards were affixed with a triangular OPEI seal.

A number of CPSC regulations went into effect in 1982. These standards called for increased safety restrictions for walk-behind power mowers, including shields to protect people from thrown objects, deflectors and drain holes to prevent

Exhibit 11 Currency Exchange Rates per U.S. Dollar, 1985, 1990–1995

Currency	1995	1994	1993	1992	1991	1990	1985
Canada (dollar)	1.35	1.31	1.29	1.21	1.15	1.17	1.32
Germany (mark)	1.38	1.74	1.61	1.51	1.49	1.68	3.15
Japan (yen)	84	112	111	127	135	145	251
Mexico (peso)*	6.29	3.10	3.10	3,089	2,948	2,683	224

* The Mexican government has revalued the country's currency a number of times during the 1980s and 1990s due to the currency's devaluation against the U.S. dollar.

Source: *The Wall Street Journal*, various years.

ignition of spilled fuel, the deadman blade control system, and labeling requirements. Mowers built after July 1, 1982, had to have blades that stopped within three seconds after the operator released a deadman control at the handle of the mower. Meeting this standard involved either installing a blade brake or the addition of a rechargeable, battery-powered electric starter. The CPSC estimated that compliance with the deadman blade control system would cost approximately $35 per unit.

Many engine manufacturers, including Briggs & Stratton, had successfully developed technology to make manual starting much easier, with engines usually starting on the first or second pull. The lawn mower industry asked Congress to amend the safety standard to allow engine stop with manual restart as a third method of compliance with the blade control requirement. President Reagan signed the amendment despite the CPSC's strong opposition. As of 1995, there were no federal regulations concerning riding mowers, and no additional regulation of walk-behind mowers had been initiated since 1982.

The industry also had to comply with the Magnuson-Moss Act of 1975 requiring that all products with a written warranty and costing the consumer $15 or more come with either a statement concerning the duration of the warranty or a limited warranty. The industry, from time to time, also faced state and local regulations concerning noise and pollution levels of outdoor power equipment.

Environmental regulations emanating from California and the U.S. Environmental Protection Agency (EPA) were of utmost concern to the industry. In 1994, the California Air Resources Board (CARB) and the EPA jointly proposed stringent national emission standards for small utility engines—those typically used in lawn mowers and other outdoor power equipment. Phase I EPA regulations enacted in 1994 required that all utility engines manufactured after August 1996 be modified to reduce the emissions of hydrocarbons and nitrogen oxides by 70 percent from 1990 levels. The California regulations were effective January 1, 1995. The EPA and CARB cited ozone formation (smog) as the motivation for Phase I regulations. In 1995, the industry was involved with the EPA in "regulatory-negotiation" of Phase II regulations that, if implemented, would ultimately require utility engines to meet the same emission standards as automobiles. Phase II regulations also concerned evaporation and spillage from gasoline tanks and containers. Phase I regulations were expected to increase the cost of utility engines by $5 to $10 per engine. In 1993, the outdoor power equipment industry incurred expenses of $10.6 million related to EPA requirements and expenses of $725,000 related to CPSC compliance.

Competition: Domestic

Competition in the OPE industry occurred mainly within two broad strategic groups—finished goods producers and components producers. The finished goods manufacturers represented the largest group of competitors. The major producers of premium-priced lawn mowers included Toro Company, Snapper, and John Deere and Company. MTD Products, Murray Ohio Manufacturing, and American Yard Products (AYP) were the chief producers of outdoor power equipment for the medium-priced and discount markets. The latter three firms also produced equipment for retailers selling OPE products under their own private label. Exhibit 12 shows the major domestic players in the OPE industry in the United States.

The largest assembler of outdoor power equipment for the premium-priced segment was the Toro Company, Inc., headquartered in Minneapolis. Toro was also the leading manufacturer of snow-throwing equipment. Toro Company had sales of $794 million and net income of $22 million in 1994. Toro's total revenue included over $300 million in commercial-grade OPE and other lawn and garden equipment such as irrigation systems. Toro had recently increased its share of the high-end segment by acquiring Wheel Horse and Lawn-Boy; Wheel Horse primarily manufactured and marketed riding mowers and garden tractors and Lawn-Boy's strength was in walk-behind lawn mowers. Lawn-Boy was one of the few vertically integrated producers and even made its own engines, designing them with a distinctive integrated look (i.e., the engine cowling lines matched the lines of the blade housing) that appealed to some consumers in the premium-priced segment. Lawn-Boy was the only domestic manufacturer to produce its own engines. Lawn-Boy models were equipped with either the brand's "in-house" two-cycle engine or Tecumseh's four-cycle engine. The two-cycle design provided additional power, which was useful for self-propelled models used on hilly terrain, but it required that gasoline and oil be mixed in the fuel tank. Lawn-Boy's top-of-the-line models were equipped with an oil injection system, where oil and gasoline were stored in separate reservoirs and then electronically mixed. Other major engine manufacturers in the industry produced four-cycle engines that required no mixing of gasoline and oil. So far, Toro had not opted to use Lawn-Boy's two-cycle engines on its Toro or Wheel Horse product lines.

The Snapper division of Actava Group, Inc., marketed a full line of premium-priced lawn mowers, tillers, and snow blowers. Snapper competed in North America and Europe and achieved sales of $248 million in 1994. Snapper emphasized after-the-sale service, and even though it had its own small sales force, it generally marketed through distributors to a network of independent lawn and garden stores. The company maintained large parts inventories and conducted factory service schools that dealers were required to attend once or twice each year.

Deere and Company, Inc., also produced top-of-the-line products. Deere's garden tractors ranged from $2,000 to $10,000 and were considered by industry rivals to have "Mercedes-Benz" quality. Much of Deere's OPE sales were in the farming segment. Deere's OPE sales in 1994 amounted to approximately $1.3 billion. For several years, Deere had chosen B&S engines to power its mowers, but recently it had signed an agreement to purchase the majority of its garden tractor engines from Kawasaki. Kawasaki gained Deere's business by supplying an engine with higher specifications and a lower price than the Briggs & Stratton engines previously used by John Deere. Deere had recently acquired the Jacobsen/Homelite division of Textron, Inc., which produced high-quality walk-behind lawn mowers, chain saws,

Exhibit 12   Selected U.S. Outdoor Power Equipment Manufacturers
(sales in millions of dollars)

Company	1994 Main OPE Sales	Products‡
American Yard Products	600*	Finished goods
Bolens/Troy-Bilt	50	Finished goods
Briggs & Stratton Corp.	1,197	Engines
John Deere & Co.	1,305†	Finished goods
Kohler Co.	200*	Engines
MTD Products Co.	700*	Finished goods
McLane Manufacturing Co.	20*	Finished goods
Murray Ohio Mfg. Co.	500*	Finished goods
Snapper	248	Finished goods
Tecumseh Products Co.	427	Engines
Toro Company Inc.	794†	Finished goods
Yazoo Mfg. Co. Inc.	25*	Finished goods

* Estimated from interviews with industry participants.
† Includes revenue from sources other than consumer OPE.
Sources: Company annual reports, Ward's Business Directory of U.S. Private and Public Companies, 1994; Standard & Poor's Register, Vol. 1, 1995.

blowers, and flexible line trimmers sold under the Homelite and Jacobsen brand names.

The producers of lower-priced mowers included the three largest U.S. lawn mower manufacturers—MTD, Murray, and AYP. MTD Products, Inc., of Valley City, Ohio, was closely held and had estimated sales of $700 million. MTD bought its engines from Briggs & Stratton and Tecumseh, manufactured the frames and housing, and assembled the units for sale. The company sold its products to private-label distributors and marketed nationally in the discount department stores and home centers under its MTD and Yardman brands. The company also marketed through lawn and garden stores under its newly acquired brands—Cub Cadet and White. MTD had the distinction of being the nation's largest producer of walk-behind lawn mowers and Briggs & Stratton's largest customer.

American Yard Products was the nation's second-largest producer of lawn mowers, with estimated sales of $600 million. AYP, a subsidiary of Electrolux, was Sears's primary supplier of Craftsman label walk-behind mowers, riding mowers, and garden tractors. The Craftsman brand accounted for approximately 25 percent of all lawn mower sales. AYP was also a private-label supplier to other discount chains and manufactured Poulan's line of lawn mowers. AYP used Tecumseh and Briggs & Stratton engines on its equipment.

The Murray Ohio Manufacturing Co., owned by British conglomerate Tomkins PLC and located in Brentwood, Tennessee, was a major producer of both OPE and bicycles for the medium-priced and discount segments. The company produced a broad line of walk-behind mowers, riding mowers, and garden tractors marketed under its Murray brand. Murray was the primary supplier to Wal-Mart until 1995, when MTD acquired the contract to supply all walk-behind and riding mowers offered by the nation's leading discounter. Murray had recently acquired Noma, a private-label manufacturer, to expand its capability to supply private-label buyers. Total corporate sales approximated $500 million in 1994. Murray, like its primary rivals MTD and AYP, sourced engines from both B&S and Tecumseh.

The single biggest cost component of lawn mowers was the engine. The three largest producers of mower engines were Briggs & Stratton, Tecumseh Products Co., and Kohler Company. Tecumseh was Briggs & Stratton's chief domestic competitor in engines ranging from 3 to 20 horsepower and had actually strengthened its position in the industry as a result of price competition in the finished goods segment of the industry. Many OPE manufacturers such as MTD, AYP, and Murray had utilized multiple sourcing as a strategy to minimize components costs. Until retailers began to pressure for lower prices, most finished goods manufacturers found it more convenient to purchase all or most of their engines from a single source—usually Briggs & Stratton.

Tecumseh Products Company was the largest U.S. producer of refrigerator compressors and the second-largest producer of small, gasoline-powered engines. The company also produced gear assemblies and related transmission parts. In 1994, Tecumseh's operating income on engine sales of $427 million (32 percent of total sales) was $41 million (32 percent of total operating income). The largest customers of Tecumseh engines were Toro Company and AYP. Tecumseh engines were used exclusively on Toro's snow-throwing equipment and on about 50 percent of Craftsman walk-behind mowers. Sears advertisements regularly touted the reliability of its Craftsman Eager-1 engines, which were all supplied by Tecumseh.

Kohler Company was privately held, had estimated sales of $1 billion, and employed 12,500 workers. The majority of the company's revenues came as a result of its plumbing fixtures business. Kohler was a distant third in small engine sales, behind B&S and Tecumseh. Kohler's engine business was strongest in segments requiring greater horsepower. Kohler engines were more commonly found on garden tractors and industrial products than on walk-behind mowers.

Competition: Foreign

Japan was the primary exporter of OPE products to the United States. The value of Japanese exports of lawn mowers and parts to the United States had increased from less than $3 million in 1978 to $36.1 million in 1985, representing 41 percent of the total value of OPE goods imported into the United States that year. As of 1992, Japanese imports still accounted for 40 percent of all outdoor power equipment imported into the United States. Most foreign imports of OPE products into the United States were high-quality walk-behind mowers and garden tractors. Garden tractors were imported as agricultural machinery and were exempted from paying U.S. tariffs. The three leading import brands of garden tractors were all Japanese: Kubota, Yanmar, and Satoh.

The Japanese small gasoline engine manufacturers—Honda, Yamaha, Kawasaki, and Suzuki—maintained their strongest foothold in the market for engines with industrial applications. Honda was widely acknowledged as the leading global supplier of industrial engines. In the lawn mower segment, Honda mowers were the only foreign brand that was a factor in the U.S. market. Competition from Japanese imports had become much less of a problem for U.S.-based manufacturers since the late 1980s because of the strong increases in the value of the yen against the dollar.

A softening of the motorcycle business in the 1980s had forced Japanese motorcycle manufacturers to look to other markets in order to maintain full use of their production facilities. All four Japanese motorcycle manufacturers (Honda, Kawasaki, Suzuki, and Yamaha) identified outdoor power products as appropriate new business opportunities.

Honda had stated publicly that it intended to become a leader in the powered products field and had transferred resources from its motorcycle division to its powered products division. In many respects, OPE products represented a natural business diversification for Honda because the company was founded in 1948 to produce small internal combustion engines. Honda's production capacity for small utility engines was about 2.1 million units a year in 1995. The company sold its mowers in the United States through a network of 2,000 established OPE lawn and garden store dealers.

Honda's U.S. Strategy

Honda had targeted the high end of the U.S. market for OPE products. Similar to Lawn-Boy, it manufactured both the lawn mower engine and the lawn mower body, which resulted in equipment having an integrated look. Honda engines were noted for their light weight and dependability. Professional users of OPE had casually dubbed Honda's engines "Briggs-Hondas" because of their dependability. Heavy users often replaced worn-out Briggs & Stratton engines with Honda engines. Honda's product strength was based on its extensive R&D expenditures and its speedy incorporation of cutting-edge technological developments. Honda marketed its products with the aid of extensive advertising and promotion and priced its products competitively, sometimes setting prices below the other premium-priced brands to gain market share. Honda had been extremely successful in both the U.S. motorcycle and automobile markets using similar strategies and possessed extensive resources to support similar efforts in the OPE market (see Exhibit 13).

In 1994, Honda sold approximately 150,000 lawn mowers in the United States—up from 10,000 mowers in 1983. Honda also sold replacement engines compatible with many makes of mowers. Until 1984, Honda lawn mowers bound for the United States had been manufactured in Japan. When its level of U.S. sales made it economical to establish a production base in the United States, Honda built a $26 million manufacturing plant for engines and lawn mowers in Sweponsville, North Carolina. The plant produced all Honda lawn mowers offered in the global market. Honda produced approximately 175,000 mowers and 200,000 engines annually and employed 350 workers in its U.S. facility. Honda had exported over 225,000 lawn mowers and engines from its Sweponsville plant to 16 countries since 1986.

Honda's products had been well received in the United States, drawing excellent ratings from consumer magazines. A list of Honda outdoor power equipment offered in the United States is provided in Exhibit 14. Comparisons with domestic models were generally quite favorable. The main disadvantages listed in a 1992 *Consumer Reports* review were difficulty of oil changes and the need to substitute blades when changing from bagging clippings to mulching. Honda mowers received high marks for convenience, performance, and safety. The starting controls were simple, easy to reach, and had an automatic choke that eliminated the need for a choke control on the throttle. The cutting performance of Honda mowers was usually rated excellent; they provided a level cut, even in tall heavy grass, and efficiently bagged clippings. Honda's mowers met or exceeded safety standards, including a deadman clutch that

Exhibit 13   Honda Motor Company: Financial Summary, 1985, 1990–1994 (in millions of U.S. dollars)

	1994	1993	1992	1991	1990	1985
Sales	$39,927	$35,798	$33,370	$30,567	$27,070	$10,753
Net income	619	220	307	540	572	532
Assets	34,708	28,526	26,374	21,005	18,018	5,974
Stockholders' equity	$11,715	$ 9,447	$ 9,085	$ 7,736	$ 6,872	$ 2,806
Number of employees	92,800	91,300	90,900	85,500	79,200	50,609

Compiled from: "The Global 500," *Fortune*, various years.

Exhibit 14   Honda Motor Company, U.S. Outdoor Power Equipment Product Line, 1995

Product	Number of Models
Lawn mowers	18
Riding mowers	3
Lawn tractors	3
Multipurpose tractors	4
Tillers	7
Generators	26
Snow blowers	6
Commercial mowers	5
Engines	69

Source: *Honda Motor Company Fact Book*.

stopped the blade one second after the control was released, well within the three-second requirement.

THE BRIGGS & STRATTON CORPORATION ————————

In 1995, Briggs & Stratton (B&S), headquartered in Wauwatosa, Wisconsin, was the world's largest producer of both small, gas-powered engines used primarily for outdoor power equipment and ignition systems and locks used by the automobile industry. B&S had an estimated 75 percent of the small engine market in the United States and over 50 percent of the worldwide market. Engines and parts accounted for 93 percent of Briggs's total revenues in 1994 (see Exhibit 15). The other 7 percent was from the sale of automotive lock and key sets through B&S Technologies. Both industries that the company competed in were characterized by strong rivalry. Briggs management decided to spin off the automobile ignition system and lock division to its shareholders in 1995. A subsidiary corporation was to be established with shares distributed to B&S shareholders as a tax-free dividend.

Exhibit 15 Briggs & Stratton's Sales of OEM and Air-Cooled Engines by End User, 1990–1994

End Uses	Percent of Engine Sales				
	1994	1993	1992	1991	1990
Lawn and garden equipment	85%	85%	86%	86%	86%
Industrial/agricultural equipment	15	15	14	14	14
All exports of engines	21	25	21	21	23
Total engine sales as a percent of corporate revenues	93%	92%	93%	93%	93%

Source: Company annual reports.

Eighty-five percent of Briggs's engine sales were to manufacturers of lawn mowers and other outdoor power equipment (shredders-grinders, snow blowers, tillers, etc.). Approximately 15 percent of its engine sales were to manufacturers of construction and agricultural equipment. Briggs's top three customers for small engines were MTD (18 percent of sales), Murray Ohio Manufacturing (12 percent of sales), and American Yard Products (12 percent of sales). Other large customers included Toro and Snapper.

In 1989, B&S's engine sales declined 4 percent, and the firm recorded its first unprofitable year in over two decades. The next year, the firm returned to profitability and sales increased at an average annual rate of 3.1 percent between 1990 and 1994. The improved performance was due in part to lower interest rates, improved housing starts, and good weather. Management expected to maintain annual growth in revenues of 3 percent during the 1995–97 period.

International Activities

B&S estimated that 35 to 40 percent of its total engine business resulted from exports, either through the company's direct sales or through the sales of U.S. OPE manufacturers who chose Briggs as a supplier. Frederick P. Stratton, the company's CEO, observed:

> The market for products powered by our engines is increasingly international. The flow of material around the world is truly amazing. For example, we know of cases where engines we ship to customers in Australia are mounted on equipment destined for Europe, and engines we ship to customers in Europe are mounted on equipment destined for the U.S.

B&S realized that simply defending its domestic market share was not sufficient and that, in the long run, new growth would come from increased sales abroad. During the past decade, B&S gradually expanded its presence in international markets. The company targeted its engines to Europe's established lawn and garden equipment market and concentrated on providing engines for agricultural, marine, and light industrial applications to developing Asian nations. The primary competitors in the overseas markets included smaller local firms and eight Japanese competitors (Honda, Kawasaki, Suzuki, Yamaha, Fuji, Mitsubishi, Kubota, and Yanmar). Tecnamotor S.p.A. of Italy was a major European competitor and was owned by Tecumseh.

In major foreign markets sales were handled by direct customer contact, whereas in smaller markets independent sales representatives were used. B&S had established sales and service offices in Switzerland, Norway, United Arab Emirates, Australia, New Zealand, and China. Wholly owned distributed centers were located in Canada, the United Kingdom, France, Germany, the Netherlands, Australia, and New Zealand.

Briggs & Stratton had used strategic alliances to establish overseas manufacturing capabilities. The first of these was a 1986 joint venture with Daihatsu Motor Co. to produce V-twin (two cylinders) overhead valve engines for B&S's Vanguard line (a premium engine line) in Osaka, Japan. This was a less expensive approach to broadening the product line than developing a new product on its own. In 1993, B&S signed a marketing agreement whereby Daihatsu would produce and market a new line of three-cylinder, water-cooled diesel and gasoline engines for the Vanguard line. Another joint venture existed with the Puling Machinery Works and the Yimin Machinery Plant in China to produce cast-iron engines for industrial/construction use in markets outside the United States. In 1992, B&S contracted with Mitsubishi Heavy Industries to supply a line of single-cylinder engines to add to B&S's Vanguard line.

Products

B&S had the widest engine product line of the small engine manufacturers located throughout the world. Briggs's most popular engines were air-cooled, four-cycle aluminum alloy engines that ran on straight gas (not mixed with oil) and ranged in size from 3 to 20 horsepower. Less than 5 percent of the company's engines were of the older air-cooled, cast-iron design, but it still made cast-iron models ranging from 9 to 16 horsepower for selected OPE products sold mainly in foreign markets. B&S also produced air- and water-cooled diesel engines ranging from 3 to 28.5 horsepower. Walk-behind lawn mowers generally were equipped with a 3- to 5.5-HP engine.

Since 1984, B&S had launched four new styles of engines to respond to changing demand and to combat increased competition from Japan. The first of these new lines was the MAX series of 3.5- to 4-HP engines offering better styling, easier starting, and quiet/low maintenance performance. This new line represented the first major engine redesign since 1967. The Quantum line was introduced two years later. It also featured low-profile styling, improved durability, and improved operating convenience—Quantum engines had fewer parts and were assembled with the aid of robotic technology. In 1987, B&S launched the Vanguard line—overhead valve engines ranging from 8 to 18 horsepower and intended for the premium-priced OPE market and for industrial applications. Subsequent additions of larger engines to this line were made through strategic alliances with two Japanese manufacturers, Daihatsu and Mitsubishi. In 1993, the Diamond series of engines was introduced for commercial lawn and garden equipment. These engines ranged from 5.5 to 20 horsepower and had extended life features for durability and rugged power.

Improvements were made to two of B&S's smaller engine lines used for lower-priced equipment. These were renamed the Classic and Sprint lines. In addition to introducing new engine lines, B&S made improvements in ignitions, noise reduction, and pollution abatement. Exhibit 16 presents B&S's track record in new product development.

Exhibit 16	Small Engine Innovations and New Product Lines Introduced by Briggs & Stratton, 1953–1993

1953	Aluminum Alloy Gasoline Engine: Reduced weight and cost of small engines.
1961	Easy Spin Starting: Engine starting effort cut in half by a simple cam-controlled, fault-proof compression release.
1962	Oil Foam Air Cleaner: Dirt banned from engine for its life by an easy-to-clean polyurethane foam filter.
1966	Syncho Balance Design: Engine and riding equipment vibrations smoothed out by a synchronized counterweight system.
1968	Automatic Vacuum Controlled Choke: Replaced manual choke, providing extra power when needed for heavy loads.
1971	12-Volt Gear-Type Starter with Dual Circuit Alternator: Provided quick starting at low temperatures. Alternator provides both D/C battery charging and A/C for light or external loads.
1977	Quiet Power: The 16-HP twin-cylinder engine prompted by noise abatement guidelines provided quiet running and low vibration levels.
1982	Magnetron Ignition: A self-contained transistor with no moving parts. Provides more consistent spark for dependable starting. Can be installed on existing engines.
1983	The small electric motor was introduced for power mowers. The new 120-volt, 1,000-watt motor weighed 11 lbs., had a 10-year life, and met CPSC standards for deadman blade control.
1984	MAX Series of 3.5- to 4-HP engines featuring improved durability and appearance.
1986	Quantum Series of 3.5- to 8-HP engines for the premium market.
1987	Vanguard OHV line of medium engines 8 to 18 horsepower for premium market and industrial/construction applications.
1993	Diamond Series of premium 5.5- to 20-HP engines for the commercial lawn care market.

Compiled from company pamphlets and annual reports.

Marketing and Promotion

For most of its history, B&S sold engines directly to OPE manufacturers, relying on its quality image and reputation to gain sales. This changed during the 80s when B&S assembled its first marketing staff to market engines to consumers and retailers of finished goods. B&S wanted consumers to ask for their engines by name when buying a lawn mower. The company began a television advertising campaign for the first time using the slogan "Briggs & Stratton: the power in power equipment." Newer versions of these ads were still being aired in the 1990s during the spring season and were shown during sporting events. However, most of B&S's advertising expenditures were devoted to paying for cooperative ads with dealers to promote OPE products equipped with B&S engines and to promote dealer-certified repair and maintenance services to owners of products with B&S engines. A 1992 survey indicated that B&S's marketing efforts had been successful, as 72 percent of the surveyed customers specified Briggs & Stratton as the engine they preferred to power their lawn and garden equipment.

Distribution and Service

B&S sold about 70 percent of its engines via annually negotiated contracts with OPE manufacturers. To attract new customers and regain former customers lost to foreign rivals, B&S abandoned its long-standing policy of a single price for all buyers, regardless of quantity purchased or other conditions. The company now offered pricing incentives to its customers who ordered standardized engines, accepted delivery during the off season, or who committed early to specific delivery times during the peak season. However, B&S was committed to its long-standing policy of not integrating forward into the finished goods market and competing with the buyers of its engines.

The growing strength of discount chain retailers had resulted in greater pressure on the prices that OPE producers and parts suppliers could command. Large retailers buying in volume were bargaining hard for favorable prices from OPE producers. Frederick Stratton observed, "For some segments it significantly reduced the price premium our brand equity could command. This increased the importance of being a low-cost producer." Briggs's network of over 25,000 authorized service centers in North America and another 7,000 overseas made B&S engines attractive to OPE producers, since the large retailers did not offer outdoor power equipment repair or service.

Production

Manufacturing and assembly of outdoor power equipment was driven by the need to deliver new lawn mowers and tractors for retail sale in early spring and summer. As a result, demand from B&S's customers was at its peak in winter and spring. Most engines were produced from December to March. Briggs & Stratton manufactured almost all of its components used in assembling engines, including aluminum and iron castings, carburetors, and ignitions. It purchased parts such as piston rings, spark plugs, valves, and smaller plastic and metal parts. Global sourcing was used for these purchases when economically feasible. Over the past few years, B&S had increased its use of recycled or recyclable material, especially steel and aluminum. Currently, 60 percent (by weight) of the firm's engines was made from recycled materials. Recycled materials tended to be cheaper and contributed to lowering material costs.

Briggs & Stratton had begun to use materials requirement planning (MRP), an inventory reduction program (EOQ), and statistical process control in its new production facilities. The purpose of the MRP system was to provide the correct parts in the right quantities when they were needed in the manufacturing process. This system took advantage of information stored in a computer for timely response and scheduling. The goal of EOQ was to cut inventory in half while still meeting demand requirements. The statistical process control system was intended to detect any trend toward making bad parts before the parts were even produced. In addition, "quality centers" were created to ensure a constant flow of ideas from the bottom up on how to improve inventory and other production management activities.

Since 1985, Briggs had begun to move its plant operations out of Wisconsin. B&S management intended to cut production costs by building state-of-the-art facilities located in nonunion areas. The company's first non-Wisconsin plant opened in 1986 in Murray, Kentucky. This fully automated plant produced the Classic and Sprint engine lines. In 1990, a new "focused factory" was opened in Poplar Bluff, Missouri, to produce the premium Quantum engine line. Both production processes and employee training at Poplar Bluff were specifically designed for this engine line to ensure the high quality demanded of premium-quality engines. B&S's largest engine factory was still located in Wauwatosa, Wisconsin. Most other engine lines as well as single-cylinder, overhead-valve Vanguard engines were produced in Wisconsin. Two other Wisconsin factories produced engines and engine parts. Other B&S engines were produced in Asia at the plants of strategic allies in Japan and China. Two foundries in West Allis, Wisconsin, produced castings for B&S engines and also sold to outside customers.

At the end of 1994, B&S employed 8,628 employees, the highest number since 1988, when employment had peaked at 9,827. Productivity per employee improved over the years. In 1985, sales per employee averaged $87,500; by the end of 1994, sales per employee averaged $148,993. Despite this improvement, B&S management still believed that the company had a labor cost disadvantage relative to its foreign and domestic rivals. In 1994, Briggs & Stratton announced a major restructuring of manufacturing operations.

As part of its low-cost strategy, the company planned to construct three new U.S. plants at an estimated cost of $112 million. The new plant construction would result in the transfer of approximately 2,000 jobs from production facilities in Milwaukee, Wisconsin, to new facilities in Statesboro, Georgia, Auburn, Alabama, and a third southern site that had not yet been determined. The plan also provided for the expansion of the Kentucky and Missouri plants and the eventual closing of some of the Wisconsin plants. B&S management anticipated that the plant relocation strategy would result in annual cost savings of approximately $12 million—primarily due to reductions in labor expenses.

Frederick Stratton stated that the hourly compensation costs at the company's Wisconsin manufacturing facilities placed it at a competitive disadvantage in regard to its ability to compete on price. B&S management estimated that its wage and benefit costs were 20 percent higher than its primary domestic rival, Tecumseh. The company had found that labor-related expenses in its new Poplar Bluff, Missouri, and Murray, Kentucky, plants were considerably lower than in the Milwaukee, Wisconsin, facility. The average wage and benefit cost in the two southern U.S. plants was approximately $11.00 per hour, whereas the hourly wage and benefit cost averaged $21.27 in Milwaukee. The Bureau of Labor Statistics estimated the 1993 U.S. average hourly compensation cost for the industry at $17.86. A contributing factor to the labor cost differential between Briggs & Stratton's plants was the reluctance by the United Paperworkers International Union to agree to productivity improvement processes that had been successful in the southern facilities. Briggs & Stratton management intended to operate the new plants on a nonunion basis.

FUTURE OUTLOOK

The threat of competition from the Japanese had made Briggs & Stratton a much stronger company. The company responded to the challenge by introducing innovative new product lines, improving product quality, and lowering its relative cost position. In addition, the company was helped by a strong U.S. economy and a strengthening Japanese yen. The economic conditions and the changes at B&S helped the company attract new customers and regain some old ones. Going into 1995, B&S had regained Toro's business that had been lost to Suzuki, gotten Snapper to switch from Fuji back to B&S, and recaptured some of John Deere's business. Frederick Stratton commented on the company's success:

> There are two ways to judge the health of a business: its current financial performance and its long-term strategic position. We believe that our recent good financial performance is to a great degree a result of strategic decisions made three to five years ago. We recognize that our financial performance three to five years from now will reflect the decisions we made in 1994.

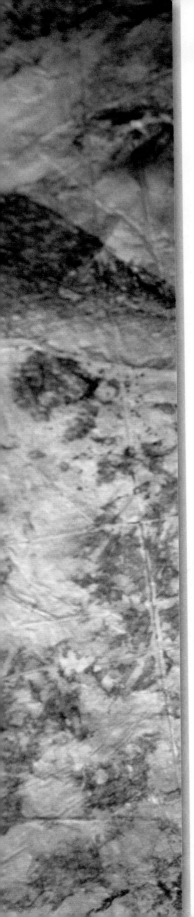

The Alabama Symphony Orchestra

Terrie Reeves, Joy R. Maples, and Woodrow D. Richardson,
all of The University of Alabama at Birmingham

The houselights were just going down as Michael Duncan, the executive director of the Alabama Symphony Orchestra (ASO), slipped into the very back seat just off the house-left aisle. Tonight's performance would be the last one of the 1991–92 season and would also be one of the last performances Maestro Paul Polivnick would conduct. Polivnick had recently announced his resignation. As the concertmaster finished tuning the orchestra and sat down, an expectant quiet came over the audience. A smiling Polivnick stepped out from stage right to loud applause as the orchestra and a few members of the audience stood. After acknowledging the audience's applause, the conductor turned to the orchestra, motioned them to be seated, gazed around them, and raised his baton. On the downbeat the lovely Mussorgsky *Prelude* filled the hall.

Although Duncan loved the music, he found his thoughts wandering to the thing he had struggled with since he became the ASO's executive director in 1990—namely, the orchestra's mounting debt. As the 1991–92 season closed, the Alabama Symphony Association (ASA), the ASO's legal and financial entity, was over $2.5 million in debt (see Exhibits 1, 2, and 3 for financial statements). Of the total debt, over $750,000 was guaranteed either by corporate contributors or by individuals, but even so, the lending banks were starting to get nervous. In addition, the ASO faced a potential conflict with the musician's union over salary. At the beginning of this season, after long negotiation, the musicians had signed a contract that decreased the number of workweeks from 45 to 42 and decreased salaries by 14 percent for the 1991–92 and 1992–93 seasons. However, the ASO would be required to restore the 14 percent for the 1993–94 season. The musicians had agreed to the salary cuts to allow the ASO to solve its financial problems, but Duncan was not at all sure the problems were solvable, let alone solvable in time to restore the musicians' salaries.

Polivnick's resignation, though significant, did not, as the local paper had written, "have quite the same emotional force as, say, the resignation of a head football coach at Ol' State U."[1] Polivnick probably would not leave until the end of the next season (1992–93), and the ASO had already hired a well-known, experienced musician/conductor for the transition period while it searched for a new conductor. Duncan

The authors thank both the ASO management and the ASO musicians for their cooperation in developing this case, which was written solely for the purpose of stimulating student discussion. All events and individuals are real, but some names have been disguised at the organization's request.

[1]Mitch Mendelson, "Symphony's Transition Provides Opportunities," *Birmingham News*, May 6, 1992.

Exhibit 1   Revenues, Alabama Symphony Orchestra, 1987–1992

	1987–88 Season	1988–89 Season	1989–90 Season	1990–91 Season	1991–92 Season
Earned revenue:					
Ticket sales	$ 793,446	$ 834,612	$1,061,380	$ 948,571	$ 942,499
Tours and area concerts	266,300	262,400	318,698	338,273	277,930
Youth orchestra concerts	52,985	42,399	46,239	50,638	34,811
Program income	42,206	42,880	0	0	0
Summer series	0	151,937	0	144,852	158,297
Special performances	39,674	56,645	14,984	0	15,206
Concert coupons	7,512	11,138	10,433	15,258	30,649
Subtotal	$1,202,123	$1,402,011	$1,451,734	$1,497,592	$1,459,392
Private contributions:					
Corporate and individual	966,973	919,835	865,676	1,348,785	1,125,708
Auxiliary	195,552	240,287	286,918	411,665	226,576
Subtotal	$1,162,525	$1,160,122	$1,152,594	$1,760,450	$1,352,284
Public grants:					
City	440,333	421,667	307,083	495,555	416,578
County	30,000	75,000	150,000	102,812	51,771
State	303,250	300,000	487,500	951,730	500,271
NEA	40,000	40,000	40,000	45,000	41,150
Other grants	206,900	53,758	79,201	198,095	81,980
Subtotal	$1,020,483	$ 890,425	$1,063,784	$1,793,192	$1,091,750
Other revenue:					
Miscellaneous	156,198	134,867	100,714	192,689	238,566
Foundation and Endowment revenues	13,181	35,213	58,297	85,420	73,119
Subtotal	$ 169,379	$ 170,080	$ 159,011	$ 278,109	$ 311,685
Total revenues, all sources	$3,554,510	$3,622,638	$3,827,123	$5,329,343	$4,215,111

Notes:

1. The 1990–91 season represents a 14-month period due to a change in the fiscal year.

2. Also in the 1990–91 season there was an anonymous individual donation of $500,000.

3. Foundation and Endowment Funds are usually large sums of money invested to earn interest income for a nonprofit organization. The actual funds are not supposed to be used by the organization, only the interest.

    There was $100,000 in the restricted endowment fund from 1987–88 through 1991–92. This fund was not touched. However, any additional endowment contributions were not restricted. These funds were used as operating fund revenues along with the interest from the restricted $100,000.

4. Miscellaneous includes educational and recording revenues.

Source: This information was adapted from the Alabama Symphony Orchestra's audited financial statements.

knew, however, that unless he came up with solutions to the ASA's financial problems, the choice of a new conductor might be purely academic.

As a late concertgoer apologetically stepped past Duncan, he realized that he was not listening to the music; rather, his mind was on how other orchestras had overcome similar financial difficulties. The ASO's plight was not unique. Other orchestras like the Denver Symphony Orchestra, the Seattle Orchestra, the St. Paul Chamber Orchestra, and the Philharmonic Orchestra of New Jersey (PONJ) dealt

Exhibit 2　Expenses, Alabama Symphony Orchestra, 1987–1992

	1987–88 Season	1988–89 Season	1989–90 Season	1990–91 Season	1991–92 Season
Artistic:					
Orchestra and conductor salaries	$2,029,817	$2,079,280	$2,111,291	$2,667,409	$2,388,593
Guest and assisting artists	257,758	398,531	392,247	477,123	402,853
Other artistic costs	0	0	3,108	4,492	0
Subtotal	$2,287,575	$2,477,811	$2,506,646	$3,149,024	$2,791,446
Concert production:					
Music and hall rental	94,281	105,338	98,728	154,200	121,428
Production salaries	135,183	153,418	161,891	220,616	203,183
Production costs	80,753	133,630	128,852	177,020	170,234
Travel	174,408	172,391	108,933	176,712	120,289
Subtotal	$ 484,625	$ 564,777	$ 498,404	$ 728,548	$ 615,134
Administration:					
Fund development	42,707	46,520	77,932	122,279	204,536
General administration	488,556	627,482	716,119	828,830	675,176
Marketing	143,620	236,018	260,941	445,950	463,546
Subtotal	$ 674,883	$ 910,020	$1,054,992	$1,397,059	$1,343,258
Other:					
Recording costs	9,257	8,783	11,674	7,345	5,645
Educational activities	138,803	151,864	141,765	194,289	209,465
Subtotal	$ 148,060	$ 160,647	$ 153,439	$ 201,634	$ 215,110
Total expenses	$3,595,143	$4,113,255	$4,213,481	$5,476,265	$4,964,948

Note: The 1990–91 season represents a 14-month period due to a change in the fiscal year.
Source: This information was adapted from the Alabama Symphony Orchestra's audited financial statements.

with similar financial problems using different means. The board wanted to hear how Duncan proposed to deal with the ASO's financial problems at its next meeting. He tried to settle back into his seat to listen to Dmitri Shostakovich's *Concerto for Violin and Orchestra*, next on the program.

SYMPHONIES IN THE UNITED STATES

The late 1980s and early 1990s were turbulent times for the orchestra industry. From 1988 to 1992, industry revenue increased 39 percent to $675 million. Unfortunately, industry expenses grew 41.5 percent over the same time period, and by 1992 the annual deficit for the industry had swelled to $23.2 million. At the same time, tax-based support for symphony orchestras in the country, adjusted for inflation, fell by more than 4 percent. Although there were 400 U.S. symphony orchestras, only 37 had budgets exceeding $4.9 million. The Wolff report, an industry publication, compiled statistics for these larger symphonies. Exhibit 4 compares ASO attendance

Exhibit 3 Funds Statements, Alabama Symphony Orchestra, 1987–1992

	1987–88 Season	1988–89 Season	1989–90 Season	1990–91 Season	1991–92 Season
Total revenues	$ 3,554,510	$ 3,622,638	$ 3,827,123	$ 5,329,343	$ 4,215,111
Total expenses	(3,595,143)	(4,113,255)	(4,213,481)	(5,476,265)	(4,954,948)
Excess (deficiency) of revenues over expenses	(40,633)	(490,617)	(386,358)	(146,922)	(749,837)
Transfer from restricted endowment fund	7,781	8,082	7,884	7,684	5,068
Prior period adjustments	0	0	(116,566)	0	0
Fund transfers	(20,424)	(5,530)	(24,287)	(4,277)	(12,431)
Fund balance at end of year	(53,276)	(488,065)	(535,095)	(158,883)	(767,336)
Fund balance at beginning of year	(570,344)	(623,620)	(1,111,685)	(1,646,780)	(1,805,663)
Accumulated fund balance at end of year	$ (623,620)	$(1,111,685)	$(1,646,780)	$(1,805,663)	$(2,572,999)

Notes:

1. The Alabama Symphony Orchestra uses a fund accounting system. Fund accounting is used by nonprofit organizations. A funds statement is similar to a for-profit organization's income statement.

2. The 1990–91 season represents a 14-month period due to a change in the fiscal year.

3. $116,566 was originally shown as an expense on the 1988–89 financials. The actual expense was incurred in 1989–90. The prior period adjustment is merely showing this change in the financials.

4. Like corporations, nonprofit organizations receive charters from the state in which they are domiciled, but they should be termed "nonstock" corporations since there are no "owners," and hence no stock. For each nonprofit organization, a board of directors or a board of trustees is set up according to the provisions of the organization's charter. This board is responsible for overseeing the operations of the organization's charter.

5. The balance in the restricted endowment fund is $100,000 from 1987–88 through 1991–92. The transfer from restricted endowment fund is the interest earned each year on the $100,000.

Source: This information was adapted from the Alabama Symphony Orchestra's audited financial statements.

and performance data to U.S. symphonies with similar or larger budgets of at least $4.9 million.[2]

During the 1991–92 season, the average cost per audience member to provide a performance was $26.17, but less than 40 percent of that cost, or only $10.26, was earned from the ticket sales that constitute concert income. The average ticket price was about $21, but most symphonies played to partially filled auditoriums. Symphonies received additional income from private contributions, government grants, and income from endowments. Industry experts believed an adequate symphony endowment should be at least three times the size of a symphony's annual budget. Exhibit 5 compares revenue and expense items for the ASO and symphonies with budgets of at least $4.9 million.[3]

SYMPHONY RESPONSES

In an effort to avoid growing deficits, some orchestras became creative in marketing and fund-raising. For example, the Philharmonic Orchestra of New Jersey (PONJ) redefined the goal of the symphony: It believed that adult music education offered in

[2]Adapted from The Wolf Organization, "The Financial Conditions of Symphony Orchestras," 1992. Commissioned by the American Symphony Orchestra League. Available from American Symphony Orchestra League, 777 14th Street NW, Washington, D.C. 20005.
[3]Ibid.

Exhibit 4   Comparative Symphony Statistics, Industry Averages versus ASO, Seasons Ending 1988–1992

	1988		1989		1990		1991		1992		Change 1988–1992	
	Industry	ASO	Industry	ASO	Industry	ASO	Industry	ASO	Industry	ASO	Industry	ASO
Total concerts	167	102	151	66	162	103	155	75	166	86	-0.5%	-16%
Number of regular season concerts	56	20	59	12	61	28	61	24	60	24	7	16
Number of pops concerts	18	16	16	6	19	16	19	16	21	16	16	0
Annual attendance for regular concerts (in thousands)	122	26	122	28	125	28	121	27	121	24	-1	-8
Annual attendance for pops concerts (in thousands)	38	28	35	36	42	36	40	30	42	31	10	10

Exhibit 5   Revenue and Expense Ratios, Industry Averages versus ASO, Seasons Ending 1988–1992

	1988		1989		1990		1991		1992		Change 1988–1992	
	Industry	ASO	Industry	ASO	Industry	ASO	Industry	ASO	Industry	ASO	Industry	ASO
Concert revenues/Total revenues	39%	34%	38%	39%	40%	38%	41%	28%	42%	35%	8%	3%
Private contributions/Total revenues	28	33	29	32	28	30	30	33	30	32	7	-3
Tax support/Total revenues	9	29	8	25	8	28	8	34	6	26	-33	-10
Other income/Total revenues	12	5	11	5	10	4	8	5	9	7	-25	40
Artistic expenses/Total expenses	50	64	50	60	50	59	51	58	51	56	2	-12
Concert production/Total expenses	16	13	15	14	16	12	16	13	17	12	6	-8
Administration/Total expenses	7	19	7	22	7	25	8	26	7	27	0	42
Other expenses/Total expenses	11	4	10	4	9	4	8	4	7	4	-36	0

convenient locations at convenient times for its target audience—baby boomers—was the key to success. This meant, first, that the PONJ offered classes in the evenings at suburban locations to attract people who commuted to New York City to work. Second, PONJ offered fewer concerts. Instead, it used its available funds for small groups of musicians to play demonstration passages of music while the conductor talked about listening to classical music for maximum enjoyment. The PONJ hired musicians at union pay scales on a per concert or per demonstration basis as needed, not on a per season contract. In addition, the PONJ had a board personally committed to fund-raising and operating in the black at all times. Many of these board members had first been introduced to classical music at the music education classes. "For an orchestra to survive today," the PONJ conductor said, "it must do things differently."[4]

Most U.S. symphonic musicians were members of the American Federation of Musicians, headquartered in New York City, with a national membership of about 155,000. As orchestras' expenses grew more quickly than revenues and musicians were pressed to accept lower increases or even decreases in pay, some symphonic musicians chose alternatives to the unions. For example, the players of the Seattle Symphony chose to drop out of the local and national musicians' union and to negotiate with the symphony directly. Thus, they gained flexibility and could negotiate outside of the provisions dictated by the union in terms of pay, hours of work, and so on, but they still had the power of being a cohesive group. After the Denver Symphony Orchestra went into Chapter 11 bankruptcy, the players formed the musician-controlled Colorado Symphony Orchestra and negotiated a profit-sharing agreement with a rock music promoter. Under this cooperative arrangement, the musicians shared in the financial risk of the orchestra. In co-ops, the musicians often provided both artistic and administrative personnel for the orchestra.

Finally, some organizations chose to downsize to a chamber orchestra consisting of 35 to 45 musicians. Most of the orchestras in the United States were full symphony orchestras consisting of 75 to 85 musicians playing all symphonic instruments. However, what is commonly called a symphony, a musical composition played in four movements, was unknown before the late 1700s. Not until well into the 1800s was a full 75-piece symphony orchestra used. Much of the music written after the late 1800s used all symphonic instruments, but much did not, and the Baroque and earlier classical musical repertoire did not require a full symphonic orchestra.[5] Thus, for many performances, a number of symphonic players were not required on stage because their instruments were not called for in the musical score.

The music chosen by the conductor for inclusion in a performance dictated the number of musicians required. Therefore, if an orchestra (such as the ASO) had all symphonic instrumental musicians under contract, some might not have to play for some performances, but most symphonic music could be played. If the orchestra was a chamber orchestra, it was restricted to music written for an orchestra of that size. Since the chamber orchestra selections tended to be somewhat shorter than symphonies, chamber orchestras such as the 37-musician St. Paul Chamber Orchestra sometimes played more concerts of shorter duration. To be easily heard, the smaller chamber orchestras usually played in smaller auditoriums.

[4]George Maull. Musical Director of PONJ, personal interview, August 12, 1993.
[5]Martin Cooper, ed., *New Oxford History of Music*, Volumes 7, 8, 9, 10 (New York: Oxford University Press, 1974).

THE BIRMINGHAM METROPOLITAN AREA ───────

The Alabama legislature incorporated the city of Birmingham on December 19, 1871. By 1890, the "Magic" city's population was 50,000, the largest in the state. As early as 1900, many of the city's leading families had moved to nice, well-to-do suburban communities on the other side of Birmingham's Red Mountain, commuting to their businesses or factories in Birmingham.

From the 1890s until the mid-1980s, Birmingham was an iron and steel town, sometimes called the "Pittsburgh of the South." During the 1970s, minimills, whose production costs were far below those of the big steel companies, grew in other parts of the United States; Birmingham's steel industry gradually withered.

Throughout the 1970s and 1980s, university, city, and business leaders worked together to change the economic base of the city. By the end of the 1980s, Birmingham had transformed itself from a dying steel town into a thriving service-sector community. Approximately 1 million people inhabited the metropolitan statistical area. However, Birmingham's population actually declined from 284,968 in 1980 to 264,968 in 1990, while the over-the-mountain communities' populations increased. Exhibit 6 compares the income and education levels of Birmingham and over-the-mountain residents.[6]

The city boasted world-class medical treatment and research, and the University of Alabama at Birmingham (UAB) became the state's largest single employer. There was also a growing financial sector and a revitalized downtown area. This "new" downtown included a Civic Center comprised of a coliseum, a hotel, facilities for conventions, museums, an exhibition hall, and a large, 3,200-seat concert hall in which the symphony performed. Located a few blocks to the north of the downtown business section on the other side of the freeway, the Civic Center took the place of dilapidated homes and warehouses and was a short walk from the library, the Art Museum, and City Hall. Despite these improvements, many area residents felt the downtown area was unsafe after dark. In addition, the logistics (leave work downtown, drive home, return to downtown) of attending downtown events for the over-the-mountain residents made evening events unappealing.

THE ARTS IN THE BIRMINGHAM AREA ───────

Using methodology developed by the National Endowment for the Arts, the Birmingham Chamber conducted a study entitled "Economic Impact of Arts and Cultural Institutions."[7] This study concluded that the visual and performing arts and educational institutions in the area had budgets totaling $20.2 million, of which 83 percent stayed in the community. The secondary economic impact, using a "conservative 3.21 turnover ratio," amounted to $53.9 million.[8] Similar earlier studies in other

---

[6]U.S. Government Printing Office, Washington, D.C. (issued in May 1992). *1990 Census of Population Housing Summary: Social, Economic and Housing Characteristics of Alabama.*

[7]Pennsylvania Economy League, "Pittsburgh Arts Organizations' Finances, Public and Private Funding and Impact on the Local Economy" (Pittsburgh: The Cultural Trust, 1989). Available from Carol R. Brown, president of the Pittsburgh Cultural Trust.

[8]Business Development & Research Division and Publications Division, "Economic Impact of the Arts: Major Cultural Land Educational Institutions on the Birmingham Metropolitan Area" (Birmingham: Cultural Affairs Committee, Birmingham Chamber of Commerce, 1992), p. 4.

Exhibit 6   Comparative Income and Education Levels of Birmingham Residents versus Residents of Suburbs

	Birmingham	Suburbs
1990 per capita income	$10,127	$27,711
Percentage of population over 25 with:		
High school education	69%	94%
College education	16%	54%

cities noted that each person who attended an arts performance spent $19.93 in addition to the price of the ticket.[9] The Birmingham report listed 34 Birmingham cultural organizations, 8 of which offered only musical performances. Eleven percent of Birmingham households ranked "attending cultural/arts events" as their top leisure activity.[10] The city recognized the importance of the arts by supporting many cultural activities, including the largest municipally owned art museum in the Southeast. The city's support for the ASO had averaged over $400,000 annually for the past five years.

COMPETING LEISURE ACTIVITIES

UAB and several other local colleges (Birmingham Southern College, Miles College, Samford University, and the University of Montevallo) all had at least one sports team. The University of Alabama in Tuscaloosa and Auburn University in Auburn were both within driving distance, and both fielded sports teams with national reputations. There was a parimutuel race track for both horse and dog racing. The metropolitan area also hosted the Chicago White Sox's AA minor league baseball team, the Birmingham Barons. Sports events (especially football) were the most popular form of entertainment in Birmingham. The city displayed banners declaring Birmingham "The football capital of the South" in the downtown area. Over 41 percent of the people in Birmingham ranked watching sports as their top leisure activity. The city's percentage of sports watchers was the 12th highest in the nation, despite being the only city in the top 12 without a professional football team.[11] All of these forms of entertainment, plus movies, night spots, and restaurants, sought an audience in the Birmingham area, and all sought some form of financial support.

THE ASO'S HISTORY

Local musicians originally formed the ASO as an amateur, volunteer orchestra whose primary support came from the blue-collar mine and steel workers of Birmingham. Posters advertising concerts outside the mines and factories attracted listeners, seats were only 25 cents, and the workers filled the concerts.

---

[9]Pennsylvania Economy League.
[10]Standard Rate and Data Service, *The Lifestyle Market Analyst*, 1991, p. 633.
[11]Ibid., p. 846.

World War II interrupted the orchestra's activities. After the war, the orchestra reformed with a new name, Birmingham Symphony Orchestra. With the help of city "bigwigs," the fourth musical director converted the orchestra to a full-time, professional group. In 1979, it became the Alabama Symphony Orchestra. The ASO hired Ed Wolff, who had a banking background, as ASO executive director in 1983, and Paul Polivnick became the musical director in 1985.

Polivnick wanted growth. "We need eight more strings," he said as he got off the plane, his brown eyes flashing. Under his musical direction, with Wolff managing operations, the number of concerts and musicians increased and the symphony recorded two compact discs. A 1988 concert in Washington, D.C.'s Kennedy Center was "kind of the pinnacle of Polivnick's time here," the chairman of the ASA board said, and "boy, we (were) feeling good."[12] Unfortunately, the increase in artistic output was not matched by equal increases in earned revenues.

Conductors had to strike a tricky balance between performing the "old friends," the musical pieces everyone knew, to keep the community happy, and letting the symphony grow by learning new works. The conductor also had to learn new repertoire to keep himself fresh. In Birmingham, Polivnick's relationship with the traditional concert audience was somewhat strained because of his emphasis on new, atonal 20th-century composers.

Although the musicians liked Polivnick's style, communications between management and orchestra members were not good during the last years of Wolff's tenure, and "there were all kinds of screaming matches."[13] Polivnick and Wolff brought the symphony artistic kudos, but when Wolff left at the start of the 1989–90 season, the deficit had swelled to $1.1 million.

MANAGEMENT: THE BOARD

The ASA board elected Mike Warren, president of a local energy company, as chairman in October 1991. He was the ASA's president and head of the fund-raising committee before becoming chairman. Although not a classical music lover himself, Warren felt strongly about the benefits of the ASO. "It (the ASO) is one of the great surprises of Alabama," he said. "We're proud of the artistic level (of the orchestra), (and) the quality of life level (in Birmingham). I love . . . the people the symphony brings to the community."[14]

With 50 volunteers, the board represented most of Birmingham's major corporations and institutions and many influential families. Warren's idea for board membership was very straightforward: Some members should represent the large organizational donors or the local banks with whom the ASA had credit lines, and some members should be true classical music lovers and/or symphony supporters who would be active in the ASO's volunteer ranks. Board members provided a strong network of the major "movers and shakers" in the community. The board provided the ASA's overall direction, but some board members viewed the responsibilities as merely social. The board delegated most administrative authority to the executive committee, which consisted of 11 members, including the executive director, the chairman, and the past chairman.

---

[12]Mike Warren, personal interview, July 9, 1993.
[13]Michael McGillivray, personal interview, August 3, 1993.
[14]Ibid.

MANAGEMENT: THE EXECUTIVE DIRECTOR AND STAFF

In September 1990, Michael Duncan, the most experienced man in the ASO's 41-year history, joined the 14-member management staff as the ASO's executive director. Duncan had 20 years experience working with symphony management. The musicians, Polivnick, and the board of directors all favored his selection. Appointed by and reporting to the board, the executive director oversaw the symphony's day-to-day operations. Several board committees, including finance, marketing, personnel, development and community relations, endowment, annual fund, and education assisted the executive director.

Duncan, seeing a need for a professional marketing staff, immediately launched a search for a marketing director and replaced the development director. By 1991, the administrative organizational chart (Exhibit 7) showed 25 people, including the executive director, on staff. To attract the best possible candidates, Duncan also increased salaries: he earned $72,000, the new development director made $60,000 (the old one had made less than $34,000), and he intended to pay the new marketing director a similar amount.

Under Ed Wolff, most communications had gone through the executive director; little communication occurred between the staff and the members of the symphony or between the staff and the board. Everyone hoped Duncan would change all that, and he did at first. At his suggestion, the board chose a member of the symphony to sit on each of the board's committees. In addition to board representation, the musicians desired greater overall input similar to that enjoyed by the Denver Symphony. They also noted that several orchestras in the country had developed special positions for "managers of orchestra personnel," whose only job was to serve the musicians so they were happy within the orchestra itself. However, as the financial position worsened, the relationships between the musicians, the management, and the board became strained. There was no move toward establishing a manager of orchestra personnel.

ARTISTIC STAFF: THE CONDUCTOR AND MUSICIANS

Before coming to Birmingham, Polivnick trained at Juilliard, worked at Tanglewood with Leonard Bernstein and with Jorge Mester at the Aspen Music Festival, and studied with Walter Susskind. He conducted in Los Angeles and served as the associate conductor of the Indianapolis and Milwaukee Symphony Orchestras. He was a dramatic conductor, urging the musicians on with theatrical gestures, seemingly wanting bigger and lusher music from them. He had sole responsibility for choosing both music and musicians as well as conducting the orchestra for most performances.

During the 1991–92 season, the artistic members of the orchestra included, in addition to Polivnick, an assistant conductor and 75 regular musicians. Occasionally, if called for in the musical score, the ASO hired additional musicians to augment specific sections of the orchestra. The sections consisted of the strings (first and second violins, violas, cellos, and basses), the woodwinds (flutes, piccolos, oboes, English horns, clarinets, bassoons, and contrabassoon), the brass (horns, trumpets, trombones, and tubas), and percussion (timpani, harp, piano, and other percussion instruments). The average ASO member was 37, made $560 per week in base pay,

Exhibit 7   Organization Chart for Alabama Symphony Association, October 1991

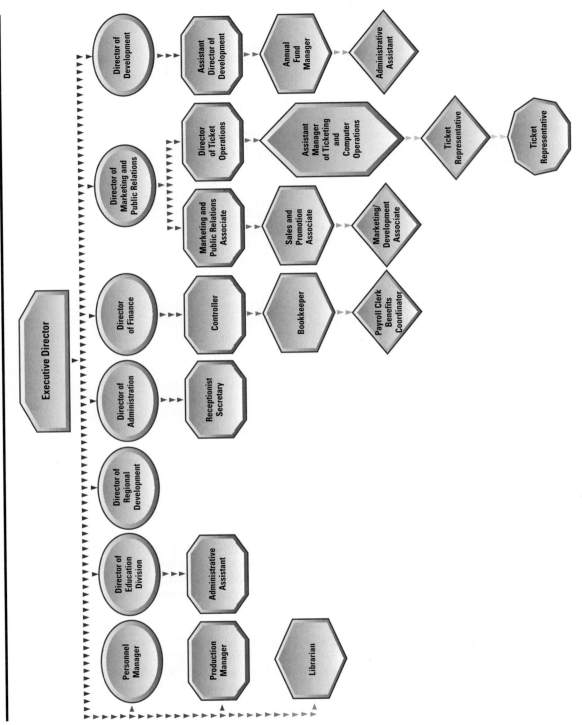

Source: Alabama Symphony Orchestra's personnel records.

and had played with the ASO for 10 years. The combined salaries and benefits for the conductor and assistant conductor were approximately $200,000.

Each musician, as a member of the local musicians' union, had a contract with the ASA. The contract specified, "Employment of ASO players is governed by a collective bargaining agreement between the musicians' union, the Birmingham Musicians' Protective Association, Local 256-733 of the American Federation of Musicians, and the Alabama Symphony Association." The 66-page contract specified the number of concerts, rehearsals, and tours allowed, the minimum amount of wages, salaries, insurance, and leave or vacation required, and the pay dates. The contract also specified notification time before each performance and rehearsal, the total amount of time a musician could play each day, the length of required breaks, and the conditions under which performance, rehearsal, recording, and broadcasting could be carried out. The contract also provided for travel conditions, concert attire, selection, tenure and removal of musicians, and grievance procedures.

All parties signed the most recent contract covering the 1991–92 season through the end of the 1993–94 season in a straightforward and relatively cordial manner. One contract clause provided that the union would not call a strike nor would the management call a lockout. Additionally, the musicians took a 14 percent salary cut for the first two years of the contract, thus putting themselves at lower salaries than any other large orchestra in the country, but still above smaller orchestras. The musicians felt that they were doing their part to help the ASA and the new executive director, and that their actions in accepting lower pay would allow the opportunity to bring the deficit under control. Duncan also made salary concessions. His original contract stipulated that his salary would increase to $81,000 over the contract period; however, he declined the increase due to the ASO's financial difficulties.

ASO PATRONS

Birmingham audiences were, on average, atypical of symphony concert audiences in two regards. The "no-show" rate among ASO Masters series season ticket holders was high: During the 1986–87 season, the no-show rate was 41.4 percent, in 1987–88 the rate was 42.2 percent, in 1988–89 the rate dropped to 31.3 percent, and during the early 1990s no-shows averaged about 30 percent compared to an industry average of 15 percent. "That's [the high no-show rate] demoralizing to the performers," Duncan said. Also, since many season ticket holders treated no-shows as a "donation" to the orchestra, the no-show rate might mean lower total donations. The Pops series experienced a lower no-show rate on average, although the worst rate in recent years was a 45 percent rate for Arthur Woodley's performance of excerpts from *Porgy and Bess*. The largest turnouts were for traditional and well-known music such as Beethoven's *Ninth Symphony*, when the no-show rate was only 21 percent.

Birmingham's audience was also more conservative than that in some other regions. They complained when Polivnick scheduled the music of modern composers. For instance, to try to reach a younger more casually dressed audience, on the Friday and Saturday evenings of one of the regular Masters series concerts, Polivnick publicly advised ticket holders to wear blue jeans if they wished. About 1,800 people attended each evening, more than normal for a Masters series concert. However, the season ticket subscriber no-show rate was even higher than normal on the blue-jeans evenings, and the orchestra management got complaint letters from many regular subscribers.

A 1992 survey of season ticket holders showed that 34.3 percent of those polled had annual incomes above $100,000, 82.7 percent had college degrees, and 23.8 percent had doctorates. Over 70 percent of the respondents attended concerts with their spouses, and 78 percent were 45 or older.

ASO PRODUCTS AND SERVICES

The ASO's major activities consisted of two concert series played at the Birmingham Concert Hall. The Masters series offered each ticket holder 12 classical music concerts performed on either Friday or Saturday evenings. On average, 991 people attended this series. Season ticket prices for the Masters ranged from $87 to $225, depending on seating assignments. The Pops series usually consisted of "popular" pieces featuring a nationally known guest musician who was not necessarily a classical musician. Usually there was a theme such as "An Evening with Rogers and Hammerstein" or "A Tribute to Paul Whiteman." When there was a guest musician, the symphony usually played alone for the first half of the program, with the guest artist appearing either alone or with the symphony after intermission. Over the past few years, such favorites as the Kingston Trio, Dizzy Gillespie, the Swingle Singers, Ray Charles, Shirley Jones, and the Harlem Boys Choir had been guest artists. Usually there were eight weekends in the Pops series. The ASO played some of the spring and fall performances in the outdoor Oak Mountain Amphitheater over-the-mountain. Attendance averaged over 1,900 for the Pops performances, with season ticket prices ranging from $88 to $199. Single-performance ticket prices for both series ranged from $10.50 to $30.50 per performance. For both series, the average ticket sold for about $20.

In addition to the season series in Birmingham, the ASO made arrangements through rural school districts to play in the state's rural areas. The ASO played for 30,000 Alabama school children across the state. The ASA received $1 million in state appropriations for this touring program to cover the musicians' salaries and other expenses associated with the tours. The symphony "set up headquarters" for a week in a centrally located place in a rural area. During the day, individual members of the orchestra visited schools to interact with students and to give demonstrations. During the evenings, the ASO performed free-to-the-public concerts combining classical and pops music. The ASO was the only symphony in the United States to carry out such a rural touring program.

In addition to the Masters, Pops, and touring concerts, occasionally the ASO gave free-to-the-public performances in city parks during the summer. The park perform-ances were not part of the musicians' ASO season contract and not all regular ASO musicians played in them. Park performance musicians' pay came from city funds.

The ASO's Education division's goal was to involve young people in Birmingham and the surrounding towns in orchestral music. The division had two programs, an instructional program and a youth orchestra. Area schools and churches served as classrooms for regular and Suzuki class lessons. A child moved on to traditional private lessons on an instrument after progression to a certain level.

The ASO, in conjunction with the Alabama School of Fine Arts, operated three youth orchestras: the Alabama Youth Symphony, the Birmingham String Orches-tra, and the Birmingham Prelude Strings. Made up of high school and college-age students, each youth orchestra had a different musical director and each performed several concerts a year in or around Birmingham. The orchestras provided an outlet for the students in the educational program and a training ground for young musicians.

FUND-RAISING

The ASO's auxiliary organizations, most of which contributed funds to the symphony, were the Women's Committee of the Alabama Symphony Association; the Decorator Showhouse, a joint project of the Women's Committee and Junior Women's Committee; the Junior Women's Committee of the Alabama Symphony Association; and the Men's Committee of the Alabama Symphony Association. Most years, these auxiliary groups contributed $250,000 to $300,000 to the symphony. The Alabama Symphony Education Committee, which oversaw the Education division and The Alabama Youth Symphony, usually contributed an additional $100,000 to $200,000 from instructional fees and youth concern proceeds. However, like most other education programs around the country, expenses incurred by the Education division usually equaled income, making its net contribution to the ASA closer to zero. The Alabama Symphony Association Trust and the Alabama Symphony Foundation usually tried to raise endowment funds, the interest from which would go to the ASO.

In 1990, at Duncan's request, the ASO hired a fund-raising consultant group to examine the ASA's community fund-raising possibilities. This "development audit" was not entirely optimistic. "Fund-raising at the Alabama Symphony suffers from fragmented strategy, lack of skilled overall direction, and a general lack of confidence," the consultants reported. They also noted that the board was not considering the true costs of doing business as a symphony; no adequate financial plan and budget was in place; volunteers and contributors had not been included in setting fund-raising goals; fund-raising personnel and volunteers did not know exactly what they were "selling" or what case they should be making when they contacted potential donors; and there was no provision for succession in the volunteer ranks, both on the board and in fund-raising.

The consultants noted that the ASO volunteers had tremendous workloads, especially the annual fund-raising chairs and the heads of the various committees and auxiliary groups. There appeared to be considerable burnout among fund-raising volunteers. As a result, in past years, the annual spring fund-raising drive normally got off to a precarious start. Year after year, the same goal, $1 million in contributions, was set but not attained. "Shore up the annual fund," the consultants urged.

The ASA held its most recent endowment fund drive in 1988, and, at only about $100,000, the endowment fell well short of industry standards. The consultants also found that the development staff, although hardworking, lacked knowledge of prospects and had no adequate system for keeping track of potential donors. There was very little communication with donors; even thank-you notes were often months late or were not sent at all. Perhaps most damaging was the development staff's apparent unfamiliarity with the business community despite ASA board connections with the area's major businesses. Because of inadequate communication between the board and the staff, the board's knowledge of potential donors never reached the staff. The development staff was also responsible for securing grants from various government agencies.

The information system further hampered the development staff's efforts. Files to provide background information and past contributions records both for individual and for corporate donors were nonexistent. Access to the computer was limited. Few staff members knew how the system worked, and the only terminal was not located on the same floor as the development office. Because the computer system configuration did not support a multiuser environment, no terminals were added. In addition, the development staff had limited access to word processing capabilities, so written follow-up with potential donors was difficult. Not surprisingly, the consultants recommended the purchase of a new computer system. Despite these limitations, in 1991–92 the development staff under Duncan's direction raised $1.1 million (a new high for the ASO).

At the end of the 1991–92 season, the ASA got a new computer system to handle all aspects of symphony management from ticket sales to musicians' payroll. The ASA purchased the database recommended by the consultants, and the first application was season ticketing. Due to problems with the new system, some 1992–93 season subscribers got their tickets late, some got duplicate tickets, and some did not even receive tickets. The local media covered the complaints about the computer problems, and it appeared total season ticket sales for the upcoming season might be down just when the symphony's finances were most precarious.

FINANCES

The Funds Statements (Exhibit 3) for 1987–92 show the increase in the ASA's accumulated deficit. Observers cited several reasons for the increase. First, during the 1989 season, the ASO booked Smokey Robinson, the Motown singer, to play with the symphony in the 17,000-seat Coliseum. Management was surprised when only about 1,100 people showed up, and the loss on that one concert was between $75,000 to $100,000. Then, during the 1988–89 season, guest artists' fees rose to $398,531, up about $140,000 from the season before, with an accompanying increase in ticket sales of only about $50,000. The president of the board argued, "we think having high-caliber guest artists will help bring people into the symphony hall,"[15] although he admitted that bringing in such performers was sometimes a gamble.

During 1990–91, there was "a series of miracles," as Warren put it. An anonymous donor gave $500,000, the state raised its contribution to over $950,000, and the bank increased its credit line. But the ASA made little effort to cut back on expenses. Faced with a deficit of about $1 million, the ASA bank borrowing totaled $1 million by the end of 1990, and the yearly debt service was about $100,000.

The ASO had four sources of revenue: earned revenue, private contributions, public grants, and endowments, as shown in Exhibit 1. The Pops series produced more in ticket sales revenues than the Masters series for the years 1987–92. The ASA produced other revenues through youth activities, special engagements including summer concerts, and miscellaneous sources such as program and coupon sales. The ASO's single largest expense was musician and conductor salaries, as shown in Exhibit 2.

For the 1992–93 season, the ASO projected revenue sources as follows: governmental grants, 22 percent; ticket sales, 36 percent, community support, 35 percent;

---

[15]Shawn Ryan, "Whither the Alabama Symphony?" *Birmingham News*, June 5, 1990.

educational activities, 5 percent; and other, 2 percent. Expenses were forecasted at 57 percent for artistic salaries and benefits, 14 percent for concert production, 4 percent for development, 8 percent for marketing, 5 percent for administration, and 12 percent for other.

As is true for many symphonies, due to lack of funds, the ASO had adopted the policy of using the proceeds of ticket sales for the upcoming season to meet current operating expenses. Season ticket money paid in for the whole season was used before the season opened. Any discrepancy between funds received from ticket sales and expenses incurred was made up by borrowing. The chairman noted, "that's 'embedded debt' we're carrying using spring ticket sales to make it through the next year."

THE FUTURE OF THE ASO

The applause from the audience suddenly brought Duncan's attention back to the concert hall. He had heard none of the *Prelude* and wondered whether he should stay for the remainder of the program or go back to his preparations for the board meeting in two weeks. What recommendation should he make to the board? He knew that some board members were unreceptive to further attempts to penetrate the market. If the ASO stayed on its current course, could earned revenues be increased enough to address the growing debt? If so, how should the marketing effort be directed? Should the target market be changed, as was done by the Philharmonic Orchestra of New Jersey? Given the debt's size, should his recommendations focus on drastically reducing expenses? Would downsizing to a chamber orchestra similar to St. Paul's be a workable solution? How would the musicians react to massive layoffs? Could expenses be cut enough in other areas to avoid layoffs? The musicians might respond to such a proposal by advocating creation of their own cooperative similar to the Colorado Orchestra.

Someone would have an objection to any of the three major alternatives: penetration, retrenchment, or cooperative. Penetration might not be realistic given the financial urgency of the ASO's situation. Musicians would object to the layoffs required by the smaller chamber orchestra. Formation of a cooperative would probably mean reorganization of the ASA and the loss of administrative staff positions, including his own. He decided the most appealing option for now was to listen to the rest of the performance.

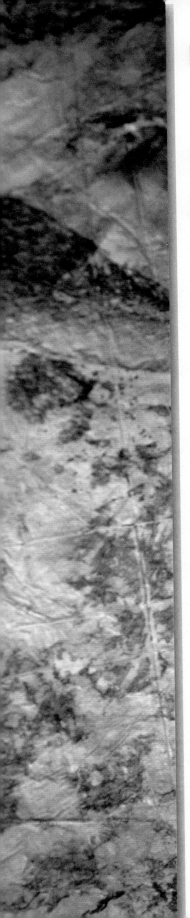

The Hue-Man Experience Bookstore

Joan Winn, University of Denver

I began telling everyone who came in the store that this was the largest African American bookstore in the country. I really didn't know if that was true, but it was the largest one I had ever seen in my travels and everyplace I go I'm always looking for bookstores. Maybe eventually I'll uncover one that's larger and I'll have to acknowledge it, but until then I won't say anything different. So I began to create that image in people's minds, nationally as well as locally.

Clara Villarosa, Owner

What began in 1984 as an attempt to set up an independent business targeted to affluent African Americans was by 1992 a 3,000-square-foot retailing establishment and north Denver community landmark. The Hue-Man Experience Bookstore specialized in books, cards, jewelry, and artwork by and for people of color (hence the "Hue" in "Human"). While most patrons lived within 5 miles of the bookstore, the Hue-Man Experience Bookstore had gained a national reputation, attracting frequent out-of-town visitors. By 1994, Clara Villarosa was looking at expansion. The availability of the building next door kindled her dream of creating an Afrocentric retail and cultural center.

HISTORY

The Hue-Man Experience Bookstore grew out of the dream of a woman who had already made her mark in corporate America. Clara Villarosa started out professionally as a psychiatric social worker, working in an out-patient (nonresidential) clinic in Chicago after she received her masters degree in social work in 1954. Like many women of her generation, she dropped out of the workforce when her children were born. In 1968, when her daughters were five and nine years old, Clara and her husband moved the family to Denver. Clara soon took a position in the department of

This case was originally presented at the Case Critique Colloquium at the Academy of Management Conference, August 1994. The author is grateful to the management and employees for their cooperation in the field research in this case, which was written solely for the purpose of stimulating student discussion. All rights reserved jointly to the author and the North American Case Research Association (NACRA). Copyright© 1994 by the *Case Research Journal* and Joan Winn.

Behavioral Sciences at Denver's Children's Hospital. By the time she left the hospital in 1980, she had become the director of the department of Behavioral Sciences, and, eventually, the assistant hospital administrator. After entering a doctoral program in social work and law, she started a consulting business.

> I wanted to help African Americans move up the corporate ladder and I thought I could sell that idea to large corporations. As a social worker I had some skills, but I didn't know how to knock on doors, to get a business off the ground. When I ran out of money I took a temporary job at United Bank. I started out in employee relations and moved quickly up the corporate ladder, becoming the Vice President of Human Resources within two years. Again I found myself in the position of being the highest African American on the payroll. But, as often happened in those times, I hit the glass ceiling. People were extremely resentful and angry about African Americans and Affirmative Action and I received a significant backlash. So I left the bank. But left the bank with some money. I think they *wanted* me to quit.

Her consulting business had taught her that she wanted to sell something tangible, and at the same time, something that would relate in a positive way to the African American community.

> And I came up with books, because I've always been a reader. My father was a reader and I grew up immersed in books. We [the African American community] had had a bookstore in Denver, but there wasn't one now, so my dream was to create the largest African American bookstore in Denver.

This time, Clara researched her market and wrote a business plan, outlining the financial and marketing requirements of her ethnic bookstore concept. With the help of two friends and her severance from the bank, she got together $35,000 and secured a lease on a two-story row house in a run-down residential/commercial area north of downtown Denver in a predominantly African American area. The Hue-Man Experience Bookstore opened in 1984. In 1986, realizing that business and friendship don't always mix well, Clara arranged to buy out her partners' shares over a two-year period by selling shares of the business to interested friends and customers. In 1993, the Hue-Man Experience Bookstore was governed by a nine-member board of directors, elected annually by Clara (who owned 58 percent) and 31 shareholders. Financial performance for the Hue-Man Experience Bookstore for 1990–93 is given in Exhibits 1 and 2.

THE BOOKSELLING INDUSTRY

In 1992, book sales in the United States exceeded $16.1 billion, according to the Association of American Publishers. The American Book Trade Directory estimated that there were about 27,000 retailers of books in the United States, 15,700 of which were privately owned independent bookstores. The largest book retailers were general bookstore chains, which had sales of $2.9 billion in 1992 from a total of 2,768 outlets. Exhibit 3 contains sales information for the largest bookstore chains in 1991–92.

Major chain expansion began in the late 1970s to mid-1980s, with 1,000- to 20,000-title mall outlets proliferating toward the end of the 1980s. As mall growth slowed, the focus changed to superstores, huge discounters that averaged 200,000 titles, 5 to 10 times the number offered by specialty or mall stores. Barnes & Noble opened its first superstore in September 1990 in a Minneapolis suburb. The 15,000-square-foot store was patterned after such well-known independent booksellers as

Exhibit 1   Hue-Man Experience Bookstore Income Statements for 1990–93

| | For the Period Ending December 31 | | | |
	1990	1991	1992	1993
Revenue:				
Books	$181,134	$216,922	$272,542	$269,751
Cards	26,024	26,517	25,811	23,106
Prints	13,503	15,579	13,994	9,616
Jewelry	3,903	2,152	1,759	1,438
Miscellaneous	17,274	16,967	14,712	7,154
Catalog	13,098	18,268	21,338	6,828
Tapes and magazines	3,924	2,724	4,342	5,310
Reimbursed postage	1,428	3,070	3,345	2,433
Total revenue	$260,289	$302,198	$357,841	$325,635
Cost of Sales:				
Books	$121,719	$143,793	$196,666	$152,104
Cards	14,613	12,769	17,603	14,583
Prints	6,146	11,100	8,487	3,453
Jewelry	956	612	1,435	325
Miscellaneous	8,942	6,396	2,665	5,946
Tapes and magazines	3,568	2,437	8,319	4,044
Catalog	3,336	5,661	779	120
Freight and postage	1,733	2,770	6,663	740
Framing supplies	1,815	590	1,379	538
Inventory (increase) decrease	(1,094)	5,617	(4,047)	8,034
Total cost of sales	$161,732	$191,743	$239,947	$189,885
Gross margin	$ 98,557	$110,455	$117,894	$135,750
Administrative expenses				
Officer salary	$ 26,000	$ 26,814	$ 29,599	$ 24,973
Salaries	20,874	27,193	27,647	26,706
Employee benefits		160	169	3,454†
Advertising	3,848	4,406	4,740	3,309
Promotional	2,677	1,364	758	13
Accounting and legal	4,008	4,101	3,389	4,256
Vehicle expense	2,822	3,010	3,433	4,517
Bank and credit card service charges	3,791	2,208	6,407	1,175
Janitorial/cleaning expenses	276	164	240	
Consulting/contract labor	2,568	2,510	328	676
Contributions	864	900	229	293
Dues and subscriptions	907	1,242	933	1,977
License and fees		10	26	95
Depreciation	3,015	4,453	4,027	3,997
Entertainment	971	257	1,409	3,299
Travel/conferences	4,011	1,530	1,576	2,082
Rent	9,078	7,677	7,350	12,495
Repairs and maintenance	869	662	2,008	2,609

Exhibit 1   Concluded

	For the Period Ending December 31			
	1990	1991	1992	1993
Security	322	520	458	556
Telephone*	5,147	7,689	9,995	7,577
Utilities	2,445	2,722	2,636	3,055
Insurance		1,462	1,164	173
Office supplies and equipment	4,082	3,345	4,259	4,667
Printing			598	2,194
Store supplies	1,686	3,681	2,722	3,264
Taxes—personal property	148	284	486	
Taxes—payroll	4,156	4,826	4,970	4,409
Freight and postage	4,242	357	1,254	5,280
Miscellaneous	1,284	319	1,254	436
Total expenses	$111,561	$113,583	$122,655	$127,755
Other income (expense):				
Interest earned	$ 348	$ 283	$ 168	$ 105
Other income	5,000	325	779	7
Interest expense	(566)	(297)	(2,145)	(155)
Bookstore net income (loss)	$ (8,222)	$ (2,817)	$ (5,960)	$ 7,952
Rental income		$ 2,066	$ 16,950	$ 19,536
Administrative expenses				
Depreciation—building		440	2,643	4,423
Repairs and maintenance		900	1,682	4,737
Utilities		125	1,046	235
Miscellaneous				575
Insurance—property			2,964	1,226
Taxes—real property		134	820	1,948
Interest income—building			35	131
Interest expenses—building		(1,140)	(2,252)	(6,001)
Total building income (expense)		(639)	(5,674)	390
Total other income (expense)	$ 4,781	$ (328)	$ 4,475	$ 347
Net income/(loss)	$ (8,222)	$ (3,456)	$ (286)	$ 8,342

† In 1993, Clara added health care coverage for the employees. Due to the prohibitive costs, this was discontinued by the end of the year, in favor of increased wages.
* Includes Yellow Pages advertising and 1-800 phone lines.

Oxford Books in Atlanta, Powell's Books in Portland, the Tattered Cover in Denver, and Waterstone's in Boston.

The hallmark of the chain superstores was discounting, selling mainly fiction, celebrity biographies, and other books that appealed to the general public. Increasing competition was coming from mail-order catalogs, warehouse clubs, discount retailers, nonbook specialty stores (such as the Nature Company, Sutton Place Gourmet, and Toys "Я" Us), and university bookstores (which have expanded their textbook holdings to include popular books and sidelines such as cards and clothing and, more

Exhibit 2   Hue-Man Experience Bookstore Balance Sheets for 1990–1993

	For the Year Ending December 31			
	1990	**1991**	**1992**	**1993**
Assets				
Current assets:				
Cash and cash equivalents	$ 6,401	$ 14,675	$ 11,891	$ 13,787
Accounts receivable—trade			681	1,998
Prepaid employee benefits			1,134	
Inventory—merchandise	61,153	55,536	59,583	65,579
Total current assets	$67,554	$ 70,211	$ 73,289	$ 81,364
Property and equipment:				
Building		$ 79,260	$ 79,260	$ 79,260
Construction in progress			8,900	8,900
Leasehold improvements	6,701	6,701	6,701	6,701
Furniture and fixtures	3,323	3,323	3,323	3,323
Machines and equipment	16,888	21,888	23,943	25,917
Less accumulated depreciation	(13,994)	(18,887)	(25,557)	(33,977)
Other assets:				
Organizational expense	5,056	5,056	5,056	5,056
Less accumulated amortization	(5,056)	(5,056)	(5,056)	(5,056)
Total fixed assets	$12,919	$ 92,286	$ 96,571	$ 90,125
Total assets	$80,473	$162,497	$169,860	$171,489
Liabilities and Stockholders' Equity				
Current liabilities:				
Accounts payable	$11,847	$ 12,060	$ 19,686	$ 14,219
Security deposits		870	870	370
Payroll taxes payable	3,429	2,960	2,606	107
Sales tax payable	2,618	3,357	4,596	3,886
Property taxes payable		806	792	2,413
Deferred revenue	100	100	2,209	100
Interest payable—SBA loan		1,140	1,140	498
Officer loans	4,400	4,400	4,400	4,400
Accrued interest—shareholder			2,097	2,383
Total current liabilities	$22,395	$ 25,694	$ 38,396	$ 28,377
Noncurrent portion—SBA loan		72,000	66,948	70,255
Total liabilities	$22,394	$ 97,694	$105,344	$ 98,631
Stockholders' equity:				
Common stock	$46,102	$ 56,282	$ 56,282	$ 56,282
Paid-in capital	47,902	47,902	47,902	47,902
Retained earnings	(23,201)	(35,925)	(39,381)	(39,669)
Dividends	(4,502)			
Net profit (loss)	(8,222)	(3,456)	(287)	8,342
Total equity	$58,079	$ 64,803	$ 64,515	$ 72,858
Total liabilities and stockholders' equity	$80,473	$162,497	$169,860	$171,489

Exhibit 3   Sales of 11 Largest U.S. Trade Bookstore Chains, 1991–1992

Chain	Ownership	1991 Sales	1992 Sales†	Percent Change	Number Stores at Year-End
Waldenbooks	Kmart	$1,139.0	$1,146.0	0.06%	1,260
Barnes & Noble	Public (in 1993)	920.9	1,086.7	18.0	916
Crown Books	Dart Group	232.5	240.7	3.5	247
Borders Books	Kmart	82.5	116.0	40.6	22§
Books-A-Million	Public	72.8	95.1	30.6	107
Encore Books	Rite-Aid Corp.	52.3	65.2	24.7	103
Lauriat's*	Chadwick-Miller	46.0	49.0	7.0	56
Tower Books*	MTS Inc.	29.0	33.0	13.8	15
Kroch's & Brentano's*	Waldenbooks	33.0	30.0‡	−9.0	20
Rizzoli Bookstores*	Private	21.0	24.0	14.3	11
Taylor's Inc.*	Private	17.5	20.0	14.3	11
Totals		$2,646.5	$2,905.7	9.8%	2,768

* Estimated sales.

† Sales in millions. Figures are for calendar 1992 or most current fiscal year.

‡ Sales estimate is a projection for year ending June 30, 1993.

§ Store totals do not include nine Basset Books transferred to Borders at year-end.

Source: *Publishers Weekly*, June 14, 1993.

recently, books targeted to young adults known as "Generation X" or "13th Gen"). Both chain and independent bookstores have been increasing their use of book catalogs and newsletters, which promote best-sellers or discount specials and also serve as promotional tools to get more people in the stores.

Profit margins among the large chains were estimated at less than 1 percent, which made volume critical to this business. The American Booksellers Association surveys independent booksellers annually for financial operating performance information. Exhibit 4 shows estimates of financial performance based on *Publishers Weekly* data compiled from Barnes & Noble, Books-A-Million, and Crown Books; and ABA's ABACUS results, based on reports from 199 bookstore operations.

Fiscal 1993 reports from the large chains showed revenue increases of 19 percent. Profit margins and operating income were similar to 1992 levels, resulting in operating margins for each of the two years at 3 percent, nearly twice the independents' 1.62 percent.

Barnes & Noble attributed a 144 percent increase in sales in 1992 to its new superstores. In 1993, 30 percent of Barnes & Noble sales were from its 135 superstores, 77 of which were added in 1993. Another 75 stores were planned for 1994 and 1995. Encore Books, which operated only one superstore in 1993, planned to open four more by mid-1994. Waldenbooks's superstore operations were under the name of Borders, a previously independent 19-store chain purchased by Kmart in the fall of 1992. Borders (which also includes Walden's Basset Book Shops) had 30 superstores in 1992 and planned to open 20 more by the end of 1993. Crown planned to increase its 22 superstores to 40 by the end of 1993. Books-A-Million, with 10 superstores in 1992, expected to open 5 more in 1993. Tower Books had 15 stores by the end of 1992; Lauriat's was positioning its new Royal Discount Bookstores as superstores.

Exhibit 4   Comparison of Independent and Chain Bookstore Revenues, Expenses, and Profits

	Chains Composite†		Sample Independents Composite	
	Dollars (in millions)	As a percent of Net Sales	Dollars (in millions)	As a percent of Net Sales
Net sales	$1,197.8	100.0%	$170.5	100.0%
Receipts from books*	1,078.1	90.0	136.4	80.0
Receipts from sidelines*	119.7	10.0	34.1	20.0
Cost of goods sold	816.3	68.2	106.4	62.4
Gross profit	381.5	31.8	64.1	37.6
Operating, selling, and administrative expense:	317.8	26.5	61.4	36.0
Occupancy costs			12.3	7.2
Advertising			4.9	2.9
Depreciation and amortization	27.6	2.3		
Operating profit	36.1	3.0	2.8	1.6
Interest expense	29.9	2.5	.34	0.2
Income before tax	6.2	0.5	2.42	1.4
Income tax	5.5	0.4	0.68	0.4*
Net income	0.7	0.1%	1.7	1.0%

* Estimate from anecdotal reports.
† Calendar year 1991 or fiscal year ending 1992. (Most independents operate on a calendar year; chains report earnings on a fiscal year basis.)
Source: *Publishers Weekly*, October 18, 1993.

Many independent bookstore owners were concerned that the industry was going the way of hardware stores and neighborhood pharmacies. According to John Mutter of *Publishers Weekly,* there was fear that superstores were creating "a concentration of power that threatens the diversity of what gets published and what is available for the public to read."[1] The American Booksellers Association was cooperating with the Federal Trade Commission in investigating business practices and pricing policies that appeared to threaten the small independent book retailers.

While chains offered cheap prices, few could offer the personal service of independents who knew their customers. This was particularly true in the growing breed of specialty bookstores. Some specialty bookstores focused on a particular subject, such as Armchair Sailor in New York, which specialized in nautical books; Victor Kamlin, Inc., in Rockville, Maryland, which specialized in Russian literature; Books of Wonder in New York, which specialized in children's books; Sports Central: The Ultimate Sports Bookstore in Palo Alto; or Books for Cooks in Baltimore. Others, like Salt of the Earth Bookstore in Albuquerque, Midnight Special in Santa Monica, California, and Odyssey Bookshop in South Hadley, Massachusetts, prided themselves on community involvement by promoting multicultural authors. Some stores focused on one particular market group, such as Charis Bookstore in Atlanta, which positioned itself as a feminist bookstore, OutBooks in Fort Lauderdale and A

[1] J. Mutter, "Heated Competition Gets Hotter," *Publishers Weekly*, January 4, 1993, p. 43.

Different Light in San Francisco, which targeted lesbians and gays, and Shrine of the Black Madonna in Detroit and Hue-Man Experience Bookstore in Denver, which catered to African American clienteles.

Bookselling and publishing by and for African Americans had surged since 1988. An increasing interest in African American culture, aided by school curriculum reforms, fueled a growth in bookstores catering to African Americans. According to Wade Hudson, who ran Just Us Books in New Jersey, "African Americans are hungry for knowledge and understanding about their experience, so they are looking for books that provide it."[2] Until recently, these books had been published by small independent publishing operations or by the authors themselves and sold out of car trunks at book conventions. More recently, the major publishers and national distributors had added African American titles to their lines, providing authors of such works easier access to booksellers through mainstream distribution channels.

"Bookstores used to assume there was no market because blacks didn't come in asking for titles like these, but that's because they assumed the stores wouldn't stock them," commented Hudson. Kassahum Checole, president of the Red Sea Press, the largest distributor of African American titles, started out in the publishing business. "The Red Sea Press now distributes titles from about 60 publishers, approximately half of them African American."[3]

Bookseller and publisher Haki Madhubuti believed that "A good 30 percent–35 percent of the people who buy our books aren't black."[4] He began the African-American Publishers and Booksellers Association in 1989, which held trade meetings and special sessions at the American Booksellers Association convention. This group became the first "specialty" segment within the ABA. As of 1992, there were several segments, such as a travel group and mystery group, that held roundtable discussions at national and regional meetings and put together newsletters, catering to specialty bookstore owners.

THE DENVER MARKET

According to the 1990 census, Colorado had almost 3.3 million residents, nearly 2 million of whom lived in the greater metropolitan Denver area. While only 4 percent of Colorado's population was black, the city of Denver was nearly 13 percent black, 60 percent of whom lived north of downtown. The Denver metropolitan area had a total African American population of nearly 100,000, 60,000 of whom lived within the Denver city limits.

According to Scarborough Research Corporation, Denver ranked 10 percent above the national average in the popularity of reading in 1993, ranking 22nd out of 209 surveyed metropolitan areas. Forty-three percent of metropolitan Denver households were considered "avid readers." Both Denver and Boulder, 35 miles away, boasted independent superstores that had been in existence for over 20 years.

The Tattered Cover was a Denver landmark, located in a former department store in Cherry Creek North, an established shopping area with nearly a million square feet of retail and service businesses. The Tattered Cover had 40,000 square feet of selling

---

[2]C. Goddard. "Aiming for the Mainstream," *Publishers Weekly*, January 20, 1992, p. 29.
[3]Ibid., p. 30.
[4]Ibid.

space on four floors and boasted over 220,000 titles. Across the street was the prestigious Cherry Creek Shopping Center, which opened in August 1990, a 1 million-square-foot mall comprised of luxury and specialty stores (including Doubleday Book Shop and Travelday's Book Shop, both owned by B. Dalton, and Brentano's, owned by Waldenbooks). Recent competitors, located in suburban areas, included five Barnes & Noble superstores, each with approximately 10,000 feet of selling space. A sixth Barnes & Noble superstore was planned in a renovated theater building about 2 miles east of the Tattered Cover.

There was a wide variation in retail lease rates in Denver, depending on the location. Rents in Cherry Creek North averaged between $17 and $28 per square foot (calculated on a yearly basis). Rates for the Cherry Creek Shopping Center, immediately south of Cherry Creek North, were estimated to be about twice that rate.

The Denver area had over 100 independent retailers of new and used books. Specialty bookstores included Murder by the Book, which specialized in mystery fiction; Astoria Books and Prints, which specialized in rare books and artwork; Hermitage Antiquarian Bookshop, which specialized in collectibles and first editions; Isis Metaphysical Bookstore, which specialized in books on metaphysics, crystals and jewelry, and New Age music; Category Six Books, specializing in gay and lesbian literature; Cultural Legacy, which specialized in books in Spanish; and numerous children's bookstores and religious specialty stores.

The Hue-Man Experience Bookstore was located on Park Avenue West, a well-traveled thoroughfare about a mile north of downtown, bordering the area known as Five Points, named for the five tramway lines that once intersected there. Five Points was one of Denver's largest residential areas, encompassing over 1,000 acres. With its close proximity to the downtown area, Five Points used to be a cultural center for African Americans, with more African American–owned businesses than any other place in the United States except for Harlem. This began to change in 1959 with the passage of Colorado's Fair Housing Act. During the 1960s and 1970s, many of the more affluent African Americans moved to other, more integrated, neighborhoods. In 1993, the area was populated with small service and retail establishments and run-down houses. According to 1990 census data, the average household income in Colorado was $36,015 (the U.S. average was $29,199). Half of the residents in the vicinity of Five Points had an annual household income under $35,000; nearly 30 percent of the households reported an annual income under $15,000.

Walking in the vicinity of Five Points was probably not advisable, especially after dark. In 1993, this area had the third-highest crime rate in Denver, 315.2 crimes reported per 1,000 population. In 1992, Five Points ranked second. The highest crime area (consistently since 1989) was North Capital Hill, which bordered Five Points to the south, with 413.2 crimes reported per 1,000 population in 1993. While these numbers included car thefts and petty robbery as well as gang violence and homicides, Five Points was generally viewed as an undesirable part of town.

THE HUE-MAN EXPERIENCE BOOKSTORE OPERATIONS/LAYOUT

The Hue-Man Experience Bookstore began operations out of a two-story row house, one of four attached residential apartments (see Exhibit 5). Within two years, Clara expanded her store into one of the adjacent row houses, convincing the landlord to do renovations to connect the two houses. With 4,200 titles occupying 3,000 square feet,

Exhibit 5   The Hue-Man Experience Bookstore, 911 Park Avenue West in Denver

Street view

Inside the store

Clara Villarosa, owner

Hue-Man Experience was, very likely, one of the largest African American book-stores in the United States.

Two cash registers, or point-of-sale (POS) computer terminals, were located just inside the door. Afrocentric greeting cards and note cards were located in a separate room adjacent to the checkout area. Afrocentric art created a backdrop for the checkout area, which was surrounded by a glass case displaying ethnic jewelry. An employee was always on hand to greet people and offer assistance. Each room was arranged around a particular theme or subject. Popular titles and classics were on the main floor, in what was once a living room. Upstairs, there were rooms devoted to sports, religion, music, and children's books.

Specialty cards, calendars, and jewelry comprised approximately 20 percent of sales. Fine art prints and ethnic artwork by local artists were displayed on the walls throughout the store and in two browsing racks. Calendars featuring African American history and African American Art were also prominently displayed. During the holiday season, two rooms upstairs were full of distinctive boxed Christmas and Kwanzaa cards. People who bought books as gifts could also purchase gift wrapping and gift bags with African designs. Like most specialty stores, these sidelines were an integral part of the store's identity, geared specifically to the African American market. Cards and jewelry typically had a bigger markup than books and brought added traffic into the store.

Industry insiders recognized that books were often an impulse purchase, bought on a whim for self-fulfillment or to be given as a gift. Both small mall boutiques and large chain stores understood the importance of lighting and displays to get people in the door to browse. Location and name recognition were important here too, especially for independent booksellers.

Because of the fixed maximum price of most items, inventory control was critical to profitability. Computerized inventory control systems attached to POS terminals were considered essential for large-store success. These computer programs ranged in price from around $400 (for software that ran on most PCs) to over $5,000 (for systems that included POS, cash registers, and scanners). Some of the most expensive computer systems available could be connected to on-line electronic ordering systems with wholesalers or major distributors to expedite reorders and returns. Others could tie into banking networks for credit card authorization and check scanning. Hue-Man Experience used a program called "Booklog," a menu-driven system that was easy to use, even for "noncomputer" people. This program kept track of purchases and sales, keeping sales histories to track fast- or slow-moving items. A customer file was kept that was used for identifying frequent buyers and sending out announcements or newsletters.

Employees were critical to the success of independent booksellers, whose customers relied on service. Many booksellers had difficulty finding competent employees, people who read and who were knowledgeable about books, people who were personable, people who were willing to work hard. Wages in most bookstores ranged from $4.50 to $5.50 per hour, far less than most full-time employment. Even in Denver's strong economy, booksellers such as the Tattered Cover and Hue-Man Experience Bookstore have had no trouble finding competent, well-educated employees. Employees at both stores were quick to indicate how much they enjoyed their jobs.

There were four full-time employees at the Hue-Man Experience Bookstore. Turnover was low, with employees typically staying over a year, a rarity in minimum-wage positions. The employees at the Hue-Man Experience Bookstore conveyed a sense of ownership, not only to the bookstore but also to the cultural community. One employee at Hue-Man Experience Bookstore, a college graduate who majored in African American Studies, had stayed at the store for over a year because she enjoyed learning more about her culture and interacting with African Americans in her community.

MARKETING

I started out with a marketing plan but there were many flaws because it was based on Anglo book purchasing behavior. We were unable to anticipate the difficulty in getting African American people to buy books. I had to go back and reevaluate my marketing strategies. We thought people would come because the idea was unique. It was an upscale store with ambiance, patterned similar to Tattered Cover, which really has a national presence. And we thought that people would come—particularly middle-class people with disposable incomes and a higher education level, because that was the population that I was close to. But it took a lot more marketing to get people in. The variable we didn't count on is that the store sold not just books, but culture. The customers we attracted have to be culturally connected.

Clara originally put out fliers and took out ads to publicize her store, but she quickly realized that she wasn't reaching her market. And she soon understood that the people who came into the store were not the well-to-do clientele that she had envisioned.

We found out that our market was the working class. So we had to direct our advertising to these people. Unfortunately, they don't belong to a lot of groups. They belong to churches but marketing from churches is very difficult because pastors do not want you to come into their congregation to sell something—other than what they sell. So we've tried to determine what our people buy and why they buy what they buy. We've studied the psychodemographics of our population and tried to create a presence in the community. And we also were trying to create a national presence because people make purchases based on prestige so the bookstore had to develop the prestige.

So Clara Villarosa began telling everyone who came in the store that this was the largest African American bookstore in the country. And she became an influential figure in the African American community. She did book reviews on the radio. She was active in community and civic affairs. She was appointed to the governor's council for business development and served on the board of directors of the Small Business Development Center and the Metro Denver Visitors and Conventions Bureau. She was a "friend of the library," she worked with the Denver Center for Performing Arts (DCPA), the Cleo Parker Robinson Dance Company, and Eulipions Cultural Center. She was willing to be involved in:

anything that's culturally related, because I enjoy ethnic events. I like the theater and the ballet and all of that, so I get involved. DCPA currently performs one black play a year, maybe someday they'll do two. I host the director and cast for a reception here in the store and I invite my customers in so that they can touch and feel the cast and it advertises the show and helps sell tickets. Cleo Parker Robinson—her dance troupe is an African American dance troupe, and I work with her and find out what she's doing. Eulipions is an African American theater company. I was a founding member of their board of directors and served for eight years. If an author—an African American author—is coming to town to make a speech or presentation, I ask if they want their book sold at the events or if they want to come to the store for a signing. Of course they will! I'm not stupid! But I really have to hustle and seek out opportunities. And so I've been nominated for a zillion awards and won most of them. I'm a small business, I'm retail, I'm a minority-owned business.

In the 10 years since the store had been opened, Clara had become much better at marketing. By the end of 1993, the only paid advertising was in the form of "courtesy ads," ads placed in local programs or newsletters. These ads generated goodwill, but she did not believe that she reached new customers with those ads. Word-of-mouth was the main source of advertising. But word-of-mouth was cultivated through sophisticated public relations. She had been featured in *Ms. Magazine, Executive Female*, and *Publishers Weekly*. She was on the board of directors of the American Booksellers Association and a member of the Mountains and Plains Booksellers Association. She was instrumental in putting together a feature exhibit entitled "Black and Read: Books by African-American Authors and Illustrators" at the ABA convention, which met in Denver in 1990.

> African Americans come to Denver for many conventions but how do I locate them? So by serving on the board [of the Denver Metropolitan Visitors and Conventions Bureau] I will be instrumental in putting together a fact sheet of things to do and places to go in Denver for African American visitors. I'm also learning about other industries—the hotel industry—all of those are what I call my marketing strategy. I'm hosting a group of African American educators here on Friday.

In 1989, at the suggestion of many out-of-town customers, Clara put together a 64-page mail-order catalog. "They said, 'Send me the booklist.' They like to read it but they don't order. It's a different motivation to pick up the phone and order a book." But the catalog appeared to create a feeling of connectedness and brought them back to the store. The book catalog was financed largely through "co-op" advertising, whereby publishers pay for most of the printing cost of ads for their books.

By 1992, Clara's book catalog was a more efficient 16 pages. The catalog was professionally produced, in a format similar to those found in upscale bookstores such as the Tattered Cover. In 1993, she began negotiating with Ingram's, a major book distributor, to jointly produce a catalog that would be distributed to other bookstores. This would be a glossy version of her newsprint catalog that other bookstore owners could use for their customers.

> My name would appear as a by-line and Ingram's would do the layout and pick up the printing costs. Individual bookstores will put their name and address on it for their own customers, which helps them publicize current titles. I know it's a lot of work to design this, but I'm already doing it for my own store. This way Hue-Man Experience will get national publicity.

She also published a quarterly newsletter, highlighting author signings and community events. A reduced copy of the newsletter appears in Exhibit 6. This newsletter was typically one page, printed on both sides, which could be mailed easily when folded and stapled. Regular customers were on the mailing list. Customers who spent at least $10 were added to this list. Clara found out the hard way that sending out unsolicited newsletters was not bringing in new customers. Regular customers were "the ones most likely to come back and most likely to come to store-sponsored events. They pay for the newsletter."

> PR is critical in this business—community connections. It's interesting, because that's what we built this store on—a community presence. Local people say that we have something of value and this creates pride and ownership. And we perpetuate that image by showing them that we care about them as individual customers and that we care about their community . . . We find that our customers expect to be treated well, everyone is greeted, everyone is treated warmly, nurtured. We have to recognize our history, based on segregation,

Exhibit 6   Sample Newsletter (front of flyer)

THE HUE-MAN READER
December, 1994

Essence Comes To Denver

Don't miss the chance to come out and hear these exceptional authors. For more information call 293-2665.

Linda Villarosa

The first and only self-help book specifically written to address Black women's physical, spiritual and emotional health concerns. Drawing from 60 Black females around the country, this book is written in clear, straightforward language with 100 illustrations and photographs.

Executive Editor
Essence Magazine

Body and Soul:
The Black Women's Guide to
Physical Health and
Emotional Well-Being

Sunday, December 11
2:00 p.m. - 4:00 p.m.

Susan L. Taylor
*Editor in Chief of **Essence Magazine***
Newly released in paperback, these inspirational writings offer life lines for living, seeds of faith and empowering messages to survive in a stress filled society.

In The Spirit

Wednesday, December 14
5:30 p.m. - 7:00 p.m.

Thank you for supporting the book store and the market place.
We strive to give you a wide variety of Afrocentric products
in a user friendly atmosphere, with good customer service
by knowledgeable staff. It gives us great pleasure
to serve and it is our good fortune to know you.
Make this holiday a celebration of family, community and culture.
Plus, each one identify a way to continue the celebration into 1995.

Happy Holidays and a spiritual prosperous New Year.
— Clara Villarosa

discrimination. You still hear of sales people demanding IDs and avoiding eye contact with African American customers. It happens every place. Not as often as before, but people are still uncomfortable around African Americans. Even in Denver, which is a city that's pretty well mixed, an integrated city . . .

> There's no central African American community because Denver was developed as an integrated city and people have dispersed to all areas of the city. People have moved to the suburbs, outlying areas, Aurora, Littleton. These people aren't inclined to drive the distance to the store very often. We have to create a destination place. There's no other traffic around here.

PLANS FOR THE FUTURE

In November 1992, Clara Villarosa bought the four houses that comprised the building that contained the bookstore, with financing backed by the U.S. Small Business Administration. She was able to buy the building for $79,000. With her track record as a successful retailer, she was able to secure a $72,000, 24-year loan on the building, which appraised for $120,000. Her store occupied two units; the other two were rented to an art gallery and an ethnic apparel retailer.

Clara viewed her business as more than a bookstore. To her, it was a cultural center. She observed, "People who come here are culturally connected." She feared that, in 1993, Denver's African American population was too dispersed to support a cultural center. She also recognized that there was strength in numbers: a larger concentration of attractive African American businesses could serve as a catalyst for cultural connections:

> I'd like to create an Afrocentric Marketplace and position it as a mini-mall. So I bought this building two years ago. The other rented spaces in this building are complementary product lines. One . . . sells African clothing and cloth and accessories and the other is [an] . . . Art Gallery. I'd eventually like to work with them to make it a coffee shop also. The rent is fixed, it's stable, so they aren't going to deal with escalating rent costs. I offer limited services, I maintain the property, but we work cooperatively. I know the bookstore is the anchor. They each have their own customer base but we feed off of each other. We want to create a synergy that will create more traffic for everyone. I'm working on joint PR [with the clothing store and the art gallery].

Around the corner from the Hue-Man Experience Bookstore was another row-house building, which faced the side street. The first floor of this building housed an artist co-op, a store that sold blues tapes, a custom hat shop, and a caterer. Rents were about $4 per square foot (per year), or $400 per month for each tenant. Three of the leases were month-to-month contracts. The second floor was boarded up and uninhabitable due to fire damage several years before.

In September 1993, this building went up for sale. By December 1993, the asking price was reduced from $150,000 to $95,000. The roof had recently been repaired but needed replacement. The building would need extensive renovation, estimated as high as $200,000, for the upstairs to be used for retail space. One prospective buyer estimated that a new floor could be put in for about $50,000 so that the upstairs could be used as storage.

The Mayor's Office of Economic Redevelopment had targeted the Five Points area for low-interest redevelopment loans. Clara believed that "There's potential for lots of retail activity in this area, but it will be slow in coming." A light rail transit system, connecting Five Points to downtown, was scheduled to open in October 1994.

> I had hoped that the catering operation [around the corner] would also serve food, but she just wants to cater; and my suspicion is that they're not stable

tenants. The top floor of the building . . . needs to be renovated for retail or office space. I think the purchase is still an option.

Clara Villarosa was confident that she could get financing for expansion without diluting her ownership in the business. Business loan rates were going for as low as 10 percent. But, even if she could obtain the building at less than the current asking price, she was not sure that this would be a prudent investment at this time. At this point in her life, Clara was particularly concerned about the income potential of any expansion effort.

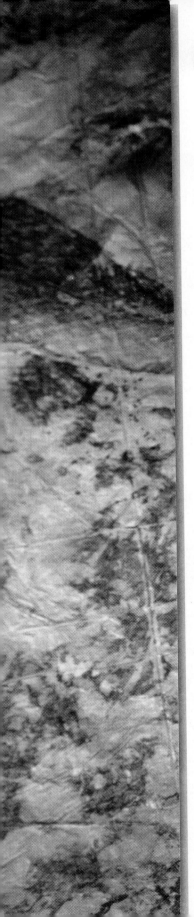

Perrigo Company

Ram Subramanian, Grand Valley State University

Mike Jandernoa, the chief executive officer and chairman of the board of Perrigo Company, was driving along Michigan State Highway 222 toward the city of Allegan, the site of the company's corporate headquarters. It was the first week of March 1993. As he passed snow-covered farmlands, Mike thought about the upcoming week-long strategic planning meeting. This was the meeting where critical long-term plans were made for the company. He smiled at the recollection of an executive who described these meetings as "5 or 6 days of pure hell." Yet, argued Mike to himself, these meetings were vital for Perrigo. The store brand industry was in a boom period, with tremendous opportunities for a company that was well positioned.

Pulling into the employee parking lot (the company had no executive parking spaces), Mike parked his car and walked briskly to his office. After greeting his executive secretary, he told her that he was not to be disturbed for the next three to four hours. He wanted to spend the time reviewing the company's present position so that he would be well prepared for the strategic planning meeting.

COMPANY HISTORY

Headquartered in Allegan, Michigan, the Perrigo Company was founded in 1887 by Luther Perrigo, who sold curative elixirs from a horse-drawn cart. In the late 1940s, William L. Tripp, grandson of Luther Perrigo, and Dr. Lem Curlin, an investor, helped guide the conversion of the company from a repacker of generic home remedies to a quality manufacturer of branded health and beauty aids.

In 1981, the founding family sold the company to a management group. The acquisition, which was a leveraged buyout, also marked the transition from a family-owned branded products company to a professionally managed maker of products for the store brand or private-label market. In 1986, the company was sold for $45 million to Grow Group, Inc., a New York-based publicly held company that owned (at that time) 23 diverse manufacturing firms. Perrigo became the largest unit of Grow Group, Inc., contributing almost one-third of total sales. In April 1988, a management group bought Perrigo from Grow Group, Inc., for $61 million through a leveraged buyout. Key management personnel, however, stayed with the company throughout these transitions.

In December 1991, the company made an initial public offering of 9.2 million shares of common stock at $16 per share. Of the more than $122 million (net of commissions) that was raised by the offering, approximately $35 million was used to acquire Cumberland-Swan, a major manufacturer of personal care products located in Smyrna, Tennessee. The rest of the proceeds was used to reduce the debt that resulted from the series of leveraged buyouts.

In September 1992, 5 million shares of common stock were sold at $32 per share by some of the existing shareholders. The company's common stock was traded in the over-the-counter (OTC) market (NASDAQ). In March 1993, approximately 40 percent of the shares were owned by institutions and the general public, while 60 percent of the shares were owned by management, together with the Hillman Company and its affiliates.

Citing a cooperative relationship with its workforce and a strong commitment to low-cost production and customer service as causes, Perrigo Company reported fiscal 1992 sales of $409.8 million and a net income of $28.6 million. It was the nation's largest supplier of over-the-counter (nonprescription) pharmaceuticals and personal care products to retailers of private-label brands as well as a leading maker of private-label vitamins. The vast majority (about 98 percent in 1992) of Perrigo's products were sold as the discounted house brands of retailers and competed with nationally advertised brand-name products. In addition, the company also marketed vitamins, personal care products, and over-the-counter pharmaceutical products under its own "Nature's Glo," "Perrigo," "Swan," and "Good Sense" labels.

THE STORE BRAND PRODUCTS INDUSTRY

In 1991, the $26 billion store brand (or private-label) industry accounted for 18.2 percent of unit volume in supermarkets and 13.7 percent of total supermarket revenue, up from 15.3 percent in units and 11.6 percent in dollars in 1988.[1] Brian Sharoff, president of the Private Label Manufacturers Association (PLMA), attributed the explosive growth of the store brand industry to good packaging, high-quality, aggressive promotion, and increased corporate commitment by retailers.[2]

Store brand products encompassed all merchandise sold under a retailer's private label. House brand products, which were usually quite comparable if not identical, to branded products, were common in such categories as food, snacks, soft drinks, canned goods, health and beauty aids, and over-the-counter drugs.

Store brand products had long been a staple offering of most supermarket and drugstore chains. Private-label goods offered customers savings of anywhere from 10 to 40 percent over national brands, depending on the item (Exhibit 1). However, despite offering significant price savings for consumers, sales of store brand products were comparatively low until the late 1980s. This was because store brands, like the low-cost generic products that mushroomed during the 1980s, had a reputation for uneven quality, drab packaging and less attractive store display. Retailer interest in store brands was rekindled in 1985 by the success a Toronto-based grocery chain, Loblaw's, enjoyed with its private-label President's Choice line.[3] The popularity of this line, coupled with the significantly higher profit margins for the retailer (approximately 10 to 20 percent for national brands versus 30 percent for store brands because of lower marketing and promotional costs), enabled the makers and sellers of private-label items to register strong sales growth in the next few years. National brands downplayed the growth in popularity of

[1] "Latest Market Statistics Show Private Label Renaissance," PLMA Press Release, May 4, 1992.
[2] Ibid.
[3] Gary Strauss, "Shoppers Find Value beyond Big Names," *USA Today*, January 7, 1993, pp. D1, 2.

Exhibit 1   Price Comparison of Selected National Brands and Their Store Brand Equivalents

Product	Typical Retail Price	Typical Retail Profit	Comparable Store Brand		Consumer Savings
			Retail Price	Retail Profit	
Advil (OTC)	$7.88	$1.55	$4.49	$2.76	43%
Head & Shoulders (personal care)	3.49	0.74	2.69	1.44	23
Centrum (vitamins)	8.99	0.99	5.75	2.25	36

Note: Advil, Head & Shoulders, and Centrum are registered trademarks.
Source: Perrigo Company.

store brands, believing that the switch was recession-driven and that customers would come back to branded products once good times returned. This was not to be, as store brand industry sales increased each year from 1988 to 1991.

The PLMA offered four explanations for the renaissance of store brand products. First, retailers saw themselves as more directly in touch with their customers than most manufacturers and therefore believed they were the ones who had the most to lose from customer dissatisfaction. They wanted to control their own destiny. Second, there was a decline in brand loyalty. Marcia Smith, the publisher of *Private Label Product News,* an industry trade magazine, talked about this decline:

> Brand loyalty is mostly dead. Consumers want quality products, they want value for their money, but they've discovered extremely good value in private labels. They've gotten smarter.[4]

The third reason was the major shift in consumer attitudes toward private labels. A 1991 Gallup poll indicated greater acceptance of store brands, primarily because retailers had improved the quality and merchandising of these products. The fourth reason offered was the internationalization of retailing. Many major U.S. supermarket chains were owned by European companies, where store brands had been accepted for a long time;[5] 1991 market share for private labels in Great Britain was around 29 percent, 24 percent in France, and 20 percent in Holland and Belgium.[6]

Exhibit 2 presents overall market size, store brands' share of the total market, and Perrigo's market share in 1992. Exhibit 3 indicates store brands' share of total market in each of the three segments where Perrigo competed.

The store brand industry was highly fragmented along product and geographic lines. Nearly 200 manufacturers vied with one another to supply retailers. Competition was driven primarily by cost and quality, though Perrigo executives constantly emphasized customer service as a key success factor. Since most players in the store brand industry were small, closely held companies, individual data about competitors was skimpy or nonexistent. Exhibit 4 profiles Perrigo's competition in

---

[4]Ibid.
[5]"A Strategic Guide to Private Label," *Discount Store News,* October 1992.
[6]"Store Brands: The Next Generation," *Progressive Grocer,* May 1992.

Exhibit 2 Overall Market Size, Store Brands' Share, and Perrigo's Market Share in 1992

Perrigo's Product Categories	Total Market Size (in billions of $)	Store Brand's Share	Perrigo's Market Share
OTC nonprescription drugs	$ 7.2	12%	65%
Personal care items	8.7	7	44
Vitamins	1.7	31	13
Total	$17.6	11%	45%

Note: Total market size includes sales of branded plus store brand product (retail value).
Source: Perrigo Company.

Exhibit 3 Store Brands' Share of Total Market, 1990–1992

Category	1990	1991	1992
OTC nonprescription drugs	9%	11%	12%
Personal care items	5	6	7
Vitamins	29	30	31

Source: Perrigo Company.

Exhibit 4 Comparative Data on Perrigo and Selected Other Competitors in the Store Brand Industry

Company	Estimated 1992 Revenues* ($ millions)	Company Participation		
		OTC Drugs	Personal Care Items	Vitamins
Perrigo	409	Yes	Yes	Yes
P. Leiner	225	Yes	Yes	Yes
Pharmarite	150	No	No	Yes
Rexall/Pennex	70	Yes	Yes	Yes
ViJon	50	No	Yes	No
Granutec	35	Yes	No	No
PFI	35	Yes	No	No
Hall Labs	35	Yes	No	Yes
American Vitamins	30	No	No	Yes

* Except for Perrigo, sales of other companies are estimates by Perrigo executives.
Source: Perrigo Company.

the OTC, personal care, and vitamin segments of the store brand industry. Perrigo considered itself to be the leader in the OTC and personal care segments and the third-biggest player in the vitamin segment of the store brand industry (both P. Leiner and Pharmavite had broader vitamin product lines and larger sales volume than Perrigo).

COMPANY PROFILE

Perrigo Company conducted its operations through three wholly owned subsidiaries. L. Perrigo Company (located in Allegan, Michigan) manufactured over-the-counter pharmaceuticals and certain lines of personal care products. Perrigo Company of South Carolina (located in Greenville, South Carolina) produced vitamins. Cumberland-Swan (in Smyrna, Tennessee) primarily produced personal care products and "wets" or traditional liquid "home remedy" products such as rubbing alcohol, hydrogen peroxide, castor oil, and witch hazel.

Michael J. Jandernoa was CEO and chairman of the board of Perrigo Company. Elected a director of the company in 1981, he became the CEO in 1986, seven years after joining the company. The other principal officers were Richard Hansen, the chief operating officer and president of L. Perrigo Company; Lonnie Smith, president of Cumberland-Swan; and M. James Gunberg, treasurer and chief financial officer. Exhibit 5 provides a condensed organizational chart for the company.

Marketing and Sales

Perrigo sought to establish close relationships with its customers, the retailers. Its marketing efforts were directed at developing customized marketing plans and programs for its customers' store brands. One important aspect of this store brand management approach was that it enabled retailers to promote their own house brand products at the point of purchase. In addition, because the cost to the retailer of a store brand product was generally significantly lower than that of a national brand product, the retailer was able to commit funds to promote its store brand products through coupons, rebates, and other individualized promotions while still realizing a higher profit margin on its store brand products than on comparable national brand products. Jeff Needham, L. Perrigo Company's vice president of marketing, talked about the company's marketing focus:

> Our customer universe is very well defined. We are doing business today in some way, shape or form with just about every retailer in the country. There are some retailers we aren't doing business with that we'd like to, but that's a pretty short list. That is not to say we're doing all the business we want to with all of our customers, obviously, but our customer universe is pretty well defined and we're talking to those people on a regular basis. So we kind of pride ourselves on understanding what's going on with all of our customers, and certainly our major customers. We have to be very well attuned to them, seeing them on a regular basis. As our customers' store brand program becomes increasingly important to them, it is necessary that they execute a well-thought-out marketing plan to support it. Perrigo's marketing role is to support our customers in helping to direct this brand management planning process and to provide the necessary programs and tools to them so that they can execute successful in-store programs. Aside from a couple of vitamin companies, Perrigo was the first company (in the store brand industry) to have invested tremendous resources in its marketing function. It clearly gives us an edge over our competitors.

Perrigo's marketing department was responsible for managing product introductions and conversions, promotional planning support, and market research. It used both primary and secondary market research (Perrigo had performed or authorized some of the largest primary and secondary market studies ever completed on store

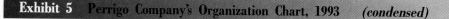

Exhibit 5 Perrigo Company's Organization Chart, 1993   (condensed)

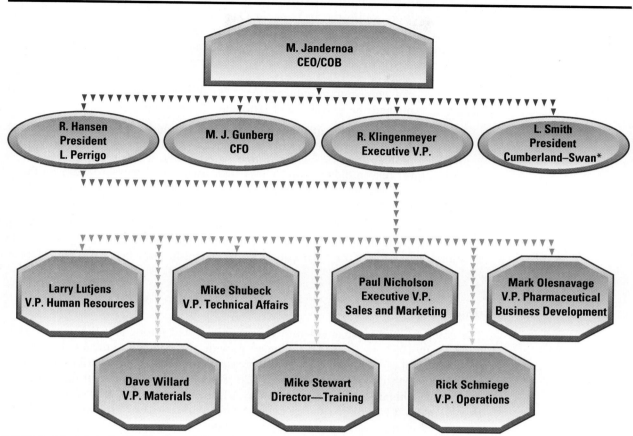

* Cumberland Swan had a functional structure similar to that of the L. Perrigo subsidiary shown above.
Source: Perrigo Company.

brand customer buying habits), monitored data and trends for products and categories, and provided market information and educational training aids to its customers.

The company's products were sold by its own sales force primarily to major retail drug, supermarket, and mass merchandise chains, and major wholesalers and to industry brokers for sales to smaller retailers. In 1992, Perrigo had approximately 2,250 customers, one of which, Wal-Mart, accounted for approximately 12 percent of total sales. According to Perrigo officials, most, though not all, retail customers sole-sourced their private-label products.

In the late 1980s, the company introduced a program to reduce retailer inventory costs while maintaining the optimum level of product on store shelves. This program, called the Minimum Inventory—Maximum Service (MIMS) program, used electronic data interchange (EDI) to allow Perrigo to monitor and manage customer inventory levels. As of 1992, about 10 percent of Perrigo's customers were involved in the MIMS program.

Exhibit 6 shows the company's product sales by class. In 1992, Perrigo offered an increased number of vitamin products to its customers. Sales of the personal care segment increased significantly over the previous year because of the Cumberland-Swan acquisition, while the increase in OTC segment sales was attributed to the introduction of several new products through the Abbreviated New Drug Application process. Exhibit 7 contains examples of products marketed by the company and their national brand equivalents. In 1993, Perrigo marketed approximately 857 store brand products to retailers.

In 1984, the company introduced the "Good Sense" brand of products. Jeff Needham explained the purpose and rationale of the program:

> About nine years ago we identified the need for a brand program, what we call the "control label" program. That was as much as anything designed to provide us with a program that we could sell to customers who weren't large enough or for whatever reason didn't want to have their own store brand program. So the Good Sense program was developed to fill that need. That business has been growing quite significantly in the last several years.

Apart from the Good Sense line, the company also manufactured and marketed Nature's Glo and Perrigo lines of natural vitamins and Swan brand "wets." In addition, the company used the Equate brand name, for which it gave Wal-Mart an exclusive license.

Operations

The company had six manufacturing facilities located throughout the country (Exhibit 8). In 1993, to support anticipated growth, the company embarked on a $60 million capital investment program to increase its production and distribution capacities. The expansion plan called for a $25 million tablet manufacturing facility at Allegan, Michigan, an $8 million mouthwash manufacturing plant at Smyrna, Tennessee, and a $3 million vitamin plant at Greenville, South Carolina. In 1992, the company's plants operated at an average 86 percent capacity.

Each of the company's six manufacturing plants was designed and equipped to allow low-cost production of a wide variety of products of different quantities, sizes, and packaging. Flexible production line changeover capabilities and reduced cycle times enabled the company to respond quickly to increases or decreases in customer orders for one item versus another.

Richard Schmiege, the vice president of operations for the L. Perrigo subsidiary, talked about the company's production function:

> Something that we constantly talk about in our regular meetings is customer service. Our goal is, as you would expect, continuous improvement. We have many programs in place to help support that objective. We meet every Monday morning in a production meeting which involves operating department managers, and we invite other people from scheduling, inventory control, purchasing, customer service—basically, anyone who wants to attend our meeting. Sometimes, we have as many as 35 people in these meetings. We report the production numbers from the previous week, we talk about the problems that we've had for the week, and assign responsibility if there's a problem that needs to be fixed. We have a very open session and talk about things that need to be done on a weekly basis. We also have many formal programs to support our objective of continuous improvement. We have installed a state-of-the-art manufacturing resource planning (MRP II) system that enables the company to develop

Exhibit 6 Perrigo Product Sales Breakdown, 1988–1992 *(in millions of $)*

	1988	1989	1990	1991	1992
Dollar Breakdown					
OTC drugs	$100.5	$144.1	$165.4	$187.7	$259.4
Personal care items	40.3	46.0	53.9	65.2	114.3
Vitamins	23.5	24.7	26.2	27.9	35.2
Total	$164.3*	$214.8	$245.5	$280.8	$408.9
Percentage Breakdown					
OTC drugs	61.2%	67.1%	67.4%	66.8%	63.4%
Personal care items	24.5	21.4	22.0	23.2	28.0
Vitamins	14.3	11.5	10.6	10.0	8.6
Total	100.0%	100.0%	100.0%	100.0%	100.0%

* The total of the three segments' sales differs from Perrigo's total reported sales because of revenues from contract work that Perrigo performs for certain national brand manufacturers. These contract sales amount to less than 1 percent of total sales. In 1992, for example, contract sales were $885,000 or 0.22 percent of total sales.
Source: Perrigo Company, 1992 Annual Report.

Exhibit 7 Examples of Perrigo Products and National Brand Equivalents

Perrigo Products	Competing National Brands
OTC Pharmaceuticals	
Ibuprofen tablets	Advil tablets
Acetaminophen tablets	Tylenol tablets
Aspirin	Bayer
Nite time cough syrup	Nyquil
Stress liquid	Pepto-Bismol
Flavored antacid tablets	Tums
Personal Care Products	
Green mouthwash	Scope
Anti-plaque rinse	Plax
Smoker's toothpaste	Topol
Shampoo plus conditioner	Pert
Antiperspirant stick	Sure
Vitamins	
Therapeutic M	Theragran M
A-shapes chewables	Flintstones
Century IV vitamins	Centrum

Source: Perrigo Company, 1992 Annual Report.

realistic and attainable production schedules and related material and capacity requirements. We have also introduced a JIT/TQC system, which we call the "Advantage" program. Our interpretation of the JIT/TQC concept led to the formation of work teams. In the past we had line workers whose job was to

Exhibit 8   Perrigo's Manufacturing Facilities

Location	Approximate Square Feet	Leased (L) or Owned (O)
Allegan, Michigan	791,000	O
Greenville, South Carolina	75,000	O
Montague, Michigan	37,000	O
Smyrna, Tennessee	580,000	L*
San Bernardino, California	68,000	L*
Holland, Michigan	101,000	O

* As part of the acquisition of Cumberland-Swan, Perrigo contracted to purchase these facilities in December 1994.
Note: The Allegan, Michigan, and Smyrna, Tennessee, facilities also housed corporate offices. Total manufacturing area was 1,467,000 square feet.
Source: Perrigo Company, 1992 Annual Report.

watch the lines to make sure they were running smoothly and to shut them down if they weren't running smoothly. We also had another set of people who would come in when machines needed to be fixed or set up. Today, we have all of the employees, including setup people, unit leaders, and line workers, doing the same thing—fixing, setting up, and running the machines as a team.

The company had a supplier certification program whose objective was to improve quality, save time, and eliminate duplication of efforts between Perrigo and its suppliers, thus reducing costs. Dave Kiddy, director of purchasing for the Allegan subsidiary, talked about the certification process:

Our supplier certification program was developed by a cross-functional team from within the company. We developed various measurements and supplier evaluation criteria that we use when auditing suppliers and their facilities. We measure quality and service for all items purchased from suppliers being considered for certification as well as those already certified. Our intent is to improve the quality and reduce our total cost of the materials we purchase by working closely with our suppliers. We attempt to clearly communicate our needs and expectations, evaluate suppliers' capabilities to meet a high standard, and take redundancy out of the system if we are confident the suppliers' processes are under control. We have been able to improve our total cost by reducing or eliminating the amount of incoming inspection, rerouting the flow of certified materials through the production departments, and reducing lead times and inventory levels. Another benefit of our certification program has been in the improvement of communication and strengthened relationships with our suppliers. I feel we are better customers to them and they are better suppliers to us because we have improved our understanding of each other's needs and capabilities. Also, multilevel relationships have been developed or enhanced during the certification process.

The certification process had been in place since 1992. Only a few of the company's suppliers had been certified by March 1993, but they represented a significant number of items and dollars spent. All of the company's certified suppliers were considered strategic suppliers.

The company did not make any of the chemicals required for production. The company was vertically integrated to the extent that it processed all the raw materials in-house before they were used in the production process. The acquisition of Cumberland-Swan gave the company a bottle blow-molding facility. In addition, the company made 75 percent of its labels and printed 35 percent of its cartons in-house.

Perrigo's Graphic Arts and Printing department was a 66,000-square-foot facility that employed 239 graphic arts experts, including 43 artists. The objective of this department was to provide excellent customer service. Extensive consumer research was used to design and produce packaging that invited comparison with national brands. In addition, the department also created point-of-sale materials custom-designed to help the retailer attract customers. Jack Godfrey, the printing manager, talked about the department's activities:

> About six years ago (in 1987) we invested in a proprietary design software that we use to design on a terminal. It is similar to designing on a Macintosh, only much larger. Our department currently runs 1,500 to 1,700 jobs per month. In designing the labels, our Regulatory Affairs department provides us with guidelines to follow.

Products were shipped from six geographically dispersed distribution facilities (Exhibit 9). Several large customers picked up their products directly from these distribution facilities. In most cases, contract or common carriers were used to deliver products.

Research and Development

The company did not seek to discover or develop new products that had not been previously sold to consumers. Instead, the company's research efforts were focused exclusively on formulating store brand equivalents of national brands and in reformulating existing products in response to changes in national brand formulas. Thirty-two employees made up this department, which spent approximately $3.4 million in 1992.

Human Resources

Larry Lutjens, vice president of Human Resources for the L. Perrigo subsidiary, described the company's labor-management situation:

> Perrigo, when I joined it in 1980, was about a $40 million company and we employed about 800 people. It was an interesting situation. The company's employees had just gone through an organizing campaign, and management had won by a very small margin. Bill Swaney, the CEO of the company after the first management-led leveraged buyout, felt that we needed to take a different approach with people here, to try to get away from an adversarial-type relationship. I wanted to start with the basics. The first thing I did was to establish some practices here so that we knew what people we had on the third shift, what people we had on the second shift, etc. We wanted to know something about the history of each employee's work experience so that when we had to make promotion decisions, we had a basis for that. The big problem we had, let's say in 1979, was favoritism. That was the biggest issue on the table at that time. Without good personnel practices, that's how it was going to be perceived. If they didn't get the job and there's no system in place, they're going to feel, "well, it's because he knew the boss."

Exhibit 9   Perrigo's Distribution Facilities

Location	Approximate Square Feet	Leased (L) or Owned (O)
Holland, Michigan	381,000	L*
Greenville, South Carolina	104,000	L*
Sacramento, California	79,000	L
Lavergne, Tennessee	311,000	L
San Bernardino, California	68,000	L†
Cranbury, New Jersey	114,000	L

Note: The San Bernardino location houses both manufacturing and distribution facilities.

* With an option to purchase all or part of the facility.

† As part of the acquisition of Cumberland-Swan, Perrigo contracted to purchase this facility in December 1994.

Source: Perrigo Company, 1992 Annual Report.

Lutjens and his group spent almost two years working on personnel practices. A committee of employees was formed to put together an employee handbook. Training sessions were conducted for supervisors on using a nonadversarial approach in the workplace. Lutjens decided that compensation was a critical area that needed to be addressed and began looking around for a plan that would motivate employees by allowing them to share the rewards of their productivity. He explained his approach:

> In looking at compensation, we tried to get away from the idea that no matter what you did, no matter what your performance, no matter how the company was doing, everybody got the same thing. At that time employees received cost of living or wage increases, maybe 3 or 4 percent each year. In 1982, we just eliminated that. We eliminated cost of living increases, and we eliminated general increases. We came across something called Improshare [a trademarked product]. It is a productivity-based bonus plan where employees receive a weekly bonus based on their productivity for that particular period. The amount of the bonus is based on performance for a particular period as compared to performance during a base period. If employees improve their productivity over a formula that is established during the base period, we pay a bonus on that and that bonus is paid weekly. Today, we are averaging about a 17 percent bonus per week. The plan is also marked by employee involvement with its implementation, active participation by employees and their supervisors in increasing productivity, and constant communication that tells employees what their bonus is for a particular period as well as why it is that particular amount.

According to Lutjens, Improshare not only improved productivity, but, more importantly, it introduced a change in the company's culture. Employees began to be more concerned about hours worked and absenteeism, not only their own but also those of others, since Improshare was a group not an individual plan. The number of job classifications was reduced from 68 (in the mid 1980s) to 8, and all employees were put on salary. Employees did not have to punch in or out of production. They maintained their own time cards. Also, to help dismantle some of the barriers between management and labor, the company instituted a policy of having no designated parking space for managers and having all employees share a common lunchroom.

Pay rates were competitive, and the company offered good benefits. More than 50 percent of the job openings were filled from within. A tuition reimbursement program encouraged employees to further their formal education.

A bimonthly newsletter acted as the forum for formal communication. In addition, Michael Jandernoa, the CEO, met with employee groups on a quarterly basis to discuss the company's performance. In 1993, the company employed a total of around 3,500 people in all its subsidiaries.

Finances

Perrigo was a high-growth company. Between fiscal 1989 (the first full year after the final management-led buyout) and fiscal 1992, the company's sales and net income grew at compounded annual rates of approximately 24 percent and 107 percent, respectively. However, the two leveraged buyouts resulted in a high long-term debt-to-equity ratio of 13.3:1 in June 1990 (before the initial public issue of its stock). Primarily as a result of the initial stock offering, this ratio decreased to 0.25:1 by June 1992. Perrigo did not break down the sales and profits of its Cumberland-Swan and South Carolina subsidiaries.

Perrigo's sales and net income had historically peaked in the second and third quarters of the fiscal year, while the first quarter had been its least profitable. Sales of cough and cold remedies traditionally peaked during the second and third fiscal quarters as customers stocked inventories for the winter months. Sales of suntan products peaked in the third and fourth quarters as customers stocked up for the summer months. To fund its rapid growth, the company did not currently pay cash dividends. Exhibits 10–13 present the company's financial statements and selected investor information.

New Product Development

Perrigo's new product development efforts had contributed to its growth and had enabled it to be among the first companies to manufacture and market certain store brand products. From the company's standpoint, new products included not only new store brand products that were comparable to newly introduced national brand products, but also variations of existing products such as new sizes, flavors, and product forms. During fiscal 1992, more than $17 million of the company's net sales (approximately 4.25 percent) were attributable to new products introduced after fiscal 1990.

Most new products introduced by Perrigo did not require prior approval of the Food and Drug Administration (FDA) for their manufacture or marketing. The company, however, sought significant opportunities for growth through the introduction of products requiring prior FDA approval using the Abbreviated New Drug Application (ANDA) process. Such products were typically those for which patent protection was expiring and/or "prescription only" status was being changed to over-the-counter status. Mark Olesnavage, vice president of Pharmaceutical Business Development for Perrigo, talked about the FDA's ANDA process:

If Merck or Sandoz or Glaxo wanted to introduce a new drug, a new chemical entity, or an old drug with a new claim, then the manufacturer has to show that the drug is effective in meeting the claim. If you want to say that you have a brand-new cure for acne, then you've got to show that it is effective in clinical studies. There are different phases in this testing process. First is usually animal testing. This is followed by a series of clinicals on humans. All such tests can

Exhibit 10   Perrigo's Balance Sheets, Fiscal Years 1991 and 1992 (in thousands of dollars)

	Years Ending June 30	
	1992	1991
Assets		
Current assets		
Cash	$ 538	$ 64
Accounts receivables (net)	50,460	31,261
Inventories	106,504	58,604
Prepaid expenses and other current assets	6,092	3,950
Total current assets	163,594	93,879
Property and equipment (at cost):		
Land	7,419	4,292
Buildings	70,515	45,975
Machinery and equipment	67,951	38,704
	145,885	88,971
Less accumulated depreciation	28,737	19,324
	117,148	69,647
Cost in excess of net assets of acquired businesses	33,177	16,412
Other	3,027	2,785
Total assets	$316,946	$182,723
Liabilities and Shareholders' Equity		
Current liabilities		
Accounts payable	$ 41,896	$ 25,989
Payroll and related taxes	8,411	5,929
Accrued expenses	16,929	9,928
Income taxes	4,358	1,718
Current installments on long-term debt	871	11,557
Total current liabilities	72,465	55,121
Deferred income taxes	14,744	12,600
Long-term debt (less current installments)	45,999	82,100
Shareholders' equity		
Common stock	132,285	10,000
Retained earnings	51,453	22,902
Total shareholders' equity	183,738	32,902
Total liabilities and shareholders' equity	$316,946	$182,723

Source: Perrigo Company, 1992 Annual Report.

take three to four years. Tests should also show that the product is safe. So the two things the manufacturer has to show are that the product is effective and that it is safe. In 1984, the Waxman-Hatch Act was passed. Prior to this act, the generic manufacturer had to conduct tests to indicate that the efficacy and safety of the generic drug matches the prescription drug. The act allowed generic drug companies (once a drug was off patent) to market a drug after getting an ANDA approval. What this meant was that the generic manufacturer

Exhibit 11 Perrigo's Income Statements, Fiscal Years 1990–1992 (in thousands of dollars)

	Years Ending June 30		
	1992	**1991**	**1990**
Net sales	$409,785	$281,265	$247,026
Cost of sales	290,626	204,614	181,699
Gross profit	119,159	76,651	65,327
Operating expenses:			
Distribution	11,369	5,305	4,375
Research and development	3,373	1,565	1,518
Selling and administrative expenses	50,585	38,057	31,646
Operating income	53,832	31,724	27,788
Interest expense	8,781	12,420	15,356
Interest before income taxes	45,051	19,304	12,432
Income taxes	16,500	7,100	4,800
Net income	$ 28,551	$ 12,204	$ 7,632

Source: Perrigo Company, 1992 Annual Report.

did not have to prove the effectiveness and safety of the drug. They just had to show that the generic drug was bioequivalent to the original drug. A typical ANDA approval takes about 18 months. We can file an ANDA application before patent expiration and the FDA can conditionally approve it, but we cannot market the product until it is off patent. Perrigo likes to introduce new products through the ANDA process because these products have typically higher margins.

Perrigo's new product group was delegated authority to file an ANDA application. Once the approval was obtained, then the top management of the company made the decision to manufacture the product. Once the decision to manufacture was made, then a cross-functional team (made up of production, marketing, and research and development people) developed specific plans for manufacturing and product introduction. The mission of the team was to take the product through introduction. Several months after launch, responsibility for the product was turned over to the regular marketing department.

By 1993, three years after the company began applying for approval of drugs through the ANDA process, Perrigo had obtained approval to market 7 formulas constituting 30 products. In January 1992, the company received approval to manufacture and market Loperamide Hydrochloride liquid—a drug used for treating acute diarrhea and comparable to the national brand Imodium AD. Olesnavage talked about how Perrigo monitored competitors' testing of new products so that it could be ready with imitative new products of its own:

The industry had never has an unsuccessful switch (from prescription to over-the-counter) yet. But I'm sure it is going to happen. Let me give you a scenario. For new products, we monitor the success of the introduction of the original product. Let's say Johnson and Johnson tested its Tylenol PM in certain markets and we think it is a great new product because the retailer

Exhibit 12 Perrigo's Statement of Cash Flows, Fiscal Years 1990–1992 (in thousands of dollars)

	Years Ending June 30		
	1992	1991	1990
Cash Flows from (for) Operating Activities			
Net income	$ 28,551	$ 12,204	$ 7,632
Depreciation	9,432	7,131	6,330
Amortization of intangible assets	2,610	2,382	1,762
Deferred income taxes	(930)	10	990
Provision for losses on accounts receivable	947	533	480
Changes in:			
Accounts receivable	(7,080)	(1,687)	(2,716)
Inventories	(27,762)	(4,957)	11,761
Prepaid expenses and other current assets	148	(681)	(316)
Accounts payable	8,901	6,208	(9,254)
Payrolls and related taxes	1,926	2,432	(223)
Accrued expenses	(260)	(439)	882
Income taxes	2,668	895	(475)
Net cash from operating activities	$ 19,151	$ 24,031	$ 16,853
Cash Flows for Investing Activities			
Additions to property and equipment	$(19,692)	$ (7,525)	$(13,964)
Acquisition of Cumberland-Swan	(35,000)	—	—
Purchase of certain assets of J. B. Laboratories	(4,900)	—	—
Other	(559)	(56)	(667)
Net cash for investing activities	$(60,151)	$ (7,581)	$(14,631)
Cash Flows from (for) Financing Activities			
Borrowings of long-term debt	—	—	$ 5,075
Repayments of long-term debt	$(80,811)	$(16,442)	$ (7,337)
Proceeds from issuance of common stock	122,285	—	—
Net cash from (for) financing activities	41,474	(16,442)	(2,262)
Net increase (decrease) in cash	474	8	(40)
Cash, at beginning of period	64	56	96
Cash, at end of period	$ 538	$ 64	$ 56

Note: Long-term debt matures as follows: 1993—$871,000; 1994—$773,000; 1995—$12.786 million; 1996—$30.3 million; 1997—$300,000, and 1998—$1.840 million (total long-term debt—$46.87 million).

Source: Perrigo Company, 1992 Annual Report.

said it was selling well in test. We develop it and it's ready to go, and all of a sudden Johnson and Johnson says "We're not going to go national." Maybe it wasn't good enough, or maybe it took too much money to support. What we've got is a formula that we've spent money on but is a skeleton in our closet. And that could happen. But that's a small risk. We stress the importance of working in partnership with our customers in developing new products.

Exhibit 13	Investor-Related Information for Perrigo Company

NASDAQ ticker symbol: PRGO
Shares outstanding at June 30, 1992: 36,568,471
Fiscal 1992 share price range: Low—20
                                                High—35¾
Market capitalization—at low price range: $731.36 million
                                —at high price range: $1.307 billion
Value Line Beta: 1.65
                    Timeliness: 3 (average)
                    Safety: 3 (average)
                    Financial strength: B++
Price–earnings ratio—fiscal 1990: 36.1
                            —fiscal 1991: 63.5

Sources: Perrigo Company 1992 Annual Report, Value Line Investment Survey.

In an effort to be among the first companies to offer comparable store brand products, in addition to selling its own ANDA products, Perrigo also entered into exclusive arrangements with various generic pharmaceutical manufacturers (some of whom were its direct competitors) to market their ANDA products. For example, prior to obtaining approval for its own ibuprofen tablets (the active ingredient in national brands such as Advil and Nuprin), the company marketed such tablets produced by another manufacturer and was the first company to market a store brand equivalent.

Subsidiaries

Until the early 1980s, Cumberland-Swan (CS) primarily manufactured and sold products under the Swan brand. Thereafter, it pursued a strategy of expansion into the store brand market. In 1991, approximately 30 percent of CS's sales came from the Swan brand and the remaining from store brands. The Swan brand enabled CS to sell products to smaller retail chains that did not have the volume for their own store brands. The acquisition of CS provided Perrigo access to such smaller retail chains (CS's own Good Sense brand had only limited penetration into such chains) as well as increased manufacturing capacity for store brand products. In addition, the acquisition helped Perrigo vertically integrate into producing bottles for its needs. However, the rate of sales growth of CS historically was lower than that of Perrigo. CS had its own group of managers (all of its top managers were long-term employees) whose president, Lonnie Smith, reported to Mike Jandernoa.

Perrigo Company of South Carolina produced and sold vitamins for the store brand market. This subsidiary was managed (except for the production function, which was local) by the L. Perrigo subsidiary from Allegan.

THE FUTURE

As Mike Jandernoa reviewed Perrigo's performance, he realized that the upcoming strategic planning meeting was important for the company. While the company did not publicly announce specific goals in terms of percentage of annual sales growth, he and his management team had set a broad objective for the company to be the

Exhibit 14   Major Drugs Losing Patent Protection 1993–1995

Brand Name	Manufacturer	Patent Expires	1989 Sales (in millions of $)
Naprosyn	Syntex	1993	$ 410
Xanax	Upjohn	1993	358
Tagamet	SmithKline	1994	570
Capoten	Squibb	1995	500
Zantac	Glaxo	1995	1,200

Source: Michael F. Conlan, "Future Is Sunny for Generics as Popular Rxs Come Off Patent," *Drug Topics*, October 22, 1990, pp. 14–16.

leader in the store brand industry through both internal product development and the introduction of items that switched from prescription to OTC status, as well as through strategic acquisitions.

A number of branded, prescription drugs were coming off patents in the next few years (Exhibit 14). Perrigo could decide to pursue the ANDA process for any of these prescription drugs and expand its marketing of generic prescription drugs, or it could decide to concentrate on providing retailers with private-label products for over-the-counter drugs and for the personal care segment.

The question Jandernoa wanted to pursue at some length at the strategic planning meeting was how best to position Perrigo to take advantage of the booming market for store brand products and generic drugs. Should the company concentrate on private-label personal care and vitamin products or private-label over-the-counter drugs or generic prescription drugs? Were the resources available to pursue all three areas simultaneously? Where would Perrigo have the best competitive advantage? What would Perrigo have to do to sustain its growth rate?

U.S. Windpower, Inc.

Murray Silverman, San Francisco State University

In 1990, Dale Osborn, president of U.S. Windpower, Inc. (USW), commented on the status of USW's centerpiece development project:

> We're in the Windplant™ business, and we intend to be a premier world-class supplier of wind plants to the utility and independent power industries. I believe our new 33M-VS turbine will be the key innovation that changes the wind industry from a push market that has largely depended on subsidies or environmental considerations to a pull market in which wind energy is fully economical at today's cost of energy from fossil fuels. We're striving for a 5 cent per kilowatt-hour (kwh) machine, but a 3 cent/kwh turbine is not out of reach.[1]

Founded in 1974, U.S. Windpower evolved from a small engineering, research, and development company into a large, fully integrated organization. In 1992, it was a subsidiary of the privately held Kenetech Corp., whose major shareholders included Allstate Insurance Co. and two investment firms, Pittsburgh's Hillman Co. and Chicago's F. H. Prince and Company.[2] Half a dozen major U.S. utilities were equity investors in various U.S. Windpower projects. Kenetech, a diversified energy corporation, employed approximately 500 employees, generated $237 million in revenue in 1991, and was involved in over $700 million worth of independent power projects.

USW, Kenetech's largest subsidiary, designed, manufactured, developed, constructed, operated, and maintained large-scale wind-driven power stations. USW's main operation and maintenance facility was in Livermore, California; senior management and the general office were located in San Francisco. USW was one of three integrated U.S. wind energy firms in the industry. USW was also the world's largest wind energy company, operating 4,100 wind turbines, logging over 50 million hours of operation, and generating over 2.7 billion kwh since 1982 (see Exhibit 1).[3]

While the future of USW appeared to be very attractive, its centerpiece development project, the Model 33M-VS wind turbine, was still being tested and was not yet on the market. USW's future hinged on the performance of this new product; however, foreign and domestic competitors were developing new wind turbines and contemplating business strategies that could erase USW's competitive advantage.

This case was written with the assistance of Douglas Eckman and John Nerfund, MBA students in the School of Business at San Francisco State University.

[1]A kilowatt or "kw" is the amount of energy required to light 10 100-watt lightbulbs, and a "kwh" is the amount of energy required to keep them burning for one hour. A megawatt or "MW" is 1,000 kw. Utilities could produce energy from conventional fossil fuel plants for 3 to 5 cents per kwh.

[2]Since 1992, Kenetech had become a public corporation; its stock was traded in the over-the-counter market (NASDAQ).

[3]"Wind Energy Evolution by PG&E," prepared by D. R. Smith and M. A. Ilyin, Pacific Gas & Electric (PG&E). August 1990.

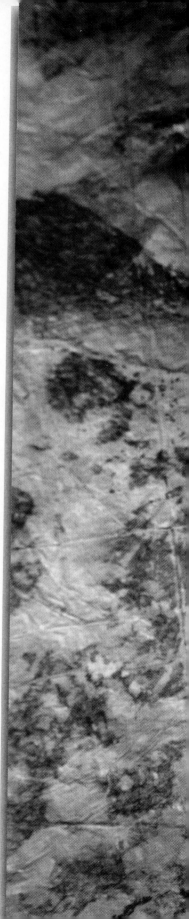

Exhibit 1   USW's Operating Experience with Wind Turbines, 1984–1990

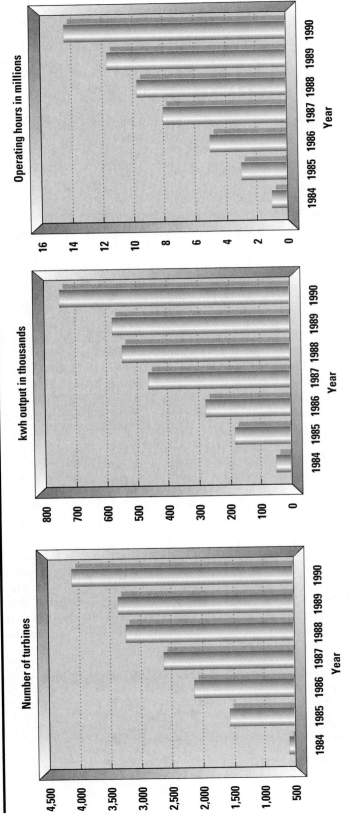

Source: U.S. Windpower internal document. By permission.

THE WIND POWER INDUSTRY

Utilization of wind energy had been a part of human history from mankind's first ventures on rivers, lakes, and seas. On land, simple vertical-axis wind power machines were used to grind grain as early as 200 B.C. in Persia. By the 14th century, the Dutch had taken the lead in improving the design of windmills and used them to drain the marshes and lakes of the Rhine River Delta. By the early 20th century, simple wind-powered machines and irrigation-pumping generators were widely used in the United States, Northern Europe, and Africa. In the early 1900s, more than 6 million less-than-1-kilowatt electricity-generation and water-pumping windmills dotted the Great Plains of the United States. These were replaced in the 1930s and 1940s when rural electric cooperatives made reliable electric service a reality in rural America. By the 1950s, electric wind generators had all but disappeared over most of the world, replaced by cheaper, more reliable central-station power plants and retail electric distribution systems.

The 1970–1985 Era

In both North America and Europe, revival of wind power generation began in the early 1970s. It was the direct result of a 300 percent increase in world oil prices in 1974 and a concomitant dramatic rise in the cost of electric energy. All types of alternative energy sources were sought to mitigate the rising prices of fuel oil, natural gas, and coal (which were the primary fuels used at power plants). In both the United States and Europe, particularly Denmark, government-sponsored research began to focus on wind energy as one alternative to conventional power plants fueled by coal, natural gas, and fuel oil. Besides direct involvement in research, nations passed legislation designed to encourage research and development in wind energy technology. In the United States, legislation took the form of investment tax credits and requirements that electric utilities purchase power supplies from alternative energy sources. Numerous independent power producers entered the market with a variety of new technologies for generating electricity. Companies promoting wind power were among the new entrants. However, the wind power companies' image suffered in the early 1980s as wind power developers raced to install thousands of small (50 to 150 kw), poorly designed and maintained wind power turbines of American and European design to take advantage of new market opportunities. Memories of the low reliability of the earliest wind energy turbines continued to act as a self-created hurdle for wind power advocates as they tried to reestablish the reliability and economics of generating electricity with wind power technology. However, those companies truly committed to fostering the growth of wind power used the new market opportunity to make major strides in advancing wind power technology.

With the Reagan administration, a markedly different philosophy regarding the role of the federal government in the energy marketplace began to emerge. When the prices of fuel oil, natural gas, and coal stopped their rapid escalation and, in the cases of fuel oil and natural gas, actually started dropping, the urgency of developing wind power technology and other alternate means of generating electricity quickly became a much lower priority. The Department of Energy's (DOE) wind energy budget in 1983 dropped from a level of about $60 million to less than $20 million.

The 1986–1992 Period

By 1986, most of the economic motivation for the development of wind power ended as oil and gas prices dropped significantly and federal government interest in alternative ways to generate electricity waned. A shake-out occurred that left only the most committed and viable wind power firms. Most of the surviving companies tended to focus their efforts on a particular segment—building wind turbines, supplying parts to turbine manufacturers, or managing wind energy "farms" and delivering wind-generated power to electric utility companies. Some companies vertically integrated into two or more of these functions. Where most early success had been with turbine sizes that generated 100 kw or less, development and deployment of larger wind-powered turbines became the goal. As manufacturers and wind plant developers moved down the experience curve, turbine and rotor equipment was upgraded to incorporate better designs, and the economics of wind power generation improved with the introduction of larger, higher-rated turbines, more sophisticated operating approaches, and better maintenance practices. Wind energy became an increasingly more economically viable option for generating electricity, particularly for power companies under pressure from state regulators to find renewable forms of electricity generation that were environmentally friendly. More than half of the wind-generating capacity in California in 1992 had been installed without federal energy tax credits because state regulators had insisted that California's electric utilities (Pacific Gas & Electric, Southern California Edison, and San Diego Gas and Electric) purchase more of their power supplies from independent power producers employing such new technologies as wind power, geothermal generation, solar generation, and plants fueled with municipal waste.

The United States still dominated the world in wind energy utilization in 1992 (accounting for 65 percent of the world's wind energy generation), but Europe was increasing its share. Since 1986, the wind electricity production had tripled in the United States but had increased by a factor of seven in Europe.[4]

WIND POWER TECHNOLOGY ————————————

Turbines

In its most elemental form, the design requirements to generate power from the wind were fairly simple. Rotors, which included the blades that were moved by the wind, turned a generator that produced electrical energy. The generator, gear box, and support systems were installed in a housing at the top of a tower (see Exhibit 2).

A wide range of turbine sizes were available from U.S. manufacturers in 1992. Very small direct current systems were available in sizes that produced a few hundred watts. These were most often used for battery charging on islands and small boats. Larger turbines (up to 20 kilowatts) were used as stand-alone, alternating current generators for agricultural uses (mostly irrigation) and remote residences. Wind turbines connected to utility power lines (for backup when the wind was not blowing) were used to produce electric power on site at residential, agricultural, commercial, and industrial facilities. These turbines had generating

---

[4]"Excellent Forecast for Wind," *EPRI Journal*, June 1990, pp. 15–25.

Exhibit 2 Sample Wind Turbine Designs and Distribution Grid

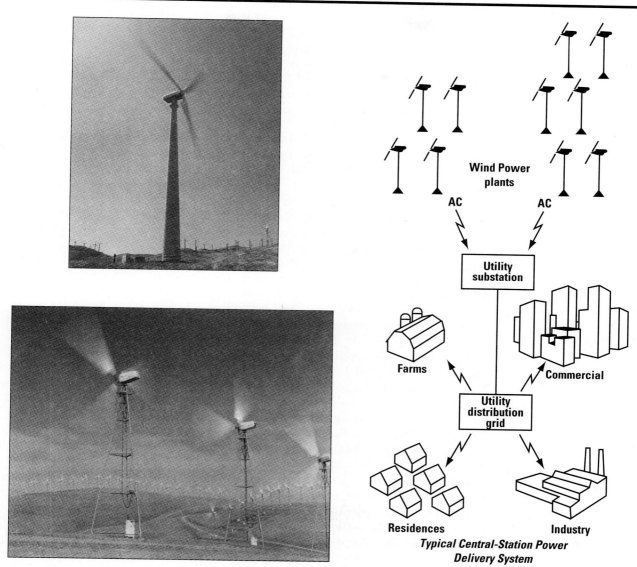

Source: U.S. Windpower materials.

capability ranging from 5 to 10 kw for residences and small farms to 100 to 200 kw (or more) for larger agricultural, commercial, and industrial loads. The electricity output of the wind turbine was fed directly into the user's distribution circuitry. When wind-generated power was available, less power was purchased from the electric utility. When more power was generated than needed, the surplus power was fed back into the utility's distribution network and purchased by the utility for resale to other customers. Hybrid wind/diesel systems in which the wind system was used as a fuel-saving device were used in thousands of islands and remote communities worldwide.

Most turbine designs, including foreign models, utilized a fixed rotor speed (the blades always turned at the same speed). This had the advantage of allowing for a constant frequency electrical output. The disadvantage was that the window of usable wind velocity (the winds speeds at which the turbine started and shut down) was limited. Also, with fixed speed rotors, the stress placed on the turbine and the tower tended to be greater in higher winds, since the blades continued to turn at a fixed rotational speed. USW had developed a variable speed turbine to control the loads and stresses that hampered fixed speed turbine operation; USW's variable speed wind turbine could also increase its power output at higher wind velocities. The disadvantages of USW's variable-speed design was that the power output frequency of the turbine was also variable. As part of the turbine development, a frequency conversion system was incorporated in the turbine to convert the variable frequency of the power to the standard electrical frequency on power company transmission lines. In 1991, USW was the only U.S. manufacturer of a variable speed turbine.

Wind turbine makers in Austria, Belgium, Britain, Denmark, Germany, Italy, Japan, and the Netherlands had already produced or were known to be developing new turbines, some with electronic controls similar to the approach used by USW in its variable speed turbine. Denmark, Germany, and the Netherlands had significant government subsidy programs for wind energy systems. Both land-based and offshore installations were being planned under these programs, with size of the subsidies tied directly to the amount of electricity generated by wind turbines. Overall government funding for wind turbine technology development in Europe was estimated to be at least 10 times that of the declining government-funded research in the United States in 1992.[5]

The initial design approach favored by U.S. wind turbine developers emphasized lightweight 50 to 100 kw turbines and incorporated such advanced technology features as variable pitched rotor blades and teetered rotors. The latter two features allowed for the maximum capture of wind energy and eventually led to turbines that outperformed foreign designs in terms of energy production per unit of area swept by the blades. For a time, though, European turbines were perceived as being better because their simple design resulted in greater reliability. Danish and Japanese firms were concentrating their developmental efforts on 250 kw turbines that were heavier and more expensive. A number of European firms claimed to have developed turbines that could produce electricity for 5 to 6 cents per kwh, but they had not yet demonstrated this capability through field tests of these turbines.

Wind power plants, or wind stations, consisted of an array of wind turbines centrally controlled that delivered electricity to a utility power grid (see Exhibit 2). There were several benefits a wind power station could offer to an independent power producer or an electric utility. A wind power station could be constructed in modular form, allowing additional generating capacity to be installed in a matter of months and in widely varying increments. For an electric utility, this could significantly decrease the financial risk of adding new capacity. Wind power plants also offered greater fuel diversity and a hedge against stringent environmental regulations being put on conventional fossil-fuel plants.

---

[5]"Proceedings: Workshop on Prospects and Requirements for Geographic Expansion of Wind Power Usage," EPRI AP-4794, Project 1996-20, November 1986, prepared by Steitz & Associates, Sun Prairie, Wisconsin.

Wind Resources

Results of a major study by Pacific Northwest Laboratories (PNL), one of the national laboratories operated for the DOE by Battelle Memorial Institute, concluded that "there was sufficient wind potential in the United States to meet not merely all of our electricity needs, but all the country's current energy needs of any kind."[6] The study provided state-by-state data after exclusions for land that was unlikely to be available for wind development, including environmentally sensitive lands, urban areas, and some forests and agricultural uses.

About 1.5 percent of the contiguous United States was characterized by Class 5 and above winds (average wind speed of 16 mph or more) with the potential to provide about 25 percent of current electric capacity. Class 3 and above winds (averaging approximately 14 mph or more) represented 14 percent of the land areas of the 48 states and had the potential to produce over 100 quads of electric energy (1 quad = 1 quadrillion Btu of energy). Total U.S. energy use in 1988 was 82 quads, with 36 percent of that devoted to the production of electricity. However, there were no unforeseen technological advances that would circumvent the laws of physics and make wind power cost-effective in low winds.

North Dakota and Wyoming had 21,000 and 20,000 average megawatts, respectively, of Class 5 potential. This was seven times North Dakota's 1990 peak requirements and four times Wyoming's. While California was the world leader in wind energy generation, with over 80 percent of the world's current installed capacity, it had only developed 20 percent of its Class 5 wind potential, even with major exclusions for competing land uses. California's installed wind capacity was about 1,500 MW in 1992, which generated 2.2 billion kwh (equivalent to more than 3.5 million barrels of oil).[7] In Pacific Gas & Electric's service territory alone, there was a potential for about 2,500 MW of wind power, of which about 800 MW was in place and operating by the end of 1990.[8] Total installed generating capacity in the United States was about 775,000 MW.

ECONOMICS OF WIND POWER

The average cost of electricity production for wind turbines had dropped from 30 cents per kwh in 1975 to about 7 cents per kwh in 1990. Operating and maintenance costs alone averaged 1.5 to 2.0 cents per kwh. The average cost to install wind turbines dropped from $3,100 per kw to $1,600 per kw in 1986. Capital costs of turbines installed in 1988 and 1989 had been estimated by industry analysts to be around $1,000 to $1,100 per kw.[9] The consensus of industry analysts was that the industry would have to reduce the cost of wind-generated energy costs to less than 5 cents per kwh by the year 2000 for wind power to be competitive with other ways to generate electricity. Department of Energy studies projected that by 2010, the costs of wind electricity at sites with moderate wind resources would fall to as little as 3.5 cents per kwh.[10]

---

[6]Press release, American Wind Energy Association, statement of Randal Swicher, executive director, American Wind Energy Association, September 25, 1990.

[7]C. J. Weinberg, "Wind Energy and the Electric Utility Industry," PG&E, 1989.

[8]"Excellent Forecast for Wind."

[9]Ibid.

[10]Carl J. Weinberg and Robert H. Williams, "Energy from the Sun," *Scientific American*, September 1990.

Wind power costs depended on a variety of interrelated factors, including the pattern and strength of wind resources at the site, the efficiency with which the turbine design recovered energy from the wind, turbine downtime for maintenance and repairs, and the turbine's capacity factor. The capacity factor was the average amount of time during the year that a turbine was generating electricity. The greater the fraction of time a turbine was generating, the more energy it produced and the lower the cost of each kilowatt-hour generated (since fixed capital costs were spread over more kwh of production). Theoretically, the capacity factor would be higher for a variable speed rotor, since the turbine would cut in at lower wind speeds and not cut out at higher wind velocities. In 1985, the California statewide capacity factor for wind turbines was 13 percent. In 1989, it was 18 percent. In 1990, it was 20 percent. However, these figures included all existing operational models. Capacity factors for newer models typically ranged between 20 and 35 percent. In 1990, one small wind power station managed 33 percent. This may have been near the maximum possible with the California wind resource. Overall wind energy output varied with the season. In California, 72 percent of the wind power generated was produced from April through September.

Poor siting or inadequate assessment of the wind resource resulted in a lower capacity factor. A 10 percent increase in wind speed equaled a 30 percent increase in generated power (because wind energy capture had a cubed relationship with wind speed). Conducting extensive wind speed measurements at specified locations and heights was thus extremely important. Accurate wind forecasting typically required at least one full year of wind measurements at different locations and different heights. This was especially important given the large effect of tower height and tower position on the wind energy available for electricity generation. A deviation of 10 feet in height or direction could result in potential wind energy differences of 5 to 10 percent. Wake effects, caused by too little spacing between wind turbines, could reduce capacity factors by over 50 percent due to reduced wind velocity below that required for turbine cut-in. Adverse wake effects had been a problem in the San Gorgonio Pass area east of Los Angeles where turbines were typically arranged in fairly close rows along flat terrain. At Altamont Pass, where siting was more along ridge lines and rolling hills, wake effects were less of a problem. Another siting consideration had to do with whether potential wind power sites were near existing transmission lines. Extending transmission lines to wind power sites was costly—approximately $500,000 to $1 million per mile depending on right-of-way costs, environmental regulations, and the terrain.

A turbine that was rarely out of service had a high availability factor, meaning that the turbine was able to generate electricity whenever adequate wind was blowing. Some turbines required substantial maintenance and some broke down frequently during operation. As of 1990, wind turbine availability factors ranged from 44 to 98 percent, with many plants routinely achieving better than 90 percent as a result of effective maintenance programs.

From a utility perspective, wind power economics also depended on whether wind availability coincided with consumers' usage of electricity. For example, the wind resource in California's Solano county had a good "fit" with Pacific Gas & Electric's load profile since the wind blew stronger and more consistently in the summer months when residential air conditioning resulted in greater demand for electricity.

Renewable Energy Technologies

Power plants fueled by coal, fuel oil, and natural gas (the so-called fossil fuels) were the major source of electricity. Over 70 percent of the electricity generating capacity in the United States utilized fossil fuels in 1990, another 15 percent came from nuclear power plants, and the balance was from renewable energy technologies such as hydroelectric dams, wind, photovoltaics, geothermal, biomass (municipal waste, wood chips, and other combustibles), and high-temperature solar thermal. The following table presents the major renewable-type fuels and the relative costs of generating electricity with plants using these fuels as of 1992:

Type of alternative energy source	Potential MW of Capacity that Renewable Fuel Could Support	Number of MW in Actual Operation In United States	1992 Cost per kwh
Hydro	146,000	72,000	4–7 cents
Geothermal	*	3,000	5–8 cents
Biomass	*	8,000	6–8 cents
Wind	*	1,400	5–9 cents
Solar thermal	*	300	8–12 cents
Photovoltaics	*	50	20–30 cents

* More than present U.S. total electric use.[11]

The costs of generating electricity at coal-fired and gas-fired power plants typically ranged between 2.5 cents and 5 cents per kwh.

Renewable fuel sources were important in the electricity-generation mix because their environmental impacts were relatively small, they reduced vulnerability to increases in fossil fuel costs and scarcities by diversifying the fuel mix for U.S. power plants, and in some cases they were the lowest cost option for electric utilities needing to add small amounts of generating capacity. (The minimum efficient scale for utility-scale fossil fuel plants was around 400 MW, although efficient scale power plants used only to cover peak demand periods could be as small as 80 MW.)

Burning fossil fuels to generate electricity contributed to air pollution, acid rain, and had been linked to global warming. A single 100 kw wind turbine, if substituted for coal-fired electricity generation, would eliminate the emission of nearly 18 tons of carbon dioxide per month. Environmentalists argued that energy prices should reflect the external social costs of energy production and use, including the dangers from air pollution, nuclear risks, and the economic, ecological, and human health costs of global climate change. In a 1988 study for the Commission of the European Communities, West German economist Olay Hohmeyer calculated that the societal cost of burning fossil fuels to generate electricity ranged between 3 cents and 7 cents per kwh. This cost included depletion of nonrenewable resources, damage to the environment, health-related services expenses brought on by pollution, and a variety of other costs.[12]

---

[11]Carl Weinberg, "Prospects for Renewable Energy, an Option for a National Energy Investment Portfolio," PG&E for the National Academy of Sciences, November 8, 1990.

[12]"Windpower Energy for a Growing World," produced under the Solar Technical Information Program at the Solar Energy Research Institute for the U.S. Department of Energy and published by the American Wind Energy Asssociation. (No date.)

Assuming Hohmeyer's calculations were accurate, and assuming electric utilities were required to include these external social costs in their decision making, wind energy would have been significantly more cost-effective than fossil fuels in many locations. While society and future generations were presently absorbing these social costs, a number of state regulatory commissions were introducing policies and requirements that would subsidize renewable types of electricity-generating plants because of their environmental advantages and the associated avoidance of social costs.

Renewables also had some negative environmental impacts. In the cases of wind power, visual impacts, noise, and birds colliding with the blades had all been cited as problems. Local opposition to the visual impact of wind power, particularly in the northern and western parts of the U.S., had limited the development of wind power farms.

LEGAL AND REGULATORY FACTORS

In 1978, the Public Utilities Regulatory Policies Act (PURPA) was passed to begin introducing more competition into the generating portion of the electric utility business. PURPA made it feasible for independent power producers (IPPs) to generate electricity and sell it directly to a customer while obligating the local electric utility to provide backup power to the customer when needed and to buy excess electricity generated at the IPP's site. PURPA also opened the door for IPPs to compete for contracts to supply power companies with needed increases in generating capacity. There probably would not have been a U.S. wind energy industry without PURPA.

Another phenomenon, supportive of the wind power industry, was the growing number of states with policies that recognized the benefits of generating plants using renewable energy sources as fuels. Some states were taking into account the estimated societal costs associated with fossil fuels. This was expected to boost growth of the wind power industry: Through the PURPA-instigated competitive bidding process for additional capacity, plants using renewable fuel sources were sometimes granted a social cost credit in the bid evaluation, or else fossil fuel plants were assessed a cost penalty based on pollutant emissions. Also, public service commissions in a few states were guaranteeing renewable fuels a specific portion of new capacity additions within their jurisdictions.

Growing regional environmental concerns, like air quality and acid rain, and global concerns, like climate change, were leading to tightening environmental standards. The National Environmental Policy Act (NEPA) and the Clean Air Act (CAA) forced the utility industry to invest billions of dollars in environmental control equipment and lengthened the time and cost to construct new power plants that used coal or natural gas. Wind stations had relatively short construction times and were competitive from a cost perspective when the external social detriments of fossil plants were factored into their costs.

The Energy Policy Act of 1992 contained tax breaks for the plants using renewable fuels, including a new 1.5 cent per kwh tax credit for electricity produced by wind power. The credit was limited to 10 years and was reduced if any part of the facility was financed or subsidized with tax-exempt financing or government grants. The tax credit was based on the avoided environmental costs of nonrenewable energy sources.

THE MARKETS FOR WIND POWER ———————————

While there was a market for small stand-alone wind turbines that generated electricity or provided pumping capabilities for private residences or isolated settings, the big market opportunity was in developing big wind power stations to mass produce electricity for distribution by traditional electric utilities.

Wind Power Markets in the United States

The U.S. electric utility industry, with its broad-based generation expertise and efficient system for dispatching power from a fleet of power plants, could readily integrate wind power into its generation and transmission system. Domestically, electric utilities were the only buyer that could utilize the electricity output from an efficient scale wind farm. However, most electric utilities were extremely cautious about making commitments to wind power chiefly because wind power was undependable—power company customers expected electricity to be available on demand, not just when the wind was blowing. Hence, power companies insisted that they needed power plants that were reliable and could produce power at whatever times customers wanted electricity.

Most U.S. electric utilities regarded wind energy skeptically because they "are used to generating plants that you can turn on and off" when desired, says Carl Weinberg, manager of R&D at Pacific Gas & Electric, which helped pioneer wind power in California.[13] PG&E and a number of other utilities in California and Hawaii were early adopters of wind energy. At PG&E, experience had shown that the wind energy profiles of Altamont Pass and Suisun Bay fit well with customers' power usage. PG&E's peak period for electricity was in the summer (heavy use of air conditioning) and this was when the wind along the coast of Northern California blew stronger. At times during late summer evenings, wind energy supplied about 7 percent of PG&E's system load.

Another obstacle to wind power from the perspective of electric utilities was transmission access. There were significant obstacles and costs associated with any effort to site and build new transmission lines almost anywhere in the United States; extending transmission lines to wind power sites was costly and not always cost-justified. This impacted decisions by the wind power industry on whether to pursue development of wind power stations at sites where transmission line extension was either not feasible or economical. Moreover, the states with large wind resources did not always have much need for additional electrical capacity, although it was sometimes feasible to wheel the extra power on transmission lines to customers in other states.

While wind was an undependable generating resource, wind power still offered utilities some important benefits. One was a more diverse mix of both generating sources and fuel sources (most utilities believed it was risky to be overly dependent on any one type of fuel source). Diversity reduced the exposure to fossil fuel scarcity or unexpected price increases. A second benefit was that the minimum efficient scale for a wind power farm was 20 to 25 MW, compared to 400 MW for a fossil fuel plant or 80 MW for a peaking plant. In addition, wind power plants could be constructed

---

[13]"Wind Farms May Energize the Midwest," David Stipp, *The Wall Street Journal*, September 6, 1991.

within a much shorter time frame than traditional power plants. Long construction times for traditional large-scale power plants created financial strains for some utilities. This, coupled with greater difficulty in forecasting future power needs and a trend toward smaller power station construction, was working in favor of the wind energy industry. Finally, the increasing cost competitiveness of wind power was making wind a more compelling option for utilities.

Some utilities, often prodded by environmentally conscious regulators, had indicated an intent to utilize wind power as a generating source and a willingness to invest in wind R&D and joint ventures. Several electric utilities were part of a consortium headed by USW to develop a new generation of wind turbines. Also, Iowa-Illinois Gas & Electric planned a joint venture with USW to develop wind plants in the midwestern United States.

European Markets

The governments of Holland, Germany, and England had made a strong commitment to wind power. Some 200 MW of wind turbine capacity had been installed in Denmark; some 20 to 30 MW of wind turbines were operating in Germany and Britain. The Netherlands' national energy policy required that at least 250 MW of wind turbine–generating capacity be installed by 1995. Industry experts estimated that 2,000 to 4,000 MW of wind turbine capacity would be installed in Europe in the 1990s.[14] While this presented a large market opportunity, in years past it had been difficult for U.S. wind turbine manufacturers to win market share at the expense of European turbine makers.

Denmark   Denmark had many small farmers and small landowners. Denmark's wind industry grew out of farm use of wind power, and it was common in Denmark to see windmills throughout the countryside. As a net energy importer, the government chose wind power as a means to avoid use of high-cost fossil fuel generation, since fossil fuels had to be imported at comparatively high cost. Because Denmark had over 5,000 miles of coastline and open agricultural land, it was a natural for the wind power market. The Danish firms that entered the wind power market had concentrated primarily on the rural home market and the farm market. Consequently, most installations were comprised of only one wind turbine. Commercial wind plants represented only one-fifth of the Danish market.

Germany   Germany was the world's fastest growing market for wind generation. In the early 1990s, total installed capacity exceeded 50 MW, and Germany was planning to install an average of 50 MW each year during the mid-1990s. With such additions, the German market would rival the Danish domestic market as the largest outside of California. The German wind program had been aided by regulations passed by the Bundeskabinet requiring utilities to purchase wind-generated electricity at 90 percent of the utilities average retail price (estimated at 10.4 cents). This price, in addition to payments given under the Germany ministry for technological development (estimated at 3.75 cents per kwh), was very attractive to wind power developers.

---

[14]"Excellent Forecast for Wind."

United Kingdom   In 1989, the United Kingdom opened its national transmission system to small generators of power. Large energy producers were then forced to subsidize alternative energy through the Non-Fossil Fuel Obligation. The United Kingdom's Department of Energy ordered 131 MW of wind power projects to be built by the end of 1993. The only British manufacturer of commercial machines was the Wind Energy Group (WEG).

SeaWest, a U.S.-based wind turbine operator, had recently entered into a joint venture with Ecogen, a Cornish developer, and Tomen, a Japanese trading company, to provide 75 MW of wind power near Wales and Cornwall. SeaWest planned to install Mitsubishi turbines for this project. Charles Davenport, SeaWest's chairman and CEO, commented:

> There is no American machine made today that I would consider buying. If all else were equal, I'd buy American, but they're not all equal. I hope someday USW or somebody will produce a machine that competes with Mitsubishi's, but it will take matching credit support and service, not just a good turbine.[15]

INDUSTRY PARTICIPANTS

There were three basic ways to participate in the industry: as a wind turbine manufacturer, a wind station operator, or a component manufacturer. The first two formed the core of the wind power industry.

Turbine Manufacturers

In the early years of the industry, turbine manufacturers sold their products to developers, who in turn installed them and financed them through individuals and limited partnerships. Investors were able to claim sizable tax credits for investments in a wind power facility. Most of the early companies were underfinanced and poorly managed and did not have wind turbines that were capable of standing up over long-term, heavy-duty use or that were adaptable to a variety of wind conditions and siting requirements.

Several U.S. corporations that had pursued development of large-scale wind turbines had exited the market. In 1983, General Electric, citing forecasts of reduced utility load growth, uncertain extension of federal wind energy tax credits, and unsuccessful efforts to interest utilities and small power producers in purchasing their turbines, concluded there was no present or near-term market for large wind turbines and withdrew from the industry. So did Boeing. GE, however, was very much a major player in manufacturing gas turbines and steam turbines for fossil fuel and nuclear plants; it, along with Westinghouse, Siemens (Germany), Asea Brown Boveri (Sweden), and Japan's Hitachi and Toshiba, were the world leaders in power-generation equipment.

During the 1980s, several turbine manufacturers decided to pursue forward vertical integration. U.S. Windpower, for example, launched a strategy that involved designing and manufacturing turbines, developing sites, installing turbines, operating and maintaining them, and selling electricity to electric utilities; its biggest utility

---

[15]"Excellent Forecast for Wind."

customer was Pacific Gas & Electric. Fayette Manufacturing Corporation (acquired by The New World Power Corporation in 1987) and FloWind Corporation also attempted to develop a fully integrated strategy. Both FloWind and The New World Power Corporation had active R&D programs, but neither had commercialized a new generation turbine since the late 1980s. In the early 1990s, USW was the sole U.S. producer of large-scale turbines capable of supplying sizable amounts of power to electric utilities.

Turbines made by foreign manufacturers had captured a large portion of the U.S. market, which as of 1990 represented 80 percent of the world market. The use of foreign-made turbines had been partially responsible for the decrease in the number of U.S. manufacturers. According to a 1990 report, about 52 percent of the total wind turbines installed in the world were Danish-built turbines, 41 percent were U.S.-built turbines, and the remaining 7 percent were supplied by companies in Belgium, the United Kingdom, Japan, and China.[16]

The 10 largest turbine manufacturers had supplied more than 86 percent of California's wind-generating capacity (see Exhibit 3). In California, U.S. manufacturers had supplied most of the wind turbines on Altamont Pass, whereas Danish turbines had primarily been used on the Pacheco, San Gorgonio, and Tehachapi passes. Mitsubishi Heavy Industries (MHI) had sold 660 of its 250 kw turbines to SeaWest, a San Diego–based company that operated wind plants in the Altamont, San Gorgonio, and Tehachapi passes.

Wind Station Operators

Some companies, such as SeaWest, had succeeded and prospered in the wind power industry solely as developers and operators of wind power stations. Wind power operators secured power contracts, obtained financing (often through an investment banker), acquired sites, and operated wind stations. Their choice of turbine was based on cost, performance, reliability, and warranty terms. The five largest wind project operators accounted for more than 76 percent of the total California wind-generating capacity (see Exhibit 4).

SeaWest was a San Diego, California–based company that focused on developing and operating alternative energy power plants. It did not manufacture wind turbines. SeaWest purchased wind turbines from foreign manufacturers in Japan and Europe. The company managed 2,543 turbines in California and 127 turbines in the United Kingdom. SeaWest was targeting markets in Europe and South America, especially Brazil. SeaWest had installed 24 Danish Bonus 300 kw turbines in Anglesey, Wales. In addition, SeaWest had begun installation of 103 Mitsubishi 300 kw turbines near Newton in Powys, Wales. According to Deborah Reyes of SeaWest, the company's strengths included being able to "use a variety of existing manufacturers' equipment to best accommodate our technical needs." SeaWest was a turnkey operator; it found investors, arranged financing, oversaw construction and setup, and managed the project. SeaWest's primary customers were electric utilities. The company was privately held and did not disclose any financial information. The company had 400 full-time employees in 1992.

Wind station operators installed performance monitoring systems so they could continuously track and monitor turbine output. Output data was valuable to operators

---

[16]"Wind Energy Evaluation by PG&E."

Exhibit 3 Ten Largest Wind Turbine Manufacturers in California, 1990

Turbine Manufacturers	Country	Cumulative Capacity (kw)	Total Number of Turbines Installed	Turbines Added in 1990
U.S. Windpower	United States	414,400	4,144	590
Vestas	Denmark	185,450	2,169	116
Fayette*	United States	135,465	1,351	0
Micon	Denmark	110,483	1,281	2
FloWind	United States	94,800	512	0
MWT (Mitsubishi)	Japan	90,000	360	240
Bonus	Denmark	81,555	838	1
Nordtank	Denmark	71,940	840	0
HMZ	Belgium	37,300	174	0
Danwin*	Denmark	36,030	233	0

* No longer manufacturing as of 1992.
Source: California Energy Commission, 1990 Annual Report, Wind Project Performance Reporting System.

Exhibit 4 Five Largest Wind Station Operators, 1990

Wind Station Operator	Cumulative Capacity (kw)	Capacity Added in 1990, (kw)	Cumulative Turbines
U.S. Windpower	419,700	59,000	4,165
SeaWest	227,112	60,000	1,901
Zond	185,550	22,050	2,204
Fayette	140,949	0	1,399
FloWind	140,040	600	863

Source: California Energy Commission, 1990 Annual Report, Wind Project Performance Report System.

in developing standards for specific sites, as it became important when operators upgraded or changed turbines on the same site. By monitoring performance, operators could decide when it made sense to trade off better performance for lower maintenance costs and longer turbine life. Turbine performance tended to vary somewhat by site location and season of the year.

DOMESTIC MANUFACTURERS

USW's chief U.S. competitors, The New World Power Corporation and FloWind Corporation, were regarded as well behind USW in developing the next generation of wind turbines. While both were experimenting with new designs, their approaches reflected attempts to incrementally improve older technologies.

The New World Power Corporation (NWP)

The New World Power Corporation (NWP), based in Connecticut and the successor to the bankrupt Fayette Company, was engaged in the production and sale of electric power from plants using renewable fuel sources. The company also provided power-generating services to owners of such plants.

NWP—through Arcadian, a subsidiary company—owned 1,500 potential wind turbine sites and had 1,187 installed wind turbines, of which only 525 were currently operational. Most of NSW's installed turbine fleet consisted of early generation models that were serviceable but relatively inefficient.

NWP's fiscal year 1992 revenues were $3.7 million. NWP was headed by essentially the same group of executives that took Catalyst Energy public in 1984. Catalyst Energy was one of the first of the public independent power companies; between 1984 and 1988, Catalyst's revenues had soared from less than $10 million to $400 million as new power plants came on line and began producing power for electric utility customers. New World Power employed 78 full-time employees.

FloWind Corporation

FloWind Corporation was a fully integrated wind power company making turbines and developing and operating wind power stations. FloWind had been in bankruptcy but emerged with a clean balance sheet after its insurance companies paid off FloWind's guarantees to customers (insurance companies had insured FloWind's first-generation turbines that did not work; when FloWind defaulted on its warranties, the insurance companies had to stand behind FloWind's warranties). In 1992, FloWind owned and operated 512 wind turbines in the Altamont Pass and the Tehachapi Pass in California. The firm was not manufacturing wind turbines in 1992 but was in the final stages of developing a new 250 kw machine. This new product, the AWT-26, was being developed in conjunction with Pacific Northwest Laboratories. After testing the AWT-26, FloWind planned to repower its existing wind turbines and develop wind stations for electric utilities. According to Al Davies, vice president of wind farm development for FloWind, the company's strengths were the existing large number of wind turbines it had in operation and low debt; management believed the company's chief weakness was its relatively small size in a very capital intensive business. The company would not disclose any financial information to the case researchers other than to say it was profitable.

KENETECH CORPORATION

Kenetech Corporation's motto was "energy that makes a difference." Kenetech, through its subsidiaries, produced energy for sale to utilities and designed, developed, constructed, operated, and maintained power-generation facilities. The company believed its primary customers, electric utilities, would soon be undergoing a fundamental restructuring that would ultimately reduce their dominance over electricity generation. Kenetech, as well as other utility experts, foresaw well-managed, independent power producers as having a major role in generating electric power in the coming years and believed that wind power sources would carve out a niche in the emerging market to supply power to electric utilities and their customers.

Kenetech had five subsidiaries. U.S. Windpower was one subsidiary, and the other four, organized into a Power Systems Group, included CNF Industries, Kenetech Energy Management, Kenetech Energy Systems, and Kenetech Facilities Management. The Power Systems Group developed, financed, constructed, operated, and managed independent electric power projects that produced electricity from wood-fired and gas-fired generating facilities for sale to electric utilities and other users.

Consolidated financial statements for Kenetech (U.S. Windpower's financials were not reported separately) are shown in Exhibits 5 and 6. The senior notes payable were due in 1997. In Exhibit 5, wind plant sales and energy sales resulted mostly from the operations of U.S. Windpower; the remaining revenues were attributable to the Power Systems Group.

Kenetech viewed the wind power business as its most important growth opportunity. However, it continued to pursue development of other types of electricity-generating projects. As of September 30, 1992, the Power Systems Group had two projects under active development and six projects under construction, ranging in size from 4 to 80 MW. In addition to being an important source of revenue for Kenetech, the Power Systems Group's skills and experience also complemented the wind power business. Kenetech was one of the largest U.S. electrical and mechanical contractors that catered to independent power projects.

CNF Industries

CNF Industries, Inc., was founded in 1910 as C. N. Flagg & Company. CNF functioned as the construction contractor for Kenetech's own independent power projects and also provided construction services to wind power developers and other independent power producers. The company employed 145 full-time employees and 249 contract/job site employees. For the year ending December 31, 1991, CNF had revenues of $96 million, down from $112 million in 1990.

Kenetech Energy Management

In January 1991, Kenetech acquired Econoler/USA and renamed it Kenetech Energy Management (KEM). KEM specialized in energy conservation—it designed, engineered, developed, procured, installed, and implemented systems that produced energy savings and better energy management in commercial and industrial buildings. KEM employed 39 full-time employees. In 1991, it had revenues of $11 million versus $8 million in 1990.

Kenetech Energy Systems

Kenetech Energy Systems initiated, developed, and managed independent electric power projects. On a recent project that KES developed, management was able to successfully obtain the necessary permits despite community opposition. KES turned around the community opposition through a novel environmental offset program that included the retirement of early model automobiles by KES and the purchase of street sweepers for the neighboring communities. In addition, KES arranged for all of the financing for KEM and USW projects. KES employed 64 full-time employees. This division's 1991 revenues were not broken out in the company's financial statements, but revenues in 1990 totaled $9 million.

Exhibit 5   Kenetech Corporation Consolidated Income Statements
(in thousands, except per share amounts)

	For Years Ended December 31		
	1991	**1990**	**1989**
Revenues:			
Construction services	$ 95,529	$111,705	$ 60,615
Windplant sales	44,274	75,396	37,455
Maintenance, management fees, and other	39,922	18,672	17,344
Energy sales	35,049	37,670	31,794
Energy management services	10,716	—	—
Interest on partnership notes and funds in escrow	12,294	14,484	15,291
Total revenue	237,784	257,927	162,499
Costs of revenues:			
Construction services	82,372	96,370	50,859
Windplant sales	28,006	51,488	24,646
Energy plant operations	53,370	47,653	44,355
Energy management services	7,570	—	—
Total costs of revenues	171,318	195,511	119,860
Gross margin	66,466	62,416	42,639
Engineering expenses	7,728	4,875	3,071
Marketing expenses	4,057	2,624	419
General and administrative expenses	25,009	25,433	15,254
Income from operations	29,672	29,484	23,895
Interest income	2,334	3,251	1,004
Interest expense	(19,374)	(21,626)	(21,609)
Income before taxes and extraordinary items	12,632	11,109	3,290
Income tax provision	3,081	3,074	883
Income before extraordinary items	9,551	8,035	2,407
Extraordinary items:			
Gain on extinguishment of debt (net of income taxes of $1,334 in 1990 and $164 in 1989)	—	7,500	796
Utilization of tax loss carryforwards	—	—	386
Net income	$ 9,551	$ 15,535	$ 3,589
Earnings per share:			
Income before extraordinary items	$ 6.74	$ 5.37	$ 1.62
Extraordinary items	—	5.01	0.79
Net income	$ 6.74	$ 10.38	$ 2.41
Weighted average number of shares used in computing per share amounts	1,417	1,497	1,490

Source: Kenetech Corporation, SEC Form S-1, October 1992.

Exhibit 6   Kenetech Corporation Consolidated Balance Sheets, December 31 (in thousands, except share amounts)

	1991	1990
Assets		
Current assets:		
Cash and cash equivalents	$ 18,917	$ 14,402
Marketable securities	2,603	4,948
Funds in escrow, net	11,653	14,447
Accounts receivable	34,565	31,624
Partnership notes and interest receivable, net	1,269	7,004
Inventories	9,631	14,866
Other	2,910	3,146
Total current assets	81,548	90,437
Accounts receivable and funds in escrow, net	17,844	10,430
Partnership notes and interest receivable, net	36,158	38,436
Property, plant, and equipment, net	93,654	77,401
Independent power plants under construction	52,722	2,272
Investments in affiliates	5,839	13,086
Other assets	5,228	5,751
Total assets	$292,993	$237,813
Liabilities and Stockholders' Equity		
Current liabilities:		
Accounts payable	$ 15,795	$ 16,400
Accrued liabilities	32,874	36,691
Bank loan payable	14,500	—
Estimated warranty costs	6,464	2,107
Current portion of other notes payable	6,790	7,266
Total current liabilities	76,423	62,464
Independent power plant construction financing	49,707	—
Senior notes payable	68,469	68,730
Other notes payable	58,497	75,125
Other long-term obligations	3,770	5,141
Total liabilities	256,866	211,460
Stockholders' equity:		
Common stock, $.01 par value:		
Series A—2,750,000 shares authorized; issued and outstanding 1991—1,354,017; 1990—1,323,041	14	13
Series B—2,750,000 shares authorized; none outstanding	—	—
Additional paid-in capital	21,655	21,103
Unearned compensation	(2,999)	(3,247)
Retained earnings	17,457	8,484
Total stockholders' equity	36,127	326,353
Total liabilities and stockholders' equity	$292,993	$237,813

Source: Kenetech Corporation, SEC Form S-1, October 1992.

Kenetech Facilities Management

Kenetech Facilities Management began operations in 1988 to provide professional management and operating and maintenance services for electric power facilities. KFM targeted small power projects that were operated by the entrepreneurs who developed the projects. The company employed 82 full-time employees. KFM's revenues for 1991 were not reported separately; the division's revenues in 1990 were $4 million.

U.S. Windpower

U.S. Windpower was formed in 1976 by Stanley Charren and Russell Wolfe to study the available windmill technology, assess its potential for the production of large amounts of electricity, and adapt the technology to mass production. In December 1980, USW sold and installed its first prototype wind plant consisting of 20 windmills. By 1983, USW had installed 800 more of Model 56-60 windmills, and by 1992 had installed 4,071 Model 56-100 windmills, making it the leading builder and operator in the industry. USW, with 4,000 turbines, produced 770 million kwh in 1990 (approximately 25 percent of all the wind energy generated in California); its turbines had a 96 percent average availability factor.

U.S. Windpower was a fully vertically integrated organization; it designed, developed, constructed, financed, operated, and maintained commercial wind plants. The company employed 341 people at the Livermore, California, facility, where it maintained 110,000 square feet of office and industrial space. Assembly of the turbines took place at the Livermore plant. USW typically contracted out the manufacture of some components used in its turbines.

USW management believed that USW's main competitors in wind turbine manufacture were FloWind, three Danish firms (Vesta, Micon, and Bonus), and Mitsubishi Heavy Industries, a Japanese maker of power-generation equipment. But, according to one USW executive:

> Mitsubishi is scratching its collective head today over an engineering problem we solved in 1984. With over 38 million turbine operation hours, USW has the most experience in properly operating and maintaining wind turbines. We're several years further up the learning curve and have a substantial competitive advantage as a U.S. marketer.[17]
>
> Our strategy is to develop a technology that is one of the lowest, if not the lowest costs of generating electric power. And we're going to compete and be successful in the marketplace whatever the definition of the marketplace is, at whatever time. If oil prices happen to go to $18 or $30 or $35 or whatever, good for us.[18]

USW's main strategic objective was to establish itself as a reliable and cost-competitive source of electricity generation that merited consideration when a commercial power producer was contemplating adding generating capacity. USW believed that its existing installations in California demonstrated that the wind plants could be commercially viable. A consortium comprised of USW, the Electric Power Research Institute, Niagara Mohawk Power Corporation, and PG&E had provided

---

[17]"Excellent Forecast for Wind."
[18] As quoted in "Nation Must Wake Up to Wind's Potential," *USA Today*, September 27, 1990.

technical and financial support for the design and development of the company's new variable speed Model 33M-VS wind turbine in return for a percentage of the revenues from future sales. USW had headed the five-year $20 million program. Management believed the economics of USW's Model 33M-VS wind turbine were cost-competitive with other types of new electricity-generating capacity. Negotiations were in varying stages with several utilities for wind power stations using the Model 33M-VS wind turbine.

Products   USW's workhorse through 1992 was the Model 56-100, a 100 kw third-generation wind turbine with 28-foot blades. The Model 56-100 was marketed from 1983 to 1991. USW claimed that with normal replacement of moving parts, these turbines would last 25 to 30 years. The Model 56-100 had an installed base of approximately 4,200 wind turbines. USW owned outright approximately 300 of the 4,200 installed turbines. The remaining 3,900 turbines were operated by USW for third-party owners. During 1992, USW stopped selling the Model 56-100 turbine, as buyers preferred to await production of the new 33M-VS turbine.

Because USW had decided to halt sales of its Model 56-100 prior to beginning production of the 33M-VS, management was planning a $100 million bond offering to bridge the revenue gap in sales, to pay off and reamortize existing debt, and to introduce the 33M-VS turbine. Of the $100 million, $27 million was earmarked for the development, production, and marketing of the 33M-VS turbine. Kenetech's investment bankers did not anticipate any problem in selling the bond issue to investors.

Scheduled to go into commercial production in early 1993, the new 33M-VS turbine was a variable speed turbine, with advanced electronic control, that allowed for increased energy capture, reduced dynamic fatigue stress, and increased siting opportunities. The power rating was 300 to 400 kw (depending on the wind resource) with a constant frequency output. The 33M-VS was expected to have a capacity factor of 23 to 35 percent. Capital costs were estimated at $735 per installed kw, with power being produced for a cost of 5 cents per kwh. The variable speed wind turbine technology and the power electronics system in the 33M-VS were protected by patents granted by the U.S. Patent Office. Patent applications were pending in Canada, Europe, and Japan.

The design cornerstone of the 33M-VS was USW's variable-speed rotor, which spun faster as the wind picked up. This enabled it to operate at higher wind speeds without experiencing the damaging stress encountered by the constant speed rotors found on most older and foreign machines. It also allowed the turbine to operate over a wider range of wind speeds than constant speed rotors. The new turbine would be able to generate power in winds as low as 8 to 9 mph and as high as 60 mph. The Model 56-100 required minimum 11 or 12 mph wind velocities to make electricity, and it shut down when winds exceeded 44 mph.

USW tested 22 preproduction units of the Model 33M-VS in California's Altamont Pass during the 1992 wind season; over 49,000 hours of operating time were logged. These machines were located on sites previously occupied by Model 56-100 wind turbines, which afforded USW a basis for performance comparisons. Based on the test results, the company made one critical change and several minor modifications to the preproduction model. All modifications made to the 33M-VS had since passed all subsequent field testing. On the other hand, while the 33M-VS represented a much-advanced technological design, some industry observers were concerned that it was too complex a machine and might break down frequently or have a shorter life than anticipated by USW.

USW intended to provide warranties with its new machines guaranteeing workmanship and design. Warranties for the Model 56-100 had included guarantees that the machines would generate specified minimum amounts of electric energy during the first three years after delivery; USW had set aside reserves on its balance sheet to provide financial backup for these warranties. These reserves had been adequate to cover all warranties on the Model 56-100. USW planned to follow a similar procedure for warranties on the new 33M-VS turbine.

Windplants[TM]   USW Windplants[TM] were multiple turbines centrally controlled and operated as a single power plant. (USW had trademarked the word *Windplant.*) They were modular in nature with short lead-time construction. They provided planning flexibility, met high power quality requirements, were nonpolluting, and were compatible with agriculture and ranching. They were configurable to withstand abrasive, corrosive, and icing-prone environments. Crews installed and maintained turbines at carefully chosen sites (USW had its own team of meteorologists). USW, through Kenetech, had acquired a service business to repair and maintain its wind turbines as well as turbines owned or operated by others.

Since April 1990, USW Windplants had employed a state-of-the-art control room that allowed controllers to monitor the performance of every one of the company's turbines at all times. If problems were encountered, operators would call up a history of the machine's performance or shut the turbine down so a field crew of "windsmiths" could make an on-site inspection. "It's a very sophisticated control system, better than anything anyone else in the industry has done," said Mary A. Ilyin of PG&E.[19]

Target Markets   Target markets in the United States were the Pacific Northwest, California, Iowa, and the East Coast. USW was also actively pursuing opportunities in Spain, Germany, the United Kingdom, and Holland.

USW's marketing strategy consisted of building relationships with key utility executives, utilizing the media to communicate USW's capabilities and products to communities and the public at large. and actively pursuing contract opportunities for new generation capacity for electric utilities. USW was diligent in presenting wind turbines as a viable, cost-effective option for generating electricity. USW management downplayed any attempt to characterize wind turbines as desirable simply because of the environmental advantages.

Opportunities for new wind power contracts often were in the form of regulatory decisions to award some generating capacity to wind or other renewables. However, with its new turbine technology, USW was hoping to compete effectively with fossil fuel technologies. In the early 1990s, USW dominated competitive bids for new wind power contracts in the United States; management believed USW's experience and technological lead gave it a significant advantage in the U.S. market over other wind turbine manufacturers and operators.

USW currently had various projects targeted for the 33M-VS (see Exhibit 7). Additional uses for the Model 33M-VS included retrofitting turbines already in operation.

---

[19]Frederic Golden, "Electric Wind, the Whirling Turbines Are Back in Power Picture," *Los Angeles Times*, December 24, 1990.

Exhibit 7   Model 33M-VS Project Development Opportunities*

Location	Utility	Projects under Development MW	Projects under Development Status	Announced Additional Opportunities (MW)
California	Sacramento Municipal Utility District	50	Agreement in principle signed February 1992	50
Netherlands	E.G.D.	25	Executed contract	25
Alberta, Canada	TransAlta Utilities Corp.	9	Executed contract	NQ
Washington	Puget Sound Power & Light Co. PacifiCorp Portland General Corp. Idaho Power Co.	50	Contract in negotiation	50
Central and South America	State-owned utilities	100	Two letters of intent signed; first power contract expected in 1992	100
Northeast	Various NEPOOL members	50	First phase contract expected last half of 1993	200
Central Midwest	Iowa-Illinois Gas & Electric Co.	50	Joint venture agreement signed; first power contract expected in 1993	200
Pacific Northwest	Several utilities	50	First phase contract expected in 1993	250
Minnesota	Northern States Power Co.	25	First phase contract award expected in 1992	75
California (BRPU)	Pacific Gas & Electric Co. Southern California Edison Co.	150 500	Bid and awards in first half of 1993	NA NA
	San Diego Gas & Electric Co.	200		NA
Western Europe	U.K. and Ireland	300	Joint venture signed; 1993 contracts expected	NQ
	Germany	35	First half of 1993	NQ
	Spain	50	Restructure existing agreement	NQ

NA = Not applicable.
NQ = Not quantified.
* Includes renewable energy opportunities as well as specific wind energy opportunities.
Source: Kenetech Corporation, SEC Form S-1, October 1992.

Iowa-Illinois Gas & Electric Co. and USW planned to jointly develop wind farms in or near Iowa to generate power for area utilities. The proposed joint venture initially would invest $200 million to $225 million to obtain rights to place wind turbines on agricultural land and to build enough turbines to generate 250 MW of power. After five years, the project could be expanded to 500 MW—the equivalent of a coal-fired generating plant. This would be the first major U.S. wind energy project outside California. The Midwest plant would be an independent power producer, selling power under contract to a host utility.

With respect to Pacific Northwest development activities, USW planned to submit bids to Puget Power, Pacific Power and Light, and Montana Power for 300 to 400

MW of new capacity. These were open competitive bids to be awarded solely on the basis of low cost and acceptable reliability; no special preferences were to be given to renewable energy sources like wind power.

Internationally, in 1992, USW sold 25 MW of wind turbine capacity to a utility in the Netherlands, a country that had vowed to meet more stringent CO_2 limits than those agreed to at the Earth Summit. Also, USW was forming joint ventures with partners in Japan and Europe. It had established a manufacturing joint venture with Spain's Abengoa to initially supply 15 MW of wind plant capacity in that country. It also had a joint venture in Britain with the Wind Energy Group (a British joint venture) for a substantial project in Wales.

In other parts of the world, USW completed a 500 kw pilot project for Inner Mongolia in late 1989. That Windplant was designed to operate in temperatures as low as −40°F and was serving as a test center for wind power in China. USW had nearly 1 MW of turbine capacity running on Okinawa in a joint marketing effort with Toyo Engineering. USW had recently entered into an agreement with Krimenergo, the Ukrainian electric utility, to provide one of the largest wind energy facilities in the world, a 500 MW wind farm on the Crimea Peninsula that would hasten the closure of the Chernobyl nuclear power plant and supply enough energy to serve about 400,000 Ukrainian households; over a five-year period, 5,000 of U.S. Windpower's 56-100 model turbines would be manufactured and installed in the Ukraine. U.S. Windpower had negotiated an interesting barter deal to cover the project financing. According to Scott Healy, director of Business Development at Kenetech, this project would be valued at over $500 million if completed in the United States. USW would act as the designer, engineer, and construction contractor on this project. In exchange, Krimenergo would manufacture and operate the wind turbines. USW would take its built-in profit out in spare parts that would be used in the already existing turbines at Altamont Pass and around the world.

Future Prospects   USW President Dale Osborn believed the United States was the biggest potential wind energy market in the world:

> We believe the ultimate customer for our product, whether it's wind-generated electricity or a wind power plant, is the American utility industry. That's why the relationship we have with EPRI and PG&E is important to us. We intend to design and produce a product that most fits the needs of utilities, so we felt it was critical to get involved with the best utility technologists we could find.[20]
>
> We have really two major marketing thrusts. One is we have got to work on this ignorance quotient of our policy-makers. And it's our responsibility to do that—both in Washington and at the state level. The second thing is that we are developing a product with the marketplace that we're going to serve, and we need to build credibility with those organizations we now serve and transfer that credibility within the industry. In Solano County, . . . it took us about 18 months of fairly solid work to get people to understand what we did, why it was important to them and why it was important to our nation. The issue is that we're developing a technology that's going to allow us to have better national security by less dependence of foreign oil. And so as we go forward, we must

---

[20]"Excellent Forecast for Wind."

get allies in the community. We must explain what we do and how we do it and why we do it well. We must be very solid community citizens.[21]

Gerald Anderson, president of Kenetech, predicted that the 1990s would be a transition decade for wind power, during which dozens of utilities would develop "relatively modest" wind projects to gather data on how they work. After that, wind power would explode, contributing as much as 10 percent of the nation's electricity by 2010 or so. The American Wind Energy Association (AWEA) believed a realistic goal for U.S. energy strategy was for wind energy to provide 20 percent of U.S. electric capacity within 20 to 30 years.

(Note: In January 1994, Kenetech changed the name of its U.S. Windpower subsidiary to Kenetech Windpower. Kenetech's stock was traded on the NASDAQ.)

---

[21]"Nation Must Wake Up to Wind's Potential."

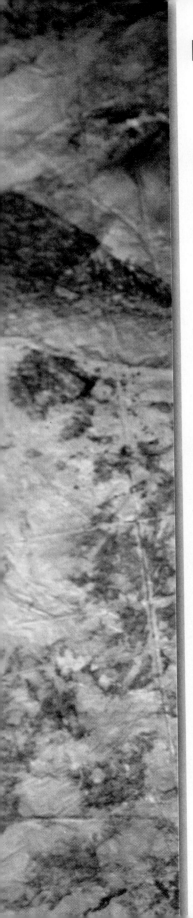

Competition in the World Tire Industry, 1995

Arthur A. Thompson, Jr., The University of Alabama
John E. Gamble, Auburn University at Montgomery

Tire manufacturing became an important industry in the first half of the 20th century as motor vehicles increasingly became the dominant mode of transportation. By 1995, manufacturers' sales of tires constituted a $55 billion market globally. Throughout most of the tire industry's history, U.S.-based tire companies had occupied leading positions in the overall world market for tires. But, during the late 1980s, the industry went through a major consolidation phase that ended U.S. domination. Five of the seven largest U.S. producers and the U.S. and European operations of the leading British producer were acquired, resulting in a shakeup of the industry's competitive structure.

Date	Deal	Purchase Price
December 1986	Sumitomo Rubber Industries (Japan) acquired control of the European operations of Dunlop Tire, the leading British-based producer. The acquisition included two plants in France and marketing rights to use the Dunlop name in Europe.	$80 million
October 1987	Continental (the leading German producer) purchased General Tire (the fourth-largest U.S. tiremaker).	$628 million
May 1988	Bridgestone Corp. (the largest Japanese-based tire manufacturer) acquired Firestone Tire and Rubber Co. (the third-largest U.S.-based tiremaker).	$2.6 billion
May 1988	Pirelli (the leading Italian producer) acquired Armstrong Tire (the fifth-largest U.S. producer).	$197 million
January 1989	Sumitomo Rubber Industries (Japan) purchased the U.S. operations of Dunlop Tire Corp. (two plants, sales of $500 million). This left the British parent of Dunlop, BTR plc, with five tire plants in Africa.	$369 million
October 1989	Yokohama Rubber (Japan) acquired Mohawk Rubber (the seventh-largest U.S. producer).	$150 million
November 1990	Groupe Michelin, a French-based producer with the biggest market share of any European tiremaker, acquired Uniroyal Goodrich Tire Co., the second-largest U.S. producer, to make Michelin the world's largest producer of tires.	$1.5 billion

Ken Tucker, Jennifer Lowry, and Andrew White assisted in researching earlier versions of this case. Copyright 1995 by Arthur A. Thompson, Jr.

Going into the 1990s, there were only two major U.S.-based producers of tires able to contend for global market leadership: Goodyear Tire (the world's largest tiremaker since the 1920s—until the acquisitions by Michelin and Bridgestone dropped it to third place) and Cooper Tire and Rubber. None of the remaining six U.S.-based tire producers had as much as $100 million in tire sales annually—all had market shares under 1 percent and competed only in restricted market niches.

The world's 11 largest tire manufacturers accounted for nearly 84 percent of worldwide tire production in 1994—see Exhibit 1. In addition to the major producers there were between 75 and 100 other producers of tires with one or more plants; the vast majority of these operated within a single national or continental market area. From a global perspective, the industry was becoming more concentrated, with the 50 biggest producers accounting for over 96 percent of world output—revenues of the 50th-largest producer amounted to about $80 million in 1993.

World production of car, truck, and bus tires in 1994 approximated 875 million units. The top tire-producing nations were the United States (27 percent), Japan (16 percent), China (7.4 percent), France (6.4 percent), Germany (5.2 percent), South Korea (5.0 percent), the Confederation of Independent States (the former USSR)—(4.6 percent), Brazil (3.3 percent), Great Britain (3.3 percent), and Italy (3.2 percent).

INDUSTRY CONDITIONS IN 1995

For the past two decades, tire companies had struggled to match production capability with market demand and overcome chronic overcapacity problems. When demand for longer-lasting radial tires started to grow rapidly in the 1965–80 period, manufacturers invested in new plants, greatly increasing output capability. Overcapacity became an ongoing problem because companies were reluctant to close down older, less efficient plants and consolidate production into fewer plants as old-style bias-ply and bias-belted tire production was phased out and tire demand matured.

Through the 1980s and 1990s, tire manufacturers invested heavily in R&D and new technology to improve tire performance, traction, and tread wear under a variety of road conditions. As a consequence, the average service life for passenger tires rose from about 24,000 miles in 1973 to almost 40,000 miles in 1994. Such dramatic increases in the number of miles driven before tires had to be replaced, coupled with maturing global demand for new motor vehicles, had dampened long-term sales growth for both original equipment and replacement tires. All these factors had combined to intensify competition among tire makers, and in recent years punishing price wars had erupted in both the U.S. and European markets.

Firestone, Uniroyal Goodrich (itself the product of a recent merger between Uniroyal Tire and BF Goodrich Tire), and General Tire were, at the time of their acquisition, struggling to restore their competitiveness. All three had fallen behind Goodyear, Bridgestone, and Michelin in tire quality, product line breadth, and brand-name reputation. All three had underutilized plants and relatively high production costs, were losing market share, and were growing weaker financially. Dunlop Tire, a respected name in tire making in Europe, had many of the same problems. Armstrong Tire and Mohawk, both second-tier U.S. producers, served limited market niches and lacked the capability to compete more broadly. When these six companies

Exhibit 1   Sales and Market Share of the World's 11 Largest Tire Producers, 1990 and 1994

Company (headquarters country)	Major Brands	1990		1994	
		Tire Sales (billions of $)	Market Share (by volume)	Tire Sales (billions of $)	Market Share (by volume)
1. Groupe Michelin (France)	Michelin, Uniroyal, BF Goodrich	$10.1	19.0%	$11.5	18.0%
2. Goodyear (U.S.)	Goodyear, Kelly-Springfield, Lee, Douglas, Monarch	8.2	16.8	10.7	16.8
3. Bridgestone Corp. (Japan)	Bridgestone, Firestone, Dayton	8.3	14.6	10.4	17.9
4. Continental (Germany)	Continental, General, Uniroyal Englebert, Semperit	3.6	6.2	4.0	7.1
5. Pirelli Group (Italy)	Pirelli, Armstrong	3.2	5.3	3.3	5.2
6. Sumitomo (Japan)	Sumitomo, Dunlop	3.0	5.3	3.4	6.1
7. Yokohama (Japan)	Yokohama, Mohawk	2.0	4.0	2.6	4.8
8. Toyo Tire (Japan)	Toyo	1.1	1.8	1.2	2.5
9. Cooper Tire and Rubber (U.S.)	Cooper, Mastercraft, Starfire	0.9	1.3	1.1	1.9
10. Hankook (South Korea)	Hankook	0.6	1.0	0.8	1.6
11. Kumho (South Korea)	Trisun	0.6	1.0	0.9	1.7
			75.3%		83.6%

Note: Yokohama had a 23.5 percent ownership stake in Hankook.
Source: Compiled from a variety of sources, including *Modern Tire Dealer, Tire Business,* and *The Economist.*

were acquired, the new owners launched extensive plant modernization projects and cost-saving, quality-enhancing changes in operations, the goal being to use the newly acquired companies' plants and customer bases to build a stronger position for competing globally in the world tire industry. Exhibit 2 shows the industry's leading brands as of 1993.

THE DEMAND SIDE OF THE TIRE MARKET

The demand for original equipment tires is directly related to the number of new motor vehicles currently produced, whereas the demand for replacement tires depends on such factors as the number of vehicles in service, the average number of miles driven per vehicle, and tire tread durability. In 1995, the replacement market was between three and four times as big as the original equipment segment; a vehicle during its useful life could require anywhere between two and six sets of replacement tires. Replacement tire sales generate much bigger profit margins for the manufacturers than original equipment sales because tire makers can command higher prices on the replacement sales through wholesale and retail channels than they could on selling tires in mass quantities to the hard-bargaining car and truck manufacturers.

Exhibit 2　Tire Industry Market Leaders, 1993

Top 10 Best-Selling Brands Worldwide

Rank	Brand	1993 Dollar Sales
1.	Goodyear	$7.25 billion
2.	Michelin	7.24
3.	Bridgestone	5.83
4.	Dunlop	3.95
5.	Firestone	2.70
6.	Pirelli	2.45
7.	Yokohama	2.40
8.	Continental	1.13
9.	Toyo	1.10
10.	Uniroyal	0.95

Company Leaders in the North American Market			Company Leaders in the European Market		
Rank	Brand	1993 Dollar Sales	Rank	Company	1993 Dollar Sales
1.	Goodyear/Kelly-Springfield	$5.15 billion	1.	Michelin	$4.50 billion
2.	Michelin/Uniroyal Goodrich	3.80	2.	Continental	1.94
3.	Bridgestone/Firestone	3.70	3.	Goodyear	1.83
4.	Continental/General	1.30	4.	Bridgestone/Firestone	1.30
5.	Cooper Tire	1.00	5.	Sumitomo/Dunlop	1.30
6.	Dunlop	0.59	6.	Pirelli	1.29
7.	Pirelli-Armstrong	0.51	7.	Yokohama	<0.25
8.	Yokohama	0.41	8.	Toyo	<0.20
9.	Toyo	0.26	9.	Vredestine (Netherlands)	0.16
10.	Kumho	0.15	10.	Nokia (Finland)	0.15
11.	Hankook	0.12			

Note: Tires carrying the Dunlop brand were produced and marketed by three different manufacturers—Sumitomo in the United States and Europe, Dunlop India (which operated two plants in India), and British-based BTR plc (which operated five tire plants in four African countries). Prior to the sale of its operations to Sumitomo and Dunlop India, BTR had been one of the world's largest tire producers.

Source: *Tire Business*, Market Data Book, November 14, 1994, pp. 12, 15; *Rubber & Plastics News*, August 15, 1994, p. 38.

The Original Equipment Market Segment

All original equipment (OE) tires were sold by the tire manufacturers factory-direct to the car and truck manufacturers. Vehicle manufacturers sourced all tires from outside suppliers; none had integrated backward into tire manufacturing as they had into other component vehicle parts. As a consequence, OE tire demand was a function of the type and number of vehicles currently being produced—each new automobile, for example, was equipped with five tires (four on the ground and a spare). World production of motor vehicles approximated 50 million units annually during the 1990s.

Since tires were such a small cost item in the overall price of new vehicles, increases or decreases in the overall industry level of OE tire prices had no appreciable effect on total OE tire demand. However, motor vehicle producers considered the price quotations of individual tire manufacturers to be a primary consideration in their tire-sourcing decisions since it was relatively easy for them to switch their OE tire purchases for particular models to tire producers with the best prices.

Tire manufacturers competed aggressively to supply OE tires to the automobile and truck manufacturers for two strategic reasons. One, tire makers believed that vehicle owners, satisfied with their OE tires, would be more likely to choose the same brand when time came for replacement. Two, OE tire sales helped achieve volume-related economies in manufacturing.

Although car and truck manufacturers were sophisticated buyers and devoted considerable time and effort to tire purchasing and to their relationships with tire manufacturers, there were two schools of thought among automakers about how tires should be purchased.

Tire Purchasing Practices of the U.S. Automakers   All the U.S. auto and truck manufacturers (General Motors, Ford, Chrysler, Navistar, and PACCAR) set detailed tire specifications for each of their car and truck models that would-be tire suppliers had to meet for their tires to be considered as original equipment. In 1995, tire makers had to meet as many as 50 specifications on a given tire, as opposed to just 10 or so in 1960. It was not unusual for U.S. auto/truck manufacturers to require higher quality standards and stricter specifications for the OE tires they purchased than for comparable replacement tire grades. However, specification differences between OE and replacement tires were narrowing, since tire manufacturers had in recent years substantially improved tire quality and performance and since vehicle manufacturers had begun relaxing "unnecessary" specifications in return for lower prices. Some automobile manufacturers regularly inspected the plants of their tire suppliers to make sure quality standards were being met, and it was not unusual for them to ask suppliers for data on costs to compare against their own independent estimates of tire-making costs.

Different-size cars and trucks were equipped with different size tires. The smallest cars had 13-inch wheelbases and required narrower tires; large luxury cars had 14-inch and 15-inch wheelbases and required wider treads. Tires for heavy-duty trucks and tractor-trailer rigs were equipped with still bigger and stronger tires, capable of withstanding heavier loads.

Vehicle manufacturers typically contracted out their tire requirements annually on a model-by-model basis, normally using several different tire suppliers to equip their full lineup of models—see Exhibits 3, 4, and 5. Using their bargaining leverage, U.S. automobile manufacturers had over the years negotiated prices for OE tires substantially below what wholesale distributors paid for comparable replacement tires with often less stringent specifications. As a result, vehicle makers obtained OE tires for roughly half the retail price commanded by replacement tires. Tire manufacturers' profit margins on OE tires rarely exceeded a couple of dollars per tire; prices at breakeven or below were not uncommon.

Tire Purchasing Practices of the Japanese Automakers   In Japan, the major Japanese vehicle manufacturers usually obtained the majority of their tires from a single supplier (often a tire supplier from the same *keiretsu* as the automaker), utilizing a long-term partnership agreement. Vehicle manufacturers worked closely with their primary suppliers, providing detailed information about their near-term and long-term requirements and emphasizing the importance of a mutually beneficial relationship. So long as the primary supplier could supply the sizes and grades

Exhibit 3 Estimated Brand Market Share for Original Equipment Passenger and Light Truck Tires in the United States and Canada, 1994

Original equipment buyer	Tire Company						
	Goodyear	Firestone	Michelin	Uniroyal Goodrich	General Tire	Dunlop	Bridgestone
General Motors	33.0%	4.0%	16.0%	32.0%	15.0%	0.0%	0.0%
Ford	25.0	36.5	25.0	2.0	11.5	0.0	0.0
Chrysler	85.0	0.0	0.0	0.0	15.0	0.0	0.0
Mazda	20.0	40.0	3.0	0.0	0.0	10.0	27.0
Honda of the United States	30.0	0.0	44.0	0.0	0.0	15.0	11.0
Toyota	22.0	17.0	11.0	0.0	1.0	33.0	14.0
Diamond Star	71.0	0.0	0.0	0.0	0.0	0.0	29.0
Nissan	26.0	22.0	22.0	6.0	15.0	9.0	0.0
Nummi (GM-Toyota)	41.0	30.0	0.0	0.0	0.0	15.0	14.0
Volvo	80.0	0.0	20.0	0.0	0.0	0.0	0.0
Saturn	0.0	100.0	0.0	0.0	0.0	0.0	0.0
Isuzu	10.0	0.0	0.0	0.0	0.0	0.0	0.0
Subaru	20.0	0.0	0.0	0.0	0.0	0.0	80.0
BMW	0.0	0.0	100.0	0.0	0.0	0.0	0.0
Overall OE market share	38.0%	16.0%	16.0%	14.0%	11.5%	2.75%	1.25%

Source: *Modern Tire Dealer*, January 1995, p. 24.

needed, Japanese vehicle makers did not seek competing bids from alternative tire makers. Only when the vehicle maker's principal tire supplier did not have the capability to provide competitively priced tires of the desired size and quality for a particular model did vehicle makers negotiate supply arrangements with other tire makers. This occurred frequently enough that Japanese automakers, despite relying heavily on one primary tire supplier, ended up using several tire suppliers to round out their total tire needs at their Japan-based plants.

The leading suppliers of the 60 million to 70 million OE tires purchased annually by the Japanese vehicle manufacturers for cars and trucks made in Japan were as follows:

Bridgestone Tires	39%
Yokohama Rubber	21
Sumitomo Rubber	17
Toyo Tire	10
Michelin	7
All others	6
	100%

The Japanese automakers placed less stress on explicit tire specifications and were less price-oriented in comparison to the U.S. automakers. Instead, they worked diligently with their tire suppliers on ways to hold down tire costs and improve tire

Exhibit 4   Trends in Tire Brand Market Shares for Original Equipment Passenger Car and Light Truck Tires, U.S./Canadian Market, 1980–1994

Producer/Brand	1980	1985	1990	1992	1993	1994
Goodyear	33.5%	32.0%	36.5%	38.0%	40.0%	40.0%
Michelin	2.0	11.2	15.7	17.0	18.0	18.0
Firestone	23.0	22.0	17.0	15.0	15.4	15.7
General	10.0	13.5	12.0	10.3	10.0	9.7
Uniroyal/Goodrich	18.0	22.5	17.0	14.0	12.0	11.5
Dunlop	—	—	1.5	2.5	2.5	2.5
Bridgestone	—	—	0.3	3.0	2.0	2.5
Others	13.5	8.8	0.0	0.5	0.1	0.1

Source: *Modern Tire Dealer,* January 1990 and January 1995 issues.

quality, and they placed great importance on timely delivery and other facets of the "just-in-time" inventory and logistics systems that they used extensively with all auto components suppliers to control purchasing, materials handling, and warehousing costs. In Japan, all of the Japanese tire manufacturing plants were located within a few miles of the assembly plants of the Japanese automakers.

However, when the Japanese automakers constructed car and truck assembly plants outside Japan (in the United States, Europe, and other parts of Asia), they tended to establish supply relationships with more than one tire maker (see Exhibits 3 and 5) and then worked gradually towards choosing a principal supplier for each plant location based on their experiences with each tire maker. Normally, it was not cost-effective for them to import Japanese-made tires from their principal tire supplier in Japan. As of 1994, the Japanese automakers were sourcing a growing portion of the tires needed at their U.S.-based assembly plants from the U.S. tire plants acquired by Bridgestone and Sumitomo—more and more models of Japanese cars and trucks made in the United States were being equipped with Bridgestone/Firestone and Dunlop/Sumitomo tires (see Exhibit 3).

The Replacement Tire Market

Replacement tires accounted for 70 to 80 percent of worldwide tire production. Unit shipments had exhibited moderate growth since 1985—see Exhibit 6 for recent volume trends in the United States by segment. Every 100-mile change in the average number of miles traveled per vehicle produced roughly a 1 million–unit change in the size of the replacement market, assuming average tread wear life of 25,000 to 30,000 miles per tire. Relatively stable gasoline prices worldwide and improving vehicle fuel economy were contributing to a rise in annual mileage driven per vehicle (in the United States, the average had risen from 9,600 miles in 1984 to 11,600 miles in 1994).

Tire manufacturers produced a large variety of grades and lines of tires for distribution under both manufacturers' brand names and private labels. Branded replacement tires were made to the tire maker's own specifications, often less rigid than those required by vehicle manufacturers for OE tires. Some private-label tires

Exhibit 5	Major Suppliers of Original Equipment Tires to Motor Vehicle Producers in Western Europe and Asia

Western Europe	Tire Suppliers
General Motors	Continental
Ford Motor Co.	Continental, Goodyear, and one other
Honda	Continental
Toyota	Continental
Mazda	Continental
Nissan Peugeot-Citroen	Continental, Michelin, Pirelli
Volvo	Goodyear, Continental
Mercedes-Benz	Michelin, Continental, Goodyear
BMW	Michelin, Continental
Volkswagen-Audi	Michelin, Goodyear, Continental, and one other
Renault	Continental, Sumitomo, Pirelli
Saab	Michelin, Continental
Fiat	Pirelli, Continental, Michelin, Goodyear
Porsche	Pirelli, Goodyear, Michelin
Asia	
Honda	Bridgestone, Sumitomo, Yokohama, and one other
Toyota	Bridgestone, Sumitomo, Toyo, Yokohama, Goodyear, Michelin, and one other
Mazda	Bridgestone, Sumitomo, Toyo, Yokohama, Goodyear, and one other
Nissan	Bridgestone, Sumitomo, Toyo, Yokohama, Goodyear, Michelin, Continental/General, and two others
Isuzu	Sumitomo, Toyo, Yokohama, Goodyear, Michelin, and one other
Mitsubishi	Bridgestone, Sumitomo, Toyo, Yokohama, Michelin, and one other
Daihatsu	Sumitomo, and one other
Hyundai (Korea)	Hankook, Kumho

supplied to wholesale distributors and large chain retailers were made to the buyer's specifications rather than to the manufacturer's standards. To those untrained in tire-making techniques or unfamiliar with tire-making practices, replacement tires appeared to be quite comparable if not exactly similar to OE tires. But there were often subtle differences in tread depth, grades of rubber, and component construction such that many, if not the majority, of replacement tires on the market were not 100 percent equal to the quality and durability of OE tires. Low-grade replacement tires had a tread life of 10,000 to 20,000 miles compared to 30,000 to 60,000 miles (or longer) for OE tires and high-grade replacement tires. As of 1995, most manufacturers provided guaranteed mileage warranties to the buyers of replacement tires. Moreover, nearly all branded replacement tires carried lifetime warranties against manufacturing defects, and all tires met certain specified safety standards regarding traction and resistance against heat buildup.

Distribution Channels   Over the years, the major brand-name tire makers had developed wholesale and retail dealer networks through which to market replacement tires to vehicle owners. Replacement tires were available from independent

Exhibit 6   Trends in U.S. Tire Shipments, 1990–1995   *(in millions of tires)*

	1990	1991	1992	1993	1994*	1995*
Passenger						
Replacement	152.3	155.4	165.8	165.2	169.0	171.0
OE	47.2	41.9	46.3	52.2	59.0	60.2
Retread	10.0	8.4	7.4	6.6	5.9	5.9
Total	209.5	205.7	219.5	224.0	223.9	237.1
Truck, light truck, bus						
Replacement	36.6	32.9	33.7	35.5	37.9	38.3
OE	7.0	5.8	7.1	8.6	10.3	10.1
Retread	22.2	22.3	22.8	22.8	23.1	23.5
Total	65.8	61.0	63.6	66.9	71.3	71.9
Farm (front and rear)						
Replacement	2.550	2.230	2.270	2.600	2.610	2.662
OE	0.955	0.796	0.755	1.000	1.000	1.050
Total	3.505	3.026	3.025	3.600	3.610	3.712
Large off-the-road						
Replacement	0.124	0.127	0.111	0.123	0.147	0.150
OE	0.060	0.049	0.051	0.064	0.074	0.076
Total	0.184	0.176	0.162	0.187	0.221	0.226
Industrial pneumatic, utility						
Replacement	2.531	2.527	2.835	3.120	3.180	3.280
OE	6.738	6.957	7.435	8.640	8.770	9.030
Total	9.269	9.484	10.270	11.760	11.950	12.310
Grand Total	288.258	279.386	296.557	306.447	310.981	325.248

* Estimated
Sources: Rubber Manufacturers Association, *Tire Retreading/Repair Journal*, Goodyear, others.

tire dealers, service stations, manufacturer-owned retail tire stores, major department stores with auto centers, retail chains (such as Wal-Mart, Sears, Kmart, and Montgomery Ward), automobile dealerships, warehouse clubs, and assorted other outlets (see Exhibit 7). In the United States alone, there were approximately 42,000 tire, battery, and accessory dealers in 1995. Independent tire dealers usually carried the brands of several different major manufacturers and a discount-priced private-label brand so as to give replacement buyers a broad assortment of brands, features, quality options, and price ranges to choose from. Retail tire outlets that were owned or franchised by the manufacturers (i.e., Goodyear Tire Stores and Firestone Auto Master Care Centers) carried only the manufacturer's name brands and perhaps a lesser-known, discount-priced line made by the manufacturer (a number of tire makers had secondary or associate brand lines that sold at a discount to their primary brand). Department stores and large retail chains tended to stock one to four brand-name lines and their own private-label brand. Exhibit 8 shows market shares of the various brands in the U.S. replacement market for 1994.

Exhibit 7 Share of Passenger Car Replacement Tire Sales in the United States, by Type of Retail Outlet, 1985 versus 1994

Type of Retail Outlet	1985	1994
Independent tire dealers	55.0%	54.0%
Chain and department stores	19.0	19.0
Tire company stores	10.0	11.5
Service stations	9.0	5.0
Warehouse clubs	2.0	8.5
Other	5.0	2.0
	100.0%	100.0%

Source: *Modern Tire Dealer*, January 1995, p. 27.

Advertising and Promotion   The major tire producers often used network TV campaigns to promote their brands, introduce new types of tires, and pull customers to their retail dealer outlets. Tire makers' network TV ad budgets commonly ran in the $10 million to $50 million range and their budgets for co-op ads with dealers were in the $20 million to $100 million range. Several tire companies sponsored auto-racing events as a way of promoting the performance capabilities of their tires.

Retailers that really pushed replacement tire sales found it advantageous to handle a broad product line so as to have tires suitable for different types of cars and trucks and to give vehicle owners a choice of tread designs, tread widths, tread durabilities, performance characteristics, and price ranges. Most car and light truck owners were unfamiliar with the different types and grades of tires available. Many ended up choosing on the basis of price, others followed the dealer's recommendation, and still others balanced price against tread wear mileage guarantees to get a tire that would last as long as they planned to keep the vehicle. The retail price of replacement tires ranged from retreaded (or recapped) tires selling for $25 to $35 each to top-of-the-line tires going for $125 to $175 each. Manufacturers' profit margins on replacement tires marketed through wholesale and retail channels were in the $5 to $10 range for passenger car and light truck tires; margins on heavy truck tires were significantly higher.

Tire dealers ran frequent price promotions to attract price-sensitive shoppers looking to buy at off-list prices. In recent years, buyers of replacement tires had become more price conscious and less brand loyal (thus eroding the importance of the strategy of the leading manufacturers to gain an edge in securing replacement sales through OE sales to the vehicle manufacturers). However, it was hard for car owners to comparison shop on the basis of tire quality and tread durability because of the proliferation of brands, lines, grades, and performance features. Manufacturers had resisted the development of standardized specifications for replacement tires, and neither tire companies nor tire retailers used common terminology in describing tire grades and construction features to the public.

Retail Competition   In most geographic areas, the retail tire market was intensely competitive. Tire retailers advertised extensively in newspapers, outdoor billboards, and occasionally on local TV to establish and maintain their market shares. Price was

Exhibit 8 Estimated Brand Shares of Replacement Market for Tires, United States, 1994

Passenger Car Tires		Light Truck Tires		Highway Truck Tires	
Goodyear	16.0%	Goodyear	13.0%	Goodyear	23.0%
Michelin	8.0	BF Goodrich	8.5	Michelin	18.0
Firestone	7.5	Firestone	6.5	Bridgestone	13.0
Sears	4.0	Michelin	7.0	General Tire	5.0
General	4.5	Cooper/Falls	5.5	Firestone	7.0
BF Goodrich	4.0	Kelly-Springfield	5.5	Kelly-Springfield	6.0
Bridgestone	3.5	Armstrong	3.0	Dunlop	4.0
Cooper	4.0	General Tire	5.0	Yokohama	7.0
Kelly-Springfield	4.0	Bridgestone	4.0	Cooper	2.0
Multi-Mile	3.0	Dunlop	3.0	Toyo	4.0
Sentry	2.0	Remington	2.0	Hankook	2.0
Uniroyal	2.5	Uniroyal	3.0	Kumho	2.0
Cordovan	2.0	Dayton	2.5	All Others	7.0
Dayton	2.0	Kumho	1.0	Total	100.0%
Dunlop	2.0	Yokohama	1.0		
Pirelli	2.0	Toyo	2.0		
Falls Mastercraft	1.5	All Others	27.5		
Hercules	1.5	Total	100.0%		
Monarch	1.0				
Montgomery Ward	1.0				
Remington	1.0				
Summit	1.5				
Yokohama	1.5				
Patriot	1.5				
Delta	1.0				
Laramie	1.0				
Lee	1.0				
Monarch	1.0				
National	1.0				
Regul	1.0				
Sigma	1.0				
Spartan	1.0				
Star	1.0				
Stratton	1.0				
Toyo	1.0				
All Others	6.5				
Total	100.0%				

Sources: *Modern Tire Dealer*, January 1995, p. 21; Market Data Book 1994, *Tire Business*, p. 12.

the dominant competitive variable. Many dealers featured and pushed their private-label "off-brand" tires because their profit margins on private-label tires were typically several percentage points greater than on the name-brand tires of major manufacturers. Dealer-sponsored private-label tires accounted for 35 to 40 percent of total replacement tire sales in the United States in 1994. Surveys showed that dealers were able to influence a car owner's choice of replacement tires, both as to brand and type of tire. Most replacement tire buyers did not have strong tire brand preferences, making it fairly easy for tire salespeople to switch customers to tire brands and grades with the highest dealer margins. Normal dealer margins on replacement tires were in the 25 to 33 percent range, but many dealers shaved margins to win incremental sales.

When tire retailers' profits started being squeezed in the mid-1970s by slowing growth in replacement tire sales and declining retail tire prices (see Exhibit 9), many tire dealers expanded into auto repair services (engine tune-ups, shock absorber and muffler replacement, and brake repair), retreading, and automobile accessories. Some tire retailers were promoting their businesses as "total car care centers." Auto service work was attractive not only as a source of revenue growth but also because gross profit margins often exceeded the margins earned on replacement tire sales. The fastest-growing tire dealers were using a strategy of opening multiple locations, providing quick tire change turnaround, employing extensive advertising, buying large quantities of tires from wholesale distributors at favorable process, and using a high volume/low margin pricing strategy based on high inventory turnover, fuller utilization of facilities and tire-changing/mounting personnel, and related volume-based economies.

TYPES OF TIRES

In 1995, virtually all car and truck tires were of radial construction. Bias-ply and bias-belted tires, once the dominant-selling types of tire, had rapidly faded from the scene during the past 20 years.

| Year | Tire Type | Passenger Tire Construction | |
		Original Equipment	Replacement
1975	Bias	34.0%	71.0%
	Radial	66.0	29.0
1985	Bias	0.0	19.0
	Radial	100.0	81.0
1994	Bias	0.0	0.3
	Radial	100.0	99.7

In 1995, bias tires were the cheapest and lowest-grade replacement tires on the market except for retreads. Radial tires were much harder and more expensive to manufacture than bias tires. In 1995, only Michelin, Goodyear, Bridgestone, and a few other tire makers had truly mastered radial tire technology to the point where they could manufacture a radial tire of superior quality for all sizes of cars and trucks. All the remaining manufacturers were striving to improve their radial tire-making skills at many of their plants; while their radial tires were of good quality, they lagged the industry leaders when it came to making superior quality radial tires for luxury/performance cars and heavy trucks. It had taken Goodyear until the mid-1980s to reach the point where its radial tire quality approached Michelin's—Michelin had pioneered radial tire technology, and its steel-belted radial tires were

Exhibit 9   Median Retail Price of Radial Tires (tire size P195/75R14), 1979–1994

Year	Median Price	Year	Median Price
1979	$69.87	1987	$51.80
1980	72.71	1988	52.85
1981	72.13	1989	54.96
1982	65.00	1990	52.70
1983	60.00	1991	54.97
1984	55.50	1992	52.25
1985	54.60	1993	53.00
1986	53.80	1994	48.68

Source: *Modern Tire Dealer*, January 1995, p. 26.

generally regarded worldwide as the best on the market. Just recently had Bridgestone gotten to the point where it could nearly match Michelin on tire quality.

Market Conversion to Radial Tires

Michelin started developing radial tire technology in the early 1940s. The company began marketing radial tires in 1948 and was the only European radial tire manufacturer until 1963. Radial tires were first marketed in Japan in the early 1950s. Radial tires became so popular in Europe and Japan that by the mid-1960s they were the dominant-selling tire. In 1972, Michelin became the first foreign manufacturer to build a tire plant in the U.S. market; it had sought to avoid locating a plant in the United States because of the higher wage rates, but European market saturation coupled with U.S. tariffs on tire imports made a U.S. plant location the most feasible way to penetrate the U.S. tire market. In its first year, Michelin sold 35 percent of all radials sold in the United States.

Michelin's dramatic success in steel-belted radial tires started a pronounced market trend away from bias tires during the 1960s in Europe and during the 1970s in the United States. Radial tires appealed to consumers because of their improved safety and puncture resistance, better skid and traction performance, added gas mileage (due to less friction with road surfaces), and longer service life. While radials were more expensive than bias tires, they delivered substantially more miles of service per dollar of cost.

A conscious decision by U.S. tire makers during the 1960s and early 1970s to pursue a slow, phased-in conversion to radial tire manufacturing opened the door for Michelin to enter the American tire market and virtually foreclosed such U.S. companies as General Tire, Uniroyal, and BF Goodrich from competing aggressively for a bigger piece of the world tire market. Tire makers in the United States were dissuaded from a strategy of rapid conversion by (1) the added costs motor vehicle manufacturers would incur to modify vehicle suspension systems, (2) the high investment costs of industry conversion to radial production (estimated in 1965 to be $700 million), and (3) an array of quality control problems and technical difficulties in making radials for larger-sized American cars. However, the market for radials in the United States took off quicker than expected, and U.S. makers were caught with too much bias tire capacity, too little radial tire capacity, and a host of radial tire production problems. All this coincided with the major European and Japanese markets for radials beginning to level off. Moreover, because of their early efforts in leading the conversion to radials, Michelin and the Japanese producers had confronted the technical difficulties of making larger-sized radial tires sooner, providing them with a technological lead and a quality edge. Even though Michelin brand tires retailed for a 15 to 30 percent premium over rival brands, Michelin made inroads into the U.S. market and built its OE and replacement market share steadily from 1970 into the mid-1980s. Japanese tire makers, especially Bridgestone, were also able to gain a foothold in the U.S. replacement tire segment because the owners of Toyotas, Hondas, and other Japanese vehicles—all of which came equipped with Japanese brand radials—constituted a ready market for replacement radials when their OE sets wore out. Among the U.S. producers only Goodyear, by virtue of its worldwide leadership position, was able to close the technology-quality gap quickly enough to compete toe-to-toe with Michelin and Bridgestone.

High-Performance Tires

In 1980, Goodyear introduced "high performance" radial tires and created one of the industry's fastest-growing segments. High-performance tires were designed for sportier high-horsepower cars with rack-and-pinion steering and four-wheel drive vehicles, vans, and pickups; they provided more safety under a variety of hazardous road conditions and were constructed to accommodate heavier loads and/or speeds above 90 miles per hour. High-performance tires retailed for as much as $30 to $40 per tire more than other premium quality tires. In 1994, speed-rated and heavy-duty performance radials accounted for about 45 percent of the OE market and 50 percent of replacement purchases. Goodyear and Michelin were regarded as the leaders in high-performance tires in 1995. Goodyear's share of the high-performance segment was an estimated 20 to 23 percent in 1994.

All-Season Tires

In 1995, over 80 percent of the radial tires on the market were designated as "all-season" because their treads were designed to deliver superior traction in both rain and snow. Sales of all-season passenger tires in the United States had grown from 1 million units in 1977 to 70 million units in 1986 to over 190 million units in 1994. All-season tread designs were popular because of the added safety, but many drivers in heavy snow areas still preferred to use snow tires on their vehicles in the winter months. Some owners of four-wheel drive sport utility vehicles preferred snow tires to all-season tires year-round because snow tires had better traction in muddy conditions on unpaved roads. Snow tires accounted for 3.5 percent of the replacement passenger tire market in 1994 and conventional tread designs accounted for the remaining 15 percent.

Private-Label Tires

Private-label and associate (or house) brand tires were usually manufactured to lesser specifications than the best-known manufacturers' brands. The leading manufacturers made tires for private labeling to utilize otherwise idle capacity; private-label production usually accounted for less than 20 percent of their tire output. Lesser-known manufacturers were often big private-label producers, with more than 50 percent of their production going to the private-label segment. Private-label tires were purchased manufacturer-direct by two types of buyers: major chain retailers and wholesale tire distributors. Tires sold directly to retail chains were typically made to the retailer's own specifications and carried a private-label brand specified by the retailer. Other private-label brands (including so-called associate or house brands) were sold in mass quantities to wholesale distributors who in turn marketed them to small and medium-sized independent tire retailers. The largest distributors of private-label and house brand tires contracted to purchase big enough volumes (sometimes as many as several million tires annually) to win a significant price break from manufacturers and passed through some of the savings to retailers. Private-label tires sold at a discount to name-brand tires and were mainly attractive to the most price-conscious vehicle owners.

Truck Tires

Truck tires and tires for specialty vehicles (motor homes, boat trailers, motorcycles, tractors, farm implements, buses, and off-the-road construction vehicles) represented a relatively small portion of industry volume (under 15 percent) but accounted for over one-fourth of industry revenues. The median price of truck tires in 1994 ranged from a low of $60 for a bias tire to over $500 for a large-size steel-belted radial. Tires for tractors and for heavy-duty earthmoving equipment ranged in price from several hundred dollars to over $5,000 per tire. Tires for earthmoving equipment had large ribbed treads for added traction and often were 6 to 10 feet in diameter. Only a limited number of tire makers made tires for heavy trucks, farm equipment, and other specialty vehicles. Goodyear produced tires for virtually every type of vehicle; in the United States and Europe Michelin dominated heavy-duty truck tire replacement with market shares in excess of 40 percent. Bridgestone was the truck tire leader in Japan.

Retreaded Tires

Retreaded tires were made from tires with worn-out treads. New treads, suitable for retreading, could be obtained from tire manufacturers or from tread manufacturers who specialized in retreading. Retreading equipment was available from several suppliers, and a small retread shop could be set up by a local dealer for an investment under $250,000. In the United States, there were about 1,600 retread plants in operation in 1995. Most cities of 50,000 or more had at least one retread shop that served the local market for passenger car and light truck retreads in competition with retreads available from wholesalers and manufacturers. Tire retreading for heavy-duty trucks was usually done by a manufacturer of retreads rather than by a local retread shop. In the United States, the leader maker of truck retreads was Bandag, with a 70 percent market share; Goodyear was second. Virtually all retailers sold replacement tires at "trade-in" prices; those worn-out tires suitable for retreading were collected and sold to retreaders.

In 1995, the passenger car retread segment was small and declining due partly to the fact that buyers could put on a new set of tires for about $100 more than the cost of retreads and partly to safety concerns. There were instances when the tread on a retreaded tire separated from the tire casing; the hazards of retreads increased with speed, heat, and rough road conditions. The trucking industry was the biggest user of retreaded tires. Radial truck tires were retreaded an average of three times, and freight companies were retreading over 80 percent of the radial tires on their trailer trucks and delivery vehicles. Retread buyers were very price conscious. The average price for passenger car retreads in 1994 was around $32, compared to an average price of $49 for new private-label passenger car tires and an average of $62 for name-brand tires. Truck retreads averaged $65 per tire for light trucks and about $105 for heavy trucks. Dealer margins on retreads were in the 30 to 45 percent range, compared to margins of 28 to 33 percent on new tires. Sales trends for retreads in the U.S. market are shown in Exhibit 6.

New Types of Tires

In 1995, three new types of tires were beginning to have a market impact: aquachannel tires, run-flat tires, and second-generation radial tires. Goodyear invented the aquachannel tire segment in 1992 when it launched its Aquatred line featuring treads with two large grooves that offered improved traction in rainy conditions combined with high performance when dry. Goodyear's Aquatred models were a solid market success, generated sales of nearly 4 million tires—primarily to safety-conscious drivers—and commanding a retail price of $95 per tire. Michelin and several other tire makers had followed Goodyear's lead in offering aquachannel models. In 1994, about 3 percent of the replacement tires sold had aquachannel tread designs.

Run-flat tires were being pioneered by Bridgestone, Michelin, and Goodyear; in 1995, run-flat tires were still in the development and experimental testing phase. Run-flat tires made by Goodyear were available on 1994 and 1995 Chevrolet Corvettes; Michelin convinced Ford to offer its run-flat tires as options on select Ford and Lincoln models in 1995. Automakers were enthusiastic about a tire that would run flat for miles because it would eliminate the need for spares; a Chrysler engineer declared, "The first company to come to market with a true run-flat tire is going to capture a dominant share of the market."[1] The tire makers' challenge was to reduce the costs of run-flat tires significantly below the current level of $375 per tire so that run-flats would be inexpensive enough to put on most or all new vehicles.

In 1995, Michelin was introducing new tire lines that it said represented "the most significant advance in tire making since we invented the radial tire." Michelin's new radial tire-making technology involved the use of a special tread compound combined with an advanced casing design that significantly increased a tire tread's grip in rain and snow, improved fuel economy, and maintained tread durability. Michelin claimed tires made with its new technology performed noticeably better in virtually every way that mattered; *European Car* magazine said, "the difference would even jump out at the inexperienced driver."[2] In 1995, Michelin tires made with its new technology were selected as original equipment for advanced luxury/performance touring models offered by BMW, Chrysler, Honda, and Mercedes-Benz.

Industry experts speculated that 21st-century "supertires" would (1) increase a vehicle's gas mileage by having low resistance to the road surface, (2) be able to run when flat, (3) have at least one channel to draw rainwater away from the tread, (4) contain computer chips to monitor tread wear, air pressure, and other performance-related factors, and (5) be durable enough to last 100,000 miles or longer.

[1] As quoted in *Barron's,* "Making Tracks," July 11, 1994, p. 17.
[2] As quoted in a Michelin ad in *Tire Business*, November 14, 1994, p. 8ff.

Tire-Grading Practices

An article in the April 1983 issue of *Consumer Reports* began with the observation:

> There are few products more mystifying to buy than a tire for your car. How can you judge which tire will last longer? Are you really getting a better tire by paying a premium price?[3]

To help U.S. consumers answer such questions, in 1980 the National Highway Traffic Safety Administration (NHTSA), acting under a congressional mandate, instituted a comparative grading system for all tires sold in the United States; tire makers were ordered to test their tires and report the grades assigned to them in three performance areas—traction, heat resistance, and tread life. The *Consumer Reports* article commented on the value of the grading system to consumers:

> Traction and heat resistance are important safety factors, but their labeling has not provided consumers with a meaningful way to choose among tires. For traction, almost all tires are rated either A or B, the two top grades. The difference between the two grades has little practical meaning. As for heat resistance, every tire sold in the U.S. must pass a Department of Transportation head-resistance test, so even a tire carrying the lowest head-resistance grade, a C, is safe.
>
> The tread-life factor, on the other hand, is an indicator of how long the tire will last before becoming hazardously bald. It thus has significant economic as well as safety relevance. The grade is represented by a number, each point of which represents 300 miles of life. Thus, a grade of 150 means tread life of 45,000 miles under the ideal test-track conditions. (In real-world driving, you might achieve considerably less, depending on how you drive and on the materials used in your state's highways.)[4]

In February 1983, NHTSA suspended indefinitely the requirement for tread-wear grading, citing statistical variability in tread-life test results and the potential for disseminating "potentially misleading information." The statistical variability stemmed from some tire makers assigning tread-wear grades based on a 95 percent confidence interval (95 percent of all tires sold would meet the assigned grade) and others adopting a more stringent 99 percent confidence interval. Moreover, inexactness in manufacturing resulted in not all samples of a particular tire performing the same in road track tests.

While the NHTSA had not reinstituted requirements for tread-wear grading as of 1995, competitive pressures in the marketplace had proved very effective in spotlighting tread-wear differences among brands and models. Motor vehicle manufacturers had pushed for and gotten tire makers to improve tread-wear mileage dramatically over the past decade. In the replacement tire segment, the battle for market share was so fierce that rival tire manufacturers had begun appealing to replacement tire purchasers on the basis of longer mileage guarantees. Michelin offered replacement tire models with tread-wear guarantees of 80,000 miles; Goodyear had models with tread-wear guarantees of 70,000 miles; and virtually all manufacturers offered replacement models with tread-wear guarantees of at least 40,000 to 50,000 miles.

---

[3]"U.S. Punctures Tire Grading," *Consumer Reports*, April 1983, p. 166.
[4]Ibid., p. 166.

TIRE MANUFACTURING ————————————————————

Tires consisted of four basic components: (1) the casing or carcass that formed the skeleton of the tire, (2) the tread (made from compounded rubber), (3) the sidewall, also made of compounded rubber, that sheathed the casing and protected it from damage, and (4) high-tensile steel bead wire that was formed into stiff loops and then embedded in parts of the sidewall and casing to give the tire added strength and to prevent the edges of the tire from stretching. Tire manufacturing was a three-stage process that included materials processing, fabrication of the component tire parts, and tire assembly.

Materials Processing

Over 200 different raw materials were used in manufacturing tires, the most important of which were natural rubber, synthetic rubber, fabric and fabric cord (nylon, rayon, polyester, and/or fiberglass), polyvinyl alcohol, sulfur, crude oil, carbon black, and high-carbon steel bead wire. Raw materials comprised about half of a tire's manufacturing cost. Crude oil and rubber were the two biggest raw material costs; since mid-1994, rubber prices had escalated 50 percent. Raw material costs for passenger car and light truck radial tires were in the $14 to $20 range in early 1995. Virtually all of the raw materials were commodities, available in bulk from a variety of sources at the going market prices. Several manufacturers had, however, many years earlier integrated backward into rubber plantations, rubber manufacturing, and tire textiles (fabrics used in tire making) and supplied all or part of their production needs for these materials. The principal functions during materials processing involved cutting the rubber, mixing the needed rubber compounds and making sheet rubber, and putting adhesive on the cord and then heat-setting the fabric.

Fabrication of Components

During this phase, several activities took place. The bead wire was rubber-coated and formed into loops. Rolls of cord fabric were treated to facilitate bonding, then cut on an angle and spliced into a continuous sheet in preparation for making the casing. Some sheet rubber stock was milled to the desired width and thickness, forced through an extruder to form tread slabs of exact dimensions and design, cooled, and the "green" treads stored until time for assembly. Other sheet rubber stock was warmed and rolled into thin sheets. Sheeted gum stocks, used for tubeless innerliner and special reinforcement, were cut to various widths in readiness for tire assembly. Belts of fabric, or steel reinforced fabric, were rubber-coated, cut into appropriate shapes, and then spliced into rolls.

Tire Assembly

This multistage process first involved assembling tire casing and sidewall components on a rotating collapsible drum called a building drum. At the next step, several workers, using a tire-building machine, added belts and the tread to produce a green tire. Green tires were sprayed with mold release lubricants, painted, inspected, and moved to the curing press. Tires assumed their final shape through the use of high pressure and high temperature in the molding press (referred to as the vulcanization process). Cured or vulcanized tires were next moved to the buffing and trimming areas where excess molding material was trimmed off and white raised letters or whitewall stripes buffed out. The completed tire was electronically tested, visually inspected, and stacked for shipment.

The materials processing and tire component fabrication stages were very similar for both bias tire and radial tire production, though there was more labor time involved for radials. The tire-building stage required substantially more labor time for radial tires than for bias production.

Improvements in the Tire-Making Process

Growing competitive pressures in the 1980s prompted tire makers to start looking for ways to simultaneously cut production costs and boost tire quality. Going into the 1990s, finding ways to build a better and better tire at a lower and lower cost was necessary for competitive survival. Reengineering of production processes to drive out costs and improve manufacturing quality had become a way of life by 1995; no aspect of plant operations was off limits. Efforts were underway to automate activities with high labor content. Aging equipment was being replaced sooner with new equipment that reduced defects, waste, and labor time. Work methods and production lines were being reorganized around teams, and shift schedules were being altered to boost productivity. Plant layouts were being reconfigured to make the manufacturing flow more efficient.

Historically, the older tire plants operated by U.S. and European companies had been laid out so that the manufacturing flow was from materials processing to component fabrication to tire assembly. Each phase had its own section of the plant and each separate activity had its own assigned area, its own stack of raw materials, and a stack of just-completed work in process. Much effort went into materials handling activities, and components could travel long distances between production steps.

Following the lead of Japanese tire makers, the latest approaches to tire-making stressed greater integration of materials processing, component fabrication, and tire assembly. Plant operations were being reorganized to create a series of production lines, with each line doing some of its materials processing and all of its own component fabrication and tire assembly. Materials processing was being centralized for those few functions where economies of scale were sizable and it was too expensive to have separate pieces of equipment for each workstation. The effect was to make the production process continuous within each workstation and to minimize materials handling and the distance traveled by each part. Such arrangements utilized one-third less space, reduced changeover costs from tire model to tire model, and shortened the lead times for production scheduling from 12 weeks to 1 week. Suppliers were being required to make just-in-time shipments of raw materials to cut back sharply on storage space requirements for inventory as well as working capital for inventory stocks. Tire producers were also working more closely with suppliers on raw materials specifications to eliminate the need for materials checking and testing when raw materials arrived. Insofar as possible, incoming raw materials were moved directly into the manufacturing flow and stocked at the workstation where they were needed. Lastly, new equipment was being introduced and work methods were being overhauled.

Labor Costs

Although tire manufacturing was relatively capital intensive (a new plant of minimum efficient size could cost as much as $250 million and plant modernization costs in the $50 million to $200 million per plant range were common), significant labor content still remained in the tire manufacturing process in the mid-1990s. Labor costs ranged from 15 to 40 percent of total costs, depending on wage rates and labor efficiency; the U.S. average was about 25 percent. Hourly compensation costs varied from country to country of manufacture (Exhibit 10); cross-country differences were the result not only of differing wage scales but also of fluctuating currency exchange rates (Exhibit 11).

South Korea, Mexico, China, India, and Brazil were considered attractive production locations for tire companies looking to compete in the world market and needing additional plant capacity. In 1994, the hot spots for new tire-making capacity were India and China (wage rates in China averaged 50 cents per hour). China's tire industry couldn't keep pace with rising tire demand and the Chinese government had imposed tariffs of up to 45 percent on tire imports to promote greater domestic production. Goodyear and Pirelli had joint venture projects going in China; Continental had initiated new projects in India and Pakistan. Shipping costs for tires made in low-wage countries and marketed elsewhere in the world were approximately $1 to $3 per tire in 1995. However, fluctuating exchange rates, import duties, governmental red tape, and trade restrictions were a barrier to locating production in low-wage countries; bureaucratic procedures and restrictive government policies were particularly burdensome in India and China, where market access had only recently been granted to foreign companies.

Virtually all of the manufacturers with tire plants in high-wage locations were working hard to reduce the labor-cost content of their tires to enable them to be more cost competitive with tires manufactured in low-wage locations. The average manufacturing costs of passenger car tires made in South Korea and Brazil were estimated to be in the $20 to $25 range in 1995. While tire plants in Japan were considered labor efficient, the rising value of the Japanese yen had undermined Japanese tire makers' use of an export strategy to capture a bigger share of the world market. In fact, the strong yen had made it economical for foreign tire makers to export tires to Japan (about 17 million in 1993).

For the most part, the high-cost producers of tires in 1995 were Continental's plants in Germany, Michelin's plants in France, Pirelli's plants in Italy, and the U.S. plants formerly owned by Firestone, Uniroyal Goodrich, General Tire, Armstrong, and Dunlop. Uniroyal Goodrich and Firestone were said to have the highest costs; at some plants labor costs approached 35 percent of total production costs.

Efforts to reduce labor costs at U.S. plants focused mainly on unionized plants and stressed efforts to boost worker productivity through automation, the elimination of costly work rules, and revamped work methods. Tire makers' relations with the United Rubber Workers Union had historically been stormy; the URW over the years had won, sometimes after long strikes, attractive wage and fringe benefit packages for its members. Each local union had also negotiated plant work rules that in many cases held down labor productivity. Labor militancy was a fact of life in most unionized plants, with grievance filings and arbitration of disputes being frequent occurrences. Younger union members, however, evidenced a greater willingness to accept proposed changes in work rules and work methods than older union members.

There were instances where tire production had been shifted from unionized plants with high labor costs to nonunion plants with lower labor costs. Eight of the nine tire plants built in the United States since 1970 were nonunion and had been located in states and communities where the threat of union organization was weak. All U.S. tire plants closed since 1970 had been unionized plants. Exhibit 12 shows how many plants the world's leading tire makers have, their geographic locations, their unionized status, and their tire-making capacities.

Exhibit 10   Hourly Compensation Costs for Production Workers in the Rubber and Plastics Industry, 1985, 1990–1993   *(in U.S. dollars)*

Country	1985	1990	1991	1992	1993
France	$ 7.80	$16.15	$16.14	$17.64	$17.15
Germany	10.11	23.06	23.77	n.a.	n.a.
Italy	8.22	19.71	20.13	21.18	17.32
Japan	7.58	15.80	18.73	20.65	23.45
Mexico	2.05	2.35	2.77	3.38	n.a.
South Korea	1.34	4.11	4.89	5.35	n.a.
United States	14.29	16.66	17.45	18.08	18.61

The figures include the impact of exchange rate fluctuations. This explains the decline in hourly compensation costs between 1992 and 1993 for both France and Italy as well as some of the large jumps in compensation between 1985–90 for France, Germany, Italy, Japan, and South Korea. In Japan's case the yen has been steadily rising in value against the dollar, thus accounting for much of the increase in hourly compensation costs in Japan for the entire 1985–93 period. Currency exchange rates are provided in Exhibit 11.

Source: U.S. Bureau of Labor Statistics, November 1994.

Exhibit 11   Currency Exchange Rates, per U.S. Dollar, 1985, 1990–1994

Country	1985	1990	1991	1992	1993	1994
Brazil (cruzeiro)	3168	8.85	161.02	1040	17020	316.27
France (franc)	8.980	5.447	5.647	5.294	5.667	5.909
Germany (mark)	2.942	1.617	1.661	1.562	1.655	1.736
Italy (lira)	1909	1198	1241	1232	1573	1713
Japan (yen)	238.5	145.0	134.6	126.8	111.1	111.6
South Korea (won)	870.0	707.8	733.4	780.6	802.7	808.1

Sources: U.S. Bureau of Labor Statistics and *The Wall Street Journal.*

COMPETITION AMONG TIRE PRODUCERS

In 1995, competition in tires centered around the variables of price and tire performance. The retail prices of tires of all types had trended downward in most world markets for over a decade (see Exhibit 9 for the price trends in the United States). Because tire makers had invested heavily in improving tread-wear mileage, traction, handling, braking, and high-speed safety, overall tire quality and tire performance was significantly better in 1995 than it had been in 1985. The rising tread life on OE and replacement tires had the potential to cut deeply into the number of sets of replacement tires needed per vehicle in service. Moreover, competition among the tire makers was increasingly global.

In the U.S. market, the tires of foreign-headquartered companies had become more visible and better known. In 1995, roughly 20 percent of all the new passenger cars sold in the United States were made at plants in Europe and Japan. Many European cars came equipped with Michelin, Pirelli, or Continental tires, and most Japanese car imports were equipped with Bridgestone, Sumitomo, Yokohama, or Toyo tires.

Exhibit 12   Plants and Estimated Production Capabilities of Major Tire Producers, 1994

Company/Plant Location	Number of Plants	Union Plants	Employees	Estimated Capacity (units per day)
Michelin				
North America	8	0	10,250	70,000
Europe	31	31	61,961	625,000
Asia	2	2	3,700	26,100
Latin America/Africa	3	n.a.	800	4,500
Total	44	33	76,711	725,600
Uniroyal Goodrich (Michelin)				
North America	7	6	9,870	136,700
Latin America (Bogota)	4	4	2,162	12,800
Totals	11	10	12,032	149,500
Goodyear				
North America	10	8	17,280	217,700
Europe	7	7	9,790	106,400
Asia/Australia/New Zealand	12	12	7,029	56,000
Latin America/Africa	11	11	11,200	84,210
Totals	40	38	45,299	464,310
Kelly-Springfield (Goodyear)				
U.S.	3	3	5,950	120,500
Totals	3	3	5,950	120,500
Bridgestone/Firestone				
North America	10	9	11,685	143,400
Europe	5	5	6,415	64,450
Asia/Australia/New Zealand	15	15	13,751	243,282
Latin America/Africa	7	7	8,568	54,139
Totals	37*	36	40,419	505,271
Continental/General				
U.S.	4	3	4,600	78,250
Europe	11	11	21,250	180,550
Pakistan	1	0	1,000	2,225
Latin America/Africa	2	2	1,250	5,856
Totals	18	16	28,100	266,881
Sumitomo/Dunlop				
U.S.	2	2	2,400	37,500
Europe	6	6	6,010	77,500
Japan	5	5	4,241	58,500
Totals	13	13	12,651	173,500

* The 1988 acquisition of Firestone included 22 plants. Eight plants were located in North America, five in Europe, one in the Philippines, one in New Zealand, and seven in Latin America/Africa.

Source: *Rubber & Plastics News*, August 15, 1994, pp. 43–49.

Exhibit 12   Concluded

Company/Plant Location	Number of Plants	Union Plants	Employees	Estimated Capacity (units per day)
Pirelli				
U.S. (Armstrong)	2	2	1,255	29,500
Europe	9	9	7,390	85,100
Latin America/Africa	8	7	5,840	54,200
Totals	19	18	14,485	168,800
Cooper Tire and Rubber				
U.S.	4	2	3,600	105,700
Totals	4	2	3,600	105,700
Yokohama				
U.S. (Mohawk)	1	1	831	18,500
Japan	6	6	6,050	75,000
Totals	7	7	6,881	93,500
Hankook				
South Korea	2	2	4,023	71,500
Totals	2	2	4,023	71,500
Kumho				
South Korea	2	2	2,860	58,200
Totals	2	2	2,860	58,200
Toyo Tire				
Japan	2	2	1,700	26,500
Totals	2	2	1,700	26,500

Bridgestone was the first Japanese tire company to produce tires in the United States; it began manufacturing truck tires in the United States in 1984, acquiring a truck tire plant from Firestone. Between 1984 and 1988, Bridgestone worked hard to expand its network of retail dealers to provide better access to replacement tire buyers. Its 1988 acquisition of Firestone gave it a six-plant production base in North America and a network of some 4,000 retail tire outlets and auto care centers.

Michelin had built a nationwide network of U.S. dealers years earlier and was represented by over 7,000 dealers in all cities and most towns—many of these dealers carried the Michelin brand as their feature line. Exhibit 13 shows the number of retail dealers handling the major brands of replacement tires in the United States. The Michelin name was well known and widely advertised in the United States, Europe, and parts of Asia. Michelin's market share in replacement tire was much lower than for OE tires because of its premium pricing strategy. The top-dollar prices for Michelin replacements were too steep for some would-be buyers, giving dealers the opportunity to switch them over to another brand in the store, often a brand carrying a larger percentage profit margin. Dealers typically earned lower profit

Exhibit 13   Number of U.S. Retail Outlets Carrying Selected Tire Brands, 1991

Tire Brand (parent company)	Number of Retail Points of Sale
Armstrong (Pirelli)	978
Bridgestone (Bridgestone Corp.)	5,960
Cooper (Cooper Tire and Rubber)	1,518
Dunlop (Sumitomo)	2,046
Firestone (Bridgestone)	4,208
General (Continental A.G.)	2,107
Goodrich (Michelin)	4,215
Goodyear (Goodyear Tire and Rubber)	7,964
Kelly-Springfield (Goodyear)	2,421
Michelin (Groupe Michelin)	7,169
Pirelli (Pirelli Group)	2,133
Uniroyal (Michelin)	2,321

Source: Market Data Book 1991, *Tire Business*, p. 14.

margins on the name-brand replacement tires of the leading manufacturers than they did on lesser-known brands and private-label brands.

Michelin, Pirelli, Bridgestone, Sumitomo, Yokohama, Toyo, and the Korean tire producers (Hankook and Kumko) were all trying to increase their market shares in North America. Recent increases in the value of the Japanese yen against U.S. and European currencies had been a driving force behind the Japanese decision to acquire tire-making facilities in the United States and Europe to support the long-term strategic objective of winning a bigger share of the global tire market. The Japanese and Korean tire makers dominated the tire market in countries in the Pacific and Southeast Asia except for New Zealand and Australia; Goodyear had a strong presence in New Zealand and Australia. Michelin had the strongest foreign presence in Japan.

Japanese efforts to penetrate the European market had not met with as much success as in the United States. Japanese cars accounted for between 10 and 12 percent of new car sales in Europe and for just under 10 percent of total car registrations, making it harder for the Japanese tire makers to enter the replacement tire segment just on the basis of selling Japanese-made replacement tires for Japanese-made cars. In terms of overall new car–truck production in Europe, U.S. manufacturers (Ford and GM) had about a 23 percent market share, the Japanese about an 11 percent share, and the European manufacturers a 66 percent share. In Europe, the market leaders in tires were Michelin, Continental, Goodyear, Bridgestone/Firestone, Pirelli, and Dunlop. Sumitomo's acquisition of Dunlop's troubled and unprofitable European operations gave it a familiar brand name to use in growing its share of the European tire market. Distribution channels for replacement tires in Europe functioned in much the same manner as in the United States, with a competitive focus on price, performance, and strong dealer networks.

In recent years, the European tire market had been characterized by a fierce price war. Between 1988 and 1991, European producers had cut prices on some tire models as much as 40 percent to win OE orders from automotive manufacturers. In 1990 alone, prices on OE tires had fallen 17 percent. Continental's CEO observed,

"We are only a handful of players. In spite of that, we are fighting each other like hell."[5] Price competition in Europe had moderated some in 1993 and 1994 but rivalry still remained very strong.

Restructuring and Diversification

Slowdowns in unit volume growth, a stiffening of competitive pressures brought on by market maturity, and declining profit prospects in tires during the 1970s had prompted the leading U.S. tire manufacturers to take a hard look at their dependence on tires and to consider just what their future course should be. Goodyear, Firestone, Goodrich, General Tire, and Uniroyal all concluded that market maturity in tires called for diversification into other businesses to open up new avenues for growth and profitability. Each began to make acquisitions. By the early 1980s, their business portfolios included investments in plastics, aerospace, flooring, footwear, rubberized roofing, petroleum production and transportation, chemicals, packaging film, and a variety of industrial products. By the mid-1980s, however, most U.S. tire manufacturers were retreating from their forays into diversification and were in a restructuring/retrenchment mode. Diversification had proved more or less disastrous, siphoning off funds that were needed to strengthen their core tire business and leaving them vulnerable to competition from foreign tire producers. In many instances, diversification had not proved to be as profitable as the tire business. In the mid-1980s, GenCorp, Inc. (the parent of General Tire) announced the sale of certain of its television stations, the closing of a bias-ply tire plant, and a significant stock repurchase program. Firestone's diversified businesses, which accounted for 25 percent of sales in 1979, made up less than 5 percent by year-end 1986; businesses that were divested included plastic resins, beer kegs, automotive seat belts, polyurethane foam, and wheels for trucks, tractors, and construction machinery. Uniroyal in the mid-1980s divested all of its nontire operations and then merged its entire tire business with the tire division of BF Goodrich to form Uniroyal Goodrich Tire Company; two years later, it was acquired by Groupe Michelin.

PROFILES OF THE LEADING COMPETITORS

In 1995, the world tire industry was struggling to emerge from the throes of a fierce price war and a global battle for market share. Late in 1994, tire manufacturers took steps to end their price war, announcing modest price increases of 2 to 4 percent; a second round of price increase announcements came in January 1995. It remained to be seen whether the announced price increases would stick. Exhibit 14 shows recent financial results for selected leading producers. Exhibit 15 presents 1993 R&D expenditures and capital investment figures for the market leaders.

Goodyear Tire and Rubber Co.

Goodyear's core business was the development, manufacture, distribution, and sale of tires throughout the world. Tires and tubes represented 86 percent of Goodyear's corporate sales of $12.3 billion in 1994; other products and businesses included an oil and gas production and pipeline subsidiary, and the manufacture of nontire

---

[5]As quoted in *Business Week*, February 27, 1990, p. 63.

Exhibit 14   Comparative Statistics on the 10 Largest Tire Manufacturers, 1985, 1990–1994

Company	Year	Sales	Net Income (Loss)	Assets	Stockholders' Equity	Number of Employees
Goodyear	1985	$ 9,897	$ 412	$ 6,954	$3,507	134,115
	1990	11,453	(38)	8,964	2,098	107,671
	1991	11,046	97	8,511	2,731	99,952
	1992	11,924	(659)	8,564	1,930	95,712
	1993	11,643	388	8,436	2,301	90,384
	1994	12,288	567	9,123	2,803	90,094
Michelin	1985	5,191	110	7,041	968	120,000
	1990	11,522	(1,089)	14,914	2,173	140,826
	1991	11,996	(124)	15,399	2,021	140,000
	1992	12,623	15	n.a.	n.a.	125,000
	1993	11,175	(698)	12,619	n.a.	124,575
	1994	12,120	246	13,142	n.a.	117,776
Bridgestone	1985	3,624	88	3,781	1,387	32,834
	1990	12,395	29	12,883	3,247	95,276
	1991	13,226	54	14,465	3,514	83,081
	1992	13,860	224	14,788	3,647	85,835
	1993	14,377	255	15,769	4,380	87,332
	1994	15,608	312	17,086	5,289	89,711
Pirelli	1985	3,650	101	3,200	1,500	61,500
	1990	6,202	(9)	6,329	2,321	68,703
	1991	6,112	(530)	5,783	1,449	64,854
	1992	5,875	(260)	5,430	1,279	45,726
	1993	5,612	248	5,017	1,531	42,132
	1994	5,495	(34)	4,933	2,077	
Continental	1985	1,699	26	1,159	229	31,673
	1990	5,301	58	4,120	1,054	51,064
	1991	5,657	(78)	4,375	906	49,877
	1992	6,202	84	4,358	905	50,581
	1993	5,666	47	4,100	863	50,974
	1994	6,585	45	4,341	1,106	49,025
Sumitomo	1985	975	9	1,052	89	6,900
	1990	3,788	8	3,713	384	21,000
	1991	4,219	30	4,267	441	22,000
	1992	4,579	48	4,408	481	23,000
	1993	4,526	41	4,881	614	22,000
	1994	n.a.	n.a.	n.a.	n.a.	n.a.
Yokohama	1985	1,264	18	1,319	119	10,775
	1990	2,963	67	3,004	481	12,722
	1991	3,310	38	3,464	687	13,346
	1992	3,429	38	3,700	707	13,888
	1993	3,598	(2)	3,983	785	13,684
	1994	n.a.	n.a.	n.a.	n.a.	n.a.

Sources: Company annual reports, Fortune Global 500 listing for various years, and Bloomberg Financial News Service.

Exhibit 14   Concluded

Company	Year	Sales	Net Income (Loss)	Assets	Stockholders' Equity	Number of Employees
Cooper Tire and Rubber	1985	522	19	295	176	4,876
	1990	896	67	616	369	6,225
	1991	1,001	79	671	440	6,545
	1992	1,175	43	797	471	7,207
	1993	1,194	102	890	550	7,607
	1994	1,406	129	1,039	662	7,815
Toyo Tire	1985	693	5	500	58	n.a.
	1990	1,757	20	1,711	334	n.a.
	1991	1,867	9	1,937	354	4,012
	1992	1,698	23	1,883	462	n.a.
	1993	1,846	5	2,035	507	n.a.
	1994	1,792	(24)	2,226	542	3,821

automotive products, synthetic rubber, chemicals, and high-technology items for aerospace, defense, and other applications. In addition to Goodyear tires, the company owned Kelly-Springfield Tire Co. and Lee Tire and Rubber Co.; both Kelly-Springfield and Lee made private-label tires in addition to their own branded tires. Until the merger–consolidation wave in 1986–1990, Goodyear had been both the world's largest tire producer and the world's largest rubber manufacturer; it had held this ranking since the 1920s.

The company operated 43 tire products plants in 28 countries and had four rubber plantations. Its major tire-making locations were North America (13 plants), Germany (2 plants), Luxembourg, Britain, and Brazil (2 plants). It had recently acquired majority interest in a small tire company in China and was negotiating to acquire tire companies in Poland. The company owned and operated almost 1,900 retail tire and service centers around the world. Goodyear and Toyo Tire were joint venture partners in a Japanese plant that produced tires for large-scale vehicles and off-the-road equipment. Goodyear in 1995 controlled about 35 percent of the tire-making capacity in North America and between 15 and 20 percent of the world's tire-making capacity. Foreign sales accounted for about 42 percent of revenues. About 40 percent of Goodyear's tire sales were to the OE market and 60 percent to the replacement market.

Goodyear had the broadest line of tire products of any manufacturer. Its reputation for tire quality was good to excellent, generally on a par with Michelin and slightly ahead of Bridgestone. Goodyear was a world leader in high-performance radial tires; its Goodyear Eagle line enjoyed a strong reputation for quality and performance, as did its Aquatred line. The strategy at Kelly-Springfield and Lee Tire was to provide dealers with an array of brands in a descending price scale below the flagship Goodyear brand; as of 1995, Kelly-Springfield and Lee were the number one producer and distributor to the private-label segment.

The Goodyear brand was the leader in both the North American market (the world's largest) and in Latin America. The company ranked number two in market share everywhere in the Asian market outside of Japan (behind Bridgestone). In

Exhibit 15 R&D Expenditures and Capital Spending of Leading Tire Manufacturers, 1993 *(in millions of U.S. dollars)*

	1993 R&D Expenditures	1993 Capital Investment
Groupe Michelin	$560.0	$ 489.4
Bridgestone	380.3	1,045.1
Goodyear	320.0	432.3
Continental	227.1	378.2
Yokohama	126.2	170.4
Sumitomo	114.5	306.6
Pirelli Tire Group	105.0	107.2
Toyo	70.3	54.1
Kumho	33.1	256.0
Hankook	31.6	110.0
Cooper Tire and Rubber	15.1	117.2

Source: *Tire Business*, November 14, 1994, p. 15.

Europe, Goodyear was challenging Continental for the number two ranking behind Michelin; going into 1995 Goodyear had the third-largest share in Europe, slightly ahead of Pirelli. Most recently, Goodyear had backed off supplying OE tires to European carmakers because of cutthroat pricing.

For over a decade, Goodyear had been aggressively pursuing cost reduction and plant modernization programs at its tire plants—the company invested $4 billion in tire plant modernization during the 1980s and plant productivity had improved substantially worldwide. Since 1985, output per worker-hour in North American plants had risen 52 percent. The workforce had been downsized by 23,000 people (20 percent) since 1987. On average, Goodyear's production costs for tires were below average worldwide. Goodyear's goal was to become a still lower cost producer.

Goodyear was active in purchasing multi-outlet retailers, and its sales force was striving to convert independent tire dealers over to the Goodyear brand and to win new accounts for Kelly-Springfield and Lee tires. Goodyear saw the replacement market as holding the biggest potential for increasing its market share. Goodyear's share of the U.S. replacement market was only 15.5 percent, well below its 38 percent share of the U.S. OE segment.

The company consistently appeared on the list of the top 50 leading national advertisers. It had maintained a high profile in auto racing for over 20 years in an effort to stress the high-performance capabilities of its tires. Goodyear promoted its tires with the slogan, "The best tires in the world have Goodyear written all around them." The name Goodyear was one of the best-known brand names in the world, and in the United States its Goodyear blimps were a prominent advertising symbol.

In June 1991, Goodyear's board of directors in a surprise move decided to replace the company's CEO; chosen as new CEO was Stanley C. Gault, who only two months earlier had retired as CEO of Rubbermaid Corporation. Gault had joined Goodyear's board in 1989 and was regarded as a very effective chief executive with a talent for product innovation and aggressive marketing. Gault immediately elevated the already high emphasis on Goodyear's companywide program to become a low-cost producer, setting a goal of reducing costs by $350 million within three years. In addition, Gault set programs in motion to boost sales by introducing new types of tires. The Aquatred line was introduced in early 1992; by 1995, 21 other new styles and models had been introduced, including a run-flat tire. To boost its stagnant share of the U.S. replacement tire segment, Goodyear recruited Sears to sell seven lines of Goodyear tires at Sears's 875 auto centers; Goodyear's research showed that some 2 million Goodyear tires a year were being replaced by tires bought at Sears. Wal-Mart and Sam's began selling Kelly-Springfield's Douglas brand tires in 1991 and Goodyear brand tires in 1993. To overcome dealer protests, Goodyear had begun reserving certain tire lines for sale only by independent dealers and company-owned outlets. Gault also boosted Goodyear's brand advertising by one-third (to $50 million annually) and increased the amount available for co-op ads with dealers. On the financial front, Gault sold off several businesses not related to tires and used the proceeds to reduce debt. Within six months, Gault had cut Goodyear's debt level from $3.7 billion to $2 billion and gotten the company out from under a crushing $1 million-a-day interest burden. By 1994, Gault's financial restructuring had resulted in debt of just $1.4 billion.

Since Gault's appointment, Goodyear's stock price had risen 400 percent. In 1994, Goodyear's earnings of $567 million were greater than its major competitors combined (see Exhibit 12).

Groupe Michelin

Groupe Michelin was a French company that had about $9.5 billion in worldwide tire sales in 1994 and total sales of $12.1 billion. Michelin's acquisition of Uniroyal Goodrich propelled it past Goodyear to be the global market share leader. Michelin operated 65 tire plants in 15 countries. Geographically, Michelin was strongest in Europe (where it had a market share of approximately 30 percent) and the United States (where its overall market share was about 21 percent).

Michelin was the acknowledged leader in radial tire technology, and its reputation for radial tire quality was the best in the world. The company was extremely secretive about its tire-making practices, and its R&D budget was the highest in the industry (see Exhibit 13). It was aggressively trying to reopen its competitive edge in radial tire technology and had recently introduced tire lines that incorporated advanced tire-making techniques. Michelin passenger car tires were generally premium priced and appealed mainly to quality-sensitive buyers who drove relatively expensive cars. Truck-owners were attracted to Michelin brand tires because of tread wear and a longer life-cycle (in terms of being retreadable); Michelin was the world leader in heavy-duty truck tires. Michelin drummed the theme to OE and replacement tire buyers that its tires deserved a price premium because they were unmatched in terms of quality and performance. In 1991, Michelin introduced a line of passenger tires guaranteed to deliver 80,000 miles of tread wear. Industry observers believed if tires with a tread-wear life of 80,000 miles worked their way into the OE market that the repercussions on the replacement market would be far-reaching. According to one official, if new vehicles came equipped with 80,000-mile tires, "by the time the owner replaces the OE tires, he won't be planning to keep the car much longer, and he won't be looking at first-line replacement tires."[6] In late 1994, Michelin began introducing tires made with its newly

---

[6] As quoted in *Tire Business*, January 13, 1992, p. 13.

developed Radial XSE technology. The company prided itself on being science and technology driven rather than marketing or customer driven.

Michelin had reported losses in three of the past four years and had debt of almost $6 billion, nearly three times its total equity. The company had downsized its workforce by 22,000 people (out of a total of 141,000) since 1990. Michelin's problems stemmed primarily from the price war in the European OE tire segment, from its Uniroyal Goodrich acquisition, and from its status as a high-cost producer. Michelin was the least efficient major producer in the industry, with wage costs equal to 41 percent of sales in 1992. Uniroyal Goodrich was also a high-cost producer, had older and less efficient plants, and was losing U.S. market share. Michelin was gradually but steadily introducing its technology and management approaches at its seven Uniroyal Goodrich plants.

During 1994, Michelin took a hardline approach with the URW in insisting on shift schedule changes and flexible work practices at its five unionized Uniroyal Goodrich plants, announcing it would close any plant that did not accept its proposal changes; ultimately, workers voted to accept the changes at all five Uniroyal Goodrich plants in the United States and Canada. So far, Michelin had not asked for cuts in wages and benefits at Uniroyal Goodrich plants, but union officials predicted that Michelin would next come to them with requests to reduce the current hourly wage of nearly $18.

Michelin had opted to maintain separate sales forces and distribution facilities for each of its three flag brands—Michelin, Uniroyal, and BF Goodrich. Michelin had positioned the Michelin brand as the top quality, premium-priced radial in both the OE and replacement markets in the United States (as well as elsewhere in the world). The BF Goodrich brand was being positioned to focus on the performance and light truck segments in the U.S. replacement market. Uniroyal brands were being aimed at the OE segment (where Uniroyal had long had a presence, chiefly as a supplier to General Motors) and at the middle of the replacement segment for vehicle owners seeking a medium-grade tire at a medium or average price. Michelin's marketing goal was to minimize competition and overlap among the three brands and to cover as wide a portion of the total U.S. market as feasible.

Bridgestone Tire

Bridgestone controlled a dominant 50 percent share of the Japanese passenger tire market and had strength in truck tires as well. It was the second-largest tire producer worldwide and it was normally the most profitable of the four largest Japanese tire makers. Bridgestone had become the leading Japanese producer following World War II using technology licensed from Goodyear. The company had made substantial technology investments of its own in recent years and was an accomplished manufacturer of radial tires.

Bridgestone had moved swiftly in 1988 to acquire Firestone when rumors surfaced of Pirelli's strong interest in buying Firestone. To block Pirelli's bid, Bridgestone offered a stunning $2.6 billion for Firestone, an amount most observers believed far exceeded Firestone's value. Following the acquisition, Bridgestone announced a three-year, $1.5 billion program to modernize Firestone's operations and to construct a new $350 million radial truck tire plant near Bridgestone's existing plant outside Nashville (acquired from Firestone in 1984). Bridgestone also renamed its Firestone unit Bridge-stone/Firestone Inc. (BFS). In 1990, BFS suffered $350 million in losses, bringing Bridgestone's overall profits down to just $29 million on sales of $12.4 billion. In mid-1991, Bridgestone replaced BFS chairman George Aucott with Yichiro Kaizaki, a

Bridgestone executive VP and top aide to Bridgestone's CEO. When Kaizaki was later promoted to CEO of Bridgestone's worldwide operations, Masatoshi Ono became BFS's CEO. BFS had recently moved its headquarters from Akron to Nashville.

In 1991, Bridgestone's subsidiaries in the United States (BFS), Latin America, and Europe (Bridgestone/Firestone Europe) posted losses of $500 million; going into 1992, only three of Bridgestone's geographic divisions were operating at a profit—its Japanese operation and its units in Thailand and Indonesia.

In Europe, Bridgestone trailed Michelin, Continental, and Goodyear. The Firestone acquisition gave Bridgestone a five-plant manufacturing base in Europe. Tires were marketed under both the Firestone and Bridgestone labels. The company's high-performance tires had been specified as original equipment on selected Jaguar, Porsche, and Ferrari models.

Bridgestone's areas of greatest market strength outside Japan and the United States were mainly in Asia, the Pacific, and South America, where Japanese cars and trucks were being heavily marketed. The company had strong market share momentum, was spending heavily on product innovation and improved facilities, and was viewed as the only company in the industry currently capable of challenging Goodyear and Michelin on a truly global scale. Bridgestone's newest truck tire plant in Warren County, Tennessee, was one of the most technologically advanced plants in the world. Bridgestone was one of the industry leaders in run-flat technology and produced over 100 million passenger and light truck tires annually.

At the time of its acquisition by Bridgestone, Firestone had foreign tire and related products facilities in Argentina, Brazil, Canada, France, Italy, Portugal, Spain, Venezuela, and New Zealand and had minority interests in tire operations in Mexico, South Africa, Thailand, Kenya, and the Philippines; the plant in Spain was the largest of Firestone's foreign operations. Additionally, Firestone owned a rubber plantation in Liberia and manufactured a major part of its requirements for synthetic rubber, rayon polyester, and nylon cord. The company produced and marketed a broad line of tires for automobiles, trucks, trailers, buses, construction vehicles, agricultural machinery, off-the-road vehicles, and other vehicles for both the OE and replacement markets. Besides Firestone brand tires, the company marketed tires under the Dayton and Road King names. In 1983, Firestone had acquired J.C. Penney automotive centers. As of 1988, Firestone owned and operated approximately 1,500 retail automotive centers, which offered a wide range of maintenance and repair services under the "MasterCare by Firestone" program and which doubled as retail tire outlets. Firestone tires were also sold through independent dealers and some service stations. Bridgestone viewed Firestone's plants and distribution channels as a major asset in building the geographic base it needed to compete globally.

In 1994, Bridgestone established new tire sales companies in Poland, Hungary, and the Czech Republic to broaden its presence in Eastern Europe. It also introduced a new snow tire line named Blizzak that delivered ice and snow traction comparable to a studded tire; initial sales were good enough to warrant claims that Bridgestone had taken a leadership role in the snow tire segment.

Pirelli Tire

Tire operations accounted for about $2.8 billion of the Pirelli Tire Company's total corporatewide sales of $5.5 billion in 1994. Pirelli's tire business worldwide had lost money every year since 1991. The price war in Europe and efforts to restructure Armstrong's tire operations in the United States had eroded its margins.

Pirelli was seen as astute at picking good tire market niches to concentrate on. Pirelli had edged Michelin for the leadership position in the European high-performance tire segment. Substantial numbers of European sports cars came equipped with Pirelli tires made at its Italian plants. In 1995, Pirelli operated 19 tire plants in 11 countries.

When Pirelli failed at acquiring Firestone, it immediately proceeded to buy Armstrong Tire and Rubber, which operated three tire plants in the United States and had sales of about $700 million. Armstrong competed only in the replacement tire market and was a major supplier of private-label tires—its biggest private-label customer was Sears. Pirelli quickly launched a four-year $200 million program to update Armstrong's plants and changed the company's name to Pirelli Armstrong. Pirelli also took immediate steps to boost the sale of its Pirelli brand in the United States by combining the sales forces and distribution efforts of the Pirelli and Armstrong brands and offering Armstrong's nearly 1,000 retail dealers a broader range of products with little overlap. The Pirelli brand was positioned at the high-performance and premium-priced end of the market (giving dealers a brand to compete against Goodyear and Michelin), while the Armstrong brand, which was strongest in the farm market, was promoted as a medium-range, more-value-for-the-dollar type of tire for price-conscious buyers. The company stopped making truck tires for the U.S. market. In early 1992, Pirelli initiated actions to convert Armstrong's newly modernized Hanford plant, where Pirelli tire-building equipment had been installed, from producing mostly Armstrong and private-label tires over to producing 100 percent Pirelli-brand production by 1995. In 1994, Pirelli sold the Pirelli Armstrong tire plant in Des Moines, Iowa, which made farm tires, to Tital Wheel International. Sale of the Des Moines plant effectively removed Pirelli from competing in the farm tire segment, once an Armstrong strength. As of 1995, Pirelli Armstrong's efforts were focused on high-performance Pirelli tires and private-label tires.

In 1994, the United Rubber Workers union (1,700 employees) struck the U.S. factories of Pirelli Armstrong because of unacceptable health care and pension plans. Pirelli Armstrong management announced that medical benefits for 3,000 retirees would be phased out, starting in October 1994. PA's management had, in addition, requested an infusion of $100 million in capital from Pirelli, its corporate parent, to cover expected losses of about $55 million in 1994 (including retiree health care expenses of about $31 million).

In 1991, Pirelli sought to merge with Continental. Pirelli's management held extensive negotiations with reluctant Continental officials over several months and spent a reported $300 million trying to put a merger together. No agreement was reached. Pirelli had argued that its Brazilian operations would complement Continental's two Mexican plants and that Pirelli's market strength in Italy and southern Europe was an ideal match with Continental's strength in Germany and northern Europe. Together, argued Pirelli, they could mount a more effective attack on the Eastern Europe and U.S. markets. Since the failed merger attempt, Pirelli had been divesting businesses unrelated to its core tire and cable operations, selling seven of the nine business units in its diversified products division. In addition, the company had downsized its tire and cable workforce by 20 percent. In tires, Pirelli was putting more focus on the replacement tire segment because margins on OE tires were nonexistent.

Continental AG

Continental was Germany's largest tire producer and the number two company, behind Michelin, in Europe. Worldwide, Continental was the fourth-largest manufacturer of radial truck tires and the fifth-largest maker of radial passenger tires. Its acquisition of General Tire made it the world's fourth-largest producer (up from sixth in 1986). Continental supplied OE tires to Mercedes-Benz, BMW, Volvo, Audi, Volkswagon, and Porsche. Continental was committed to product development and research. Its tires were viewed as premium quality and it offered independent tire dealers attractive profit margins. In 1995, Continental had 22 tire plants in 14 countries; 13 of the company's tire plants were in Europe and 6 were in the United States and Mexico. Tires were marketed under nine brands.

In 1987, when Continental acquired General Tire, it said that the relationships between Continental and General brands in the United States would be patterned after its European approach, where its flag brands (Continental, Uniroyal Englebert, and Semperit) all competed with each other for market share. However, in 1991, Continental decided to merge its sales force for the Continental and General brands under General Tire management. The plan was to position General Tires in the mainstream portion of the market and target Continental brands for the upscale and high-performance segments, thus ending brand overlap and offering dealers more models to better cover the price-quality spectrum.[7] Continental believed this approach would encourage more dealers to carry both brands—as of 1992 only 20 percent of the combined dealer network carried both brands. The new program also offered dealers the advantages of combined delivery, common purchase terms, the ability to avoid duplicating inventories on sizes and models, and more economical co-op advertising packages.

Meanwhile, on the production side, Continental launched a five-year, $670 million program to modernize General's U.S. and Canadian plants, improve efficiency, and eliminate a host of chronic quality problems. Although Continental had expected its General Tire operations to break even in 1993, sales of the General brand proved weaker than expected and the unit lost $21 million in 1993. In late 1993, General replaced or eliminated 8 of its 19 vice presidents and reorganized sales and management; to cover the division's losses, Continental injected $100 million in new capital. Since Continental's acquisition in 1987, General Tire's sales had remained flat in the $1.3 to $1.4 billion range, the unit had lost money in four out of the last seven years, and combined net earnings for the 1988–94 period were a *negative* $300 million. Even though General's management believed in 1994 that its quality problems were finally licked, Continental's management was beginning to question whether the company could prosper in the North American market with operations that were only 10 percent the size of Goodyear. In 1994, Continental assigned a German executive to run General's tire business, the fourth president to attempt a turnaround since 1987. Besides the General Tire division in the United States, Continental also engaged in a joint venture with Yokohama and Toyo in a $200 million truck tire plant in Mount Vernon, Illinois.

Continental had strengthened its access to the replacement market by buying a 400-unit retail chain in Great Britain and buying minority interests in 400 additional retail outlets in Germany, Scotland, Canada, and the United States. To overcome its handicap of having the highest labor costs of any tire producer in Europe (and among the highest in the world), Continental had cut its German and U.S. workforce by over 20 percent (12,000 employees) since 1991 and moved about one-fourth of its tire production to the Czech Republic, Slovenia, Poland, and Portugal. In addition, management was working with its unions in Germany to reduce its costly benefit

---

[7]*Tire Business*, November 4, 1991, p. 12.

package and was instituting total quality management processes, team-based production methods, workforce downsizing of 4 percent, and leaner operating practices. The company's CEO had expressed a desire for Continental to remain independent but said, "if we don't do better, all options of new alliances are open."[8]

Sumitomo Rubber Industries

Sumitomo had the third-largest share of the Japanese tire market and was the world's sixth-largest tire maker. Following World War II, Sumitomo acquired tire-making technology under an ongoing licensing agreement with Uniroyal. In 1986, Sumitomo acquired the European tire business of Dunlop Tire, making it the first Japanese producer to establish a major European base; the acquisition involved two tire plants in France and the use of the Dunlop brand name in Europe.[9] A few years later, Sumitomo purchased Dunlop's two U.S. tire plants in Buffalo, New York, and Huntsville, Alabama; in the United States, Dunlop supplied some OE tires and had a 2.5 percent share of the replacement market. Going into 1992, Sumitomo operated 18 tire plants in 7 countries.

Sumitomo was trying to increase its share in OE tires in the United States and Europe via its Dunlop brand and was marketing both its Sumitomo and Dunlop brands in the replacement tire segment. It sold replacement tires through wholesale distributors in the United States, who in turn marketed them to independent tire dealers as a second or third line. Sumitomo had recruited dealers by offering them above-average margins and, as early as 1991, had started providing buyers of its replacement tires with a written 60,000-mile guarantee, something few other tire makers were willing to do at that time.

In recent years, Sumitomo had invested over $250 million to modernize the Dunlop tire plants in the United States and Europe and to boost labor productivity. In 1990, output per worker at the two U.S. Dunlop plants was only 60 percent of that at Sumitomo's plants in Japan. In 1994, Sumitomo's two U.S. plants were struck by the URW.

Yokohama Tire Corporation

Yokohama was the second-largest tire company in Japan and the seventh-largest in the world. In 1994, Yokohama operated six tire plants in Japan and one in the United States (the Mohawk tire plant in Salem, Virginia, acquired in 1989). It was also in a joint venture with Toyo and General in a truck tire plant in Illinois. Years ago, Yokohama had entered into a technology licensing agreement with BF Goodrich; in exchange for its technology BFG received a minority ownership position in Yokohama Tire. Yokohama's strategic objective was to become the world's fifth-largest manufacturer. Yokohama was concentrating its R&D efforts on advanced designs, better engineering, and innovation. In 1986, it introduced a new-style asymmetrical tire for the high-performance tire segment, and it offered truck tires that delivered proven fuel savings, retreadability, and long tread life.

---

[8]As quoted in *Fortune*, June 13, 1994, p. 118.

[9]British-based Dunlop had also divested itself of two tire plants in India (the new owners retained use of the Dunlop name in India). The company, BTR plc, still had controlling interest in five tire plants in Africa (Nigeria, Zambia, Zimbabwe, and South Africa), which marketed under the Dunlop name. The Dunlop brand was the world's fourth best-selling brand (see Exhibit 2) when worldwide sales of all tires carrying the Dunlop name were combined.

In the United States, Yokohama was one of the suppliers of tires to "price club" and "warehouse club" retail outlets. Warehouse clubs accounted for 8.5 percent of passenger tire replacements in 1994, up from 2 percent in 1985.

Cooper Tire and Rubber Co.

Cooper Tire and Rubber was the ninth-largest tire producer and marketer in the world. The company had total sales of $1.4 billion in 1994, tires sales of $1 billion, and four tire plants, all in the United States. Based on tire-making capacity, Cooper was the fourth-largest of 15 tire producers in North America. During the 1990s, Cooper Tire had the biggest overall net profit margins on tire sales (net income as percentage of total sales) of any major tire manufacturer. It was the lowest cost producer in North America and one of the lowest cost producers in the world. The company's sales had more than tripled since 1980. It produced car tires, light truck tires, and medium truck tires.

Cooper marketed only through replacement tire channels. Its two biggest brands, Cooper and Mastercraft, were distributed through independent tire stores. About half of Cooper's production was devoted to making private-label tires for oil companies, mass merchandise retailers, and independent buying groups. Cooper's 10 largest customers accounted for 53 percent of sales. Because of its low-cost position, Cooper offered its distributors, dealers, and private-label customers low wholesale prices and the highest gross margins in the industry (about 33 percent versus the industry average of 28 percent). In recent years, Cooper had begun exporting tires to Canada and countries in Latin America, Western Europe, the Middle East, Asia, Africa, and Oceania; in 1994, tire exports to 80 countries accounted for 6 percent of Cooper's sales. The company had recently added a major customer in Japan.

All Cooper Tire employees were on an incentive plan. Hourly workers could more than double their base rate through incentives; salaried workers could earn bonuses of up to 7.5 percent based on the return on assets achieved in their area of responsibility. Executive compensation was tied to performance benchmarks and provided for cuts as well as raises of up to 30 percent. In 1994, wages and benefits averaged $48,850 per employee. The company was regarded as having excellent labor relations and a motivated workforce; it had two unionized plants and two nonunion plants. As a rule, all four plants operated at maximum capacity. Cooper's management was committed to improving manufacturing methods, expanding its tire-making capacity, and continuing its excellent reputation for customer service. In 1994, Cooper introduced 67 new and improved tire models, including an aquachannel model, a touring radial with a 60,000-mile warranty, an economy all-season radial with a 40,000-mile warranty, and new light truck radials for sports utility vehicles, vans, and pickup trucks.

Korean Tire Producers

Hankook and Kumho each had two plants located in South Korea. They were the dominant suppliers of OE tires to the growing and ambitious Korean auto producers. Kumho had one of the world's 10-largest tire manufacturing plants; the recently built plant was outfitted with advanced equipment and was among the lowest cost tire plants in the world. Kumho supplied over 100 countries with a full line of bias and steel radial tires for everything from small passenger cars to off-the-road earthmoving equipment. The company was diversified into petrochemicals, rubber, electrical products, lubricants, and finance; it had 1994 sales totaling about $1.1 billion, about $900 million of which was from tires.

Hankook had total 1994 sales of about $900 million, 90 percent of which came from tires. Hankook's stated objective was to become one of the world's top seven tire makers by the end of the 1990s using a four-part strategy based on product innovation, increased production capacity, greater distribution capability in overseas markets, and reinforced sales and R&D activities. Over 50 percent of Hankook's sales were derived from tire exports. North America was Hankook's single largest overseas market.

Both Hankook and Kumho had built capacity aggressively on the expectation that the Korean car export business would grow rapidly. However, when Korean car exports grew slower than expected during the 1990s, Kumho and Hankook started using their excess capacity and their low-cost producer position to supply replacement tires to wholesale distributors and tire dealers in the United States and in other Pacific Rim markets. Hankook was constructing a new $1.6 billion plant in South Korea with capacity to make 5 million tires for cars, light and heavy trucks, and buses.

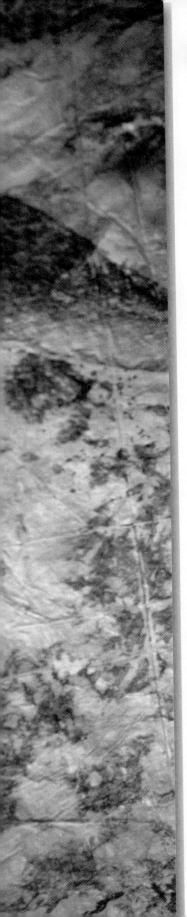

Whirlpool Corporation

Arthur A. Thompson, The University of Alabama
Bryan Fuller, The University of Alabama,

In 1995, Whirlpool Corporation was the world's leading producer and marketer of major home appliances. The company had manufacturing plants in 12 countries and marketed products in over 120 countries under such brands as Whirlpool, Kitchen-Aid, Roper, Estate, Bauknecht, Ignis, Laden, Inglis, Brastemp, Consul, and Semer. Whirlpool was also the principal supplier to Sears Roebuck and Co. of many major home appliances that Sears sold under its own private-label Kenmore brand.

Since 1988, Whirlpool had embarked on a strategy to globalize its home appliance business and to lead the industry's transformation from a collection of national markets and national competitors to a global market with global competitors. The strategy was the product of an assessment by Whirlpool's management of the appliance industry worldwide, of Whirlpool's current position as a North America–only producer and marketer, and of what Whirlpool's long-term strategic direction should be. The assessment, led by newly appointed CEO David Whitwam in 1987, produced several conclusions. First, profitable growth opportunities in the North American market were scarce. Competition was fierce and margins wafer-thin. Where once there had been several dozen North American appliance manufacturers, now there were four large, dominant players—Whirlpool, General Electric, Maytag, and White/Frigidaire, all positioned to do battle in a price-driven market characterized by relatively high saturation rates for major household appliances and up-and-down annual sales volumes.

Second, to continue to grow and flourish in the major home appliance business, Whirlpool would have to enter foreign markets and eventually become a global competitor. Just as had occurred in North America, the appliance industry in Europe was starting to consolidate, thus presenting Whirlpool with opportunities to enter the European market via acquisition. Moreover, with the advent of the European Common Market, management thought it was probable that the European market for appliances would evolve toward a single market with similar home appliances and away from its present state as a group of individual country markets with distinctly different home appliances. Latin America was seen as a region with enormous growth potential, given the low saturation rates of major home appliances. And Asia, by the year 2000, was expected to become the world's largest market for home appliances. Hence, to participate in the industry's future growth, management argued, Whirlpool would have to be a global player.

Third, Whirlpool's management concluded that global success would require a strong customer focus combined with best-cost, best-quality production and that

Whirlpool's North American home market would have to be profitable enough to provide much of the financial means for Whirlpool to invest in a long-term strategy to build a globally competitive position. Since the 1987 assessment, Whirlpool's management had not wavered in its commitment to an aggressive global strategy.

THE WORLD MARKET FOR HOME APPLIANCES

Major home appliances (often referred to as "white goods") consisted of kitchen appliances (ranges, cooking tops, ovens, refrigerators, freezers, garbage disposals, dishwashers, compactors, and microwaves), laundry appliances (washers and dryers), and to a lesser extent comfort appliances (room air conditioners and dehumidifiers). Appliance manufacture represented one of the world's largest consumer goods industries. Worldwide shipments of home appliances totaled about 194 million units in 1994, equal to a wholesale market of $55 to $60 billion. Market conditions varied significantly across the appliance industry's four most important geographic regions: North America, Europe, Latin America, and Asia.

The North American Appliance Market

Total appliance shipments in North America approximated 50 million units annually, recently accounting for between 25 and 30 percent of the world total. Exhibit 1 shows shipments by product category. Except for Mexico, the market was mature, growing less rapidly on average than the economy. Shipments were projected to increase 1 to 3 percent annually through the year 2000. Overall appliance demand varied from year to year depending on saturation levels, replacement needs, housing starts, and general economic conditions. Each of these sales-determining factors affected the various appliance product categories differently. Sales of ranges, dishwashers, compactors, and built-in ovens and microwaves, for example, were heavily affected by changes in new housing starts. Refrigerators, which had the highest saturation rate of any appliance (some households had more than one), were minimally affected by housing starts and depended chiefly on the decisions of households to replace their present refrigerator. Washer and dryer sales were least dependent on housing starts but washers had a much higher saturation rate than dryers, making replacement decisions a bigger sales driver for washers than for dryers. Since household saturation rates for dishwashers, laundry appliances, and freezers were lower than for other appliances (ranges or refrigerators), there was an initial purchase market for them independent of replacement demand and new housing starts. Low saturation levels sometimes resulted in big gains in sales volumes; for example, in the 1980s, when consumers decided microwaves were a "must have" appliance, unit volumes soared. Exhibit 2 shows saturation rates by product type. General economic conditions were a driver of appliance sales because of their effects on housing starts, the current ability of households to afford either initial or replacement purchases, and the tendency of households to postpone buying discretionary items like appliances during recessions—home appliances were the epitome of a cyclical durable goods industry.

Each appliance category had its own life span. According to the Association of Home Appliance Manufacturers, ranges had a life span of 10 to 30 years, laundry appliances 10 to 16 years, refrigerators and freezers 10 to 20 years, and dishwashers

Exhibit 1   Shipments of Major Household Appliances in North America, 1990–1994 *(in thousands of units)*

Product Category	1990	1991	1992	1993	1994
Kitchen appliances, total	30,218	29,019	31,226	32,597	35,839
Cooking, total	13,862	12,630	13,685	14,222	16,057
Electric ranges	3,444	3,309	3,574	3,848	4,159
Gas ranges	2,429	2,401	2,614	2,755	2,951
Microwave ovens/range	8,126	7,012	7,588	7,703	9,030
Food waste disposers	4,137	4,002	4,195	4,436	4,789
Trash compactors	185	129	126	125	120
Automatic dishwashers	3,637	3,571	3,820	4,099	4,572
Freezers	1,296	1,414	1,639	1,609	1,690
Refrigerators	7,101	7,273	7,761	8,109	8,611
Laundry appliances, total	10,512	10,510	11,232	11,867	12,325
Dryers, total	4,320	4,313	4,717	5,074	5,332
Electric	3,318	3,295	3,563	3,853	4,033
Gas	1,002	1,018	1,154	1,229	1,299
Washers	6,192	6,197	6,515	6,793	6,993
Total appliances	40,730	39,529	42,457	44,463	48,164

Source: *Appliance Manufacturer*, 1995.

7 to 14 years—see Exhibit 2 for average life expectancy by appliance type. About 75 percent of all appliance purchases in North America were made to replace another appliance. While appliance purchases could be accelerated or postponed, their functional necessity in the life-styles of households limited the deferral period. Except when they had had a bad experience, U.S. consumers exhibited strong brand loyalty on replacement purchases.

While there were no major new home appliance products in the development stage, appliance manufacturers were introducing a variety of new features to stimulate faster replacement and spur new demand. Such features included user-friendly electronic controls that were more durable and easier to see, easier to clean components, quieter operation, greater energy efficiency, programmable controls, larger capacity, more efficient use of space, and the cosmetics of color and styling.

In the United States, recently enacted federal standards called for 25 percent increases in the energy efficiency of appliances; the Department of Energy's goal was to reduce energy usage in appliances by 25 percent every five years. Manufacturers were beginning to promote the reduced energy usage of their new appliances because the energy cost savings were significant enough in some cases to pay for early replacement. For instance, refrigerators purchased in the 1960s and 1970s could use as much as $15 to $20 of electricity per month; those purchased in 1995 used as little as $5 per month. Federal regulations regarding the phase-out of ozone-depleting chlorofluorocarbons had also had an impact on the design of refrigerators and freezers; however, when a few manufacturers moved early to introduce models with CFC-free technology in 1994, rivals quickly followed and the new standards were being met ahead of schedule.

Exhibit 2 Major Appliance Product Saturation Levels in the United States, 1973–1994 *(percent of households with appliance)*

Product	1973	1983	1990	1991	1992	1993	1994	Average Life Expectancy (years)
Kitchen appliances								
Dishwasher	34	45	52	48	50	51	52	9
Microwave oven	1	3	84	85	85	86	89	10
Electric range	47	58	61	57	57	58	59	15
Gas range	52	43	45	46	46	45	45	18
Disposer	35	50	52	47	50	51	52	9
Freezer	31	43	44	33	38	40	40	12
Refrigerator	100	100	100	100	99	99	100	15
Laundry appliances								
Electric dryer	41	49	49	51	51	53	54	13
Gas dryer	10	15	17	16	18	17	18	14
Washer	68	74	73	73	74	74	75	13

Source: Standard & Poors Industry Surveys; *Appliance*, September 1995.

Wholesale and Retail Distribution During the past two decades there had been major consolidation among appliance distributors and retailers. In 1995, about 50 percent of total appliance volume was accounted for by the 10 leading retailers. Sears, with a 25 percent market share, was the biggest of the appliance mega-retailers, followed by Montgomery Ward, Circuit City, and Silo. A number of smaller retailers and distributors had exited the business because of inability to match the prices and bargaining power of large-volume dealers and because manufacturers were bypassing distributors with factory-direct strategies. Large chain retailers had increased their demands for service from manufacturers in addition to wrangling price concessions.

To meet these demands and still eke out a profit, appliance manufacturers were revamping their shipping and warehousing systems to shorten delivery times, stream-line order processing, and reduce the need for large retailer inventories. Whirlpool, for example, had begun replacing its system of independent distributors with a factory-direct distribution system that would permit delivery of all its products to retailers within 24 hours. General Electric had instituted a "Direct Connect" program for its retail dealers that allowed stores to operate with virtually zero inventory.[1] With Direct Connect, GE dealers utilized computer software giving them on-line access to GE's distribution warehouse inventories 24 hours a day; they could use the system to check model availability and place orders for next-day delivery. Dealers got GE's lowest prices, regardless of order size, plus consumer financing through GE Credit with the first 90 days free of interest. In exchange, GE dealers agreed to (1) promote sales of nine different GE appliances, while stocking only microwaves and

---

[1]Michael Treacy and Fred Wiersema, *The Discipline of Market Leaders* (Reading, MA: Addison-Wesley Publishing, 1995), pp. 33–34.

air conditioners for customer carryout, (2) guarantee that GE products account for at least 50 percent of sales, and (3) pay GE through electronic funds transfer on the 25th of the month. With Direct Connect, dealer profit margins on GE products increased since dealer costs for inventory were virtually eliminated and dealers did not have to order full-truckload lots to get GE's best price. Manufacturers' efforts to speed delivery and streamline distribution activities not only permitted dealers to function as appliance showrooms but also facilitated the creation of manufacturer–dealer partnerships that cut both partners' costs and improved the service provided to household appliance buyers.

Competition   Since 1980, the manufacturing portion of the North American appliance industry had gone through several rounds of merger/acquisition activity that reduced the field from 15 competitors to a market dominated by 5 major players:

Company	Major Brands	Overall Market Share
Whirlpool	Whirlpool, KitchenAid, Roper, Estate, Inglis	33.6%
General Electric	General Electric (GE), Hotpoint	27.7
Electrolux/Frigidaire	Frigidaire, Tappan, Kelvinator, White-Westinghouse, Gibson	16.9
Maytag	Maytag, Jenn-Air, Magic Chef, Admiral, Norge, Hardwick	14.6
Raytheon/Amana	Amana, Speed Queen, Caloric/Modern Maid	5.5
		98.3%

There were several other participants that competed in specialized segments: the Japanese and Korean producers in microwave ovens (Matsushita/Panasonic, Sharp, Sanyo, Toshiba, Samsung, and Goldstar), Emerson Electric (In-Sink-Erator waste disposals and Emerson room air conditioners), Thermador-Waste King (high-end ranges, ovens, refrigerators, compactors, and garbage disposals), and a few makers of room air conditioners and dehumidifiers. Industry consolidation had been driven by the competitive needs to provide distributors and dealers with a broad product line (in terms of both price ranges and appliance categories) and to achieve volume-related operating economies. Given the maturity of the North American appliance market and continuing inability to increase prices (fierce competition had kept appliance prices flat for almost a decade), manufacturers saw revenue and volume growth as being dependent on a wider product line, acquisition, and a larger market share.

GE and Whirlpool had been the overall market share leaders in North America for over two decades. Market share by appliance category varied among the major competitors—see Exhibit 3. Competition centered around price, the introduction of attractive new product features, product performance and quality, appearance and styling, the range and caliber of services offered to distributors and dealers, and brand-name reputation. Exhibit 4 provides a profile of Whirlpool's North American competitors.

While GE and Whirlpool were generally regarded as the overall lowest-cost U.S. appliance manufacturers, in 1995 virtually all of the remaining U.S. producers operated comparatively efficient, cost-competitive plants. The minimum efficient scale plant for ranges, refrigerators, dishwashers, and washer-dryers was about

Exhibit 3 U.S. Market Shares of Major Appliance Manufacturers by Product Category, 1988–1994

Product/Manufacturers	Market Share (%)				Product/Manufacturers	Market Share (%)			
	1994	1992	1990	1988		1994	1992	1990	1988
Washers					**Ranges (Gas)**				
Whirlpool	52	52	52	50	Maytag	24	27	21	24
GE	17	16	15	17	Electrolux (Frigidaire)	24	25‡	20‡	7
Maytag	17	17	17	16	Raytheon (Caloric)	20	22	20	15
Electrolux (Frigidaire)	12	10	9	10	GE	27	19§	34§	II
Raytheon (Speed Queen)	2	4	4	4	Brown	2	3	1	4
Others	—	3	3	3	Perrless-Premier	2	3	1	3
					Tappan	—	—	—	25
Dryers (gas)					Roper	—	—	—	15
Whirlpool	53	53	55	52	Others	1	1	3	7
Maytag	15	17	16	12					
GE	14	14	13	16	**Ranges (Electric)**				
Electrolux (Frigidaire)	12	10	9	11	GE	37	30§	47§	30
Raytheon (Speed Queen)	5	4	3	3	Whirlpool	25	30	15	13
Norge	—	—	—	2	Maytag	14	17	11	10
Others	1	2	4	4	Electrolux (Frigidaire)	17	15‡	19‡	15
					Raytheon (Caloric)	6	7	6	7
Dryers (electric)					Thermador	1	1	2	n.a.
Whirlpool	52	52	52	52	Roper	—	—	—	14
GE	17	18	19	16	Tappan	—	—	—	7
Maytag	15	15	15	12	Others	—	—	—	4
Electrolux (Frigidaire)	14	12	8	11					
Raytheon (Speed Queen)	2	3	4	3	**Microwave Ovens**				
Norge	—	—	—	2	Sharp	25	20	15	17
Others	—	—	2	4	Samsung	21	18	18	18
					Matsushita	15	17	12	13
Refrigerators					Electrolux	7	10	7	5
GE	35	35	36	35	Goldstar	10	10	18	19
Whirlpool	25	25	27	28	Sanyo	5	7	7	5
Electrolux (Frigidaire)	18	17	19	21	Maytag	8	6	5	2
Maytag (Admiral)	13	13	7	10	Raytheon	2	4	4	6
Raytheon (Amana)	7	8	9	5	Whirlpool	1	3	2	2
Others	2	2	2	1	Toshiba	—	1	3	2
					Others	6	4	9	11

Note: Market share figures include units made for private-label retailers as well as those sold under manufacturers' brand names.   (*continued*)

n.a.—not available.

* No longer makes freezers.

† Includes sales of Design and Manufacturing (acquired by Electrolux).

‡ Includes Tappan, an Electrolux unit.

§ Includes Roper, a GE unit.

II Not in gas range manufacturing.

Sources: *Appliance Manufacturer*, April 1990–94.

500,000 units annually. The recent wave of mergers had permitted companies to consolidate production into an efficient number of plants, combine purchasing activities and gain more bargaining leverage with suppliers, share technology and R&D

Exhibit 3   **Concluded**

Product/Manufacturers	Market Share (%)				Product/Manufacturers	Market Share (%)			
	1994	1992	1990	1988		1994	1992	1990	1988
Freezers					**Disposers**				
Electrolux (Frigidaire)	73	76	32	32	In-Sink-Erator	65	65	62	60
W.C. Wood	17	14	n.a.	n.a.	Electrolux	17	17	23	30
Maytag (Admiral)	*	*	22	22	Waste King	10	10	8	5
Raytheon (Amana)	5	5	6	6	Whirlpool (KitchenAid)	3	2	n.a.	n.a.
Whirlpool	5	5	36	36	Maytag	1	2	1	1
Others	—	—	4	4	Watertown Metal	2	2	5	2
					Others	2	2	1	2
Dishwashers					**Compactors**				
GE	40	40	35	40	Whirlpool	82	70	74	67
Whirlpool	31	31	34	19	GE	—	14	16	14
Electrolux (Frigidaire)	20†	20†	19†	7	Broan	18	14	5	6
Maytag	8	8	11	7	Thermador	—	1	3	3
Thermador	1	1	1	1	Emerson	—	—	—	8
Design and Manufacturing	—	—	—	20	Others	—	1	2	2
Emerson	—	—	—	5					
Others	—	—	—	1					

n.a.—not available.

* No longer makes freezers.

† Includes sales of Design and Manufacturing (acquired by Electrolux).

‡ Includes Tappan, an Electrolux unit.

§ Includes Roper, a GE unit.

‖ Not in gas range manufacturing.

Sources: *Appliance Manufacturer,* April 1990–94.

across plant and product categories, and eliminate costly excess capacity. While cost differences still remained, the gaps were narrower and related more to differences in design, quality, performance features, and degree of vertical integration (in-house manufacture of parts and components versus outsourcing) than to differences in plant efficiency.

Manufacturing was essentially an assembly-line operation. Labor costs were typically under 10 percent of total costs. Parts and components averaged 30 to 45 percent of total costs, depending on the appliance. Cost fluctuations were chiefly a function of changes in the prices of raw materials and components; unit costs also depended on the percentage utilization of manufacturing capacity. High-volume manufacturers often had significant purchasing power leverage with parts and components suppliers and, in recent years, had been able to procure needed supplies from outside parts specialists with world-scale plants at better prices than appliance manufacturers who had integrated backward into parts and components manufacture.

High-end appliances carried greater profit margins than medium- and low-priced models. Company profit margins were thus a reflection of a more or less profitable product mix, as well as operating efficiency. For instance, Maytag's overall margins eroded slightly when it purchased Magic Chef, a maker of medium- and low-end

Exhibit 4 Profile of Whirlpool's North American Competitors

Maytag

Headquartered in Iowa, Maytag had 1994 sales of $3.4 billion and profits of $148 million. Maytag was best known for its top-quality washers and dryers. To compete more broadly, Maytag in the late 1980s acquired the Magic Chef, Jenn-Air, Norge, and Admiral appliance lines and purchased Chicago Pacific, owner of Hoover vacuum and several European plants that manufactured home appliances sold under the Hoover brand name. Maytag's strategy was to offer a wider selection of brand-name appliances at various price points: Jenn-Air at the high end, Maytag in the middle to upper range, Admiral and Magic Chef in the medium to low range, and Norge on the low end. Maytag expanded Jenn-Air's line of cooking tops and ranges to include refrigerators and dishwashers, the Maytag line of washing equipment to include cooking equipment, dishwashers, and refrigerators, and the Magic Chef line of cooking equipment to include dishwashers and refrigerators. Maytag then developed "focus factories" whereby all brands of the same appliance (dishwashers, refrigerators, and cooking equipment) would be produced at the same plant. By jointly sharing technologies and production facilities, Maytag hoped to improve designs and increase manufacturing efficiencies; Maytag also produced more parts and components in-house than most other appliance makers. Maytag created two sales force organizations to market the five brands: one was responsible for the Jenn-Air line, the Magic Chef line, and the low-end Norge line; the other handled the Maytag line and the medium-priced Admiral line.

The Hoover acquisition included a large European subsidiary that manufactured laundry appliances, dishwashers, and vacuum cleaners and provided a vehicle for entering the European appliance market; as of 1994, over 15 percent of Maytag's sales were derived from foreign markets. In 1995, Maytag consisted of nine company subsidiaries with 22 manufacturing plants in the United States and six European countries. So far, Maytag's foray in Europe had not been profitable.

General Electric

General Electric was the sixth-largest industrial enterprise in the United States, with 1994 sales of $60.1 billion and profits of $4.7 billion. GE was broadly diversified; its biggest businesses were power generation equipment, aircraft engines, lighting products, appliances, TV broadcasting (it owned NBC), medical equipment and services, plastics, and financial and credit services. GE Appliances had 1994 sales of $6 billion and operating profits of $683 million. The division was a low-cost producer; it had modern, efficient manufacturing plants and operated its own distribution network to serve retail dealers. GE's strongest appliance lines were cooking tops, built-in ovens and microwaves, refrigerators, and dishwashers. GE had an extensive network of U.S. retail dealers, plus it had recently begun selling its appliances through Sears's Brand Central store format. GE also supplied its appliances directly to builders for installation in new homes and apartments. In 1994, GE Appliances introduced more than 300 new appliance models, led by a 30-cubic-foot side-by-side refrigerator-freezer (the world's largest capacity) that fit in the same space as 27-cubic-foot models and a new high-performance model that used no ozone-depleting chloroflurocarbons (CFCs) in the compressor refrigerant and had greater storage capacity. The division had made major capital investments in its refrigerator and laundry equipment plants and had a world-class dishwasher plant.

Although sales were heavily concentrated in North America, GE Appliances had recently begun putting more emphasis on export sales to increase its presence in the fastest-growing global markets, particularly India, China, Southeast Asia, and South America. It had developed a number of new models specifically for export to foreign country markets. GE's international strategy had two main parts: export sales of products manufactured in North America and strategic alliances with strong local appliance manufacturers. In 1995, GE appliances were sold on every continent, with domestically produced appliances being exported to more than 50 countries. Export sales were biggest in Europe and Asia; distribution in the Middle East, South America, and Africa was established in 1992. GE had about a 25 to 30 percent share of the U.K. appliance market but was a niche player in most other foreign markets. Its most important strategic alliances were in Mexico (with MABE) and in India (with Godrej and Boyce, India's largest appliance maker). The joint venture with Godrej and Boyce was established in February 1993 to develop, manufacture, and market a range of selected home appliances to meet the growing demands of India's expanding middle-income population. Godrej-GE's objective was to increase revenues 10-fold by the year 2000.

Electrolux

Swedish-based Electrolux was the world's second-largest manufacturer of white goods. It was the European market leader. It had entered the U.S. market in 1986 when it acquired White Consolidated Industries, the third-largest U.S. producer, for $780 million. White Consolidated was a company recently created by merging the businesses of a number of lesser-known appliance brands; White's biggest-selling appliance lines were Frigidaire refrigerators, freezers, washers, and dryers. Electrolux had also acquired Tappan (best known for its gas cooking ranges) and Design and Manufacturing, the principal supplier of dishwashers sold under Sears's Kenmore label. In 1991, Electrolux had changed the name of its WCI Major Appliance Group to Frigidaire Company. Since the acquisition, Electrolux had invested over $600 million in Frigidaire, improving production methods and equipment, modernizing and expanding existing factories, and building new refrigerator and dishwasher plants. Like Whirlpool, Electrolux was restructuring its appliance business along global lines. Frigidaire's design engineers had been consolidated into a single unit; the unit worked closely with Electrolux's appliance design centers in Sweden and Italy, endeavoring to coordinate and

Exhibit 4   Concluded

Electrolux (*continued*)

standardize designs where possible. Frigidaire was paring its list of suppliers and establishing long-term relationships with those who could mesh their efforts with Frigidaire's to make a competitive difference. Electrolux was moving to coordinate its procurement worldwide.

Electrolux, Whirlpool's biggest rival in Europe, was broadly diversified and had acquired 200 companies during the 1980s. During the 1990s, Electrolux had focused greater attention on its core appliance business. So far, its Frigidaire division had been only marginally profitable. However, Electrolux's strategic intent was to raise consumer awareness of the Frigidaire brand name to a level equal to GE and Whirlpool and to reposition Frigidaire as a high-end brand. In 1995, Frigidaire introduced its new Gallery line of refrigerator-freezers, ranges, dishwashers, and washer-dryers to appeal to high-end consumers; the expertise of Electrolux's global design center was used to develop the new line. Frigidaire launched a $20 million ad campaign (the biggest national print and TV advertising blitz in the company's history) to launch the Gallery line. Frigidaire management believed that, since all U.S. manufacturers made good-quality appliances, successful differentiation of the Frigidaire brand depended on being a leader on styling and performance features.

Raytheon/Amana

Raytheon was a diversified, technology-based company that ranked among the 100 largest U.S. corporations and was best known as the maker of Patriot missiles. Raytheon consisted of five business groups, one of which was major home appliances. The appliance group had sales of just over $1 billion and consisted of three brands: Amana, Speed Queen, and Caloric/Modern Maid. Amana was positioned in the upper end of the appliance market; the brand's best-selling models were refrigerators, freezers, smooth-top cooking equipment, and microwaves. Caloric was a maker of gas and electric ranges. Speed Queen was the leading supplier of washers and dryers for the coin-operated segment and for hotels, hospitals, prisons, and other commercial operations; it had significant exports, with sales in 95 countries. In 1991, the three brands, which formerly had operated as independent subsidiaries, were consolidated into a single operation under the Amana umbrella. Downsizing, consolidation of marketing and other functions, and plant upgrading ensued. Speed Queen became the laundry equipment supplier for both the Speed Queen and Amana brands; Amana washer-dryer models were positioned in the mid- to high-end segment, and Speed Queen–branded models were targeted to the lower and mid-market segments. Amana washers and dryers offered stainless steel baskets and drums (which the company said were preferable to porcelain or plastic in terms of wear and tear on clothing), were quiet, and carried the longest warranties in the industry; dryer models could be easily adjusted with a screwdriver to open from the right or left and had a moisture sensor that signaled the dryer to stop as soon as the fabric was dry.

appliance products. And Whirlpool's margins benefited from its acquisition of KitchenAid, a producer of high-end appliances.

All manufacturers were experiencing pressure on profit margins. Appliance prices had risen less than 10 percent on average since the early 1980s. By way of comparison, the consumer price index had risen 40 percent during the same period.

The European Appliance Market

Total appliance shipments across all of Europe were around 50 million units annually, up from 44 million units in 1988 and 35 million units in the early 1980s. The five best-selling appliances were refrigerators, washers, cooking equipment, microwave ovens, and freezers. In general, appliance saturation rates were lower in Europe than in the United States (see Exhibits 2 and 5), but rates varied significantly from country to country even for the same appliance. Whereas nearly all West European households had refrigerators, in many countries in Eastern Europe refrigerators were a luxury. Only 1 in 3 European households had dishwashers, ranging from 2 in 5 in Germany and France to just 1 in 10 in Britain. Appliance sales were expected to grow 2 to 3 percent annually in Europe throughout the 1990s. Sales in the former communist block of European countries were expected to flourish after 2000, as these countries strengthened their economies and household purchasing power increased; Eastern Europe accounted for 5 to 10 percent of world appliance sales. European consumers paid a higher percentage of

Exhibit 5 Estimated Appliance Saturation Rates outside North America, 1994

Geographic Region	Appliance	Estimated 1994 Saturation Rate
Western Europe	Refrigerators	99%
	Cooking	97
	Washers	82
	Dryers	18
	Dishwashers	30
	Microwave ovens	40
	Freezers	40
Latin America	Refrigerators	70
	Cooking	90
	Washers	40
	Microwave ovens	6
	Room air conditioners	10
Asia	Refrigerators	30
	Washers	20
	Microwave ovens	7
	Room air conditioners	8

Source: Whirlpool's 1994 Annual Report.

household income for appliances than did U.S. households. European consumers often paid up to twice as much for appliances as U.S. consumers when cost was measured by number of hours worked.

The European appliance market was complex because of varying consumer preferences in choosing appliances, varying mechanical differences, and varying electrical standards. The French preferred top-loading washing machines, whereas front-loading washers were preferred in most other European countries. German and U.K. washing machines spun at a faster rate during the spin cycle than those in Italy and other southern European countries because drying clothes took longer in Northern climates. Northern Europeans wanted large refrigerators because they tended to shop once a week in supermarkets; southern Europeans got by on small refrigerators because they shopped almost daily in open-air markets. Northern Europeans liked refrigerators with freezer units on the bottom; southern Europeans were accustomed to freezers on the top. British households, which were heavy consumers of frozen foods, insisted on units with 60 percent freezer space. Italian households preferred cooking on elegantly designed gas ranges, whereas German households preferred practical electric cooking equipment. British households used either gas or electric cooking equipment, depending on which tended to be most economical in their community. In France, where cooking practices relied heavily on special sauces and baking, self-cleaning ovens were very popular; in Italy, where much of the food was grilled, the self-clean function was not as popular.

Manufacturers coped with the country-to-country differences in sizes, shapes, and styles by developing flexible assembly lines that could handle small runs for many different models and styles in a cost-effective manner. An Italian refrigerator plant, for example, produced 935 variations of 54 basic models. Electrolux produced 1,500 variations of 120 basic appliance designs to accommodate the diverse market conditions in Europe. Some manufacturers believed, however, that as European economic integration proceeded, the fragmented and heterogeneous makeup of the European appliance market would gradually give way to greater homogeneity, reducing the need to produce so many variations of the same appliance. Other producers were skeptical about whether consumer preferences would converge rapidly.

The appliance market in Europe was also more driven by environmental factors. Relatively high electricity prices made the energy efficiency of appliances an important consumer concern. Washers were designed to economize on water usage, a concern in European locations like Germany where water was expensive. European manufacturers were considered to be leaders in energy efficient appliances, low water usage, and built-in models (a desirable feature, given the comparatively small size of European kitchens and living quarters).

Distribution   In Europe, home appliances were retailed through about 40,000 dealers. As in the North American market, the distribution sector was becoming more concentrated. Large retail chains were selling a growing fraction of appliances, both under manufacturers' brands and their own private labels. Many European manufacturers produced appliances for sale under a distributor's own private label. Retail chains in Europe had been able to exert considerable bargaining leverage over manufacturers with idle factory capacity.

Because the European appliance market was so fragmented, many brands were country-specific within Europe. In addition, language and cultural differences made it more troublesome to advertise the same brand across the entire continent. Whirlpool was having difficulty establishing the Whirlpool brand in several European countries because Whirlpool was virtually unpronounceable in certain languages.

Competition   Although the manufacturing side of the European appliance market was consolidating, there were still 35 appliance makers in Western Europe and another 50 or so in Eastern and Central Europe. Most were small companies that either specialized in making a single appliance line (stoves or laundry equipment) or competed in just a single country (due to differing product designs, consumer preferences, electrical standards, or trade restrictions). Fewer than eight appliance manufacturers competed broadly across most of Europe with a fairly complete lineup of appliance products. The market leaders in 1995 were:

Company	Major Brands	Overall Market Share
Electrolux	Electrolux, Zanussi, Zoppas, Euroflair, Arthur Martin, Faure, Zanker, Juno	25%
Bosch-Siemens	Bosch, Siemens, Constructa, Neff	15
Whirlpool	Whirlpool, Bauknecht, Ignis, Laden	13
Elfi/Brandt	Brandt, Ocean, eight others	10
Merloni	Ariston, Indesit, Scholtes, New World	9
Candy	Candy, Zerowatt, Rosieres, LEC	7
General Electric	GE, Hotpoint	1
Maytag	Hoover	1

Source: *Appliance Manufacturer,* April 1995; July 1994.

In 1989, the top five manufacturers accounted for 57 percent of the market; in 1994, they had a combined market share approaching 70 percent.

Exhibit 6 provides a profile of Whirlpool's major European competitors. European manufacturers also faced competition from Japanese and South Korean manufacturers in the microwave oven segment. As in the North American market, competition was focused on price, performance features, styling, dealer networks, brand image and reputation, and energy consumption.

Rival appliance manufacturers were pursuing ways to reduce manufacturing costs, improve product quality, add attractive new features, and revamp designs to permit reduced energy and water consumption, recyclability of appliance components, and greater standardization of parts and components. Whirlpool, for example, had introduced a new automatic washer line in Europe that retained fewer than 1 percent of the parts and components of its predecessor.

Whirlpool and Electrolux were both employing strategies to compete all across Europe; both believed that a convergence of European life-styles would ultimately lead to a more uniform appliance market in Europe. Both were pursuing ways to consolidate and integrate their European operations while still accommodating the market imperatives for country-specific product designs in certain locations. According to Leif Johnson, Electrolux's president:

> I want to be a good Frenchman in France and a good Italian in Italy. My strategy is to go global only when I can and stay local when I must.[2]

The Latin American Appliance Market

The Latin American market consisted of 37 South American, Central American, and Caribbean countries with a combined population of 380 million people. In 1994 alone, appliance shipments were up over 15 percent. Brazil accounted for about 8 million of the 17 million appliances sold in Latin America in 1994. Brazil had a relatively young population, with between 600,000 and 700,000 new households expected to be formed before 2000. The five best-selling appliances were automatic washers, microwave ovens, ranges, refrigerators, and room air conditioners; saturation rates for all five were quite low except for ranges (see Exhibit 5). Even though many Latin American countries had low-income economies, the sales of appliances were expected to grow 6 to 7 percent annually as prosperity spread through the region—see Exhibit 7. Recent trade agreements among nine South America countries had made cross-border marketing of home appliances easier, and lower tariffs in Venezuela, Brazil, and Argentina were spurring buyer demand.

With its joint venture partners, Whirlpool was the clear market leader in Latin America, with a market share of about 27 percent. None of its major competitors— Refripar, Continental Dako, and Madosa—had as much as a 10 percent market share. Altogether, there were approximately 65 home appliance manufacturers in the region. Competition in the Latin American region centered around product features, price, product quality and performance, service, warranties, advertising, and dealer promotion.

---

[2]As quoted in *Fortune*, September 20, 1993, p. 82.

Exhibit 6   Profile of Whirlpool's European Competitors

AB Electrolux (Sweden)

Electrolux was the market share leader in Europe and had made several acquisitions to build its position: Arthur Martin (France, 1976), Zannusi (Italy, 1986), Lehel (Hungary, 1991), and AEG Hausgerate (Germany, 1994). The Zannusi acquisition marked the beginning of Electrolux's strategy to lead the transition from a series of separate country markets for appliances to more of a pan-European market for appliances. Increased penetration of the Eastern European market, which accounted for approximately 10 percent of the global appliance market, was the most recent component of Electrolux's strategy to eventually dominate the European appliance market. The Lehel acquisition provided the vehicle for establishing Electrolux products in Russia, Poland, the Czech Republic, Slovakia, Hungary, and Turkey. The company's goal was to double Eastern European sales by 1999 by establishing wholly or partially owned companies in the region. The AEG Hausgerate acquisition gave Electrolux a market share in Germany roughly equal to Bosch-Siemens (Germany accounted for the largest white goods volume of any European country and was the country where consumers placed the biggest emphasis on styling and sophisticated product features). The AEG Hausgerate acquisition also gave Electrolux market leadership in all of Europe's major geographic segments and allowed the company to offer a comprehensive product range across Europe. Thus, with the addition of the AEG brand, Electrolux had three pan-European brands—AEG's sales were primarily in central Europe, while the Electrolux and Zannusi brands were strong in both southern and northern Europe. The Zannusi brand was also established in every North African country. Electrolux had integrated its three international product divisions and numerous local marketing companies into a single organization to achieve greater scale economies in product development and production and to facilitate coordinated marketing across countries and continents. Electrolux reported $13.8 billion in sales for 1994 and $712 million in operating profits (household appliances accounted for 60 percent of the company's business).

Bosch-Siemens (Germany)

Bosch-Siemens Hausegeraete GmbH was established in 1965 as a 50–50 joint venture between Robert Bosch GmbH and Siemens AG; Siemens was Germany's second-largest industrial enterprise (its main products were power-generation equipment, electrical and electronics products, and telecommunications equipment) and Bosch was the country's eighth-largest industrial manufacturer (its primary businesses were auto parts and communications technology products). As of 1994, Bosch-Siemens had sales of $4.8 billion and profits of $224 million. Sales outside Germany in 1993 accounted for approximately 42 percent of total sales. The company had subsidiaries in 20 countries in Western and Eastern Europe (including Russia) and Scandinavia. Bosch-Siemens had manufacturing facilities in Germany (5), Spain (5), Greece (1), Slovenia (1), and Poland (1). Appliances were marketed under such brands as Bosch, Siemens, Constructa, Balay, Baby, Lynx, Crolls, and Neff. The company was the market leader in Germany with a 30 percent market share. Bosch-Siemens had acquired two Spanish appliance manufacturers in 1989, Balay SA and the Safel Group. Output from a new facility in Poland was expected to increase sales in Eastern Europe from $299 million in 1994 to $359 million in 1999. In Eastern Europe and Russia Bosch-Siemens had positioned its products in the middle and lower-end segments; elsewhere, it concentrated on the middle and high-end segments where it had developed a reputation for innovation and technological sophistication. Management had planned to grow the company's European market share to 18 to 19 percent by 1999, largely through acquisitions in the United Kingdom, France, and Italy where its market shares were low. Bosch-Siemens management had stated that current differences in the appliance preferences of European consumers would be slow to change, and that to be successful, manufacturers would have to offer a large number of regional variations. Bosch-Siemens was also interested in increasing its sales in the Asian market and recently acquired a majority interest in Wuxi Little Swan Co., a leading Chinese manufacturer of laundry appliances. Management was also involved in negotiations to establish a washer production joint venture in China; 1994 export sales to Asia were in the $50 million range.

Elfi/Brandt Electromenager (Italy)

In late 1992, the Italian holding company Elfi (Elletrofinanziaria) acquired the last French domestic appliance group, Thomson Electromenager (TEM). Elfi's management believed TEM's sales outside of France were well below what was possible with TEM's resources. The TEM acquisition gave Elfi a 10 percent share of the European market, roughly the same as Merloni, and marked the first step in Elfi's strategy to establish a pan-European appliance manufacturing and sales group. Shortly after the acquisition, Elfi announced a major restructuring plan that first grouped appliance operations under a new organization, Brandt Electromenager; the move put the brands gained in the TEM acquisition (Brandt, De Dietrich, Sauter, Thermor, Thomson, and Vedette) and Elfi's four brands (Ocean, CGA, Blomberg, and Elektra Bregenz) under common management. Brandt Electromenager was divided into three divisions (washing, refrigeration, and cooking) to consolidate operations across its plants in Italy, Germany, and France. Since the reorganization, Brandt had maintained but not expanded its dominant share of the French appliance market (28 to 30 percent) and was intent on expanding its share of the European market. In 1995, Brandt's management indicated that it was considering entering the Polish appliance market.

Exhibit 6   Concluded

Merloni Elettrodomestici (Italy)

Based in Fabriano, Italy, Merloni was the fifth-largest European appliance manufacturer with 1994 sales of $1.1 billion. Merloni's sales consisted of washers and dishwashers (35 percent), refrigerators and freezers (34 percent), and ovens/stoves (31 percent). The company had subsidiaries in 11 European countries, as well as in the Cayman Islands and Argentina. As of 1994, Merloni's overseas operations accounted 9 percent of total sales. European sales were concentrated in Italy (28 percent), France (20 percent), UK (13 percent), and Turkey (11 percent). Since 1980, the company's growth strategy was driven by a need to gain critical mass and access to other European countries in the European market consolidated. Merloni's growth in the European market was largely due to acquisition, namely Indesit and Scholtes in 1988, and several lesser operations in Portugal, Turkey, and Argentina. In 1995, Merloni bought New World Domestic Appliances, a leading U.K. gas range manufacturer. New World had a 24 percent share of the U.K. market for freestanding gas ranges (24 percent), and a 14 percent share of the U.K. market for built-in gas ranges (second only to Whirlpool's 18 percent share). In Western Europe, Merloni's sales had grown an average of 17 percent annually since 1980. The company's brand names included Ariston, Indesit, New World, and Scholtes. Merloni management believed Eastern Europe was key to the company's future success. The company had recently built a refrigerator and freezer manufacturing facility in Russia, as well as a 1.5 million-unit compressor plant. In 1994, Merloni sold over 60,000 appliances in Russia (20 percent share of the import market), generating sales of approximately $25 million. Merloni opened an office in Singapore in 1993 and was developing plans to enter the Chinese market.

Candy Elettrodomestici (Italy)

Candy specialized in the manufacture of washing machines, dishwashers, and refrigerators. In 1993, Candy posted sales of $249 million and profits of $1.7 million. Candy's market share in Italy was 11 percent, trailing only Merloni (21 percent) and Zannusi (26 percent). Almost 50 percent of Candy's total sales were in its home market of Italy, with the remaining half coming from European countries, countries formerly comprising Russia, and North Africa. Candy's cross-border operations had increased its European market share from 2 percent in 1980 to 6 percent in 1993, most of which had been achieved through acquisition: Zerowatt (Italy), Rosieres (France), and LEC (U.K.). In 1992, Candy announced construction of a manufacturing plant in Libya. Candy had also aggressively targeted the Russian market since the collapse of the old communist regime. By early 1995, Candy and Merloni were supplying approximately 50 percent of washing machine sales in Russia.

General Electric

GE's Hotpoint brand commanded a 28 percent share of the U.K. market for cleaning appliances (washers, dryers, dishwashers, and vacuum cleaners) where it had a manufacturing presence. GE was a niche player in the rest of Europe, with most of its sales being supplied from U.S. plants.

Maytag

The acquisition of Hoover in 1989 not only gave Maytag a substantial share of the appliance market in the United Kingdom but also manufacturing operations as well. By 1994, Hoover's share of the appliance market in the United Kingdom was 15 percent, second only to Hotpoint. Hoover Europe's 1994 sales totaled $399 million; profits were a meager $420,000 but 1994 was the division's first profitable year since its acquisition. In the rest of Europe, Maytag was a niche player. Maytag formed an alliance in 1992 with Bosch-Siemens to extend its presence in the European market. Maytag's alliance with Bosch-Siemens included technology sharing and collaborative product development.

The Asian Appliance Market

Asia consisted of two very different appliance markets—Japan and the rest of the region (China, Thailand, Indonesia, Malaysia, India, Australia, New Zealand, Taiwan, Hong King, and Singapore). The appliance market in Japan was virtually closed to outsiders; Matsushita, Sharp, Toshiba, Sanyo, and a few other Japanese appliance makers accounted for close to 100 percent of the market, and their control over distributor–dealer networks made any foreign incursion into the Japanese market formidable and expensive. But elsewhere, the Japanese manufacturers lacked such a stronghold. Outside Japan, Matsushita was the market leader; yet, its market share was less than 10 percent. Whirlpool was the leading non-Japanese competitor with a market share of just over 1 percent. Other key players outside Japan included Sharp,

Exhibit 7   The Global Market for Major Home Appliances, by Geographic Region, 1994–2004

Geographic Region	Population	Annual Market Demand (in units)		Estimated Compound Average Growth Rate
		1994	2004 (est.)	
North America	380 million	46 million	63 million	3.6%
Europe (including Eastern Europe, Middle East, and Africa)	1.1 billion	75 million	94 million	2.5
Western Europe only	325 million	51 million	63 million	2.4
Latin America	380 million	17 million	30 million	6.5
Asia	2.9 billion	56 million	120 million	8.8
World total	5.1 billion	245 million	370 million	4.7%

Source: Whirlpool's 1994 Annual Report.

Sanyo, Samsung, and Goldstar. Exhibit 8 provides profiles of Whirlpool's chief competitors in Asia. Competition was based on local production capabilities, product features, price, product quality, and product performance. Many of the better-known Asian manufacturers had integrated backward, making a sizeable fraction of the parts and component systems needed for their appliances. Whirlpool, however, was following a different path; Lee Ross, manufacturing vice president of Whirlpool's Asian Appliance Group, explained:

> We're going to focus on our core competencies, then outsource the rest. You can't be world-class at everything. I think the rapid expansion of business in Asia is also increasing the number of quality suppliers. So vertical integration is less necessary today than when these other companies started manufacturing.[3]

As a rule, appliance plants in Asia were less automated because low wage rates made it more cost-effective to use labor-intensive production methods to perform many of the work steps.

Asia was the fastest-growing region within the global home appliance industry (Exhibit 7) and had also become the world's largest home appliance market, accounting for nearly 23 percent of shipments in 1994. The best-selling appliances in Asia were refrigerators, washers, microwave ovens, and room air conditioners (see Exhibit 5 for saturation rates). More refrigerators were sold in China in 1994 than in any country worldwide; only about 10 percent of Chinese households had refrigerators. In 1994, appliance sales in China totaled about 20 million units, about 40 percent of the total Asian market and 10 percent of the world market. Demand for major home appliances in China was expected to reach 60 million units annually by 2004, equal to about 50 percent of the Asian market and 20 percent of the world market. Chinese retailers of home appliances preferred to deal with one manufacturer for all the products they carried. Home appliance demand in India, the world's second most populous country, was also rising strongly.

---

[3]As quoted in *Appliance Manufacturer*, February 1995, p. W-31.

Exhibit 8   Profile of Whirlpool's Asian Competitors

Matsushita Electrical Industrial Co. (Japan)

Matsushita, one of the world's largest conglomerates, earned $911 million on consolidated 1994 sales of $70 billion. Since 1989, Matsushita's sales outside Japan had grown from 42 percent to 49 percent of total revenues. Matsushita had manufacturing plants in 38 countries and produced a wide variety of electronics and appliance products. Matsushita's appliance products were sold under the Panasonic brand overseas and the National brand in Japan. Over the years, Matsushita had built a strong domestic retail appliance network that had enabled the company to maintain a market leading position in Japan for many of the product lines, including refrigerators and air conditioning. In 1993, Matsushita opened what was billed as the "largest microwave oven factory in the world" in Chicago, Illinois. Outside of Japan, Matsushita was the acknowledged leader of the appliance market in Asia, although in 1995 its Asian share amounted to less than 10 percent. Management believed that expansion of Matsushita's presence in the Chinese appliance market would increase its leading share of the Asian market. Matsushita participated in 16 Chinese joint ventures and had plans to build 30 appliance manufacturing plants in China.

Sanyo Electric Co., Ltd. (Japan)

The Sanyo Group consisted of 60 manufacturing companies, 33 sales companies, and 15 other companies operating in 28 different countries. Sanyo manufactured a broad range of consumer electronic products, industrial equipment, and household appliances. In the early 1990s Sanyo had formed an equity joint venture in China to produce up to 400,000 washing machines. Sanyo's management expected the Chinese market for washers to grow from 900,000 units in 1994 to 2.4 million units by 1997. Home appliances accounted for almost 20 percent of Sanyo's 1994 sales of $16.4 billion. However, Sanyo's appliance sales were stagnant; its $2.8 billion in appliance sales in 1993 represented a five-year low.

Toshiba Corporation (Japan)

Toshiba was one of Japan's leading producers of semiconductors, electronics, and electrical appliances. Due to the rising value of the yen in the world currency market in the 1990s, Toshiba's management believed that it had become necessary to begin relocating its appliance manufacturing operations outside Japan. In 1993 Toshiba began to develop its manufacturing operations in Thailand and planned eventually to make Thailand Toshiba's primary appliance production base for Indochina. In 1994, Toshiba pulled out of the U.K. microwave oven market despite its 14 percent market share, citing profit margin pressures from cheaper Korean and Chinese products. Toshiba reported consolidated sales of $48.2 billion and profits of $450 million for its fiscal year ending March 31, 1995.

Hitachi Limited (Japan)

Hitachi was one of the world's 15 largest diversified corporations, with 1994 revenues of $76.4 billion, profits of $1.1 billion, and 330,000 employees. Hitachi manufactured telecommunications products, power generation equipment, industrial machinery, appliances, and consumer electronics products. The company's appliance products had captured sizable market shares in several Asian countries, an example being Thailand where Hitachi held a leading 20 percent share of the refrigerator market in 1994. Late in 1994, Hitachi's management announced the introduction of a new low-end appliance brand for its home market to complement the high-end Hitachi brand. The company did not have plans to market the new low-end products outside of Japan. In 1994 Hitachi also entered into the Chinese appliance market by forming a joint venture to produce air conditioners.

Sharp Corporation (Japan)

A private company established in 1912, Sharp manufactured consumer electronics, information and office automation equipment, electrical devices and home appliances. In 1994, the company posted sales of $16.3 billion and profits of $448 million.

Sharp's "New Life" strategy, begun in the mid-1970s, focused on developing products that appealed to diverse consumer tastes. The "New Life" strategy also promoted new consumer lifestyles by emphasizing color and design. The strategy was successful enough that Sharp's appliance business posted growth rates over 10 percent through the early 1980s (versus an industry average for the same period of 3 percent). The "New Life" strategy continued into the 1990s, and was particularly popular with younger consumers. However, Sharp's appliance group was growing more slowly than other Sharp divisions and accounted for only 17.5 percent of total corporate revenues.

In the 1970s Sharp established manufacturing joint ventures in Taiwan, Brazil, Korea and Malaysia in response to the appreciation of the yen. In the early 1990s, Sharp built more overseas manufacturing plants to reduce its production costs. A market leader in the microwave oven segment, the company had built a microwave oven plant in Thailand with a capacity of 1 million units per year. Sharp also had a subsidiary in China that produced 200,000 air conditioners a year, and the company had plans to initiate a joint venture in Shanghai to produce a variety of household appliances.

Exhibit 8 Concluded

Samsung Electronics Company, Ltd. (Korea)

Samsung was South Korea's largest producer of consumer electronics and had 1994 sales of $14.6 billion and profits of $1.2 billion. In the early 1990s Samsung began aggressively expanding its Asian appliance division. In 1994, Samsung formed a joint venture with Trade Import Export Electronics Co. in Vietnam to produce refrigerators and washing machines and committed to investing $500 million in appliance manufacturing facilities in Suzhou, China. Also in 1994, Samsung announced a contract to export approximately $33 million in washing machines to India's Voltas Company and to provide Voltas with Samsung's washer manufacturing technology for an additional $7 million. Samsung and Voltas planned to extend the technology transfer agreement to include microwaves, air conditioners, and refrigerators. In 1995 Samsung expanded its manufacturing operations in Thailand, building a washing machine manufacturing plant (100,000 unit capacity). The company planned to invest an additional $20 million in the Thailand complex to include production of refrigerators and microwave ovens.

Goldstar (Korea)

A multinational conglomerate, Goldstar manufactured a wide variety of products, including consumer electronics, semiconductors, and household appliances. In the 1980s, Goldstar's share of the Korean market had declined and the company had lost its No. 1 position to Samsung. A change of management in 1991 resulted in a reorganization of Goldstar into 9 strategic business units including 29 operating groups that were run by multidisciplinary teams (designers, engineers, factory workers, and marketing people). Production operations were simplified to reduce costs (the average length of a microwave assembly line was reduced from 200 to 65 meters). By 1994 average output per employee had doubled, and Goldstar had regained its dominant position in the Korean appliance market, surpassing Samsung's sales in refrigerators and washing machines. Management then adopted a two-pronged strategy to build its global position: (1) Goldstar began shifting production of low-end products to China and Vietnam, and (2) Goldstar began to develop strategic alliances with leading technology companies (appliances—GE). Three new joint ventures in China were established by Goldstar in 1994. By 1997, Goldstar's management planned for overseas production to account for 25 percent of its total appliance output, up from 10 percent in 1994. As of 1995, Goldstar's 8 percent share of the imported appliance market in Russia was second only to Samsung's (10 percent).

AB Electrolux (Sweden)

Electrolux's management believed expansion of its market share in Asia to be the primary component of its growth strategy heading into the 21st century. The company planned to double its 1994 Asian market revenues by 1999, and was building five new manufacturing facilities in the region. The company planned to compete on quality, technology, and range of product offerings. Electrolux designed new product lines for the Asian market (for instance, cold wash–only washers for countries with limited electric power supplies or populations with low buying power) and set product prices 10 to 15 percent above comparable Japanese products. The company intended to spend approximately $30 million between 1994 and 1997 to introduce and promote the Electrolux brand name in Asia. Electrolux's management believed China was the growth market of the future, and in 1994 opened its second joint venture factory in Tianjin, China.

Like other regions in the world, the Asian appliance market had features unique to certain countries, consumer segments, and product categories. The electric power supply in many Asian countries was unreliable; in addition to frequent outages, there were wide swings in voltages and frequencies. In India, for example, appliances had to be designed to handle anywhere from 170 to 270 volts; this meant adding more windings to motors and other coil components to protect against failure. Much of the region had high humidity and many metropolitan areas were near salty seacoast air, making corrosion resistance and protection of controls from moisture a critical quality issue. The typical Asian residence didn't have the ductwork to accommodate central air conditioning and consumers disliked room air conditioners that took up scarce window space; the preferred product was a split system where the condensing unit was located outside, the evaporating unit with fan was installed high on an outside wall, and remote controls were used to regulate operation.

Clothes dryers and dishwashers were niche market items because Asian incomes were too low for many households to afford them. Because little baking was done in Asia and kitchens were small, there was little demand for ranges with ovens. Most cooking was done on portable two-top burners that could be stored when meals were finished. Asian consumers wanted clothes washers to be portable and easily moved because most residences had no place to keep one permanently hooked up to a water supply and drain; often they were stored in an outside hallway or porch and moved into the kitchen or bathroom for use. A lack of space also affected refrigerator size; some were only 4 feet high so the top could be used for something else. Moreover, because refrigerators were a status symbol for families rising up the economic ladder, they were sometimes placed in the living room, which led to a preference for stylish designs and colors—in India, for example, refrigerators were sold in bright blue or red. In one part of China, freezer capacity was important; in another part, households preferred large crispers for fresh vegetables. There were technology variations as well. In China, all three types of clothes washers (horizontal-axis, vertical-axis, and twin-tub) were being marketed as well as both direct-cool refrigerators (the dominant type in Europe) and forced-air refrigerators (the dominant type in the United States). In Hong Kong there was a preference for European-style appliances, but Taiwan households preferred larger American-style appliances.

WHIRLPOOL'S GLOBAL STRATEGY

Whirlpool's decision in the late 1980s to formulate and pursue a global strategy was based on management's conclusion that the major home appliance industry would, in time, be dominated by a handful of global players and that global expansion was Whirlpool's best route to less cyclical performance, greater shareholder value, and long-term viability. According to Whirlpool's CEO David Whitman:

> Several other possibilities were considered first, including the idea of diversifying away from appliances, forward and backward integration, and a major financial restructuring. But when we looked at the global marketplace, it quickly became clear that the only reason we were defining our industry as "slow growing" was because we were defining the industry as North American. When we looked at the world appliance market, we saw an industry that had significant growth prospects.[4]

Whirlpool's strategic approach quickly evolved into one of not only participating in, but leading, the industry's globalization. Between 1987 and 1995, Whirlpool broadened its stable of brands in North America, established a major position in Europe, entered the Latin American market by partnering with several Latin American producers and constructing plants in Brazil and Argentina, and began building a base for competing aggressively in Asia. Exhibit 9 shows the global presence Whirlpool had developed by 1995. It was the only manufacturer that was an active player in all four regions of the global appliance industry. Exhibit 10 shows Whirlpool's revenues by product category.

Whirlpool's Strategy and Position in North America

To put itself in position to offer consumers a wide selection of brand-name appliances at various price points, Whirlpool made four acquisitions in the late 1980s:

- KitchenAid, a high-end manufacturer of dishwashers and food mixers.

---

[4]As quoted in Jay Palmer, "Oh Boy, a Washer," *Barron's*, September 26, 1994, p. 17.

Exhibit 9   Whirlpool's Global Presence by Geographic Region, 1994

Geographic Region	Manufacturing Plants	Sales Offices	Subsidiaries, Joint Ventures, and Affiliates
North America	13	20	2
Europe	10	20	0
Latin America	5	0	6
Asia	4	6	6

Source: Whirlpool's 1994 Annual Report.

Exhibit 10   Whirlpool's Revenues by Product Category, 1992–1994 (in millions of dollars)

Product Category	1992	1993	1994
Laundry appliances (washers and dryers)	$2,489	$2,481	$2,610
Refrigerators, freezers, and room air conditioners	2,525	2,588	2,900
All other home appliances	2,083	2,299	2,439
Total	$7,097	$7,368	$7,949
Whirlpool Financial Services	204	165	155
	$7,301	$7,533	$8,104

Source: Whirlpool's 1994 Annual Report.

- Roper, a maker of low-end appliances and one of Sears's suppliers of Kenmore brand appliances.
- Inglis, the leading Canadian appliance maker.
- A 49 percent ownership stake in Vitromatic, the second-largest appliance maker in Mexico.

Responsibility for the acquired businesses, along with Whirlpool's other U.S. operations, was then consolidated under a single unit, the North American Appliance Group (NAAG). NAAG had 1994 sales of $5.05 billion and operating profits of $522 million (see Exhibit 11). Sears was NAAG's biggest customer, accounting for about 19 percent of sales each year since 1990.[5]

NAAG's strategy was to build market position by giving customers compelling reasons beyond price to select Whirlpool appliances. The objective was to create a "dominant consumer franchise" in home appliances such that consumers would

---

[5]Whirlpool had been Sears's principal supplier of laundry equipment for over 75 years and of room air conditioners for over 30 years. During the three decades following World War II, most of Whirlpool's business consisted of supplying Kenmore appliances to Sears; Sears had a sizable ownership stake in Whirlpool (as it did in several other of its key suppliers). However, Sears elected to divest its Whirlpool ownership stake when it became apparent that Sears could obtain Kenmore appliances from Whirlpool at even lower costs if Whirlpool pursued scale economies by increasing sales of Whirlpool brand appliances at the same time it supplied private-label goods to Sears.

Exhibit 11	Whirlpool's Revenues and Operating Profits by Geographic Region

	1993	1994
Net Sales Revenue		
North America	$4,559	$5,048
Europe	2,225	2,373
Latin America	303	329
Asia	151	205
Operating Profits		
North America	$ 474	$ 522
Europe	139	163
Latin America	43	49
Asia	(5)	(22)
Operating Profit Margin		
North America	10.4%	10.3%
Europe	6.3	6.9
Latin America	14.2	14.9
Asia	(3.3)	(10.7)

Source: Whirlpool's 1994 Annual Report.

insist on Whirlpool's brands for reasons other than price, view Whirlpool product as clearly superior to other appliances, and demonstrate strong brand loyalty in future purchase decisions. To create this degree of consumer support, management believed that NAAG's appliance lineup would increasingly have to include functional and attractive products, that the company would have to operate from a platform of both high quality and low cost, and that constant product innovation and superior service would have to permeate its operations. To open the door to greater imagination and innovation, management had reconceptualized its business, switching from a product-dominated definition—the refrigerator business, the washing machine business, or the range business—to a functional definition—the food preservation business, the fabric care business, and the food preparation business. David Whitwam believed that the design issues changed dramatically when the business definition was keyed to the function that consumers wanted the product to accomplish:

> The microwave couldn't have been invented by someone who assumed he or she was in the business of designing a range. Such a design breakthrough required seeing the opportunity is "easier, quicker food preparation," not "a better range."[6]

NAAG was cultivating different images and themes for its three major brands: KitchenAid, style and substance; Whirlpool, products to help people run their home; and Roper, a quality value brand.

The KitchenAid line of food mixers epitomized the sort of dominant consumer franchise that Whirlpool was trying to create all across its major home appliance

---

[6]"The Right Way to Go Global," *Harvard Business Review*, March–April 1994, p. 143.

lines. KitchenAid food mixers dominated the premium end of the category in both North America and Europe, selling for prices substantially above the industry average because they delivered superior styling, performance, reliability, and service. Annual sales had increased fivefold over the past eight years. NAAG had plans to begin introducing the KitchenAid food mixer line in Latin America and Asia.

The Whirlpool refrigerator division was selected by a consortium of electric utilities to produce a chlorofluorocarbon-free, superefficient refrigerator in 1992; the division received a $30 million award for submitting the winning design. The new no ozone–depleting models were introduced in 1994 and not only featured much lower use of electricity but also a new exterior look and new bins, shelves, crispers, and interior controls. To build the new models, Whirlpool used insulation technology from its European operations, compressor technology developed by its Brazilian affiliates, and manufacturing and design expertise supplied by NAAG. Starting in 1995, CFC refrigerants were eliminated from all KitchenAid, Whirlpool, and Roper refrigerators and freezers. Surveys indicated that Whirlpool's new side-by-side refrigerator-freezer was the best in the industry. A new clothes washer that used one-third of the water and energy of conventional washers was scheduled for 1996. Whirlpool's European technology was being used in a line of new, quieter dishwashers.

All told, more than two-thirds of NAAG's product lineup was new in 1995, and hundreds of additional models were scheduled for 1996. NAAG's work in new product development was not confined to North America. The LaVergne (Tennessee) Division had designed and produced a room air conditioner that was being sold in Asia and would eventually be sold worldwide.

The North American Appliance Group's manufacturing plants were all implementing factory master plans that would enable them to produce more models in smaller runs each day, thus allowing production to be matched closely to current dealer sales. Whirlpool, like General Electric, had eliminated independent distributors and was supplying retail dealers factory-direct. Surveys of retail dealers indicated that Whirlpool's "Quality Express" product-delivery system was clearly superior in terms of on-time delivery, driver courtesy, responsiveness, and overall ability to met dealer needs. The plants were also on track to reduce warranty service rates by 90 percent. A five-year quality improvement plan had been implemented in 1992, and by 1994 Whirlpool's studies showed that interim warranty service targets were being met. Whirlpool's market research indicated that service repair frequencies for its appliances were the lowest in the industry in 1994.

The role of the North American Appliance Group in Whirlpool's global strategy was to maintain sufficient profitability and cash flow to fund the company's expansion into markets in the rest of the world. During the 1990s, NAAG had been able to generate between $100 million and $200 million annually to help finance such activities.

Whirlpool's Strategy and Position in Europe

Whirlpool's entry into Europe was accomplished in two stages. In 1989, Whirlpool acquired 53 percent of the major home appliance division of Dutch-based N.V. Philips for $470 million; Philips was Europe's third-largest appliance producer, with sales of about $2 billion. In 1991, Whirlpool spent $600 million to buy out the remaining 47 percent interest in Philips's major home appliance business. Whirlpool Europe B.V. (WEBV) was formed to manage Whirlpool's activities in Europe, the Middle East, and Africa. Philips's appliance business had been floundering for several years prior to its acquisition by Whirlpool; Philips had employed a multi-country strategy in Europe, with virtually no cross-border coordination. Philips's washing machines made in Germany did not even have one screw in common with the washers made at its Italian plant. WEBV management promptly initiated a Europeanwide approach in all areas of operation: procurement, technology and component standardization, manufacturing, marketing, and dealer support activities. David Whitwam explained the rationale for a uniform strategy even though no one shape or style of appliance would sell in all of Europe's national and regional markets:

> The basic technology and the basic components are still very similar, market to market. The adaptations needed to meet local preferences can be done very late in the production cycle. We can leverage the similarities.[7]

Early on, Whirlpool initiated a brand-transfer program, putting the Philips-Whirlpool brand on all Philips brand appliances and eliminating several of the national brand names Philips used in specific European countries. WEBV earmarked $110 million to promote the Whirlpool name with consumers over a five-year period. Starting in 1995, the Philips name was dropped entirely from all labels and advertising. Recent consumer surveys showed that Whirlpool was Europe's most-recognized appliance brand, and in 1994 Whirlpool was the largest-selling appliance brand in Europe.

Product development was carried out at two regional technology centers, both of which worked closely with Whirlpool's other technology centers worldwide. The goal was to achieve more commonality of components and more modularity in assembly. Procurement at the 10 European plants was increasingly being performed by the company's global procurement organization. WEBV maintained a growing database, tracking cost and quality of manufacturing practices at each of its plants to ensure that best practices were recognized and transferred.[8] To reduce costs and improve efficiency, WEBV was planning to eliminate 2,000 positions, realizing cost savings of $80 million annually by 1996. Since 1990, WEBV had improved productivity by 25 percent and reduced first-year warranty service rates by one-third. However, WEBV's operating margin of 5.6 percent was still far from its goal of 10 percent.

As in the North American market, Whirlpool was utilizing a multibrand strategy to cover all price segments. Bauknecht brand appliances were positioned in the medium- to high-price range; Whirlpool brand appliances were positioned to appeal to the broad middle market segment, and Ignis brand products were value-priced for budget-conscious buyers. Laden brand appliances were sold in France, in addition to the other three brands.

To strengthen Whirlpool's brands with the approximately 40,000 European appliance dealers stocking one or more of WEBV's brands, WEBV took a road show across Europe in 1994 to provide dealers with product information, explaining how the benefits of product features could be communicated to consumers, giving product demonstrations, and offering training to dealer salespeople. A major accounts group was created to coordinate sales and marketing to transnational dealer buyer groups (the four largest represented a combined total of nearly 6,000 dealers) and to the

---

[7]Palmer, "Oh Boy, a Washer," p. 17.
[8]"Around the World with Whirlpool: Europe," *Appliance Manufacturer*, February 1995, p. W-12.

major retail appliance chains. As of 1995, WEBV's top 70 accounts accounted for over half of its sales.

To provide European consumers with service levels comparable to those provided in the United States, WEBV had formed a consumer service operation consisting of 1,000 consumer service representatives and field service technicians at locations throughout Europe. Six customer assistance centers were in operation in Germany, the United Kingdom, Belgium, Holland, Austria, and Switzerland, and five others were planned for Poland, Hungary, Slovakia, Greece, and the Czech Republic. The centers booked repair calls, responded to customer complaints, provided product information, facilitated the ordering and invoicing of spare parts, processed warranty claims, and handled extended service contracts. Through Whirlpool Financial Corporation, WEBV was leasing appliances to consumers in the former communist countries of Central and Eastern Europe.

A new clothes dryer model and a new family of microwave ovens were introduced in 1994. Other whole new generations of Bauknecht, Whirlpool, and Ignis brand appliances were being developed, including six new lines in 1995. By 1998, about 85 percent of sales in Europe were expected to come from models that didn't exist in 1993. WBEV's new automatic washer design retained fewer than 1 percent of the parts and components of its predecessor.

WEBV's 1994 sales were approximately 8 million units, up 1.5 million units since 1990. The division's share of the European market had gone up for five consecutive years. About 10 percent of WEBV's sales were to countries in Central and Eastern Europe. WEBV's line of VIP microwave ovens was the best-selling microwave oven in Europe and the recipient of eight awards for superior performance. Whirlpool executives believed WEBV was in a favorable position relative to competitors because it had an experienced dealer network in Western Europe, balanced sales throughout the Western European market under well-recognized brand names, manufacturing facilities located in different countries, and the ability to customize its products to met the preferences of diverse buyers in different country and regional markets. According to Jeff Fettig, president of WEBV:

> We are successfully eliminating the geographical borders as the basis for defining our markets. It's the consumer segments and not the borders that are significant.[9]

Whirlpool's Strategy and Position in Latin America

Whirlpool first entered the Latin American market in 1958 when it bought an equity interest in Multibras S.A. of Brazil, a manufacturer of major appliances. By 1995, Whirlpool had expanded its position to include equity interests in Embraco S.A., a maker of compressors, and Brasmotor S.A., a Brazilian holding company with interests that included Multibras and Brasmotor. It also bought control of SAGAD S.A. in Argentina, a transaction that completed the acquisition of Philips Electronics' worldwide appliance business; SAGAD was renamed Whirlpool Argentina. In 1995, Whirlpool Argentina was marketing a full line of appliances produced locally and in Brazil by Multibras, as well as by Whirlpool plants in North America and Europe. Whirlpool's Brazilian partners also exported appliances to the Middle East, Africa, and North America. Exhibit 12 summarizes Whirlpool's moves to establish a market presence in Latin America.

---

[9]As quoted in *Appliance Manufacturer*, February 1995, p. W-6.

Exhibit 12 Summary of Whirlpool's Strategic Moves to Establish a Market Presence in Latin America

1958	Whirlpool invests in Latin America through purchase of an equity interest in Multibras S.A., a part of the Brasmotor holding company in Brazil. Multibras is later renamed Brastemp S.A.
1976	Brasmotor S.A. acquires Consul, a Brazilian manufacturer of refrigerators/freezers and room air conditioners. Consul was founded in 1950 as a manufacturer of kerosene-powered refrigerators.
1976	Whirlpool increases its investment in Brazil through purchases of equity interests in Consul and Embraco S.A., a maker of compressors.
1984	Semer, a Brazilian manufacturer of stoves, is acquired by Brastemp. Semer broadens its product line to include semiautomatic clothes washer/dryers and countertop dishwashers.
1992	Whirlpool acquires the control of SAGAD S.A., from Philips Electronics N.V., and renames it Whirlpool Argentina.
1992	South American Sales Co. (SASCO) is formed as a sales and marketing joint venture with Brasmotor to manage export sales to Latin America.
1993	Whirlpool sells 40 percent of its interest in Whirlpool Argentina to Brasmotor.
1994	Brastemp, Consul, and Semer are merged and renamed Multibras S.A.
1994	Embraco acquires Whirlpool's Italian refrigerator-compressor business. The transaction involves a plant in Riva di Chieri, Italy, which manufactures Aspera-brand compressors.

Source: *Appliance Manufacturer*, February 1995, p. W-39.

While the majority of appliance products made by Whirlpool's Brazilian affiliates and Whirlpool Argentina were for the medium and high ends of the Latin American market, efforts were underway to strengthen Whirlpool's presence in the low end of the price spectrum. Eight brands were currently being sold in the Latin American market. For high-end buyers, there were U.S.-made KitchenAid and Whirlpool models, Brazilian-made Brastemp models, and European-made Bauknecht models. Positioned in the middle of the price spectrum were Brazilian-made Consul models, European-made Ignis models, and Whirlpool Argentina's Eslabon de Lujo brand. At the low end were the Brazilian-made Semer brand and a substantial selection of Eslabon de Lujo brand models. Brastemp offered a full line of appliances and exported its models to Africa and the Middle East. The Consul line included refrigerators, freezers, microwave ovens, and room air conditioners; Consul models were exported to Africa, the Middle East, North America, Singapore, Australia, and Switzerland. The Semer brand included ranges, semiautomatic washers (no spin cycle), dryers, and countertop dishwashers; Semer appliances were sold in 50 countries in Latin America, Africa, and the Middle East. In Brazil, sales of the Brastemp, Consul, and Semer brands combined resulted in Whirlpool/Multibras having the leading market share. Whirlpool Argentina had an 18 percent share of the 3 million–unit Argentine market; 40 percent of its appliance sales were made locally and sold under the Whirlpool brand name.

Whirlpool utilized 60 distributors in 37 countries to access the large numbers of small independent appliance retailers. Pleasing appliance distributors was a critical success factor because Latin American distributors were typically responsible for servicing and maintaining product warranties, as well as importing, warehousing, and marketing the various product lines to local retailers. Distributors were the main vehicle for educating retailers on product features and benefits; Whirlpool regional sales managers and professional trainers worked closely with the 60 distributors to facilitate dealer training and education.

The region's four Brazilian plants and one Argentinean plant each had factory master plans to incorporate best practice manufacturing methods. Plant teams had visited North American and European plants to study and share manufacturing and quality control approaches. Initiatives to erase operating distinctions between the various Latin American organizations and to more fully connect with Whirlpool worldwide were underway in 1995. Processes, systems, technology, and people were being shared freely among the operating units of Whirlpool's Latin America Appliance Group.

Whirlpool's Strategy and Position in Asia

While Whirlpool had exported appliances to Asia for many years, it did not establish an operating base in Asia until 1989 when several sales offices were opened. Management decided to truly understand Asian consumers preferences and life-styles and the trade channels to access the marketplace before deciding where to put factories and what products to build in Asia. During the 1990s, as its knowledge of the market increased, Whirlpool added sales locations and began putting together a manufacturing base, usually with local partners, with Whirlpool maintaining a majority interest.

In 1987, Whirlpool entered into a joint venture with a company in India to manufacture automatic and semiautomatic washers and twin-tub washers for the Indian market; the venture, called TVS Whirlpool, sold its products under the brand name of TVS. In 1993, a technology center was established in Singapore to coordinate product development in the region. In early 1994, Whirlpool partnered with Great Teco Trade Co. in Taiwan to form a large distributorship for Whirlpool appliances in Taiwan. Over the next 12 months, a flurry of moves were made to develop Asian manufacturing capability:

- Whirlpool acquired a controlling interest in Kelvinator of India, Ltd., the second largest manufacturer and marketer of refrigerators in India. Kelvinator of India had 3,000 retail dealers handling its product line.

- Whirlpool purchased a majority interest in the largest Chinese producer of microwave ovens; the company had annual sales of 500,000 units in China (about a 50 percent market share) and exported another 500,000 units to Asian, European, and Latin American markets. (This acquisition, together with Whirlpool's microwave operations in Europe, made Whirlpool one of the world's five largest makers of microwave ovens.)

- Whirlpool entered into a joint venture with Beijing Snowflake Electric Appliance Group, a state-owned enterprise that produced refrigerators and freezers. Whirlpool had majority ownership. Beijing Snowflake's operations produced 120,000 units annually, and an expansion was underway to increase production to 500,000 units annually by 1997.

- Discussions for two other joint ventures in China, one to make room air conditioners and the other to make clothes washers, were underway. Both involved partners who were the leading Chinese manufacturers in their respective product categories.

By early 1995, Whirlpool's strategy in Asia had seven key elements: partnering with solid local companies (usually with Whirlpool having a controlling interest), transferring best practices from Whirlpool's other operations worldwide to Asia, developing the manufacturing skills of the workforces at the various Asian plant locations, making the Whirlpool brand the centerpiece of the Asian marketing plan and effectively positioning other brands around it, leveraging the company's global size in procurement of parts and components (the company's best suppliers in other regions were being encouraged to work with Whirlpool in Asia), designing products around a common platform that allowed modifications for specific areas within the Asian market, and concentrating on four specific appliance products—refrigerators, clothes washers, microwave ovens, and room air conditioners. Ranges were not on Whirlpool's product priority list because of small kitchens, less baking of goods, and widespread use of portable, two-burner tabletop units. Where demand for ranges, cooking tops, and ovens existed (Australia and New Zealand, for example), the market was supplied by Whirlpool plants in other global locations.

The company's Asian managers were spending considerable time promoting a one-company vision and developing rapport between once-independent operations. In 1994, Whirlpool sold about 700,000 appliance products in Asia; in 1995, the total was expected to be about 2.8 million units. At the end of 1994, Whirlpool had about 800 employees in the Asia region; management foresaw that it could have close to 10,000 by year-end 1995. Whirlpool executives believed that the most critical driver of success in Asia was having strong local talent, only a small percentage of which could come by transferring people from other Whirlpool operations to Asia.

India and China were the primary targets for locating manufacturing plants. Recent changes in government policy in both countries had made it possible for foreign corporations to own a controlling interest in local manufacturing companies; in many other Asian countries, governments insisted on majority control, exercised strong policy-making roles, or imposed dividend restrictions; in addition, there were significant trade barriers in Asia that made locating large-scale plants in countries with small local markets a risky proposition (since exports were necessary to fully utilize capacity). Robert Frey, head of the Whirlpool Asia Appliance Group, observed:

> In both India and China, you can afford to build a world-class, global scale, million-unit-a-year factory and be fairly certain that the plant can be fully utilized just satisfying the demands of the local market. The size of these markets lets you start operating at a competitive level.
>
> In some places you have to balance your foreign exchange or achieve a certain level of exports. Sometimes there are import tariffs on key components. So you have to understand all the rules and carefully manage all the logistics they require.[10]

Whirlpool had ambitious plans for its Asian operations. According to Robert Frey:

> First of all, we expect to stay ahead of the pack in terms of Western players. And within 10 years, we expect to achieve a leadership position in Asia. By leadership position, I mean having a strong market share, more than 10 percent,

---

[10]As quoted in *Appliance Manufacturer*, February 1995, p. W-24.

having a presence in all key markets, and having the level of influence such that all major retailers want Whirlpool's products in their stores.

Whirlpool's expansion into Asia was a move that was anticipated nine years ago when the company adopted a vision of world leadership. We need to be a leader in Asia. It is imperative to survival in the appliance industry. We don't believe you will be a major player in the appliance industry in 10 years if you aren't a major player in Asia. So this is a natural next step. This is not just an Asian strategy, but a key part of Whirlpool's global strategy.[11]

The World Washer

In 1990, Whirlpool began production of a "world washer." The concept was to make a compact, affordable washer that handled small loads, that could be built at various locations with local labor and local materials, that required low investment in facilities and equipment, and that could be assembled with flexible manufacturing methods, thereby permitting models to be customized as needed for various markets throughout the world. For the time being, Whirlpool had assigned production of the world washer to Brastemp in Brazil, TVS Whirlpool in India, and Vitromatic in Mexico. The world washer's unique design specifications called for the unit to be built in modules, with 15 to 20 percent fewer parts than conventional washers. Modular components were tested during assembly to ensure a quality end product and to eliminate the need for service bays at the end of the line to rework defective units. Plants were given the authority to utilize different components to cut costs or to satisfy consumer preferences in specific country or regional markets. For instance, stainless steel baskets were used at the plants in Brazil and India because they required no welding and no operator to complete the assembly; while stainless steel was more expensive than porcelain, the two plants were able to avoid investing several million dollars in additional equipment. In Mexico, however, Vitromatic was associated with a porcelain producer and found it more economical to use porcelain baskets instead of stainless steel ones. World washer units sold in areas that lacked sophisticated plumbing were modified so that wash water could be loaded by hand and discharged directly onto the ground.

World washer models were introduced in the United States in 1993. A Whirlpool official explained the strategic thinking behind the move:

> The number of persons living alone in this country has more than doubled in the past 20 years. The average number of people in a household has dropped from 3.1 to 2.6. Statistics like this suggest there's a growing number of folks out there who would be interested in buying compact machines that take up less space and handle small loads efficiently. It's not a huge market, but we sure can't afford to ignore it.[12]

All of Whirlpool's design personnel and technology centers were looking increasingly toward global parts, component systems, and products. The goal was to leverage Whirlpool's technological expertise and capabilities on a global scale. Ed Eisele, vice president of technology for Whirlpool's Asian Appliance Group, said:

> There are certain core technologies you want to capitalize on when you design certain products. Obviously you have to differentiate some things . . . but

---

[11]Ibid.
[12]As quoted in *Dealerscope*, October 1992, p. 61.

where technologies are similar, you want to borrow on the strong existing experience within the Whirlpool organization rather than start from scratch every time.[13]

Another Whirlpool technology executive noted:

The world is shrinking. We see Whirlpool globally getting into product platforms that have applicability in a lot of different markets. In some cases, if volumes justify it, a product may be manufactured in more than one region, just like the world washer being manufactured in India, Brazil, and Mexico. In other cases, a product may be made in one location to serve several different world markets. So product design will become more global in nature.[14]

WHIRLPOOL'S FINANCIAL PERFORMANCE

Although senior management exuded confidence that Whirlpool's global strategy was timely and well matched to industry and competitive conditions, the company's financial performance seven years after the strategy's launch was still lackluster at best. Since the beginning of 1988, Whirlpool had invested nearly $2 billion in new capital pursuing its strategy, yet net earnings were lower in 1993 and 1994 than in 1984, 1985, and 1986, the three years immediately preceding the decision to compete globally. The company's 10-year trend in earnings per share was uninspiring. Operating profit margins, return on assets, and return on stockholder's equity were all lower throughout the 1990s than they had been in the mid-1980s—see the 11-year financial review in Exhibit 13. Some Whirlpool shareholders were concerned whether Whirlpool's strategy to become the global market leader in major home appliances was working. When would they begin to see a real bottom-line payoff?

---

[13]As quoted in *Appliance Manufacturer*, February 1995, p. W-32.
[14]As quoted in *Appliance Manufacturer*, February 1995, p. W-29.

Exhibit 13 Eleven-Year Consolidated Statistical Review, Whirlpool Corp. *(millions of dollars, except share data)*

	1994	1993	1992	1991	1990	1989	1988	1987	1986	1985	1984
Consolidated Operations											
Net sales	$7,949	$7,368	$7,097	$6,550	$6,424	$6,138	$4,306	$4,104	$3,928	$3,465	$3,128
Financial services	155	165	204	207	181	136	107	94	76	67	63
Total revenues	8,104	7,533	7,301	6,757	6,605	6,274	4,413	4,198	4,004	3,532	3,191
Operating profit	$ 397	$ 482	$ 479	$ 393	$ 349	$ 411	$ 261	$ 296	$ 326	$ 295	$ 288
Earnings from continuing operations before income taxes and other items	292	375	372	304	220	308	233	280	329	321	326
Earnings from continuing operations before accounting change[1]	158	231	205	170	72	187	161	187	202	182	190
Net earnings[2]	158	51	205	170	72	187	94	192	200	182	190
Net capital expenditures	418	309	288	287	265	208	166	223	217	178	135
Depreciation	246	241	275	233	247	222	143	133	120	89	72
Dividends paid	90	85	77	76	76	76	76	79	76	73	73
Consolidated Financial Position											
Current assets	$3,078	$2,708	$2,740	$2,920	$2,900	$2,889	$1,827	$1,690	$1,654	$1,410	$1,302
Current liabilities	2,988	2,763	2,887	2,931	2,651	2,251	1,374	1,246	1,006	781	671
Working capital	90	(55)	(147)	(11)	249	638	453	444	648	629	632
Property, plant, and equipment—net	1,440	1,319	1,325	1,400	1,349	1,288	820	779	667	514	398
Total assets	6,655	6,047	6,118	6,445	5,614	5,354	3,410	3,137	2,856	2,207	1,901
Long-term debt	885	840	1,215	1,528	874	982	474	367	298	125	91
Total debt—appliance business	965	850	1,198	1,330	1,026	1,125	441	383	194	64	53
Stockholders' equity	1,723	1,648	1,600	1,515	1,424	1,421	1,321	1,304	1,350	1,207	1,096
Per Share Data											
Earnings from continuing operations before accounting change	$ 2.10	$ 3.19	$ 2.90	$ 2.45	$ 1.04	$ 2.70	$ 2.33	$ 2.61	$ 2.72	$ 2.49	$ 2.59
Net earnings	2.10	0.67	2.90	2.45	1.04	2.70	1.36	2.68	2.70	2.49	2.59
Dividends	1.22	1.19	1.10	1.10	1.10	1.10	1.10	1.10	1.03	1.00	1.00
Book value	22.83	22.80	22.67	21.78	20.51	20.49	19.06	18.83	18.21	16.46	14.97
Closing stock price—NYSE	50¼	66½	44⅝	38⅞	23½	33	24¾	24⅜	33⅞	24 11/16	23¼

Exhibit 13 Continued

	1994	1993	1992	1991	1990	1989	1988	1987	1986	1985	1984
Key Ratios											
Operating profit margin	4.9%	6.4%	6.6%	5.8%	5.3%	6.6%	5.9%	7.1%	8.1%	8.4%	9.0%
Pretax margin[3]	3.6%	5.0%	5.1%	4.5%	3.3%	4.9%	5.3%	6.6%	8.2%	9.1%	10.2%
Net margin[4]	2.0%	3.1%	2.8%	2.5%	1.1%	3.0%	3.6%	4.4%	5.0%	5.1%	5.9%
Return on average stockholders' equity[5]	9.4%	14.2%	13.1%	11.6%	5.1%	13.7%	12.3%	14.1%	15.8%	15.8%	18.3%
Return on average total assets[6]	2.8%	4.0%	3.3%	2.9%	1.4%	4.9%	4.9%	6.2%	8.0%	9.1%	10.6%
Current assets to current liabilities	1.0	1.0	0.9	1.0	1.1	1.3	1.3	1.4	1.6	1.8	1.9
Total debt—appliance business as a percent of invested capital[7]	34.4%	31.6%	41.7%	46.1%	37.6%	39.2%	20.5%	19.3%	—	2.8%	2.7%
Price-earnings ratio	23.9	20.8	15.4	15.9	22.6	12.2	18.2	9.1	12.5	9.9	9.0
Fixed charge coverage[8]	3.0	3.2	2.6	2.3	1.8	2.7	3.5	5.4	7.7	10.7	11.9
Other Data											
Number of common shares outstanding (in thousands):											
Average	75,490	72,272	70,558	69,528	69,443	69,338	69,262	71,732	73,831	73,285	73,171
Year-end	73,845	73,068	70,027	69,640	69,465	69,382	69,289	69,232	74,128	73,325	73,234
Number of shareholders (year-end)	11,821	11,438	11,724	12,032	12,542	12,454	12,521	12,128	11,297	11,668	8,912
Number of employees (year-end)	39,016	39,590	38,520	37,886	36,157	39,411	29,110	30,301	30,520	25,573	22,757
Total return to shareholders (five-year annualized)[9]	12.0%	25.8%	17.0%	6.7%	2.8%	11.3%	4.4%	6.2%	26.8%	26.6%	26.6%

[1] Accounting changes: 1993—accounting for postretirement benefits other than pensions, 1987—Accounting for income taxes, and 1986—accounting for pensions.
[2] The company's kitchen cabinet business was discontinued in 1988.
[3] Earnings from continuing operations before income taxes and other items, as a percent of revenue.
[4] Earnings from continuing operations before accounting change, as a percent of revenue.
[5] Earnings from continuing operations before accounting change divided by average stockholders' equity.
[6] Earnings from continuing operations before accounting change, plus minority interest, divided by average total assets.
[7] Cash, debt, minority interests, and stockholders' equity.
[8] Ratio of earnings from continuing operations (before income taxes, accounting change, and interest expense) to interest expense.
[9] Stock appreciation plus reinvested dividends.

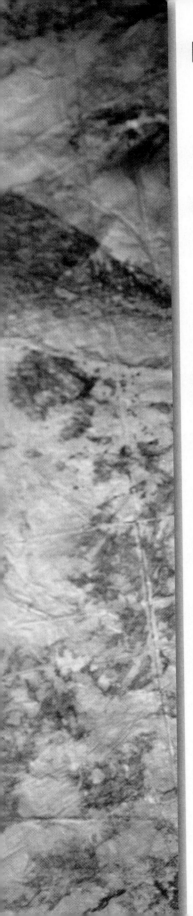

The Black & Decker Corporation

Arthur A. Thompson, Jr., University of Alabama
John E. Gamble, Auburn University at Montgomery

In 1992, the Black & Decker Corporation was a diversified global manufacturer and marketer of household, commercial, and industrial products. The company operated 61 manufacturing plants, 32 in the United States and 29 in 14 other countries; its products were marketed in over 100 countries. Black & Decker was the world's largest producer of power tools, power tool accessories, and security hardware. Its small-appliance business was the U.S. leader, and the company was among the leaders in the global market for small household appliances. B&D's plumbing subsidiary was the fastest growing maker of kitchen and bathroom faucets in the United States. Black & Decker was also the worldwide leader in golf club shafts and glass container–making equipment and was among the major global suppliers of fastening systems.

Surveys showed Black & Decker was the seventh most powerful consumer brand name in the United States (behind Coca-Cola and Kodak but ahead of Levi's and Hershey's) and was in the top 20 in Europe. The company's brand names were recognized worldwide, and it enjoyed a reputation for quality, design, innovation, and value. The company had paid a dividend on its common stock every quarter of every year since 1937.

COMPANY BACKGROUND

Black & Decker was incorporated in 1910. Over the next 70 years, the company established itself as the dominant name in power tools and accessories, first in the United States and then across a broad global front but particularly in Europe. Growth was achieved by adding to its lineup of power tools and accessories and by increasing its penetration of more and more foreign markets.

Diversification into Small Household Appliances

Black & Decker began to pursue diversification because of growing maturity of its core power tools business. In 1984, Black & Decker acquired General Electric's housewares business for $300 million. GE's brands had about a 25 percent share of the small-appliance market and generated annual revenues of about $500 million. GE sold its small-appliance division, despite its number one market position, because of the division's low profitability. GE's strong suit was in irons and toaster ovens where its share was close to 50 percent; sales of GE irons totaled about $250 million. Among the other 150 GE products acquired by Black & Decker were coffee makers, hair dryers and hair curlers, food mixers and processors, toasters, electric skillets, can openers, waffle irons, and blenders.

Also in 1984, Black & Decker purchased three European tool manufacturers to fill in product gaps and strengthen its manufacturing base; the acquisition involved a Swiss manufacturer of portable electric woodworking tools for professional users, the leading European manufacturer of drill bits, and a German producer of hobby and precision power tools.

The acquisition of GE's housewares division launched Black & Decker on a course to transform the company from a power tools manufacturer into a consumer products company. In early 1985, the firm changed its name from Black & Decker Manufacturing Co. to Black & Decker Corp. to reflect its new emphasis on "being more marketing driven" rather than being merely engaged in manufacturing.

Failed Acquisition Attempts

In early 1988, Black & Decker began an unsolicited takeover bid for American Standard Inc., a diversified manufacturer of bathroom fixtures, air-conditioning products, and braking systems for rail and automotive vehicles. American Standard had revenues of $3.4 billion and earnings of $127 million in 1987 (compared to revenues of $1.9 billion and earnings of almost $70 million for Black & Decker). After several months of negotiations, the takeover effort failed and B&D withdrew from the battle to win control of American Standard.

In January 1989, Black & Decker negotiated a deal with Allegheny International to purchase its Sunbeam/Oster Appliance division for about $260 million. Sunbeam/Oster was a leading manufacturer and marketer of small household appliances—blenders, can openers, food mixers, electric skillets, steam irons, and other kitchen items. However, in February, Allegheny International backed out of the sale and merged with another company.

The Emhart Acquisition

A month later, in March 1989, Black & Decker agreed to acquire Emhart Corporation for $2.8 billion, rescuing the firm from a hostile takeover bid. Emhart had 1988 sales of $2.8 billion, earnings of $127 million, assets of $2.4 billion, and shareholders' equity of $971 million. Emhart was a diversified manufacturer of industrial products (1988 sales of $1.6 billion), information and electronic systems (1988 sales of $654 million), and consumer products (1988 sales of $547 million). Approximately 40 percent of Emhart's sales and earnings came from foreign operations, the majority of which were concentrated in Europe. Exhibit 1 provides a profile of Emhart's business portfolio. Exhibit 2 provides data on the financial performance of Emhart's business units in the years preceding its acquisition by B&D.

In the days after the announcement of Black & Decker's friendly plan to acquire Emhart, B&D's stock price dropped about 15 percent. There was considerable skepticism over the wisdom of the acquisition, both from the standpoint of whether Emhart's business had attractive strategic fit with B&D's businesses and whether Black & Decker could handle the financial strain of making such a large acquisition. Emhart was significantly larger than Black & Decker:

1988 Financials	Emhart Corp.	Black & Decker Corp.
Sales revenues	$ 2.76 billion	$ 2.28 billion
Net earnings	126.60 million	97.10 million
Assets	2.43 billion	1.83 billion
Stockholders' equity	970.90 million	724.90 million
Long-term debt	674.30 million	277.10 million

The acquisition agreement called for Black & Decker to purchase 59.5 million shares (95 percent) of Emhart Corp. common stock at $40 per share—almost three times book value per share ($14.32). Black & Decker had to secure $2.7 billion in financing to acquire Emhart. To come up with the funds, Black & Decker entered into a credit agreement with a group of banks that consisted of term loans due in 1992 through 1997 and a revolving credit loan of up to $575 million. The loans carried an interest rate of ¼ percent above whatever the prevailing prime rate was. Scheduled principal payments on the term loans were as follows:

1992	$201,217,000
1993	274,287,000
1994	275,221,000
1995	743,923,000
1996	401,318,000

The credit agreement included covenants that required Black & Decker to achieve certain minimum levels of cash flow coverage of its interest obligations and not to exceed specified leverage (debt to equity) ratios during the term of the loan:

Fiscal Year	Maximum Leverage Ratio	Minimum Cash Flow Coverage Ratio
1992	3.25	1.35
1993	2.75	1.50
1994	2.25	1.55
1995 and thereafter	1.50	1.60

Note: The leverage ratio was calculated by dividing indebtedness, as defined by the credit agreement, by consolidated net stockholders' equity. The cash flow coverage ratio was calculated by dividing earnings before interest, taxes, depreciation, and amortization of goodwill minus capital expenditures by net interest expense plus cash income tax payments and dividends declared.

Other covenants in the credit agreement limited Black & Decker's ability to incur additional indebtedness and to acquire new businesses or sell assets.

Black & Decker recorded the excess amount of its purchase price for Emhart over the book value of Emhart's net assets as goodwill to be amortized on a straight-line basis over 40 years. This resulted in Black & Decker having increased depreciation and amortization charges of about $45 million annually.

Exhibit 1   Emhart Corporation's Business Portfolio in 1989 *(at the time of the company's acquisition by Black & Decker)*

Business and Product Categories	Trademarks/Names	Primary Markets/Customers
Industrial Businesses (1988 sales of $1.6 billion)		
Capacitors, audible signal devices	Emhart, Mallory, Sonalert, Arcotronica	Telecommunications, computer, automotive, and electronic components industries
Electromechanical devices, solid-state control systems, hydrocarbon leak detection systems	Emhart, Mallory, Pollulert	Appliance, automotive, and environmental controls manufacturers
Commercial door hardware, electronic locking systems	Emhart, Carbin, Russwin	Commercial, institutional building construction, and original equipment manufacturers
Footwear materials (insoles, toe puffs, shanks, eyelets, tacks, and nails)	Emhart, Texon, Aquiline	Manufacturers of footwear
Fastening systems (rivets, locknuts, screw anchors, adhesive systems, sealants, and grouts)	Emhart, Molly, Warren, Gripco, Bostik, Kelox, Dodge, Heli-Coil, POP	Appliance, construction, electronics, furniture/woodwork, packaging, automotive, and other transportation industries
Glass container machinery	Emhart, Hartford, Powers, Sundsvalls	Producers of glass containers for beverage, food, household, and pharmaceutical products
Printed circuit board assembling machinery	Emhart, Dynapert	Electronics industry
Information and Electronic Systems (1988 sales of $654 million)		
Technology-based systems and services (including computer-based systems), scientific research services, program management	Emhart, PRC, Planning Research Corp., PRC System Services, PRC Environmental Management, PRC Medic Computer Systems, Nova, Stellar	Governmental units and agencies, real estate multiple listing services, group medical practices, and public utilities
Consumer Products Businesses (1988 sales of $547 million)		
Door hardware, including lock sets, high-security locks, and locking devices	Emhart, Kwikset	Residential construction
Nonpowered lawn and garden equipment, landscape lighting	Garden America, True Temper	Do-it-yourself homeowners
Underground sprinkling and watering systems	Lawn Genie, Drip Mist, Irri-trol	Landscape specialists, do-it-yourself consumers
Golf club shafts, bicycle-frame tubing	True Temper, Dynamic Gold, Black Gold	Golf club manufacturers
Bathroom and kitchen faucets	Price Pfister, The Pfabulous Pfaucet with the Pfunny Name	Residential and commercial construction
Adhesive, sealants	Bostik, Thermogrip	Residential and commercial construction, do-it-yourself consumers
Fasteners, staplers, nailers	Blue-Tack, POP, Molly	Residential and commercial construction

Exhibit 2   Financial Performance of Emhart's Business Groups, 1986–1988 (in millions of dollars)

	1988	1987	1986A*	1986B
Revenues				
Industrial				
Components	$ 641.8	$ 671.9		$ 653.9
Fastening systems	640.5	638.8		576.3
Machinery	279.0	291.1		419.2
	$1,561.3	$1,601.8		$1,649.4
Information and electronic systems	653.7	438.3		39.3
Consumer	547.5	414.4		405.6
Total	$2,762.5	$2,454.5		$2,094.3
Operating Income (Loss)				
Industrial				
Components	$ 63.8	$ 65.7	$ 48.2	$ (5.4)
Fastening systems	74.8	78.7	68.3	24.8
Machinery	42.7	34.1	44.4	3.9
	$ 181.3	$ 178.5	$160.9	$ 23.3
Information and electronic systems	37.2	22.3	2.0	2.0
Consumer	84.8	68.3	60.4	51.7
	$ 303.3	$ 269.1	$223.3	$ 77.0
Corporate expense	(35.0)	(32.9)	(30.3)	(34.0)
Total	$ 268.3	$ 236.2	$193.0	$ 43.0
Identifiable Assets				
Industrial				
Components	$ 457.8	$ 472.0		$ 400.3
Fastening systems	428.4	428.2		409.7
Machinery	167.8	164.8		297.2
	$1,054.0	$1,065.0		$1,107.2
Information and Electronic Systems	546.7	361.3		334.5
Consumer	702.7	225.1		266.1
	$2,303.4	$1,651.4		$1,707.8
Corporate	123.2	378.5		148.9
Total	$2,426.6	$2,029.9		$1,856.7

* 1986 before provision for restructuring.
Source: Emhart 1988 Annual Report.

Divestitures

Senior management at Black & Decker realized early that as much as $1 billion of Emhart's business assets would have to be sold to reduce B&D's interest expenses and debt obligations and enable it to meet its covenant agreements. According to accounting rules, these assets had to be sold within a year or be consolidated with the rest of B&D's assets—a move that could cause B&D to fail to meet its maximum leverage covenant. The Emhart businesses that were identified for sale within one year from the acquisition date included footwear materials, printed circuit board assembly equipment (Dynapert), capacitors, chemical adhesives (Bostik), and the entire information and electronic systems business unit (PRC).

During 1989 and early 1990, Black & Decker sold the Bostik chemical adhesives division to a French company for $345 million, the footwear materials business to the United Machinery Group for approximately $125 million, and its Arcotronics capacitors business to Nissei Electric of Tokyo for about $80 million; the net proceeds from these sales were used to reduce debt. In early 1990, when the one-year period expired, Black & Decker was forced to put about $566 million of the unsold assets on its books, boosting the goodwill on its balance sheet by $560 million and raising annual amortization charges by $14 million. To keep from violating the maximum debt/equity ratio allowed under its credit schedule, Black & Decker was forced to issue $150 million in new preferred stock, $47 million of which was purchased with money from its 401(k) employee thrift plan when no other buyers came forward.

Throughout 1991, Black & Decker continued to struggle to meet its covenant agreements. The company divested Emhart's Garden America business unit and the Mallory Controls operations in North America and Brazil for a combined total of about $140 million. The company also sold its True Temper Hardware unit, its PRC Medic unit, and its U.S. capacitors business for a combined total of nearly $110 million. The prices that B&D got for the Emhart businesses it sold were generally below management's expectations, partly because oncoming recessionary effects reduced what buyers were willing to pay.

Nonetheless, these divestitures (described by B&D management as "nonstrategic assets") and the sale of $150 million in preferred stock allowed Black & Decker to reduce its total debt from a peak of $4 billion following the Emhart acquisition in April 1989 to $2.9 billion at year-end 1991. Even so, Black & Decker was still hard pressed to generate enough cash to meet its debt repayment schedule, a problem compounded by the 1990–92 recession, which hit the company's tool and household goods businesses fairly hard. The company's stock price fell from the mid-20s at the time of the Emhart acquisition to a low of $11 to $12 in early 1991—many observers believed the fundamental cause of B&D's financial plight was that it had paid too much for Emhart. There was also concern whether there was enough strategic fit between Emhart and B&D. By early 1992, Black & Decker's stock price had recovered to the low 20s, partly because a decline in the prime rate from 10 percent to 6.5 percent had lowered B&D's interest burden substantially.

Exhibit 3 provides a 10-year summary of Black & Decker's financial and operating performance.

BLACK & DECKER'S CEO, NOLAN D. ARCHIBALD

The chief architect of Black & Decker's foray into diversification was Nolan D. Archibald. Black & Decker hired Archibald as president and chief operating officer in 1985, soon after the acquisition of GE's small household appliance business. Before joining Black & Decker, Archibald was president of the $1.7 billion consumer durables group at Beatrice Companies, where he was responsible for such business units as Samsonite luggage, Culligan water treatment products, Del Mar window coverings, Stiffel lamps, and Aristocraft kitchen cabinets.

At the time he was hired, Archibald was 42; he was chosen from a pool of some 50 candidates for the position and turned down offers to be president at two other

Exhibit 3 Summary of Black & Decker's Financial and Operating Performance, 1982–1991 (in thousands of dollars except for per common share data)

	1991	1990	1989[d]	1988[e]	1987	1986	1985[f]	1984[g]	1983	1982
Summary of Operations										
Total revenues	$4,636,954	$4,832,264	$3,172,540	$2,280,923	$1,934,799	$1,791,194	$1,732,278	$1,532,883	$1,167,752	$1,160,233
% change	(4.0)	52.3	39.1	17.9	8.0	3.4	13.0	31.3	0.6	(6.8)
Operating income	$ 401,414	$ 486,394	$ 259,170	$ 159,115	$ 112,473	$ 55,325	$ 93,287	$ 150,428	$ 91,781	$ 84,958
% of total revenues	8.7	10.1	8.2	7.0	5.8	3.1	5.4	9.8	7.9	7.3
% change	(17.5)	87.7	62.9	41.5	103.3	(40.7)	(38.0)	63.9	8.0	(37.4)
Earnings (loss) from continuing operations before income taxes and extraordinary item	$ 107,531	$ 123,495	$ 62,926	$ 125,695	$ 69,766	$ 34,743	$ (159,825)	$ 140,804	$ 38,451	$ 55,481
% of total revenues	2.3	2.6	2.0	5.5	3.6	1.9	(9.2)	9.2	3.3	4.8
% change	(12.9)	96.3	(49.9)	80.2	100.8	—	—	266.2	(30.7)	(44.1)
Income taxes (benefits)	$ 54,500	$ 72,400	$ 32,900	$ 28,600	$ 14,200	$ 7,200	$ (1,400)	$ 45,400	$ 10,300	$ 14,800
Effective tax (benefit) rate	50.7%	58.6%	52.3%	22.8%	20.4%	20.7%	(0.9)%	32.2%	26.8%	26.7%
Earnings (loss) from continuing operations before extraordinary item	$ 53,031	$ 51,095	$ 30,026	$ 97,095	$ 55,566	$ 27,543	$ (158,425)	$ 95,404	$ 28,151	$ 40,681
% change	3.8	70.2	(69.1)	74.7	101.8	—	—	238.9	(30.8)	(44.3)
Earnings (loss) from discontinued operations	—	—	—	—	—	—	—	—	$ 16,000	$ (117,283)
Net earnings (loss) before extraordinary item	$ 53,031	$ 51,095	$ 30,026	$ 97,095	$ 55,566	$ 27,543	$ (158,425)	$ 95,404	$ 44,151	$ (76,602)
% change	3.8	70.2	(69.1)	74.7	101.8	—	—	116.1	—	—
Extraordinary item	—	—	—	—	—	$ (21,239)	—	—	—	—
Net earnings (loss)	$ 53,031	$ 51,095	$ 30,026	$ 97,095	$ 55,566	$ 6,304	$ (158,425)	$ 95,404	$ 44,151	$ (76,602)
% change	3.8	70.2	(69.1)	74.7	781.4	—	—	116.1	—	—

Exhibit 3 Concluded

Per Common Share Data[a]

Earnings (loss):										
Continuing operations	$ 0.81	$ 0.84	$ 0.51	$ 1.65	$ 0.95	$ 0.49	$ (3.11)	$ 1.95	$ 0.65	$ 0.97
Discontinued operations	—	—	—	—	—	(.38)	—	—	0.37	(2.79)
Extraordinary item	—	—	—	—	—	—	—	—	—	—
Total	0.81	0.84	0.51	1.65	0.95	0.11	(3.11)	1.95	1.02	(1.82)
Cash dividends	0.40	0.40	0.40	0.40	0.40	0.58	0.64	0.58	0.52	0.76
Stockholders' equity	14.18	14.94	12.24	12.38	11.12	10.61	9.94	13.58	11.79	10.70

Other Data[b]

Number of employees	38,600	43,400	38,600	20,800	19,700	21,700	22,400	23,000	14,500	15,700
Total assets	$5,532,769	$5,889,534	$6,258,089	$1,825,109	$1,668,045	$1,580,571	$1,452,146	$1,473,448	$ 985,358	$ 995,329
Long-term debt	$2,625,833	$2,755,634	$2,629,718	$ 277,091	$ 250,578	$ 195,544	$ 334,501	$ 279,540	$ 150,108	$ 263,864
Total debt	$2,870,365	$3,268,345	$4,057,473	$ 492,574	$ 478,536	$ 407,426	$ 371,983	$ 303,763	$ 179,515	$ 306,239
Stockholders' equity	$1,027,163	$ 920,693	$ 720,721	$ 724,868	$ 649,114	$ 616,659	$ 504,848	$ 683,507	$ 554,416	$ 450,419
Capital expenditures	$ 107,667	$ 112,968	$ 112,103	$ 98,404	$ 58,766	$ 82,375	$ 118,299	$ 91,835	$ 75,759	$ 80,837
Depreciation and amortization	$ 202,324	$ 210,063	$ 130,978	$ 93,488	$ 99,036	$ 107,370	$ 93,338	$ 66,211	$ 51,973	$ 48,444
Working capital	$ 356,045	$ 221,146	$ 679,596	$ 555,786	$ 450,650	$ 355,128	$ 344,684	$ 461,545	$ 423,809	$ 406,542
Current ratio	1.3	1.1	1.3	1.7	1.6	1.5	1.7	2.2	2.8	2.8
Total revenues to average total assets	0.81	0.80	0.78	1.31	1.19	1.18	1.18	1.25	1.18	1.09
% return on average stockholders' equity[c]	5.4	6.3	4.2	14.1	8.8	1.1	(26.7)	15.4	5.2	8.1

aBased on the average number of shares of common stock outstanding during each year, except stockholders' equity, which is based on stockholders' equity, excluding preferred equity, divided by common shares outstanding at year-end.

bNumber of employees, capital expenditures, and depreciation and amortization relate to continuing operations of the corporation.

cCalculated on total stockholders' equity on an "as reported" basis for 1984 through 1991. For years 1982 and 1983, a pro forma basis was used with earnings from continuing operations and stockholders' equity adjusted to exclude portions allocable to operations sold.

dIncludes Emhart operations acquired on April 27, 1989.

eThe corporation adopted Statement of Financial Accounting Standard No. 96 in 1988. Accordingly, tax benefits recorded since 1988 as a result of utilizing net operating loss carryforwards are included as a reduction of income tax expense rather than as an extraordinary item.

fOperating results for 1985 include a restructuring charge of $215,000 before tax ($205,000 after tax).

gIncludes housewares operations acquired on April 27, 1984.

companies to take the B&D job. Archibald had been at Beatrice since 1977 and was successful in engineering turnarounds in three of Beatrice's businesses. Before that, he had headed a turnaround of Conroy Inc.'s Sno-Jet snowmobile business. Archibald spent two years of his youth winning converts as a Mormon missionary, was an All-American basketball player at Utah's Dixie College, became a standout player at Weber State College in Utah, earned his MBA degree at Harvard Business School, and tried out (unsuccessfully) for the Chicago Bulls professional basketball team. Corporate headhunters rated Archibald as a good strategic thinker who was personable, versatile, and sensitive to people.

According to one Black & Decker dealer, before Archibald took over as president in September 1985, "Black & Decker had been coasting along for quite a few years like a ship without a captain."[1] Archibald wasted little time in reorganizing Black & Decker's worldwide manufacturing operations. Within three months, Archibald initiated a restructuring plan to close older, inefficient plants and boost factory utilization rates by consolidating production within B&D's newest and biggest plants. Approximately 3,000 jobs were eliminated, including a number of high-level managerial positions. In 1985, B&D took a $215 million write-off for plant shutdowns and other cost-saving reorganization efforts.

Before 1985, the company had pursued a decentralized, multicountry strategy. Each geographic area of the world had its own production facilities, its own product-design centers, and its own marketing and sales organizations to better cater to local market conditions. Over the years, this had resulted in short production runs at scattered production sites, reduced overall manufacturing efficiency, and prevented achievement of scale economies—for example, there were about 100 motor sizes in B&D's product line. Archibald set the company on a more globalized approach to product design and manufacturing, with much greater communication and coordination between geographic operating units. Production at plants was organized around motor sizes, the number of product variations reduced, and production runs lengthened. From 1984 to 1989, seven plants were closed. Archibald also insisted more emphasis be put on quality control—during the early 1980s, B&D's reputation in power tools had been tarnished by shoddy product quality.

Meanwhile, Archibald put additional resources into new product development and redesign of the company's power tools and small-appliance lines. The company introduced a line of men's hair blowers, toasters with wider slots, a line of cordless power tools, and a heavy-duty power saw with a blade that moved back and forth for tasks such as cutting through plaster walls. Archibald set a goal for the tool division to come up with more than a dozen new products each year—more than B&D had introduced in the five years before his arrival. To help get new product ideas, Archibald created 10 panels of dealers and end-users to provide suggestions. Work on a new line of cordless kitchen appliances was accelerated.

Archibald's biggest marketing challenge was transferring consumers' brand loyalty for GE small appliances over to Black & Decker. Some observers believed Black & Decker would have trouble because B&D's traditional customers were men, and buyers of houseware products were usually women—as a *Wall Street Journal* article headline put it, "Would You Buy a Toaster from a Drillmaker?"

B&D executives believed, however, many women were familiar with the Black & Decker name because they bought power tools as gifts for men and because B&D had

---

[1]As quoted in *Business Week*, July 13, 1987, p. 90.

pioneered the development of household appliances powered by rechargeable batteries. Black & Decker's handheld Dustbuster vacuum cleaner was the market leader with a 45 percent share. B&D also had been marketing a cordless rotary scrub brush, a cordless rechargeable shoe shiner, and a rechargeable flashlight. Even before acquiring GE's houseware's business, B&D had planned to introduce a line of cordless kitchen appliances, but gaining ample retail shelf space was often a hit-and-miss proposition. What made the GE acquisition attractive to B&D was the extra clout that offering retailers a full line of housewares would have in competing for shelf space.

Black & Decker's competitors in small appliances saw the brand-name transition from GE to Black & Decker as an opportunity to gain market share that once was GE's. Sunbeam Appliance quadrupled its 1985 ad budget to $42 million because it wanted to replace GE as the best-known brand in small appliances. Norelco launched a new line of irons and handheld can openers powered by rechargeable batteries to wrest share away from GE/Black & Decker. Hamilton Beach introduced a battery-operated carving knife. Nearly all small-appliance producers were rumored to be trying to develop cordless adaptations of irons, coffee makers, handheld mixers, and electric carving knives.

Archibald responded to the brand transfer challenge with a series of actions. Since Black & Decker had until 1987 to put its own name on all the GE products it acquired, it led off the transfer process by first putting its name on GE's innovative, expensive, high-margin Spacemaker products that were mounted under kitchen cabinets—a line that was not as strongly identified with the GE name. Then B&D introduced a new iron (invented by GE) that shut off automatically when it sat too long or was tipped over; B&D's TV ads for the iron showed an elephant walking away from an iron that had been left on, with a tag line: "Even elephants forget." The brand transfer was accomplished product by product, in each case accompanied by heavy advertising. Under Archibald, Black & Decker spent approximately $100 million during the 1985–87 period to promote the brand transition. The company also organized a large team of brand transition assistants to hang paper tags on display models of newly rebranded products in about 10,000 retail stores across the United States—the tags stated GE previously sold products now made by Black & Decker. Most analysts regarded Archibald's brand transfer program as successful; a Harvard Business School professor stated, "It is almost a textbook example of how to manage a brand transition."[2]

By year-end 1988, Archibald was widely credited with engineering another impressive turnaround, having boosted Black & Decker's profits to $97.1 million—up sharply from the loss of $158.4 million posted in 1985 (see Exhibit 3). Archibald was promoted to chairman, president, and chief executive officer in 1986.

BLACK & DECKER'S BUSINESS PORTFOLIO IN 1992

In 1992, Black & Decker Corp. was a diversified multinational enterprise; its business portfolio consisted of:

- Power tools and power tool accessories for both do-it-yourselfers and professional tradespeople.
- Household appliance products.

[2]Ibid.

- Consumer-use fastening products.
- Security hardware for both residential and commercial use.
- Lawn and garden care products.
- Outdoor recreational products.
- Plumbing products.
- Commercial fastening products.
- Machinery for making glass containers.
- Machinery for manufacturing printed circuit boards.
- Information services.

Exhibit 4 provides a more detailed listing of the products produced and marketed by each of these businesses. Exhibit 5 provides financial performance data by business group and by geographic area. A brief description of each business group follows.

Power Tools and Accessories

Black & Decker was the world's largest manufacturer, marketer, and servicer of power tools and accessories. In 1991 alone, the power tools division introduced 50 new products; over the past five years, B&D had introduced more than 200 new and redesigned power tool products. B&D's approach to product development and manufacturing reflected a global outlook, although global strategies were modified to local country requirements as needed. B&D had formed "global business teams" to achieve worldwide coordination in power tool design, manufacturing, and marketing and to bring new power tool products to market quickly and efficiently. More than 200 companies had visited Black & Decker's power tools plant in Great Britain; the plant had won the Queen's Award for high standards and practices in quality, design, technology, and production. Most of the company's products carried a two-year warranty.

Industry Growth and Competition   Demand for power tools and accessories was regarded as mature and cyclical. Volume was influenced by residential and commercial construction activity, by consumer expenditures for home improvement, and by the overall level of manufacturing activity (a number of manufacturers used power tools in performing certain production tasks—automotive and aerospace firms, for example, were heavy users of power tools). The 1990–92 recession in the United States had produced a slump in power tool sales. However, rising demand for cordless tools was a significant sales plus. During the 1992–97 period, the power tool industry in the United States was expected to grow at a compound annual rate of 1.5 percent in constant dollars. Demand in Europe was expected to grow faster due to sales opportunities to users in the newly democratic countries in Eastern Europe. Worldwide, the biggest percentage growth was projected to occur in developing countries where use of power tools was still rather limited. Worldwide sales of power tools and accessories were an estimated $6 billion in 1991.

Market Segments   There were two distinct groups of buyers for power tools: professional users and do-it-yourselfers. Professional users included construction workers, electricians, plumbers, repair and maintenance workers, auto mechanics,

Exhibit 4   Black & Decker's Business Portfolio in 1992

Consumer and Home Improvement Products Group

Power tools (1991 sales: $1.095 billion)
- Drills
- Screwdrivers
- Saws
- Sanders
- Grinders
- Car care and automotive products
- Workmate workcenters

Power tool accessories (1991 sales: $32 million)
- Drill bits
- Screwdriver bits
- Saw blades

Consumer-use fastening products (1991 sales: $185 million)
- Blind fasteners
- Wall anchors
- Rivets and rivet guns
- Staple and glue guns

Security hardware (1991 sales: $454 million)
- Lock sets
- Deadbolts
- Door closers
- Exit devices
- High-security locks
- Master keying systems

Plumbing products (1991 sales: $148 million)
- Faucets and fixtures
- Valves
- Fittings

Household products (1991 sales: $723 million)
- Cordless vacuum cleaners
- Cordless flashlights
- Cordless scrub brushes
- Cordless shoe shiners
- Irons
- Toasters
- Toaster ovens
- Coffee makers
- Can openers
- Food mixers
- Food processors and choppers
- Blenders

Lawn and garden care products (1991 sales: $198 million)
- Hedge and lawn trimmers
- Edgers
- Electric lawn mowers
- Blowers and vacuums
- Thatchers
- Shredders
- Electric chain saws

Outdoor recreational products (1991 sales: $100 million)
- Golf club shafts
- Tubing for bicycle frames
- Kayak paddles

Commercial and Industrial Products Groups

Fastening systems (1991 sales: $371 million)
- Rivets and riveting tools
- Threaded inserts
- Stud welding fastening systems
- Lock nuts
- Self-drilling screws
- Construction anchors

Glass container–making machinery
(1991 sales: about $180 million)

Assembly equipment for making printed circuit boards
(1991 sales: about $180 million)

Information Systems and Services Group

This group consisted entirely of the business of PRC, Inc. (1991 sales: $684 million), an information technology firm that contracted with customers to provide the following:
Systems integration
Software development and computer services
Data network development
Engineering and management services
Scientific research services
Environmental engineering and consulting services
Real estate multiple listing services
Computer-aided emergency dispatch systems

Exhibit 5   Black & Decker's Financial Performance by Business Segment and Geographic Area, 1989–1991

Business Segments

1991	Consumer and Home Improvement Products	Commercial and Industrial Products	Information System and Services
Sales to unaffiliated customers	$3,224,372	$ 728,206	$684,376
Operating income before goodwill amortization	307,232	113,278	35,432
Goodwill amortization	53,089	17,698	3,125
Operating income	254,143	95,580	32,307
Identifiable assets	4,605,945	1,574,051	380,563
Capital expenditures	80,096	12,816	12,708
Depreciation	92,577	16,155	12,098
1990			
Sales to unaffiliated customers	$3,425,703	$ 887,509	$519,052
Operating income before goodwill amortization	355,533	143,463	28,279
Goodwill amortization	48,918	17,062	2,344
Operating income	306,615	126,401	25,935
Identifiable assets	4,792,075	1,532,318	327,839
Capital expenditures	85,455	16,413	9,891
Depreciation	102,067	21,959	9,894
1989			
Sales to unaffiliated customers	$2,856,599	$ 315,941	—
Operating income before goodwill amortization	236,594	43,408	—
Goodwill amortization	20,261	5,111	—
Operating income	216,333	38,297	—
Identifiable assets	4,567,007	1,045,510	—
Capital expenditures	101,082	7,444	—
Depreciation	85,873	8,212	—

Geographic Areas

1991	United States	Europe	Other
Sales to unaffiliated customers	$2,599,436	$1,409,478	$628,040
Sales and transfers between geographic areas	223,022	143,630	164,310
Total sales	$2,822,458	$1,553,108	$792,350
Operating income	$ 188,427	$ 163,968	$ 27,868
Identifiable assets	3,479,143	2,391,445	595,472
1990			
Sales to unaffiliated customers	$2,785,980	$1,371,585	$674,699
Sales and transfers between geographic areas	213,860	150,283	187,330
Total sales	$2,999,840	$1,521,868	$862,029
Operating income	$ 249,932	$ 166,184	$ 45,771
Identifiable assets	3,583,638	2,296,307	782,687
1989			
Sales to unaffiliated customers	$1,734,525	$ 935,560	$502,455
Sales and transfers between geographic areas	112,317	73,494	233,594
Total sales	$1,846,842	$1,009,054	$736,049
Operating income	$ 114,119	$ 92,837	$ 47,674
Identifiable assets	3,259,304	1,654,185	698,428

Source: 1991 annual report.

and manufacturing workers. Professional users were very quality conscious and features conscious; they tended to buy only tools that were durable, functional, dependable, and precision capable. They tended to be very knowledgeable and informed as compared to do-it-yourselfers, many of whom were first-time buyers and used power tools infrequently.

Because the needs of professional users and do-it-yourself consumers tended to be sharply different, some manufacturers had a heavy-duty professional line and a consumer/do-it-yourselfer line while others catered to just one segment. Professional users tended to purchase their tools through jobbers, contractor supply firms, industrial supply houses, and some building supply centers. Tools for the consumer segment were sold at home improvement centers (such as Home Depot and Lowe's), building materials centers, mass merchandisers (Sears), discount chains (Wal-Mart, Kmart), and hardware stores.

Until the late 1980s, the consumer tool segment was growing at a faster clip than the professional segment. But narrowing price differentials and a rising interest on the part of gung-ho do-it-yourselfers in professional quality tools had, in the U.S. market, spurred demand for heavy-duty professional tools. The professional tool segment in the United States was a $400 million market, compared to $1.5 billion to $1.6 billion for the consumer tools segment. B&D believed sales of power tools and power tool accessories to professional users in North America (Canada, Mexico, and the United States) represented a $1 billion market.

Competition Power tool manufacturers competed on such variables as price, quality, product design, product innovation, brand-name reputation, size and strength of retail dealer networks, and after-sale service. All makers were working to bring out new products that were lightweight, compact, cordless, less noisy, prone to less vibration, strong, and fit easily and comfortably in users' hands. The major manufacturers had sales forces whose main task was to expand and strengthen the network of retail dealers carrying their line of tools. Salespeople signed on new dealers and called on major accounts—wholesale distributors, discount chains, home improvement centers, and other mass merchandisers—to win better access to shelf space in their retail outlets, help with promotion and display activities, and upgrade dealers' product knowledge and sales skills. Some manufacturers offered training seminars and provided training videos to dealers/distributors. Manufacturers that concentrated on the professional segment engaged in limited advertising and promotion activities, spending their dollars for trade magazine ads, trade shows, and in-store displays. Those that concentrated on the consumer segment, like Black & Decker, spent rather heavily for TV and magazine ads and also for co-op ad programs with dealers.

Black & Decker's Competitive Position In 1992, Black & Decker was the overall world leader in the world power tool industry, followed by Japanese maker Makita and Germany's Robert Bosch Power Tools, a division of Robert Bosch Corp.—one of Germany's leading companies (1991 sales of $20 billion) and a major global supplier of automotive components, electronics products, and small household appliances. Black & Decker's strength was in the consumer tools segment (see Exhibit 6); it was the market leader in the United States, Europe (where it had had a presence since the 1920s), and many other countries outside Europe. No other manufacturer came close to matching B&D's global distribution capabilities in the do-it-yourself segment. Makita, along with Ryobi, were the leaders in Japan and several other Asian

Exhibit 6 Estimated U.S. Sales and Market Shares of Power Tool Manufacturers, 1979 and 1991 (dollar values in millions)

Company	Consumer Tools 1979 Dollar Sales	Consumer Tools 1979 Percent Share	Consumer Tools 1991 Dollar Sales	Consumer Tools 1991 Percent Share	Professional Tools 1979 Dollar Sales	Professional Tools 1979 Percent Share	Professional Tools 1991 Dollar Sales	Professional Tools 1991 Percent Share	Total Tools 1979 Dollar Sales	Total Tools 1979 Percent Share	Total Tools 1991 Dollar Sales	Total Tools 1991 Percent Share	Accessories 1991 Dollar Sales	Accessories 1991 Percent Share
Black & Decker	$169	44.5%	$325	39.7%	$205	42.1%	$125	17.9%	$374	43.1%	$450	29.6%	$110	10.0%
Sears/Ryobi	107	28.2	280	34.0	9	1.8	50	7.1	116	13.4	330	21.7	20	1.8
Makita	2	0.5	43	5.2	22	4.5	160	22.9	24	2.8	203	13.4	157	14.3
Milwaukee	6	1.5	4	0.5	89	18.2	145	20.7	95	10.9	149	9.8	146	13.3
Skil	52	13.7	82	10.0	54	11.1	40	5.7	106	12.2	122	8.0	128	11.6
Porter Cable	—	—	—	—	NA	NA	50	7.1	NA	NA	50	3.3	50	4.5
Delta	—	—	—	—	NA	NA	40	5.7	NA	NA	40	2.6	50	4.5
Bosch	—	—	—	—	25	5.1	30	4.3	25	2.9	30	2.0	—	—
Hitachi	—	—	—	—	NA	NA	20	2.9	NA	NA	20	1.3	5	0.5
Others	44	11.6	86	10.6	84	17.2	40	5.7	128	14.7	126	8.3	434	39.5
Total	$380	100.0%	$820	100.0%	$488	100.0%	$700	100.0%	$868	100.0%	$1,520	100.0%	$1,100	100.0%

NA = not available.
Source: Compiled by the case researchers from a variety of sources, including telephone interviews with company personnel; data for 1979 is based on information in Skil Corporation, Harvard Business School, case #9-389-005.

countries. Bosch was strongest in Europe. In late 1991, Bosch announced that Robert Bosch Tools would merge with Skil, a subsidiary of Emerson Electric, to form a 50-50 joint venture to manufacture and market power tools.

In consumer tools, Black & Decker's strongest U.S. competitor was Sears, which marketed tools under the Sears Craftsman label. Sears' longtime supplier of tools was Singer; Singer's tool manufacturing operations had recently been acquired by Japan's Ryobi. Singer/Ryobi supplied Sears with 80 to 90 percent of its tool requirements. Skil's strength was in power saws; its joint venture with Robert Bosch Power Tools was expected to give the two partners more clout in gaining shelf space and greater global coverage capabilities.

Although surveys showed consumers associated the Black & Decker name with durable power tools, trade professionals viewed B&D tools as products for do-it-yourselfers. The company's charcoal-gray professional line was not seen by professional users as sufficiently differentiated from B&D's traditional black line of consumer tools. Professionals preferred tools made by Makita, Skil, and Milwaukee (a U.S. tool manufacturer with a reputation for quality, heavy-duty tools). However, no toolmaker currently held the largest share in every tool category. During the 1970s and 1980s, Makita had steadily increased its share of the professional segment and as of 1992 was the brand most used by professionals.

In 1991, B&D executives formed a team, headed by the president of B&D's power tools division, to come up with a new strategy for the professional market. The team elected to create a new line of industrial-grade tools for professional users under the DeWalt brand, a name borrowed from a 65-year-old maker of high-quality stationary saws acquired by B&D in 1960. The team changed the tool's color from gray to industrial yellow because it was easy to see, signaled safety, and was a color pros liked. Every product in B&D's professional line was redesigned based on input from professionals, dealers, and B&D engineers. The redesigned versions were all tested by professional users; every item had to meet or beat Makita's tools in user tests before going into production.

The new DeWalt line was introduced in March 1992. As part of the introduction, B&D created a fleet of demonstration booth vans, which were parked near major retailers or construction sites. The company also instituted a policy of offering professional users the loan of a DeWalt power tool when waiting for their equipment to be fixed at any of the company's 117 U.S. service centers. There were also DeWalt demonstration booths at each of the service centers. Initial response to the DeWalt line was excellent. B&D officials expected DeWalt to be a $100 million to $200 million brand and have a 25 to 50 percent market share in the United States within three years. Archibald's goal was for DeWalt's revenues to equal or exceed Makita's revenues in the U.S. market by 1996.

In addition to its 117 service and repair centers in the United States, Black & Decker had 123 foreign service centers, primarily in Canada, Mexico, Europe, Latin America, and Australia. Although recessionary influences caused a drop in 1991 power tool sales in the United States, Australia, and Brazil, B&D had record sales and operating profits in Europe in 1991.

To gain distribution for its products in Japan and begin to challenge Makita and Ryobi in their home market, B&D had recently entered into a joint venture with a Japanese distributor of power tools. B&D had more than doubled its sales of power tool accessories (particularly drill bits, screwdriver bits, and saw blades) in North America over the past five years. The company had a just-in-time procurement, inventory management, and distribution program to shorten the cycle of supplying customers; this "quick response" system received sales data electronically from the top retailers and processed orders automatically.

In 1991, B&D was named Vendor of the Year by Lowe's, a large North American home center chain; it also received the Partners in Progress award from Sears (Sears began selling Black & Decker products when it implemented its "brand central" theme of stocking many name-brand items as well as traditional Sears' brands).

Household Products

As of 1992, Black & Decker's household products business had established itself as a worldwide leader in products used for home cleaning, garment care, cooking, and food and beverage preparation. It had the largest market share of any full-line producer of household appliance products in the United States, Canada, Mexico, and Australia and a growing presence in Europe, Southeast Asia, and Latin America. The household products division was using the worldwide distribution network and brand-name recognition that had been established by the tools division to gain greater global penetration in household appliances. In 1992, B&D's irons and Dustbuster cordless vacuums were being marketed in more than 100 countries. To accelerate international expansion, B&D had formed global business teams to focus the corporation's technical expertise and marketing capabilities on (1) launching new houseware products in foreign countries where B&D already had a presence and (2) expanding into new countries.

Industry Growth and Competition   Like power tools, the market for small household appliances was both mature and cyclical. Growth opportunities existed mainly in the form of creating innovative new products and in increasing market penetration in the countries of Eastern Europe and other developing nations where household appliance saturation rates were low. Sales of small household appliances in the United States had fluctuated between $2.2 billion and $2.7 billion for the past five years, with no evident trend. Exhibit 7 shows the makeup and size of the market for small household appliances in the United States. The global market for small appliances (excluding electric fans and vacuum cleaners) was approximately $6 billion to $8 billion. Industry experts projected growth of 1.5 to 2.5 percent (in constant dollars) during the 1992–96 period, with potential for a bigger near-term rebound since recessionary influences in the United States and Australia had produced a sales downturn in 1992. Sales of household appliances tended to be greatest during the Christmas shopping period.

Black & Decker's Competitive Position   Black and Decker was the market leader in most product categories in the U.S. market (see Exhibit 8 for market shares of the major competitors by product category). *Consumer Reports* gave Black & Decker products generally high ratings for various household appliances. Black & Decker confronted different competitors in different product categories and in different areas of the world. In irons, for example, B&D's strongest U.S. competitors were Wear-Ever/Proctor-Silex and Sunbeam, but in Europe its strongest competitor was German maker Rowenta. In food processors, B&D's strongest competitor in the United States was Hamilton Beach, but its strongest U.S. competitor in can openers was Rival. B&D's brand awareness in the United States and Canada was twice that of its nearest competitor in small appliances.

Exhibit 7   Size and Makeup of the Small Household Appliance Market in the United States, 1990

	1990 Sales of Small Household Appliances in the United States			1990 Estimated Unit Volume of Small Household Appliances	
	Dollar Sales (millions)	Percent Share		Units (thousands)	Percent Share
Electric housewares	$5,065	80.29%	Clocks	40,530	22.80%
Vacuum cleaners	1,680	26.63	Coffee makers	17,740	9.98
Household fans	1,075	17.04	Irons	16,950	9.54
Food processors	500	7.93	Electric grills/skillets/fryers	11,100	6.25
Coffee makers	450	7.13	Vacuum cleaners, nonhandheld	10,960	6.17
Cookware	450	7.13	Smoke detectors	10,000	5.63
Irons	225	3.57	Toasters	8,900	5.00
Toasters	220	3.48	Can openers	6,200	3.49
Can openers	100	1.59	Timers	5,850	3.29
Corn poppers	30	0.48	Blenders	5,600	3.15
Other housewares	335	5.31	Vacuums, handheld rechargeable	5,000	2.81
Other appliances	1,243	19.71	Food processors	4,760	2.68
Total	$6,308	100.00%	Hand mixers	4,400	2.48
			Slow cookers	4,160	2.34
			Air purifiers	3,800	2.14
			Corn poppers	2,900	1.63
			Toaster ovens	2,800	1.58
			Vacuums, handheld electric	2,500	1.41
			Ice cream makers	1,530	0.86
			Electric knives	1,420	0.80
			Bag sealers	1,400	0.79
			Mixers, stand-type	1,100	0.62
			Coffee grinders	800	0.45
			Intrusion systems	800	0.45
			Juicers	410	0.23
			Floor polishers	175	0.10
			Convection ovens	125	0.07
			Bread makers	105	0.06
			Other small appliances	5,755	3.20
			Total	177,770	100.00%

Sources: Compiled by the case researchers from data presented in *American Metals Market*, September 30, 1991, p. 4, and *Appliance*, April 1991, p. 27.

Black & Decker was using its quick response system to good advantage in household appliances as well as power tools. B&D had electronic point-of-sale linkage with many of its retail customers to speed order processing, manage inventories, and plan its own production more efficiently. It also supplied modular in-store displays for retailers to use in showcasing the features of B&D's new household appliance products. In 1992, B&D received Vendor of the Year awards from its two most important customers, Wal-Mart and Target. Survey data showed B&D's household products were ranked ahead of all other brands that retailers preferred to sell.

Exhibit 8   Market Shares of Major Small Appliance Competitors, 1990

Company	Blenders	Can Openers	Coffee Makers	Food Processors	Hand Mixers	Irons	Smoke Detectors	Toaster Ovens	Toasters	Vacuum Cleaners	Handheld Vacuums
Black & Decker	9%	26%	20%	25%	34%	50%	—	57%	16%	—	45%
Wear-Ever	—	6	16	—	—	21	—	19	35	—	—
Sunbeam	—	8	—	13	25	17	—	—	6	—	—
Mr. Coffee	—	—	28	—	—	—	—	—	—	—	—
Hamilton Beach	27	7	3	21	14	3	—	13	—	—	—
Toastmaster	—	2	—	—	—	—	—	13	27	—	—
Rival	—	33	—	—	12	—	—	—	—	—	—
Braun	17	—	9	3	—	—	—	—	—	—	—
Oster	35	3	—	5	—	—	—	—	—	—	—
Hoover	—	—	—	—	—	—	—	—	—	34%	5
Eureka	—	—	—	—	—	—	—	—	—	23	3
Singer	—	—	—	—	—	—	—	—	—	11	—
Royal	—	—	—	—	—	—	—	—	—	3	37
Pittway	—	—	—	—	—	—	60%	—	—	—	—
Jameson	—	—	—	—	—	—	25	—	—	—	—
Others	12	15	24	33	15	9	15	11	16	29	10
Total	100%	100%	100%	100%	100%	100%	100%	100%	100%	100%	100%

Source: Compiled by the case researchers from data presented in *Appliance*, April 1991.

Security Hardware

B&D's security hardware business was the world leader in door hardware for homes and businesses. Its Kwikset brand was the best-selling U.S. brand of residential door locks and hardware. The Kwikset brand was particularly favored by do-it-yourselfers; B&D had boosted Kwikset's sales by providing retailers with a videotape that took the mystery out of changing locks for do-it-yourselfers. In Europe, B&D had recently introduced new lines of garage door locks, fire-resistant locks, and high-security key cylinders for the German, Dutch, and Italian markets.

This business, acquired from Emhart, had achieved significant cost savings by integrating its purchasing, distribution, and marketing activities with B&D's other consumer products businesses. B&D's worldwide distribution network was also providing the hardware group wider geographic sales opportunities. In many instances, door hardware was sold in the same retail channels as B&D's power tools and accessories.

Plumbing Products

B&D's plumbing products business, Price Pfister, had gained market share since the Emhart acquisition, though it trailed the market leaders in kitchen and bathroom faucets. Price Pfister had benefited from access to B&D's retail distribution network and its corporate support systems (quick response), gaining more shelf space in home improvement centers. Price Pfister had also introduced fashionable but affordably-priced new designs and new lines that had become popular with plumbing wholesalers and plumbing contractors. Price Pfister had increased its brand recognition with TV ads, using the theme "The Pfabulous Pfaucet with the Pfunny Name." Price Pfister's major competitors were American Standard, Kohler, and Delta, all of which had bigger market shares of the approximately $1.5 billion U.S. market for sink, tub, shower, and lavatory plumbing hardware.

Recreational Outdoor Products

B&D's True Temper Sports business unit was the leading global producer of golf club shafts, supplying major golf club manufacturers around the world. Nine out of 10 golf professionals used clubs with True Temper shafts. The sales of this unit had declined significantly in 1991 as recessionary influences in several major markets produced a general slowdown in golf equipment sales. However, the golf industry had enjoyed record growth during the 1986–90 period, and demographic trends pointed to renewed expansion since golf was growing in popularity among the increasingly populous 45 to 75 age group in the United States, Europe, and Japan. Golfers were also upgrading their golf equipment in response to manufacturers' introduction of high-tech golf clubs with graphite, boron, and titanium shafts; the new shafts had much bigger profit margins than conventional steel shafts.

The 1992 Olympic Summer Games marked the third consecutive Olympics at which U.S. cyclists competed on True Temper bicycle frames. Olympic kayakers also used True Temper paddles (three 1988 gold medalists had used True Temper paddles).

Lawn and Garden Equipment

Black & Decker's lawn and garden products unit introduced nine new products in 1991. This business unit also utilized the same distribution channels as the power tools business, and the buyers of B&D's lawn and garden equipment could get items repaired at B&D's 240 company-owned service centers worldwide and several hundred other authorized service centers operated by independent owners. It was also employing the quick response system. Where feasible, B&D's lawn and garden products had a global design.

Fastening Systems

This business unit marketed 11 brands of fastening products. To link their identities, B&D in 1991 began marketing them under the banner of Emhart Fastening Teknologies. Management believed this would leverage its brand names and enhance the unit's ability to market to industrial users on a more global scale. Joining the marketing activities of these brands under a single banner to create more of a full line of fastening products was considered vital to get the business of industrial customers, who preferred to deal with a limited number of suppliers. Recently, the fasteners unit had introduced new stud welding and assembly systems that boosted its sales to automotive manufacturers worldwide by 25 percent. A "total quality" initiative had been launched throughout the Emhart Fasteners Teknologies group. The Warren division was selected by Honda of America from among 300 suppliers for Honda's 1991 Quality Performance Award and 1991 Delivery Performance Award—Warren achieved 100 percent on-time delivery and zero rejections per million pieces. The Gripco division received Ford's Q1 Award, Chrysler's QE Award, and GM's Mark of Excellence award in 1991.

The fasteners unit had seven U.S. plants and two European plants and marketed to customers in the United States, Europe, and the Far East. Principal customers were automotive, electronics, aerospace, machine tool, and appliance companies. Products were sold directly to users and also through distributors and manufacturer's representatives. Competition centered around product quality, performance, reliability, price, delivery, and ability to provide customers with technical and engineering services. Competition came from many manufacturers in several countries. B&D management believed the Emhart Fasteners Teknologies group was among the global leaders in the fasteners industry.

Glass Container–Making Machinery

Several U.S. manufacturers and a number of foreign firms competed with B&D's glass container–making machinery business. However, B&D's Emhart Glass/Powers division was considered the global leader and offered the world's most complete line of glass container–making equipment. Important competitive factors were price, technological and machine performance features, product reliability, and technical and engineering services. An increasing worldwide preference for recyclable glass packaging was expected to produce steady growth in demand for glass container–making equipment. Glass container–making equipment was in 24-hour use in virtually all plants worldwide, creating a predictable need for servicing and rebuilding; over two-thirds of the unit's revenues came from rebuilding and repair services and technology upgrades. The business reported sales and profit gains in 1991 and entered 1992 with a substantial order backlog.

Dynapert

The Dynapert business unit provided automated equipment for assembling printed circuit boards to electronics customers around the world. The equipment was among the most complex computer-controlled machinery being used in any industrial application. Dynapert had two manufacturing plants (one in the United States and one in England) and sales and service facilities throughout the world. The unit had launched a "total quality" program and implemented just-in-time manufacturing techniques.

Sales were made directly to users by an employee sales force and independent sales representatives. Dynapert faced competition from both U.S. and foreign manufacturers. Competition centered around technological and machine performance features, price, delivery terms, and provision of technical services. The Dynapert division, which generated annual sales of about $180 million, had been put on the market for sale shortly after the Emhart acquisition, but so far a buyer willing to pay an acceptable price had not been found.

Information Systems and Services

This segment consisted of a single business unit known as PRC, Inc., headquartered in McLean, Virginia. PRC and its predecessors had been in business since the mid-1970s. A majority of PRC's business came from contracts with various agencies and units of the federal government. Approximately 40 percent of PRC's 1991 revenues were from contracts with the Department of Defense. In addition, PRC was the leading provider of on-line printed residential real estate multiple listing systems and computer-aided emergency dispatch systems.

The types of services PRC provided were highly competitive, and strategic defense expenditures were expected to decline given the end of the Cold War. Many of PRC's competitors were large defense contractors with significantly greater financial resources. As the Department of Defense's expenditures for weapons programs continued to decline, these large contractors were expected to bid more aggressively for the types of contract work done by PRC.

PRC had also been put on the market for sale after the Emhart acquisition. In 1991, PRC had sales of $684 million and pretax operating earnings of $32.3 million. In mid-1991, B&D appointed a new person to head PRC; shortly thereafter, PRC launched an initiative to pursue new markets. The objective was to shift PRC's business mix so that half came from U.S. customers and half from overseas customers.

BLACK & DECKER'S FUTURE OUTLOOK

Black & Decker outperformed competitors and gained market share in most of its major businesses in 1991—even in businesses where difficult economic conditions resulted in sales declines. Nolan Archibald believed the company was in position to prosper when market conditions improved. Archibald's two top objectives were to reduce B&D's debt still further, selling nonstrategic assets if necessary, and to increase net income 20 percent annually over the next several years.

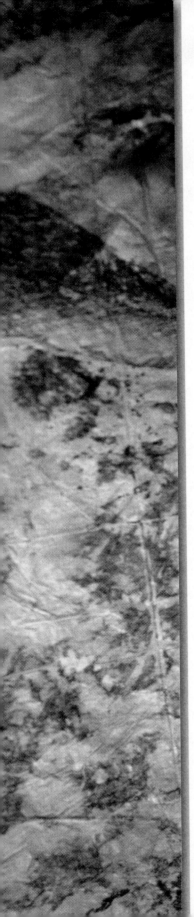

Campbell Soup Company

John E. Gamble, Auburn University at Montgomery
Arthur A. Thompson, Jr., The University of Alabama

Campbell Soup Company is one of the world's leading manufacturers and marketers of branded consumer food products. In 1995, the company had approximately 45,000 employees, total revenues of $7 billion, 80 manufacturing plants in 12 nations, and over 1,000 products on the market. Its major products were its flagship red-and-white label canned soups, Prego spaghetti sauces, LeMenu frozen dinners, Pepperidge Farms baked goods, Mrs. Paul's frozen foods, Franco-American canned spaghettis, Vlasic Pickles, and its newly acquired Pace Mexican foods.

Founded in 1869 by Joseph Campbell, a fruit merchant, and Abram Anderson, an icebox maker, the company was originally known for its jams and jellies. In 1891, it was incorporated as the Joseph Campbell Co. in Camden, New Jersey. In 1899, John T. Dorrance, a brilliant 24-year-old with a Ph.D. from MIT, developed a process for canning soup in condensed form. He was also a master salesman who came up with the idea of attaching snappy placards to the sides of New York City streetcars as a way of promoting the company's products. From 1900 to 1954, the company was owned entirely by the Dorrance family. It was incorporated as the Campbell Soup Company in 1922.

When John Dorrance died in 1930 after running the company for 16 years, he left an estate of over $115 million, the third largest at that time. He also left a company devoted to engineering, committed to providing good products (in recessions it would rather shave margins than cut back product quality or raise price), and obsessed with secrecy. His successor, John T. Dorrance, Jr., headed the company for the next 24 years (1930–54) and few, if any, important decisions were made at Campbell without his approval. In 1954, the company went public, with the Dorrance family retaining majority control. In 1995, the Dorrance family still owned about 58 percent of Campbell's stock and, despite having relinquished direct management control, still exerted a powerful shareholder influence. In 1984, John T. Dorrance III became a member of the board.

Over the years Campbell had diversified into a number of food and food-related businesses—Swanson frozen dinners, Pepperidge Farm bakery products, Franco-American spaghetti products, Recipe pet food, fast-food restaurant chains, Godiva chocolates, and even retail garden centers. Still, in 1995, almost 40 percent of the company's revenues came from the sale of its original stock-in-trade: canned soup. Traditionally, most of Campbell's top executives had come up through the production ranks of the Soup division—most had engineering training and good track records in achieving better manufacturing efficiency. One such person, Harold A. Shaub, a

We gratefully acknowledge the contribution of Sharon Henson in researching and helping develop an earlier (1985) version of this case.

30-year veteran of the company, was named president in 1972. An industrial engineer, Shaub placed a premium on controlling production costs while maintaining acceptable product quality. There were occasions when Shaub, during unannounced plant inspection tours, had ordered a halt to production when he spotted things that didn't measure up to the strict standards he demanded.

During his tenure Shaub restructured the company into divisions built around major product lines. In 1978, concluding that Campbell's marketing skills were subpar, he brought in management outsiders to revitalize the company's marketing capabilities. That same year Shaub engineered Campbell's acquisition of Vlasic Foods, Inc., the largest producer of pickles in the United States. Also in 1978 Campbell launched Prego spaghetti sauce products, the first major new food item introduced by Campbell in 10 years. Prior to Prego's introduction, it was Campbell's policy to require that a new product have the potential to recover development costs and introductory expenses within a year. But because the policy resulted in many new product ideas being canceled, Shaub set a goal of introducing two additional products each year, and he approved the Prego line introduction despite an expected three-year investment payback period.

Given Campbell's long-standing practice of selecting production-oriented CEOs, everyone expected Shaub's successor to come from production. Thus, it came as a surprise to Gordon McGovern, president of Campbell's Connecticut-based Pepperidge Farm subsidiary and a marketing man, when Shaub called him into his office and said, "I'd like you to come down here and take my place."[1] McGovern became Campbell's president and CEO on December 1, 1980.

THE GORDON MCGOVERN ERA: 1980–1989

McGovern was in business school when Margaret Rudkin, founder of Pepperidge Farm, spoke to his class. She told how she had built her bread company from scratch in an industry dominated by giants. McGovern was impressed. He wrote to Rudkin for a job, received it in 1956, and began his climb through Pepperidge Farm's ranks. When Campbell acquired Pepperidge Farm in 1961, it had sales of $40 million. When McGovern became Pepperidge Farm's president in 1968, sales had reached $60 million. When he was named president of Campbell in 1980, Pepperidge Farm had sales of $300 million. McGovern implemented several key elements of Pepperidge's strategy when he took over at Campbell: creativity and a willingness to experiment, emphasis on new product development, and building a strong competence in marketing.

McGovern's Corporate Strategy

During the McGovern years, Campbell's strategic focus was on the consumer. The consumer's "hot buttons" were identified as nutrition, convenience, low sodium, attractive price, good quality, and unique products—and managers were urged to press those buttons. Business unit managers were expected to be responsive to consumer perceptions, needs, and demands regarding nutrition, safety, flavor, and convenience. Key business unit strategies included (1) improving operating efficiency,

---

[1]As quoted in *Forbes*, December 7, 1981, p. 44.

(2) developing new products to capitalize on consumer trends, (3) updating advertising for new and established products, and (4) continuing Campbell's long-standing emphasis on high production standards and premium-quality products.

Early in his tenure, McGovern developed a five-year plan that featured four financial performance objectives: a 15 percent annual increase in earnings, a 5 percent increase in volume, a 5 percent increase in sales (plus inflation), and an 18 percent return on equity by 1986. The two cornerstones of McGovern's growth strategy were (1) developing and introducing new products and (2) making acquisitions every two years that would bring in $200 million in annual sales. Campbell's acquisition strategy was to look for small, fast-growing food companies strong in product areas where Campbell had no presence and companies on the fast track that were in rapidly growing product categories or industries. Under McGovern, Campbell made a number of acquisitions:

1982

- Mrs. Paul's Kitchens, Inc., a processor and marketer of frozen prepared seafood and vegetable products, with annual sales of approximately $125 million; acquired at a cost of $55 million.
- Snow King Frozen Foods, Inc., engaged in the production and marketing of a line of uncooked frozen specialty meat products, with annual sales of $32 million.
- Juice Bowl Products, Inc., a Florida producer of fruit juices.
- Win Schuler Foods, Inc., a Michigan-based producer and distributor of specialty cheese spreads, flavored melba rounds, food-service salad dressings, party dips, and sauces, with annual sales of $6.5 million.
- Costa Apple Products, Inc., a producer of apple juice retailed primarily in the eastern United States, with annual sales of $6 million.

1983

- Annabelle's restaurant chain of 12 units in the southeastern United States.
- Triangle Manufacturing Corp., a manufacturer of physical fitness and sports medicine products.

1984

- Mendelson-Zeller Co., Inc., a California distributor of fresh produce.

1985

- Continental Foods Company S.A. and affiliated companies, which produced sauces, confectioneries, and other food products in Belgium and France; the cost of the acquisition was $17 million.
- A 20 percent ownership interest in Arnott's, Ltd., an Australian producer of cookies and crackers.

1988

- Freshbake Foods Group, a British producer of baked goods.

Campbell's Business Portfolio under McGovern

During the McGovern era Campbell Soup Company was organized into six business units—Campbell U.S., Pepperidge Farm, Vlasic Foods, Mrs. Paul's Kitchens, Other United States, and International. Sales and profit performance by division are shown in Exhibit 1.

Campbell U.S.   In 1989, the Campbell U.S. division was the company's largest operating unit, accounting for just over 50 percent of corporate revenues. The Campbell U.S. division was divided into eight profit centers: soup, frozen foods, grocery, beverage, food service, poultry, fresh produce, and pet foods. Exhibit 2 shows the brands Campbell had in this division and the major competitors each brand faced during most of the 1980s.

The soup business group alone accounted for more than 25 percent of the company's consolidated sales (as compared to around 50 percent in the 1970s)—Campbell's flagship brands of soup accounted for 80 percent of the $1 billion-plus annual canned soup market; in 1989, Campbell offered grocery shoppers over 50 varieties of canned soups. Heinz was the second largest soup producer, with 10 percent of the market. Heinz had earlier withdrawn from producing Heinz-label soups and shifted its production over to making soups for sale under the private labels of grocery chains; Heinz was the leading private-label producer of canned soup, holding almost an 80 percent share of the private-label segment.

Although the soup business was relatively mature (McGovern preferred to call it underworked), Campbell's most ambitious consumer research took place in this unit. McGovern opted to grow Campbell's soup sales by turning out a steady flow of new varieties in convenient packages: "Ethnic, dried, refrigerated, frozen, microwave—you name it, we're going to try it."[2] In 1985, Campbell entered the $290 million dry-soup-mix market dominated by Thomas J. Lipton Inc., a business unit of Unilever. Dry-soup sales in the United States were growing faster than sales of canned soup. Lipton's aggressive response to test-marketing of an early Campbell dry-soup product resulted in Campbell's rushing a six-flavor line into national distribution ahead of schedule.

In 1982, McGovern caused a stir when he declared publicly that Campbell's Swanson TV-dinner line was "junk food . . . It was great in 1950, but in today's world it didn't go into the microwave; it didn't represent any variety or a good eating experience to my palate."[3] Over the past five years, Swanson's sales volume had slipped 16 percent. McGovern maintained that consumers had discovered better quality options to the TV-dinner concept. Campbell's frozen foods group answered the challenge by creating a new frozen gourmet line, LeMenu. Campbell committed about $50 million in manufacturing, marketing, and trade promotion costs when initial market tests of the LeMenu line proved encouraging.

LeMenu—served on round heatable plates and consisting of such delicacies as chicken cordon bleu, al dente vegetables, and sophisticated wine sauces—produced 21 percent growth in the frozen meal unit with sales of $150 million during its first year of national distribution (1984), double Campbell's sales projection. In addition, the Swanson line of TV-dinners was overhauled, with less salt and more meat stock in gravies, new desserts and sauces, and new packaging and a redesigned logo.

---

[2]As quoted in *Business Week*, December 24, 1984, p. 67.
[3]Ibid.

Exhibit 1   **Performance of Campbell's Divisions under Gordon McGovern, 1980–1989** *(in millions of dollars)*

	1989	1988	1987	1986	1985	1984	1983	1982	1981	1980
Campbell U.S.										
Sales	$2,776	$2,584	$2,445	$2,507	$2,500	$2,282	$1,987	$1,773	$1,678	$1,608
Operating earnings	175	272	284	302	292	278	250	211	190	205
Pepperidge Farm										
Sales	548	495	459	420	426	435	433	392	329	283
Operating earnings	54	58	54	46	39	35	43	41	35	29
Vlasic Foods										
Sales	441	353	283	263	199	193	168	149	137	130
Operating earnings	39	30	22	24	16	14	13	12	10	8
Mrs. Paul's Kitchens										
Sales	140	150	153	141	138	126	108	—	—	—
Operating earnings	0.4	(4)	10	8	11	14	10	—	—	—
Other United States*										
Sales	—	—	59	76	81	84	64	56	27	35
Operating earnings	—	—	(2)	(7)	(3)	(2)	(1)	(1)	(1)	1
International										
Sales	1,527	1,037	898	766	716	624	599	643	694	512
Operating earnings	(81)	58	69	(61)	35	34	33	46	46	33

* Division eliminated in 1988 and replaced with a new division called Campbell Enterprises.
Source: Campbell annual reports.

The grocery business unit's star was Prego Spaghetti Sauce. By 1984, the Prego brand had captured 25 percent of the still growing spaghetti sauce market, becoming the number two sauce, behind Ragu. A Prego Plus Spaghetti Sauce line was introduced in 1985.

Pepperidge Farm   Pepperidge Farm was Campbell's third largest division in 1989, with 10 percent of the company's consolidated sales. Although the division was one of Campbell's best performers during the late 1970s (with sales rising at an average compound rate of 14 percent), by the mid-1980s growth had slowed and a number of newly introduced products had produced disappointing results (Star Wars cookies, Vegetables in Pastry). To remedy the division's weak performance, a number of steps were taken:

- The Costa Apple Products unit, acquired in 1982, was transferred to the Campbell U.S. beverage group.
- Pepperidge divested itself of operations that no longer fit into its strategic plan, including Lexington Gardens, Inc., a garden center chain.
- Deli's Vegetables in Pastry went back into research and development to improve quality.
- A new management team was put in place and a comprehensive review of each product was initiated.

Exhibit 3 shows Pepperidge Farm's product portfolio during the 1980s.

Exhibit 2   The Campbell U.S. Division; Products, Rival Brands, and Competitors as of 1985

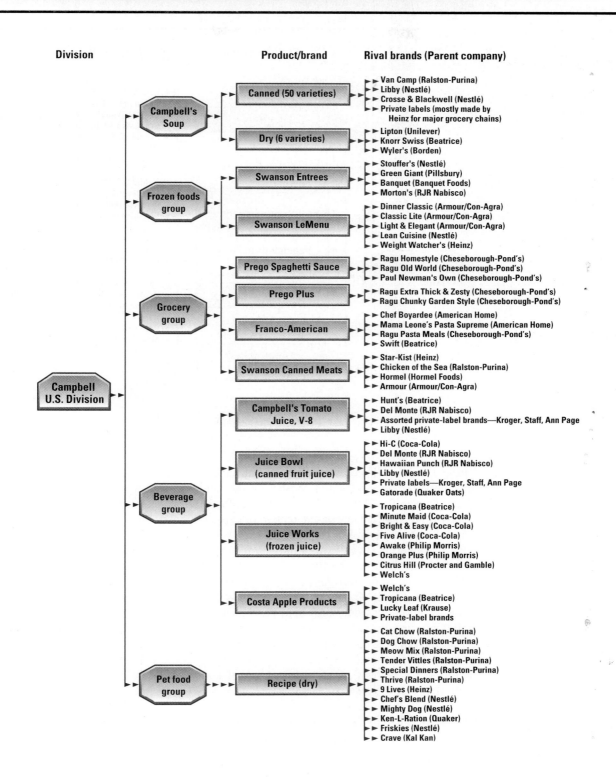

Division	Product/brand	Rival brands (Parent company)

Campbell U.S. Division

Campbell's Soup
- Canned (50 varieties)
  - ► Van Camp (Ralston-Purina)
  - ► Libby (Nestlé)
  - ► Crosse & Blackwell (Nestlé)
  - ► Private labels (mostly made by Heinz for major grocery chains)
- Dry (6 varieties)
  - ► Lipton (Unilever)
  - ► Knorr Swiss (Beatrice)
  - ► Wyler's (Borden)

Frozen foods group
- Swanson Entrees
  - ► Stouffer's (Nestlé)
  - ► Green Giant (Pillsbury)
  - ► Banquet (Banquet Foods)
  - ► Morton's (RJR Nabisco)
- Swanson LeMenu
  - ► Dinner Classic (Armour/Con-Agra)
  - ► Classic Lite (Armour/Con-Agra)
  - ► Light & Elegant (Armour/Con-Agra)
  - ► Lean Cuisine (Nestlé)
  - ► Weight Watcher's (Heinz)

Grocery group
- Prego Spaghetti Sauce
  - ► Ragu Homestyle (Cheseborough-Pond's)
  - ► Ragu Old World (Cheseborough-Pond's)
  - ► Paul Newman's Own (Cheseborough-Pond's)
- Prego Plus
  - ► Ragu Extra Thick & Zesty (Cheseborough-Pond's)
  - ► Ragu Chunky Garden Style (Cheseborough-Pond's)
- Franco-American
  - ► Chef Boyardee (American Home)
  - ► Mama Leone's Pasta Supreme (American Home)
  - ► Ragu Pasta Meals (Cheseborough-Pond's)
  - ► Swift (Beatrice)
- Swanson Canned Meats
  - ► Star-Kist (Heinz)
  - ► Chicken of the Sea (Ralston-Purina)
  - ► Hormel (Hormel Foods)
  - ► Armour (Armour/Con-Agra)

Beverage group
- Campbell's Tomato Juice, V-8
  - ► Hunt's (Beatrice)
  - ► Del Monte (RJR Nabisco)
  - ► Assorted private-label brands—Kroger, Staff, Ann Page
  - ► Libby (Nestlé)
- Juice Bowl (canned fruit juice)
  - ► Hi-C (Coca-Cola)
  - ► Del Monte (RJR Nabisco)
  - ► Hawaiian Punch (RJR Nabisco)
  - ► Libby (Nestlé)
  - ► Private labels—Kroger, Staff, Ann Page
  - ► Gatorade (Quaker Oats)
- Juice Works (frozen juice)
  - ► Tropicana (Beatrice)
  - ► Minute Maid (Coca-Cola)
  - ► Bright & Easy (Coca-Cola)
  - ► Five Alive (Coca-Cola)
  - ► Awake (Philip Morris)
  - ► Orange Plus (Philip Morris)
  - ► Citrus Hill (Procter and Gamble)
  - ► Welch's
- Costa Apple Products
  - ► Welch's
  - ► Tropicana (Beatrice)
  - ► Lucky Leaf (Krause)
  - ► Private-label brands

Pet food group
- Recipe (dry)
  - ► Cat Chow (Ralston-Purina)
  - ► Dog Chow (Ralston-Purina)
  - ► Meow Mix (Ralston-Purina)
  - ► Tender Vittles (Ralston-Purina)
  - ► Special Dinners (Ralston-Purina)
  - ► Thrive (Ralston-Purina)
  - ► 9 Lives (Heinz)
  - ► Chef's Blend (Nestlé)
  - ► Mighty Dog (Nestlé)
  - ► Ken-L-Ration (Quaker)
  - ► Friskies (Nestlé)
  - ► Crave (Kal Kan)

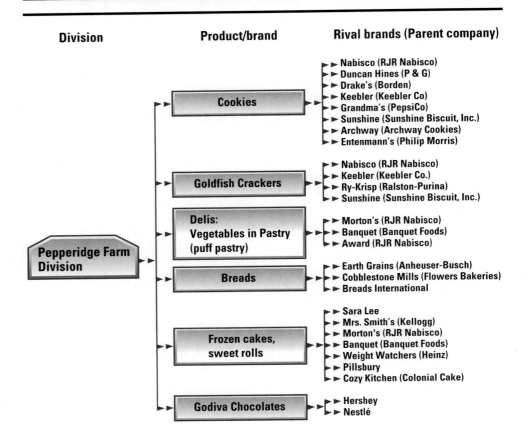

Exhibit 3   The Pepperidge Farm Division: Products, Rival Brands, and Competitors in 1985

Vlasic Foods   Vlasic, Campbell's fourth largest division, was the leading producer and marketer of pickles and relishes in the United States with a 31 percent market share. During the 1982–84 period, Vlasic also had responsibility for the Win Schuler Foods unit, a Michigan-based maker of cheese spreads, melba rounds, party dips, sauces, and salad dressings. Win Schuler was purchased in 1982, and its products were marketed in several states in the upper Midwest. When sales of the Win Schuler unit flattened in 1984, partly due to a sagging Midwest economy, McGovern transferred the unit to the refrigerated foods group in the Campbell U.S. business division.

In 1985, Vlasic implemented new labels that used color bands and a new flavor scale to help consumers find their favorite tastes quickly on the supermarket shelf. Following up on marketing research indicating consumer desires for new and interesting flavors, Vlasic had introduced Zesty Dills and Bread and Butter Whole Pickle lines in 1985. Heinz was Campbell's leading national competitor in this area, but there were a number of important regional and private-label brands that competed with Heinz and Vlasic for shelf space.

Mrs. Paul's Kitchens   This business unit, acquired in 1982, produced frozen fish entrees, frozen breaded vegetables, and frozen chicken nuggets. When Campbell acquired Mrs. Paul's in 1982, it was rumored that Heinz and Pillsbury, among others, were considering the same acquisition. Shortly after the acquisition, the Mrs. Paul's division responded to consumer preferences for convenience seafood products that were nutritious, low in calories, microwavable, and coated more lightly by introducing Light & Natural Fish Fillets in 1983. Quality improvements were also made in existing products, and a promising new product, Light Seafood entrees, was introduced in 1984. Market share increased about 25 percent over 1983, and Light Seafood Entrees went national in 1985. This line, which featured seven varieties of low-calorie, microwavable, seafood dishes, accounted for 11 percent of 1985's volume. However, sales of the company's established product lines of breaded seafood items eroded in the years following acquisition because they had to be fried in cooking oil prior to serving. Revenues had dropped in both 1988 and 1989 and the division was barely profitable in 1989 (see Exhibit 1).

Campbell's Other U.S. Business Division   Grouped into the Other U.S. Business division were Triangle Manufacturing Corp., a health and fitness products manufacturer; Campbell Hospitality, a restaurant unit that operated 59 Pietro's restaurants, 15 Annabelle's restaurants, and 6 H.T. McDoogal's restaurants; and Snow King Frozen Foods, Inc., a manufacturer of frozen specialty meat products. Triangle's best-known product line was The Band wrist and ankle weights, which had the number two position in its market category with a market share of 14 percent. Triangle was trying to build on its strength by entering the exercise equipment market and by selling its products internationally. The Hospitality division struggled through most of the 1980s to sustain sales and earnings growth. Snow King was also a weak performer. In 1988, this division was reorganized and renamed the Campbell Enterprises division; it included Triangle Manufacturing, Godiva International, V8 and Campbell juices, Campbell Food Services, Snow King Frozen Foods, and Pietro's, Annabelle's, and H.T. McDoogal's restaurant chains. All three restaurant chains were divested in 1989.

Campbell's International Business Unit   This division was Campbell's second largest division throughout the 1980s, and accounted for about one-fifth of corporate revenues in 1989. Campbell International had subsidiaries in about 12 foreign countries as of 1989 and had plans to expand further. The division was reorganized in 1985 to build a more solid base for sales and earnings growth. McGovern's goal was for the International division to contribute 25 percent of Campbell's corporate sales and earnings. His strategy was to develop and strengthen Campbell's presence in international markets and to make Campbell a premier international company.

A number of acquisitions were completed in 1989 to strengthen Campbell's international competitive position. The Habitant soup and pickle brands, the Laura Secord brand of jams, and a refrigerated distribution company were all acquired by Campbell's Canadian subsidiary. In Europe, Campbell acquired a German specialty food importer and an Italian producer of institutional foods. Also during 1989, the company increased its ownership in Australia's leading cookie company, Arnotts Limited, to 32 percent, acquired 50 percent ownership in an Australian juice manufacturer, and obtained complete ownership of Melbourne Mushrooms. The International division's three biggest profit contributors in 1989 were Campbell Soup Canada, the European food and confectionery group, and the operations in Australia.

Even though the company had a number of successes internationally, Campbell management had encountered some difficulties. Campbell's Italian business suffered losses during 1989 as a result of excessive costs brought on by an aggressive and poorly controlled attempt to build market share. Campbell was also having difficulty making its recently acquired Freshbake Foods unit profitable. The U.K. food processing company was struggling to absorb a number of acquisitions that it had made prior to its acquisition by Campbell in 1988. Campbell management found it necessary to institute an extensive restructuring process at Freshbake, including closing a number of plants.

McGovern's Approach to Managing Campbell's Business Portfolio

Every Saturday morning McGovern did his family's grocery shopping, stopping to straighten Campbell's displays and inspect those of competitors, studying packaging and reading labels, and trying to learn all he could about how and what people were eating. He encouraged his managers to do the same. Several board meetings were held in the back rooms of supermarkets so that afterwards, directors could roam the store aisles interviewing customers about Campbell products.

McGovern's style of management was innovative to a company known in business circles as much for its conservative policies and corporate culture as for its red-and-white soup can. For decades, Campbell Soup had operated under strict rules of decorum. Eating, smoking, and drinking coffee were not permitted in the office. Managers had to share their offices with their secretaries, and an unwritten rule required executives to keep their suit coats on in the office. Finding the atmosphere at headquarters stifling, McGovern made a point of being a different kind of CEO and role model.

McGovern wandered the corridors of Campbell's headquarters and visited Campbell's plants, mingling easily among the employees. McGovern's voluble personality and memory for names made him popular with many employees. But not everyone was won over by McGovern's style. Some production managers were suspicious of his marketing background. Others believed that his grocery trips and hobnobbing with employees were ploys calculated to win him support and a reputation. Still, McGovern pressed forward with several internal initiatives to change Campbell's corporate culture: (1) a day care center for the children of employees (complete with Campbell's Kids posters on the wall), (2) a health program including workouts in a gymnasium, and (3) an unusual new benefit program that covered adoption expenses up to $1,000 and gave time off to employees who adopted children—in the same way that women were given maternity leave. He appointed the first two women vice presidents in the company's history; one of these, a former director of Good Housekeeping Institute, was hired to identify consumers' food preferences and needs. In 1992, three years after McGovern's retirement, *The Wall Street Journal* named Campbell Soup Company the nation's third best employer because of the generous benefit package provided women and families.

McGovern decentralized Campbell management to facilitate entrepreneurial risk-taking and new product development, devising a new compensation program to reward these traits. He restructured the company into some 50 autonomous units, each with the leeway to develop new products even if the new product ideas were closely related to another business unit's products. Thus, the Prego spaghetti sauce unit—not the frozen food group—initiated frozen Mexican dinners. And although it wasn't his job, the director of market research created "Today's Taste," a line of refrigerated entrees and side dishes. "It's like things are in constant motion," the director said. "We are overloaded but it's fun."[4]

---

[4]As quoted in *The Wall Street Journal*, September 17, 1984, p. A10.

McGovern believed the new structure encouraged managers of business units, who had to compete for corporate funding, to be more creative and venturesome in developing promising products:

> These business divisions allow the company to really get its arms around chunks of the business. The managers are answerable to the bottom line—to their investments, their hiring, their products—and it's a great motivation for performance.[5]

As part of this motivation, Campbell began annually allotting around $30 million to $40 million to support new ventures and the creation of new products families; it often took $10 million to develop and test new products. In addition, it took $10 million to $15 million in advertising and couponing to launch a new brand. McGovern believed a special new product venture fund was needed to encourage managers to think big in terms of new product development. He emphasized that it was no disgrace to fail if the effort was a good one. High failure rates were common in the industry—only about 20 percent of new products lasted more than one year on the market—but Campbell's failure rate on new product introductions was running even higher. In fact, during the 1980s, only about one out of eight new Campbell products reaching the market was successful.

Every Friday morning, McGovern held meetings to discuss new products. The fact-finding sessions were attended by financial, marketing, engineering, and sales personnel. Typical McGovern questions included: "Would you eat something like that?" "Why not?" "Have you tried the competition's product?" "Is there a consumer niche?" The marketing research director noted that in Shaub's meetings, the question had been "can we make such a product cost-effectively?"[6]

McGovern's New Product Development and Marketing Strategies

McGovern instituted a number of internal changes to make Campbell's new product development strategy produce the desired results. Much revolved around efforts to enhance the sophistication of Campbell's corporate marketing strategies and approach to marketing research. Under McGovern, Campbell's market research unearthed several findings and projections that drove the company's new product development effort:

- Women comprised 43 percent of the work force (with a level of 50 percent projected by 1990).
- Two-income marriages represented 60 percent of all U.S. families and accounted for 60 percent of total family income.
- Upper-income households would grow 3.5 times faster than the total household formations.
- More than half of all households consisted of only one or two members; 23 percent of all households contained only one person.
- More and more consumers were exhibiting a growing preference for refrigerated and fresh produce over canned and frozen products.
- The percentage of meals eaten at home was declining.

---

[5]*Advertising Age*, January 3, 1983, p. 38.
[6]*The Wall Street Journal*, September 17, 1984, p. A10.

- Nearly half of the adult meal planners in the United States were watching their weight.
- Poultry consumption had increased 26 percent since 1973.
- Ethnic food preparation at home was increasing, with 40 percent, 21 percent, and 14 percent of households preparing Italian, Mexican, and Oriental foods, respectively, at home from scratch.
- There was a growing consumer concern with food avoidance: sugar, salt, calories, chemicals, cholesterol, and additives.
- The "I am what I eat" philosophy had tied food into life-styles that embraced exercise machines, hot tubs, jogging, racquet ball, backpacking, cross-country skiing, and aerobic dancing.

In response to growing ethnic food demand, Campbell began marketing ethnic selections in regions where consumer interests for particular food types were strong. For instance, it marketed spicy Ranchero Beans only in the South and Southwest and its newly acquired Puerto Rican foods were marketed in New York City and Florida (which had sizable Puerto Rican populations).

Campbell's product development guidelines emphasized convenience, taste, flavor, and texture. The strategic themes McGovern stressed were:

- Concentrate on products that represent superior value to consumers and constantly strive to improve those values.
- Develop products that help build markets.
- Develop products that yield a fair profit to Campbell.

In pursuing these guidelines, Campbell adopted several operating practices:

- Using ongoing consumer research to determine eating habits, and checking home menus, recipes, and food preparation techniques to learn which food items were served together.
- Studying meal and snack eating occasions to learn which household members participated so that preliminary estimates of volume potential could be made for possible new products and product improvement ideas.
- Testing new or improved products in a large enough number of households across the United States that reliable national sales projections could be made. Once a product met pretest standards, testing in a sample of supermarkets and sales outlets was conducted.
- Rolling out the new products on a regional or national plan and using test-market data to establish the sequence in which area markets should be entered.

A key part of McGovern's product development strategy was the "Campbell in the Kitchen" project, consisting of some 75 homemakers across the country. Three to five times a year, Campbell asked this "focus group" to try different products and give opinions. McGovern regularly dispatched company executives to the kitchens of these homemakers to observe eating patterns and how the meals were prepared. He sent Campbell's home economists into some homes to work with meal preparers on a one-on-one basis.

By 1983, McGovern's strategy had turned Campbell into the biggest new products generator in the combined food and health and beauty aids categories, with a total of 42 new products. Exhibit 4 shows Campbell's leading new products from 1982

Exhibit 4 Campbell's Leading New Products for Fiscal 1985 *(total $600 million in sales)*

1985 Ranking	Year Introduced
LeMenu Frozen Dinner	1982
Prego Spaghetti Sauce	1982
Chunky New England Clam Chowder	1984
Great Starts breakfasts	1984
Prego Plus	1985

Source: *The Wall Street Journal,* August 14, 1985.

through 1985. Meanwhile, Campbell's marketing budget grew from $275 million in 1982, to $488 million in 1985, and to $552 million in 1989. Ad expenditures jumped from $67 million in 1980 to $197 million in 1989. Prior to McGovern, Campbell often trimmed ad spending at the end of a quarter to boost earnings.

In 1982, McGovern was named *Advertising Age*'s Adman of the Year for his efforts in transforming Campbell into "one of the most aggressive market-driven companies in the food industry today."[7] *Advertising Age* cited the company's emphasis on nutrition and fitness as opposed to the former "mmm, mmm, good" emphasis on taste. Print ads featured government research studies concerning soup's nutritional values and a new slogan, "Soup is good food."

Production, Quality, and Cost Considerations during the McGovern Era

Gordon McGovern also stressed the importance of high production quality; a 1984 article in *Savvy* quoted him as saying, "I want zero defects. If we can't produce quality, we'll get out of the business." That same year, Campbell held its first Worldwide Corporate conference dedicated to quality. Hundreds of Campbell managers from all levels and most company locations spent three days at this conference. Management believed that the ultimate test of quality was consumer satisfaction, and the company's goal was to instill a strong quality-conscious attitude among employees in every single operation throughout the company.

Before McGovern took over, Campbell used to adjust the design of new products so that they could be produced with existing equipment and plant facilities. For example, a square omelet was specified for Swanson's breakfasts because it was what the installed machine would make. After McGovern's appointment, although low-cost production was still a strategic factor, market considerations and consumer trends—not existing machinery and production capabilities—were deciding factors in production, packaging, and labeling. The company spent between $150 million and $300 million annually throughout the 1980s for improved equipment, new plants and plant expansions, better packaging technology, and distribution facilities.

Campbell executives believed the company's key strengths during the 1985–89 period were: (1) a worldwide system for obtaining ingredients, (2) a broad range of

---

[7]*Advertising Age*, January 3, 1983, p. 38.

food products that could be used as a launching pad for formulating, producing, and marketing new products, and (3) an emphasis on low-cost production.

Campbell's Performance under Gordon McGovern

McGovern's campaign for renewed growth via new product introduction and acquisition produced good results early on. By year-end 1984, sales were up 31 percent—to $3.7 billion—and earnings had risen by 47 percent—to $191 million. During McGovern's 10-year reign as CEO, Campbell introduced 922 new items—more than any other food processing company. By the late 1980s, however, there were signs that Campbell's brand managers had become so involved in new product development that they had neglected the old stand-by products as well as slighting cost-control and profit margin targets. According to one Campbell executive:

> We became fat cats. We said, "We can't fail." We began to throw things against the marketplace that had long paybacks and were in processes, packaging, and distribution that we didn't understand.[8]

Campbell's growth in operating earnings for fiscal years 1985–89 fell short of McGovern's 15 percent target rate (Exhibit 5), and McGovern in 1989 initiated several internal restructuring moves to eliminate many of the inefficiencies and cost excesses that had crept into the company's operations and new product development efforts.

THE DORRANCE FAMILY FIGHT

From the day he became chief executive officer, Gordon McGovern feared a takeover of Campbell Soup. He made a number of attempts to bond the Dorrance heirs to the company. McGovern invited the family shareholders to company picnics, made sure they felt welcome to visit the Camden, New Jersey, headquarters whenever they wished, and provided quarterly results to the family members over the phone. Prior to McGovern's tenure as CEO, most of John T. Dorrance's heirs (Exhibit 6) did not attempt to become involved in company matters. John T. (Jack) Dorrance, Jr., and John T. (Ipy) Dorrance III were the only real exceptions. Jack Dorrance had actually run the company before it was taken public and later served as chairman when the family turned day-to-day operations over to nonfamily professionals. Ipy Dorrance was a board member, and his name was proposed to McGovern as a candidate to head Campbell's International division in 1986.

Even though McGovern had courted the approval of the Dorrance family, he wasn't pleased with what he considered to be Jack and Ipy Dorrance's undue involvement in company matters. A former company executive recalled that McGovern complained that Jack Dorrance "basically wasn't smart."[9] He promptly killed the idea of Ipy becoming president of the International division; he also closed the executive dining room where Jack regularly enjoyed his lunch shortly after his 1984 retirement as chairman.

---

[8]As quoted in *Financial World*, June 11, 1991, p. 53.
[9]*The Wall Street Journal*, February 7, 1990, p. A12.

Exhibit 5   Financial Summary, Campbell Soup Company, 1985–1994   *(in millions, except per share amounts)*

	1994	1993	1992	1991	1990	1989	1988	1987	1986	1985
Net sales	$6,690.0	$6,586.0	$6,263.0	$6,204.0	$6,205.0	$5,672.0	$4,868.0	$4,490.0	$4,286.0	$3,916.0
Earnings before taxes	963.0	519.8	779.3	667.4	179.4	106.5	388.6	417.9	387.2	333.7
Earnings before cumulative effect of accounting change	630.0	257.2	490.5	401.5	4.4	13.1	241.6	247.3	223.2	197.8
Net earnings	630.0	8.2	490.5	401.5	4.4	13.1	274.0	247.3	223.2	197.8
Taxes on earnings	333.0	262.6	308.8	265.9	175.0	93.4	147.0	170.6	164.0	135.8
Interest—net	64.0	73.8	86.6	90.2	94.0	55.8	20.7	22.2	28.6	32.1
Earnings per share	$ 2.51	$ 0.03	$ 1.95	$ 1.58	$ 0.02	$ 0.05	$ 0.93	$ 0.95	$ 0.86	$ 0.77
Dividends per share	1.09	0.92	0.71	0.56	0.49	0.45	0.41	0.35	0.33	0.31
Weighted average shares outstanding	250.7	251.9	251.7	254.0	259.2	258.5	258.9	259.8	258.9	258.3
Capital expenditures	$ 421.0	$ 371.3	$ 361.5	$ 371.1	$ 397.3	$ 302.0	$ 261.9	$ 328.0	$ 251.3	$ 212.9
Depreciation and amortization	n.a.	242.2	216.2	208.6	200.9	192.3	170.9	144.6	126.8	119.0
Assets	4,992.0	4,897.0	4,353.0	4,149.0	4,115.0	3,932.0	3,609.0	3,097.0	2,762.0	2,437.0
Stockholders' equity	1,989.0	1,704.0	2,027.0	1,793.0	1,691.0	1,778.0	1,895.0	1,736.0	1,538.0	1,382.0

Source: Campbell annual reports.

Exhibit 6   The Dorrance Family Tree

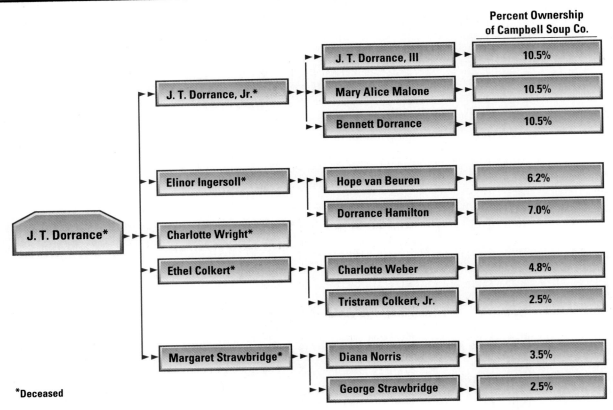

Source: *The Wall Street Journal*, February 7, 1990, p. A12.

In March 1989, Chairman of the Board Robert J. Vlasic, who owned 2.1 percent of Campbell's stock, informed Dorrance family members that he had been approached by the Quaker Oats Company to explore a merger between the two companies. A month later, Jack Dorrance died of a heart attack. Jack Dorrance's nieces and nephews quickly let Vlasic know that they were receptive to the merger, assuming the proper share price could be attained. However, Jack Dorrance's three children, who at the time each received over $13 million per year in dividends from their Campbell stock holdings, notified Vlasic that they would block any merger attempt. Vlasic quickly backed off of merger negotiations once it became apparent that such a move lacked the support of these three stockholders. Even so, the dissident faction of the Dorrance family publicly announced that their stake in the company was for sale even though the Quaker Oats merger was off.

McGovern's Resignation and the Hiring of a Replacement

Disenchanted with the family squabble and stung by outspoken criticism of his performance by family members, Gordon McGovern resigned as CEO and took early retirement in November 1989. Campbell's search for a replacement, spearheaded by

Ipy Dorrance and Robert Vlasic, quickly focused on Gerber's CEO, David Johnson, as best candidate to replace McGovern. A native of Australia, David Johnson had a bachelor's degree in economics from the University of Sydney and an MBA from the University of Chicago. Starting out as a management trainee with the International division of Colgate-Palmolive in Australia, he moved up through the ranks to become managing director of Colgate's South African operations in 1967. In 1973, he moved to Hong Kong as president of Warner-Lambert/Parke Davis Asia; there, exposed to the Orient's fundamentally different customs and approaches, he came to appreciate that if managers were creative enough to look beyond accepted solutions to business problems, it was easy to find innovative answers. Looking back on his Hong Kong experiences, Johnson observed that he gained, "an elasticized mind, opened to a greater run of possibilities than I'd ever known before."[10] Warner-Lambert brought Johnson to the United States in 1976 as president of its Personal Products division; a year later, he was promoted to president of the company's American Chicle division. When Warner-Lambert acquired Entenmann's in 1979, Johnson took over as head; he then moved to General Foods when GF acquired Entenmann's from Warner-Lambert in 1982. As Entenmann's chief executive from 1979 to 1987, he engineered the company's drive from a regional to a national provider of bakery products, more than quadrupling sales and profits. In 1987, Johnson left Entenmann's to become CEO of Gerber Products, a company whose performance had been lackluster for several years. He proceeded to craft a turnaround strategy for Gerber that involved divesting seven business divisions (toys, furniture, trucking) and refocusing Gerber's attention on its core baby foods business. By 1990, 27 months after Johnson became CEO, Gerber's sales were up 30 percent, profits were up 50 percent, and the stock price had tripled. With the Dorrance family's blessing, Campbell lured Johnson away from Gerber as McGovern's successor.

THE DAVID JOHNSON ERA: 1990–PRESENT ————

David Johnson became chairman and CEO of Campbell Soup Company in January 1990. He saw his first priority as crafting a strategy for Campbell that would grow earnings and win the confidence of the Dorrance heirs. While at Gerber, Johnson had viewed Campbell, a competitor of Gerber's in some product categories, as an underperforming company that was a likely target for corporate raiders, once even commenting, "Boy, that's a troubled company. I could really run that one."[11] But in interviewing for the job at Campbell, he came to believe that the arguments and differences between the Dorrance family and Campbell's prior management were more a function of "poor results" than of activist family members wanting to meddle in company affairs and the desire of some to sell out their stake and invest their inheritance elsewhere. Johnson deemed the challenge worthy because he saw rich resources and vast potential at Campbell; he observed:[12]

> It was a company that was founded on incredible strength on which you could build. I knew that it had excellent R&D. I knew it had terrific brands. It had lost its direction, lost its focus, was underperforming, and I knew that it could be

---

[10]Jeffrey Zygmont, "In Command at Campbell," *Sky Magazine*, March 1993, p. 60.
[11]As quoted in *Fortune*, September 9, 1991, p. 143.
[12]As quoted in *Sky Magazine*, March 1993, p. 54.

refocused and reorganized within six months, and that we could really get it going very quickly.

Johnson concluded that it was imperative to boost Campbell's performance quickly, not only to pacify disgruntled shareholders but also to get the company's stock price high enough to discourage would-be acquirers from launching a takeover attempt:

> Under those circumstances, when you come in, it's not the pretties of "Here is my vision. Let me explain the principles from the book." When you move in, you've got to do it in an exciting fashion, lay down the challenge—Boom! Strike! Crash! It's short term focus. You know that dirty word we're all accused of? "Short term" Isn't it terrible? Under those circumstances, if you don't win the first year, if you don't win in the short term, you're dead.[13]

Johnson's Turnaround Strategy

To direct Campbell's managers in their efforts to rejuvenate the company's performance, Johnson set financial objectives of 20 percent earnings growth, 20 percent return on equity, and 20 percent cash return on assets: "I used to say, if perfect human vision is 20–20, then perfect business vision is 20–20–20, which was shorthand for earnings, return and cash."[14] This was followed by the establishment of four corporate-level strategic principles to guide the creation of business and functional strategies in each divisional unit:

- The primary purpose of the corporation is to *build shareholder wealth*. It is imperative to provide dividend growth and long-term stock appreciation to reward the stockholders of the corporation.

- Campbell must exploit its *brand power*. Campbell's strong brands have been the basis of the company's strengths over the past 90 years and should be the focal point for the future.

- Campbell's ability to sustain its brand power and build on its powerful brands is only possible through *people power*. The company's employees have to be responsible for maintaining the existing brands, for building on these brands, and for finding new markets for these brands. Campbell should encourage individual risk-bearing and teamwork with rewards linked to results.

- It is important to *preserve the company's independence*. Management needs to preserve the heritage of Campbell Soup Company and resist any outside thrust for control through delivery of superior performance on building long-term shareholder wealth.

Johnson differed with McGovern's view that Campbell's growth should come primarily from the acquisition of small, fast-growing food companies and from the introduction of new products that served some niche of the food industry. Instead, Johnson believed that Campbell Soup should concentrate on growing sales of its best-known brands—the red-and-white soup line, Prego, Pepperidge Farm, Vlasic, and Swanson—and to increase its U.S. market share in these product categories.

---

[13]As quoted in *Fortune*, December 14, 1992, p. 112.
[14]Ibid.

Over the past decade, for example, Campbell's tonnage in canned soups had risen a paltry 1 percent annually, and Campbell's market share of the U.S. soup market, according to Wall Street estimates, had slipped from a lofty 80 percent in the 1950s and 1960s to 70 percent in the mid-1980s to around 65 percent in 1990. Johnson also decided to press even harder than McGovern had on gaining increased penetration of foreign markets.

While McGovern had pursued ways to reduce costs and eliminate inefficiencies during his 1989 restructuring, Johnson saw opportunities to achieve further economies and better profit margins, principally by eliminating unprofitable and slow-selling items from Campbell's product lineup and by divesting peripheral lines of businesses that did not complement the company's strengths or bolster the market power of its flagship brands. Consequently, the strategy Johnson crafted to boost Campbell's performance incorporated five major initiatives:

- Divesting poorly performing and nonstrategic business units and reorganizing Campbell's six divisions.
- Eliminating weak items from the company's product lineup.
- Requiring that new product introductions exploit Campbell Soup's strengths, core competencies, and organizational capabilities as well as have the potential to achieve the three 20–20–20 financial performance targets.
- Focusing on the global marketing of the company's competencies and capabilities.
- Installing and expanding low-cost business systems at the corporate level to support the operations of the business divisions.

Exhibit 7 shows the business lines that were divested—Johnson saw all of them as nonstrategic, unrelated to Campbell's core competencies, or chronic money losers. This pruning of Campbell's portfolio resulted in the sale of 8 plants and the shutdown of 12 plants worldwide plus a workforce reduction of 8,000 people during Johnson's first 18 months as CEO. As the remaining plants bid to absorb the production of the closed plants, overall capacity utilization rose from 60 percent to 80 percent; Campbell's Maxton, North Carolina, plant was able to increase its output 50 percent and become Campbell's first canned-soup plant to drive manufacturing costs below 50 percent of the retail price of its products. Included among the plant closings was the company's 131-year-old Camden, New Jersey, plant with its distinctive water towers painted to look like giant Campbell Soup cans.

Revised New Product Development and Marketing Strategies

Johnson instituted a more cautious approach to new product development. New product ideas were more heavily researched and tested before they were put on the market. Moreover, new products were expected to provide quicker paybacks on investment; potential products that held little promise for near-term profitability and for meeting the 20–20–20 financial performance standards were tabled. The search for new product ideas was limited to areas where Campbell had production and marketing expertise; as one executive put it, "We want to be in areas we know we are good at and in processes we are good at."[15] Despite the more conservative

---

[15] As quoted in *Financial World*, June 11, 1991, p. 53.

Exhibit 7 Divested Campbell Soup Company Businesses, 1990–1993

- Fried chicken plant in Sumpter, South Carolina.
- Salmon Farms.
- Snow King Frozen Foods—frozen meat products.
- Triangle Manufacturing Corporation—health and fitness products manufacturer.
- Mushroom farms.
- Menderson-Zeller, Inc.
- Recipe Pet Food.
- D. Lazzaroni Cookie Company (Italy).
- Win Schuler Foods, Inc.
- Juice Bowl.
- Juice Works.
- The fresh produce and frozen vegetable portions of the U.K. Freshbake Foods Group (acquired for $450 million in 1988)—the frozen entree portion of Freshbake was retained.

approach to new product development, Campbell introduced nearly 50 new products in 1991, 121 in 1992, and 96 in 1993. New items included cream of broccoli soup (which became the first new soup since 1935 to rank in the top five best-selling soups), broccoli cheese soup, Light 'n Tangy V8, Swanson Kids Fun Feast frozen dinners, Prego pizza sauce, more varieties of Pepperidge products, a relaunch of LeMenu LightStyle (renamed LeMenu Healthy). The company's long-time "soup is good food" slogan was abandoned and, instead, Campbell began aggressively promoting individual soups for kids, healthy soups for adults, and soups for cooking.

To meet Johnson's 20–20–20 financial targets, Campbell initiated price hikes for a number of product lines, including canned soups, Pepperidge Farm Goldfish crackers, and the Franco-American pasta line. Critics were concerned that the price hikes unduly held back gains in volume; one analyst observed, "They're sowing the seeds of future problems by milking their brands instead of investing in them and investing in new brands."[16] Campbell executives acknowledged the price increase could pinch volume growth in the short term, but believed that the effects would be short-lived and that the price increases were overdue given the expected short-term gains in profitability.

Johnson's Corporate Reorganization

Johnson's reorganization effort aimed at capturing strategic fit benefits among related products and product families. Johnson concluded that McGovern's 50 autonomous units had resulted in lack of communication and cooperation between the different business units. For example, the U.S. soup division once ran a promotion with Nabisco crackers even though Pepperidge Farm produced a competing product. Also, U.S. tomato paste plants did not share technology with Mexican tomato paste plants since the Mexican plants were in a different division. Exhibit 8 compares the groups and brands associated with each division under the structure established by McGovern with Johnson's three-division structure: Campbell U.S.A., Campbell Biscuits and Bakery, and Campbell International. Johnson believed the new alignment allowed for

---

[16]As quoted in *Business Week*, June 17, 1991, p. 57.

Exhibit 8   Comparison of Campbell's Business Unit Structure under Gordon McGovern and David Johnson

Campbell's Structure under Gordon McGovern		Campbell's Structure under David Johnson	
Division	**Example Brands/Services**	**Division**	**Example Brands/Services**
Campbell U.S.		**Campbell U.S.A.**	
• Soup group	Red-and-white, Healthy Request, Chunky	• U.S. Soup group	Dry and canned soup, Franco-American
• Frozen Food group	Swanson, LeMenu	• Beverage group	V8, Campbell's tomato juice
• Grocery group	Prego, Franco-American, Swanson canned meats	• Meal Enhancement group	Marie's salad dressing, Open Pit barbecue sauce, Vlasic, Prego, food service
• Beverage group	Campbell's Tomato Juice, V8, Juice Bowl, Juice Works	• Frozen Foods group	Swanson, LeMenu, Mrs. Paul's
• Pet Food group	Recipe		
Pepperidge Farm	Pepperidge Farms breads, cookies, Godiva chocolates, Costa apple juice, Deli's frozen entrees	**Campbell Biscuit and Bakery**	Arnotts Ltd., Pepperidge Farm, Delacre
Vlasic	Pickles and relishes		
Mrs. Paul's	Frozen fish, frozen chicken, frozen vegetables		
Other U.S.	Triangle Manufacturing Corp.—fitness products Campbell Hospitality—restaurants Snow King Frozen Foods—frozen meats		
Campbell International	Soup—Canada and Mexico Freshbake Foods Group (Britain)—baked goods	**Campbell International**	
		• International Soup group	Red-and-white canned soup, Sanwa Foods
		• International Specialty Foods group	Godiva, Fray Bentos, Lacroix, Swift, Lutti

more communication and technology-sharing between businesses in similar product categories and geographies. He also saw the new alignment as helping Campbell Soup put more emphasis on the company's international businesses.

Johnson's International Push

Johnson was convinced a sizable fraction of Campbell Soup's growth should come from international expansion because the world market for processed food products was projected to grow over twice as fast as the 1 percent growth rate projected for the $200 billion U.S. food processing industry. By the year 2000, Johnson wanted at least one-half of Campbell's revenues to come from outside the United States. Already, Campbell marketed its soups in Mexico, Canada, Argentina, Poland, Hong Kong, and China, and its baked goods in Europe under the Delacre, Freshbake, and Pepperidge Farm brands. In Europe, Pepperidge Farm products were rebranded Biscuits Maison to enhance appeal to European consumers. In 1993, Campbell increased its 33 percent ownership of Australia's Arnott's Ltd. to 58 percent to gain an organizational base for increasing its long-term presence in baked goods in the Pacific Rim and Asia. To help familiarize himself with Campbell's international operations and to better gauge the company's potential for foreign expansion, Johnson had all of Campbell's top international executives report directly to him for the first 12 months he was at Campbell.

International marketing of prepared foods was complicated. Taste preferences varied significantly from country to country (and sometimes within countries), prompting international producers to employ multicountry strategies to gear product characteristics to local preferences and eating habits. Campbell's 1988 acquisition of Britain's Freshbake Foods Group never performed up to expectations partly because Campbell management didn't cater adequately to the taste preferences of British consumers. Also, Campbell's penetration of the European soup market had proven more difficult than originally expected because the predominant form of store-bought soups on the continent were dry soups and ready-to-serve soups; demand for Campbell's mainstay condensed soups was virtually nonexistent in Europe, and consumers had to be persuaded of the merits of switching to a different preparation technique.

Campbell management opened a Hong Kong taste kitchen in 1991 as part of the company's effort to ensure that the products it introduced would appeal to Asia's 2 billion consumers, whose average per capita soup consumption averaged six bowls per week. The Hong Kong kitchen proved to be a success, having a role in creating such popular sellers as scallop, watercress, duck-gizzard, and ham soups. The kitchen experimented with other soup varieties made from pork, dates, figs, and snake.

Campbell had been successful in Mexico with spicy soups such as Crema de Chile Poblano and had captured 10 percent of Argentina's $50 million soup market within one year of introducing nine varieties of its red-and-white canned soup. A summary of Campbell Soup's geographic performance under Johnson is displayed in Exhibit 9.

Johnson and Campbell Soup were supporters of the North American Free Trade Agreement that effectively established a North American common market. Johnson saw more potential in a single North American market of 364 million people (with projections of 400 million people by the year 2000) than in the European market of 325 million people. It was in anticipation of NAFTA's approval that Johnson created Campbell North America by consolidating the company's U.S. businesses, Canadian operations, and Mexican subsidiaries into a single business division.

Johnson's Approach to People Management[17]

David Johnson saw corporations as a collection of people in possession of resources directed toward a common purpose. To get corporations to achieve the common purpose as fully as possible, Johnson believed that company executives had to exhibit three traits:

> First, the confidence to make risk-bearing decisions, particularly of a strategic nature. Next, you've got to have the humility to trust the organization to implement them; let the controls go to them. And then, you cannot claim strong leadership if you don't have a track record of results that supports your decision-making. What matters is the results, the record, the scoreboard.

---

[17]This section is based on information contained in Zygmont, "In Command of Campbell," pp. 52–64.

Exhibit 9 Sales and Earnings of Campbell Soup Company, by Geographic Region, 1991–1994 (millions of dollars)

	1994	1993	1992	1991
United States				
Net sales	$4,639	$4,744	$4,649	$4,496
Earnings before taxes	854	715	809	695
Europe				
Net sales	1,041	1,050	1,043	1,149
Earnings before taxes	64	(170)	45	49
Other countries				
Net sales	1,011	917	652	656
Earnings before taxes	154	99	70	55

Source: Campbell annual reports.

Good corporate performance, in Johnson's view, depended on effectively motivating, guiding, and encouraging workers at all levels; he saw corporate leadership as a requirement for all corporate executives, not just the CEO:

> All my officers have to also be disciples for the company. I want people who are convinced, who are good communicators, coaches, going out there and getting the message and the sharing down through the entire organization.

Understanding that encouraging words alone were not enough, Johnson implemented comprehensive pay-for-performance incentives for Campbell managers and employees. All workers participated in the "Savings Plus" program, which paid cash bonuses based on company financial performance and industry ranking. A larger share of employees' total compensation was tied to incentives and performance bonuses and thus put "at risk." Bonuses were based strictly on how an individual performed against well-defined measures. According to Johnson:

> Today, nobody gets money for nothing. Nobody gets money for being a good negotiator, or appealing to subjective criteria. Nothing. But then, it's got to work both ways; if somebody has a run that's unbelievable, you pay them every cent they have earned.

In many instances, employee bonuses were paid in the form of shares of Campbell common stock to encourage people to think like owners and risk-bearers.

JOHNSON'S THREE-UNIT BUSINESS STRUCTURE

Campbell U.S.A.

In 1995, Campbell U.S.A. was Campbell's largest operating unit, accounting for almost 60 percent of the company's total consolidated sales. Sales and earnings contributions by division are shown in Exhibit 10. Although the soup business was relatively mature, soup volume alone was up 5.5 percent in 1993 as 10 new varieties were added. Much of the increase was due to the sales boost provided by

Exhibit 10   Sales and Earnings of Campbell Soup Company, by Division, 1991–1994   (millions of dollars)

	1994	1993	1992	1991
Campbell U.S.A.*				
Sales	$4,000	$4,123	$4,457.8	$4,308.5
Operating earnings	783	780†	790.1	671.2
Campbell Biscuit and Bakery				
Sales	1,200	998	808.6	788.5
Operating earnings	153	106†	90.6	91.2
Campbell International				
Sales	1,550	1,580	999.6	1,113.3
Operating earnings	136	111†	43.2	36.2

* 1991 and 1992, sales and earnings data include contributions from operations in Canada, Mexico, and South America. Contributions from these operations were allocated to Campbell International for the years 1993 and 1994.

† Before special charges of $175 million for Campbell U.S.A., $5 million for Campbell Biscuit and Bakery, and $173 million for Campbell International.

Source: Campbell annual reports.

noodle soups resulting from the acquisition of Sanwa Foods, Inc. Campbell also had strong market share growth in its Healthy Request soup varieties, much of which was due to consumers switching from varieties with higher fat and sodium content. Healthy Request's rising 6.1 percent 1992 market share helped push the market shares of the Home Cookin' and Chunky lines down from 8.5 to 7.4 percent and from 14.6 to 12.6 percent, respectively, between 1991 and 1992. Campbell attributed some of the overall increase in soup sales to its "contraseasonal" marketing strategy that focused on increasing the consumption of soup in summer months. Traditionally, soup sales during summer months were only about 50 percent of the winter month volume. Campbell's historical share of the U.S. canned soup market approached 80 percent. In 1993, Campbell's standard red-and-white brands alone generated sales of $1.1 billion, equal to 48.9 percent of the $2.3 billion U.S. canned soup market.

Frozen food group earnings had recently suffered because of strong price competition and trade promotions by the leading brands. Most participants in the segment were offering 2-for-1 sales and 25 percent off-the-entire-line promotions. These discounts made it exceedingly difficult for higher priced lines, such as LeMenu, to compete; deep price-cutting was seen as responsible for a 5 percent decline in dollar sales of the $2.88 billion frozen food entree segment. LeMenu, introduced by Campbell in 1982 with a $4 price, was successful throughout its first 10 years, but had experienced a dramatic decline in dollar volume in 1993 as sales of the premium-priced line fell by 41.5 percent. Campbell's lower-cost Swanson line was better positioned to compete on price. Exhibit 11 indicates the ranking of frozen dinner competitors.

Campbell Soup acquired Mrs. Paul's Kitchens in 1982 under Gordon McGovern's acquisition strategy to acquire small, fast-growing companies that were strong in areas that Campbell was not. The unit performed well initially, but since the mid-1980s, sales of Mrs. Paul's breaded frozen fish and vegetable products had been

Exhibit 11   Top 10 Frozen Dinner Brands, 1991–1995

Brand	1991 share of the market	1992 share of the market	1994 share of the market	1995 share of the market
Stouffers	13.5%	14.2%	13.9%	13.5%
Swanson	11.2	12.1	11.1	11.6
Healthy Choice	12.5	11.5	13.7	16.1
Budget Gourmet	12.3	11.3	11.4	10.0
LeMenu*	9.4	11.0	—	—
Weight Watchers	8.0	9.4	9.4	6.7
Banquet	6.5	7.6	6.0	6.5
Lean Cuisine	5.0	3.4	13.1	14.9
Tyson	2.8	2.9	2.0	1.8
Marie Callendar	1.2	2.3	2.5	3.3
All others	17.6	14.4	16.9	15.6
Total market in millions of dollars	$3,033.0	$2,884.9	$3,311.2	$3,424.2

* Brand dropped in 1994.

Source: IRI as reported in *Advertising Age*, September 29, 1993 and *Frozen Food Age*, 1995.

eroding despite product reformulations that permitted baking and microwaving. Frozen fish sales were also competitively affected by the actions of many supermarkets to introduce fresh fish counters in the meat department.

The beverage group and meal enhancement group both achieved volume gains during the 1990s. Prego Spaghetti Sauce had increased its market share substantially since 1985 when it held 25 percent of the market. However, Prego was still the number two brand behind Ragu; competition in prepared spaghetti sauces had increased as several recently introduced brands attracted consumer interest. Campbell was exploiting the strength of its Prego brand by adding pizza sauce. Under Johnson, Vlasic continued to hold the leading U.S. market share in the pickle category.

In 1992, Campbell decided to get into the business of producing private-label products for supermarket chains. The company announced that it would offer almost everything it made—except canned soup and bakery products—for store brand programs. The president of Campbell North America and South America explained the decision:

> If there's business in private label, and you have excess capacity that's keeping the cost of your branded goods up, you've got a decision to make. We won't make private-label soup, and we won't do private label in categories where we have significant share. If we make private-label products, we ask the retailer to give us preferential treatment in that category; for instance, all their pickles will be our pickles, whether Vlasic or the store brand.[18]

However, by late 1993, Campbell management had found it difficult to achieve sufficient margins in its private-label business without lowering the quality of the product substantially.

[18]*Advertising Age*, April 12, 1993, pp. 4 and 5.

Campbell Biscuit and Bakery

Campbell Biscuit and Bakery had 1994 sales of $1.2 billion and operating earnings of $153 million, up from $778 million and $91 million, respectively, in 1991. The division, which included Pepperidge Farm in North America, Delacre in Europe, and Arnott's in the Pacific Rim/Asia, was ranked as the fourth largest biscuit and cracker maker in the world. Pepperidge Farm's operating earnings declined 4 percent during 1992 and had not really experienced any growth since the early 1980s, when the division enjoyed a 14 percent compound annual growth rate. Under Johnson, management had moved to revitalize PF through production line extensions, such as goldfish cookie packs, frozen garlic bread, and Pepperidge Farm gravy and rolls. Management was planning to introduce Pepperidge Farm brand products in Canada and Mexico. Campbell held a strong position in Europe with Delacre, the leader in the European cookie market.

Campbell management believed that a controlling interest in Arnott's, Ltd., would yield a competitive advantage in the $3 billion Asian cookie and cracker market. Arnott's was the world's seventh largest cookie and cracker brand, had access to low-cost ingredients, and had efficient manufacturing processes. Arnott's Australian location also provided a shipping cost advantage for products exported to the entire Asian/Pacific Rim region.

Campbell International

Campbell International in 1994 had sales of $1.55 billion, marginally below the $1.58 billion level of 1991. In 1993, Campbell acquired Fray Bentos, Britain's leading brand of premium canned meats, which contributed significantly to 1994 sales growth in the United Kingdom. Campbell developed a competence in heat-process technology that was being utilized in canned soups and in its Swift meat-processing business in Argentina. Campbell had introduced its soups in various international markets, but was far from achieving the market dominance it enjoyed in the United States. In 1993, for example, Campbell held only a 3 percent market share of Japan's $540 million "Western" soup market. To bolster its brand-name recognition in foreign markets, Campbell began affixing the Campbell name to a growing number of products it sold in Europe and Asia.

A Major Acquisition

In late 1994, Johnson engineered Campbell's biggest acquisition ever—a $1.12 billion purchase of Pace Foods, the leading U.S. producer and marketer of Mexican salsa. The cash price paid for Pace represented five times sales and 20 times earnings. A number of companies, including Heinz and Lea & Perrin, had been attempting to buy the private company for a number of years, but owner Kit Goldsbury was not interested. The chief operating officer of Pace Foods stated that Goldsbury agreed to the sale to Campbell because he could identify with and liked the company's management team.[19]

As a product category, the spicy blend of jalapenos, tomatoes, onion, and garlic surpassed ketchup in 1991 as the best-selling condiment. The salsa category grew at

---

[19]*Wall Street Journal*, November 29, 1994, p. A3.

just under a 13 percent compound annual growth rate from 1988 to 1993 as sales increased from $325 million to $700 million. The growth in popularity of the product was attributed to its unique characteristics, a spicy flavor and low fat content—a jar of Pace contained no fat and only 70 calories. Market shares for salsa brands during 1993 and 1994 are listed in Exhibit 12.

BACKGROUND ON THE FOOD PROCESSING INDUSTRY

In the early 19th century, small incomes and low urban population greatly limited the demand for packaged food. In 1859, one industry—grain milling—accounted for over three-fifths of the total U.S. food processing. Several industries were in their infancy: evaporated milk, canning, candy, natural extracts, and coffee roasting. From 1860 to 1900, the food processing industry entered a period of development and growth that made food processing the leading manufacturing industry in the United States. The driving forces behind this growth were increased urbanization, cheaper rail transport, and the advent of the refrigeration and tin can manufacturing.

At the beginning of the 20th century, the food processing industry was highly fragmented—the thousands of local and regional firms were too small to capture economies in mass production and distribution as was occurring in other industries. During the 1920s, industry consolidation via acquisition and merger began. The process was evolutionary, not revolutionary, and continued on into the 1960s and 1970s. Companies such as Del Monte and Kraft, whose names have since become household words, were established, as were the first two multiline food companies—General Foods and Standard Brands. With consolidation came greater production cost efficiency and national market coverage. Following World War II, the bigger food companies moved toward more product differentiation and increased emphasis on advertising. Some became multinational in scope, establishing subsidiaries in many other countries. Starting in the 1960s, the industry went through more consolidation. This time the emphasis was on brand diversification and product-line expansion. Acquisition-minded companies shopped for smaller companies with products having strong brand recognition and brand loyalty.

Then, in the 1980s, giants began acquiring other giants. In 1984, Nestlé acquired Carnation for $3 billion. In 1985, R. J. Reynolds purchased Nabisco Brands for $4.9 billion (and then changed its corporate name to RJR Nabisco), and Philip Morris acquired General Foods Corporation for $5.7 billion, and later, Kraft foods for $6 billion. During the 1990s, most food processing companies shifted their acquisition strategy to focus on nondomestic acquisition targets. With a growth rate of 1 percent in the $200 billion U.S. food industry, food processing companies saw international expansion as one of the few ways to achieve growth in the industry.

A significant shift occurred during the 1990s in regard to where and how people shopped for food. In 1980, there were 96,000 small grocery stores in the United States whose annual sales were less than $2 million each. By 1992, this number had decreased to 53,000 and the number of these mom-and-pop stores were expected to decline to 39,000 by 1997. During this same period, the number of warehouse clubs increased from 920 stores to 2,100 stores in 1992. By 1993, over 12 percent of grocery sales had moved from supermarkets to warehouse clubs and discount stores such as Wal-Mart. This trend reflected the efforts of value-conscious consumers to shop at locations offering brand-name and good-quality private-label products at a low price. A survey of shoppers who purchased private-label processed foods indicated that only 15 to 25 percent of the shoppers would accept lower quality in return for a lower price.

Faced with the introduction of new rivals and consumers' demands for value, supermarket chains were forced to hold prices. Supermarkets and discounters alike responded to decreased margins by introducing store brand—private-label—alternatives to national brands. Store brands offering acceptable quality gained acceptance by the consumer and provided supermarkets with leverage in their relationships with processed food companies. A president of a marketing strategy firm explained the role of private-label products in the relationship between supermarkets and food processors:

> It's a major battle between the private-label brands and the outside brands. And the reason the balance of power is shifting is because the retailers own their shelf space like real estate.[20]

In 1993, private-label brands accounted for approximately 17 to 20 percent of all supermarket sales. Exhibit 13 details store brand share of selected food

Exhibit 12 Market Shares of the Leading Salsa Brands, 1993 and 1994

Manufacturer	Brand	1994	1993
Pace Foods	Pace	27.1%	28.8
Pet	Old El Paso	18.8	18.8
Frito-Lay	Chunky Salsa	12.7	11.8
Hormel	Chi-Chi's	8.5	n.a.
RJR Nabisco	Ortega	7.8	n.a.

Source: Information Resources and Nielsen North America, as reported by *The Wall Street Journal.*

Exhibit 13 Private-Label Market Share (by volume) in Selected Food Categories

Category	1993 Market Share	1992 Market Share
Cold cereal	8.2%	7.8%
Chips and snacks	8.9	9.2
Ice cream	35.1	36.9
Cookies	13.2	12.6
Soup	9.3	9.6
Carbonated beverages	20.8	19.2

Source: *Brandweek*, May 2, 1994, p. 56.

---

[20]*Mediaweek*, September 20, 1993, p. 23.

categories. In order to maintain premium pricing on brand-name products, the leading processed food companies were striving to differentiate their name-brand products from the high-quality store brands. Cobranding was one successful marketing strategy to differentiate branded products from store brands. Examples of cobranded products were Campbell's Mrs. Paul's fish sticks with Pepperidge Farm breading, Kellogg's Pop-Tarts with Smucker's fruit filling, and RJR Nabisco's Cranberry Newtons with Ocean Spray cranberries. Exhibits 14 and 15 show the largest food products companies based on revenues and the number of new food product introductions.

Exhibit 14   **The 25 Largest Food Products Companies, Ranked by 1993 Food and Beverage Sales**   *(in millions of dollars)*

Company	1992	1993
1. Philip Morris	$33,024	$34,526
2. ConAgra Inc.	16,201	16,499
3. PepsiCo	13,738	15,665
4. Coca-Cola	13,039	13,937
5. IBP Inc.	11,128	11,671
6. Anheuser-Busch	10,741	10,792
7. Sara Lee	6,622	7,206
8. H. J. Heinz	6,582	7,103
9. RJR Nabisco	6,707	7,025
10. Campbell Soup	6,263	6,586
11. Kellogg	6,191	6,295
12. Quaker Oats	5,576	5,731
13. CPC International	5,502	5,636
14. General Mills	5,234	5,397
15. Seagram Company	5,214	5,227
16. Tyson Foods	4,169	4,707
17. Ralston Purina	4,558	4,526
18. Borden Inc.	4,056	3,674
19. Hershey Foods	3,220	3,488
20. Procter & Gamble	3,709	3,271
21. Dole Foods	3,120	3,108
22. Hormel Food	2,814	2,854
23. Chiquita Brands	2,723	2,533
24. Dean Foods	2,220	2,243
25. International Multifoods	2,281	2,224

Source: The Food Institute.

Exhibit 15   New Food Product Introductions, by Company, 1992 and 1993

Company	1992	1993
1. Nestlé	114	186
2. Philip Morris	256	170
3. ConAgra Inc.	151	114
4. Campbell Soup	121	96
5. Wessanen USA	81	93
6. H. J. Heinz	99	91
7. Grand Met	74	88
8. RJR Nabisco	67	72
9. General Mills	61	70
10. Pet*	11	70
11. Unilever	53	66
12. Hormel Foods	50	64
13. PepsiCo*	34	62
14. Sara Lee	60	62
15. Specialty Brands*	33	48
16. E. J. Brach	71	46
17. J. M. Smucker*	30	45
18. Borden	44	43
19. M&M/Mars	40	39
20. Spice Hunter	41	37
Total	1,491	1,562

* Not in 1992 top 20.
Source: *Prepared Foods* magazine.

Bombardier Ltd. (B)

Joseph Lampel, New York University
Jamal Shamsie, New York University

I want a company with a continuous flow, that is not subject to the drastic fluctuations of being in just one business.[1]

These were the words of Laurent Beaudoin, chairman of Bombardier, during the early 1980s as he contemplated his company's dramatic rise to prominence. The Canadian company's name had been at one point synonymous with snowmobiles. Its pioneering efforts in the development and the launching of the Ski-Doo had been handsomely rewarded. By the late 1960s, Bombardier controlled close to 50 percent of the snowmobile market, about three times as much as its closest competitor.

Notwithstanding this success, Laurent Beaudoin came to believe that the potential of the snowmobile market was limited and that Bombardier should take steps to insulate itself from the uncertainties of the recreational market. Throughout the 1970s and the 1980s, Beaudoin led his company on an aggressive strategy of diversification into other areas of leisure and transportation.

As the company moved into the 1990s, its revenues had grown considerably beyond the $28 million in sales that it had generated from snowmobiles some 30 years earlier. The company had grown into a vast, publicly traded conglomerate with factories in seven countries and a labor force of over 34,000 employees. However, while Bombardier's revenues had grown dramatically, its profits had hardly kept up. Each year, solid performances by some of its businesses did not sufficiently compensate for unexpected losses elsewhere (see Exhibits 1 through 5 for Bombardier's financial picture and organization). For example, the transportation group had just reported a loss of $72.6 million, representing the single largest loss that any Bombardier business had ever incurred. The stable stream of profits on which Bombardier's strategy depended was proving to be more elusive than Beaudoin had expected.

GROWING WITH SNOWMOBILES

Birth of the Snowmobile

Work on the snowmobile was first started in the mid-1920s by Joseph-Armand Bombardier in his father's garage at Valcourt, Quebec. But it took until 1935 before Joseph-Armand had built the first snowmobile. It consisted of a large plywood body

---

Note: This case is a revised and thoroughly updated follow-on to a case developed by the same authors in 1988. Copyright © 1994, by the authors.
[1] "Bombardier: Making a Second Leap from Snowmobiles to Mass Transit," *Business Week*, February 23, 1981.

Exhibit 1   Bombardier's Income Statements, 1989–1993   (in millions of Canadian dollars)

	For the year ended January 31				
	1993	**1992**	**1991**	**1990**	**1989**
Net sales	$4,448.0	$3,058.6	$2,892.3	$2,143.3	$1,426.0
Cost of sales	4,180.2	2,828.2	2,672.5	1,974.4	1,298.9
Operating income	267.8	230.4	219.8	168.9	127.1
Interest on long-term debt	46.7	28.7	17.3	7.5	5.3
Other interest expenses	32.3	23.9	35.9	51.7	13.0
Other expenses	37.9	56.4	46.1		
Pretax income	150.9	121.4	120.5	117.2	108.8
Income taxes	18.1	13.7	20.4	25.7	39.2
Extraordinary loss	—	—	—	—	1.3
Net income	$ 132.8	$ 107.7	$ 100.1	$ 91.5	$ 68.3

Source: Bombardier annual reports.

Exhibit 2   Bombardier's Sales, by Class of Business, 1989–1993   (in millions of Canadian dollars)

	For the year ended January 31				
	1993	**1992**	**1991**	**1990**	**1989**
Aerospace	$2,228.4	$1,519.1	$1,382.9	$ 840.6	$ 630.7
Defense	366.5	366.2	358.3	214.7	143.9
Transportation	1,237.6	725.6	697.1	639.5	311.3
Consumer products	555.8	391.5	398.0	399.0	310.3
Capital group	59.7	56.2	56.0	49.5	29.8
Total	$4,448.0	$3,058.6	$2,892.3	$2,143.3	$1,426.0

Source: Bombardier annual reports.

set on caterpillar tracks and driven by a heavy, conventional internal combustion engine.

These early snowmobiles were hand-assembled in versions intended to accommodate from 5 to 25 passengers. In each case, the machine was individually adapted for a specific use according to the wishes of different customers. By 1942, Joseph-Armand had incorporated his garage to form Bombardier Snowmobile Limited and was producing snowmobiles to serve doctors, missionaries, woodsmen, foresters, trappers, and farmers in outlying districts of Quebec.

With the advent of World War II, the basic snowmobile design was adapted to produce an amphitrack armored carrier called the Penguin for use by Canadian troops. Subsequently, the demonstrated durability and ruggedness of the snowmobile also led to the development and production of various forms of specialized industrial equipment. These consisted of machines that were especially suited for use in forestry, logging, oil exploration, and snow removal.

Exhibit 3   Bombardier's Profits from Operations, by Class of Business, 1989–1993   (in millions of Canadian dollars)

	For the year ended January 31				
	1993	1992	1991	1990	1989
Aerospace	$180.6	$137.2	$112.9	$ 69.8	$ 34.8
Defense	6.9	2.0	28.5	17.8	7.4
Transportation	(72.6)	3.5	20.1	16.5	46.3
Consumer products	28.6	(9.1)	(29.5)	10.1	14.6
Capital group	7.4	(12.2)	(11.5)	3.0	5.7
Total	$150.9	$121.4	$120.5	$117.2	$108.8

Source: Bombardier annual reports.

Exhibit 4   Bombardier's Balance Sheets, 1989–1993   (in millions of Canadian dollars)

	For the year ended January 31				
Assets	1993	1992	1991	1990	1989
Cash and term deposits	$ 235.1	$ 179.2	$ 87.5	$ 84.0	$ 150.0
Accounts receivable	380.4	360.1	413.7	428.8	174.0
Financing receivables	942.1	640.8	491.3	458.0	307.5
Inventories	1,803.1	1,215.7	992.7	583.5	220.2
Prepaid expenses	19.6	13.6	9.5	12.2	9.9
Fixed assets	834.5	626.8	533.5	335.7	262.1
Other assets	55.2	34.5	35.3	34.8	27.0
Total assets	$4,270.0	$3,070.7	$2,563.5	$1,937.0	$1,150.7
Liabilities and Shareholders' Equity					
Short-term loans	884.9	640.1	558.2	376.8	153.2
Accounts payable	1,311.6	883.2	818.1	671.1	341.5
Income taxes payable	69.3	18.2	13.7	13.3	5.7
Long-term debt	698.5	381.2	265.9	147.0	70.6
Other liabilities	112.0	54.9	68.0	55.6	54.5
Convertible notes	209.6	193.8	145.4	50.4	—
Preferred shares	34.1	35.7	37.4	157.7	158.3
Shareholders' equity	950.0	863.6	656.8	465.1	366.9
Total liabilities and shareholders' equity	$4,270.0	$3,070.7	$2,563.5	$1,937.0	$1,150.7

Source: Bombardier annual reports.

Eventually, Joseph-Armand and his son Germain tackled the challenge of developing and producing a smaller and lighter version of the basic snowmobile design intended to carry one or two persons. The key to the new design was the coupling of a recently introduced two-cycle motor-scooter engine with an all rubber track that had internal steel rods built in for added strength. By 1959, the first snowmobile directed at the individual user was introduced into the market. Initially, Joseph-Armand thought of calling his invention the Ski-Dog, but he decided in favor of a more bilingual name, the Ski-Doo.

Exhibit 5　Bombardier's Business Unit Organization, 1993

Aerospace and Defense	Transportation Equipment	Motorized Consumer Products
Aerospace Group North America	**Transportation Equipment Group North America**	**Motorized Consumer Products Group**
Canadair (Canada)	Transportation Equipment Group (Canada, U.S.)	Sea-Doo/Ski-Doo Division (Canada)
de Havilland (Canada)	UTDC Systems Division (Canada, U.S.)	Bombardier-Rotax GmbH (Austria)
Learjet Inc. (U.S.)	Bombardier S.A. de C.V. (Mexico)	Scanhold Oy (Finland)
	Auburn Technology (U.S.)	Industrial Equipment Division (Canada)
Short Group	**Bombardier Eurorail**	
Short Brothers PLC (United Kingdom)	BN Division (Belgium)	
	Societe ANF-Industrie S.A. (France)	
	Bombardier-Wien A.G. (Austria)	
	Bombardier Prorail Limited (United Kingdom)	

Source: Bombardier annual reports.

Development of the Snowmobile

When he died in 1964, Joseph-Armand left behind a company that had 700 employees and a product that was enjoying increasing popularity—16,500 Ski-Doos had been sold and demand was clearly on the rise. Joseph-Armand's son Germain took over as president but shortly thereafter relinquished his post for reasons of health. The company passed into the hands of son-in-law Laurent Beaudoin, a chartered accountant and one of the first management graduates of the University of Sherbrooke. Beaudoin realized that certain factors were standing in the way of the development of the full potential of the snowmobile:

> There were two fundamental problems arising from the nature of the company's beginnings. First, there was no research and development department because it had all taken place in the mind of Joseph-Armand Bombardier. Second, the company which he created was, very naturally, a production-oriented company. It produced machines to fill a market need, which was mainly for large machines to do practical jobs, rather than creating and seeking out new markets.[2]

Beaudoin introduced an R&D section, set up an integrated marketing system, and geared up facilities for efficient mass production. Extensive research confirmed that an untapped snowmobile market existed not only for transport but also for recreation and sport. Bombardier invested heavily in the development of this potential market.

---

[2]"Bombardier Skids to Success," *International Management*, January 1972.

Over the next several years, massive advertising, combined with the establishment of a dealership network, culminated in the setting up of 18 regional sales groups covering Canada, the United States, and Europe. These efforts resulted in making Bombardier a leader in the snowmobile market and turned the Ski-Doo trademark into a generic term for snowmobiles.

But the success of Bombardier also brought about the entry of new producers of snowmobiles. Most of the new competition came from U.S. companies that had been closely watching the development of the snowmobile business. Beaudoin, however, was not fazed at the prospect of more competition. He was confident about the capabilities of his company to maintain its leadership:

> It's an industry that looks very simple. Everybody looks and says: "Gee, we can get in tomorrow morning and grab everything." But it's not that simple. The advantage we have over all those companies is that we eat snow, we know snow, and are snowmobilers ourselves.[3]

In order to ensure that it could meet this growing competition, Beaudoin also decided to start acquiring almost all of his suppliers, most of which were situated within the province of Quebec. These acquisitions led to the development of a series of subsidiaries and affiliates that manufactured parts or accessories related to snowmobile production (see Exhibit 6). This push for acquisitions eventually climaxed in the $30 million purchase of Rotax-Werk. Located in Austria, Rotax-Werk manufactured the two-stroke engine used in the Ski-Doo. By 1970, Bombardier's own production facilities, or those of its subsidiaries and affiliates, were supplying over 90 percent of the 1,400 parts that went into the manufacturing of the Ski-Doo. Beaudoin saw these moves as a necessary precaution against an eventual intensification of competition, in particular the likely outbreak of price wars: "If there is any price war, we will be in a position to face it. This has been our first idea."[4]

Shortly thereafter, Bombardier moved to buy out its largest competitor. In 1971, it finalized the acquisition of Moto-Ski from its U.S. parent Giffin Industries. This acquisition consolidated Bombardier's domination of the snowmobile market. By this time, the achievements and stature of Bombardier were acclaimed as a product of Canadian imagination and entrepreneurial vigor. An article, published at the beginning of 1972, bestowed praise on the company:

> Not many companies can claim to have started an entirely new industry—fewer still to have done so and stayed ahead of the pack. Bombardier Ltd. has done just that . . . It is a company owned and managed by Canadians, which several foreign companies would dearly love to own. It is the largest Quebec-owned company operating in the province, and is one of the 200 most profitable public companies in Canada.[5]

The Crunch for Snowmobiles

The early 1970s saw an increasing number of companies competing in the snowmobile market. In addition to new American and Canadian firms, Bombardier had to contend with the entry of Swedish, Italian, and Japanese manufacturers. Yet while the number of competitors was increasing, market growth in snowmobiles was slowing down.

---

[3]"Snow Job?" *Forbes*, February 1, 1970.
[4]Ibid.
[5]"Bombardier Skids to Success."

Exhibit 6   Bombardier's Acquisitions, 1957–1992

Consumer Products	Transportation Equipment	Aerospace and Defense
1957 Rockland Industries* Location: Kingsbury, Quebec Business: Rubber parts	1970 Lohner-Werke Location: Vienna, Austria Business: Streetcars	1973 Heroux# Location: Longueuil, Quebec Business: Aeronautical parts
1968 La Salle Plastic* Location: Richmond, Quebec Business: Plastic parts	1976 Montreal Locomotive Works# Location: Montreal, Quebec Business: Locomotives, diesel engines	1986 Canadair Location: Montreal, Quebec Business: Aerospace
1969 Roski* Location: Roxton Falls, Quebec Business: Fiberglass products	1984 Alco Power Location: Auburn, N.Y. Business: Locomotives, diesel engines	1989 Short Brothers Location: Belfast, Northern Ireland Business: Aerospace
1970 Rotax-Werk Location: Gunskirchen, Austria Business: Engines	1986 BN Constructions Location: Bruges, Belgium Business: Mass transit products	1990 Learjet Location: Wichita, Texas Business: Business jets
1970 Walker Manufacturing* Location: Montreal, Quebec Business: Sportswear	1986 Pullman Technology Location: Chicago, Illinois Business: Mass transit products	1992 de Havilland Location: Toronto, Ontario Business: Commuter aircraft
1970 Drummond Automatic Plating† Location: Drummondville, Quebec Business: Chrome plating	1989 ANF-Industrie Location: Paris, France Business: Mass transit products	
1970 Jarry Precision‡ Location: Montreal, Quebec Business: Transmissions	1990 Procor Engineering Location: Wakefield, England Business: Railcars	
1971 Moto-Ski§ Location: LaPocatiere, Quebec Business: Snowmobiles	1992 Carros de Ferrocarril (Concarril) Location: Mexico City, Mexico Business: Mass transit products	
1972 Ville Marie Upholstering‖ Location: Beauport, Quebec Business: Foam seats	1992 UDTC Location: Kingston, Ontario Business: Mass transit products	
1989 Scanhold Oy Location: Rovaniemi, Finland Business: Snowmobiles		

* Disposed of in 1983.
† Disposed of in 1976.
‡ Closed down in 1973.
§ Dissolved in 1975.
‖ Disposed of in 1979.
Disposed of in 1989.
Source: Financial Post Corporation Service.

Several reasons were advanced for the softening of snowmobile sales. The main blame was put on the stagnant economy, which was seen as the principal cause of the decline in demand. Snowmobiles constituted a type of purchase that was often postponed by consumers during a downturn in the economy. Other reasons were more peculiar to the snowmobile market. Poor winters, with late snow and unusually low precipitation, reduced the recreational use of snowmobiles. At the same time, newspaper stories of crashes and injured or killed riders led to a mounting concern over safety of snowmobiles. Finally, environmentalists were vocal in their criticism of the high noise levels generated by snowmobiles, particularly in wilderness areas.

There was growing awareness that stricter legislation covering the design and use of snowmobiles was likely to be forthcoming. Bombardier attempted to meet these concerns by trying to design better safety features and special mufflers for their upcoming snowmobile models. It also produced films, slides, and brochures on safety measures and the proper use of the snowmobile. Furthermore, a newly created public relations department tried to involve the various levels of government and different types of businesses in the creation of a system comparable to the one found in the ski industry. This was to include the development of snowmobile trails, snowmobile weekends, and snowmobile resorts.

The market for snowmobiles dropped sharply through most of the 1970s before it began to stabilize at around 100,000 units a year during the 1980s (see Exhibit 7). In order to adjust to these lower level of sales, Bombardier gradually sold off the various firms that were producing parts and accessories for snowmobiles. Apart from assembling the snowmobiles, Bombardier's actual manufacture of the vehicle was limited to the engine, which was still supplied by the company's Rotax division in Austria.

Beaudoin attributed the gradual dismantling of the manufacturing operations to the general state of the snowmobile industry. But eventually he acknowledged that Bombardier's position in the depressed snowmobile market had also been slipping. From a 45 percent share during the early 1970s, the company's share had declined to about 25 percent by the late 1980s. The competition had been closing in on Bombardier's leadership, causing it to have second thoughts about the merits of the industry that it had pioneered.

MOVING AWAY FROM SNOWMOBILES

In 1974, Bombardier seized on an opportunity to bid on a four-year $118 million contract to build 423 new cars for the proposed extension of the Montreal subway system. The bid represented a major departure from the core business of the company. It was not, however, the first time that Bombardier had ventured away from snowmobiles.

Early Diversification Moves

Even before the snowmobile market was developed, Bombardier had been producing all-terrain tracked and wheeled vehicles for different kinds of industrial use. The company had continuously developed and marketed many basic types or sizes of vehicles for work in swamps, forests, and snow. The earliest of these were the Muskeg series of carriers, tractors, and brushcutters that were used in logging, construction, petroleum, and mining. Later developments included the SW series for urban snow removal, the Skidozer line for grooming snowmobile trails and ski slopes, and the Bombi carrier for transporting people over snowy or marshy terrain.

A further departure from snowmobiles came as a result of Bombardier's acquisition of suppliers (see Exhibit 6). Originally, the acquisitions were undertaken in order

Exhibit 7　Snowmobile Market Statistics, 1971–1992

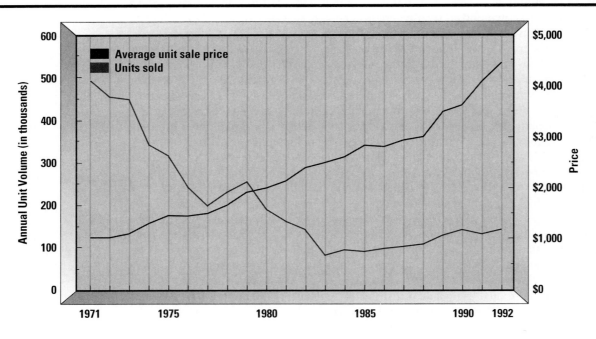

Source: International Snowmobile Manufacturers Association.

to consolidate the company's position in the snowmobile market. Once made, they presented attractive opportunities. For example, Rotax-Werk was acquired in 1970 because it produced the engines that were used in Ski-Doos. But it also manufactured engines for boats and motorcycles. Another acquired subsidiary proceeded to develop and introduce a new type of fiberglass sailboat, followed by a canoe and a catamaran.

In addition, the success of the snowmobile created other ancillary markets. For instance, traveling on snowmobiles at 40 miles per hour in subfreezing temperatures required specialized clothing. Beaudoin saw this new type of market as a promising opportunity:

> Someone was going to have to supply wet-proof clothing that was warm enough to prevent our customers from freezing to death on our machines. We decided it might as well be us.[6]

Consequently, Bombardier acquired an apparel manufacturer in order to introduce snowmobile clothing. This led the company into the sportswear market because the acquired manufacturer was already engaged in the production and marketing of several other types of sportswear. Said Beaudoin: "We are in the leisure business."[7]

In other instances, Bombardier sought to enter markets not directly related to its core snowmobile business. In 1970, the company introduced a new product called the

[6]Ibid.
[7]Ibid.

Sea-Doo, which was a kind of snowmobile on water. This was marketed most heavily in Florida and California. Unfortunately, the Sea-Doo was found to rust in salt water and production was suspended after a couple of years. A more technically successful product was the Can-Am motorcycle, which was test-marketed by Bombardier in 1973. The idea for the motorcycle originated with the development of a new engine by Bombardier's new Rotax subsidiary in Austria. The result was a light, high-performance motorcycle that quickly gained recognition after it won several races in Canada, the United States, and Europe.

A Bold Thrust

It was around this time that Bombardier began to see mass transit as a potentially lucrative market. The decision to move into mass transit was facilitated by overtures to Bombardier from the French-based Compagnie Industrielle de Materiel de Transport (CIMT). CIMT had been involved in a partnership with Canadian Vickers Limited on a previous order for the Montreal subway system. Charles Leblanc, who was vice president, administration, for the company at the time stated:

> CIMT came to us. They said don't be afraid of it. They pointed out that the same manufacturing steps were needed for subway cars as for snowmobiles. So we went ahead and bid.[8]

The award of this substantial contract represented Bombardier's entry into the mass transit market. There were strong doubts whether Bombardier had the necessary capabilities to complete the order. Up to this point, the company's involvement in mass transit products had been limited to trams and streetcars produced by its Austrian subsidiary. But trams and streetcars are light rail vehicles, substantially different in design from subway cars.

The company moved to convert the Moto-Ski snowmobile plant at La Pocatiere to handle production of subway cars. The complexity of making a subway car is several orders of magnitude greater than that of a snowmobile. A subway car has 8,000 parts and 14 kilometers of electric wiring, compared to only 2,000 parts in a snowmobile. The shift to subway cars required a considerable retraining of the labor force. It was also costly in terms of physical facilities. The estimated cost of conversion was about $5 million, of which $1 million was provided by a grant from the Canadian government.

Bombardier did experience some problems in production, due in part to a labor strike in its newly converted plant. Nevertheless, the company began to make deliveries of subway cars to the city of Montreal late in 1976. By this time, Bombardier had also begun to receive orders for commuter cars from the United States and for subway cars from Mexico. But the firm made its biggest splash in 1982, landing a large and prestigious order of about $1 billion for 825 subway cars from the Metropolitan Transportation Authority of New York. The company managed to acquire the technology that it needed for these subway cars from Kawasaki, the Japanese firm that had manufactured the previous batch of New York subway cars. A low-interest export financing scheme from the Canadian federal government also helped to clinch the sale.

Encouraged by its success in attracting orders, Bombardier bought out the mass transit activities of Pullman and Budd companies. Between them, these companies

---

[8]"Why Bombardier Is Trying Out Mass Transit," *Business Week*, March 10, 1975.

accounted for the designs of 85 percent of the vehicles operating in the United States and Canada. By 1988, the company had also acquired almost all of the stock of a Belgian mass transit company that had supplied the technology to develop and build the streetcars that it had already delivered to Portland, Oregon. The acquired firm, BN Constructions Ferroviares et Metalliques S.A., had three factories in Belgium, one in England, and one in France. Besides streetcars, BN manufactured subway cars, electric railcars, passenger coaches, and freight cars.

During the next two years, Bombardier followed up with two more acquisitions to increase its presence in Europe. In France, it spent $23.5 million to acquire ANF-Industrie, one of the largest suppliers of railcars and coaches to the French railway industry. ANF was already working with Bombardier's BN subsidiary on a contract worth $650 million for the design and manufacture of shuttle train cars for the English Channel tunnel project. Across the channel from France, Bombardier purchased Procor Engineering Limited, a major British manufacturer of passenger and freight cars for the railway.

During 1992, Bombardier picked up two more manufacturers of mass transit equipment in North America. In Mexico, the company acquired Carros de Ferrocarril (Concarril), the largest manufacturer of rail cars. Besides paying $27 million to the Mexican government, it assumed $55 million of the debt that Concarril had accumulated when operations were suspended a few months earlier. Back home, Bombardier added to its Canadian production capacity by purchasing Toronto-based UTDC from the Ontario government for $34 million. Additionally, it was able to negotiate a $17 million subsidy from the provincial government in return for a commitment to maintain employment and invest up to $30 million in new plant and equipment.

Reflecting back on Bombardier's growing position in mass transportation products, Beaudoin stressed the role of Lohner-Werke, the Austrian firm that made tramways that had come along with the purchase of Rotax. Bombardier had at one point shopped around for firms that would buy Lohner-Werke but had found few takers. Beaudoin commented:

> Everyone thinks we're great strategists but it was by chance that Bombardier got involved in rail transportation . . . The decision to hold onto the Austrian subsidiary was the turning point. It taught us how to operate a company abroad, and it developed our expertise in the rail sector.[9]

A Stab at Related Diversification

Shortly after its entry into mass transit, Bombardier tried to find new acquisitions that would help it to become a significant competitor in the transportation business. According to Beaudoin, Bombardier's move into mass transit products had done much to ameliorate the company's dependence on recreational products such as the snowmobile. He summed up his company's goals in the following terms:

> Our goal is to develop some equilibrium between transportation and recreation. The transportation and recreation cycles are different. Recreational products are strong when the economy is strong. It's the reverse for transportation because of energy problems.[10]

---

[9]"Trains, Planes and Snowmobiles," *CA Magazine*, November 1992.
[10]"Snowmobiles to Subways: Bombardier Maps Out its Route," *Financial Post*, September 13, 1980.

In 1976, Bombardier succeeded in purchasing the Montreal Locomotive Works (MLW) from its U.S. parent for a cash payment of $16.8 million. Bombardier was given much needed financial help from the Quebec government in finalizing this deal. The diesel-electric locomotives produced by MLW were mostly in the lighter category, ranging from 1,000 to 2,000 horsepower. The main markets for such locomotives were mainly the operators of railways in developing countries.

Bombardier's purchase of MLW was largely motivated by its growing interest in developing the Light, Rapid and Comfortable (LRC) passenger train. Its partners in this project were Alcan and Dofasco. The Canadian government also contributed development grants through its program for the advancement of industrial technology. The new train was designed to run at constant high speeds on existing North American tracks. Both Via Rail in Canada and Amtrack in the United States began to make test runs of the new LRC trains during the late 1970s and early 1980s. Bombardier vice president Henry Valle, who had previously headed MLW, talked about the distinctive features of the LRC:

> We think the LRC is as good or better than anything comparable on the market anywhere. And we don't think anyone anywhere knows any more about high-speed trains than we do.[11]

Bombardier also made substantial investments to upgrade the MLW facilities for the production of diesel locomotives. In 1984, the company sought to expand its capacity and obtain new customers through the $30 million acquisition of Alco Power, located in Auburn, New York. However, Alco's production capabilities were also limited to the lighter category of diesel-electric locomotives that were similar to those offered by MLW.

At the same time, Bombardier was being forced to reevaluate its potential orders for passenger locomotives that would result from the sales of its LRC train. The company had believed that it would eventually make worldwide sales of 150 locomotives and 750 coaches. But by 1986, after the sale of only 31 locomotives and 100 coaches to Canadian-based Via Rail, there were no more orders on hand. Even Via Rail had declined to exercise its options for further orders because of mechanical and electrical problems it had experienced with equipment already delivered.

Bombardier also began to realize that it was not likely to build a viable position in the locomotive market unless it developed and produced locomotives with greater horsepower, such as those presently manufactured by General Electric and General Motors. The company explored the possibility of linking up with existing large competitors such as General Electric or Kawasaki in order to gain better access to the technology that would be required to develop higher powered locomotives. Having failed in this direction, Bombardier decided to terminate the production of new locomotives and to focus primarily on the servicing of existing locomotives. Most of this work was subsequently channeled into the Alco facility in New York state. In 1989, the MLW facility was finally sold off to the Canadian division of General Electric. Raymond Royer, soon to become Bombardier's president, expressed the company's disappointment over the sale: "It has been very painful for us. It's a major decision to take, but if we can't make a profit, we have to act as good managers."[12]

---

[11]"Bombardier Looks to Amtrack to Open Doors to U.S. Inter-City Market," *Globe & Mail*, November 16, 1977.

[12]"Locomotives to Be Dropped," *Globe & Mail*, July 13, 1985.

LEAVING SNOWMOBILES BEHIND ─────────────────

As Bombardier moved into the 1980s, it was becoming increasingly aware of the volatility in the orders for its newly developed mass transit business. As the company was completing deliveries on the large order of subway cars for New York City, it was not sure when other orders of a comparable size would become available. Mass transit orders do not tend to follow any predictable cycles, seasons, or patterns. Consequently, Bombardier began to look for businesses that could insulate it from the uncertainties of the mass transit business. The search led the company to look beyond mass transit to automobiles and aerospace, both of which were industries whose size could provide it with considerable scope for further expansion. However, entry into either of these would represent the first major shift in business focus since Bombardier's entry into mass transit.

Exploration of Entry into Small Car Manufacture

Since 1983, Bombardier had been actively exploring the possibility of introducing into the North American market a small car designed to carry two persons that would retail for about $7,000. The company had concluded an agreement with Daihatsu Motor Company of Japan to obtain the technology that was going to be used in the design of the car. Daihatsu, which was partly owned by Toyota, was the smallest producer of cars in Japan. Talks between Bombardier and Daihatsu focused on a joint venture framework for development and production of the new car.

As a first step, Bombardier would begin production of the Daihatsu three-cylinder car that was already marketed in Asia and Europe. The next step would be for Bombardier and Daihatsu to jointly design a front-wheel-drive version of this car for the North American market. The car would be produced by Bombardier at Valcourt, where the company had sufficient spare factory space. The facilities were deemed to be sufficient to handle production of about 200,000 cars annually. Sales and service were to be carried out by the 350 snowmobile dealers that Bombardier had developed throughout Canada and the United States.

Supported by generous grants from the various levels of the Canadian government, Bombardier spent about $15 million developing and testing four prototypes. Although prototype testing had gone well, there were still strong doubts within the company about the size of the potential market for such a small car. Since the car was to be powered by a three-cylinder engine, it would offer a maximum speed of about 55–65 miles per hour. It would therefore have to be targeted as a second car, used mainly for driving within the urban and suburban areas.

In 1987, Laurent Beaudoin finally announced that the company had decided to abandon the proposed joint venture to assemble small cars. Among other factors, Beaudoin cited the rising value of the yen, which made the cost of imported parts from Japan—notably the power train—much too expensive to meet the company's profitability objectives. In his words: "We saw there was no realistic way to attain an acceptable profit in the medium term."[13]

─────────

[13]"Bombardier, Daihatsu Abandon Venus Project," *Globe & Mail*, June 24, 1987.

Diversifying in Another Direction

Even as Bombardier was getting ready to abandon small cars, it was actively exploring an opportunity that emerged when the Canadian government expressed its intention to sell Canadair, an aerospace company located in Montreal. Canadair had run into difficulty after spending in excess of $1 billion to develop the Challenger, a business jet that earned praise from industry observers for being spacious, quiet, and fuel efficient. Unfortunately for Canadair, projected sales of the aircraft showed that it was unlikely to cover initial development costs.

When the financial condition of Canadair could no longer be concealed from the public, the government decided to absorb the development costs and sell the company. As a Canadian company based in Quebec, Bombardier was favorably positioned to take advantage of the government's predicament. After a brief negotiation period, the Canadian government agreed to sell Canadair to Bombardier for $120 million, provided it continued to develop Canadair's assets. In addition to its highly regarded business jet, these assets also included the CL-215 water bomber. The CL-215 had been the mainstay of the company during the 1970s while the Challenger was being developed. Although it offered excellent firefighting capabilities, Canadair was having difficulty obtaining new orders for the plane.

Immediately after its acquisition, Bombardier moved to turn Canadair around by reducing management hierarchy and cutting operating costs. With the encouragement of Bombardier's top management, Canadair also decided to further exploit its existing technological capabilities. It announced plans to adapt the Challenger design to create an extended 50-seat short-haul regional jet. This commuter version was designed to serve the growing traffic in short-haul routes, particularly in the United States and in Europe. The $300 million development project received substantial financial help from both the federal and provincial levels of the Canadian government.

In 1989, Bombardier expanded its aerospace business to Europe, acquiring Short Brothers PLC from the British government. Bombardier paid $60 million for the company and undertook to maintain its operations in Belfast, Northern Ireland, running for at least four years. In return, the British government agreed to write off $1.3 billion of the company's debt and provide grants totaling more than $200 million. The deal gave Bombardier control of a firm with $1.5 billion in orders and entry into the lucrative European aviation industry. Short produced Tucano trainer aircraft and C-23 Sherpa aircraft for European military outfits. However, the major share of its revenues came from supplying aircraft components to other aircraft manufacturers such as Boeing and Fokker. Bombardier also began to use Short's expertise to design and manufacture several components for the regional jet under development by Canadair.

Shortly after acquiring Short Brothers, Bombardier moved again to acquire Learjet Corporation, a financially troubled U.S. manufacturer of small jets. Learjet was purchased for $75 million in cash and assumption of $38 million of outstanding debt from its parent, which had filed for protection under the bankruptcy code. The company produced several models of light jets such as the 31A and 35A, both of which seat 9 or 10 passengers, compared to the 12 to 19 passengers that could be carried by the Challenger models. By 1991, Learjet had begun to adapt the existing Learjet designs to develop a model 60, which would accommodate more passengers and be able to fly longer distances. Beaudoin commented on Bombardier's strategy to exploit the technology that it had obtained from the Canadair, Short, and Learjet acquisitions: "First acquire the outside technology, then improve on it to become competitive."[14]

In 1992, Bombardier acquired 51 percent of Boeing's ailing de Havilland division, with an option to buy out the rest of the company from the Ontario provincial government after four years. De Havilland produced the Dash 8-100 and Dash 8-300 lines of propeller-driven commuter aircraft seating 37 to 40 passengers each. Beaudoin felt that these would complement the Challenger regional jet that was currently being developed by the company's Canadair division. Although de Havilland had been a consistent money loser for Boeing, Bombardier was protected from any losses during the first four years of operations by a $300 million reserve fund set up by the Canadian federal and provincial governments.

Asked to explain how Bombardier would be able to turn around ailing aerospace companies that others had failed to revive, Beaudoin answered:

> The main difference is we're very close to those operations. We have a very quick decision-making process. We encourage entrepreneurship among our people. We delegate responsibility to them. And we support them in their decision-making process.[15]

Growth of Auxiliary Markets

The acquisition of Canadair also resulted in Bombardier's entry into the defense industry. Canadair was a major producer of airborne surveillance systems, and it also possessed a fully developed capability for servicing military aircraft. Shortly after Bombardier's acquisition of Canadair, the Canadian government awarded the company a lucrative contract for the maintenance of the CF-18 fighter that would eventually result in more than $1 billion of revenues. This contract led to further technical services, including full-scale fatigue tests for the CF-5 and CF-18, as well as maintenance of other aircraft used by the Canadian armed forces.

In addition to these contracts, Canadair was also involved in the design and manufacture of unmanned or remotely piloted air surveillance systems. Its CL-89 surveillance systems had already been purchased by several NATO countries. The company had recently completed work on a more advanced CL-289 system and was planning to start work on a CL-227 Sentinel system.

Bombardier's activities in the defense sector expanded considerably as a result of its subsequent acquisition of Short Brothers. Short Brothers had developed military aircraft, notably the older Tucano military trainer and the more recently developed Sherpa C-23 transport. The company had long-term contracts for providing technical support for the fleet of Tucano trainers and Sherpa cargos operated by, among others, the British Air Force.

Furthermore, Short was also engaged in the production and delivery of short-range defense systems for the British armed forces. The first of these systems was the high-velocity Starstreak missile system that had been under development since 1987. More recently, this system had been complemented by the introduction of a more advanced laser-guided Starburst missile system. The company was also exploring many possible export markets in Europe, the United States, and the Far East.

---

[14]"Planes, Trains and Snowmobiles," *Enroute*, March 1991.
[15]"On the Move," *Montreal Gazette*, November 1, 1993.

BOMBARDIER'S CURRENT BUSINESS PORTFOLIO ⸻

By 1993, Bombardier's operations fell into four different business sectors, consisting of 16 different divisions or subsidiaries (see Exhibit 5). While the transportation equipment sector included the largest number of divisions, the bulk of sales came from the aerospace and defense sector. A fourth sector, the Bombardier Capital Group, provided credit and financing services for all other sectors. Although Bombardier was moving to bring its various divisions and subsidiaries under centralized control, they continued to be managed as separate administrative and financial entities. Each division or subsidiary was headed by a chief executive who possessed a considerable degree of autonomy. However, these chief executives were expected to work more closely with the member of Bombardier's corporate management team that had lead oversight for their particular business sector.

Bombardier's top management worked mostly out of the company's corporate headquarters in Montreal. Except for a brief period, the position of chairman and chief executive officer had been occupied by Laurent Beaudoin. Joseph-Armand's son Andre Bombardier, and son-in-law Jean-Louis Fontaine, held positions as vice chairmen of the company. Finally, Raymond Royer, who was hired away from a rival snowmobile manufacturer by Beaudoin in the early 1970s, was currently president and chief operating officer.

Aerospace and Defense Group

Although Bombardier was a relatively new entrant into the aerospace industry, its string of acquisitions quickly elevated it to the status of seventh largest manufacturer of civil aircraft in the world. Furthermore, its extensive range of turboprops and jets made the company one of the most diversified aerospace manufacturers in the world (see Exhibit 8). Over the last three years, revenues from Bombardier's aerospace and defense segment accounted for just over 60 percent of the company's total sales. Aerospace and defense products were also the only significant contributors to the firm's overall pretax profits.

Bombardier's financial performance in the aerospace sector had been achieved in the face of growing difficulties in securing sufficient orders for its products. The shortage of orders was particularly evident in the market for commuter aircraft where the company's Canadair division had recently launched the newly developed Challenger regional jet, the first commercial jet liner on the market with fewer than 70 seats. When the $275 million project was launched with great fanfare in early 1989, it had more than 100 tentative orders. Despite a worldwide marketing offensive, only 36 of these had been converted into firm orders. The company had not received any new orders for well over a year. Regional airlines had been noticeably slow to sign up for a unique jetliner in spite of the fact that it was designed especially with this market in mind.

There was a similar shortage of orders for the lower priced propeller-driven Dash 8 lines of commuter aircraft offered by the newly acquired de Havilland subsidiary. The company was considering shutting down most of its operations for two months in the summer months, temporarily laying off 2,000 of its 2,800 employees. The closure was being forced by the cancellation of an order for 22 of the Dash 8 turboprops by an Irish aircraft leasing firm that was experiencing financial difficulties.

Exhibit 8   Bombardier's Aerospace Products

Large Business Aircraft

Canadair Challenger

Major competitors: Gulfstream models and Dassault's Falcon business jet line

Small Business Aircraft

Learjet 31 and 35A
Learjet 60

Major competitors: Cessna's Citation line, British Aerospace models, and Beech's BeechJet

Commuter Aircraft

Canadair Regional Jet RJ-100
de Havilland Dash 8 100 and 300

Major competitors: British Aerospace Jetstream lines, Saab, and Fokker's regional aircraft lines

Amphibious Aircraft

Canadair CL-215 and CL-415

Military Aircraft

Short's Sherpa
Short's Tucano

Source: Business and Commercial Aviation 1992 Handbook.

Beaudoin attributed the problems with orders to excess capacity, fare wars, and record losses in the commercial airline industry. He was confident that the sales of commuter jets would pick up as industry conditions improved. A Stanford University study commissioned by Bombardier forecast that there would be demand for 7,000 aircraft in the 20- to 90-seat category between 1994 and 2010, propelled by the growth of smaller, regional airlines, particularly in the United States and Europe. Bombardier management saw few aircraft on the horizon that could provide strong competition for its products. Saab of Sweden was planning to introduce a 50-seat turboprop in 1994, but Fokker's new 70-seat jet was not expected to be ready before 1995.

Most of the remaining sales in this sector came from the company's business jets. Canadair's Challenger business jet had managed to gain about 25 to 30 percent of the market for such large business jets in spite of strong competition from Gulfstream and Dassault. Canadair had just introduced a longer range version of the Challenger and was hoping to build sales in international markets with a Global Express high-speed business jet that would cover the distance between New York and Tokyo without refuelling. This luxury jet would contain a fully equipped office, main cabin, bedroom, and a bathroom with a shower. However, both Gulfstream and Dassault had also begun to develop competing models that were likely to be introduced at around the same time.

With the acquisition of Learjet, Bombardier added small business jets to its product line. The Learjet 31A and 35A models could seat up to 10 people and had a range of just under 1,500 nautical miles. The newly developed model 60 extended that range to almost 3,000 nautical miles, making it comparable in range to the larger Challenger business jets. Nevertheless, Learjet had relatively few orders in a market that was heavily dominated by Textron's Cessna division. With seven different models available, Cessna controlled almost 60 percent of the market for small business jets. In order to improve its market position, Learjet had recently announced the development of a new Learjet 45 based on a completely new design offering more cabin space, greater range, and better fuel efficiency at a more competitive price.

Bombardier had tried to use the excess capacity in its aerospace divisions to build components for the larger aircraft manufacturers. However, declining orders for larger aircraft were likely to reduce the work that Short Brothers and Canadair did on components for such companies as Boeing, Airbus, and Fokker. As a result, Bombardier had sought to spread the risk faced by its subsidiaries by reducing each division's reliance on a single product line. Instead of making only the Dash 8, for instance, de Havilland was also doing engine modifications on Canadair-built CL-215T waterbombers, designing the wings for the new Learjet 45, and painting the Challenger regional jet.

Transportation Equipment Group

Bombardier's transportation products included a wide variety of heavy, conventional, and light-rail vehicles. The expansion into different transportation products was achieved through a combination of licensing agreements and related acquisitions (see Exhibit 9). As a result of this product expansion, Bombardier ranked among the top 10 producers of mass transit equipment in the world. During the last three years, revenues from this segment accounted for about 25 percent of the company's total sales. But the sector had shown low levels of profits in recent years, culminating in a loss of $72.6 million before taxes during the last year.

Bombardier's recent acquisitions in Belgium, France, and England had also given the company greater access to the larger European market for mass transit equipment. Its presence in several European countries allowed it to neutralize pressure on governments to award mass transit jobs to local companies. Bombardier had won several large contracts from the Belgian and French railways, but it had only a 7 percent share of the orders for mass transit equipment in Europe. In part, this was the result of stiff competition the company faced from several large multinationals such as Asea Brown Boveri, GEC-Alsthom, AEG-Westinghouse, and Siemens.

Bombardier's European operations had been plagued by chronic cost overruns on several of the contracts that its various divisions had succeeded in winning. The biggest such problem occurred with the $700 million contract by the Belgian subsidiary to provide 250 high-speed shuttle train cars to the consortium building the English Channel tunnel. Bombardier had filed a lawsuit claiming that repeated changes in design specifications for the rail cars resulted in $450 million of additional costs.

The company's purchase of Concarril from the Mexican government in 1992 was turning out to be a disappointment. Concarril had recently lost on two important subway contracts that it had bid for and was still waiting to hear about the outcome on a third bid. Beaudoin argued that since the acquisition of the Mexican unit was relatively inexpensive, it could afford to wait. He claimed that these operations gave Bombardier a presence in each of the countries covered by the North American free-trade agreement and a gateway to South America.

In general, Bombardier had fared much better in the North American market north of Mexico. The company believed it had a 30 percent share of the mass transit orders in this market. It had just delivered the first set of technologically advanced subway cars to the New York City Transit Authority and was presently also working on orders for subway cars for the transit authorities in other cities such as Toronto and Boston. Through its newly acquired UTDC subsidiary based in Toronto, Bombardier

Exhibit 9   Bombardier's Mass Transit Products

Heavy Rail	**Technology Source**
Rubber-tired subway cars	License from CIMT France
	Acquired through BN and ANF
Steel-wheeled subway cars	License from Kawasaki
Conventional Rail	
Commuter and rail cars	Acquired through Pullman
	Acquired through BN and ANF
Shuttle-train cars	Acquired through BN and ANF
LRC railcars	Developed with Alcan and Dofasco
TGV railcars	License from GEC-Alsthom
Light Rail	
Light rail vehicles	Acquired through BN and UTDC
Streetcars	Acquired through Rotex
Monorail	License from Disney
PeopleMover	License from Disney

Source: Financial Post Corporation Service.

had also obtained an order for 108 subway cars for Ankara as part of a fully automated subway project for the Turkish capital.

Beaudoin estimated that the North American demand for new subway and rail cars would surpass 4,000 during the next five years, and hundreds more would need to be refurbished. Bombardier's major competition in North America came from few firms, chiefly Morris Knudsen and Asea Brown Boveri. However, the company expected to face stiffer competition in the future as giant U.S. defense contractors entered this business in the transition to civilian production. Recently, Bombardier had to bid against new entrants such as Lockheed Corporation, Hughes Aircraft, and Rockwell International to obtain a contract supplying mass transportation vehicles for Los Angeles.

Finally, Bombardier was aggressively searching for clients since its acquisition of the exclusive North American rights for France's TGV trains from GEC-Alsthom. It had spent millions trying to persuade governments on both sides of the Canada–U.S. border of the merits of electrified fast trains, but so far it had little to show for this investment. A proposed TGV link joining Dallas and Houston was in limbo, and hopes for an estimated $7 billion TGV line connecting Montreal and Toronto, had been dashed by cash-short governments.

Motorized Consumer Products Group

The original lines of snowmobiles and a revived Sea-Doo represented the bulk of the sales of motorized consumer products currently offered by Bombardier. Although the company was still one of the largest manufacturers of snowmobiles in 1993, revenues from this segment accounted for only 13 percent of the company's total sales during the 1990s. Furthermore, consumer products had just rebounded with a pretax profit of $29 million in the last year, after two successive years of losses.

During the 1980s, Bombardier lost the leadership in the snowmobile market that it had originally pioneered. Its market share declined as other competitors continued to develop stronger technological and manufacturing advantages. In the early 1990s, the company moved aggressively to update its product lines, increase its product quality, and reduce its production costs. By 1993, the company had regained some of its lost market share, attaining almost 25 percent of North American sales. But Bombardier was still in second position, just behind U.S.-based Polaris Industries and just ahead of Japanese-based Yamaha.

Bombardier had increased its product line to 20 models of snowmobiles that were geared toward six different types of users. These included family models developed for greater comfort and safety, as well as sporty models designed for higher speed and better performance. It revamped its distribution system to introduce new models earlier in the year and began to produce on order rather than for inventories.

In 1992, Bombardier acquired full ownership of Scanhold Oy, producer of the Lynx line of snowmobiles and utility vehicles. While Scanhold already dominated the snowmobile market in the Scandinavian countries, the proximity of its plant to the potentially massive Russian market was promising. Bombardier had hired Soviet hockey legend Vlasislav Tretiak to help promote its machines, after its Ski-Doo and Lynx snowmobiles had finished one-two in an international snowmobile race in Moscow in 1992.

Apart from snowmobiles, the company had experienced considerable success with a revival of its Sea-Doo watercraft. Its launch in 1987 was a result of three years of research and development, including the development of a new Rotax engine. In spite of growing competition, the Sea-Doo had been well received and its market share had grown to almost 37 percent of the sit-down segment of the North American light watercraft market. During 1992, Bombardier added other models, including a three-passenger GTX model and a jet-powered Explorer runabout.

With the exception of the Rotax engines, most of the company's consumer products were manufactured in a shared production facility in Valcourt where the company was first started. Its assembly line was capable of producing several hundred snowmobiles and watercraft daily. Part of the facilities had been expanded or adapted for the manufacturing of industrial and logistic equipment, with rates of production that could vary from three to six units per day.

LOOKING TOWARD THE FUTURE

> I don't mean to downplay my own contribution but I have always followed the conservative management principle that was behind Joseph-Armand Bombardier's success: Stick to what you know.[16]

Beaudoin had always argued that the change in Bombardier during the 1970s and 1980s was more than merely a shift in the company's products and markets. For him, the expansion in the company's scope was motivated by the need to spread risk. By 1993, Bombardier's sales had reached $4.4 billion, up from $1.4 billion of only four years earlier. Its profits had risen to $132.8 million from $68.3 million during the same time period. Furthermore, the company had a backlog of orders worth just over $8 billion. The backlog, which was spread over aerospace and transportation equipment, was at the highest level ever recorded.

---

[16]"Trains, Planes and Snowmobiles."

In spite of this promising performance, Bombardier chairman Laurent Beaudoin had to reassure stockholders during the company's annual meeting in June 1993. Bombardier's stock had wobbled in recent months, falling under $11.75, well below its 1992 peak of $17.25. The company had also been forced to cancel plans to raise $150 million through the issue of a new class of shares. The souring of the market was attributed to the Bombardier's inconsistent performance as reflected in the fluctuating profits generated by its various sectors.

During his speech to shareholders, Beaudoin stressed that while individual sectors within Bombardier had had good and bad years, the sectors that performed well more than compensated for those that did not. He pointed to the rebound in the consumer products sectors, which had posted profits after the success of the new Ski-Doo and the Sea-Doo models. He also predicted that the transportation sector would reverse its losses in 1994 once the contract dispute over the English Channel project was resolved.

Looking farther ahead, Beaudoin confidently predicted that his transportation giant would double its revenue over the next five years. In addition, he vowed that the growth would come from the businesses that the company presently owned and not through acquisitions of new ones. According to Beaudoin, the company already sold its products in 50 countries around the world and expected to gradually tap into emerging markets in South America, Asia, central and eastern Europe, and the countries of the former Soviet Union.

But analysts who had tracked Bombardier's performance over the years noted the company had largely grown through acquiring companies, often at bargain-basement prices and usually with generous government help. This had led to some serious concerns about the distorting effects that subsidies had on the company's profitability, particularly in the extremely important aerospace sector. Many of these subsidies were expected to run out in 1994.

The company thus faced the challenging task of consolidating its recent string of acquisitions while at the same time generating enough cash to finance the next round of product development. Beaudoin downplayed the problems that some analysts attributed to the diversity and range of businesses into which his company had expanded. He recently commented:

> What does Bombardier do, essentially? It assembles metal parts. It welds. It uses professionals and trades that revolve around this key activity. If you look at it from this angle, you can see that there isn't a big difference between a railcar and an aircraft fuselage. For a welder or a machinist, in fact, it's simply a question of millimeters or fractions of millimeters.[17]

---

[17]Ibid.

Motorola, Inc.

Dean Aluzio, University of Connecticut
Michael Lubatkin, University of Connecticut

Motorola is one of the world's leading diversified electronics manufacturers, providing wireless communications equipment (cellular telephones and systems, pagers, and two-way radios), semiconductor products (computer chips, integrated circuits, and microprocessor units), and advanced electronics equipment and services for worldwide markets. Motorola has competed quite successfully in markets where many U.S. competitors have exited; over the past 11 years, revenues grew an average of 14.5 percent annually, from just under $5 billion in 1983 to $22.2 billion in 1994. According to former CEO George Fisher, "I see no reason why we can't maintain that pace throughout the 1990s."[1] In 1994, Motorola employed approximately 132,000 people worldwide and ranked 28th among the 500 largest U.S. companies in terms of total sales.

One of the factors that made Motorola's sales gains particularly impressive was the competitors that Motorola went up against. In its two main markets, semiconductors and communications, Motorola competed with the elite of Japanese companies in industries that the Japanese government had targeted for nationally supported development. Yet Motorola was the worldwide leader in cellular phones, pagers, two-way radios, and advanced dispatch systems for commercial fleets. In wireless telecommunications equipment, Motorola alternated between the number one and number two spots, while competing with AT&T and Sweden-based Ericsson. In microprocessors (MPUs), Motorola was second only to Intel. Motorola endeavored to compete for a leadership position in these markets with innovative products and the most advanced technology. In the words of one observer, "Its excellence lies in good part in a deeply bred ability to continually move out along the curve of innovation, to invent new, related applications of technology as fast as older ones become everyday, commodity type products."[2]

COMPANY HISTORY AND BACKGROUND

Paul V. Galvin established the Galvin Manufacturing Corp. in Chicago in 1928. The company first produced a "battery eliminator" that allowed customers to operate radios directly from household current instead of the batteries supplied with early models. Although this venture eventually failed, Galvin was more fortunate in the

---

[1]H. Garret DeYoung, "Motorola's Strength Comes from Growth by Renewal," *Electronic Business*, July 9, 1990, p. 30.
[2]Gary Slutsker, "The Company That Likes to Obsolete Itself," *Forbes*, September 13, 1993, p. 140.

1930s, when another venture successfully commercialized car radios under the brand name *Motorola*, a word that suggested sound in motion by combining *motor* with *Victrola*. During the 1930s, the company also established home radio and police radio departments, instituted pioneering personnel programs, and began national advertising. In the 1940s, the company started to do work for the government and opened a research laboratory in Phoenix, Arizona, to explore solid-state electronics. The name of the company was changed to Motorola, Inc., in 1947.

By the time of Paul Galvin's death in 1959, Motorola was a leader in military, space, and commercial communications, had built its first semiconductor production facility, and was a growing force in consumer electronics. Under the leadership of Paul's son, Robert W. Galvin, Motorola expanded into international markets in the 1960s, setting up sales and manufacturing operations around the world. In the 1970s, the company faced increasing Japanese competition, especially in consumer electronics. The company shifted its focus away from consumer electronics, selling off businesses such as color television. Motorola's management staked the company's future on high-technology electronic products for commercial, industrial, and government customers and on its ability to renew itself. The company instituted a participative management program that linked the needs and interests of employees more closely with the needs and interests of the company. In 1979, management began the journey toward total quality in Motorola's operations and products. The company's ongoing commitment to quality later resulted in Motorola winning the coveted Malcolm Baldrige Quality Award in 1988, the first year the award was given.

George Fisher, CEO from 1988 until late 1993, continued to concentrate Motorola's energies on high-technology markets in commercial, industrial, and government fields and engineered the development of a global customer base and Motorola's strong position across a portfolio of related electronic product lines. Under Fisher's guidance, Motorola became a recognized world leader in the manufacture of communications and electronic equipment. Fisher left Motorola in October 1993 to accept the CEO position at Eastman Kodak, leaving a company well positioned to exploit some of the future's most promising markets. He was succeeded by Gary Tooker, who moved up from the president and COO position.

Exhibit 1 provides a summary of Motorola's recent financial performance.

MOTOROLA'S BUSINESS LINES

Motorola operated in four interdependent arenas of electronics—components, communications equipment, semiconductors, and control devices. Businesses within and across these arenas were managed as highly decentralized sectors, groups, or divisions, depending on size. In 1994, Motorola had four business sectors (Semiconductor Products; Land Mobile Products; General Systems; and Messaging, Information, and Media), and two business groups (Government and Space Technology; Automotive, Energy, and Controls). The company also had a New Enterprises division that served as an incubator for new businesses. The overarching theme of Motorola's corporate strategy was to maintain, develop, and exploit expertise and technology to be the world's best manufacturer of products within its traditional arenas while continually developing new products and technologies that expanded, extended, and bridged these arenas.

Exhibit 1 **Five-Year Summary of Motorola's Financial Performance, 1990–1994** *(in millions, except per share amounts and other data)*

	Years Ended December 31				
	1994	**1993**	**1992**	**1991**	**1990**
Operating Results					
Net sales	$22,245	$16,963	$13,303	$11,341	$10,885
Manufacturing and other costs of sales	13,760	10,351	8,395	7,134	6,787
Selling, general, and administrative expenses	4,381	3,776	2,951	2,579	2,509
Depreciation expense	1,525	1,170	1,000	886	790
Interest expense, net	142	141	157	129	133
Total costs and expenses	19,808	15,438	12,503	10,728	10,219
Earnings before income taxes and cumulative effect of change in accounting principle	2,437	1,525	800	613	666
Income taxes provided on earnings	877	503	224	159	167
Net earnings before cumulative effect of change in accounting principle	$ 1,560	$ 1,022	$ 576	$ 454	$ 499
Net earnings	$ 1,560	$ 1,022	$ 453	$ 454	$ 499
Net earnings before cumulative effect of change in accounting principle as a percent of sales	7.0%	6.0%	4.3%	4.0%	4.6%
Net earnings as a percent of sales	7.0%	6.0%	3.4%	4.0%	4.6%
Per Share Data (in dollars)*†					
Fully diluted:					
Net earnings before cumulative effect of change in accounting principle	$ 2.65	$ 1.78	$ 1.05	$ 0.84	$ 0.93
Cumulative effect of change in accounting principle	—	—	(0.22)	—	—
Net earnings	$ 2.65	$ 1.78	$ 0.83	$ 0.84	$ 0.93
Average common and common equivalent shares outstanding	592.7	583.7	567.1	558.5	555.7
Dividends declared per share	$ 0.310	$ 0.220	$ 0.198	$ 0.190	$ 0.190
Balance Sheet Data					
Total assets	$17,536	$13,498	$10,629	$ 9,375	$ 8,742
Working capital	3,008	2,324	1.883	1,424	1,404
Long-term debt	1,127	1,360	1,258	954	792
Total debt	2,043	1,915	1,695	1,806	1,787
Total stockholders' equity	$ 9,096	$ 6,409	$ 5,144	$ 4,630	$ 4,257
Other Data					
Current ratio	1.51	1.53	1.56	1.46	1.46
Return on average invested capital before cumulative effect of change in accounting principle	17.5%	15.3%	9.4%	7.8%	9.4%
Return on average invested capital	17.5%	15.3%	7.5%	7.8%	9.4%
Return on average stockholders' equity before cumulative effect of change in accounting principle	21.0%	17.8%	11.7%	10.2%	12.3%
Return on average stockholders' equity	21.0%	17.8%	9.4%	10.2%	12.3%
Fixed asset expenditures	$ 3,322	$ 2,187	$ 1,442	$ 1,387	$ 1,371
% to sales	14.9%	12.9%	10.8%	12.2%	12.6%
Research and development expenditures	$ 1,860	$ 1,521	$ 1,306	$ 1,133	$ 1,030
% to sales	8.4%	9.0%	9.8%	10.0%	9.5%
Year-end employment (in thousands)	132	120	107	102	105

* All earnings per share, dividends, and outstanding shares data have been restated to reflect the 1994 and 1992 two-for-one stock splits.

† Primary earnings per common and common equivalent share were the same as fully diluted for all years shown except in 1994 and 1991, when primary earnings per share were 1 cent higher than fully diluted. Average primary common and common equivalent shares outstanding for 1994, 1993, 1992, 1991, and 1990 were 591.7, 582.6, 565.6, 555.6, and 555.7, respectively.

Source: Company annual report.

The Semiconductor Products Sector

This strategic unit designed and produced a broad line of discrete semiconductors and integrated circuits (including microprocessors, microcomputers, memories, and sensors) to serve the advanced systems needs of the computer, consumer, automotive, industrial, federal government/military, and telecommunications markets. The segment accounted for 31 percent of Motorola's 1994 sales. Motorola was the second-largest semiconductor manufacturer in North America and the fifth-largest in the world behind Intel and Japan's Hitachi, NEC, and Toshiba. Although some observers doubted Motorola's ability to keep pace in semiconductors while investing heavily in its other businesses, management had stated that its semiconductor business would not be sacrificed. The company's portfolio of over 50,000 components was the broadest product line in the industry, and Motorola was particularly strong in eight-bit microcontrollers, digital signal processing, logic devices, discrete semiconductors, RISC microprocessors, and 16- and 32-bit microprocessors (see Exhibit 2 for a list of Motorola's chief products). Its MPUs were the standard in products such as Apple Computers, SEGA Game systems, and most new cars rolling out of Detroit. And in a joint venture with IBM and Apple, Motorola was producing the PowerPC family of microprocessing units, which competed against Intel's Pentium line of PC chips. The company's MOS-11 fabrication plant in Austin, Texas, was the world's first commercial semiconductor facility to manufacture 8-inch wafers, which allowed a higher yield of chips per wafer.

The Semiconductor Products Sector, like other Motorola businesses, was expanding its sales to foreign-based customers, particularly in Asia, the region with both the highest demand for semiconductors and the fastest growth in demand. About 10 to 15 percent of Motorola's semiconductor sales were to Japanese customers, and roughly half were outside the United States. Overall, the corporation's Asian sales were growing 2 to 3 times faster than sales in the United States and Europe. According to Motorola's director of international operations, Rick Younts, Asia was expected to become Motorola's largest source of revenue within a decade. Motorola's success in penetrating Asian markets was a result of a long-term commitment to the region. The company had been manufacturing for over 20 years in Korea, Taiwan, and Malaysia, seeing the enormous growth potential of the emerging Asian markets before the rest of the world realized their long-term importance. Motorola was doing business in China before China started to open up to Western business and was one of the first U.S. companies to compete with the Japanese in Japan and in their sphere of economic influence in Asia. Efforts to compete with the Japanese triggered the quality revolution and organizational renewal that transformed the company in the late 1970s and early 1980s. Younts observed, "the Japanese were our benchmark for quality." Competing with the Japanese in their domestic market meant that Motorola had to have comparable quality and service; Younts said, "the Japanese customer is the most demanding in the world—he does not accept poor service or poor quality."

In businesses like semiconductors where volume was the key to success, Motorola quickly found itself competing with Intel, Hitachi, NEC, and Toshiba in most of the world's key country markets. Motorola's international strategy was "to understand local culture and market conditions, to be an insider in the markets in which the company operated, and to ultimately contribute to the betterment of the welfare and society of those markets." To become an insider, Motorola located the activities of its Semiconductor Products Sector in many different countries, including China, France, Germany, the Philippines, Malaysia, Singapore, Japan, Hong Kong, Korea, Mexico,

Exhibit 2 Motorola's Products by Sector and Group, 1994

• Semiconductor Products Sector

Bipolar, BiCMOS, and MOS digital ICs
Bipolar, BiCMOS, CMOS, and combined technology
  semicustom circuits
Custom and semicustom semiconductors
Customer defined arrays
Data conversion circuits
Digital signal processing
Fiber optic active components
Field effect transistors (FETs)
Industrial control circuits
Interface circuits
Microcomputers and peripherals
Microcontroller ICs
Microprocessors and peripherals
Microwave transistors
MOS and bipolar memories

Motor control circuits
Open architecture CAD systems
Operational amplifiers
Optoelectronics components
Power supply circuits
Pressure and temperature sensors
Rectifiers
RF modules
RF power and small signal transistors
SMARTMOS™ products
Telecommunications circuits
Thyristors and triggers
TMOS and bipolar pair products
Voltage regulators and circuits
Zener and tuning diodes

• Land Mobile Products Sector

Automatic vehicle locations systems
Communications control centers
Communications system installation and maintenance
Emergency medical communications systems
FM two-way radio products:
  Base station and repeater products
  Mobile products
  Portable products

FM two-way radio systems:
  Advanced conventional systems
Digital voice protection systems:
  Communication systems
  Trunked radio systems
HF single sideband communications systems
Integrated security and access control systems
Signaling and remote control systems

• General Systems Sector

Cellular mobile, portable, transportable, and personal
  subscriber products
Cellular radiotelephone systems
Electronic mobile exchange (EMX) series
HD, LD, and HDII series cellular base stations

Microcomputer (VME) board level products
Multiuser super microcomputer systems and servers
Software for workgroup and network computing
  communications
Wireless in-building network products

• Messaging, Information, and Media Sector

Codex Corporation Products

Network management:
  Integrated network management that supports emerging
  international standards and complements key de facto
  industry standards
Digital transmissions:
  DSU/CSUs, digital platforms, ISDN terminal adapters
Analog transmission:
  V.32 and other dial modems, leased line modems
Data and data voice networking:
  T1 and subrate multiplexers, x.25 switches and PADs,
  statistical multiplexers
LAN internetworking:
  LAN/WAN bridges

UDS Products

Modems
Multiplexers
High-speed digital communication products
ISDN terminal adapters
Micro-to-mainframe plug-in boards
Network management services
Custom data comm products

Paging and Wireless Data Products

Pagers and components
CT2 (telepoint systems)
Radio paging systems
Mobile data systems:
  Data radio networks
  Portable and mobile data terminals
  RF modems

Exhibit 2   Concluded

- **Government and Space Technology Group**

Fixed and satellite communications systems
Space communication systems
Electronic fuse systems
Missile guidance systems
Missile and aircraft instrumentation
Secure telecommunications
Drone and target command and control systems

Video processing systems and products
Intelligent display terminals and systems
Electronic positioning and tracking systems
Satellite survey and positioning systems
Surveillance radar systems
Tracking and command transponder systems
Tactical communications transceivers

- **Automotive, Energy, and Controls Group**

Agricultural vehicle controls
Antilock braking systems controls
Automotive and industrial sensors
Automotive body computers
Gasoline and diesel engine controls
Ignition modules
Instrumentation
Keyless entry systems
Motor controls

Multiplex systems
Power modules
Solid state relays
Steering controls
Suspension controls
Transmission controls
Vehicle navigation systems
Vehicle theft alarm modules
Voltage regulators

- **New Enterprises Organizations**

EMTEK health care systems
DASCAN

Taiwan, Great Britain, and the United States (seven plants). The company began opening design and manufacturing centers around the world to stay close to customers and competitors. Hong Kong was chosen as a regional business center and semiconductor manufacturing site because of its potential one day to rival Silicon Valley's mutually profitable alliance between industry and academia. In Japan, Motorola Nihon succeeded in getting Motorola components designed into Japanese products. Motorola worked with Canon to develop the microprocessor controls for a new type of auto focus on Canon's 35mm cameras. Motorola also teamed up with Toshiba, a leading producer of memory chips, in a joint venture named Tohoku Semiconductor Corp., to build a $727 million plant in Sendai to produce 16K memory chips. The venture was making about 9 million components monthly, including DRAMs, MPUs, and microcontrollers, and had been used by the two companies to develop chips for high-definition TV applications and for Toyota car engines.[3]

Motorola's Semiconductor Products Sector consisted of the following products and organizational business units:

- Asia-Pacific Semiconductor Group.
- Communications, Power, and Signal Technologies Group.
- European Semiconductor Group.
- Logic and Analog Technologies Group.
- Microcontroller Technologies Group.

---

[3]"Motorola, Toshiba Joint Venture Plans to Build Chip Plant," *The Wall Street Journal*, June 24, 1993, p. B7.

- Microprocessor and Memory Technologies Group.
- Semiconductor Products Division (Nippon Motorola Limited).

The Land Mobile Products Sector

The land mobile unit designed, manufactured, and distributed two-way radios and other forms of analog and digital communications systems for customers, including agriculture, commercial, construction, education, state, government, health care, mining, petroleum, utilities, and transportation companies. The company's involvement in these products started in World War II, when Motorola made walkie-talkies for the U.S. Army. Motorola was the leading supplier in the largest segment of this industry, two-way private mobile radio, such as those used by taxicabs, police and fire departments, trucking companies, and service businesses that had a fleet of vehicles. This sector's products were made in Iowa, Illinois, Florida, Germany, Ireland, Israel, and Malaysia. Organizationally, the Land Mobile Products Sector consisted of four business/product groups:

- Network Services and Business Strategies Group.
- Radio Network Solution Group.
- Radio Parts and Service Group.
- Radio Products Group.

The General Systems Sector

The General Systems Sector designed and manufactured computer-based cellular telephones and systems, personal communications systems, computers, microcomputer boards, and information processing and handling equipment. Motorola was the world's largest producer of mobile and portable cellular phones, winning more contracts to supply cellular equipment than any other manufacturer. More than half of Motorola's cellular revenues came from sales to customers outside the United States. Motorola was a supplier of cellular equipment to Japan's Nippon Telephone and Telegraph (NTT).

Cellular technology was an area where Motorola had made many advances. Motorola spent 15 years and $150 million developing cellular technology before there was any significant demand. The investment paid off; going into 1995, Motorola was regarded as a world leader in cellular technology and cellular products. In the last four years, cellular phones had outsold conventional cord phones, and Motorola's customer base of 15 million was growing rapidly. Motorola management was convinced that the company had barely scratched the surface of this market. Chris Galvin, Motorola's president and COO, and son of retired CEO Bob Galvin, believed that "at some point during this decade, 20 percent of all POTS [plain old telephone services] will be portable. That's a tremendous market."[4] The company claimed the widest product line of any producer, offering cellular and portable phones as well as related infrastructure, test equipment, and reseller services. Since the average cellular subscriber required about $1,500 in support equipment and services above the price of the phone, this market represented an incredible growth opportunity for Motorola, especially in developing countries where it was easier and cheaper to build cellular phone systems than to build traditional wired telephone systems.

---

[4]DeYoung, "Motorola's Strength Comes from Growth by Renewal," p. 32.

Motorola's entrance into cellular products and equipment provided a representative example of how the company spins off new technologies and businesses. In the early days of cellular, Edward Staiano saw that emerging technology was being treated like a stepchild by the communications group, which back then was mainly involved in two-way radio systems. Motorola gave Staiano free rein to develop the technology independently. Says Staiano, "So I moved out of the building with a few people, got a building down the road, and we ran basically like a startup. Motorola is one of the few big companies where you have a pretty good chance of starting up your own business and running it."[5] Staiano led Motorola's drive to become the world leader in cellular products and later became the president and general manager of the General Systems Sector.

Motorola's cellular strategy was to maintain its leadership by continuously developing new products and entering markets ahead of the competition. One notable product innovation was the MicroTac™ cellular phone Motorola introduced in 1989 as the world's smallest portable cellular phone. The MicroTac was an instant success, and it took 18 months for major competitors like NEC, Fujitsu, Mitsubishi, and LM Ericsson to counter with imitative products. According to Motorola CEO Gary Tooker, the MicroTac illustrated how Motorola anticipated customer needs and introduced products that were ahead of their time: "When we formed the MicroTac team, no one was demanding this product."[6]

Motorola also created demand by developing new markets. The General Systems Sector was investing in cellular network services to create cellular infrastructures in countries where wired telephone systems were either undeveloped or unreliable and outdated. Cellular was expected to become the primary system in these countries because of the huge investments needed to connect a country through traditional wired phone lines; cellular systems provided a lower-cost technological substitute. Motorola first got involved in cellular network services in Hong Kong in 1987. According to Staiano, cellular did not exist in the colony, so he decided that Motorola should jump-start it by taking a 30 percent equity position in a newly created cellular network company. Motorola originally had decided not to compete with equipment customers, and thus did not invest in cellular networks in the United States. Realizing what those missed opportunities had cost Motorola, Staiano launched a strategy for Motorola to build and operate cellular systems in six countries (with Motorola equipment); by 1994, the company's network ventures in foreign markets were among Motorola's most profitable and fastest-growing operations.[7] Motorola also controlled radio frequencies previously used for dispatch systems and had the technology to convert these analog systems into high-traffic digital networks that could compete with cellular. But according to some Motorola executives, these ventures were just vehicles to promote equipment sales, and the long-term strategy was to exit these businesses once the market was developed.

Motorola's involvement in the European and Japanese markets was seen as strategically important for cellular products because it was expected that Japan and Europe would move more quickly to advanced digital systems than the United States. Motorola had won several contracts from NTT, Japan's chief telecommunications company, and for the Pan-European digital cellular network, or GSM. Motorola had

---

[5]Slutsker, "The Company That Likes to Obsolete Itself," p. 141.
[6]DeYoung, "Motorola's Strength Comes from Growth by Renewal," p. 33.
[7]Slutsker, "The Company That Likes to Obsolete Itself," p. 143.

provided validation systems in several countries and had been chosen to supply operating systems in Sweden, Spain, and the United Kingdom.

As of 1995, the General Systems Sector consisted of the:

- Cellular Infrastructure Group.
- Cellular Subscriber Group.
- Computer Group.
- Network Ventures Division.
- Personal Communications Systems Division.

Manufacturing facilities were located in China, Germany, Israel, the United Kingdom, and the United States (one plant in Arizona and four in Illinois).

The Messaging, Information, and Media Sector

This strategic business unit designed, manufactured, and distributed messaging products, including pagers and paging systems, wireless and wireline data communications products, equipment, systems, and services worldwide. Motorola was the world leader in pagers and paging systems. Pagers received one-way messages that ranged from a simple beep to words and numbers that could be stored and displayed on a screen. Used traditionally to contact personnel in the field and prompt a phone call, customers were finding more innovative uses for Motorola's pagers. Restaurants were using pagers to let waitpersons know when orders were ready to be served. In China, where the telephone infrastructure was not well developed, pagers were being used to send coded messages to field personnel, instructing them on their next task.

Motorola's paging operations previously had been combined with land mobile products to form the Communications Sector, which accounted for 29 percent of 1992 sales. The sector was split in 1993, and the paging and wireless data operations became its own group. The primary reason for the new organizational structure was to encourage the development of wireless data technology, which was being hindered by the dominant focus of the Communications Sector on land mobile products.

There were about 300,000 users of wireless data systems in 1994, including United Parcel Service (UPS), whose 50,000 drivers transmitted package tracking data from Motorola equipment in their trucks. Revenues from wireless data services were still small, about $192 million in 1993 and $303 million in 1994, according to Ira Brodsky of Datacomm Research.[8] But Robert Growney, executive vice president and general manager of the Paging and Wireless Data Group, expected that the worldwide market would reach 26 million users by the year 2000.[9] At the forefront of this market was the development of personal digital assistants (PDAs), small palmtop computers that had the potential to revolutionize the way individuals organized and communicated information while on the go. Motorola had licensed two PDA formats: Apple Computer's Newton Operating System and General Magic's operating system. Motorola had also established a joint venture with Samsung of Korea to manufacture portable palmtop computers and was competing with a GE–Ericsson joint venture and AT&T to supply the wireless modems to make PDAs and the new generation of laptop computers feasible. Hewlett-Packard's 95LX palmtop was one

---

[8]Andrew Collier and Dan Cray, "Wireless Data Market Still Up in the Air?" *Electronic News*, July 27, 1992, p. 19.

[9]Slutsker, "The Company That Likes to Obsolete Itself," p. 142.

of the first PDAs to be introduced, and Motorola furnished it with DataStream™, a nationwide broadcasting service supported by a miniature data transceiver.[10]

Like the General Systems Sector, the Messaging, Information, and Media Sector had expanded into network development in order to stimulate demand for equipment. The International Networks unit had set up paging operations in countries like Brazil, where such services were in their infancy, and established wireless messaging networks in the United States, such as Ardis™, a joint venture with IBM, and Embarc™, a receive-only electronic mail network.

The Information Systems Group within this sector provided the elements for distributed data and voice networks for the communication of data through telephone lines, from basic modems to network management systems. The Group was also involved in developing a wide range of products for the new digital equipment operated by local and long-distance telephone companies, including high-speed terminal adapters and products developed in conjunction with Northern Telecom.

The Messaging, Information, and Media Sector consisted of the Paging Products Group, the Wireless Data Group, the Multimedia Group, the Information Systems Group, and the International Networks Division. Manufacturing facilities were located in India, China, Singapore, Ireland, Puerto Rico, and the United States (Alabama, Illinois, Florida, Texas, and Massachusetts).

The Government and Space Technology Group

This unit specialized in research, development, and production of electronic systems and equipment for the U.S. Department of Defense and other government agencies. Motorola had developed a number of products for government projects. Motorola equipment had been on board virtually all U.S. space missions. The first words transmitted from the Moon to the Earth came through a Motorola transponder. The 1988 photos of Neptune taken by the Voyager II were also sent back to Earth by Motorola equipment.

The group was currently involved in the Iridium satellite-based communication project, an ambitious attempt to make portable communication possible from any location in the world. The foundation of this global network was 77 satellites in circular orbits around the Earth. While the service was expected to be too expensive for cost-conscious users of wire and cellular phone service, the Iridium system would provide needy travelers or inhabitants of remote locations with a means of instant communication to anywhere in the world via portable phone. Motorola had spun off Iridium as an independent entity, selling equity in the project to international consortiums, companies, and governments. But the company retained a 15 percent share and was supplying the equipment necessary to make the system work. The $3.4 billion network was scheduled to begin operations in 1998.[11]

The Automotive, Energy, and Controls Group

This business unit designed and manufactured a broad range of electronic components, modules, and integrated systems and products for the automotive, industrial, transportation, navigation, communications, energy, and lighting markets. High-technology

---

[10]Samuel Weber, "Anatomy of Competition," *Electronics*, August 1991, p. 37.
[11]"Japanese Consortium to Take a 15% Stake in Motorola Project," *The Wall Street Journal*, April 2, 1993, p. B1.

automotive applications included power-train and chassis electronics, power controls, and sensors. Building on a dominant position in certain types of automotive sensors, the group planned to develop new automotive applications and then leverage the learning and production volume advantages to enter more lucrative markets in medical applications. Some of the newer product development efforts involved engine management controls, antilock braking system controls, truck instrumentation, agricultural monitoring systems, and automotive theft alarms. Motorola was also positioned to develop electronics for the car of the future, such as voice activated in-dash navigation systems and multiplex systems.

The New Enterprises Division

This division managed Motorola's entry into emerging, high-growth, and high-technology areas. It served as Motorola's outlet for entrepreneurial activity, giving Motorola an organizational vehicle to capitalize on the initiative of its people with ideas to create new businesses in areas not directly related to existing operations. Two recent ventures were DASCAN and EMTEK Health Care Systems. DASCAN designed and produced supervisory control and data acquisition (SCADA) systems and cell controller systems used by electric utility companies. EMTEK provided clinical information management systems for hospital intensive care units. Successful start-up operations were either put under the umbrella of whatever sector or group had the best strategic fit or else divested, often by selling them to the very managers who were engineering the start-up operation.

Exhibit 3 provides recent data on the financial performance of Motorola's business sectors.

APPROACHES TO MANAGING MOTOROLA'S BUSINESS PORTFOLIO

Until late 1993, when CEO George Fisher resigned to go to Eastman Kodak, Motorola management was headed by a three-person office of the chief executive, made up of CEO George Fisher, President and COO Gary Tooker, and Senior Executive Vice President and Assistant COO Chris Galvin. The three members of the office of the chief executive shared responsibility for operations, geographic areas, and concerns/initiatives. George Fisher had responsibility for human resources, law, strategy, technology, and external relations. He also had regional responsibility for Japan and such special projects and corporate activities as U.S. government relations, trade, corporate goals, women and minority development, the trade policy committee, the company's total quality management program, and product development. Gary Tooker had responsibility for the Semiconductor Sector, the Land Mobile Sector, and the Government Group; finance, quality, and corporate manufacturing reported to him. His geographic responsibilities encompassed the rest of Asia and the Americas. He was also the company's lead executive for the Iridium satellite telecommunications project, cycle time, technology transfer, management incentive programs, product improvement, employee empowerment, and the environment. Chris Galvin was responsible for General Systems, the Paging and Wireless Group, the Automotive Group, the Information Systems Group, and New Enterprises. He had geographic responsibility for Europe, the Middle East, and Africa, and directed acquisitions, consumer products, personal communications, and the premier employee program.

Exhibit 3   Recent Performance of Motorola's Business Sectors and Groups, 1992–1994

INDUSTRY SEGMENT INFORMATION

Years Ended December 31	Net Sales			Operating Profit/Operating Profit Margin					
	1994	1993	1992	1994		1993		1992	
General Systems products	$ 8,613	$ 5,236	$ 3,662	$ 1,214	14.1%	$ 718	13.7%	$ 420	11.5%
Semiconductor products	6,936	5,707	4,475	996	14.4	801	14.0	464	10.4
Communications products	5,776	4,834	3,906	589	10.2	354	7.3	192	4.9
Government and space technology products	829	858	650	(55)	(6.6)	(17)	(2.0)	(7)	(1.1)
Other products	2,434	1,762	1,452	156	6.4	95	5.4	77	5.3
Adjustments and eliminations	(2,343)	(1,434)	(842)	(29)	—	(11)	—	(4)	—
Industry segment totals	$22,245	$16,963	$13,303	2,871	12.9%	1,940	11.4%	1,142	8.6%
General corporate expenses				(292)		(274)		(185)	
Interest expense, net				(142)		(141)		(157)	
Earnings before income taxes and cumulative effect of change in accounting principle				$ 2,437	11.0%	$ 1,525	9.0%	$ 800	6.0%

Years Ended December 31	Assets			Fixed Asset Expenditures			Depreciation Expense		
	1994	1993	1992	1994	1993	1992	1994	1993	1992
General Systems products	$ 4,470	$ 3,223	$ 2,108	$ 621	$ 453	$ 334	$ 327	$ 227	$ 171
Semiconductor products	5,886	4,507	3,618	1,640	1,120	666	683	529	429
Communications products	4,319	3,202	2,925	451	363	263	265	238	207
Government and space technology products	565	304	312	41	31	24	35	33	33
Other products	905	957	826	315	120	101	152	89	106
Adjustments and eliminations	(72)	(24)	(32)	—	—	—	—	—	—
Industry segment totals	16,343	12,169	9,757	3,068	2,087	1,388	1,462	1,116	946
General corporate	1,193	1,329	872	254	100	54	63	54	54
Consolidated totals	$17,536	$13,498	$10,629	$ 3,322	$ 2,187	$ 1,442	$ 1,525	$ 1,170	$ 1,000

GEOGRAPHIC AREA INFORMATION

Years Ended December 31	Net Sales			Operating Profit/Operating Profit Margin					
	1994	1993	1992	1994		1993		1992	
United States	$16,297	$12,924	$10,232	$ 1,932	11.9%	$ 970	7.5%	$ 624	6.1%
Other nations	12,758	10,066	8,017	1,292	10.1%	1,164	11.6%	706	8.8%
Adjustments and eliminations	(6,810)	(6,027)	(4,946)	(353)	—	(194)	—	(188)	—
Geographic totals	$22,245	$16,963	$13,303	2,871	12.9%	1,940	11.4%	1,142	8.6%
General corporate expenses				(292)		(274)		(185)	
Interest expense, net				(142)		(141)		(157)	
Earnings before income taxes and cumulative effect of change in accounting principle				$ 2,437	11.0%	$ 1,525	9.0%	$ 800	6.0%

December 31	Assets		
	1994	1993	1992
United States	$10,750	$ 7,731	$ 6,297
Other nations	5,943	4,674	3,668
Adjustments and eliminations	(350)	(236)	(208)
Geographic totals	16,343	12,169	9,757
General corporate assets	1,193	1,329	872
Consolidated totals	$17,536	$13,498	$10,629

1993 and 1992 have been reclassified to reflect the realignment of various business units. Source: Company annual report.

Despite the coordinative and supervisory importance of the office of the chief executive, Motorola was a highly decentralized company that pushed operating and strategic authority down to the business level. Motorola relied on financial controls to monitor individual business unit performance and avoid unexpected bottom-line surprises. The finance departments of business units reported directly to corporate staff, with dotted line relationships to the operating divisions. Finance, research, strategic planning, and quality functions were handled by small staff groups at the corporate level. Corporate staff took responsibility for having expertise in functions that could not be justified on an individual business level. Businesses drew on this expertise as needed. Motorola had been careful not to become top heavy; it maintained a good balance between oversight by corporate support staff and decentralized decision making at the business level. One executive explained the rationale for a small corporate staff, "It keeps staff small, running tight, and in demand. They can't be running around with time on their hands looking for things to do. If they are, then they are either overstaffed or not staffed with the right people." According to a line manager, "there is not a lot of hands-on day-to-day involvement by corporate staff. We look to the corporate staff for guidance, advice, and counseling on the future."

Corporate staff in the legal, environmental, quality, human relations, and strategy departments developed and disseminated new ideas and set policy guidelines consistent with Motorola's mission, values, and history. The corporation's mission helped unify and guide business strategy:

In each of our chosen areas of the electronics industry, we will grow rapidly by providing our world-wide customers what they want, when they want it, with Six-Sigma quality and best-in-class cycle time, as we strive to achieve our fundamental corporate objective of Total Customer Satisfaction, and to achieve our stated goals of increased global market share, best-in-class people, products, marketing, manufacturing, technology and service, and superior financial results.

Motorola businesses had the autonomy to develop their own strategies subject to staying within the corporate mission, corporate policies, and corporate guidelines.

Participative Management Program   The cornerstone of Motorola's informal, first name–only culture was the company's Participative Management Program (PMP).[12] Building on the highly participative style of founder Paul Galvin, Motorola management created a system in the 1970s and 1980s in which employees were given a significant decision-making latitude in their respective areas of operation.

The key building blocks of the PMP were work teams of 50 to 250 workers. Each employee shared in a common bonus pool with his or her team members. The people in the pool were responsible for their own performance—as measured by the production costs and materials used that were controllable by the team, by quality standards, by targeted production levels, by inventory stock and finished goods, by housekeeping standards, and by safety records. Whenever an idea proposed by a team led to cost reduction or to production that exceeded target, all team members shared in the gains through bonuses. The average bonus varied between 8 and 12 percent of base salary, with a top range of 40 percent.

[12]Description of the Participative Management Program adapted, in part, from James O'Toole, *Vanguard Management*, Doubleday (Garden City, NY: 1985).

Motorola management had documented many instances of how the PMP program had increased worker productivity. In one case, an assembly worker in a Fort Worth, Texas, plant discovered that 1 of every 10 screws she used to assemble a radio would break. Instead of just throwing the screws away, or reporting the problem to a supervisor, the employee called the vendor. After the initial conversation, the work team got together with the vendor and they collectively solved the problem. It turned out that if the screws had proper heat treatment, they wouldn't break. Another example of the trimming of waste involved the use of gold in producing semiconductors. Before the PMP, something like 40 percent of the gold used was wasted. After two months of analysis, Motorola employees identified some 50 spots in the process where gold was being lost; ultimately, they reduced waste to zero.

To make the PMP work at a company as large and diversified as Motorola, management had established a series of steering committees for businesses, divisions, groups, and sectors to communicate issues up and down the organization structure. Each team had one of its members on a steering committee at the next higher level in the company (which, in turn, had a member on another committee at the subsequent higher level). The steering committees performed several critical functions:

1. *Coordination*—acting on ideas that required one team or business to work in cooperation with one or more business units, divisions, groups, or sectors.

2. *Lateral communication*—disseminating ideas or practices of one working group to other groups, thus facilitating organizational learning.

3. *Downward communication*—ensuring that each work team (or business, division, group, or sector) had all the managerial information needed to do its job.

4. *Upward communication*—passing information up to the next level steering committee (which in turn reported to top management); shop floor issues reached Motorola executives after going through only four levels in the hierarchical chain.

5. *Control*—negotiating output standards and performance measures with the work teams that report to it. This was a continuing process in which trust was built by establishing clear performance criteria against which work teams were to be measured.

6. *Evaluation*—assessing the record of the work teams and allocating rewards based on the negotiated measures of performance.

While originally intended for production workers, Motorola had extended PMP across the entire organization. Professional, clerical, marketing, research, and other staff people were also organized into teams. The PMP system was supplemented with Motorola's "I Recommend" plan. Every work area in the company had a bulletin board on which employees could post questions or recommendations. The questions and recommendations could either be signed or anonymous. Either way, the supervisor responsible for the area was required to post a reply within 72 hours. In those cases where it was not feasible to obtain an answer that quickly, the supervisor had to post the name of the person who was working on obtaining the information, along with the date by which a final answer would be posted.

The PMP had, over the years, become a cornerstone of Motorola's culture. A big reason why Motorola had been able to institutionalize a level of participation usually found only in smaller companies or Japanese companies was, according to former Chief Operating Officer William Weisz, because "of our set of assumptions about human behavior." In Motorola's employee handbook on PMP, the discussion begins with a recitation of the company's assumptions about workers and work—see Exhibit 4.

Quality Programs

Motorola was an avid practitioner of total quality management and gave its corporate quality department a major role in the organization. Motorola had adopted quality as the cornerstone of everything the company did. Its goal was to achieve Six Sigma quality—3.4 defects per million. Motorola had achieved this target in certain processes and products and had begun efforts to double the amount of quality improvement every two years. Although quality was the responsibility of line businesses, corporate staff played an important part in coordinating its development and maintenance across the organization. Their role within the company was to teach quality and champion its cause, make sure material and techniques were up-to-date, measure customer satisfaction, and serve as the customer's advocate. Corporate quality staff were important participants in the semiannual review meetings. Motorola championed TQM and the need for quality outside the company as well as inside; it responded favorably to requests from other companies to provide information about its programs and practices.

Motorola's quality revolution started in 1979 at a meeting of corporate executives, when one of the attendees put it bluntly: "The real problem around here is that quality stinks." This started the dialogue on quality that would eventually force Motorola executives to face up to the fact that some of its products and operations did not make the grade.

According to Motorola CEO Gary Tooker, top executives faced a choice: Go back to the fundamentals or continue to lose customers to Japanese competitors with better quality.[13] Going back to the fundamentals meant assuming final responsibility for quality at corporate headquarters. "No one wants to do a lousy job," said Richard Buetow, vice president and director of quality. "If a company has a quality problem, 95 percent of the fault is with management." So top management began to infuse a strong concern for quality into Motorola's operations, aided by a participative management style that made quality everybody's responsibility. To help workers do their jobs better, Motorola initiated employee training programs and insisted that every worker take a one-week company course in a job-related subject. In recent years, Motorola had spent about $100 million annually on sustaining its training effort and managing its total quality programs. Management believed that the effort had paid off in better products, more satisfied customers, and increased market share; it had also eliminated the need for inspection and testing—a saving estimated at 3 to 4 percent of the cost of sales.[14]

Cycle Time

Aside from managing ongoing efforts to constantly improve quality, Motorola's quality department had turned to new ways to help businesses reach their goal of total customer satisfaction. One important new initiative was the cycle time reduction

---

[13]DeYoung, "Motorola's Strength Comes from Growth by Renewal," p. 32.
[14]Ibid.

Exhibit 4   Summary of Motorola Assumptions about Workers

1. Employee behavior is a consequence of how they are treated.
2. Employees are intelligent, curious and responsible.
3. Employees need a rational work world in which they know what is expected of them, and why.
4. Employees need to know how their jobs relate to the jobs of others and to company goals.
5. There is only one class of employee, not a creative management group and a group of others who carry out orders.
6. There is no one best way to manage.
7. No one knows how to do his or her job better than the person on the job.
8. Employees want to have pride in their work.
9. Employees want to be involved in decisions that affect their own work.
10. The responsibility of every manager is to draw out the ideas and abilities of workers in a shared effort of addressing business problems and opportunities.

Source: James O'Toole, *Vanguard Management*, Doubleday (Garden City, NY: 1985).

program. The program was originally a response to customer dissatisfaction with Motorola's long lead times for product design and manufacturing. Based on environmental scanning, contact with line businesses, and surveys of customer satisfaction, corporate staff documented the need to shorten Motorola's design-to-market cycle. After the idea was approved by the office of the chief executive, the corporate quality department took responsibility for an organizationwide program to reduce cycle time, first in manufacturing and product design and then eventually in all areas of the company's operations. It was not first executed as a pilot program but instead was implemented across the whole organization simultaneously. In a two-day meeting, corporate staff introduced the problem and initiated discussion on how to reduce cycle times among the 180 to 200 corporate officers responsible for running line businesses. Eventually, corporate quality staff and line business personnel developed a methodology to attack the problem: First the process was mapped, then it was examined to determine which steps were critical and which were not. Next, nonvalue-adding steps were eliminated and the process was simplified. Then attention was focused on shortening the time needed to perform critical value-adding activities.

Intraorganizational Relationships

Although corporate headquarters staff could try to proactively solve problems, they avoided meddling in line affairs. Corporate staff expected problems to be solved at the business level, with expertise and information supplied as necessary. Proactive involvement often took such forms as the cycle time initiative, or recommendations from the acquisitions office to make strategic investments in other companies. The contribution of the corporate staff was to try to look at the company and the environment from a broader perspective than line managers, intervening only when necessary and beneficial. In one instance, a regional Bell System company had ordered some equipment from the cellular division for a major showcase in Baltimore. Due to the fact that the equipment was not in production yet and was still being assembled by engineers, the cellular division was not going to be able to supply by the deadline. The Bell company thought that the division was holding back on them in order to give priority to equipment Motorola was using to set up its own showcase. They complained to Executive Committee Chairman and retired CEO Bob Galvin that the deck was being stacked against them. Galvin intervened, and the result was that 15 engineers from each of the other operating divisions were commandeered and temporarily put on the project so that the deadline could be honored.

Relationships between Motorola's businesses tended to be like any vendor–customer relationship. While equipment divisions purchased from the components divisions when it was the best value, they did not hesitate to go outside the company for vendors. But divisions were highly motivated to win internal orders. While in-house customers were a valuable source of feedback on product quality and performance, Motorola tried to be close to all of its customers, conducting semiannual customer surveys and stressing regular customer contact. Equipment divisions had liaisons with the Semiconductor Sector. There was some cooperative technology development, such as the Integrated Circuit Applications Research Lab (ICAR), which tried to develop future applications of integrated circuits through cooperation with internal users. But the real coordination of independent businesses came from shared R&D resources and the Management Technology Review process.

Research and Development

As a corporation, Motorola spent $1.86 billion dollars on research and development activities in 1994 (Exhibit 1). Research was a mix of centralized and decentralized facilities. Operating units bought R&D time from various research organizations throughout the company to work on projects they were interested in. Relationships between businesses, projects, and R&D personnel could become semipermanent. Divisions also had specific research and development activities funded and performed within their own organization. The corporation sponsored general research in critical technologies such as radio systems and in new technologies such as voice coding that could one day have application in several businesses. Corporate involvement in R&D aimed not only at ensuring a steady stream of developments but also at imposing discipline: George Fisher once observed, "We're like kids in a candy shop. There are so many opportunities, but we know we can't pursue everything."[15]

Management Technology Review

The Management Technology Review was a distinctive Motorola management practice aimed at integrating the multiple streams of technology at the company. Semiannually, corporate staff did a business management review and a technology management review of each business. Although issues often got intertwined, the two reviews were conducted separately so that conflicting issues did not detract from the review process. In the technology review process, Motorola charted out the expected evolution of products and technology on a technological roadmap and did a forecast of future technological advancement, with interim technological milestones, product destinations, and delineated routes to these destinations. It was an interactive process, and technical people at every level participated. All

---

[15]DeYoung, "Motorola's Strength Comes from Growth by Renewal," p. 35.

employees with technical knowledge were involved in generating the initial fore-casts and in implementing the plan based on these forecasts. The reviews were always attended by senior staff, often a member of the CEO office, the directors of quality, strategy, and R&D, and senior people from other businesses. The participation of experts from various Motorola businesses was important because they often had firsthand knowledge of where the required technology was within Motorola, possible outside sources, other possible applications for it, and opportunities to invest or license. During the review, attention was paid to the strength of competitors, experience curves, sales history, and Motorola's own core competencies, organizational capabilities, and strategic interests. From this evaluation, a long-term product plan was created to indicate when and where to introduce new products and when to take existing products out of production.[16]

The review process pinpointed what each division expected in terms of technological progress from company and industry R&D efforts. Since technical progress in one division was often partly dependent on the technical developments of other divisions and outside suppliers, this review/mapping process served as a key coordinative mechanism between different operating divisions. An example of the cross-division benefits of requesting or anticipating technical breakthroughs in related areas was when one of the communications equipment divisions called for the development of a new kind of chip from the semiconductor division in order to make a new product feasible. By designating future technological needs, the corporation could then make sure someone in the targeted division was given responsibility for meeting these needs. To request breakthroughs from other divisions, Motorola managers had to make coherent arguments of why the breakthrough was important and why it was possible. According to one General Systems Sector executive, Motorola's technologists usually knew where to expect the next breakthroughs, and the technology review process stimulated those breakthroughs by having business units demanding them for new product applications and product improvements.

The Management Technology Review was also an important opportunity for corporate management to realign businesses strategically. Products developed in one division were sometimes transferred to another division or spun off on their own. Usually this occurred because a business could not fund the development of a certain type of technology that would play only a limited role in its current business domain. When the corporation identified a promising technology in danger of being cut, it might decide to accept responsibility for nurturing and developing that technology, giving it time to grow without the profit requirements that constrained the line businesses.

Corporate headquarters staff learned about these opportunities through the network of reporting lines, the review process, and informal contact. Businesses were supposed to let it all hang out during the review, an outcome encouraged by Motorola's culture of frank, forthright discussion and debate to resolve issues. A hallmark of Motorola culture that aided communication was informality. If executives had a question, they were likely to talk directly to the person involved, not the person's boss. George Fisher explained, "I know technologists throughout the company. We all understand how the company works, so that nobody's toes get stepped on when I call an engineer to find out how something really works or what his opinion is."[17]

---

[16]O'Toole, *Vanguard Management*, p. 177.
[17]Slutsker, "The Company That Likes to Obsolete Itself," p. 143.

Spinoffs

Because creating new products and technologies was the modus operandi at Motorola, employees were very conscious of the career and business opportunities that new products and technology breakthroughs afforded. There were big payoffs for success, and creating a new business was seen as a primary way to climb the corporate ladder. The corporation nurtured the exercise of entrepreneurial initiative by giving financial support to promising projects outside of a particular business's mission, or by transferring responsibility for them to more suitable locations. Many managers had become vice presidents by growing a new business.

Spinoffs came about because autonomous initiatives within business units could result in products unrelated to the domain of the business where they were developed. Such products, if they had promising market potential, became candidates for special organizational arrangements to facilitate further development. Pressure from customers who were not satisfied with specific products within a division were also a driver for new product spinoffs. And if outside consultants or industry experts pointed out a new technology as being a critical area in the future, Motorola might move to establish a strategic foothold in the area by establishing a spinoff operation in the area, usually under the umbrella of the New Enterprises division.

Managers placed in charge of a spinoff that hit a dead end were not forced to leave the company. While there were no guarantees that they would return to their old position, part of the risk/reward balance of the venture was still having a position somewhere within the company.

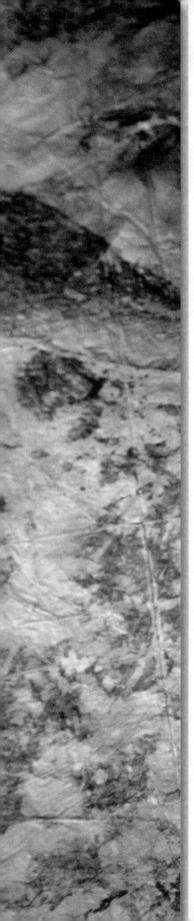

Robin Hood

Joseph Lampel, New York University

It was in the spring of the second year of his insurrection against the High Sheriff of Nottingham that Robin Hood took a walk in Sherwood forest. As he walked he pondered the progress of the campaign, the disposition of his forces, the Sheriff's recent moves, and the options that confronted him.

The revolt against the Sheriff had begun as a personal crusade. It erupted out of Robin's conflict with the Sheriff and his administration. However, alone Robin Hood could do little. He therefore sought allies, men with grievances and a deep sense of justice. Later he welcomed all who came, asking few questions and demanding only a willingness to serve. Strength, he believed, lay in numbers.

He spent the first year forging the group into a disciplined band, united in enmity against the Sheriff and willing to live outside the law. The band's organization was simple. Robin ruled supreme, making all important decisions. He delegated specific tasks to his lieutenants. Will Scarlett was in charge of intelligence and scouting. His main job was to shadow the Sheriff and his men, always alert to their next move. He also collected information on the travel plans of the rich merchants and tax collectors. Little John kept discipline among the men and saw to it that their archery was at the high peak that their profession demanded. Scarlock took care of the finances, converting loot to cash, paying shares of the take, and finding suitable hiding places for the surplus. Finally, Much the Miller's son had the difficult task of provisioning the ever-increasing band of Merrymen.

The increasing size of the band was a source of satisfaction for Robin, but also a source of concern. The fame of his Merrymen was spreading, and new recruits poured in from every corner of England. As the band grew larger, their small bivouac became a major encampment. Between raids the men milled about, talking and playing games. Vigilance was in decline, and discipline was becoming harder to enforce. "Why," Robin reflected, "I don't know half the men I run into these days."

The growing band was also beginning to exceed the food capacity of the forest. Game was becoming scarce, and supplies had to be obtained from outlying villages. The cost of buying food was beginning to drain the band's financial reserves at the very moment when revenues were in decline. Travelers, especially those with the most to lose, were now giving the forest a wide birth. This was costly and inconvenient to them, but it was preferable to having all their goods confiscated.

Robin believed that the time had come for the Merrymen to change their policy of outright confiscation of goods to one of a fixed transit tax. His lieutenants strongly resisted this idea. They were proud of the Merrymen's famous motto: "Rob the rich to give to the poor." "The farmers and the townspeople," they argued, "are our most important allies." "How can we tax them, and still hope for their help in our fight against the Sheriff?"

Robin wondered how long the Merrymen could keep to the ways and methods of their early days. The Sheriff was growing stronger and becoming better organized. He now had the money and the men and was beginning to harass the band, probing for its weaknesses. The tide of events was beginning to turn against the Merrymen. Robin felt the campaign must be decisively concluded before the Sheriff had a chance to deliver a mortal blow. "But how," he wondered, "could this be done?"

Robin had often entertained the possibility of killing the Sheriff, but the chances for this seemed increasingly remote. Besides, killing the Sheriff might satisfy his personal thirst for revenge, but it would not improve the situation. Robin had hoped that the perpetual state of unrest, and the Sheriff's failure to collect taxes, would lead to his removal from office. Instead, the Sheriff used his political connections to obtain reinforcement. He had powerful friends at court and was well regarded by the regent, Prince John.

Prince John was vicious and volatile. He was consumed by his unpopularity among the people, who wanted the imprisoned King Richard back. He also lived in constant fear of the barons, who had first given him the regency but were now beginning to dispute his claim to the throne. Several of these barons had set out to collect the ransom that would release King Richard the Lionheart from his jail in Austria. Robin was invited to join the conspiracy in return for future amnesty. It was a dangerous proposition. Provincial banditry was one thing, court intrigue another. Prince John had spies everywhere, and he was known for his vindictiveness. If the conspirators' plan failed, the pursuit would be relentless and retributions swift.

The sound of the supper horn startled Robin from his thoughts. There was the smell of roasting venison in the air. Nothing was resolved or settled. Robin headed for camp promising himself that he would give these problems his utmost attention after tomorrow's raid.

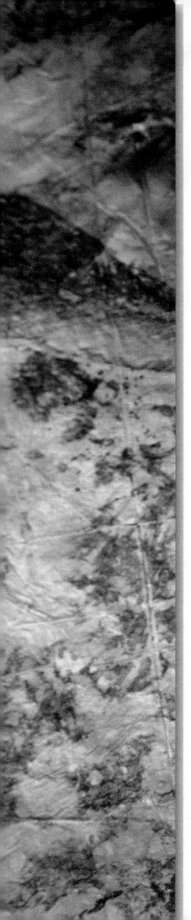

Bama Pie, Limited

Raymond E. Belford, Oklahoma City University

Bama Pie, Limited's phenomenal growth over the past 24 years of its 65-year history was due directly to the growth of its major customer, McDonald's, and a fanatical commitment to quality. As the single-source supplier of pies to McDonald's U.S. operations, Bama was testimony to how a small, aggressive, and creative company could succeed competing with much larger organizations. By providing top-quality pie products and "never missing an order," Bama had been able to expand its core pie business by landing 50 percent of McDonald's oven-ready, prebaked frozen biscuit needs. Its new role as a supplier of McDonald's breakfast biscuit requirements was expected to allow Bama to increase total sales to approximately $100 million in 1992. Bama Pie's actual financial information was closely guarded since it was a privately held, family-owned limited partnership; the company's CEO was 38-year-old Paula Marshall-Chapman, who had succeeded her father and grandfather as head of the business.

Bama Pie produced more than 1 million pies per day from facilities in Tulsa, Oklahoma, for McDonald's. In 1968, the firm was producing only 500 pies per day. In 1991, the company completed a $38 million facility in Tulsa to produce the biscuits for McDonald's, arranging the bank financing within about six weeks. The new facility, in early 1992, was producing more than 120,000 biscuits per hour.

Other major customers included Pizza Hut (for which Bama was producing approximately 25 percent of its bread stick requirements), TCBY, and Braum's (an Oklahoma-based ice cream chain).

The company, in an effort to lessen its dependence on McDonald's, had begun seeking business with other major fast-food and convenience food companies. In 1992, more than 70 percent of Bama's business was with McDonald's. Less than 10 percent of the company's revenues came from products carrying the Bama Pie brand, the best-known of which was a 3-inch pecan pie. Of the McDonald's business, about 4 percent was exported to McDonald's operations in Hong Kong and Taiwan. In early 1992, Bama was working toward establishing a joint venture in Hong Kong to provide pies to McDonald's in Hong Kong, the People's Republic of China, and Taiwan. Bama also had a licensing arrangement in Canada with a Canadian baker that provided pies to McDonald's Canadian operations.

The firm considered itself responsible for McDonald's pies worldwide. Marshall-Chapman's father, Paul Marshall, began providing technical assistance to McDonald's in the early days as he, Ray Kroc (McDonald's founder), and Fred Turner (early president of McDonald's) worked together. The technical assistance in helping establish local bakeries in McDonald's global enterprise had always been provided at no cost to McDonald's. "We see it as part of our service," said Marshall-Chapman.

In 1991, Bama competed in the national Baldrige awards for quality and made the fourth cut. The companies that reached the fifth cut were chosen for the prestigious award. The company was under consideration in 1992 for the award. Marshall-Chapman was named Quality Fanatic of the Year in 1989 by Philip Crosby of the Quality College.

The word most often heard around Bama Pie headquarters in Tulsa was *quality*. Marshall-Chapman had attended numerous quality conferences and had spoken to international groups about commitment to quality. The company had dropped the traditional mission statement (see Exhibit 1) for "Bama's Quality Circle." According to Marshall-Chapman, "We had a very nice mission statement of a traditional nature—very wordy, very flowery, like most progressive companies. If you've read most mission statements, they tend to be written for Wall Street or people outside the organization. We felt the mission should be written for our employees. Our Quality Circle is very simple and keeps us focused." (See Exhibit 2 for a description of the Quality Circle.)

The company also had a values statement (Exhibit 3) that reinforced "quality as a way of life" at Bama. The company's quality statement was read before every meeting held in the company. "It helps keep us focused," Marshall-Chapman explained.

COMPANY HISTORY

The history of Bama Pies dates to 1927 when Henry C. Marshall decided to utilize the pie-baking talents of his wife, Cornelia Alabama Marshall (who went by the name Bama), to provide employment for himself after a lengthy period of being out of work. Bama Marshall began baking pies for the lunch counter at the Woolworth's in Dallas. Her talents created a market for her pies that topped 75 per day (including take-home purchases), and the local owner of Woolworth's expanded his lunch counter to 75 stools to handle customer volume.

Bama was soon baking up to 300 pies per day for Woolworth's, and business at the lunch counter was booming. Bama was spending so much time at her work, Henry began to think she was being unfaithful to him and was "carrying on" with the owner of the Woolworth's. He sent his son, Paul, down to "spy" on Bama. When Paul reported back that the reason the owner "liked Mama so much is because of the pies she was making," Henry came up with an idea.

The following passage from *A Piece of the Pie* by Paul Marshall describes the event.[1]

> I heard Papa ask Mama something that made me cringe.
>
> "Blanchie, how are things at Woolworth's?"
>
> That question sounded innocent enough, but I knew Papa was fishing for an answer that would drive him into the rage which he had been holding in for weeks. (Paul still thought his father believed his mother was having an affair.) I looked over at Mama and saw her relaxed manner. She had no idea what was happening with Papa.
>
> "I'm working harder these days, that's for sure. A man from the head office came down this week."
>
> She stopped talking there. I guess she wanted to see if Papa was interested in her news or just making conversation.

---

[1] Paul Marshall with Brian and Sandy Miller, *A Piece of the Pie* (Tulsa: Walsworth Press, 1987).

Papa looked over at Mama and said, "So?"

"So he told me what a good job I was doing and how he wished more employees worked as well as I did. Then he asked me if I would be willing to move to Amarillo and be in charge of the lunch counter at the new store there."

I got even more worried right then. Papa didn't say anything right at first. I must have held my breath for at least 10 minutes waiting for Papa to blow.

But he never did. When he finally broke the silence, he spoke in a soft voice. "Blanchie, if you can make pies for Mr. Tanner to sell, why can't you make pies for me to sell?"

Mama looked over at him, surprised like.

"What do you mean?" she asked.

"Just that. If Mr. Tanner can make money on your pies, why can't we? I've been thinking about this for weeks now. I'm not talking foolishness. You make some pies and I'll carry them around the area here and sell them."

Mama just rolled her head back, shut her eyes, and moaned a sigh. It was more like she was tired than anything else.

Papa didn't pay her any mind. He just kept on talking. "I've been looking at those Hubig pies in the stores. They make the smaller seven-inch pies thin so they look larger. They could cost a quarter of what the big nine-inch family pies cost," Papa's voice was getting stronger. He wasn't looking at Mama anymore, but looking out above the rooftops across the street.

"I've checked on prices. Dried fruit runs about 5 cents a pounds and that's the most expensive part of the pie. How many pies could you make with a pound of dried fruit?"

Mama didn't answer. Papa didn't seem to be expecting an answer, either, because he just kept talking and even started gesturing with his arms, swinging this way and that.

Exhibit 2   Bama's Quality Circle

BUZZINGS

The Busy B's • Bama Pie Ltd. • BTC • Bama Pailet • Base Inc. • Bama Sweets • Bama Foods • January 1992

BAMA'S QUALITY CIRCLE

OUR QUALITY FUTURE

1991 was a transition year for our Quality culture. You may have not been aware it was because "Quality" is a way of life at Bama—but subtle changes have been occurring. As a company, in our sixth year involved with the Quality Process, our needs are very different. We have matured with Crosby's principles and now is the time to adopt our own values. In 1992 we will be building a solid quality foundation based on these principles.

- ► People
- ► Products
- ► Services
- ► Profits
- ► Continuous Improvement

Our mission is to consistently strive to improve all processes, through continuous improvement, to ensure total customer satisfaction.

—Paula Marshall-Chapman

"Your pies taste a hundred times better than Hubig's. Why, before long we'll be selling pies all over Dallas, then the whole country."

Papa stopped suddenly and turned to Mama who was wilted next to him. I think she must have been wishing he'd calm down and start talking about the smell of fresh cut grass or something.

"I've even come up with a name for the company." It was too dark to tell, but his voice sounded like there must have been a gleam in his eyes.

"Now you know I've always called you Blanchie because I didn't like Cornelia Alabama, or even 'Bama' like your family called you. But for a company, 'Bama' is just fine. In fact, I like it real good. 'The Bama Pie Company,' how does that sound Blanchie?"

I couldn't see Mama right then, but hearing the swing squeaking, I figured she sat up in her seat before she answered Papa.

"Well, I . . ."

I think Mama was surprised at how excited Papa was at the idea of starting a business selling her pies. From hearing her hesitate, I knew Papa would be selling Mama's pies before long.

"The idea sounds all right. But we don't have much of a place to make pies or enough pans and equipment. We . . ."

"Don't worry about a thing, Blanchie. Tell me what you need and I'll get it for you."

"Well, I'll have to think about it for a while. I . . ."

"Fine," Papa said. "We'll start tomorrow."

Exhibit 3   The Bama Pie Values Statement

Customers
Bama will provide our customers with products and services that conform to their requirements and deliver them on time, at a competitive price.

Suppliers
Bama will encourage open and honest communication with our "partners" and reward those who have adopted and demonstrated use of the continuous improvement process. We will also encourage the sharing of ideas.

Passion
Bama will conduct our business with integrity and professionalism and with a strategy of continuous improvement. This will provide increased profits and create worldwide awareness of our products. We will continue to focus on being a "Corporate Good Citizen" by being active in our community.

Quality

Products and Services
Product quality and product safety will be the responsibility of every employee. We will sell quality products and services at a fair value. We will anticipate and react to our customers' needs. We will take pride in all products and services which we perform.

People
Bama will attract result-oriented people, provide a safe work environment, operate as an equal opportunity employer, focus on employee development and retention, develop mutual trust and respect for each other, and support promotion from within. We will inspire new ideas and innovation by creating the environment whereby we create employee satisfaction.

Through continuous improvement our name will represent QUALITY to our customers, our suppliers, and ourselves. We believe that if we live by these values we will establish the Bama Companies as world class and will achieve our long-range objectives.

Thus, the Bama Pie Company was born, according to Paul Marshall's recounting of the event. The next day, Henry took $1.67 and went out to obtain what was needed. He talked a bakery goods supplier into granting credit with the $1.67 paid down on an order that totaled more than $25. He obtained the rest of what was needed on credit from the grocery store where the family had shopped and was known. That evening, the family pitched in to make pies, and the following day, Henry set out to sell the first Bama Pies. The first day's sales far exceeded expectations, and the company began to grow.

Soon the sales route had expanded to the delivery of two baskets of pies per day. When sales were slow, Henry Marshall would walk farther and extend the route until all the pies were sold each day. One day, as evening was approaching and he had a few pies left, he spotted a grocery store across the street from where he was. He approached the grocer and asked if he could leave the pies on consignment, promising to service the store daily with fresh products. The grocer agreed and thus began a new phase; Bama Pie became a wholesale distributor.

Soon a car was purchased and modified to carry the pies; and the company established routes in the Dallas area. All the Marshall children became involved in the business, including Paul. The company tried to expand into Waco in 1931, but was unsuccessful because of the Depression.

In the mid-1930s, Paul Marshall observed the operation of Bama's major competitor, Hubig Pies. He was overwhelmed with the modern, high-volume, machine-aided production. Seeing the operation made him aware of how small and old-fashioned Bama was. He attempted to convince his father of the need to purchase new equipment, but to no avail. The company continued to produce pies in a highly labor-intensive process. Paul's dream had become bigger than his father's; he saw the need to change to high-volume, machine-production methods as the way to expand the company. This conflict became a source of disagreement over the years between Paul and his father.

During the next few years, the older Marshall children opened other Bama Pie operations, including one in Oklahoma City started by Paul's sister Grace and her husband. In a move for independence, Paul moved to Oklahoma City and began working for his sister as a route salesman. It was in Oklahoma City that Paul met and eventually married Lilah Drake, who worked in the kitchen of the pie company. Both had the dream of opening their own Bama Pie shop and looked toward Tulsa as a potential market; they began saving for the future.

In the meantime, Paul's brother, Henry, who had reopened the Bama Pie store in Waco, decided to leave the Waco operation and move to Tulsa. While Paul understood his dad's rule that whoever established a territory first had rights to it, he was disappointed that Tulsa would be taken. When Paul and Lilah discovered Henry was simply going to walk away from the Waco business, they decided to take over the Waco operation. Within a year, Waco was profitable and expanding. In January 1937, Paul's father told him his brother would like to return to Waco, which was closer to his wife's family. Paul and his brother agreed to trade operations, and on February 6, 1937, Paul and Lilah, with their new son John, arrived in Tulsa.

The company struggled through 1937, and a decision to buy a large quantity of new "soft wheat flour" from General Mills nearly did the company in. The new flour was developed for pies, but the formula worked best with baked pies, not the fried pies that made up the bulk of Bama's sales. After discovering the problem and restoring lost customer confidence, the company had grown to six drivers and 14 women assisting Lilah in the bakery by the spring of 1938.

The company continued to prosper as the United States entered World War II, and Paul was given a draft classification of 4-F (which exempted him from being called to duty) since the company was a major supplier to the military.

In December 1943, the owner of Mrs. Marshall's Pies offered to sell his company to Paul Marshall. Paul recounted the meeting in his book:

"Paul, I just wanted to meet another damned fool named Marshall who was in the pie business."

I laughed and decided I like Archie Marshall.

We talked shop for a while, then Archie asked. "Would you like to buy my business?"

My eyes popped wide open. Who did he think I was, Rockefeller or something? I was almost embarrassed to answer him. But I wanted him to know who he was dealing with from the beginning. I wasn't going to play the high roller. "Archie," I said, "I couldn't buy the spare tire off of your Cadillac."

Archie didn't look at me right then. He just swung his feet back and forth under the table and stared out the window for a few seconds. Then he turned to me and said, "I didn't ask you if you *could* buy my business. I asked you if you would *like* to buy my business."

Well, it was a fact that I would love to have his business, but I didn't understand what he was talking about. "Sure, Archie, I'd like to have your business, but I don't have the kind of money you're looking for. I can tell you that right now."

"I'll work that out," Archie said.

They worked out a deal, and Bama Pie Company acquired Mrs. Marshall's Pies. One of the major contributions of the acquisition was an understanding of quality. Paul Marshall said, "The most valuable asset we acquired was a 10-cent calendar advertising Karo syrup. On that calendar was a phrase that became our slogan, 'Keep your eye on the key to success, QUALITY.' "

By the end of 1945, Bama Pies was a well-established and profitable operation. But over the next few years, the company was beset with major union organizing problems that left Paul Marshall with a bitter resentment of unions. He fought the union's attempt to unionize his company despite threats on his life and the members of his family. He endured beatings of his drivers, threatening calls at 2 AM, stink bombs that ruined products, smashed pies in the grocery stores, boycotts, and other forms of harassment.

He called national attention to his plight when he had a welder friend create a rotating track with a department store manikin fitted to it to put on the front of his bakery as a "counter-picket." He dressed the manikin in a suit and placed an American flag in its hands. The manikin moved continuously back and forth on a track above the street while the union's live picket walked back and forth below. Since the bakery was on heavily traveled U.S. Route 66, the counter-picket attracted national attention with photos appearing in *Life* and other magazines. One day a group of kids who had gathered to watch Duke (as the manikin was called) started calling the live union picket a "dummy." The union picket picked up a rock and threw it at one of the kids. This brought a barrage of rocks from the kids and he was driven off. That ended the picketing, but not the harassment.

As the union eroded Bama Pie's markets among grocery stores and hotel restaurants, Paul Marshall began to look for new markets immune from union pressures. At a Chicago bakery equipment auction in 1951, he encountered a refrigerated truck carrying frozen pies. In May 1953, he got into the frozen pie business when he contracted to provide pies for five new Howard Johnson's restaurants being constructed on the new Turner Turnpike linking Tulsa with Oklahoma City. Once in the frozen pie business, he quickly saw that the future of Bama Pies was in frozen pies— with frozen pies there were no stale pies to pick up, no more waste.

Bama supplied the Howard Johnson's restaurants until mid-1955, when Marshall was informed by the head office that Howard Johnson's was going to begin making its own pies. Bama Pie then trained its efforts on large supermarkets. By the late 1950s, the company was working on a frozen turnover fried pie that could be sold in restaurants. By the beginning of 1960, all the other Bama Pie operations owned and operated by Paul's brothers and sisters had gone out of business, leaving only the Tulsa operation.

Another major turning point for Bama Pies occurred in 1965 when Paul Marshall landed the account of Sandy's restaurant chain (later purchased by Hardee's). In his book, Paul describes the event as follows:

> I couldn't wait to get back to Tulsa so I could tell our employees about the orders we'd have coming in.
>
> For 30 miles I nearly broke my arm patting myself on the back for landing the Sandy's account. I thought over what we had said in our meeting and grinned to myself. Then suddenly the sobering truth of our agreement hit home.
>
> During my chat with Mr. Andres (president of Sandy's) he had pointed out all of the Sandy's locations on a wall map. And like some dunce, I was only thinking of the pies we would be selling to all those locations. The little red pins on the map were spread out over the midwest, from Arizona to Ohio. But I only saw inches between pins.
>
> The reality of what those pins meant hadn't registered on me at the time, but now it was hitting me full force. Our trucks would have to drive 100 to 500

miles between stops! There wouldn't be any way my company could survive with shipping costs gobbling our profits.

By the time I was on the outskirts of Bloomington, I had come up with a plan to make it all work. I decided the only way to justify delivering pies to such spread-out markets was to acquire more fast-food customers and establish distribution points. The thought never occurred to me to call off the deal with Sandy's.

It was 11 o'clock when I reached Bloomington. The McDonald's hamburger store had just opened so, after I parked in their lot, I grabbed one of our sample frozen pies out of the dry-ice cooler in the trunk and then walked in and ordered coffee.

"You got any pie?" I asked the manager as he served my coffee.

"No, but I wish we did," he said.

Marshall discovered that individual McDonald's units were not allowed to make menu decisions and was told he needed to go to McDonald's headquarters in Chicago. He decided to make a cold call immediately and headed his car toward Chicago with his remaining frozen pies. Surprisingly, he was able to see the frozen-food buyer and arranged to leave some samples for a dinner of McDonald's executives that evening. He then headed back to Tulsa.

When he called to see how the pies fared, he was told they weren't bad, but were not what McDonald's was looking for. He convinced Al Bernardin, the McDonald's buyer, to allow him to attempt to develop a pie that McDonald's would want.

Bernardin told Marshall, "Well, Paul, we'd be willing to work with you on developing a good pie. But I'm certainly not going to promise anything. And I'll warn you, if you work for 10 years trying to come up with a pie that fits our needs, you still might not get the order."

The next attempt to make a pie that McDonald's would accept brought an unexpected response. The quality wasn't good enough. He was told the crust needed to be lighter and the apples needed to be sliced, rather than chipped.

"We want a quality product, not a cheap one. I promise you that we will pay the price for quality," Bernardin told him. Marshall was surprised that a low-priced, high-volume restaurant chain would be more interested in quality than price, but he was happy for the opportunity to develop the high-quality product McDonald's demanded.

For more than a year, Marshall traveled almost weekly between Tulsa and Chicago until he finally produced a product that McDonald's was satisfied with.

The pies were test-marketed in Joplin and Springfield, Missouri, and soon amounted to nearly 7 percent of each store's sales. Soon, Marshall was called to Chicago to meet with the top executives of McDonald's. To supply McDonald's more than 600 restaurants on a national basis would require a significant investment for Bama Pies, and Marshall was concerned about coming up with the $250,000 he estimated would be needed.

When Fred Turner, McDonald's president, asked him if he was ready to begin supplying McDonald's on a national basis, Marshall had to tell the truth and admit he probably couldn't.

In his book, he describes the event:

"How much money would you need to get ready to supply McDonald's?" Turner asked.

I was glad I had done some figuring on that question already. "It would cost us $250,000 to build a line that would produce 20,000 pies an hour."

"Can you get that kind of money?" he asked, his eyes never wavering from mine.

Mr. Turner was questioning me like a judge who wanted to know if I was guilty or not—there was no discussion called for.

"I don't know," I said, feeling weak in the pit of my stomach. I figured Mr. Turner was wondering why we Oklahoma hicks were wasting his time. I had hoped our meeting would be real casual, just friends sitting down to talk over what would be needed to make McDonald's pies. I wasn't prepared for the rapid-fire questions and piercing eyes of Mr. Turner.

"How long have you been doing business at your bank?" Mr. Turner asked.

"Probably 25 years or so," I replied, hoping he wasn't going to ask our credit limit.

"Do you owe them anything?"

"Not much. Our mortgage is paid down quite a bit."

"Fine," he said. "I'll send a couple of men down to Tulsa to talk with your banker and see if we can make this pie business work."

"Thank you, sir."

"What kind of contract would you like?" Mr. Turner asked.

"If we can't give you the quality and service you need, Mr. Turner, a contract won't help either of us. But if we can, we won't need one."

"I like your way of thinking, Paul," Mr. Turner said. He reached out and shook my hand, then Johnny's hand and marched out the door.

A couple of days later, two McDonald's executives visited Marshall's bank, and the next day one of the bank's officers called and said, "Paul, I understand you could use a quarter of a million dollars?"

Thus began a long-term relationship with McDonald's that allowed Bama Pies to grow along with McDonald's as one of its key suppliers. During the 1970s and 1980s, Paul and Lilah traveled worldwide with McDonald's officials as consultants to assist local bakers in supplying fruit pies for McDonald's far-flung global enterprise. In 1987, Bama Pies received an award for being a 20-year vendor to McDonald's.

PAULA MARSHALL-CHAPMAN

Paula Marshall-Chapman succeeded her father in 1985 as chief executive officer of the company and immediately made quality her top priority. "To be honest, we almost lost the account in the mid-80s because we had let our quality fall a bit as we struggled to keep up with our growth," Marshall-Chapman said. She said her father was ready to retire and was almost becoming a problem. "Someone would call from McDonald's about a problem, and he might tell them just what they could do with it. He really didn't relate to the younger technical staff that McDonald's was sending around. He might tell one of them that they didn't know anything about the pie business and that he was 'buddies with Ray Kroc and had been making pies since before they were in diapers.'"

"When I took over, I spent a lot of time just listening," she said.

Taking over the company was not an automatic thing for Marshall-Chapman—she had to earn her way to the top. Paula first joined the company in 1970; she recalled: "My ideas of going off to college were sidetracked when I was a senior in high school. I got pregnant. I first went to work in the thrift stores (Bama Pie's retail operation for picked up and damaged products) and began learning about the business. I learned how to meet and talk to customers, how to display merchandise, how I could increase sales by providing samples, and I also learned how much poor quality costs. We were selling pies for a nickel in the thrift store that could be sold for 50 cents if the product had not been damaged."

After a few years, Paula moved to the central office and learned how to manage the company's fleet of 35 trailer trucks. (The company in 1992 operated more than 90 trucks through Bama Pie Trucking, a subsidiary.) She said that job provided a learning experience in the areas of government regulation, fuel costs, and record keeping and generally broadened her view of the company.

In the mid-1970s, Bama decided to computerize, and Paula was selected to make the purchase. As a result, she was the person trained to run the new system, and in that capacity she learned the value of training people and helping people solve problems. Since she also had to set up the company's systems on the computer, she learned about costs, payables, invoicing, and again expanded her knowledge about the company. "In my position, I got to be known as Bama's problem solver," she recalled.

Her father noticed her management talents but had been grooming her older brother, Johnny, to take over the company. Paula remembered, "Dad began to say things to me like: 'You really like this business, don't you?' 'Why don't you want to do more?' 'Women probably don't need to be in a CEO role.' Like most kids, when a parent says you can't do something, that's what you decide you want to do just to show them they are wrong."

Paula began her college education during this time, attending Tulsa Junior College and working full time. In 1982, her older brother had a serious illness and her other brother "got into a fight" with her father, so her father came to her and said, "You're going to have to be the one, or we're going to have to sell the company."

For the next three years, she traveled with her father everywhere. She said when her father first presented her as the future CEO to some of the McDonald's officials, they laughed. "During that time I learned a lot," she says. Some of the best advice her father gave her included: "Always have a good work ethic. Be committed to what you are doing. Commitment is what gets through hard times and there will always be hard times."

In 1985, Paul Marshall handed over the reins of the company to Paula and retired to Naples, Florida. According to other Bama executives, when he left, he left. He let her run the company and stayed out of the way. The company, which had been incorporated, was reorganized as a partnership in 1985 to allow Paula's parents to cash out their equity. Paula then became a general partner.

Between 1985 and 1992, Paula reshaped the company. She recruited a young, professional executive staff. She also completed a bachelor's degree through Oklahoma City University's Competency Based Degree Program and was recognized as a distinguished alumna of that program in 1989.

Employees described Paula as a "unique chief executive." One marketing representative who had previously worked for Pizza Hut in the PepsiCo organization was asked to compare what it was like at Pizza Hut and Bama. He said:

> At PepsiCo, everything was numbers driven. You either made the numbers, or you were gone. You didn't feel like you were treated as a person. Big companies are like that. You worked for an organization. Here you work for a human being who treats you as a human being. Paula is more concerned about long term. She doesn't look for someone to blame when a problem arises, she only wants to look for what caused the problem and find a way to fix the problem. I've never seen her blame anyone for anything.

MANAGEMENT IN 1992

Marshall-Chapman reshaped the management team significantly after she took control of the company and assembled a highly professional staff with an average age under 40.

John Davsco, 45, was vice president of operations. He joined Bama Pie in 1989 after 19 years of high-level operations management with Pillsbury. A graduate of St. Louis University in 1968, he also had a brief career as a major league baseball pitcher with the St. Louis Cardinals and Cincinnati Reds.

William L. Chew, 35, vice president of finance, joined the firm in 1987 after two years as controller of a real estate management and development company and seven years with Price Waterhouse in Chicago. He was a 1978 graduate of the University of Illinois and a certified public accountant.

Kay White, 46, vice president of human resources, joined Bama Pie in 1976 as a line worker in production. She was promoted to supervisor and then plant manager and served 2½ years as operations director.

Brenda Rice, 31, vice president for quality assurance systems, joined the company in 1989. She previously was employed in McDonald's R & D Division and worked with Bama Pies in developing the biscuit for McDonald's. She also worked as product development technologist with Magic Pantry Foods (Canada). She received an associate degree in food science from Humber College, Toronto, Canada, in 1981.

With more than 70 percent of the company's business coming from McDonald's, Bama had never developed a fully functioning marketing department. During 1991, the company began establishing a marketing strategy and hired Lynn Dickson, previously associated with Pizza Hut, to begin developing a professional marketing function within the company. Exhibit 4 presents an organization chart for the company.

PRODUCTS

The products Bama Pies produced included 3-ounce pies and 3-inch biscuits for McDonald's, bread sticks for Pizza Hut, 9-inch graham cracker pie shells, 3-inch and 9-inch pecan pies, and soft cookies.

The 3-ounce pies supplied to McDonald's were provided frozen as either ready to fry or bake, with the bulk of the volume having apple or cherry fillings. The company could also produce pies with lemon, peach, and apricot fillings. The original pies supplied to McDonald's were fried turnovers. The baked product was an optional choice in the restaurants in the McDonald's organization and had been increasing in popularity.

The 3-inch biscuit was processed in the new 135,000-square-foot facility in Tulsa and was prebaked to a ready-to-bake stage, frozen, and then baked off in the individual restaurant. The product took several years to develop, with McDonald's, Bama Pies, and Quaker Oats (the other 50 percent supplier) jointly working on the project. Currently, Bama supplied operations west of the Mississippi, and Quaker supplied restaurants east of the Mississippi. During the development of the product, the group experimented with more than 200 recipes.

According to Marshall-Chapman, the reason McDonald's wanted a ready-to-bake product was to ensure a consistent product at all its units. When biscuits first began

Exhibit 4 Bama Pie, Ltd., Corporate Organization as of September 1990

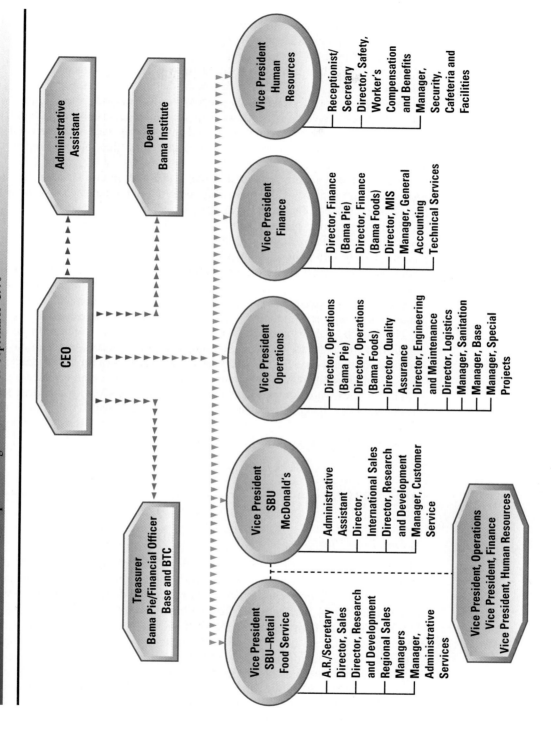

appearing in restaurants, they were made from mixes. "Our customer has 8,000 domestic restaurants and, thus, 8,000 biscuit bakers. That means a lot of variation is possible," Marshall-Chapman said.

The long development time resulted from McDonald's insistence that the frozen product be equal in quality to fresh-baked, made-from-scratch products. To provide the product, a carefully controlled process was developed. The biscuits were essentially 90 percent baked, frozen, and then shipped to distribution centers for delivery to the restaurants. The product, packaged in a baking bag, was then finished off in convection ovens at the local restaurant to give that "just baked" appearance, taste, and texture.

The bread sticks were produced in the 11th Street plant of Bama Pies and were a frozen dough product, made under a confidential agreement with Pizza Hut with the recipe kept secret. The dough was processed, rolled to a specific thickness, and shipped frozen in flat pieces about 9 inches by 12 inches. The dough was thawed and the sticks cut at the restaurant before baking.

The 3-inch and 9-inch pecan pies were a mainstay of Bama Pies and had been produced for almost the entire 65 years of operation. The recipe was virtually unchanged from the original developed by Marshall-Chapman's grandmother. The pies were fully baked, packaged in single wraps, and then boxed in a variety of quantities. Customers included Wal-Mart and Sam's Wholesale Clubs.

The 9-inch graham cracker shells were produced for retail sale and were also provided to TCBY and Braum's. The shells came in a metal pie pan ready to be filled with a customer's own filling. The shells were often used for cheesecake and ice box pies or could be filled with ice cream or yogurt to provide an ice cream pie product.

The cookies were soft products that competed directly with the large soft cookies produced under the Grandma's label by Frito-Lay, a PepsiCo subsidiary. The cookies were packaged individually and boxed for retail sale. See Exhibit 5 for a comparison of the ingredients used in these products.

OPERATIONS

McDonald's Pies

The 3-ounce pies for McDonald's were processed in the 11th Street Plant. Ingredients were mixed in two different areas. The dough was prepared in large mixers that fed a moving conveyor system that rolled the dough out on two separate belts approximately 24 inches wide. The filling was prepared in large, heated mixing bowls with real fruit added. This mixture was pumped through seven separate hoses that streamed filling on the bottom conveyor of dough. The top layer was then placed on top of the filling, and the pies were then cut and sealed in a two-step operation. The pies were sent to a spiral freezer where they were frozen. The process was basically the same whether the pie was a fried product or a baked product. The dough mixture was different for each product, and the baked product had slits cut in the top of each pie.

After freezing, the pies were processed slightly differently. The fried product was dipped in a liquid that immediately froze to the pie and caused the finished pie to have a bubbly, flaky texture. The pies were then hand-packed 12 to a tray, with six trays then boxed in an automated operation. Four boxes were packaged with

| Exhibit 5 | Bama Pie's Use of Ingredients in Its Products, 1984 versus 1991 |

Description	1984 Pounds (in millions)	1991 Pounds (in millions)
Frozen apples	3.5	9.2
Frozen cherries	3.0	1.6
Flour	2.0	11.0
Shelled pecans	2.0	0.3
Shortening	1.5	4.2
Sugar	1.0	2.6
Shelled eggs	0.9	0.4

Note: Reduction in cherries is because the cherry pie is now optional at McDonald's restaurants. In 1984, it was a required menu item. Reduction in pecans and eggs is due to reduced number of pecan pies being sold, an outcome attributed to increased weight and health concerns.

shrink-wrap before moving into the storage freezer. The baked pies were processed similarly, but instead of being dipped when exiting the freezer, they were sprayed with water and dusted with cinnamon before packaging.

Each hour, samples were taken from the production process to the test kitchen where the same ovens and fryers used by McDonald's were installed. The product was finished off and tested to ensure specifications were being met. Each line was capable of producing 40,000 pies per hour, and more than 1 million pies were produced daily at the plant.

McDonald's Biscuits

The McDonald's biscuit was produced in a new facility that *Baking & Snack* magazine called "world class."[2] The facility contained two parallel production lines that included 250-foot ovens. The dough was mixed and laid down on a flour-dusted conveyor belt that transferred the dough through a series of rollers until it was a 50-inch-wide sheet. The dough was then cut and passed through a metal detector before dropping into the baking pans. The biscuit pans passed three wide through the oven where modular construction and nine heating zones transformed the dough into a biscuit ready for freezing in about 15 minutes. The highly automated line removed the pans, cleaned them, re-oiled them, and returned them for reuse. The biscuits were then cartoned and put through a spiral freezer after cooling to 90 degrees. After freezing, the biscuits were wrapped and passed through another metal detector before being boxed for shipment and moved into the storage freezer.

Graham Shells

The graham shells were produced on a highly automated line that was installed in 1991 and put into operation in early 1992. The graham meal was mixed and fed into a hopper that dumped an exact measurement of meal into an aluminum pie pan and

---

[2]Laurie Gorton, "World Class: Bama Creates a Flexible Plant Dedicated to Making Ready-to-Bake Biscuits," *Baking & Snack*, November 1991.

was then automatically pressed and formed. The shell moved through a process where the clear plastic cover was pressed into place and sealed to the pan. Next, the shells were automatically stacked and boxed for shipment.

Pizza Hut Bread Sticks

Using the secret recipe from Pizza Hut, the dough was mixed and fed onto a conveyor belt into a series of rollers that reduced the sheet of dough to the proper thickness and width. The dough was then run through a cutter that produced sheets of dough approximately 9 inches by 12 inches. These sheets were then frozen in a spiral freezer before packaging and boxing. The bread stick line was located in the 11th Street plant.

Pecan Pies

The 3-inch and 9-inch pecan pies were also produced in the 11th Street plant. The dough was prepared and rolled and fed onto a conveyor line where it was cut and dropped into the aluminum pie shell. The dough was then automatically formed inside the shell. The pies continued on and were filled with pecans and pie filling before entering an oven approximately 200 feet long. Once the pies were baked, they were conveyed back to packaging by passing through a cooling tunnel where they went through automated packaging machines and were hand-packed and boxed.

Cookies

The soft-batch cookies were processed in much the same manner as the pecan pies. The batter was measured and dropped onto a conveyor belt that took the cookies through the oven and returned them through a cooling tunnel for packaging.

THE MCDONALD'S RELATIONSHIP

The relationship with McDonald's was unusual in that Bama had been the company's principal supplier of pies for 24 years and had never had a contract. Moreover, Bama did not sell directly to McDonald's. McDonald's selected and approved suppliers, but the actual sales were made to independently owned distribution centers that supplied the McDonald's restaurants around the country.

The company did not have a contract for the biscuit product either. "When a couple of banks heard we wanted to borrow $40 million to build a biscuit plant and didn't have a contract to even buy one biscuit, they ran away," Marshall-Chapman said. McDonald's put the company in touch with Texas Commerce Bank in Houston, and Bama found a bank that was actively seeking to develop a business relationship with McDonald's. In fact, the bank had formed a special group of McDonald's specialists. The bank understood that McDonald's developed "partnership arrangements" with suppliers and that contracts were not a part of the business. "They (both the bank and McDonald's) were eager to help, and we completed the deal at extremely favorable rates," Marshall-Chapman said.

COMMITMENT TO QUALITY AND STAYING PRIVATE ──────

Favorable lending rates were extremely important to Bama Pie, since the company and Marshall-Chapman were committed to remaining private. Marshall-Chapman believed going public would ruin the company: "Public companies have to run the business for Wall Street. They have to think quarterly. I want to run our business for my customers and my employees. I want to concentrate on developing the business, not worrying about what is happening to my stock price."

Decisions were made based on what the management team thought was best. A commitment to quality was evident in everything the company did. Marshall-Chapman believed that not having to answer to stockholders allowed the company to focus on quality; she indicated the company was ahead of the people who were teaching total quality management: "They (the Quality College and others) are now calling us and asking us what we've done new and what we're currently working on."

Bama insisted on quality from its suppliers. Suppliers were expected to ship random samples of product runs due for Bama in advance so they could be pretested. "We want to know if there is a problem before the shipment leaves their plant," Marshall-Chapman said. Vendors were willing to cooperate because it was much less expensive to provide the samples and get preapproval for shipment than to risk having a whole order rejected after shipment and returned.

The company had instilled a total quality management discipline in its approximately 600 employees through extensive training and educational programs offered through the in-house Bama Institute. Getting employees involved in all aspects of quality permeated everything, including internal record keeping. Within a year's time, inventory adjustments based on physical counts had dropped from between $50,000 and $70,000 per month to less than $3,000 per month and was still improving. "One month we'd have a negative adjustment, the next a positive adjustment," William Chew, vice president of finance said. At a time when the company was attempting to refine its cost system and implement standard costs under an activity-based cost system, the inventory problem was major. Chew commented, "Even our fork truck operators have gotten involved in helping solve the inventory adjustments problem."

To support the quality program and refine data for decision making, the company purchased a new computer system using Prism software on an IBM AS/400 mainframe. The conversion was implemented within one year. "We were able to do it because Paula released people from some of their regular jobs and put them on the project," Chew said. According to the consultants working with Bama, no company had ever been able to accomplish such a conversion in such a short period. The result was a system with world-class manufacturing software that supported an activity-based standard cost accounting system and electronic data interchange transactions.

DRUG POLICIES ──────────────────────

Bama was a "drug-free" workplace; all applicants for employment were screened for drugs. According to company officials, approximately one in five applicants tested positive. In addition, all employees (including Paula) had been drug tested and random drug testing was administered within the company. The random sampling for drug tests was determined by a computer program. Urine samples were taken and tested in a lab. A positive result was grounds for immediate dismissal.

According to Marshall-Chapman, the company's drug policy was mainly aimed at reducing accidents. Since the program had been implemented, accidents had declined significantly. Any employee involved in an accident at work was automatically drug tested.

BEBOPP

In 1990, Bama instituted the Bama Employees' Bonus on Profit Plan (BEBOPP) to provide bonus incentives to all employees in the company. The plan was based on an annual return on sales objective that was established by Marshall-Chapman. The goal was expressed as a percentage, and for each 0.5 percent above the target all employees shared in a bonus pool. The pool began at 2 percent of payroll and increased for each 0.5 percent above the target. For example, if Bama's return on sales topped the goal by 2 percent, the bonus pool would equal 3.5 percent of payroll. Even though the program was based on annual sales, quarterly payments were made to employees. All eligible employees received equal amounts from the pool.

FUTURE PROSPECTS

The company was attempting to decrease its reliance on McDonald's. The biscuit plant, which was also capable of producing cookies and other bread-type products, had underutilized capacity plus room for expansion. The main plant also had open capacity.

Opportunities for new business were coming in faster than the company could deal with them. John Davsko, vice president of operations, said, "We have people calling us all the time asking if we are interested in developing a product for them. Our reputation is bringing business. We had one potential customer referred to us by one of our suppliers."

However, there were problems with expansion. Management believed any expansion had to come mainly from new product development. Bama believed it could not seek additional customers for its fast-food pie product without putting its McDonald's account at risk. Likewise, it would be unwise to seek another customer for biscuits or bread sticks. According to Marshall-Chapman, about the only negative thing Paul Marshall had said regarding how Paula had handled the business since he left is, "He thinks we're expanding too fast, and he doesn't like us borrowing money."

Perdue Farms Inc.

George C. Rubenson, Salisbury State University
Frank M. Shipper, Salisbury State University
Jean M. Hanebury, Salisbury State University

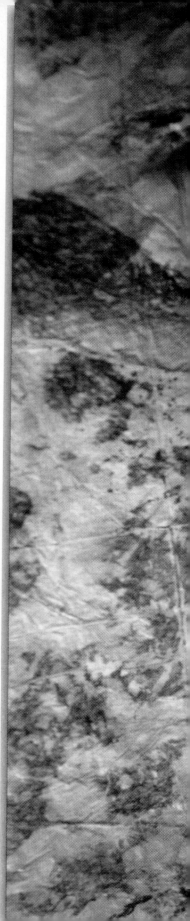

I have a theory that you can tell the difference between those who have inherited a fortune and those who have made a fortune. Those who have made their own fortune forget not where they came from and are less likely to lose touch with the common man.[1]

In 1917, Arthur W. Perdue, a Railway Express agent and descendent of a French Huguenot family named Perdeaux, bought 50 leghorn chickens for a total of $5 and began selling table eggs near the small town of Salisbury, Maryland. A region immortalized in James Michener's *Chesapeake*, it is alternately known as the "Eastern Shore" or the "Delmarva Peninsula" and includes parts of Delaware, Maryland, and Virginia.

Initially, the business amounted to little more than a sideline chore for "pin money," raising a few "biddies" in a cardboard box behind the wood stove in the kitchen until they were old enough to fend for themselves in the barnyard. But, in 1920, when Railway Express asked "Mr. Arthur" to move to a station away from the Eastern Shore, at age 36 he quit his job as Salisbury's Railway Express agent and entered the egg business full time. His only child, Franklin Parsons Perdue, was born that same year.

Mr. Arthur soon expanded his egg market and began shipments to New York. Practicing small economies such as mixing his own chicken feed and using leather from his old shoes to make hinges for his chicken coops, he stayed out of debt and prospered. He tried to add a new chicken coop every year. By the time young Frank was 10, he had 50 chickens or so of his own to look after, earning money from their eggs. He worked along with his parents, not always enthusiastically, to feed the chickens, clean the coops, dig the cesspools, and gather and grade eggs. A shy introverted country boy, he went for five years to a one-room school, eventually graduated from Wicomico High School, and attended the State Teachers College in Salisbury for two years before returning to the farm in 1939 to work full time with his father.

By 1940, it was obvious to father and son that the future lay in selling chickens, not eggs. But the Perdues made the shift to selling broilers only after careful

The authors are indebted to Frank Perdue, Jim Perdue, and the numerous associates at Perdue Farms Inc. who generously shared their time and information about the company. In addition, the authors would like to thank the anonymous librarians who routinely review area newspapers and file articles about the poultry industry—the most important industry on the Delmarva Peninsula. Without their assistance, this case would not be possible. Copyright © 1995 by the case authors. Used with permission.
[1]Bill Sterling, "Just Browsin'," *Eastern Shore News*, March 2, 1988.

attention to every detail—a standard Perdue procedure in the years to come. In 1944, Mr. Arthur made his son Frank a full partner in what was then A. W. Perdue and Son, Inc., a firm already known for quality products and fair dealing in a toughly competitive business. In 1950, Frank took over leadership of Perdue Farms, a company of 40 employees. By 1952, revenues were $6 million from the sale of 2 million broilers.

By 1967, annual sales had increased to about $35 million but it was becoming increasingly clear that additional profits lay in processing chickens. Frank recalled in an interview for *Business Week* (September 15, 1972) "processors were paying us 10 cents a live pound for what cost us 14 cents to produce. Suddenly, processors were making as much as 7 cents a pound."

A cautious, conservative planner, Arthur Perdue had not been eager for expansion, and Frank Perdue himself was reluctant to enter poultry processing. But economic forces dictated the move and, in 1968, Perdue Farms became a vertically integrated operation, hatching eggs, delivering the chicks to contract growers, buying grain, supplying the feed and litter, and finally, processing the broilers and shipping them to market.

The company bought its first plant in 1968, a Swift and Company operation in Salisbury, renovated it, and equipped it with machines capable of processing 14,000 broilers per hour. Computers were soon employed to devise feeding formulas for each stage of growth so birds reached their growth potential sooner. Geneticists were hired to breed larger-breasted chickens and veterinarians were put on staff to keep the flocks healthy, while nutritionists handled the feed formulations to achieve the best feed conversion.

From the beginning, Frank Perdue refused to permit his broilers to be frozen for shipping, a process that resulted in unappetizing black bones and loss of flavor and moistness when cooked. Instead, Perdue chickens were (and some still are) shipped to market packed in ice, justifying the company's advertisements at that time that it sold only "fresh, young broilers." However, this policy also limited the company's market to those locations that could be serviced overnight from the Eastern Shore of Maryland. Thus, Perdue chose for its primary markets the densely populated towns and cities of the East Coast, particularly New York City which consumed more Perdue chicken than all other brands combined.

During the 1970s, the firm entered the Baltimore, Philadelphia, Boston, and Providence markets. Facilities were expanded rapidly to include a new broiler processing plant and protein conversion plant in Accomac, Virginia; a processing plant in Lewiston, North Carolina; a hatchery in Murfreesboro, North Carolina; and the acquisition of several Swift and Company facilities, including a processing plant in Georgetown, Delaware; a feedmill in Bridgeville, Delaware; and a feedmill in Elkin, North Carolina.

In 1977, Mr. Arthur died at the age of 91, leaving behind a company with annual sales of nearly $200 million, an average annual growth rate of 17 percent compared to an industry average of 1 percent a year, the potential for processing 78,000 broilers per hour, and annual production of nearly 350 million pounds of poultry per year. Frank Perdue said of himself, without a hint of self-deprecation, "I am a B-minus student. I know how smart I am. I know a B-minus is not as good as an A." Of his father he simply said, "I learned everything from him."

Stew Leonard, owner of a huge supermarket in Norwalk, Connecticut, and one of Perdue's top customers, described Frank Perdue as "What you see is what you get. If you ask him a question you will get an answer." Perdue disapproved of the presence of a union between himself and his associates, saying, "The absence of unions makes for a better relationship with our associates. If we treat our associates right, I don't think we will have a union." On conglomerates, he stated, "Diversification is the most dangerous word in the English language." His business philosophy was quality-driven: "I'm interested in being the best rather than the biggest. Expansion is OK if it has a positive effect on product quality. I'll do nothing that detracts from product quality."

Frank Perdue was known for having a temper. He was as hard on himself, however, as he was on others, readily admitting his shortcomings and even his mistakes. For example, in the 70s, he apparently briefly discussed using the influence of some unsavory characters to help alleviate union pressure. When an investigative reporter in the late 1980s asked him about this instance, he admitted that it was a mistake, saying "it was probably the dumbest thing I ever did."

In 1981, Frank Perdue was in Massachusetts for his induction into the Babson College Academy of Distinguished Entrepreneurs, an award established in 1978 to recognize the spirit of free enterprise and business leadership. Babson College President Ralph Z. Sorenson inducted Perdue into the academy which, at that time, numbered 18 men and women from four continents. Perdue had the following to say to the college students:

> There are none, nor will there ever be, easy steps for the entrepreneur. Nothing, absolutely nothing, replaces the willingness to work earnestly, intelligently towards a goal. You have to be willing to pay the price. You have to have an insatiable appetite for detail, have to be willing to accept constructive criticism, to ask questions, to be fiscally responsible, to surround yourself with good people and most of all, to listen.[2]

The early 1980s proved to be a period of further growth as Perdue Farms broadened its product line and market. New marketing areas included Washington, D.C.; Richmond, Virginia; and Norfolk, Virginia. Additional facilities were opened in Cofield, Kenly, Halifax, Robbins, and Robersonville, North Carolina. The firm broadened its line to include value-added products such as "Oven Stuffer" roasters and "Perdue Done It!" a new brand of fresh, prepared chicken products featuring cooked chicken breast nuggets, cutlets, and tenders. James A. (Jim) Perdue, Frank's only son, joined the company as a management trainee in 1983.

But the latter 1980s also tested the mettle of the firm. Following a period of considerable expansion and new product additions, a consulting firm was brought in to recommend ways to cope with the new complexity. Believing that the span of control was too broad, the consulting firm recommended that strategic business units, responsible for their own operations, be formed. In other words, the firm should decentralize.

Soon after, the chicken market leveled off and eventually began to decline. At one point, the firm was losing as much as $1 million a week; in 1988, Perdue Farms experienced its first year in the red. Unfortunately, the decentralization had created duplication of duties and enormous administrative costs. Management information system (MIS) costs, for example, had tripled. The firm's rapid plunge into turkeys and other food processing, where it had little experience, contributed to the losses. Waste and inefficiency had permeated the company. Characteristically, Frank Perdue took the firm back to basics, concentrating on efficiency of operations, improving communications throughout the company, and paying close attention to detail.

---

[2]Frank Perdue, speech at Babson College, April 28, 1981.

On June 2, 1989, Frank celebrated 50 years with Perdue Farms Inc. At a morning reception in downtown Salisbury, the governor of Maryland proclaimed "Frank Perdue Day." The governors of Delaware and Virginia did the same.

During the early 1990s the company pursued market expansion into North Carolina; Atlanta, Georgia; Pittsburgh, Pennsylvania; Cleveland, Ohio; Chicago, Illinois; and Florida. New products included fresh ground chicken, fresh ground turkey, sweet Italian turkey sausage, turkey breakfast sausage, fun-shaped chicken breast nuggets in star and drumstick shapes, and BBQ and oven-roasted chicken parts in the "Perdue Done It!" line. A new "Fit 'n Easy" label was introduced as part of a nutrition campaign using skinless, boneless chicken and turkey products.

In 1991, with 12,500 associates and 3,000 producers company revenues approximated $1.2 billion. Frank was named chairman of the Executive Committee and Jim Perdue became chairman of the board. Sitting in the small unpretentious office that had been his dad's for 40 years, Jim looked out the window at the house where he had grown up, the broiler houses Frank had built in the 1940s, his grandfather's homestead across the road where Frank was born, and a modern hatchery and said to the case researchers, "Dad would come home for dinner, then come back here and work into the early hours of the morning. There's a fold-out cot behind that credenza. He got by on three or four hours of sleep a night."

Jim, Frank, and Mr. Arthur Perdue . . . three generations of Perdue Farms leadership.

MISSION STATEMENT AND STATEMENT OF VALUES

From the beginning, Mr. Arthur's motto had been to "create a quality product, be aware of your customers, deal fairly with people, and work hard, work hard, work hard." In a speech in September 1991 to the firm's leaders, accountants, and Perdue associates, Frank Perdue reiterated these values, saying:

> If you were to ask me what was the biggest factor in whatever success we have enjoyed, I would answer that it was not technology, or economic resources, or

organizational structure. It . . . has been our conscious decision that, in order to be successful, we must have a sound set of beliefs on which we premise all our policies and actions . . . Central to these beliefs is our emphasis on quality . . . Quality is no accident. It is the one absolutely necessary ingredient of all the most successful companies in the world.

The quality theme was prominent in the company's mission statement and its statement of values. To help communicate the company's mission, quality policy, values, and annual goals to organizational members, the company printed and distributed a fold-up, wallet-size card with the relevant information (see Exhibit 1).

SOCIAL RESPONSIBILITY

To live up to its corporate statement of values, Perdue Farms strived to be a good corporate citizen. Two areas in which this was especially clear were its code of ethics and its efforts to minimize the environmental damage it caused.

Code of Ethics

Perdue Farms set forth explicitly the ethical standards it expects all associates to follow. Specifically, the code of ethics calls on associates to conduct every aspect of business in the full spirit of honest and lawful behavior. Further, all salaried associates and certain hourly associates are required to sign a statement acknowledging that they understand the code and are prepared to comply with it. Associates are expected to report to their supervisor dishonest or illegal activities as well as possible violations of the code. If the supervisor does not provide a satisfactory response, employees are expected to contact either the vice president for human resources or the vice president of their division. The code notes that any Perdue manager who initiates or encourages reprisal against any person who reports a violation commits a serious violation of the code.

Minimizing Environmental Damage

Historically, chicken processing has been the focus of special interest groups whose interests range from animal rights to repetitive-motion disorders to environmental causes. Perdue Farms accepted the challenge of striving to maintain an environmentally friendly work place as a goal, which required the commitment of all of its associates, from Frank Perdue down. Frank Perdue stated it best: "We know that we must be good neighbors environmentally. We have an obligation not to pollute, to police ourselves, and to be better than EPA requires us to be."

For example, over the years, the industry had explored many alternative ways of disposing of dead birds. Perdue research provided the solution—small composters on each farm. Using this approach, dead birds are reduced to an end product that resembles soil in a matter of a few days. This has become a major environmental activity. Another environmental challenge was the disposal of hatchery

Exhibit 1   Perdue Farms' Mission, Values, Goals, and Quality Policy, 1995

MISSION STATEMENT

Our mission is to provide the highest quality poultry and poultry-related products to retail and food service customers.

We want to be the recognized industry leader in quality and service, providing more than expected for our customers, associates, and owners.

We will accomplish this by maintaining a tradition of pride in our products, growth through innovation, integrity in the management of our business, and commitment to Team Management and the Quality Improvement Process.

QUALITY POLICY

We shall produce products and provide services at all times which meet or exceed the expectations of our customers.

We shall not be content to be of equal quality to our competitors.

Our commitment is to be increasingly superior.

Contribution to quality is a responsibility shared by everyone in the Perdue organization.

STATEMENT OF VALUES

Our success as a company, and as individuals working at Perdue, depend upon:

- Meeting customer needs with the best quality, innovative food and food-related products and services.
- Associates being team members in the business and having opportunities to influence, make contributions, and reach their full potential.
- Working together as business partners by implementing the principles of the QIP so that mutual respect, trust, and a commitment to being the best are shared among associates, customers, producers, and suppliers.
- Achieving the long-term goals of the company and providing economic stability and a rewarding future for all associates through well-planned, market-driven growth.

- Being the best in our industry in profitability as a low-cost producer, realizing that our customers won't pay for our inefficiencies.
- Staying ahead of the competition by investing our profits to provide a safe work environment to pay competitive wages; to maintain up-to-date facilities, equipment, and processes; and to create challenging opportunities for associates.
- Serving the communities in which we do business with resources, time, and the creative energies of our associates.

1995 COMPANY GOALS

People—Provide a Safe, Secure, and Productive Work Environment

- **Improve workplace safety.** Measurements include reduction in lost-time accidents and per-capita workers compensation cost.
- **Improve associate satisfaction.** Goal is completion of associate survey throughout the company.

Products—Provide the Highest Quality Products and Services at Competitive Costs

- **Improve consumer satisfaction.** Measured by consumer rating of the brand.
- **Improve the "Customer Service Satisfaction Index" (CSI).** Each division has an individual improvement goal.
- **Improve Perdue quality spread over competition.** Measurements include plant weighted ranking scores and quality consistency scores.

Profitability—Grow Profitably

- **Achieve planned ROE target.**
- **Improve competitiveness.** Measurement is Agrimetrics IOE deviation in Fresh Poultry, Perdue Foods, and Turkey.

wastes. Historically, manure and unhatched eggs that make up these wastes were shipped to a landfill. Perdue produced about 10 tons of this waste per day! However, Perdue reduced the waste by 50 percent by selling the liquid fraction to a pet food processor who cooks it for protein. The other 50 percent is recycled through a rendering process. In 1990, Perdue spent $4.2 million to construct a state-of-the-art wastewater treatment facility at its Accomac, Virginia, plant. This facility uses forced hot air heated to 120 degrees to cause the microbes to digest all traces of ammonia, even during the cold winter months. In April 1993, the company took a major step with the creation of the Environmental Steering Committee. Its mission is "to provide all Perdue Farms work sites with vision, direction, and leadership so that they can be good corporate citizens from an environmental perspective today and in the future." The committee oversees how the company is doing in such environmentally sensitive areas as wastewater, stormwater, hazardous waste, solid waste, recycling, biosolids, and human health and safety.

Jim Perdue summed it up as follows: "we must not only comply with environmental laws as they exist today, but look to the future to make sure we don't have any surprises. We must make sure our policy statement is real, and that there's something behind it, and that we do what we say we're going to do."

MARKETING

In the early days, chicken was sold to groceries as a commodity—that is, producers sold it in bulk and butchers cut and wrapped it. The consumer had no idea what company grew the chicken. Frank Perdue was convinced that higher profits could be made if Perdue's products were premium quality so that they could be sold at a premium price. But the only way the premium quality concept would work was if consumers asked for it by name—and that meant the product must be differentiated and "branded" to identify what the premium qualities were. Hence, the emphasis over the years on superior quality, a higher meat-to-bone ratio, and a yellow skin (the result of mixing marigold petals in the feed) which was an indicator of bird health.

In 1968, Perdue spent $40,000 on radio advertising. In 1969, the company spent $80,000 on radio, and in 1970 spent $160,000, split 50–50 between radio and television. The advertising agency had recommended against television advertising, but the combination worked. TV ads increased sales and Frank Perdue decided the old agency he was dealing with did not match one of the basic Perdue tenets: "The people you deal with should be as good at what they do as you are at what you do."

That decision set off a storm of activity on Frank's part. In order to select a new ad agency, Frank studied intensively and personally learned more about advertising than any poultry man before him. He began a 10-week immersion on the theory and practice of advertising. He read books and papers on advertising. He talked to sales managers of every newspaper and radio and television station in the New York City area, consulted experts, and interviewed 48 ad agencies. On April 2, 1971, Perdue Farms selected Scali, McCabe, Sloves as its new advertising agency. As the agency tried to figure out how to successfully "brand" a chicken—something that had never been done—it realized that Frank Perdue was their greatest ally. "He looked a little like a chicken himself, and he sounded a little like one, and he squawked a lot!" Ed McCabe, partner and chief copywriter of the firm, decided that Frank Perdue should be the firm's spokesperson. Initially Frank resisted. But in the end, he accepted the role, and the campaign based on "It takes a tough man to make a tender chicken" was born. Frank set Perdue Farms apart by educating consumers about chicken quality. The process catapulted Perdue Farms into the ranks of the top poultry producers in the country.

The firm's very first television commercial showed Frank on a picnic in the Salisbury City Park saying:

A chicken is what it eats . . . And my chickens eat better than people do . . . I store my own grain and mix my own feed . . . And give my Perdue chickens nothing but pure well water to drink . . . That's why my chickens always have that healthy golden yellow color . . . If you want to eat as good as my chickens, you'll just have to eat my chickens . . . Mmmm, that's really good!

Additional ads, touting superior quality and more breast meat, proclaimed:

Government standards would allow me to call this a grade A chicken . . . but my standards wouldn't. This chicken is skinny . . . It has scrapes and hairs . . . The fact is, my graders reject 30% of the chickens government inspectors accept as grade A . . . That's why it pays to insist on a chicken with my name on it . . . If you're not completely satisfied, write me and I'll give you your money back . . . Who do you write in Washington? . . . What do they know about chickens?

Never go into a store and just ask for a pound of chicken breasts . . . Because you could be cheating yourself out of some meat . . . Here's an ordinary one-pound chicken breast, and here's a one-pound breast of mine . . . They weigh the same. But as you can see, mine has more meat, and theirs have more bone. I breed the broadest breasted, meatiest chicken you can buy . . . So don't buy a chicken breast by the pound . . . Buy them by the name . . . and get an extra bite in every breast.

The ads paid off. In 1968, Perdue Farms supplied about 3 percent of the New York City market. By 1972, one out of every six chickens eaten in New York City was a Perdue chicken. Fifty-one percent of New Yorkers recognized the label. Scali, McCabe, Sloves credited Frank Perdue's "believability" for the success of the program. "This was advertising in which Perdue had a personality that lent credibility to the product." In 1994 Perdue Farms supplied 50 percent of the chickens consumed in New York City.

Frank had his own view. As he told a Rotary audience in Charlotte, North Carolina, in March 1989, "the product met the promise of the advertising and was far superior to the competition. Two great sayings tell it all: 'nothing will destroy a good product as quickly as poor advertising' and 'a gifted product is mightier than a gifted pen!' "

The responsibilities of the company's marketing department included deciding (1) how many chickens and turkeys to grow, (2) what the advertising and promotion pieces should look like, where they should run, and how much the company should spend, and (3) which new products the company would pursue. The marketing plan was derived from the company's five-year business plan and included goals concerning volume, return on sales, market share, and profitability. To round out the company's marketing effort, the marketing staff utilized the services of several outsiders:

- Lowe & Partners/SMS—advertising campaigns, media buys.
- R. C. Auletta & Co.—public relations, company image.
- Gertsman & Meyers—packaging design.
- Group Williams—consumer promotional programs.
- Various research companies for focus groups, telephone surveys, and in-home tests.

OPERATIONS

Two words have characterized the Perdue approach to operations—quality and efficiency, with emphasis on the first over the latter. Perdue, more than most companies, lives by the total quality management (TQM) slogan: "Quality, a journey without end." Some of the key events are listed in Exhibit 2. The pursuit of quality began with Arthur Perdue in 1924 when he purchased breeding roosters from Texas for the princely sum of $25 each. For comparison, typical wages in 1925 were $1 for a 10-hour workday. Frank Perdue's own pursuit of quality was legendary. One story was told in 1968 by Ellis Wainwright, the state of Maryland grading inspector, during start-up operations at Perdue's first processing plant. Frank had told Ellis that the standards that he wanted were higher than the Government Grade A standard. The first two days had been pretty much disastrous. On the third day, as Wainwright recalls:

We graded all morning, and I found only five boxes that passed what I took to be Frank's standards. The rest had the yellow skin color knocked off by the picking machines. I was afraid Frank was going to raise cain that I had accepted so few. Then Frank came through and rejected half of those.

To benchmark whether Perdue was actually leading the industry in quality, it bought about 2,000 pounds of competitors' products a week. Inspection associates graded these products, and shared the results with the highest levels of management. In addition, the company's quality policy was displayed in all operating locations and taught to all associates in quality training (Exhibit 1).

Company policy mandated that nothing artificial be fed or injected into its birds. The company took no shortcuts in pursuit of "the perfect chicken." A chemical- and steroid-free diet is fed to the chickens. Young chickens are vaccinated against disease. Selective breeding was used to improve the quality of the chickens sold. Chickens were bred to yield more breast meat because that was what consumers wanted.

Efficiency was improved through careful management of key activities. As a vertically integrated producer of chickens, Perdue performed all the strategy-critical value chain activities internally, including breeding and hatching its own eggs, selecting growers, building Perdue-engineered chicken houses, formulating and manufacturing its own feed, overseeing care and feeding, operating its own processing plants, distributing

Exhibit 2	Milestones in the Quality Improvement Process at Perdue Farms

1924	Arthur Perdue buys leghorn roosters for $25.
1950s	Adopts the company logo of a chick under a magnifying glass.
1984	Frank Perdue attends Philip Crosby's Quality College.
1985	Perdue recognized for its pursuit of quality in A Passion for Excellence. 200 Perdue managers attend Quality College. Adopted the Quality Improvement Process (QIP).
1986	Established Corrective Action Teams (CATs).
1987	Established Quality Training for all associates. Implemented Error Cause Removal Process (ECR).
1988	Steering Committee formed.
1989	First Annual Quality Conference held. Implemented Team Management.
1990	Second Annual Quality Conference held. Codified values and corporate mission.
1991	Third Annual Quality Conference held. Customer satisfaction defined.
1992	Fourth annual Quality Conference held."How to" implement customer satisfaction explained for team leaders and QITs.

via its own trucking fleet, and marketing. Improvements were measured in fractional cents per pound. Ways were found to minimize waste. Chicken feet that once had been thrown away were being processed and sold in the Orient as a barroom delicacy.

Frank's knowledge of details was also legendary. He not only impressed people in the poultry industry but those in others as well. At the end of one day, the managers and engineers of a new Grumman plant in Salisbury, Maryland, were reviewing their progress. Through the door unannounced came Frank Perdue. The Grumman managers proceeded to give Frank a tour of the plant. One machine was an ink-jet printer that labeled parts as they passed. Frank said he believed he had some of those in his plants. He paused for a minute and then he asked them if it clogged often. They responded yes. Frank exclaimed excitedly, "I am sure that I got some of those!" To promote attention to detail, eight measurable items—hatchability, turnover, feed conversion, livability, yield, birds per man-hour, utilization, and grade—were tracked.

Frank Perdue credited much of his success to listening to others. He agreed with Tom Peters that "Nobody knows a person's 20 square feet better than the person who works there." To facilitate the transmission of ideas through the organization, the company was undertaking a cultural transformation, beginning with Frank (Exhibit 3). He described the transition from the old to the new culture and himself as follows:

> We also learned that *loud and noisy* were worth a lot more than mugs and pens. What I mean by this is, we used to spend a lot of time calling companies to get trinkets as gifts. Gradually, we learned that money and trinkets weren't what really motivated people. We learned that when a man or woman on the line is going all out to do a good job, that he or she doesn't care that much about a trinket of some sort; what they really want is for the manager to get up from behind his desk, walk over to them and, in front of their peers, give them a hearty and sincere "thank you."
>
> When we give recognition now, we do it when there's an audience and lots of peers can see. This is, I can tell you, a lot more motivating than the "kick in the butt," that was part of the old culture—*and I was the most guilty!*"

Changing the behavioral pattern from writing-up people who did something wrong to recognizing people for doing their job well still produced some setbacks. For example, the company started what it called the "Good Egg Award," which was good

Exhibit 3   Culture Change at Perdue Farms

New Culture

1. Team management
2. Focused message from senior management
3. Long-range planning
4. Expanded commitment to quality
5. Focus on people, products, and profitability
6. Recognition is a way of life
7. Commitment to training
8. Long-term productivity improvements
9. Continuous improvement
10. Delighted customers

Old Culture

1. Top-down management
2. Poor communications
3. Short-term planning
4. Commitment to quality
5. Profitability focus
6. Limited associate recognition
7. Limited associate training
8. Short-term cost reduction
9. Annual goals as end target
10. Satisfied customers

for a free lunch. Managers in the Salisbury plant were all trained and asked to distribute the awards by "catching" someone doing a good job. When the program manager checked with the cafeteria the following week to see how many had been claimed, the answer was none. A meeting of the managers was called to see how many had been handed out. The answer was none. When the managers were asked what they had done with their award certificates, the majority replied they were in their shirt pockets. A goal was set for all managers to hand out five a week.

The following week, the program manager still found that very few were being turned in for a free lunch. When employees were asked what they had done with their awards, they replied that they had framed them and hung them up on walls at home or put them in trophy cases. The program was changed so that the "Good Egg Award" consisted of both a certificate and a ticket for a free lunch.

Perdue also implemented a suggestion program called "Error Cause Removal." It averaged better than one submission per year per three employees. Although that was much less than the 22 suggestions per employee per year of companies in Japan, it was significantly better than the national average in the United States of one per year per five employees. According to Frank Perdue, "We're 'one up' . . . because with the help of the quality improvement process and the help of our associates, we have *thousands* of 'better minds' helping us."

MANAGEMENT INFORMATION SYSTEMS (MIS)

In 1989, Perdue Farms employed 118 IS people who spent 146 hours per week on IS maintenance—"fix it" jobs. By 1994 the entire department consisted of only 50 associates who spent a total of 52 hours per week fixing problems and 94 percent of their time building new systems or reengineering old ones. Moreover, a six-year backlog of projects had been eliminated and the average "build-it" cost for a project had dropped from $1,950 to $568—an overall 300 percent increase in efficiency.

According to Don Taylor, director of MIS, this was the payoff from a significant management reorientation. A key philosophy was that a fix-it mentality was counterproductive. MIS personnel were now being asked to determine the root cause of the problem and reengineer the program to eliminate future problems.

Developer–user partnerships—including a monthly payback system—were developed with five functional groups: sales and marketing, finance and human resources, logistics, quality assurance, and fresh-poultry and plant systems. Each has an assigned number of IS hours per month and defines its own priorities, permitting it to function as a customer.

In addition, a set of critical success factors (CSFs) were developed. These included the following: (1) automation is never the first step in a project—it occurs only after superfluous business processes are eliminated and necessary ones simplified; (2) senior management sponsorship—vice presidents for the business units must sponsor major projects in their area; (3) limited size, duration, and scope—IS has found that small projects have more success and a cumulative bigger payoff than big ones, so all major projects are broken into 3- to 6-month segments with separate deliverables and benefits; (4) precise definition of requirements—the team must determine up front exactly what the project will accomplish; and (5) there must be commitment of both the IS staff and the customer to work as a team.

Management considers IS key to the operation of its business. For example, IS developed a customer ordering system for the centralized sales office (CSO). This system automated key business processes that link Perdue with its customers. The CSO has 13 applications, including order entry, product transfers, sales allocations, production scheduling, and credit management.

In taking orders, a Perdue salesperson negotiates the specifics of the sale directly with the buyer in the grocery chain. Next, the salesperson sends the request to a dispatcher, who determines where the various products are located and designates a specific truck to make the required pickups and delivery, all within the designated one-hour delivery window that has been granted by the grocery chain. Each truck is even equipped with a small satellite dish that is connected to the LAN so that a trucker on the New Jersey Turnpike headed for New York can call for a replacement tractor if his rig breaks down.

Obviously, a computer malfunction has potential for disaster. Four hours of downtime are equivalent to $6.2 million in lost sales. Thus, Perdue has back-up systems and processes in place to avoid such problems. In addition to maximizing on-time delivery, the system gives the salespeople more time to discuss wants and needs with customers, handle customer relations, and resolve key marketing issues such as Perdue shelf space and location.

On the other hand, management had learned that computer automation is not the answer to all problems. For example, it was decided that electronic monitoring in the poultry houses was counterproductive and not cost-effective. While it was possible to develop systems to monitor and control almost every facet of the chicken house environment, management was concerned that doing so would weaken the invaluable link between the farmer and the livestock—the belief was that poultry producers need to be personally involved with conditions in the chicken house in order to maximize quality and spot problems or health challenges as soon as possible.

RESEARCH AND DEVELOPMENT ───────────────

The company is an acknowledged industry leader in the use of technology to provide quality products and service to its customers. A list of some of its technological accomplishments is given in Exhibit 4. As with everything else he did, Frank Perdue has tried to leave nothing to chance. Perdue employs 25 people full time in the industry's largest research and development effort, including five with graduate degrees. It has specialists in avian science, microbiology, genetics, nutrition, and veterinary science. Because of its research and development capabilities, the company is often involved in USDA field tests with pharmaceutical suppliers. Knowledge and experience gained from these tests hold the potential for competitive advantage. For example, Perdue Farms has the most extensive and expensive vaccination program among its breeders in the industry. As a result, Perdue growers raise more disease resistant chickens and have one of the lowest mortality rates in the industry.

According to Dr. Mac Terzich, veterinarian and laboratory manager, Perdue management has really pushed for creativity and innovation. Currently, the company works with and studies some European producers who use different operating methods.

HUMAN RESOURCE MANAGEMENT ──────────────

When entering the Human Resource department at Perdue Farms, the first thing one sees is a prominently displayed set of human resource corporate strategic goals (see Exhibit 5). Besides these human resource corporate strategic goals, Perdue sets annual company goals that deal with "people." FY 1995's strategic people goals centered on providing a safe, secure, and productive work environment. The specific goals were included on the wallet-size, fold-up card mentioned earlier (see Exhibit 1).

Strategic human resource planning was still developing at Perdue Farms. According to Tom Moyers, vice president for Human Resource Management, "Every department in the company has a mission statement or policy which has been developed within the past 18 months . . . Department heads are free to update their goals as they see fit . . . Initial strategic human resource plans are developed by teams of three or four associates . . . These teams meet once or twice a year companywide to review where we stand in terms of meeting our objectives."

To keep associates informed about company plans, Perdue Farms holds "state of the business meetings" for all interested associates twice a year. For example, during May 1994, five separate meetings were held near various plants in Delmarva, the Carolinas, Virginia, and Indiana. Typically, a local auditorium is rented, overhead slides are prepared, and the company's progress toward its goals and its financial status is shared with its associates. Discussion revolves around what is wrong and what is right about the company. New product lines are reviewed with those attending, and opportunities for improvement are discussed.

Upon joining Perdue Farms, each new associate attends an extensive orientation that begins with a thorough review of the "Perdue Associate Handbook." The handbook details Perdue's philosophy on quality, employee relations, drugs and alcohol, and its code of ethics. The orientation also includes a thorough discussion of the Perdue benefit plans. Fully paid benefits for all associates include (1) paid vacation, (2) eight official paid holidays, (3) health, accident, disability, and life

Exhibit 4   Perdue Farms Inc. Technological Accomplishments

- Breeds chickens with 15 percent more breast meat.
- First to use digital scales to guarantee weights to customers.
- First to package fully cooked chicken products on microwaveable trays.
- First to have a box lab to compare quality of boxes from different suppliers.
- First to test both its chickens and competitors' chickens on 52 quality factors every week.
- Improved on-time deliveries 20 percent between 1987 and 1993.

Exhibit 5   Human Resource Corporate Strategic Goals

- Provide leadership to the corporation in all aspects of human resources, including safety, recruitment and retention of associates, training and development, employee relations, compensation, benefits, communication, security, medical, housekeeping, and food services.
- Provide leadership and assistance to management at all levels in communicating and implementing company policy to ensure consistency and compliance with federal, state, and local regulations.
- Provide leadership and assistance to management in maintaining a socially responsible community image in all of our Perdue communities by maintaining positive community relations and encouraging Perdue associates to be active in their community.
- Provide leadership and assistance to management in creating an environment wherein all associates can contribute to the overall success of the company.
- Be innovative and cost efficient in developing, implementing, and providing to all associates systems which will reward performance, encourage individual growth, and recognize contribution to the corporation.

insurance, (4) savings and pension plans, (5) funeral leave, and (6) jury duty leave. The company also offers a scholarship program for children of Perdue associates.

Special arrangements can be made with the individual's immediate supervisor for a leave of absence of up to 12 months in case of extended nonjob-related illness or injury, birth or adoption of a child, care of a spouse or other close relative, or other personal situations. Although the Family and Medical Leave Act of 1993 was opposed by many companies because its requirements went well beyond the benefit packages they currently offered their employees, it had little impact on Perdue Farms since existing leave of absence policies were already more generous than the new Federal law required.

Perdue Farms is a nonunion employer. The firm has had a long-standing open door policy, and managers are expected to be easily accessible to other associates, whatever the person's concern. The open door policy is supplemented by a formal peer review process. While associates are expected to discuss problems with their supervisors first, they are urged to pursue peer review of supervisory decisions if they remain dissatisfied.

Wages and salaries, which are reviewed at least once a year, are determined by patterns in the poultry industry and the particular geographic location of the plant. Changes in the general economy and the state of the business are also considered.

Informal comparisons of turnover statistics among poultry producers indicate that Perdue Farms' turnover numbers are among the lowest in the industry. Perdue also benchmarked workers' compensation claims with its competitors, and its incidence rates (for accidents) are also among the lowest in the industry. Supervisors initially train and coach all new associates about the proper way to do their jobs. Once trained, the philosophy is that all associates are professionals and, as such, should make suggestions about how to make their jobs even more efficient and effective. After a 60-day employment trial, the associate is awarded seniority based on the starting date of employment. Seniority is the determining factor in promotions where qualifications (skill, proficiency, dependability, work record) are equal. Also, when the workforce needs to be reduced, seniority is used as the determining factor in layoffs.

A form of management by objectives (MBO) is used for annual performance appraisal and planning review. The format involves a four-step process:

1. Establish accountability, goals, standards of performance, and their relative weights for the review period.
2. Conduct coaching sessions throughout the review period, and document these discussions.
3. Evaluate performance at the end of the review period, and conduct appraisal interview.
4. Undertake next review period planning.

The cornerstones of human resources development includes extensive training and management development plus intensive succession planning and career pathing. The essence of the company's approach to human resource management is captured in Frank Perdue's statement:

> We have gotten where we are because we have believed in hiring our own people and training them in our own way. We believe in promotion from within, going outside only when we feel it is absolutely necessary—for expertise and sometimes because our company was simply growing faster than our people development program. The number one item in our success has been the quality of our people.

FINANCE

Perdue Farms Inc. is a privately held firm and considers financial information to be proprietary. Hence, available data is limited. The majority of the stock is owned by the family and a limited amount by Perdue management. Industry observers pegged Perdue Farm's revenues for 1994 at about $1.5 billion and the number of associates at 13,800.

The firm's compound sales growth rate slowly decreased during the past 20 years, mirroring the industry, which was experiencing market saturation and overproduction. However, Perdue had compensated for slower industry growth by stressing increased labor productivity to enhance its competitiveness and boost revenues. For example, in the early 1970s, a 1 percent increase in associates resulted in a 1.3 percent increase in revenue. In 1994, a 1 percent increase in associates resulted in a 2.5 percent increase in revenues (see Exhibit 6).

Perdue Farms has three operating divisions: Retail Chicken (62 percent of sales—growth rate 5 percent), Foodservice Chicken and Turkey (20 percent of sales—growth rate 12 percent), and Grain and Oilseed (18 percent of sales—growth rate 10 percent). Thus, the bulk of sales came from the sector—retail chicken—with the slowest growth rate. Part of the reason for the company's slow sales growth in retail chicken sales

Exhibit 6	Perdue Farms' Annual Compound Growth Rate in Revenues and Associates	
	Revenue Growth	**Associate Growth**
Past 20 years	13%	10%
Past 15 years	11	8
Past 10 years	9	5
Past 5 years	5	2

stemmed from Perdue Farm's policy of selling only fresh—never frozen—chicken. This limited the company's markets to cities that could be serviced overnight by truck from production facility locations—New York, Boston, Philadelphia, Baltimore, and Washington, D.C.—which were pretty well saturated. (Other cities where sales were being pursued included Chicago, Cleveland, Atlanta, Pittsburgh, and Miami.) On the other hand, the company's foodservice and grain and oilseed divisions had no such distance constraints and could serve customers nationwide as well as export customers in Eastern Europe, China, Japan, and South America.

Perdue Farms had been profitable every year since its founding with the exception of 1988. Company officials believed the loss in 1988 was caused by a decentralization effort begun during the early 80s. At that time, there was a concerted effort to push decisions down through the corporate ranks to provide more autonomy. When the new strategy resulted in higher costs, Frank Perdue responded quickly by returning to the basics, reconsolidating, and downsizing. In 1994 the goal was to constantly streamline and protect profit margins with continuous improvements in efficiency.

Perdue Farms had a conservative approach to financial management, using retained earnings and cash flow to finance asset replacement projects and normal growth. Long-term debt was used to fund expansion projects or acquisitions. The target debt limit was 55 percent of equity. Debt financing was normally provided by domestic and international bank and insurance companies. The debt strategy was to match asset lives with liability maturities and have a mix of fixed rate and variable rate debt. Management believed that it took about $1 in new investment capital to fund $2 in new revenue growth.

THE U.S. POULTRY INDUSTRY

U.S. per capita consumption of poultry had risen dramatically during the past 40 years, from 26.3 pounds per year in 1950 to almost 80 pounds in 1990. Consumption continued to grow through 1993, according to a broiler industry survey of the largest integrated broiler companies. Production of ready-to-cook chicken increased 5.8 percent in 1991, 5.3 percent in 1992, and 6.0 percent in 1993 to 476 million pounds per week.

Recent growth stemmed largely from consumers moving away from red meat due to health concerns and the industry's continued development of ready-to-serve products such as precooked or roasted chicken and chicken parts. Unfortunately, recent sales growth had not been accompanied by higher profits due to chronic overcapacity throughout the industry that has pushed down wholesale prices. The industry had experienced cyclical troughs before and experts expected future improvement in both sales and profits. Still, razor-thin margins required producers to pursue absolute efficiency.

Fifty-four integrated broiler companies have accounted for approximately 99 percent of ready-to-cook production in the United States. While slow consolidation of the industry appeared to be taking place, it was still necessary to include 22 companies to get to 80 percent of production. Concentration had been fastest among the top four producers. For example, since 1986, market share of the top four had grown from 35 to 40.5 percent (see Exhibit 7).

Although the Delmarva Peninsula (home of Perdue Farms Inc.) has long been considered the birthplace of the commercial broiler industry, recent production gains have been most rapid in the Southeast. Arkansas, Georgia, and Alabama were the largest poultry producing states—a result of abundant space and inexpensive labor. The Southeast accounted for approximately 50 percent of the $20 billion U.S. chicken industry, employing 125,000 across the region. Still, Delmarva chicken products accounted for about 10 percent of all broilers grown in the United States. This was due largely to the region's proximity to Washington, D.C., Baltimore, Philadelphia, New York, and Boston. Each weekday, more than 200 tractor-trailers loaded with fresh-dressed poultry left the Delmarva area headed for these metropolitan markets.

Eight integrated companies operated 10 feed mills, 15 hatcheries, and 13 processing plants on Delmarva, employing approximately 22,000 people and producing approximately 10 million broilers each week (see Exhibit 8).

THE FUTURE

Considering Americans' average annual consumption of chicken (almost 80 pounds annually per person in 1990), many in the industry wondered how much growth was left. For example, after wholesale prices climbed from 14 cents per pound in 1960 to 34 cents per pound in 1990, the recession and a general glut in the market caused prices to fall back (see Exhibit 9). In real terms, the price of chicken was at an all-time low in 1994. A pound of chicken was down from costing 30 minutes of an average worker's 1940 wage to costing only 4.5 minutes of a 1990 wage.

While the low prices were partly justified by improved production efficiencies, prices in 1994 were clearly depressed because of continuing overcapacity in the industry. In 1992, ConAgra, Inc., temporarily stopped sending chicks to 30 Delmarva growers to prevent an oversupply of chickens, and several chicken companies started to experiment with producing other kinds of meats—from pork to striped bass—to utilize excess processing capability.[3]

Consumer demand was shifting away from whole chickens to skinless, boneless parts. Perdue had responded with its line of "Fit 'n Easy" products with detailed nutrition labeling. It was also developing exports of dark meat to Puerto Rico and chicken feet to China. Fresh young turkey and turkey parts had become an important product, and the "Perdue Done it!" line had been expanded to include fully cooked roasted broilers and Cornish hens and parts. Recently, the company expanded its lines to include ground chicken and turkey sausage.

Frank Perdue reflected recently that "we have a very high share of the available supermarket business in the Middle Atlantic and Northeastern United States, and if

---

[3]Kim Clark, "Tender Times: Is Sky Falling on Chicken Boom?" *The Sun*, July 4, 1993, p. 4F.

Exhibit 7 Top Four Broiler Companies in the U.S., 1993*

	Million Head	Million Pounds
1. Tyson Foods, Inc.	26.50	84.15
2. ConAgra, Inc.	11.25	40.53
3. Gold Kist, Inc.	12.60	39.70
4. Perdue Farms Inc.	7.51	28.28

* Based on average weekly slaughter; *Broiler Industry Survey*, 1993.

Exhibit 8 Integrated Broiler Producers Operating on Delmarva Peninsula*

	National Rank
1. Tyson Foods, Inc.	1
2. ConAgra, Inc.	2
3. Perdue Farms Inc. (Headquarters in Salisbury, Maryland)	4
4. Hudson Foods, Inc.	7
5. Townsend, Inc. (Headquarters in Millsboro, Delaware)	9
6. Showell Farms, Inc. (Headquarters in Showell, Maryland)	10
7. Allen Family Foods, Inc. (Headquarters in Seaford, Delaware)	17
8. Mountaire Farms of Delmarva, Inc. (Headquarters in Selbyville, Delaware)	28

*Delmarva Poultry Industry, Inc., 1993 fact sheets.

we were to follow that course which we know best—selling to the consumer through the retailer—we'd have to consider the Upper Midwest—Pittsburgh, Chicago, Detroit, with 25 to 30 million people."

PUBLIC SOURCES OF INFORMATION

Barmash, Isadore. "Handing Off to the Next Generation." *New York Times*, July 26, 1992, Business, p. 1.

Bates, Eric, and Bob Hall. "Ruling the Roost." *Southern Exposure*, Summer 1989, p. 11.

Clark, Kim. "Tender Times: Is Sky Falling on the Chicken Boom?" *The Sun*, July 4, 1993, p. 4F/Business.

"Facts about the DelMarVa Broiler Industry—1973." Industry Bulletin, Feb. 25, 1974.

"Facts about the DelMarVa Poultry Industry," DelMarVa Poultry Industry, Inc., July 28, 1994.

Fahy, Joe. "All Pain, No Gain." *Southern Exposure*, Summer 1989, pp. 35–39.

Flynn, Ramsey. "Strange Bird." *The Washingtonian*, December 1989, p. 165.

Gale, Bradley T. "Quality Comes First When Hatching Power Brands." *Planning Review*, July–August, 1992, pp. 4–48.

"Golden Jubilee! Company Honors Frank Perdue for His 50 Years of Service." *Perdue Courier (Special Edition)*, July 1989.

Goldoftas, Barbara. "Inside the Slaughterhouse." *Southern Exposure*, Summer 1989, pp. 25–29.

Hall, Bob. "Chicken Empires." *Southern Exposure*, Summer 1989, pp. 12–19.

"In the Money: Downhome Retailer Is Nation's Richest, Forbes Says." *The Washington Post*, October 14, 1986.

MacPherson, Myra. "Chicken Big." *The Washington Post, Potomac Magazine*, May 11, 1975, p. 15.

"Perdue Chicken Spreads Its Wings." *Business Week*, September 16, 1972, p. 113.

Perdue Farms Incorporated—Historical Highlights. Perdue Farms publication, September 1992.

Perdue, Frank. Speech at Babson College, April 28, 1981.

Perdue, Frank. Speech to firm's lenders, accountants, and Perdue Associates, September 1991.

Exhibit 9 · Price per Pound of Live Broilers as Received by Farmers

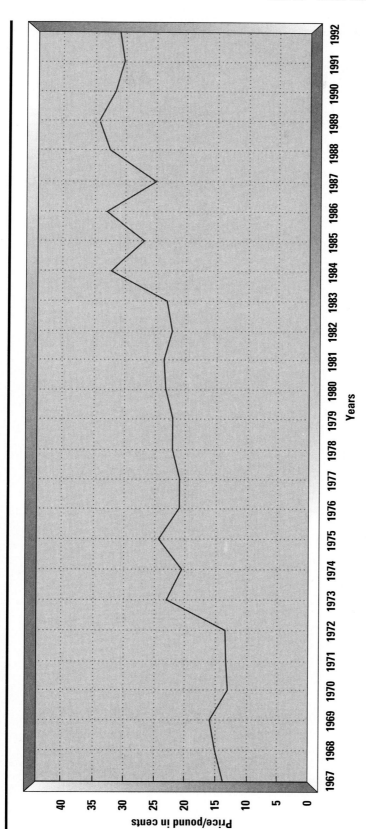

Poultry Industry file—miscellaneous newspaper clippings from 1950 to 1994. The Maryland Room, Blackwell Library, Salisbury State University.

Santosus, Megan. "Perdue's New Pecking Orders." *CIO*, March 1993, pp, 60–68.

Scarupa, Henry. "When Is a Chicken Not a Football?" *The (Baltimore) Sun Magazine*, March 4, 1973, pp. 5–12.

"Silent Millionaires in America." *Economist* 270, no. 7072, March 17, 1979.

Sterling, Bill. "Just Browsin' " *Eastern Shore News*, March 2, 1988.

"The Perdue Story: And the Five Reasons Why Our Consumers Tell It Best." Perdue Farms Inc. Publication, October 1991.

Thornton, Gary. "Data from Broiler Industry," Elanco Poultry Team, partner with the Poultry Industry, December 1993.

Yeoman, Barry. "Don't Count Your Chickens." *Southern Exposure*, Summer 1989, pp. 21–24.

Carmike Cinemas, Inc., in 1995

Tracy Robertson Kramer, George Mason University
Marilyn L. Taylor, University of Missouri at Kansas City

During the spring of 1995, Michael W. Patrick, the 45-year-old president and chief executive officer of Carmike Cinemas, Inc., sat before the blinking computer screen in his office evaluating the performance of the company's 445 theaters. During his 13 years as president of the company, Patrick had been the driving force behind the company's explosive growth. The company had grown from 265 screens and total annual revenues of $47 million in 1982 to 1,942 screens and $327 million in 1994. In 1995, about 45 percent of the movie screens in the United States were operated by the 10 largest theater companies (see Exhibit 1). Carmike was the second-largest theater chain in the United States, with 2,035 screens.

The company was formed during a leveraged buyout led by Mike Patrick's father in 1982. In 1986, the Patrick family took the company public. The company completed its initial public offering coincident with its first sizable acquisition, the Essantee Theater chain, which added 209 screens in Virginia and the Carolinas. Its stock was initially traded on the NASDAQ over-the-counter market but moved to trading on the New York Stock Exchange in December 1992.

Mike Patrick had been uncertain about taking the company public, fearing the scrutiny by stockholders would limit his ability to take risks and manage the company as he saw best:

> I have to know where my capital is. I run this company from this book containing every financial thing you want to know about Carmike—construction coming up, everything we are going to spend, sources of cash, where it's going to go, everything. One of the critical things we are thinking about is how to expand. I know that if business goes bad, within 90 days, three or four more circuits are going to come up for sale. I must be in a position to buy them and I must have the knowledge to do it with. I will not bet the store on any deal.

Despite Patrick's wariness, the company did not come under the spotlight of unhappy shareholder scrutiny. Stockholders' equity increased from $50 million in 1991 to nearly $172 million in 1994. Exhibit 2 summarizes the company's performance from 1988 through 1994. The company was not without its detractors, however. Some cited Carmike's highly leveraged position as a cause for concern (see Exhibit 2 for financial highlights of Carmike Cinemas). Others were not pleased with the company's policy of not paying dividends and plowing all earnings into the expansion of the business. Additionally, there was the concern that the market was already saturated with theater screens and that growth could not continue.

Mike Patrick was less worried about shareholder concerns than he was about the future of the industry, since the Patrick family collectively had about 70 percent of the voting stock through ownership of 100 percent of the company's 10 votes per share of class B stock. Additionally, the company's stock value had steadily increased over the

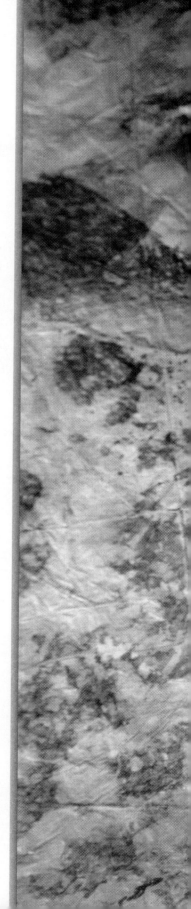

Exhibit 1   Largest Theater Chains in the United States and Canada, 1994

Rank	Chain	Parent Company	Number of Screens
1	United Artists*	United Artists Theater Circuits, Inc.	2,204
2	Carmike Cinemas	Carmike Cinemas, Inc.	2,035
3	Cineplex Odeon†	Cineplex Odeon Corp.	1,643
4	American Multi-Cinema	AMC Entertainment	1,636
5	General Cinema Theatres	GC Companies	1,221
6	Cinemark‡	Cinemark USA	1,214
7	Sony Theaters	Sony Corp.	912
8	National Amusements§	National Amusements, Inc.	848
9	Regal Cinemas	Regal Cinemas, Inc.	722
10	Act III Theaters	Act III Communications	568
11	Hoyts	Hoyts Corp.	519
12	Famous Players‖	Viacom Inc.	441
13	Cinamerica Theatres L.P.	Viacom Inc. and Time Warner	341

* Includes some screens in Hong Kong.

† About 43 percent owned by Matsushita Electric Industrial Co. Ltd. Includes about 575 screens in Canada.

‡ May include some theaters outside of the United States and Canada.

§ Includes some screens in the United Kingdom.

‖ All screens located in Canada.

Sources: *Hollywood Reporter, Variety;* Dow Jones; company reports.

years (see Exhibit 3). However, sustaining Carmike's growth in a flat market was getting harder to achieve. The company was experimenting with a new source of revenue—a joint venture in which Carmike would receive annual fees for managing a chain of theaters. There was the possibility that this arrangement would lead to similar deals in the future, but Patrick was always searching for new opportunities for Carmike Cinemas.

In sizing up the industry, Patrick provided the following observations:

We compete with other theaters, of course, but we also compete for the entertainment dollar, especially against other movie related businesses such as cable direct TV, HBO, videocassette rentals, and so on. We must differentiate our product from these ancillary markets as much as possible by building theater auditoriums and installing the newest digital sound equipment. We want to make going to the movies an event. The public does not want to stay home and people are looking for ways to spend their entertainment dollar. Competition from the ancillary markets does take away some of our patrons. On the other hand, it also helps pay for the costs of making these movies because the revenues generated from cable showings, rentals, and tape sales put more money back into Hollywood and stimulate additional movie production. The ancillary markets, along with the "electronic highway," are giving studios more outlets for their products, so for the first time, the theaters are not having to pay for the entire cost of a movie. This is having two positive effects. One, more movies are being made, and two, if a movie is just so-so at the theaters it still has a chance of breaking even or making a little money when revenues from all the viewing categories are added up. All this makes the motion picture studios more financially sound.

As far as other theater circuits are concerned, there will always be competition from specific locations but there are no other circuits with our strategy of

Exhibit 2   Selected Financial Data, 1988–1994   *(in thousands, except per share data)*

	Years Ended December 31						
	1994	**1993**	**1992**	**1991**	**1990**	**1989**	**1988**
Income Statement Data							
Revenues:							
Admissions	$232,134	$167,294	$119,408	$ 99,110	$ 86,378	$ 64,996	$ 54,973
Concessions	95,485	74,504	52,570	46,686	41,042	34,448	29,503
Total revenues	327,619	241,798	171,978	145,796	127,420	99,444	84,476
Costs and expenses:							
Cost of operations	254,756	186,778	135,204	113,000	97,582	73,391	64,010
General and administrative	5,092	4,710	3,897	3,828	3,674	3,239	3,126
Depreciation and amortization	22,544	16,255	11,134	9,437	7,612	5,342	5,664
Total operating expenses	282,392	207,713	150,235	126,265	108,868	81,972	72,800
Operating income	45,227	34,055	21,743	19,531	18,552	17,472	11,676
Interest expense:	17,028	14,282	11,623	9,914	8,038	6,927	6,312
Income before income taxes	28,199	19,773	10,120	9,617	10,514	10,545	5,364
Income taxes	11,246	7,912	4,008	3,902	4,221	4,304	2,044
Net income	$ 16,953	$ 12,251	$ 6,112	$ 5,715	$ 6,293	$ 6,241	$ 3,320
Earnings per common share:	$ 2.00	$ 1.50	$ 0.80	$ 0.75	$ 0.84	$ 1.22	$ 0.66
Balance Sheet Data							
Cash and equivalents	$ 17,872	$ 10,649	$ 16,842	$ 9,528	$ 17,762	$ 2,470	$ 2,496
Total assets	377,598	327,024	230,291	184,085	178,670	134,895	111,779
Total long-term debt	158,434	193,120	120,234	91,605	94,022	59,105	45,093
Convertible subordinated debenture	3,051	2,819	0	0	0	25,999	26,000
Shareholders' equity	$171,956	$ 93,856	$ 75,728	$ 69,177	$ 63,329	$ 32,770	$ 26,034

specializing in noncompetitive secondary markets. No other circuits have an internal computer system like our IQ-Zero, which allows us to operate with a small local staff, as well as lower home office costs. This gives us a great advantage over other theater chains.

The multiplex theater offers the public a variety of movies to view. We have two types of patrons. There's the movie buff who has to see a movie the first week it opens. High profile hits will bring these patrons out in droves. Then there are patrons who go to the movies when they have the time, and the multiplex allows us to hold a movie for four to six weeks, so that it will be there when they decide to take in a movie. Movies such as *Bridges of Madison County* will hold well but will never give us the opening grosses that a *Batman Forever* or *Pocahontas* will. We have to be able to attract both types of patrons in our small markets as well as our large markets.

THE EARLY YEARS

Carmike Cinemas' origins stem from Martin Theaters, a circuit that was founded in 1912 by the Martin family. Carl L. Patrick joined Martin Theaters in 1945 and was instrumental in the company's growth. In 1969, Martin Theaters was acquired by

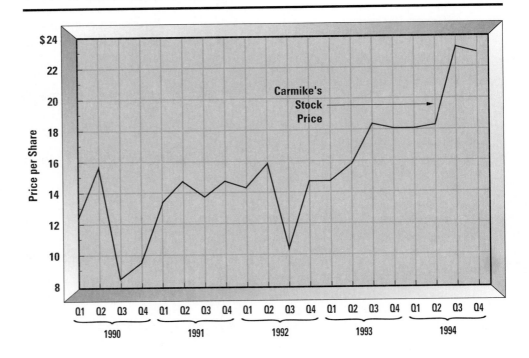

Exhibit 3 Carmike Cinemas Stock Value, 1990–1994

Fuqua Industries, a diversified company based in Atlanta. Patrick served as president of Fuqua from 1970 to 1978 and as vice chairman of the board of directors of Fuqua from 1978 to 1983. Carmike—named for Patrick's two sons, Carl, Jr., and Michael—was created in 1982 when Carl Patrick, Sr., led a leveraged buyout and acquired the 265-screen Martin Theaters from Fuqua for $25 million.

Even though financing arrangements for purchasing Martin Theaters were very favorable, the purchase of the theaters was highly leveraged. Early efforts were directed toward improving the company's cash flow to reduce outstanding debt. At the same time, the company had significant capital improvement requirements. To make the venture viable, the Patricks undertook a number of changes in operations. Success was by no means assured, as Mike Patrick explained:

> When we bought Martin, Martin was going downhill. It looked bad. And I want you to know that it looked pretty bad for us for a while. I mean it really did. For a while there we were asking ourselves, "Why are we in this mess?" Not only were we leveraged 100 percent, but we realized that we had to spend some-where in the neighborhood of $25 million more to renew the company.

At the time they purchased the Martin Theater circuit, the Patricks were well aware that some of the theaters were losing money and that many of Martin's facilities were becoming outmoded. A 1981 consulting report on Martin underscored that during the 1970s Martin had not aggressively moved to multiplexing. In addition, one of the previous presidents had put a number of theaters into "B-locations" where there were "great leases . . . but the theaters were off the beaten track." Mike Patrick explained the approach he took to pulling off a turnaround:

I looked at all the markets we were in, the big markets where the money was to be made, and I said, "Here's what we will do. First, let's take the losers and make them profitable." At the time the losing theaters were a $1.2 million deficit on the bottom line. So I decided to experiment . . . Phenix City is a perfect example. I took the admission price from $3.75 to $0.99. Everybody said I was a fool. The first year it made $70,000 which I thought was a great increase over the $26,000 it had been making. The next year what happened was—the people in Phenix City are poor, very poor, blue-collar workers, but the theater is as nice as anything I have over here in Columbus—so as word of mouth got going, it kept getting better and better. Now it sells out every Friday, Saturday, and Sunday. And I still charge $0.99. That theater today makes over $200,000 a year.

As Patrick put it, the conversion to dollar theaters was "a new concept. No one else is doing that." By 1986, Carmike had 20 99-cent theaters. The company also offered a discount in admission prices on Tuesdays and discount ticket plans to groups. Two facilities called "Flick 'n' Foam" had restaurants and bar services in the theater.

CARMIKE CINEMAS' MARKET FOCUS

Carmike targeted secondary markets, small cities and towns with populations between 40,000 and 200,000 people. Unlike rivals Cineplex Odeon and AMC Entertainment, which focused on populated metropolitan areas, Carmike located its facilities where competition, if it existed at all, was less intense, overhead expenses were lower, and profit margins wider. The company was the sole theater operator in 55 percent of its locations and the dominant operator in another 25 percent. According to Mike Patrick, "Our goal is to dominate the second-tier cities, areas with populations of 100,000 to 250,000 . . . We think there is a lot of opportunity in these markets."[1] Carmike's strategy of avoiding locations in the urban areas preferred by rival theater chains had resulted in Carmike being labeled by *Forbes* as "a Wal-Mart for the movies."

As potential markets for expansion, Carmike managers targeted rural communities that had insufficient screens (usually fewer than one for every 10,000 persons) with older, deteriorated facilities that lacked customer appeal. Once an area was identified, the company would either buy out the existing theaters at bargain-basement prices or construct new state-of-the-art facilities with 5 to 11 screens adjoining a popular shopping complex to outcompete the local theater rival.

With this approach, Carmike was able to realize several advantages, not the least of which was reduced competition. "Many of the towns we're going into are so small that once we're there, there won't be any potential for other chains," said Mike Patrick.[2] In fact, Patrick referred to his major competition in most markets as the local Friday night high school football game.

Carmike Cinemas' small-town strategy also allowed it to blunt the bargaining power of film producers. Theater revenues were film product–driven—that is, they were dependent on commercially successful "hit" movies being available from major film

---

[1]*Forbes*, August 22, 1988, p. 60.
[2]Ibid., p. 61.

producers. Typical film cost arrangements called for the film distributor to receive approximately 70 percent of the film's gross box office receipts in its first week, 60 percent in the second week, and so on down to about 30 percent in the subsequent weeks. Ideally, the film would draw large audiences for several weeks, increasing the theater's revenues. Carmike's theaters, because of their less competitive rural locations, often were able to schedule longer runs of each film, thereby capturing a bigger overall percentage of ticket revenues.

In 1980, the number of theater screens in the United States was 17,675; this number had increased to over 26,000 by 1994. However, the average number of hit films had not increased nor had the number of moviegoers. Film makers were able to use the rising demand of theater owners for films to show on the expanding number of screens to increase their take of the box office gross and to force theaters to bid against one another for first rights to exhibit hit movies. Since negotiations for film exhibition privileges took place city by city, large theater chains had no special advantages over chains with few theater locations in bargaining with film makers for first-run hits. Carmike, as the sole or dominant player in most of its markets, was less vulnerable to the threat that film makers would bid up the fees by offering the first-run rights to Carmike rivals.

CARMIKE CINEMAS' GROWTH AND ACQUISITIONS

In only 12 years, Carmike Cinemas grew from 265 screens in 1982 to 2,035 screens in early 1995. In 1982, Martin Theaters was the seventh-largest U.S. theater circuit; in 1994, Carmike was the second-largest motion picture exhibitor, operating 445 theaters in 31 states with approximately 8,000 employees. Headquartered in Columbus, Georgia, the company's theaters were located primarily in the Southeast, the Midwest, and the West—see Exhibit 4. Carmike Cinemas had achieved its 20 percent compound annual growth rate from 1982 through 1994 through a combination of acquisitions and construction. Nearly 84 percent of the growth was via acquisitions (see Exhibit 5). A chronological listing of Carmike's acquisition history is presented in Exhibit 6. The company acquired 224 screens in 1994 alone, and nearly 60 percent of all of acquisitions since the initial buyout had taken place in the last three years, several from financially struggling, large operators such as Cineplex Odeon and AMC Entertainment.

Mike Patrick was very candid about not overpaying for acquisitions. In fact, he negotiated the purchase of 96 screens in the Carolinas and Tennessee from Cineplex Odeon in 1990 based on six times the 1990 cash flow—approximately half the going rate in acquisitions by Cineplex. Mike Patrick talked about his acquisition strategy, beginning with the first acquisition of Video Independent Theaters, Inc., in 1983:

> During the 1970s Martin had not been aggressive. In our industry if you are not on the attack you are being attacked. Then you are subject to what the industry does. We believe in making things happen.
>
> Video was owned by a company which had bought Video for its cable rights. In the mid-1970s the management was killed in an air crash. I went up and talked to the guy in charge. He told me the parent company wasn't interested in theaters.
>
> The circuit had a lot of singles and some drive-ins. We borrowed $1 million as a down payment and the parent accepted a note for the remainder due in three equal yearly installments. Right off the bat, we sold two of the drive-ins

Exhibit 4   Partial Listing of Carmike Cinemas Theater Locations (eight most important states)

State	Theaters	Screens
North Carolina	84	295
Tennessee	46	213
Alabama	30	151
Texas	38	121
South Carolina	24	95
Georgia	16	66
Oklahoma	18	64
Virginia	10	43

Exhibit 5   Growth in Screens, 1982–1995

Screens at time of leveraged buyout, 1982	265
Acquisitions	1,096
Newly Constructed by Carmike	475
Disposed of/closed	199
Screens in operation as of June 1, 1995	2,035

for about $1.5 million and immediately paid back the down payment. We used the cash flow from the remaining theaters to meet the installment payments and the depreciation to rebuild the circuit.

In 1995, Carmike's acquisition strategy remained basically unchanged. Mike Patrick commented on how he targeted his acquisitions:

We have compiled a list of over 100 circuits in the United States. Some are as large as 2,000 screens and some as small as 25 screens. We've identified those that are owned by people who are nearing retirement or may have reasons to sell. Each owner or management team has its own goals and reasons for selling or disposing of a portion of their circuits. I am the number one person who follows companies' financial situations and I have a pretty good idea of which ones are going to be in financial trouble.

A few offers come our way but most of them we initiate or are brought to us by financial brokers. We have mapped the locations of most of the circuits and we know who fits the best regionally with our circuits.

In 1948, the Paramount Consent Degree made the Hollywood studios sell their theater chains. Many of these theaters were bought by individuals who are now reaching their mid-70s. If the owner does not have an heir who wants to run the circuit of theaters, then it's time for them to sell. We do get calls from families who are interested in selling, but most of our deals come from big circuits who have strategies that are different from Carmike or need the money. We have a good reputation which has paid off. We bought two groups of theaters from General Cinemas, one from United Artists, two from AMC, one from Loews, and three from Cineplex Odeon.

Exhibit 6   Carmike's Acquisitions, 1982–1994

		Number of Screens
1982	Martin Theaters, Inc.	265
1983	Video Independent Theaters, Inc.	85
1986	Essantee Theaters, Inc.	209
1989	Consolidated Theaters, Inc.	116
1990	Various theaters from United Artists and Plitt	137
1991	Various AMC theaters	45
1992	Various Plitt, AC, and Cinamerica theaters	150
1993	Westwynn Theatres, Inc.	355
	Manos Enterprises	80
1994	Various General Cinema theaters	48
	Cinema World	176

> We bought Consolidated Theatres and Excellence Theatres that were both in financial trouble, but we also buy parts that don't fit other circuits either geographically or strategically. Many of the larger circuits are focusing on the larger domestic markets and the larger foreign markets; they don't want to keep the theaters they have in small and medium-sized towns. When they buy a theater circuit that has several big-city theaters that they really want, but a bunch of smaller-town theaters they don't want to keep, I'll buy them. I'm buying a bunch of Cineplex-owned theaters in Georgia and Alabama right now because I know these units don't fit its strategy.

Mike Patrick stated that acquisitions would always be a part of Carmike's strategy:

> Even though we have increased our new theater construction program, I believe that acquisitions will be our main thrust of expansion.
>
> By July 1995, we will have bought 254 screens since the first of the year, and should buy at least another 100 before the year is out. In January of this year, we were in discussions to buy two different circuits; however, when the Republicans began to talk about a capital gains tax cut, the deals went on the back burner. As soon as the capital gains issue is put to bed, we expect a few more circuits to be put on the block. We have set a goal of 6,000 screens for Carmike Cinemas and, given enough time, I believe it is feasible.

In October 1991, Carmike entered into a joint venture with the owners of the former Excellence Theatres chain, creating a new company called Westwynn Theatres. Carmike contributed cash and assets to Westwynn through the purchase of preferred stock (representing a 49 percent ownership position) and formed an agreement to manage the chain of 367 theaters. This venture promised to yield a 10-year revenue stream of a minimum annual fee of $1.5 million (adjusted annually for increases in the consumer price index) plus a percentage of theater cash flows. In 1993, Carmike acquired Westwynn (see Exhibit 6).

MIKE PATRICK'S MANAGEMENT STYLE

Mike Patrick had first worked in Martin Theaters as a high school student in Columbus, Georgia, and later in Atlanta as a student at Georgia State. Still later, back in Columbus, he worked at Martin while he finished his studies in economics at

Columbus College. He explained these time periods in his life and how he became acquainted with the business:

> Movie theaters was the only business in which I really wanted to work . . . it's a fun business. If you are in construction, no one cares about your business. But if you tell someone that you are in the theater business, then everybody has seen a movie. Everyone has something they want to talk about. So it's an entertaining industry. Plus when I got into it, I was in the night end of it. I wasn't into administrative. So I got captured, as I called it. If you have never worked at night then you don't understand. I really went to work at 8 AM and got off at 10 AM and then went back at 2 PM and got off at 11 PM at night. So your whole group of friends is a total flip-flop. You have nighttime friends. Before you know it, you are trapped into this life. All your friends work at night. So your job becomes a little more important to you because that's where you spend all your time. Working in a theater . . . is a lot of fun. It really is, especially when you are 19 and get to handle the cash. A theater is a cash business.
>
> My father was president of Martin. In 1970 he became president of Fuqua and moved to Atlanta. My father wanted to sell the house in Columbus and my mother did not want to. I was very homesick for Columbus . . . So I said, "I will go back to Columbus College and I will live in the house." I moved back here in the summer of 1970 and worked in the accounting department because I wanted to understand the reports, why I filled out all these forms, and where they went. I learned then that the treasurer of the accounting department did not understand the paper flow at all.

When Carmike purchased Martin Theaters in early 1982, Mike Patrick became president. He explained the advantage of working so long in the company:

> I had done every job in this company except that of Marion Jones, our attorney. But my brother is an attorney, so I have someone in the family to talk to if I have a question. No one can put one over on me . . . I've fired them too, and I want to tell you something—I do my own firing . . . and firing a man who is incompetent when he doesn't know it is hard. He breaks down because he thinks he's good. When I first became president there was a family member who had to go. The other management noticed that.

In considering the purchase of Martin, Mike Patrick had described the firm to his father as "fat." Mike Patrick described what he did after Martin was purchased.

> It appeared that each layer of management got rid of their responsibilities to the next echelon down. For example, I could not figure out what the president, Sam Fowler (Ron Baldwin's successor) did . . . I kept looking at management trying to figure out what they did. I sort of took an approach like you call zero-base budgeting. Instead of saying my budget was $40,000 last year and I need 10 percent more this year, I required that an individual had to justify everything he did. For example, there is now only one person in our financial department. The young man in there makes less than the guy that had the job as vice president of finance three years ago and the current guy does not have a subordinate. The advertising department went from a senior vice president level to a clerk. You are talking about a difference between an $80,000 salary and a $19,000 salary.

Approximately 75 percent of the employees were paid minimum wage. The company was totally nonunion and only about 8 percent of the employees worked in a managerial capacity. Employee relationships were generally good. The company did not have a policy discouraging nepotism. Indeed, Mike Patrick encouraged the hiring of family members. Especially in smaller towns where there might be several family members in visible positions, hiring family was a deterrent to theft. As Mike Patrick explained:

> I will let them hire family for two reasons: One, they don't want to quit me. They're married to me as much as they are to the family. Second, you get people who just would not steal. They have more to lose than just the job. None of the family will steal from me because it would have a direct bearing on the father, the uncle, the whole family. I am in a lot of little towns and in a small town a son is either going to work on a farm, a grocery store, a filling station, or a theater, 'cause there is no industry there. The cleanest job in town is the theater manager. Also, in a small town we allow the manager to look like he owns the theater. 'Cause I don't go in and act like "Here's the boss," and all that.

Mike Patrick's hands-on approach extended to his acquisitions, as well. When the company acquired a group of theaters, it expected the new theaters—its assets and its managers and staff—to fit quickly into the Carmike system. Because of Carmike's proprietary management information system, IQ-Zero, assimilating new theaters was relatively simple. Patrick described how this was done:

> First, we begin to install IQ-Zero into each theater so we can have a "hands-on" operation and begin to analyze and fine-tune the theater operation. Most of the theater employees stay, as they are part-time employees. The managers, however, are different. It seems that managers who work for larger circuits in the bigger markets transfer to other locations, so we bring in our own people. In the medium and smaller markets, the managers stay. As we fine-tune the operation, we do lose some of the managers who are used to a desk job and have a hard time adjusting to our operation.
>
> Other circuits do not have anything like IQ-Zero. When we install our system, we eliminate almost all of the paperwork, such as "payroll," film exchange copies, concession reports, etc. These managers are comfortable doing the paperwork, which is eliminated by IQ-Zero, so it is a major change for them. We want them to focus on the patron and theater needs, not paperwork. It also switches them from working a normal 9-to-5 job since we expect them to run their theater and to be there when it is busy, which is usually at night, and help maximize the performance of the theater. It is a complete change for some managers.

COST CONTROL SYSTEMS

Carmike executives put considerable emphasis on budgeting and cost control. As Mike Patrick explained, "I was brought up on theater P&L's." The systems he set in place for Carmike theaters were straightforward. Every theater was treated as a profit center and had its own profit and loss statement. Results came across Patrick's desk monthly; theater performances were printed out in descending order of amount of profit generated for that month. A monthly statement of expenses was generated for each administrative department. Every department head received a recap each week. Charges for business lunches appeared on the statement of the person who signed the bill. Patrick checked the reports and required explanations for anything out of line; he explained why he made a point of scrutinizing the theater expenses authorized by each district manager:

All district managers want their facilities to look brand new. You can write them letters, you can swear, you can cuss. It makes no difference. They are in that theater and that's the only thing they see. It's their world. They want new carpet every week. They want a new roof every week. They want a new projector and a new ticket machine every week . . . the government says you have to capitalize improvements. I hate to capitalize these kind of expenses. If the air conditioning breaks, the IRS makes me capitalize the cost to fix it. Horse feathers! I wrote the check for $18,000. The money is gone. What I do is give every district manager a repair report. It shows anything charged to repairs.

Patrick's ability to maintain tight controls resulted from his decision in 1982 to develop a proprietary management information system for tracking individual theater operations and for planning purposes. Carmike's IQ-Zero system captured point-of-sale revenue data at each theater and transmitted it directly to Carmike's headquarters. The system was considered one of Carmike's secret weapons and it was continuously being upgraded, refined, and improved. IQ-Zero provided information such as the number of tickets sold for each show on each screen and concession sales by product category and show time. Patrick observed, "We can tell you how many Raisinets every theater sold last night."[3]

IQ-Zero also tracked staffing levels at the individual theaters. Data was uploaded each evening to headquarters where it was compiled into summary reports for analysis. P&L statements were generated weekly. Carmike also used the system to maintain a historical database by picture type (such as comedy, western, etc.) and by market to provide information on the type of film that performed best in each market. Analysis of the information was then used to plan theater scheduling for upcoming releases.

Carmike's multiscreen format also helped the company realize cost savings. By 1992, the company no longer owned drive-ins and had only two single-screen theaters left. The multiscreen concept enabled the company to stagger show times, thus using one set of ushers, concession stand attendants, and restrooms to serve all auditoriums. Cost savings were also realized when several films could be promoted in the same newspaper ads.

The company had implemented improved technology to trim the number of employees. Mike Patrick explained what happened in one city when the firm switched to totally automated projection booths:

I called our attorney in and I asked him, "What is the recourse if I fire projectionists?" He said, "You must reinstate them and pay them the back pay if you lose in court." I said, "You mean there is no million dollar fine?" He replied, "No, you've just got to worry about back pay." He went on to ask, "Well, why are you going to get rid of them?" I said, "There is equipment for showing movies that will work very similar to an eight-track tape player so I don't need projectionists to do something that the machine can do just as well."

The city had a code which said to be a projectionist you must take a test from the electrical board to be certified. That law was put in about 1913 because back in the old days, they didn't have lightbulbs. You used two carbon arcs and it was a safety issue because back then film was made out of something that burned. That was before my time that film burned like that and you had a fire in the lamp house. Now we have Zenow bulbs. The projectionists hadn't gone and gotten their cards for years. But the rule was on the books. So I figured the only problem we had was the city. As soon as we fired projection-ists, they went to the council and had the police raid my theater. I sued the City of Nashville . . . In the meantime, we sent an engineer from Columbus up and started teaching all our theater managers how to pass the test. As they began to pass the board's test, it became a moot question.

Carmike had already leased and installed all the equipment needed to automate the film projection process except for a simple lens adjustment that could easily be done manually in a few seconds. The equipment made it possible to get the theater managers to cooperate in eliminating the projectionist's job:

> I told our managers that I would give them a raise consisting of 40 percent of whatever the projectionist had made. So all of a sudden the manager went from being against the program to where I got a flood of letters from managers saying, "I'm now trained. Fire my projectionist."

Carmike was equally aggressive in managing construction activities in a cost-efficient manner. In 12 years of operation, Carmike Cinemas had constructed theaters with a total of 475 screens. New theaters, either replacements or additions, were usually constructed and financed through build, sell, and leaseback agreements. Carmike paid close attention to cost control in construction; Mike Patrick explained the approach and rationale:

> A small town does not have the population to support the $3 to $4 million cost of a new 10-plex theater. It is impossible for a small market to give a decent return on this kind of investment. Yet even a small market needs to offer enough variety to satisfy the moviegoing public and keep the movie habit alive. The cost of a theater can be broken into three parts: land, building and equip-ment. The land is usually not very expensive in a small market, but the cost of construction and equipment is the same as in a larger market.
>
> We brought in our architectural staff to design a package of auditoriums to attach to a smaller existing theater. This is not as simple as it sounds since the fire codes and building regulations differ so much from place to place.
>
> Our first project of this type was in Cartersville, Georgia. We took an old twin and added six screens to give us an eight-plex. The total cost was $650,000. After the first year, we realized a 30 percent return on investment. We then took a 4-plex in Cookville, Tennessee, and added 6 screens to give us a 10-plex. The first year of operation is not up yet, but it looks like it will do even better than Cartersville.
>
> To get the construction costs even further down, we are building four of these at the same time just two weeks apart using the same construction crew. We have one contractor but he moves his subs from one job to the next. It gives him volume and us a lower cost per theater unit.
>
> It seems that in every major acquisition we get theaters in one or two small markets that produce very little cash flow. So with this plan, we can take a twin or triple and, with a reasonable investment, turn it into a larger cash generator with six to eight screens.

Mike Patrick built his first theater in 1982 at a cost of $26 per square foot. At the time, the industry average was around $31. He noted that even his insurance com-pany had questioned him when he turned in his replacement cost estimate. Patrick had come up with several innovative ways to keep construction costs to a minimum.

When a shopping center firm built a theater for Carmike to lease, Patrick insisted on having a clause in the lease specify that if construction costs exceeded a certain amount, Carmike had the option of building the theater. Without that specification,

Patrick explained, there was no incentive for the development firm to contain costs. Carmike's lease payment was based on a return on investment to the development firm. On a recent theater, the estimated costs came in at $39 per square foot versus the $41 per square foot that the lease specified. Mike Patrick had convinced the development company to use one of his experienced contractors who helped achieve the cost savings. Carmike's cost per square foot for new theater construction in early 1995 was between $32 and $45—a third to half the going rate in major markets.

Recently, the company had opened its own maintenance department in Columbus. With 1,942 auditoriums to be serviced, the company found that the costs of equipment maintenance could be reduced and controlled by centralizing the maintenance function. The company was hoping to achieve cost savings by rebuilding and repairing seats and sound and projection equipment in-house. Mike Patrick discussed why he brought the maintenance function in-house:

> You cannot repair or renovate a theater auditorium cost-efficiently using local contractors because there are so few around that no one has all the specialized equipment and know-how to just go in and do it. To do a drape in an auditorium is not the same thing as doing one at your house. I mean you've got to get the scaffolding in, you've got to get people who understand how to go that high and know how to handle it. To refurbish a theater, you've got to have people who can repair your screen, people who can repair your projectors, people to repair your seats. That just cannot be done locally because there aren't businesses set up to do that kind of stuff.
>
> Since we have our own refurbishing department at Carmike, the task of reducing the cost of the equipment was assigned to it. We rebuild and refurbish approximately 2,000 chairs a month. New, thick larger chairs cost $120 each, whereas we can refurbish existing chairs for around $25. We also rebuild projectors, platters, sound heads and special equipment for all theaters. We have plenty of surplus equipment, so the basic cost for furnishing a complex with rebuilt equipment is more than reasonable. We're starting our own drapery department this month.

NEW MANAGEMENT STRUCTURE

As the company grew, Mike Patrick's hands-on approach became less and less feasible. While many functions were still centralized, the company eventually added new layers of management to handle the day-to-day operation of the business. Mike Patrick discussed how he managed the current structure:

> My style of management has been described as very hands on; however, let me point out that I work through departments. The difference is that our computer system gives me all the information that each department gets; so all the information is at my fingertips and not filtered by the individual department. I get the information as soon as they do. This enables me to make the decision *with* each department and not be overly influenced by them. From my office, I can tell you who worked each concession stand, how much they sold, and how many Raisinets each theater sold last night. We have a system unlike anyone else, unique and built just for the theater business. This would have been impossible to have 20 years ago.

Mike Patrick had organized the company geographically into four operating divisions, each with a division manager, and fourteen operating districts (see Exhibit 7). Each district had approximately 130 screens with a district manager who supervised

Exhibit 7   Organizational Chart for Carmike Cinemas, 1995

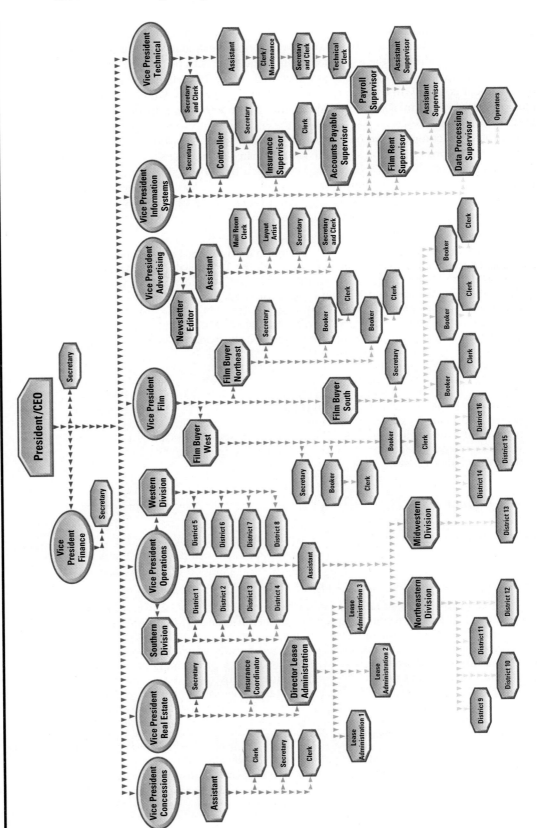

the individual theater managers. Fred Van Noy, vice president and general manager, was in charge of all theater operations for Carmike. The division managers, responsible for implementing the operating policies of the company, also reported to Van Noy. Gary Green was the Western division manager and he had four district managers under his authority. There were three district managers in the Midwestern division headed by James Zimmerman and Shirley Barnes, and Frank Elkins was the Northeast division manager with four district managers reporting to him. Louis Hourvany was the Southern division manager with three district managers under his jurisdiction.

John O. Barwick III functioned as the company's vice president of Finance and treasurer. Barwick administered control of the company finances and supervised relations with financial institutions and shareholders. Matt Citrin, controller, handled all the details of closing the books every month, tax planning and return preparation, and dealt with auditors. Larry Adams, vice president of Informational Systems, along with his four department heads, established and supervised the computer systems that oversaw the operation of IQ-Zero. Marilyn Grant was vice president of Advertising and supervised the advertising of all pictures playing in Carmike's 1,942 auditoriums. Grant worked with the advertising departments of all film companies to create a "want to see" atmosphere for every attraction. Matt Shirley, vice president of Concessions, ensured that all concession stands, equipment, and products met the company's standards for quality and that concessions continued to be a very profitable part of theater operations. Tony Rhead, vice president of Film, bought and booked the pictures for all of Carmike's screens. Rhead, along with two deputies, was responsible for evaluating all pictures being released, determining how long they should play on various Carmike screens, and negotiating terms with the film companies. Lamar Fields, vice president of Development, and his staff of four, handled all real estate transactions, new construction, and leases. The company's technical director was James Davis, who bought and maintained in peak operating efficiency all of the state-of-the-art equipment for Carmike, including seats, projection equipment, and sound systems. Dorothy Moore was the firm's director of Human Relations. It was her job to assist each department in hiring and training Carmike's employees.

CARMIKE'S PERFORMANCE

In 1982, Carmike Cinemas was the seventh-largest theater circuit in the United States and Canada; a decade later, it was the third-largest chain. Going into 1995, the company was the second-largest theater chain and was closing in fast on the number one position. Although industry average ticket prices had steadily increased over the past 12 years, total admission dollars and admission revenues had peaked in 1984 and remained flat at approximately $1 billion annually in the years since (Exhibit 8). Carmike was well below the industry averages in admission price, admission revenues per screen, and attendance per screen (Exhibit 9). This reflected, in part, the company's pricing strategy of keeping admission prices in line with local cost-of-living indexes, incomes, and economic conditions. Carmike's admission prices rose from $2.77 in 1987 to $3.47 in 1992, almost 25 percent. In 1994, the company increased admission and concession prices an average of 6.5 percent, greatly increasing the company's margins. The company had a target of $1.40 in concession sales per moviegoer and was moving steadily toward that goal.

Carmike's recent financial statements are provided in Exhibits 10, 11, and 12. The company's financial performance was a testimony to its ability to craft and

Exhibit 8   Theater Industry Statistics, 1980–1992

Year	Attendance (millions)	Admission (millions of $)	Average Price per Ticket	Screens	Annual Attendance per Screen	Annual Admission Revenues per Screen
1980	1,022	$2,749	$2.69	17,675	57,793	$155,530
1981	1,067	2,960	2.77	18,144	58,807	163,139
1982	1,175	3,445	2.93	18,295	64,247	188,303
1983	1,197	3,766	3.15	18,884	63,382	199,428
1984	1,199	4,031	3.36	19,589	61,213	205,779
1985	1,056	3,749	3.55	21,097	50,055	177,703
1986	1,017	3,778	3.71	22,665	44,880	166,689
1987	1,089	4,252	3.91	23,555	46,211	180,514
1988	1,085	4,458	4.11	23,129	46,902	192,745
1989	1,133	5,033	4.44	22,921	49,409	219,580
1990	1,057	5,021	4.75	23,814	44,369	210,842
1991	982	4,803	4.89	24,639	39,851	194,935
1992	964	4,871	5.05	NA	NA	NA

NA = not available

Exhibit 9   Selected Operating Statistics for Carmike Cinemas, 1987–1992

	1992	1991	1990	1989	1988	1987
Theaters	394	362	263	225	211	218
Screens	1,570	1,400	979	813	692	666
Average theaters	280	262	245	208	212	224
Average screens	1,112	1,002	897	693	667	664
Average screens per theater	4.0	3.8	3.7	3.3	3.1	3.0
Annual attendance (in thousands)	34,415	29,126	26,215	21,767	20,072	20,489
Admission (in thousands of $)	$119,408	$ 99,060	$ 86,378	$ 64,996	$ 54,973	$ 56,759
Concessions (in thousands of $)	$ 44,101	$ 38,066	$ 33,406	$ 27,214	$ 22,634	$ 21,288
Average admission price	$ 3.47	$ 3.40	$ 3.29	$ 2.99	$ 2.74	$ 2.77
Average concession sale	$ 1.28	$ 1.31	$ 1.27	$ 1.25	$ 1.13	$ 1.04
Average combined sale	$ 4.75	$ 4.71	$ 4.57	$ 4.24	$ 3.87	$ 3.81
Average attendance per screen	30,949	29,068	29,225	31,410	30,093	30,857
Average attendance per theater	122,911	111,168	107,000	104,649	94,679	91,469
Average admission per screen	$107,381	$ 98,862	$ 96,297	$ 93,789	$ 82,418	$ 85,480
Average admission per theater	$426,457	$378,092	$352,563	$312,481	$259,307	$253,388
Average concession sales per screen	$ 39,659	$ 37,990	$ 37,242	$ 39,270	$ 33,934	$ 32,060
Average concession sales per theater	$157,504	$145,290	$136,351	$130,837	$106,764	$ 95,036
Average annual revenue per screen	$147,040	$136,852	$133,538	$133,059	$116,352	$117,541
Average annual revenue per theater	$583,961	$523,382	$488,914	$443,317	$366,071	$348,424
Average cash flow per theater	$ 59,450	$ 57,832	$ 56,755	$ 55,688	$ 42,377	$ 37,027

Source: Company annual reports.

Exhibit 10   Income Statement for Carmike Cinemas, Inc., 1990–1994   *(in thousands of $)*

	1994	1993	1992	1991	1990
Revenues:					
Admissions	$232,134	$167,294	$119,408	$ 99,110	$ 86,378
Concessions and other	95,485	74,504	52,570	46,686	41,042
	327,619	241,798	171,978	145,796	127,420
Cost and expenses:					
Cost of operations	254,756	186,778	135,204	113,000	97,582
General and administrative	5,092	4,710	3,897	3,828	3,674
Depreciation and amortization	22,544	16,255	11,134	9,437	7,612
Total operating expenses	282,392	207,743	150,235	126,265	108,868
Operating Income	$ 45,227	$ 34,055	$ 21,743	$ 19,531	$ 18,552
Interest expense	17,028	14,282	11,623	9,914	8,038
Income before taxes and changes in accounting	28,199	19,773	10,120	9,617	10,514
Income taxes	11,246	7,912	4,008	3,902	42,221
Income before changes in accounting	16,953	11,861	6,112	5,715	6,293
Cumulative effect of change in accounting	0	390	0	0	0
Net income	$ 16,953	$ 12,251	$ 6,112	$ 5,715	$ 6,293
Weighted average common shares outstanding	$ 8,477	$ 7,917	$ 7,672	$ 7,648	$ 7,491
Earnings per share:					
Income before change in accounting	$ 2.00	$ 1.50	$ 0.80	$ 0.75	$ 0.84
Cumulative effect of accounting change	$ 0.00	$ 0.05	$ 0.00	$ 0.00	$ 0.00
Net income per share	$ 2.00	$ 1.55	$ 0.80	$ 0.75	$ 0.84

Source: 1994 annual report.

implement a successful strategy. While revenues and incomes had grown steadily, the company had managed to reduce general and administrative expenses to 1.6 percent of total revenues. In 1994, the company raised $58 million in new equity through the sale of common stock. It also put in place a new $100 million revolving line of credit. These actions significantly strengthened the company's capital structure, providing liquidity and the financial flexibility to continue its expansion strategy. Some observers viewed the company's cash position as a veritable war chest for acquisition opportunities.

FUTURE OUTLOOK

In 1995, Carmike Cinemas was poised to take advantage of a wide variety of opportunities. Mike Patrick was interested in making them happen rather than waiting for them to come his way. He dismissed the idea that he might someday in the not-too-distant future consider selling control of Carmike, stating, "I'm having too much fun to even think of doing something else."[4] In the spring of 1995, industry

---

[4]*Business Week*, July 2, 1990, p. 37.

Exhibit 11   Carmike Cinemas, Inc., Balance Sheets, 1991–1994   *(in thousands of $)*

	1994	1993	1992	1991
Assets				
Current Assets:				
Cash and cash equivalents	$ 17,872	$ 10,649	$ 16,842	$ 9,528
Short-term investments	4,815	22,004	15,263	14,434
Accounts and notes receivable	3,814	4,406	3,644	5,782
Inventories	1,939	1,563	995	618
Prepaid expenses	5,025	3,626	2,234	2,383
Total current assets	$ 33,465	$ 42,248	$ 38,978	$ 32,745
Other assets:				
Investments in and advances to partnerships	$ 4,631	$ 2,098	$ 9,496	$ 9,245
Other	2,375	2,575	2,452	1,381
Total other assets	$ 7,006	$ 4,673	$ 11,948	$ 10,626
Property and Equipment:				
Land	$ 31,835	$ 26,717	$ 17,671	$ 15,749
Buildings and improvements	88,500	76,866	54,371	49,271
Leasehold improvements	107,155	86,095	61,459	55,314
Leasehold interests	42,581	36,624	29,967	11,079
Equipment	111,780	90,775	57,643	48,243
	381,851	317,077	221,111	179,656
Accumulated depreciation	(87,880)	(67,527)	(53,206)	(43,471)
	$293,971	$249,550	$167,905	$136,185
Excess of purchase price over net assets of businesses acquired	$ 43,156	$ 30,553	$ 11,460	$ 4,502
Total assets	$377,598	$327,024	$230,291	$184,058
Liabilities and Shareholders' Equity				
Current liabilities:				
Accounts payable	$ 23,478	$ 20,757	$ 17,864	$ 9,747
Accrued expenses	11,327	8,265	7,430	5,204
Current maturities of long-term debt, senior notes, and capital leases	9,352	8,207	2,049	2,033
Total current liabilities	$ 44,157	$ 37,229	$ 27,343	$ 16,987
Long-term debt, less current	$ 3,495	$ 35,376	$ 7,402	$ 8,066
Senior notes	$118,182	$125,000	$100,000	$ 75,000
Capital lease obligations, less current	$ 19,245	$ 17,441	$ 12,832	$ 8,539
Convertible subordinated debt	$ 3,051	$ 2,819	$ 0	$ 0
Deferred income taxes	$ 17,512	$ 15,303	$ 6,986	$ 6,292
Shareholders' equity:				
Class A common stock*	$ 292	$ 201	$ 199	$ 197
Class B common stock†	43	43	43	43
Paid-in capital	99,763	39,621	35,519	35,082
Retained earnings	71,858	54,905	42,654	36,542
Treasury stock	0	(914)	(2,687)	(2,687)
Total stockholders' equity	$171,956	$ 93,856	$ 75,728	$ 69,177
Total liabilities and stockholders' equity	$377,598	$327,024	$230,291	$184,058

* Class A common stock, $0.03 par value, authorized 15,000,000 shares; issued 9,738,101 (1994), 6,724,901 (1993), 6,631,811 (1992), and 6,574,686 (1991).
† Class B common stock, $0.03 par value, authorized 5,000,000 shares; issued and outstanding 1,420,700 shares.
Source: 1994 annual report.

Exhibit 12 Carmike Cinemas Statement of Cash Flows, 1992–1994 (in thousands of $)

	Years Ended December 31		
	1994	1993	1992
Operating Activities			
Net income	$ 16,953	$ 12,251	$ 6,112
Adjustments to reconcile net income to net cash provided by operating activities			
Depreciation and amortization	22,544	16,255	11,134
Deferred income taxes	1,674	691	194
Gain on sales of property and equipment	(122)	(932)	(388)
Changes in operating assets and liabilities:			
Accounts and notes receivable	592	(909)	2,138
Inventories	(376)	(300)	(377)
Prepaid expenses	(1,399)	(911)	149
Accounts payable	2,721	2,929	8,378
Accrued expenses	3,597	(2,908)	1,965
Net cash provided by operating activities	$ 46,184	$ 26,166	$ 29,305
Investing Activities			
Purchases of property and equipment	(29,096)	(33,466)	(13,298)
Purchases of assets from other theater operations	(51,050)	(11,200)	(38,083)
Acquisition of remaining interest in Westwynn Theatres, Inc., net of cash acquired	0	(8,774)	0
Proceeds from sales of property and equipment	860	1,466	1,197
Decrease (increase) in:			
Short-term investments	17,189	(3,506)	(829)
Other	(2,493)	(1,304)	(62)
Net cash used in investing activities	$(64,590)	$(56,784)	$(51,075)
Financing activities			
Debt and other liabilities:			
Additional borrowings	110,950	29,275	30,844
Repayments	(146,468)	(5,656)	(2,199)
Issuance of Class A common stock	61,147	806	439
Net cash provided by financing activities	$ 25,629	$ 24,425	$ 29,084
Increase (decrease) in cash and equivalents	$ 7,223	$ (6,193)	$ 7,314
Cash and equivalents at beginning of year	$ 10,649	$ 16,842	$ 9,528
Cash and equivalents at end of year	$ 17,872	$ 10,679	$ 16,842

analysts were unconcerned that Mike Patrick would opt out of the theater industry. Rather, they were speculating on what deals he was concocting to take over the industry leadership position.

When asked if he had plans to be the largest theater circuit in the world, Mike Patrick had the following to say:

Doing business in a foreign country would be different than in the United States. Each country has its own set of laws and culture. In Italy, for example, each town is allocated a number of seats. If the town already has that number, a new theater cannot be built. Then there is the currency problem. I would hate to have invested dollars in Mexico before the peso fell. For us to go into another country, we would have to have a strategic partner to guide us through the local customs and regulations.

It would have to be a perfect fit. We designed IQ-Zero with the thought of going to a foreign country and transmitting the information from that theater to our home office by satellite, just like we do here. But we are in no rush to build theaters outside the United States.

Carmike was considering some limited types of diversification in the company's future as well:

Because we are not diversified, we have been able to keep our G&A expenses extremely low and focus on our business. As we get larger, we could diversify in two different ways. Number one, we are about to open a drapery company to replace drapes in our theaters, as needed, at a cheaper price than we could have an outside firm do the job. We will also do drapery work outside of Carmike Cinemas for other businesses and other theater circuits. We may also do something like this in the concession business. We may distribute our own concession supplies and may choose to service other theater circuits or businesses.

The second type of diversification will come as we focus on entertainment. At some of the bigger towns, some other companies are going to build big entertainment centers. Game rooms and other businesses in a miniature-mall type setup—it's all entertainment. We've been in one of these before. If the individual businesses are run well and are good businesses, they work. But having a bad restaurant next to a theater does not make the restaurant work. If the food's not good, after about two months no one goes. If the arcade games are inferior or not what the public wants, they stop going after about a month. The individual businesses have to some degree stand on their own.

The entertainment idea, having it all in one area, does have benefits. We're already looking to see what would fit Carmike's operation. We're looking at what might fit the theater business real well and not be an inventory business. We've looked at putting a putt-putt and theater together; we've looked at putt-putt's, go-carts, and theaters together. But we haven't found the mix yet that's perfect for us. Maybe one day we'll try a couple in this line. But right now, we just haven't found the ingredients that fit us like a glove and it's going to have to fit like a glove.

Carmike's management was very optimistic about the company's future. Carl L. Patrick, Sr., and Mike Patrick said the following in their letter to shareholders in the company's 1994 annual report:

We are delighted to report that 1994 was the best year in Carmike's history in all categories—revenues, net income, and cash flow.

We are aware this did not happen by accident or plain luck. It happened first by good planning, second by hard work, and third by the enthusiastic efforts of Carmike's management team.

While the nature of our business creates fluctuations in the short term due to the availability of popular pictures, we believe that proper planning and management skills will ensure that the pace-setting accomplishments of the past will continue into the future.

The management of Carmike is optimistic about the future of the industry and about continuing Carmike's strategy of growth through acquisition and construction of new screens. We are just as eager to grow today as we were 10 years ago.

W. L. Gore & Associates, Inc.

Frank Shipper, Salisbury State University
Charles C. Manz, Arizona State University

To make money and have fun.
W. L. Gore

On July 26, 1976, Jack Dougherty, a newly minted MBA from the College of William and Mary, dressed in a dark blue suit and bursting with resolve, reported for his first day at W. L. Gore & Associates. He presented himself to Bill Gore, shook hands firmly, looked him in the eye, and said he was ready for anything.

What happened next was one thing for which Jack was not ready. Gore replied, "That's fine, Jack, fine. Why don't you look around and find something you'd like to do." Three frustrating weeks later he found that something, dressed in jeans, loading fabric into the mouth of a machine that laminated the company's patented Gore-Tex membrane to fabric. By 1982, Jack had become responsible for all advertising and marketing in the fabrics group. This story was part of the folklore that was heard over and over about W. L. Gore. By 1991, the process was slightly more structured. New associates took a journey through the business before settling into their own positions, regardless of the position for which they were hired. A new sales associate in the Fabric Division might spend six weeks rotating through different areas before concentrating on sales and marketing. Among other things, he or she might learn how Gore-Tex fabric was made, what it could and could not do, how Gore handled customer complaints, and how it made investment decisions.

Anita McBride related her early experience at W. L. Gore & Associates this way:

> Before I came to Gore, I had worked for a structured organization. I came here, and for the first month it was fairly structured because I was going through training and this is what we do and this is how Gore is and all of that, and I went to Flagstaff for that training. After a month I came down to Phoenix, and my sponsor said, "Well, here's your office, and here's your desk," and walked away. And I thought, "Now what do I do," you know? I was waiting for a memo or something, or a job description. Finally after another month I was so frustrated, I felt, "What have I gotten myself into?" And so I went to my sponsor and I said, "What the heck do you want from me? I need something from you." And he said, "If you don't know what you're supposed to do, examine your commitment and your opportunities."

BACKGROUND

W. L. Gore & Associates evolved from the late Wilbert L. Gore's experiences personally, organizationally, and technically. He was born in Meridian, Idaho, near Boise in 1912. By age six, he claimed he had become an avid hiker in the Wasatch

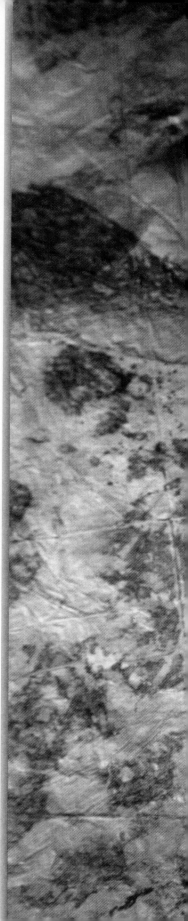

Mountain Range in Utah. In those mountains, at a church camp, he met Genevieve (called Vieve by everyone), his future wife. In 1935, they got married, which was, in their eyes, a partnership—a partnership that lasted a lifetime.

He received both a bachelor of science degree in chemical engineering in 1933 and a master of science in physical chemistry in 1935 from the University of Utah. He began his professional career at American Smelting and Refining in 1936, moved to Remington Arms Company in 1941, and moved once again to E. I. du Pont de Nemours in 1945 where he held positions of research supervisor and head of operations research. While at Du Pont, he worked on a team to develop applications for polytetraflurothylene, frequently referred to as PTFE in the scientific community and known as Teflon by consumers. On this team, Wilbert Gore, called Bill by everyone, felt a sense of excited commitment, personal fulfillment, and self-direction. He followed the development of computers and transistors and believed that PTFE had the ideal insulating characteristics for use with such equipment.

He tried a number of ways to make a PTFE-coated ribbon cable without success. A breakthrough came in his home basement laboratory. He was explaining the problem to his son, Bob. Bob saw some PTFE sealant tape made by 3M and asked his father, "Why don't you try this tape?" His father then explained to his son, "Everyone knows you can not bond PTFE to itself." So, Bob went on to bed.

Bill Gore remained in his basement lab and proceeded to try what everyone knew would not work. About 4 AM, he woke his son waving a small piece of cable around, saying excitedly, "It works, it works." The following night father and son returned to the basement lab to make ribbon cable coated with PTFE.

For the next four months, Bill Gore tried to persuade Du Pont to make a new product—PTFE-coated ribbon cable. By this time in his career, Bill Gore knew some of the decision makers at Du Pont. After talking to a number of decision makers, it became clear that Du Pont wanted to remain a supplier of raw materials and not a fabricator.

Bill began to discuss with his wife the possibility of starting their own insulated wire and cable business. On January 1, 1958, their wedding anniversary, they founded W. L. Gore & Associates, which they viewed as another partnership. The basement of their home served as their first facility. After finishing dinner on their anniversary, Vieve turned to her husband of 23 years and said, "Well, let's clear up the dishes, go downstairs, and get to work."

Bill Gore was 45 years old with five children to support when he left Du Pont. He left behind a career of 17 years and a good and secure salary. To finance the first two years of the business, they mortgaged their house and took $4,000 from savings. All of their friends cautioned them against taking the risk.

The first few years were rough. In lieu of salary, some of their employees accepted room and board in the Gore home. At one point, 11 employees were living and working under one roof. Then came the order from the City of Denver's water department that put the company on a profitable footing. One afternoon, Vieve answered a phone call while sifting PTFE powder. The caller indicated he was interested in the ribbon cable, but wanted to ask some technical questions and asked for the product manager. But Bill was out running some errands, so Vieve explained that he was out at the moment. Next he asked for the sales manager and, finally, the president. Vieve explained that they were also out. The caller became outraged and hollered, "What kind of company is this anyway?" With a little diplomacy, the Gores eventually secured an order for $100,000. This order put the company over the hump and it began to take off.

W. L. Gore & Associates continued to grow and develop new products primarily derived from PTFE, including its best-known product, Gore-Tex. In 1986, Bill Gore died while backpacking in the Wind River Mountains of Wyoming. Before he died, however, he had become chairman and his son, Bob, president. Vieve remained as the only other officer, secretary-treasurer.

THE OPERATING COMPANY

W. L. Gore & Associates was a company without titles, hierarchy, or any of the conventional structures associated with enterprises of its size. The titles of president and secretary-treasurer were used only because they were required by the laws of incorporation. In addition, Gore did not have a corporatewide mission or code of ethics statement; Gore neither required nor prohibited its business units from developing such statements for themselves. Thus, the associates of some business units who felt a need for mission or ethics statements developed them. The majority of business units within Gore did not have such statements. When questioned about this issue, one associate stated, "The company belief is that its four basic operating principles cover ethical practices required of people in business; besides, it will not tolerate illegal practices." The management style at W. L. Gore was often referred to as unmanagement. The organization had been guided by Bill's experiences on teams at Du Pont and had evolved as needed.

For example, in 1965, W. L. Gore & Associates was a thriving and growing company operating a facility on Paper Mill Road in Newark, Delaware, with about 200 employees. One warm Monday morning in the summer, Bill Gore was taking his usual walk through the plant. All of a sudden he realized he did not know everyone in the plant. In his mind the team had become too big. As a result, the company established a policy that no facility would have over 150 to 200 employees. Thus was born the expansion policy of "Get big by staying small." The purpose of maintaining small plants was to accentuate a close-knit and interpersonal atmosphere.

By 1991, W. L. Gore & Associates consisted of 44 plants worldwide with over 5,300 associates. In some cases, the plants were clustered together on the same site as in Flagstaff, Arizona, with four plants on the same site. Twenty-seven of those plants were in the United States and 17 were overseas. Gore's overseas plants were located in Scotland, Germany, France, Japan, and India.

PRODUCTS

The products that W. L. Gore made were organized into eight divisions—electronic, medical, waterproofing fabrics, fibers, industrial filtration, industrial seals, coatings, and microfiltration.

The electronic products division produced wire and cable for various demanding applications in aerospace, defense, computers, and telecommunications. The wire and cable products had a reputation for unequaled reliability. Most of the wire and cable was used where conventional cables could not operate. For example, Gore wire and cable assemblies were used in the space shuttle Columbia because they would stand the heat of ignition and the cold of space. Gore wire was used in the moon vehicle shuttle that scooped up samples of moon rocks, and Gore's microwave coaxial assemblies opened new horizons in microwave technology. On Earth, the electrical wire products helped make the world's fastest computers possible because electrical signals could travel through them at up to 90 percent of the speed of light. Because of the physical properties of the Gore-Tex material used in their construction, the electronic products were used extensively in defense systems, electronic switching for telephone systems, scientific and industrial instrumentation, microwave communications, and industrial robotics. Reliability was a watchword for all Gore products.

In medical products, reliability was literally a matter of life and death. Gore-Tex–expanded PTFE was an ideal material used to combat cardiovascular disease. When human arteries were seriously damaged or plugged with deposits that interrupted the flow of blood, the diseased portions could often be replaced with Gore-Tex artificial arteries. Gore-Tex arteries and patches were not rejected by the body because the patient's own tissues grew into the grafts' open porous spaces. Gore-Tex vascular grafts came in many sizes to restore circulation to all areas of the body. They had saved limbs from amputation and saved lives. Some of the tiniest grafts relieved pulmonary problems in newborns. Gore-Tex was also used to help people with kidney disease. Associates were developing a variety of surgical reinforcing membranes, known as Gore-Tex cardiovascular patches, which could literally mend broken hearts, by patching holes and repairing aneurysms.

Through the waterproof fabrics division, Gore technology had traveled to the top of the world on the backs of renowned mountaineers. Gore-Tex fabric was waterproof and windproof, yet breathable. Those features had qualified Gore-Tex fabric as essential gear for mountaineers and adventurers facing extremely harsh environments. The PTFE membrane blocked wind and water but allowed sweat to escape. That made Gore-Tex fabric ideal for anyone who worked or played hard in foul weather. Backpackers had discovered that a single lightweight Gore-Tex fabric shell would replace a poplin jacket and a rain suit and dramatically outperform both. Skiers, sailors, runners, bicyclists, hunters, fishermen, and other outdoor enthusiasts had also become big customers of garments made of Gore-Tex fabric. General sportswear and women's fashion footwear and handwear of Gore-Tex fabric were as functional as they were beautiful. Boots and gloves, both for work and recreation, were waterproof thanks to Gore-Tex liners. Gore-Tex was even becoming government issue for many military personnel. Wet suits, parkas, pants, headgear, gloves, and boots kept the troops warm and dry in foul-weather missions. Other demanding jobs also required the protection of Gore-Tex fabric because of its unique combination of chemical and physical properties.

The Gore-Tex fibers products, like the fabrics, ended up in some tough places. The outer protective layer of NASA's spacesuit was woven from Gore-Tex fibers. Gore-Tex fibers were in many ways the ultimate in synthetic fibers. They were impervious to sunlight, chemicals, heat, and cold. They were strong and uniquely resistant to abrasion.

Industrial filtration products, such as Gore-Tex filter bags, reduced air pollution and recovered valuable solids from gases and liquids more completely than alternatives; they also did it more economically. They could make coal-burning plants smoke free, contributing to a cleaner environment.

The industrial seals division produced joint sealant, a flexible cord of porous PTFE that could be applied as a gasket to the most complex shapes, sealing them to prevent leakage of corrosive chemicals, even at extreme temperature and pressure. Steam valves packed with Gore-Tex valve stempacking never leaked and never needed to be repacked.

The coatings division applied layers of PTFE to steel castings and other metal articles by a patented process. Called Fluoroshield protective coatings, this fluorocarbon polymer protected chemical processing vessels from corrosion during production.

Gore-Tex microfiltration products were used in medical devices, pharmaceutical manufacturing, and chemical processing. These membranes removed bacteria and other microorganisms from air or liquids, making them sterile.

FINANCIAL INFORMATION

W. L. Gore was a closely held private corporation. Financial information was as closely guarded as proprietary information on products and processes. Eighty percent of the stock was held by the Gore family and veteran associates, 10 percent by current associates, and 10 percent by others.

According to Shanti Mehta, an associate, Gore's return on assets and equity ranked it among the top 5 percent of major companies. According to another source, W. L. Gore & Associates was performing well by any financial measure. It had had 27 straight years of profitability and positive return on equity. The compounded growth rate for revenues at W. L. Gore over the past 20 years had been over 18 percent discounted for inflation.[1] In 1969, total sales were $6 million; in 1982, $125 million; in 1983, $160 million; in 1985, $250 million; in 1987, $400 million; in 1988, $426 million; and in 1989, $600 million. This growth had largely been financed without debt.

ORGANIZATIONAL STRUCTURE

Bill Gore wanted to avoid smothering the company in thick layers of formal "management." He believed they stifled individual creativity. As the company grew, he knew a way had to be devised to assist new people to get started and to follow their progress. This was seen as particularly important when it came to compensation. W. L. Gore & Associates developed what it called the "sponsor" program to meet these needs. When people applied to W. L. Gore, they were initially screened by personnel specialists as in most companies. For those who met the basic criteria, there were interviews with other associates. Before anyone was hired, an associate must have agreed to be that person's sponsor. The sponsor was expected to take a personal interest in the new associate's contributions, problems, and goals. The sponsor was both a coach and an advocate. The sponsor tracked the new associate's progress, helping and encouraging, dealing with weaknesses and nurturing strengths. Sponsoring was not a short-term commitment. All associates had sponsors and many had more than one. When individuals were hired, they had a sponsor in their immediate work area. If they moved to another area, they also had a sponsor in that work area. As associates' responsibilities grew, they could acquire additional sponsors.

Because the sponsoring program looked beyond conventional views of what made a good associate, some anomalies occurred in the hiring practices. Bill Gore proudly

---

[1] In comparison, only 11 of the 200 largest companies in the Fortune 500 had positive ROEs each year from 1970–88 and only two other companies missed only one year. The revenue growth rate for these 13 companies was 5.4 percent compared to 2.5 percent for the entire Fortune 500.

told the story of "a very young man" of 84 who walked in, applied, and spent five very good years with the company. The individual had 30 years of experience in the industry before joining Gore. His other associates had no problems accepting him, but the personnel computer did. It insisted his age was 48.

An internal memo by Bill Gore described three kinds of sponsorship and how they might work as follows:

1. *Starting sponsor*—a sponsor who helps a new associate *get started* on the job. Also, the sponsor who helps a present associate get started on a new job.

2. *Advocate sponsor*—a sponsor who sees to it the associate being sponsored *gets credit* and recognition for contributions and accomplishments.

3. *Compensation sponsor*—a sponsor who sees to it that the associate being sponsored is *fairly paid* for contributions to the success of the enterprise.

An associate could perform any one or all three kinds of sponsorship. Quite frequently, a sponsoring associate was a friend. Often (perhaps usually) two associates sponsored each other as advocates.

W. L. Gore & Associates had not only been described as unmanaged, but also as unstructured. Bill Gore referred to the structure as a lattice organization. A lattice structure is portrayed in Exhibit 1. The characteristics of this structure were:

1. Direct lines of communication—person to person—with no intermediary.
2. No fixed or assigned authority.
3. Sponsors, not bosses.
4. Natural leadership defined by followership.
5. Objectives set by those who must "make them happen."
6. Tasks and functions organized through commitments.

The structure within the lattice was described by the people at Gore as complex and a function of interpersonal interactions, self-commitment, group-known responsibilities, natural leadership, and group-imposed discipline.

Bill Gore once commented on the structure saying, "Every successful organization has an underground lattice. It's where the news spreads like lightning, where people can go around the organization to get things done." Another feature of the lattice structure was heavy reliance on cross-functional teams to perform the work. When a puzzled interviewer told Bill he was having trouble understanding how planning and accountability worked, Bill replied with a grin, "So am I. It works every which way."

The lattice structure did have some similarities to traditional management structures. For instance, a group of 30 to 40 associates who made up an advisory group met every six months to review marketing, sales, and production plans. As Bill Gore conceded, "The abdication of titles and rankings can never be 100 percent."

The lattice structure was criticized by some associates for its lack of quick response times and decisive action. But Bill Gore stated, "I'm told from time to time that a lattice organization can't meet a crisis well because it takes too long to reach a consensus when there are no bosses. But this isn't true. Actually, a lattice, by its very nature, works particularly well in a crisis. A lot of useless effort is avoided because there is no rigid management hierarchy to conquer before you can attack a problem."

Exhibit 1   The Lattice Structure

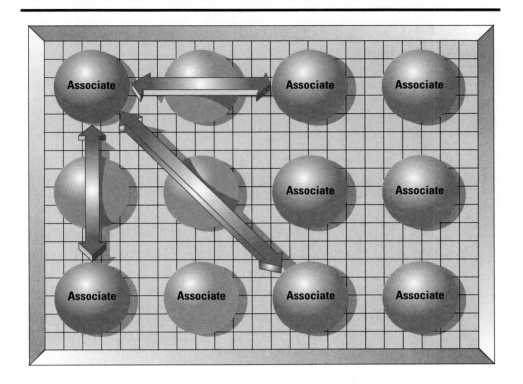

The lattice had been put to the test on a number of occasions. For example, in 1975, Dr. Charles Campbell, a University of Pittsburgh medical school's senior resident, reported a Gore-Tex arterial graft in a patient had developed an aneurysm. (An aneurysm is a bubble-like protrusion that is life-threatening.) If it continued to expand, it would explode. Obviously, this kind of problem had to be solved quickly and permanently.

Within only a few days of Dr. Campbell's first report, he flew to Newark to present his findings to Bill and Bob Gore and a few other associates. The meeting lasted two hours. Bill Hubis, a former policeman who had joined Gore to develop new production methods, had an idea before the meeting was over. He returned to his work area to try some different production techniques. After only three hours and 12 tries, he had developed a permanent solution. In other words, in three hours, a potentially damaging problem to both patients and the company was resolved. Furthermore, Hubis's redesigned graft went on to win widespread acceptance in the medical community. By 1991, it dominated the market with a 70 percent share.

One critic, Eric Reynolds, founder of Marmot Mountain Works Ltd. of Grand Junction, Colorado, and a major Gore customer, said, "I think the lattice has its problems with the day-to-day nitty-gritty of getting things done on time and out the door. I don't think Bill realizes how the lattice system affects customers. I mean after you've established a relationship with someone about product quality, you can call up one day and suddenly find that someone new to you is handling your problem. It's frustrating to find a lack of continuity." He went on to say, "But I have to admit that

I've personally seen at Gore remarkable examples of people coming out of nowhere and excelling."

Bill Gore was asked a number of times if the lattice structure he employed might work at other companies. His answer was, "No, established companies would find it very difficult. Too many hierarchies would be destroyed. When you remove titles and positions and allow people to follow who they want, it may very well be someone other than the person who has been in charge. The lattice works for us, but it's always evolving. You have to expect problems." He maintained the lattice system worked best when put in place in start-up companies by organizationally creative entrepreneurs.

ORGANIZATIONAL CULTURE

In addition to the sponsor program, Gore associates were asked to follow four guiding principles:

1. Try to be fair.
2. Use your freedom to grow.
3. Make your own commitments, and keep them.
4. Consult with other associates before any action that may hurt the reputation or financial stability of the company.

The four principles were often referred to as fairness, freedom, commitment, and discretion. The last principle was also often referred to as the waterline principle. The terminology was drawn from an analogy to ships. If someone poked a hole in a boat above the waterline, the boat would be in relatively little real danger. But if someone poked a hole below the waterline, the boat would be in immediate danger of sinking.

In practice, the fourth principle provided associates with a great deal of discretion. For example, W. L. Gore had no travel policy, no request for travel forms, no prohibition against first-class travel, and no expense reports. The associate called an internal travel consultant and gave the individual his or her requirements. All tickets issued to Gore travelers were accompanied by a note that stated, "The normal coach fare is X, you've saved Y." Upon return, the associate could file a travel investment report and be reimbursed for his or her savings investment.

According to Debbie Sharp, "Very few people take advantage of this. It's only the infrequent travelers who sometimes get carried away. If we see expenses that stand out, we'll call the traveler and ask him to be more careful next time. But no one ever pays money back on an investment report."

The travel consultant also had a high amount of discretion. For example, W. L. Gore had been doing business with three different rental car companies when one became more expensive. The travel consultant dropped that firm and picked up another without checking with anyone else.

The operating principles were put to a test in 1978. By this time, the word about the qualities of Gore-Tex were being spread throughout the recreational and outdoor markets. Production and shipment had begun in volume. At first, a few complaints were heard. Next, some of the clothing started coming back. Finally, a great deal of the clothing was being returned. The trouble was that fabric treated with supposedly waterproof Gore-Tex was leaking. Waterproofing was one of the two major properties responsible for Gore-Tex's success. The company's reputation and credibility were on the line.

Peter W. Gilson, who led Gore's fabric division, said, "It was an incredible crisis for us at that point. We were really starting to attract attention, we were taking off—and then this." Peter and a number of his associates in the next few months made a number of those below-the-waterline decisions. First, the researchers determined certain oils in human sweat were clogging the pores in Gore-Tex and altering the surface tension of the membrane. Thus, water could pass through. They also discovered a good washing could restore the waterproof property. At first this solution, known as the "Ivory Snow Solution," was accepted.

A single letter from "Butch," a mountain guide in the Sierras, changed the company's position. Butch wrote how he had been leading a group and, "My parka leaked and my life was in danger." As Gilson said, "That scared the hell out of us. Clearly our solution was no solution at all to someone on a mountaintop." All of the products were recalled. As Gilson said, "We bought back, at our own expense, a fortune in pipeline material. Anything that was in store, at the manufacturers, or anywhere else in the pipeline."

In the meantime, Bob Gore and other associates set out to develop a permanent fix. One month later, a second generation Gore-Tex formula had been developed. Gilson told dealers that if at any time a customer returned a leaky parka, they should replace it and bill the company. The replacement program cost Gore roughly $4 million.

One thing that might strike an outsider in the meetings and the other places in the Gore organization was the informality and amount of humor. One of the most common words often heard in meetings was "Bullshit!" In contrast, other commonly heard words were "responsibilities" and "commitments." This was an organization that seemed to take what it did very seriously, but its members did not take themselves too seriously.

Gore, for a company of its size, had a very short organizational pyramid. The pyramid consisted of Bob Gore, the late Bill Gore's son, as president, and Vieve, Bill Gore's widow, as secretary-treasurer. All the other members of the Gore organization were referred to as associates. Words such as employees, subordinates, and managers were taboo in the Gore culture.

Gore did not have any managers, but it did have many leaders. Bill Gore described in an internal memo the kinds of "leaders" and their company roles:

1. *The associate who is recognized by a team as having a special knowledge or experience* (for example, this could be a chemist, computer expert, machine operator, salesman, engineer, lawyer). This kind of leader gives the team *guidance in a special area.*

2. *The associate the team looks to for coordination of individual activities to achieve the agree-on objectives of the team.* The role of this leader is to persuade team members to *make the commitments* necessary for success (commitment seeker).

3. *The associate who proposes necessary objectives and activities and seeks agreement and team consensus on objectives.* This leader is perceived by the team membership as having a good grasp of how the objectives of the team fit in with the broad objective of the enterprise. This kind of leader is often also the "commitment seeking" leader.

4. *The leader who evaluates the relative contribution of team members (in consultation with other sponsors) and reports these contribution evaluations to a compensation committee.* This leader

may also participate in the compensation committee on relative contribution and pay and *reports changes in compensation* to individual associates. This leader is then also a compensation sponsor.

5. *Product specialists* who coordinate the research, manufacturing, and marketing of one product type within a business, interacting with team leaders and individual associates who have commitments regarding the product type. They are respected for their knowledge and dedication to their products.

6. *Plant leaders* who help coordinate activities of people within a plant.

7. *Business leaders* who help coordinate activities of people in a business.

8. *Functional leaders* who help coordinate activities of people in a "functional" area.

9. *Corporate leaders* who help coordinate activities of people in different businesses and functions and who try to promote communication and cooperation among all associates.

10. *Intrapreneuring associates who organize new teams* for new businesses, new products, new processes, new devices, new marketing efforts, new or better methods of all kinds. These leaders invite other associates to "sign up" for their project.

It is clear that leadership is widespread in our lattice organization and that it is continually changing and evolving. The situation that leaders are frequently *also* sponsors should not confuse that these are different activities and responsibilities. Leaders are not authoritarians, managers of people, or supervisors who tell us what to do or forbid us doing things; nor are they "parents" to whom we transfer our own self-responsibility. However, they do often advise us of the consequences of actions we have done or propose to do. Our actions result in contributions, or lack of contribution, to the success of our enterprise. Our pay depends on the magnitude of our contributions. This is the basic discipline of our lattice organization.

Many other aspects were arranged along egalitarian lines. The parking lot did not have any reserved parking spaces except for customers and the handicapped. There was only one area in each plant in which to eat. The lunchroom in each new plant was designed to be a focal point for employee interaction. As Dave McCarter of Phoenix explained, "The design is no accident. The lunchroom in Flagstaff has a fireplace in the middle. We want people to like to be here." The location of the plant was also no accident. Sites were selected based on transportation access, a nearby university, beautiful surroundings, and climate appeal. Land cost was never a primary consideration. McCarter justified the selection by stating, "Expanding is not costly in the long run. The loss of money is what you make happen by stymying people into a box."

Not all people functioned well under such a system, especially initially. For those accustomed to a more structured work environment, there were adjustment problems. As Bill Gore said, "All our lives most of us have been told what to do, and some people don't know how to respond when asked to do something—and have the very real option of saying no—on their job. It's the new associate's responsibility to find out what he or she can do for the good of the operation," The vast majority of the new associates, after some initial floundering, adapted quickly.

For those who required more structured working conditions and could not adapt, Gore's flexible workplace was not for them. According to Bill, for those few, "It's an unhappy situation, both for the associate and the sponsor. If there is no contribution, there is no paycheck."

As Anita McBride, an associate in Phoenix, said, "It's not for everybody. People ask me do we have turnover, and yes we do have turnover. What you're seeing looks like utopia, but it also looks extreme. If you finally figure the system, it can be real exciting. If you can't handle it, you've got to go. Probably by your own choice, because you're going to be so frustrated."

Associates had also encountered criticism from outsiders who had problems with the idea of no titles. Sarah Clifton, an associate at the Flagstaff facility, was being pressed by some outsiders as to what her title was. She made one up and had it printed on business cards—SUPREME COMMANDER. When Bill Gore learned what she did, he loved it and recounted the story to others.

In rare cases, an associate "is trying to be unfair," in Bill's own words. In one case, the problem was chronic absenteeism and in the other the individual was caught stealing. "When that happens, all hell breaks loose," said Bill Gore. "We can get damned authoritarian when we have to."

Over the years, Gore & Associates faced a number of unionization drives. The company neither tried to dissuade an associate from attending an organizational meeting nor retaliated when fliers were passed out. Each attempt was unsuccessful. None of the plants had been organized to date. Bill believed no need existed for third-party representation under the lattice structure. He asked the question, "Why would associates join a union when they own the company? It seems rather absurd."

Overall, the associates appeared to have responded positively to the Gore system of unmanagement and unstructure. Bill estimated the year before he died that, "The profit per associate is double" that of Du Pont.

ASSOCIATE DEVELOPMENT

Ron Hill, an associate in Newark, said W. L. Gore "will work with associates who want to advance themselves." Associates were offered many in-house training opportunities. Most were technical and engineering focused because of the type of organization W. L. Gore was, but the company also offered in-house programs in leadership development. In addition, the company had cooperative programs with associates to obtain training through universities and other outside providers in which Gore picked up most of the educational costs for the associates. The emphasis in employee development, as in many parts of W. L. Gore, was that the associate must take the initiative.

COMPENSATION

Compensation at W. L. Gore & Associates took three forms—salary, bonus, and an Associates' Stock Option Program (ASOP).[2] Entry-level salary was in the middle of the range for comparable jobs. According to Sally Gore, daughter-in-law of the founder, "We do not feel we need to be the highest paid. We never try to steal people

---

[2]Gore's ASOP is similar legally to an ESOP (Employee Stock Option Plan). Gore simply does not use the word *employee* in any of its documentation.

away from other companies with salary. We want them to come here because of the opportunities for growth and the unique work environment." Associates' salaries were reviewed at least once a year and more commonly twice a year. The reviews were conducted by a compensation team for most workers in the facility in which they work. The sponsors for all associates acted as their advocate during this review process. Before meeting with the compensation committee, the sponsor checked with customers or whoever used the results of the person's work to find out what contribution had been made. In addition, the evaluation team considered the associate's leadership ability and willingness to help others to develop to their fullest.

Besides salaries, W. L. Gore had a bonus and ASOP profit-sharing plan for all associates. The bonus consisted of 15 percent of the company's profits distributed among all associates twice a year. In addition, the firm bought company stock equivalent to 15 percent of the associates' annual income and placed it in an (ASOP) retirement fund. An associate became a stockholder after being at Gore for one year. Bill wanted all associates to feel they were the owners.

The principle of commitment was seen as a two-way street. W. L. Gore & Associates tried to avoid layoffs. Instead of cutting pay, which was seen at Gore as disastrous to morale, the company had used a system of temporary transfers within a plant or cluster of plants and voluntary layoffs.

RESEARCH AND DEVELOPMENT

Research and development activities, like everything else at Gore, were unstructured. There was no formal research and development department. Yet the company held over 150 patents, although most inventions were held as proprietary or trade secrets. Any associate could ask for a piece of raw PTFE, known as a silly worm, with which to experiment. Bill Gore believed all people had it within themselves to be creative.

The best way to understand how research and development worked was to see how inventiveness had previously occurred at Gore. By 1979, the wire and cable division was facing increased competition. Bill Gore began to look for a way to straighten out the PTFE molecules. As he said, "I figured out that if we ever could unfold those molecules, get them to stretch out straight, we'd have a tremendous new kind of material." He thought that if PTFE could be stretched, air could be introduced into its molecular structure. The result would be greater volume per pound of raw material without affecting performance. Thus, fabricating costs would be reduced and the profit margins would be increased. Going about this search in a scientific manner with his son Bob, the Gores heated rods of PTFE to various temperatures and then slowly stretched them. Regardless of the temperature or how carefully they stretched them, the rods broke.

Working alone late one night in 1969 after countless failures, Bob, in frustration, yanked at one of the rods violently. To his surprise, it did not break. He tried it again and again with the same results.

The next morning, Bob demonstrated his breakthrough to his father, but not without some drama. As Bill Gore recalled, "Bob wanted to surprise me so he took a rod and stretched it slowly. Naturally, it broke. Then he pretended to get mad. He grabbed another rod and said, 'Oh the hell with this,' and gave it a pull. It didn't break—he'd done it." The new arrangement of molecules changed not only the wire and cable division, but also led to the development of Gore-Tex and what is now the largest division at Gore plus a host of other products.

Initial field-testing of Gore-Tex was conducted by Bill and Vieve in the summer of 1970. Vieve made a hand-sewn tent out of patches of Gore-Tex. They took it on their annual camping trip to the Wind River Mountains in Wyoming. The very first night in the wilderness, they encountered a hail storm. The hail tore holes in the top of the tent, but the bottom filled up like a bathtub from the rain. As Bill Gore stated, "At least we knew from all the water that the tent was waterproof. We just needed to make it stronger, so it could withstand hail."

The second largest division began on the ski slopes of Colorado. Bill was skiing with his friend Dr. Ben Eiseman of the Denver General Hospital. As Bill Gore told the story, "We were just to start a run when I absentmindedly pulled a small tubular section of Gore-Tex out of my pocket and looked at it. 'What is that stuff?' Ben asked. So I told him about its properties. 'Feels great,' he said, 'What do you use it for?' 'Got no idea,' I said. 'Well give it to me,' he said, 'and I'll try it in a vascular graft on a pig.' Two weeks later, he called me up. Ben was pretty excited. 'Bill,' he said 'I put it in a pig and it works. What do I do now?' I told him to get together with Pete Cooper in our Flagstaff plant, and let them figure it out." Now hundreds of thousands of people throughout the world walk around with Gore-Tex vascular grafts.

Every associate was encouraged to think, experiment, and follow a potentially profitable idea to its conclusion. For example, at a plant in Newark, Delaware, a machine that wrapped thousands of yards of wire a day was designed by Fred L. Eldreth, an associate with a third-grade education. The design was done over a weekend. Many other associates had contributed their ideas through both product and process breakthroughs.

Even without a research and development department, innovations and creativity worked very well at Gore & Associates. The year before he died, Bill Gore claimed, "The creativity, the number of patent applications and innovative products, is triple" that of Du Pont.

MARKETING STRATEGY

Gore's marketing strategy was geared toward offering premium products that delivered superior value and was predicated on the beliefs that people in that marketplace appreciated what it manufactured and that Gore could become a leader in its areas of expertise. The operating procedures used to implement the strategy followed the same principles as other functions at Gore.

First, the marketing of a product revolved around a leader who was referred to as a product champion. According to Dave McCarter, "You marry your technology with the interests of your champions as you've got to have champions for all these things no matter what. And that's the key element within our company. Without a product champion you can't do much anyway, so it is individually driven. If you get a person interested in a particular market or a particular product for the marketplace, then there is no stopping them."

Second, a product champion was responsible for marketing the product through commitments with sales representatives. Again according to McCarter, "We have no quota system. Our marketing and our salespeople make their own commitments as to what their forecasts are. There is no person sitting around telling them that that is not high enough, you have to increase it by 10 percent, or whatever somebody feels is necessary. You are expected to meet your commitment, which is your forecast, but nobody is going to tell you to change it . . . There is no order of command, no chain involved. These are groups of independent people who come together to make unified commitments to do something and sometimes when they can't make those agreements . . . you may pass up a marketplace, . . . but that's OK because there's much more advantage when the team decides to do something."

Third, the sales representatives were on salary. They were not on commission. They participated in the profit sharing and ASOP plans in which all other associates participated.

As in other areas of Gore, the individual success stories came from diverse backgrounds. McCarter related one of these success stories as follows:

> I interviewed Sam one day. I didn't even know why I was interviewing him actually. Sam was retired from AT&T. After 25 years, he took the golden parachute and went down to Sun Lakes to play golf. He played golf a few months and got tired of that. He was selling life insurance.
>
> I sat reading the application; his technical background interested me . . . He had managed an engineering department with 600 people. He'd managed manufacturing plants for AT&T and had a great wealth of experience at AT&T. He said, "I'm retired. I like to play golf, but I just can't do it every day so I want to do something else. Do you have something around here I can do?" I was thinking to myself, this is one of these guys I would sure like to hire, but I don't know what I would do with him.
>
> The thing that triggered me was the fact that he said he sold insurance and here is a guy with a high degree of technical background selling insurance. He had marketing experience, international marketing experience. So the bell went off in my head that we were trying to introduce a new product into the marketplace that was a hydrocarbon leak protection cable. You can bury it in the ground and in a matter of seconds it could detect a hydrocarbon [gasoline, etc.]. I had a couple of other guys working on it who hadn't been very successful with marketing it. We were having a hard time finding a customer.
>
> Well, I thought that kind of a product would be like selling insurance. If you think about it, why should you protect your tanks? It's an insurance policy that things are not leaking into the environment. That has implications, big-time monetary. So, actually, I said, "Why don't you come back Monday? I have just the thing for you." So he did. We hired him; he went to work, a very energetic guy. Certainly a champion of the product, he picked right up on it. Ran with it single-handed . . . Now it's a growing business. It certainly is a valuable one too for the environment.

In the implementation of its marketing strategy, Gore relied on cooperative and world-of-mouth advertising. Cooperative advertising was especially used to promote Gore-Tex fabric products, which were sold through a number of clothing manufacturers and distributors, including Apparel Technologies, Lands' End, Austin Reed, Timberland, Woolrich, North Face, Grandoe, and Michelle Jaffe. Gore engaged in cooperative advertising because the associates believed positive experiences with any one product would carry over to purchases of other and more Gore-Tex fabric products. Apparently, this strategy was paying off. Richard Zuckerwar, president of the Grandoe Corporation, said about his company's introduction of Gore-Tex gloves, "Sports activists have had the benefit of Gore-Tex gloves to protect their hands from the elements . . . With this handsome collection of gloves . . . you can have warm, dry hands without sacrificing style."

The power of informal marketing techniques extended beyond consumer products. According to McCarter, "In the technical end of the business, company reputation probably is most important. You have to have a good reputation with your company."

He went on to say that without a good reputation, a company's products would not be considered seriously by many industrial customers. In other words, the sale was often made before the representative called. Gore had been very successful using its marketing strategies to secure a market leadership position in a number of areas ranging from waterproof outdoor clothing to vascular grafts.

ACKNOWLEDGMENTS

A number of sources were especially helpful in providing background material for this case. The most important sources were the W. L. Gore associates who generously shared their time and viewpoints about the company. We especially appreciate the input received from Anita McBride, who spent hours with us sharing her personal experiences as well as providing many resources including internal documents and videotapes. In addition, Trish Hearn and Dave McCarter also added much to this case through sharing their personal experiences as well as ensuring that the case accurately reflected the Gore company and culture.

REFERENCES

Aburdene, Patricia, and John Nasbitt. *Reinventing the Corporation.* New York: Warner Books, 1985.

Angrist, S. W. "Classless Capitalists," *Forbes*, May 9, 1983, pp. 123–24.

Franlesca, L. "Dry and Cool," *Forbes*, August 27, 1984, p. 126.

Hoerr, J. "A Company Where Everybody Is the Boss," *Business Week*, April 15, 1985, p. 98.

Levering, Robert. *The 100 Best Companies to Work for in America.*

McKendrick, Joseph. "The Employees as Entrepreneur," *Management World*, January 1985, pp. 12–13.

Milne, M. J. "The Gorey Details," *Management Review*, March 1985, pp. 16–17.

Posner, B. G. "The First Day on the Job," *Inc.*, June 1986, pp. 73–75.

Price, Kathy. "Firm Thrives without Boss," *AZ Republic*, February 2, 1986.

Rhodes, Lucien. "The Un-Manager," *Inc.*, August 1982, p. 34.

Simmons, J. "People Managing Themselves: Un-Management at W. L. Gore Inc." *Journal for Quality and Participation*, December 1987, pp. 14–19.

"The Future Workplace," *Management Review*, July 1986, pp. 22–23.

Trachtenberg, J. A. "Give Them Stormy Weather," *Forbes*, March 24, 1986, pp. 172–74.

Ward, Alex. "An All-Weather Idea," *The New York Times Magazine*, November 10, 1985, sec. 6.

Weber, Joseph. "No Bosses. And Even 'Leaders' Can't Give Orders," *Business Week*, December 10, 1990, pp. 196–97.

"Wilbert L. Gore," *Industry Week*, October 17, 1983, pp. 48–49.

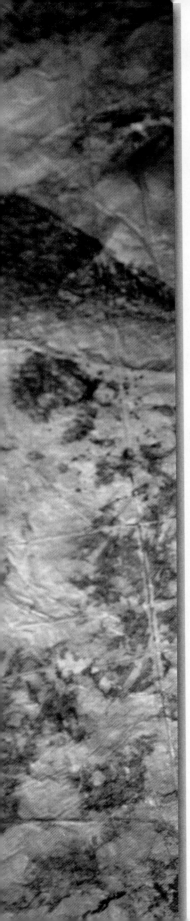

Rubbermaid Inc. in 1993

Bernard A. Deitzer, University of Akron
Susan Hanlon, University of Akron
Alan G. Krigline, University of Akron
Thomas C. Peterson, University of Akron

On May 1, 1991, Stanley Carleton Gault ended a 10-year successful relationship with Rubbermaid when he retired as chairman of the board and chief executive officer. Gault planned to maintain his long-time association with Rubbermaid, stating, "I certainly won't be running the company anymore, but I'll be around to talk about it."[1] He was awarded a two-year consulting contract, an office at Rubbermaid headquarters, and membership on Rubbermaid's board of directors until he turned 70.[2]

However, within a matter of weeks, Akron, Ohio–based Goodyear Tire and Rubber company's board persuaded Gault to become chairman and CEO of Goodyear and lead Goodyear's efforts to retain its long-held leadership status in the intensely competitive world tire industry.

Rubbermaid's board of directors selected Walter W. Williams, former chief operating office and vice chairman of the board, to succeed Gault as chairman of the board and chief executive officer. Eighteen months later, in November 1992, Williams resigned for personal reasons.

Following Williams's brief leadership, the board elected Wolfgang R. Schmitt as cochairman of the board of directors, chief executive officer, and president of the Rubbermaid Corporation. The Rubbermaid board persuaded Stanley Gault to step into the role of cochairman of the board. Stanley Gault commented on his new role at Rubbermaid: "The company [Rubbermaid] doesn't need me to run it. It has very top-notch people. I'm available as an adviser as I was [available] as a director. I will serve as a lead director in assisting the board to fulfill its role and responsibilities to shareholders. I am not going to be involved in running Rubbermaid."[3]

COMPANY HISTORY

Rubbermaid's origins can be traced to events that transpired in the 1920s. In early May 1920, the Wooster Rubber Company began manufacturing its first product—the Sunshine brand of toy balloons. In the mid-1920s, Horatio B. Ebert and Errett M. Grable, executives of the Wear-Ever Division, Aluminum Company of America, purchased Wooster Rubber as a personal investment. They engaged Clyde C. Gault,

[1]Alecia Swasy, *The Wall Street Journal*, April 2, 1990, p. 26.
[2]Yalinda Rhoden, "Sans Gault," *The Beacon Journal* (Akron, Ohio), April 22, 1991, p. D2.
[3]Yalinda Rhoden, "Gault Says Rubbermaid Role Limited," *The Beacon Journal* (Akron, Ohio), November 22, 1992, p. A10.

Stanley Gault's father, who had been general manager of Wooster Rubber, to continue managing the business. By 1928, the company had prospered sufficiently to build a new factory and office building. However, the Great Depression caused sales to plummet.

Meanwhile, James R. Caldwell, a New Englander who had developed a rubber dustpan, was forced into selling it door-to-door since department store buyers turned it down, saying, "We have no calls for a $1 rubber dustpan. We can sell metal dustpans for 39 cents." Persistence paid off, and eventually Caldwell, the door-to-door entrepreneur, persuaded department store buyers to carry rubber dustpans. He adopted the brand name Rubbermaid and developed three other rubber items; a drain board mat to protect countertops, a soap dish, and a sink stopper.

During this period, Ebert, while calling on New England department stores, saw and became interested in Caldwell's rubber housewares products. Subsequently, the two combined businesses, and in July 1934, the manufacture of rubber housewares products began at the Wooster Rubber Company.

During World War II, civilian use of rubber was frozen by the government. The company's consumer business became nonexistent. Survival came in the form of subcontracts to produce components for self-sealing fuel tanks for military aircraft, life jackets, and medical tourniquets. Following the war, the company resumed production and sale of rubber housewares products. Since coloring materials were not yet available, all products were produced in black. In 1950, the company established an operation in Canada. In 1995, it issued its first public offering of stock, which traded on the over-the-counter market.

The first plastic product, a dishpan, was introduced in 1956. In 1957, the firm officially changed its corporate name to Rubbermaid Incorporated to capitalize on an already widely accepted brand name. In 1958, a salesman was assigned to call on hotels and motels to sell doormats and bathtub mats. Thus was the beginning of today's successful institutional business, established as Rubbermaid Commercial Products Inc. in 1967.

When Caldwell retired as president in 1958, Donald E. Noble, who had joined Rubbermaid in 1941, was elected chief executive officer, serving first as president and later as chairman of the board. During Noble's 39 years of service, new businesses were entered, physical facilities were expanded, and an operation in West Germany was established. Rubbermaid's rite of passage from a small, rural Ohio company to a multinational firm with one of America's best-known brand names was under way.

RUBBERMAID'S BUSINESS AND MISSION

Rubbermaid in 1993 manufactured and marketed plastic and rubber products for the consumer, commercial, industrial, agricultural, office, marine, automotive accessories, contract, and children's markets. The company's product line included kitchenware, laundry and bath accessories, food storage containers, office products, juvenile products, home horticultural products, decorative coverings, leisure and recreational products, and those used in food service, health care, and sanitary maintenance. The company's business mission is presented in Exhibit 1.

Products were marketed by company sales personnel and independent sales reps to a broad range of retailers that included mass merchandisers, wholesalers, and distributors serving institutional markets.

Exhibit 1   Rubbermaid's Mission

Our mission is to be the leading world-class creator and marketer of brand-name, primarily plastic products which are creatively responsive to global trends and capable of earning a leading market share position. We will achieve this mission by creating the best value available for the consumer, commercial, and industrial markets.

We will think, plan, experiment, operate and manage strategically. We will monitor, interpret and respond to changing trends to pursue the following avenues of growth:

- *Continuous Value Improvement:* Make our products a better value
- *Market Penetration:* Sell more of our current products
- *Product Enhancement:* Revitalize our current products
- *Product Line Extensions:* Expand our current products
- *New Product Lines:* Add lines to strengthen current market positions
- *New Technology:* Aggressively utilize new materials and processes
- *Retailing:* Utilize our retail outlets to learn and expand globally

- *Global Expansion:* Think and compete internationally
- *Service:* Make our products easy to buy, easy to handle, and easy to sell
- *Franchising:* Create business with partners
- *Licensing:* Leverage our and our partners' brand names
- *Acquisitions:* Add complementary businesses
- *Joint Ventures and Alliances:* Capitalize upon synergistic expertise
- *Rubbermaid Resources:* Utilize the full resources of Rubbermaid

Source: Rubbermaid corporate document, 1992.

Corporate headquarters as well as the home products and specialty products divisions were located in Wooster, Ohio. The company employed over 11,000 employees and had approximately 25,000 stockholders.

THE RUBBERMAID MYSTIQUE

Rubbermaid, according to business analysts, enjoyed an enviable reputation. Overwhelmingly market-driven, the firm offered exceptional value to its consumers with high-quality, nonfaddish, and cost-competitive products, excellent distribution, and a highly focused customer orientation.

Rubbermaid's fundamental corporate strengths served it effectively over the years, with widely recognized and respected brand names, high-quality innovative products, a peerless financial performance, dedicated associates, and focused direction for growth and profitability.[4]

Redesigned versions of the early and ordinary dustpan, along with drain board mats, sink mats, and soap dishes, were among the most popular of the company's portfolio of rubber and plastic products. What set Rubbermaid products apart was the company's ability to transform mundane and colorless kitchen utensils into appealing, colorful, upscale housewares. Customers recognized Rubbermaid's brand name and equated it with quality household products.

Rubbermaid's business philosophy, core principles and values, and objectives are presented in Exhibits 2, 3 and 4.

---

[4]*The Wall Street Transcript*, March 23, 1987, p. 84964.

Exhibit 2   Rubbermaid's Business Philosophy and Beliefs

We believe that partnerships with our consumers, customers, suppliers, communities, government, shareholders, and Rubbermaid associates will most effectively and efficiently enable us to reinvent and improve the value we create.

We believe that value is comprised of quality, service, cost, timeliness, and innovation.

We believe that internal partnerships, meaningful teamwork and personal development will instill in every Rubbermaid associate the skills, the understanding, and the desire to achieve continuous improvement of our value.

We believe in partnerships which strive for:

- A relationship of mutual respect, recognition and reward for performance
- A commitment to a high degree of integrity
- An observance of ethical standards

- A dedication to safety and the environment
- A fair return on investment

We believe that through this partnership and teamwork philosophy, the enterprise will be greater than the sum of its parts.

We believe that the consistent, profitable growth of Rubbermaid as an independent enterprise will be met by delivering increasingly better value to meet the changing needs of our customers and consumers.

Source: Rubbermaid corporate document, 1992.

THE GAULT YEARS, 1980–1991

Stanley Gault, whose name eventually became synonymous with Rubbermaid itself, joined the company after a successful 31-year career at General Electric where he served as senior vice president and senior executive of the industrial products and components sector. He decided to leave GE when he realized he was not being considered in the selection process for GE's new CEO.

When Gault became CEO of Rubbermaid in 1980, revenues were climbing steadily. However, while sales totaled $309 million from continuing operations, earnings had dipped to $14 million. In Gault's view, Rubbermaid was a slow-growth company with a growing overhead, a declining rate of productivity, and personnel that had grown comfortable and unaccustomed to change.[5] "Our product development lagged, our retail customers claimed we were arrogant, and our profit margins had fallen," summarized the new CEO.[6]

Gault immediately began to restructure the firm and its in-place management, stating, "You have to set the tone and pace, define objectives and strategies and demonstrate through personal example what you expect from others."[7] He reshuffled, hired, and fired. Ten percent of all salaried personnel were dismissed. Some two years later, only 2 of 172 Rubbermaid managers still held their original jobs.

While the housewares and commercial products divisions generated over 96 percent of total corporate income, the remaining units were "six weak soldiers." All

[5]Kenneth Labich, "The Seven Keys to Business Leadership," *Fortune*, October 24, 1988, p. 60.
[6]Patricia Sellers, "Does the CEO Really Matter?" *Fortune*, April 22, 1991, p. 86.
[7]Labich, "The Seven Keys."

Exhibit 3   Rubbermaid's Principles and Core Values

For Our Associates

We will strive to
- Have management lead by example
- Provide an environment which is positive and reinforces initiative
- Reinforce experimentation, listening and risk taking
- Nurture diversity and variety of thought
- Develop with them a learning contract
- Empower to the fullest extent with appropriate accountability
- Offer equal opportunity for career growth and advancement
- Create focused, decentralized operating units
- Provide rewards and opportunity consistent with their contribution
- Develop a global view of customers, consumers, vendors and opportunities

For Everyone

We will strive to
- Ensure that every Rubbermaid associate acts with high integrity and observes our shared ethical standards

For Our Shareholders

We will strive to
- Continually reinvent our people, products, plans, processes and plants
- Optimize the full resources of the organization
- Provide superior management depth and continuity
- Provide leadership which is proactive and demands excellence
- Balance our incremental and leap growth strategies
- Provide an attractive and consistent return on investment
- Communicate effectively the company's performance on a timely basis

For Our Communities and Government

We will strive to
- Support the economy and general welfare
- Conduct business in an ethical and responsible manner
- Encourage our associates to participate actively with them
- Be a good corporate citizen
- Communicate the many benefits of the free enterprise system

Source: Rubbermaid corporate document, 1992.

operations were subsequently and rigorously evaluated to determine their strengths, weaknesses, and opportunities. Early on, Gault dramatically informed the organization he was aiming for 12 to 15 percent average annual growth in sales, profits, and earnings per share, plus $1 billion in sales revenues by 1990.[8]

Gault's first strategic step in restructuring was to review Rubbermaid's eight lines of business and to cut out half of them. One casualty was its in-home party plan operation. Gault perceived that current demographics and the changing life-styles of working women allowed little time for after-hours housewares parties. Besides, Rubbermaid did not have a presence commensurate with its competitive arch rival, Tupperware.

In addition, Rubbermaid sold its domestic car mat and auto accessories business. Gault believed auto accessories were a commodity business with stiff price- and volume-elastic competition where automakers tended to pressure suppliers.[9]

[8]Ibid.
[9]James Braham, "The Billion Dollar Dustpan," *Industry Week*, August 1, 1988, p. 47.

Exhibit 4   Rubbermaid's Objectives

Associates
- Stress open and frequent communications
- Invest consistently in growing our capabilities
- Train associates consistent with Continuous Value Improvement and Creative Innovation goals
- Create a global competitive capability
- Recognize, reinforce and reward teamwork, results and excellence

Growth
- Double sales every five years
- Maintain 33 percent of yearly sales from new products introduced in the previous five-year period
- Enter a new market every 12 to 18 months
- Attain 25 percent of sales outside the United States by year 2000
- Create leading distinctive brands worldwide

Profit
- Double earnings per share every five years
- Achieve a 20 percent return on average shareholders' equity
- Average 13 percent return on assets employed
- Deliver a 5 percent continuous value improvement on productivity
- Utilize profits for people and productivity improvement, growth and dividends

Leadership
- Achieve and maintain the best value position
- Continuously create competitive advantages by benchmarking worldwide
- Be proactive on environmental and safety issues
- Internalize the process of change
- Be recognized for excellence by customers, business, government, communities and all of our financial constituencies

Technology
- Utilize supplier research and technology
- Enhance our applied and basic research capabilities
- Encourage experimentation and learning
- Use common management information systems as a competitive advantage

Competencies
- Recognize and strengthen the core competencies of:
  - Corporate associates
  - Individual business units
  - Business teams
  - Project, process, partner and self-directed teams

Shareholders
- Consistently deliver a superior return on investment

Source: Rubbermaid corporate document, 1992.

Rubbermaid's Corporate Goals under Gault

Under Gault's leadership, Rubbermaid became widely recognized as an innovative company. His new product goal was for Rubbermaid to have 30 percent of sales each year come from products not in its product line five years earlier. Over 1,000 new products were introduced between 1985 and 1990.

Rubbermaid also strived to be the lowest-cost, highest-quality producer in the household products industry. From 1981 through 1990, over $612 million was invested in equipment and facilities that increased productivity, enhanced quality, added the capacity needed for new products, and moved it closer to world-class manufacturing status.

Gault's performance targets for Rubbermaid during the 1990s were to increase sales, earnings, and earnings per share 15 percent per year while achieving a 20 percent return on average shareholders' equity. He planned to pay approximately 30 percent of current year's earnings as dividends to shareholders, with the remainder used to fund future growth opportunities. Moreover, each year, 30 percent of sales was to come from new products introduced over the previous five years. An entirely new market was to be entered every 18 to 24 months.

In 1989, Gault had set a goal for achieving $2 billion in annual sales five years from 1987, the year in which Rubbermaid had reached sales of $1 billion. In 1991, Gault believed Rubbermaid could reach the $2 billion mark by the last quarter of 1992 simply by following its present course:

> We project our growth to come from a combination of areas. We'll see growth occur in the core product lines of Rubbermaid's domestic business; the effort under way to grow business internationally; from new product development in all our businesses; new product categories being added to existing business; and growth through a selective acquisition program.[10]

RUBBERMAID'S ACQUISITION STRATEGY DURING GAULT'S TENURE

[handwritten margin note: Related Acquisitions]

Gault's relentless and unyielding commitment to growth prompted a number of acquisitions. Gault looked for small companies that were number one or two in their product category, could benefit from Rubbermaid's manufacturing and marketing expertise, complemented Rubbermaid's product families, and matched up well with the company's distribution channels. Exhibit 5 lists the company's acquisitions and joint ventures.

As Gault emphasized, "We are definitely receptive to good acquisition opportunities. We have made numerous acquisitions; they have all been top-notch companies. We want them to be companies that are well managed and where the management will want to stay and be part of the growing Rubbermaid family."[11]

RUBBERMAID'S GROWTH STRATEGIES DURING THE GAULT YEARS

[handwritten margin note: Incremental—Good long term planning, leap growth—Short term shot in the arm]

Gault strongly believed in developing strategies to control and direct new product activities to meet two types of ambitious growth objectives. The first was *incremental growth*, defined as growth stemming from concentrating on doing what Rubbermaid did best—only better. The second approach was *leap growth*, which involved moving aggressively into new product markets with big sales growth potential and carried a higher degree of risk—the company won big or lost big. Within these two major classifications, there were eight strategic elements; four applied to incremental growth and four entailing leap approaches:[12]

Gault's Incremental Growth Strategies

- To increase the volume of Rubbermaid's existing products. The key to this growth area is in providing value to dealers, distributors, and consumers in the form of quality, low cost, and service.

---

[10]*Rubbermaid Annual Report*, 1990.
[11]*The Wall Street Transcript*, April 18, 1988, p. 89116.
[12]Adapted from remarks by Stanley C. Gault, chairman of the board and chief executive officer, Rubbermaid Incorporated, before the Conference Board of Canada's 15th Annual Marketing Conference, Hilton International, Toronto, Canada, March 29, 1990.

Exhibit 5	Rubbermaid's Acquisitions, Joint Ventures, and Divestments, 1981–1993

1981	Acquired Con-Tact Brand self-adhesive decorative coverings.
1984	Acquired The Little Tikes Company—leading quality manufacturer of preschool children's products.
1985	Acquired Gott Corporation—high-quality consumer recreational products.
1986	Acquired SECO Industries—leading manufacturer of maintenance products.
	Acquired MicroComputer Accessories—accessories for the microcomputer market.
1987	Acquired Viking Brush Limited—household brushes.
	Acquired The Little Tikes Company (Ireland).
	Acquired MicroComputer Accessories Europe S.A.—computer-related accessories
1989	Formed Rubbermaid Allibert—joint venture to make resin furniture for the North American market.
1990	Acquired Curver Rubbermaid Group, Breda, the Netherlands (40 percent joint venture)—manufactures plastic and rubber housewares and resin furniture.
	Acquired EWU AG, Switzerland—producer of floor care supplies and equipment.
	Acquired Eldon Industries—distributor of molded plastic office products and equipment.
1992	Acquired CIPSA—leading plastic housewares manufacturer and marketer in Mexico.
	Divested Ungar Electronics of Hungary (acquired with Eldon in 1990).
	Dissolved Rubbermaid Allibert—the joint venture was dissolved and Rubbermaid formed a strategic alliance with its former joint venture partner.
	Acquired Commercial Products, Cleburne, Texas (acquired to expand capacity).
	Acquired Iron Mountain Forge Corporation, Farmington, Missouri—playground systems and outdoor furniture.
	Formed Curver Rubbermaid Group, Breda, the Netherlands—joint venture with Panoplastic Group, headquartered in Debrecen, Hungary.

Source: Rubbermaid annual reports, 1991–1992.

- To upscale existing products to meet today's consumer and new designs preferences. Upscaling includes introducing new colors to existing lines.
- To extend existing lines to capitalize on product successes, increase retail shelf space, and boost sales volume.
- To expand Rubbermaid's international business as a significant growth opportunity during the 1990s.

Gault's Leap Growth Strategies

- To develop new products and have at least 30 percent of annual sales coming from new products introduced during the past five years.
- To hone product lines and optimize the number of stock units retained to keep the lines manageable and provide proper customer service levels.
- To enter new markets.
- To engage in joint ventures or acquisitions to enter new markets by combining the capabilities of a strong outside partner with the many strengths of Rubbermaid.

GAULT'S FOCUS ON QUALITY

Rubbermaid's hallmark during the Gault years was product quality. Senior executives stressed the importance of turning out top-quality products on a consistent basis and were willing to personally lead the company's drive to achieve product superiority.

Stanley Gault did not hesitate to phone and placate disgruntled dealers. He functioned as Rubbermaid's top quality controller. Precise and methodical, Gault visited several stores a week to see how Rubbermaid products were displayed and to see that Rubbermaid's products on store shelves met his standard for quality and workmanship. If Gault spotted an ill-fitting lid or wrinkled label, he bought the offending goods and then later summoned his senior managers for a lecture. "He gets livid about defects," commented Walter Williams, Gault's successor.[13]

When confronted by the claim that plastic was once synonymous with junk, Gault launched into an energetic speech on the mixture of polyethylene that Rubbermaid used and the intricacies of Rubbermaid's injection molding process. Gault, when comparing Rubbermaid's enormously popular garbage cans to flimsier competing versions, remarked, "On quality I'm a sonofabitch. No one surpasses our quality. We use more and better resin. We don't buy any scrap resin. And we use a thick gauge."[14] Sales of Rubbermaid's big garbage cans jumped 20 percent when Gault suggested to the design engineer that the cans be made in a shade of blue instead of chocolate brown.

Gault's Leadership Style and Approach to Management

Stanley Gault's leadership philosophy reflected an ingrained belief that a leader has to be a living example, inspire the organization, and be part of the team while still being the manager. In Gault's view, leaders should be supportive and, when sensing the need for change, genuinely communicate the need for it. Highly interactive and strong on interpersonal communications, Gault regularly toured Rubbermaid factories to talk one-on-one with managers and workers alike. Gault favored a lean and flat organization structure, believing, "Any incoming chief executive will need to be able to run a flatter organization. As companies continue to cut costs further, middle managers will be eliminated and the CEO will have more people reporting directly to him."[15]

Gault was regarded as a tireless, energetic leader who expected and rewarded hard work from his subordinates. He was an affable person, well liked by his staff despite the demands he placed on them. His personal schedule often included 12- to 14-hour workdays, six days a week. Gault was described by his associates as being a very involved manager who wanted to know everything that was going on in each of Rubbermaid's businesses.

Gault believed successful CEOs should set strategic direction, align employees behind that strategy so they would carry it out, and enforce high performance standards. "I am very demanding and I know it. But I'm demanding of myself, first. I set high standards and I expect people to meet them. I want all the business we can get, provided we get it fairly. If people can't meet my standards after training and counseling, then a change has to be made. That's not saying they aren't good people but they are not cut out for the particular job."[16]

Rubbermaid sought out managers with a strong work ethic who were entrepreneurial, enthusiastic, competent, and ambitious. The company wanted its managers to

---

[13]Brian O'Reilly, "Leaders of the Most Admired Corporations," *Fortune*, January 29, 1990, p. 43.
[14]Ibid.
[15]Jennifer Reese, "CEO's: More Churn at the Top," *Fortune*, March 11, 1991, p. 13.
[16]Braham, "The Billion Dollar Dustpan," p. 48.

be good team players as well as hardworking. Bonuses were based on both increases in profit and increases in the firm's shareholder value.

Hourly workers generally mirrored a belief that the Rubbermaid family came first and that there was no other way. Regularly enjoying profit sharing since 1944, workers had offered over 12,000 cost-cutting suggestions in housewares alone. In 1987, the housewares and specialty products division saved $24.7 million by adopting worker suggestions.[17] Relations with the United Rubber Workers were good. In 1987's negotiations, a new contract froze wages for three years in return for the company's pledge to maintain existing jobs.[18] While doubling sales, Rubbermaid increased its workforce by only 50 percent and halved its number of sales representatives. It had held the line on prices; revenue and profit gains came mainly from increased volume and productivity improvement.[19]

THE WALTER WILLIAMS ERA

After 31 years with General Electric, Williams, 59, joined Rubbermaid in September 1987 as president and chief operating officer. Named vice chairman of Rubbermaid in 1990, Williams, hand-picked by Gault, became chairman and CEO following Gault's retirement in May 1991.

Williams' laid-back often unreserved and gregarious style contrasted markedly with that of his predecessor. "I fully recognized the challenge of following a guy like Stan. I expect comparisons but I have my own style.[20] It may be that it's easier to grow a company in trouble and show improvements but it's a bigger challenge to go to an extremely successful company and continue to make it grow."[21]

Under Walter Williams, Rubbermaid's financial objectives remained largely the same: to increase sales, earnings, and earnings per share by 15 percent per year and to achieve a 20 percent return on shareholders' equity. Williams wanted to pay out approximately one-third of earnings as dividends to shareholders and use the remainder to fund future growth opportunities.

Williams also stuck with Gault's objective of striving to have 30 percent of Rubbermaid's sales revenues come from products introduced during the previous five years. Williams's marketing objectives were to consistently offer the best value to customers (meaning the highest-quality products at a reasonable price), have a continuous flow of new products, and provide exceptional service to customers. Other Rubbermaid objectives during Williams's tenure as CEO are shown in Exhibit 4.

Rubbermaid's Financial Performance under Williams

In Williams's first year, ending December 31, 1991, Rubbermaid's sales reached $1.67 billion, a 9 percent increase from 1990's $1.53 billion. Earnings for 1991 increased 13 percent to $162.6 million or $1.02 per share. The previous year's earnings were $143.5 million or 90 cents a share. Return on average shareholders'

---

[17]Ibid.

[18]Ibid.

[19]Ibid.

[20]Yalinda Rhoden, "Learning to Relax at Rubbermaid," *The Beacon Journal* (Akron, Ohio), April 27, 1992, p. D1.

[21]Ibid.

equity in 1991 was 19.7 percent, a 2.5 percent decrease from the previous year. Long-term debt was $28 million (4 percent of capitalization)—a decrease of 1 percent over the previous year. "Our philosophy is that we're in business to increase our shareholders' wealth," Williams stated.[22]

WOLFGANG R. SCHMITT: COCHAIRMAN, CEO, AND PRESIDENT, 1992–PRESENT

Wolfgang Schmitt, 49, prior to succeeding Walter Williams in late 1992, was president and chief operating officer and, before that, an executive vice president as well as a director of Rubbermaid since 1987. Earlier, from 1984 until 1990, he served as president and general manager of the Home Products Division, the firm's largest operating unit. Previously, he was vice president of marketing and director of research and development for that division.

Schmitt, a native of Germany, came to Smithville, Ohio, at age 10 to be near relatives. A graduate of Otterbein College, Westerville, Ohio, he joined Rubbermaid's management training program in 1966. Described as a tenacious, hard-driving, hands-on marketing man, Schmitt was viewed as being much like Stanley Gault. In an interview with the media soon after his appointment as CEO, Schmitt attested "My challenge is to continue the tradition of Rubbermaid in the tradition of former chairmen Donald Noble, Stanley Gault, and Walter Williams. Their hallmark is constant growth in sales and profits and continual new products."[23]

Schmitt's Goals and Strategies for Rubbermaid

In early 1993, Schmitt was optimistic that Rubbermaid would enjoy another successful year as one of America's most recognized consumer product businesses:

> Our expectations for 1993 continue to be optimistic, although they are tempered with a concern about the strength of the economic recovery. Our strategies emphasize continued cost controls, new product introductions, aggressive use of technology, and strengthened partnerships with our customers. We are committed to delivering another record performance this year.[24]

Additionally, Schmitt stressed that Rubbermaid planned to squeeze out as much growth as possible during the sluggish economy. Managers and employees were attempting to "reinvent" the company, with more than 600 employee teams analyzing everything from catering services to financial measures. Top management had accelerated strategies to introduce products at a faster clip and enter new markets more rapidly.[25] New product markets were to be entered every 12 to 18 months as against earlier intentions of 18 to 24 months. Moreover, Schmitt upped Rubbermaid's goal of having 30 percent of its revenues come from products launched in the past five years to 33 percent.

[Handwritten margin note: Change of mgt. style to one of employee Teams & involvement]

---

[22]Rhoden, "Learning to Relax."

[23]Sallie Cash, "Taking Charge of Rubbermaid," *The Beacon Journal* (Akron, Ohio), November 15, 1992, p. A1.

[24]Rubbermaid Corporate Press Release, April 13, 1993.

[25]Robert Fernandez, "For Investors: A Hit, a Miss," *The Beacon Journal* (Akron, Ohio), April 28, 1993, p. B8.

By the year 2000, Schmitt wanted 25 percent of Rubbermaid's sales to come from outside the United States, up from about 18 percent in 1992.[26] Schmitt, in describing Rubbermaid's growth strategies, envisioned 11 potential avenues to growth. The first five dealt with incremental or near-term growth strategies. The remaining six avenues were leap strategies, which were expected to result in major growth gains during the next century—see Exhibit 6.

The Reinvention Strategy   Rubbermaid's reinvention strategy, according to Schmitt, was a vehicle certain to implement incremental growth. Rubbermaid's culture, moreover, nurtured reinvention and accommodated the process of change. The company had an internal environment that encouraged experimentation and fostered diversity and variety of thought.

In 1992, Schmitt began implementing the reinvention strategy via the use of new technology, product innovation, team participation, customer and supplier partnerships, associate education, global planning, capacity expansion, operations restructuring, and productivity improvement. Over 600 internally trained teams were involved in reinvention. Process teams, project teams, business teams, partner teams, and self-directed work teams all looked for ways to create better value for customers and consumers. These efforts were aimed at realizing big gains in quality improvement, customer service, cost reduction, and time savings. Schmitt said, "Our teams are as nimble as entrepreneurs. The teams can reach anywhere in the company for resources."[27]

Schmitt cited two processes critical to the reinvention program: continuous value improvement and creative innovation. The aim of continuous value improvement was to achieve incremental productivity improvement. This evolutionary process, declared Schmitt, involved intensive training and development for every associate in team dynamics and participation, brainstorming, statistical process control, and communication skills. In partnerships with associates, Rubbermaid offered educational opportunities to improve their potential for advancement and achieving genuine job security.

As a catalyst to reinvention and to create better value products, Rubbermaid had been building better working relationships not only with associates but also with its customers, consumers, suppliers, and communities. Relationships with customers, for example, had evolved from selling items, to selling lines, to selling categories, to developing strategic business partnerships. Business discussions involved concrete operational issues: how to distribute products most effectively; how to keep shelves in stock; how to harness management information through centralization; how to best utilize electronic data interchange and point-of-sale information to reduce costs and improve service.

Creative innovation, according to Schmitt, provided a foundation for helping Rubbermaid master major leaps in its growth or improvement. Creative innovation involved new uses of technology, new business development, new product break-throughs, strategic thinking, and planning for each business.

Rubbermaid management had developed "10 Imperatives" to help ensure that the reinvention strategy produced the desired outcomes—see Exhibit 7.

---

[26]Ibid., p. B8.
[27]*Fortune*, March 6, 1995, p. 56.

Exhibit 6   Schmitt's Growth Strategies for Rubbermaid

Incremental Growth Strategies	Leap Growth Strategies
• Value improvement of existing lines • Market penetration, to sell more of existing lines • Product enhancement by upscaling designs, adding features and enhancing a product's capabilities • Product line extensions to capitalize upon successes with new sizes, capacities or allied products • Development of new products for existing markets	• Entry into new markets adjacent to current markets • Leveraging new material and process technology to gain competitive advantage • Global expansion, high on list of priorities for each business • Joint ventures and alliances with other organizations which offer significant opportunities to utilize the resources and expertise of both partners • Acquisitions of complementary businesses, products, and skills which can provide synergy • Utilization of the full resources of Rubbermaid and its associates

Source: Rubbermaid corporate document, 1992.

RUBBERMAID'S SALES AND DISTRIBUTION STRATEGY

One of Gault's first moves on assuming leadership in 1980 was to revamp Rubbermaid's sales and marketing strategy. The key, according to Gault, was strict adherence to fundamentals. At the time, Rubbermaid's sales force traditionally sold every product category—sinkware, household containers, space organizers—to all customers. Gault severed the field sales function from marketing and put sales strategies in place to cover each market segment.

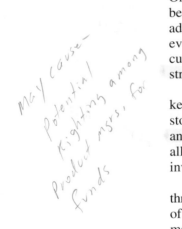

As Gault earlier explained it, "A distribution channel that would serve supermarkets and drugstores would not necessarily work for mass merchants or hardware stores or catalog showrooms." Marketing was organized around product categories, and a product manager was put in charge of each category. Rubbermaid believed this allowed effective specialization and permitted a "more intense level of management involvement with customers."[28]

In 1992, Gault's revamped strategies were still operational. Products were distributed through Rubbermaid's sales representatives and independent sales reps to a broad range of retailers, mass merchandisers, wholesalers, and distributors serving institutional markets. Wal-Mart accounted for 14 percent of Rubbermaid's net sales in 1992.

ADVERTISING AND PROMOTION

Rubbermaid supported its products with national television and radio commercials and magazine ads, along with allowances for promotion and co-op advertising. The company had boosted the number of outlets carrying Rubbermaid products from

---

[28]Christy Marshall, "Rubbermaid, Yes, Plastics," *Business Week*, December 1988, p. 38.

Exhibit 7   Rubbermaid's 10 Reinvention Imperatives, with Examples of Actions Taken to Generate New Products

1. **Extend Product Line Usage**
   Find everyday products and turn them upside down. Rubbermaid launched a durable polypropylene composter to satisfy composing needs in a capacity-filled landfill environment.

2. **Attention to Demographic Changes**
   An aging population prompted plastic storage crates and plastic two-wheel carts. A new 10-gallon storage box emerged for children's rooms.

3. **Dominate the Retail Market**
   A retail partnership effort, called "Everything Rubbermaid," created a store within a store that comprises the firm's full line of housewares.

4. **Penetrate Global Markets**
   Falling trade barriers and a globalized culture assist global efforts. Dustpans may need to be redesigned for smaller kitchens in Japan—but there's no need to redesign a lunch kit.

5. **Innovate Entrepreneurially**
   Product groups are broken down along product lines. Each line has a new product team, including product managers, market researchers, advertising managers, product designers, materials engineers, package designers, and manufacturing and financial people.

6. **Critique and Evaluate**
   Every new product's design is critiqued to ensure customer satisfaction. Focus groups analyze and evaluate products for possible flaws.

7. **Improve Product Features**
   Teams update existing products by adding design features. Example: Enlarging a Drain Tainer 12-quart oil pan and adding a screw-on lid—to prevent spilling, and a spigot—for easy pouring.

8. **Extend the Product**
   Certain products have multiple personalities. The Action-Packer, a two-tone polypropylene crate for storing auto gear, became a white box for storing ropes, life vests, and other marine equipment. Colored teal with a lime or pink lid, it is suitable for college students.

9. **Glorify Product Color**
   Former colors were brown, blue, and pink. Today's product colors are fashionably varied for product uses and trends. Soap dishes are now ruby red, sapphire, emerald, and onyx. Children's products are lagoon green, periwinkle, pink pearl, and aqua.

10. **Create Cross Promotion**
    Apply spin on creative cross promotion. Example: Memorial Day's Indianapolis 500 featured TV scenes that showed pit crews using Rubbermaid Action-Packer storage crates.

Source: Adapted from Jon Berry, "The Art of Rubbermaid," *Advertising Marketing Week*, March 16, 1992.

60,000 in 1980 to over 100,000 in 1993. While Rubbermaid's prices tended to be higher than those of competitors, the company had a wider range of promotable products that commanded more shelf space and delivered better overall value.

Exhibit 8 shows Rubbermaid's advertising and promotion budgets for the years 1989 through 1992.

CUSTOMER RESEARCH

While the firm employed demographic and life-style analysis techniques to identify trends, the core product development activity at Rubbermaid resided in the insights provided by consumer research. Qualitative and quantitative methods were used to

| Exhibit 8 | Rubbermaid's Promotion Budgets, 1989–1992 |

Year	Advertising Budget	Sales	Advertising Budget as Percent of Sales
1989	$52 million	$1.45 billion	3.6%
1990	63 million	1.53 billion	4.1
1991	65 million	1.67 billion	3.9
1992	68 million	1.81 billion	3.8

Source: Prudential Securities.

learn more about shopper preferences. Rubbermaid never test-marketed its products. Instead, it tested color preferences year-round through fact-finding consumer focus groups in five cities, and it regularly quizzed people in shopping malls. The company extensively used buyer panels, brand awareness studies, and diaries that consumers filled with notations about product use.[29]

Rubbermaid had some 150 competitors in home products alone, but no one rival competed with Rubbermaid across its entire product line. Rubbermaid was the only broadly recognized brand name. Since competing products often were not imprinted with the manufacturer's name, it was not unusual for Rubbermaid to receive complaints about some other manufacturer's product. Gault took advantage of this. "We're the only name they can think of, so they write *us* their complaint letters." It was Gault's practice to respond with a letter to the disgruntled writer, "Please make certain that every time you buy a plastic product you look for our name. If we make it, our name is on it. But because you did mean to buy ours and made a mistake and will not do so in the future, here, have one on us."[30]

PRODUCT DEVELOPMENT AT RUBBERMAID

Rubbermaid practiced the team approach to product development and product innovation. In 1987, Rubbermaid considered developing the so-called auto office, a portable plastic device that straps onto a car seat and holds files, pens, and other articles and provides a writing surface. A cross-functional team composed of engineers, designers, and marketers was assembled. They did field research to determine what features customers desired. Rubbermaid brought the new product to the market in 1990; initial sales ran 50 percent above projections.[31]

As a vice president of marketing put it, "It's a misnomer that Rubbermaid is 'marketing-driven.' We're 'market-driven.'" Toward this end, the marketing department was charged with coordinating and managing business teams that focused on an individual business. "We're teamed cross-functionally. Each team has finance, manufacturing, purchasing, sales and marketing, and R&D representation."[32]

---

[29]Alex Taylor III, "Why the Bounce at Rubbermaid?" *Fortune*, April 13, 1987, p. 78.
[30]Ibid.
[31]Brian Dunmaine, "Who Needs a Boss," *Fortune*, May 7, 1990, p. 53.
[32]Seth Lubove, "Okay, Call Me a Predator," *Forbes*, February 16, 1993, p. 151.

In 1992, Rubbermaid introduced, on average, a new product every day of the year. The underlying reasons for developing so many new products, according to management, were to ascertain and develop new categories that allowed Rubbermaid to enter new markets and new sections within a retail store. New lines, it was claimed, kept Rubbermaid's product offerings fresh, up-to-date, and highly salable. The company had installed a new generation of computer-aided design (CAD) workstations that reduced new product design time from months to days. "New product obsession is what defines us," Schmitt professes. "It creates excitement, momentum, and growth."

[handwritten margin note: strength — continuous & rapid product development & fast to mkt.]

THE EVERYTHING RUBBERMAID STORE

In August 1993, Rubbermaid opened "Everything Rubbermaid," a four-floor retail outlet in downtown Wooster. "It's a laboratory store and it gives us the opportunity to experiment," Schmitt said. "It would be one way of getting our brand flag planted in other countries."[33] The 21,000-square-foot Everything Rubbermaid offered shoppers 2,500 products made by Rubbermaid's divisions and subsidiaries.

Rubbermaid's management believed the store would set a national trend for how general merchandise, deep discounters, and specialty-niche stores could work together to open new markets. Modeled after a factory outlet store, but without discount prices, it was not intended as a format to draw consumers away from stores already selling Rubbermaid products. Everything Rubbermaid also served as a facility to survey consumers and have focus groups evaluate Rubbermaid products.

RUBBERMAID'S RESEARCH AND DEVELOPMENT EFFORTS

Adept at searching out ways to grow, Rubbermaid's designers continually tweaked and twisted mature products to spark incremental sales. The firm's formula for R&D success was to study consumer behavior and markets regularly and keenly. Management believed the key to effective research was acute attention to changing demographics and current trends and carefully listening to customers' stated and perceived needs.

[handwritten margin note: Ambitious goals — long term plan should allow for mkt. maturity]

Keeping a stream of new products and product improvements flowing required a solid commitment to research and development. Each of Rubbermaid's operating divisions had its own R&D team, and some divisions were expected to enter a new market segment every 18 to 24 months under Gault and more recently every 12 to 18 months under Schmitt.

[handwritten margin note: Cost of being leader quite high]

Rubbermaid launched more than 250 new products in both 1989 and 1990, with a success rate of 90 percent. In 1992, about 350 new products were introduced. The company's goal of 30 percent of sales each year coming from products less than five years old had been consistently met and often exceeded since 1985. Rubbermaid's R&D expenditures had risen from $6.6 million in 1985 to $17.4 million in 1990 to $23.2 million in 1991 and $25.1 million in 1992.

---

[33]Lornet Trumbull, "Store to Be One of a Kind," *The Beacon Journal* (Akron, Ohio), August 6, 1993, p. B3.

RUBBERMAID MANUFACTURING AND POLYMERS[34] ———————

Historically, new product development at Rubbermaid had closely tracked the development of new raw materials and new production technology. In its early years, Rubbermaid was one of the first users of the then new material vulcanized rubber.

Most recently, Rubbermaid's new product development had been closely linked to new material development and process enhancements occurring within the polymer industry. Polymers were man-made molecules strung together to arrive at various forms of materials generally referred to as plastics. Plastics varied according to how elastic or inelastic they were; the challenge was to create a plastic product that was inelastic enough to retain its shape, yet not brittle enough to crack, shatter, or break due to use, pressure, or low temperatures. The potential for materials and products made from individual polymers and strings of polymers was vast and had barely been touched.

Rubbermaid maintained very close relationships with the suppliers of the plastics it used as raw materials. It participated in technical exchange meetings and programs on a regular basis with its vendors. Rubbermaid was always looking, and waiting, for vendors to develop new plastics with properties that would allow it to manufacture new products. Rubbermaid always had a list of potential products waiting for the right material—this led to a constant exchange with polymer producers. Vendors were quite anxious to bring new plastics to Rubbermaid because Rubbermaid had a reputation for being able to quickly apply a material to a new product and get the product produced and into the marketplace. Also, the potential high volume of output of any product Rubbermaid manufactured and marketed was quite attractive to a polymer vendor.

Polymer-Related Manufacturing Issues: Color, Recycling, and Cooperation

Color was a key factor in the production of plastic goods. Some of Rubbermaid's most significant successes related to the innovative use of color. However, adding color to plastics and thus to the resulting goods was often a difficult and costly process. In fact, it could be the most expensive element of the production process. Still, Rubbermaid was very committed to being a leader in the use of color in plastic products. Management viewed the ability to lead in the use of color as a strategic factor in maintaining a competitive edge in almost all of the company's product areas.

Rubbermaid wanted to see the color problem studied and solved. The ideal solution was to add color to molten plastic right before it came out of the nozzle to be used in production machines, presses, or molds. By doing this a significant savings would result, mainly in the form of reduced time, labor, energy, and downtime associated with having to totally flush out an entire plastic "line" every time there was to be a switch in color. A color change could sometimes take 24 hours due to the need to repeat the flushing so that none of a previous color remained to contaminate the next color of plastic that went through the line.

---

[34]The material in this section is based on personal interviews with Rubbermaid senior managers—Michael E. Naylor, Sr., VP Technology and Environment; and Norman J. DeCost, VP Product Processes/Process Technology.

RUBBERMAID'S CAPITAL INVESTMENT PROGRAM ⸺

Between 1981 and 1991, Rubbermaid invested over $600 million to expand manufacturing and distribution facilities, modernize equipment, install process control systems and automatic packaging systems, purchase new tooling for new products, and increase capacity for existing products. During 1991, while many companies curtailed capital investments, Rubbermaid invested $122.5 million to accelerate productivity improvements, expand facilities, enter new markets, and develop new products. In 1992, Rubbermaid invested a record $134.5 million; projected capital spending in 1993 was $141.7 million. By upgrading plants, worker productivity had increased from 300 units per day in 1952 to 500 in 1980 and, under Gault's leadership, had risen beyond 900 units.[35]

RUBBERMAID'S APPROACH TO GLOBAL EXPANSION ⸺

Rubbermaid's top management placed the primary responsibility for global expansion within each operating division. In 1992, each operating division had an international vice president concentrating on global opportunities. Rubbermaid's corporate role was to develop, in conjunction with the core businesses, organizational and operating plans and priorities. Also, to improve efficiencies in the new country markets being targeted, staff functions were centralized while line functions were decentralized to each core business.

Conflict of interests?

Rubbermaid saw expanding into foreign markets as one of the firm's greatest opportunities. Significant growth potential existed because of the functional utility of its products, their universal acceptability, and the prolific introductions of new items. As of 1993, Rubbermaid's products were distributed in over 100 countries.

Rubbermaid used several approaches to pursue sales growth in international markets. To maximize returns on existing plant investments, Rubbermaid exported from existing manufacturing facilities in the United States, Mexico, Canada, and Europe. Licensing arrangements were used in those markets where the costs of importing were prohibitive and where company-owned manufacturing was not economically justifiable.

In 1992, Rubbermaid acquired CIPSA, the leading plastic housewares manufacturer and marketer in Mexico. That same year, a new joint venture in Hungary by Curver Rubbermaid Group broadened Rubbermaid's global capacity and sales momentum.

By the year 2000, Schmitt wanted 25 percent of Rubbermaid's total revenues to come from outside the United States. Since Rubbermaid wanted to double its sales every five years, this translated into a foreign market goal of $1.5 billion, an amount almost the size of Rubbermaid itself in 1992.

Rubbermaid was concentrating on four primary strategic spheres of opportunity: North America, Europe, the Far East, and South America:

> *Europe:* The Curver Rubbermaid Group European joint venture represented the housewares and specialty product segments of the business. Rubbermaid viewed the impending economic unification in Western Europe and the

---

[35]Alex Taylor, "Why the Bounce at Rubbermaid?"

new-found freedoms of the Eastern European countries as creating a giant market and significant opportunities.

Little Tikes, commercial products, and office products operated their own businesses, with European distribution facilities supported by imports from North America (including Mexico) and licensed local companies.

Far East: This sphere of opportunity posed the greatest challenge to Rubbermaid. However, where relationships had been established—for example, in Japan—results so far had been impressive. As more emphasis was directed toward the Orient, rapid acceptance of Rubbermaid products was anticipated.

South America: To serve South America, the remainder of Latin America, and the Caribbean, Rubbermaid exported products from North America (including Mexico) and licensed local companies.

North America: Rubbermaid anticipated rapid sales expansion as North America evolved into a more homogeneous market. In Canada, the company had manufacturing and or distribution facilities for all operations. The addition of CIPSA by the Home Products Division expanded the Mexican housewares market. All other North American Rubbermaid businesses utilized Mexican distributors.

New Markets: Countries in the Pacific Rim such as China, Malaysia, Indonesia, and India offered opportunities to experiment and learn new means and ways for expansion.

RUBBERMAID'S CORPORATE REPUTATION

In January 1993, Rubbermaid was ranked second among *Fortune's* "America's Most Admired Corporations." It was the eighth consecutive year Rubbermaid had ranked in the top 10. Rubbermaid and Merck (number one) were the only two companies to be included among the top 10 over the prior eight surveys. The *Fortune* ranking was based on a survey of over 10,000 senior executives, outside board members, and financial analysts. The ranking was based on eight attributes: quality of management, quality of products and services, financial soundness, value as a long-term investment, use of corporate assets, innovativeness, community or environmental responsibility, and ability to attract, develop, and keep talented people.

Exhibit 9 presents an 11-year review of Rubbermaid's performance.

Exhibit 9 Summary of Rubbermaid's Performance, 1982–1992 *(dollars in thousands except per share amounts)*

	1992	1991	1990	1989	1988	1987	1986	1985	1984	1983	1982
Operating Results											
Net sales	$1,805,332	$1,667,305	$1,534,013	$1,452,365	$1,291,584	$1,096,055	$864,721	$747,858	$676,660	$555,789	$462,792
Cost of sales	1,200,651	1,102,685	1,014,526	967,563	886,850	727,927	554,421	488,169	458,803	366,425	306,190
Realignment costs	27,500	—	—	—	—	—	—	—	—	—	—
Other operating expenses	310,410	307,780	286,647	268,148	221,497	199,145	166,954	140,203	118,915	103,608	90,336
Net earnings	$ 164,095*	$ 162,650	$ 143,520	$ 124,984	$ 106,858	$ 90,723	$ 75,000	$ 62,288	$ 54,129	$ 44,825	$ 32,819
Per common share	$1.02*	$1.02	$0.90	$0.78	$0.67	$0.57	$0.47	$0.40	$0.34	$0.29	$0.22
As a percentage of sales	9.1%*	9.8%	9.4%	8.6%	8.3%	8.3%	8.7%	8.3%	8.0%	8.1%	7.1%
Return on average shareholders' equity	19.5%/17.5%*	19.7%	20.2%	20.6%	20.6%	20.8%	20.5%	20.0%	20.4%	20.1%	17.3%
Financial Position											
Current assets	$ 699,650	$ 663,999	$ 602,697	$ 567,307	$ 452,639	$ 418,563	$332,655	$309,336	$270,989	$232,226	$169,879
Property, plant, and equipment, net	517,096	461,375	405,520	379,107	347,677	310,017	248,224	210,929	171,836	138,078	138,003
Intangible and other assets, net	109,823	119,157	106,033	38,591	42,389	45,748	45,780	13,041	9,826	8,151	8,112
Total assets	$1,326,569	$1,244,531	$1,114,250	$985,005	$842,705	$774,328	$626,659	$533,306	$452,651	$378,455	$315,994
Current liabilities	$ 223,246	$ 245,500	$ 235,300	$ 215,121	$ 197,431	$ 209,771	$156,456	$133,116	$114,970	$ 87,061	$ 65,342
Deferred taxes and other liabilities	95,395	85,479	71,555	67,114	47,471	47,585	40,013	28,713	23,172	19,317	17,166
Long-term debt	20,279	27,812	39,191	50,294	39,023	40,042	35,668	34,071	27,559	28,589	29,873
Shareholders' equity	987,649	885,740	768,204	652,476	558,780	476,930	394,522	337,406	286,950	243,488	203,613
Total liabilities and shareholders' equity	$1,326,569	$1,244,531	$1,114,250	$985,005	$842,705	$774,328	$626,659	$533,306	$452,651	$378,455	$315,994
Long-term debt as a percent of capitalization	3%	4%	5%	8%	7%	8%	9%	10%	9%	11%	13%
Working capital	$ 476,404	$ 418,499	$ 367,397	$ 352,186	$ 255,208	$ 208,792	$176,199	$176,220	$156,019	$145,165	$104,537
Current ratio	3.13	2.70	2.56	2.64	2.29	2.00	2.13	2.32	2.36	2.67	2.60

* Results after the cumulative effect of changing the method of accounting for postretirement benefits other than pensions.

Exhibit 9   Concluded

	1992	1991	1990	1989	1988	1987	1986	1985	1984	1983	1982
Other Data											
Average common shares outstanding (000)	160,207	160,126	159,688	159,250	158,928	158,468	158,064	157,588	157,240	153,934	149,444
Cash dividends paid	$ 56,477	$ 49,643	$ 42,621	$ 35,975	$ 29,520	$ 24,581	$ 19,771	$ 15,907	$ 13,224	$ 11,277	$ 9,995
Cash dividends paid per common share	$ 0.3525	$ 0.31	$ 0.27	$ 0.23	$ 0.19	$ 0.16	$ 0.13	$ 0.113	$ 0.098	$ 0.088	$ 0.079
Shareholders' equity per common share	$ 6.16	$ 5.53	$ 4.80	$ 4.10	$ 3.52	$ 3.01	$ 2.50	$ 2.15	$ 1.83	$ 1.57	$ 1.38
NYSE stock price range (high-low)	$ 37-27	$ 38-19	$ 23-16	$ 19-13	$ 14-11	$ 18-10	$ 14-8	$ 9-5	$ 6-4	$ 6-4	$ 4-2
Additions to property, plant, and equipment	$ 134,528	$ 122,513	$ 103,720	$ 89,787	$ 87,333	$ 104,429	$ 71,587	$ 71,665	$ 55,615	$ 29,275	$ 21,433
Depreciation expense	$ 69,919	$ 62,650	$ 55,346	$ 57,341	$ 46,134	$ 44,155	$ 34,135	$ 31,607	$ 23,473	$ 20,054	$ 18,450
Number of shareholders—year-end	20,255	15,429	13,305	11,225	10,482	10,104	8,379	6,332	5,722	5,168	4,775
Average number of associates	11,296	9,754	9,304	9,098	8,643	7,512	6,509	5,934	5,374	4,815	4,645

Source: Rubbermaid Incorporated, 1992 Annual Report.

Plant Barry and the International Brotherhood of Electrical Workers

Faculty of Global Utility Institute, Samford University

In the fall of 1990, the management of The Southern Company, one of the largest electric utilities in the United States, adopted a vision statement to give direction to the company's several operating units (Georgia Power Co., Alabama Power Co., Gulf Power Co., Mississippi Power Co., Savannah Electric, and SEI). The vision statement contained commitments to customer satisfaction, efficiency, participative management, openness, and a business-mindedness that previously had been relatively underemphasized in The Southern Company.

One group's interpretation of the vision statement gave rise to a total quality initiative (TQI) at Alabama Power Company's Plant Barry. The TQI at Plant Barry began with the combined efforts of Ed Covington, plant manager, his management team, and members of the International Brotherhood of Electrical Workers (IBEW or "the Brotherhood"). The individuals who created and promoted TQI replaced a management style and organizational structure that had characterized Plant Barry and The Southern Company for several decades. An indication of these changes was reflected in a goal statement developed by the Barry Design Team, a team of IBEW and non-IBEW employees:

> Our goal is to redesign Barry Steam Plant into an empowered, team-based, value adding organization, charged with increasing net customer value, and with continuously improving the processes involved.

BARRY STEAM PLANT CHARTER

This case traces the beginnings of the transformation of the 380 employees at Barry Steam Plant (Plant Barry) into an "empowered" organization and explores the individual and group changes that made it possible. Plant Barry, a coal-fired generating plant with a capacity exceeding 1,500 megawatts (1500 MW), is located 25 miles northwest of Mobile, Alabama. The changes at Plant Barry raise several issues concerning the introduction and facilitation of change and its effects on people and organizations. Among them:

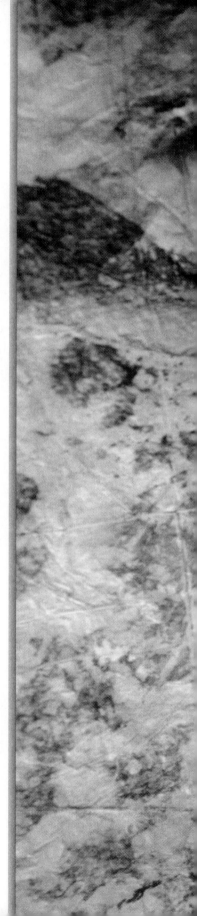

1. What personal changes are needed for a leader to initiate fundamental changes in fellow workers and their relationships?

2. How does one enlist the enthusiastic participation of employees in seeking ways to increase efficiency and effectiveness in the midst of a company environment that threatens security?

3. Can an organization sustain changes of this significance when one or more of the principal sponsors leaves the organization?

Origins of Change in Fuel Handling

In late summer 1990, the management of Plant Barry and the leaders of the Brotherhood forged a new alliance with the undertaking of a major safety-improvement initiative. The safety initiative was the responsibility of Plant Barry's safety committee. The safety committee extensively used employee involvement to identify and implement safety practices that, for the first time in many years, resulted in significant reductions in accidents and injuries. Jerry Pack, an internal consultant with Alabama Power Company, was recognized as the facilitator of the worker involvement found in the safety committee.

Concurrently, Alan Reaves, superintendent of fuel handling, sought in another program to dislodge the deeply ingrained authoritarian management style of the foremen in the department. With the assistance of Bill Bruckel, an external change consultant, a training program was developed and offered to the foremen. Shortly after the training sessions began, Alan was transferred to Miller Steam Plant. The project was continued by Alan's successor, Greg Long.

As the Fuel Handling Project moved through its initial stages, Ed Covington and Ron Campbell (assistant plant manager) explored ways to expand the positive outcomes of employee participation. Ed and Ron wanted to capitalize on the safety initiative in other joint actions with the Brotherhood. Ed and Ron asked Greg Long, Jerry Pack, and Bill Bruckel to implement a pilot project of "self-directed work teams" in the fuel handling department.

In October 1991, Long, Pack, and Bruckel met with Ed Covington and Ron Campbell to recommend total quality management (TQM) as the model for change in fuel handling. Ed and Ron endorsed the approach and recognized it as a complement to the teamwork previously developed between management and the Brotherhood.

The next step was to select a process for implementing TQM. From three well-established approaches to TQM, the management of Plant Barry selected the one offered by the Miller Consulting Group of Atlanta. The Miller Group's program was entitled "Design for Quality." Design for Quality emphasized the need for radical change in the organization—technical structure, social structure, and culture—as a prerequisite to positive long-term results.

Training in Design for Quality began in December 1991, when Ron Campbell and four senior officers of the Brotherhood (Andy Grantham and Wayne Sheffield, president and vice president of Local 345; and L. C. Studdard and Jeff Blanton, business agent and assistant business agent of the IBEW System Council U-19) attended a three-day seminar presented by the Miller Group. Ed Covington attended the seminar a few weeks later.

Following the seminars, meetings were held at Plant Barry with groups of employees to explain management's intention to create and implement change in the culture and structure of the organization. The meetings emphasized the linkage between success in The Southern Company's competitive environment and teamwork in day-to-day operations. The satisfaction of both external and internal customers was the key to success.

Work-process analysis was introduced. Work-process analysis is the study of work to find means of restructuring or "mapping" it into more productive designs. The idea was for all members of the workforce to understand all work processes. In these meetings, a new vocabulary was introduced to Plant Barry: *empowerment, self-direction, teamwork, customer satisfaction, whole-process ownership, continuous improvement*, and *paradigm shifts.*

The Project Expanded to the Entire Plant

Ed Covington and his staff became convinced that quality could not be attained anywhere without change everywhere, and they decided to expand the initiative to the entire plant. With this in mind, Ed, Greg Long, Jerry Pack, and Bill Bruckel sought approval from Harold Jones, senior vice president, Fossil and Hydro Generation, Alabama Power Company, to expand the TQM effort to the entire plant. Jones stipulated that the project must observe all corporate policies governing contracts, finances, and legal requirements. In addition, Jones suggested that interaction with other plants and departments be undertaken with careful consideration of how they operate.

In late February 1992, Jones authorized Plant Barry to be the pilot project for the introduction of TQM in Fossil and Hydro Generation. Jones hinted that if the project at Plant Barry was successful, he would encourage the same approach for other plants in Alabama Power Company.

The Plant Barry team initiated the project immediately. The Miller Group's approach called for the formation of a steering committee that would have the power to make changes and negotiate, when necessary, with the company and the Brotherhood. The steering committee was formed in March 1992, with five members of management, four members of the IBEW, and one nonexempt employee. Representing the IBEW on the steering committee were Buddy Black, Jr., plant control operator; Wayne Sheffield, welder and vice president of the Local; John Dean, helper; and Joe Isbell, I&E journeyman.

Following John Dean's transfer to the Mobile division and Joe Isbell's death, Carl Elmore, welder, and Tommy Hunt, electrician, were selected to fill the vacancies. Members of management on the steering committee were Ed Covington; Gary Lewis, administrative manager; Ron Campbell; John Huggins, technical manager; and Lewis Jeffers, maintenance manager. Will Harrison, chemical technician, filled the nonexempt employee position.

The steering committee was responsible for initiating and setting business and organizational goals for the quality process. These responsibilities were divided into two significant elements: (1) forming the design team and (2) writing the charter for Plant Barry. The design team focused on plantwide organizational change. The charter identified the values and operating principles for the plant and established directions and limits to guide the design team.

By late March 1992, the design team was formed with six representatives from management and six from the Brotherhood. For one week in April, the steering committee and the design team participated in a combined training activity to discuss the change process and to clearly identify their respective objectives and responsibilities. The design team was assigned the tasks of analyzing all major work processes, refining them to eliminate waste, establishing "expert teams" to own each process, and empowering the expert teams to be responsible for continuously improving processes.

Following the publication of the Barry Steam Plant Charter on May 6, 1992, the design team participated in a training effort to learn four project-critical skills: (1) team building, (2) data collection, (3) data analysis, and (4) process mapping.

As the design team undertook the work of mapping processes within Plant Barry, management conducted orientation sessions for other plant personnel. Management prepared and delivered a three-day workshop with superintendents and foremen. This workshop involved interactive sessions in which issues of competition, quality, customer awareness, the state of the industry, the future of the company, and the future of the staff were discussed.

By July 1992, the design team had begun mapping the major systems (customer, supplier, technical, and social) of the plant and had completed extensive mapping in the fuel handling department.

Contract Negotiations Cause a Snag

In August 1992, Alabama Power Company and the IBEW were in the process of completing negotiations for contract renewal. The two sides had a long history of an adversarial or win–lose relationship. Among the issues discussed in 1992 was management's desire to have greater flexibility in work assignments across several job classifications. The bargaining sessions became strained and the negotiating committee felt that they had been ill-treated by management. The effects of these tensions were felt at Plant Barry.

In mid-August, it was agreed to suspend the design team's activity until negotiations were concluded. After much effort, an agreement was reached, and a contract was signed in late August. However, the persistence of bad feeling led the Local's leadership to encourage the Brotherhood at Plant Barry to withdraw from noncontract-specified activities. The Brotherhood interpreted this to mean noninvolvement in the TQI.

Ed Covington and his management team faced a dilemma—how to conclude the work of the design team by January 1993 without the assistance of the Brotherhood's representatives. Three alternative courses of action were considered: (1) reform the design team without representatives from the Brotherhood, (2) reform the design team with replacements for the Brotherhood's members, and (3) restart the work of the design team without the union members but openly invite them to participate.

The first alternative appealed to some members of the management team because it was a familiar behavior—unilateral management action. From experience, Barry's management knew that they could reach consensus on issues affecting the plant and its workforce more quickly without Brotherhood participation, but that violated principles of the TQI. The second alternative was rejected because of the time required to train new members of the design team. The third alternative was similar to the first, except that the Brotherhood was welcome to rejoin the process at any time.

The management team chose the third course of action and resumed the work of the design team, with the positions for Brotherhood members remaining open in the hope that they would return to participate. By this action, management demonstrated to the Brotherhood that the management team was serious about the TQI and wanted IBEW participation.

During this period, the Brotherhood's leadership attended steering committee meetings only in their capacity as IBEW representatives. They explored management's options as it became known that the design team would resume its work. The Local feared that management might resort to its old practices of exclusion and unilateral decision making.

The Process Resumes

After a short period of estrangement, the Brotherhood's leadership could see that it was more beneficial to participate and encouraged the members to resume normal activities. In mid-September 1992, the Brotherhood resumed its participation in the design team.

From the earlier three-day workshop facilitated by management with foremen and superintendents, a volunteer team of 18 foremen had decided to continue the process by conducting similar sessions with all plant employees. During the period that the Brotherhood's design team members were absent, the team of foremen decided to "roll-out" the employee involvement meetings to the whole plant. Their first step was to approach members of the Brotherhood for input. In addition to providing valuable input, Brotherhood members were encouraged by the leadership to help develop and facilitate sessions. The actions of the Brotherhood's leadership was a clear signal to the rest of the Brotherhood members that the TQI was something the leadership considered valuable and participation was encouraged.

The organization of Plant Barry conceived by the design team and implemented by management is shown in Exhibit 1. The design was a hub-and-spoke organization. At the center of the organization was the leadership team. The leadership team included four Brotherhood members, the plant's management group, and two other members. The accomplishments were significant. After fuel handling, the team turned its attention to fuel maintenance, auto garage, tractor garage, and yard crew (each area mapped, analyzed, and refined). Following fuel, the work had progressed to warehouse, then to chemical and results, and finally to operations and maintenance, the largest and most complex component of Plant Barry's workings. By March 1993, the plant's organization had been redesigned.

Ed Covington and Ron Campbell Look Back

"Ron, do you think we would have started the total quality initiative if we had known what we were going to have to go through?" Ed asked Ron as they sat in Ed's office.

Ron responded, "I've been thinking about that, too. It is really difficult sometimes. I miss getting into things myself and making sure people are doing things right. Standing, watching, and having to just sit there and listen when I feel like I'm being attacked has really been tough. I start to doubt whether I'm really in control."

Ed stated, "For my first 30 years with this company, from the time I was a construction laborer in 1958 until recently, the company wanted managers who were 'strong' and who knew what to do and who did it, without questioning."

Ron interjected with a smile, "I've not been at it as long as you have, but when I started with Florida Power in 1973, management told me what to do and I followed orders and ordered others to follow my orders. There were no ifs, ands, or buts about it."

Ed continued, "When I was a new plant manager, in 1986, I was described as a 'watch over the shoulder, kick ass and take names boss' and I was good at it. Now

Exhibit 1   Barry Electric Generating Plant Organization Design

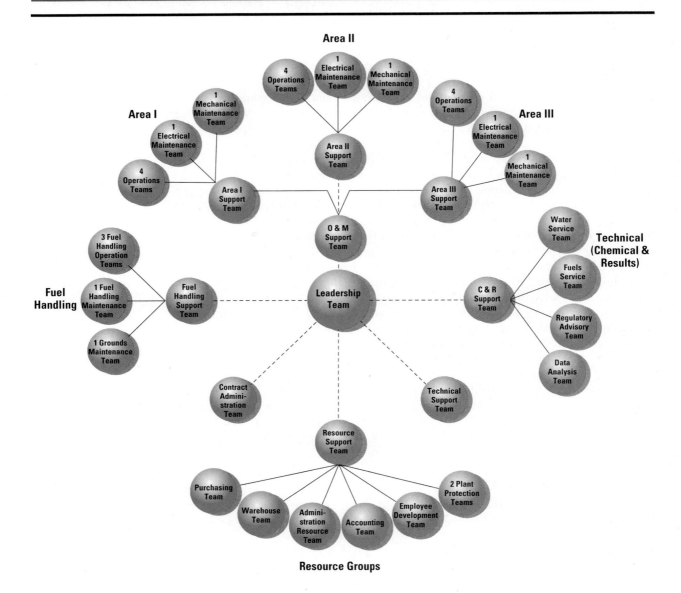

with the quality initiative, employees kid me about the past. I want badly at times to make decisions and get on with it."

Ron replied, "There were times when the design team was bogged down, I wanted to say 'do it this way and let's move on.' It was so hard sometimes to be restrained."

"I sure wanted to retaliate when we were going through the Brotherhood problems," said Ed. "I share your frustration. But when I can remember what it is we are trying to accomplish it makes it easier to change. Everyone has responded when we are supportive and serve as a role model like we did in the employee involvement orientation sessions."

"We have a new challenge the leadership team needs to act on, and it concerns me," said Ron. "There is a question of what roles belong to the leadership team, support teams, and what roles still belong to the managers. How can we make sure we have the right balance?"

Ed answered, "I think it will be a struggle and will evolve. I realize that the older employees, especially the foremen, are beginning to feel frustrated. They are losing their sense of security. The rest of the folks want some security, too. They want to do what we have laid out—participate in decision making, have more control over their future, and show what they can do."

Ron nodded in agreement. As he rose to leave the room, he turned and said to Ed, "What do you think would happen to Barry if you and I were transferred to other locations?" Ed paused thoughtfully, but before he could respond, Ron had left the room.

Epilogue

Ed Covington died suddenly in July 1993, just prior to being transferred to the Miller Steam Plant. Ron Campbell became plant manager of Barry Steam Plant.

Ron talked about his role and hopes for the future of Plant Barry and The Southern Company.

> Being plant manager now gives me some sense of apprehension—learning how to respond to challenges of the future and knowing that I have the responsibility for how well Plant Barry operates. Before my promotion to plant manager, I always felt that I had input into decisions that were made, but ultimately, the final decision was made by the plant manager. Now, I am the one seeking input from others and I have responsibility for those final decisions. As one might imagine, I have had something of a paradigm shift with the job change.
>
> There are several other things that come to mind as I think about being plant manager and setting the tone for the future of Barry. First, and foremost, is being able to communicate to everyone my vision of how different from the past I want the future to be. A lot of these differences are in people treating the business like they are owners, because they are, and not just employees. I think as an owner you have a different mindset about how you conduct yourself and that different mindset will make everyone's job easier and will result in us being more cost effective.
>
> I want to remove as much fear about the future as I can. The nature of our business right now creates a lot of fear that is keeping us from focusing on the changes that we need to make. The fear of the loss of jobs and lack of advancement is keeping us from moving forward as fast as we need to. We need to change more rapidly than we are, but we must help people get ready to change in order for us to be able to move forward.
>
> My biggest desire is for us—I am referring to all employees of The Southern Company—to realize that if we all pull the wagon in the same direction, it will roll a lot easier, we will get to where we need to go quicker, and all of our jobs will be more enjoyable. I firmly believe that together we can find a better solution than if we develop solutions independently.

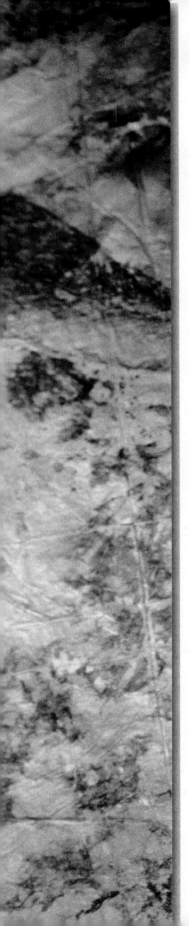

Titeflex Corporation:
The turnaround challenge
Ravi Ramamurti, Northeastern University

On December 1, 1988, Jon H. Simpson, 41, became president and CEO of Titeflex Corporation, a firm that sold $45 million worth of high-performance hoses to the aerospace, industrial, and automotive sectors. Simpson had worked for many years in the R&D department of the 3M Company. More recently, he had been VP (Operations) in CHR Industries, which, like Titeflex, was a part of the Bundy Group of companies. In January 1988, when Bundy brought in the Boston Consulting Group (BCG) to study Titeflex's operations, Jon Simpson was asked to get involved with the project. Within a year, two important events occurred: first, the British engineering conglomerate Tube Investments (TI) acquired the Bundy Group; second, TI assigned Jon Simpson to manage the Titeflex subsidiary.

The promotion transformed Simpson's life. Suddenly, he found himself in Springfield, Massachusetts, managing a new division under a new set of (British) bosses. Simpson noted that it felt good to have been promoted but admitted that the task before him in Titeflex was daunting: To be sure, the company was profitable and its sales were growing, but competitors were nibbling away at Titeflex's market share, production was slow, deliveries were more often late than on time, and relations between management and Titeflex's union were abysmal.

Sir Christopher Lewinton, who was the TI Group's CEO, had divested nearly 70 percent of the group's assets and bought nearly a billion dollars worth of new companies since becoming TI's head in 1985. He wanted TI's 70 companies to be worldwide leaders in technology and market share in their respective niches. Lewinton believed in giving his companies a great deal of autonomy, but he expected their sales and profits to grow at 15 percent per annum while yielding at least a 15 percent return on sales and a 30 percent return on net assets before interest and taxes.

As CEO, Simpson said he felt sandwiched between irate customers, warring employees, and demanding superiors. How should he deal with his customers? What could he do to improve Titeflex's operations and relations with the union? Would he be able to change the culture within Titeflex? How should he handle his bosses in England? It seemed there was so much to do and so little time. Simpson wondered what his priorities ought to be, where he ought to begin, and how he ought to proceed.

BRIEF HISTORY OF TITEFLEX

Titeflex was founded in 1916 by Westinghouse Corporation. At that time, flexible hoses were made either from metal or natural rubber. Titeflex introduced a hose made from interlocking brass strips tacked with string. These early hoses were used in industrial and automotive applications as well as in World War I aircraft engines. With the advent in the 1930s of synthetic rubber and plastics that could withstand the corrosive effects of fuels and oils, Titeflex shifted its emphasis to shielded metal conduits. During World War II, every B-17 and B-24 was equipped with a Titeflex ignition harness. In the late 1950s, Titeflex began developing metal hose products with inner cores made of Teflon for use in fuel and oil systems in jet engines. In 1971, Titeflex reentered the industrial hose market, and, in 1978, the automotive market. In 1978, Bundy Corporation added Titeflex to its Performance Plastics Group.

MARKETING AND SALES

According to customers that Simpson met in his first few days at the company, Titeflex had a reputation for producing "pricey" products of excellent quality. A total of 100,000 different hoses varying in size, shape, fittings, and type of protective sleeving were offered by Titeflex. Customers for these hoses were concentrated in three market segments: aerospace (50 percent of sales), industrial (30 percent of sales), and automotive (20 percent of sales).

Aerospace

Titeflex's Marketing department estimated that with 35 percent of the market in the early 1980s, Titeflex ranked second in market share in this segment. Its customers included all aircraft engine and airframe manufacturers worldwide. Titeflex and two other firms accounted for 90 percent of all sales, with the remainder shared by several smaller competitors. Few competitors existed in this segment because of the long time required to demonstrate effectiveness in usage and the need to get certified as a qualified supplier. While the number of pieces sold was small (10 units per day), the parts were highly customized for each client and involved large margins. Some complex hoses went through all 44 manufacturing departments, traveling two-and-a-half miles from start to finish. In recent years, Titeflex's market share had declined to approximately 25 percent; in 1988, sales to this segment were expected to be 10 percent below the 1987 level. Indeed, two of Titeflex's largest customers told Simpson that they were seriously considering dropping Titeflex as a supplier.

While products for the aerospace segment were highly engineered, the rate of technological change was small until a new series of aircraft was announced. Then, the technological change was substantial. Continued success in the market depended largely on delivery and price for existing products and on technological advances for future products.

Demand in this market had boomed in the 1980s, thanks to the defense build-up in the United States and the growth of the commercial airline industry. However, the outlook for the future was somewhat bleak due to the thaw in East–West relations and the shake-out occurring in the airline industry.

Industrial

Industrial application of hoses ranged from oil field equipment to refrigeration equipment. Half of all sales were to equipment OEMs and the other half to distributors. Many firms participated in this segment, including a number that competed primarily on price. Titeflex held only 1 to 2 percent of the overall market for industrial hoses but as much as 20 percent of the market for the high-pressure/high-temperature segment, where price was less important than quality and reliability.

A key feature in the replacement portion of this market was rapid response to customer requests. On the other hand, meeting delivery schedules, rather than immediate response, was important for the OEM segment. Product customization was not as critical as in the aerospace market, and unit demand was roughly twice as large. Titeflex's marketing department estimated that demand would grow in line with the general economy.

Automotive

As automobiles and their engines became smaller, engine temperatures and vibration effects increased dramatically. Titeflex had a technological advantage when entering this market because these problems had been solved 10 years earlier in aerospace applications. Demand was somewhat seasonal because of the automotive companies' production schedules and cyclical according to the performance of the overall economy.

Price competition was intense. Margins were low in contrast to those in the other two markets, but there was little variety in products. A customer might expect 2,000 hoses to be shipped per day. Late deliveries could shut down an engine assembly or components plant, and customers would not accept early delivery. Technological change was continuous, although changes were small when compared to those encountered in aerospace. Of the three markets served by Titeflex, the automotive segment was expected to grow the fastest.

Sales and Marketing Organization

Titeflex had separate sales and marketing departments for the aerospace segment and the industrial and automotive segments, both based in Springfield (see Exhibit 1 for Titeflex's organization structure in 1988). Salespersons were paid a base salary plus commission. The sales department was the principal contact point with customers, and other forms of contact between customers and Titeflex employees were strongly discouraged. For instance, when customers visited the company to follow up on orders, they were whisked away to a small room in the sales department and not permitted to wander around the offices or on the shop floor.

Competitors

Titeflex's strongest competitor in high-performance hoses was Aeroquip Corporation, based in Jackson, Michigan, which was also the leading supplier to the aerospace segment. The other major competitor, Stratoflex, was based in Dallas, Texas, and had become increasingly aggressive after it was acquired by Parker Hannifin, which invested heavily in the firm's modernization. Both companies were reducing their

Exhibit 1   Titeflex Organization Structure and Staffing, December 1988

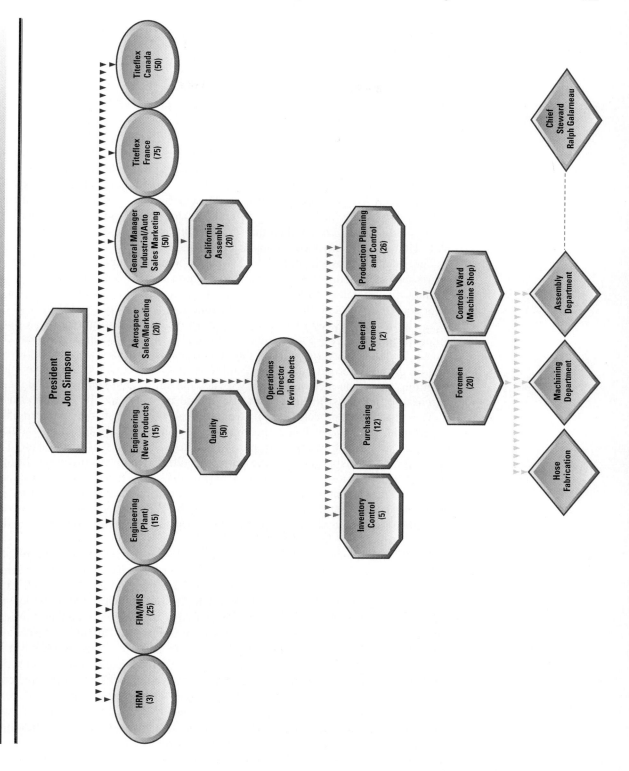

costs and improving customer service at a brisk pace. As of 1988, no foreign competitor of any significance had emerged.

ORGANIZATION AND OPERATIONS AT SPRINGFIELD ————

In 1988, Titeflex employed about 750 people, including nearly 600 in its largest facility in Springfield, Massachusetts, with the rest in plants and offices located in Canada and France. About half the employees at Springfield were shop floor workers, while the rest worked in "front offices:" operations planning, engineering, quality control, sales, finance/MIS, R&D, and human resource management (see Exhibit 1). Bundy had invested significant sums to expand and modernize the Springfield plant and strengthen the MIS system. However, Bundy had not tampered with Titeflex's organization or management methods.

The sales department took 3 to 5 weeks for order entry and processing, while operations took about 7 to 10 weeks to manufacture a standard, "made to stock" product, for a total of 10 to 15 weeks from order receipt to shipment—provided all went according to plan. In the operations function, there were five to six levels in the hierarchy from the head of the department to the shop floor employee. A purchase order for a bearing to fix a machine might require seven or eight signatures. Departmental loyalties were strong, and interdepartmental coordination was achieved primarily through formal meetings. Said one busy executive: "We have morning meetings, afternoon meetings, quality review meetings, engineering review meetings, purchasing meetings, make–buy meetings, and meetings to schedule meetings!"

The production process for an average hose began with the plant engineering department, which developed the drawings required for manufacture—unless the customer supplied drawings with the order. The basic hose was manufactured in the hose fabrication department, while parts and fittings were manufactured in the machining department. Each of these departments had a handful of very expensive pieces of equipment that were common to the manufacture of all parts. In the assembly department, hoses and fittings made by these departments were assembled with outside parts to make finished products for the aerospace, industrial, and auto-motive markets.

In all departments, workers and equipment were organized by type of activity rather than type of hose or type of customer. For instance, the same machine or worker might be used to fabricate a $10,000 hose for a jet engine as well as a $50 exhaust-recovery hose for a car. Material handlers moved work from one location to the next; the company had designed special carts to minimize damage during such transportation. Indirect workers of this sort accounted for about 20 percent of the shop floor workforce. Most direct workers were paid on a piecework basis.

Shipments were frequently held up for want of outside parts or internal production bottlenecks, leading in some cases to delays of several weeks and infuriated customers. To alleviate this problem, Titeflex built up inventories of parts and work-in-process at all stages; by 1988, inventories had risen to four months of sales. A modern, computerized Materials Requirement Planning (MRP) system introduced in the mid-1980s at a cost of nearly $1 million generated very detailed reports on schedules, inventories, and manufacturing costs (by order, by department, etc.). In addition, Production Planning and Control (PPC) held periodic meetings to review the status of various jobs. When all else failed, the "sales action" group in the PPC department shepherded high-priority orders through the production maze to placate angry customers. Yet, in 1988, only a fourth of all industrial orders and a tenth of all aerospace orders were delivered on time.

Titeflex had the reputation of shipping high-quality products. A large quality department, which reported to the engineering department rather than the operations manager, inspected parts and subassemblies at every stage of the production process, sending anything that fell short of specifications for rework. Typically, 25 percent of the output had to be reworked. A competent 15-person new products engineering department was engaged in R&D; lately, it had been downsized and was quite heavily focused on new products for the automotive industry.

Several of the most senior executives were included in an incentive plan that awarded bonuses at the end of the year based on the company's overall performance. The accounting system yielded cost data on individual departments and generated profit numbers for the company as a whole. Titeflex had no scheme for employee stock ownership, although a few senior executives were believed to own Bundy stock. John Makis, who headed Titeflex from 1980 to 1988, had been with the company for more than 30 years and was described by a colleague as "conservative and cautious."

MANAGEMENT–UNION RELATIONS AT SPRINGFIELD

Ralph Galarneau, 42, was chief steward of Titeflex's Springfield union. Galarneau joined Titeflex at age 19, following in the footsteps of his father, who was himself a union leader in Titeflex. Although workers voted (over his objections) in 1976 to join the Teamsters Union rather than remain an independent union, Galarneau remained an influential member of the union, eventually becoming its head. Like Galarneau, the average Titeflex worker was about 40 years old, had been with the organization 20 years, and had at least a few relatives working in the company.

Historically, union contracts had been negotiated annually, usually through a contentious process that involved a one- or two-week strike. In addition, workers went on wildcat strikes from time to time. The contract stipulated work rules in detail, including who could perform which tasks: for instance, only welders could weld, and only material handlers could move materials. For the first time, in 1987, management and the union signed a three-year contract, one that would expire in April 1990. Although Ralph Galarneau represented workers at contract negotiations, it was the local Teamsters' Union's business agent that formally signed the contract.

Kevin Roberts, head of operations, represented management in contract negotiations. A subordinate described him as "brilliant," while another noted that Roberts had a large following among the supervisory staff within operations. According to one employee, "Kevin and Ralph play cat and mouse day in and day out." Roberts expected his foremen to take disciplinary action against troublemakers on a regular basis; in turn, Galarneau filed grievances with Kevin Roberts at the rate of at least one per day, and often pursued individual cases for as long as possible. Workers were subject to "progressive discipline"—that is, they could be fired only after a long series of prior warnings and hearings. Typically, only one or two workers were fired every year. However, when demand slackened, layoffs were permitted on a reverse seniority basis. Reflecting on the work environment, Chris Ward, a supervisor, said: "It's unfortunate, but true, that in this company to get work out of your guys and to keep your bosses happy you've got to be an s.o.b.!"

Once signed, the contract became the primary basis for union–management relations. As one employee put it, "Both management and union walk around with copies of the contract in their back pockets." There was minimal interaction between front office people, such as engineers and salespersons, and shop floor workers. Although in the 1960s and 1970s management and workers had celebrated special times like Christmas together, in recent years each had organized its own parties on such occasions.

JON SIMPSON

Jon Simpson earned degrees in polymer chemistry from Duke University and the University of Arizona before joining the 3M Company in 1969 as a bench chemist. Eleven years later, he had become supervisor of an R&D lab employing 70 scientists. In 1980, he left 3M to become vice president of R&D at CHR Industries, a Bundy company within the Performance Plastics Group based in New Haven, Connecticut. CHR made high-performance pressure-sensitive tapes and silicone rubber products for the aerospace and electronics industries. Like Titeflex, CHR worked with Teflon technology and served some of the same end-users. In 1982, Simpson became VP (Operations) of CHR, with continued responsibility for R&D. CHR workers were members of the United Rubber Workers Union. Describing his stint as VP (Operations) at CHR, Jon Simpson said:

> At 3M, I was used to managing professionals doing R&D. It was always very gentlemanly. At CHR, they ate me alive when I tried managing in that style. So, I turned into a Genghis Khan. At the end of the day, my blood pressure was high, theirs was high, and we all went home with knots in our stomach. But I fought and I won every goddamn battle with the unions. And I won it bloody and I won it dirty, but I won every battle. I wouldn't even let 'em win the small ones!

In 1988, when Bundy brought in the Boston Consulting Group (BCG) to study Titeflex's operations, Jon Simpson was asked to get involved with the project. Over a period of nine months, he spent two days a week in Springfield serving as an internal consultant to the BCG team, whose mission was to flowchart organizational processes in every area to identify how efficiency and speed of response could be improved. In August 1988, Bundy transferred Simpson to Titeflex with the intention of making him head of Titeflex's industrial and automotive businesses, leaving the aerospace/marine business under the charge of another general manager. This plan went astray when Tube Investments (TI) bought Bundy and announced its decision to divest all four subsidiaries in Bundy's Performance Plastics Group, including CHR Industries and Titeflex. After further study, however, TI pulled Titeflex out of the divestment package because its technology was seen as having value for Bundy's automotive business as well as for TI's flourishing aerospace business. Christopher Lewinton then made Jon Simpson president and CEO of all of Titeflex.

THE TASK AHEAD

In 1988, Titeflex earned a 5 percent margin on $45 million in sales and a return on net assets[1] before interest and taxes of 20 percent. (See Exhibit 2 for the trend in several performance indicators in the two years prior to Simpson's arrival at Titeflex). In recent years, sales had grown at 6 to 7 percent per year, with growth in the

---

[1]Gross fixed assets less accumulated depreciation.

Exhibit 2   Trends in Performance Indicators, 1988 versus 1987 (1987=100)*

Indicator	1987	1988‡
Sales		
Aerospace	100	89.5
Industrial	100	113.1
Automotive	100	146.3
Total	100	107.4
Quality		
Returns	100	102.3
Rework	100	105.4
Inventory	100	116.5
Overhead/Sales ratio	100	110.0
Pretax return on net assets† before interest (EBIT/NA)	100	94.6
Return on sales	100	87.3

* As Titeflex did not report divisional financial results, the actual amounts are not shown in this table; only changes in each item in 1988 relative to 1987 (base year) are shown. Thus, the table gives some idea of the trends in performance at the time Simpson took over as head of Titeflex (December 1988).

† Net assets equal gross fixed assets less accumulated depreciation.

‡Estimates as of December 1988.

automotive segment offsetting sluggish growth in the industrial sector and negative growth in the aerospace market. Meanwhile, Titeflex's costs were rising faster than sales. Customers were also beginning to expect their suppliers to provide more and better service for less money.

Simpson estimated that Titeflex had a 15 to 20 percent cost disadvantage relative to its major competitors because of its location in Massachusetts, where taxes and wages were higher than in other parts of the country. At the same time, moving to a different location could be an expensive proposition; among other things, a new facility would have to be recertified before it could supply the aerospace industry. Besides, Simpson believed the workforce in western Massachusetts was highly skilled and had a strong work ethic.

Simpson wondered what course of action he ought to take in the coming weeks and months.

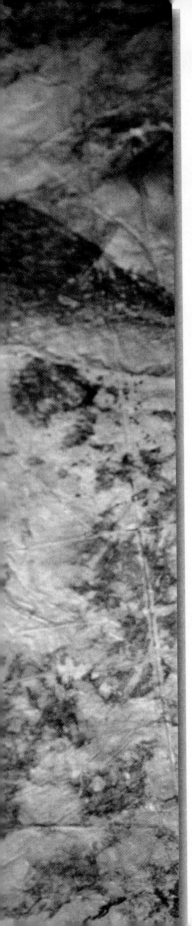

Singapore Airlines:
Continuing service improvement

Francesca Gee, INSEAD Euro-Asia Centre
Todd D. Jick, INSEAD Euro-Asia Centre*

Since its early days in 1972, the management at Singapore International Airlines (SIA) had seen superior service as the company's only possible source of competitive advantage. "We selected the two-letter airline code SQ to remind our people that an SQ flight is not just an ordinary flight, it's a quality flight," explained ground services senior manager Vijendran Alfreds. At the outset SIA had no domestic network and a small customer base among Singapore's population of 2 million, few of whom could afford air travel. The Singapore government made it clear that the airline had to stand on its own feet: Although a flag carrier, it would receive no subsidies.

According to a favorite piece of company lore, the first flight of SIA's predecessor, Malayan Airlines (from Singapore to a road near Ipoh in Malaysia in 1947) saw the beginning of in-flight service: The pilot picked up a thermos flask of iced water from under his seat and passed it around to his five passengers. A few years later, the carrier was the first to offer free drinks and headsets, as well a choice of quality meals for economy-class passengers.

AN INFLIGHT EXPERIENCE ON SINGAPORE AIRLINES

The slim, impeccably groomed stewardess in traditional Malay costume smiled at the Denver family as they entered the aircraft and quickly glanced at their boarding cards. "Good afternoon, Mrs. Denver," she said. "Let me show you to your seats."

"Isn't she pretty?" Marsha whispered to Tamara. "Do you remember this dress?" She was pointing to the long-skirted sarong kebaya, a figure-hugging outfit made of flowery batik cloth. Designed by Pierre Balmain, it combined the charm of traditional Asian wear with the elegance of French haute couture. But Tamara looked uncertain. "Of course you remember!" said Marsha. "We saw it at Madame Tussaud's!"

Constant attention to training had turned the stewardesses into symbols of Asian charm, grace, and hospitality. So successful was the "Singapore Girl" advertising concept that Madame Tussaud's, the London wax museum, had chosen it as an emblem of international travel. And the outfit, on sale at most Singapore souvenir

---

*Todd Jick is currently Managing Partner, Center for Executive Development, Cambridge, Massachusetts.

shops, was almost as popular as the "Girls" themselves, an indication that the stewardesses were also emblems of the island-state.

But Marsha, a professional woman who believed in equal opportunities, wasn't sure that she approved of the Singapore Girl concept altogether. SIA hostesses had to retire before they turned 35, unless promoted to a higher position: This policy would be illegal in many Western countries because of age discrimination laws.

Female flight attendants were given five-year contracts, with a maximum of three contracts, and were not taken back as cabin crew after they had given birth to a child, although they could find a ground job with the airline. Stewards were regular, not contract, employees and worked until they reached the normal retirement age in Singapore.

The young woman's gestures were graceful but precise as she advanced down the aisle with a tray of scented towels. "Would you like a hot towel, Mrs. Denver?" she asked. And to Tamara: "Be careful, you could burn your hands!" But Paul Denver was mildly annoyed when she woke him up some minutes later to offer him a glass of champagne. The stewardess seemed to follow established procedures rather automatically, oblivious to the fact that he was asleep. Neither of the Denvers, however, had any gripes about the smiling steward who, shortly afterwards, brought the children kits of games and small toys. After lunch (a choice of three main courses, exotic desserts, fresh fruit, fine cheese, and vintage port or a liqueur), he came back to ask whether they needed help with the baby. By then Janice was asleep—mercifully.

"The Most Modern Fleet"

As Marsha Denver settled down for the 13-hour, nonstop flight to Singapore, she surveyed appreciatively the newly fitted Raffles-class cabin with its tasteful decor in subtle shades of purple. She was sitting on the top deck of a Boeing 747-400 "Megatop," the fastest 747 with the largest stretched upper deck. Not quite as glamorous as the supersonic Concorde that SIA used to fly on the London-Bahrain-Singapore route in the 1970s, but nonetheless very comfortable, she thought. "No wonder Singapore Airlines comes so often on top in magazine surveys," she remarked to her husband as she activated the comfortable, 60-degree leg rest with adjustable calf support and stretched her legs across the 42-inch pitch.

The 747-400, the jumbo jet's fourth generation, played a crucial role in the expansion of airlines from the Asia–Pacific region. Its range, the longest ever for a commercial jet, enabled airlines to carry 410 passengers nonstop from Singapore to London or Hong Kong to San Francisco. In 1993, SIA's fleet was composed of 42 Boeing aircraft (18 of them Megatops) and 20 Airbus jets. The airline, which planned to double the total size of its fleet by the end of the decade, had 34 aircraft on firm order and options on 28 more. Because it frequently brought in the latest models, the average age of SIA's aircraft was five years and one month, well below the industry's average of nearly 12 years.

Flight SQ319 was equipped with Celestel, the world's first international on-board telephone service, which SIA had introduced in September 1991. The installation cost, Paul had read somewhere, was about US$60,000 per aircraft. He asked a chief stewardess, recognizable in her red sarong kebaya, whether it would be possible to send a fax from the aircraft. Certainly, she answered, reminding him that SIA had been the first airline to offer inflight facsimile facilities. It was about to introduce individual interactive video screens, she added. These would enable passengers to access real-time news, play computer games, make telephone calls, or order items for sale on board, she said. This way, businesspeople could keep up-to-date with stock exchange or money market prices as well as work on their portable computers and transmit data to their companies or to customers on the ground without leaving their seats.

"Outstanding Service on the Ground"

The holiday on Bali had been a success. The children had enjoyed the white sand at Sanur beach while their parents watched temple ceremonies and the popular wayang kulit *Balinese shadow plays or bought batik in countless patterns and colors. The Denvers were now at Ngurah Rai airport in Denpasar, checking in for a one-day layover in Singapore on their way back to Paris. Paul pointed first to a single brown leather suitcase, then to the jumble of bags and sports gear on the cart. "This one we'll need in Singapore tomorrow," he told the check-in officer. "Could SIA hold on to the rest of our luggage in Singapore and put it on our plane to Paris?" The agent replied, "I'm not sure we can do this. I'll have to ask the supervisor."*

While the Denvers waited for him to return, Paul gazed at the poster on the wall that declared: "Singapore Airlines Ground Services. We're with you all the way." "We'll soon find out about that," he thought. On a previous leg, from Manila to Singapore, Denver had asked whether one bag could be separated from the rest of his luggage and checked in at the left luggage counter in Singapore while he flew on the Denpasar. The SIA supervisor in Manila had gone to great pains to oblige, sending a telex to Singapore's Changi Airport to ask staff there to retrieve the bag, carry it to the security clearance area for a bomb search, and finally check it in at the left luggage office.

In 1986, SIA decided to complete its strategy of impeccable service on board state-of-the-art aircraft by adding a third pillar: ground service. The Outstanding Service on the Ground (OSG) campaign was launched, focusing on improving service at reservation, ticket offices and, most importantly, at each airport SIA flew to.

Making customers' perception of ground service as positive as their perception of inflight service was a challenge. Typically, passengers interacted with sales or check-in staff for a few seconds or minutes, and tended to remember them only when something went wrong. And while inflight service was provided by Singapore-based staff recruited, trained, motivated, and rewarded by SIA, ground service was provided by handling agents spread across 70 stations around the world. These were often direct competitors (for example, British Airways handled SIA flights at Heathrow Airport).

Each airport unit was given standards in terms of punctuality, baggage handling, speed and friendliness of check-in, efficiency of seat assignment, number of compliments and complaints from customers, and professionalism in handling delays. An additional standard for Changi, the region's largest hub, was efficiency of transfers. At every airport, the station manager was held accountable for achieving these standards; awards were given to stations that did well.

The campaign, implemented at an initial cost of S$4 million, was aimed at instilling three principles: "Show You Care" through body language evidencing interest and attention, "Dare to Care," and "Be Service Entrepreneurs," which meant displaying creativity to exceed customers' expectations. It involved motivational seminars, "booster training," reminders and reinforcement through monthly reports by country managers, a dedicated newsletter, *Higher Ground*, as well as monitoring and recognition. Posters carrying slogans such as "Go Near Not Away" or "An Impossible Situation Is a Disguised Opportunity" decorated staff quarters.

INGREDIENTS OF SUCCESS

The "three pillars" all contributed to SIA's undeniable prosperity. For years, the airline had topped carrier profitability tables as its pretax profit rose from S$69 million in 1983 to S$1,161 million in 1990 (see Exhibit 1 for recent profitability trends). Behind this success were policies—and practices—deliberately and systematically developed by management. These included long-standing guiding principles such as long-term planning, steady growth, a diversified route network, a decision to stick to core competencies, and helping attract visitors to Singapore.

A Policy of Steady Organic Growth

Managers rejected the idea that consolidation would lead to an industry consisting of a handful of megacarriers and a few niche players by the year 2000. They were nervous that SIA would grow too fast and were generally suspicious of acquisitions despite SIA's strong cash position. They did, however, make an unsuccessful bid for a 25 percent stake in Australia's Qantas in 1992. "Our goal is to continue to operate a successful airline," said Michael Tan, deputy managing director (Commercial). "If we have to grow to do that, we grow. But we never set out to be a megacarrier." Because of its long-term vision, SIA did not let what one senior manager described as "the slumps and bumps in the business cycle" disrupt its investment plans. In fact, it placed its largest-ever order for planes during the 1979–80 post–oil shock recession. It tried to diversify its network so as not to be dependent on any one market or route but remained focused on its core activity—commercial travel and its supporting services.

"We wish to retain our individuality," said Joseph Pillay, SIA's chairman since 1972, "and to expand at a measured pace that permits us to retain those essential qualities that have made SIA one of the foremost carriers in the world in terms of quality of service, depth of commitment to employees, technical prowess, and financial strength." SIA's response to what Pillay called "the challenge of globalization" was its 1989 alliance with Delta Airlines and Swissair. "Wherever possible, we shall cooperate with other carriers to widen our reach, to strengthen our product, and to improve our services to the traveling public. We shall particularly seek out airlines such as Delta and Swissair that share many common traits with SIA," said Pillay.[1] The three airlines, bound together through cross-equity stakes of 5 percent, reaped advantages that included sales benefits from dovetailed schedules, discounts on coordinated aircraft purchases, savings from shared ground facilities and sales and check-in offices, as well as flexibility from exchanging cabin crew.

A Strong Corporate Culture

One reason not to grow through acquisitions was to protect SIA's idiosyncratic culture, which managers saw as a hybrid of East and West reminiscent of the former colony's long-standing role as a regional crossroads. "The Singapore Girl is a cross between Western and Asian stewardesses," reflected personnel director Syn Chung Wah. "Typical Western service is lots of communication and talk while Asian service is shy and distanced. Our people are fairly confident and they are unique in Asia in

---

[1] "Responding to the Global Challenge," *Outlook*, January 1990.

Exhibit 1   Financial Performance Summary, Singapore Airlines, 1988–1993

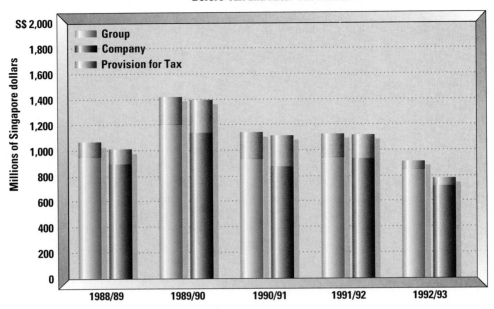

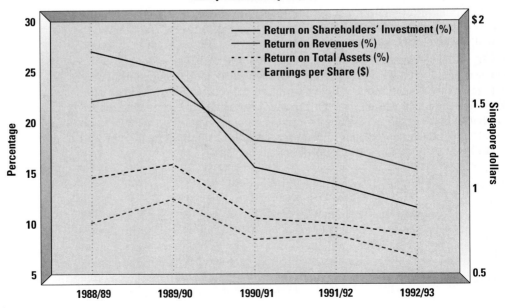

Note: As of August 31, 1993, the exchange rate for the Singapore dollar was US$1 = S$1.61.

Exhibit 1 (concluded)

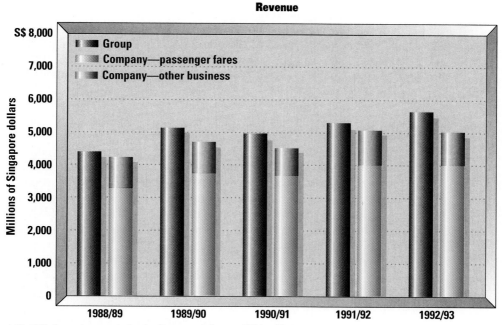

Note: As of August 31, 1993, the exchange rate for the Singapore dollar was US$1 = S$1.61.

not suffering from a language barrier when talking with international travelers, since English is Singapore's official language."

The importance of the Chinese Confucian ethic of filial piety and deference for hierarchy was limited. "We expect loyalty to the company and the country," said Prush Nadaisan, assistant director of personnel. "But we don't give seniority a lot of value. People move up according to performance. Singapore in general operates on meritocracy. And a lot of our operations are overseas; inevitably we imbibe a lot of Western values." However, the majority of SIA's employees were Singaporeans with shared values and concerns, and SIA's management saw the importance of this unity. "We are a cohesive group and we work together as a team with the same culture, attitudes, and motivation," said one senior executive.

Recruitment

The service concept required total commitment from all front-line staff, whom SIA saw as its interface with passengers and greatest asset. "The only way to guarantee that customers are satisfied is by making sure that those who serve them are satisfied with their jobs and have a positive attitude," explained a senior manager. "A key element in a service organization is the motivation of the employee," said director of flight operations Maurice de Vaz. But years of fast growth presented SIA with a major challenge when it came to recruiting in Singapore's dwindling labor market. Between 1972 and 1993, staff had grown from 6,200 to 14,819 for the airline, and to 24,600 for the group. Hiring the right front-line staff was thus a major priority.

Recruitment of cabin crew in particular was highly selective. Applicants, who had to be under 25, were screened for a positive attitude towards work and good appearance, posture, and language skills. "Character molding and positive mental attitude are essential components of a successful cabin crew," said Michael Tan. To try to eliminate uncertainty, a psychological test known as the Personal Profile System was developed with outside consultants to determine the service aptitude of applicants. "Crew must anticipate passengers' needs," explained T. O. Thoeng, director of marketing services. "That means being attentive. This is something people must have in them to begin with, you can't change attitude. That's why SIA has the PPS test."

Training

Nearly 12 percent of SIA's payroll was devoted to training, and every front-line employee was expected to attend at least one course a year. In 1992, the company opened a S$80 million training complex where 230 professionals conducted specially designed courses and workshops on product orientation, customer awareness, supervisory skills, and other service enhancement skills. The emphasis was on soft skills such as attitude and style rather than on technical or product knowledge (see Exhibit 2 on SIA's training philosophy).

Cabin crew underwent a four-month full-time course, longer than those provided by SIA's competitors. While noting the importance of technical aspects of cabin service, Michael Tan warned crew against becoming overdependent on procedures. "Of course we need good systems and procedures," he said. "But what has distinguished us from other airlines all these years is the human touch." The crew were taught little tricks such as memorizing the names of Raffles-class and first-class passengers at boarding, or learning to spot which flyers wanted to chat and which wanted to be left alone.

The commercial training department trained SIA staff and handling agents around the world. All new front-line ground staff attended an orientation program and an OSG seminar that were held in Singapore and in regional centers every three months. Within one year all new staff went to Singapore for product training. "We teach the staff that customers are our bread and butter," explained a training manager. "We say things like, 'Don't think of customers as nuisances. They are our employers.' We tell them to be customer champions."

The methods used included experiential learning such as problem-solving games, case studies of real-life situations, and role-playing, where staff were asked to put themselves in the shoes of a frequent traveler, a first-time flyer, or a mother with small children. There was "rescripting," where shy participants were told to convince themselves that they were customer champions. Training also involved brainstorming, with staff asked to think of what they could do to solve an actual problem in their station. Outdoor activities and even boot camp training were also among SIA's varied training resources (see Exhibit 3 for a description of an OSG course).

Leadership Development

Particular attention was paid to the "field commanders": front-line supervisors. By motivating them and instilling leadership qualities into them, SIA believed it could facilitate the handing down of its distinctive culture to a new generation of staff. An

Exhibit 2   SIA's Training Philosophy

SIA's training philosophy

One, training is a necessity, not an option. It is not to be dispensed with when times are bad, nor postponed for operational expediency.

Two, training is for everyone. It covers all aspects of the Group's operations, and it embraces everyone from the office assistant to the managing director.

Three, we do not skimp on training. We don't waste, but we don't penny-pinch, and we'll use the best in training software and hardware that money can buy.

Four, training is systematic and structured. An individual follows a training path that parallels his career progress.

Five, training is both specialised and general. We give technical training to pilots, engineers . . . but we also teach employees how to manage and supervise, how to communicate properly and relate to others.

Here (at STC), staff from different sections of the SIA Group, and different parts of the Airline's network, will learn together and from one another. There should emerge a better understanding of the diverse activities of the Group, and a stronger camaraderie among its people.

Our spirit is strong and eager, simply because training is so much a part of the corporate ethos. The SIA Training Centre will be a symbol of that ethos.

— Managing Director SIA Dr Cheong Choong Kong at the foundation stone-laying ceremony of the $80-million STC in January 1991.

Source: *Outlook*, February 1993, p. 9 (a company publication).

ambitious development program for senior cabin crew was aimed at making them feel that they were part of management, and at boosting their commitment. A similar program, "Take the Lead," was developed for ground service supervisors. "We're training them to be OSG leaders, to play a more active role and provide better guidance to their subordinates," explained customer affairs manager Ong Boon Khim. "We don't want them to depend on the head office. We want them to take the initiative." Being a service entrepreneur meant being assertive and resourceful, he said. "We say to them, 'There will always be opportunities for you, in your dealings with customers, to establish a certain impression so that they will come back and fly SIA again.' "

Exhibit 3   An OSG Course at Singapore Airlines *(as portrayed in an employee publication)*

'We are ready to give,' say SATS OSG participants

Trainee Passenger Services Agent (PSA) *Michelle Koh,* who was in a batch of trainee PSAs from SATS to attend the Outstanding Service on the Ground Programme, gives a first-person account of her experience.

"I CARE." That is the OSG (Outstanding Service on the Ground) motto my class — Batch 140 — picked up very early in the one-day programme held on 8 May.

First, we chanted it as a group. Later, we discovered its meaning on a more personal level when we were taught how to "stroke" each other positively to bring out the best in each person. We learnt how effective positive stroking could be through an exercise in which we sent complimentary messages to one another. Initial shyness overcome, this exercise became easy and fun.

However, when asked to state our own strengths, most of us were hesitant. Yet, there was virtually no reservation in highlighting our weaknesses. Perseverance in this exercise provided some self discoveries.

Now that we knew ourselves a little better, we embarked on a very important project: teamwork and cooperation. I must admit, though, that I was very puzzled on

seeing plastic chains, cane hoops and wooden blocks on the stage in the auditorium where our training was being held.

What had all these items to do with teamwork and cooperation? I was soon to find out. In the "centipede activity," our class was divided into two teams. With ankles shackled to one another, each team was expected to move forward and backward, and up and down a flight of stairs in the shortest time possible.

Yes, this exercise certainly

called for teamwork and cooperation. When we did not move together, ankles hurt, tempers flared, and someone fell down!

One of the other exercises taught us that careful planning was necessary if we wanted to do our jobs well. This was where the hoops came in. The objective was to get each member through the hoops, without using a hoop twice and without the members coming into contact with the hoops. Sounds confusing, but we had to do it. With some

planning, agility and strength, we managed.

We rounded up the day with the "Trust" activity. It entailed a participant throwing himself backwards into the arms of his team mates. I remember thinking at the time that any sane person would hesitate to do this if he had the slightest doubt about the person who was to catch him. But then, at the OSG course, we were doing rather "insane" things, were we not? I held my breath and . . . my team mates caught me — a lesson in trust indeed.

At the start of the course, Instructor Clara Nai had warned us that it would not be all fun and games. She was right. It was also quite tiring, both mentally and physically. But the unanimous verdict at the end of the day was: "We are ready to give!"

Source: Company employee communications publication.

Staff Recognition and Reward

SIA recognized staff for outstanding customer service and for good ideas, and kept them informed of company problems and plans through the glossy in-house magazine, *Outlook*, various divisional newsletters, and frequent meetings and briefings. A sizable part of all employees' earnings, as much as three extra months of pay in a good year, came through a profit-sharing scheme. Examples of rewards included the following:

- S-I-A Staff Ideas in Action, which awarded cash prizes of up to S$9,700 for good ideas.

- Winning Ways, for cabin crew who had received a minimum of three compliment letters and no complaints over three months. One winner had received 23 letters.
- Managing Director's Awards: introduced in 1987, they recognized front-line staff who went beyond the call of duty in providing ground service. Selection criteria included both consistency in performance and outstanding acts of service (see Exhibit 4).
- Health for Wealth: a S$3,000 prize given out every month to a ground service employee at Changi airport to encourage all staff to stay fit. The incidence of sick leave among check-in and other ground service staff, who had to work shifts 24 hours a day, was high.

An OSG Feedback Competition tested staff's grasp of front-line issues. "Each question consisted of a scenario and three possible answers," explained customer affairs manager Ong. "They have to think it through, maybe get together with their peers to deliberate. It encourages staff to think about these issues." The 20 winners each received a S$1,000 shopping voucher.

Monitoring Customer Satisfaction

Much effort went into monitoring compliments and complaints from customers, which were examined at weekly meetings of SIA's complaints and compliments committee. On average, cabin crew received nine letters of compliment for every complaint, but ground staff, whose transactions with customers were quite different, had nearly as many criticisms as they had praise. "On board we're pouring champagne and giving out caviar," said Ground Services' Alfreds. "In ground service we take your money and your coupon, we check your passport." Each complaint was investigated and answered in writing. Any lessons drawn were passed on to the trainers and departments concerned and a selection of both praise and criticism was published regularly in in-house publications. (Exhibit 5 has examples of both sorts of letters.)

Trends in customer satisfaction were carefully analyzed. An in-hour Service Performance Index survey continuously tracked SIA service. Every quarter, 18,000 passengers' ratings of 30 factors, such as eye appeal of meals or friendliness of check-in staff, were analyzed. Index movements were carefully studied for early indications of how SIA was meeting passengers' expectations. The index improved year by year. By 1991, ground services sometimes received compliments when flights were delayed, so professional were ground staff in service recovery.

Management Style

SIA's management made conscious efforts to delegate authority to the lowest possible level. Employees described SIA as a democratic company where top management welcomed new ideas, criticisms, and decision making from the lower echelons and encouraged them to speak out, make suggestions, and generally express their opinion. "We try to keep reporting lines as short as possible," said Michael Tan. "We are not a formal organization."

SIA tried hard to become a flat organization, spinning off business units as soon as they were self-sustaining. "We're trying to stay small," explained managing director Cheong Choong Kong. "We are creating many small, autonomous divisions to keep

Exhibit 4   Employees Receiving Managing Director's Awards, 1992

Maite Losada
Cargo Supervisor, BRU

Lena Kellens
Reservations/Ticketing Officer, BRU

Maite and Lena were on holiday when their SQ flight was diverted to AMS. Although they were on leave, they spontaneously helped their working colleagues manage the disruption. They helped passengers with their rebookings, distributed meals and newspapers on the coach to AMS, assisted passengers at AMS, and helped them with their transfer flights in SIN. They assisted layover passengers, looked after them at the hotel, and helped them with their onward flights the next day. On arrival at MEL, they again helped the passengers before catching their own flight to BNE.

Over 36 hours and over three continents, Maite and Lena displayed many OSG qualities. They went beyond the call of duty to help the affected passengers throughout the journey, they sacrificed their own time, displayed initiative, and showed they cared. They truly embody the OSG spirit "We're with you all the way."

Kalyan Subramanyam
Customer Services Agent, MAA

During the year 1991–92 Kalyan received 15 written compliments. In all these cases, he repeatedly showed that he cares for our passengers. The passengers were impressed not just by his acts of assistance but also by his high standard of service and the kindness he displayed.

For example, he helped a sick and elderly passenger who was booked to fly on another airline. His selfless act for a competitor's airline passenger so impressed the passenger's relative that the relative said in his letter of compliment that he would in future travel on SIA.

Kalyan wins the award for consistently giving outstanding service to our passengers.

Tadashi Yakumaru
Customer Services Officer, NRT

Tadashi received four written compliments and numerous verbal compliments in the year.

For example, Tadashi voluntarily gave a distraught passenger, who had no cash in local currency, the money he required for his airport tax. The passenger, who turned out to be a priority passenger, later wrote in to compliment Tadashi and to return the money.

In another case, a couple were delayed in arriving at the airport due to a traffic jam, and had to park their car at the terminal instead of their prearranged car park. Tadashi offered to drive the car to the other car park and looked after the car until they returned.

The many compliments Tadashi received were testimony of his consistent helpfulness beyond the call of duty.

Ron Jensen
Reservations Agent (Rate Desk), LAX

As a reservations agent (Rate Desk), Ron has few face-to-face contacts with passengers and hence, less opportunity to show his outstanding service. Yet in the year he received four written compliments for his professionalism, courtesy, and helpfulness.

Ron displayed initiative, thoroughness, and persistence in handling a difficult and urgent ticketing case. He dared to make decisions to overcome problems and followed up with all the details of the case from his home during the weekend. Subsequently, when there was a problem with the payment, he also took it upon himself to solve the problem, and even drove to the airport to pick up the check.

Ron is an outstanding model worker for all our office staff.

London Station
Station Award

SQ19 was diverted to Gatwick because of bad weather at Heathrow, causing a delay of 12 hours. On the same day, another incoming flight was diverted to MAN causing a delay of 16 hours. SQ19 was handled under very difficult conditions as the base of operations had to be shifted to Gatwick. Staff and handling agents, and airport, hotel and transport facilities were all stretched to the limit. London Station took many proactive steps to minimize the inconvenience to passengers.

Another delayed flight, SQ21, was also handled with flying colors. Good teamwork, decisive planning and attention to detail were displayed. 60% of passengers rated the overall handling "excellent" and 37.5% rated it "good."

For the outstanding handling of these two disrupted flights, the Station Award went to London Station. Senior Traffic Officer Phillip Parker, who was actively involved in handling both flights, represented the station at the Awards Presentation.

Source: *Higher Ground*, November–December 1992.

decision making down." When a new engineering subsidiary was formed in April 1992, top management pointed to several benefits, saying it would increase accountability, enhance *esprit de corps*, encourage innovation and entrepreneurship, and reap the benefits of competitive advantage in the high-growth engineering maintenance business. Next on the list were computer services and cargo.

Exhibit 5 Sample Compliments and Complaints from Passengers, Singapore Airlines, 1992

Customer Comments on Ground Service . . .

Our flight was disabled due to mechanical problems and we were stuck in Jakarta airport without access to a telephone or a fax machine for most of the day. The ground crew in Jakarta promised to send fax messages on our behalf . . . these messages were not transmitted.

They attempt to arrange alternative bookings for us but . . . these arrangements were never completed. We did suggest that as the delay had caused us to miss our connection in Singapore and because it was not possible to book an alternative flight with Qantas, we should be put on the Singapore–Darwin flight on 4 July. We were told this was not possible as the flight was fully booked in economy and although business class seats were available we would only be able to upgrade if we paid the extra fare.

On arriving in Singapore . . . we were given vouchers for hotel accommodation and meals, but, although our luggage had not arrived in Singapore, were not given an allowance to purchase toiletries, etc. . . . Our luggage had still not been traced when we boarded SQ223 and we were told that it was probably still in Jakarta. When we arrived in Perth, however, we found our things had in fact been loaded. Although it was a relief to see the luggage, I find the fact that it had been loaded but not recorded on the flight manifest most disturbing.

As you can imagine the experience was most upsetting and extremely tiring. In addition, as a consequence of the missed connection we "lost" several days from a holiday which had been planned for over a year.

**R.C.P.
Surrey**

When we returned to San Francisco, my wife removed two of our four bags from the carousel while I was in the rest room. At our hotel I discovered that one bag was not ours. After many phone calls, I contacted the Singapore Airline baggage person and learned that my bag was at the airport and that I had a bag of a man who was going to Honduras. I was surprised that it was not suggested that the bag would be delivered to the hotel and the bags would be exchanged. Having flown all night and being 76 years of age, I was quite tired after the 12-hour flight. Nevertheless, I got a taxi, returned the bag to the airport and retrieved mine. My friends tell me that in similar circumstances they have had their bags returned to them at the hotel by the airline.

**F.A.G.
Texas**

It was indeed our pleasure to see you last week at the Singapore Airlines counter at Brussels Airport. Our children have always traveled alone, but were never as happy as they were with your company. They were very well looked after, and also at N.Y. the ground staff were very helpful and courteous. We take this opportunity to thank you, and your airline for the excellent service, and it's surely not for nothing that you are known as the best!

My husband is a nonresident Singaporean, and we are happy that you have started this service to N.Y. and hope to use it more often.

**D. & P.M.
New York**

Source: *Higher Ground,* November–December, 1992.

The group had a policy of management mobility, rotating managers and directors every three to five years. This prevented managers from becoming jaded and fostered team spirit, according to assistant director of personnel Nadaisan. "Loyalty to a function or a division is not as great. It's difficult to say, 'I'm a marketing man,' when tomorrow you may be in finance. It forces you to look at the company as a whole." Managers also moved between the airline and the various subsidiaries. In the same spirit, SIA encouraged multidivisional task forces.

SIA'S DEMANDING CUSTOMERS IN THE 1990S ———————

In Denpasar, the check-in officer at Ngurah Rai airport had returned with the SIA supervisor. "I am sorry, sir," the supervisor said. "Our procedures require that your luggage travel to only one location. You can send it to Singapore or to Paris but not both." His tone was courteous, but strained. Paul Denver launched into a lengthy explanation, pointing to the fact that a week earlier in Manila his request to split his luggage at check-in had been accepted quite easily. Then he realized he was wasting his time and shut up, but decided to complain in writing. His letter read as follows:

> I thought that Singapore Airlines was committed to service, in particular to improving ground service. I was pleased with check-in staff in Manila, who went out of their way to help me. This is the kind of service I expected from SIA. What I cannot understand is why your man in Denpasar was so uncooperative.

Competitive Pressures

In 1993, the world of air travel was in the throes of its worst-ever recession, which had drained first-class and business-class cabins of full-fare payers. The *Financial Times* wrote:

> The desperation of airlines to lure back the lucrative business traveler can be reflected in one simple statistic: in the past two years, carriers worldwide have managed to lose every penny of profit made since the Second World War—an estimated total of about £7 billion. It is against that background—and the knowledge that business class provides about 50 percent of profits while taking just 20 percent of the space—that airlines have been waging a fierce battle for the hearts and wallets of the executive traveler.[2]

Airlines felt threatened by information technology advances such as video conferencing that could reduce businesspeople's need to travel. But the biggest menace was corporations' decisions to slash travel costs, requiring executives to travel less or to fly economy class. Customers began to take perks such as frequent flyer programs (FFPs) for granted in this increasingly competitive marketplace. The success of FFPs, in which regular passengers accumulated points that could be exchanged for free flights or upgrades, was enormous: According to one estimate, U.S. members had accumulated more than 600 billion miles of free travel. SIA, long reluctant to give out free flights, finally created its own FFP, *Passages*, in 1993. In terms of strategic response, airlines roughly fell into three camps:

- The Traditionalists, who continued to raise standards, even though this meant maintaining high prices and perhaps frightening off cash-strapped customers, and who advertised heavily. The logic was simple: Surveys showed that 88 percent of business and first-class travelers rated the size of their seat as their "preferred aspect of business class travel," and that what they feared most on long-haul routes was physical discomfort.
- The Old-Style Entrepreneurs, who competed on price, even though this put at risk the perceived quality of their product and hurt revenue per seat. Their target was the budget-conscious traveler.

---

[2] "Fierce Battle for Hearts and Wallets," *Financial Times*, April 19, 1993.

- The Radical Entrepreneurs, who were prepared to abolish the traditional class structure of aircraft and try to sell something entirely new—offering, for instance, a combination of first-class seats and business-class levels of service and prices.[3]

Even Southeast Asian airlines were feeling the crunch after enjoying an unprecedented boom throughout the 1980s. According to the International Air Transport Association (IATA), Asia-Pacific, which accounted for 25 percent of the world's passenger traffic in 1985, would be close to 40 percent at the turn of the century. But the region's airlines also faced more aggressive competition. SIA itself posted a 15 percent drop in pretax profits for the first half of 1993–94, while leading competitor Cathay Pacific of Hong Kong reported a 46 percent fall in interim earnings. More than ever, controlling costs appeared to be a necessity for SIA.

Internal Pressures

The Labor Shortage in Singapore   The economic success of Singapore had at least one unwanted consequence for SIA. Until 1993, almost all its stewardesses had been Singaporeans and Malaysians, the only exceptions a few nationals of Japan, Taiwan, or Korea recruited for linguistic reasons. But the labor shortage was making it increasingly difficult for the airline to recruit the home-grown hostesses who had been its main marketing tool for two entire decades: In its advertising, it exclusively used its own stewardesses. The number of cabin crew was expected to grow from 5,000 in 1993 to 8,000 or 10,000 by the end of the decade.

SIA clearly saw that it would have to recruit beyond the borders of the tiny island-state and neighboring Malaysia. But could the Singapore Girl be Thai or Indian or even Caucasian? This move would erode a key difference with Cathay Pacific, which cultivated a cosmopolitan image with multiethnic cabin crew fluent in a variety of languages besides English. While SIA's leadership saw some advantages in heterogeneity, they thought it made it harder to have shared values and dedication to service. "Cathay has problems with the assimilation of different nationalities: They have a hard time getting them to work as teams," said one senior manager.

The "Young Turks"   Traditionally, SIA staff had felt a strong attachment to the company. "We're almost like Communists, we believe in a cause," joked one senior manager. "I want the company to do well. I don't see it as an employer." But the new generation, whom one executive described as "the young Turks," had somewhat different expectations. As the republic became more affluent, individual values tended to replace the Confucian tradition of respect for authority, and some managers felt the young generation lacked dedication and a service spirit.

Young Singaporeans were better educated, more mobile, and readier to challenge. While proud of working for Singapore's most prestigious employer, they also expected higher standards of living. As a result, unions were becoming more militant. "In the early years, we were like a small family," said managing director Cheong. "As we grow bigger, the relationship between management and unions is becoming more formalized and there's a greater degree of tension."

---

[3]Adapted from "A Time for Fresh ideas," *Financial Times*, April 19, 1993.

Strategies for Satisfying the Demanding Customer

Michael Tan's analysis of the competitive situation ran as follows:

> Since the early 1980s, a number of governments have been divesting their shares in airlines in an effort to encourage competition. They are giving a wider choice to consumers, creating competition and therefore improvements in quality. As a result, more and more airlines are trying to duplicate the causes of SIA's success. Even if the world economy picks up, the good old days are over. The industry will be fitter. Competitors are doing away with excess manpower and looking at their route structure. The bottom line is becoming more important, the aircraft more reliable, the staff more motivated. There is structural change, as well as mental change, among airline executives.

This is how he saw the challenge for SIA:

> SIA is changing all the time. We start off telling ourselves we must continually improve. There is no such thing as, We have nothing more to learn. But we're not talking about changing people, we're talking about strengthening what we have. We encourage our people to look for new ways of doing things. SIA's image is strong: That is not easy to keep up unless you continue to strengthen your operations, you come up with new ways of doing things. We never sacrificed quality, even in the last two years. If you try to save by cutting down on what you give the customer, people feel it straight away. We won't allow cost-cutting to affect what we've built over the years. For instance, we're looking for ways to prepare the food ahead of time, but that is to give cabin crew more time to look after our passengers, not to reduce the number of crew.

The challenge for SIA was to train front-line staff to anticipate customers' needs in order to satisfy them before the passengers even realized they had those needs. One answer was to be flexible, explained inflight services senior manager George Lee:

> Demand is evolving, and one of our strategies is to provide flexibility, especially in first class and business class. For instance, on long trips you can have your meals at any time you like. We encourage our people to be flexible. They have to be on the watch-out to do more things that will remain ingrained in passengers' minds, and turn any negative impression into a positive one. As long as the company continues to see itself as its main competitor, it will continue to improve and innovate.

RESPONDING TO THE CUSTOMER: TWO APPROACHES ———

In practice, customers' demands were analyzed at weekly meetings of SIA's complaints and compliments review committee. Paul Denver's letter provided an interesting test of the airline's approach to continuous service improvement: One of its demanding customers was challenging it to go farther. Two major views emerged at the meeting. The first, underlining the importance of safety, standards, and consistency, could be summarized as follows:

> First and foremost we have considerations of security, cost and efficiency: There are lots of security regulations on the handling of luggage. Secondly, the Manila supervisor incurred a lot of expense for the company: If we were to have this as a standard procedure, it would mean tremendous costs. Thirdly, the risk of mishandling would be a lot higher. We are proud of our low rate of mishandled luggage, by far the lowest among major airlines. Passengers far

prefer to have their bags with them in a normal situation. But of course we tell our staff that OSG means going beyond, finding a way to satisfy the passenger. This is a classic dilemma. I'm not saying it would be impossible to satisfy Mr. Denver, but it is a choice we'd have to make. I certainly wouldn't tell off our people in Denpasar for refusing the passenger's request. In this industry, in the final analysis the safety and security of the passenger are more important, and this means procedures. I don't want to compromise on that.

A second view stressed the need for staff to use their judgment and make considered decisions, rather than follow established guidelines:

We need a balance between the soft part, people's judgment, and the system of rules. We need the system of course, but only as a guide. More emphasis must now be placed on judgment, responsibility, and entrepreneurship.

At first glance, the Manila agent should be congratulated for his decision. We encourage staff, even junior staff, to take considered decisions. The Manila agent took a decision and he took responsibility for it. He went out of his way to help a passenger. The Bali agent didn't show any courage, he just played by the rules. We've been telling our people, "Go beyond the rules. We dare you to innovate." We've asked them to use their judgment. He was probably worried about giving away the "company store." We must show him what was missing in his thought process: If he tries to accommodate a passenger, we will support him.

I want all our people to show that they can think through a situation and make judgments on behalf of customers, whether they're traveling economy, business, or first class. The pressure is on the front line. The pressure is also on us to coach and counsel. If we determine that the Bali agent did make a mistake, he should discuss the issue with his staff. In that case, we would congratulate the Manila agent, and also recommend discussion there. The issue would be mentioned in the Manila agent's annual performance review, but the Bali agent would not be penalized.

In fact, the issue is more complex. What we really need to understand is the thinking behind both decisions. What led each of them to his decision? Saying "No" to a passenger is more difficult than saying "Yes." But did the Bali agent just fall back on regulations, or was there a basis for his judgment? What about the Manila agent? Did he say "Yes" to make it easy? How did he arrive to his judgment? Front-line staff must put themselves in the customer's shoes and determine whether a request is reasonable, genuine, or whether someone is trying to take advantage of the airline. The Bali agent did not have to copy the Manila agent's decision if his conclusions were different. Consistency is to do well all the time, not consistently to say "No" or "Yes": This is what SIA is trying to instill.

This debate was part of a larger set of issues for SIA. Could the airline contain costs without sacrificing service? Could it grow, yet maintain its high service standards? And could it in fact further improve its already high quality of service? Meanwhile, Paul Denver awaited an answer to his letter.

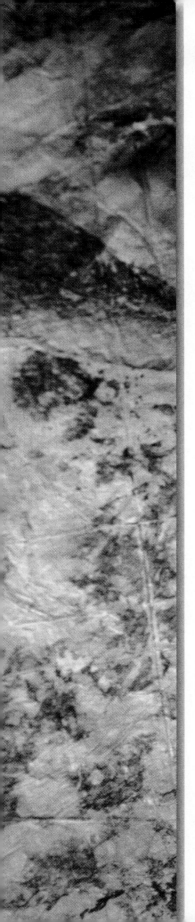

Zetor Tractors (A)

Karen L. Newman, Georgetown University
Stanley D. Nollen, Georgetown University

Jan Otoupalík, the 60-year-old managing director of State Plant Zetor, reviewed his company's situation in early 1992. The tractor and bearings concern, his employer for over 35 years, was fighting for its life. The 1989 "Velvet Revolution"[1] had brought freedom and democracy to the Czech and Slovak Republics, but it was creating unprecedented challenges for his company. Sales were down, production was at less than 60 percent of capacity, receivables and payables were growing, and it was not possible to obtain bank credit. He wondered how much longer Zetor could stay in business. As he surveyed the strengths and weaknesses of his firm, he realized that Zetor would have to change quickly if it was to survive the transition to a market operation. "In its current form the enterprise will not be able to continue," he reflected.

THE COMPANY AND ITS BUSINESS

Zetor tractors were the first produced in 1945. The company was established in 1952 by the Czechoslovakian government in the Moravian city of Brno. Most of the current manufacturing facility was built in the 1960s. The most recent expansion was an assembly facility completed in 1988.

Brno is the second-largest city in the Czech Republic, with a population of approximately 400,000. It is located 200 kilometers southeast of Prague and 130 kilometers north of Vienna and Bratislava (see Exhibit 1). Though easily accessible by car and train, Brno had no commercial airport until 1993. Zetor was Brno's biggest employer, and it was one of the Czech and Slovak Republics' biggest

The authors are indebted to Roman Motyka, Jan Otoupalík, and the Deputy Directors of Zetor s.p. for their informative cooperation. Thanks are also owed to Miloslava Zbořilová for translation and interpretation. The research was supported in part by the Georgetown University City for International Business Education and Research, the Georgetown School of Business and the Graduate School, and the University of Pittsburgh. All events and individuals are real.

[1]The Velvet Revolution occurred in late November and early December 1989 in Czechoslovakia, a few months after the fall of the Berlin Wall. The name Velvet Revolution comes from the fact that the existing Communist government resigned without bloodshed, after massive peaceful demonstrations in Prague, giving way to a democracy almost overnight. The first post-Communist government was led by Václav Havel, a playwright who had been imprisoned under the former regime for his political views. Havel, though inexperienced in government, was a strong symbol of the moral underpinnings of the Velvet Revolution and the future for Czechoslovakia. One of the first orders of business was rapid transformation of the economy (one of the 10 largest in the world between World Wars I and II) from the most thoroughly state owned of all Soviet-bloc economies to a market economy based on private ownership of property.

Exhibit 1   Europe in 1992

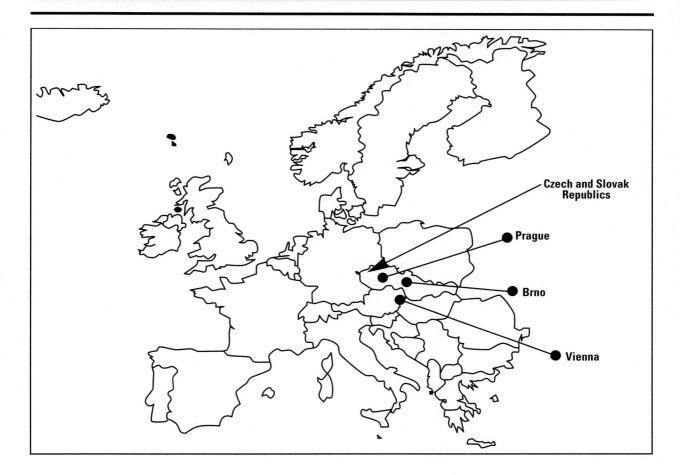

enterprises. The company's gross revenue at the time of the Velvet Revolution was nearly Kč 4 billion annually (or $267 million at the 1989 exchange rate of 15 Czech crowns per U.S. dollar—15 Kč/US$) but only Kč 2.8 billion in 1992 ($93 million at the new exchange rate of 30 Kč/US$). Zetor employed 10,000 people in Brno.

Products and Plants

Zetor manufactured three types of products: tractors (its main business), roller bearings, and forgings and castings. Prior to the Velvet Revolution, Zetor produced 28,000 tractors per year in its Brno plant.

In early 1992, Zetor's main tractor products were medium-sized tractors used in agriculture. The smallest tractor was a four-cylinder 42-horsepower model that sold for about Kč 200,000. The largest tractor was a four-cylinder 95-horsepower model that sold for about Kč 340,000. (At the time, the average industrial wage in the Czech Republic was about Kč 48,000, or $1,600 per year.) Tractors were produced on one of two assembly lines, neither of which used sophisticated automation. A variety of tools could be attached to the tractors to customize them for specific applications, but Zetor did not manufacture attachments.

Until the early 1970s, Zetor also produced a two-cylinder, 28-horsepower model but found that it was too small for most of its customers (annual sales were about 1,000 units in 1973) and could not be produced profitably. In 1973, Zetor entered into a license agreement permitting an Indian firm to produce the two-cylinder model. A similar arrangement existed with a larger model made by a Slovakian firm and marketed under the Zetor name.

Zetor established a factory in Iraq to assemble tractors under the brand name Antar in 1970. About 80 percent of all parts were manufactured in Brno and shipped to Iraq, where the remaining parts were manufactured and final assembly was accomplished. Zetor was the monopoly producer of midsized tractors in Iraq, selling 6,000 units per year prior to the Velvet Revolution (Exhibit 2). Apart from these arrangements, all other tractors with the Zetor brand name were manufactured at the Brno plant.

According to industry analysts, Zetor tractors were well designed, technologically simple yet up-to-date, rugged, simple to repair, and reliable. Up to 60 percent of the tractor parts were interchangeable from one model to another. This feature was a major product concept for Zetor, enabling the company to call its tractors the "Unified Series." In many cases Zetor tractors could be repaired on-site by the farmers themselves. The average productive life of a Zetor tractor was over 15 years.

The company also produced large, sophisticated spherical roller bearings of various sizes that were used in diverse industrial applications. In 1989, Zetor produced about 500,000 of these bearings, one-third for export. Sales in this business were Kč 280 million ($18.7 million) in 1989. The bearings produced by Zetor were a separate business and were not used in the manufacture of its tractors.

Finally, Zetor had a metallurgical works that made forgings and castings for tractor components, bearing rings, and other industrial applications. About 35,000 tons of castings and 20,000 tons of forgings were produced annually. The foundry began production in 1964 and was last upgraded in 1986.

Zetor operated a respected research and development institute for tractors, one of a few Czech enterprises to have extensive research and development capability in-house. It also had its own training center with apprenticeship programs that allowed the company to train its employees on new equipment and manufacturing techniques. Between 300 and 400 students were enrolled in the apprenticeship program at any time. Most of the students were Zetor employees, but a few worked in smaller firms in Brno that had no apprenticeship program.

As was true of most large state enterprises in the Czech and Slovak Republics, Zetor had social service assets as well, including a medical clinic, flats for employees, and a recreation center for use by employees.

DOING BUSINESS UNDER CENTRAL PLANNING

Since its inception, Zetor had operated primarily as an arm of the state in Czechoslovakia's centrally planned economy. The ramifications could be seen in many areas, as Zetor embraced many business approaches that differed from those typically observed in a market economy.

Exhibit 2   Selected Changes at Zetor between 1989 and 1991

	1989	1991
Number of employees	10,000	8,800
Average hours worked per week	37	34
Annual tractor production (units)	27,700	14,500
Annual tractor exports (units)		
Iraq	6,500	0
Eastern Europe	8,600	4,000
Western Europe and other	7,200	7,400
Domestic tractor sales (units)	5,400	3,100
Tractor inventory; completed units in excess of 10 days' supply	0	500
Tractor plant capacity (units)	30,000	30,000
Gross revenue (millions of current Kč)	4,000	5,000
Tractors	3,400	3,900
Bearings	280	660
Other	350	410
Net income (millions of current Kč)	−167	405
Tractors	−157	16
Bearings	−14	245
Other	3	144
Assets (millions of current Kč)	8,200	10,700
Average age (in days) of receivables	230	355
Average selling price of a tractor (Kč)	120,000	250,000

Source: Data provided by Zetor's director of finance.

Marketing and Sales

Marketing and sales were normally not necessary in-house business functions because central planners told the enterprise what and how much to produce and to whom it was to be delivered. Performance was measured in units produced against a plan, not in revenues or profitability or market share. Every manager's goal was to produce the required number of units. Quality and customer satisfaction were not considerations. As one manager said, "Customers did not complain. They were happy to get any tractor at all."

Annual and five-year plans were negotiated by company management with the appropriate central government ministry officials. Profits went to the state, and losses were made up by the state. Some firms doing business in hard-currency foreign countries, including Zetor, were allowed to sell their products at below-market prices because of the state's need for the hard currency. It was not possible to determine whether Zetor's export prices to the West were lower than costs of production because costs and prices were the result of negotiations, not market forces. Costs were not measured at all in most large firms.

The Domestic Market   Zetor tractors for the domestic market were distributed through Agrozet, a separate state-owned enterprise that was responsible for supplying the equipment needs of the country's collective and cooperative farms. Agrozet was the link between production firms such as Zetor and agricultural users, delivering tractors, stocking and selling spare parts, and providing service that could not be done on the farm.

Exports   About 75 percent of Zetor's production was for export, half of which went to Western Europe and North America. Zetor tractor products were exported directly to 40 countries and could be found in use in over 90 countries in 1989. In 1989, exports to North America were about 1,000 tractors per year.

Zetor's international distribution was handled by another separate state company, Motokov. As one of Czechoslovakia's largest foreign trade companies, Motokov had handled the worldwide distribution of products for all of Czechoslovakia's automotive industries (cars, trucks, tires, tractors, motorcycles, even bicycles) before the Velvet Revolution. Motokov had employees who were familiar with the techniques of exporting located in various branch offices around the world. Motokov also handled after-sales service and parts through the dealer network, though parts and service were a very low priority.

From the standpoint of export customers, Zetor tractors were low in price and thus represented good value for money. Zetor competed favorably in Europe with other tractor brands such as Massey-Ferguson, Ford, and Case-IH, selling at 30 to 60 percent less than technically equivalent tractors manufactured in the West. Zetor enjoyed a 30 percent market share in countries as diverse as Sweden and Greece. The brand name was well regarded in Europe.

Production

In planned economies, most firms were specialized to produce one narrow product line or one component of a finished product made in another firm. Zetor was no exception. The company produced many of the parts for its tractors at its Brno headquarters and at two smaller plants in Moravia. However, Zetor bought all of the engines for its tractors from Zbrojovka, a separate Brno state enterprise, that in turn was dependent on Zetor for 80 percent of its engine business. Zetor also bought tractor cabs and tires from other single-product companies. In the case of engines and cabs, Zetor did all of the development and design for the components. The suppliers produced to Zetor's specifications.

The Czechoslovak centrally planned economy, like most command economies, developed localized shortages frequently. Component parts were sometimes not available. Equipment used in manufacturing was sometimes slow to be replaced or repaired. As a result, company management learned to get by without the right parts and equipment. Purchasing managers were notorious for stockpiling, bartering, and bribing to maintain adequate supplies of materials. At one point, Zetor had 600 tractors fully assembled and ready for shipment in their inventory lot, all missing the steering wheel. Tire sizes were substituted frequently, depending on availability. Tractors were not produced to customer specifications. They were produced to best available quality, given the materials available.

Finance

Economic objectives, the amount and method of finance, and the costs and prices of supplies and products were determined in negotiations with the Ministry of Industry. There was no clear relationship between costs negotiated with the ministry and the market price of a good. There existed little capability for Western-style finance or accounting within Zetor. There was a division of "economy" that kept track of costs and prices, but it had no real control over either. Performance was measured as actual production (in units) against the plan for production. The most important finance function was to ensure that adequate funds were on hand to pay employees.

Management and Organization

Prior to 1990, top management was appointed by the state (the Communist Party). Production plans were developed by the State Planning Commission, via various ministries, through a process of negotiation. In Zetor's case, the primary ministry was the Ministry of Industry, Office of Heavy Engineering.

As in most centrally planned economies, the two major purposes of the business were meeting its production quotas and providing jobs for citizens. Full employment was guaranteed by the state. Firms such as Zetor were expected to provide enough work opportunities to achieve full employment of the citizenry.

In 1991, Zetor was organized by function (see Exhibit 3). Membership in the Communist Party was usually necessary to obtain a top position, and nearly all of the division heads were Party members. Most high-level managers had technical educations from the Technical University in Brno or another technically oriented university in the country. A few were educated in economics.

About one-third of all employees were engaged in direct production. Another 40 percent were "overhead," or indirect production, including maintenance and service. The remaining employees were administrative.

PRIVATIZATION

One major task during 1990 and 1991, for Zetor as well as much of the Czechoslovakian economy, was to prepare for privatization—the transfer of ownership of enterprises from the state to the private sector.

The Privatization Process

Most of the large state-owned enterprises in the Czech Republic were privatized between 1991 and 1994 using an innovative voucher scheme. The government's objective was to transfer most of the country's larger goods-making and service-producing enterprises to widespread private ownership quite quickly. Because local citizens did not have the financial resources to "buy the economy" overnight, much of it was being "given away."

Under voucher privatization, each adult citizen was entitled to buy a book of vouchers containing 1,000 points at a price of Kč 1,000 (which in early 1992 was an average week's wages). The voucher holder could bid for shares of individual companies or could spend voucher points on mutual funds that in turn bought shares of companies.

Voucher privatization was not the only means of transferring ownership to the private sector, but it was the most common for large companies. Other methods of privatization included auction (usually for smaller firms); tender offers (usually with conditions regarding maintaining a particular employment level); management buyouts; direct sale to a predetermined buyer; transfer at no cost to a municipality,

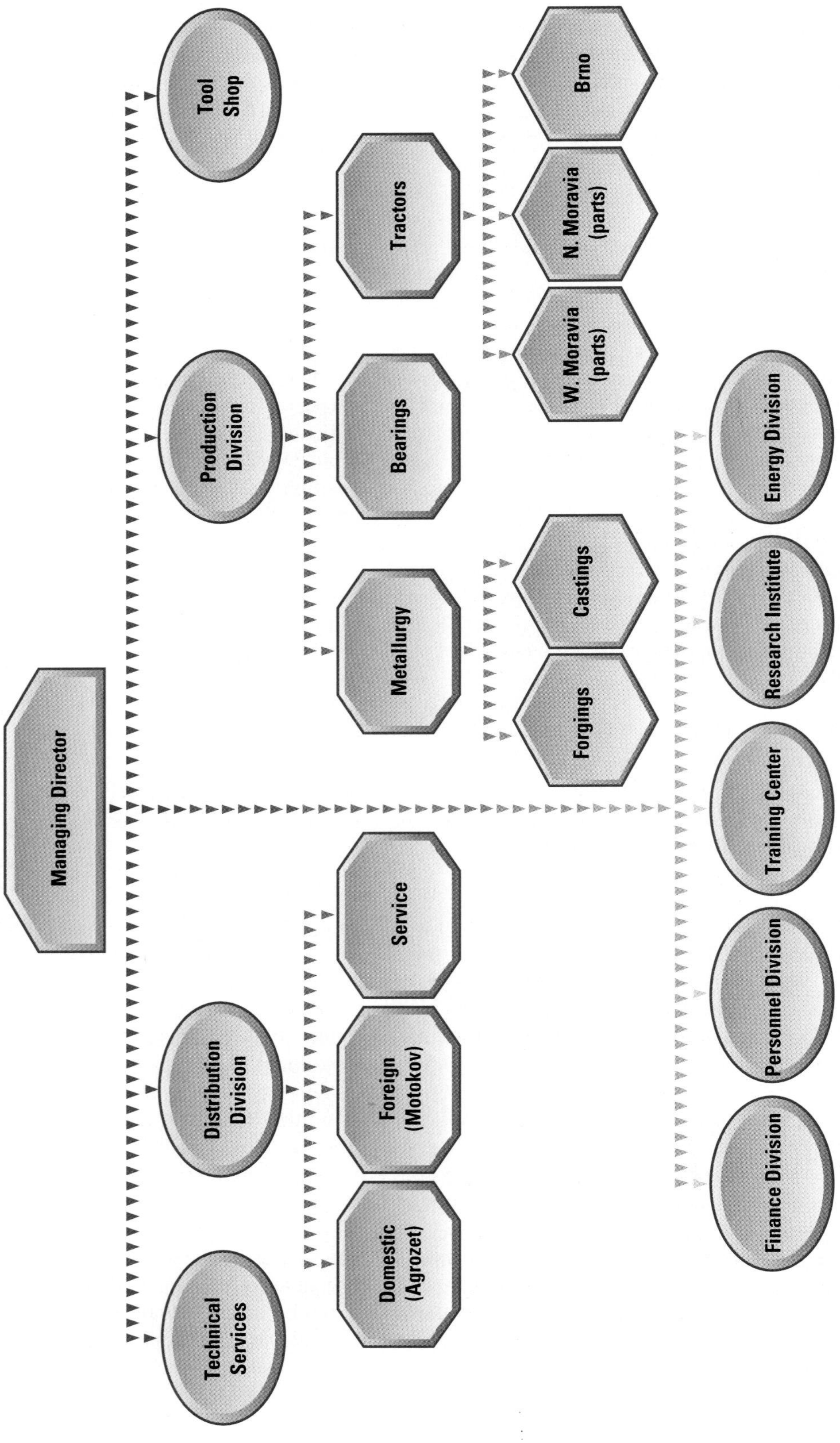

Exhibit 3 Organizational Structure of State Plant Zetor, 1991

pension fund, or bank; and restitution to the family from which the property had been confiscated by the state (where heirs were clearly identified and uncontested).

Companies prepared for privatization by publishing an official "project" that was essentially a proposed business plan. Financial information such as fixed assets, capital, and debt was combined with a five-year strategic plan and submitted to representatives from the Ministries of Privatization, Finance, and Industry for consideration. For the privatization of large firms, people outside the company were also encouraged to submit competing projects. The "best" project was followed during the early stages of privatization, and in most cases it was the project produced by company insiders.

Projects for privatization of large companies had some common features. First, all set aside 3 percent of shares to help pay restitution claims. Second, most set aside 20 to 30 percent of shares for voucher privatization. Third, the remaining shares were usually set aside for the National Property Fund to purchase. The National Property Fund, a state entity supervised by the Ministry of Privatization, was the temporary owner of shares of large firms that were too large for full voucher privatization and for which no other buyer had been found.

The privatization process in the Czech Republic was a combination of a company-initiated "bottom-up" approach and a central government strategy involving the Ministries of Privatization, Industry, and Finance. This was in contrast to the policy in Poland and Hungary, where the appropriate ministry hand-picked companies or industrial sectors for privatization. Firms in the Czech Republic had some influence over when and how they were to be privatized, though the final decision always rested with the ministries.

Privatization Results

Motokov, the separate company that handled Zetor's international distribution, was privatized in 1992. Zetor bought a 10 percent stake in the new firm. Other supplier firms bought a total of 30 percent, and the special government fund bought the remaining 60 percent to hold for further privatization or direct sale in the future.

Zetor's engine supplier was also privatized in 1992 as Brno Diesel. A majority of its shares were held by the National Property Fund pending further privatization. Agrozet, Zetor's domestic distributor, was privatized in 1992. Its local offices were sold directly to buyers as dealerships.

Zetor was not scheduled to be privatized until mid-1993. According to Jan Otoupalík, Zetor decided to wait until later to privatize so that discussions could take place with foreign firms regarding partnership arrangements. Otoupalík believed in 1991 that Zetor would need an infusion of foreign capital to be competitive and felt it was better to achieve agreement with a foreign firm prior to privatization.

DOMESTIC BUSINESS CONDITIONS: 1990–1991

The transition in the Czech Republic was accompanied by a drop in industrial production of 27 percent in 1990–91 (see Exhibit 4). The Czechoslovak crown was devalued twice in late 1990 from Kč 15/US$ to Kč 30/US$. Price inflation surged to 58 percent in 1991. The breakup and economic collapse of the Soviet Union in 1991 meant that one of the large export markets for products made by Czech companies had disappeared.

Exhibit 4 Economic Conditions in Czechoslovakia, 1989–1991

Indicator	1989	1990	1991
Gross domestic product, real % change	0.7†	−3.5	−15.0
Industrial production, real % change	0.9	−3.7	−23.1
Price inflation, % (consumer prices)	1.4	10.0	57.8
Interest rate, %*	5.5	6.2	15.4
Exchange rate, Kč/$ (annual average)	15.1	18.0	29.5
Unemployment rate, %	n.a.	0.3	6.8

† Net material product.

* Lending rate to state enterprises for working capital.

Sources: Economist Intelligence Unit, *Country Report: Czech Republic and Slovakia*, 2nd quarter 1994, 2nd quarter 1993, 2nd quarter 1990, London, 1994, 1993, 1990. International Monetary Fund, *International Financial Statistics*, January 1994 and March 1994. Washington, D.C., 1994.

Business conditions in the Czech Republic proved to be a major challenge for Zetor and other firms. The country lacked the legal and financial infrastructure taken for granted in Western countries with market economies. There were few laws on the books about bankruptcy, contracts, and property rights. Capital was scarce. Interest rates were over 15 percent. Banks were unaccustomed to checking accounts, letters of credit, and wire transfers, not to mention use of more sophisticated financial instruments found common in the West. One banker said, "It takes one day to move money from London to Prague and three weeks to move it from Prague to Brno."

Telecommunications were also unreliable, especially during business hours when demand was at its peak. After the Velvet Revolution, demand for telecommunications increased markedly, much faster than capacity. Waiting time for new telephone lines was as long as 2½ years in some parts of the country. Plans for laying new fiber-optic cable had yet to materialize, and the system was close to gridlock in Prague on some days.

Finally, because there was little or no bank credit available, firms began financing each other by extending trade credit, creating a huge inventory of nonperforming interfirm debt. Most large firms had payables and receivables exceeding 150 days in late 1991. Banks also held a large inventory of nonperforming loans, most of which had been made prior to the Velvet Revolution at nominal interest rates and with no historic expectation of repayment.

ZETOR'S BUSINESS: 1990–1991

Management Changes

Almost immediately after the Velvet Revolution there was an exodus from Zetor of top managers who had gained their positions more because of Party membership than job-relevant skills. These top officials of the Communist Party left Zetor and began private businesses or retired. Their replacements came from a variety of places, most importantly from the ranks of those who were on the losing side during the "Prague

Spring" liberalization movement of 1968. These people were known as "sixty-eighters."

Jan Otoupalík, the managing director, was a sixty-eighter. He started working at Zetor in 1956 after completing his studies at the Economic University in Brno. Within four years he was promoted to deputy director. Between 1960 and 1966 he held positions of deputy director for planning and deputy director for economy. Between 1966 and 1970 he was deputy director, commercial, the number two person in the firm. During this time he was also an active member of the Communist Party.

In the mid-1960s, Otoupalík was involved in discussions with Massey-Ferguson and John Deere about cooperative ventures, including a tractor plant that John Deere later located in Mexico. Zetor won an international competition for the joint venture with Deere. Zetor was to produce a two-cylinder 25-horsepower tractor in Mexico and market it under the brand name John Deere-Zetor. Unfortunately, the crackdown following the failure of Prague Spring intervened. The agreement was canceled. Otoupalík was found guilty of conspiring with Western firms. He was removed from the Party and from his position and assigned to work in the Zetor factory as a technician.

Later, he was instrumental in the technology transfer of Zetor's two-cylinder capability to India and setting up the assembly plant in Iraq. Very shortly after the Velvet Revolution, Otoupalík was elected by workers' representatives to be the managing director. As one of his colleagues said privately, "There is no one else quite like Otoupalík. No one is ready to take his place."

The story of Emil Filouš, the deputy director for production and number two person in the firm, was similar. A friend of Otoupalík's since grammar school, Filouš joined Zetor in 1962 after working for seven years in Slovakia manufacturing tanks. He started at Zetor as a dispatcher, and within two years had been named director of tractor production. He, too, was removed from his position and from the Party in 1970 and remained at the factory as a technician. In 1986, having been completely rehabilitated by the Party, he became managing director of Zetor. However, in 1988, Filouš was again on the wrong side of a political dispute and found himself back in the factory as a technician. In 1990, he was promoted to his deputy director position.

Similar stories abounded at Zetor. Of the top managers, only the deputy director for bearings was unchanged from before the Velvet Revolution. He had been a member of the Communist Party prior to the revolution, but, in his words, "I did nothing wrong. There was no reason for me to go."

Domestic Sales

The agricultural industry, with its large state-owned and cooperative firms, was slated for reorganization, but in late 1991 no one knew what shape the organization would take. The result was that farm managers were uncertain about their future needs for tractors. Even if farmers had the money to purchase new tractors, they did not know what size tractor to buy because nobody knew how large the farms would be; methods for privatizing cooperative and state-owned farms had not been decided.

At the same time, the attempt by the European Community to reduce high levels of government support to farmers contained in the old Common Agriculture Policy caused farm managers to expect that real prices for farm output would go down in the future. As a result, domestic sales of Zetor tractors dropped from 5,400 units in 1989 to about 3,100 units in 1991 (see Exhibit 2).

Export Sales

Export sales fell sharply from over 22,000 tractors in 1989 to 11,400 in 1991. Two events explain much of this decline: the Persian Gulf War with Iraq in early 1991, and import tariffs imposed by Poland.

- Zetor's Iraqi business had developed over many years, and by 1989 was responsible for annual sales of over 6,000 tractors. The United Nations embargo against all trade with Iraq that began in August 1990 brought Zetor's exports to Iraq to zero. Receivables from Iraq stood at about Kč 3 billion ($100 million) at the end of 1991.
- Poland imposed a 30 percent tariff against the import of tractors in 1991, seeking to protect its own tractor industry, which was operating at one-third capacity. As a consequence, export of Zetor tractors to Poland fell dramatically. Though Poland had agreed to remove its protective tariffs, the ones covering tractors were to be removed last.

The combination of much lower domestic and export sales resulted in 1991 production of less than 60 percent of plant capacity. The workforce was smaller by about 12 percent in 1991 than it had been in 1989 (Exhibit 2). Average hours worked per week had dropped from 37 to 34.

Otoupalík felt a joint venture might solve Zetor's excess capacity problem. He began negotiations with an Italian firm, Samé, to produce small tractors. "However," noted Otoupalík, "we have to be careful with joint ventures. These are our competitors. We do not want to sell our markets to them." He went on to say, "Our problems are temporary. This is just a matter of timing. Our sales should recover in the second half of next year."

THE TRADE CREDIT PROBLEM

Even when Zetor sold a tractor, payment was by no means assured. Zetor's receivables were averaging 355 days old in 1991. Zetor's tractor receivables from Motokov in late 1991 stood at nearly Kč 1 billion. Domestic tractor receivables were Kč 200 million. Receivables from the bearings business were also high, about Kč 300 million.

Receivables from the domestic trading organization reflected Agrozet's own problems with its receivables. Agrozet used the payment it got from retail customers for Zetor tractors to finance its own receivables. In essence, trade credit, which in functioning market economies was financed through banks, was instead being financed ad hoc, as firms "borrowed" from their suppliers by not paying bills on time.

Competition

Zetor faced the end of its domestic monopoly. The trade and investment liberalization that accompanied the change of government meant that foreign tractor companies were free to export products to Czech customers and to invest in local production facilities. Either action meant new competition for Zetor. John Deere, Massey-Ferguson, Case I-H, and Ford of Europe had shown interest in doing business in the Czech Republic. Nevertheless, the low labor wage rates in the region made it difficult for foreign imports to compete on a price basis with Zetor in its home market.

Otoupalík was aware that he had to make some strategic choices about the company and its operation if Zetor was to survive these turbulent times. But he was unsure about the right direction for Zetor. What company strengths or weaknesses would make a difference as he moved ahead? What opportunities did Zetor have for competing in a market economy? What were the most immediate problems Zetor had to address? How should the company be organized for competition in the global economy?

Procuring Goods from Manufacturers in India:

A conscience or a competitive edge (A)

Kate Button, journalist, and Christopher K. Bart, McMaster University

The plane touched down at the Bombay airport precisely on time. Olivia Jones made her way through the usual immigration bureaucracy without incident and was finally ushered into a waiting limousine, complete with uniformed chauffeur and soft black leather seats. Her already considerable excitement at being in India for the first time was mounting. As she cruised the dark city streets, she asked her chauffeur why so few cars had their headlights on at night. The driver responded that most drivers believed that headlights use too much petrol! Finally, she arrived at her hotel, a black marble monolith, grandiose and decadent in its splendor, towering above the bay.

The goal of her four-day trip was to sample and select swatches of woven cotton from the mills in and around Bombay, to be used in the following season's youthwear collection of shirts, trousers, and underwear. She was thus treated with the utmost deference by her hosts, who were invariably Indian factory owners or British agents for Indian mills. For three days she was ferried from one air-conditioned office to another, sipping iced tea or chilled lemonade, poring over leather-bound swatch catalogs, which featured every type of stripe and design possible. On the fourth day, Jones made a request that she knew would cause some anxiety in the camp. "I want to see a factory," she declared.

After much consultation and several attempts at dissuasion, she was once again ushered into a limousine and driven through a part of the city she had not previously seen. Gradually, the hotel and the Western shops dissolved into the background and Jones entered downtown Bombay. All around was a sprawling shantytown, constructed from sheets of corrugated iron and panels of cardboard boxes. Dust flew in spirals everywhere among the dirt roads and open drains. The car crawled along the unsealed roads behind carts hauled by man and beast alike, laden to overflowing with straw or city refuse—the treasure of the ghetto. More than once the limousine had to halt and wait while a lumbering white bull crossed the road.

Finally, in the very heart of the ghetto, the car came to a stop. "Are you sure you want to do this?" asked her host. Determined not to be faint-hearted, Jones got out of the car.

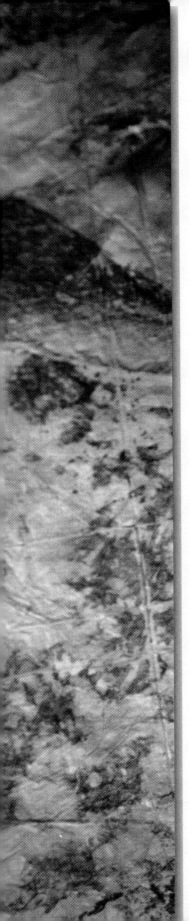

White-skinned, blue-eyed, and blond, clad in a city suit and stiletto-heeled shoes, and carrying a briefcase, Jones was indeed conspicuous. It was hardly surprising that the inhabitants of the area found her an interesting and amusing subject, as she teetered along the dusty street and stepped gingerly over the open sewers.

Her host led her down an alley, between the shacks and open doors and inky black interiors. Some shelters, Jones was told, were restaurants, where at lunchtime people would gather on the rush mat floors and eat rice together. In the doorway of one shack there was a table that served as a counter, laden with ancient cans of baked beans, sardines, and rusted tins of a fluorescent green substance that might have been peas. The eyes of the young man behind the counter were smiling and proud as he beckoned her forward to view his wares.

As Jones turned another corner, she saw an old man in the middle of the street, clad in a waist cloth, sitting in a large tin bucket. He had a tin can in his hand with which he poured water from the bucket over his head and shoulders. Beside him two little girls played in brilliant white nylon dresses, bedecked with ribbons and lace. They posed for her with smiling faces, delighted at having their photograph taken in their best frocks. The men and women moved around her with great dignity and grace, Jones thought.

Finally, her host led her up a precarious wooden ladder to a floor above the street. At the top Jones was warned not to stand straight as the ceiling was just 5 feet high. There, in a room not 20 feet by 40 feet, 20 men were sitting at treadle sewing machines, bent over yards of white cloth. Between them on the floor were rush mats, some occupied by sleeping workers awaiting their next shift. Jones learned that these men were on a 24-hour rotation, 12 hours on and 12 hours off, every day for 6 months of the year. For the remaining 6 months they returned to their families in the countryside to work the land, planting and building with the money they had earned in the city. The shirts they were working on were for an order she had placed four weeks earlier in London, an order of which she had been particularly proud because of the low price she had succeeded in negotiating. Jones reflected that this sight was the most humbling experience of her life. When she questioned her host about these conditions, she was told that they were typical for her industry—and for most of the Third World, as well.

Eventually, she left the heat, dust, and din of the little shirt factory and returned to the protected, air-conditioned world of the limousine.

"What I've experienced today and the role I've played in creating that living hell will stay with me forever," she thought. Later in the day, she asked herself whether what she had seen was an inevitable consequence of pricing policies that enabled the British customer to purchase shirts at £12.99 instead of £13.99 and at the same time allowed the company to make its mandatory 56 percent profit margin? Were her negotiating skills—the result of many years of training—an indirect cause of the terrible conditions she had seen?

Once Jones returned to the U.K., she considered her position and the options open to her as a buyer for a large, publicly traded, retail chain operating in a highly competitive environment. Her dilemma was twofold: Can an ambitious employee afford to exercise a social conscience in his or her career? And can career-minded individuals truly make a difference without jeopardizing their future?

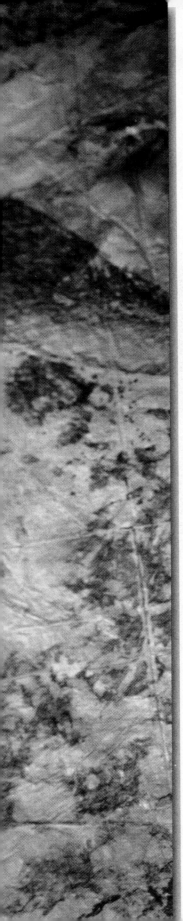

Martha McCaskey

Bart J. van Dissel, Harvard Business School

Martha McCaskey felt both elated and uneasy after her late Friday meeting with Tom Malone and Bud Hackert, two of the top managers in Praxis Associates' Industry Analysis Division (IAD). Malone, the division's de facto COO, had said that upon successful completion of the Silicon 6 study, for which McCaskey was project leader, she would be promoted to group manager. The promotion would mean both a substantial increase in pay and a reprieve from the tedious field work typical of Praxis's consulting projects. Completing the Silicon 6 project, however, meant a second session with Phil Devon, the one person who could provide her with the information required by Praxis's client. Now, McCaskey reflected, finishing the project would likely mean following the course of action proposed by Hackert and seconded by Malone: to pay Devon off.

Praxis's client, a semiconductor manufacturer based in California, was trying to identify the cost structure and manufacturing technologies of a new chip produced by one of its competitors. McCaskey and the others felt certain that Phil Devon, a semiconductor industry consultant who had worked in the competitor's West Coast operation some 12 years earlier, could provide the detailed information on manufacturing costs and processes required by their client (see Exhibit 1 for a summary of the required information). Her first interview with Devon had caused McCaskey to have serious doubts both about the propriety of asking for such information and about Devon's motivation in so eagerly offering to help her.

Malone suggested that she prepare an action plan over the weekend. Ty Richardson, head of the Industry Analysis Division, would be in town on Monday to meet with Malone and the two group managers, Bud Hackert and Bill Davies. McCaskey could present her plan for completing the Silicon 6 project at that meeting. Malone said all of them would be extremely interested in hearing her ideas. Silicon 6 was turning out to be a very important project. The client currently accounted for 15 to 20 percent of the division's revenues. In a meeting earlier that day, the marketing manager representing the client had offered to double the fee for the Silicon 6 project. He had also promised that there would be 10 more projects for the division to do that would be just as lucrative if they could come through on Silicon 6.

By Saturday afternoon, McCaskey had worked up several approaches to completing the Silicon 6 project. With the additional funds now available from the client, she could simply have Devon provide analyses of several alternatives for manufacturing state-of-the-art chips, including the one used at the competitor's Silicon 6 plant. The extra analyses would be expensive and time-consuming, but Devon most likely

Exhibit 1   Summary of Information Required by Praxis's Client

Project

Develop a competitive profile, in detail, of the Silicon 6 semiconductor manufacturing facility, obtaining:

1. Detailed cost information per 1,000 chips
   - Utilities
   - Scrap
   - Depreciation
   - Other materials
2. Salaries for professionals
3. Number of people in each category of hourly workers
4. How overhead is split out between the different chips
5. Equipment
   - Description, including capacities
   - Operating temperatures
   - Actual production rates and expenses
   - Do they use the same lines for different chips?
6. Raw materials
   - Source
   - Price
   - Long-term contracts?
   - How to account for captive raw materials—transferred at cost or cost plus?
7. Marketing and service expenses

would not suspect what she was after. Another option was to hand the project over to Chuck Kaufmann, another senior associate. Chuck handled many of the division's projects that required getting information that a competitor, if asked, would consider proprietary.

McCaskey felt, however, that no matter which option she chose, completing the Silicon 6 project would compromise her values. Where do you draw the line on proprietary information, she wondered? Was she about to engage in what one of her friends at another consulting firm referred to as "gentleman's industrial espionage"? McCaskey reflected on how well things had gone since she joined the Industry Analysis Division. Until the Silicon 6 project, she felt that she had always been able to maintain a high degree of integrity in her work. Now, McCaskey wondered, would the next step to success mean playing the game the way everyone else did?

PRAXIS ASSOCIATES

Praxis was a medium-sized consulting firm based in Chicago, with offices in New York, Los Angeles, and San Francisco. Founded in 1962 by three professors who taught accounting in Chicago-area universities, the firm had grown to nearly 350 employees by 1986. Over this period, Praxis had expanded its practice into four divisions: Management Control and Systems (which had been the original practice of the firm), Financial Services, General Management, and Industry Analysis. These expansions had taken place within a policy of conservative, controlled growth to ensure that the firm maintained a high-level quality of services and an informal, think-tank atmosphere. Throughout its history, Praxis had enjoyed a reputation for high technical and professional standards.

Industry Analysis was the newest and smallest of Praxis's four divisions. It had been created in 1982 in response to increasing demand for industry and competitive analysis by clients of the firm's Financial Services and General Management divisions. Industry and competitive analysis involved an examination of the competitive forces in industries and then identifying and developing ways in which firms could create and sustain competitive advantage through a distinctive competitive strategy.

Unlike the other three divisions, the Industry Analysis Division was a separate, autonomous unit operating exclusively out of San Francisco. The other divisions were headquartered in Chicago, with branch operations in New York and Los Angeles. The Industry Analysis Division had been located in San Francisco for two reasons: (1) much of Praxis's demand for competitive analysis came from clients based in California, and particularly in Silicon Valley, and (2) Ty Richardson, the person hired to start the division, was well-connected in Northern California and had made staying in San Francisco part of his terms for accepting the job. Richardson reported directly to Praxis's executive committee. Richardson had also insisted on hiring all his own people. Unlike the rest of Praxis's divisions, which were staffed primarily by people who were developed internally, the Industry Analysis Division was staffed entirely with outsiders.

The Industry Analysis Division

By 1986, the Industry Analysis Division consisted of 15 professionals, 12 analysts (called associates), and 6 clerical staff. In addition to Richardson (who was a senior vice president), the division had one vice president (who served as Richardson's chief of operations) and two group managers. The remaining 11 professionals formed two groups of senior associates that reported to the two group managers. (See Exhibit 2 for a complete chart showing names and positions of members of both groups.)

The two groups of senior associates were distinctly different. The senior associates who reported to Bud Hackert were referred to as the "old guard." Several years earlier, they had all worked for Richardson when he had run his own consulting firm in Los Angeles. In contrast to the old guard, the senior associates reporting to Bill Davies all had MBAs from well-known schools. Consequently, the "new guard" had significantly higher starting salaries. Another difference between the two groups was that members of the new guard tended to spend their time equally between individual and team projects. The old guard worked strictly on individual projects.

Senior associates and group managers received their project assignments from Tom Malone, Richardson's chief of operations. For the most part, however, roles and reporting relationships among the professional staff were loosely defined. Senior associates often discussed the status of their projects directly with Malone or Richardson rather than with the group managers. Both group managers and senior associates served as project leaders. On team projects, it was not unusual for the group manager to be part of a team on which a senior associate was project leader. The assignment of associates to projects, determined by a process of informal bargaining among associates and project leaders, served to further blur the distinction between senior associates and group managers.

Malone and the two group managers also had previously worked with Richardson. Hackert and Richardson met when Richardson, who had a PhD in business

Exhibit 2   Praxis Associates—Staffing in the San Francisco Office

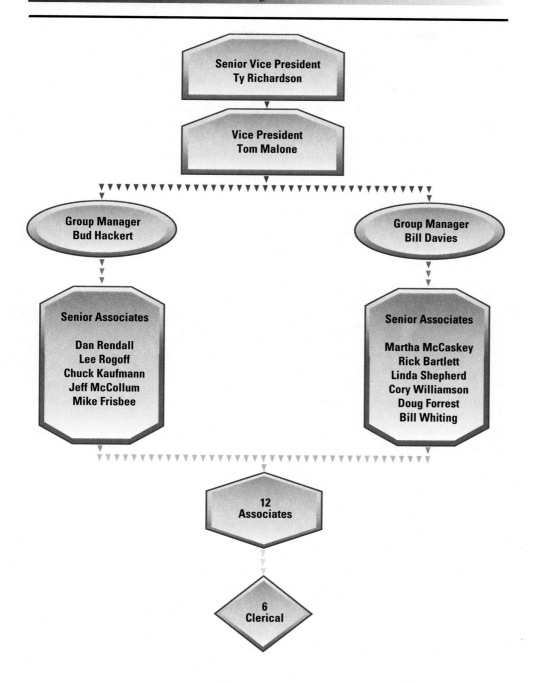

administration, left academia to join the Los Angeles branch of a well-known consulting firm. Richardson left shortly thereafter to start his own firm in Los Angeles, consulting to high-tech industries. Malone had managed Richardson's Los Angeles operation.

Clients and employees alike described Richardson as an exceptional salesperson. Very sharp in all his dealings, he had a folksy way with people that was both disarming and charismatic. Richardson was also a highly driven person who rarely slept more than four hours a night. He had taken major risks with personal finances, making and losing several fortunes by the time he was 35. Some of these ventures had involved Hackert, who had not made it in his previous employer's up-or-out system and had gone to work for a major Los Angeles real estate developer. By age 40, the demands both of being an entrepreneur and running his own consulting business had played havoc with Richardson's personal life. At his wife's insistence, Richardson switched careers and moved to San Francisco, where his wife started her own business and he accepted a high-level job with a major international consulting firm. Within the year, though, Richardson had grown restless. When Praxis agreed to let Richardson run his own show in San Francisco, he left the consulting firm, taking Bill Davies and several of the new guard with him.

MARTHA MCCASKEY

Martha McCaskey, 29 years old and single, had been with Praxis for 18 months. She joined the firm in 1985, shortly after completing her MBA at Harvard. Prior to the MBA, McCaskey had worked at a major consumer electronics firm for three years, after graduating from CalTech with a degree in electrical engineering. In the summer between her two MBA years, McCaskey worked as a consultant to a young biomedical firm in Massachusetts that specialized in self-administered diagnostic tests. While there, she developed product strategy and implementation plans for a supplement to one of the project lines and assisted in preparation of the firm's second equity offering. McCaskey thoroughly enjoyed the project orientation of the summer work experience and her role as consultant. The firm indicated a strong interest in hiring her upon completion of the MBA. McCaskey, however, had decided to pursue a career in consulting. In addition, she had grown up in the Bay area, and wanted to return there if possible.

Praxis was one of several consulting firms with whom McCaskey interviewed. Her first interview at the San Francisco branch was with Tom Malone, the division's vice president. Malone told her that the Industry Analysis Division was a wonderful place to work, especially emphasizing the collegial, think-tank environment. He said that they were experiencing tremendous growth. He also said they were just beginning to get involved in some very exciting projects. The interview ended before McCaskey could push him on specifics, but she wasn't sure that such questions would have been appropriate. Malone had impressed her as very dynamic and engaging. Instead of interrogating her, as she expected, McCaskey commented later that he had made her feel "pretty darn good."

The rest of her interviews were similar. Although she grilled the other people she met, they all told her what a terrific place the IAD was. McCaskey was surprised that many of the senior associates—and even the two group managers—did not seem as sharp as she had expected. In one of the interviews, McCaskey was also surprised to see Jeff McCollum, a former classmate she had known slightly at CalTech.

Upon returning to Boston, McCaskey had a message from Ty Richardson, who had called to say he would be in town the following night and was wondering if she could meet him. Over dinner at one of Boston's most expensive restaurants, Richardson told her he was quite impressed with what he had heard about her. They were looking for people like her to help the business grow and to handle the exciting new projects they were getting. He also said that, for the right people, the Industry Analysis Division offered rapid advancement—more so than she would likely find at the other firms with whom she was interviewing.

The next day Richardson called McCaskey with a generous offer. Later that afternoon she received a call from Jeff McCollum, who once again told her what a great place Praxis was to work, and how Richardson often would take everybody out for drinks Friday afternoon when he was around. In fact, Jeff laughed, there had been a golf outing the day before McCaskey's interview, and everyone had still been a little hung over when she arrived.

McCaskey called Richardson early the next week to accept the offer.

WORKING IN THE INDUSTRY ANALYSIS DIVISION ————

McCaskey's First Assignment

McCaskey's first day at work started with a visit from Malone. He explained that the division was experiencing a bit of a crunch just then, and they needed her help on a competitive analysis study. In fact, she would have to do the project by herself. It was unusual to give a new person his or her own project, Malone continued, but he had arranged for Bill Davies, her group manager, to provide backup support if she needed it. McCaskey reflected on her first project:

> It was relatively easy and I was lucky; it was a nice industry to interview in. Some industries are tough to interview because they tend to be very close-mouthed. Some industries are easier. The consumer electronics industry, for example, is pretty easy. Other industries, like the electronic chemicals areas, can be really tough. People making chips are very secretive.

Although it was her first assignment, McCaskey gave the client presentation and wrote a formal report detailing her analysis and recommendations. A few days later, Richardson dropped in on a working lunch among Davies's group to compliment McCaskey on her handling of the project. He went so far as to say that both he and Malone felt that her analysis was the best they had yet seen by anyone in the division.

McCaskey's Second Assignment

Two weeks later, McCaskey was assigned to a major project involving a competitive analysis for a company that made printed circuit boards. As with her first assignment, she was to work alone on the study, consulting Davies if and when she needed help. It was during this period that Malone began suggesting that she talk with two members of the old guard, Dan Rendall and Chuck Kaufmann, about sources of information. The project involved gathering some fairly detailed information about a number of competitors, including one Japanese and two European firms. The old guard handled many of the projects that involved gathering sensitive information on target firms (i.e., the client's competitors). This was always information that was not publicly available—information that a target firm would consider proprietary. It appeared to McCaskey that Dan Rendall and Chuck Kaufman were the real producers in this group, often taking on projects when other members of the old guard had difficulty obtaining sensitive information.

Rendall was the recognized leader of the old guard. He could often be seen coming and going from Richardson's office on the infrequent occasions that Richardson was in town. Recently, Richardson had been spending about 80 percent of his time on the road. When McCaskey approached Rendall, however, she felt him to be difficult and uncooperative. McCaskey found subsequent attempts to talk with Rendall equally unproductive. Chuck Kaufmann was out of town on assignment for two weeks and thus was unable to meet with McCaskey.

Given her difficulty in following through on Malone's recommendation to work with the old guard, McCaskey developed her own approach to the printed circuit board project. The project turned out to be extremely difficult. Over a period of six months, McCaskey conducted nearly 300 telephone interviews, attended trade shows in the United States, Japan, and Europe, and personally interviewed consultants, distributors, and industry representatives in all three places. Toward the end, McCaskey remembered working seven days a week, 10 to 15 hours a day. Her European contacts finally came through with all the necessary information just three days before the client presentation. Despite the results that her efforts produced, McCaskey felt that Richardson and Malone disapproved of how she handled the project, that it could have been completed with less time and effort:

> The presentation went really well. Towards the end, I began to relax and feel really good. I was presenting to a bunch of guys who had been in the business for 30 years. There were a few minor follow-up questions, but mostly a lot of compliments. I was really looking forward to taking a break. I had been with the company at this point for nine months, and never taken a day of vacation, and I was exhausted. And then, Richardson got up and promised the client a written report in two weeks.
>
> Davies was very good about it. We got in the car to go back to the airport, and he asked me wasn't I planning to take a vacation in the near future? But it went right by Richardson. Davies didn't press it, of course. Even though he had an MBA from Stanford, he was a really laid-back California type. That sometimes made for problems when you needed direction on projects or firm policy.
>
> The next day, I was a basket case. I should have called in sick, I really should have. I managed to dictate about one page. Richardson came by at the end of the day and said, "Well, what's the hold-up?" I was so mad, I got the report done in 10 days.

The rate at which McCaskey wrote the report was held up by Malone as a new standard for Industry Analysis projects.

McCaskey's handling of the written report on her next project led to an even tighter standard for the division's projects. Hoping to avoid a similar bind on the project, McCaskey planned to write the report before the client presentation. Malone had told her she would not have any other responsibilities while on the project because the deadline was so tight. Two weeks later, however, Richardson asked her to join a major project involving the rest of Davies's group.

> He kind of shuffled into my office and said something like, "Damn, you know, ah, gee Martha, we really admire you. I'd really like to have you on this team. We're a little behind schedule and we could really use your expertise. I've also

asked Chuck Kaufmann to join the team and I'd like the two of you to work on a particularly challenging piece of the project.''

Despite the dual assignment, McCaskey managed to complete the report on her original project before the client presentation. That also became a standard within the division.

The Environment at IAD

In mid-1986, several senior associates left the firm. Bill Whiting and Cory Williamson took jobs with competing firms. Doug Forrest was planning to take a job with one of Praxis's clients. Jeff McCollum left, complaining that he was burned out and that he planned to take several months off to travel before looking for work. Over the previous six months there also had been high turnover among the associates. It had become a running joke that Tuesday's edition of *The Wall Street Journal*, which carried the job advertisements, should be included in the set of industry journals that were circulated around the office.

While some of the turnover could be attributed to the increasing work load and performance expectations, a number of people had also been upset over the previous year's bonuses. Richardson and Malone had met with each senior associate prior to Christmas and explained that the division was going through a growth phase and wasn't the cash generator everybody seemed to think it was. They were all then given the same bonus and told how valuable they were to the firm, regardless of the length of time they had been with the firm or what they had accomplished. But, as McCaskey recalled, what really got to people was when Richardson and Malone showed up at the New Year's office party, each in a brand new Mercedes.

Chuck Kaufmann had gone to see Malone about the personnel situation. He warned Malone that unless something was done to improve things, several more people would leave. Malone responded that he could put an ad in the paper and get 10 new people any time he wanted. Chuck was shocked. For McCaskey, however, Malone's response was not surprising. In the lighter moments of working on team projects, conversation among members of the new guard had naturally drifted to views on Richardson and Malone and on what made them so successful:

> Malone was good-looking, married, with two kids. He usually drove a Ferrari instead of the Mercedes. He was very aggressive. You could hear this man all over the building when he was on the phone. We decided he was just really driven by money. That's all there was . . . he'd go whip someone and tell them to get work out by the end of the month so we could bill for it—and have no qualms about doing it—all right, 'cause he's counting his bucks. He was also a very smart man. If you spent a couple of hours with him in the car or on a plane explaining a business to him, he'd have it. The man had amazing retention.
>
> Both he and Richardson were great salesmen. Malone could be an incredible bullshitter. At times, though, you wondered how much credibility you could put in these people. They kept saying they wanted you to be part of the management team. But then they'd turn around and wouldn't even tell us where or when they would go on a client call, so you really couldn't make a contribution.

Chuck's shock at Malone's response to the personnel question was also typical. McCaskey had worked with Chuck on a number of team projects and found him to be different from most of the old guard. He was working on his MBA in the evening program at Berkeley and really seemed to enjoy being with the new guard.

McCaskey knew that Chuck also had a reputation for working on what were referred to as the "sleaze" projects in the office: projects that involved questionable practices in contacting and interviewing people who could provide very detailed information about target companies. Even so, McCaskey felt that he did this work mainly out of a sense of loyalty to Richardson and Malone:

> Chuck was always torn between doing the job and feeling, "These guys need me to help them run their business, because I'm going to be a group manager someday, and they really need me." He was torn between that and trying to be, not diplomatic, but objective about his situation, saying, "They're paying me less than anybody else, but look what these guys are asking me to do."
>
> He wanted to do good in the eyes of people he looked up to, whether it's Richardson and Malone or peers like Dan or myself, because he has that personal attachment and can't step back and say, "They're screwing me to the wall." He just could not make that distinction.

Chuck had been fun to work with, though. McCaskey had observed that many of their team projects had required increasingly detailed information about a client's competitors. These projects had given rise to discussions among McCaskey and her colleagues about what constituted proprietary information and what, if anything, they should do if they found they had to obtain such information. While there was some discussion about the appropriateness of such projects, McCaskey recalled a particular conversation that characterized how the issue was typically handled:

> We were on a quick coffee break and Linda Shepherd said she really needed to get psyched up for her next call. Linda was a member of the new guard whom I liked and respected. She had an MBA from Berkeley and had been there about a year longer than I had. We became good friends soon after I arrived and ended up working together a lot on team projects.
>
> I said, "Yeah, I know what you mean. I tried to get some discounting information from a marketing manager this morning and all he would give me was list price. As usual, I started out with general questions, but as soon as I tried to get specific he was all over me. Like pulling teeth. Invariably, they slap it back at you. What information do you have? You know, and you don't want to give away the pot because then he'd know what you're doing."
>
> Chuck's advice was pretty funny. He said that he was working on a project that was so slimy he had to take a shower every time he got off the phone, and maybe that's what we ought to do, too.

As was the norm on most of the division's projects, McCaskey usually identified herself as a representative of a newly formed trade journal for the particular industry in which she was interviewing. To McCaskey, that was not nearly as dishonest as visiting a target company on the pretense of interviewing for a job, as a friend of hers who worked for another consulting firm had done.

All in all, McCaskey felt that she had been given the freedom to do her work with integrity and quality. It was also clear that her performance was recognized by Richardson. Of the senior associates, Richardson spent the most time with Dan Rendall, McCaskey, or Chuck. While Dan often could be seen in Richardson's office, Richardson seemed to make a point of dropping in on Chuck and McCaskey. For McCaskey, these visits also seemed to be more social than work-related. Richardson's comments at a recent consumer electronics marketing research association convention were a typical example of how these meetings went. Martha described that evening:

We had gone to the dinner but decided not to hang around for the speeches. Instead, he asked me if I'd like to have a nightcap. I said sure. So we went to a bar, and he spent the evening giving me all these warm fuzzies—about how he really enjoyed having me with the company, how I was an important member of the management team of the company, how everything was wonderful with me there, and that he hoped that I would be with them for a long time. And on and on.

At the end of 1986 McCaskey received a substantial increase in pay. She also received a $10,000 bonus. Most of the other senior associates had received much smaller bonuses—in many cases equivalent to what they had received the previous year.

THE SILICON 6 PROJECT

In January 1987 both Richardson and Malone met with McCaskey to talk about a new assignment. The project was for one of Praxis's oldest clients in the high-tech electronics field. Since its inception, the Industry Analysis Division had done a lot of work for this client. The project involved a new type of computer chip being produced by one of the client's prime competitors—a company that also had once been one of Praxis's major clients. The project had originally been assigned to Lee Rogoff, a senior associate who reported to Hackert. The client was interested in detailed information about manufacturing processes and costs for the new computer chip. Although Lee had made numerous calls to the target company's clients and distributors, he had been unable to obtain any of the required information.

Normally, Dan Rendall would have been asked to take over the project if it had previously been handled by a member of the old guard. Instead, Malone explained, he and Richardson had decided to approach McCaskey because of her background in electrical engineering. (McCaskey had in fact done some coursework on chip design at CalTech.) Malone also told her that they had been impressed with her creativity and success in obtaining difficult, detailed information on previous projects. Malone added that there was one constraint on the project. The client had insisted that Praxis not contact the target company, to avoid potential allegations of price fixing.

The project was code-named Silicon 6 after the plant at which the chip was produced—the sixth building of an industrial cluster in Silicon Valley. McCaskey began by contacting the Silicon 6 plant's equipment manufacturers. They were unusually close-mouthed. She was unable to get them even to say what equipment the plant had ordered, never mind its operating characteristics. McCaskey also contacted raw materials suppliers to semiconductor manufacturers. Again, she was unsuccessful in obtaining any information. She held meetings nearly every day with Malone (standard operating procedure for problem projects). For McCaskey, the meetings soon began to have a monotonous quality to them:

How's it going? Well, OK. Let's retrench. Did you try this tack? Do you try that tack? Did you try this customer base? Did you try this group of calls?

Malone was especially interested in whether she was having any luck identifying ex-employees. On several of the projects McCaskey had worked on, particularly those requiring detailed data, the best source of information had been ex-employees of target companies. McCaskey had generally found these people quite willing to talk, sometimes out of vengeance, but also at times because there was a sympathetic, willing listener available. People love to talk about their "expertise," she often thought.

Industry consultants had been another good source of detailed information. It was not unusual for the Industry Analysis Division to hire consultants for $1,000 or $2,000 a day on specific projects. McCaskey felt that some of the senior associates had been rather creative in their use of this practice. Several months earlier, Chuck Kaufmann had confided to her that he had hired an ex-employee of a target company as a "consultant" to provide him with a list of software contracts for that target company. He said that this was something that Dan Rendall had done regularly on his projects. In one case, Dan had paid an ex-employee of a target company a "consulting" fee of $2,000 for a business plan and spreadsheets of the target company's upcoming new product information. Bud Hackert was there when Chuck had asked Dan if such information wasn't proprietary. Hackert had a reputation as a tough, no-nonsense manager who prided himself on running a tight shop and on his ability to get the job done, no matter what it took. Hackert said that if someone was willing to talk about it, then it wasn't proprietary.

McCaskey had mentioned this incident to Linda Shepherd. They both agreed that Dan's behavior, and Hackert's response, only confirmed what they had suspected all along about members of the old guard: they routinely paid ex-employees of target companies to obtain highly sensitive information for Praxis's clients. Linda ended the conversation with a comment that, given such behavior, the old guard wouldn't last long when the division really took off and headquarters became more interested in the San Francisco operation.

Many consulting firms had formal, written policies regarding the solicitation and performance of contracts. For example, some consulting firms required that their employees identify themselves as working for the firm before beginning an interview. The Industry Analysis Division did not have any written, formal policies as such. Richardson occasionally had given lunchtime talks concerning the division's policies, but, as McCaskey recalled, these tended to be quite vague and general. For example, for McCaskey, the bottom line in Richardson's "ethics" talk was quite simply, we don't do anything unethical. Besides, McCaskey knew from her friends at highly reputable firms that people occasionally broke the rules even when formal, written policies existed. After her discussion with Linda, McCaskey considered raising the old guard's use of ex-employees with Richardson, but he was out of the office for a couple of weeks. By the time he returned, she was in the middle of several large projects and had all but forgotten about it.

McCaskey's only lead on the Silicon 6 project occurred through a seemingly random set of events. Working through a list of academics involved in semiconductor research, she found a professor at a small East Coast engineering school who actively consulted with several European manufacturers of semiconductors. When she called him, McCaskey found that he could not provide her with any of the information on the list. Malone had suggested, however, that she fly out and interview him because he might have some gossip on the new chip. The interview served to clarify McCaskey's understanding of the manufacturing processes involved but, as she had suspected, did not provide her with any new information. He did suggest, however, that she get in touch with Phil Devon, a consultant in southern California. He did not know Devon personally but knew that Devon recently had been involved in the design and start-up of a plant for one of the European firms.

Upon returning to San Francisco, McCaskey called Devon to set up an interview. During the call she learned that he had been a vice president at the target company some 12 years earlier. When she told Malone about Devon, he was ecstatic. He congratulated her on once again coming through for the division, letting her know that both he and Richardson felt she was the one person they could always count on when the chips were down.

McCaskey Meets with Devon

McCaskey met with Devon the following Friday. He was in his mid-forties, very distinguished looking, and relaxed in his manner. McCaskey's first impression of Devon was that he was both professional and fatherly. Even before getting into the interview, she began to have qualms about asking for detailed information on the Silicon 6 plant. Feeling uneasy, McCaskey opened the interview by saying that she represented an international concern that was interested in building a semiconductor manufacturing plant in the United States. Devon responded by saying that he couldn't understand why anybody would want to build another plant, given the current global overcapacity for semiconductor production. He added, however, that he was willing to help her in whatever way he could.

McCaskey then suggested that they talk about the cost structure for a plant that would be employing state-of-the-art technology. Devon responded that he would need more information to work with if he was going to be of help to her. He explained that there were several new technologies available or under development, and it would make a difference which one they chose. It briefly crossed McCaskey's mind that this was an opportunity to talk about the Silicon 6 plant. Instead, she suggested that they might try to cover each of the options. Devon responded that it would involve an awful lot of work, and that it would be helpful if she could narrow things down. He then asked what kind of chips they intended to produce and whether there would be several products or just a single line. He added that if he knew whom she was representing, it would help him to determine what type of facility they might be interested in.

McCaskey felt increasingly uncomfortable as the interview progressed. She felt that Devon was earnestly trying to help her. He seemed to have an excellent technical background and to know what he was doing. It was clear that Devon took pride in doing what he did and in doing it well. By mid-morning, McCaskey began to feel nauseated with herself and the prospect of asking Devon to give her proprietary information on the Silicon 6 plant. As she talked with him, she couldn't help thinking, "This is a guy who's trying to do good in the world. How can I be doing this? I have an EE degree from CalTech, an MBA from Harvard, and here I am trying to sleaze this guy."

At this point, McCaskey settled on a scheme to end the interview but keep open the option of a second interview with Devon. From the morning's discussion, she was convinced that he had access to the information she needed to complete the Silicon 6 project. Instead of probing for the information, she told Devon that her client had not supplied her with adequately detailed information to focus on a specific technology and plant cost structure. She added that his questions had helped her learn a lot about what she needed to find out from her client before she came back to him. She suggested, however, that if they could put together a representative plant cost structure, it would be useful in going back to her client. Once again, Devon said that he was willing to help her in whatever way he could. He said he had recently helped set up a state-of-the-art facility in Europe that might be similar to the type of plant her client was considering. At this point, McCaskey began to feel that perhaps Devon was being too helpful. She wondered if he might be leading her on to find out who she was working for.

As the morning progressed, Devon provided her with background on the European plant, including general information about its cost structure and other items on McCaskey's list. McCaskey was so uncomfortable about deceiving him about the purpose of her visit that she barely made it through lunch, even though she had contracted with him for the full day. After lunch, she paid Devon the full day's fee and thanked him. McCaskey said that she would get in touch with him after meeting with her client to see if they could focus on a particular plant design. Devon thanked her, said that he wished he could have been more helpful, and that he looked forward to seeing her again.

McCaskey Meets with Malone

A meeting on the Silicon 6 project was scheduled with the client for the following Friday. McCaskey worked over the weekend and through the early part of the next week putting together her slides and presentation. As she worked, she continued to reflect on her meeting with Devon. Devon had seemed so professional. She wasn't really sure how he would have responded to specific questions about the Silicon 6 plant. She felt sure he could have provided her with all the information they needed. On the other hand, although it sounded far-fetched, it seemed just possible that Devon was so straight he might have called the police had she asked him for the information. Or, given his prior employment at the target company, Devon might have called someone there about McCaskey's interest in the Silicon 6 plant.

On Wednesday, McCaskey met with Malone to provide him with an update on her meeting with Devon and to review her presentation. She told Malone that she was unable to get the information they needed. To her surprise, Malone did not press her to try to get more information from Devon. Instead, he asked McCaskey to go through her presentation. When she came to a slide titled "Representative Plant Cost Structure," Malone stopped her, saying that the title should read "Plant Cost Structure." When McCaskey asked him what he meant, Malone told her to cross out the word "Representative." They would conduct the presentation as if this was data they had gathered on the actual Silicon 6 plant. When McCaskey objected, Malone pointed out that the analysis was general enough that no one would know the difference.

McCaskey Meets with the Client's Plant Managers

Going into the presentation Friday morning, McCaskey had only 30 slides. On other projects she typically had used in excess of 100 slides. To McCaskey's surprise, all of the client's senior plant managers were present for the presentation. She had been under the impression that the meeting was to be a dry run for a more formal presentation later on. The plant managers were courteous but stopped her 15 minutes into the presentation to say that she was not telling them anything new. If this was all she had, they said, it would be pointless to meet with senior management on the Silicon 6 project, although such a meeting was scheduled for the following month. They then asked her to identify all the sources she had contacted. McCaskey did not mention Devon, but the plant managers seemed satisfied with her efforts. Malone then explained that the lack of detailed information was due to the constraint of not being able to contact the target company.

The marketing manager in charge of the Silicon 6 project then asked his secretary to take McCaskey and Malone to his office while he held a brief meeting with the plant managers. Upon joining McCaskey and Malone, the marketing manager expressed his disappointment with Praxis's handling of the Silicon 6 project. Specifically, he said that his firm had never had any trouble getting such information before. Further, he pointed out how much business they provided for the Industry Analysis Division and that he had hoped the relationship could continue. Given the progress made by Praxis on the Silicon 6 project, however, he had doubts. Malone then brought up the possibility of still being able to successfully complete the project. Without mentioning Devon's name, he said that they had just made contact with an ex-employee who could provide them with the necessary information if provided with the proper incentives.

McCaskey was struck by how the marketing manager immediately brightened and told them that he didn't care how they got the information, as long as they got it. He then doubled the original fee that the Industry Analysis Division would be paid on completion of the project, adding that the additional funds should provide their source with an adequate incentive. He also told them that if they could come through on Silicon 6, he had 10 more projects just like it for them that would also be just as lucrative.

As they climbed into Malone's Ferrari for the ride back to the office, McCaskey felt stunned by the turn of events. First, there had been the unexpected importance of the presentation; then, the marketing manager's proposition; and, now, Malone's enthusiasm for it. Malone could barely contain himself, delighting in how Richardson would react upon hearing how things had worked out. McCaskey just looked at him, shook her head and said "You're amazing!" Malone agreed with her, complimented McCaskey in return, and promised her she would be promoted to group manager as soon as she completed Silicon 6.

When they got back, Malone called Hackert into his office with McCaskey and briefed him on the meeting. Hackert's response was that it would be a "piece of cake." All they'd have to do is figure out how to handle Devon. Hackert then suggested that, given the importance of the project, Devon be offered a per diem consulting fee of $4,000 instead of the standard $2,000. Malone responded that he was unsure if that was how they should approach it, but he did agree that they should make it worthwhile to Devon to provide the necessary information. He then turned to McCaskey and suggested she think about how to proceed with Devon. He also told her not to overlook the option of having someone else, such as Chuck, meet with Devon. She could still manage the overall project. He grinned and said it would be good training for her upcoming promotion.

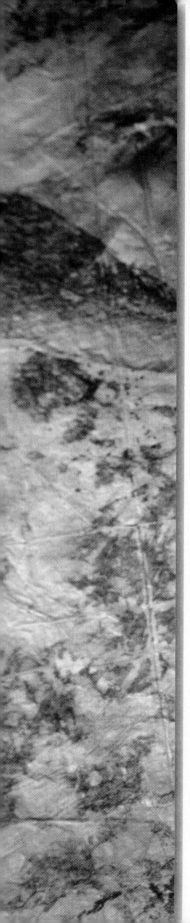

Nintendo versus SEGA (C):
Sex, violence, and videogames

Romuald A. Stone, James Madison University

Violence in America in 1994 was considered by many people to have reached epidemic proportions. All across the United States—in cities and towns large and small—citizens were increasingly fearful and concerned that violence was out of control. What was causing this violent behavior? There was no easy answer. But many experts said that the pervasive violence in television programming, films, and videogames was one seed that promoted physical aggression in some individuals and helped create a culture tolerant of violence.

Just as television emerged as a powerful social and cultural force in the early 1950s, videogames were said to be emerging as a potentially powerful influence on children's behavior in the 1990s. While the impact of the growing violence in videogames was debatable, the years of research on violence in television programming provided instructive warning. According to Parker Page, president of the Children's Television Resource and Education Center, "years of research indicate that children who watch a steady diet of violent programming increase their chances of becoming more aggressive towards other children, less cooperative and altruistic, more tolerant of real life violence and more afraid of the world outside their homes."[1] The advent of virtual reality technology in videogame programming led Page to express a special concern in his testimony before a joint Senate subcommittee hearing held in December 1993.

> Mortal Kombat is simply the first in a new generation of video games that allows software designers to combine high levels of violence with fully digitalized human images. No more cute hedge hogs or cartoonish Super Mario Brothers—increasingly, the characters that a young player beheads, disembowels or crushes will look more and more like the kids at school, the neighbor who lives down the street or the young woman heading for aerobics class.[2]

Alarmed by the violent content of many videogames, parents and concerned citizens started lobbying for a comprehensive, industrywide videogame rating system that would give parents the information they needed to make informed choices. To address these concerns, Senators Lieberman and Kohl sponsored legislation to establish the National Independent Council for Entertainment in Video Devices as an independent agency of the federal government to oversee the development of

[1] U.S. Senate, Violence in Videogames: Joint Hearing of the Judiciary Subcommittee on Juvenile Justice and Government Affairs Subcommittee on Regulation and Government Information (testimony of Parker Page, PhD), 103rd Cong., 1993.
[2] Ibid.

"voluntary" standards to alert parents to the content of videogames. In his testimony before the hearing, Robert Chase, vice president of the National Education Association, expressed the collective concern of educators, children's advocates, and parents:

> America's children are faced with a bewildering set of messages from television, movies, music, electronic games, and print media. Too often, the almost unrelenting assault on the senses encouraging aggression and irresponsibility are in direct opposition to the values families hope to instill and the mores our society struggles to preserve. Parents, social scientists, and the community at large share deep trepidation about the fruits of this ever widening dispersal of negative images. The explosion of media in the latter half of this century has made the problem all the more pervasive and the challenges for parents and community leaders all the more difficult.[3]

At the same hearing, the Software Publishers Association (SPA) provided a counter argument:

> In our attempt to protect our children from those relatively few video games which contain unacceptable violence, however, we must not lose sight of the fact that the vast majority of videogames are appropriate for children, and have the potential for developing many important and socially desirable skills. As stated so eloquently by Bob Keeshan, otherwise known as Captain Kangaroo, "Video games . . . provide the potential for heretofore unknown opportunities for information, education and delightful entertainment . . . The technology is to be encouraged because, used appropriately, such games can be a tool for education as well as entertainment."[4]

The SPA indicated in its testimony that the software entertainment industry was committed to moving quickly and decisively on this issue. The SPA was in the process of working with a coalition of concerned parties to establish a rating system that would be easy for consumers to understand and one that the industry could implement. Nintendo and SEGA had also initiated moves toward a rating system.

NINTENDO'S POSITION

When Nintendo entered the U.S. videogame industry in 1985, the company established written Game Content Guidelines requiring games marketed under the Nintendo Seal of Quality to meet the following standards:

- No sexually suggestive or explicit content.
- No sexist language or depictions.
- No random, gratuitous, or excessive violence.
- No graphic illustration of death.
- No domestic violence or abuse.
- No excessive force in sports games.
- No ethnic, racial, religious, or sexual stereotypes.
- No profanity or obscenity.

[3]Ibid. (testimony of Robert Chase).
[4]Ibid. (testimony of Ilene Rosenthal).

- No use of drugs, smoking materials, or alcohol.
- No subliminal political messages or overt political statements.

As an example of Nintendo's pledge to control and monitor its game content, the company insisted that one of its largest licensees, Acclaim Entertainment, remove objectionable material from the controversial arcade game "Mortal Kombat." In its original form, the game included scenes in which characters' heads were ripped off, their spines were pulled out, they were impaled on spikes, and they splurted blood when hit. All of these graphics were deemed unacceptable and removed from the Nintendo version of the game. SEGA released the game in its entirety.

Some games had been simply rejected outright, since no amount of modification would make them acceptable to Nintendo. One such game was "Night Trap," which contained full motion videos of young, scantily-clad females being attacked by hooded men who drilled holes in their bodies to suck out blood.

Howard Lincoln, Nintendo's then senior vice president (and later chairman), reiterated his company's continued commitment to wholesome family entertainment that was both challenging and exciting to youth while remaining nonoffensive to parents:

> This will remain our philosophy despite the fact we have been criticized by both video game players and others in our industry for taking what we feel is the only responsible approach . . . we believe our game guidelines have served us and our customers well for the past eight years. And we have no intention of abandoning this approach.[5]

However, Nintendo apparently decided to moderate its position following a raft of angry letters from users. Nintendo's 1994 holiday season new version of the "Mortal Kombat" game was just as gruesome as the arcade version.

SEGA'S POSITION[6]

In 1993, SEGA established a three-pronged approach designed to help parents determine the age-appropriateness of its stable of interactive video software. It included a rating classification system, a toll-free hotline, and an informational brochure. Building on the motion picture industry model, the SEGA rating system applied one of three classifications to each interactive video program it released:

GAF For general audiences.

MA-13 For mature audiences age 13 and over.

MA-17 Adult appropriate, not suitable for those under age 17.

SEGA's toll-free hotline was staffed by professionals who could supplement the rating classification by informing parents about the specific content of each SEGA product. SEGA also offered its "Everybody Wins" brochure that provided additional information to shoppers at more than 2,800 retail stores. In addition, SEGA formed an independent Videogame Rating Council consisting of experts in the areas of psychology, sociology, cinema, and education to evaluate games and

---

[5]Ibid. (testimony of Howard C. Lincoln).
[6]Ibid. (testimony of William White, vice president, SEGA of America Inc.).

Exhibit 1   Rating Guidelines

Interactive Digital Software is using five categories by age to rate video game cartridges such as Nintendo, Sega, Atari. They are:
- Early childhood, ages 3 and up
- Kids to adult, ages 6 and up
- Teen, ages 13 and up
- Mature, ages 17 and up
- Adults only

The Software Publishers Association is using a label that shows the level of violence, sex, and strong language used in a computer software or CD-ROM game. Games with no offensive material receive a "Suitable for all audiences" label.

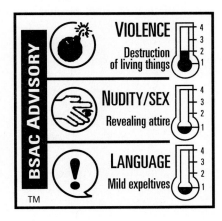

Source: *The Washington Post.*

assign appropriate rating classifications. By the end of 1993, 173 SEGA titles had been rated with the following distribution: 86 percent rated for general audiences (GA); 10 percent earned an MA-13 rating; and only 4 percent were targeted for exclusively adult (MA-17) audiences. To make SEGA's rating system work, the company decided that products bearing the MA-17 label should not be distributed to retail toy stores.

PROGRESS REPORT[7]

In July 1994, the U.S. Senate subcommittee endorsed rating guidelines issued by an industry trade group, the Interactive Digital Software Association (IDSA)—see Exhibit 1. The IDSA ratings provided age guidance with five categories similar to those used by the Motion Picture Association of America. The ratings were expected to appear on videogame packages by mid-November, in time for the holiday season. Retailers who rent games planned to adhere to the ratings guidelines. Some mass merchants

---

[7]M. Moran, "Retailers See Videogame Ratings as a Helpful Guide," *Video Business* 14, no. 32 (1994), pp. 12, 16.

(Sears, Wal-Mart, Toys "Я" Us) had vowed to carry only rated videogames. An informal survey of retailers, however, revealed that large numbers of unrated games were on retailers' shelves for the 1994 seasonal buying rush.[8] Although the IDSA had rated more than 280 titles, the ratings were apparently completed after game packages were printed.

The SPA encountered similar problems. At the end of 1994, only 40 CD-ROM and other software game titles had been rated. Exhibit 1 depicts SPA rating guidelines. Ken Wasch, executive director of the SPA, commented: "I wish more had been rated, but it took longer than we expected to get products submitted, to get them rated, and to get them out to the stores."[9]

There was no agreement among game producers on an industrywide rating system. Some observers believed the existence of several rating systems would confuse consumers. There also appeared to be a debate emerging whether widespread dissemination of rated products would ultimately hurt or help sales.

[8]P. Farhi, "A Waiting Game for Rating Games," *The Washington Post*, December 24, 1994, p. D1.
[9]Ibid.

NAME INDEX

CASE INDEX